2600 Special Topics
- AS 2601: Consideration of an Entity's Use of a Service Organization
- AS 2605: Consideration of the Internal Audit Function
- AS 2610: Initial Audits—Communications Between Predecessor and Successor Auditors

2700 Auditor's Responsibilities Regarding Supplemental and Other Information
- AS 2701: Auditing Supplemental Information Accompanying Audited Financial Statements
- AS 2705: Required Supplementary Information
- AS 2710: Other Information in Documents Containing Audited Financial Statements

2800 Concluding Audit Procedures
- AS 2801: Subsequent Events
- AS 2805: Management Representations
- AS 2810: Evaluating Audit Results
- AS 2815: The Meaning of "Present Fairly in Conformity with Generally Accepted Accounting Principles"
- AS 2820: Evaluating Consistency of Financial Statements

2900 Post-Audit Matters
- AS 2901: Consideration of Omitted Procedures After the Report Date
- AS 2905: Subsequent Discovery of Facts Existing at the Date of the Auditor's Report

Auditor Reporting

3100 Reporting on Audits of Financial Statements
- AS 3101: Reports on Audited Financial Statements
- AS 3110: Dating of the Independent Auditor's Report

3300 Other Reporting Topics
- AS 3305: Special Reports
- AS 3310: Special Reports on Regulated Companies
- AS 3315: Reporting on Condensed Financial Statements and Selected Financial Data
- AS 3320: Association with Financial Statements

Matters Relating to Filings Under Federal Securities Laws

- AS 4101: Responsibilities Regarding Filings Under Federal Securities Statutes
- AS 4105: Reviews of Interim Financial Information

Other Matters Associated with Audits

- AS 6101: Letters for Underwriters and Certain Other Requesting Parties
- AS 6105: Reports on the Application of Accounting Principles
- AS 6110: Compliance Auditing Considerations in Audits of Recipients of Governmental Financial Assistance
- AS 6115: Reporting on Whether a Previously Reported Material Weakness Continues to Exist

IAASB Standards

- ISA 200 *Overall Objectives of the Independent Auditor and the Conduct of an Audit in Accordance with International Standards on Auditing*
- ISA 210 *Agreeing the Terms of Audit Engagements*
- ISA 220 *Quality Control for an Audit of Financial Statements*
- ISA 230 *Audit Documentation*
- ISA 240 *The Auditor's Responsibilities Relating to Fraud in an Audit of Financial Statements*
- ISA 250 *Consideration of Laws and Regulations in an Audit of Financial Statements*
- ISA 260 *Communication with Those Charged with Governance*
- ISA 265 *Communicating Deficiencies in Internal Control to Those Charged with Governance and Management*
- ISA 300 *Planning an Audit of Financial Statements*
- ISA 315 *Identifying and Assessing the Risks of Material Misstatement through Understanding the Entity and Its Environment*

AICPA Standards

(Continued on back cover endsheets)

11TH EDITION

AUDITING

A RISK-BASED APPROACH

JOHNSTONE | GRAMLING | RITTENBERG

CENGAGE

Australia • Brazil • Mexico • Singapore • United Kingdom • United States

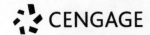

Auditing: A Risk-Based Approach, 11e

Karla M. Johnstone, Audrey A. Gramling and Larry E. Rittenberg

Senior Vice President: Erin Joyner

Product Director: Jason Fremder

Product Manager: Matt Filimonov

Content Developer: Emily Lehmann

Product Assistant: Aiyana Moore

Digital Content Specialist: Timothy Ross

Manufacturing Planner: Doug Wilke

Project Management and Composition: SPi Global

Sr. Art Director: Michelle Kunkler

Text Designer: Ke Design/Trish Knapke

Cover Designer: Stratton Design

Intellectual Property

   Analyst: Reba Frederics

   Project Manager: Kelli Besse

Cover Image: cozyta/Shutterstock.com, Orhan Cam/Shutterstock.com, islavicek/Shutterstock.com, Gardeazabal/Shutterstock.com

For product information and technology assistance, contact us at
Cengage Customer & Sales Support, 1-800-354-9706

For permission to use material from this text or product, submit all requests online at **www.cengage.com/permissions**
Further permissions questions can be emailed to
permissionrequest@cengage.com

Library of Congress Control Number: 2017960519

ISBN: 978-1-337-61945-5

Cengage
20 Channel Center Street
Boston, MA 02210
USA

Cengage is a leading provider of customized learning solutions with employees residing in nearly 40 different countries and sales in more than 125 countries around the world. Find your local representative at **www.cengage.com.**

Cengage products are represented in Canada by Nelson Education, Ltd.

To learn more about Cengage platforms and services, visit **www.cengage.com**

To register or access your online learning solution or purchase materials for your course, visit **www.cengagebrain.com**

Printed in Mexico
Print Number: 03   Print Year: 2018

Brief Contents

Contents

6 Audit Evidence   222

7 Planning the Audit: Identifying, Assessing, and Responding to the Risk of Material Misstatement   278

11 Auditing Inventory, Goods and Services, and Accounts Payable: The Acquisition and Payment Cycle   568

12 Auditing Long-Lived Assets and Merger and Acquisition Activity   642

13 Auditing Debt, Equity, and Long-Term Liabilities Requiring Management Estimates   700

Preface

The auditing environment continues to change in significant ways. University graduates entering the auditing profession today should be prepared for a high standard of responsibility, should be ready to serve the public interest, and should recognize the emerging issues and continuing points of focus facing auditors. Examples of today's emerging issues and continuing points of focus facing the profession include:

- New accounting guidance from the Financial Accounting Standards Board on *leases* and *revenue recognition*.
- Increased need for *critical thinking* and *professional skepticism*.
- Increased and growing use of *data analytics tools*.
- Continued and increasing importance of *ethical and professional decision making*.
- Continued efforts toward *international convergence of auditing standards* of the American Institute of Certified Public Accountants (AICPA) and the International Auditing and Assurance Standards Board (IAASB).
- *Reorganization of the Public Company Accounting Oversight Board (PCAOB) auditing standards* to provide auditors and others with a logical framework and easy access to the standards governing the conduct of audits of public companies.
- The *IAASB's issuance of new and revised auditor reporting standards*, which require auditors to provide more transparent and informative reports on the companies they audit, including the disclosure of *key audit matters*.
- The *PCAOB's adoption of a new auditing standard on the auditor's report*, including the disclosure of *critical audit matters*.

The eleventh edition of *Financial Statement Auditing: A Risk-Based Approach* represents the most up-to-date professional auditing guidance available and reflects the many emerging issues and continuing points of focus in the profession. This text provides students with the tools they need to understand the full range of issues associated with conducting a quality financial statement audit in an evolving national and global context.

Revision Themes and New Enhancements in the Eleventh Edition

Coverage of Emerging Data Analytics Tools. Data analytics tools include qualitative and quantitative techniques and processes that auditors use to enhance their productivity and effectiveness in terms of extracting, categorizing, identifying, and analyzing patterns in their client's data. Emerging data analytics tools facilitate testing 100% of a population, enabling the auditor to focus on potentially erroneous transactions or risky areas of the audit. These emerging tools also include sophisticated data visualization tools, for example, Tableau. Data analytics tools also include familiar platforms such as Excel, ACL, and IDEA; the landscape is changing dramatically and quickly in this space, so instructors and students must be adaptive to fast-paced change. We introduce key terms and explain data analytics tools in an expanded *Chapter 8*, with an entirely new section, "Using Data Analytics Tools to Obtain and Evaluate Evidence." We also include end-of-chapter problems to reinforce opportunities to employ data analytics tools within *Chapter 8* and the following cycle chapters (e.g., data analytics in the revenue cycle in *Chapter 9*).

Auditing Standards Exhibit–PCAOB, AICPA, and IAASB–appears inside the front cover of this textbook. This exhibit allows for easy access to relevant standards, and provides a platform for relative comparisons across each of the standards-setting bodies. End-of-chapter problems require students to review and apply the material in the *Auditing Standards Exhibit*. These problems provide students with practice completing task-based simulations similar to what they will see on the CPA exam; we highlight these problems with an identifying icon.

Three New Learning Engagement Features. Students today demand more than case facts and standard lectures. They require opportunities to engage with the instructor and classmates on important topics facing the profession.

- *"Why It Matters" feature.* This feature helps students see beyond the factual insights provided in the chapters. Elements include for example, extensions based on in-the-news examples that illustrate fundamental features and applications of text facts, professional standards in foreign jurisdictions, and interesting points that may be tangential to the text facts, but that should facilitate students' deep engagement with the chapter. Certain of these features are noted as relating to an International Focus.
- *"Prompt for Critical Thinking—It's Your Turn!" feature.* This feature encourages students to engage in critical thinking as they acquire knowledge relevant to each chapter. This feature is intentionally creative in form and substance, and varies widely in structure based upon the learning objective to which it is related. As an example of one such prompt, students are asked to consider auditors' responsibilities with respect to internal controls around the Foreign Corrupt Practices Act.
- *"What Do You Think?—For Classroom Discussion" feature.* This feature provides an avenue by which instructors can facilitate preparation for class, cognitive engagement, and critical thinking through discussions with other students. Like the *Prompt for Critical Thinking* feature, *What Do You Think?* is creative in form and substance and varies in unexpected ways to spark students' interest in engagement with the chapter topic. This feature is an ideal way for instructors to facilitate an interesting class discussion using a flipped-classroom approach (either involving the entire class or within small teams).

Below we provide examples of each of these three new learning engagement features that appear in *Chapter 14* ("Completing a Quality Audit") with respect to the learning objective "Obtaining Remaining Audit Evidence on Noncompliance with Laws and Regulations."

- The *Why It Matters* feature articulates the motivation for and provisions of the Foreign Corrupt Practices Act (FCPA).
- The *Prompt for Critical Thinking* feature extends this discussion by prompting students to think about corruption, how to measure it, and its variation across different jurisdictions.
- The *What Do You Think?* feature encourages students to consider the applicability of the FCPA in today's business and auditing environment.

Compliance with the Foreign Corrupt Practices Act (FCPA) of 1977

Why It Matters

This feature highlights an important law that many companies have failed to comply with.

The FCPA was written to respond to SEC investigations in the 1970s revealing that over 400 companies had made questionable or illegal payments of over $300 million to foreign officials, politicians, and political parties. The payments involved bribery of foreign officials to facilitate business operations in their respective foreign countries. The main provisions of the FCPA include:

- No U.S. person or company that has securities listed on U.S. markets may make a payment to a foreign official for the purpose of obtaining or retaining business. This provision is commonly called the anti-bribery provision of the FCPA.

- Companies that have securities listed on U.S. markets must make and keep financial records that accurately and fairly reflect the transactions of the company and must design and maintain an adequate system of internal accounting controls.

- Certain payments to foreign officials are acceptable. These include grease payments, which are payments made to an official to expedite the performance of the duties that the official would already be bound to perform.

Prompt for Critical Thinking

Before reading this text, had you heard of the Transparency International corruption perception index? Think critically about what you know about the political and economic structure of the following countries. In the spaces below, (1) rank the six countries from most corrupt to least corrupt just from what you know, and (2) guess what their ranking is on a scale from 0–100 on the corruption perception index from 0 (highly corrupt) to 100 (very clean):

Country (in alphabetical order)	Rank (1 = most to 6 = least corrupt among this list)	Estimated corruption perception index (0 − 100)
Belgium		
Brazil		
New Zealand		
Somalia		
South Korea		
United States of America		

After ranking the countries, visit Transparency International and compare your answers and estimates against theirs:

https://www.transparency.org/news/feature/corruption_perceptions_index_2016#table

What are your reactions to what you have learned? What rankings surprised you? How accurate were your rankings?

What Do You Think?   For Classroom Discussion

The FCPA of 1977 was enacted a LONG time ago!

1. Do you think it is still relevant today? Why or why not?
2. Review the following SEC website:

https://www.sec.gov/spotlight/fcpa/fcpa-cases.shtml What are your impressions? What surprises you? What companies on this list are well-known? Focus on one of the enforcement actions (perhaps at the discretion of your instructor) and explain how the company violated the FCPA.

Updates to "Focus on Fraud" Feature. The authors continue their use of this learning engagement feature, which provides compelling examples of recent frauds, and the role of the auditor in preventing, detecting, or (sometimes) *not* detecting those frauds. Below we provide an example of this learning feature that appears in *Chapter 14* ("Completing a Quality Audit") with respect to the learning objective "Obtaining Remaining Audit Evidence on Noncompliance with Laws and Regulations."

Focus on Fraud   Triton Energy and Noncompliance with Laws and Regulations

This feature describes a historically important case involving noncompliance with the Foreign Corrupt Practices Act (FCPA) of 1977.

Triton Energy engages in the exploration and production of crude oil and natural gas in many areas around the world. Triton has traditionally operated in relatively high-risk, politically unstable areas where larger and better-known producers do not operate. Top Triton Indonesia officials (President, CFO, Commercial Manager, and Controller) were investigated by the SEC for violations of the Foreign Corrupt Practices Act. These violations included:

- Improper payments were made to a middleman who used the funds to reduce Triton Indonesia's tax liability.

- Improper payments were made to a middleman who used the funds to ensure a favorable governmental audit.

- Improper payments were made to a middleman who used the funds to obtain corporate tax refunds from government officials.

- The recording of false journal entries by Triton Indonesia's Commercial Manager and Controller were made to cover up the improper payments.

These improper payments and false journal entries were facilitated because Triton's CEO, Bill Lee, was an aggressive top manager who provided weak tone at the top in terms of his failure to encourage compliance with applicable laws and regulations, failure to discourage improper payments, and failure to implement internal controls to deter improper payments. Triton was ultimately fined $300,000 related to the scandal.

For further details, see the SEC's Securities Exchange Act of 1934 Release No. 38343 and Accounting and Auditing Enforcement Release No. 889, February 27, 1997.

- To help students prepare for the CPA exam, MindTap for Auditing includes two pre- and post-tests using author-selected multiple-choice questions from Becker Professional Education, all tailored to this edition's critical learning objectives.

- *"Check Your Basic Knowledge" feature.* To enhance and expand on the *Becker CPA Exam Questions* feature, each chapter includes additional true-false and multiple-choice questions *within the chapter text itself.*

Following the discussion of each learning objective within the chapters, we challenge students to answer four questions (two true-false and two multiple-choice) to alert students to their effective learning, or alternatively, to their lack of understanding (which should encourage students to more carefully acquire the concepts relating to each particular learning objective). Taken collectively, the Becker CPA Exam Questions and Check Your Basic Knowledge questions ensure that students have the opportunity to challenge themselves during reading the chapter, thereby tracking their learning, and after reading the chapter.

- *Updated and Expanded Chapter Examples and End-of-Chapter* problems, including *"Review Questions and Short Cases," "Application Activities,"* along with more extensive longer cases: *"Fraud Focus: Contemporary and Historical Cases."* To help instructors identify these problems, the text includes the following icons that highlight overall themes: *Ethics, Fraud, Professional Skepticism, International Issues, and Auditing Standards Application Activities.* We also rely extensively on using facts from SEC Accounting, Auditing, and Enforcement Releases (AAERs) and PCAOB Enforcement Actions in the cases to illustrate the regulatory implications of auditors' judgments and decisions. For most chapters, we have updated the *Academic Research Cases*, providing instructors with an opportunity to introduce students to the relevance of academic research to the auditing profession.

Examples of Selected Cases by Chapter include:
Longtop Financial Technologies (Ch. 1), Bentley's Brisbane Partnership (Ch. 1), Wells Fargo (Ch. 2), Weatherford International (Ch. 2), Lime Energy (Ch. 2), U.S. Department of Defense (Ch. 3), Diamond Foods (Ch. 3), Chesapeake Petroleum and Supply (Ch. 3), Florida Department of Financial Services (Ch. 4), Toshiba (Ch. 4), Boeing (Ch. 5), ContinuityXSolutions, Inc. (Ch. 7), Ag Feed Industries (Ch. 9), China Media Express Holdings (Ch. 9), Monsanto Corporation (Ch. 9), Agricultural Bank of China (Ch. 10), MagnaChip (Ch. 11), Miller Energy Resources (Ch. 12), Soyo Group (Ch. 13), Logitech (Ch. 13), 2GO (Ch. 14), Chelsea Logistics Holding Corp. (Ch. 14), Suiss Finance (Ch. 14), ImmunoGen, Inc. (Ch. 15), Rolls Royce (Ch. 15), and Westmoreland Coal Company (Ch. 15).

Expanded View of "Users." In prior versions, our user-emphasis was on shareholders, bondholders, regulators, and standards-setters as primary actors. While of course critical, we now incorporate discussion of the role that analysts play (e.g., in incentivizing managers, and therefore affecting the judgments and decisions of users), along with stock market reactions to both financial accounting and auditing information disclosures. As an illustration of one such view, we include the following discussion in *Chapter 9* (the revenue cycle), embedded in a *Why It Matters* feature.

This feature provides insight into the role that stock analyst following and consensus analyst earnings per share calculations play in affecting managements' incentives to commit fraud.

Stock analysts follow companies and issue earnings per share and revenue forecasts they anticipate for the companies they follow.

To understand this concept better, see the analysts' forecast report for Ford Motor Company as of June 2017, which we reproduce below.

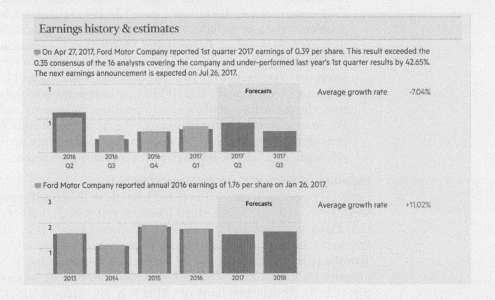

Earnings history & estimates

On Apr 27, 2017, Ford Motor Company reported 1st quarter 2017 earnings of 0.39 per share. This result exceeded the 0.35 consensus of the 16 analysts covering the company and under-performed last year's 1st quarter results by 42.65%. The next earnings announcement is expected on Jul 26, 2017.

Ford Motor Company reported annual 2016 earnings of 1.76 per share on Jan 26, 2017.

This report shows that 16 analysts together, that is, by consensus predict Q1 2017 earnings per share of $0.35 per share, and that the actual results were better than that at $0.39 per share. It also shows that the annual earnings per share for 2016 was $1.76; analysts make predictions about both quarterly and annual earnings per share. Managers do not want to "disappoint" the market by having their earnings results come in "under forecast," which creates the incentive for earnings manipulation.

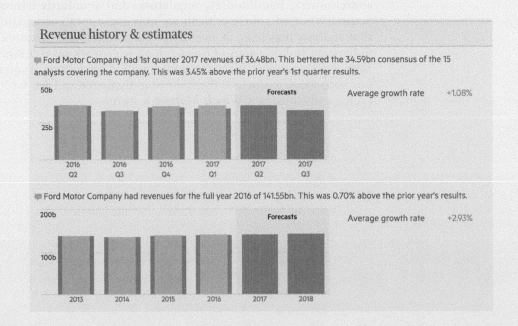

Revenue history & estimates

Ford Motor Company had 1st quarter 2017 revenues of 36.48bn. This bettered the 34.59bn consensus of the 15 analysts covering the company. This was 3.45% above the prior year's 1st quarter results.

Ford Motor Company had revenues for the full year 2016 of 141.55bn. This was 0.70% above the prior year's results.

This report shows that 15 analysts together, that is, by consensus predict Q1 2017 revenues at $34.59 billion, while the actual revenue that Ford reported exceeded that estimate, coming in at $36.48 billion. Managers do not want to "disappoint" the market by having their revenue results come in "under forecast," which creates the incentive for fraudulently overstated revenue amounts.

What does the term "analyst consensus forecast" mean?

It means the average earnings per share or revenue based on all the analysts that are following the company. If a company is at or near its consensus forecast and the auditor proposes a material, income decreasing audit adjustment, client management may resist because they do not want to report a negative earnings surprise.

What is a negative earnings surprise or a negative revenue surprise?

It is a negative departure from the consensus analyst earnings forecast or the revenue forecast, for example, lower actual earnings per share amount compared to the consensus or lower revenue compared to the consensus expectation.

For further details, see

https://markets.ft.com/data/equities/tearsheet/forecasts?s=F:NYQ

Hallmark Pedagogical Features

Articulating an audit opinion formulation process to help organize students' acquisition of the technical material in each chapter. A chapter-opening figure helps students identify the major phases in the audit process and see how the steps within that process relate to specific chapters. The textbook describes how auditors go through a structured judgment process to issue an audit opinion. We refer to this process as the *Audit Opinion Formulation Process*, and it serves as the foundation for this textbook.

The process consists of five phases. Phase I concerns client acceptance and continuance. Once a client is accepted (or the audit firm decides to continue to provide services to a client), the auditor needs to perform risk assessment procedures to thoroughly understand the client's business (or update prior knowledge in the case of a continuing client), its industry, its competition, and its management and governance processes (including internal controls) to determine the likelihood that financial accounts might be materially misstated (Phase II). In some audits, the auditor also obtains evidence about internal control operating effectiveness through testing those controls (Phase III). Much of what most people think of as auditing, obtaining substantive evidence about accounts, disclosures, and assertions, occurs in Phase IV. The information gathered in Phases I through III greatly influences the amount of testing auditors perform in Phase IV. Finally, in Phase V, the auditor completes the audit and makes a decision about what type of audit report to issue.

Also fundamental to students' understanding is the framework's inclusion of the auditing profession, audit quality, quality judgments, ethical decisions, and professional liability. Further fundamentals highlighted in the *Audit Opinion Formulation Process* include discussion of a framework for obtaining audit evidence, as depicted below.

Recognizing that professional judgment, sufficient appropriate evidence, and quality decisions are critical to conducting a quality financial statement audit. In addition to the focus on professional judgment throughout the text, numerous exercises emphasize this key auditing skill, including examples and end-of-chapter materials based on the business press, PCAOB enforcement actions, SEC filings, and company proxy statements. Further, the end-of-chapter materials help ensure that students understand the link between mandatory financial reporting and auditing, risk assessment, transaction cycles, and analytical procedures.

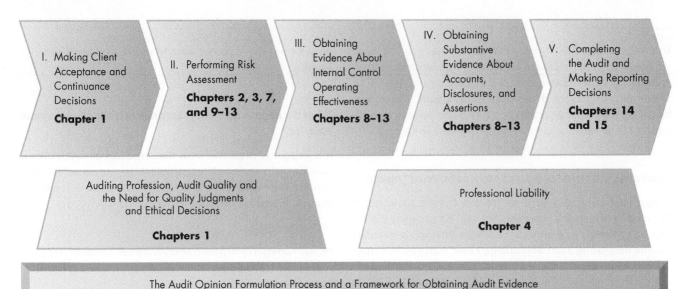

Emphasizing that professional skepticism, which can be challenging to maintain, is at the heart of auditor judgments. This emphasis provides students with the tools to learn how to apply the concept of professional skepticism. We include conceptual discussion of this topic in *Chapter 1*, with substantial reinforcement through the remaining chapters in the text, as well as in end-of-chapter materials (highlighted with an identifying icon for ease of identification). This emphasis helps students see the practical application of professional skepticism, as well as provides practical insights as to downside risks when auditors fail to maintain appropriate levels of skepticism.

Using data analytics tools and analytical procedures to improve the effectiveness and efficiency of the audit. The text contains a new focus on data analytics around "big data" that will become an evolving hallmark pedagogical feature over subsequent editions. The text covers planning, substantive, and review-related analytical procedures, and provides ways in which auditors can use data analytics tools to perform these procedures. *Chapter 6* and *Chapter 7* outline the theory of analytical procedures, and discuss appropriate processes and best practices. Various end-of-chapter problems provide examples of using analytical procedures. *Chapters 9, 11,* and *13* contain an extensive practice case (set in the pharmaceutical industry, complete with data based on three real companies) that would be ideal for a semester team project to enforce concepts around analytical procedures.

Employing specific learning objectives, which we introduce at the outset of each chapter in a "What You Will Learn" feature and summarize at the end of each Chapter with a "Let's Review" feature. We reinforce these objectives throughout the chapter materials, along with linking the objectives to specific end-of-chapter materials, including links to academic research cases to enhance students' appreciation for the theoretical underpinnings of the learning objectives. These learning objectives help to shape students' cognitive architecture as they integrate their preliminary understanding of chapter topics with the theory, examples, and accompanying discussion that follow.

Providing and applying professional decision-making and ethical decision-making frameworks. Decision-making frameworks, introduced in *Chapter 1*, require students to think about real-life professional and ethical decisions associated in each chapter. End-of-chapter materials continue the use of these professional and ethical decision-making frameworks to help students address contemporary issues. Further, we identify these problems as part of the last learning objective in each chapter.

Acquiring hands-on experience through a practice-oriented audit case. On the CengageNOW website, you will find a tool that allows students to engage in a practice-oriented audit case. Brony's Bikes is an auditing case that encompasses a complete auditing scenario spanning from Performing Risk Assessment (Phase II of the Audit Opinion Formulation Process) to making reporting decisions (Phase V of the Audit Opinion Formulation Process). The case includes 13 modules that address specific activities included in the Audit Opinion Formulation Process. The authors have structured these 13 modules so that each can be undertaken independently of the other modules. For example, Module I, *Assessment of Inherent Risk*, takes the students through the audit planning process based on AU-C 200 *Overall Objectives of the Independent Auditor and the Conduct of an Audit in Accordance with Generally Accepted Auditing Standards*, AU-C 300 *Planning an Audit*, and AU 315-C *Understanding the Entity and Its Environment and Assessing the Risks of Material Misstatement*. Module I can be assigned on a stand-alone basis or along with any or all of the other modules at the instructor's discretion.

Students gain experience with auditing documentation including many working papers. Analytical procedures are performed in Excel worksheets requiring conclusions and recommendations.

Other Resources

MindTap: Empower Your Students

MindTap is a platform that propels students from memorization to mastery. It gives you complete control of your course, so you can provide engaging content, challenge every learner, and build student confidence. Customize interactive syllabi to emphasize priority topics, then add your own material or notes to the eBook as desired. This outcomes-driven application gives you the tools needed to empower students and boost both understanding and performance.

Access Everything You Need in One Place

Cut down on prep with the preloaded and organized MindTap course materials. Teach more efficiently with interactive multimedia, assignments, quizzes, and more. Give your students the power to read, listen, and study on their phones, so they can learn on their terms.

Empower Students to Reach their Potential

Twelve distinct metrics give you actionable insights into student engagement. Identify topics troubling your entire class and instantly communicate with those struggling. Students can track their scores to stay motivated toward their goals. Together, you can be unstoppable.

Control Your Course—and Your Content

Get the flexibility to reorder textbook chapters, add your own notes, and embed a variety of content including Open Educational Resources (OER). Personalize course content to your students' needs. Students can even read your notes, add their own notes, and highlight key text to aid their learning.

Get a Dedicated Team, Whenever You Need Them

MindTap isn't just a tool; it's backed by a personalized team eager to support you. We can help set up your course and tailor it to your specific objectives, so you'll be ready to make an impact from day one. Know we'll be standing by to help you and your students until the final day of the term.

Becker CPA Exam Questions

To help students prepare for taking the CPA exam, for each chapter, students have access to four or five representative multiple-choice questions from the Becker test bank, tailored to each chapter's most critical learning objectives.

ACL analytics and audit software with updated cases.

This edition integrates ACL software into end-of-chapter materials. An ACL Appendix and tutorial is located at the end of the text. The ACL Appendix contains an overview of the basic functions of ACL followed by a brief, illustrated tutorial to help students learn how to use the basic features of the ACL Analytics. Access to the software can be provided by Instructors who are enrolled in the ACL Academic Network program.

ACL cases include the following:

1. *Pell Grants*, a fraud investigation case related to this student grant program. (*Chapter 6*)
2. *Husky Accounts Receivable*, which includes exercises in which students identify unpaid invoices and sales made over credit limits, perform cutoff analyses, conduct aging analyses, and identify procedures to be performed based upon their results. (*Chapter 9*)
3. *FloorMart Sales and Inventory*, which requires students to identify store locations in which data appear to indicate potential inaccuracies, and to identify procedures to gather additional evidence. (*Chapter 9*)
4. *Husky Inventory*, which includes exercises in which students identify potentially obsolete inventory, calculate inventory turnover, consider possible write-downs, and prepare a report based on their results. (*Chapter 11*)
5. *Benford's Law Case*, a fraud case dealing with employee expense reimbursements and the application of Benford's Law of numbers. (*Chapter 14*)

Organization of the Eleventh Edition

The demand for quality auditing: Chapter 1.

Chapter 1 provides the foundation for students to understand the economic context in which financial statement auditing exists. The chapter defines the objective of financial statement auditing and describes its role in meeting society's demands for reliable financial and internal control information. *Chapter 1* introduces the Financial Reporting Council's *Audit Quality Framework*, and identifies professional conduct requirements that help auditors achieve high quality. This chapter also provides frameworks for professional and ethical decision making. *Chapter 1* also describes the process by which audit firms make client acceptance and continuance decisions, and recognizes that this process is important to achieving audit quality.

Risk assessment with a focus on fraud and internal controls over financial reporting: Chapters 2 and 3.

Chapter 2 defines fraud, describes the fraud triangle, and provides examples of recent financial reporting frauds. The chapter discusses users' expectations of auditors' fraud-related responsibilities, explains how various requirements of the Sarbanes-Oxley Act of 2002 help prevent fraud, and discusses the importance of corporate governance in relation to quality auditing.

Chapter 3 articulates the importance of internal control over financial reporting, defines internal control, identifies and describes the components and principles of internal control, and describes management's responsibility related to internal control. *Chapter 3* also explains how to distinguish between material weaknesses, significant deficiencies, and control deficiencies in internal control over financial reporting.

Important elements of the professional environment and the audit opinion formulation process: Chapters 4, 5, and 6.

Chapter 4 discusses the liability environment in which auditors operate, explores the effects of lawsuits on audit firms, identifies laws from which auditor liability is derived, and describes possible remedies, sanctions, and auditor defenses.

Chapter 5 identifies and compares auditing standards that provide audit guidance on the audit opinion formulation process, and discusses the foundational principles underlying these standards. The chapter lists the phases and related activities in the audit opinion formulation process, explains the concept of accounting cycles, describes the assertions that are inherent to financial statements, defines audit evidence and the purpose and types of audit procedures used to obtain audit evidence, and discusses the importance of audit documentation.

Chapter 6 discusses the importance of evidence sufficiency and appropriateness, illustrates professional judgments about the type and timing of audit procedures, discusses the use and application of substantive analytical procedures, identifies issues relating to audit evidence needed for accounts involving management estimates, and discusses evidence issues involving specialists and related party transactions. *Chapter 6* also describes the characteristics of quality audit documentation and explains the nature, design, and purposes of audit programs.

Planning the audit and employing appropriate audit tools: Chapters 7 and 8.

Chapter 7 defines the concept of material misstatement and discusses the importance of materiality judgments in the audit context. The chapter also identifies the risks of material misstatement and describes how they relate to audit risk and detection risk. *Chapter 7* illustrates how auditors respond to assessed risks of material misstatement.

In planning how to respond to assessed risk of material misstatements, auditors need to determine which of the available specialized tools they will use. *Chapter 8* describes how auditors can use sampling techniques and data analytics tools to gather and evaluate sufficient appropriate audit evidence. The chapter explains the objectives of sampling for testing controls and account balances, compares and contrasts nonstatistical and statistical sampling, describes attributes sampling, describes the sampling process used to gather evidence about misstatements in account balances and assertions, describes monetary unit sampling, and explains how to use data analytics tools to obtain and evaluate audit evidence.

Performing Audits Using the Transaction Cycle Approach: Chapters 9, 10, 11, 12, and 13.

These five chapters focus on the application of concepts developed earlier for assessing risk, identifying and testing controls designed to address those risks, and using substantive approaches to testing account balances. Each chapter:

- identifies significant accounts, disclosures, and relevant assertions
- explains the process of identifying and assessing inherent risks, fraud risks, and control risks

- describes planning analytical procedures that the auditor can use to identify potential material misstatement
- articulates appropriate responses to identified risks of material misstatement, including appropriate tests of controls and considering results of tests of controls
- and identifies how to apply substantive audit procedures.

Completing a quality audit and issuing the audit report: Chapters 14 and 15.

Chapter 14 discusses the procedures that auditors conduct while completing the audit. These procedures include reviewing activities relating to detected misstatements, loss contingencies, disclosure adequacy, noncompliance with laws or regulations, review analytical procedures, going-concern matters, and subsequent events. The chapter also distinguishes between a management representation letter and a management letter, identifies procedures that are part of an engagement quality review, and identifies issues the auditor should communicate to the audit committee and management.

Once these activities are completed, the auditor makes a reporting decision, which is described in *Chapter 15*. This chapter identifies the principles underlying audit reporting on financial statements, describes the information that is included in an unqualified/unmodified audit report, and describes financial statement audits resulting in an unqualified/unmodified audit opinion with report modifications. The chapter describes financial statement audits resulting in a qualified opinion, an adverse opinion, or a disclaimer of opinion. *Chapter 15* describes the emerging critical audit matters (PCAOB) and key audit matters (IAASB) disclosures that auditors will, or already are, including in the auditor's report. The chapter also describes the information that is included in a standard unqualified audit report on internal control over financial reporting and identifies the appropriate audit report modifications for situations requiring other than an unqualified report on internal control over financial reporting. *Chapter 15* concludes with a discussion of how auditors should respond to situations in which omitted procedures come to light after the audit report has been issued.

Supplements

Companion Site: Instructors and students can find most of the textbook's support materials online at login.cengage.com., including the solutions manual, PowerPoint slides, ACL data spreadsheet files, and other resources.

Solutions Manual: The solutions manual contains the solutions to all end-of-chapter assignments. It is available on the instructor's page at www.cengagebrain.com.

PowerPoint Slides: Instructors can bring their lectures to life with engaging PowerPoint slides that are interesting, visually stimulating, and paced for student comprehension. These slides are ideal as lecture tools and provide a clear guide for student study and note-taking. We have purposely provided *more* slides rather than *less*! We encourage instructors to tailor down the slides to meet their own, individual instructional preferences.

Test Bank: Cengage Learning Testing Powered by Cognero is a flexible, online system that allows you to:

- author, edit, and manage test bank content from multiple Cengage Learning solutions,
- create multiple test versions in an instant,
- deliver tests from your LMS, your classroom, or wherever you want. The test bank is also available in Microsoft Word.

The eleventh edition integrates the use of ACL software into both homework and cases. An appendix and tutorial located at the end of the textbook provide guidance for students unfamiliar with the software. Access to the software can be provided by instructors who are enrolled in the ACL Academic Network program.

Access to the software for qualified instructors and their students can be arranged with ACL through the Academic Network program: http://info.acl.com/Academic-Network-for-Professors.html and http://info.acl.com/Academic-Network-Program_Professor-Sign-up.html. The signup process may take a few weeks to process so first-time instructors should sign-up for the program in advance of their teaching semester.

Once instructors join the Academic Network, they will have access to:

- ACL GRC - a cloud-based platform for audit management (including electronic workpapers)
- ACL Analytics
- ACL Launchpad - the single access point for ACL GRC, ACL Analytics, as well as support, ScriptHub, and ACL Academy
- Analytical Procedures: A Case in the Context of the Pharmaceutical Industry (*Chapters 9, 11,* and *13*): The case contains online Excel files that students download and analyze. The case enables students to practice developing and conducting planning and substantive analytical procedures. We developed the case using the published financial statements of three prominent companies in this industry, with adaptations to make the case suitable for classroom use. Students will access an Excel file on the companion site at login. cengage.com. The Excel file contains financial data and information from footnote disclosures. We view these exercises as one type of data analytic technique – one that individual instructors may be more comfortable using than emerging data analytics such as Tableau or other similar platforms.

Acknowledgments

We are grateful to members of the staff at Cengage for their help in developing the eleventh edition: Matt Filimonov, Senior Product Manager; Emily Lehmann, Associate Content Developer; Sangeetha Vijay, Content Project Manager at SPi Global; and Emily McLellan, Marketing Manager.

Karla M. Johnstone
Audrey A. Gramling
Larry E. Rittenberg

About the Authors

Karla M. Johnstone

Karla M. Johnstone, Ph.D., CPA, is the Ernst & Young (EY) Professor of Accounting and Information Systems at the University of Wisconsin–Madison, School of Business. She teaches auditing, and her research investigates a broad range of auditing topics, including: curriculum enhancements in auditing, along with auditor decision making; client acceptance and continuance decisions; how fraud risk and fraud brainstorming affect audit planning and audit fees; client–auditor negotiation; competitive bidding; audit budget-setting processes; and governance responses to various negative corporate events such as fraud or internal control material weakness disclosures. Professor Johnstone serves on the editorial boards of numerous academic journals and is active in the Auditing Section of the American Accounting Association (AAA). She recently completed a term as the President of the Auditing Section. Before beginning her coursework for her Ph.D., Karla worked as a corporate accountant and as a staff auditor and was a doctoral fellow in residence at Coopers & Lybrand. Importantly, Karla's research and interactions with practice—both in the U.S., and abroad (e.g., the Foundation for Audit Research in the Netherlands)—demonstrate a significant commitment to the theory and practice of auditing, along with associated regulatory and standards-setting activities.

Audrey A. Gramling

Audrey A. Gramling, Ph.D., CPA, CIA is the Accounting Department Chair and Professor at Colorado State University. Previously, she held the Treece Endowed Chair and was Accounting Department Professor and Chair at Bellarmine University. She has been on the accounting faculty at Kennesaw State University, Georgia State University, Wake Forest University, and University of Illinois at Urbana-Champaign. Audrey's research investigates both internal and external auditing issues, with a focus on decision behavior of auditors, external auditor independence, internal control reporting, and other factors affecting the market for audit and assurance services. Prior to earning her Ph.D. at the University of Arizona, Audrey worked as an external auditor at a predecessor firm of Deloitte and as an internal auditor at Georgia Institute of Technology. She has also served a one-year appointment as an Academic Accounting Fellow in the Office of the Chief Accountant at the U.S. Securities and Exchange Commission. She is a past-President of the Auditing Section of the American Accounting Association and has served in an advisory role to the Committee of Sponsoring Organizations (COSO). In February 2018 she began serving as a member of the AICPA's Auditing Standards Board. For over three decades, in recognition of the valuable role of auditing as a key component of corporate governance, Audrey has been committed to both the practice and theory of quality auditing.

Larry E. Rittenberg

Larry E. Rittenberg, Ph.D., CPA, CIA, is Professor Emeritus, Department of Accounting and Information Systems, at the University of Wisconsin–Madison, where he taught courses in auditing, risk management, and corporate governance. He is also Chair Emeritus of the COSO of the Treadway Commission, where he provided oversight of the development of the COSO Enterprise Risk Management Framework, the COSO Guidance for Smaller Businesses, and was instrumental in developing the Framework for COSO 2013. He has served as Vice-Chair of Professional Practices for the Institute of Internal Auditors (IIA) and President of the IIA Research Foundation, and has been a member of the Auditing Standards Committee of the AAA Auditing Section, the NACD Blue Ribbon Commission on Audit Committees, the IIA's Professional Practices Committee, and Vice-President and Treasurer of the AAA. He recently retired as audit committee chair and board member of Woodward Governor, a publicly traded company, and has consulted on audit committee, risk, and control issues with Petro China – the largest public company in China. Professor Rittenberg served as a staff auditor for Ernst & Young and has co-authored five books and monographs and numerous research articles.

Recommendations from Instructors Who Have Used Our Textbook Previously

Professor Tim Bell, University of North Florida. I have used [this] text for seven years now and it has been an outstanding resource for teaching my students the fundamentals of contemporary auditing. Text discussions and end-of-chapter applications help me to develop students' critical analysis and judgment skills, sensitivity and responses to ethical dilemmas, and understanding and appreciation of the essential role of professional skepticism in auditing.... My impression based on use of successive editions of the text is that the authors have worked very hard to ensure it is up-to-date as auditing standards and related guidance evolve and audit-relevant events occur in the rapidly-changing business environment. Without reservation, I highly recommend this text.

Professor Veena L. Brown, University of Wisconsin-Milwaukee. This textbook is ideal for my students as it presents a good mix of theory and practice using the integrated audit approach. The authors do a great job portraying the auditing concepts in a deceptively simple manner. The Exhibits and the Professional Judgment in Context presented in each chapter helps students better grasp the sometimes-elusive auditing concepts. I have successfully used this textbook for the past six years and look forward to exploring the next edition with my students.

Professor Barry J. Bryan, Southern Methodist University. I selected this textbook because I believe that it presents a realistic approach to the integrated audit. Having worked with several of the Big Four firms, it is evident to me that the authors have been diligent in writing a book that mirrors the risk-based approach to the audit. In addition, my students have enjoyed outstanding success on the AUD Exam having used this text as their primary study resource.

Professor Sean Dennis, University of Kentucky. I use this book because it has it all... detailed (yet intuitive!) explanations, challenging review questions for students, and detailed cases that are both timely and relevant. The authors have organized the material in a way that helps students build an understanding of risk and the audit process from the ground up. The questions and cases at the end of the chapters also help create engaging discussions among students that lead to productive critical thinking. In fact, my favorite thing about this book is that the authors continually update the cases at the end of the chapters. This has really helped my students relate to the course material – and I use these cases in class as much as I can!

Professor Denise Hanes Downey, Villanova University. The beauty of this textbook is that it facilitates an appreciation for the many nuances and complexities of auditing without overwhelming students. The authors appropriately balance necessary details with illustrations and *recent* examples to guide students' understanding. As a result, students come into class ready to engage in higher level discussions – having mastered the fundamentals on their own. From a course design perspective, I appreciate how the chapters stand-alone allowing professors to select chapters they find to be of particular importance without requiring additional chapters be added to the syllabus for clarity.

Professor Kim Westermann, California Polytechnic State University. As a former auditor and current audit professor, I find the book very easy to follow and well written. The content is organized in a similar fashion to the audit process itself, which I think is essential for students' understanding. The authors also include topics that I have not found in any other auditing textbook (e.g., an entire chapter on corporate governance, sections on upcoming changes or changes soon to be integrated into the profession). This textbook simply feels more up to date about current events in auditing.

How Can You Learn by Leveraging the Features of this Textbook?

Follow these ten steps:

1. Before you even begin, go online to MindTap via login.cengage.com and complete the first **Becker CPA Exam Pre-test**, which the authors have personally tailored to the chapters and learning objectives in this textbook. There is a 25-question Pre-test relating to Chapters 1–8, and another 25-question Pre-test relating to Chapters 9–15. In addition, these same tests are available online as **Becker CPA Exam Post-tests**, so that you can track your knowledge progress both within this course, as well as relating to the upcoming CPA exam.

2. For each chapter, start by viewing the **Audit Opinion Formulation Process** diagram at the outset of the chapter. Relevant chapter topics are highlighted for your reference so that you can track your progress through learning about all of the phases of conducting a quality audit.

3. Take a few minutes to read the **What's Covered** feature in the chapter, which briefly describes the main themes of the chapter. Then, review the **Learning Objectives**. Just as you begin to read the chapter, quickly read the **What You Will Learn** questions. Engaging in these simple and quick actions will help you know what to expect out of each chapter, which research shows will help you organize your knowledge and recall it later (during exams!).

4. To help set the practical application for each chapter, read the **Why It Matters** feature at the outset of each chapter. This feature will help you see beyond the factual insights provided in the chapters. Elements include for example, extensions based on in-the-news examples that illustrate fundamental features and applications of text facts, professional standards in foreign jurisdictions, and interesting points that may be tangential to the text facts, but that should facilitate your deep engagement with the chapter. In addition, we highlight some of these features as relating to an **International Focus**.

Continued

5. The 15 chapters are split into a variety of clearly articulated learning objectives, each containing its own important insights. Within these objectives, you will encounter the following helpful learning take-aways that we intend to engage your critical thinking about the conceptual contents of each chapter:

   "Prompt for Critical Thinking—It's Your Turn!" feature. This feature encourages you to engage in critical thinking as you acquire knowledge relevant to each chapter. This feature is intentionally creative in form and substance, and varies widely in structure based upon the learning objective to which it is related. We also provide potential answers to these prompts at the end of the chapter so that you can compare your thoughts about these prompts to those that the authors provide.

   "What Do You Think?—For Classroom Discussion" feature. This feature provides an avenue by which you can expect that the will use to facilitate preparation for class, encourage cognitive engagement, and facilitate critical thinking through discussions with other students. You have the opportunity to learn by preparing for these discussions, and engaging with the instructor and your classmates.

   Your employers and their clients will take as a given that you are proficient in your technical knowledge; what will set you apart from other young professionals is to express clearly articulated perspectives on the matters at hand; use these features as practice in rising to this challenge!

6. At the conclusion of each learning objective, complete the ***Check Your Basic Knowledge*** feature, which contains two true-false questions and two multiple-choice questions. Your instructor will provide you with answers to these questions, so you can compare your existing knowledge with the correct facts as you expand your understanding of textbook materials.

7. Fraud prevention and detection is one of the most important roles that auditors play in providing assurance with respect to financial reporting. Carefully read and be prepared to discuss in class the examples of auditors' roles in this regard in the ***Focus on Fraud*** feature.

8. Attend to the Exhibits and Figures! These lists and diagrams will be very helpful to you as you organize your knowledge in preparation for both the exams in this class, as well as the CPA exam.

9. Examine the ***Let's Review*** feature at the end of each chapter to ensure that you have a solid understanding of the basic concepts of the chapter. Review the ***Significant Terms*** list and use it as a way to review your understanding of the material that you have read about within the chapter. As you do this review, develop a set of questions for any topics whereby you lack understanding. Impress your instructor by drafting some formative questions whereby you can challenge the in-class lecture on these topics.

10. Complete the ***End-of-Chapter Review Questions, Cases, and Application Activities*** that your instructor requires, and view them not as a burden, but rather as an opportunity for you to thoughtfully engage these topics. Doing so will enable you to properly categorize these ideas for later retrieval and use, both in the CPA exam and in your professional job.

1 Quality Auditing: Why It Matters

The Audit Opinion Formulation Process

I. Making Client Acceptance and Continuance Decisions
Chapter 1

II. Performing Risk Assessment
Chapters 2, 3, 7, and 9–13

III. Obtaining Evidence About Internal Control Operating Effectiveness
Chapters 8–13

IV. Obtaining Substantive Evidence About Accounts, Disclosures, and Assertions
Chapters 8–13

V. Completing the Audit and Making Reporting Decisions
Chapters 14 and 15

Quality Auditing and the Need for Quality Auditor Judgments and Ethical Decisions
Chapter 1

Professional Liability
Chapter 4

The Audit Opinion Formulation Process and a Framework for Obtaining Audit Evidence
Chapters 5 and 6

Decision makers need reliable information to make many types of decisions, including investing and lending decisions. If these decision makers receive unreliable information, they may lose confidence in the information, make poor decisions, and lose money. External auditors help enhance the reliability of the information used by these decision makers by performing a quality financial statement audit.

Learning Objectives

LO 1 Describe decision makers' needs for reliable financial and internal control information, and discuss how a financial statement audit helps meet those needs.

LO 2 Define audit quality and list drivers of audit quality provided in the Financial Reporting Council's *Audit Quality Framework*.

LO 3 Identify professional conduct requirements that help auditors achieve audit quality.

LO 4 Describe and apply frameworks for professional and ethical decision making.

LO 5 Describe factors considered by audit firms making client acceptance and continuance decisions.

The Importance of Conducting a Quality Audit and Complying with Professional Requirements

Why It Matters: An International Perspective

This feature highlights that audit quality is an international issue.

In March 2017, the Public Company Accounting Oversight Board (PCAOB) announced sanctions against a former partner of PricewaterhouseCoopers Auditores Independentes in Brazil for audit failures and violations of PCAOB rules and standards.

Wander Rodrigues Teles was the lead partner for PwC-Brazil's audit work in connection with the audits of Sara Lee's FYE 2007 through FYE 2011 consolidated financial statements. U.S.-based PricewaterhouseCoopers LLP ("PwC-US") prepared and issued the audit reports on Sara Lee's consolidated financial statements, which were filed with the U.S. Securities and Exchange Commission. In 2012, Sara Lee restated its 2010 and 2011 financial results, citing accounting irregularities in its Brazil operations, including the overstatement of accounts receivable.

The PCAOB found that Teles failed to adequately respond to indications that one of Sara Lee's subsidiaries may have overstated its accounts receivable. When conducting the audit, Teles knew that a material amount of the subsidiary's accounts receivable was overdue and disputed by customers. He was also aware that the subsidiary was extending the due dates of overdue receivables. The re-aging of receivables in this manner could cause overdue receivables to appear current. The PCAOB found that Teles failed to adequately respond to these risks with **due professional care** and **professional skepticism**, and failed to obtain sufficient evidence to support his audit conclusions.

In the settled disciplinary order, Teles was censured, fined $10,000, and barred for two years from associating with a registered public accounting firm.

In discussing this case, PCAOB Chairman James R. Doty noted, "Audit quality is a global issue. As this order demonstrates, the Board is committed to investigating and disciplining auditors who present risks to investors in the U.S. markets, regardless of where the audit is conducted."

For further details, see PCAOB Release No. 105-2017-007.

What You Will Learn

- What is a financial statement audit, and how does it provide financial statement users with enhanced information reliability? (LO 1)

- What skills and knowledge do auditors need? (LO 1)

- What is audit quality, and why is it vital to perform an audit in a quality manner? (LO 2)

- What professional conduct requirements aid auditors in conducting a quality audit? (LO 3)

- What frameworks can auditors use to make professional and ethical decisions? (LO 4)

- Why are client acceptance and continuance decisions important to audit quality? (LO 5)

LO 1

Describe decision makers' needs for reliable financial and internal control information, and discuss how a financial statement audit helps meet those needs.

An Overview of External Auditing

Decision Makers' Need for Reliable Information and the Role of a Financial Statement Audit

External auditors perform an important task. While managers within organizations produce financial statements and design internal control systems, external auditors performing a **financial statement audit** provide independent assurance on the reliability of the financial statements and, as part of an **integrated audit**, provide independent assurance on internal control effectiveness.

Decision makers need information that is transparent and unbiased—information that does not favor one user over another. However, the interests of the various users can conflict. Current shareholders might want management to use accounting principles that result in higher levels of reported income, while lending institutions might prefer management to use a conservative approach to valuation and income recognition. *Exhibit 1.1* identifies potential financial statement users and the decisions they make based on financial and internal control information.

Why do financial statement users need independent assurance on reliability of information provided by management? Shouldn't users expect management

Exhibit 1.1
Users of Audited Financial Statements

User	Types of Decisions
Management	Review performance, make operational decisions, and report results to capital markets
Stockholders	Buy or sell stock
Bondholders	Buy or sell bonds
Financial institutions	Evaluate loan decisions, considering interest rates, terms, and risk
Taxing authorities	Determine taxable income and tax due
Regulatory agencies	Develop regulations and monitor compliance
Labor unions	Make collective bargaining decisions
Court system	Assess the financial position of a company in litigation
Vendors	Assess credit risk
Retired employees	Protect employees from surprises concerning pensions and other post-retirement benefits

to provide reliable information? The need for independent assurance arises from several factors:

- *Potential bias*—Management might have incentives to bias financial information to convey a better impression of the financial data than circumstances would merit. For example, when management's compensation is tied to profitability or stock price, managers may be tempted to "bend" generally accepted accounting principles (GAAP) to make the organization's performance look better.
- *Remoteness*—An organization and the users of its financial information are often remote from each other, both in terms of geographic distance and the extent of information available to the both parties. Most users cannot interview management, tour a company's plant, or review its financial records; instead, they must rely on financial statements to communicate the results of management's performance. These factors can tempt management to keep information from users or bend GAAP so the organization looks better.
- *Complexity*—Transactions, information, and processing systems are often very complex, so it can be difficult to determine their proper presentation. This factor provides an opportunity for management to mislead users.
- *Consequences*—When financial information is not reliable, investors and other users lose a significant source of information that they need to make decisions that have important consequences. Without reliable financial information, users may invest in securities or may lend money to a company that is committing a fraud, and once the fraud is revealed users are in a position of losing significant amounts of money.

Financial statement audits help increase the confidence that users can place on management-prepared information. Users of audited information need to have confidence in the objectivity and accuracy of the opinions provided by external auditors. Thus, external auditors need to be independent when performing a financial statement audit. Independence, often referred to as the *cornerstone* of the auditing profession, requires objectivity and freedom from bias. Without independence, audits lack value.

Auditors must not only be independent *in fact*, but they must act in a manner that ensures that they are independent *in appearance*. For example, if an audit partner's uncle was the CEO at the partner's client company, users could reasonably worry about a conflict of interest. It is entirely possible that the audit partner has, in fact, an independent mental attitude. However, the audit partner would not appear to be independent in this scenario. Further complicating

Auditors Must Be Mindful of their Role as Guardians of the Capital Markets

Why It Matters

This feature makes the point an auditor should make decisions in the public interest rather than in the interest of management.

Auditors are hired by their clients, so in some sense they owe an allegiance to clients' interests. However, the most critical role that auditors play is providing independent assurance to investors, lenders, workers, and others who make decisions based on the client's financial and internal control information. Auditors, therefore, need the highest level of technical competence, freedom from bias, and concern for the integrity of the financial reporting process.

Why It Matters

Does Owning Stock in an Audit Client Affect Auditor Independence?

This feature provides an interesting example of an audit senior violating auditor independence rules.

In 2005, Susan Birkert was an audit senior working for KPMG on the audit engagement of Comtech Corporation. One of Susan's friends asked her whether she thought that Comtech stock was a good investment. She responded that, indeed, it was a good investment. At that point, her friend asked if she would like him to purchase Comtech stock on her behalf. She agreed and gave her friend $5,000 to make the purchase under his name rather than hers. She did so because she was aware that owning stock in one's audit client is not allowed because of independence concerns. If auditors own stock in their audit clients, they are not independent of their clients because they are part owners. Therefore, rather than acting in an unbiased manner during the conduct of the audit, they might make judgments that favor the client company rather than external users of the financial statements. Even if the auditor does not actually behave in a biased manner and is independent in fact, external users may *perceive* an independence conflict—the auditor would not be independent in appearance.

Susan continued working on the Comtech engagement well into 2006, and she lied when she responded to KPMG's yearly written requirements to comply with the firm's independence policies. Prompted by an anonymous tip later in 2006, KPMG launched an internal investigation into the matter and terminated her employment. The PCAOB barred her from serving as an external auditor for a period of at least one year.

For further details, see PCAOB Release No. 105-2007-003.

matters, management and the audit committee expect cost-effective audits. Auditors face many pressures—keeping fees low, making careful decisions regarding independence, and conducting a quality audit.

What Is a Financial Statement Audit?

A financial statement audit is a

> systematic process of objectively obtaining and evaluating evidence regarding assertions about economic actions and events to ascertain the degree of correspondence between those assertions and established criteria; and communicating the results to interested users.[1]

The overall objective of an audit is to obtain reasonable assurance about whether the financial statements are free from material misstatement and to report on the financial statements based on the auditor's findings. To accomplish these objectives, the auditor:

- Complies with relevant ethical and professional conduct requirements
- Conducts the audit in accordance with professional auditing standards
- Exercises professional judgment, professional skepticism, and critical thinking
- Obtains sufficient appropriate evidence, via a structured process, on which to base the auditor's opinion

We refer to the structured process used by auditors to accomplish their objectives as the *audit opinion formulation process. Exhibit 1.2* presents that process.

Phase I addresses client acceptance and continuance decisions. Auditors are not required to perform audits for any organization that asks; *auditors* choose whether to perform each individual audit. Audit firms have procedures to help them ensure that they are not associated with clients where management integrity is in question or where a company might otherwise present the audit firm with unnecessarily high risk (such as client financial failure or regulatory action against the client).

Exhibit 1.2
The Audit Opinion Formulation Process

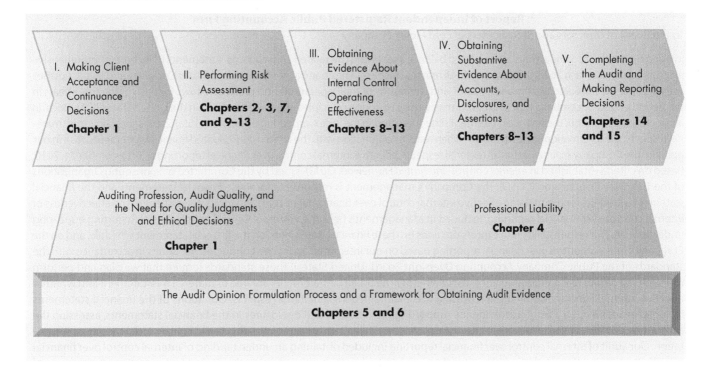

Next, in Phase II the auditor performs risk assessment procedures to thoroughly understand the client's business (or update prior knowledge in the case of a continuing client), its industry, its competition, and its management and governance processes (including internal controls) to determine the likelihood that financial accounts might be in error. These assessments also include the risk of fraud. In some audits, the auditor also obtains evidence about internal control operating effectiveness through testing those controls (Phase III).

In Phase IV, the auditor obtains substantive evidence about accounts, disclosures, and assertions. The information gathered in Phases I through III greatly influences the amount of testing performed in Phase IV. Finally, in Phase V the auditor will complete the audit and make a decision about what type of audit report to issue.

Exhibit 1.2 notes that the five phases occur in an environment where auditors conducting a quality audit need to make quality judgments and ethical decisions, and are subject to legal liability. The foundation for the audit opinion formulation process relies on obtaining audit evidence to support the audit opinion.

When the auditor has no objections about management's financial statements or internal controls, the auditor issues an **unqualified audit report**. *Exhibit 1.3* provides an example of this type of report. *Exhibit 1.3* indicates that the audit firm, PricewaterhouseCoopers, has provided two opinions. One opinion states that the audit firm has confidence that the financial statements of Ford are fairly stated. The other opinion states that PricewaterhouseCoopers has confidence that Ford's internal control over financial reporting was effective as of Ford's year-end, December 31, 2016.

PricewaterhouseCoopers provided these opinions after going through a systematic process of objectively obtaining and evaluating sufficient appropriate

Report of Independent Registered Public Accounting Firm

To the Board of Directors and Stockholders of Ford Motor Company

In our opinion, the accompanying consolidated balance sheets and the related consolidated statements of income, comprehensive income, equity and cash flows present fairly, in all material respects, the financial position of Ford Motor Company and its subsidiaries at December 31, 2016 and December 31, 2015, and the results of their operations and their cash flows for each of the three years in the period ended December 31, 2016 in conformity with accounting principles generally accepted in the United States of America. In addition, in our opinion, the financial statement schedule listed in the index appearing under Item 15(a)(2) presents fairly, in all material respects, the information set forth therein when read in conjunction with the related consolidated financial statements. Also in our opinion, the Company maintained, in all material respects, effective internal control over financial reporting as of December 31, 2016, based on criteria established in *Internal Control - Integrated Framework (2013)* issued by the Committee of Sponsoring Organizations of the Treadway Commission (COSO). The Company's management is responsible for these financial statements and the financial statement schedule, for maintaining effective internal control over financial reporting and for its assessment of the effectiveness of internal control over financial reporting, included in Management's Report on Internal Control over Financial Reporting appearing under Item 9A. Our responsibility is to express opinions on these financial statements, on the financial statement schedule, and on the Company's internal control over financial reporting based on our integrated audits. We conducted our audits in accordance with the standards of the Public Company Accounting Oversight Board (United States). Those standards require that we plan and perform the audits to obtain reasonable assurance about whether the financial statements are free of material misstatement and whether effective internal control over financial reporting was maintained in all material respects. Our audits of the financial statements included examining, on a test basis, evidence supporting the amounts and disclosures in the financial statements, assessing the accounting principles used and significant estimates made by management, and evaluating the overall financial statement presentation. Our audit of internal control over financial reporting included obtaining an understanding of internal control over financial reporting, assessing the risk that a material weakness exists, and testing and evaluating the design and operating effectiveness of internal control based on the assessed risk. Our audits also included performing such other procedures as we considered necessary in the circumstances. We believe that our audits provide a reasonable basis for our opinions.

A company's internal control over financial reporting is a process designed to provide reasonable assurance regarding the reliability of financial reporting and the preparation of financial statements for external purposes in accordance with generally accepted accounting principles. A company's internal control over financial reporting includes those policies and procedures that (i) pertain to the maintenance of records that, in reasonable detail, accurately and fairly reflect the transactions and dispositions of the assets of the company; (ii) provide reasonable assurance that transactions are recorded as necessary to permit preparation of financial statements in accordance with generally accepted accounting principles, and that receipts and expenditures of the company are being made only in accordance with authorizations of management and directors of the company; and (iii) provide reasonable assurance regarding prevention or timely detection of unauthorized acquisition, use, or disposition of the company's assets that could have a material effect on the financial statements.

Because of its inherent limitations, internal control over financial reporting may not prevent or detect misstatements. Also, projections of any evaluation of effectiveness to future periods are subject to the risk that controls may become inadequate because of changes in conditions, or that the degree of compliance with the policies or procedures may deteriorate.

/s/ PricewaterhouseCoopers LLP

PricewaterhouseCoopers LLP
Detroit, Michigan
February 9, 2017

Source: *http://shareholder.ford.com/~/media/Files/F/Ford-IR/annual-report/2016-annual-report.pdf.*

NOTE: The format of this report for public companies will be different effective for fiscal years ending on or after December 15, 2017. We discuss the new report formats in Chapter 15.

evidence. If the auditor had objections about the fair presentation of the financial statements, the audit report would be modified to explain the nature of the auditor's objections (for further details, see *Chapter 15*). If the auditor had reservations about the effectiveness of the client's internal controls, the auditor would issue an **adverse opinion** on internal controls.

Parties Involved in Preparing and Auditing Financial Statements

Various parties are involved in preparing and auditing financial statements and related disclosures; *Exhibit 1.4* describes these parties and their roles. Management has responsibilities for: (a) preparing and presenting financial statements in accordance with the applicable financial reporting framework; (b) designing, implementing, and maintaining internal control over financial reporting; and (c) providing auditors with information relevant to the financial statements and internal controls.

The internal audit function provides management and the audit committee with assurance on internal controls and reports. The audit committee, a subcommittee of the organization's board of directors, oversees both management and the internal auditors; they also hire and oversee the external auditor.

The external auditor's job is to obtain reasonable assurance about whether management's statements are materially accurate and to provide a publicly available report. External auditors conduct their procedures and make judgments in accordance with professional standards (for further details, see *Chapter 5*). Those who have an interest in the organization will use the audited financial statements for various purposes.

Providers of External Auditing Services

The external auditing profession includes sole-practitioner firms, local and regional firms, and large multinational professional services firms such as the Big 4. The Big 4 firms are KPMG, Deloitte Touche Tohmatsu (Deloitte in the United States), PricewaterhouseCoopers (PwC), and EY. The organizational structure of these firms is quite complex. For example, each of the Big 4 firms is a network of member firms. Each of the member firms enters into agreements to share a common name, brand, and quality standards. In most cases, member firms organize as a partnership or limited liability corporation within each country.

Some smaller firms also practice internationally through an affiliation with a network of firms. For example, a number of regional or local firms belong to an

Exhibit 1.4
Parties Involved in Preparing and Auditing Financial Statements

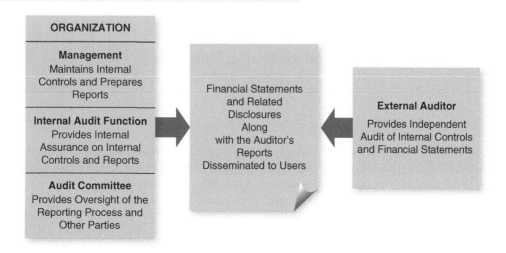

affiliation of such firms under the name of Moore Stephens, and another group operates under the name of Baker Tilly.

Many public accounting firms have also organized their practices along industry lines. Common industry lines include financial services, retailing, not-for-profit, manufacturing, and government.

The organizational hierarchy of audit firms is structured with partners (or owners) at the top level; these individuals are responsible for the overall conduct of each audit. Next in the hierarchy are managers, who review the audit work performed by seniors and staff personnel. Seniors are responsible for overseeing the day-to-day activities on a specific audit, and they oversee staff auditors and interns who perform many of the basic auditing procedures. Partners and managers are simultaneously responsible for many audit engagements, whereas seniors and staff are usually assigned to fewer audits at one time.

Skills and Knowledge Needed by External Auditors

The requirements for external auditors are demanding. Auditors complete tasks requiring considerable technical knowledge and expertise; auditors must understand accounting and auditing authoritative literature, develop industry and client-specific knowledge, develop and apply computer skills, evaluate internal controls, and assess and respond to fraud risk.

In addition to having appropriate technical knowledge, auditors need well-developed skills in leadership, teamwork, communication, decision-making, **critical thinking**, and general professionalism.

In terms of general professionalism, auditors make presentations to management and audit committee members, exercise logical reasoning, communicate decisions to users, manage and supervise others by providing meaningful feedback, act with integrity and ethics, interact in a team environment, collaborate with others, and maintain a professional presence.

A credential that auditors use to let the public know that they have the appropriate knowledge and skills to conduct an audit is the CPA license. A **CPA** is a certified public accountant who is licensed by a state board of accountancy. A CPA license is the profession's highest standard of competence, a symbol of achievement and assurance of quality. A CPA license holds its owner to a high standard of ethical conduct, no matter where the individual is in his or her career. To earn a CPA license, you are required to demonstrate knowledge and competence by meeting high educational standards, passing the CPA exam, and completing a specific amount of general accounting experience.

Why It Matters   The Need for Critical Thinking

This feature emphasizes the need for auditors to be critical thinkers throughout the audit opinion formulation process.

Critical thinking is a rational response to questions that cannot be answered definitively and for which all the relevant information may not be available. Critical thinking is an investigation whose purpose is to: (1) analyze a problem, (2) arrive at a conclusion that integrates all available information, and (3) justify that conclusion convincingly to others.

Auditors make many decisions throughout the audit that require critical thinking. These decisions including assessing the risk associated with a client, determining the appropriate audit procedures to perform, evaluating the sufficiency of evidence collected, and resolving detected misstatements in the client's financial statements.

Check Your Basic Knowledge

1-1 When the auditor has no reservations about management's financial statements or internal controls, the auditor will issue an unqualified audit opinion.   (T/F)

1-2 The sole responsibility of management with regard to financial reporting involves preparing and presenting financial statements in accordance with the applicable financial reporting framework.   (T/F)

1-3 Which of the following are the responsibilities of the external auditor in auditing financial statements?
a. Maintaining internal controls and preparing financial reports.
b. Providing internal assurance on internal control and financial reports.
c. Providing internal oversight of the reporting process.
d. Providing independent assurance on the financial statements.

1-4 Which of the following factors does not create a demand for external audit services?
a. Potential bias by management in providing information.
b. Requirements of the state boards of accountancy.
c. Complexity of the accounting processing systems.
d. Remoteness between a user and the organization.

For Classroom Discussion

What Do You Think?

External auditing is a "special function" as described by Chief Justice Warren Burger in a 1984 Supreme Court decision:

> By certifying the public reports that collectively depict a corporation's financial status, the independent auditor assumes a public responsibility transcending any employment relationship with the client. The independent public accountant performing this special function owes ultimate allegiance to the corporation's creditors and stockholders, as well as to the investing public. This "public watchdog" function demands … complete fidelity to the public trust.[2]

Auditors serve a number of parties. Which party is the most important? Do you agree with Chief Justice Burger's characterization of the auditor as a public watchdog?

LO 2

Define audit quality and list drivers of audit quality provided in the Financial Reporting Council's *Audit Quality Framework*.

Achieving Audit Quality

Financial statement users expect a quality audit. What is a **quality audit**? One definition describes a quality audit as one performed "in accordance with **generally accepted auditing standards** (GAAS) to provide reasonable assurance that the audited financial statements and related disclosures are (1) presented in accordance with GAAP and (2) are not materially misstated whether due to errors or fraud."[3]

The Financial Reporting Council's *Audit Quality Framework* identifies five primary drivers of audit quality, including (1) audit firm culture, (2) the skills and personal qualities of audit partners and staff, (3) the effectiveness of the audit process, (4) the reliability and usefulness of audit reporting, and (5) factors outside the control of auditors that affect audit quality. *Exhibit 1.5* contains an overview of the FRC's *Audit Quality Framework* that recognizes effective audit processes, by themselves, are not sufficient to achieve audit quality. Rather, a combination of five factors influences audit quality.

Who Are They?   FRC

The Financial Reporting Council (*https://www.frc.org.uk/*) is the United Kingdom's independent regulator responsible for promoting investment in securities through good corporate governance and financial reporting. The FRC sets standards for corporate reporting and audit practice. It monitors and enforces accounting and auditing standards.

Audit Firm Culture

Audit firm culture contributes positively to audit quality when the leadership of the audit firm:

- Creates a work culture where audit quality is valued and rewarded
- Emphasizes that "doing the right thing" is appropriate from a public interest perspective, and that doing the right thing helps develop and maintain both individual and audit firm reputation
- Ensures that audit firm employees have enough time and resources to address difficult issues that may arise
- Ensures that monetary considerations do not adversely affect audit quality
- Promotes the benefits of having audit partners seek guidance on difficult issues and supporting their professional judgment
- Ensures that the audit firm has quality systems in place for making client acceptance and continuation decisions
- Fosters evaluation and compensation practices that promote personal characteristics important to quality auditing
- Ensures that audit quality is monitored within the audit firm and that appropriate consequences are taken when audit quality is found to be lacking

Exhibit 1.5
Drivers of Audit Quality

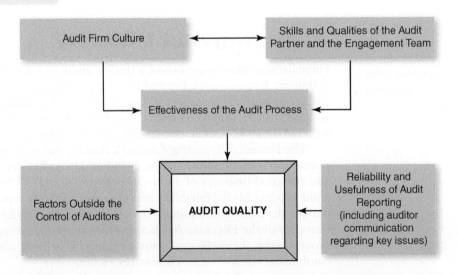

This feature highlights a recent disclosure requirement for auditing firms.

The skills and qualities of the engagement team are important to audit quality. Beginning in 2017, the PCAOB requires disclosure of the names of engagement partners for all public company audits. Further, many audit engagements are conducted with the assistance of other audit firms. Information about other audit firms participating in an audit must also be disclosed for all public company audits. These disclosures appear in PCAOB Form AP.

These disclosures recognize that one important way investors can assess the quality of an audit is to know who conducted that audit. If you are interested in learning the engagement partners and audit firms participating in an audit, you can find a searchable public database with this information at *https://pcaobus .org/Pages/AuditorSearch.aspx*

Skills and Qualities of the Engagement Team

Auditors positively contribute to audit quality when they:

- Understand the client's business and adhere to auditing and ethical standards
- Exhibit professional skepticism and address issues identified during the audit
- Ensure that staff performing audit work have appropriate levels of experience and that they are properly supervised by their superiors
- Ensure that partners and managers provide lower-level staff with mentoring and on-the-job training opportunities
- Participate in training intended to aid in understanding audit, accounting, and industry specialist issues

Effectiveness of the Audit Process

The audit process contributes in a positive way to audit quality when:

- The audit methodology is well structured and:
  - Encourages partners and managers to work diligently in planning the audit
  - Provides a framework and the procedures to obtain sufficient appropriate audit evidence in an effective and efficient manner
  - Requires appropriate audit documentation
  - Provides for complying with auditing standards but does not inhibit professional judgment
  - Ensures that audit work is effectively reviewed
  - Includes audit quality-control procedures that are effective, understood, and applied
- Quality technical support is available when auditors encounter unfamiliar situations requiring assistance or guidance.
- Ethical standards are communicated and achieved, thereby aiding auditors' integrity, objectivity, and independence.
- Auditors' evidence collection is not constrained by financial pressures.

Reliability and Usefulness of Audit Reporting

Audit reporting contributes positively to audit quality when:

- Audit reports are written in a way that clearly and unambiguously conveys the auditor's opinion on the financial statements and addresses the needs of users of financial statements

- Auditors appropriately conclude as to the truth and fairness of the financial statements (e.g., in the United States, concluding that the financial statements are fairly presented in accordance with GAAP)
- The auditor communicates with the audit committee about:
  - Audit scope (in other words, what the auditor is engaged to accomplish)
  - Threats to auditor objectivity
  - Important risks identified and judgments that were made in reaching the audit opinion
  - Qualitative aspects of the client's accounting and reporting and possible ways of improving financial reporting

Factors Outside the Control of Auditors

The FRC recognizes that some factors affecting audit quality are outside of the direct control of the external auditor, such as client corporate governance. Good corporate governance includes audit committees that are robust in dealing with

What Do You Think?   For Classroom Discussion

The Financial Reporting Council's *Audit Quality Framework* is one of many frameworks of audit quality. The profession worldwide is committed to providing quality audits.

The Center for Audit Quality (CAQ) has published *Approach to Audit Quality Indicators*, which lays out perspectives regarding which indicators of audit quality may be most relevant and how and to whom they should be communicated. The indicators represent four thematic elements of audit quality: firm leadership and tone at the top; engagement team knowledge, experience, and workload; monitoring; and auditor reporting. You can find this publication at *http://www.thecaq.org/caq-approach-audit-quality-indicators*

The International Auditing and Assurance Standards Board (IAASB) has published *A Framework for Audit Quality: Key Elements* *that Create an Environment for Audit Quality*. This *Framework* describes the different input, process, and output factors relevant to audit quality at the engagement, firm, and national levels. Further, the *Framework* demonstrates the importance of various contextual factors, such as laws and regulations, the litigation environment, corporate governance, and the financial reporting framework to audit quality. You can find this publication at *https://www.ifac.org/publications-resources/framework-audit-quality-key-elements-create-environment-audit-quality*

Review these two frameworks. Compare and contrast them with the FRC's framework. Which framework do you think might be most helpful to an auditor who wants to conduct a quality audit?

Who Are They?   CAQ and IAASB

Center for Audit Quality

The Center for Audit Quality (CAQ, *http://www.thecaq.org/about-us*) is a public policy organization based in Washington, DC. The CAQ is dedicated to enhancing investor confidence and public trust in the global capital markets. The CAQ engages in many activities including providing thought leadership on proposed rules and standards, as well as webcasts, events, and tools for the profession and other members of the financial reporting supply chain. While conducting its own research, the CAQ works closely with the academic community to facilitate independent research relevant to the auditing profession.

International Auditing and Assurance Standards Board

The International Auditing and Assurance Standards Board (IAASB, *www.ifac.org/iaasb*) is a part of the International Federation of Accountants (IFAC), a global organization for the accounting profession. The IAASB sets International Standards on Auditing (ISAs) and facilitates the convergence of national and international auditing standards.

1-5 Audit quality is achieved when the audit is performed in accordance with GAAS and when it provides reasonable assurance that the financial statements have been presented in accordance with GAAP and are not materially misstated due to errors or fraud.   (T/F)

1-6 One of the key drivers of audit quality is the gross margin achieved by the audit firm and the ability of the engagement partner to maintain those margins over the duration of the audit engagement.   (T/F)

1-7 Audit quality involves which of the following?
   a. Performing an audit in accordance with GAAS to provide reasonable assurance that the audited financial statements and related disclosures are presented in accordance with GAAP and providing assurance that those financial statements are not materially misstated whether due to errors or fraud.
   b. Performing an audit in accordance with GAAP to provide reasonable assurance that the audited financial statements and related disclosures are presented in accordance with GAAS and providing assurance that

those financial statements are not materially misstated whether due to errors or fraud.
   c. Performing an audit in accordance with GAAS to provide absolute assurance that the audited financial statements and related disclosures are presented in accordance with GAAP and providing assurance that those financial statements are not materially misstated whether due to errors or fraud.
   d. Performing an audit in accordance with GAAS to provide reasonable assurance that the audited financial statements and related disclosures are presented in accordance with GAAP and providing assurance that those financial statements contain no misstatements due to errors or fraud.

1-8 Which of the following factors is <u>not</u> a driver of audit quality as discussed by the FRC?
   a. Audit firm culture.
   b. Skills and personal qualities of client management.
   c. Reliability and usefulness of audit reporting.
   d. Factors outside the control of auditors.

issues and a greater emphasis by the client on getting things right as opposed to getting done by a particular date (for further discussion, see *Chapter 2*).

LO 3

Identify professional conduct requirements that help auditors achieve audit quality.

Professional Conduct Requirements that Help Auditors Achieve Audit Quality

To achieve audit quality, auditors should adhere to relevant codes of professional conduct and related guidance on professional responsibilities. Organizations providing such guidance for U.S. auditors include the AICPA SEC, and PCAOB.

AICPA, SEC, and the PCAOB

American Institute of Certified Public Accountants

The **American Institute of Certified Public Accountants** (AICPA, *www.aicpa.org*) has long served as the primary governing organization of the public accounting profession. That role changed with the establishment of the PCAOB as the body for setting auditing standards for the audits of public companies. However, the AICPA

continues to develop standards for audits of nonpublic companies. The ACIPA is responsible for a peer review program in which registered firms are subject to periodic peer review of their nonpublic audits. The AICPA also provides continuing education programs, and through its Board of Examiners, prepares and administers the Uniform CPA Examination.

Securities and Exchange Commission

The **Securities and Exchange Commission** (SEC, *www.sec.gov*) was established by Congress in 1934 to regulate the capital market system. The SEC has oversight responsibilities for the PCAOB and for all public companies that are traded on U.S. stock exchanges. The SEC has the authority to establish GAAP for companies whose stock is publicly traded, although it has generally delegated this authority to the Financial Accounting Standards Board (FASB).

Actions by the SEC have important implications for public company auditors. For example, the SEC has a responsibility to prosecute public companies and their auditors for violating SEC laws, including fraudulent accounting. In recent years, the SEC has brought actions against companies and auditors including: (a) Dell for failing to disclose material information and for improper accounting related to the use of "cookie jar" reserves, (b) Lucent for inappropriate revenue recognition, (c) a former Deloitte & Touche partner for a lack of independence, (d) Ernst & Young for allowing premature revenue recognition and improper deferral of costs in its audits of Bally Total Fitness Holding Corporation, and (e) a former KPMG partner for insider trading.

Public Company Accounting Oversight Board

The **Public Company Accounting Oversight Board** (PCAOB, *www.pcaobus.org*) is a private sector, nonprofit organization that oversees auditors of public companies. The overall goal of the PCAOB is to protect the interests of investors and further the public interest in the preparation of informative, fair, and independent audit reports.

The PCAOB has four primary responsibilities related to auditors of public companies: (1) registering audit firms that audit public companies; (2) periodically inspecting registered audit firms; (3) establishing auditing and related standards for registered audit firms; and (4) investigating and disciplining registered audit firms for violations of relevant laws or professional standards. Firms that provide audits of U.S. public companies must register with the PCAOB.

The PCAOB is comprised of five board members. No more than two board members may be Certified Public Accountants (CPAs); this requirement helps ensure that members of the external auditing profession do not dominate the Board. This helps assure users of audited financial statements that the PCAOB is representing the broad interests of users, not just serving the preferences of the external auditing profession.

AICPA Requirements: Code of Professional Conduct

The AICPA has a code of professional conduct to aid auditors in conducting a quality audit. The *Code* applies to professional services performed by AICPA members. Compliance with the *Code* depends primarily on the voluntary cooperation of AICPA members and secondarily on public opinion, reinforcement by peers, and ultimately, on disciplinary proceedings. Disciplinary proceedings are initiated by complaints received by the AICPA's Professional Ethics Division. A disciplinary proceeding may result in the suspension or revocation of an auditor's CPA license by the state board of accountancy. Without that license, one is legally prohibited from issuing an audit report on financial statements. The state board may also require additional continuing education to retain or reinstate the CPA certificate.

The AICPA's *Code of Professional Conduct* consists of a set of **principles of professional conduct** which we summarize in *Exhibit 1.6*. These principles apply to all members of the AICPA.

The *Code* also includes a conceptual framework for members in public practice. This framework incorporates a "threats and safeguards" approach to help auditors analyze relationships and circumstances that the *Code* does not specifically address. *Exhibit 1.7* provides a flowchart of the steps in the conceptual framework.

Threats are circumstances that could result in an auditor lacking independence in fact or in appearance. Threats to independence include:

1. *Self-review threat*—occurs when the audit firm also provides nonaudit work for the client, such as preparing source documents used to generate the client's financial statements. Self-review threatens independence because it may appear that the auditor is reviewing his or her own work.
2. *Advocacy threat*—occurs when the auditor acts to promote the client's interests, such as representing the client in tax court. Advocacy threatens

Exhibit 1.6
AICPA Principles of Professional Conduct

Responsibilities In carrying out their responsibilities as professionals, members should exercise sensitive professional and moral judgments in all their activities.

Public interest Members should accept the obligation to act in a way that will serve the public interest, honor the public trust, and demonstrate commitment to professionalism.

Integrity To maintain and broaden public confidence, members should perform all professional responsibilities with the highest sense of integrity.

Objectivity and independence A member should maintain objectivity and be free of conflicts in discharging professional responsibilities. A member in public practice should be independent both in fact and in appearance when providing auditing and other attestation services. A member not in public practice does not need to maintain independence.

Due care A member should observe the profession's technical and ethical standards, strive continually to improve competence and the quality of services, and discharge professional responsibility to the best of the member's ability.

Scope and nature of services A member in public practice should observe the principles of the *Code* in determining the scope and nature of services to be provided.

Source: *http://www.aicpa.org/Research/Standards/CodeofConduct/DownloadableDocuments/2014December15ContentAsof2016August31 CodeofConduct.pdf*

Exhibit 1.7
Steps of the Conceptual Framework

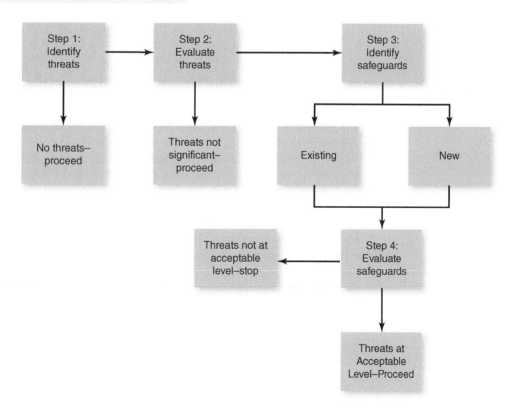

Source: *www.aicpa.org/InterestAreas/ProfessionalEthics/Resources/DownloadableDocuments/ToolkitsandAids/ConceptualFramework ToolkitForMembersInPublicPractice.docm*

independence because it may appear that the auditor cares more about the client than external users of the financial statements.

3. *Adverse interest threat*—occurs when the auditor and the client are in opposition to each other, such as when either party has initiated litigation against the other. Adverse interest threatens independence because the auditor may take actions that are intended to weaken the client's chances in the litigation and may appear to care more about the audit firm and its interests rather than those of the company or external users of the financial statements.

4. *Familiarity threat*—occurs when the auditor has some long-standing relationship with an important person associated with the client. Examples include:
   - The audit partner's close relative is employed in a key position at the client.
   - The audit partner has been assigned to the client for a long period of time and has developed very close personal relationships with top management.
   - A member of the audit team has a close personal friend who is employed in a key position at the client.
   - A member of the audit team was recently a director or officer at the client.

   In each of these examples, familiarity threatens independence because the auditor may act in a way that favors the client or individual employed at the client rather than external users of the financial statements.

5. *Undue influence threat*—occurs when client management attempts to coerce or provide excessive influence over the auditor. Examples include:
   - Top management threatens to replace the auditor or the audit firm because of a disagreement over an accounting issue.
   - Top management pressures the auditor to reduce the amount of work he or she does on the audit in order to achieve lower audit fees.
   - An employee of the client gives the auditor a gift that is clearly significant or economically important to the auditor.

   In each of these examples, undue influence threatens independence because the auditor may act in a way that favors the client or individual employed at the client rather than external users of the financial statements.

6. *Self-interest threat*—occurs when the auditor has a direct financial relationship with the client, such as owning stock in the client company, owing money to the client company, or when the audit client makes up the vast majority of the audit firm's total revenue. Self-interest threatens independence because the auditor's judgment may be unduly influenced by their own financial interests rather than acting in the best interests of external users of the financial statements.

7. *Management participation threat*—occurs when the auditor takes on the role of management or completes functions that management should reasonably complete, such as establishing internal controls or hiring/firing client employees. Management participation threatens independence because the auditor is acting as management; therefore, the auditor would, in essence, be reviewing his or her own work.

Safeguards are actions or other measures that may eliminate a threat or reduce a threat to an **acceptable level**. These safeguards include:

1. *Safeguards created by the profession, legislation, or regulation.* Examples include:
   - Education, continuing education, and training requirements
   - Professional standards and disciplinary punishments

- External review of audit firms' quality-control systems
- Legislation concerning independence requirements
- Audit partner rotation requirements for publicly traded companies, which include mandatory partner rotation after five years of service
- Nonaudit (e.g., consulting) work not allowed for companies for which the auditor provides external audit work

2. *Safeguards implemented by the audit client.* Examples include:
- Client personnel with expertise to adequately complete necessary management and accounting tasks without the involvement or advice of the auditor
- Appropriate tone at the top of the client
- Policies and procedures to ensure accurate financial reporting
- Policies and procedures to ensure appropriate relationships with the audit firm

3. *Safeguards implemented by the audit firm.* Examples include:
- Audit firm leadership that stresses the importance of independence
- Audit firm quality-control policies and procedures
- Audit firm monitoring processes to detect instances of possible independence violations
- Disciplinary mechanisms to promote compliance with independence policies and procedures
- Rotation of senior engagement personnel

The *Code* also consists of specific rules of conduct. The rules and related interpretations address many situations; however, they cannot address all relationships or circumstances that may arise. In the absence of a rule or interpretation addressing a particular relationship or circumstance, auditors evaluate whether that relationship or circumstance would lead a reasonable and informed third party who is aware of the relevant information to conclude that there is a threat to compliance with the rules that is not at an acceptable level. When making that evaluation, auditors should apply the conceptual framework approach discussed earlier and highlighted in *Exhibit 1.7*.

The evaluation includes identification of threats to compliance with the rules, evaluation of the significance of the threats, and identification and application to safeguards. When an auditor identifies threats, the auditor must demonstrate that safeguards were applied that eliminated or reduced significant threats to an acceptable level.

One of the critical rules is the Independence Rule, which we discuss below. We summarize rules applicable to members in public practice in *Exhibit 1.8*.

Independence Rule

The Independence Rule requires that a member in public practice be independent in the performance of professional services as required by standards promulgated by bodies designated by the AICPA.

Covered Member An important point concerning the Independence Rule is that it only applies to a **covered member**. A covered member includes:

a. An individual on the engagement team
b. An individual in a position to influence the engagement
c. A partner, partner equivalent, or manager who provides more than 10 hours of nonattest services to the audit client within any fiscal year
d. A partner or partner equivalent in the office in which the lead engagement partner or partner equivalent primarily practices in connection with the engagement

Exhibit 1.8

AICPA Rules of Conduct for Members in Public Practice

Rule Section Number and Topic	Guidance	What You Should Know
100 *Integrity and objectivity*	In the performance of any professional service, a member shall maintain objectivity and integrity, shall be free of conflicts of interest, and shall not knowingly misrepresent facts or subordinate his or her judgment to others.	You are required to act with integrity and objectivity when performing all services. If you offer a gift to a client or accept gifts or entertainment from a client that is not reasonable, *self-interest, familiarity, or undue influence threats* to your compliance with this rule may exist. A conflict of interest creates *adverse interest and self-interest threats* to your compliance with this rule. *Self-interest, familiarity, and undue influence threats* to your compliance with this rule may exist when you and your supervisor or any other person within your organization have a difference of opinion relating to the application of accounting principles; auditing standards; or other relevant professional standards, including standards applicable to tax and consulting services or applicable laws or regulations. An *advocacy threat* to compliance with this rule may exist when a you or your firm is engaged to perform nonattest services, such as tax and consulting services, that involve acting as an advocate for the *client* or to support a *client's* position on accounting or financial reporting issues.
200 *Independence*	A member in public practice shall be independent in the performance of professional services as required by standards promulgated by bodies designated by Council.	The existence of unpaid audit fees for professional services previously rendered to an audit client may create self-interest, undue influence, or advocacy threats to the covered member's compliance with this rule. In some circumstances, no safeguards can reduce an independence threat to an acceptable level. For example, as discussed earlier, the *Code* specifies that a covered member may not own even an immaterial direct financial interest in an audit client because there is no safeguard to reduce the *self-interest threat* to an acceptable level. As another example, threats to the covered member's compliance with this rule could not be reduced to an acceptable level by the application of safeguards if the unpaid fees are for any previously rendered professional service provided more than one year prior to the date of the current-year report. Accordingly, independence would be impaired.

300 General Standards	A member shall comply with the following standards and with any interpretations thereof by bodies designated by Council. *Professional Competence.* Undertake only those professional services that the member or the member's firm can reasonably expect to be completed with professional competence. *Due Professional Care.* Exercise due professional care in the performance of professional services. *Planning and Supervision.* Adequately plan and supervise the performance of professional services. *Sufficient Relevant Data.* Obtain sufficient relevant data to afford a reasonable basis for conclusions or recommendations in relation to any professional services performed.	This rule requires you to comply with general standards and interpretations by standards setters such as the FASB, the PCAOB, and the AICPA.
310 Compliance with Standards	A member who performs auditing, review, compilation, consulting, tax, or other professional services shall comply with standards promulgated by bodies designated by Council.	This rule requires you to comply with general standards and interpretations by standards setters such as the FASB, the PCAOB, and the AICPA.
320 Accounting Principles	A member shall not (1) express an opinion that the financial statements or other financial data of any entity are presented in conformity with generally accepted accounting principles or (2) state that he or she is not aware of any material modifications that should be made to such statements or data in order for them to be in conformity with generally accepted accounting principles, if such statements or data contain any departure from an accounting principle promulgated by bodies designated by Council to establish such principles that has a material effect on the statements or data taken as a whole. If, however, the statements or data contain such a departure and the member can demonstrate that due to unusual circumstances the financial statements or data would otherwise have been misleading, the member can comply with the rule by describing the departure, its approximate effects, if practicable, and the reasons why compliance with the principle would result in a misleading statement.	This rule requires you to comply with general standards and interpretations by standards setters such as the FASB, the PCAOB, and the AICPA.
400 Acts Discreditable	A member shall not commit an act discreditable to the profession.	Examples of discreditable acts include violation of an antidiscrimination law, failure to file a tax return, the preparation and presentation of false information in financial statements due to negligence, and failure to follow the accountancy laws, rules, and regulations on use of the CPA credential in any of the jurisdictions in which the CPA practices. As a student, you may be interested to learn that solicitation or knowing disclosure of CPA exam questions or answers is a discreditable act.

(Continues)

Exhibit 1.8 *Continued*

Rule Section Number and Topic	Guidance	What You Should Know
510 *Contingent Fees*	A member in public practice shall not: (1) perform for a contingent fee any professional services for, or receive such a fee from a client for whom the member or the member's firm also performs: (a) an audit or review of a financial statement, or (b) a compilation of a financial statement when the member expects, or reasonably might expect, that a third party will use the financial statement and the member's compilation report does not describe a lack of independence, or (c) an examination of prospective financial information, or (2) prepare an original or amended tax return or claim for a tax refund for a contingent fee for any client. This prohibition applies during the period in which the member or the member's firm is engaged to perform any of the services listed above and the period covered by any historical financial statements involved in any such listed services.	A contingent fee is a fee established for the performance of any service in which a fee will not be collected unless a specified finding or result is attained, or in which the amount of the fee depends on the finding or results of such services. An example of a contingent fee is a consulting firm agreeing to perform an information systems project for a fee of 50% of the defined cost savings attributable to the system for a period of three years. Contingent fees are prohibited from any client for whom the auditor performs audit services. However, an auditor's fees may vary, depending on the complexity of services rendered or the time taken to perform the services. Contingent fees have not been prohibited for services provided to nonaudit clients; however, the auditor must still be sure that the use of such fees does not impair the auditor's objectivity or ability to uphold the public trust.
520 *Commissions and Referral Fees*	Prohibited Commissions. A member in public practice shall not for a commission recommend or refer to a client any product or service, or for a commission recommend or refer any product or service to be supplied by a client, or receive a commission, when the member or the member's firm also performs (attestation services referred to in Rule 302) for the client. This prohibition applies to the period covered by the attestation service and the related historical financial statements. Disclosure of Permitted Commissions. A member in public practice who is not prohibited by this rule from performing services for or receiving a commission and who is paid or expects to be paid a commission shall disclose that fact to any person or entity to whom the member recommends or refers a product or service to which the commission relates. Referral Fees. Any member who accepts a referral fee for recommending or referring any service of a CPA to any person or entity or who pays a referral fee to obtain a client shall disclose such acceptance or payment to the client.	Many types of commissions are prohibited. For permitted commissions, appropriate disclosures must be made. Referral fees, which are distinct from commissions, are permitted, but must be disclosed.

600 Advertising and Other Forms of Solicitation	A member in public practice shall not seek to obtain clients by advertising or other forms of solicitation in a manner that is false, misleading, or deceptive. Solicitation by the use of coercion, over-reaching, or harassing conduct is prohibited.

This rule prohibits false, misleading, or deceptive advertising. Examples include:

- Creating false expectations about outcomes
- Suggesting the ability to influence relevant parties
- Providing representations that would cause one to be deceived

During the course of an audit, the auditor develops a complete understanding of the client and obtains confidential information, such as its operating strengths, weaknesses, and plans for financing or expanding into new markets. To assure a free flow and sharing of information between the client and the auditor, the client must be assured that the auditor will not communicate confidential information to outside parties.

700 Confidential Client Information	A member in public practice shall not disclose any confidential client information without the specific consent of the client.

The exceptions to this general rule are that auditors are not precluded from communicating information for any of the following purposes:

- To assure the adequacy of accounting disclosures required by GAAP
- To comply with a validly issued and enforceable subpoena or summons or to comply with applicable laws and government regulations
- To provide relevant information for an outside quality review of the firm's practice under PCAOB, AICPA, or state board of accountancy authorization
- To initiate a complaint with, or respond to an inquiry made by the AICPA's professional ethics division or by the trial board or investigative or disciplinary body of a state CPA society or board of accountancy

800 Form of Organization and Name	A member may practice public accounting only in a form of organization permitted by state law or regulation whose characteristics conform to resolutions of Council. A member shall not practice public accounting under a firm name that is misleading. Names of one or more past owners may be included in the firm name of a successor organization. A firm may not designate itself as "Members of the American Institute of Certified Public Accountants" unless all of its CPA owners are members of the Institute.

An audit firm name should not be misleading. If the firm name contains any representation that would be likely to cause a reasonable person to misunderstand, or be confused about, what the legal form of the firm is or who the owners or members of the firm are, the firm name would be misleading.

Firms within a network sometimes share the use of a common brand or share common initials as part of the firm name. The sharing of a common brand name or common initials of a network as part of the member's firm name would not be considered misleading, provided the firm is a network firm.

Source: http://www.aicpa.org/Research/Standards/CodeofConduct/DownloadableDocuments/2014December15ContentAsof2016August31CodeofConduct.pdf

e. The firm, including the firm's employee benefit plans
f. An entity whose operating, financial, or accounting policies can be controlled by any of the individuals or entities described in items a–e or two or more such individuals or entities if they act together

Financial Interests   Auditors and their immediate family should not have any direct or material indirect financial interest in that client. A **direct financial interest** is a financial interest owned directly by, or under the control of, an individual or entity or beneficially owned through an investment vehicle, estate, or trust when the beneficiary controls the intermediary or has the authority to supervise or participate in the intermediary's investment decisions. For example, a covered member may not own bonds of a client.

An **indirect financial interest** occurs when the beneficiary neither controls the intermediary nor has the authority to supervise or participate in the intermediary's investment decisions. The concept is that a covered member may have some limited financial interests in clients as long as the interests are not direct and not material (to either the member or the client). For example, suppose an auditor has an investment in a mutual fund that has an investment in an audit client. The auditor does not make the decisions to buy or sell the security held by the mutual fund. Ownership of mutual fund shares is a direct financial interest. The underlying investments of a mutual fund are indirect financial interests. If the mutual fund is diversified, a covered member's ownership of 5% or less of the outstanding shares of the mutual fund would not be considered to constitute a material indirect financial interest in the underlying investments. For purposes of determining materiality, the financial interests of the covered member and immediate family should be aggregated.

Independence would be considered impaired in the following situations involving financial interests:

- A covered member has a material joint, closely held investment with a client. For example, the member cannot own a vacation home or time share with a key office or principal shareholder of a client.
- A partner or professional employee of an audit firm owns more than 5% of client.
- One or more partners or professional employees have a relationship with a client as an officer, director, manager, employee, etc.

Employment of Family Members   A covered member's independence would be impaired if an immediate family member was employed by an audit client in a key position in which he or she can exercise influence over the contents of the financial statements. Key positions typically include the CEO, CFO, chief accountant, member of the board of directors, chief internal audit executive, or treasurer. Independence is impaired if a covered member has a close relative who has a key position with the client or has a material financial interest in the client of which the CPA has knowledge. An immediate family member may be employed by the client in a position that is not key to the organization.

Loans   There are limits on the types and amounts of loans covered members may obtain from a financial institution that is also an audit client. Essentially, auditors cannot obtain large loans, or loans for investment purposes, from a client. However, auditors may obtain loans through normal lending procedures if they are at standard terms, such as automobile loans.

Performing Other Nonaudit Services   Independence may be impaired if auditors provide certain *non*audit services to an audit client. In particular, independence is impaired when an auditor assumes management responsibilities for an audit client.

The AICPA's *Code* does not necessarily prohibit auditors from performing other services such as bookkeeping, payroll processing, consulting, tax preparation, or business risk advisory services for their private clients, but auditors must take care to assure that working too closely with the client does not compromise the appearance of independence. If, for example, the auditor does bookkeeping, prepares tax returns, and performs management consulting services, the appearance of independence has disappeared, even if independence, in fact, remains. A fundamental premise in these standards is that management must not concede decision-making authority to the accountant or auditor. For example, it is acceptable for the auditor of a nonpublic company to design, install, or integrate a client's information system, provided the client makes all management decisions. It is not acceptable to supervise client personnel in the daily operation of a client's information system.

Network Firms   To enhance their capabilities to provide professional services, firms frequently join larger groups, which typically are membership associations that are separate legal entities and otherwise unrelated to their members. The associations facilitate their members' use of association services and resources. An association would be considered a network if, in addition to cooperation among member firms and other entities to enhance their capabilities to provide professional services, member firms and other entities share one or more additional characteristics such as brand name, common business strategy, or common quality-control procedures. A **network firm** is required to comply with the Independence Rule with respect to the financial statement audit clients of the other network firms.

SEC and PCAOB: Other Guidance on Professional Responsibilities

The SEC and PCAOB have independence requirements that apply only to auditors of public companies. These two organizations have complementary independence requirements. The following summarizes the SEC's commitment to independence:

> The independence requirement serves two related, but distinct, public policy goals. One goal is to foster high-quality audits by minimizing the possibility that any external factors will influence an auditor's judgments. The auditor must approach each audit with professional skepticism and must have the capacity and the willingness to decide issues in an unbiased and objective manner, even when the auditor's decisions may be against the interests of management of the audit client or against the interests of the auditor's own accounting firm.
>
> The other related goal is to promote investor confidence in the financial statements of public companies. Investor confidence in the integrity of publicly available financial information is the cornerstone of our securities market. . . . Investors are more likely to invest, and pricing is more likely to be efficient, where there is greater assurance that the financial information disclosed by issuers is reliable . . . [that] assurance will flow from knowledge that the financial information has been subjected to rigorous examination by competent and objective auditors.[4]

The SEC has taken a principles-based approach in dealing with independence issues. All of the SEC statements on independence follow from four basic principles that define when an auditor is in a position that impairs independence. Those principles dictate that auditor independence is impaired when the auditor has a relationship that:

- Creates a mutual or conflicting interest between the accountant and the audit client
- Places the accountant in the position of auditing his or her own work
- Results in the accountant acting as management or an employee of the audit client
- Places the accountant in a position of being an advocate for the audit client[5]

Why It Matters

Audit Partner Rotation Required for Public Company Audits

This feature provides an interesting example of a violation of audit partner rotation requirements.

The PCAOB found that an audit firm (Jeffrey & Company) and the firm's sole owner and managing partner (Robert G. Jeffrey, CPA) violated the provisions of federal securities laws and PCAOB rules and auditing standards that require auditor independence. The firm and partner were not independent with respect to two public company clients because Jeffrey served as the lead audit partner for more than five consecutive years. In addition, the firm and Jeffrey were not independent as to a third client because Jeffrey served as the lead audit partner for that client within five years of previously serving for the maximum permitted period.

Disciplinary actions resulting from this case include Robert Jeffrey being barred from associating with a firm registered with the PCAOB and the firm having its PCAOB registration revoked.

For further details, see PCAOB Release No. 105-2014-005.

Auditors of public companies have additional requirements for professional conduct that extend beyond those of the AICPA, including preapproval of services, fee disclosures, audit partner rotation, and prohibited services.

Preapproval of Services

Audit committees should typically preapprove services performed by auditors, including all audit services and permissible nonaudit services. The audit committee cannot delegate this authority to management.

Fee Disclosures

Public companies must disclose the fees paid to its auditors. The disclosure is typically in a company's proxy statement or annual filing. The disclosure provides fees for four types of services: audit, audit-related, tax, and other.

Audit Partner Rotation

Lead and concurring audit partners on public clients must rotate every five years, and must have a five-year cooling off period. A **cooling off period** is the number of years after which the individual auditor may resume providing service to the audit client. During the cooling off period, the individual auditor may not engage in any meaningful audit-related interactions with the client. Other audit partners on the engagement are required to rotate every seven years, with a two-year cooling off period.

Prohibited Services

The types of nonaudit services that audit firms can provide to their public company audit clients are more restricted than those that can be provided to non-public companies. Prohibited nonaudit services for public company audit clients include:

- Bookkeeping or other services related to the accounting records or financial statements of the audit client
- Financial information systems design and implementation
- Appraisal or valuation services, fairness opinions, or contribution-in-kind reports
- Actuarial services
- Internal audit outsourcing services
- Management functions or human resources
- Broker or dealer, investment adviser, or investment banking services
- Legal services and expert services unrelated to the audit
- Any other service that the PCAOB determines, by regulation, is impermissible

International Professional Requirements That Help Auditors Achieve Audit Quality

Code of Ethics for Professional Conduct

The International Ethics Standards Board for Accountants (IESBA) (under the International Federation of Accountants) outlines fundamental principles that should guide auditors' ethical decision making. The IESBA *Code of Ethics for Professional Accountants* applies to all professional accountants, whether in public practice, in business, education, or the public sector. The IESBA *Code* serves as the foundation for codes of ethics developed and enforced by members of the International Federation of Accountants (IFAC). No member body of IFAC or audit firm issuing reports in accordance with standards of the International Auditing and Assurance Standards Board can apply less stringent standards than those stated in the IESBA *Code*. The *Code of Ethics for Professional Accountants* requires auditors to adhere to five fundamental principles[6]:

- *Integrity*—A professional accountant should be straightforward and honest in performing professional services.
- *Objectivity*—A professional accountant should not allow bias, conflict of interest, or undue influence of others to override professional or business judgments.
- *Professional Competence and Due Care*—A professional accountant has a continuing duty to maintain professional knowledge and skill at the level required to assure that a client or employer receives competent professional service based on current developments. A professional accountant should act diligently and in accordance with applicable technical and professional standards when providing professional services.
- *Confidentiality*—A professional accountant should respect the confidentiality of information acquired as a result of professional and business relationships and should not disclose any such information to third parties without proper and specific authority unless there is a legal or professional right or duty to disclose. Confidential information acquired as a result of professional and business relationships should not be used for the personal advantage of the professional accountant or of third parties.
- *Professional Behavior*—A professional accountant should comply with relevant laws and regulations and should avoid any action that discredits the profession.

In addition to these five principles, the *Code* contains specific standards addressing many of the same topics contained in the AICPA's *Code of Professional Conduct*.

IESBA and IFAC   *Who Are They?*

International Ethics Standards Board for Accountants

The International Ethics Standards Board for Accountants (IESBA, *https://www.ethicsboard.org/*) is an independent, standard-setting body that serves the public interest by setting robust, internationally appropriate ethics standards, including auditor independence requirements, for professional accountants worldwide.

International Federation of Accountants

The International Federation of Accountants (IFAC, *http://www.ifac.org/*) is the global organization for the accountancy profession dedicated to serving the public interest by strengthening the profession and contributing to the development of strong international economies. IFAC is comprised of over 175 members and associates in more than 130 countries and jurisdictions, representing almost 3 million accountants in public practice, education, government service, industry, and commerce.

Check Your Basic Knowledge

1-9 The AICPA's principles of professional conduct articulate auditors' responsibilities and their requirements to act in the public interest, to act with integrity and objectivity, to be objective and independent, to exercise due care, and to perform an appropriate scope of services. (T/F)

1-10 Per the AICPA's *Code*, independence would be impaired if his or her immediate family member were employed by the audit client in any capacity or personnel level. (T/F)

1-11 Which of the following is <u>not</u> a threat to auditor independence?
   a. Self-review threat.
   b. Advocacy threat.
   c. Adverse interest threat.
   d. Regulatory interest threat.

1-12 Which of the following statements is <u>false</u>?
   a. An auditor in public practice shall be independent in the performance of professional services.
   b. In performing audit services, the auditor shall maintain objectivity and integrity, be free of conflicts of interest, and not knowingly misrepresent facts or subordinate his or her judgment to others.
   c. In performing audit services, the auditor may accept only contingent fees for publicly traded audit clients.
   d. An auditor in public practice shall not seek to obtain clients by advertising or other forms of solicitation in a manner that is false, misleading, or deceptive.

What Do You Think?   For Classroom Discussion

In the U.S. there is a requirement for audit partner rotation, but no requirement for audit firm rotation. Requirements differ internationally. For example, European Union Countries have mandatory audit firm rotation.

Deloitte has been the audit firm used by Procter & Gamble since 1890. In fact, as of January 2017, 13 public companies have engaged the same auditor for at least a century. Should investors be concerned about the remarkable length of these relationships and the ability of an audit firm to be independent when conducting the audit? Does a relationship of this length improve or diminish audit quality? Should there be a requirement for mandatory firm rotation for audit firms of U.S. public companies?

LO 4

Describe and apply frameworks for professional and ethical decision making.

Frameworks for Professional and Ethical Decision Making

A Framework for Professional Decision Making

To achieve audit quality, auditors need to make quality decisions throughout the audit. Quality decisions are unbiased, meet the expectations of reasonable users, comply with professional standards, and incorporate sufficient appropriate evidence to justify the decisions made by the auditors. For example, auditors make decisions about the types of evidence to gather, how to evaluate that evidence, when to gather additional evidence, and what conclusions are appropriate given the evidence they have obtained. Ultimately, auditors have to decide whether the client's financial statements contain any material departures from generally accepted accounting principles that would affect the judgment of users of the financial statements.

Exhibit 1.9
A Framework
for Professional
Decision Making

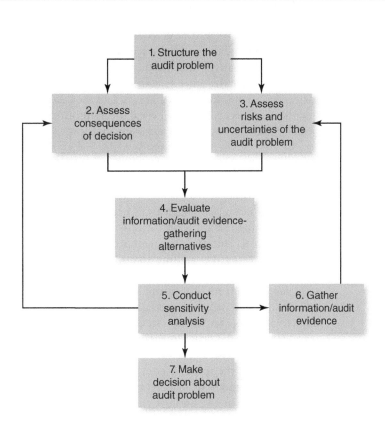

Source: Adapted from *Judgment and Choice* by Robin Hogarth.

This type of decision-making situation is common among professionals. Consider a doctor trying to diagnose the illness of a patient. The doctor must decide what tests to order, how to interpret the test results, and when to order additional tests (how many and what type), and must ultimately diagnose any potential illness in the patient. In order to make complex, difficult, and important decisions such as these, professionals can benefit from a structured approach to their decision making, as depicted in *Exhibit 1.9*.

In **Step 1**, the auditor structures the problem by considering the relevant parties to involve in the decision process, identifying various feasible alternatives, considering how to evaluate the alternatives, and identifying uncertainties or risks. To illustrate these tasks, consider a common decision that auditors face—determining whether a client's inventory values are fairly stated in accordance with generally accepted accounting principles. In terms of identifying relevant parties, auditors work within an organizational hierarchy with clearly defined roles about appropriate types of auditors that should participate in inventory testing (e.g., less experienced auditors may conduct inventory test counts, but industry experts may consider the valuation of complex inventory items). In addition, auditors consider which individuals at the client are most qualified to assess inventory values. Auditors also identify feasible alternatives about the inventory balance. For example, is it fairly stated, overstated, or understated? Consideration will also be given to the evidence necessary to determine accurate inventory valuation (such as observing the inventory, consulting outside prices of the inventory, and evaluating potential obsolescence). Auditors also have to evaluate the risk that the evidence they collect may not necessarily be diagnostic of the true, underlying value of the inventory. In other words, there is a risk that despite the work that they perform, their conclusions may be incorrect.

In **Step 2,** the auditor assesses the consequences of the potential alternatives. Considerations at this stage include determining the dimensions on which to evaluate the alternatives and how to weigh those dimensions. Continuing the preceding example, the auditor will have to consider the consequences of various inventory valuation alternatives and whether a particular valuation alternative is more or less appropriate than the other available alternatives. If the auditor decides that the inventory is properly valued, and that is in fact the case, then there are no negative consequences to the decision. However, if the auditor reaches an incorrect conclusion, then stakeholders may be misled, exposing auditors to litigation and reputation damage.

In **Step 3,** the auditor assesses the risks and uncertainties in the situation. Those risks and uncertainties are related to (a) the risks the audit client faces, (b) the quality of evidence the auditor gathers, and (c) the sufficiency of audit evidence gathered. In other words, there are risks related to a particular client, and there are risks in gathering sufficient audit evidence. All of these risks need to be assessed in determining the appropriate audit evidence to gather.

In **Step 4,** the auditor evaluates the various information/audit evidence-gathering alternatives against an appropriate decision rule. For auditors, decision rules are often articulated in terms of generally accepted accounting principles or generally accepted auditing standards. In our example, inventory valuation rules under generally accepted accounting principles may provide necessary guidance to assist in the decision-making process. Further, generally accepted auditing standards articulate rules regarding appropriate evidence-gathering strategies that must be followed when auditing inventory values.

In **Step 5,** the auditor considers the sensitivity of the conclusions reached in Steps 2, 3, and 4 to incorrect assumptions. It may be, given the results of the earlier steps, that the auditor can determine enough evidence has been gathered to support (or not support), at a convincing level of certainty, and that the audit problem being evaluated can be answered appropriately. Continuing the preceding example, it may be that the auditor's initial evidence gathering and risk analysis enable a definitive conclusion. In that case, the auditor can move on to **Step 7,** and make a final decision.

However, there may still be significant uncertainties to resolve. For example, in the case of inventory, there may be variation in available market values used to value the client's inventory. As such, the true inventory value may fall within a range, so the auditor will have to use **professional judgment** to determine a value that is most reflective of economic reality. In such a situation, the auditor will move to **Step 6** of the process.

In **Step 6,** the auditor gathers information and audit evidence in an iterative process that affects considerations about the consequences of potential alternatives and the uncertainties associated with those judgments. Importantly, the auditor considers the costs and benefits of information acquisition, knowing that gathering additional

Why It Matters   **What Is Professional Judgment?**

This feature emphasizes the importance of auditors using professional judgment throughout the audit opinion formulation process.

Professional judgment involves applying relevant professional knowledge and experience to unique and potentially uncertain facts and circumstances in order to reach a conclusion or make a decision. Thus, professional judgment begins with determining when the auditor has sufficient appropriate evidence to make a decision. Then, when an auditor makes quality professional judgments, he or she competently applies auditing and/or accounting principles and makes decisions that are appropriate given the evidence. Professional judgment is an important element to conducting a quality audit.

evidence requires time, effort, and money. Given that an audit firm is a for-profit enterprise, cost–benefit considerations in evidence gathering are particularly important. A good auditor knows "when to say when"—to stop collecting evidence at the right time. In contrast, some auditors stop evidence collection too soon, thereby yielding inadequate evidence on which to make a decision. Still others continue evidence collection even though the current evidence is sufficient and appropriate, thereby contributing to inefficiency and reduced profitability in the audit.

The auditor iterates through Steps 1 through 6 repeatedly until satisfied that a decision can prudently be made.

Finally, in **Step 7**, the auditor makes the difficult determination of whether the problem has been sufficiently analyzed and whether the risk of making an incorrect decision has been minimized to an acceptable level. Ultimately, the auditor makes and documents the decision reached.

Importance of Professional Skepticism in Making Professional Judgments

The auditor must exercise professional skepticism when completing the steps in *Exhibit 1.9*. Professional skepticism is an attitude that includes a questioning mind and a critical assessment of audit evidence. Without professional skepticism, auditors are susceptible to accepting weak or inaccurate audit evidence. By exercising professional skepticism, auditors are less likely to overlook unusual circumstances, to overgeneralize from limited audit evidence, or to use inappropriate assumptions in determining the nature, timing, and extent of audit procedures. An auditor who is professionally skeptical will:

- Critically question contradictory audit evidence
- Carefully evaluate the reliability of audit evidence, especially in situations in which fraud risk is high and/or only a single piece of evidence exists to support a material financial accounting transaction or amount
- Reasonably question the authenticity of documentation, while accepting that documents are to be considered genuine unless there is reason to believe the contrary
- Reasonably question the honesty and integrity of management, individuals charged with governance, and third-party providers of audit evidence

A difficulty auditors face when exercising professional skepticism is one inherent in being human—we trust others and accept information and assertions as truth. Further, if an auditor did not trust management, for example, that auditor would presumably cease to perform audit services for the client. These difficulties sometimes cause auditors to be less professionally skeptical than is appropriate. So how can audit firms and individual auditors be sure that they maintain and exercise appropriate professional skepticism? At the audit firm level, firm leaders must ensure that auditors receive training on how to be skeptical, and they must create firm policies and procedures to encourage skepticism. At the individual auditor level, the following tips can encourage a skeptical mindset:

- Be sure to collect sufficient evidence so that judgments are not made in haste or without adequate support.
- When evidence is contradictory, be particularly diligent in evaluating the reliability of the individuals or processes that provided that evidence.
- Generate independent ideas about reasons for unexpected trends or financial ratios rather than simply relying on management's explanations.
- Question trends or outcomes that appear "too good to be true."
- Wait to make professional judgments until all the relevant facts are known.
- Have confidence in your own knowledge or in your own ability to understand complex situations; do not assume that the client's explanation for unexpected trends or financial ratios simply reflects your lack of understanding.

Focus on Fraud   Poor Professional Judgment and Low Audit Quality

This feature provides a recent example of how a lack of professional judgment can have significant consequences.

In 2016, the Securities and Exchange Commission suspended an auditor for conducting a faulty audit of the financial statements of a public company that was committing fraud. The firm where the accountant was a partner at the time, EFP Rotenberg LLP, was prohibited from accepting new public company clients for one year.

According to the SEC's order, the publicly traded company, ContinuityX Solutions, claimed to sell internet services to businesses. In September 2015, the SEC charged its executives for allegedly engineering a scheme to grossly overstate the company's revenue through fraudulent sales.

During the audits of ContinuityX, EFP Rotenberg and the accountant, Nicholas Bottini, failed to perform sufficient procedures to detect the fraudulent sales in the company's financial statements.

EFP Rotenberg and Bottini also failed to obtain sufficient audit evidence over revenue recognition and accounts receivable, to identify related-party transactions, to investigate management representations that contradicted other audit evidence, to perform procedures to resolve and properly document inconsistencies, and to exercise due professional care.

The firm was ordered to pay a $100,000 penalty, and before the firm could begin accepting new clients an independent consultant had to certify that the firm had corrected the causes of its audit failures. The audit partner agreed to pay a $25,000 penalty in addition to being permanently suspended from appearing and practicing before the SEC as an accountant, which includes not participating in the financial reporting or audits of public companies.

For further details, see SEC Accounting and Auditing Enforcement Release No. 3790.

A Framework for Ethical Decision Making

The auditing profession has worked hard to gain the public trust, and the profession benefits from that trust as the sole legally acceptable provider of audit services for companies and other organizations. To maintain that trust and economic advantage, it is essential that professional integrity be based on personal moral standards and reinforced by codes of conduct. Whenever a scandal surfaces, the profession is diminished and auditors' reputations may be tarnished beyond repair. It is not difficult to find oneself facing an ethical dilemma without realizing it.

Auditors using the framework in *Exhibit 1.9* will encounter decisions that have ethical implications. For example, consider a situation in which your senior on the engagement is already worried about the time that it has taken you to complete your work. Would you take the time needed to diligently follow up on evidence suggesting that something might be wrong with the financial statements? Would you consider concluding that a client's decision to extend the life of its assets is appropriate, even if you have serious reservations about this decision? Auditing professionals often face these types of difficult ethical decisions. In such situations, a defined methodology is helpful in resolving the situation in a thoughtful, quality manner. An **ethical dilemma** occurs when there are conflicting moral duties or an individual is ethically required to take an action that may conflict with his or her immediate self-interest. Complex ethical dilemmas do not lend themselves to simple "right" or "wrong" decisions. Ethical theories are helpful in assisting individuals in dealing with ethical dilemmas. Two such theories—utilitarian theory and rights theory—have helped develop codes of conduct that can be used by professionals in dealing with ethically challenging situations.

Utilitarian Theory
Utilitarian theory holds that what is ethical is the action that achieves the greatest good for the greatest number of people. Actions that result in outcomes that fall short of the greatest good for the greatest number and those that represent

inefficient means to accomplish such ends are less desirable. Utilitarianism requires:

- An identification of the potential problem and possible courses of action
- An identification of the potential direct or indirect impact of actions on each affected party (often referred to as **stakeholders**) who may have a vested interest in the outcome of actions taken
- An assessment of the desirability (goodness) of each action
- An overall assessment of the greatest good for the greatest number Utilitarianism requires that individuals not advocate or choose alternatives that favor narrow interests or that serve the greatest good in an inefficient manner. There can be honest disagreements about the likely impact of actions or the relative efficiency of different actions in attaining desired ends. There are also potential problems in measuring what constitutes "the greatest good" in a particular circumstance. One problem with the utilitarian theory is the implicit assumption that the "ends achieved" justify the means to attain those ends. Unfortunately, such an approach can lead to disastrous courses of actions when those making the decisions fail to adequately measure or assess the potential costs and benefits. Thus, ethicists generally argue that utilitarian arguments should be mitigated by some "value-based" approach. Rights theory presents such a framework.

Rights Theory

Rights theory focuses on evaluating actions based on the fundamental rights of the parties involved. However, not all rights are equal. In the hierarchy of rights, higher-order rights take precedence over lower-order rights. The highest order rights include the right to life, to autonomy, and to human dignity. Second-order rights include rights granted by the government, such as civil rights, legal rights, rights to own property, and license privileges. Third-order rights are social rights, such as the right to higher education, to good health care, and to earning a living. The fourth-order rights relate to one's nonessential interests or one's personal tastes.

Rights theory requires that the "rights" of affected parties be examined as a constraint on ethical decision making. The rights approach is most effective in identifying outcomes that ought to be automatically eliminated, such as the "Robin Hood approach" of robbing from the rich to give to the poor; in these situations, the utilitarian answer is at odds with most societal values.

Applying the Ethical Decision Making Framework

Exhibit 1.10 contains a framework derived from the utilitarianism and rights theories that can help individuals resolve ethical dilemmas in a quality manner. We present a situation in Column 2 of *Exhibit 1.10* as an application of this framework to an auditing situation.

The court case used to develop the example in *Exhibit 1.10* is *Consolidata Services v. Alexander Grant*. In that case, the court found the audit firm guilty of providing confidential information to its other clients. Alexander Grant (now Grant Thornton) performed tax work for Consolidata Services, a company that provided computerized payroll services to other companies. On learning that Consolidata was in financial trouble, Grant warned some of its other clients, who were also Consolidata customers. Consolidata sued Grant, charging that the audit firm's disclosures effectively put it out of business. The jury ruled in favor of Consolidata. Grant was also found guilty of providing the information only to selected parties; that is, it provided the information only to its clients—not all customers of Consolidata.

Exhibit 1.10
An Application of the Framework for Ethical Decision Making

Steps in Framework	Application
Step 1 Identify the ethical issue(s).	The external auditor for Payroll Processors, Inc. believes that the company might go bankrupt. Several clients of the audit firm use the payroll processing services of Payroll Processors. Should the other clients be provided with this **confidential information** prior to the information being publicly available through the audit report—which might be delayed as auditors further assess the potential for bankruptcy?
Step 2 Determine the affected parties and identify their rights.	The relevant parties to the issue include the following: • Payroll Processors and its management • Payroll Processors' current and prospective customers, creditors, and investors • The audit firm and its other clients • The external auditing profession Some of the rights involved: • Company management has the right to assume that confidential information obtained by its auditors will remain confidential unless disclosure is permitted by the company or is required by accounting, auditing, or legal standards. • Payroll Processors' current and prospective customers, creditors, and investors have a right to receive reliable information and not be denied important information that could adversely affect their operations. • The audit firm has the right to expect its employees to follow the professional standards. However, some may argue that the firms' existing clients have a right to information that might protect them from financial crises. • The external auditing profession has the right to expect all its members to uphold relevant codes of professional conduct (described in the following section of the chapter) and to take actions that enhance the general reputation and perception of the integrity of the profession.
Step 3 Determine the most important rights.	Many auditors would assess that the rights listed in order of importance are: (1) the client to not have confidential information improperly disclosed, (2) other affected parties to receive important information that will affect their operations, and (3) the profession to retain its reputation for conducting quality audits.
Step 4 Develop alternative courses of action.	The possible courses of action are: (1) share the confidential information with the other clients of the audit firm prior to issuing an audit opinion on the client's financial statements, or (2) do not share that information prior to issuing an audit opinion on the client's financial statements. The audit firm was performing audit work, and the professional standards require that the reservations about Payroll Processors remaining a going concern in their audit report, not in private information given to selected entities.
Step 5 Determine the likely consequences of each proposed course of action.	These could include: *Prior to Issuing the Audit Opinion.* Sharing this information with the other clients prior to issuing an audit report with a going-concern reservation may cause these other clients to take their business away from Payroll Processors, thus increasing the likelihood of bankruptcy for Payroll Processors. It might also increase the possibility of the audit firm being found in violation of the rules of conduct and being sued by Payroll Processors or others for inappropriately providing confidential information to selected parties outside of the public role that external auditors fulfill. The auditor may also have his or her license suspended or revoked. Other Payroll Processors' clients who do not receive the information because they are not the audit firm's clients will be put at a competitive disadvantage, and they may sue the auditor because of discriminatory disclosure. *Do Not Share the Information Until the Audit Report Has Been Issued.* If the information is not shared with the other clients, those clients might take their audit business elsewhere if they find out the auditors knew of this problem and did not share it with them. Other clients of Payroll Processors may suffer losses because of the financial problems of Payroll Processors.
Step 6 Assess the possible consequences, including an estimation of the greatest good for the greatest number. Determine whether the rights framework would cause any course of action to be eliminated.	Sharing the information may help other clients move their payroll processing business to other service providers in a more orderly manner and more quickly than would happen if they had to wait until the audit opinion was issued. However, other Payroll Processors' customers may be placed at a disadvantage if Payroll Processors does go bankrupt and their payroll processing is disrupted. Payroll Processors' employees will lose their jobs more quickly, and its investors are likely to lose more money more quickly. Its right to have confidential information remain confidential will be violated. There may be less confidence in the profession because of discriminatory or unauthorized disclosure of information. Management of other companies may be reluctant to share other nonfinancial information with audit firms. After assessing the relative benefits of disclosing versus not disclosing the information prior to issuing the audit opinion, it appears that the greatest good is served by not sharing the information selectively with current audit clients, but to complete the audit and issue the audit opinion in a timely manner.
Step 7 Decide on the appropriate course of action.	The auditor should not share the information prior to issuing the audit opinion. The auditor may encourage Payroll Processors to share its state of affairs with its clients but cannot dictate that it do so. The need for equity and confidentiality of information dictates that the auditor's primary form of communication is through formal audit reports associated with the financial statements.

1-13 Utilitarian theory holds that what is ethical is the action that achieves the greatest good for the most important people.   (T/F)

1-14 In rights theory, the highest order rights are those granted by the government, such as civil rights, legal rights, rights to own property, and license privileges.   (T/F)

1-15 Which of the following statements related to rights theory is <u>false</u>?
   a. The highest order rights include the rights to life, autonomy, and human dignity.
   b. Second-order rights include rights granted by the government, such as civil rights and legal rights.
   c. Third-order rights include social rights, such as the right to higher education, to good health care, and to earning a living.

   d. Fourth-order rights include one's essential interests or personal tastes.

1-16 Utilitarianism does <u>not</u> require which of the following actions when a person considers how to resolve an ethical dilemma?
   a. Identification of the potential problem and courses of action.
   b. Identification of the potential direct or indirect impact of actions on each affected party who has an interest in the outcome.
   c. Identification of the motivation of the person facing the ethical dilemma.
   d. Assessment of the desirability of each action for each affected party.

For Classroom Discussion

If auditors are not appropriately skeptical, then their opinions lose value to investors and other decision makers. Auditors who are not appropriately skeptical might be seen as seeking only to corroborate management's assertions or rationalize evidence that doesn't make sense.

What circumstances do you think might impede an auditor's application of professional skepticism? Do you think that auditors can trust clients and be skeptical at the same time?

LO 5

Describe factors considered by audit firms making client acceptance and continuance decisions.

Importance of Client Acceptance and Continuance Decisions to Audit Quality

Conducting a quality audit begins with client acceptance and continuance decisions. Such decisions are part of an audit firm's overall portfolio management activities. One can view an individual audit client as an individual stock in an investment portfolio. That is, some stocks (clients) are more risky, but yield better returns; some stocks (clients) are less risky, but yield weaker returns. Still other stocks (clients) do not present a clear picture of their risk-return profile.

In the context of auditing, better returns do not only relate to audit fees. Better returns may include other considerations such as the upside potential of a client that may become publicly traded or the reputational visibility that an audit firm gains when they audit a superior and well-known company. Portfolio management, of which client acceptance and continuance decisions are just one part, is the key to an

Exhibit 1.11

Audit Firm Portfolio Management

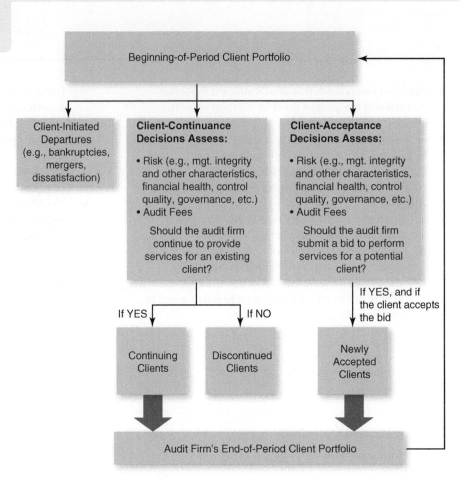

audit firm's long-run survival and its ability to offer quality audit services to its clients. Audit firm culture plays a role in audit firm portfolio management, in that some audit firms are more willing to provide service to risky clients than are other audit firms.

As depicted in *Exhibit 1.11*, an audit firm begins each period with a given number of clients in its portfolio. Some clients voluntarily depart from the audit firm, such as in the case of a company going bankrupt or merging with another company; other reasons for departure include fee issues, service issues, changes in location, or poor working relationships. New clients become part of an audit firm's portfolio based on the **client acceptance decision**, which includes an evaluation of the client's relative risk and audit fee profile. The audit firm makes a proposal (and in some cases a formal bid) to the client if the audit firm decides the client is acceptable; if the client accepts, the audit firm adds the client to its portfolio.

Existing clients are organizations for which the audit firm provided audit services in the preceding period. Each year, the audit firm makes a **client continuance decision** to determine whether the audit firm should continue to provide services in the next period. The engagement partner and the audit firm must decide, based on what they know about the client, whether it is worthwhile to retain the client in the firm's portfolio. Similar to the client acceptance decision, the client continuance decision is based on a consideration of the client's relative risk and audit fee profile. Discontinued clients are those the audit firm decides to eliminate from its portfolio. The audit partner informs client management that the firm will no longer perform audit services for the client after issuing the current period audit report. Continuing clients are those clients for whom the audit firm will continue to provide audit services.

Audit firm portfolio management decisions are critical to achieve audit quality. If an audit firm provides audit services to a potentially problematic client such as a client that is in very weak financial condition, a client that has very poor internal controls, a client that is perpetrating a fraud, or a client with poor management integrity, it may be difficult for the audit firm to provide a quality audit. For example, a client in weak financial condition may be unable to pay a reasonable audit fee, and so the audit firm may find itself in a position of not having enough budgeted audit hours to do a quality audit. A client with weak internal controls may be difficult to audit because of unreliable financial data. Similarly, a client perpetrating a fraud, or one with weak management integrity, may present financial information that is intentionally unreliable, and so again the audit may be difficult to conduct in a way that results in an accurate audit opinion.

An important consideration in client acceptance and continuance decisions involves the audit firm's growth strategy. Audit firms may discontinue serving a client because the client does not fit the complement the portfolio the firm is hoping to achieve. For example, a Big 4 firm may discontinue serving a smaller client because the client is not sufficiently profitable, or the client may not be in an industry the firm wants to emphasize.

Risks Considered in Client Acceptance and Continuance Decisions

Audit firms consider many key risks when making client acceptance and continuance decisions. Types of key risks, and an example of each, follow:

- *Client entity characteristics:* History of earnings management
- *Independence risk factors:* Audit engagement partner has a business relationship with the client CEO
- *Third-party/due diligence risk factors:* Reason for changing auditors is negative relationships between the client and the previous auditor
- *Quantitative risk factors:* Client is in significant financial distress
- *Qualitative risk factors:* Client's business model is weak
- *Entity organizational or governance risk:* Client management lacks integrity
- *Financial reporting risk:* Management records unusual transactions at the end of each quarter

---

Accepting a New Audit Client

Why It Matters

This feature highlights the importance of communicating with a predecessor auditor prior to accepting a new client.

Before accepting a new audit client, the auditor should request that management authorizes the predecessor auditor to respond to the auditor's inquiries on issues that will assist the auditor in determining whether to accept the new client. If management refuses to authorize the predecessor auditor to respond or limits the response, the auditor should inquire about the reasons and consider the implications in deciding whether to accept the engagement.

The communication with the predecessor auditor may be either written or oral, although obtaining the communication in writing is better. Matters addressed include:

- Information that might bear on the integrity of management
- Disagreements with management about accounting policies, auditing procedures, or other similarly significant matters
- Communications to those charged with governance regarding fraud and noncompliance with laws or regulations by the entity
- Communications to management and those charged with governance regarding significant deficiencies and material weaknesses in internal control
- Understanding about the reasons for the change of auditors

Prompt for Critical Thinking #1   It's Your Turn!

For each of the types of key risks just presented, provide several additional examples.

•   **Client entity characteristics**

   _____, _____

   _____, _____

•   **Independence risk factors**

   _____, _____

   _____, _____

•   **Third-party/due diligence risk factors**

   _____, _____

   _____, _____

•   **Quantitative risk factors**

   _____, _____

   _____, _____

•   **Qualitative risk factors**

   _____, _____

   _____, _____

•   **Entity organizational or governance risk**

   _____, _____

   _____, _____

•   **Financial reporting risk**

   _____, _____

   _____, _____

Why It Matters   Deciding Whether to Continue Providing Audit Services to a Client

This feature provides an example of a firm that resigned from a client because of independence considerations.

KPMG notified its client Herbalife on April 8, 2013, that KPMG was resigning as Herbalife's audit firm. KPMG had concluded that it was not independent because of alleged insider trading in Herbalife's securities by one of KPMG's former partners who had served as the KPMG engagement partner on Herbalife's audit.

KPMG noted that it resigned as Herbalife's independent accountant solely due to the impairment of KPMG's independence resulting from the alleged unlawful activities and not for any reason related to Herbalife's financial statements, its accounting practices, the integrity of Herbalife's management, or for any other reason.

Because KPMG's independence had been impaired, it had no option but to withdraw its audit reports on Herbalife's financial statements for the fiscal years ended December 31, 2010, 2011, and 2012 and the effectiveness of internal control over financial reporting as of December 31, 2010, 2011, and 2012. The reports could not be relied upon due to KPMG's lack of independence created by the insider trading circumstances.

In 2014, the audit partner involved in the insider trading situation was sentenced to 14 months in federal prison for giving confidential information about his firm's clients to a golfing buddy, who used it to make more than $1 million in profits trading stocks. The partner was also ordered to pay a $100,000 fine.

Other Considerations

Auditors are not required to perform audits for any organization that asks. An audit firm should not perform an audit that it is not qualified to perform. Small growing firms may be tempted to perform an audit for which they are not qualified or not large enough to perform. Firms should not provide audit services if they do not have the size or expertise to serve the client as the client grows larger, becomes more geographically dispersed, or increases in complexity.

As a further consideration, auditors should provide audit services only when the preconditions for an audit are present. These preconditions include:

- *Management's use of an acceptable financial reporting framework.* Without an acceptable financial reporting framework (e.g., GAAP or IFRS), management does not have an appropriate basis for the preparation of the financial statements, and the auditor does not have suitable criteria for auditing the financial statements.
- *The agreement of management that it acknowledges and understands its responsibilities.* These responsibilities include the preparation and fair presentation of the financial statements, along with the design, implementation, and maintenance of internal control over financial reporting. Further, management needs to agree to provide the auditor with access to all relevant information, such as records, and documentation, and unrestricted access to persons within the organization.

Engagement Letters

When an audit firm agrees to provide a client with audit services, the firm should prepare an **engagement letter** stating the scope of the audit work to be performed. This letter documents the expectations agreed to by the auditor and the client. The engagement letter, which includes the audit fee, also includes a description of the timing of the external auditor's work and of documentation that the client is expected to provide to the external auditor. The engagement letter should describe the degree of responsibility the auditor takes with respect to discovering fraud and misstatements. If a client wants its auditors to go beyond the requirements of the auditing standards, the auditors should have their attorneys review the wording to make sure that it says not only what is intended, but also what is possible. An example of an engagement letter is provided in *Chapter 14*.

Items in the engagement letter typically include:

- The objective and scope of the audit of the financial statements
- The responsibilities of the auditor
- The responsibilities of management
- A statement that because of the inherent limitations of an audit, together with the inherent limitations of internal control, an unavoidable risk exists that some material misstatements may not be detected, even though the audit is properly planned and performed in accordance with relevant auditing standards
- The identification of the applicable financial reporting framework for the preparation of the financial statements
- A reference to the expected form and content of any reports to be issued by the auditor and a statement about circumstances that may arise in which a report may differ from its expected form and content

Check Your Basic Knowledge

1-17 Existing clients for which the audit firm provided services in the preceding period are evaluated by the audit firm and by the individual engagement partner at the completion of the audit to determine whether the audit firm should continue to provide services again in the next period. The process by which this evaluation occurs is called the client continuance decision.   (T/F)

1-18 Audit firms may discontinue serving a client because the client does not fit the profile or growth strategy of the audit firm.   (T/F)

1-19 With regard to client acceptance/continuance decisions, which of the following is <u>false</u>?
   a. Client acceptance/continuance decisions are one part of the audit firm's overall portfolio management activities.
   b. The primary driver of the client acceptance/continuance decision is the level of audit fees that the audit firm can charge the client.
   c. One can view an individual audit client as analogous to an individual stock in an investment portfolio.
   d. Audit firms are not required to provide audit services for all organizations requesting an audit.

1-20 Which of the following factors is <u>not</u> an example of a risk relevant to the client continuance decision?
   a. Client entity characteristics.
   b. Independence risk factors.
   c. Third-party/due diligence risk factors.
   d. Advocacy threat.

What Do You Think? For Classroom Discussion

Assume that you are the owner of a small audit firm. A prospective client calls in late November asking, "Can you audit my company? We have a December 31 year-end, and we need the audit report by March 31."

After some discussion, you think the fee will be around $125,000, which should provide your firm with a nice profit. You have auditors with the appropriate knowledge needed to conduct the audit. After some preliminary analysis, you believe that this client would be a good addition to your client portfolio. Your audit staff is already working more than 60 hours a week during this time of the year, and it is not very likely that you will be able to hire additional auditors. Should you take the engagement? What factors will influence your decision?

Let's Review

• Decision makers need information that is transparent and unbiased—information that does not favor one user over another. However, the interests of the various users can conflict. Current shareholders might want management to use accounting principles that result in higher levels of reported income, while lending institutions might prefer management to use a conservative approach to valuation and income recognition. (LO 1)

• Managers within organizations produce financial statements and design internal control systems. External auditors performing a financial statement audit provide independent assurance on the reliability of the financial statements and, as part of an integrated audit, provide independent assurance on internal control effectiveness. (LO 1)

- A financial statement audit is systematic process of objectively obtaining and evaluating evidence regarding assertions about economic actions and events to ascertain the degree of correspondence between those assertions and established criteria; and communicating the results to interested users. (LO 1)

- Auditors need technical knowledge and expertise; auditors must understand accounting and auditing authoritative literature, develop industry and client-specific knowledge, develop and apply computer skills, evaluate internal controls, and assess and respond to fraud risk. In addition to having appropriate technical knowledge, auditors need well-developed skills in leadership, teamwork, communication, decision making, critical thinking, and general professionalism. (LO 1)

- A quality audit is an audit performed in accordance with generally accepted auditing standards (GAAS) to provide reasonable assurance that the audited financial statements and related disclosures are: (1) presented in accordance with GAAP and (2) are not materially misstated whether due to errors or fraud. For an audit to have value for its users, it must be conducted in a quality manner. (LO 2)

- To achieve audit quality, auditors need to adhere to relevant codes of professional conduct and related guidance on professional responsibilities. Codes of conduct include principles and specific rules of conduct. One of the critically important rules requires auditors to be independent when conducting an audit. (LO 3)

- To achieve audit quality, auditors need to make quality decisions throughout the audit. Quality decisions are unbiased, meet the expectations of reasonable users, comply with professional standards, and incorporate sufficient evidence to justify the decision that is rendered. Two ethical theories—utilitarian theory and rights theory—have helped develop codes of conduct that can be used by professionals in making decisions in ethically challenging situations. (LO 4)

- Conducting a quality audit begins with client acceptance and continuance decisions. If an audit firm provides audit services to a potentially problematic client such as a client that is in very weak financial condition, a client that has very poor internal controls, a client that is perpetrating a fraud, or a client with poor management integrity, it may be difficult for the audit firm to provide a quality audit. (LO 5)

Significant Terms

Acceptable level In connection with independence, an acceptable level is a level at which a reasonable and informed third party who is aware of the relevant information would be expected to conclude that a member's independence is not impaired. When used in connection with any rule except for the Independence Rule, an acceptable level is a level at which a reasonable and informed third party who is aware of the relevant information would be expected to conclude that a member's compliance with the rules is not compromised.

Adverse opinion An adverse opinion should be expressed when the auditor believes that the financial statements taken as a whole are *not presented fairly* in conformity with GAAP or when the auditor believes that the client's internal control over financial reporting is not effective.

American Institute of Certified Public Accountants (AICPA) A professional organization for CPAs that develops professional standards for the conduct of nonpublic company audits and other services performed by its members. The organization also serves to self-regulate the profession performing nonpublic audits.

Audit quality Performing an audit in accordance with generally accepted auditing standards (GAAS) to provide reasonable assurance that the audited financial statements and related disclosures are presented in accordance with GAAP and providing assurance that those financial statements are not materially misstated whether due to errors or fraud.

Center for Audit Quality (CAQ) An organization affiliated with the AICPA that is dedicated to enhancing investor confidence and trust in the financial markets.

Client acceptance decision   The process by which a new client is evaluated by the audit firm and individual engagement partner prior to being accepted into the audit firm's portfolio of clients.

Client continuance decision   The process by which existing clients for which the audit firm provided services in the preceding period are evaluated by the audit firm and the individual engagement partner at the completion of the audit to determine whether the audit firm should continue to provide services again in the next period.

Confidential information   Information obtained during the conduct of an audit related to the client's business or business plans; the auditor is prohibited from communicating confidential information except in very specific instances defined by the *Code* or with the client's specific authorization.

Cooling off period   Number of years after which the individual auditor may resume providing service to the audit client.

Covered member   A covered member includes:
a. An individual on the engagement team
b. An individual in a position to influence the engagement
c. A partner, partner equivalent, or manager who provides more than 10 hours of nonattest services to the audit client within any fiscal year
d. A partner or partner equivalent in the office in which the lead engagement partner or partner equivalent primarily practices in connection with the engagement
e. The firm, including the firm's employee benefit plans
f. An entity whose operating, financial, or accounting policies can be controlled by any of the individuals or entities described in items a–e or two or more such individuals or entities if they act together

CPA   A certified public accountant who is licensed by a state board of accountancy.

Direct financial interest   A financial interest owned directly by, or under the control of, an individual or entity or beneficially owned through an investment vehicle, estate, or trust when the beneficiary controls the intermediary or has the authority to supervise or participate in the intermediary's investment decisions.

Due professional care   A standard of care expected to be demonstrated by a competent professional in his or her field of expertise, set by GAAS but supplemented in specific implementation instances by the standard of care expected by a reasonably prudent auditor.

Engagement letter   A communication between the audit firm and the audit committee that states the scope of the work to be done on the audit so that there can be no doubt in the mind of the client, external auditor, or the court system as to the expectations agreed to by the external auditor and the client.

Ethical dilemma   A situation in which moral duties or obligations conflict; an ethically correct action may conflict with an individual's immediate self-interest.

Financial Reporting Council   The United Kingdom's independent regulator responsible for promoting investment in securities through good corporate governance and financial reporting.

Financial statement audit   A systematic process of objectively obtaining evidence regarding assertions about economic actions and events to ascertain the degree of correspondence between those assertions and established criteria and communicating the results to interested users.

Generally accepted auditing standards (GAAS)   GAAS refers to professional external auditing standards that are followed by auditors when conducting a financial statement audit. Throughout the book, when we refer to professional external auditing standards, we will use the term GAAS (generally accepted auditing standards). GAAS are set by several bodies, including the AICPA, the IAASB, and the PCAOB.

Indirect financial interest A financial interest in which the beneficiary neither controls the intermediary nor has the authority to supervise or participate in the intermediary's investment decisions.

Integrated audit Type of audit provided when an external auditor is engaged to perform an audit of the effectiveness of internal control over financial reporting (the audit of internal control over financial reporting) that is integrated with an audit of the financial statements.

International Auditing and Assurance Standards Board (IAASB) A part of the International Federation of Accountants that is responsible for issuing auditing and assurance standards. Its goal is to harmonize auditing standards on a global basis.

International Ethics Standards Board for Accountants (IESBA) An independent, standard-setting body that serves the public interest by setting robust, internationally appropriate ethics standards, including auditor independence requirements, for professional accountants worldwide.

International Federation of Accountants (IFAC) The global organization for the accountancy profession dedicated to serving the public interest by strengthening the profession and contributing to the development of strong international economies.

Network firm A firm or other entity that belongs to a network. This includes any entity (including another firm) that the network firm, by itself or through one or more of its owners, controls, is controlled by, or is under common control with.

Objectivity An impartial, unbiased attitude.

Principles of professional conduct Broad principles that articulate auditors' responsibilities and their requirements to act in the public interest, to act with integrity and objectivity, to be independent, to exercise due care, and to perform an appropriate scope of services.

Professional judgment The application of relevant professional knowledge and experience to the facts and circumstances in order to reach a conclusion or make a decision.

Professional skepticism An attitude that includes a questioning mind and critical assessment of audit evidence.

Public Company Accounting Oversight Board (PCAOB) A quasi-public board, appointed by the SEC, to provide oversight of the firms that audit public companies registered with the SEC. It has the authority to set auditing standards for the audits of public companies.

Rights theory An ethical theory that identifies a hierarchy of rights that should be considered in solving ethical dilemmas.

Safeguards Actions or other measures that may eliminate a threat or reduce a threat to an acceptable level.

Securities and Exchange Commission (SEC) The governmental body with the oversight responsibility to ensure the proper and efficient operation of capital markets in the United States.

Threats Relationships or circumstances that could compromise compliance with the rules.

Unqualified audit report The standard audit report that describes the auditor's work and communicates the auditor's opinion that the financial statements are fairly presented in accordance with GAAP.

Utilitarian theory An ethical theory that systematically considers all the potential stakeholders who may be affected by an ethical decision and seeks to measure the effects of the decision on each party; it seeks to facilitate decisions resulting in the greatest amount of good for the greatest number of people.

Prompt for Critical Thinking

Prompt for Critical Thinking #1

- *Client entity characteristics*. For example, a history of earnings management or of making unrealistic promises to analysts; failing to meet market expectations or consistently just meeting those expectations; difficulties in relationships with prior professional service providers, such as attorneys; and high-risk business models, such as online gaming.
- *Independence risk factors*. For example, the engagement partner has a business or family relationship with the client; client management was a former employee of the audit firm; the client purchases consulting services from the audit firm; or the audit firm has some other independence-related conflict with the client.
- *Third-party/due diligence risk factors*. For example, the reason for the client to change auditors is unknown or is due to negative relationship factors, the predecessor audit firm is unwilling to discuss the reasons for the client's departure, there have been significant changes in the ownership structure of the entity or evidence that key members of management have prior histories of financial fraud or other types of legal difficulties.
- *Quantitative risk factors*. For example, the client is in significant financial stress, is having difficulty raising capital or paying its existing debts, or is experiencing significant cash flow problems.
- *Qualitative risk factors*. For example, the industry in which the client operates is either in the early development stage or in the late stage of its product life cycle; there are minimal barriers to entry to the client's business model; the business model is weak or untested; there are low profit margins; the client's products have multiple viable substitutes; there are significant supply chain risks; there is significant production or operational complexity; or there are risks related to strong union presence.
- *Entity organizational or governance risks*. For example, the organizational structure is inappropriate for the business operations of the entity, there are weak internal controls, there is weak governance, management is unqualified or lacks integrity, and the internal audit function is weak or nonexistent.
- *Financial reporting risks*. For example, the client uses inappropriate estimates in its financial reporting judgments, management has a history of misrepresentations or unwillingness to correct detected misstatements, the financial statement line items involve a significant amount of judgment or complexity, there are large or unusual transactions that management records at quarter or year-end, or the prior audit report is other than an unqualified report.

Review Questions and Short Cases

NOTE: Completing *Review Questions and Short Cases* does not require the student to reference additional resources and materials.

NOTE: We make special note of problems addressing fraud, international issues, professional skepticism, and ethics.

1-1 **LO 1** What is the objective of external auditing? Describe the role of external auditing in meeting demands for unbiased financial statement and internal control information.

1-2 **LO 1** What is the special function that auditors perform? Whom does the external auditing profession serve in performing this special function?

1-3 **LO 1** What factors create a demand for an independent external audit?

1-4 **LO 1** How does an audit enhance the quality of financial statements and management's reports on internal control? Does an audit guarantee a fair presentation of a company's financial statements?

1-5 **LO 1** Why is it important that users perceive auditors to be independent? What is the difference between *being independent in fact* and *being independent in appearance*?

1-6 **LO 1** Auditors must be independent because audited financial statements must serve the needs of a wide variety of users. If the auditor were to favor one group, such as existing shareholders, there might be a bias against another group, such as prospective investors.

a. What steps has the external auditing profession taken to minimize potential bias toward important users and thereby encourage auditor independence?

b. Refer to *Exhibit 1.1* and describe the users of audited financial statements and the decisions that they need to make based on reliable information.

ETHICS

1-7 **LO 1** Refer to the *Why It Matters* feature "Does Owning Stock in an Audit Client Affect Auditor Independence?"

a. Describe the unethical actions of Susan Birkert.

b. Compare and contrast the ideas of *independence in fact* and *independence in appearance* in the context of this case.

c. Do you think that Susan's punishments were appropriate? Explain your answer.

1-8 **LO 1** McIver's Swimwear Distributors is a relatively small, privately held swimwear distribution company that operates in the Midwest and handles several product lines, including footwear, clothing, and swim team supplies. It sells directly to swimwear shops and does not sell to the big retailers. It has approximately $8 million in sales and wants to grow at about 20% per year for the next five years. It is also considering a takeover or a merger with another swimwear distributorship that operates in the same region.

a. Explain why management might want an independent audit of its financial statements.

b. What are the factors that McIver's might consider in deciding whether to seek an audit from a large national audit firm, a regional audit firm, or a local firm?

c. What types of users might be interested in McIver's financial results?

1-9 **LO 1** Refer to *Exhibit 1.4* and identify the primary parties involved in preparing and auditing financial statements, and briefly describe their roles.

1-10 **LO 1** List the various types of audit service providers. What types of audit firms are best suited for auditing large multinational companies versus small, regional companies that are not publicly traded?

1-11 **LO 1** What types of skills and knowledge do professionals entering the external auditing profession need to be successful?

INTERNATIONAL

1-12 **LO 2** Define audit quality and identify drivers of audit quality as specified by the Financial Reporting Council's *Audit Quality Framework*.

INTERNATIONAL

1-13 **LO 2** Refer to *Exhibit 1.5*.

a. How does positive audit firm culture, along with expert skills and qualities of both the audit partner and the engagement team, affect audit quality?

b. What factors outside the control of the external auditor affect audit quality?

c. Why do users care about audit quality? Are there certain users who might care more about audit quality than others? Explain.

1-14 LO 2, 3   Refer to the various *Who Are They?* features throughout the chapter and describe the roles of the following organizations that affect the external auditing process, and the nature of those effects.
  a. Public Company Accounting Oversight Board (PCAOB)
  b. Securities and Exchange Commission (SEC)
  c. American Institute of Certified Public Accountants (AICPA)
  d. Center for Audit Quality (CAQ)
  e. International Auditing and Assurance Standards Board (IAASB)
  f. Financial Reporting Council (FRC)

1-15 LO 3   Distinguish between the roles of the PCAOB and the AICPA in: (a) setting audit standards and (b) setting accounting standards.

1-16 LO 3   The PCAOB has the authority to set auditing standards for audits of public companies registered in the U.S. The AICPA continues to set auditing standards for nonpublic companies through its Auditing Standards Board (ASB).
  a. What are the pros and cons of having potentially different auditing standards for both public and nonpublic companies?
  b. In what ways might you expect auditing standards for audits of nonpublic companies to differ from the standards for public companies?

1-17 LO 3   Refer to the *Who Are They?* feature that describes the PCAOB. Why is there a requirement that no more than two of the board members are CPAs?

1-18 LO 3   Codes of conduct followed by auditors emphasize the importance of independence to achieving audit quality. Explain why independence is considered the cornerstone of the auditing profession.

1-19 LO 3   Describe why maintaining auditor independence can help achieve audit quality.

1-20 LO 3   Describe the seven threats to independence articulated in the AICPA's independence conceptual framework, and provide examples of each.

1-21 LO 3   Describe the safeguards to independence articulated in the AICPA's independence conceptual framework, and provide examples of each.

1-22 LO 3   Summarize the five fundamental principles of ethics as articulated by the International Ethics Standards Board for Accountants (IESBA).

1-23 LO 3   Refer to *Exhibit 1.6*. Describe the AICPA's six principles of professional conduct.

1-24 LO 3   The issue of independence is important to the profession.
  a. Are auditors of publicly traded clients required to be independent?
  b. Are auditors of privately held clients required to be independent?
  c. The AICPA's Rules applies only to covered members. What does it mean to be a covered member?
  d. What is the difference between a direct financial interest and an indirect financial interest?
  e. What services does the Sarbanes-Oxley Act of 2002 prohibit auditors from performing for their publicly traded clients?

1-25 LO 3   Refer to *Exhibit 1.8*. Read the description of the rule related to Integrity and Objectivity. What does this rule require?

1-26 `LO 3`   Refer to *Exhibit 1.8*. Read the description of the rule related to Confidential Client Information.
  a. What is confidential information?
  b. Normally, the external auditor must keep client information confidential. Identify those circumstances in which this does not apply.

1-27 `LO 3`   Refer to *Exhibit 1.8*. Read the description of the rule related to Contingent Fees.
  a. What is a contingent fee?
  b. Why are external auditors not allowed to accept contingent fees?

1-28 `LO 3`   Describe the various ways in which the AICPA's *Code* is enforced.

1-29 `LO 3`   Would a CPA violate the AICPA's *Code* by serving as an auditor and legal counsel to the same client? Explain your answer.

1-30 `LO 3`   The following are a number of scenarios that might constitute a violation of the AICPA's *Code of Professional Conduct*. For each of the five scenarios, indicate which principle or rule would be violated, or if none would be violated.
  a. Tom Hart, CPA, does the bookkeeping, prepares the tax returns, and performs various management services for Sanders, Incorporated, but does not do the audit. One management service involved the assessment of the computer needs and the identification of equipment to meet those needs. Hart recommended a product sold by Computer Company, which has agreed to pay Hart a 10% commission if Sanders buys its product.
  b. Irma Stone, CPA, was scheduled to be extremely busy for the next few months. When a prospective client asked if Stone would do its next year's audit, she declined but referred them to Joe Rock, CPA. Rock paid Stone $2,000 for the referral.
  c. Nancy Heck, CPA, has agreed to perform an inventory control study and recommend a new inventory control system for Ettes, Incorporated, a new client. Currently, Ettes engages another audit firm to audit its financial statements. The financial arrangement is that Ettes will pay Heck 50% of the savings in inventory costs over the two-year period following the implementation of the new system.
  d. Brad Gage, CPA, has served as the auditor for Hi-Dee Company for several years. In addition, Gage has performed other services for the company. This year, the financial vice president has asked Gage to perform a major computer system evaluation.
  e. Due to the death of its controller, an audit client had its external auditor, Gail Klate, CPA, perform the controller's job for a month until a replacement was found.

1-31 `LO 4`   Refer to *Exhibit 1.9*. Briefly explain the seven steps in the framework for professional decision making. Provide an example of a professionally oriented decision that you have recently made, and relate it to the seven steps (one example might be a decision about whether to apply to a graduate program).

1-32 `LO 4`   Refer to the *Why It Matters* feature "What Is Professional Judgment?" Explain the term *professional judgment*.

PROFESSIONAL SKEPTICISM

1-33 `LO 4`   Explain why professional skepticism is important in making professional judgments. What are the types of actions that a professionally skeptical auditor will take?

FRAUD

1-34 **LO 4** Refer to the *Focus on Fraud* feature "Poor Professional Judgment and Low Audit Quality."
a. Identify the indicators of poor professional judgment in this case.
b. What do you think was the auditor's motivation for this conduct?
c. Why were auditor's actions potentially harmful to external users of the audited financial statements?

ETHICS

1-35 **LO 4** Describe utilitarian theory. What are the weaknesses of utilitarian theory?

ETHICS

1-36 **LO 4** Describe rights theory and list the four levels of rights. In what way is rights theory particularly helpful?

ETHICS

1-37 **LO 4** Refer to *Exhibit 1.10*. Briefly explain the seven steps in the framework for ethical decision making. Provide an example of a difficult ethical decision that you have recently made, and use the framework to help you make a decision using the seven steps. (An example might be a decision to challenge a friend who has done something wrong or a decision to report on a person that you know was cheating on an exam.)

ETHICS

1-38 **LO 4** As the auditor for XYZ Company, you discover that a material sale ($500,000 sale; cost of goods of $300,000) was made to a customer this year. Because of poor internal accounting controls, the sale was never recorded. Your client makes a management decision not to bill the customer because such a long time has passed since the shipment was made. You determine, to the best of your ability, that the sale was not fraudulent. Using the framework for ethical decision making, determine whether the auditor should require either a recording or a disclosure of the sales transaction. Explain your reasoning.

ETHICS

1-39 **LO 4** You have worked as a staff auditor for two and one-half years and have mastered your job. You will likely be promoted to a senior position after this busy season. Your current senior was promoted about a year ago. He appreciates your competence and rarely interferes with you. As long as he can report good performance to his manager on things she wants, he is satisfied. The manager has been in her position for three years. She is focused on making sure audits run smoothly and is good at this. She is not as strong on the softer skills. Although she is approachable, her attention span can be short if what you are saying does not interest her. You are aware that she expects her teams to perform excellently during this busy season and she hopes to be promoted to senior manager as a result, bringing her closer to her goal of making partner early.

The audit engagement on which you are working has become increasingly difficult since last year because of some complicated accounting transactions that the client made. There has also been unexpected turnover in accounting personnel at the client. This has made interacting with the client and getting the information you need in a timely manner problematic. However, the engagement time budget and the audit fee remain the same as last year's. Further, four staff auditors are assigned to the engagement, and there are no additional staff available to transfer in to ease the workload. Your senior now tells you that the manager has requested that you, he, and the other staff auditors do an additional analysis of a potential misstatement in one of the client's accounts. Even with your team's current workload, there is significant danger that the engagement will run over budget. You know that if you do the analysis thoroughly, it will further endanger meeting the time budget the manager had planned. The more time you spend on the engagement, the less profitable it will be for the audit firm, which clearly will displease the manager and her superiors.

As a group, the staff auditors discuss the situation and express their concerns regarding the perceptions that running over budget will create and the reputational issues that short-circuiting the analysis could create. When your senior stops by to discuss the new plan, the group raises its concerns. He talks to the group and implies that he would be satisfied if the team did either of the following: complete the analysis and simply not record the hours (doing so would prevent the reported audit hours from going too far over budget) or do a minimal job on the analysis, which would save time and avoid having to question the client too much. You and a few other staff members express discomfort with both of these strategies. It is suggested that the ramifications of the new order be made clear to the manager. The senior wants nothing to do with this. He says, "She doesn't want to hear these details so just use one of the ideas I have already given you." When he leaves, several staff members start griping about what they are being asked to do. A couple say they are going to leave the firm after this busy season, so they don't really care about this issue. Another says, "We've been told what to do. Let's just get on with it."

a. Using the framework for ethical decision making, decide what you would do. Explain your rationale.

b. How can you do what you think is the right thing without undermining your senior or undermining the manager's confidence in your ability to get a job done?

1-40 **LO 5** Describe how individual audit clients are both similar to and different from individual stocks in an investment portfolio. What is the difference between a client acceptance decision and a client continuance decision? In which decision-making setting does the auditor have the benefit of deeper knowledge of the client?

1-41 **LO 5** Refer to *Exhibit 1.11.* What are the three possibilities that may happen to the clients in the audit firm's beginning-of-period client portfolio? What are the two main factors that auditors consider in making client acceptance and continuance decisions?

1-42 **LO 5** The following are the key types of risk that audit firms consider when they make client acceptance and continuance decisions. Provide examples of each of these types of risks.

- Client entity characteristics
- Independence risk factors
- Third-party/due diligence risk factors
- Quantitative risk factors
- Qualitative risk factors
- Entity organizational or governance risks
- Financial reporting risks

Fraud Focus: Contemporary and Historical Cases

FRAUD

INTERNATIONAL

NOTE: Completing *Fraud Focus: Contemporary and Historical Cases* may require students to reference additional resources and materials.

1-43 **LONGTOP FINANCIAL TECHNOLOGIES, DELOITTE (LO 5)**

Deloitte audited the financial statements of Longtop Financial Technologies (Longtop) both before and after the company's 2007 initial public offering. In May 2011, Deloitte resigned from the Longtop engagement, citing concerns about management fraud. The allegations are that Longtop's top management, including the chief operating officer, interfered with the audit confirmation process. In fact, there is currently widespread concern that significant collusion has been taking place between Chinese companies and their banks, including evidence that banks are signing false confirmations of their clients' cash accounts. The reason for the false confirmations is that the Chinese companies, including Longtop, had been recording fictitious revenues and fictitious inflows of cash to agree with the revenues. When Deloitte personnel confronted Longtop management, the auditors were subject to seizure of their audit workpapers and were faced with physical threats to try to prevent the auditors from leaving the property.

Read the resignation letter below that Deloitte sent to Longtop management describing their reasons for resigning from the engagement. Briefly describe Deloitte's main complaints. Deloitte and other large audit firms would like very much to operate in the China market. What risks do you think might be unique to accepting and retaining clients in a foreign country that is not necessarily supportive of U.S. interests?

Following is the resignation letter from Deloitte Shanghai to the Longtop Audit Committee on May 22, 2011:

BY EMAIL & BY REGISTERED MAIL
The Audit Committee
Longtop Financial Technologies Limited
No. 61 Wanghai Road, Xiamen Software Park
Xiamen, Fujian Province
People's Republic of China
Attention: Mr. Thomas Gurnee, Chairman of the Audit Committee

Dear Sirs,

Longtop Financial Technologies Limited (the "Company") and together with its subsidiaries (the "Group") Audit for the Year Ended 31 March 2011

We hereby give you formal notice of our resignation as auditor of the Company.

Background and significant issues encountered by Deloitte Touche Tohmatsu CPA Ltd. (China) ("Deloitte")

As part of the process for auditing the Company's financial statements for the year ended 31 March 2011, we determined that, in regard to bank confirmations, it was appropriate to perform follow up visits to certain banks. These audit steps were recently performed and identified a number of very serious defects including: statements by bank staff that their bank had no record of certain transactions; confirmation replies previously received were said to be false; significant differences in deposit balances reported by the bank staff compared with the amounts identified in previously received confirmations (and in the books and records of the Group); and significant bank borrowings reported by bank staff not identified in previously received confirmations (and not recorded in the books and records of the Group).

In the light of this, a formal second round of bank confirmation was initiated on 17 May. Within hours however, as a result of intervention by the Company's officials including the Chief Operating Officer, the confirmation process was stopped amid serious and troubling new developments including: calls to banks by the Company asserting that Deloitte was not their auditor; seizure by the Company's staff of second round bank confirmation documentation on bank premises; threats to stop our staff leaving the Company premises unless they allowed the Company to retain our audit files then on the premises; and then seizure by the Company of certain of our working papers.

In that connection, we must insist that you promptly return our documents.

Then on 20 May the Chairman of the Company, Mr. Jia Xiao Gong called our Eastern Region Managing Partner, Mr. Paul Sin, and informed him in the course of their conversation that "there were fake revenue in the past so there were fake cash recorded on the books". Mr. Jia did not answer when questioned as to the extent and duration of the discrepancies. When asked who was involved, Mr. Jia answered: "senior management".

We bring these significant issues to your attention in the context of our responsibilities under Statement on Auditing Standards No. 99 "Consideration of Fraud in a Financial Statement Audit" issued by the American Institute of Certified Public Accountants.

Reasons for our resignation

The reasons for our resignation include: 1) the recently identified falsity of the Group's financial records in relation to cash at bank and loan balances (and also now seemingly in the sales revenue); 2) the deliberate interference by the management in our audit process; and 3) the unlawful detention of our audit files. These recent developments undermine our ability to rely on the representations of the management which is an essential element of the audit process; hence our resignation.

Prior periods' financial reports and our reports thereon

We have reached the conclusion that we are no longer able to place reliance on management representations in relation to prior period financial reports. Accordingly, we request that the Company take immediate steps to make the necessary 8-K filing to state that continuing reliance should no longer be placed on our audit reports on the previous financial statements and moreover that we decline to be associated with any of the Company's financial communications during 2010 and 2011.

Our consent

We hereby consent to a copy of this letter being supplied to the SEC and the succeeding auditor to be appointed.

Section 10A of the Securities Exchange Act of 1934 (U.S.)

In our view, without providing any legal conclusion, the circumstances mentioned above could constitute illegal acts for purposes of Section 10A of the Securities Exchange Act of 1934. Accordingly, we remind the Board of its obligations under Section 10A of the Securities Exchange Act, including the notice requirements to the U.S. Securities and Exchange Commission. You may consider taking legal advice on this.

Yours faithfully,

/s/ Deloitte Touche Tohmatsu CPA Ltd.
c.c.: The Board of Directors

Postscript: Ultimately, the SEC delisted Longtop because the company failed to file its annual report for FYE March 31, 2011. Similar delistings occurred at other Chinese companies with stock traded in U.S. markets, including Advanced Battery Technologies, China MediaExpress Holdings, and Shengda Tech. These examples serve as a serious warning to audit firms as they enter high-risk international markets and as they make their client continuance decisions.

Source: Deloitte Shanghai, May 22, 2011.

1-44

THOMAS FLANAGAN, DELOITTE
(LO 3, 4)

Thomas Flanagan was an audit partner and key member of management (vice chairman) at Deloitte LLP, based out of the firm's Chicago office. During the latter part of his career, he managed a large number of public company audit engagements. Based on knowledge obtained from key members of management of one of his audit clients, Flanagan learned that the client would soon be purchasing another company. Knowing that the value of the acquired company would rise upon the news of the purchase, Flanagan purchased stock in the acquired company. As such, he engaged in insider trading. As the subsequent investigation would reveal, Flanagan traded in securities of at least 12 of his audit clients during 2005–2008. In fact, he made more than 300 trades in shares of the firm's clients over this period. He concealed his actions by lying on his independence disclosure filings with Deloitte, not revealing the existence of several of his brokerage accounts that would have identified his actions. Ultimately, the SEC uncovered his actions and notified Deloitte. Flanagan resigned from the firm, and Deloitte subsequently sued him for breach of fiduciary duty, fraud, and breach of contract based upon his misconduct. The firm ultimately won a judgment against him. As part of a legal settlement with the firm, Flanagan gave up about $14 million in pension and deferred compensation, according to court papers filed by his attorney. A spokesperson for the firm stated "Deloitte unequivocally condemns the actions of this individual, which are unprecedented in our experience. His personal trading activities were in blatant violation of Deloitte's strict and clearly stated policies for investments by partners and other professional personnel."

In August 2010, the SEC charged Thomas Flanagan and his son with insider trading in the securities of several of the firm's audit clients. The SEC alleged that Flanagan's illegal trading resulted in profits of more than $430,000. On four occasions, Flanagan shared the nonpublic information with his son, who then traded based on that information for illegal profits of more than $57,000. The SEC also instituted administrative proceedings against Thomas Flanagan, finding that he violated the SEC's auditor independence rules on 71 occasions between 2003 and 2008. The Flanagans agreed to pay more than $1.1 million to settle the SEC's charges.

In October 2012, Flanagan was given 21 months in prison for trading on insider information about the accounting firm's clients. Flanagan, who pleaded guilty to a single count of securities fraud in August 2012, was also sentenced to one year of supervised release and fined $100,000. Securities fraud carries a maximum punishment of 20 years in prison. Flanagan's plea agreement called for a term of three to four years in prison, and prosecutors sought at least 37 months.

a. Why is owning stock in one's client considered inappropriate?
b. Why is it important that auditors be independent of their clients?
c. Why did Deloitte take Flanagan's actions so seriously?
d. What do you think might have led Flanagan to make such poor professional and ethical decisions?
e. Assume that you were working on one of Flanagan's engagements and you discovered that insider trading was occurring. What procedures should the audit firm have in place to encourage you to report the inappropriate behavior and yet protect your career?

Source: The description of this case is based, in part, on facts disclosed in the case Deloitte LLP v. Thomas P. Flanagan, Court of Chancery of the State of Delaware, No. 4125-VCN and SEC Accounting and Auditing Enforcement Release No. 3164.

1-45

FRAUD

ETHICS

DELOITTE, ADELPHIA COMMUNICATIONS (LO 3, 4)

In 2005, Deloitte & Touche agreed to pay a $50 million settlement concerning its failed audit of Adelphia Communications. The settlement was the largest ever to that date, with a record penalty of $25 million. Individual auditors found to be unqualified, unethical, or in willful violation of any provision of the federal securities laws can be disciplined by the SEC. Actions taken by the SEC in these types of situations are described in *Accounting and Auditing Enforcement Releases (AAER), Litigation Releases, and Administrative Proceedings* available at *www.sec.gov*.

a. Read AAER 2326 (September 30, 2005; Administrative Proceeding File No. 3-12065) and AAER No. 2842 (June 25, 2008; Administrative Proceeding File No. 3-12065), available at *www.sec.gov*. These releases relate to the actions of William E. Caswell, CPA, who served as a director and held the most senior, nonpartner position on the Adelphia engagement. What type of improper professional conduct was William E. Caswell, CPA, engaged in? Identify at least one rule of conduct in the AICPA's *Code* that Caswell likely violated. In 2005, what was the SEC's response to his behavior? What was the SEC's response in 2008?

b. Consider Caswell's failure to make sure that Adelphia's disclosure of its liabilities related to the co-borrowing credit facilities was sufficient. Use the framework for ethical decision making to assess Caswell's actions related to this disclosure.

1-46

FRAUD

PROFESSIONAL SKEPTICISM

INTERNATIONAL

PCAOB, BENTLEYS BRISBANE PARTNERSHIP (LO 1, 2, 3, 5)

On December 20, 2011, the Public Company Accounting Oversight Board (PCAOB) revoked the ability of Bentleys Brisbane Partnership (an external audit firm) to perform public company audits, and the Board imposed a monetary penalty of $10,000 on Robert Forbes, the audit partner in charge of the audit of Alloy Steel International. These penalties were imposed because the PCAOB concluded that Bentleys and Forbes failed to exercise due professional care (a standard of care expected to be demonstrated by a competent auditing professional), failed to exercise professional skepticism (an attitude that includes a questioning mind and critical assessment of audit evidence), and failed to obtain sufficient evidence necessary to issue an audit opinion on the financial statements of Alloy Steel's 2006 fiscal year-end financial statements. The PCAOB also concluded that Bentleys violated PCAOB quality-control standards because the firm did not develop policies to ensure that the work performed by its personnel met PCAOB auditing standards, and the Board said that the firm did not undertake audits that the firm could reasonably expect to be completed with professional competence.

Alloy Steel International is an American company headquartered in Malaga, Australia. Alloy's stock was traded on the Over-the-Counter Bulletin Board, and as such was subject to the Securities and Exchange Commission's (SEC) rules and requirements. Its auditors were subject to the PCAOB's rules and requirements. On the audit of Alloy, Bentleys and Forbes made a number of critical mistakes. Bentleys and Forbes used an unregistered audit firm in Australia to actually perform the audit work, rather than performing the audit work themselves. Bentleys' and Forbes' involvement on the engagement was limited to reviewing the unregistered audit firm's workpapers. The unregistered audit firm's personnel had no training or experience in conducting audits that complied with PCAOB standards. Despite these factors, Bentleys and Forbes issued and signed an unqualified audit report on Alloy's 2006 financial statements.

For further details, see PCAOB disciplinary proceedings in Release No. 105-2011-007.

Robert Forbes was the audit partner in charge of the Alloy Steel engagement, and he made several critical mistakes that adversely affected audit quality.

a. What is the objective of external auditing, and how did Forbes' and Bentley's actions fail to achieve that objective?

b. Why did Alloy Steel require an independent audit on its financial statements?

c. Which parties are likely users of Alloy Steel's financial statements? How might they have been adversely affected by Forbes' actions?

d. In most situations, we would worry about fraud in terms of the client, not the audit firm. In this case, Robert Forbes essentially committed fraud in that he signed the audit report knowing that he did not do the work required of him. What skills and knowledge were required to do a quality audit of Alloy Steel's financial statements? How did the individuals who actually performed the audit work on the Alloy Steel engagement fail in this regard?

e. Refer to *Exhibit 1.5.* Explain how the facts in this case relate to each of the drivers of audit quality identified in *Exhibit 1.5.* If a particular driver is not applicable to this case, state why.

f. Should Bentleys and Forbes have agreed to conduct this audit in the first place?

Application Activities

NOTE: Completing *Application Activities* requires students to reference additional resources and materials.

1-47 **PCAOB** **(LO 3)** Access the PCAOB website at *www.pcaobus.org.*

a. List the members of the Board and describe their backgrounds. What are their professional qualifications?

b. Identify the most recent auditing standard issued by the PCAOB. Describe the nature of the standard and discuss the reason that the Board issued the standard.

1-48 **AICPA** **(LO 3)** Access information about the Auditing Standards Board on the AICPA website at *www.aicpa.org.*

a. Identify the members of the Board and describe their backgrounds. What are their professional qualifications?

b. Identify the most recent auditing standard issued by the AICPA. Describe the nature of the standard and discuss the reason(s) that the Board issued the standard.

1-49 **IAASB** **(LO 3)** Access the IAASB website at *www.ifac.org/ auditing-assurance.*

INTERNATIONAL

a. List the members of the Board and describe their backgrounds. What are their professional qualifications?

b. Identify the most recent auditing standard issued by the IAASB. Describe the nature of the standard and discuss the reason(s) that the board issued the standard.

PROFESSIONAL SKEPTICISM

1-50 **PCAOB (LO 3)** In April 2010, the PCAOB issued a disciplinary order instituting disciplinary proceedings, making findings, and imposing sanctions in the case of Robert T. Taylor, CPA (both the firm and the individual auditor). The order can be found in PCAOB Release No. 105–2010–006 at *www.pcaobus.org.* (*Hint*: Search in the "Enforcement" section of the website, then go to "settled disciplinary orders," then search to see the disciplinary order against Taylor.)

a. Who is the PCAOB and what authority does it have to issue disciplinary orders and impose sanctions?
b. What is the PCAOB's source of potential violations of law or PCAOB rules?
c. The order in the case of Robert T. Taylor recognizes that PCAOB standards require that an auditor exercise due professional care, exercise professional skepticism, and obtain sufficient evidence on which to base an opinion on the financial statements. Describe instances in which the respondents in the order did not adhere to these requirements, resulting in low audit quality.
d. What sanctions were imposed in this case? Do the sanctions seem appropriate?

Academic Research Cases

NOTE: Completing *Academic Research Cases* requires students to reference additional resources and materials.

SEARCH HINT

It is easy to locate academic research articles! Use a search engine such as Google Scholar or an electronic research platform such as ABI Inform, and search using the author names and part of the article title.

1-51 **LO 5** Locate and read the article listed below.

Hsieh, Y., and Lin, C. (2016). Audit firms' client acceptance decisions: Does partner-level industry expertise matter? *Auditing: A Journal of Practice and Theory* 35(2): 9–120.

a. What is the purpose of the study?
b. Describe the design/method/approach used to conduct the study.
c. What are the primary findings of the study?

1-52 **LO 2** Locate and read the article listed below.

Pickerd, J. S., Summers, S. L., & Wood, D. A. (2015). An examination of how entry-level staff auditors respond to tone at the top vis-à-vis tone at the bottom. *Behavioral Research in Accounting* 27(1): 79–98.

a. What is the purpose of the study?
b. Describe the design/method/approach used to conduct the study.
c. What are the primary findings of the study?

The Auditor's Responsibilities Regarding Fraud and Mechanisms to Address Fraud: Regulation and Corporate Governance

The Audit Opinion Formulation Process

I. Making Client Acceptance and Continuance Decisions

Chapter 1

II. Performing Risk Assessment

Chapters 2, 3, 7, and 9–13

III. Obtaining Evidence About Internal Control Operating Effectiveness

Chapters 8–13

IV. Obtaining Substantive Evidence About Accounts, Disclosures, and Assertions

Chapters 8–13

V. Completing the Audit and Making Reporting Decisions

Chapters 14 and 15

Quality Auditing and the Need for Quality Auditor Judgments and Ethical Decisions

Chapter 1

Professional Liability

Chapter 4

The Audit Opinion Formulation Process and a Framework for Obtaining Audit Evidence

Chapters 5 and 6

There are various types of fraud and many incentives, opportunities, and rationalizations explaining why people perpetrate fraud. When conducting a quality audit, auditors are responsible for considering the possibility of fraud at their clients. Auditors should expect their clients to have implemented a corporate governance process by which owners and creditors of the client exert control and demand accountability for the resources they entrusted to the organization.

Learning Objectives

LO 1 Define the various types of fraud that affect organizations.

LO 2 Define the fraud triangle and describe its three elements.

LO 3 Describe implications for auditors of instances of fraudulent financial reporting and related fraud findings.

LO 4 Discuss auditors' fraud-related responsibilities and users' fraud-related expectations.

LO 5 Explain how various requirements in the Sarbanes-Oxley Act of 2002 help prevent fraud.

LO 6 Define corporate governance, identify the parties involved, and describe their respective activities.

Examples of Theft and Financial Reporting Frauds

This feature provides several examples of fraud at U.S. and international companies.

Milwaukee-based Koss Corporation reported an embezzlement of funds of approximately $31 million orchestrated by its chief financial officer (CFO) over a five-year period when the company's reported earnings were only $26 million. The CFO used the funds for personal goods, such as expensive coats, jewelry, and other personal items, which were mostly kept in storage facilities. Interestingly, the CFO was neither an accountant nor a certified public accountant (CPA); the chief executive officer (CEO) had a college degree in anthropology; most of the board members had served on the board for 20–30 years; and the company made highly technical products that were in very competitive markets.

In another fraud, a senior benefits executive at Hitachi America, Inc. diverted approximately $8 million from Hitachi by creating a separate bank account that included the Hitachi name, but was controlled by him. The funds that were diverted included payments from health providers and insurance companies intended for Hitachi's employee benefit plans. The executive used the $8 million in the new account to purchase an expensive vacation home and a new Lexus automobile, among other items.

In addition to outright thefts, fraud can also involve fraudulent financial reporting. For example, WorldCom orchestrated its fraud, in part, by capitalizing items that should have been recorded as expenses, thereby increasing current-period income. Charter Communications inflated revenue by selling control boxes back to its supplier and then repurchasing them later. Dell, Inc. admitted to manipulating its reported income by not accurately disclosing payments that it received from computer-chip maker Intel. The payments were in exchange for Dell's agreement not to use chips from Intel's rival, Advanced Micro Devices. These payments accounted for 76% of Dell's operating income in early 2007. Dell also covered earnings shortages by dipping into reserves and claimed that the seemingly strong financial results were due to high-quality management and efficient operations.

In 2014, the Securities and Exchange Commission (SEC) alleged that Diamond Foods engaged in financial reporting fraud to overstate the company's income by delaying the recording of costs paid to the company's walnut growers. Diamond Foods was facing significant gross margin declines because of steep price increases for the company's main raw material, and by delaying the recording of costs the company was able to exceed analysts' earnings expectations.

In an international setting, Sino-Forest fraudulently asserted that it owned vast amounts of timberland in China, when in fact the company did not have sufficient proof of ownership. The Ontario Securities Commission began investigating allegations of the fraud in 2012, and the company ultimately was delisted and entered bankruptcy shortly thereafter.

What You Will Learn

- What are the major types of fraud? What are the typical characteristics of fraud that auditors should consider? (LO 1, 2)
- What are the implications of financial reporting fraud, and what types of financial reporting frauds are common? (LO 3)
- To what extent should the auditor be responsible for identifying the risk of fraud, and then determining whether material fraud exists? (LO 4)

- How can a quality audit prevent or detect these types of frauds? (LO 4)
- How can society as a whole, and the external auditing profession in particular, act to prevent and detect fraud? (LO 4, 5, 6)
- What is corporate governance, and how can effective corporate governance prevent these types of frauds? (LO 6)

LO 1

Define the various types of fraud that affect organizations.

Fraud Defined

Fraud is an intentional act involving the use of deception that results in a misstatement of the financial statements. Two types of misstatements are relevant to auditors' consideration of fraud: (a) misstatements arising from misappropriation of assets and (b) misstatements arising from fraudulent financial reporting. Intent to deceive is what distinguishes fraud from errors. Auditors routinely find financial errors in their clients' books, but errors are *not* intentional.

Misappropriation of Assets

Asset misappropriation occurs when a perpetrator steals or misuses an organization's assets. Asset misappropriations are the primary fraud scheme in small businesses, and the perpetrators are usually employees. Asset misappropriations include embezzling cash receipts, stealing assets, or causing the organization to pay for goods or services that the organization did not receive. Asset misappropriation happens, for example, when employees steal assets such as inventory or equipment and manipulate financial accounts to cover it up or steal cash by writing checks to fake vendors (whose bank accounts they control). A well-known example of asset misappropriation is the famous Madoff Ponzi scheme, which *Exhibit 2.1* describes.

Fraudulent Financial Reporting

The intentional manipulation of reported financial results is called **fraudulent financial reporting**. The perpetrator of such a fraud generally seeks gain through the rise in stock price and the commensurate increase in personal wealth. Sometimes the perpetrator does not seek direct personal gain, but instead uses the fraudulent financial reporting to "help" the organization avoid bankruptcy or to avoid some other negative financial outcome. Three common means to accomplish fraudulent financial reporting include manipulation, falsification, or alteration of accounting records or supporting documents, misrepresentation or omission of events, transactions, or other significant information, and/or intentional misapplication of accounting principles.

Common types of fraudulent financial reporting include improperly recognizing revenue, improperly deferring expenses, improperly valuing assets, concealing liabilities, and making misrepresentations or omissions in the financial statement footnotes or the Management Discussion and Analysis (MD&A).

Exhibit 2.1

The Bernie Madoff Ponzi Scheme

A **Ponzi scheme** occurs when a fraudster uses deposits of new investors to pay returns on the deposits of previous investors; no real investment is happening. A Ponzi scheme will collapse if new investors do not join, or their deposits are too small to pay an adequate return to previous investors. Ponzi schemes are based on trust and greed. The fraudster develops trust by building a relationship with the investors. The fraudster usually gains trust through their actions, their professional, social, or religious affiliations, and through personal references. Fraudsters exploit the greed of their investors, who see an opportunity to obtain higher than usual returns. Because the investors trust the fraudster, they do not perform their normal due diligence.

In March 2009, Madoff pleaded guilty to 11 federal crimes and admitted to turning his broker-dealer business into a massive Ponzi scheme that defrauded thousands of investors of billions of dollars. Federal investigators believe that the fraud began as early as the 1980s and that the investment operation may never have been legitimate. The amount missing from client accounts, including fabricated gains, was almost $65 billion. On June 29, 2009, Madoff was sentenced to 150 years in prison, the maximum allowed. He is still in prison.

Madoff built a veil of trust by running a legitimate brokerage firm, and at one time he was the chair of NASDAQ. He often appeared on CNBC talking about the securities industry. Madoff took advantage of his ties to the investment community to encourage further investment, and he always sold the idea of an investment into his company as one of "special privilege." He conducted the scheme by hiring individuals who were paid commissions to bring in more investors. Obviously, the scheme can only work as long as the funds brought into the scheme in future years are sufficient to continue to pay all the previous investors. Ponzi schemes eventually become too big and collapse. However, until the collapse, Madoff led an extremely lavish lifestyle.

Madoff conducted the scheme by keeping all of the transactions off his formal books. He employed a CPA firm to audit the books, but the audit was a sham; that is, it did not exist. In fact, the CPA was also an investor in the fund, which clearly violates independence requirements. For a fund of its size, it would normally be the case that a very large, high-quality audit firm would conduct the audit. This is where greed comes into play: the investors felt they were part of something special, and they enjoyed earning high returns. They trusted Madoff, so they didn't require typical due diligence information of which an external audit is an important part.

Although not verified, it is alleged (as reported on a CNBC Primetime Special) that Madoff chose to surrender and plead guilty because one of the investors was with the Russian mob and Madoff feared for both his life and that of his sons. Many have speculated that his sons helped him orchestrate the fraud: one committed suicide two years after the fraud was revealed, and the other died of natural causes a bit afterward. As a result of this fraud, the Public Company Accounting Oversight Board (PCAOB) began requiring broker-dealers to obtain audits using firms registered with the PCAOB, and the PCAOB now sets standards for audits of broker-dealers.

The Great Salad Oil Swindle of 1963

Focus on Fraud

The feature is a classic example of fraudulent financial reporting. This historically relevant fraud has practical application today, because fraud perpetrators continue to use similar types of inventory manipulation to commit fraud.

The Great Salad Oil Swindle was one of the first large-scale fraudulent financial reporting scandals. Top managers at Allied Crude Vegetable Oil in New Jersey were the fraudsters. Their concept was simple: The company could overstate its financial position by claiming that it had more inventory than it actually had. Overstated ending inventory yields an understated cost of goods sold, thereby resulting in overstated net income. The fraud cost creditors and suppliers about $150 million (over $1 billion in current dollars).

The fraud was fairly simple. The company stored salad oil in large tanks. It issued numerous receipts all showing that it owned a large amount of salad oil inventory. The auditor did observe part of the inventory, but did so by checking the various tanks one after another. The company accomplished the fraud by doing the following:

- First, it filled the tanks with a large container of water on the inside.

- Second, it created an outer layer with salad oil, so if the auditor checked the oil from an opening on top, the auditor would find oil.

- Third, the company pumped the oil underground from one tank to another in anticipation of the auditor's planned inspection route.

Check Your Basic Knowledge

2-1 The Great Salad Oil Swindle of 1963 is an asset misappropriation fraud. (T/F)

2-2 The Koss Corporation fraud is a fraudulent financial reporting fraud. (T/F)

2-3 What is the primary difference between fraud and error in financial statement reporting?
   a. The materiality of the misstatement.
   b. The intent to deceive.
   c. The level of management involved.
   d. The type of transaction effected.

2-4 Which of the following examples best represents an example of fraudulent financial reporting?

   a. The transfer agent issues 40,000 shares of the company's stock to a friend without authorization by the board of directors.
   b. The controller of the company inappropriately records January sales in December so that year-end results will meet analysts' expectations.
   c. The in-house attorney receives payments from the French government for negotiating the development of a new plant in Paris.
   d. The accounts receivable clerk covers up the theft of cash receipts by writing off older receivables without authorization.

What Do You Think?   For Classroom Discussion

Given that many frauds ultimately are discovered, and that there exists very significant negative consequences to the fraudsters themselves, in addition to their victims, why do you think that both theft and financial reporting fraud continue to be prevalent in our society?

LO 2

Define the fraud triangle and describe its three elements.

The Fraud Triangle

Career criminologist Don Cressey introduced the term **fraud triangle** in the 1950s. Cressey identified three factors that are generally present when fraud occurs, and a large body of research validates it.

The three elements of the fraud triangle, as shown in *Exhibit 2.2*, include an **incentive** to commit fraud, the **opportunity** to commit and conceal the fraud, and **rationalization**—the mindset of the fraudster—to justify committing the fraud.

We illustrate the fraud triangle with a simple example from a fraud that took place in a construction company. The company did paving, sewer, and gutter work. It started small but grew to about $30 million in annual revenue. The construction work was performed at various locations throughout Michigan and Colorado. The company often purchased supplies at the job location, which were signed for by a construction employee and forwarded to the accountant for payment.

Exhibit 2.2
The Fraud Triangle

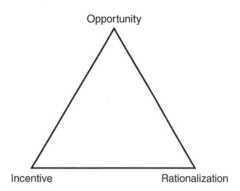

The company had one accountant, but the president of the company approved all payments and formally signed off on them. When the president retired, his son replaced him, and the son spent more time growing the paving business than on accounting. He trusted the accountant because of the work the accountant had done for his father; therefore, he spent considerably less time in reviewing and signing off on payments than his father had done. The essence of the fraud was that the accountant prepared bogus invoices for a bogus vendor, set the account up in his name, and prepared receiving slips and purchase orders to gain approval for the payments.

Now consider how the fraud triangle worked in this case. First, what were the *incentives* for the fraud? Like many similar situations, the accountant faced considerable personal financial problems, mostly associated with taking care of his elderly parents, who had unpaid medical bills. Second, because the new president no longer reviewed items for payment, the *opportunity* (deficiencies in controls) presented itself. Third, the *rationalization* was a little more complex. Like most frauds, the fraudster thought that it would be a one-time extra payment to get him over the difficult times, and like most frauds, when the fraud was not detected, there was a further opportunity to grow it. The other part of the rationalization was more subtle. When the new president furnished all of the vice-presidents and job supervisors with new pickup trucks, the accountant did not receive one, nor did he receive a very substantial bonus, as compared to the job superintendents. The accountant felt that the amount of money he was taking was no different than what the job superintendents and vice-presidents were getting. In other words, he rationalized his actions to himself by believing that he 'deserved' the payments.

On each audit engagement, when the auditor estimates the likelihood of fraud— through either misappropriation of assets or fraudulent financial reporting—the auditor should start by carefully considering the three elements of the triangle, and the most likely areas for fraud to occur. Factors associated with the fraud triangle are called fraud risk factors or **red flags**.

Incentives or Pressures to Commit Fraud

Possible incentives for fraudulent financial reporting include:

- Management compensation schemes
- Financial pressures for either improved earnings or an improved balance sheet
- Debt covenants

Prompt for Critical Thinking #1   It's Your Turn!

Identify other *incentives* for fraudulent financial reporting.

- _____
- _____
- _____
- _____
- _____

Opportunities to Commit Fraud

For fraud to happen there must be opportunity for fraud to be committed. Although this may sound obvious—that is, "everyone has an opportunity to commit fraud"—certain factors provide enhanced opportunities. Opportunities include a lack of controls or complex transactions such that the perpetrator assesses the risk of being caught as low. Other opportunities include:

- Significant related-party transactions
- A company's industry position, such as the ability to dictate terms or conditions to suppliers or customers that might allow individuals to structure fraudulent transactions
- Management's inconsistency involving subjective judgments regarding assets or accounting estimates

Prompt for Critical Thinking #2   It's Your Turn!

Identify other *opportunities* for fraudulent financial reporting.

- _____
- _____
- _____
- _____
- _____

Rationalizing the Fraud

Rationalization is a crucial component in most frauds. Rationalization involves a person reconciling unlawful or unethical behavior, such as stealing, with the commonly accepted notions of decency and trust. For fraudulent financial reporting, the rationalization can range from "saving the company" to personal greed and includes thoughts such as:

- This is a one-time thing to get us through the current crisis and survive until things get better.
- Everybody cheats on the financial statements a little; we are just playing the same game.
- We will be in violation of all of our debt covenants unless we find a way to get this debt off the financial statements.
- I will lose everything (family, home, car, and so on) if I don't take the money.

Prompt for Critical Thinking #3

Identify other *rationalizations* for fraudulent financial reporting.

- _____
- _____
- _____
- _____
- _____

Check Your Basic Knowledge

2-5 The three elements of the fraud triangle include incentive, opportunity, and rationalization.   (T/F)

2-6 Management compensation schemes that heavily emphasize stock-based compensation primarily affect the opportunity to commit fraud.   (T/F)

2-7 Which of the following factors creates an opportunity for fraud to be committed in an organization?
   a. Management demands financial success.
   b. Poor internal control.
   c. Commitments tied to debt covenants.
   d. Management is aggressive in its application of accounting rules.

2-8 Which of the following is a common rationalization for fraudulent financial reporting?
   a. This is a one-time transaction and it will allow the company to get through the current financial crisis, but I'll never do it again.
   b. I am only borrowing the money; I will pay it back next year.
   c. Executives at other companies are getting paid more than I am, so I deserve the money.
   d. The accounting rules don't make sense for our company, and they make our financial results look weaker than is necessary. Therefore, we have good reason to record revenue using a non-GAAP method.
   e. Both (a) and (d).

What Do You Think? **For Classroom Discussion**

The three elements of the fraud triangle include incentive, opportunity, and rationalization. Are each alone significant enough to enable the fraudster to perpetrate the fraud? If you had to rank the three in terms of importance, what would that ranking be, and what is your rationale for that ranking?

LO 3

Describe implications for auditors of instances of fraudulent financial reporting and related fraud findings.

History of Fraudulent Financial Reporting

Examples of Recent Frauds and Implications for External Auditors

Exhibit 2.3 contains examples of notable instances of fraudulent financial reporting over the last two decades. The patterns evident across the frauds in *Exhibit 2.3* yield the following implications for auditors:

- The auditor should be aware of the pressure that analyst following and earnings expectations create for top management.
- If there are potential problems with revenue, the auditor cannot complete the audit until there is sufficient time to examine major year-end transactions.
- The auditor must understand complex transactions to determine their economic substance and the parties that have economic obligations.
- The auditor must clearly understand and analyze weaknesses in an organization's internal controls in order to determine where and how a fraud may take place.
- The auditor must develop audit procedures to address specific opportunities for fraud to take place.

These examples also illustrate that auditors must exercise professional skepticism in analyzing the possibility of fraud and must be especially alert to trends in performance, or results that are not consistent with other companies, in determining the audit procedures that should be performed. When there are red flags, suggesting a heightened risk of fraud, the auditor uses audit procedures targeted at discovering the potential fraud.

Insights from COSO Studies

The Committee of Sponsoring Organizations (COSO) has published several studies on fraudulent financial reporting. These studies provide insights based on companies that have been cited in an SEC Accounting and Auditing Enforcement Release (AAER). Some major findings include:

- The total amount of fraud during the 1998–2007 time period was more than $120 billion spread across just 300 companies.
- The median size of the company perpetrating the fraud rose tenfold to $100 million during the 1998–2007 period (as compared to the previous ten years).

Exhibit 2.3
Important Cases of Fraudulent Financial Reporting

Company	Nature of the Fraud
Enron (2001)	Considered by many to be one of the most significant frauds of the early 2000s, Enron was initially a utility company that management converted into an energy trading company. When energy trades went bad, management covered up financial problems by: • Shifting debt to off–balance sheet special entities • Recognizing revenue on impaired assets by selling them to special-purpose entities that they controlled • Engaging in round-tripping trades, which are trades that eventually found the assets returning to Enron after initially recognizing sales and profits • Numerous other related-party transactions
WorldCom (2002)	In what would end in one of the largest bankruptcies of all time, WorldCom was the second-largest U.S. long-distance phone company (after AT&T). The company pursued an aggressive growth strategy of acquiring other telecommunications companies. When the financial results of these acquisitions faltered, management decreased expenses and increased revenues through the following: • Recording bartered transactions as sales; for example, trading the right to use lines in one part of the world to similar rights to another part of the world • Using restructuring reserves established through acquisitions to decrease expenses; for example, over-accruing reserves upon acquiring a company and later "releasing" those reserves to decrease expenses of future periods • Capitalizing line costs (rentals paid to other phone companies) rather than expensing them as would have been appropriate
Parmalat (2003)	Parmalat is an Italian multinational company specializing in milk, fruit juice, and other food products. In the late 1990s, the company acquired various international subsidiaries and funded the acquisitions with debt. Ultimately, the fraud led to the largest bankruptcy in Europe. The company siphoned cash from subsidiaries through a complex scheme that: • Overstated cash and included the false recording of cash ostensibly held at major banks • Understated debt by entering into complex transactions with off-shore subsidiaries in tax-haven places such as countries in the Caribbean
HealthSouth (2003)	HealthSouth runs the largest group of inpatient rehabilitation hospitals in the United States. Top management directed company employees to grossly exaggerate earnings in order to meet shareholder and analyst expectations. A wide variety of schemes were used, including: • Billing group psychiatric sessions as individual sessions; for example, with ten people in a group session, billing for ten individual sessions instead of one group session • Using adjusted journal entries to both reduce expenses and enhance revenues
Dell (2005)	Dell is a U.S. computer maker that ultimately was forced to pay the SEC $100 million to settle fraud charges against the company. The fraud included various disclosure inaccuracies, including: • Misleading investors by miscategorizing large payments from Intel, which were essentially bribes to ensure that Dell would not use central processing units manufactured by Intel's main rival • Misrepresenting the Intel payments as involving operations, thereby enabling the company to meet its earnings targets • Failing to disclose the true reason for the company's profitability declines that occurred after Intel refused to continue making the payments
Koss Corp. (2009)	Koss Corporation is a U.S. headphone manufacturer. The CFO misappropriated approximately $31 million of funds for her personal use during a period of time in which reported earnings was $26 million. Ultimately, she had to pay $34 million in restitution and was given an eleven-year prison sentence. She perpetrated the fraud through a process consisting of: • Intimidation of lower-level employees • Sole approval for large expenditures made through American Express and other corporate credit cards • Lack of supervisory review and approval by the CEO • Lack of audit committee oversight • Lack of an effective internal audit function

Exhibit 2.3 *Continued*

Company	Nature of the Fraud
Olympus (2011)	Olympus is a large multinational manufacturer involved in the medical, life science, industrial, and imaging industries. Its top-level executives and boards: • Concealed large losses related to securities investments for over two decades • Switched audit firms during the period because company management clashed with their external auditor over accounting issues • Committed fraud, which was eventually revealed when the company's president was fired after discovering and objecting to accounting irregularities
Longtop Financial Technologies (2011)	Longtop Financial Technologies was the first Chinese software company to be listed on the New York Stock Exchange (NYSE) and was the leading software development provider in the financial services industry in that country. This fraud highlighted the risks that investors face when investing their money in Chinese companies with weak corporate governance. The company: • Exaggerated profit margins by shifting staffing expenses to another entity • Recorded fake cash to cover up fake revenue that had been previously recognized • Threatened the audit firm personnel and tried to physically retain the audit firm's workpapers when the auditors uncovered the fraud
Peregrine Financial Group (2012)	Peregrine Financial Group was a financial futures firm whose founder and sole shareholder, Russell Wasendorf, embezzled over $200 million during a 20-year period. Wasendorf concealed the fraud by: • Assuming complete and sole control over the bank statements • Forging the bank statements when they were reviewed by the firm's auditor Just before the fraud was discovered, the futures industry transitioned to an electronic confirmation system for bank statements that enabled the auditor to view the true bank statements. Knowing that the fraud would be uncovered in a few days, Wasendorf unsuccessfully attempted suicide and was ultimately sent to prison.
Sino-Forest Corporation (2012)	Sino-Forest Corporation is a China-based company in the timber production and wood-fiber industry. The company's top-level management orchestrated a financial reporting fraud and personally benefited by engaging in lucrative transactions between Sino-Forest and other companies that were secretly controlled by top-level management of Sino-Forest. The fraudulent actions perpetrated by management included: • Significantly overstating the valuation of timber assets • Making false public statements about the company's performance in order to manipulate stock price • Convincing suppliers and intermediaries in timber products transactions to hinder the investigation into the fraud
Diamond Foods, Inc. (2014)	Diamond Foods, Inc. is a large producer of snack food and culinary nut products. Walnuts are one of the company's primary raw materials. During 2010, the price of walnuts rose dramatically, which threatened to reduce the company's net income. The company's CFO, Steven Neil, orchestrated a fraudulent financial reporting scheme that involved the following activities and outcomes: • He instructed accounting personnel to delay recording the cost of walnuts acquired during 2010, thereby overstating earnings by $10.5 million. • He again instructed accounting personnel to delay recording the cost of walnuts acquired during 2011, this time overstating earnings by $23.6 million. • As a result, the company exceeded analyst earnings targets, leading to increases in the company's stock price to over $90 per share. • The company raised $181 million in a stock offering when the share price was artificially high. • Once the fraud was revealed, the stock price fell to just $17 per share, representing a market capitalization loss of about $1.7 billion.
Wells Fargo (2016)	Wells Fargo is a large and well-known federal savings bank, worth about $250 billion. Top management was not implicated. Rather, bank employees created phony PIN numbers and fake email addresses to enroll customers in online banking services. Employees created more than 1.5 million deposit accounts. Here is how it worked: • Employees moved funds from existing customer accounts into new accounts that they did not know about. Because the money was no longer in their existing accounts, they were charged for insufficient funds or overdraft fees. • Employees also submitted applications for over 565,000 credit card accounts without customers' knowledge or consent. To fully appreciate the extent of the fraud, about 14,000 of those credit cards incurred $400,000 in annual fees, interest charges, and overdraft fees. • The employees' motivation was greed. They used the fake accounts to boost their sales figures and bonuses. • Wells Fargo had to pay fines of $185 million, along with refunding $5 million to customers.

Company	Nature of the Fraud
Weatherford Int'l (2016)	Weatherford Int'l is an oil services company whose top management fraudulently understated its tax expenses. Weatherford management began boasting to its investors, starting in 2007, that the company was particularly strategic with respect to their accounting for income taxes, and that management was able to produce excellent earnings performance by aggressively employing such strategies.
	• Weatherford's executives in charge of tax reporting strategically used one tax accounting standard instead of another (more applicable) standard.
	• The executives intentionally reversed accounting entries that had been correctly entered into the company's accounting system, using a post year-end closing entry that reduced the reported tax expense by $440 million. To accomplish the fraud, they used **top-side journal entries**, which are entries not automatically recorded using the company's book-keeping software; rather, these entries are manually entered by an individual outside of the regular course of producing the financial statements.
	• The company's auditors, Ernst & Young, knew that the company's tax strategy was risky, and also knew of the company's failure to properly document its tax reporting and the errors in that reporting. The firm received an AAER (#3814) and were required to pay the SEC $11.8 million settlement.
	• Weatherford was also required to pay the SEC a large settlement, totaling $140 million.
Lime Energy Company (2016)	Lime Energy Company provides clean energy services to yield energy savings to utility clients under Small Business Direct Install (SBDI) programs. Their clients are small businesses who want help in designing and implementing energy efficiency projects.
	• The following executed the fraud: the Executive VP of Operations, the Corporate Controller, the Director of Operations, and the Vice President of Operations. The CEO and the CFO were not implicated, but ultimately gave up cash bonuses and stock awards that they had received during the fraud period.
	• Their motivation was to meet company-wide revenue and earnings targets, thereby enabling them to achieve bonuses.
	• Following a restatement of its results from 2008-2011 in 2013, the company disclosed it had recognized $17.4 million in revenue earlier than was appropriate under GAAP, and that it had also reported outright fictitious revenue of $14.2 million.

- There was heavy involvement in the fraud by the CEO and/or CFO, with at least one of them named in 89% of the cases.
- The most common fraud involved revenue recognition—60% of the cases during the latest period compared to 50% in previous periods.
- One-third of the companies changed auditors during the latter part of the fraud (with the full knowledge of the audit committee) compared to less than half that amount of auditor changes taking place with the nonfraud companies.
- The majority of the frauds took place at companies that were listed on the over-the-counter (OTC) market, rather than those listed on the NYSE or NASDAQ.

Commonly cited motivations for the frauds described in the COSO reports include the need to meet internal or external earnings expectations, an attempt to conceal the company's deteriorating financial condition, the need to increase the stock price, the need to bolster financial performance for pending equity or debt financing, or the desire to increase management compensation based on financial results.

The Enron Fraud

Enron is perhaps one of the most well-known frauds of the early 2000s, representing almost everything that was wrong at the time with corporate governance, accounting, financial analysts, banking, and the external auditing profession. How did it happen?

Why It Matters — The Crucial Role of Professional Skepticism

This feature provides various perspectives on professional skeptcisim.

What is **professional skepticism**, and how does an auditor maintain proper professional skepticism in an environment in which the auditor's personal experiences might consist only of audits in which no fraud was ever found? After all, we are all products of our experiences, and many times our audit experience will tell us that we spent extra time investigating something that showed nothing was wrong, resulting in increased audit time, but no discovery of wrongdoing. How do we approach each situation as something unique, and not the total culmination of our past experiences?

The Center for Audit Quality (CAQ), in its 2010 report on fraud, describes professional skepticism as follows:

Skepticism involves the validation of information through probing questions, the critical assessment of evidence, and attention to inconsistencies. Skepticism is not an end in itself and is not meant to encourage a hostile atmosphere or micromanagement; it is an essential element of the professional objectivity required of all participants in the financial reporting supply chain. Skepticism throughout the supply chain increases not only the likelihood that fraud will be detected, but also the perception that fraud will be detected, which reduces the risk that fraud will be attempted.

In a subsequent report, the CAQ (2014) articulates what it means for an audit client to be a fraud resistant organization:

"While there is no way to guarantee an organization will not fall victim to fraud, research on the qualities of, and techniques employed by, fraud-resistant organizations yields three themes:

- A tone at the top that encourages an ethical culture
- The presence of skepticism
- The engagement of all participants in the financial reporting supply chain, with all relevant parties understanding and effectively performing their roles with respect to the company's financial reporting" (p. 13).

For further details, see http://www.thecaq.org/fraud-resistant-organization

Similar to the CAQ (2010) report, International Standards on Auditing defines professional skepticism as follows:

Professional skepticism is an attitude that includes a questioning mind and a critical assessment of audit evidence.

Professional skepticism requires an ongoing questioning of whether the information and audit evidence obtained suggests that a material misstatement due to fraud may exist. (ISA 240, para. 23)

The Standard goes on to state:

The auditor's previous experience with the entity contributes to an understanding of the entity. However, although the auditor cannot be expected to fully disregard past experience with the entity about the honesty and integrity of management and those charged with governance, the maintenance of an attitude of professional skepticism is important because there may have been changes in circumstances. When making inquiries and performing other audit procedures, the auditor exercises professional skepticism and is not satisfied with less-than-persuasive audit evidence based on a belief that management and those charged with governance are honest and have integrity. With respect to those charged with governance, maintaining an attitude of professional skepticism means that the auditor carefully considers the reasonableness of responses to inquiries of those charged with governance, and other information obtained from them, in light of all other evidence obtained during the audit. (ISA 240, para. 25)

The report by the Global Public Policy Committee, "Enhancing Auditor Professional Skepticism" (November 2013), articulates a variety of definitions of professional skepticism and introduces a professional skepticism continuum. The skepticism continuum is founded on the belief that professional skepticism is related to a questioning mind, and that an individual may range from a neutral mindset, to a presumptive doubt mindset, to complete doubt. Complete trust would be outside the range on the continuum of professional skepticism. The continuum then relates to evidence collection, whereby lower skepticism is associated with less audit evidence and documentation and higher skepticism is associated with more audit evidence and documentation.

Taken together, these definitions highlight that the key elements to successfully exercising professional skepticism include obtaining strong evidence and analyzing that evidence through critical assessment, attention to inconsistencies, and asking probing (often open-ended) questions. The essence of auditing is to bring professional skepticism to the audit and to be alert to all of the possibilities that may cause the auditor to be misled.

For Classroom Discussion

What Do You Think?

After reading these various descriptions and definitions of professional skepticism, consider someone in your life that you view as particularly skeptical. Who is that person? How do you know him or her? What characteristics does he or she possess that influence your view about his or her relative skepticism? What factors in his or her life and experiences do you think made that person particularly skeptical? Do you think that you could exhibit professional skepticism when conducting an audit?

Enron was a utility company that developed a new concept and rode the new concept to unbelievable stock market highs. Just prior to its collapse, it had a stock value of $90 per share, which eventually became worthless. The concept:

> It would increase market efficiency by developing the most sophisticated system in the world to trade electricity, natural gas, and related resources. It would separate the production of energy—a capital-intensive process—from the trading and use of the resources. It would improve market efficiency by increasing the scope of energy production and expanding the output of the local utility to the nation and the world. Energy would flow where the highest market bid for it, which is a fundamental concept of economics.

Enron hired MBA traders and provided them with lucrative bonuses for meeting profit objectives. Competition among the traders was encouraged, and risks were encouraged; but most of all, reported profits were rewarded. However, much of the company, at its heart, remained a utility. It needed heavy amounts of cash to support its trading positions, and it needed to continually report higher profits to sustain stock market valuations. Most of the top executives of the company were compensated primarily through stock.

The fraud was widespread. Much of the fraud involved special-purpose entities (SPEs), partnerships that often involved substantial loans from banks to be secured by assets transferred to the SPE, partners dominated by Enron executives,

COSO

Who Are They?

The **Committee of Sponsoring Organizations of the Treadway Commission** (COSO, *www.coso.org*) is a recognized provider of guidance on internal control, enterprise risk management, and fraud deterrence. COSO is sponsored by five organizations, including the Financial Executives International, the American Institute of Certified Public Accountants, the American Accounting Association, the Institute of Internal Auditors, and the Association of Accountants and Financial Professionals in Business (IMA). COSO provides the internal control framework that serves as the benchmark for auditors who assess the effectiveness of their client's internal controls.

What Do You Think?   For Classroom Discussion

An example of a current SEC AAER can be found at *https://www .sec.gov/litigation/admin/2017/33-10286.pdf*

Read the AAER and consider the following questions: (1) What is the company involved in the fraud and what is their line of business? (2) What was the nature of the fraud? (3) How did the fraud come to light? Who was the person that led to its discovery? (4) It does not appear that the audit firm was charged in this case, but the company and its CFO, Myles Itkin, were charged. Why do

you think the auditing firm avoided SEC punishment for failing to detect the fraud in a timely manner?

If you are curious and want to challenge yourself, locate other recent AAERs on the SEC's website. Here's how to get there:

Go to *www.sec.gov*

Click on the Enforcement link.

Click on the Accounting and Auditing link.

Click on any current or prior year to retrieve the AAERs.

and a small outside interest (exceeding 3% per the accounting rule). The company transferred devalued assets to the SPEs and recognized gains on the books. It kept borrowing off the books by having the SPEs borrow from banks and purchase Enron assets. It even recognized over $100 million in anticipated sales that it hoped would occur with a joint venture with Blockbuster on rental movies over the Internet. The SPEs were used such that Enron's balance sheet looked healthy because it minimized the debt on the balance sheet; the SPEs also increased reported income by hiding all losses.

What were the failures that allowed the Enron fraud to occur? Unfortunately, the answer is that the failures were widespread and include problems in the following areas:

- *Management Accountability.* Management was virtually not accountable to anyone as long as the company showed dramatic stock increases justified by earnings growth. Company management had a "good story," and anyone who questioned them was viewed as being stupid. Compensation was based on stock price. Apparently, stock valuation was based on a good story and fictitious numbers.

- *Corporate Governance.* Although the board appeared to be independent, most of the board members had close ties to management of the company through philanthropic organizations. Some board members hardly ever attended a meeting, and they certainly did not ask hard questions. Finally, the board waived a conflict-of-interest provision in their code of ethics that allowed Andy Fastow, the treasurer of the company, to profit handsomely from related-party transactions.

- *Accounting Rules.* Accounting became more rule oriented and complex. Accountants used obscure pronouncements, such as those dealing with SPEs that were designed for leasing transactions, and applied them to other entities for which such accounting was never intended. Accounting was looked at as a tool to earn more money and not as a mechanism to portray economic reality.

- *The Financial Analyst Community.* Financial analysts who were riding the bubble of the dot-com economy concluded that they did not have tools to appropriately value many of the emerging companies. Rather than analyze the underlying fundamentals, the analysts relied too much on earnings guidance provided by management. Managers who achieved the projected guidance were rewarded; those who did not were severely punished. Analysts came to accept pro forma accounting statements, more aptly described as what would occur as long as nothing bad happened.

- *Banking and Investment Banking.* Many large financial institutions were willing participants in the process because they were rewarded with large underwriting fees for other Enron work. Enron management was smart enough to know that the investment bankers were also rewarded on the amount of fees they generated.

- *The External Auditing Profession and Arthur Andersen.* At the time of Enron, the largest five external audit firms referred to themselves as professional service firms with diverse lines of business. All of the firms had large consulting practices. Arthur Andersen performed internal audit work for Enron, in addition to performing the external audit. The consulting fees of many clients dramatically exceeded the audit fees. Partners were compensated on revenue and profitability. Worse yet, auditors were hired by management that sometimes succeeded in pressuring auditors to acquiesce to aggressive financial reporting preferences. In short, there is a perception that audit quality was low during this period of time. The final straw for Arthur Andersen was that when federal authorities began investigating the bankruptcy of Enron, the Houston office auditors on the Enron engagement began aggressively destroying documentation and evidence related to their failed audit. Ultimately, this action was what enabled federal authorities to force the downfall of Arthur Andersen.

Check Your Basic Knowledge

2-9 In the Enron fraud, one of the ways that management covered up the fraud was to shift debt off the balance sheet to SPEs. (T/F)

2-10 Professional skepticism related to detecting possible fraud involves the validation of information through probing questions, critical assessment of evidence, and attention to inconsistencies. (T/F)

2-11 Which of the following types of transactions did WorldCom management engage in as part of that company's fraudulent financial reporting scheme?
   a. Recorded barter transactions as sales.
   b. Used restructuring reserves from prior acquisitions to decrease expenses.
   c. Capitalizing line costs rather than expensing them.

   d. All of the above.
   e. None of the above.

2-12 Which of the following is an implication resulting from the *results of the* COSO studies?
   a. The most common frauds involve outright theft of assets.
   b. The individuals most often responsible for fraud include low-level accounting personnel, such as accounts payable clerks.
   c. The majority of frauds take place at smaller companies listed on the OTC market rather than at larger companies listed on the NYSE.
   d. All of the above.
   e. None of the above.

LO 4

Discuss auditors' fraud-related responsibilities and users' fraud-related expectations.

Fraud: Auditors' Responsibilities and Users' Expectations

Auditors' fraud-related responsibilities are important to improving the external auditor's contribution to society and to gaining respect for the auditing profession. However, preventing and detecting fraud cannot be the job of the external auditor alone; all the parties involved in preparing and opining on audited financial statements need to play a role in preventing and detecting fraud. Management, the audit committee, internal auditors, external auditors and regulatory authorities need to:

- Acknowledge that there needs to exist a strong, highly ethical tone at the top of an organization that permeates the corporate culture, including an effective fraud risk management program.
- Exercise professional skepticism, a questioning mindset that strengthens professional objectivity, in evaluating and/or preparing financial reports.
- Remember that strong communication among those involved in the financial reporting process is critical.

Fraud-Related Requirements in Professional Auditing Standards

Auditing standards historically have reflected a belief that it is not reasonable to expect auditors to detect cleverly implemented frauds. However, the general public expects auditors to be responsible for detecting and reporting on material frauds, as noted here:

> The mission of the PCAOB is to restore the confidence of investors, and society generally, in the independent auditors of companies. There is no doubt that repeated revelations of accounting scandals and audit failures have seriously damaged public confidence. The detection of material fraud is a reasonable expectation of users of audited financial statements. Society needs and expects assurance that financial information has not been materially misstated because of fraud. *Unless an independent audit can provide this assurance, it has little if any value to society.*

Professional auditing standards require the auditor to plan and perform an audit that will detect material misstatements resulting from fraud. As part of that requirement, auditors begin an audit with a brainstorming session focusing on how and where fraud could occur at the client. Auditors also need to communicate with the audit committee and management about the risks of fraud, and how the audit plan will address those risks.

Exhibit 2.4 provides details on the PCAOB, the American Institute of Certified Public Accountants (AICPA), and the International Auditing and Assurance Standards Board (IAASB) standards on audit considerations regarding fraud. The guidance from the AICPA and IAASB is essentially identical, with just minor wording differences in the standards. The PCAOB standard differs in terms of wording, but the substance of the guidance is the same.

Exhibit 2.4
Professional Standards on Audit Considerations Regarding Fraud

Considerations Regarding Fraud	PCAOB AS 2401	AICPA AU-C 240 and IAASB ISA 240
Management's responsibilities	Management is responsible for designing and implementing programs and controls to prevent, deter, and detect fraud.	The primary responsibility for the prevention and detection of fraud rests with both those charged with governance of the entity and management.

Considerations Regarding Fraud	PCAOB AS 2401	AICPA AU-C 240 and IAASB ISA 240
The auditor's responsibilities	The auditor is responsible for planning and performing the audit to obtain reasonable assurance about whether the financial statements are free of material misstatement, whether caused by error or fraud. The standard acknowledges that there is an unavoidable risk that some material misstatements may be undetected, even if the audit is properly planned and performed.	The auditor is responsible for obtaining reasonable assurance that the financial statements as a whole are free of material misstatement, whether caused by error or fraud. The standard acknowledges that there is an unavoidable risk that some material misstatements may be undetected, even if the audit is properly planned and performed.
Professional skepticism	Furthermore, professional skepticism requires an ongoing questioning of whether the information and evidence obtained suggests that a material misstatement due to fraud has occurred. In exercising professional skepticism in gathering and evaluating evidence, the auditor should not be satisfied with less-than-persuasive evidence because of a belief that management is honest.	The auditor should maintain professional skepticism, regardless of the auditor's past experience with honesty and integrity of management and those charged with governance. The auditor should investigate when management or those charged with governance provide unsatisfactory responses (e.g., inconsistent, vague, or implausible) to questions. The auditor may accept records and documents as genuine but should investigate if the auditor believes that such an assumption is not appropriate.
Risk assessment	The auditor should formally assess fraud risk through a discussion among the engagement team members (commonly referred to as **fraud brainstorming**). The auditor should identify unusual or unexpected relationships in performing analytical procedures that might indicate fraud.	The auditor should formally assess fraud risk through a discussion among the engagement team members (commonly referred to as *fraud brainstorming*). The auditor should identify unusual or unexpected relationships in performing analytical procedures that might indicate fraud.
Risk response	The auditor must respond to identified fraud risks. Responses should include ensuring that audit personnel are adequately trained and supervised, evaluating whether subjective or complex transactions may indicate fraud, and incorporating an element of unpredictability in the nature, timing, and extent of audit procedures.	The auditor must respond to identified fraud risks. Responses should include ensuring that audit personnel are adequately trained and supervised, evaluating whether subjective or complex transactions may indicate fraud, and incorporating an element of unpredictability in the nature, timing, and extent of audit procedures.

Check Your Basic Knowledge

2-13 The investing public generally recognizes that it is very difficult for auditors to detect fraud, so investors do not hold auditors accountable when auditors fail to detect fraud.   (T/F)

2-14 The mission of the SEC is to restore the confidence of investors, and society generally, in the independent auditors of companies.   (T/F)

2-15 Which of the following statements is <u>true</u> regarding the deterrence and detection of fraud in financial reporting?
   a. Preventing and detecting fraud is the job of the external auditor alone.
   b. An effective fraud risk management program can be expected to prevent virtually all frauds, especially those perpetrated by top management.
   c. Communication among those involved in the financial reporting process is critical.
   d. All of the above.
   e. None of the above.

2-16 Which of the following statements is <u>true</u>?
   a. Unless an independent audit can provide reasonable assurance that financial information has not been materially misstated because of fraud, it has little, if any, value to society.
   b. Repeated revelations of accounting scandals and audit failures related to undetected frauds have seriously damaged public confidence in external auditors.
   c. A strong ethical tone at the top of an organization that permeates corporate culture is essential in mitigating the risk of fraud.
   d. All of the above.
   e. None of the above.

What Do You Think? For Classroom Discussion

Auditors are held accountable for their ability to detect fraud, facing severe consequences sometimes for not detecting fraud. However, management may collude, lie to the auditors, and cover up a fraud. Do you think the auditors' negative consequences, both in monetary and reputation terms, are unfair as a result?

LO 5

Explain how various requirements in the Sarbanes-Oxley Act of 2002 help prevent fraud.

The Sarbanes-Oxley Act of 2002 as a Regulatory Response to Fraud

The financial scandals and associated stock market declines in the early 2000s dramatically illustrate the costs of various parties' bad ethical decisions, weak corporate governance, low audit quality, and insufficient auditor independence. The bankruptcy of Enron and the subsequent collapse of its auditing firm, Arthur Andersen, were such dramatic events that Congress was compelled to respond, and it did so in the form of the **Sarbanes-Oxley Act of 2002**.

The Act only applies to publicly traded companies. *Exhibit 2.5* summarizes selected provisions most relevant to auditors and the audit opinion formulation process of the Sarbanes-Oxley Act (to access the entire Act, see *www.sec.gov/about/laws/soa2002.pdf*).

Exhibit 2.5

Significant Audit-Related Provisions of the Sarbanes-Oxley Act of 2002

TITLE I: Public Company Accounting Oversight Board

101   *Establishment and administrative provisions.* The Board:

- Is a nonprofit corporation, not an agency of the U.S. government
- Will have five financially literate members who are prominent individuals of integrity and reputation with a commitment to the interests of investors and the public
- Has authority to set standards related to audit reports and to conduct inspections of registered public accounting firms

102   *Registration with the Board.* Accounting firms auditing public companies must register with the PCAOB.

103   *Auditing, quality control, and independence standards and rules.* The Board will:

- Establish or adopt rules regarding the conduct of audits and regarding audit firm quality-control standards
- Require audit firms to describe the scope of testing of issuers' internal control structure

104   *Inspections of registered public accounting firms.* The Board will:

- Inspect annually registered accounting firms that audit 100 or more issuers
- Inspect at least every three years registered accounting firms that audit fewer than 100 issuers
- Publicly report results of its inspections

105   *Investigations and disciplinary proceedings.* The Board will:

- Adopt procedures for disciplining registered accounting firms
- Require registered accounting firms to provide documentation and testimony that the Board deems necessary to conduct investigations
- Be able to sanction registered accounting firms for noncooperation with investigations

106   *Foreign public accounting firms.* Foreign accounting firms must comply with the same rules related to the PCAOB as domestic accounting firms.

107   *Commission oversight of the Board.* The SEC has oversight and enforcement authority over the Board, including in processes involving standards setting, enforcement, and disciplinary procedures.

108   *Accounting standards.* The SEC will recognize as "generally accepted" accounting principles that are established by a standard setter that meets the Act's criteria.

109   *Funding.* Registered accounting firms and issuers will pay for the operations of the Board.

TITLE II: Auditor Independence

201   *Services outside the scope of practice of auditors.* There are a variety of services that registered accounting firms may not perform for issuers, such as bookkeeping, systems design, appraisal services, and internal auditing, among others. Tax services may be performed, but only with preapproval by the audit committee.

202   *Preapproval requirements.* All audit and nonaudit services (with certain exceptions based on size and practicality) must be approved by the audit committee of the issuer.

203   *Audit partner rotation.* The lead partner and reviewing partner must rotate off the issuer engagement at least every five years.

204   *Auditor reports to audit committees.* Registered accounting firms must report to the audit committee issues concerning:

- Critical accounting policies and practices
- Alternative treatments of financial information within generally accepted accounting principles that have been considered by management, as well as the preferred treatment of the accounting firm
- Significant written communications between the accounting firm and management

205   *Conforming amendments.* This section details minor wording changes between the Sarbanes-Oxley Act and the Securities Act of 1934.

206   *Conflicts of interest.* Registered accounting firms may not perform audits for an issuer whose CEO, CFO, controller, chief accounting officer, or other equivalent position was employed by the accounting firm during the one-year period preceding the audit. This is known as a **cooling-off period**.

207   *Study of mandatory rotation of registered public accounting firms.* The Comptroller General of the United States shall conduct a study addressing this issue.

TITLE III: Corporate Responsibility

301   *Public company audit committees.*

- Audit committees are to be directly responsible for the appointment, compensation, and oversight of the work of registered accounting firms.
- Each audit committee member shall be independent.
- Audit committees must establish whistle-blowing mechanisms within issuers.
- Audit committees have the authority to engage their own independent counsel.
- Issuers must provide adequate funding for audit committees.

302   *Corporate responsibility for financial reports.* The signing officers (usually the CEO and CFO):

- Will certify in quarterly and annual reports filed with the SEC that the report does not contain untrue statements of material facts and that the financial statements and disclosures present fairly (in all material respects) the financial condition and results of operations of the issuer
- Must establish and maintain effective internal controls to ensure reliable financial statements and disclosures
- Are responsible for designing internal controls, assessing their effectiveness, and disclosing material deficiencies in controls to the audit committee and to the registered accounting firm

Exhibit 2.5   *Continues*

Exhibit 2.5 *Continued*

303   *Improper influence on conduct of audits.* Officers of issuers may not take action to fraudulently influence, coerce, manipulate, or mislead the registered accounting firm or its employees.

TITLE IV: Enhanced Financial Disclosures

401   *Disclosures in periodic reports.*

- Financial reports must be in accordance with generally accepted accounting principles and must reflect material correcting adjustments proposed by the registered accounting firm.
- Material off-balance sheet transactions and other relationships with unconsolidated entities or persons must be disclosed.
- The SEC must issue new rules on pro forma figures and must study the issues of off-balance sheet transactions and the use of SPEs.

402   *Enhanced conflict of interest provisions.* Issuers may not extend credit to directors or executive offers.

403   *Disclosures of transactions involving management and principal stockholders.* Requires that any director, officer, or shareholder who owns more than 10% of the company's equity securities publicly disclose that fact.

404   *Management assessment of internal controls.*

- Annual reports must state the responsibility of management for establishing and maintaining an adequate internal control structure and procedures for financial reporting.
- Annual reports must contain an assessment of the effectiveness of the internal control structure and procedures of the issuer for financial reporting.
- Each registered accounting firm must attest to and report on the assessment made by the management of the issuer, and such attestation must not be the subject of a separate engagement (in other words, requires an integrated audit).

406   *Code of ethics for senior financial officers.* The SEC must issue rules requiring issuers to disclose whether or not the issuer has adopted a code of ethics for senior financial officers (and if not, the issuer must explain the rationale).

407   *Disclosure of audit committee financial expert.* The SEC must issue rules to require issuers to disclose whether or not the audit committee of the issuer includes at least one member who is a financial expert (and if not, the issuer must explain the rationale).

Title I removes self-regulation of the auditing profession and replaces it with independent oversight by the PCAOB. Section 201 prevents audit firms from providing many consulting services to audit clients, which was an issue cited as a significant driver of the failed audits of Enron. Sections 204, 301, and 407 significantly expand the power, responsibilities, and disclosures of corporate audit committees, thereby addressing concerns over weak corporate governance. Audit committees are directly responsible for the oversight of the company's external auditors and have the power to hire and fire the auditors.

Section 404 requires management assessment and external audit firm attestation regarding the effectiveness of internal control over financial reporting—a key structural problem in many organizations experiencing fraud.

What Do You Think?   For Classroom Discussion

Read the various sections of the Sarbanes-Oxley Act at *https://www.sec.gov/about/laws/soa2002.pdf*

Which provisions strike you as the most important/influential in preventing potential fraud? Which provisions surprise you or change your view of the auditing profession and regulation? Explain why.

2-17 The AICPA wrote the Sarbanes-Oxley Act of 2002 to address problems revealed in frauds that were committed in the late 1980s.   (T/F)

2-18 An important change resulting from the Sarbanes-Oxley Act is that auditors are no longer allowed to provide most consulting services for their public company audit clients.   (T/F)

2-19 Refer to *Exhibit 2.5*. The Sarbanes-Oxley Act enacted which of the following provisions relevant to auditors and the audit opinion formulation process?

    a. The PCAOB was established, and it has the power to conduct inspections of public company audits.

    b. The lead audit partner and reviewing partner must rotate off the audit of a publicly traded company at least every 10 years.

    c. In the annual report, management must acknowledge that they are required to have the company's

internal audit function attest to the accuracy of the annual reports.

    d. All of the above.

    e. None of the above.

2-20 Which of the following statements is <u>true</u> regarding the PCAOB?

    a. The PCAOB is a nonprofit corporation, not an agency of the U.S. government.

    b. The PCAOB will have five financially literate members who are prominent individuals of integrity and reputation with a commitment to the interests of investors and the public.

    c. The PCAOB has authority to set standards related to public company audit reports and to conduct inspections of registered external audit firms.

    d. All of the above.

    e. None of the above.

For Classroom Discussion

One part of Section 302 of the Sarbanes-Oxley Act states that the CEO and CFO:

    "Will certify in quarterly and annual reports filed with the SEC that the report does not contain untrue statements of material facts and that the financial statements and

disclosures present fairly (in all material respects) the financial condition and results of operations of the issuer."

If top management is committing a fraud, do you think that they will refuse to certify the annual reports? What do you think that they will do when faced with that requirement?

Corporate Governance Defined

LO 6

Define corporate governance, identify the parties involved, and describe their respective activities.

Corporate governance is a process by which the owners (stockholders) and creditors of an organization exert control and require accountability for the resources entrusted to the organization. The owners elect a board of directors to provide oversight of the organization's activities and accountability to stakeholders.

Exhibit 2.6 identifies the parties involved in corporate governance. Governance starts with the owners delegating responsibilities to management through an elected **board of directors**—including a subcommittee of the board that serves as an **audit committee**. In turn, responsibilities are given to operating units, with oversight and assistance from internal auditors. The board of directors and its audit committee oversee management, and, in that role, are to protect the stockholders' rights and ensure that controls exist to prevent and detect fraud. However, it is important to recognize that management is part of the governance framework; management can influence who sits on the board and the audit committee, as well as other governance activities.

Exhibit 2.6

Overview of Corporate Governance Responsibilities and Accountabilities

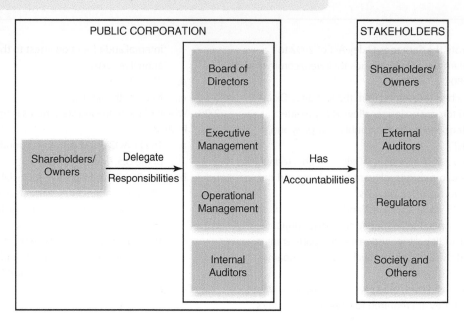

In return for the responsibilities (and power) given to management and the board, governance demands accountability back through the system to the owners and other stakeholders. **Stakeholders** include anyone who is affected, either directly or indirectly, by the actions of a company. Management and the board have responsibilities to act within the laws of society and to meet various requirements of creditors and employees and other stakeholders.

Exhibit 2.7 describes the responsibilities of major parties involved in corporate governance. These parties each have unique responsibilities, but rely on the other parties to help ensure quality financial reporting through effective corporate governance. The term **corporate governance mosaic** refers to the fact that each of these parties has complementary roles and specific responsibilities; no one party is completely responsible.

Exhibit 2.7

Corporate Governance Responsibilities

Party	Overview of Responsibilities
Stockholders	Provide effective oversight through election of board members, through approval of major initiatives (such as buying or selling stock), and through annual reports on management compensation from the board
Board of Directors	Serve as representatives of stockholders; ensure that the organization is run according to the organization's charter and that there is proper accountability **Specific activities include:** • Selecting management • Reviewing management performance and determining compensation • Declaring dividends • Approving major changes, such as mergers • Approving corporate strategy • Overseeing accountability activities

Party	Overview of Responsibilities
Management	Manage the organization effectively; provide accurate and timely accountability to shareholders and other stakeholders
	Specific activities include:
	• Formulating strategy and risk management
	• Implementing effective internal controls
	• Developing financial and other reports to meet public, stakeholder, and regulatory requirements
	• Managing and reviewing operations
	• Implementing an effective ethical environment
Audit Committees of the Board of Directors	Provide oversight of the internal and external audit function and over the process of preparing the annual financial statements and public reports on internal control
	Specific activities include:
	• Selecting the external audit firm
	• Approving any nonaudit work performed by the audit firm
	• Selecting and/or approving the appointment of the chief audit executive (internal auditor)
	• Reviewing and approving the scope and budget of the internal audit function
	• Discussing audit findings with internal and external auditors, and advising the board (and management) on specific actions that should be taken
Regulators and Standards Setters (PCAOB, SEC, AICPA, FASB, IAASB, IASB)	Set accounting and auditing standards dictating underlying financial reporting and auditing concepts; set the expectations of audit quality and accounting quality
	Specific activities include:
	• Establishing accounting principles
	• Establishing auditing standards
	• Interpreting previously issued standards
	• Enforcing adherence to relevant standards and rules for public companies and their auditors

Accounting Standards and Accounting Standards Setting Organizations

Who Are They?

Generally Accepted Accounting Principles (GAAP) in the United States have traditionally been set by the **Financial Accounting Standards Board** (FASB, *http://www.fasb.org/home*) with approval by the SEC.

International accounting standards (**IFRS—International Financial Reporting Standards**) are set by the International Financial Reporting Standards Foundation of the **International Accounting Standards Board** (IASB, *http://www.ifrs.org/About-us/IASB/Pages/Home.aspx*).

For Classroom Discussion

What Do You Think?

Consider the roles and responsibilities of each of these parties with corporate governance responsibilities. Which party do you think is most responsible for *preventing* fraud? Which party do you think is most responsible for *detecting* fraud?

Characteristics of Effective Corporate Governance

What characteristics and actions on the part of organizations are important to quality corporate governance? In 2010, a commission sponsored by the NYSE issued a report identifying key core governance principles. The report includes both broad principles related to boards and management, along with very specific corporate governance guidelines.

Broad Principles

The board's fundamental objective should be to build long-term sustainable growth in shareholder value for the corporation. Successful corporate governance depends upon successful management of the company, as management has the primary responsibility for creating a culture of performance with integrity and ethical behavior. Effective corporate governance should be integrated with the company's business strategy and not viewed as simply a compliance obligation. Transparency is a critical element of effective corporate governance, and companies should make regular efforts to ensure that they have sound disclosure policies and practices. Independence and objectivity are necessary attributes of board members; however, companies must also strike the right balance in the appointment of independent and nonindependent directors to ensure an appropriate range and mix of expertise, diversity, and knowledge on the board.

NYSE corporate governance guidelines

- Boards need to consist of a majority of independent directors.
- Boards need to hold regular executive sessions of independent directors without management present.
- Boards must have a nominating/corporate governance committee composed entirely of independent directors.
- The nominating/corporate governance committee must have a written charter that addresses the committee's purpose and responsibilities, and there must be an annual performance evaluation of the committee.
- Boards must have a compensation committee composed entirely of independent directors.
- The compensation committee must have a written charter that addresses the committee's purpose and responsibilities, which must include (at a minimum) the responsibility to review and approve corporate goals relevant to CEO compensation, to make recommendations to the board about non-CEO compensation and incentive-based compensation plans, and to produce a report on executive compensation; there must also be an annual performance evaluation of the committee.
- Boards must have an audit committee with a minimum of three independent members.
- The audit committee must have a written charter that addresses the committee's purpose and responsibilities, and the committee must produce an audit committee report; there must also be an annual performance evaluation of the committee.
- Companies must adopt and disclose corporate governance guidelines addressing director qualification standards, director responsibilities, director access to management and independent advisors, director compensation, director continuing education, management succession, and an annual performance evaluation of the board.
- Companies must adopt and disclose a code of business conduct and ethics for directors, officers, and employees.
- Foreign companies must disclose how their corporate governance practices differ from those followed by domestic companies.

- CEOs must provide an annual certification of compliance with corporate governance standards.
- Companies must have an internal audit function, whether housed internally or outsourced.

NYSE

Who Are They?

According to Wikipedia: "The **New York Stock Exchange** (abbreviated as **NYSE** and nicknamed "The Big Board"), is an American stock exchange located at 11 Wall Street, Lower Manhattan, New York City, New York. It is by far the world's largest stock exchange by market capitalization of its listed companies at US $19.3 trillion as of June 2016."

The NYSE came into existence on May 17, 1792, with 24 stockbrokers and five available securities for purchase and sale (three government bonds and two bank stocks). The NYSE is a highly liquid capital market, and is considered one of the most demanding, high-quality markets in which to trade.

You may wish to review its website at *https://www.nyse .com/index*

As an example of what you can learn on the NYSE's website, you can read about its fascinating business model: "The NYSE's unique market model combines leading technology with human judgment to prioritize price discovery and stability over speed for our listed companies. Coupled with our electronic markets, we believe nothing can take the place of human insight and accountability. It's the human element at NYSE that results in lower volatility, deeper liquidity and improved prices" (see *https://www.nyse .com/market-model*).

For Classroom Discussion

What Do You Think?

In 2014, the New York Stock Exchange (NYSE) provided an updated report with further details on stakeholder perspectives about corporate governance, viewpoints on the composition and structure of the Board of Directors, key challenges for boards and management, shareholder activism, and international "hot button" issues. To access a complete copy of the report, go to *https://www.nyse.com/publicdocs/nyse/listing/ NYSE_Corporate_Governance_Guide.pdf*

An emerging trend in corporate governance and stock trading is the concept of shareholder activism. After reading the Guide, define shareholder activism. Why is it important? Why do you think there exist more shareholder activists today as compared to in the past?

Responsibilities of Audit Committees

Section 301 of the Sarbanes-Oxley Act outlines the responsibilities of audit committee members for publicly traded companies. Audit committees are to be directly responsible for the appointment, compensation, and oversight of the work of audit firms. Audit committees must be independent, they must establish whistleblowing mechanisms within the company, they must have the authority to engage their own independent counsel, and they must provide adequate funding for audit committees.

In addition to these broad responsibilities, the NYSE has mandated certain specific responsibilities of audit committees, including:

- Obtaining an annual report by the external auditor that addresses the company's internal control procedures, any quality-control or regulatory problems, and any relationships that might threaten the independence of the external auditor

- Discussing the company's financial statements with management and the external auditor
- Discussing in its meetings the company's earnings press releases, as well as financial information and earnings guidance provided to analysts
- Discussing in its meetings policies with respect to risk assessment and risk management
- Meeting separately with management, internal auditors, and the external auditor on a periodic basis
- Reviewing with the external auditor any audit problems or difficulties that they have had with management
- Setting clear hiring policies for employees or former employees of the external auditor
- Reporting regularly to the board of directors

Further, in many organizations the audit committee also has the authority to hire and fire the head of the internal audit function, set the budget for the internal audit activity, review the internal audit plan, and discuss all significant internal audit results. Other responsibilities might include performing or supervising special investigations, reviewing policies on sensitive payments, and coordinating periodic reviews of compliance with company policies such as corporate governance policies.

Why It Matters

Audit Committee Members' Liability for Preventing and Detecting Fraud

This feature illustrates SEC action on enforcing penalties on audit committee members who fail to perform their duties.

Two enforcement actions by the SEC against audit committee members highlight the potential liability that audit committee members face if they do not perform their duties responsibly in the presence of fraud red flags. These cases illustrate the importance that financial statement users and regulators attach to the role of audit committee members and highlight the downside risks to such individuals should they fail to adequately attend to their responsibilities.

The first case involves an enforcement action against the entire three-member audit committee of DHB Industries, a manufacturer of body armor used by the police and military. Top management of DHB committed a variety of illegal acts including financial reporting fraud, conspiracy, misappropriation of corporate funds, and insider trading. What is notable about the case, however, is that in addition to pursuing charges against management, the SEC also vigorously pursued charges against each of the audit committee members (Jerome Krantz, Cary Chasin, and Gary Nadelman). The investigation revealed that these individuals were not independent of top management, they deliberately ignored fraud red flags, allowed top management to attempt to thwart

the external auditor's and SEC's investigations, and participated in various aspects of the fraud. The three audit committee members were ultimately barred from serving as an officer or director of a public company and they paid a total of $1.6 million in fines.

For further details, see http://www.sec.gov/litigation/litreleases/2011/lr21867.htm and http://www.sec.gov/news/press/2011/2011-238.htm

The second case involves an enforcement action against the audit committee chair of InfoUSA, a sales and marketing firm that compiles and sells business and consumer databases. Similar to the DHB case, top management committed a variety of illegal acts, including inappropriate personal use of corporate assets. The audit committee chair, Vasant Raval, was informed of various aspects of the fraudulent activity by the head of internal audit and legal counsel. The board of directors requested that Raval investigate allegations of fraud. Raval wrote a report, but it was incomplete and he never challenged top management. He was ultimately fined $50,000 and received a five-year bar from serving as an officer or director of a public company.

For further details, see http://www.sec.gov/litigation/complaints/2010/comp21451-raval.pdf

For Classroom Discussion

To view the full set of NYSE listing requirements for companies wishing to access this capital market, see *http://nysemanual.nyse.com/LCM/*

How many sections of requirements exist? Why do you think there are so many specific requirements? How do these requirements help companies that are seeking capital? How do these requirements make it difficult for companies that are seeking capital?

Note that requirement 103.01B states that a company must meet an "earnings test," which requires that pre-tax earnings from continuing operations must total at least $100,000,000 in the aggregate for the last three fiscal years with a minimum of $25,000,000 in each of the most recent two fiscal years.

What are the implications of an earnings test in terms of companies' access to capital on the NYSE? How does an earnings test protect investors? How does the existence of an earnings test provide an incentive for management to commit financial reporting fraud?

2-21 Corporate governance is the process by which the owners and creditors of an organization exert control over and require accountability for the resources entrusted to the organization.   (T/F)

2-22 The term corporate governance mosaic refers to the fact that each of the parties involved in corporate governance has complementary roles and specific responsibilities; no one party is completely responsible.   (T/F)

2-23 Audit committee activities and responsibilities include which of the following?
   a. Selecting the external audit firm.
   b. Approving corporate strategy.
   c. Reviewing management performance and determining compensation.
   d. All of the above.
   e. None of the above.

2-24 Which of the following audit committee responsibilities has the NYSE mandated?
   a. Obtaining a report each year by the internal auditor that addresses the company's internal control procedures, any quality-control or regulatory problems, and any relationships that might threaten the independence of the internal auditor.
   b. Discussing in its meetings the company's earnings press releases as well as financial information and earnings guidance provided to analysts.
   c. Reviewing with the internal auditor any audit problems or difficulties that they have had with management.
   d. All of the above.
   e. None of the above.

For Classroom Discussion

Audit committee members have significant responsibilities, and can be held responsible should they fail to execute those responsibilities. They also can be held responsible for making poor judgments and/or making bad decisions that negatively affect the company on whose board they serve.

Go to the following link, which provides Ford Motor Company's 2017 Proxy Statement: *http://shareholder.ford.com/~/media/Files/F/Ford-IR/annual-report/2017-proxy-statement.pdf*

Locate the information about the audit committee member in the proxy. To find it efficiently, search on the name of the Audit Committee Chair, Stephen Butler. Who are Ford's four audit committee members? Search for their bios; what are their backgrounds? What are their responsibilities? Locate their compensation information. Notice that the Chairman of the Audit Committee makes $125,000 in cash alone for serving in that role. Do you think that compensation is sufficient or excessive?

Let's Review

- The major types of fraud include misappropriation of assets (i.e., theft) and financial reporting fraud. The major characteristics of fraud are best represented by the fraud triangle, including incentive, opportunity, and rationalization. (LO 1, 2)

- Fraud raises important concerns for external auditors, as external auditors have professional obligations to perform an audit that provides reasonable assurance that the financial statements are free from material misstatement, including fraud. Fraud studies indicate that fraud is most common in the revenue cycle and the acquisition/payment cycle. The median size of the company perpetrating the fraud rose tenfold to $100 million during the 1998–2007 period (as compared to the previous 10 years). The CEO and/or CFO are often implicated in the fraud. The majority of the frauds take place at companies listed on the over-the-counter (OTC) market, rather than those listed on the NYSE or NASDAQ. (LO 3)

- To mitigate fraud, organizations need a strong, highly ethical tone at the top that permeates the corporate culture, including an effective fraud risk management program. Auditors must exercise professional skepticism, a questioning mindset that strengthens professional objectivity, in evaluating and/or preparing financial reports. Auditor should take care to remember that strong communication among those involved in the financial reporting process is critical. (LO 4)

- Knowing that auditors will be evaluating the financial statements may prevent fraud because managers know that they are accountable. Auditing standards historically have reflected a belief that it is not reasonable to expect auditors to detect cleverly implemented frauds. However, the public expects that auditors have a responsibility to detect and report on material frauds. (LO 4)

- All parties in the corporate governance mosaic have a responsibility to monitor for fraud. The Sarbanes-Oxley Act of 2002 provides various requirements intended to strengthen controls, prevent fraud, and improve audit quality. (LO 4, 5, 6)

- Governance starts with the owners delegating responsibilities to management through an elected board of directors—including a subcommittee of the board that serves as an audit committee. In turn, responsibilities are handed to operating units with oversight and assistance from internal auditors. The board of directors and its audit committee oversee management, and, in that role, are expected to protect the stockholders' rights and ensure that controls exist to prevent and detect fraud. However, it is important to recognize that management is part of the governance framework; management can influence who sits on the board and the audit committee, as well as other governance controls that might be put into place. (LO 6)

Significant Terms

Asset misappropriation   A fraud that involves the theft or misuse of an organization's assets. Common examples include skimming cash, stealing inventory, and payroll fraud.

Audit committee   A subcommittee of the board of directors responsible for monitoring audit activities and serving as a surrogate for the interests of shareholders; it should be composed of outside members of the board, that is, members who are independent of the organization.

Board of directors   The major representative of stockholders to help ensure that the organization is run according to the organization's charter and that there is proper accountability.

Committee of Sponsoring Organizations of the Treadway Commission (COSO)   A joint initiative among five private-sector organizations to combat corporate fraud by guiding executive management and those involved in governance in terms of business ethics, internal control, enterprise risk management, fraud, and financial reporting.

Cooling-off period   A one-year period of time during which registered accounting firms may not perform audits whose CEO, CFO, controller, chief accounting officer or other equivalent position was employed by the accounting firm.

Corporate governance   A process by which the owners and creditors of an organization exert control and require accountability for the resources entrusted to the organization. The owners (stockholders) elect a board of directors to provide oversight of the organization's activities and accountability to stakeholders.

Corporate governance mosaic   Each of the parties with responsibilities in terms of corporate governance has complementary roles and specific responsibilities; no one party is completely responsible.

Financial Accounting Standards Board (FASB)   The independent, private-sector, not-for-profit organization that establishes financial accounting and reporting standards for public and private companies and not-for-profit organizations that follow Generally Accepted Accounting Principles (GAAP).

Fraudulent financial reporting   The intentional manipulation of reported financial results to misstate the economic condition of the organization.

Fraud   An intentional act involving the use of deception that results in a material misstatement of the financial statements.

Fraud brainstorming   A formal discussion among the audit engagement team members about the possibility of fraud, including a fraud risk assessment.

Fraud triangle   A model that recognizes that incentives, opportunities, and rationalization are elements typically associated with fraud.

Generally Accepted Accounting Principles (GAAP)   GAAP refers to generally accepted accounting principles for financial reporting. Throughout the book we recognize that the criteria may be developed by either the FASB or the IASB. GAAP has general acceptance and provides criteria by which to assess the fairness of a financial statement presentation.

Incentive   The underlying reason for a fraudster to commit fraud.

International Accounting Standards Board (IASB)   An independent, private-sector body that develops and approves International Financial Reporting Standards (IFRSs). The IASB was formed in 2001 and replaced the International Accounting Standards Committee.

International Financial Reporting Standards (IFRSs)   A set of accounting standards developed by an independent, not-for-profit organization called the International Accounting Standards Board (IASB).

Opportunity   The internal control weakness that enables the fraudster to commit and conceal the fraud.

Ponzi scheme   This type of fraud occurs when the deposits of current investors are used to pay returns on the deposits of previous investors; no real investment is happening.

Professional skepticism   An attitude that includes a questioning mind, being alert to conditions which may indicate possible misstatement due to error or fraud, and a critical assessment of audit evidence.

Rationalization   The mental process that fraudsters employ to 'live with themselves' as they try to convince themselves that what they are doing is *not* wrong or is in some way justifiable.

Red flags   Risk factors suggesting a heightened risk of fraud.

Sarbanes-Oxley Act of 2002   Broad legislation mandating new standard setting for audits of public companies and new standards for corporate governance.

Stakeholders   Anyone who is influenced, either directly or indirectly, by the actions of a company; stakeholders extend beyond the shareholders of a company.

Top-side journal entries   These are adjusting journal entries that are not automatically recorded using the company's book-keeping software; rather, these entries are manually entered by an individual outside of the regular course of producing the financial statements.

Prompts for Critical Thinking

Prompt for Critical Thinking #1

- Pending retirement or stock option expirations
- Personal wealth tied to either financial results or survival of the company

- Greed—for example, the backdating of stock options was performed by individuals who already had millions of dollars of wealth through stock
- Personal factors, such as severe financial difficulties
- Pressure from family, friends, or the culture to live a more lavish lifestyle than one's personal earnings enable
- Addiction to gambling or drugs

Prompt for Critical Thinking #2

- Simple transactions that are made complex through an unusual recording process
- Complex or difficult-to-understand transactions, such as financial derivatives or special-purpose entities
- Ineffective monitoring of management by the board, either because the board of directors is not independent or effective, or because there is a domineering manager
- Complex or unstable organizational structure
- Weak or nonexistent internal controls, especially a lack of segregation of duties

Prompt for Critical Thinking #3

- We need a higher stock price to acquire company XYZ, or to keep our employees through stock options, and so forth.
- Fraud is justified to save a family member or loved one from financial crisis.
- No help is available from outside.
- This is "borrowing," and I intend to pay the stolen money back at some point.
- The organization owes me because others are treated better.
- I simply do not care about the consequences of my actions or of accepted notions of decency and trust; I have to look out for myself.

Review Questions and Short Cases

NOTE: Completing *Review Questions and Short Cases* does not require the student to reference additional resources and materials.

NOTE: We make special note of problems addressing international issues, professional skepticism, and ethics. *We do not make special note of fraud-related problems in this chapter because of the heavy emphasis on that topic throughout this chapter.*

2-1 **LO 1** Define fraud and explain the two types of misstatements that are relevant to auditors' consideration of fraud.

2-2 **LO 1** What are the most common approaches that perpetrators use to commit fraudulent financial reporting? What are the common types of fraudulent financial reporting?

2-3 **LO 1** Assume that you are interviewed by a student newspaper regarding the nature of accounting fraud. The reporter says, "As I understand it, asset misappropriations are more likely to be found in small organizations, but not in larger organizations. On the other hand, fraudulent financial reporting is more likely to be found in larger organizations." How would you respond to the reporter's observation?

2-4 **LO 1** Refer to *Exhibit 2.1*
  a. What is a Ponzi scheme?
  b. Describe the key elements of the Bernie Madoff fraud.
  c. Is this fraud primarily a case of asset misappropriation or fraudulent financial reporting?

2-5 **LO 1, 2** Refer to the *Focus on Fraud* feature "The Great Salad Oil Swindle of 1963."
  a. How did management perpetrate the fraud?
  b. What was management's incentive to perpetrate the fraud?
  c. Is this fraud primarily a case of asset misappropriation or fraudulent financial reporting?

2-6 **LO 2** The fraud triangle identifies incentives, opportunities, and rationalizations as the three elements associated with frauds. Describe how these elements relate to the occurrence of fraud.

2-7 **LO 2** List some common incentives for managers to commit fraudulent financial reporting.

2-8 **LO 2** Identify several factors (red flags) that would be strong indicators of opportunities to commit fraud.

2-9 **LO 2** Is the ability to rationalize the fraud an important aspect to consider when analyzing a potentially fraudulent situation? What are some of the common rationalizations used by fraud perpetrators?

2-10 **LO 2** Each of the following scenarios is based on facts in an actual fraud. Categorize each scenario as primarily indicating: (1) an incentive to commit fraud, (2) an opportunity to commit fraud, or (3) a rationalization to commit fraud. State your reasoning for each categorization.

a. There was intense pressure to keep the corporation's stock from declining further. This pressure came from investors, analysts, and the CEO, whose financial well being was significantly dependent on the corporation's stock price.

b. A group of top-level management was compensated (mostly in the form of stock options) well in excess of what would be considered normal for their positions in this industry.

c. Top management of the company closely guards internal financial information, to the extent that even some employees on a need-to-know basis are denied full access.

d. Managing specific financial ratios is very important to the company, and both management and analysts are keenly observant of variability in key ratios. Key ratios for the company changed very little even though the ratios for the overall industry were quite volatile during the time period.

e. In an effort to reduce certain accrued expenses to meet budget targets, the CFO directs the general accounting department to reallocate a division's expenses by a significant amount. The general accounting department refuses to acquiesce to the request, but the journal entry is made through the corporate office. An accountant in the general accounting department is uncomfortable with the journal entries required to reallocate divisional expenses. He brings his concerns to the CFO, who assures him that everything will be fine and that the entries are necessary. The accountant considers resigning, but he does not have another job lined up and is worried about supporting his family. Therefore, he never voices his concerns to either the internal or external auditors.

f. Accounting records were either nonexistent or in a state of such disorganization that significant effort was required to locate or compile them.

2-11 **LO 1, 3** Refer to *Exhibit* 2.3 and briefly describe the frauds that were perpetrated at the following companies. For each company, categorize the fraud as involving primarily: (1) asset misappropriation or (2) fraudulent financial reporting.

a. Enron
b. WorldCom
c. Parmalat
d. HealthSouth
e. Dell
f. Koss Corporation
g. Olympus

h. Longtop Financial Technologies
i. Peregrine Financial Group
j. Sino-Forest Corporation
k. Diamond Foods, Inc.
l. Wells Fargo
m. Weatherford Int'l
n. Lime Energy

PROFESSIONAL SKEPTICISM

2-12 **LO 3** Refer to the *Why It Matters* feature "The Crucial Role of Professional Skepticism."
a. What is professional skepticism?
b. Why is professional skepticism helpful for detecting fraud?
c. What are the key behaviors needed to successfully exercise professional skepticism during the performance of the audit?
d. Why is it sometimes difficult for auditors to exercise appropriate levels of professional skepticism in practice?
e. Imagine that you are working on an audit engagement. What are the personal characteristics and behaviors of management or other client employees that might make you skeptical about whether or not they are providing you accurate audit evidence? Aside from personal observations, what publicly available information about management or other client employees could you obtain to determine whether you should exercise heightened professional skepticism in your dealings with these individuals?

PROFESSIONAL SKEPTICISM

2-13 **LO 3** For each of the following situations indicating heightened fraud risk, discuss how a professionally skeptical auditor might interpret the situation.
a. The company is not as profitable as its competitors, but it seems to have good products. However, it has a deficiency in internal control over disbursements that makes it subject to management override.
b. The company is doing better than its competitors. Although sales are about the same as competitors, net income is significantly more. Management attributes the greater profitability to better control of expenses.
c. The company is financially distressed and is at some risk of defaulting on its debt covenants. The company improves its current ratio and other ratios by making an unusually large payment against its current liabilities, accompanied by highly discounted sales if their customers paid before year end.
d. A smaller public company has a CFO who has centralized power under her. Her style is very intimidating. She is not a CPA, and she has limited accounting experience. The company has not been able to increase profitability during her time with the company.

2-14 **LO 3** Describe some major findings regarding financial reporting frauds that the COSO studies reveal.

2-15 **LO 2, 3** Many consider the Enron fraud to be one of the most significant frauds of the early 2000s.
a. Describe the various failures and environmental characteristics during this time that enabled the Enron fraud to happen.
b. What elements of the fraud triangle seem most relevant to the Enron fraud?

2-16 **LO 4** What is the responsibility of the external auditor to detect material fraud?

2-17 **LO 4** The text notes three ways in which individuals involved in the financial reporting process (management, audit committee, internal audit, external audit, and regulatory authorities) can mitigate the risk of fraudulent financial reporting. Describe these three ways. Do you think that these three approaches will be effective, given your knowledge of frauds discussed in the text (such as Enron, WorldCom, Parmalat, and Koss)?

2-18 **LO 5** Refer to *Exhibit 2.5*.
a. (Sections 101, 104, and 105) How does the establishment and operation of the PCAOB help to ensure quality external audits? How will audit firm inspections and investigations by the PCAOB help ensure high audit quality?
b. (Sections 201–203) How do Sections 201–203 address auditor independence concerns?
c. (Section 206) What is a cooling-off period, and how does it address auditor independence concerns?
d. (Section 301) How do the audit committee requirements help ensure effective corporate governance?
e. (Section 302) How do the officer certification requirements help to address the risk of fraud in publicly traded organizations? What is the likelihood that a CFO who is committing fraudulent financial reporting would sign the certification falsely, and what are your reactions to that possibility?
f. (Section 401) How does this section relate to the Enron fraud?
g. (Section 404) How do the management assessment and auditor attestation of internal controls contained in this section help to address the risk of fraud in publicly traded organizations?
h. (Section 407) Why is it important that at least one member of the audit committee be a financial expert? What are the financial reporting implications if the audit committee does not have any individuals serving on it who possess financial expertise?

2-19 **LO 5** Are nonpublic organizations required to adhere to the requirements of the Sarbanes-Oxley Act? Explain.

2-20 **LO 6** Corporate governance is the process by which the owners and creditors of an organization exert control over and require accountability for the resources entrusted to the organization. Refer to *Exhibits 2.6* and *2.7*.
a. List the major parties involved in corporate governance.
b. Describe the general roles and activities for each party.

2-21 **LO 6** Describe the broad key principles of effective corporate governance articulated in the 2010 report of the NYSE.

2-22 **LO 6** Following is a summary of the NYSE corporate governance requirements of companies listed on this stock exchange. For each requirement, state how it is intended to address the risk of fraud in publicly traded organizations.
a. Boards need to consist of a majority of independent directors.
b. Boards need to hold regular executive sessions of independent directors without management present.
c. Boards must have a nominating/corporate governance committee composed entirely of independent directors.
d. The nominating/corporate governance committee must have a written charter that addresses the committee's purpose and responsibilities, and there must be an annual performance evaluation of the committee.

e. Boards must have a compensation committee composed entirely of independent directors.

f. The compensation committee must have a written charter that addresses the committee's purpose and responsibilities, which must include (at a minimum) the responsibility to review and approve corporate goals relevant to CEO compensation, make recommendations to the board about non-CEO compensation and incentive-based compensation plans, and produce a report on executive compensation; there must also be an annual performance evaluation of the committee.

g. Boards must have an audit committee with a minimum of three independent members.

h. The audit committee must have a written charter that addresses the committee's purpose and responsibilities, and the committee must produce an audit committee report; there must also be an annual performance evaluation of the committee.

i. Companies must adopt and disclose corporate governance guidelines addressing director qualification standards, director responsibilities, director access to management and independent advisors, director compensation, director continuing education, management succession, and an annual performance evaluation of the board.

j. Companies must adopt and disclose a code of business conduct and ethics for directors, officers, and employees.

k. Foreign companies must disclose how their corporate governance practices differ from those followed by domestic companies

l. CEOs need to provide an annual certification of compliance with corporate governance standards.

m. Companies must have an internal audit function, whether housed internally or outsourced.

2-23 **LO 6** Following is a summary of the NYSE listing requirements for audit committee responsibilities of companies listed on this stock exchange. For each requirement, state how it is intended to address the risk of fraud in publicly traded organizations.

a. Obtaining an annual report by the external auditor that addresses the company's internal control procedures, any quality-control or regulatory problems, and any relationships that might threaten the independence of the external auditor

b. Discussing the company's financial statements with management and the external auditor

c. Discussing in its meetings the company's earnings press releases, as well as financial information and earnings guidance provided to analysts

d. Discussing in its meetings policies with respect to risk assessment and risk management

e. Meeting separately with management, internal auditors, and the external auditor on a periodic basis

f. Reviewing with the external auditor any audit problems or difficulties that they have had with management

g. Setting clear hiring policies for employees or former employees of the external auditors

h. Reporting regularly to the board of directors

2-24 **LO 6** Audit committees are an important element of corporate governance and have taken on additional responsibilities following the passage of the Sarbanes-Oxley Act.

a. Describe the changes in audit committee membership, and list duties mandated by the Sarbanes-Oxley Act. Also, describe any other increased responsibilities of audit committees following the passage of the Sarbanes-Oxley Act.

b. The audit committee now has ownership of the relationship with the external auditor. What are the implications of this change for the audit committee and for the external auditor?

c. Assume that management and the auditor disagree on the appropriate accounting for a complex transaction. The external auditor has conveyed the disagreement to the audit committee and provided an assessment that the disagreement is on the economics of the transaction and has nothing to do with earnings management. What is the responsibility of the audit committee? What skills of audit committee members do you think might be helpful in this type of situation?

2-25 **LO 6** The following factors describe a potential audit client. For each factor, indicate whether it is indicative of poor corporate governance. Explain the reasoning for your assessment. Finally, identify the risks to reliable financial reporting that are associated with each factor.

a. The company is in the financial services sector and has a large number of consumer loans, including mortgages, that are outstanding.

b. The CEO's and CFO's compensation is based on three components: (a) base salary, (b) bonus based on growth in assets and profits, and (c) significant stock options.

c. The audit committee meets semiannually. It is chaired by a retired CFO who knows the company well because she had served as the CFO of a division of the firm. The other two members are local community members—one is the president of the Chamber of Commerce and the other is a retired executive from a successful local manufacturing firm.

d. The company has an internal auditor who reports directly to the CFO and makes an annual report to the audit committee.

e. The CEO is a dominating personality—not unusual in this environment. He has been on the job for six months and has decreed that he is streamlining the organization to reduce costs and centralize authority (most of it in him).

f. The company has a loan committee. It meets quarterly to approve, on an ex-post basis, all loans over $300 million (top 5% for this institution).

g. The previous auditor has resigned because of a dispute regarding the accounting treatment and fair value assessment of some of the loans.

Fraud Focus: Contemporary and Historical Cases

PROFESSIONAL SKEPTICISM

ETHICS

2-26   **KOSS CORPORATION, GRANT THORNTON** (LO 1, 2, 3, 4, 6)

In the *Why It Matters* feature "Examples of Theft and Financial Reporting Frauds" at the beginning of the chapter, we introduced you to the Koss Corporation fraud. In this problem, we provide you with further details about that fraud. During the fall of 2009, Koss Corporation, a Wisconsin-based manufacturer of stereo headphone equipment, revealed that its vice president of finance (Sujata "Sue" Sachdeva) had defrauded the company of approximately $31 million over a period of at least five years. Grant Thornton LLP was the company's auditor, and the firm issued unqualified audit opinions for the entire period in which they worked for Koss. According to reports, Sachdeva's theft accelerated over a period of years as follows:

FY 2005	$2,195,477
FY 2006	$2,227,669
FY 2007	$3,160,310
FY 2008	$5,040,968
FY 2009	$8,485,937
Q1 FY 2010	$5,326,305
Q2 FY 2010	$4,917,005

To give you a sense of the magnitude of the fraud, annual revenues for Koss Corporation are in the range of $40 to $45 million annually. Previously reported pre-tax income for fiscal years 2007 through Q1 2010 was as follows:

FY 2007	$8,344,715
FY 2008	$7,410,569
FY 2009	$2,887,730
Q1 FY 2010	$928,491

How could Sachdeva have stolen so much money and fooled so many people over a long period? It is thought that Sachdeva hid the theft in the company's cost-of-goods-sold accounts, and that weak internal controls and poor corporate governance and oversight enabled her to conceal the theft from corporate officials. Certainly, there must have been questions raised about the company's deteriorating financial condition. But any number of excuses could have been used by Sachdeva to explain the missing money. For example, she might have blamed higher cost of goods sold on a change in suppliers or rising raw materials prices. Another contributing factor in Sachdeva's ability to conceal her thefts was that top management of Koss had a high degree of trust in her, so they did not monitor the accounts that she controlled at the company.

Sachdeva's total compensation for fiscal year 2009 was $173,734. But according to published reports, Sachdeva was known for her unusually lavish lifestyle and shopping sprees. It is reported that she spent $225,000 at a single Houston, Texas, jewelry store. Another report describes a $1.4 million shopping spree at Valentina Boutique in Mequon, Wisconsin. People familiar with her spending habits assumed that she used family money and that her husband's job as a prominent pediatrician funded her extravagant lifestyle. The fraud was ultimately uncovered because American Express became concerned when it realized that Sachdeva was paying for large balances on her personal account with wire transfers from a Koss Corporation account. American Express notified the FBI and relayed its concerns.

Upon learning of the fraud, Koss Corporation executives fired Sachdeva, along with the company's audit firm, Grant Thornton LLP. About 22,000 items—including high-end women's clothing, shoes, handbags, and jewelry—have been recovered to date. Sachdeva stored the bulk of the items she purchased in rented storage units in order to conceal the items from her husband.

Sue Sachdeva was released from prison after serving 6 years of an 11-year sentence. For details, see *http://www.jsonline.com/story/money/ business/2017/04/06/sachdeva-out-prison-after-serving-six-years- stealing-34-million-koss-corp/100129710/*

a. Why might Koss management have placed so much trust in Sachdeva, along with providing only minimal supervision and monitoring?

b. What was Grant Thornton's obligation to uncover the fraud?

c. Why should Sachdeva's lavish lifestyle have raised suspicions? Why might it have been ignored or explained away by her professional colleagues?

d. How could the other members of management, the audit committee, and the auditors have been more professionally skeptical in this situation?

e. What was the audit committee's responsibility in noticing that something looked amiss in the financial statements?

f. Sachdeva paid for her purchases using corporate credit cards. What internal controls could the company have used to prevent inappropriate use of the credit cards?

g. Some reports have described Sachdeva as having a very dominating personality, and revelations were made about the fact that she would often be verbally abusive of her subordinates in front of top-level managers at Koss. How should top-level managers have responded to this behavior? What actions could the subordinates have taken to respond to this behavior? Why might this behavior be a red flag indicating a heightened risk of fraud?

2-27 **KOSS CORPORATION**
(LO 3, 5, 6)

Read the facts of the case in *Problem 2-26* to become familiar with the fraud involving Koss Corporation. From the company's October 7, 2009, proxy statement (Def 14A filing with the SEC), we know the following facts about the company's audit committee and its members:

Thomas L. Doerr 65, has been a director of the company since 1987. In 1972, Mr. Doerr co-founded Leeson Electric Corporation and served as its president and CEO until 1982. The company manufactures industrial electric motors. In 1983, Mr. Doerr incorporated Doerr Corporation as a holding company for the purpose of acquiring established companies involved in distributing products to industrial and commercial markets. Currently, Mr. Doerr serves as president of Doerr Corporation. Mr. Doerr owns no stock in Koss Corporation and received $24,000 in cash compensation during 2009 to serve on the audit committee.

Lawrence S. Mattson 77, has been a director of the company since 1978. Mr. Mattson is the retired president of Oster company, a division of Sunbeam Corporation, which manufactures and sells portable household appliances. Mr. Mattson is the designated audit committee financial expert. Mr. Mattson owns no stock in Koss Corporation and received $23,000 in cash compensation during 2009 to serve on the audit committee.

Theodore H. Nixon 57, has been a director of the company since 2006. Since 1992, Mr. Nixon has been the CEO of D.D. Williamson, which is a manufacturer of caramel coloring used in the food and beverage industries. Mr. Nixon joined D.D. Williamson in 1974 and was promoted to president and chief operating officer in 1982. Mr. Nixon is also a director of the Nonprofit Center for Quality of Management. Mr. Nixon owns 2,480 shares of common stock of the company (less than 1% of outstanding shares) and received $21,000 in cash compensation during 2009 to serve on the audit committee.

John J. Stollenwerk 69, has been a director of the company since 1986. Mr. Stollenwerk is the chairman of the Allen–Edmonds Shoe Corporation, an international manufacturer and retailer of high-quality footwear. He is also a director of Allen–Edmonds Shoe Corporation; Badger Meter, Inc.; U.S. Bancorp; and Northwestern Mutual Life Insurance Company. Mr. Stollenwerk owns 13,551 shares of common stock of the company (less than 1% of outstanding shares) and received $23,000 in cash compensation during 2009 to serve on the audit committee.

Audit Committee

- The Audit committee met three times during the fiscal year ended June 30, 2009. The external auditors (Grant Thornton LLP) were present at two of these meetings to discuss their audit scope and the results of their audit.
- Koss claims that each member of the audit committee is independent as defined in NASDAQ Marketplace Rule 4200.
- The proxy statement describes the responsibilities of the audit committee as follows: "The audit committee, among other things, monitors the integrity of the financial reporting process, systems of internal controls, and financial statements and reports of the company; appoints, compensates, retains, and oversees the company's independent auditors, including reviewing the qualifications, performance and independence of the independent auditors; reviews and preapproves all audit, attests and reviews services and permitted nonaudit services; oversees the audit work performed by the company's internal accounting staff; and oversees the company's compliance with legal and regulatory requirements. The audit committee meets twice a year with the company's independent accountants to discuss the results of their examinations, their evaluations of the company's internal controls, and the overall quality of the company's financial reporting."

  a. Does the description of the audit committee members warrant a conclusion that its members appear to be professionally qualified for their positions? Do they meet enough times during the year to accomplish their responsibilities? What additional information might you need to answer this question, and how would the auditor obtain that information?

  b. Who was the audit committee financial expert? Do you think that the experiences of this individual as described should ensure that he is truly a financial expert capable of fulfilling his roles in this regard? Why is financial expertise important for audit committee members in general?

  c. In your opinion, was the compensation that the audit committee members received for their services adequate?

  d. Based on the information that you have learned in Parts a., b., and c. of this problem, what weaknesses in the audit committee governance structure existed at Koss Corporation immediately preceding the discovery of fraud?

PROFESSIONAL SKEPTICISM **2-28** | **DELL, INC.**
(LO, 1, 3, 4, 6)

In August 2010, Michael Dell, Dell, Inc.'s CEO and chairman of the board, was reelected to Dell's board of directors by Dell's shareholders. However, not all of the shareholders were happy with Mr. Dell's reappointment. Specifically, two labor groups that own shares of Dell stock wanted Mr. Dell removed from the board because of an action and settlement of the SEC involving the company and Mr. Dell. The SEC complaint alleged various accounting manipulations that called into question Dell's reported financial success from 2002 to 2006. In July 2010, Dell, Inc. agreed to pay $100 million to settle SEC charges, without admitting or denying guilt. Mr. Dell agreed to pay a $4 million fine, also without admitting or denying guilt.

a. What principles of corporate governance appear to have been missing at Dell?

b. Given the apparent actions of Mr. Dell, along with his management and board roles, should Dell's external auditor expect the corporate governance at Dell to be effective?

    c. How might Dell's external auditor respond to concerns about the quality of governance at Dell?

    d. Given the SEC settlement, should Dell's board have an independent chair?

    e. Given the SEC settlement, should Mr. Dell be removed from his CEO position?

Application Activities

PROFESSIONAL SKEPTICISM

NOTE: Completing *Application Activities* requires students to reference additional resources and materials.

2-29   **PCAOB, W.T. UNIACK CPA**
         (LO 4)

Obtain a copy of the PCAOB's enforcement Release No. 105-2017-028 (May 24, 2017), with respect to the matter of W.T. Uniack CPA and the audit of Bravo Multinational incorporated. To find it, go to the PCAOB website, look under "Enforcement" and "Settled Disciplinary Orders."

    a. While we often think of client management as committing fraud, is it possible that auditors commit fraud by neglecting their professional duties?

    b. How did William Uniack, CPA, neglect his professional duties?

    c. Auditing firms heavily rely on their reputation to attract clients. Why might Bravo Multinational Incorporated have sought to purchase the auditing services of W.T. Uniack CPA? What does it mean to perform a "sham audit"?

PROFESSIONAL SKEPTICISM

2-30   **DELOITTE, BEAZER HOMES**
         (LO 3, 4)

In June 2009, Deloitte agreed to pay almost $1 million to settle a class action lawsuit related to its audits of Beazer, a homebuilding company. The lawsuit claims that Deloitte should have noticed that the homebuilder was issuing inaccurate financial statements as the housing market began to decline. A spokesperson for Deloitte indicated that the firm denies all liability and settled to avoid the expense and uncertainty of continued litigation.

    a. Using online sources, research this case and identify fraud risk red flags that the auditor should have been aware of in these audits. One source that can get you started is *www.cfo.com/article .cfm/13612963?f=search*

    b. If these fraud risk red flags were indeed present during Deloitte's audit, what were the auditors' responsibilities in conducting the audit?

    c. What is your reaction to the fact that Deloitte settled the case rather than going to court? Do you think that implies that they are admitting their guilt? Or are they just trying to avoid the negative publicity of a trial? Does it seem fair that Beazer was committing a fraud, concealing it from Deloitte, and yet Deloitte was still penalized?

PROFESSIONAL SKEPTICISM

2-31   **CAQ**
         (LO 3, 4)

Obtain a copy of the report by the Global Public Policy Committee, "Enhancing Auditor Professional Skepticism" (November 2013) at *http://www.thecaq.org/enhancing-auditor-professional-skepticism*

    a. Explain the professional skepticism continuum. How does it relate to the extent of audit evidence collection and audit documentation?

b. What are some threats to individual auditor professional skepticism? How can these threats be mitigated?

c. What are some common human judgment tendencies that can weaken individual auditor professional skepticism?

2-32 **PCAOB**
(LO 4, 5)

Obtain a copy of the PCAOB's report titled "Observations on Auditors' Implementation of PCAOB Standards Relating to Auditors' Responsibilities with Respect to Fraud." You can use any search engine or go to *https://pcaobus.org/Inspections/Documents/2007_01-22_Release_2007-001.pdf http://pcaobus.org/Inspections/Documents/2007_01–22_Release_2007–001.pdf*

The PCAOB's report summarizes findings from inspections of audit engagements as they relate to the performance of fraud detection audit procedures. The PCAOB report comments on auditor deficiencies in each of the following six areas:

a. Auditors' overall approach to the detection of fraud

b. Brainstorming sessions

c. Auditors' responses to fraud risk factors

d. Financial statement misstatements

e. Risk of management override of controls

f. Other areas to improve fraud detection

Summarize the PCAOB's concerns with respect to problems its inspection teams have noted in auditors' performance in each of the areas listed.

2-33 **PCAOB**
(LO 5)

The development of the PCAOB is a significant component of the Sarbanes-Oxley Act of 2002. Go to the PCAOB's website *www.pcaobus.org* to learn more about the organization.

a. Identify the responsibilities of the PCAOB as described in the web site. How does the inspection process performed by the PCAOB likely affect the practice of external auditing?

b. The PCAOB can have no more than two CPAs among its five members. Read the biographies of the current board members and note which have the CPA designation. What might be the rationale for such a requirement? What are the advantages and disadvantages of the limitation concerning CPA members on the board?

c. Do the auditing standards set by the PCAOB apply to audits of nonpublic companies? Explain.

2-34 **SEC**
(LO 5, 6)

The Sarbanes-Oxley Act mandates that the audit committee of the board of directors of public companies be directly responsible for the appointment, compensation, and oversight of the external auditors. In addition, the audit committee must preapprove all nonaudit services that might be performed by the audit firm.

a. Discuss the rationale for this mandate, as opposed to the alternative of letting the shareholders, CFO, or CEO have these responsibilities.

b. What factors should the audit committee consider in evaluating the independence of the external auditor?

c. Locate the proxy statement for a publicly traded company of your choice. To do so, go to the SEC's website *https://www.sec.gov*. Search for your company's filings using the EDGAR data system on the website. Once you have located your company's filings, you may narrow your search by typing in the phrase "Def 14A," which is the proxy filing. Once you have found the proxy, read and summarize the disclosures provided concerning the audit committee members, their compensation, their responsibilities, and their activities.

2-35 **(LO 5, 6)**

Select either a public company or a company that is near your university and perform a preliminary review of its corporate governance. Identify all the sources of evidence for your conclusion regarding corporate governance. Identify the strengths and weaknesses of the governance and describe the implications of the governance structure for the auditor.

INTERNATIONAL   **2-36** **(LO 6)**

Corporate governance is not just an issue for U.S. companies; companies throughout the world need to focus on corporate governance issues. However, the principles and challenges of corporate governance vary across countries.

Select a country and research the corporate governance issues in that country. A good starting point is the website of the Organisation for Economic Co-operation and Development (OECD) (*www.oecd.org*) or the World Bank (*www.worldbank.org*), which provides corporate governance information by country. Also, Transparency International (*www.transparency.org/*) provides country-specific metrics on corruption and bribery—activities that could be associated with fraud.

Using information from these websites, along with other resources, prepare a report that addresses the following issues for your selected country: (1) compare and contrast the corporate governance principles of your selected country with the United States, (2) identify the relevant corporate governance parties and their roles, (3) describe recent challenges related to the corporate governance for your selected country, and (4) list and describe recent corporate governance activities in your selected country.

Academic Research Cases

NOTE: Completing *Academic Research Cases* requires students to reference additional resources and materials.

SEARCH HINT

It is easy to locate academic research articles! Use a search engine such as Google Scholar or an electronic research platform such as ABI Inform, and search using the author names and part of the article title.

2-37 **LO 4**   Locate and read the article listed below.

Dennis, S. A., and K. M. Johnstone. (2016). A field survey of contemporary brainstorming practices. *Accounting Horizons* 30(4): 449–472.

a. What is the purpose of the study?
b. Describe the design/method/approach used to conduct the study.
c. What are the primary findings of the study?

2-38 **LO 6**   Locate and read the article listed below.

Tanyi, P. N., and D. B. Smith. (2015). Busyness, expertise, and financial reporting quality of audit committee chairs and financial experts. *Auditing: A Journal of Practice and Theory* 34(2): 59–89.

a. What is the purpose of the study?
b. Describe the design/method/approach used to conduct the study.
c. What are the primary findings of the study?

3

Internal Control Over Financial Reporting: Responsibilities of Management and the External Auditor

The Audit Opinion Formulation Process

I. Making Client Acceptance and Continuance Decisions

Chapter 1

II. Performing Risk Assessment

Chapters 2, 3, 7, and 9–13

III. Obtaining Evidence About Internal Control Operating Effectiveness

Chapters 8–13

IV. Obtaining Substantive Evidence About Accounts, Disclosures, and Assertions

Chapters 8–13

V. Completing the Audit and Making Reporting Decisions

Chapters 14 and 15

Quality Auditing and the Need for Quality Auditor Judgments and Ethical Decisions

Chapter 1

Professional Liability

Chapter 4

The Audit Opinion Formulation Process and a Framework for Obtaining Audit Evidence

Chapters 5 and 6

Internal control is an important part of an organization's corporate governance. Effective internal control over financial reporting enhances the reliability of financial statements. Management has the responsibility to design, implement, and maintain effective internal control over financial reporting. Management of public companies evaluates and publicly reports on the effectiveness of the company's internal control.

The external auditor needs to understand a client's internal control over financial reporting. For large public companies, the external auditor will also issue an opinion of the effectiveness of the client's internal control over financial reporting.

Learning Objectives

LO 1 Articulate the importance of internal control over financial reporting for organizations.

LO 2 Define internal control as presented in COSO's 2013 *Internal Control–Integrated Framework* and identify the components of internal control.

LO 3 Describe the control environment component of internal control, list its principles, and provide examples of each principle.

LO 4 Describe the risk assessment component of internal control, list its principles, and provide examples of each principle.

LO 5 Describe the control activities component of internal control, list its principles, and provide examples of each principle.

LO 6 Describe the information and communication component of internal control, list its principles, and provide examples of each principle.

LO 7 Describe the monitoring component of internal control, list its principles, and provide examples of each principle.

LO 8 Identify management's responsibilities related to internal control over financial reporting.

LO 9 Distinguish between material weaknesses, significant deficiencies, and control deficiencies in internal control over financial reporting.

LO 10 Articulate the importance of internal control over financial reporting for the external audit and apply the concepts related to management's and the auditor's assessments of internal control effectiveness.

The Inability of the Department of Defense (DOD) to Produce Auditable Financial Statements

This feature provides an interesting example of ineffective internal controls.

The U.S. DOD has an incredibly important mission in keeping American citizens safe. Its annual budget averages about $600 billion. You will likely be surprised to learn that the organization does not have adequate internal controls in place to enable an audit of its financial statements. For example, in his 2014 message in the DOD Agency Financial Report, Deputy Secretary Robert Work stated (p. v):

> This report also includes a brief update on our financial management improvement initiatives, including our audit readiness efforts and actions to resolve material

weaknesses in our business controls necessary to support a financial audit. As Defense Secretary Chuck Hagel has stated, audits will demonstrate that the Department of Defense manages its money with the same confidence and precision that we bring to our military organizations. In the final analysis, mission readiness and audit readiness are two sides of the very same coin.

The Report acknowledges that the DOD cannot produce auditable financial statements (p. 21):

> At present, the Department cannot produce auditable financial statements and management cannot provide unqualified assurance as to the effectiveness of our

internal controls over financial reporting. The Department currently lacks the ability to prove reliable and well-controlled business processes and consistently provide supporting documentation to auditors in a timely manner.

The Report goes on to say how the DOD is working to improve its systems of internal control over financial reporting (p. 15):

The National Defense Authorization Act of 2010 mandated that the Department have audit-ready financial statements by 2017; accordingly, the Department made this requirement a priority goal. Achieving audit readiness means that the Department has strengthened internal controls and improved financial practices, processes, and systems so there is reasonable confidence the information can withstand review by an independent auditor.

The 2015 Report also notes that the DOD cannot produce auditable financial statements, citing the complexity and scope of its operations as one source of the difficulties. Some metrics related to the complexity and scope include:

Description	FY 2015
Number of Pay Transactions	135.7 million
Number of Commercial Invoices Paid	11.8 million
Number of Travel Payments	5.7 million
Number of General Ledger Accounts Managed	190.6 million
Amount Disbursed	$477 billion
Amount of Military Retirement and Health Benefits Funds Managed	$834 billion
Foreign Military Sales Cases Reimbursed by Foreign Governments	$455 billion

As of mid-2017, the financial statements for the DOD's 2016 fiscal year were not available.

What You Will Learn

- Why is internal control over financial reporting important to an organization? (LO 1)

- How does internal control help an organization achieve reliable financial reporting? (LO 1)

- What is internal control over financial reporting, and what are its components? (LO 2, 3, 4, 5, 6, 7)

- What are management's responsibilities related to internal control over financial reporting? (LO 8)

- What is a material weakness in internal control over financial reporting? (LO 9)

- Why does an external auditor need to understand a client's internal control over financial reporting? (LO 10)

LO 1

Articulate the importance of internal control over financial reporting for organizations.

Importance of Internal Control Over Financial Reporting

Internal control helps an organization mitigate the risks of not achieving its objectives. Examples of objectives include achieving profitability, ensuring efficient operations, manufacturing high-quality products or providing high-quality services, adhering to governmental and regulatory requirements, conducting operations and employee relations in a socially responsible manner, and providing users with reliable financial information.

Organizations face many risks of not achieving reliable financial reporting. For example, a salesperson may overstate sales to improve the likelihood of receiving a bonus. Employees in the receiving area may be too busy to accurately record the delivery of inventory. Management may misapply judgment and overvalue intangible assets.

Management needs to identify the risks to its organization of not achieving reliable financial reporting. Once management identifies these risks, management implements controls to provide reasonable assurance that material misstatements do not occur in the financial statements.

For Classroom Discussion

What Do You Think?

Consider the internal control situation at the DOD. What risks to reliable financial reporting are likely present at the DOD? How might their ineffective internal controls adversely affect the organization? How is a lack of effective controls at the DOD possibly detrimental to the safety of U.S. citizens and other people throughout the world?

Check Your Basic Knowledge

3-1 Effective internal control over financial reporting allows for more informed decisions by internal and external users of the financial information.   (T/F)

3-2 Management needs to understand its risks to reliable financial reporting before determining which internal controls would be most helpful to achieving its goal of reliable financial reporting.   (T/F)

3-3 Which of the following are affected by the quality of an organization's internal controls?
  a. Reliability of financial data.
  b. Ability of management to make informed business decisions.
  c. Ability of the organization to remain in business.
  d. All of the above.
  e. Only a and c.

3-4 Which of the following creates an opportunity for committing fraudulent financial reporting in an organization?
  a. Management demands financial success.
  b. Poor internal control.
  c. Commitments tied to debt covenants.
  d. Management is aggressive in its application of accounting rules.

LO 2

Define internal control as presented in COSO's 2013 *Internal Control–Integrated Framework* and identify the components of internal control.

Internal Control Defined

Just as a U.S. company might refer to generally accepted accounting principles (GAAP) as a framework for determining whether its financial statements are fairly presented, companies need to refer to a framework of internal control when assessing the effectiveness of internal control over financial reporting. The most widely used framework in the United States and around the world is the *Internal Control–Integrated Framework* published by the Committee of Sponsoring Organizations of the Treadway Commission (COSO).

The sponsoring organizations first came together in the 1980s to address the increasing fraudulent financial reporting that was occurring at that time. COSO released the original *Internal Control–Integrated Framework* in 1992. The framework gained widespread acceptance following the financial failures of the early 2000s. In 2013, COSO updated, enhanced, and clarified the framework. Today, the **COSO Internal Control–Integrated Framework** (often referred to simply as

"COSO") assists management and others in developing, implementing, and maintaining an effective system of internal control. COSO defines **internal control** as:

a process, effected by an entity's board of directors, management, and other personnel, designed to provide reasonable assurance regarding the achievement of objectives relating to operations, reporting, and compliance.

Important elements of the definition recognize that internal control is:

- A *process* consisting of ongoing tasks and activities.
- *Effected by people* and is not just about policy manuals, systems, and forms. People at every level of the organization, ranging from shipping clerks to the internal auditor to the chief financial officer (CFO), chief executive officer (CEO), and the board of directors, impact internal control.
- *Able to provide reasonable assurance*, but not absolute assurance, regarding the achievement of objectives. Limitations of internal control preclude absolute assurance. These limitations include faulty human judgment, breakdowns because of mistakes, circumventing controls by collusion of multiple people, and management ability to override controls.
- *Geared toward the achievement of multiple objectives*. The definition highlights that internal control provides reasonable assurance regarding three categories of objectives. However, the external auditor is primarily interested in the objective related to the reliability of financial reporting.

For further details, see https://en.wikipedia.org/wiki/Committee_of_Sponsoring_Organizations_of_the_Treadway_Commission

COSO identifies five components of internal control that support an organization in achieving its objectives. These components, shown in *Exhibit 3.1*, include:

1. **Control Environment** is the set of standards, processes, and structures that provides the basis for carrying out internal control across the organization. It includes the tone at the top regarding the importance of internal control and the expected standards of conduct. The control environment has a pervasive impact on the overall system of internal control.
2. **Risk Assessment** involves the process for identifying and assessing the risks that may affect an organization from achieving its objectives.
3. **Control Activities** are the actions that have been established by policies and procedures. They help ensure that management's directives regarding internal control are carried out.
4. **Information and Communication** recognizes that information is necessary for an organization to carry out its internal control responsibilities. Information can come from internal and external sources. Communication is the process of providing, sharing, and obtaining necessary information. Information and communication help all relevant parties understand internal control responsibilities and how internal controls are related to achieving objectives.
5. **Monitoring** is necessary to determine whether the controls, including all five components, are present and continuing to function effectively.

What Do You Think?   **For Classroom Discussion**

How do you view the relationship between internal controls and the likelihood of: (a) misappropriation of assets, and (b) fraudulent financial reporting? How might controls differ in terms of preventing these two types of fraud?

Exhibit 3.1
COSO Framework for Internal Control

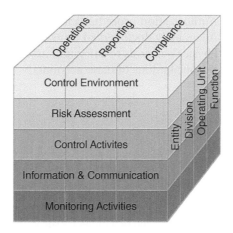

Effective internal control requires that all five components be implemented and operate effectively. Specifically, the controls need to: (1) be effectively designed and implemented and (2) operate effectively; that is, the operation of the controls is consistent with the design of the controls.

Entity-Wide Controls and Transaction Controls

Some components of internal control operate across an entity, and we refer to these as **entity-wide controls**. Entity-wide controls affect multiple processes, transactions, accounts, and assertions. The following are typically considered entity-wide controls:

- Controls related to the control environment
- Controls over management override
- The organization's risk assessment process
- Centralized processing and controls, including shared service environments
- Controls to monitor results of operations
- Controls to monitor other controls, including activities of the internal audit function, the audit committee, and self-assessment programs
- Controls over the period-end financial reporting process
- Policies that address significant business control and risk management practices

To illustrate why these controls are described as entity-wide, consider controls over management override. If the CFO is able to override controls, the CFO could record erroneous transactions in multiple processes affecting multiple accounts. Thus, controls over management override have an entity-wide effect.

In contrast, other controls such as control activities typically affect only certain processes, transactions, accounts, and assertions. We refer to these types of controls as **transaction controls**, and they are not expected to have a pervasive effect throughout the organization. For example, an organization might require that a supervisor approve an employee expense report after reviewing it for reasonableness and compliance with policy. This control provides assurance about employee expenses but will not provide assurance on other types of transactions and accounts throughout the entity. The following are common examples of transaction controls:

- Segregation of duties over cash receipts and recording
- Authorization procedures for purchasing
- Adequately documented transaction trail for all sales transactions
- Physical controls to safeguard assets such as inventory
- Reconciliations of bank accounts

Prompt for Critical Thinking #1   It's Your Turn!

Think about a work experience that you have had in which you or another person in the organization handled cash, had control over inventory, or had access to fixed assets. Identify internal controls that the organization had in place related to these areas.

- _____
- _____
- _____
- _____

Check Your Basic Knowledge

3-5 The purpose of internal control is to provide absolute assurance that an organization will achieve its objective of reliable financial reporting.   (T/F)

3-6 Organizations use the GAAP framework of internal control as a benchmark when assessing the effectiveness of internal control over financial reporting.   (T/F)

3-7 What are the components of internal control per COSO's *Internal Control–Integrated Framework?*

   a. Organizational structure, management philosophy, planning, risk assessment, and control activities.

   b. Control environment, risk assessment, control activities, information and communication, and monitoring.

   c. Risk assessment, control structure, backup facilities, responsibility accounting, and natural laws.

   d. Legal environment of the firm, management philosophy, organizational structure, control activities, and control assessment.

3-8 Which of the following statements regarding internal control is *false*?

   a. Internal control is a process consisting of ongoing tasks and activities.

   b. Internal control is primarily about policy manuals, forms, and procedures.

   c. Internal control is geared toward the achievement of multiple objectives.

   d. A limitation of internal control is faulty human judgment.

   e. All of the above statements are true.

LO 3

Describe the control environment component of internal control, list its principles, and provide examples of each principle.

Control Environment

The control environment is the foundation for all other components of internal control. It starts with the leadership culture of the organization, including the board of directors, the audit committee, and management, and can be described as the **tone at the top**. The board of directors and management establish the tone regarding the importance of internal control and expected standards of conduct. These expectations should be reinforced throughout the organization. A strong control environment is an important line of defense against the risks related to financial statement reliability. *Exhibit 3.2* summarizes the principles associated with the control environment.

Deficiencies in the control environment, including weak board oversight, are associated with many financial frauds that are likely familiar to you, including Enron and Madoff, among others. Indicators of a weak control environment include:

- An ineffective board of directors dominated by top management
- Management teams driven to increase the stock price as a basis for either expanding the organization or personally enriching themselves through stock compensation
- A low level of control consciousness within the organization
- An audit committee that does not have independent members
- The absence of an ethics policy or a lack of reinforcement of ethical behavior within the organization
- An audit committee that is not viewed as the client of the external auditor
- A management that overrides controls over accounting transactions
- Personnel who do not have the competencies to carry out their assigned tasks

Exhibit 3.2
Principles Associated with the Control Environment

1. The organization demonstrates a commitment to integrity and ethical values.
2. The board of directors demonstrates independence from management and exercises oversight of the development and performance of internal control.
3. Management establishes, with board oversight, structures, reporting lines, and appropriate authorities and responsibilities in the pursuit of objectives.
4. The organization demonstrates a commitment to attract, develop, and retain competent individuals in alignment with objectives.
5. The organization holds individuals accountable for their internal control responsibilities in the pursuit of objectives.

Focus on Fraud   Ethical Values and the Control Environment at HealthSouth

This feature describes how a weak control environment enables fraud to occur.

In testimony before the House Subcommittee in October 2003, the director of internal audit of HealthSouth testified that she had inquired about expanding her department's work and that she needed access to corporate records. She reported directly to the HealthSouth CEO, Richard Scrushy. She told a congressional committee that Mr. Scrushy reminded her that she did not have a job before she came to HealthSouth, and she should do the job she was hired to do. When asked by a congressman whether she had thought about reporting rumors of fraud to Ernst & Young (HealthSouth's external auditors), she indicated that she had run

her concerns through the chain of command within the company and had done all she could do. Unfortunately, the chain of command was controlled by the CEO.

The internal auditor did not follow up with Ernst & Young. Others testified to the same effect—if they wanted to keep their jobs, they continued to do the work they were hired to do and let management take care of other items. The tone at the top sent a clear message: "Don't question management!" In the case of HealthSouth, it did not matter that the organization had a code of ethics for its employees. The company and its board were dominated by management. The unwritten message was stronger than any written message: "Do what we want you to do or lose your job."

What Do You Think?   For Classroom Discussion

Consider each of the indictors of a weak control environment presented in the *Focus on Fraud* feature above. What financial statement errors might occur because of such weaknesses?

Commitment to Integrity and Ethical Values (COSO Principle 1)

An organization demonstrates its commitment to integrity and ethical values through the tone set by the board and management throughout the organization. Do the directives, actions, and behaviors of the board and management highlight the importance of integrity and ethical values? An organization should have standards of conduct regarding expectations for integrity and ethical values and have processes in place to determine if individuals are performing in accordance with expected standards of conduct. Deviations in expected conduct should be identified and addressed in an appropriate, timely, and consistent matter.

The Board of Directors Exercises Oversight Responsibility (COSO Principle 2)

Members of the board of directors are the elected representatives of shareholders. Typically, the board has committees that specialize in certain areas. A board and its committees are most effective when they can provide unbiased oversight consisting of evaluations, guidance, and feedback.

The audit committee of the board oversees management, has responsibility for the overall reliability of financial reporting, and oversees the external auditor. The board, primarily through the audit committee, exercises objective oversight for the development and performance of internal control. For example, the board, as part

Inappropriate Tone Regarding Internal Controls
Leads to Other Deficiencies at NutraCea

Why It Matters

This feature describes how a weak control environment can lead to other internal control deficiencies.

Management at NutraCea identified the following material weaknesses in the company's internal control over financial reporting as of December 31, 2008:

The Company did not maintain an effective control environment based on the criteria established in the COSO framework. The Company failed to design controls to prevent or detect instances of inappropriate override of, or interference with, existing policies, procedures, and internal controls. The Company did not establish and maintain a proper tone as to internal control over financial reporting. More specifically, senior management failed to emphasize, through consistent communication and behavior, the importance

of internal control over financial reporting and adherence to the Company's code of business conduct and ethics, which, among other things, resulted in information being withheld from, and improper explanations and inadequate supporting documentation being provided to the Company's Audit Committee, its Board of Directors, and independent registered public accountants.

Presumably, the weak control environment led to other material weaknesses in internal control. For example, NutraCea management failed to properly analyze, account for, and record significant sales contracts. The company also failed to retain the resources necessary to analyze significant transactions, prepare financial statements, and respond to regulatory comments in a timely manner.

of its oversight responsibilities, might require discussions with senior management on areas where controls have not been operating effectively. The board should have relevant expertise to fulfill its oversight responsibilities. This expertise might include market and company knowledge, financial expertise, legal and regulatory expertise, knowledge of systems and technology, and problem-solving skills. Importantly, the board needs a sufficient number of members who are independent of the organization to help ensure the board's objectivity.

Management Establishes Structure, Authority, and Responsibility (COSO Principle 3)

Effective internal control requires an organization to have an appropriate structure and clearly defined lines of responsibility and authority. Everyone in the organization has some responsibility for the effective operation of internal control. COSO identifies the following internal control responsibilities:

- *The board of directors* has authority over significant decisions and reviews management's assignments.
- *Senior management* establishes directives, guidance, and controls to help employees understand and carry out their internal control responsibilities.
- *Management* guides and facilitates senior management's directives.
- *Personnel* understand internal control requirements relative to their position in the organization.
- *Outsourced service providers* adhere to management's definition of the scope of authority and responsibility for all nonemployees engaged.

The Organization Demonstrates Commitment to Competence (COSO Principle 4)

An organization needs to attract, develop, and retain competent individuals. Competence is the knowledge and skills necessary to accomplish tasks that define the individual's job. An organization demonstrates this commitment through policies and procedures to attract, train, mentor, evaluate, and retain employees.

Why It Matters

KPMG Fires Five Audit Partners and the Head of Its Audit Practice

This feature makes an important point: Audit firms expect their clients to have effective internal control. It is also imperative that audit firms themselves have effective internal control.

In April 2017, KPMG announced that an unprecedented event led to the firing of five audit partners, including the head of its audit practice, Scott Marcello. An interesting aspect of this event is that it was initiated by a disgruntled PCAOB employee.

Many PCAOB employees leave that organization and step back into public accounting; public accounting firms value the insights PCAOB employees gain about the inspection process. In this case, a *former* PCAOB employee (who was currently working for KPMG) learned from a *current* PCAOB employee the names of particular KPMG audit engagements that the PCAOB would be inspecting. Marcello and his colleagues "either had improper

advance warnings of engagements to be inspected by the PCAOB, or were aware that others had received such advance warnings and had failed to properly report the situation in a timely manner."

Upon learning this information, Marcello should have reported the situation to the PCAOB and/or to his superiors at KPMG. He did not. Some speculate that the pressure that Marcello felt to use the confidential PCAOB inspection planning information was related to the fact that in the past few years, KPMG was the auditing firm that received the most negative inspection findings by PCAOB inspection teams. KPMG and the PCAOB enforced accountability by bringing the event to light, and by firing those individuals involved in it.

For more details, see http://ww2.cfo.com/finance-risk-management/2017/04/kpmg-replaces-audit-chair-wake-pcaob-leaks/

The Organization Enforces Accountability (COSO Principle 5)

An organization should hold individuals accountable for their internal control responsibilities. Accountability mechanisms include establishing and evaluating performance measures and providing appropriate incentives and rewards. Management and the board should be sensitive to pressures that could cause employees to circumvent controls or undertake fraudulent activity. Excessive pressures could include unrealistic performance targets or an imbalance between short-term and long-term performance measures. For example, pressures to generate unrealistic levels of sales might cause sale managers to book fraudulent sales entries, thereby reducing the reliability of financial reporting.

Check Your Basic Knowledge

3-9 The control environment component of internal control is a pervasive or entity-wide control because it affects multiple processes and multiple types of transactions.　(T/F)

3-10 The control environment is seen as the foundation for all other components of internal control.　(T/F)

3-11 Which of the following principles would <u>not</u> be considered a principle of an organization's control environment?
　a. Independence and competence of the board.
　b. Competence of accounting personnel.
　c. Structures, reporting lines, and authorities and responsibilities.

　d. Commitment to integrity and ethical values.
　e. They would all be considered principles of the control environment.

3-12 Which one of the following components of internal control over financial reporting sets the tone for the organization?
　a. Risk assessment.
　b. Control environment.
　c. Information and communication.
　d. Monitoring.

LO 4

Describe the risk assessment component of internal control, list its principles, and provide examples of each principle.

Risk Assessment

Organizations face risks of material misstatement in their financial reports. Risk is the possibility that an event will adversely affect the organization's achievement of its objectives. Risk comes from both internal and external sources. Examples of internal risks include changes in management responsibilities, changes in information technology, and a poorly conceived business model. Examples of external risks include economic recessions, increases in competition, the development of substitute products or services, and changes in regulation.

An organization that ignores these risks subjects both the organization and its auditors to potential bankruptcy or litigation. Client's risk assessment is a robust process for identifying and assessing the risks associated with the objective of reliable financial reporting. This process requires considering how changes either in the external environment or within the organization may affect the controls necessary to mitigate risk. *Exhibit 3.3* summarizes the principles associated with risk assessment.

Management Specifies Relevant Objectives (COSO Principle 6)

An organization has many reasons for having reliable financial reporting as one of its objectives. Reliable financial reporting is important for accessing capital markets, obtaining sales contracts, and having relationships with vendors, suppliers, and other third parties. When specifying this objective, management should take steps so that the financial reporting reflects the underlying transactions and events of the organization. Financial reporting objectives should be consistent with the accounting principles that are suitable for the organization. As appropriate, the broad reporting objective should be cascaded down to various business units.

Management should consider the level of materiality when specifying objectives. For example, management might have an objective to report revenue accurately. Management does not likely mean that revenue needs to be accurate to the nearest dollar. Rather, management's objective would likely be that any misstatements in revenue not be material, or important, to the overall financial statement presentation. For example, if the revenue account of a large company had an error that overstated revenue by $1,000, most users of the financial statements would not consider that misstatement as material, or important, to their decisions. Materiality is a topic that we explore further in *Chapter 7*.

Exhibit 3.3
Principles Associated with Risk Assessment

6. The organization specifies objectives with sufficient clarity to enable the identification and assessment of risks relating to objectives.

7. The organization identifies risks to the achievement of its objectives across the entity and analyzes risks as a basis for determining how the risks should be managed.

8. The organization considers the potential for fraud in assessing risks to the achievement of objectives.

9. The organization identifies and assesses changes that could significantly impact the system of internal control.

The Organization Identifies and Analyzes Risk (COSO Principle 7)

This principle highlights the importance of an organization identifying the risks that it will not achieve its financial reporting objective and serves as a basis for determining how the risks should be mitigated. Appropriate levels of management need to be involved in the identification and analysis of risk. Risk identification should include both internal and external factors. For example, economic changes may impact barriers to competitive entry, or a new financial reporting standard may require different or additional reporting. Internally, a change in management responsibilities could affect the way certain controls operate, or the expiration of labor agreements can affect the availability of competent personnel. Identified risks—whether internal or external—should be analyzed to include an estimate of the potential significance of the risks and consideration of how each risk should be addressed.

The Organization Assesses Fraud Risk (COSO Principle 8)

As part of assessing risks, an organization considers fraud risks—risks related to misappropriation of assets and fraudulent financial reporting (as discussed in *Chapter* 2). Assessment of fraud risk considers ways that fraud could occur and fraud risk factors that impact financial reporting, including incentives and pressures that might lead to fraud in the financial statements, opportunities for fraud, and whether employees might rationalize fraud activities—that is, the fraud triangle.

The Organization Identifies and Analyzes Significant Change (COSO Principle 9)

As internal and external conditions change, an organization's internal controls may need to change. Internal control that is effective in one condition may not be effective when that condition changes. For example, when an organization alters its lines of business or business model, new controls may be needed because the organization may have taken on new risks. Another example of change that impacts controls would be the introduction of new information system technologies. The organization also needs to consider changes in management and other personnel and their respective attitudes and philosophies on the system of internal control. Overall, the key principle is that an organization needs a process for identifying and assessing changes in internal and external factors that can affect its ability to produce reliable financial reports.

Prompt For Critical Thinking #2   It's Your Turn!

Obtain Ford Motor Company's 10-K on the SEC's Edgar website. Read the Management Discussion and Analysis section (Item1A, Risk Factors). Identify some of the most important risks that Ford is facing. Think about why these risks are important from both operational and financial reporting perspectives.

- _____
- _____
- _____
- _____

Ineffective Internal Control Over Financial Reporting Leads to Embezzlement at Citigroup

Focus on Fraud

This feature highlights the importance of identifying fraud risks as a basis for determining the controls necessary to mitigate such risks.

Gary Foster was a mid-level accountant in Citigroup's Long Island City office, with an annual salary of about $100,000. He embezzled about $19 million from the company. It appears that Foster transferred money from various Citigroup accounts to his personal bank account at JPMorgan Chase. He did so by making adjusting journal entries from interest expense accounts and debt adjustment accounts to Citigroup's main cash accounts. Then, on at least eight occasions, he transferred the money to a personal bank account at Chase. To conceal the transactions, he used a false contract number in the reference line of the wire transfer. This series of actions continued for at least a year, undetected by the company's internal controls. During that time, Foster traveled extensively internationally, owned six expensive homes, and acquired Maserati and BMW automobiles.

Contemplate the following question relating to this situation:

Which is worse from a societal perspective? Embezzlement resulting in declines in people not trusting one another in society, or financial reporting fraud resulting in declines in market capitalization of stock? (Note: there is no right answer!) Or, alternatively, how are each detrimental, but in different ways?

Check Your Basic Knowledge

3-13 Only organizations in high-risk industries face a risk that they will not achieve their objective of reliable financial reporting. (T/F)

3-14 An organization's risk assessment process should identify risks to reliable financial reporting from both internal and external sources. (T/F)

3-15 Which of the following statements is <u>false</u> regarding the risk assessment component of internal control?
   a. Risk assessment includes assessing fraud risk.
   b. Risk assessment includes assessing internal and external sources of risk.
   c. Risk assessment includes the identification and analysis of significant changes.
   d. Economic changes would not be considered a risk that needs to be analyzed as part of the risk assessment process.

3-16 Which of the following is not part of management's fraud risk assessment process?
   a. The assessment considers ways the fraud could occur.
   b. The assessment considers the role of the external auditor in preventing fraud.
   c. Fraud risk assessments serve as an important basis for determining the control activities needed to mitigate fraud risks.
   d. The assessment considers pressures that might lead to fraud in the financial statements.

Control Activities

LO 5

Describe the control activities component of internal control, list its principles, and provide examples of each principle.

Control activities are the actions established through policies and procedures that help ensure that management's directives regarding controls are accomplished. Control activities are performed within processes (e.g., segregation of duties required in processing cash receipt transactions) and over the technology environment. They may be preventive or detective, and they may be manual or automated in nature. *Exhibit 3.4* summarizes the principles associated with control activities.

Exhibit 3.4
Principles Associated with Control Activities

10. The organization selects and develops control activities that contribute to the mitigation of risks to the achievement of objectives to acceptable levels.

11. The organization selects and develops general control activities over technology to support the achievement of objectives.

12. The organization deploys control activities through policies that establish what is expected and in procedures that put policies into action.

The Organization Selects and Develops Control Activities (COSO Principle 10)

Although some control activities are present in many organizations—segregation of duties, independent reconciliations, authorizations and approvals, and verifications—no universal set of control activities is applicable to all organizations. Rather, organizations select and develop control activities that are specific to the risks they identify during risk assessment. For example, highly regulated organizations generally have more complex control activities than less-regulated entities. As another example, an organization with decentralized operations and an emphasis on local autonomy and innovation will have different control activities than an organization whose operations are consistent across locations and highly centralized. Control activities are present within each of an organization's business processes (e.g., purchasing or sales) and help mitigate transaction-processing risks within each of those processes.

Transaction Controls

Transaction controls (also referred to as **application controls**) are implemented to provide assurance that all transactions that occurred are recorded (e.g., were all accounts payable recorded as liabilities?), that the transactions are recorded in an accurate and timely manner, and that only valid transactions are recorded (e.g., were any fictitious sales recorded as revenue?).

Exhibit 3.5 illustrates three types of transactions that have a significant effect on the quality of data in the financial statements and associated disclosures. They include business process transactions, accounting estimates, and adjusting, closing, or unusual entries.

What Do You think?   For Classroom Discussion

A common internal control includes segregation of duties over cash receipts and recording, i.e., no one person can both have physical custody of cash and the ability to record journal entries. Imagine that an accountant works for a nonprofit organization, such as the Boys & Girls Club. Imagine also that the accountant lacks segregation of duties. What could go wrong?

Many frauds happen at nonprofit organizations because they lack the resources to establish a strong system of internal control, and instead rely on trust. Use the Internet to locate a fraud in a local nonprofit and to learn how the fraud was perpetrated.

Be prepared to discuss the logistics and monetary impact of the fraud. Also, be prepared to discuss how you think the discovery of this fraud affected the community. What concerns would you have about donating to a nonprofit with weak internal controls?

Exhibit 3.5
Transaction Processing

During transaction processing, an organization wants reasonable assurance that the information processing is complete, accurate, and valid. The organization wants to achieve the following control objectives:

- Recorded transactions exist and have occurred.
- All transactions are recorded.
- Transactions are properly valued.
- Transactions are properly presented and disclosed.
- Transactions relate to rights or obligations of the organization.

Transaction controls performed within specific business processes—such as purchasing and sales—are developed and implemented to provide reasonable assurance that these processing objectives are achieved. Control activities related to business transaction processing include verifications such as computer matching or reasonableness checks, reconciliations such as checking for agreement between detailed subsidiary accounts and control accounts, and authorizations and approvals such as a supervisor approving an expense report.

Accounting estimates, such as those used in developing the allowance for doubtful accounts, pension liabilities, environmental obligations, and warranty reserves, are subject to significant management judgment. Management should base these estimates on underlying processes and data that have been successful in providing accurate estimates in the past. Management should ensure that controls around the processes are in place to provide reasonable assurance that the data are accurate, the estimates are faithful to the data, and the underlying estimation model reflects current economic conditions and has proven to provide reasonable estimates in the past.

Controls over adjusting, closing, or other unusual entries include:

- Documented support for all entries
- Reference to underlying supporting data with a well-developed **transaction trail** that includes the documents and records that allow a user (or auditor) to trace a transaction from its origination through to its final disposition or vice versa
- Review by the CFO or controller

Automated and Manual Transaction Controls

Transaction controls include manual control activities, automated control activities, and a combination of the two. An example of an automated application control activity is an automated matching and edit check to examine data entered online. If the data do not match or are entered in the wrong format, the system provides feedback so that personnel can make appropriate corrections. In some cases, that feedback and correction occur automatically. In other cases, a combination of manual and automated controls is present such that the system automatically detects the data transmission error, but an individual is needed to manually retransmit the data. Transaction controls, whether automated or manual, mitigate risks associated with data input, processing, and output.

Input controls are designed to ensure that authorized transactions are correct and complete and that only authorized transactions can be input. Two common types of input controls are **input validation tests** and **self-checking digits**. Input validation tests are often referred to as **edit tests** because they are control tests built into an application to examine or edit input data for obvious errors. Input validation tests are designed to review transactions much like experienced personnel do in manual systems in which an employee would know, for example, that no one worked more than 70 hours in the past week. If an item entered online does not meet the required criteria, the user is notified and a correction is made or a decision is made about whether the transaction should be processed or reviewed further before processing. Self-checking digits are a type of input validation test that have been developed to test for transposition errors associated with identification numbers. Self-checking digits operate by computing an extra digit, or several digits, that are added (or inserted) into a numeric identifier. The algorithms are designed to detect common types of mistakes. Whenever the identifier is entered into the system, the application recalculates the self-checking digit to determine whether the identifier is correct.

Processing controls are designed to provide reasonable assurance that the correct program is used for processing, all transactions are processed, and the transactions update appropriate files. For example, processed payroll transactions should update the payroll subledger.

Output controls are designed to provide reasonable assurance that all data are completely processed and that output is distributed only to authorized recipients. Typical controls include reconciliation of control totals, output distribution schedules and procedures, and output reviews. For critical data, the user may perform a detailed review and reconciliation of the output data with the input to determine the completeness of a crucial process. The organization should also develop policies for protecting privacy and retaining records.

Other Important Control Activities

Other important control activities include **segregation of duties** and **physical controls over assets**. Segregation of duties is an important control activity that is designed to protect against the risk that an individual could both perpetrate and cover up a fraud. Proper segregation of duties requires that at least two employees be involved in processing transactions such that one does not have (a) the authority and ability to process transactions, and (b) custodial responsibilities. Separating these functions prevents someone from authorizing a fictitious or illegal transaction and then covering it up through the accounting process. Separating record keeping and physical custody of assets is designed to prevent someone with custodial responsibilities from taking assets and covering it up by making fictitious entries to the accounting records.

Physical controls are necessary to protect and safeguard assets from accidental or intentional destruction and theft. Examples of physical controls include security locks to limit access to inventory warehouses, vaults, safes, and similar items to limit access to cash and other liquid assets. An additional control is a periodic count of the physical assets, such as inventory, and a reconciliation of this count with recorded amounts.

The Importance of Internal Control for Safeguarding
Assets at Chesapeake Petroleum and Supply, Inc.

Focus on Fraud

This feature provides an example of a situation where segregation of duties was lacking, thereby enabling an individual to misappropriate assets.

Most organizations, presumably, have reliable financial reporting as one of their objectives. This objective would include safeguarding assets. However, to achieve this objective, organizations need to have effective controls in place. Such controls were not in place at Chesapeake Petroleum and Supply, Inc., where the CFO pled guilty to embezzling more than

$2.7 million. The CFO—employed by Chesapeake Petroleum for 30 years—authorized and signed company checks made payable to him and to the bank that held the mortgage on one of his properties. The CFO had both authorizing and signing control over company checks. This executive also had exclusive control over petty cash and stole thousands of dollars from the company's petty cash fund. These situations represent classic examples of control deficiencies related to an inadequate segregation of duties.

Preventive and Detective Controls

The appropriate mix of control activities includes both preventive and detective controls. **Preventive controls** are designed to prevent the occurrence of a misstatement. For example, edit tests may prevent some inappropriate transactions from being recorded. Preventive controls are usually the most cost efficient. **Detective controls** are designed to discover errors that occurred during processing. For example, continuous monitoring techniques detect transactions that should not have been processed.

Management Selects and Develops General Controls Over Technology (COSO Principle 11)

Nearly all organizations depend on information technology to facilitate reliable financial reporting. As part of selecting control activities, management needs to determine the extent to which automated control activities and **general computer controls** are part of the mix of control activities. For automated application controls to work properly, an organization needs to have effective general computer controls (sometimes referred to as **information technology general controls**). General computer controls are pervasive control activities that affect multiple types of information technology systems, from mainframe computers, to desktop computers, to laptop computers, to the mobile devices that you use to organize your everyday life. General computer controls include control activities—either manual or automated—over technology infrastructure, security management, and technology acquisition, development, and maintenance.

Technology Infrastructure

Technology infrastructure provides the support for information technology to effectively function. It includes the communication network that links technologies together, the computing resources needed for applications to operate, and even the electricity needed to power the technology. Control activities are necessary to check the technology for any problems and take corrective action as necessary. Two other important control activities related to the infrastructure include backup procedures and disaster recovery plans.

Security Management

Security management includes control activities that limit access to technologies. These control activities include policies that restrict authorized users to applications that are related to their job responsibilities, update access when employees change jobs or leave the organization, and require a periodic review of access rights to determine if they remain appropriate. Security controls over technology protect the organization from inappropriate and unauthorized access, thereby protecting data and program integrity.

Important considerations in security management related to user access include:

- Access to any data item is limited to those *with a need to know*.
- The ability to change, modify, or delete a data item is restricted to those *with the authorization to make such changes*.
- The access control system has the *ability to identify and verify any potential users* as authorized or unauthorized for the data item and function requested.
- *A security department should actively monitor* attempts to compromise the system and prepare periodic reports to those responsible for the integrity of data and access to the data.

Techniques for controlling user access include passwords, cards with magnetic strips (often combined with a password requirement), and required identification on the basis of physical characteristics (e.g., fingerprint or retina scan).

Technology Acquisition, Development, and Maintenance

An organization needs to select and develop control activities over the acquisition, development, and maintenance of technology. Some organizations may develop their technology in-house, while other organizations may obtain their technology through packaged software or through outsourcing arrangements. If an organization chooses to use packaged software, it should have policies about selecting and implementing these packages. If an organization develops and maintains its technology in-house, the organization should have policies on documentation requirements, approval requirements, authorization of change requests, appropriate protocols, and testing of whether changes are made properly.

The Organization Deploys Control Activities Through Policies and Procedures (COSO Principle 12)

An important principle of control activities is that an organization needs to have policies outlining what is expected and procedures that put the policies into action. For example, a policy might require monthly reconciliations of all bank accounts by appropriate personnel who do not have access to cash. The procedure would be the reconciliation itself. Policies are communicated orally or in writing, and should establish clear responsibility and accountability. Further, appropriate and competent personnel should perform the procedures diligently, consistently, and in a timely manner.

3-17 There is one standard set of control activities that all organizations should implement. (T/F)

3-18 Control activities include both preventive and detective controls. (T/F)

3-19 Which of the following scenarios provides the best example of segregation of duties?
   a. Employees perform multiple jobs, and have access to related records.
   b. The internal audit function performs an independent test of transactions throughout the year and reports any errors to departmental managers.
   c. The person responsible for reconciling the bank account is responsible for cash disbursements but not for cash receipts.
   d. The payroll department cannot add employees to the payroll or change pay rates without the explicit authorization of the Human Resources Department.

3-20 Which of the following statements about application controls is <u>true</u>?
   a. Organizations can have manual application controls or automated application controls, but not a combination of the two.
   b. Application controls are intended to mitigate risks associated with data input, data processing, and data output.
   c. Application controls are a part of the monitoring component of internal control.
   d. Self-checking digits are an output control.

Information and Communication

LO 6

Describe the information and communication component of internal control, list its principles, and provide examples of each principle.

An organization needs information, from both internal and external sources, to carry out its internal control responsibilities. Communication is the process of providing, sharing, and obtaining information. Information is communicated internally throughout the organization, and there should be two-way communication with relevant parties external to the organization. Information and communication refers to the process of identifying, capturing, and exchanging information in a timely fashion to enable accomplishment of the organization's objectives. It includes the organization's accounting system and methods for recording and reporting on transactions, as well as other communications such as key policies, code of conduct, and strategies. *Exhibit 3.6* summarizes the principles associated with information and communication.

The Organization Uses Relevant Information (COSO Principle 13)

An organization needs to identify and obtain relevant internal and external information to support its internal control and achieve its objective of reliable financial reporting. For example, an organization may conduct a periodic survey of its employees to determine whether employees have been asked to behave in a

Exhibit 3.6

Principles Associated with Information and Communication

13. The organization obtains or generates and uses relevant, quality information to support the functioning of internal control.

14. The organization internally communicates information, including objectives and responsibilities for internal control, necessary to support the functioning of internal control.

15. The organization communicates with external parties regarding matters affecting the functioning of internal control.

manner inconsistent with the organization's standards of conduct, such as, recording a journal entry without adequate supporting documentation. The survey results produce information about the functioning of the control environment and can be used to determine if other controls are needed. Other sources of internal information include the accounting system, internal emails, minutes from meetings, and time reporting systems. Examples of external sources of information include industry research reports, whistleblower hotlines, and competitor earnings releases.

The Organization Communicates Internally (COSO Principle 14)

Internal communication of information occurs throughout the organization including up, down, and across the organization. For example, all personnel should receive a clear message that internal control responsibilities should be taken seriously. This communication could occur through periodic newsletters, posters in the break rooms, or more formal communications from senior management and the board. In some cases, a special line of communication is needed for anonymous or confidential communications, particularly when an employee is concerned that something is inappropriate in the organization's operations. This is referred to as a **whistleblower function** and often includes processes such that reporting can be anonymous.

Further, employers should not be permitted to take adverse actions against employee whistleblowers. The whistleblower function should include a process to bring important ethical and financial issues to the audit committee.

The Organization Communicates Externally (COSO Principle 15)

Organizations have a need for two-way communication with parties external to the organization, including shareholders, business partners, customers, and regulators. Management's external communication should send a message about the importance of internal control and the organization's values and culture. Organizations should also have mechanisms so that external parties can provide information to the organization. For example, customers may provide feedback about product quality and vendors may have questions about payments for goods sold or complaints about possibly inappropriate behavior. As another example, large retailers often have relationships with many vendors. Many of these retailers establish a hotline where a vendor can communicate directly with the internal audit department or other appropriate party if the vendor finds any inappropriate action by a purchasing agent of the organization; for example, a suggestion of a kickback if the vendor places a large order.

What Do You Think?   For Classroom Discussion

The SEC has been actively trying to incentivize people who know about financial misreporting to come forward and disclose that information to the SEC. Learn more about the SEC's whistleblowing function by visiting the following link: *https://www.sec.gov/whistleblower*

Be prepared to discuss any recent whistleblowing activities described on the SEC website. The SEC website makes it clear that the SEC will provide financial rewards to whistleblowers. What are some potential downside risks to whistleblowing?

William and Flora Hewlett Foundation: Policy Regarding Reporting of Financial, Auditing, or Governance Improprieties

Why It Matters

This feature provides an example of a whistleblower policy highlighting the importance of employee involvement and the absence of any fear of retaliation for being a whistleblower employee.

The William and Flora Hewlett Foundation is committed to facilitating open and honest communications relevant to its governance, finances, and compliance with all applicable laws and regulations. It is important that the Foundation be apprised about unlawful or improper behavior including, but not limited to, any of the following conduct:

- theft;
- financial reporting that is intentionally misleading;
- improper or undocumented financial transactions;
- improper destruction of records;
- improper use of Foundation assets;
- violations of the Hewlett Foundation's conflict of interest policy; and
- any other improper occurrence regarding cash, financial procedures, or reporting

We request the assistance of every employee who has a reasonable belief or suspicion about any improper transaction. The Foundation values this input, and each employee should feel free to raise issues of concern, in good faith, without the fear of retaliation. Employees will not be disciplined, demoted, lose their jobs, or be retaliated against for asking questions or voicing concerns about conduct of this sort.

We encourage any employee who has a concern regarding an action concerning the Foundation's governance, finances, or compliance with all applicable laws and regulations to raise the concern with a supervisor, human resources, the president, the general counsel, the treasurer, the chair of the Board of Directors or of the Audit Committee, or any other Board member.

If for any reason the employee does not believe these channels of communication are adequate or safe, the concern should be reported immediately to [*name of outside counsel and firm*]. [*Name of outside counsel*] has been retained specifically to be an independent agent to collect any such reports and to assure that they are looked into and that corrective action is taken when appropriate. Anonymous reports will also be accepted, and all reports will be handled on a confidential basis. [*His/Her*] contact information is:

[*Name, address, email, telephone for outside counsel*] Mark envelope: "TO BE OPENED BY ADDRESSEE ONLY PERSONAL AND CONFIDENTIAL"

[*Name of outside counsel*] and the Chair of the Audit Committee will coordinate the investigation and the Foundation will then take appropriate action as it deems justified by the circumstances.

Source: Used with permission of the William and Flora Hewlett Foundation.

For Classroom Discussion

What Do You Think?

Target Corporation has a particularly helpful *Business Conduct Guide*, which outlines various whistleblowing features and hotlines. Read the Guide at the following link:

https://corporate.target.com/_media/TargetCorp/csr/pdf/ business-conduct-guide-2016.pdf

One particularly powerful point in the *Guide* states:

Target promotes a culture of smart risk taking, ethical conduct and a commitment to compliance. This Business Conduct Guide outlines expectations of conduct for all team members

and focuses on the integrity and high ethical standards that are part of Target's culture. The cornerstone of our strong ethical culture is our team members' dedication to and ownership of compliance. Target's Board of Directors promotes this commitment as well, and has approved this Business Conduct Guide.

What do you think the term 'smart risk taking' means? What does the *Guide* say about retaliation?

Check Your Basic Knowledge

3-21 An organization's accounting system is part of its information and communication component of internal control.   (T/F)

3-22 An organization needs information from both internal and external sources to achieve its objectives.   (T/F)

3-23 Which of the following is an effective implementation of the information and communication component of COSO's *Internal Control–Integrated Framework?*

   a. The organization has one-way communication with parties external to the organization.

   b. The organization has a whistleblower function that allows parties internal and external to the organization to communicate concerns about possible inappropriate actions in the organization's operations.

   c. The organization has a robust process for assessing risks internal and external to the organization.

   d. The organization builds in edit checks to determine whether all purchases are made from authorized vendors.

   e. All of the above.

3-24 Which of the following is not a principle of the information and communication component of COSO's *Internal Control–Integrated Framework?*

   a. The organization identifies, obtains, and uses relevant information.

   b. The organization communicates internally.

   c. The organization communicates externally.

   d. All of the above are principles of the information and communication component of COSO's *Internal Control–Integrated Framework.*

LO 7

Describe the monitoring component of internal control, list its principles, and provide examples of each principle.

Monitoring

Monitoring is a process that provides feedback on the effectiveness of each of the five components of internal control. Management selects a mix of ongoing evaluations, separate evaluations, or some combination of the two to accomplish monitoring. Monitoring requires that identified deficiencies in internal control are communicated to appropriate personnel and follow-up action be taken. *Exhibit 3.7* summarizes the principles associated with monitoring.

The Organization Conducts Ongoing and/or Separate Evaluations (COSO Principle 16)

Ongoing evaluations are procedures built into the normal recurring activities of an entity. Computerized monitoring of transactions is an approach many organizations take to review a large volume of transactions at a relatively low cost. An

---

Exhibit 3.7
Principles Associated with Monitoring

16. The organization selects, develops, and performs ongoing and/or separate evaluations to ascertain whether the components of internal control are present and functioning.

17. The organization evaluates and communicates internal control deficiencies in a timely manner to those parties responsible for taking corrective action, including senior management and the board of directors, as appropriate.

organization may use software to automate the review of all payment transactions and identify anomalies to investigate further.

Separate evaluations are conducted periodically, typically by objective management personnel, internal auditors, or external consultants. For example, an organization's internal auditors may perform an annual audit of all disbursements at selected operating units. As part of that audit, the internal auditors will identify instances in which a control is not operating effectively. Consider an organization that has a policy requiring approvals from appropriate personnel for disbursements over a certain dollar amount. During its periodic audit, the internal auditor might find several instances of disbursements made without the required approval.

As separate evaluations take place periodically, they are not as timely as ongoing evaluations in identifying control deficiencies. However, separate evaluations do allow for a fresh, objective look at control effectiveness.

Monitoring Controls in Fast-Food Franchises

Why It Matters

This feature provides an example of ongoing evaluations, which is one type of monitoring.

The owner of a franchise such as Wendy's or McDonald's that serves fast-food across many locations must be able to monitor the workings of its controls at each location. The franchise will have written policies and procedures dealing with control issues ranging from product acceptance (must be from authorized vendor), waste disposal, recording sales (must offer a cash register receipt or the meal is free), and employee supervision. The franchise will have standardized procedures for counting cash, reconciling cash with the cash register, depositing the cash daily, and transferring cash to corporate headquarters. Assume that from previous statistics and industry averages, the franchise owner knows that food costs should equal approximately 37% of revenue.

The franchise owner then develops a performance-monitoring process that results in daily and weekly reports on:

- Store revenue compared with expected revenue and previous year's revenue for the same week

- Special promotions in effect
- Gross margin

The franchise owner then uses the monitoring reports to follow up with local stores and to determine which stores, if any, need further investigation. For example, assume that the franchise owner identifies a group of stores—all managed by one person—for which store revenue is lower than expected; but more important, the gross margin is significantly less than expected (63% expected, but 60% attained). The monitoring report indicates that one of the following explanations may represent the problems at the stores: (a) not all revenue is being recorded, (b) product is unnecessarily wasted, (c) product is diverted to other places (or stolen), or (d) some combination of these. Although the original focus is on operating data, the implication is that a breakdown of internal controls exists at those specific locations. The monitoring of performance has led to the monitoring of controls. The report will then lead the franchise owner to determine the cause of the problem and to take corrective action.

Management Evaluates and Communicates Deficiencies (COSO Principle 17)

Control deficiencies identified through monitoring or other activities should be communicated to appropriate personnel such as management or the board of directors so that appropriate corrective action can be taken. Recall the previous example in which internal auditors, conducting a separate evaluation, identified a deficiency in controls over disbursements. Internal audit should provide this information to parties responsible for taking appropriate corrective action. Included in this principle is the need for an organization to implement a system to track whether deficiencies are corrected on a timely basis.

Check Your Basic Knowledge

3-25 As part of monitoring, an organization will select either ongoing evaluations or separate evaluations, but not both.   (T/F)

3-26 Communicating identified control deficiencies is a principle of monitoring.   (T/F)

3-27 Which of the following is <u>not</u> an effective implementation of the monitoring component of COSO's *Internal Control–Integrated Framework*?

   a. Internal audit periodically works to improve internal controls.

   b. Management reviews current economic performance against expectations and investigates to determine causes of significant deviations from the expectations.

   c. The organization implements software that captures all instances in which the underlying program identifies processed transactions that exceed company-authorized limits.

   d. The organization builds in edit checks to determine whether all purchases are made from authorized vendors, and flags those that are not.

3-28 Which of the following is the most accurate statement related to the monitoring component of COSO's *Internal Control–Integrated Framework*?

   a. Monitoring is a process that is relevant only to the control activities component of COSO's *Internal Control–Integrated Framework*.

   b. Separate evaluations are more timely than ongoing evaluations in identifying control deficiencies.

   c. Monitoring is a process that provides feedback on the effectiveness of each component of internal control.

   d. Monitoring includes automated edit checks to determine whether all purchases are made from authorized vendors.

LO 8

Identify management's responsibilities related to internal control over financial reporting.

Management's Responsibilities for Internal Control Over Financial Reporting

Management provides the first line of defense in achieving reliable financial reporting. Management is responsible for designing, implementing, and maintaining effective internal control over financial reporting. Further, management should maintain adequate documentation related to internal control over financial reporting. Management of U.S. public companies also has a responsibility to provide a report on the effectiveness of the organization's internal control over financial reporting.

Management Documentation of Internal Control

Management needs sufficient and appropriate documentation of the internal controls they have designed and implemented to achieve the objective of reliable financial reporting. This documentation communicates standards and expectations related to internal control. Documentation is also useful in training new employees or serving as a reference tool for all employees. Further, documentation provides evidence that the controls are operating, enables proper monitoring activities, and supports reporting on internal control effectiveness. Further, for clients like Ford Motor Company where the external auditor issues an opinion on the effectiveness of the client's controls, management will need to provide the auditor with documentation supporting management's assessment, and the auditor may use that documentation as part of the audit evidence. The nature and extent of internal control documentation will vary across organizations.

In terms of documentation supporting controls over transactions, an organization should have documentation, for example, that provides evidence of the authorization of transactions, the existence of transactions, the support for journal entries, and the financial commitments made by the organization. The documentation can be either paper or electronic. The information technology system may have an automated application programmed to pay for merchandise when an electronic copy of receipt of merchandise is available. The computer program compares receipts with a purchase order and may or may not require a vendor invoice before payment.

Some guidelines for developing reliable documentation—either paper or electronic—related to internal control include:

- *Prenumbered paper or computer-generated documents* facilitate the control of, and accountability for, transactions and are crucial to the completeness assertion.
- *Timely preparation* improves the credibility and accountability of documents and decreases the rate of errors on all documents.
- *Evidence of authorization* of a transaction.
- A *transaction trail* should exist such that a user (or auditor) can trace a transaction from its origination through to its final disposition or vice versa. A transaction trail serves many purposes, including providing information in order to respond to customer inquiries and identify and correct errors. *Exhibit 3.8* provides an overview of important aspects of an electronic transaction trail.

Management Reporting on Internal Control Over Financial Reporting

The Sarbanes-Oxley Act of 2002 requires public company management to annually report on the design and operating effectiveness of the organization's internal control over financial reporting. The U.S. Securities and Exchange Commission (SEC) has provided guidelines to assist management in its evaluation of the effectiveness

Exhibit 3.8

Important Aspects of an Electronic Transaction Trail

Unique identification of transaction—Examples include assigning a unique number by the computer. The unique identifier could be assigned sequentially or could consist of a location identifier and unique number within a location. Sales invoices, for example, are sequentially numbered by the computer application.

Date and time of transaction—These could be automatically noted by the computer application.

Individual responsible for the transaction—The log-in to the system identifies the party authorizing or initiating the transaction.

Location from which the transaction originated—The log-in to the system identifies the source of the transaction.

Details of the transaction—These should be noted in a system log. Essentially, all the details normally found in a paper document, such as the quantities ordered and back-order provisions, can also be captured and saved as an electronic trail.

Cross-reference to other transactions—When applicable, all cross-referencing to other transactions should be captured. For example, if a payment cross-references a specific invoice, the information needed to complete the cross-reference should be captured.

Authorization or approval of the transaction—If the transaction requires authorization by a party other than the one initiating the transaction, the proper electronic authorization should be captured.

of internal controls over financial reporting. The SEC guidelines require that suitable criteria, for example, COSO, be used as the benchmark in assessing internal control effectiveness. Determining whether internal control is effective requires an assessment of whether each of the five internal control components, and their principles, are present and operating effectively.

Exhibit 3.9 provides an example of a management report from Ford Motor Company. Note that management, including the CEO and CFO, both supervised and participated in the evaluation of internal controls. Further, they concluded that their internal control over financial reporting was effective as of December 31, 2016. A review of *Exhibit 3.9* highlights important features of management's report. Management's report:

- Provides a statement that management is responsible for internal control
- Includes a definition of internal control
- Discusses the limitations of internal control
- Identifies the criteria (COSO) used in assessing internal control
- Concludes as to the effectiveness of internal control at a point in time (year-end)
- References the report on internal control provided by the company's external auditors

Exhibit 3.9
Ford Motor Company Management Report on Internal Control Over Financial Reporting (2017)

ITEM 9A. Controls and Procedures

Evaluation of Disclosure Controls and Procedures. N. Joy Falotico, our Chairman of the Board and Chief Executive Officer ("CEO"), and Marion B. Harris, our Chief Financial Officer ("CFO") and Treasurer, have performed an evaluation of the Company's disclosure controls and procedures, as the term is defined in Rule 13a-15(e) of the Securities Exchange Act of 1934, as amended (the "Exchange Act"), as December 31, 2016, and each has concluded that such disclosure controls and procedures are effective to ensure that information required to be disclosed in our periodic reports filed under the Exchange Act is recorded. processed, summarized, and reported within the time periods specified by SEC rules and forms, and that such information is accumulated and communicated to the CEO and CFO to allow timely decisions regarding required disclosures.

Management's Report on Internal Control Over Financial Reporting. Our management is responsible for establishing and maintaining adequate internal control over financial reporting, as such term is defined in Exchange Act Rule 13a-15(f). The Company's Internal control over financial reporting is a process designed to provide reasonable assurance regarding the reliability of financial reporting and the preparation of financial statements for external purposes in accordance with generally accepted accounting principles.

Because of its inherent limitations, internal control over financial reporting may not prevent or detect misstatements. Also, projections of any evaluation of effectiveness to future periods are subject to the risk that controls may become inadequate because of changes in conditions or because the degree of compliance with policies or procedures may deteriorate.

Under the supervision and with the participation of our management, including our CEO and CFO, we conducted an assessment of the effectiveness of our internal control over financial reporting as of December 31, 2016. The assessment was based on criteria established in the framework *Internal Control – Integrated Framework (2013)*, issued by the Committee of Sponsoring Organizations of the Treadway Commission. Based on this assessment, management concluded that our internal control over financial reporting was effective as of December 31, 2016.

The effectiveness of the Company's internal control over financial reporting as of December 31, 2016, has been audited by PricewaterhouseCoopers LLP ("PwC"), an independent registered public accounting firm, as stated in its report which appears herein.

Changes in Internal Control Over Financial Reporting. There were no changes in internal control over financial reporting during the fourth quarter of 2016 that have materially affected, or are reasonably likely to materially affect, our internal control over financial reporting.

For further details, see http://otp.investis.com/clients/us/ford_motors/SEC/sec-show.aspx?Type=html&FilingId=11834820&CIK =0000037996&Index=10000

Evaluating Internal Control Over Financial Reporting

What does management need to do to provide a report on internal control effectiveness? The SEC's guidance for management encourages a risk-based approach to evaluation. *Exhibit 3.10* summarizes the steps involved in management's evaluation of internal control over financial. Management begins by identifying the significant risks to reliable financial reporting. For example, a manufacturer of semiconductor devices would likely consider inventory to be a **significant account** because of the materiality of the inventory account. Further, the substantial judgment required in valuing the inventory (due to obsolescence) suggests that valuation is a particularly **relevant assertion**. Thus, for this example, there is a significant risk that the financial reporting related to inventory may not be reliable.

Management then focuses on the design effectiveness of the controls intended to mitigate the risks to reliable financial reporting for the significant accounts and their relevant assertions. Management will likely conduct a **walkthrough**, following a transaction from origination to when it is reflected in the financial records. A walkthrough helps management determine whether the controls are effectively designed and have been implemented.

Management then gathers evidence through various testing procedures (e.g., inquiry, observation, review of documentation, and reperformance) as to whether the controls are operating effectively. For example, within its purchasing process, an organization may require approvals for all purchases over a stated dollar amount. As part of its testing, management could inquire of personnel who provide such approval and review documentation for an indication of the

Exhibit 3.10

Steps in Management's Evaluation of Internal Control Over Financial Reporting

Identify Financial Reporting Risks and Controls Implemented to Mitigate those Risks
Identify financial reporting risks
Identify controls that mitigate financial reporting risks
Assess design effectiveness (possibly via walkthroughs)

↓

Evaluate the Operating Effectiveness of Internal Control over Financial Reporting
Select and perform testing procedures to evaluate the operating effectiveness
Document operating effectiveness

↓

Provide Report on Effectiveness of Internal Control over Financial Reporting
Evaluate control deficiencies
Provide public disclosure of management report, including any material weaknesses

Exhibit 3.11

Examples of Approaches to Management Testing of Operating Effectiveness of Controls

Control to Be Tested	Possible Management Testing Approach
As part of the organization's risk assessment process, formal forecasts are prepared and updated during the year to reflect changes in conditions, estimates, or current knowledge.	Obtain and review the most recent corporate budget, including current forecasts. Inquire of those who are responsible for preparing and updating the forecasts.
The organization has a documented and approved disaster recovery plan, which includes off-site storage controlled by a third-party vendor.	Review disaster recovery plan and third-party vendor contract. Confirm off-site storage arrangement with third-party vendor. Obtain evidence of approval of the disaster recovery plan.
The organization has a policy requiring that a revenue recognition review be performed by the revenue accountant before revenue from complex contracts is recorded.	Review the policy. For selected transactions, review documentation that substantiates the review or reperform the review.
Surveys of internal users of financial reports are conducted to obtain information on user satisfaction with the reliability and timeliness of the reporting.	Obtain and review user surveys. Interview users.

required approval by appropriate personnel. *Exhibit 3.11* provides other examples of approaches management might use to test the operating effectiveness of various controls. After management completes testing, management then evaluates any identified control deficiencies.

Check Your Basic Knowledge

3-29 Management of U.S. public companies may provide a public report on the effectiveness of their organization's internal control over financial reporting, but management is not required to do so.   (T/F)

3-30 As part of a walkthrough, management will follow a transaction from origination to when it is reflected in the financial records to determine whether the controls are effectively designed and have been implemented.   (T/F)

3-31 Which of the following statements is <u>false</u> regarding management's documentation of internal control over financial reporting?
  a. Management needs to maintain sufficient and appropriate documentation of the internal controls they have designed and implemented to achieve the objective of reliable financial reporting.

  b. Internal control documentation is useful in training new personnel or serving as a reference tool for all employees.
  c. Management only needs to maintain documentation if the company's auditors will be providing an opinion on internal control effectiveness.
  d. Documentation provides evidence that the controls are operating.

3-32 Which of the following is <u>not</u> included in management's report on internal control?
  a. A statement that management is responsible for internal control.
  b. A definition of internal control.
  c. A discussion of the limitations of internal control.
  d. The criteria used in assessing internal control.
  e. A description of the work that the internal auditors performed.

Assessing Deficiencies in Internal Control Over Financial Reporting

LO 9

Distinguish between material weaknesses, significant deficiencies, and control deficiencies in internal control over financial reporting.

As part of its evaluation, management may become aware of deficiencies in internal control design or operating effectiveness. A **control deficiency** is some shortcoming in internal control such that the objective of reliable financial reporting may not be achieved. A deficiency in *design* exists when a control necessary to meet the control objective is missing, or when an existing control is not properly designed so that, even if the control operates as designed, the control objective would not be met.

A deficiency in *operation* exists when a properly designed control does not operate as designed, or when the person performing the control does not possess the necessary authority or competence to perform the control effectively. Management will assess all identified control deficiencies. When assessing a control deficiency, management assesses both the *likelihood* (whether there is a reasonable possibility) of misstatement and the *magnitude* of potential misstatement. *Exhibit 3.12* identifies factors affecting these two assessments.

Management's assessment will result in the deficiency being described as a control deficiency, a significant deficiency, or a material weakness.

Significant Deficiency in Internal Control

A **significant deficiency** is a deficiency, or a combination of deficiencies, in internal control over financial reporting that is less severe than a material weakness, yet important enough to merit attention by those responsible for oversight of the organization's financial reporting. A significant deficiency is important enough that it should be brought to the attention of management and the audit committee, but it does not need to be reported to external users. Significant deficiencies would not be included in management's report on internal control effectiveness.

Material Weakness in Internal Control

A **material weakness** is a deficiency, or a combination of deficiencies, in internal control over financial reporting, such that there is a *reasonable possibility* that a *material misstatement* of the company's annual or interim financial statements will not be prevented or detected on a timely basis.

For these deficiencies, the likelihood and magnitude of potential misstatement are such that the company cannot conclude that its internal control over financial reporting is effective. A material weakness does not mean the control deficiency resulted in a material, or even immaterial, misstatement in the financial statements.

Exhibit 3.12
Assessing Likelihood and Magnitude of Potential Misstatements

Factors affecting the *likelihood* that a deficiency, or a combination of deficiencies, will result in a misstatement include:

- Nature of the financial statement accounts, disclosures, and assertions involved
- Susceptibility of the related asset or liability to loss or fraud
- Subjectivity, complexity, or extent of judgment required to determine the amount involved
- Interaction or relationship of the control with other controls, including whether they are interdependent or redundant
- Interaction of the deficiencies
- Possible future consequences of the deficiency

Factors affecting the *magnitude* of a potential misstatement resulting from a deficiency or a combination of deficiencies include:

- Financial statement amounts or total of transactions exposed to the deficiency
- Volume of activity in the account balance or class of transactions exposed to the deficiency that has occurred in the current period or that is expected in future periods

What Do You think?   For Classroom Discussion

If a deficiency is *significant*, shouldn't users of the financial statements know about it? Why do you think the PCAOB decided not to require significant deficiencies to be transparent to the market and users? How do you think that auditors and management would react to requiring that significant deficiencies be transparent, i.e., disclosed to users of the financial statements?

Rather, there is a reasonable possibility that this type of control deficiency *could* lead to a material misstatement. However, when management has to restate published financial statements because of a material misstatement, management will likely conclude that a material weakness in internal control existed.

An organization that has one or more material weaknesses will issue a report indicating that internal control over financial reporting is not effective. The report will describe the identified material weaknesses. *Exhibit 3.13* provides examples of internal control material weaknesses that have been provided in actual management reports. Note that the material weaknesses can be in either the design or operation of the control. *Exhibit 3.13* highlights material weaknesses primarily related to control activities; however, material weaknesses are found in other components of internal control, including the control environment, risk assessment, information and communication, and monitoring.

Exhibit 3.13
Examples of Material Weaknesses in Internal Control Over Financial Reporting

Weaknesses in the Design of Controls

- Absence of appropriate segregation of duties over important processes
- Absence of appropriate reviews and approvals of transactions, accounting entries, or systems output
- Inadequate controls to safeguard assets
- Absence of controls to ensure that all items in a population are recorded
- Inadequate processes to develop significant estimates affecting the financial statements; for example, estimates for pensions, warranties, and other reserves
- Undue complexity in the design of the processing system that obfuscates an understanding of the system by key personnel
- Inadequate controls over access to computer systems, data, and files
- Inadequate controls over computer processing
- Inadequate controls built into computer processing

Weaknesses in the Operation of Controls

- Independent tests of controls at a division level indicate that the control activities are not working properly; for example, purchases have been made outside of the approved purchasing function.
- Controls fail to prevent or detect significant misstatements of accounting information.
- Misapplication of accounting principles.
- Credit authorization processes overridden by the sales manager to achieve sales performance goals.
- Reconciliations (a) not performed on a timely basis or (b) performed by someone independent of the underlying process.
- Testing reveals evidence that accounting records have been manipulated or altered.
- Evidence of misrepresentation by accounting personnel.
- Computerized controls leading to items identified for nonprocessing that are systematically overridden by employees to process the transactions.
- The completeness of a population, for example, prenumbered documents or reconciling items logged on to the computer with those processed, not accounted for on a regular basis.

For Classroom Discussion

What Do You Think?

In its 2016 FYE 20-F filing, Trivago (an online hotel comparison website) noted that it had identified material weaknesses in its internal controls (p. 16):

> We have identified a material weakness in our internal control over financial reporting and may identify additional material weaknesses in the future that may cause us to fail to meet our reporting obligations or result in material misstatements of our financial statements.
>
> If we fail to remediate our material weakness or if we fail to establish and maintain an effective system of internal control over financial reporting, we may not be able to report our financial results accurately or to prevent fraud. Any inability to report and file our financial results accurately and timely could harm our business and adversely impact the trading price of our securities" … "We have already hired two experienced employees for Financial Reporting and an SEC in-house counsel…
>
> Additionally, we will expand our accounting policies and procedures as well as provide additional training to our accounting and finance staff. While we are working to remediate the material weakness as quickly and efficiently as possible and expect to have remediated the material weakness during the year ending December 31, 2017, at this time we cannot provide an estimate of costs expected to be incurred in connection with implementing this remediation plan. These remediation measures may be time consuming, costly, and might place significant demands on our financial and operational resources.

> If we are unable to successfully remediate this material weakness, and if we are unable to produce accurate and timely financial statements, our financial statements could contain material misstatements that, when discovered in the future, could cause us to fail to meet our future reporting obligations and cause the price of our ADSs to decline.

Management goes on to state (p. 17):

> For as long as we are an "emerging growth company" under the JOBS Act, our independent registered public accounting firm will not be required to attest to the effectiveness of our internal controls over financial reporting pursuant to Section 404 of the Sarbanes-Oxley Act. An independent assessment of the effectiveness of our internal controls could detect problems that our management's assessment might not.

As of mid-2017, Trivago had 30 million shares outstanding, a share price of approximately $20/share and a market capitalization of over $4.2 billion.

- Given the facts about the existence of material weaknesses relating to its ability to produce accurate financial reports, what do you think about the market's apparent lack of concern about the material weaknesses?
- Would you buy stock in Trivago? Why or why not?
- What is your opinion about the facet of the JOBS Act that does not require Trivago's auditor to assess its internal control over financial reporting?

The following situations would suggest that there is a material weakness in internal control:

- Identification of fraud, whether or not material, on the part of senior management
- Multiple control deficiencies affecting the same financial statement account
- Significant deficiencies from the previous management report that the organization has not remediated
- Restatement of previously issued financial statements to reflect the correction of a material misstatement

Material Weakness or Significant Deficiency?

Management uses professional judgment in assessing whether identified control deficiencies rise to the level of a significant deficiency or material weakness. Management considers the specific facts and circumstances surrounding the identified deficiency. *Exhibit 3.14* describes two control deficiencies—one that would likely be assessed as a material weakness and one that would likely be assessed as a significant deficiency.

Exhibit 3.14
Assessing Identified Control Deficiencies

Likely Material Weakness

An organization has a new product line whereby the total annual revenue for this product line is large enough that a misstatement in the revenue account could be material to the financial statements overall. The revenue from this product line is based on contracts that have complex multi-element arrangements. The organization initiates a significant number of new contracts for this product line each week across multiple regions. When preparing these new contracts, a standard contract is used, and modifications to the standard contract are made based on the specific characteristics of the transaction.

When a new contract is entered into the computerized billing system, client accounting personnel at the regional office are to verify that revenue recognition conforms to GAAP. As part of the control procedure, the client accounting personnel who perform the verification are to complete and sign off on a revenue checklist. It appears that the control is effectively designed. However, when management tested the control they found that these control procedures had not been consistently documented or performed for the new product line. The control had not been operating effectively. Based only on these facts, management would likely determine that this deficiency represents a material weakness for the following reasons: (1) the magnitude of a financial statement misstatement resulting from this deficiency could reasonably be expected to be material as many new significant sales transactions occur each week, and (2) the total sales transactions over the year are material. Management could conclude that the likelihood of material misstatements occurring is reasonably possible. Taken together, the magnitude and likelihood of misstatement that could occur in the financial statements resulting from this internal control deficiency meet the definition of a material weakness.

Likely Significant Deficiency

Consider the same scenario as described previously with the following additional facts. The organization has implemented an additional procedure whereby the revenue accounting manager at the company headquarters verifies the revenue recognition provisions of a random sample of new contracts on a weekly basis. The manager examines documents that indicate that regional accounting personnel have verified the revenue recognition provisions. The manager also reperforms the verification procedure to ensure that revenue recognition provisions have been properly entered into the billing system. A test of this control by management indicates that the additional control has been operating effectively. Based only on these facts, management now would likely determine that the deficiency represents a significant deficiency because the weekly verifications by the revenue accounting manager constitute a compensating control that is likely to detect and prevent material misstatements in revenue recognition. Thus, the control deficiency should likely be reported to the audit committee, but does not rise to the level of a material weakness.

Check Your Basic Knowledge

3-33 If management identifies even one material weakness in internal control, then management will conclude that the organization's internal control over financial reporting is not effective. (T/F)

3-34 Management will classify a control deficiency as a material weakness only if there has been a material misstatement in the financial statements. (T/F)

3-35 Assume that an organization sells software. The sales contracts with the customers often have nonstandard terms that impact the timing of revenue recognition. Thus, there is a risk that revenue may be recorded inappropriately. To mitigate that risk, the organization has implemented a policy that requires all nonstandard contracts greater than $1 million to be reviewed on a timely basis by an experienced and competent revenue accountant for appropriate accounting, prior to the recording of revenue. Management tested this control and found several instances in which the control was not working. Management has classified this deficiency as a material weakness. Which of the following best describes the conclusion made by management?

a. There is more than a remote possibility that a material misstatement could occur.
b. The likelihood of misstatement is reasonably possible.
c. There is more than a remote possibility that a misstatement could occur.
d. There is a reasonable possibility that a material misstatement could occur.
e. There is a reasonable possibility that a misstatement could occur.

3-36 Which of the following scenarios represents a control deficiency?
a. A missing control that is required for achieving objectives.
b. A control that operates as designed.
c. A control that provides reasonable, but not absolute assurance, about the reliability of financial reporting.
d. An immaterial individual misstatement in internal control.

LO 10

Articulate the importance of internal control over financial reporting for the external audit and apply the concepts related to management's and the auditor's assessments of internal control effectiveness.

Importance of Internal Control to the External Audit

Professional auditing standards require the auditor, as part of planning an audit, to identify and assess a client's risk of material misstatement, whether due to fraud or error. This assessment requires an understanding of the organization and its environment, including its internal control over financial reporting. The auditor needs to understand a client's internal controls in order to anticipate the types of material misstatements that may occur and then develop appropriate audit procedures to determine whether those misstatements exist in the financial statements.

If a client has ineffective internal controls, the auditor will plan the audit with this in mind. For example, if an auditor notes that a client does not have effective controls to provide reasonable assurance that all sales are recorded in the correct period, then the auditor needs to develop sufficient appropriate audit procedures to test whether sales and receivables are materially misstated because of the absence of effective controls.

Auditors of large public companies have an additional interest in their client's internal controls. When conducting a financial statement audit for these companies, the auditor performs an integrated audit, which includes providing an opinion on the effectiveness of the client's internal control over financial reporting in addition to the opinion on the financial statements.

Application: Assessing Control Design Effectiveness, Implementation, and Operating Effectiveness

To illustrate the concepts related to internal control introduced in this chapter, we provide an abbreviated example focusing on cost of goods sold, inventory, and accounts payable. We assume that the organization purchases and distributes products; the organization is not a manufacturer, but it does hold a material amount of inventory. We focus our example on the purchasing cycle and the significant accounts of *accounts payable, inventory,* and *expenses*.

Management Assessment of Controls

Management has identified the significant accounts and relevant assertions in the process of purchasing goods and recording the related accounts payable and inventory. After selecting and testing controls designed to mitigate risk of misstatement in these accounts, management identifies the following control deficiencies:

- *Segregation of duties*: At one location, there is no proper segregation of duties. This represents a design deficiency. The location is very small, accounting for less than 1% of purchases.
- *Required approval*: At a second location that handles 62% of the organization's purchases, management found that approximately 17% of the purchase orders did not contain proper approval. The reason for the lack of approval was the rush to procure material in a timely fashion to meet a contract requirement. This represents an operating deficiency.

In deciding whether to categorize a deficiency as a significant deficiency or material weakness, management considers the following factors:

- The risk that is being mitigated and whether other controls operate effectively to mitigate the risk of material misstatement
- The materiality of the related account balances

- The nature of the deficiency
- The volume of transactions affected
- The subjectivity of the account balance that is subject to the control
- The rate at which the control fails to operate

Management concludes that the first deficiency (related to segregation of duties) did not rise to the level of either a significant deficiency or a material weakness. However, management decides to use this deficiency as a motivation to centralize purchases at headquarters.

The second deficiency (related to lack of approval) is more of a problem. Management determines this is a significant deficiency based on the following rationale:

- It is a major departure from an approved process.
- It could lead to the purchase of unauthorized goods.
- The unauthorized goods could lead to either: (a) inferior products or (b) potential obsolescence.
- Those making the purchases could cause them to be shipped elsewhere (fraudulently) and could lead to a material misstatement in the financial statements.

Management determines that other controls are in place that test for inferior products and obsolescence and that cycle counting of inventory would discover goods that are shipped to a different location. Accordingly, management believes that because of these controls, any potential misstatements in the financial statements would not be material. Management tests these controls and determines that they are operating effectively. If these other controls were not in place and operating effectively, then management would have assessed the control deficiency as a material weakness.

Auditor Assessment of Controls

After determining significant accounts and relevant assertions, the auditor reviews management's documentation of its internal control and management's evaluation and findings related to internal control effectiveness. The auditor had previously reviewed and tested the control environment and other entity-wide controls and had evaluated them as effective. The auditor then determined that the following were the important controls in this process (for discussion purposes, we will again concentrate on the purchasing process and assume that the auditor did not find any material weaknesses in the other processes):

- Only authorized goods are purchased from authorized vendors.
- Purchase prices are negotiated by contract or from bids.
- All purchases are delivered to the organization and received by a separate receiving department.
- All purchases are recorded in a timely fashion and are appropriately classified.
- Payments are made only for goods that are received.
- Payments are made consistent with the purchase orders or contracts.
- Payments are made in a timely fashion.

The auditor gathers evidence on the operating effectiveness of these controls as of the client's year-end for the opinion on internal control effectiveness and on operating effectiveness throughout the year for the financial statement audit. Because much of the process is computerized, the auditor performs computer security tests to assure that access controls are working properly and there is adequate control over program changes. The auditor determines that those controls are effective.

The auditor takes a sample of fifty purchase orders to examine whether purchases are authorized and processed properly. The auditor's sample size is influenced by previous information about the operation of the control. Although management had also taken a random sample of purchases and tested the operating effectiveness, the auditor needs to independently determine that the controls are working (or not working). The sample is randomly chosen, and the auditor traces the transactions through the system to determine that the objectives identified previously are addressed by controls.

The auditor's testing of controls identified the same two deficiencies identified by management. Management viewed the deficiency related to lack of approval as a *significant deficiency* because: (a) the organization has a good ethical climate and (b) management's tests confirmed that all goods were delivered to the organization. The auditor's tentative conclusion is that this deficiency is a *material weakness* because:

- The location was responsible for ordering 62% of all of the organization's products.
- Management's tests showed a failure rate of over 17%.

The fact that all the goods were delivered to the organization is important and a testament to the ethical culture of the organization. However, not all individuals are ethical; someone with a lower commitment to ethical behavior could be in the purchasing position. Stated another way, a material weakness in internal control can exist even if there are no errors in processing and no misstatements in the current period. The potential for misstatement is high because the auditor believes that existing controls do not mitigate the risk of material misstatement.

More specifically, the auditor notes the following related to the auditor's tests of controls:

- One of the 50 purchases was made from an unauthorized vendor. Investigation reveals that the vendor was subsequently authorized and it was a timing problem; that is, the vendor should have been authorized earlier.
- Seven of the 50 did not have proper authorization, corroborating the earlier finding by management.
- Three of the 50 purchases were paid even though there was no receiving report.
- All of the other controls were found to work properly.

The auditor is concerned that the system allowed a purchase to be made before the vendor was authorized. The auditor's analysis is focused primarily on the risks that may be caused by unauthorized purchases. The auditor believes that unauthorized purchases could lead to a material misstatement of inventory; that is, goods were ordered and paid for, with no proof that they were actually received, and may have been delivered elsewhere. Based on this concern, the auditor decides that the deficiency related to lack of approval warrants a material weakness designation.

Check Your Basic Knowledge

3-37 The auditor needs to understand a client's internal controls in order to anticipate the types of material misstatements that may occur in the financial statements and then develop sufficient appropriate audit procedures to determine whether those misstatements exist in the financial statements. (T/F)

3-38 While understanding a client's internal control over financial reporting may help the external auditor plan the audit, the external auditor is not required to obtain this understanding for all audit engagements. (T/F)

3-39 Which of the following is a reason that the auditor obtains an understanding of the client's internal control over financial reporting?
   a. This understanding is required by professional auditing standards.
   b. Understanding of internal control is needed to properly plan the audit.
   c. This understanding helps an auditor assess a client's risk of material misstatement.
   d. All of the above are reasons why the auditor obtains an understanding of the client's internal control over financial reporting.

3-40 Which of the following statements is <u>true</u> regarding the auditor's assessment of a client's internal control over financial reporting?
   a. The auditor reviews management's documentation of its internal control and management's evaluation and findings related to internal control effectiveness.
   b. The auditor's assessments of control deficiencies will be the same as management's assessment of the same deficiencies.
   c. In testing controls, the auditor is only concerned about the client's control environment and risk assessment.
   d. All of the above are true.

Let's Review

- Organizations need effective internal control over financial reporting so they can produce reliable financial statements that are free from material misstatement. By producing reliable financial statements, users can trust their accuracy, and managers can make better decisions because they are making decisions based on reliable data. (LO 1)

- Implementing the components (control environment, risk assessment, control activities, information and communication, and monitoring) and principles of the COSO framework enables organizations to achieve reliable financial reporting. (LO 1)

- Internal control is a process, effected by an entity's board of directors, management, and other personnel, designed to provide reasonable assurance regarding the achievement of objectives relating to operations, reporting, and compliance. The COSO components include the control environment, risk assessment, control activities, information and communication, and monitoring. (LO 2, 3, 4, 5, 6, 7)

- Management provides the first line of defense in achieving reliable financial reporting. Management is responsible for designing, implementing, and maintaining effective internal control over financial reporting and addressing risks to reliable financial reporting. Further, management should maintain adequate documentation related to internal control over financial reporting. Management of U.S. public companies also has a responsibility to provide a report on the effectiveness of the organization's internal control over financial reporting. (LO 8)

- A material weakness in internal control is a deficiency, or a combination of deficiencies, in internal control over financial reporting such that there is a reasonable possibility that a material misstatement of the company's annual or interim financial statements will not be prevented or detected on a timely basis. A material weakness is more severe than a significant deficiency in internal controls, which is a deficiency, or a combination of deficiencies, in internal control over financial reporting that is less severe than a material weakness, yet important enough to merit attention by those responsible for oversight of the company's financial reporting. (LO 9)

- Professional auditing standards require the auditor, as part of planning an audit, to identify and assess a client's risks of material misstatement, whether due to fraud or error. The auditor bases this assessment on an understanding of the organization and its environment, including its internal control over financial reporting. The auditor needs to understand a client's internal controls in order to anticipate the types of material misstatements that may occur and then develop appropriate audit procedures to determine whether those misstatements exist in the financial statements. (LO 10)

Significant Terms

Application controls   See *transaction controls*.

Control activities   The component of internal control that includes control actions that have been established by policies and procedures. They help ensure that management's directives regarding internal control are carried out.

Control deficiency   A shortcoming in internal controls such that the objective of reliable financial reporting may not be achieved.

Control environment   The component of internal control that includes the set of standards, processes, and structures that provides the basis for carrying out internal control across the organization. It includes the "tone at the top" regarding the importance of internal control and the expected standards of conduct.

COSO Internal Control–Integrated Framework   A comprehensive framework of internal control used to assess the effectiveness of internal control over financial reporting, as well as controls over operational and compliance objectives.

Detective controls   Controls designed to discover errors that occur during processing.

Edit tests   See *input validation tests*.

Entity-wide controls   Controls that operate across an entity and affect multiple processes, transactions, accounts, and assertions.

General computer controls   Pervasive control activities that affect multiple types of information technology systems and are necessary for automated application controls to work properly (also referred to as *information technology general controls*).

Information and communication   The component of internal control that refers to the process of identifying, capturing, and exchanging information in a timely fashion to enable accomplishment of the organization's objectives.

Information technology general controls   See *general computer controls*.

Input controls   Controls designed to ensure that authorized transactions are correct and complete and that only authorized transactions can be input.

Input validation tests   Control tests built into an application to examine input data for obvious errors (also referred to as *edit tests*).

Internal control   A process, effected by an entity's board of directors, management, and other personnel, designed to provide reasonable assurance regarding the achievement of objectives relating to operations, reporting, and compliance.

Material weakness   A deficiency, or a combination of deficiencies, in internal control over financial reporting such that there is a reasonable possibility that a material misstatement of the company's annual or interim financial statements will not be prevented or detected on a timely basis.

Monitoring The component of internal control that determines whether the controls, including all five components, are present and continuing to function effectively.

Ongoing evaluations Monitoring procedures that are built into the normal recurring activities of an entity.

Output controls Controls designed to provide reasonable assurance that all data are completely processed and that output is distributed only to authorized recipients.

Physical controls over assets Controls designed to protect and safeguard assets from accidental or intentional destruction and theft.

Preventive controls Controls designed to prevent the occurrence of a misstatement.

Processing controls Controls designed to provide reasonable assurance that the correct program is used for processing, all transactions are processed, and the transactions update appropriate files.

Relevant assertion A financial statement assertion, for a given account, is most relevant to determining whether there is a reasonable possibility that the account could contain a material misstatement, without considering the effect of internal controls.

Risk assessment The component of internal control that is the process for identifying and assessing the risks that may affect an organization from achieving its objectives.

Segregation of duties A control activity that is designed to protects against the risk that an individual could both perpetrate and cover up a fraud.

Self-checking digits A type of input test that has been developed to test for transposition errors associated with identification numbers.

Separate evaluations Monitoring procedures that are conducted periodically, typically by objective management personnel, internal auditors, or external consultants.

Significant account An account that has a reasonable possibility of containing a material misstatement, without considering the effect of internal controls.

Significant deficiency A deficiency, or a combination of deficiencies, in internal control over financial reporting that is less severe than a material weakness, yet important enough to merit attention by those responsible for oversight of the company's financial reporting.

Tone at the top The leadership culture of the organization, including the board of directors, the audit committee, and management.

Transaction controls Control activities implemented to mitigate transaction-processing risk that typically affect only certain processes, transactions, accounts, and assertions. These are controls that do not have an entity-wide effect.

Transaction trail Includes the documents and records that allow a user (or auditor) to trace a transaction from its origination through to its final disposition or vice versa.

Walkthrough A process whereby management (or the auditor) follows a transaction from origination through the organization's processes until it is reflected in the organization's financial records. This process includes a combination of inquiry, observation, inspection of documentation making up the transaction trail, and reperformance of controls.

Whistleblower function A special line of communication that is needed for anonymous or confidential communications, particularly when an employee is concerned that something is inappropriate in the organization's operations.

Prompts for Critical Thinking

Prompt for Critical Thinking #1

- Physical controls over inventory and fixed assets
- Reconciliations between sales records and cash
- Reconciliations between inventory on hand as compared to sales (i.e., checking for stolen/misplaced inventory)

Prompt for Critical Thinking #2

Some examples include the following (but many more are included in the 10-K):

- Decline in industry sales volume, particularly in the United States, Europe, or China, due to financial crisis, recession, geopolitical events, or other factors.
- Lower-than-anticipated market acceptance of Ford's new or existing products or services, or failure to achieve expected growth.
- Market shift away from sales of larger, more profitable vehicles beyond Ford's current planning assumption, particularly in the United States.
- Continued or increased price competition resulting from industry excess capacity, currency fluctuations, or other factors.

Review Questions and Short Cases

NOTE: Completing *Review Questions and Short* Cases does not require the student to reference additional resources and materials.

NOTE: We make special note of problems addressing fraud and ethics.

3-1 LO 1 How does internal control benefit an organization?

3-2 LO 1 How are the concepts of risk and internal control related?

3-3 LO 2 Using COSO's *Internal Control–Integrated Framework*, define internal control and describe important elements of the definition.

3-4 LO 2 Refer to *Exhibit 3.1*. Identify and describe the components of internal control.

3-5 LO 2 Distinguish between entity-wide and transaction controls. Which components of internal control are typically entity-wide controls? Which components of internal control are typically transaction controls?

ETHICS **3-6** LO 3 Refer to *Exhibit 3.2*. List the principles representing the fundamental concepts of the control environment component.

ETHICS **3-7** LO 3 Refer to *Exhibit 3.2*. For each control environment principle, provide an example of how an organization might apply that principle.

ETHICS **3-8** LO 3 What functions do an organization's board of directors and the audit committee of the board of directors perform in promoting an effective internal control environment?

FRAUD **3-9** LO 3 As part of assessing the control environment, management might consider the compensation programs that the organization has in place. Why would management consider these programs?

FRAUD **3-10** LO 4 Refer to *Exhibit 3.3*. List the principles representing the fundamental concepts of the risk assessment component.

FRAUD

3-11 **LO 4** Refer to *Exhibit 3.3*. For each risk assessment principle, provide an example of how an organization might apply that principle.

3-12 **LO 5** Refer to *Exhibit 3.4*. List the principles representing the fundamental concepts of the control activities component.

3-13 **LO 5** Refer to *Exhibit 3.4*. For each control activities principle, provide an example of how an organization might apply that principle.

3-14 **LO 5** Refer to *Exhibit 3.5*. Describe the three types of transactions subject to transaction-processing risk. For each type of transaction, indicate a control activity that could be implemented to mitigate that risk.

3-15 **LO 5** What are the important considerations in security management related to user access?

3-16 **LO 5** What are general computer controls? What is the relationship between general computer controls and application controls? Why is management concerned about the effectiveness of these controls?

3-17 **LO 5** Brown Company provides office support services for more than 100 small clients. These services include supplying temporary personnel, providing monthly bookkeeping services, designing and printing small brochures, copying and reproduction services, and preparing tax reports. Some clients pay for these services on a cash basis, some use thirty-day charge accounts, and others operate on a contractual basis with quarterly payments. Brown's new office manager was concerned about the effectiveness of control procedures over sales and cash flow. At the manager's request, the process was reviewed by conducting a walkthrough. The following facts were identified. Review the identified facts (listed as A through L) and complete the following.

a. What is a *walkthrough*, and why would it be useful for assessing controls over sales and cash flow?

b. List at least eight elements of ineffective internal control at Brown Company.

c. List at least six elements of effective internal control at Brown Company.

   A. Contracts were written by account executives and then passed to the accounts receivable department, where they were filed. Contracts had a limitation (ceiling) on the types of services and the amount of work covered. Contracts were payable quarterly in advance.

   B. Client periodic payments on contracts were identified on the contract, and a payment receipt was placed in the contract file.

   C. Periodically, a clerk reviewed the contract files to determine their status.

   D. Work orders relating to contract services were placed in the contract file. Accounting records showed Debit Cost of Services; Credit Cash or Accounts Payable or Accrued Payroll entry.

   E. Monthly bookkeeping services were usually paid for when the work was complete. If not paid in cash, a copy of the financial statement (marked "Unpaid _____") was put into cash-pending file. It was removed when cash was received, and accounting records showed Debit Cash; Credit Revenue entry.

   F. Design and printing work was handled like bookkeeping's work. However, a design and printing order form was used to accumulate costs and compute the charge to be made to the client. A copy of the order form served as a billing to the client and, when cash was received, as a remittance advice.

G. Reproduction (copy) work was generally a cash transaction that was rung up on a cash register and balanced at the end of the day. Some reproduction work was charged to open accounts. A billing form was given to the client with the work, and a copy was put in an open file. It was removed when paid. In both cases, when cash was received, the accounting entry was Debit Cash; Credit Revenue.

H. Tax work was handled like the bookkeeping services.

I. Cash from cash sales was deposited daily. Cash from receipts on account or quarterly payments on contracts was deposited after being matched with the evidence of the receivable.

J. Bank reconciliations were performed using the deposit slips as original data for the deposits on the bank statements.

K. A cash log of all cash received in the mail was maintained and used for reference purposes when payment was disputed.

L. Monthly comparisons were made of the costs and revenues of printing, design, bookkeeping, and tax service. Unusual variations between revenues and costs were investigated. However, the handling of deferred payments made this analysis difficult.

3-18 **LO 5** The following items represent errors that often occur in an automated environment. For each error (listed as A through I), identify a control activity that could be effective in either preventing or detecting the error.

A. The selling price for all products handled by a particular company salesperson was reduced from authorized prices by 25% to 40%. The salesperson was paid commission on gross sales made. Subsequently, management found that other sales personnel also reduced prices in order to meet sales targets.

B. Duplicate paychecks were prepared for all employees in the company's warehouse for the week ended July 31. This occurred because the data-processing department processed employee time cards twice.

C. An employee in the sales order department who was upset about an inadequate pay raise copied the client's product master file and sold it to a competitor. The master file contained information on the cost and sales price of each product, as well as special discounts given to customers.

D. An individual in the sales department accessed the product master file and, in an attempt to change prices for a specific customer, ended up changing prices for the products for all customers.

E. A nonexistent part number was included in the description of goods on a shipping document. Fortunately, the individual packing the item for shipment was able to identify the product by its description and included it in the order. The item was not billed, however, because it was not correctly identified in the system.

F. A customer account number was transposed during the order-taking process. Consequently, the shipment was billed to another customer. By the time the error was identified, the original customer decided to take its business elsewhere.

G. An accounts receivable clerk with access to entering cash remittances misappropriated the cash remittances and recorded the credit to the customer's account as a discount.

H. An employee consistently misstated his time card by returning at night and punching out then, rather than when his shift was over at 3:30 p.m. Instead of being paid for 40 hours per week, he was paid, on average, for over 60 hours per week for almost one year. When accused of the error, he denied any wrongdoing and quit.

I. A customer order was filled and shipped to a former customer who had already declared bankruptcy and already owed a large amount to the company that was most likely uncollectible. The company's standard billing terms are 2%, 10 days, or net 30.

FRAUD

3-19 **LO 5** Authorization of transactions is a key control in most organizations. Authorizations should not be made by individuals who have incompatible functions. For each transaction (listed as A through I), indicate the individual or function (e.g., the head of a particular department) that should have the ability to authorize that transaction. Briefly provide a rationale for your answer.

A. Writing off old accounts receivable.
B. Committing the organization to acquire another company that is half the size of the existing company.
C. Paying an employee for overtime.
D. Shipping goods on account to a new customer.
E. Purchasing goods from a new vendor.
F. Temporarily investing funds in common stock investments instead of money market funds.
G. Purchasing a new line of manufacturing equipment to remodel a production line at one of the company's major divisions (the purchase represents a major new investment for the organization).
H. Replacing an older machine at one of the company's major divisions.
I. Rewriting the company's major computer program for processing purchase orders and accounts payable (the cost of rewriting the program will represent one quarter of the organization's computer development budget for the year).

FRAUD

3-20 **LO 5** For each of the following situations (indicated A through E), evaluate the segregation of duties implemented by the company and indicate the following:

a. Any deficiency in the segregation of duties described. (Indicate "None" if no deficiency is present.)
b. The potential financial statement misstatements that might occur because of the inadequate segregation of duties.
c. Additional controls that might mitigate potential misstatements.
   A. The company's payroll is computerized and is handled by one person in charge of payroll who enters all weekly time reports into the system. The payroll system is password protected so that only the payroll person can change pay rates or add/delete company personnel to the payroll file. Payroll checks are prepared weekly, and the payroll person batches the checks by supervisor or department head for subsequent distribution to employees.
   B. A relatively small organization has segregated the duties of cash receipts and cash disbursements. However, the employee responsible for handling cash receipts also reconciles the monthly bank account.
   C. Nick's is a small family-owned restaurant in a northern resort area whose employees are trusted. When the restaurant is very busy, any of the servers have the ability to operate the cash register and collect the amounts due from the customer. All

orders are tabulated on "tickets." Although each ticket has a place to indicate the server, most do not bother to do so, nor does management reconcile the ticket numbers and amounts with total cash receipts for the day.

D. A sporting goods store takes customer orders via a toll-free phone number. The order taker sits at a terminal and has complete access to the customer's previous credit history and a list of inventory available for sale. The order clerk has the ability to input all the customer's requests and generate a sales invoice and shipment with no additional supervisory review or approval.

E. The purchasing department of Big Dutch is organized around three purchasing agents. The first is responsible for ordering electrical gear and motors, the second orders fabrication material, and the third orders nuts and bolts and other smaller supplies that go into the assembly process. To improve the accountability to vendors, all receiving slips and vendor invoices are sent directly to the purchasing agent placing the order. This allows the purchasing agent to better monitor the performance of vendors. When approved by the purchasing agent for payment, the purchasing agent must forward (a) a copy of the purchase order, (b) a copy of the receiving slip, and (c) a copy of the vendor invoice to accounts payable for payment. Accounts payable will not pay an invoice unless all three items are present and match as to quantities, prices, and so forth. The receiving department reports to the purchasing department.

FRAUD

3-21 **LO 5** Sports Life World is a catalog retailer emphasizing outdoor gear, with a focus on fishing and hunting equipment and clothing. It prints an annual catalog containing over 200 pages of products, as well as approximately six special sale catalogs during the year. Products range from fishing lures retailing for just over $1.00 to boat packages for over $25,000. Sports Life World also has both a significant Internet presence and a number of large retail locations. Purchases can be made through the mail, on the company's website, or at the retail store. There will sometimes be online specials that are not available elsewhere (e.g., closeouts). Merchandise can be paid for by personal check, credit card, or cash. Customers can (a) order online, (b) mail in their order (with check or credit card information included), or (c) place an order by calling the company's toll-free number. Focusing on catalog operations, assume the company has implemented an order-entry system by which computer operators take the customer order, check the availability of items for shipment, and confirm the invoice amount with the customer. Once an order is taken, the system generates a shipping-and-packing document, places a hold on the inventory, and prepares an invoice (and recording of sales) when items are shipped.

a. Identify the application control procedures (including edit controls) you would recommend for orders coming in over the Internet or through calls to the online order taker.

b. Briefly indicate how control procedures might differ for the orders that are made through the company's website.

c. For each control procedure identified in your response to (a), briefly indicate the potential types of misstatements that could occur because the control is not present or is not operating effectively.

3-22 `LO 6` Refer to *Exhibit 3.6*. List the principles representing the fundamental concepts of the information and communication component.

3-23 `LO 6` Refer to *Exhibit 3.6*. For each information and communication principle, provide an example of how an organization might apply that principle.

3-24 `LO 7` Refer to *Exhibit 3.7*. List the principles representing the fundamental concepts of the monitoring component.

3-25 `LO 7` Refer to *Exhibit 3.7*. For each monitoring principle, provide an example of how an organization might apply that principle.

3-26 `LO 7` Companies can improve internal control effectiveness by implementing effective ongoing monitoring of their internal control processes. Identify ongoing monitoring procedures that an organization might use in assessing its controls over revenue recognition in each of the following situations:
a. A convenience store such as 7-Eleven.
b. A chain restaurant such as Olive Garden.
c. A manufacturing division of a larger company that makes rubberized containers for the consumer market.

3-27 `LO 8` What are management's responsibilities related to internal control over financial reporting?

3-28 `LO 8` Refer to *Exhibit 3.8*. What is a transaction trail? List important aspects of an electronic transaction trail. What are management's responsibilities related to maintaining a transaction trial?

3-29 `LO 8` Refer to *Exhibit 3.9*. What are the important features of management's report on internal control over financial reporting?

3-30 `LO 8` Refer to *Exhibit 3.10* and *Exhibit 3.11*. Describe management's process for evaluating internal control over financial reporting. For the control environment principles, identify evidence that management might obtain to assess the operating effectiveness of the control environment.

ETHICS

3-31 `LO 8` Should management's assessment of internal control over financial reporting consider all of the COSO components, or could it be based only on the controls over the processing of transactions? Explain.

3-32 `LO 8` One principle of the control environment is the organization's commitment to develop, attract, and retain competent individuals. How would management evaluate the competency of accounting department personnel and the competencies of those making judgments on financial reporting issues?

3-33 `LO 9` Assume that management had determined that its organization's audit committee is not effective. How do the weaknesses in audit committee affect management's evaluation of internal control over financial reporting? Would an ineffective audit committee constitute a material weakness in internal control over financial reporting? State the rationale for your response.

3-34 `LO 9` Refer to *Exhibit 3.12* and *Exhibit 3.13*. Define the terms *significant deficiency* and *material weakness*. What factors does management consider when assessing identified control deficiencies?

3-35 `LO 9` Assume that management is gathering evidence as part of its process for assessing the effectiveness of internal control over financial reporting. The company is a manufacturer of high-dollar specialized machines used in the medical profession. The following table identifies important controls that management is testing regarding accounts related to revenue recognition, accounts receivable, and other sales-related activities. The first column describes the control, and the second column describes the test results. Based on the test results, determine the conclusion that management should likely make about the deficiency. (Is it a control deficiency, a significant deficiency, or a material weakness?)

Control Testing Over Revenue

Control Tested	Test Results
A. All sales over $10,000 require computer check of outstanding balances to see if approved balance is exceeded.	Tested throughout year with a sample size of thirty. Only three failures, all in the last quarter, and all approved by sales manager.
B. The computer is programmed to record a sale only when an item is shipped.	Sampled ten items during the last month. One indicated that it was recorded before it was shipped. Management was aware of the recording.
C. All prices are obtained from a standardized price list maintained within the computer and accessible only by the marketing manager.	Management selected forty invoices and found five instances in which the price was less than the price list. All of the price changes were initiated by salespeople.
D. Sales are shipped only upon receiving an authorized purchase order from customer.	Management selects fifteen transactions near the end of each quarter. On average, three to four are shipped each quarter based on salesperson's approval and without a customer purchase order.

3-36 **LO 9** The following scenario describes PPC, a small plastics producer with $250 million in revenue and approximately 300 employees. PPC is a public company that first became listed three years ago. Its sales have dropped from $1,375 million to $1,250 million over that period. It is barely profitable and is just meeting some of its most important debt covenants. During the past year, John Slade, CEO and owner of 22% of the company's shares, has taken the following actions (listed as A through I) to reduce costs. For each action, complete the following:

a. Would the action be considered an operational issue and not a control deficiency, or would it likely constitute a material weakness or significant deficiency in internal control? Provide a brief rationale for your assessment. If additional information is needed in order to assess whether the item is a control deficiency, briefly indicate what information would be required.

b. Considering all of the indicated actions (A through I), how has the risk related to the objective of reliable financial reporting changed during the year?

    A. Laid off approximately 75 factory workers and streamlined receiving and shipping to be more efficient.

    B. Cut hourly wages by $3 per hour.

C. Reduced the size of the board by eliminating three of the four independent directors and changed the compensation of remaining board members to 100% stock options to save cash outflow. The company granted options to the remaining six directors with a market value of $100,000 per director, but no cash outlay.

D. Eliminated the internal audit department at a savings of $450,000. The process owners (e.g., those responsible for accounts payable) are now required to objectively evaluate the quality of controls over their own areas and thus to serve as a basis for management's report on the effectiveness of internal control.

E. Changed from a Big 4 audit firm to a regional audit firm, resulting in an additional audit savings of $300,000. This is the first public company audit for the new firm.

F. Because internal audit no longer exists, the CEO relies on monitoring as the major form of control assessment. Most of the monitoring consists of comparing budget with actual results. Management argues this is very effective because the CEO is very much involved in operations and would know if there is a reporting problem.

G. Set tight performance goals for managers and promised a bonus of 20% of their salary if they meet the performance objectives. The performance objectives relate to increased profitability and meeting existing volumes.

H. The purchasing department has been challenged to move away from single-supplier contracts to identify suppliers that can significantly reduce the cost of products purchased.

I. Put a freeze on all hiring, in spite of the fact that the accounting department has lost its assistant controller. This has required a great deal of extra overtime for most accounting personnel, who are quite stressed.

3-37 **LO 10** When testing internal controls, does the auditor test the same transactions that management tested, or does the auditor test different transactions? Explain your rationale.

3-38 **LO 10** Why do external auditors need to understand their client's internal control over financial reporting?

Fraud Focus: Contemporary and Historical Cases

FRAUD

3-39 **Chesapeake Petroleum and Supply, Inc.**
(LO 1, 2, 5)

Refer to the *Focus on Fraud* feature "The Importance of Internal Control for Safeguarding Assets at Chesapeake Petroleum and Supply, Inc." which describes the embezzlement at Chesapeake Petroleum and Supply.

a. Why is internal control important to an organization?

b. How does internal control help an organization achieve reliable financial reporting?

c. Why does an external auditor need to know about a client's internal control?

d. What is internal control over financial reporting and what are its components?

e. What type of control is segregation of duties and what risks is that control intended to mitigate?

f. What controls could Chesapeake have implemented that may have prevented the embezzlement?

FRAUD

3-40 | **Diamond Foods, Inc.**
(LO 8, 9)

In February 2012, the *Wall Street Journal* reported that Diamond Foods, Inc. fired its CEO and CFO, and would restate financial results for two years. The restatement was required after the company found that it had wrongly accounted for crop payments to walnut growers. The investigation focused primarily on whether payments to growers in September 2011 of approximately $60 million and payments to growers in August 2010 of approximately $20 million were accounted for in the correct periods. Shareholders suing the company allege the payments may have been used to shift costs from a prior fiscal year into a subsequent fiscal year. In a February 2012 filing with the SEC, the audit committee stated that Diamond had one or more material weaknesses in its internal control over financial reporting. In January 2014, the SEC charged Diamond Foods and two former executives for their roles in the accounting scheme to falsify walnut costs in order to boost earnings and meet estimates by stock analysts. Diamond Foods agreed to pay $5 million to settle the SEC's charges.

a. Does the restatement suggest that the company's internal controls contained a material weakness? Explain your rationale.

b. In September 2011, the company filed its annual report with the SEC for its fiscal year ended July 31, 2011. As part of that filing, the company maintained that it had effective internal controls over financial reporting as of its year-end date. Do you believe that management's report on internal control over financial reporting was accurate?

c. In February 2012, the audit committee indicated that the company had ineffective internal controls. What types of material weaknesses do you think might exist at Diamond?

Application Activities

NOTE: Completing *Application Activities* requires students to reference additional resources and materials.

3-41 | **KPMG, PCAOB**
(LO 1, 2)

ETHICS

Refer to the *Why It Matters* feature "KPMG Fires Five Audit Partners and the Head of Its Audit Practice." Recall that this incident initially involved a former and a current PCAOB employee, with the latter supplying information about upcoming PCAOB inspections of various KPMG audit client engagements.

The incident *could have stopped there*, if the KPMG employee either did not act upon the information, or s/he notified a superior, who then did the right thing and notified the PCAOB of the breach. Of course, we now know that the chain of events *did not stop there*. Instead, the breached information made its way up the organization all the way to Scott Marcello, the head of the entire audit practice of KPMG.

a. How, if at all, could the PCAOB have internal controls in place to prevent an employee from leaking inspection information?

b. How, if at all, could KPMG have internal controls in place to prevent a former PCAOB employee who now works for the Firm have inappropriate communication with current PCAOB employees?

    c. What changes can you think of that could prevent a breach such as this?

    d. Scott Marcello had a 38-year career with KPMG, and now he has been disgraced and fired. Speculate as to his potential incentives and rationalizations.

3-42 (LO 2, 5)

Select a company where you have worked part-time or an organization in which you have some acquaintance (relative or friend) and therefore have access. Choose one area of operations (cash receipts, sales, shipping, receiving, or payroll) for review. For the area selected:

    a. Identify the major transactions processed.

    b. Select a representative transaction and perform a walkthrough of the transaction to gain an understanding of how the transaction is processed and the controls implemented to mitigate the risks to reliable financial reporting.

    c. Document the important controls and the risks they were intended to mitigate.

    d. Identify additional controls you would recommend to improve the organization's internal controls.

3-43 (LO 7)   Companies are using data analytics tools to develop continuous monitoring approaches to identify control problems early and to take corrective action on a timely basis.

    a. Explain how the concept of continuous monitoring might be applied in a computerized application that processes sales orders and records sales.

    b. Select one of the following websites:

        www.oversightsystems.com

        www.acl.com

    Explain the types of products that each company provides and how the products might help other companies implement effective monitoring over computer operations. To what extent are the software products (1) another control to be implemented versus (2) an approach to control monitoring? Explain.

3-44 **SEC, Diamond Foods, Inc.**

    (LO 8, 9)   At the SEC website, obtain Management's Report on Internal Control provided by Diamond Foods, Inc. for the year-end July 31, 2013. (See p. 79 of Form 10-K, via EDGAR at *www.sec.gov*)

    a. Identify the material weaknesses that management described in its report on internal control.

    b. Why would management consider these deficiencies to be material weaknesses?

    c. Are misstatements necessary for management to conclude that a control deficiency is a material weakness? Explain.

    d. What process would Diamond's management have gone through to identify these material weaknesses?

3-45 (LO 8, 9)   Using the business press (i.e., financial news articles), identify a company that has restated it published financial statements. Describe the nature of the restatement. What types of deficiencies in internal control likely existed such that the financial statements were materially misstated? Should management now conclude that it has a material weakness in internal control over financial reporting?

3-46 **Ford Motor Company**

(LO 1, 2, 10) At the SEC website, obtain Management's Report on Internal Control provided by Ford Motor Company for the year-end December 31, 2016. (See p. 100 of Form 10-K, via EDGAR at *www.sec.gov*.)

a. Ford management comments on the fact that internal control over financial reporting has "inherent limitations." What are those inherent limitations?

b. Locate the CEO certification toward the end of Ford's 10K (Exhibit 3.9). Summarize the main components of the certification. Why should users of the financial statements be assured by the statements made in the certification?

c. How does management obtain comfort that internal control does not contain any material weaknesses?

d. From a conceptual point of view, assume that two companies are the same size, participate in the same industry, and have the same reported net income. However, one has a material weakness in internal control over financial reporting and the other does not have any material weaknesses. Should the stock price of the two be different? What is the rationale for your answer?

Academic Research Cases

NOTE: Completing *Academic Research Cases* requires students to reference additional resources and materials.

SEARCH HINT

It is easy to locate these academic research articles! Use a search engine such as Google Scholar or an electronic research platform such as ABI Inform, and search using the author names and part of the article title.

3-47 **(LO 9, 10)** Locate and read the article listed below.

Gramling, A. A., E. F. O'Donnell, and S. D. Vandervelde. (2013). An experimental examination of factors that influence auditor assessments of a deficiency in internal control over financial reporting. *Accounting Horizons* 27(2): 249–269.

a. What is the purpose of the study?
b. Describe the design/method/approach used to conduct the study.
c. What are the primary findings of the study?

3-48 **(LO 3, 8, 9)** Locate and read the article listed below.

Choi, J. H., S. Choi, C. E. Hogan, and J. Lee. (2013). The effect of human resource investment in internal control on the disclosure of internal control weaknesses. *Auditing: A Journal of Practice & Theory* 32(4): 169–199.

a. What is the purpose of the study?
b. Describe the design/method/approach used to conduct the study.
c. What are the primary findings of the study?

The Audit Opinion Formulation Process

I. Making Client Acceptance and Continuance Decisions

Chapter 1

II. Performing Risk Assessment

Chapters 2, 3, 7, and 9–13

III. Obtaining Evidence About Internal Control Operating Effectiveness

Chapters 8–13

IV. Obtaining Substantive Evidence About Accounts, Disclosures, and Assertions

Chapters 8–13

V. Completing the Audit and Making Reporting Decisions

Chapters 14 and 15

Quality Auditing and the Need for Quality Auditor Judgments and Ethical Decisions

Chapter 1

Professional Liability

Chapter 4

The Audit Opinion Formulation Process and a Framework for Obtaining Audit Evidence

Chapters 5 and 6

You might be surprised to learn that audit firms spend a large percentage of their revenues on litigation-related costs, including insurance, legal fees, and litigation settlements. Litigation-related costs have caused some of the world's largest audit firms to go out of business.

Learning Objectives

LO 1 Discuss the liability environment in which auditors operate and the effects of litigation on audit firms.

LO 2 List the three types of law most relevant to auditor liability, describe the causes of legal action against auditors, and identify parties that can file suit against auditors.

LO 3 Describe auditor liability under contract law, common law, and statutory law, and discuss possible defenses, remedies, and sanctions.

Violation of Federal Securities Laws

This feature provides an example of the implications to an auditor for attempting to evade federal securities laws.

The U.S. Securities and Exchange Commission sanctioned a Boca Raton, FL, auditor for trying to evade a federal law that requires lead audit partners to periodically rotate off their audit engagements with a public company.

Eliot Berman, the owner of accounting firm Berman & Co., was the lead partner in audits of Issuer A, a publicly traded biotech company, for its fiscal year audits from 2006 to 2010. After the 2010 audit, Berman was required to rotate off the assignment under a law that prohibits auditors from performing lead audit partner services for the same issuer for more than five consecutive fiscal years.

Instead, Berman appointed a firm employee who was not a CPA as the "lead" partner for the client's 2011 audit. Berman improperly continued performing many of the lead partner functions. In effect, Berman attempted to undermine the independence rules. He basically concocted a sham by naming an unqualified employee of the firm to serve as a token lead audit partner while Berman continued to serve as the actual lead partner.

As part of a settlement that preempted filing of formal charges, Berman agreed to pay a $15,000 penalty and to a suspension of at least one year from practicing as an accountant on behalf of any publicly traded company or other entity regulated by the SEC.

For further details, see SEC AAER Release No. 3592 / October 24, 2014.

What You Will Learn

- What aspects of the liability environment lead to lawsuits against audit firms and individual auditors? (LO 1)
- Who can file suit against auditors? (LO 2)
- What types of law are relevant to auditor liability? (LO 2)
- What types of auditor actions could lead to litigation? (LO 2, 3)
- What are possible sanctions and penalties that auditors could face for violating federal securities laws? (LO 3)

LO 1

Discuss the liability environment in which auditors operate and the effects of litigation on audit firms.

The Legal Environment and the Effects of Lawsuits on Audit Firms

Litigation is costly for audit firms—whether they win or lose. Litigation results in monetary losses, consumes time of audit firm members, and can hurt the reputation of the audit firm. Audit firms have reported that litigation-related costs, such as insurance, legal fees, and litigation settlements, are the second-highest costs faced by audit firms, behind only employee compensation costs. Most audits are quality audits, where auditors comply with principles of professional conduct, employ professional judgment and professional skepticism, make ethical decisions, comply with auditing standards, and issue appropriate opinions.

If an audit firm issued an inaccurate audit opinion and failed to comply with the auditing standards, most auditors and financial statement users would consider that audit to be an **audit failure**. In instances of an audit failure, litigation is likely an appropriate response. However, audit firms experience litigation when it is not clear that an audit failure occurred. Incentives for this litigation include:

- Legal liability doctrines that include joint and several liability statutes permitting a plaintiff to recover the full amount of a settlement from an audit firm, even though that firm is found to be only partially responsible for the loss (often referred to as the **deep-pocket theory**, which is the practice of suing a party not based on the level of that party's fault in a legal action, but based instead on the perceived ability of that party to pay damages)
- Class action lawsuits and associated user awareness of the possibilities and rewards of litigation
- Contingent-fee compensation for law firms, especially in class action lawsuits
- Viewing the audit as an insurance policy against investment losses

Liability Doctrines

Auditors facing lawsuits may be subject to either joint and several liability or proportionate liability. For lawsuits filed in federal court, proportionate liability generally applies. However, if the auditor knowingly participated in the fraud or had knowledge of the fraud, joint and several liability would apply. For lawsuits filed in state court, state laws determine whether proportionate liability or joint and several liability applies.

Under **proportionate liability**, a defendant pays a proportionate share of the damage, which depends on the degree of fault determined by the judge or jury. In federal cases, the amount of liability can be increased to 150 percent of the amount determined to be proportionate to the defendant in situations when the primary defendant is insolvent.

Joint and several liability provides more protection to users who experience losses because of misplaced reliance on materially misstated financial statements. Sometimes those primarily responsible for the losses, such as client management, do not have the monetary resources to compensate users who experienced losses. Under joint and several liability, users experiencing a loss are able to recover full damages from any defendant, including an audit firm, regardless of the level of fault of the party. For example, if a jury decided that management was 80% at fault and the auditor was 20% at fault, the damages would be apportioned 80% to management and 20% to auditors. In many lawsuits involving auditors, the client is in bankruptcy, management has few monetary resources, and the auditor is the only party left with adequate resources to pay the damages. Joint and several liability then apportions the damages over the remaining defendants in proportion to the relative damages. Under joint and several liability, if management has no resources and there are no other defendants, 100% of the damages will be apportioned to the audit firm.

Accounting-Related Class Action Lawsuits

Why It Matters

This feature makes the point that class action lawsuits have increased over recent years.

The number of accounting-related securities class action filings increased for the third year in a row in 2015. There were 71 filings with accounting allegations in 2015. Accounting case settlement dollars reached $2.6 billion in 2015. The total settlement value for cases with accounting allegations in 2015 was almost three times the level for 2014.

In 2016, there were again increases. The number of accounting-related securities class action filings was 93. Settlement dollars reached $4.8 billion in 2016.

In 2015, the number of accounting cases against companies with headquarters outside the United States increased 43 percent to its second highest level in the last 10 years. Accounting cases against companies headquartered in China increased 75 percent from 2014 to 2015.

While these numbers do not specifically indicate auditor liability, audit firms are likely named in at least some of these lawsuits. In fact, audit firms were co-defendants in four securities class actions in 2016, three of which included allegations against a Big Four accounting firm.

Class Action Lawsuits

Class action lawsuits help prevent multiple lawsuits for the same case that might result in inconsistent judgments. Class action lawsuits also encourage litigation when no individual plaintiff has a claim large enough to justify the expense of litigation. These types of lawsuits can be especially appropriate for securities litigation because they enable a number of shareholders to combine claims that they could not afford to litigate individually. Often in these cases, the lawyers work on a contingent fee basis and will work very diligently to identify every potential member of the class. Damages to audit firms in such cases can be extremely large.

Federal class action filings with an accounting firm co-defendant are rarer today than prior to the 2008 financial crisis. This decrease can be attributed, in part, to changes in the legal environment related to accounting co-defendants. These changes included two U.S. Supreme Court rulings. The Supreme Court's Janus decision in 2011 restricted the ability of plaintiffs to sue parties not directly responsible for misstatements (*Janus Capital Group, Inc., et al. v. First Derivative Traders* (Docket No. 09-525)), thus making it less appealing to sue audit firms. Further, the Court's Stoneridge decision in 2008 (*Stoneridge Investment Partners v. Scientific-Atlanta, Inc.* (Docket No. 06-43)) limited the scope of liability of secondary actors, such as lawyers and accountants, for securities fraud under the Securities Exchange Act of 1934.

Contingent-Fee Compensation for Lawyers

Contingent fees for lawyers have evolved in our society to allow individuals who cannot afford high-priced lawyers to seek compensation for their damages. Lawyers take **contingent-fee cases** with an agreement that a client who loses a case owes the lawyer nothing; however, if the lawyer wins the case, the lawyer receives an agreed-upon portion (usually one-third to one-half) of the damages awarded. This arrangement protects the underprivileged and encourages lawsuits by a wide variety of parties. The plaintiffs have little to lose, while the lawyers have a large incentive to successfully pursue such cases.

Why It Matters:
An International Perspective

Class Action Lawsuits Are Global

This feature notes that class action lawsuits are not just a U.S. issue.

Class action suits against large audit firms occur throughout the world. Examples include:

• As of 2012, the biggest class action settlement in Australia was a $203-million case that named audit firm PricewaterhouseCoopers (PwC) as one of the defendants. The firm paid about a third of the sum.

• In 2012, Ernst & Young paid about $118 million in Canada's largest class action settlement against an auditor.

• In 2017, the Ontario (Canada) Court of Appeal (OCA) certified a class-action lawsuit against an accounting firm involving international investors who lost money in an investment in a Chinese livestock company. The class action lawsuit alleges negligence and negligent misrepresentation related to a "clean" audit report that the investors claim to have relied upon when deciding to invest.

The Audit Viewed as an Insurance Policy: The Expectations Gap

An audit report accompanying a financial statement is not a guarantee that an investment in the audited company is free of risk. Some investors mistakenly view the unqualified audit report as an insurance policy against losses from a risky investment. These investors believe that when they suffer losses, they should be able to recover their losses from the auditor. This misperception represents an **expectations gap**, whereby shareholders believe that they are entitled to recover losses on investments for which the auditor provided an unqualified opinion on the financial statements. This misperception, coupled with joint and several liability, class action lawsuits, and contingent-fee compensation for lawyers, encourages large lawsuits against auditors, even for cases in which the auditor is only partially at fault or is not at fault.

Check Your Basic Knowledge

4-1 Litigation costs are the largest single cost faced by audit firms.   (T/F)

4-2 The expectations gap includes a misperception by shareholders that they are entitled to recover losses on investments for which the auditor provided an unqualified opinion on the financial statements.   (T/F)

4-3 Which of the following factors is not a reason that audit firms experience litigation for business failures, rather than audit failures?
   a. Joint and several liability statutes.
   b. Class action lawsuits.
   c. Contingent-fee compensation for audit firms.
   d. A misunderstanding by some users that an unqualified audit opinion represents an insurance policy against investment losses.

4-4 The shareholders of a bank sue Karen Frank, CPA, for malpractice due to an audit failure that preceded the bank's financial failure. The jury determines that Frank is 60% at fault and that management is 40% at fault. The bank has no financial resources, nor does its management. Under joint and several liability, what is the likely percentage of damages that Frank will pay?
   a. 100%.
   b. 50%.
   c. 40%.
   d. None of the above.

Do you think it is appropriate for audit firms to be subject to joint and several liability? Would your answer change if you were answering this question from the perspective of an investor? Why or why not?

LO 2

List the three types of law most relevant to auditor liability, describe the causes of legal action against auditors, and identify parties that can file suit against auditors.

Applicable Laws and Causes of Legal Action

Types of Law and Legal Actions Relevant to Auditors

The three types of law most relevant to auditor liability include:

- **Contract law**—Liability occurs where there is a breach of contract. The contract is usually between the external auditor and the client for the performance of the financial statement audit. Contract law is governed by common law.
- **Common law**—Auditors have liability, based on ordinary negligence, gross negligence, or fraud, to third parties under common law. Third parties can include stockholders, employees, creditors, and vendors. Common law is a tradition-based but constantly evolving set of laws that is mostly judge-made, from court decisions over the years.
- **Statutory law**—Statutory law refers to laws that have been passed by governmental units and includes federal securities laws and state statutes. Important federal statutes for the auditing profession are the Securities Act of 1933 (1933 Act), the Securities Exchange Act of 1934 (1934 Act), and the Sarbanes-Oxley Act of 2002.

Lawsuits against auditors usually allege that the auditors did not meet the standard of due care in performing the audit. Recall that the AICPA *Principles of Professional Conduct* describe a member acting with due care as a member who observes the profession's technical and ethical standards, strives to improve competence and the quality of services, and discharges professional responsibility to the best of the member's ability. Auditors are responsible for due care. The specific responsibility in a particular case depends on whether there is a breach of contract, ordinary negligence, gross negligence, or fraud.

Breach of contract occurs when a person fails to perform a contractual duty. As an example, consider an auditor who was hired to find a material fraud. If reasonable procedures would have detected the fraud and the auditor failed to uncover the fraud, the auditor would have breached the contract. As another example, if the auditor agreed to provide the audit report by a certain date, but did not, the auditor would have breached the contract.

Ordinary negligence is the failure to exercise reasonable care, thereby causing harm to another or to property. If an auditor, for example, did not detect an embezzlement scheme because of a failure to follow up on evidence that would have brought it to light, but a prudent auditor would have performed such follow-up, the auditor is negligent. The profession's standards require that audits be conducted in accordance with professional auditing standards; thus, a failure to meet these standards could be considered negligence on the part of the auditor.

Gross negligence is the failure to use even minimal care, a reckless disregard for the truth, or reckless behavior. Expressing an opinion on a set of financial statements with careless disregard of professional auditing standards is an example of gross negligence. Gross negligence is more than failing to comply with professional standards; it is such complete disregard for due care that judges and juries are allowed to infer intent to deceive, even though there may be no direct evidence of intent to deceive.

Fraud is an intentional concealment or misrepresentation of a material fact that causes damage to those deceived. In an action for fraud, scienter must generally be proved. **Scienter** means knowledge on the part of a person making false representations, at the time they are made, that they are false. An auditor perpetrates a fraud on investors, for example, by expressing an unqualified opinion on financial statements that the auditor knows are not fairly presented. In such a situation, the purpose of expressing the unqualified audit opinion is to deceive.

Parties that May Bring Suit Against Auditors

Generally, anyone who can support a claim that damages were incurred based on misleading audited financial statements can bring a lawsuit against the auditor. These parties typically include the client and third-party users. They may accuse the auditor of breach of contract or of a tort. A **tort** is a civil wrong, other than breach of contract, based on ordinary negligence, gross negligence, or fraud. Unlike actions for breach of contract, tort actions do not require an agreement between the parties to a lawsuit. *Exhibit 4.1* lists the parties to whom the external auditor is liable, and outlines the applicable law.

Focus on Fraud　　　　　CPA Knowingly Issues Wrong Opinion

This feature provides an interesting example of the implications to an auditor who commits fraud.

Marc Wieselthier, CPA, participated in a scheme to help a client obtain millions of dollars in loans by making false statements and providing false and fraudulent documents to commercial banks concerning the financial condition of one of his clients.

From 2007 through 2014, the client's executives persuaded the banks to lend them millions of dollars by repeatedly making false and misleading statements about their company's financial condition. The company inflated its sales and accounts receivable in financial statements audited by Wieselthier, which were provided to the banks. The company used the falsely inflated sales and accounts receivable to mislead the banks about the company's true financial performance so the company could secure and draw down millions of dollars in revolving loans from the banks that the company would not otherwise have been entitled to receive.

As part of the scheme, Wieselthier, the partner on the engagement, issued unqualified audit reports on an annual basis falsely certifying that the company's financial statements fairly, and in all material respects, reflected the true financial condition of the company and were in conformity with U.S. GAAP. At the time he issued those "clean opinions," he allegedly knew the company's financial statements falsely overstated accounts receivable and understood that the banks would rely upon those false financial statements in loaning money to the company.

In March 2014, the company defaulted on the loans. At the time, the company's outstanding balance on the loans was more than $4.8 million. In 2015, Wieselthier pled guilty to one count of conspiracy to commit bank fraud. In 2016, Wieselthier received a 27-month prison sentence. He was also hit with a $161,000 forfeiture and $4.9 million in restitution for the fraud.

For more details, see USA v. Cohen et al., case number 1:15-cr-00396, in the U.S. District Court for the Southern District of New York.

Exhibit 4.1
Overview of Auditor Liability

(AUDITOR HELD LIABLE? Y = YES, N = NO, NA = NOT APPLICABLE)

Who Can Sue?	**Client**	**3rd Party**		
Under What Law?	**Contract Law**	**Common Law**	**Statutory Law**	
			1933 Act	**1934 Act**
For What?				
Breach of contract	Y	NA	NA	NA
Ordinary negligence	Y	*	NA	N
Gross negligence	Y	Y	NA	Unclear
Fraud	Y	Y	NA	Y

*Depends on the test used:
- Identified User
- Foreseen User
- Foreseeable User

Check Your Basic Knowledge

4-5 The three laws most relevant to auditor liability include common law, contract law, and statutory law. (T/F)

4-6 Negligence occurs when a person fails to perform a contractual duty. (T/F)

4-7 Which of the following statements is <u>false</u>?
- a. Breach of contract occurs when a person competently performs a contractual duty.
- b. Negligence is the failure to exercise reasonable care, thereby causing harm to another person or to property.
- c. Gross negligence is operating with a reckless disregard for the truth, or the failure to use even minimal care.
- d. Fraud is an intentional concealment or misrepresentation of a material fact with the intent to deceive another person, causing damage to the deceived person.

4-8 An audit client can sue the auditor under contract law for which of the following?
- a. Breach of contract.
- b. Negligence.
- c. Gross negligence.
- d. Fraud.
- e. All of the above.

For Classroom Discussion

What Do You Think?

Refer to the *Focus on Fraud* feature "CPA Knowingly Issues Wrong Opinion." Why do you think Marc Wieselthier knowingly participated in a scheme to help a client obtain millions of dollars in loans by making false statements and providing false and fraudulent documents? Do you think that his sentence was appropriate? Why or why not?

LO 3

Describe auditor liability under contract law, common law, and statutory law and discuss possible defenses, remedies, and sanctions.

Auditor Liability under Contract Law, Common Law, and Statutory Law

Contract Law: Liability to Clients

When a client contracts with an auditor to perform specific services, the parties draw up a contract indicating that the auditor will perform the services in accordance with professional auditing standards and in a timely basis. Auditors can be held liable to clients under contract law for breach of contract, ordinary negligence, gross negligence, and fraud. An example of a potential claim is a client suing an auditor for not discovering a material fraud when conducting the audit.

Breach of contract may occur when there is non-performance of a contractual duty. Causes for action against the auditor for breach of contract may include, but are not limited to, the following:

- Violating client confidentiality
- Failing to provide the audit report on time
- Failing to discover a material error or employee fraud
- Withdrawing from an audit engagement without justification

A client seeking to recover damages from an auditor in an action based on negligence must show that the auditor had a duty not to be negligent. In determining this duty, courts use as criteria the standards and principles of the profession, including professional auditing standards and financial accounting principles. Liability may be imposed for lack of due care either in performing the audit or in presenting financial information. The auditor must have breached that duty by not exercising due professional care. The client must show there was a causal relationship between the negligence and damage. The client must prove actual damages. The amount of damages must be established with reasonable certainty, and the client must demonstrate that the auditor's acts or omissions were the cause of the loss.

The auditor can use the following defenses against a breach of contract suit:

- *The auditor did not have a duty to perform the service* (e.g., the level of service outlined in the contract did not require the auditor to uncover the immaterial misstatement)
- *The auditor exercised due professional care in accordance with the contract* (e.g., the audit was performed in accordance with professional auditing standards)
- *The client was contributorily negligent* (e.g., the client provided the auditor with false documents)
- *The client's losses were not caused by the breach of contract* (e.g., the reason the bank did not provide a loan to the client was not due to the auditor breaching the contract by providing the audit report after the agreed-upon date)

Remedies

The remedies for breach of contract include:

- Requiring specific performance of the contract agreement
- Granting an injunction to prohibit the auditor from doing certain acts, such as disclosing confidential information
- Providing for recovery of amounts lost as a result of the breach

When specific performance or an injunction is not appropriate, the client is entitled to recover compensatory damages. In determining the amount of damages, courts try to put the client in the position in which it would have been, had the auditor performed the contractual duties as promised.

Moss Adams and the Meridian Mortgage Funds Fraud

Focus on Fraud

This feature illustrates the serious litigation risk that audit firms face when their clients are acting fraudulently and when the audit firm conducts the audits in a way that allows those relying on the financial statements to question audit quality.

Although management is responsible for the preparation of financial statements, it is possible that the statements contain material misstatements that the auditor should have discovered. For example, the auditor may have failed to discover a fraud that management perpetrated against the company. The auditor will usually argue that the client was negligent because client management contributed to the fraud in some way (e.g., the auditor might argue that the damage was intentional or was at least in part caused by management's carelessness or lack of internal controls). Nonetheless, clients have brought litigation against auditors when financial statements were misleading or frauds were not detected.

As an example, the trustee for the bankrupt Meridian Mortgage Funds sued the audit firm Moss Adams for $150 million for failing to detect the founder's Ponzi scheme. The founder, Frederick Berg, pleaded guilty, admitting to stealing about $100 million of Meridian's funds for personal use and to perpetuating the Ponzi scheme. Moss Adams had issued unqualified audit opinions for the funds, and the trustee argued that a series of low-quality audits allowed the Ponzi scheme to continue undetected. The trustee alleged that Moss Adams acted intentionally and recklessly. The trustee also argued that the audit firm was not independent, as Berg was paying the firm large sums of money to perform consulting and personal tax services for him.

Common Law: Liability to Third Parties

In most audit engagements, the auditor does not know specifically who will be using the audited financial statements, but is aware that third parties will be using them. The courts generally have held auditors liable to injured third parties when the auditor has been found guilty of gross negligence or fraud. Courts differ, however, as to what third parties the auditor should be held liable to for ordinary negligence. Common law has developed through court decisions, custom, and usage without written legislation.

To win a claim against the auditor, third parties suing under common law must generally prove that:

- They suffered a loss
- The loss was due to reliance on misleading financial statements
- The auditor knew, or should have known, that the financial statements were misleading

Defenses available to auditors for third party lawsuits under common law include:

- The auditor did not have a duty to perform the service
- The auditor exercised due professional care
- Losses were not caused by the auditor's actions

The auditor's liability to third parties depends on the jurisdiction of the case, along with whether the auditor could foresee that different types of users would be relying upon the audit report and audited financial statements.

Foreseeability and Negligence

The fundamental issue is whether the plaintiff has to prove ordinary negligence or gross negligence to obtain damages from an auditor. Courts in different jurisdictions have taken different approaches to determining a plaintiff's standing to bring a suit for negligence. The critical point in determining the type of claim against the auditor is the likelihood that an auditor could reasonably foresee that a user might have relied upon the audited financial statements. Generally, less foreseeable plaintiffs need to establish a gross negligence claim, whereas foreseeable users, in some jurisdictions, have to establish only a negligence claim.

The Ultramares Case: The Third-Party Beneficiary Test

The landmark case of *Ultramares Corporation v. Touche*, decided by the New York Court of Appeals in 1931, set the precedent for an auditor's liability to third parties. The court held that auditors are liable to third parties for fraud and gross negligence, but not for ordinary negligence. For liability to be established, a **third-party beneficiary** must be specifically identified in the engagement letter as a user for whom the audit is being conducted. If, for example, a bank requires an audit as part of a loan application and is named in the engagement letter, the auditor may be held liable to the bank for negligence. If the bank had not been named in the engagement letter, however, such liability would not exist. This precedent dominated judicial thinking for many years and many jurisdictions still follow it.

Expansion of Ultramares: The Identified User Test

In the 1985 case of *Credit Alliance Corp. v. Arthur Andersen & Co.*,[1] the New York Court of Appeals extended auditor liability for ordinary negligence to identified users. An **identified user** is a specific third party whom the auditor knows will use the audited financial statements for a particular purpose, even though the identified user is not named in the engagement letter.

Foreseen User Test

The 1965 Restatement (Second) of Torts[2] expanded auditor liability for ordinary negligence to identified users and to any individually unknown third parties who are members of a known or intended class of third parties, called **foreseen users**. The client must have informed the auditor that a third party or class of third parties intends to use the financial statements for a particular transaction. The auditor does not have to know the identity of the third party. For example, the client tells the auditor that it plans to include the audited financial statements in an application to some financial institutions for a loan. The auditor would be liable to the bank that ultimately makes the loan, even though its identity was not known at the time of the audit.

Foreseeable User Test

Some courts have extended auditor liability to **foreseeable users** (as opposed to foreseen users) of audited financial statements. In *Citizens State Bank v. Timm, Schmidt & Co.*, the Wisconsin Supreme Court extended auditor liability to creditors who could foreseeably use the audited financial statements.[3] A similar position was taken in *Rosenblum, Inc. v. Adler,* where the New Jersey Supreme Court noted that the nature of the economy had changed since the *Ultramares* case and that auditors are indeed acting as if a number of potential users rely on their audit opinion.

Exhibit 4.2 provides a summary of foreseeability concepts under common law, along with practical examples. The current liability status depends on the state and court involved and on the precedent the court determines is appropriate.

This court made it clear that for liability to be established, foreseeable users must have obtained the financial statements from the client for proper business purposes,[4] but this is not true in all jurisdictions.

Statutory Law: Liability to Third Parties

Public companies are required to include audited financial statements in information provided to current and prospective investors. The Securities Act of 1933 and the Securities Exchange Act of 1934 are two important federal statutes affecting auditor liability for public clients. These laws help assure that investors in public companies have access to full and adequate disclosure of relevant information.

Exhibit 4.2

Foreseeability Concepts for Auditor's
Common Law Liability to Third Parties

FORSEEABLE USER		
FORSEEN USER		
IDENTIFIED USER		
The auditor knows the user's identity and specific transaction involved.	The user is a member of a limited class of users for a specific transaction. Identity of the specific user may or may not be known to the auditor.	The user is a member of a group who could foreseeably use the financial statements.
Example: The auditor knows that the First National Bank wants audited financial statements as part of the client's application for a loan.	*Example:* The auditor knows that the client wants audited financial statements to obtain a loan from one of several possible banks.	*Example:* The auditor knows that current and prospective creditors and stockholders are likely to use the audited statements.

Securities Act of 1933

The Securities Act of 1933 requires companies to file registration statements with the SEC before they may issue new securities to the public. A registration statement contains, among other things, information about the company, lists of its officers and major stockholders, and plans for using the proceeds from the new securities issue. The registration statement, called the **prospectus**, includes audited financial statements. For the auditor, an important liability section of the 1933 Act is Section 11, which imposes penalties for misstatements contained in registration statements.

For purposes of Section 11, the accuracy of the registration statement is determined at its effective date, which is the date the company can begin to sell the new securities. Because the effective date may be several months after the end of the normal audit work, the auditors must perform certain audit procedures covering events between the end of the normal audit work and the effective date.

Anyone receiving the prospectus may sue the auditor based on damages due to alleged misleading financial statements or inadequate audits. Purchasers need to prove only that they incurred a loss and that the financial statements were materially misleading or not fairly stated. Purchasers do not need to prove reliance on the financial statements, that such statements had been read or even seen, or that the auditors were negligent.

In terms of defenses, the burden of proof rests with the auditors, who must prove their innocence. Defenses include: (1) they used due professional care, (2) the statements were not materially misstated, or (3) the purchaser did not incur a loss caused by the misleading financial statements.

Securities Exchange Act of 1934

The 1934 Act regulates the trading of securities after their initial issuance. Regulated companies are required to file periodic reports with the SEC and stockholders. The following are the most common periodic reports:

- *Annual reports* to shareholders and *10-Ks*, which are annual reports filed with the SEC, both containing audited financial statements. 10-Ks must be filed within 60 to 90 days of the end of the fiscal year. Smaller companies have up to 90 days to file; larger companies must file within 60 days.

- *Quarterly financial reports* to shareholders and *10-Qs*, which are quarterly reports filed with the SEC. 10-Qs must be filed within 40 to 45 days of the end of each of the first three quarters and must be reviewed by the auditors. Smaller companies have up to 45 days to file; larger companies must file within 40 days.
- *8-Ks*, which are reports filed with the SEC describing the occurrence of important events, such as a change in auditors. Other important events required to be reported include changes in the company's business and operations, changes in financial status (such as an acquisition or disposal of assets), and major changes in corporate governance elements (such as the departure of a senior member of management), among others. These disclosures generally must occur within four business days of the event.

For the auditor, an important liability section of the 1934 Act is Section 10, and specifically Rule 10b-5. This rule prohibits material misrepresentations or omissions and fraudulent conduct and provides a general antifraud remedy for purchasers and sellers of securities. Under the 1934 Act, an auditor may be held liable for fraud when a plaintiff alleges that in making decisions on purchasing or selling securities, it was misled by misstatements in financial statements. The Act explicitly makes it unlawful to make any untrue statement of a material fact or to omit to state a material fact that is necessary for understanding the financial statements. To bring a successful case for securities fraud, a private party must prove six basic elements: (1) a material misrepresentation or omission, (2) fraudulent conduct in connection with the purchase or sale of a security, (3) a wrongful state of mind, known as scienter, when making the misrepresentation or omission, (4) reliance upon the fraudulent conduct, (5) measurable monetary damages, and (6) a causal connection between the misrepresentation or omission and the economic loss. Each of these elements has been interpreted by the courts over the years; court decisions continue to shape how the elements are applied.

In *Herzfeld v. Laventhol, Krekstein, Horwath & Horwath* (1974), the auditors were liable under the 1934 Act for failing to fully disclose the facts and circumstances underlying their qualified opinion. The judge on the case stated that the auditor cannot be content merely to see that the financial statements meet minimum requirements of GAAP, but that the auditor has a duty to inform the public if adherence to GAAP does not fairly portray the economic results of the company being audited. More specifically, the trial court judge stated:

> The policy underlying the securities laws of providing investors with all the facts needed to make intelligent investment decisions can only be accomplished if financial statements fully and fairly portray the actual financial condition of the company. In those cases where application of generally accepted accounting principles fulfills the duty of full and fair disclosure, the accountant need go no further. But if application of accounting principles alone will not adequately inform investors, accountants, as well as insiders, the auditor must take pains to lay bare all the facts needed by investors to interpret the financial statements accurately.[5]

Federal courts have struggled with the negligence standard implied by the 1934 Act. The standard of holding auditors responsible for gross negligence had essentially eroded to a standard of ordinary negligence. In 1976, the U.S. Supreme Court provided greater guidance in its review of *Ernst & Ernst v. Hochfelder*. The Court held that under the 1934 Act, Congress had intended the plaintiff to prove that an auditor acted with scienter in order to hold the auditor liable. The Court reserved judgment as to whether reckless disregard for the truth (gross negligence) would be sufficient to impose liability.

Available auditor defenses for lawsuits under the 1934 Act include:

- The auditor did not have a duty to perform the service
- The auditor exercised due professional care
- Losses were not caused by the auditor's actions

Possible Auditor Sanctions and Criminal Penalties

Auditors found to be unqualified, unethical, or in willful violation of any provision of the federal securities laws can be disciplined by the SEC and the PCAOB. Possible sanctions include:

- Temporarily or permanently revoking a firm's registration with the PCAOB, meaning that the SEC will not accept that firm's audit reports
- Imposing civil monetary penalties
- Requiring special continuing education of firm personnel
- Suspending individuals from serving as officers or directors of securities issuers or participating in the securities industry
- Prohibiting a firm from accepting new public company clients for a stated period of time

Both the 1933 and 1934 Acts provide for criminal actions against auditors who wilfully violate provisions of either Act and related rules or regulation. Criminal actions are pursued against auditors who know that financial statements are false and misleading and who issue inappropriate opinions on such statements.

Further, the Sarbanes-Oxley Act of 2002 makes it a felony to destroy or create documents as a means of obstructing a federal investigation. Those who alter or destroy documents in violation of the Sarbanes-Oxley Act can face fines and imprisonment of up to 20 years.

Check Your Basic Knowledge

4-9 Examples of breach of contract include violating client confidentiality, failing to provide the audit report on time, and failing to discover material error or material employee fraud.   (T/F)

4-10 To win a claim against the auditor, third parties suing under common law must generally prove that they suffered a loss, that the loss was due to lack of reliance on misleading financial statements, and that the auditor knowingly participated in the financial misrepresentation.   (T/F)

4-11 The remedies for breach of contract include which of the following?
  a. Requiring specific performance of the contract agreement.
  b. Granting an injunction to prohibit the auditor from doing certain acts, such as disclosing confidential information.
  c. Providing for recovery of amounts lost as a result of the breach.
  d. All of the above.

4-12 Which of the following scenarios includes an example of a foreseen user?
  a. The auditor knows that the First National Bank wants audited financial statements as part of the client's application for a loan.
  b. The auditor knows that the client needs audited financial statements because it wants to obtain a loan from one of several possible banks.
  c. Current and prospective creditors and stockholders are likely to use the audited financial statements.
  d. None of the above.

For Classroom Discussion

What Do You Think?

Do you think it is appropriate for the burden of proof to rest with auditors, who must prove their innocence, when faced with litigation under the Securities Act of 1933? Why do you think that the Act requires this?

Let's Review

- Incentives in the liability environment leading to lawsuits against audit firms and individual auditors include joint and several liability statutes, class action lawsuits coupled with user awareness of the possibilities and rewards of litigation, contingent-fee compensation for law firms, especially in class action lawsuits, and a perspective that the audit is an insurance policy against investment losses. (LO 1)

- Generally, anyone who can support a claim that damages were incurred based on misleading audited financial statements can bring a lawsuit against the auditor. These parties typically include the client and third-party users. (LO 2)

- Three types of law most relevant to auditor liability include contract law, common law, and statutory law. (LO 2)

- Lawsuits against auditors usually allege that the auditors did not meet the standard of due care in performing the audit. Clients can sue for breach of contract; this type of litigation occurs when there is non-performance of a contractual duty. Third party users can sue under common law and statutory law. (LO 2, 3)

- Possible sanctions for violating federal securities laws include revoking a firm's registration with the PCAOB, imposing civil monetary penalties, and requiring special continuing education of firm personnel. Criminal penalties include imprisonment and fines, and are pursued against auditors who know that financial statements are false and misleading and who issue inappropriate opinions on such statements. (LO 3)

Significant Terms

Audit failure   An audit firm issues an inaccurate audit opinion and fails to comply with the auditing standards.

Breach of contract   Failure to perform a contractual duty that has not been excused; for audit firms, the parties to a contract normally include clients and designated third-party beneficiaries.

Class action lawsuits   Lawsuits that are brought on behalf of a large group of plaintiffs to consolidate suits and to encourage consistent judgments and minimize litigation costs; plaintiff shareholders may bring suit for themselves and all others in a similar situation, that is, all other shareholders of record at a specific date.

Common law   Liability concepts are developed through court decisions based on negligence, gross negligence, or fraud.

Contingent fee   A fee established for the performance of any service in which a fee will not be collected unless a specified finding or result is attained, or in which the amount of the fee depends on the finding or results of such services.

Contingent-fee cases   Lawsuits brought by plaintiffs with compensation for their attorneys being contingent on the outcome of the litigation.

Contract law   Liability occurs where there is a breach of contract. The contract is usually between the external auditor and the client for the performance of the financial statement audit.

Deep-pocket theory   The practice of suing another party not based on the level of their true fault in a legal action, but based instead on the perceived ability of that party to pay damages.

Expectations gap   A misunderstanding whereby shareholders mistakenly believe that they are entitled to recover losses on investments for which the auditor provided an unqualified opinion on the financial statements.

Foreseeable user Those not known specifically by the auditor to be using the financial statements, but recognized by general knowledge as current and potential creditors and investors who will use them.

Foreseen user Individually unknown third parties who are members of a known or intended class of third-party users who the auditor, through knowledge gained from interactions with the client, can foresee will use the statements.

Fraud Intentional concealment or misrepresentation of a material fact with the intent to deceive another person, causing damage to the deceived person.

Gross negligence Failure to use even minimal care or evidence of activities that show recklessness or careless disregard for the truth; evidence may not be present, but may be inferred by a judge or jury because of the carelessness of the defendant's conduct.

Identified user Third-party beneficiaries and other users when the auditor has specific knowledge that known users will be utilizing the financial statements in making specific economic decisions.

Joint and several liability A type of liability that apportions losses among all defendants who have an ability to pay for the damages, regardless of the level of fault.

Ordinary negligence Failure to exercise reasonable care, thereby causing harm to another or to property.

Proportionate liability Payment by an individual defendant based on the degree of fault of the individual.

Prospectus The first part of a registration statement filed with the SEC, issued as part of a public offering of debt or equity and used to solicit prospective investors in a new security issue containing, among other items, audited financial statements. The Securities Act of 1933 imposes liability for misstatements in a prospectus.

Scienter Knowledge on the part of the person making the representations, at the time they are made, that they are false; intent.

Statutory law Laws developed through legislation, such as the Securities Act of 1933 and the Securities Exchange Act of 1934.

Third-party beneficiary A person who was not a party to a contract but is named in the contract as one to whom the contracting parties intended that benefits be given.

Tort A civil wrong, other than breach of contract, based on negligence, constructive fraud, or fraud.

Review Questions and Short Cases

FRAUD

NOTE: Completing *Review Questions and Short Cases* does not require the student to reference additional resources and materials.

NOTE: We make special note of problems addressing fraud, international issues, professional skepticism, and ethics.

4-1 **LO 1** Describe the elements in the litigation environment that provide incentives to pursue litigation against audit firms.

4-2 **LO 2** Compare and contrast breach of contract, ordinary negligence, gross negligence, and fraud.

4-3 **LO 2** Distinguish between the development of common law and statutory law.

4-4 **LO 3** What are some potential causes of action against an auditor under a breach of contract lawsuit?

4-5 **LO 3** What are some remedies for a breach of contract?

4-6 **LO 3** What defenses might an auditor use in successfully defending a suit brought:
a. Because of breach of contract?
b. Under statutory law?

4-7 **LO 3** Refer to the *Focus on Fraud* feature "Moss Adams and the Meridian Mortgage Funds Fraud."
a. Why was Moss Adams sued by the trustee for the bankrupt Meridian Mortgage?
b. What would the trustee have to prove in order for the courts to hold Moss Adams liable for damages?

4-8 **LO 3** Three tests have been used by various courts in common-law decisions to determine which third-party users can successfully bring a suit against the auditor for negligence. Identify each of these tests and describe the parties that are defined in each of these tests.

4-9 **LO 3** What are some sanctions the SEC can bring against auditors who have violated statutory law?

4-10 **LO 3** Briefly explain the primary purpose of the:
a. Securities Act of 1933
b. Securities Exchange Act of 1934

4-11 **LO 3** How does the auditor's liability to third parties differ under the 1933 Act and the 1934 Exchange Act? What is the importance of the *Hochfelder* case as it relates to the 1934 Act?

4-12 **LO 3** Is there a conceptual difference between an error on the part of the auditor and ordinary negligence? Explain.

4-13 **LO 3** What precedent was set in the *Ernst & Ernst vs. Hochfelder* case? What actions would be necessary to change the precedent?

4-14 **LO 3** An auditor was sued and found guilty of negligence.
For each of the following situations, indicate the likelihood the plaintiff would win if the plaintiff is:
a. A financial institution that the auditor knew was the primary beneficiary of the audit, suing under common law.
b. A stockholder suing under common law.
c. A financial institution that was unknown to the auditor loaned money to the client based on the audit financial statements, but the auditor knew only that the client would use the statements to obtain a loan from some financial institution. The plaintiff is suing under common law.
d. An investor suing under the 1934 Securities Exchange Act.
e. An investor suing under the 1933 Securities Act.

4-15 **LO 3** Compare an auditor's liability to third parties for negligence under *Ultramares, Credit Alliance, 1965 Restatement (Second) of Torts,* and *Rosenblum.* Then indicate which approach you think auditors prefer, and why. Which approach do you think is best for society? Why?

4-16 **LO 3** An auditor issued an unqualified opinion on financial statements that failed to disclose that a significant portion of the accounts receivable was uncollectible. The auditor also failed to follow professional auditing standards with respect to inventory. The auditor knew that the client would use the financial statements to obtain a loan. The client subsequently declared bankruptcy. Under what concepts might a creditor, who loaned money to the client based on the financial statements, recover losses from the auditor?

4-17 **LO 3** An investor is suing an auditor for issuing an unqualified opinion on the financial statements of Duluth Industries, which contained a material misstatement. The auditor was negligent in performing the audit. The investor had reason to believe the statements were wrong prior to purchasing stock in the company. In the subsequent period, Duluth Industries sustained operating losses, the stock price went down by 40%, and the investor sold the stock at a loss. During the period that the investor held this stock, the Dow Jones Industrial Average declined 10%. What defenses might the auditor use against the investor's lawsuit to recover losses?

FRAUD

4-18 **LO 3** An audit client applied for a bank loan from First Bank. In connection with the loan application, the client engaged its auditor to audit its financial statements, and the auditor issued an unqualified opinion. Based on those statements, First Bank loaned money to the client. Shortly thereafter, the client filed for bankruptcy, and First Bank sued the auditor for damages. The audit documentation showed negligence and possible other misconduct in performing the audit.

a. Under what circumstances is First Bank an identified user?

b. What exceptions to the identified user test might First Bank argue?

FRAUD

4-19 **LO 3** Monicker Co. engaged the audit firm of Gasner & Gasner to audit its financial statements that Monicker was going to use in connection with a public offering of its securities. Monicker's stock regularly trades on the NASDAQ. The audit was completed and the auditor issued an unqualified opinion on the financial statements, which Monicker submitted to the SEC along with the registration statement. Three hundred thousand shares of Monicker common stock were sold to the public at $13.50 per share. Eight months later, the stock fell to $2 per share when it was disclosed that several large loans to two "paper" companies owned by one of the directors were worthless. The loans were secured by the stock of the borrowing corporation and by Monicker stock owned by the director. These facts were not disclosed in the financial statements. The director and the two corporations are insolvent. Considering these facts, indicate whether each of the following statements is true or false, and briefly explain the rationale for your choice.

a. The Securities Act of 1933 applies to the preceding public offering of securities.

b. The audit firm has potential liability to any person who acquired the stock described in connection with the public offering.

c. An investor who bought shares in Monicker would make a reasonable case if he or she alleged that the failure to explain the nature of the loans in question constituted a false statement or misleading omission in the financial statements.

d. The auditors could avoid liability if they could show that they were not fraudulent in the conduct of the audit.

e. The auditors could avoid or reduce the damages asserted against them if they could establish that the drop-in price was due in whole or in part to other causes.

f. The SEC would establish contributory negligence as a partial defense for the auditor because the SEC approved the registration statement.

FRAUD

4-20 **LO 3** To expand its operations, Dark Corporation raised $4 million by making a private interstate offering of $2 million in common stock and negotiating a $2 million loan from Safe Bank. The common stock was properly offered pursuant to securities rules, which exempt the offering from the 1933 Act, but not the antifraud provisions of the Federal Securities Acts.

In connection with this financing, Dark engaged Crea, CPAs to audit Dark's financial statements. Crea knew that the sole purpose for the audit was so that Dark would have audited financial statements to provide to Safe Bank and the purchasers of the common stock. Although Crea conducted the audit in conformity with its audit program, Crea failed to detect material fraud committed by Dark's president. Crea did not detect the embezzlement because of its inadvertent failure to exercise due care in designing its audit program for this engagement.

After completing the audit, Crea rendered an unqualified audit opinion on Dark's financial statements. Purchasers of the common stock relied on the financial statements in deciding whether to purchase the shares. In addition, Safe Bank approved the loan to Dark based on the audited financial statements. Within 60 days after selling the common stock and obtaining the loan from Safe Bank, Dark was involuntarily petitioned into bankruptcy. Because of the president's embezzlement, Dark became insolvent and defaulted on its loan to Safe Bank. Its common stock became virtually worthless. Actions have been commenced against Crea by the purchasers of the common stock (who have asserted that Crea is liable for damages under the Securities Exchange Act of 1934) and Safe Bank, based on Crea's negligence.

a. Discuss the merits of the actions commenced against Crea by the purchasers of the common stock and by Safe Bank, indicating the likely outcomes and the reasoning behind each outcome.

b. How would your answer be different if the client filed a registration statement and the purchasers of the common stock were able to bring suit under the 1933 Act?

4-21 **LO 3**   The common stock of Wilson, Inc. is owned by 20 stockholders. Doe & Doe, CPAs audited Wilson's financial statements as of December 31, 2017. The audit firm rendered an unqualified opinion on the financial statements. Relying on Wilson's financial statements, which showed net income for 2017 of $1,500,000, Peters purchased 10,000 shares of Wilson stock for $200,000 on April 10, 2018. Wilson's financial statements contained material misstatements. Because Doe & Doe did not carefully follow professional auditing standards, it did not discover that the statements failed to reflect unrecorded expenses, which reduced Wilson's actual net income to $800,000. After disclosure of the corrected financial statements, Peters sold his shares for $100,000, which was the highest price he could obtain. Peters has brought an action against Doe & Doe under federal securities law and common law.

Answer the following, setting forth reasons for your conclusions:

a. Will Peters prevail on his federal securities-law claims?

b. Will Peters prevail on his common-law claims?

4-22 **LO 3**   Able Corporation decided to make a public offering of bonds to raise needed capital. It publicly sold $2,500,000 of 8% debentures in accordance with the registration requirements of the Securities Act of 1933. The financial statements filed with the registration statement contained the unqualified opinion of Baker & Baker, CPAs. The financial statements overstated Able's net income and net worth. Through negligence, Baker & Baker did not detect the overstatements. As a result, the bonds, which originally sold for $1,000 per bond, have dropped in value to $700. Ira is an investor who purchased $10,000 of the bonds. He promptly brought an action against Baker & Baker under the Securities Act of 1933.

Answer the following, providing reasons for your conclusions:

a. Will Ira likely prevail on his claim under the Securities Act of 1933?

b. Identify the primary issues that will determine the likelihood of Ira's prevailing on the claim.

Fraud Focus: Contemporary and Historical Cases

FRAUD

4-23 **KPMG**
(LO 1, 2, 3)

KPMG LLP served as the external auditor for some of the largest sub-prime mortgage lenders in the U.S. leading up to and during the housing market crisis of the mid to late-2000s. The audits of two of their largest lending clients, New Century Financial Corporation and Countrywide, ultimately led the firm to settle litigation charges in 2010 for $44.7 and $24 million, respectively. The business model of these two subprime mortgage lenders consisted of providing loans to borrowers with weak credit histories. The business model had begun to fail during 2007, when the economy weakened, borrowers began defaulting, and home prices declined drastically. New Century filed for bankruptcy and Countrywide was purchased by Bank of America, which subsequently suffered massive losses related to business failures at Countrywide.

Just before the housing crash of 2007 put the companies in severe financial crises, KPMG had given both companies unqualified audit opinions. In both cases, KPMG was subsequently accused of violating professional standards, lacking independence, and being negligent. KPMG defended itself by arguing that its audits were not the cause of the financial woes at New Century and Countrywide. Rather, the firm contended that the failed business model of the two companies led to investor losses.

a. How does the economic environment affect the litigation risk faced by audit firms?

b. Should auditors be held liable if their client's business fails or if the financial statements contain a fraud that the auditors did not detect?

c. What defenses do auditors use in response to litigation?

d. What actions can auditors take to minimize litigation exposure?

FRAUD

INTERNATIONAL

4-24 **Toshiba, EY**
(LO 1, 2, 3)

In 2015, the business press reported that Japan's Toshiba Corp. overstated its operating profit by 151.8 billion yen ($1.22 billion) over several years through accounting irregularities involving top management. This overstatement represents approximately one-third of Toshiba's pre-tax profits during the misstatement period. Toshiba had a corporate culture in which one could not go against the wishes of superiors. An investigation report noted that when top management presented 'challenges', division presidents, line managers and employees below them continually carried out inappropriate accounting practices to meet targets in line with the wishes of their superiors. Improper accounting included overstatements and booking profits early or pushing back the recording of losses or charges, and such steps often led to even higher targets being set for divisions in the following period.

The report said much of the improper accounting, stretching back to fiscal year 2008, was intentional and would have been difficult for auditors to detect. The audit firm during this misstatement period was EY (Ernst & Young ShinNihon) who incurred significant reputational damage after they were accused of failing to detect the misstatement and fined $17.4 million by Japanese regulators.

The investigation into Toshiba's accounting practices was initially limited to its home country. However, in 2016 the U.S. Justice Department and the Securities and Exchange Commission began looking into the case since part of the alleged fraud involved a Toshiba unit based in the US (Westinghouse Electric Company).

a. Based on this limited information, does this case represent a business failure, an audit failure, or both?

b. Should auditors be held liable if their client's business fails or if the financial statements contain a fraud that the auditors did not detect?

c. Under what law would the SEC be likely to pursue this case?

Application Activities

FRAUD

PROFESSIONAL SKEPTICISM

NOTE: Completing *Application Activities* requires students to reference additional resources and materials.

4-25 **Deloitte, Beazer Homes (LO 1, 2, 3)**

In June 2009, Deloitte agreed to pay almost $1 million to settle a class action lawsuit related to its audits of Beazer, a homebuilding company. The lawsuit claimed that Deloitte should have noticed the homebuilder was issuing inaccurate financial statements as the housing market began to decline. A spokesperson for Deloitte indicated that the firm denies all liability and settled to avoid the expense and uncertainty of continued litigation.

a. Research this case and identify fraud risk red flags that the auditor should have been aware of in these audits. One source that can get you started is: www.cfo.com/article.cfm/13612963?f=search

b. If these fraud risk red flags were indeed present during Deloitte's audit, what were the auditors' responsibilities in conducting the audit?

c. Comment on Deloitte's willingness to settle the case, while at the same time denying liability.

4-26 **Deloitte, Florida Department of Financial Services (LO 1, 3)**

In 2015, a jury ruled that Deloitte & Touche LLP wasn't liable in Florida's biggest-ever insurance-company collapse. The Florida Department of Financial Services did not prove its claims that Deloitte was negligent in its audits for three insurance companies that collapsed after a string of hurricanes hit the state in 2004 and 2005. The state was seeking up to $850 million in damages. Deloitte had maintained that the insurance companies' collapses were caused by an unprecedented string of hurricanes, not by an audit failure.

Research this case to learn further details.

a. How was Deloitte allegedly connected to the damages in this case?

b. Why did the Florida Department of Financial Services decide to sue Deloitte?

Academic Research Case

SEARCH HINT

It is easy to locate academic research articles! Use a search engine such as Google Scholar or an electronic research platform such as ABI Inform, and search using the author names and part of the article title.

4-27   **LO 1, 2, 3**   Locate and read the article listed below.

Rasso, J. T. (2014). Apology accepted: The benefits of an apology for a deficient audit following an audit failure. *Auditing: A Journal of Practice & Theory* 33(1): 161–176.

a.   What is the purpose of the study?
b.   Describe the design/method/approach used to conduct the study.
c.   What are the primary findings of the study?

5 Professional Auditing Standards and the Audit Opinion Formulation Process

The Audit Opinion Formulation Process

I. Making Client Acceptance and Continuance Decisions

Chapter 1

II. Performing Risk Assessment

Chapters 2, 3, 7, and 9–13

III. Obtaining Evidence About Internal Control Operating Effectiveness

Chapters 8–13

IV. Obtaining Substantive Evidence About Accounts, Disclosures, and Assertions

Chapters 8–13

V. Completing the Audit and Making Reporting Decisions

Chapters 14 and 15

Quality Auditing and the Need for Quality Auditor Judgments and Ethical Decisions

Chapter 1

Professional Liability

Chapter 4

The Audit Opinion Formulation Process and a Framework for Obtaining Audit Evidence

Chapters 5 and 6

Professional auditing standards provide guidance on the judgments and decisions auditors make throughout the audit opinion formulation process. These standards help auditors properly plan, perform, document, and supervise audits. Auditors conduct a quality audit when they follow these standards. This chapter will help you identify the relevant auditing guidance to use each time you perform an audit task.

Learning Objectives

LO 1 Identify and compare the auditing standards that provide guidance on the audit opinion formulation process.

LO 2 List and discuss the foundational principles underlying the auditing standards.

LO 3 List the phases and related activities in the audit opinion formulation process.

LO 4 Explain the concept of accounting cycles and discuss their importance to the audit opinion formulation process.

LO 5 Describe the assertions integral to the financial statements and explain their importance to the audit opinion formulation process.

LO 6 Define audit evidence and describe the purpose of audit procedures used to obtain audit evidence.

LO 7 Discuss the importance of audit documentation and provide examples.

LO 8 Discuss audit activities in each of the five phases of the audit opinion formulation process.

LO 9 Apply the frameworks for professional decision making and ethical decision making for decisions made when conducting an audit.

Implications of Not Adhering to Professional Auditing Standards: The Case of Daniel Millmann, Lisa Hanmer, and RSM

This feature illustrates examples of not adhering to professional auditing standards.

Neglecting to adhere to the professional auditing standards heightens the risk that the auditor will provide an unqualified audit opinion on financial statements that are materially misstated. This lesson is highlighted in an audit performed by RSM for the audit of Madison Capital Energy Income Fund I (hereafter, Fund I), which audit partner Daniel Millmann (hereafter, Millmann) led.

In the SEC's summary of the weaknesses that they uncovered while evaluating the quality of the audit, the SEC claims that Millmann repeatedly violated professional standards, including failing to conduct the audit in conformity with GAAS. He did not adequately plan and assess the risk of the Fund I audit before beginning fieldwork. He had not previously had experience working on an oil and gas fund audit, and he was not approved to work on the audit before he began doing so. As a result, the Fund I financial statements did not separately report the fair value of the investment in each oil and gas royalty interest held by Fund I, as required by GAAP.

Lisa Hanmer (Hanmer), the RSM engagement manager for the Fund I audit, knew that the auditing procedures were inadequate with respect to the fair value of the investment in the royalty interests, and she concealed this fact from RSM personnel, including Millmann. Like Millmann, Hanmer also had no experience in auditing a company such as Fund I. Millmann also did not complete the report release workpaper, which requires that he satisfy himself that all review comments on the audit are adequately resolved before releasing the audit report.

The SEC was dissatisfied with the fact that Millmann essentially delegated most of his responsibilities to Hanmer. In addition to criticizing Millmann and Hanmer individually, the SEC also levelled a variety of criticisms against RSM as a firm, including with respect to client acceptance decisions, risk assessment, training, and competence of employees.

While Millmann's actions were passively unprofessional and related more to a dereliction of duties in allowing Hanmer to conduct most of the audit on her own (she was in the process of going up for partner at the time, so he probably felt that she was capable), Hanmer's actions were actively unethical and in violation of professional standards.

For example, the concurring review partner on the engagement detected the GAAP violation and asked her to remedy it. Instead, she acquiesced to client pressure to release the Fund I report. She disregarded her concurring partner's request, sent the final audit report to the client, and then provided the concurring partner with a different schedule of investments that purported to incorporate the concurring partner's comment, but in fact included fictitious fair values for individual royalty interests.

For further details, see Securities and Exchange Commission Accounting and Auditing Enforcement Release Nos. 3870 and 3871 (May 23, 2017).

What Do You Think?   For Classroom Discussion

It seems that in the SEC case against RSM and its employees, Millmann and Hanmer, there were failures on the part of many parties to fulfil their professional obligations in a variety of ways. Think about RSM as a whole. Why would it neglect basic rules of professionalism in terms of client acceptance, risk assessment, and training of its personnel? Think about Millmann. Why would he essentially delegate the audit partner responsibilities to an audit manager who also did not have experience auditing these kinds of funds? Think about Hanmer. She was in the process of going up for partner at RSM, and yet knowingly subverted the legitimate comments of the concurring partner reviewer. Why would she engage in such unethical behavior at such a critical juncture in her career?

What You Will Learn

- What are the three standards setting bodies relevant to conducting an audit in the United States? When are each relevant to a particular audit client? (LO 1)

- What are the foundational principles underlying the auditing standards? (LO 2)

- What are the phases of the audit opinion formulation process? (LO 3)

- What are accounting cycles, and how is thinking about accounts within accounting cycles helpful to conducting a quality audit? (LO 4)

- What assertions does management make when they present the unaudited statements to the external auditor for evaluation? (LO 5)

- What audit evidence is necessary for opining on a client's financial statements? (LO 6)

- How does audit documentation provide evidence related to audit quality? (LO 7)

- What audit activities do auditors conduct to provide reasonable assurance about a client's financial statements? (LO 8)

Professional Auditing Standards

Auditors in the United States follow auditing guidance issued by the American Institute of Certified Public Accountants (AICPA), the Public Company Accounting Oversight Board (PCAOB), and the International Auditing and Assurance Standards Board (IAASB). When to use each of these alternative standards depends on the public trading status of the client and the location of the exchange on which its securities trade.

- The auditor of a private U.S. company will use AICPA standards.
- The auditor of a publicly traded company whose securities trade on, e.g., the New York Stock Exchange (NYSE) will use PCAOB standards.
- The auditor of a publicly traded company whose securities trade on, e.g., the London Stock Exchange (LSE) will use IAASB standards.

Auditing standards set by these various authorities have a common objective—to provide reasonable assurance to financial statement users that audits are conducted in a quality manner. Auditing standards apply to the auditor's task of developing and communicating an opinion on financial statements and, as part of an integrated audit, on a client's internal control over financial reporting.

Refer to the *Auditing Standards Exhibit* inside the front cover of this textbook for a listing of auditing standards by topic for each standard setter. As an example, you will see that the standards related to consideration of fraud in a financial statement audit include:

- AICPA: AU-C 240 *Consideration of Fraud in a Financial Statement Audit*
- IAASB: ISA 240 *The Auditor's Responsibilities Relating to Fraud in an Audit of Financial Statements*
- PCAOB: AS 2401 *Consideration of Fraud in a Financial Statement Audit*

Auditing Standards Issued by the AICPA, IAASB, and PCAOB

AICPA and IAASB Standards

The AICPA and IAASB have worked to converge, i.e., jointly coordinate the format and organization of their standards. Both standards setters use the following format for auditing standards:

- *Introduction* explains the purpose and scope of the standard.
- *Objective* defines the context in which the requirements are set.
- *Definitions* include, where relevant, specific meanings of terms in the standards.
- *Requirements* identify what the auditor is required to do to achieve the objective of the standard. Requirements are expressed using the words *the auditor should* or *the auditor must.*
- *Application and Other Explanatory Material* include cross-references to the requirements and provide further guidance for applying the requirements of the standard.

PCAOB Standards

The PCAOB's standards do not necessarily attempt to converge with the AICPA and the IAASB. Rather, their standards are organized by topical areas that follow the flow of the audit opinion formulation process. For example, the PCAOB organizes auditing standards that apply to procedures performed near the beginning of the audit in one area of the standards, and those performed near the end of the audit in another area. The PCAOB's numbering convention is purposely different from the convention used by the AICPA and IAASB. The PCAOB's intent in this regard is to help avoid the potential for confusion between its standards and those of other standard setters.

Comparing the Auditing Standards

While the PCAOB does not formally attempt to harmonize with the activities of the AICPA or IAASB, there still exists a great deal of commonality among the auditing standards. After all, the standards are all aimed at achieving audit quality and underlying audit tasks don't really differ based upon most client characteristics. All of the standards start from fundamental principles on how an audit engagement should be planned and performed and how the results should be communicated. *Exhibit 5.1* contains an overview of these auditing standards.

Exhibit 5.1

Comparison of U.S. and International Auditing Standards

	IAASB	PCAOB	AICPA
Authority	International Federation of Accountants, and as agreed upon by countries who abide by these standards	U.S Congress, as expressed in the Sarbanes–Oxley Act of 2002	Historical, as a self-regulatory profession
Terminology	International Standards on Auditing (ISA)	Auditing Standards (AS)	Statements on Auditing Standards (AU-C)
Scope of applicability of standards	Audits in countries for which international standards are required, including most of Europe and many emerging markets	Audits of U.S. public companies	Audits of most U.S. nonpublic entities
Convergence of auditing standards	Committed to international convergence	Does not currently have a mandate for international convergence	Committed to international convergence

What Do You Think? For Classroom Discussion

While the AICPA and IAASB are committed towards convergence, the PCAOB's standards do not necessarily attempt to converge with the standards of the AICPA and the IAASB.

- Why do you think that the PCAOB might not focus on convergence?

- What barriers might there be to a more harmonized structure for the three sets of auditing standards?

- Do you think that the PCAOB's responsibilities for inspections and enforcement might affect their decision not to attempt to converge their standards with those of the AICPA and IAASB?

- What challenges might the existence of multiple standards have on audit firms, students, and instructors?

5-1 Auditors of U.S. public companies should follow the PCAOB's auditing standards. (T/F)

5-2 There is not much overlap; i.e., things in common among the auditing standards set by the PCAOB, AICPA, and IAASB. (T/F)

5-3 Which of the following statements is <u>true</u> regarding auditing standard setting in the United States?
   a. The AICPA is responsible for setting auditing standards for audits of nonpublic entities.
   b. The PCAOB is responsible for setting auditing standards for audits of public companies.
   c. The AICPA is responsible for setting auditing standards for audits of both public and nonpublic companies.
   d. The SEC sets auditing standards for auditors of public and nonpublic companies.
   e. Both (a) and (b) are correct.

5-4 The following describes a situation in which an auditor has to determine the most appropriate standards to follow.

   The audited company is headquartered in Paris but has substantial operations within the United States (60% of all operations) and has securities registered with the SEC and is traded on the New York Stock Exchange (NYSE). The company uses International Financial Reporting Standards (IFRS) for its accounting framework.

   What would be the most appropriate set of auditing standards to follow?
   a. PCAOB.
   b. Either PCAOB or AICPA.
   c. Either IAASB or AICPA.
   d. Only the AICPA standards would be appropriate.

LO 2

List and discuss the foundational principles underlying the auditing standards.

Principles Underlying the Auditing Standards

The PCAOB, AICPA, and IAASB each have somewhat different underlying principles and objectives. While the specific wording differs across standards setters, the fundamental tenant is that audits must be conducted in a quality manner.

PCAOB Guidance—Five Topical Categories of Standards

The individual PCAOB standards fall into the following five topical categories:

1. *General Auditing Standards*—Standards on broad auditing principles, concepts, activities, and communications;
2. *Audit Procedures*—Standards for planning and performing audit procedures and for obtaining audit evidence;
3. *Auditor Reporting*—Standards for auditors' reports;
4. *Matters Relating to Filings Under Federal Securities Laws*—Standards on certain auditor responsibilities relating to U.S. Securities and Exchange Commission ("SEC" or "Commission") filings for securities offerings and reviews of interim financial information; and
5. *Other Matters Associated with Audits*—Standards for other work performed in conjunction with an audit of an issuer or of a broker or dealer.

Within the General Auditing Standards category, the PCAOB provides the following guidance about the responsibilities and functions of the independent auditor:

The objective of the ordinary audit of financial statements by the independent auditor is the expression of an opinion on the fairness with which they present, in all material respects, financial position, results of operations, and its cash flows in conformity with generally accepted accounting principles. The auditor's report is the medium through which he expresses his opinion or, if circumstances require, disclaims an opinion.

The General Auditing Standards category also notes the need for auditors to:

- Exercise due professional care, including professional skepticism
- Obtain *reasonable assurance* about whether the financial statements are free of material misstatement, whether caused by error or fraud, or whether any material weaknesses exist as of the date of management's assessment
- Maintain an independence in mental attitude
- Have the appropriate professional qualifications

AICPA Guidance: Principles Governing an Audit

The AICPA articulates seven fundamental principles, within four categories, that govern audits.

Purpose of an Audit and Premise Upon Which an Audit is Conducted

1. The purpose of an audit is to enhance the degree of confidence that users can place in the financial statement. This purpose is achieved when an auditor expresses an opinion on the financial statements.
2. An audit is based on the premise that management has responsibility to prepare the financial statements, maintain internal control over financial reporting, and provide the auditor with relevant information and access to personnel.

Responsibilities

3. Auditors are responsible for having the appropriate competence and capabilities to perform the audit, should comply with ethical requirements, and maintain professional skepticism throughout the audit.

Performance

4. The auditor needs to obtain reasonable assurance as to whether the financial statements are free from material misstatement.
5. Obtaining reasonable assurance requires the auditor to plan and supervise the work, determine materiality levels, identify risks of material misstatement, and design and implement appropriate audit responses to the assessed risks.
6. An audit has inherent limitations such that the auditor is not able to obtain absolute assurance about whether the financial statements are free from misstatement.

Reporting

7. The auditor expresses an opinion as to whether the financial statements are free of material misstatement or states that an opinion cannot be expressed.

IAASB Guidance: Objectives of an Audit

The IAASB's guidance is somewhat general (and described fully in ISA 200, *Overall Objectives of the Independent Auditor and the Conduct of an Audit in Accordance with International Standards on Auditing*):

In conducting an audit of financial statements, the overall objectives of the auditor are as follows:

a. To obtain reasonable assurance about whether the financial statements as a whole are free from material misstatement, whether due to fraud or error, thereby enabling the auditor to express an opinion on whether the financial statements are prepared, in all material respects, in accordance with an applicable financial reporting framework; and
b. To report on the financial statements, and communicate as required by the ISAs, in accordance with the auditor's findings.

5-5 The AICPA's and PCAOB's standards underlying an audit are the same, and each contain four categories of standards.   (T/F)

5-6 The purpose of an audit is to enhance the degree of confidence that users can place on the financial statements.   (T/F)

5-7 Which of the following statements is <u>false</u>?

a. The purpose of an audit is to enhance the degree of confidence that managers can place in the financial statements, thereby facilitating their decision making.

b. Auditors are responsible for having the appropriate competence and capabilities to perform the audit, should comply with ethical requirements, and maintain professional skepticism throughout the audit.

c. The auditor needs to obtain reasonable assurance as to whether the financial statements are free from material misstatement.

d. An audit has inherent limitations such that the auditor is not able to obtain absolute assurance about whether the financial statements are free from misstatement.

5-8 Which of the following is included as part of the AICPA's principles governing an audit?

a. Auditors need to obtain a high level of assurance that the financial statements are free of all misstatements.

b. An audit has inherent limitations such that the auditor cannot provide absolute assurance about whether the financial statements are free of misstatement.

c. Auditors need to maintain professional skepticism only on audits where there is a high risk of material misstatement.

d. All of the above are included as part of the AICPA's principles governing an audit.

LO 3

List the phases and related activities in the audit opinion formulation process.

Overview of the Audit Opinion Formulation Process

An important starting point for the audit opinion formulation process is the client's responsibilities related to internal control and the financial statements.

Exhibit 5.2 provides an overview of the client's preparation of its financial statements and management report on internal control. The quality of internal control, which is the responsibility of the client, affects the reliability of the client's financial statement data. If controls over input, process, and output activities are effective, there is a higher likelihood that the financial statements are free from material misstatement. This relationship has important implications for planning and performing the audit.

The *Audit Opinion Formulation Process* diagram presented at the beginning of this chapter summarizes the phases of an audit performed for purposes of providing an opinion on the client's financial statements and internal control effectiveness. These phases include:

Phase I	Making Client Acceptance and Continuance Decisions
Phase II	Performing Risk Assessment
Phase III	Obtaining Evidence About Internal Control Operating Effectiveness
Phase IV	Obtaining Substantive Evidence About Accounts, Disclosures, and Assertions
Phase V	Completing the Audit and Making Reporting Decisions

Within each of these phases, the auditor performs various activities, most of which are the same whether the auditor is performing a financial statement only audit or an integrated audit. *Exhibit 5.3* lists these activities. When performing these activities, the auditor is to make quality professional judgments and ethical decisions.

Exhibit 5.2

Overview of the Client's Preparation of
Financial Statements and Management
Report on Internal Control

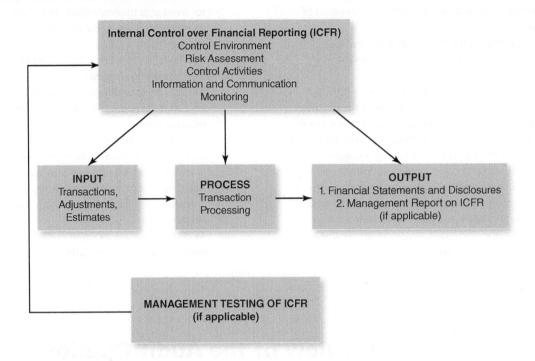

Exhibit 5.3

Activities Within Each Phase of the
Audit Opinion Formulation Process

Phase of the Audit Opinion Formulation Process	Activities Within the Phase
Phase I—Making Client Acceptance and Continuance Decisions	• Assess whether management uses an acceptable financial reporting framework • Assess whether management acknowledges and understands its responsibilities • Assess management's competence and ethics
Phase II—Performing Risk Assessment	• Identify and assess risks of material misstatement • Plan the audit to respond to identified risks of material misstatement
Phase III—Obtaining Evidence About Internal Control Operating Effectiveness, if applicable	• Select controls to test, if applicable • Perform appropriate tests of controls, if applicable • Consider the results of tests of controls, if applicable
Phase IV—Obtaining Substantive Evidence About Accounts, Disclosures, and Assertions	• Perform appropriate substantive procedures
Phase V—Completing the Audit and Making Reporting Decisions	• Complete review and communication activities • Determine the type(s) of opinion(s) to issue

5-9   An important precursor to implementing the audit opinion formulation process includes management's acknowledgement that they have important responsibilities for internal control over financial reporting and the financial statements.   (T/F)

5-10   The audit opinion formulation process consists of five phases, all of which must be performed on every audit engagement, regardless of the client's public trading status.   (T/F)

5-11   Which of the following statements is <u>true</u> about the audit opinion formulation process presented in this chapter?

   a.   The audit opinion formulation process is different for the financial statement only audit and the integrated audit.

   b.   The audit opinion formulation process is based on the premise that management has responsibility to prepare the financial statements and maintain internal control over financial reporting.

   c.   The audit opinion formulation process is comprised of seven phases.

   d.   All of the above are true statements regarding the audit opinion formulation process.

5-12   Which of the following activities is <u>not</u> part of the activities within the audit opinion formulation process?

   a.   The auditor develops a common understanding of the audit engagement with the client.

   b.   The auditor determines the appropriate nonaudit consulting services to provide to the client.

   c.   The auditor identifies and assesses risks of material misstatements and then responds to those identified risks.

   d.   The auditor determines the appropriate audit opinion(s) to issue.

LO 4

Explain the concept of accounting cycles and discuss their importance to the audit opinion formulation process.

Audit Opinion Formulation Process: Accounting Cycles

Financial statements are comprised of accounts, such as revenue or accounts receivable, and they represent a summary of an organization's transactions. Similar transactions linked by procedures and controls that affect related accounts are often grouped together for analysis (and audit) purposes and are referred to as an **accounting cycle** (or process). For example, the revenue cycle includes transactions related to revenue, beginning with an initial customer order that flows through to an invoice, a recording of a receivable and a sale, and eventually the collection of cash. The cycle concept provides a convenient way to break the audit up into manageable sections of related accounts. Individual auditors or teams of auditors are typically assigned to audit a particular accounting cycle. *Exhibit 5.4* lists two cycles and their related accounts.

Exhibit 5.4

Examples of Transaction Cycles and Related Accounts

Cycle	Related Accounts
Acquisitions and Payments for Inventory, Goods, and Services	Accounts Payable
	Inventory
	Expenses
	Other Assets
	Cash
Acquisitions and Payments for Long-Lived Assets	Equipment
	Accumulated Depreciation
	Depreciation Expense
	Gain or Loss on Disposal
	Impairment Loss

Prompt for Critical Thinking #1   It's Your Turn!

Refer to *Exhibit 5.4*. Identify typical accounting cycles *not* listed in *Exhibit 5.4* and list their associated accounts.

For a particular cycle, the auditor focuses on the flow of transactions within that cycle, including how transactions are initiated, authorized, recorded, and reported. The auditor identifies points in the cycle where material misstatements can occur and controls that have been designed and implemented to mitigate those risks.

Understanding the risks and controls within each cycle helps the auditor determine the specific audit procedures to use and the specific audit evidence to obtain. We cover the following cycles in this book:

- Revenue (*Chapter 9*)
- Cash and Marketable Securities (*Chapter 10*)
- Inventory, Goods and Services, and Accounts Payable (*Chapter 11*)
- Long-Lived Assets (*Chapter 12*)
- Long-Term Liabilities and Stockholders' Equity (*Chapter 13*)

Check Your Basic Knowledge

5-13   The cycle approach to auditing provides a way for breaking the audit up into manageable components.   (T/F)

5-14   Within a particular cycle, the auditor focuses on the flow of transactions within that cycle, including how transactions are initiated, authorized, recorded, and reported.   (T/F)

5-15   Which of the following is a reason that the auditor uses an accounting cycle approach when performing an audit?
   a.   The accounting cycle approach allows the auditor to focus exclusively on either the balance sheet or the income statement.
   b.   COSO internal control components are based on the accounting cycles.
   c.   The accounting cycles provide a convenient way to break the audit up into manageable pieces.
   d.   The auditor needs to be able to provide an opinion related to each accounting cycle.

5-16   Which of the following accounts would not be included in the Acquisition and Payment for Long-Lived Assets Cycle?
   a.   Revenue
   b.   Depreciation expense
   c.   Gain on disposal
   d.   Equipment

LO 5

Describe the assertions integral to the financial statements and explain their importance to the audit opinion formulation process.

Audit Opinion Formulation Process: Financial Statement Assertions

Within each cycle, the audit is designed around management's assertions inherent in the financial statements. For example, if an organization asserts that it has property, plant, and equipment (PPE), net of depreciation of $42 million, the assertions being made by management include:

1. PPE is physically present (*existence*).
2. All purchases of PPE are fully recorded (*completeness*).

3. It owns the PPE and has title to the equipment (*rights and obligations*).
4. The PPE is properly valued at cost with applicable allowances for depreciation (*valuation*).
5. The PPE is appropriately classified and described (*presentation and disclosure*)

These five assertions are the ones we refer to throughout the textbook. The AICPA and IAASB have a similar conceptual structure for their assertions, although in some cases the wording differs somewhat from this wording.

The auditor's job is to obtain evidence related to these management assertions for each significant account and disclosure in the financial statements. As part of this process, auditors identify the most **relevant assertions** associated with the significant accounts and disclosures. Relevant assertions are those having a meaningful bearing on whether a financial statement account is fairly stated.

While multiple assertions likely have a bearing on a financial statement account or disclosure, certain financial statement assertions are "more" relevant than others for particular financial statement accounts. For example, valuation is not particularly relevant to the cash account, unless currency translation is involved. However, existence would be considered very relevant to the cash account. As another example, valuation is especially relevant for the inventory account.

The type of account influences the assertions considered most relevant. In general, assets and revenues are more likely to be overstated, so existence/occurrence is the more relevant assertion for those accounts. In contrast, completeness would be the more relevant assertion for liabilities and expenses, as management would be more likely to understate these accounts. Accounts that require subjective judgments by management (such as allowance for loan loss reserve or allowance for inventory obsolescence) will usually have valuation as a more relevant assertion, as the valuation assessment is subject to management bias.

Existence or Occurrence Assertion

Assertions about existence address whether all assets and liabilities recorded in the financial statements exist. For example, an auditor wants assurance that all of the property and equipment included in the client's balance sheet actually exists.

Assertions about occurrence address whether all transactions recorded in the financial statements have occurred. For example, an auditor wants assurance that all of the recorded sales transactions have occurred.

The existence/occurrence assertion is generally most relevant for accounts where the auditor is concerned that management has an incentive to *overstate the ending balance*.

Consider a situation in which management asserts that the sales revenue recorded in the income statement represents all valid sales transactions that occurred during the period. The auditor is concerned that management may have an incentive, e.g., financial performance-based executive compensation, to overstate sales revenue. A common method for overstating sales revenue would be for management to record the first week's sales in 20X1 in the current period 20X0, i.e., accelerating the recognition of sales revenue. The revenue from the first week's sales in 20X1 did not occur during the current period, thus management violated the occurrence assertion.

Common accounts for which the existence or occurrence assertion is relevant include revenue and assets (e.g., inventory, fixed assets).

Completeness Assertion

Assertions about completeness address whether all transactions and accounts that should be included in the financial statements are included. Has anything been left out of the financial statements? This assertion is generally most relevant for accounts for which the auditor is concerned that management has an incentive to *understate the ending balance*.

Consider a setting in which management asserts that accounts payable in the balance sheet includes all accounts payable that the organization owes. The auditor is concerned that management may have an incentive, perhaps based upon debt covenants with their bank, to understate short-term liabilities, e.g., accounts payable. A common method for understating accounts payable would be for management to neglect recording the last week's accounts payable for the current period 20X0 until the first week of 20X1, i.e., delaying recording the liability.

Common accounts for which the completeness assertion is relevant include expenses and liabilities (e.g., accounts payable).

Rights and Obligations Assertion

Assertions about rights address whether recorded assets are the rights of the organization. The auditor is concerned that management may have an incentive, e.g., financial performance-based executive compensation, to improperly claim that they have a right to a revenue or asset.

Consider a situation in which management asserts that they own inventory that is in their warehouse. The auditor's concern is that while the inventory *does physically exist* (i.e., the existence assertion), it is *not actually owned* by the organization. This situation could arise when management fraudulently includes goods in its ending inventory for which they do not have legal title (e.g., goods that are on consignment, or goods that they have 'borrowed' and will return to their original owner after the ending inventory count has been taken). *Exhibit 5.5* illustrates this situation. Management recorded an ending inventory amount, indicating that their organization owned the inventory. If the misstatement is intentional, a fraud exists because the organization does not have legal title, or rights, to the inventory. The result is a classic inventory fraud, whereby management acts in some way to overstate ending inventory and thereby overstate financial reporting profitability.

Exhibit 5.5
Effect of a Fraudulent Overstatement of Ending Inventory on Reported Profitability: Importance of the Rights Assertion

Correct Ending Inventory based on what the oragnization actually owns: $100,000

Fraudulently overstated Ending Inventory: $120,000

Correct Income Statement			Fraudulent Income Statement		
Revenue:		$500,000	Revenue:		$500,000
minus, Cost of Goods Sold (COGS):			*minus*, Cost of Goods Sold (COGS):		
Beginning Inventory	$75,000		Beginning Inventory	$75,000	
plus, Purchases	$200,000		*plus*, Purchases	$200,000	
minus, Ending Inventory	**$100,000**		*minus*, Ending Inventory	**$120,000**	
Equals COGS	$175,000		Equals COGS	$155,000	
Revenue minus COGS:			Revenue minus COGS:		
Gross margin =		**$325,000**	Gross margin =		**$345,000**

The profitability effect of overstating Ending Inventory

Notice that by overstating ending inventory, cost of goods sold is lower, and therefore, profitability is higher. This is an example of a situation in which management is violating the rights assertion; they do not really have a right to the asset, and by fraudulently asserting that they do have that right, they are able to achieve a higher level of reported profitability.

The Importance of Appropriate Disclosures About Long-Term Liabilities at Boeing

Why It Matters

This feature illustrates the usefulness of appropriate disclosures.

Take a guess…how much long-term debt does a large, capital intensive company such as Boeing Airlines have? Below, review Boeing's disclosure of its various elements of long-term debt. Management is asserting that its disclosures of this long-term debt are accurate; it is the auditor's job to conduct the audit to ensure that, indeed, those disclosures are accurate.

Think for a moment as you review this disclosure. What is the implication for the accuracy of the financial disclosures if an interest rate percentage is stated incorrectly, e.g., understated for the cost of borrowing? What is the implication for potential debt covenants if the portion of the debt that is short-term versus long-term is misallocated between the two-time horizons for which the debt is due?

Note: All $ values are stated in millions.

Note 13 – Debt

On May 18, 2016, we issued $1200 of fixed rate senior notes consisting of $400 due June 15, 2023 that bear an annual interest rate of 1.875%, $400 due June 15, 2026 that bear an annual interest of 2.25%, and $400 due June 15, 2046 that bear an annual interest rate of 3.375%. The notes are unsecured senior obligations and rank equally in right of payment with our existing and future unsecured and unsubordinated indebtedness. The net proceeds of the issuance totaled $1,170, after deducting underwriting discounts, commissions and offering expenses.

Interest incurred including amounts capitalized was $535, $497 and $504 for the years ended December 31, 2016, 2015 and 2014, respectively. Interest expense recorded by BCC is reflected as

Boeing Capital interest expense on our Consolidated Statements of Operations. Total Company interest payments were $523, $488 and $511 for the years ended December 31, 2016, 2015 and 2014, respectively.

We have $5,000 currently available under credit line agreements, of which $2,480 is a 364-day revolving credit facility expiring in November 2017, $2,370 expires in November 2021, $90 expires in November 2019 and $60 expires in November 2017. The 364-day credit facility has a one-year term out options which allows us to extend the maturity of any borrowings one year beyond the aforementioned expiration date. We continue to be in full compliance with all covenants contained in our debt or credit facility agreements.

Short-term and current portion of long-term debt at December 31 consisted of the following:

	2016	2015
Unsecured debt securities	**$255**	$1,004
Non-recourse debt and notes	**33**	36
Capital lease obligations	**57**	53
Other notes	**39**	141
Total	**$384**	$1,234

Note: To access Boeing's 10-K, which contains this disclosure on p. 85 of its 2016 FYE financial statements, go to the SEC's website at www.sec.gov and search the Edgar filings for Boeing. You may also access the financial statements at the following website (p. 84 of the 10-K): https://www.sec.gov/Archives/edgar/data/12927/000001292717000006/a201612dec3110k.htm

Assertions about obligations address whether recorded liabilities are the obligations of the organization. In some cases, a client may intentionally overstate a liability (and related expense) to avoid paying taxes. The auditor needs to understand the client's motivations to assess whether such a risk is present.

Common accounts for which the rights and obligation assertion is relevant include assets and liabilities.

Valuation or Allocation Assertion

Assertions about valuation or allocation address whether accounts have been included in the financial statements at appropriate amounts. The auditor is concerned that management may have an incentive, e.g., financial performance-based executive compensation, to improperly value revenues, expenses, assets, and liabilities.

As an example, management might improperly undervalue bad debt expense and the allowance for doubtful accounts in order to show higher, i.e., more favorable net accounts receivable.

Common accounts for which the valuation or allocation assertion is relevant include revenue, expenses, assets, and liabilities (everything!).

Presentation and Disclosure Assertion

Assertions about presentation and disclosure address whether components of the financial statements are properly classified, described, and disclosed. For example, management might assert that obligations classified as long-term liabilities in the balance sheet will *not* mature within one year. The auditor is concerned that the liabilities will mature within a year and that the organization's presentation on the face of the balance sheet does not conform with GAAP requirements. In addition, the auditor will test the disclosure assertion by examining the footnotes to the financial statements for the long-term liability balance and the relevance and appropriateness of management's disclosures.

Check Your Basic Knowledge

5-17 The completeness assertion is typically the more relevant assertion for assets and revenue. (T/F)

5-18 A classic inventory fraud involves management understating ending inventory, thereby yielding a reduction in cost of goods sold and an overstatement of profitability. (T/F)

5-19 Which of the following is not a management assertion?
a. Completeness.
b. Existence.
c. Rights and obligations.
d. Valuation.
e. Placement.

5-20 Which management assertion is usually most relevant for liability accounts?
a. Completeness.
b. Existence.
c. Rights and obligations.
d. Presentation and disclosure.
e. None of the above.

LO 6

Define audit evidence and describe the purpose of audit procedures used to obtain audit evidence.

Audit Opinion Formulation Process: Audit Evidence and Audit Procedures

Audit evidence is information obtained by the auditor to support the audit opinion. Most of the auditor's work in forming an opinion consists of obtaining and evaluating audit evidence through performing **audit procedures**. Audit procedures fall into three categories:

1. **Risk assessment procedures**. Procedures performed by the auditor to obtain information for identifying and assessing the risks of material misstatement in the financial statements whether due to error or fraud. Risk assessment procedures by themselves do not provide sufficient appropriate evidence on which to base an audit opinion but the auditor uses for purposes of planning the audit.
2. **Tests of controls**. Procedures performed to evaluate the operating effectiveness of internal controls in preventing, or detecting and correcting, material misstatements.
3. **Substantive procedures**. Procedures performed to detect material misstatements in account balances.

The auditor has a responsibility to design and perform audit procedures to obtain **sufficient appropriate audit evidence** that supports the auditor's opinion. The auditor obtains evidence by performing audit procedures including inspection of documentation, inspection of assets, observation, external confirmation, recalculation, reperformance, analytical procedures, scanning, and inquiry. Auditors summarize the various procedures they perform in a document referred to as an **audit program**.

Evidence Example: Substantive Audit Procedures to Obtain Evidence About Management's Valuation Assertion

The auditor selects audit procedures and evidence based on the accounts and assertions being tested. Consider an audit of property, plant, and equipment (PPE) and the following valuation assertion implied in an organization's financial statements:

> The equipment shown on the financial statements is properly valued at cost, with applicable allowances for depreciation.

> This assertion can be broken down into four major components:

- The valuation of new assets added this year
- The valuation of assets that were acquired in previous years
- The proper recording of depreciation
- Potential impairment of the existing assets

For illustration purposes, we focus on whether the current year's additions to equipment are properly valued. Substantive audit procedures that would address this assertion include:

- *Testing Additions to PPE Through Inspection of Documentation*—Take a sample from the file containing additions to property, plant, and equipment, verify the cost through vendor invoices, and determine that cost is accurately recorded. If there is a high risk that the valuation may be misstated, the auditor may choose to take a larger sample.
- *Assessing the Potential Impairment of the Asset Additions Through Inquiry of Management and Inspection of Assets*—These procedures help the auditor determine if the assets should be written down to an impaired value. Current economic information and independent evidence as to the current market price of the assets can be used to corroborate management's statements.

Important elements in these audit procedures highlight the following:

- *Select a sample of items to test.* The auditor needs to take a representative sample because it is often too costly to examine all additions to PPE. The sample size could be increased in order to respond to a heightened risk of misstatement. We fully discuss sampling in *Chapter 8*.
- *Inspect documentary evidence of cost.* The auditor examines external, objective evidence of the amount paid and the nature of the equipment purchased, for example, an invoice.
- *Inquire of management and corroborate with evidence obtained from other procedures.* While the auditor will likely inquire of management to obtain some audit evidence, it is important that the auditor corroborate what management has said by obtaining complementary evidence, such as inspection of documentation or assets.

Check Your Basic Knowledge

5-21 Risk assessment procedures provide sufficient appropriate audit evidence on which to base an audit opinion.   (T/F)

5-22 The auditor's selection of audit procedures depends on the accounts and assertions the auditor is testing.   (T/F)

5-23 Audit procedures fall into three categories. Which of the following is <u>not</u> a category of audit procedures?
   a. Risk assessment procedures.
   b. Tests of risks.
   c. Tests of controls.
   d. Substantive procedures.
   e. All of the above are categories of audit procedures.

5-24 Which of the following is a <u>true</u> statement regarding audit evidence and audit procedures?
   a. The auditor has a responsibility to design and perform audit procedures to obtain sufficient appropriate audit evidence.
   b. Inquiry is a type of audit procedure that typically does not require the auditor to perform additional procedures.
   c. Substantive procedures are performed to test the operating effectiveness of a client's internal control.
   d. Risk assessment procedures alone provide sufficient appropriate audit evidence on which to base an audit opinion.

LO 7

Discuss the importance of audit documentation and provide examples.

Audit Opinion Formulation Process: Audit Documentation

The auditor prepares **audit documentation** to provide evidence that the audit was planned and performed in accordance with auditing standards. The terms *working papers* or *workpapers* are sometimes used to refer to audit documentation.

The audit team should document everything done on the audit. It is difficult to persuade a jury or a regulator such as the PCAOB that a procedure was performed if it wasn't documented. The PCAOB considers adequate documentation critically important. Their perspective can be best characterized with a belief in the following phrase: "Not Documented...Not Done!"

Audit documentation should clearly show evidence of supervisory review, particularly in those areas with the greatest potential for improprieties, such as inventories, revenue recognition, and accounting estimates. The documentation should indicate what tests were performed, who performed them, the audit evidence examined, any significant judgments made (along with the rationale for those judgments), and the conclusions reached with respect to relevant financial statement assertions. Auditing standards note that audit documentation serves other purposes, including:

• Assisting the engagement team in planning and performing the audit
• Assisting members of the engagement team responsible for supervising and reviewing the audit work
• Retaining a record of matters of continuing significance to future audits of the same organization
• Enabling internal or external inspections of completed audits
• Assisting auditors in understanding the work performed in the prior year as an aid in planning and performing the current engagement

Examples of audit documentation include:

• Audit programs summarizing the procedures performed by the auditor
• Analyses prepared by the client or the auditor

It's Your Turn!

Prompt for Critical Thinking #2

Develop a list of additional examples of audit documentation.

- _____
- _____
- _____
- _____
- _____

Check Your Basic Knowledge

5-25 The PCAOB, but not the AICPA, requires auditors to prepare audit documentation. (T/F)

5-26 Audit checklists and audit programs are examples of audit documentation. (T/F)

5-27 Which of the following information should be included in audit documentation?
 a. Procedures performed.
 b. Audit evidence examined.
 c. Conclusions reached with respect to relevant financial statement assertions.
 d. All of the above should be included.

5-28 Which of the following statements is <u>false</u> regarding audit documentation?
 a. An audit program is an example of audit documentation.
 b. The only purpose of audit documentation is to provide evidence that the audit was planned and performed in accordance with auditing standards.
 c. Audit documentation helps facilitate internal and external inspections of completed audits.
 d. Audit documentation is required on all audit engagements.

LO 8

Discuss audit activities in each of the five phases of the audit opinion formulation process.

Five Phases of the Audit Opinion Formulation Process

Phase I—Making Client Acceptance and Continuance Decisions

Auditors are not required to perform audits for any organization that asks for an audit. Recall from *Chapter 1* that audit firm portfolio management decisions (client acceptance and continuance decisions) occur on an ongoing basis and are critical to achieve audit quality.

An audit firm's portfolio of clients changes because of many factors. These factors include clients departing from the firm's portfolio—either voluntarily or involuntarily (e.g., because they merged with another entity, went bankrupt, or voluntarily changed firms for some other reason) and clients being newly accepted by the firm (either because of seeking an audit for the first time or those switching from their previous audit firm to the new audit firm).

What Do You Think? **For Classroom Discussion**

Review the data below that details information from the Audit Analytics database about auditor and client changes based on audit firm portfolio management and client decision making.

AUDIT ANALYTICS®

Client Gains & Losses
January 1, 2017 - March 31, 2017

Firm		Big Four				Global & National Firms							Totals					
		Deloitte	KPMG	E&Y	PwC	BDO USA	GT	RSM US	Crowe	EisnerAmper	Marcum[1]	BKD	Big Four	Global & National	Regional & Local	N/A	Total	Net
Deloitte	Gains	--	4	3	3	2	1	-	-	-	-	-	10	3	1	-	13	9
	Losses	--	1	1	1	-	-	-	-	-	-	-	3	0	1	-	4	
KPMG	Gains	1	--	1	-	1	-	-	-	-	-	-	2	1	1	-	4	-7
	Losses	4	--	-	2	1	-	-	1	-	-	-	6	2	1	2	11	
EY	Gains	1	-	--	-	2	1	-	-	-	-	-	1	3	1	-	5	-4
	Losses	3	1	--	-	-	1	1	-	-	1	-	4	3	2	-	9	
PwC	Gains	1	1	-	--	-	-	-	-	-	-	-	2	0	-	-	2	-7
	Losses	3	-	1	--	-	1	3	-	-	-	-	4	4	1	-	9	
BDO USA	Gains	-	1	-	-	--	1	1	-	-	-	-	1	2	2	-	5	-4
	Losses	2	1	2	-	--	1	-	1	-	-	-	5	2	2	-	9	
GT	Gains	2	-	1	1	1	--	-	-	-	-	-	2	1	1	-	4	-2
	Losses	1	-	2	-	1	--	-	-	-	-	-	3	1	1	1	6	
RSM US	Gains	-	-	1	3	-	-	--	-	-	-	-	4	0	-	-	4	1
	Losses	-	-	-	-	-	1	--	-	-	-	-	0	1	2	-	3	
Crowe	Gains	-	1	-	-	-	-	-	--	-	-	-	1	0	4	-	5	5
	Losses	-	-	-	-	-	-	-	--	-	-	-	0	0	-	-	0	
EisnerAmper	Gains	-	-	-	-	1	-	-	-	--	-	-	0	1	2	-	3	3
	Losses	-	-	-	-	-	-	-	-	--	-	-	0	0	-	-	0	
Marcum[1]	Gains	-	-	2	-	-	-	-	-	-	--	-	2	0	1	-	3	0
	Losses	-	-	-	-	-	-	-	-	-	--	-	0	0	2	1	3	
BKD	Gains	-	-	-	-	-	-	-	-	-	-	--	0	0	-	-	0	0
	Losses	-	-	-	-	-	-	-	-	-	-	--	0	0	-	-	0	

[1] Comprised of Marcum LLP & Marcum Bernstein Pinchuk LLP

Source: AuditAnalytics.com
Editor's note: AuditAnalytics.com is a premium online intelligence service delivering audit, regulatory and disclosure analysis to the accounting, legal and academic communities. For information, call (508) 476-7007, email info@auditanalytics.com or visit www.auditanalytics.com.

As an example of how to interpret this data, it appears that in the first quarter of 2017, Deloitte has attracted nine publicly traded clients, while each of the other Big 4 have lost 18, with notable gains by Crowe and EisnerAmper.

• Why might a client shift from one Big 4 firm to another?

• Why might a client shift from a non-Big 4 firm to a Big 4 firm?

• Why might a client shift from a Big 4 firm to a non-Big 4 firm?

• Speculate as to potential auditing pricing differences (or lack thereof) based on these client shifts in the audit firm market. Should an audit cost the same regardless of the audit firm that provides it?

• What are potential implications of the fact that Deloitte has gained nine publicly traded clients in this period as compared to its competitors?

Note: You can access the full Audit Analytics report at the following website: http://www.auditanalytics.com/blog/auditor-changes-roundup-q1-2017/

In making client acceptance and continuance decisions, the auditor will perform various procedures in assessing the client, including:

• Inquire of client and audit firm personnel whether there are any potential independence-impairing relationships
• Obtain background checks on management to assess management integrity
• Perform a review of any questionable accounting policies that might indicate management's lack of commitment to GAAP
• Review regulatory filings and inquire of management about any internal control deficiencies
• Analyze client and industry financial statements to assess the possibility of business failure
• Assess the background and experience of the potential client's accounting personnel

5-29   Audit firm portfolio management decisions are influenced only by audit fee considerations.   (T/F)

5-30   Auditors are required to perform an audit for any organization that needs one.   (T/F)

5-31   Which of the following factors would an auditor typically <u>not</u> consider when making a client acceptance decision?
   a.   Any potential independence-impairing relationships.
   b.   Any internal control deficiencies.
   c.   Management's commitment to GAAP.
   d.   Management integrity.
   e.   An auditor would consider all of the above factors.

5-32   Which of the following statements regarding client acceptance/continuance decisions is <u>false</u>?
   a.   An audit firm's client portfolio is impacted by both audit firm decisions and client decisions.
   b.   It would not be appropriate for audit firms to perform background checks on management of a potential client.
   c.   Auditors are not required to perform audits for any organization that asks for an audit.
   d.   Auditors should assess the background and experience of accounting personnel of a potential client.

One of the most important factors of a quality audit is the client acceptance/continuance decision. It is important that the auditor make these decisions in a way that results in the appropriate portfolio of clients for the firm.

Phase II—Performing Risk Assessment

Once the audit firm accepts a new client (or the audit firm decides to retain a continuing client), the auditor needs to thoroughly understand the client, with a focus on understanding the risks of material misstatement—due to either fraud or errors—in the financial statements and related disclosures. For continuing clients, much of the information is available from the previous year's audit and can be updated for changes. For new clients, this process is more time consuming.

Risk assessment underlies the entire audit process; identifying the risks of material misstatement is essential to planning an audit. A starting point for risk assessment is the identification of significant accounts, disclosures, and relevant assertions. Because the focus is on identifying material misstatements in the financial statements, the auditor establishes a materiality level for the financial statements overall and for specific accounts and disclosures. Materiality relates to the importance or significance of an amount, transaction, or discrepancy. Misstatements are material if they could reasonably be expected to influence the decisions of users made on the basis of the financial statements. Materiality considerations are the same for a financial statement audit and an integrated audit. *Exhibit 5.6* identifies sources of risk of material misstatement that the auditor should consider.

The auditor assesses the risk of material misstatement at both the financial statement level and the account and assertion levels. Risks at the financial statement level could potentially affect multiple accounts and assertions. In reviewing

For Classroom Discussion

What Do You Think?

We can probably all agree that risk assessment during the planning phase of the audit is important, because that assessment determines the auditors' planned procedures to address assessed risk. But, what are the implications if the audit team "gets it wrong" and assesses client risks inaccurately—either too low or too high?

Exhibit 5.6

Examples of Sources of Risk of Material Misstatement

BUSINESS RISK
- Economic and competitive changes
- Changes in fair market values of assets/liabilities
- Regulatory risks and changes

MANAGEMENT MOTIVATIONS
- Compensation/reward structure for all levels
- Stock market performance and debt covenants
- Short-term actions to enhance current performance

PROCESSES AFFECTING MATERIAL ACCOUNT BALANCES
- Transaction processing of high volumes of material transactions
- IT risks and vulnerabilities
- Processes affecting major estimates and adjusting entries

Assessment of Risk of Material Misstatement

Exhibit 5.6, consider the presence of declining economic conditions and management pressure for good stock performance. These risks could affect the existence of sales, the valuation of receivables, and the completeness of expenses. At the assertion level, the auditor will consider both inherent and control risks.

Inherent risk refers to the susceptibility of an assertion about a class of transaction, account balance, or disclosure to a misstatement that could be material, either individually or when aggregated with other misstatements, before consideration of any related controls. For example, the valuation of the loan loss reserve for a financial institution will likely have a high level of inherent risk due to its susceptibility of misstatement resulting from management bias.

Control risk refers to the risk that a misstatement, which could occur in an assertion about a class of transaction, account balance, or disclosure, and which could be material, either individually or when aggregated with other misstatements, will not be prevented, or detected and corrected, on a timely basis by the organization's internal control. For example, a small, nonprofit client with few accounting personnel is likely to have a high level of control risk because of the lack of resources. Control risk is a function of the effectiveness of the design, the implementation of internal control, and the operation of internal control.

Risk Assessment Procedures

Risk assessment procedures typically include:

- Inquiries of management and others within the entity who may have information to assist in identifying risks of material misstatement due to fraud or error
- Planning analytical procedures
- Observation (such as watching an organization's operations, facilities, or premises) and inspection of documentation (e.g., reviewing business plans, internal control manuals, or management reports)

Assessing Internal Control Design Effectiveness and Implementation An important aspect of risk assessment is obtaining an understanding of internal control over financial reporting. The quality of internal control directly affects the risk of material misstatement. During Phase II, the auditor focuses on the design effectiveness and implementation of internal control, and includes entity-wide controls, transaction-specific controls, and fraud-related controls.

The auditor assesses control design effectiveness and implementation by determining whether the organization's controls, if they are operated as designed by persons possessing the necessary authority and competence, can reasonably prevent or detect material misstatements in the financial statements. This understanding will allow the auditor to make a preliminary control risk assessment.

The auditor performs various procedures to assess design effectiveness, including inquiry of appropriate personnel, observation of the organization's operations, and inspection of relevant documentation. Auditors also perform walkthroughs, as discussed in *Chapter 3*, to evaluate design effectiveness and implementation.

Controls to Address Fraud Risk   *Focus on Fraud*

This feature provides examples of fraud-related controls.

The PCAOB has identified the following as specific types of controls that the auditor should consider in evaluating whether or not an organization has sufficiently addressed fraud risk. The baseline for quality financial reporting is that the organization will have controls over:

- Significant, unusual transactions, particularly those that result in late or unusual journal entries

- Journal entries made by top management, i.e., adjustments made in the period-end financial reporting process, which are sometimes called **top-side journal entries**
- Related-party transactions
- Significant management estimates

Organizations should also have controls that mitigate incentives for, and pressures on, management to falsify or inappropriately manage financial results.

For Classroom Discussion   *What Do You Think?*

- Why is it important that an organization have controls around top-side journal entries?
- How could top management perpetrate financial reporting fraud through top-side journal entries?

- How do you think auditors gain comfort that, indeed, any top-side journal entries that top management makes are not relating to fraud, but are instead being used to record valid transactions?

Why It Matters

Documenting the Auditor's Understanding of an Organization's Internal Controls

This feature explains how the auditor should document the preliminary assessment of control design and the basis for that assessment, and why doing so is important.

The auditor's documentation should clearly identify each important control and the auditor's assessment of the design and implementation of that control. The auditor may base the audit documentation on documentation prepared by the client. The assessment of design effectiveness and implementation is the basis for the auditor's preliminary control risk assessment. The documentation of the understanding of internal control is often captured with narratives and flowcharts that describe the control processes. Some audit firms also use questionnaires to assist in identifying important areas where controls are expected. There is no one right approach; each audit firm chooses an approach that fits the nature of its technology, its clients, and its clients' risks. Once the overall internal control process has been initially documented, in subsequent years many audit firms focus only on changes in the system and the effectiveness of monitoring controls to signal potential breakdowns in the overall control design.

Based on obtaining an understanding of internal control through the various procedures and review of management's documentation, the auditor assesses control risk ranging from high (weak controls) to low (strong controls). Assessing control risk as high means the auditor does not have confidence that internal controls will prevent or detect material misstatements; assessing control risk as low has the opposite implication.

This preliminary assessment, based on the auditor's understanding of the design and implementation of the controls, is important because it drives the planning for the rest of the audit. If control risk is assessed as high, the auditor cannot plan on relying on the controls to reduce substantive procedures for account balances. Therefore, the auditor will not perform tests of controls; instead, the auditor must plan for substantive procedures, with no reliance being placed on the client's internal controls. If control risk is assessed as low, the auditor will plan to test the operating effectiveness of those controls (see Phase III) in an effort to reduce substantive testing related to account balances.

Responding to Identified Risks of Material Misstatement

Once the auditor completes risk assessment, the next step is to determine the mix of tests of controls and substantive procedures for Phases III and IV of the audit opinion formulation process. The purpose of risk assessment is to identify the risks of material misstatement, determine where misstatements in the financial statements might possibly occur, and design the appropriate audit strategy (audit procedures) to respond.

For a financial statement audit where the auditor wants to rely on controls as part of the basis for the audit opinion, the auditor designs a **controls reliance audit**—an audit that includes tests of controls and substantive procedures. For some audits, the auditor may determine that it is not efficient or effective to rely on the client's controls in forming the audit opinion. In those audits, the auditor designs a **substantive audit**—an audit that includes substantive procedures and does not include tests of controls. Within the same audit, the auditor can take different approaches across different cycles. For example, a controls reliance approach might be taken when auditing cash, but a substantive approach might be taken when auditing revenue.

In addition to selecting specific audit procedures to respond to identified risks, the auditor should consider the following overall responses to identified risks:

- Assembling an audit team that has the knowledge, skill, and ability needed to address the assessed risks of material misstatement
- Emphasizing to the audit team the need for professional skepticism
- Providing the level of supervision that is appropriate for the assessed risks of material misstatement
- Incorporating elements of unpredictability in the selection and timing of audit procedures to be performed

An Analogy for Responding to Identified Risks of Material Misstatement   It can be helpful to view the response to identified risks of material misstatements as accumulating boxes of audit evidence. Two key considerations are the size of each evidence box and what type of evidence goes into each box. Accounts, disclosures, and assertions that have a higher level of identified risk of material misstatement would require larger boxes of evidence. Consider the three boxes in Panel A of *Exhibit 5.7*. An assertion with a low risk of material misstatement might require only enough evidence to fill Box A; an assertion with a high level of risk of material misstatement might require enough evidence to fill Box C; an assertion with a moderate level of risk of material misstatement might require enough evidence to fill Box B. There is not one right box size for every assertion. The appropriate size of the box is based on the level of assessed risk of material misstatement.

The evidence that goes into each box will also vary. Consider an assertion where the auditor has assessed the risk of material misstatement as moderate. Again, referring to *Exhibit 5.7*, the auditor needs to fill Box B in Panel A with audit evidence. Panel B illustrates alternative approaches that the auditor could use in filling that box. First, assume that the auditor has determined that the controls for that assertion are well designed. The auditor can fill the box with evidence from tests of controls and from substantive procedures (a controls reliance audit).

For example, 50% of the evidence may come from tests of controls and 50% from substantive procedures. In contrast, assume that the auditor has determined that the controls related to that assertion are not well designed. The auditor should

Exhibit 5.7
Responding to Identified Risks
Through Evidence Decisions

PANEL A: EXTENT OF EVIDENCE

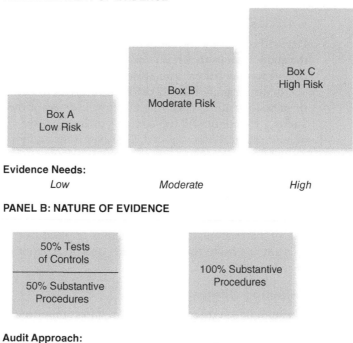

Check Your Basic Knowledge

5-33 In conducting a substantive audit, the auditor uses only substantive procedures, and does not rely on tests of internal controls. (T/F)

5-34 The auditor assesses the risk of material misstatement at only the account level. (T/F)

5-35 Which of the following statements is <u>true</u> regarding the design of controls related to credit limits?
   a. The effectiveness of the control design is contingent on the credit manager's process for establishing and reviewing credit limits.
   b. Because the process of establishing credit limits is fairly time consuming, the control should be designed so that the marketing manager has the ability to approve sales on an ad hoc basis while waiting for the credit approval.

   c. The control should be designed so that the sales manager has final approval regarding credit limits.
   d. All are true statements regarding the design of controls related to credit limits.

5-36 The baseline for quality financial reporting is that the organization will have controls over which of the following?
   a. Significant, unusual transactions, particularly those that result in late or unusual journal entries.
   b. Top-side journal entries.
   c. Related-party transactions.
   d. Significant management estimates.
   e. All of the above.

not obtain any evidence on the operating effectiveness (why bother testing the operating effectiveness of a control that is poorly designed?), but instead should fill Box B with only evidence from substantive procedures (a substantive audit). That is, 100% of the evidence will come from substantive procedures. These same types of evidence decisions would also occur for assertions where the risk of material misstatement is high (Box C in Panel A of *Exhibit 5.7*) or low (Box A in Panel A of *Exhibit 5.7*).

Phase III—Obtaining Evidence About Internal Control

Phase III is relevant for integrated audits and for financial statement audits where the auditor wants to rely on controls as part of the evidence about the reasonableness of account balances and disclosures (in other words, a controls reliance audit).

In an integrated audit, the auditor needs to opine on internal control effectiveness—including operating effectiveness—as of the client's year-end. For these audits, the auditor will test controls throughout the year, with an increased focus on testing controls at year end. However, if the auditor wants to rely on controls as part of the audit evidence about account balances for the financial statement audit, the auditor needs to know whether controls were operating effectively throughout the year. To determine whether controls are operating effectively—either at year-end or throughout the year—the auditor tests controls that are important to the conclusion about whether the organization's controls adequately address the risk of material misstatement. There is no need to test every control related to a relevant assertion; the auditor tests only those controls that are most important in reducing the risk.

Selecting Controls to Test

The auditor selects controls that are most important to the organization's ability to adequately address the risk of material misstatement. The auditor selects both entity-wide and transaction controls for testing. The selection of transaction controls to be tested will depend, in part, on the results of testing the selected entity-wide controls. Effective entity-wide controls may reduce the number of control activities selected for testing. Overall, risks associated with significant accounts,

Exhibit 5.8
Assertions and Examples of
Controls to Test Assertions

Financial Statement Assertion	Examples of Controls That Might Be Selected for Testing
Existence or occurrence	• Shipments recorded are reconciled with shipping documents daily. • Items cannot be recorded without underlying source documents and approvals.
Completeness	• Prenumbered shipping documents are used and reconciled with shipments recorded daily. • A list of cash receipts is developed when cash is collected and is reconciled with cash deposits and the debit to cash daily.
Valuation or allocation	• Preauthorized sales prices are entered into the computer pricing table by authorized individuals. • Sales prices can be overridden only on the authorization of key management personnel. A record of overrides is documented and independently reviewed by management, internal audit, or other parties performing control analysis.

disclosures, and relevant assertions should lead to the identification of important controls that need to be tested.

In determining which controls to select for testing, the auditor should explicitly link controls and assertions. *Exhibit 5.8* links the assertions of existence, completeness, and valuation to possible controls that the auditor may test.

Performing Tests of Controls

To obtain evidence about whether a control is operating effectively, the auditor directly tests the control in operation. The following tests of controls are presented in the order of their rigor, from the least to the most rigorous:

- Inquiry
- Observation
- Inspecting relevant documentation
- Reperforming a control

Inquiry alone does not provide sufficient evidence to support a conclusion about the effectiveness of a control; the auditor must perform other procedures. The type of test of control used varies with the process, the materiality of the account balance, and the control. For example, computerized edit controls built into a computer application could be tested by submitting test transactions. For manual controls, such as authorizations, the auditor might select a number of transactions to determine if there is documented evidence that proper authorization has taken place.

For the reconciliation of shipments with recorded sales, the auditor could select a number of daily sales and review documentation to determine whether the reconciliations were performed appropriately. If a more rigorous test was needed because of the materiality of the account related to the reconciliation, the auditor may choose to reperform the reconciliation.

In selecting approaches to test controls, the auditor needs to consider the type of control being tested including computerized controls, manual controls, controls over adjusting entries, and controls over accounting estimates. *Exhibit 5.9* provides examples of possible tests of controls.

Exhibit 5.9
Types of Controls and Tests of Controls

Types of Controls	Possible Tests of Controls
Computerized controls	**Audit Objective:** *Determine whether there have been changes to important computer applications during the year.* • Determine if there are changes in the computer program. If there are, test the integrity of the controls after the changes (inspection of relevant documentation and reperformance of control). • Consider submitting test transactions through the system to determine that it is working properly (reperformance of control). • Take a random sample of transactions and determine that (a) key controls are operating and (b) processing is complete (reperformance of control). • Review exception reports to determine that (a) proper exceptions are being noted and that (b) exceptions go to authorized personnel and there is adequate follow-up for proper processing (inspection of relevant documentation).
Manual controls	**Audit Objective:** *Determine whether there is documented evidence that a control is operating effectively.* • Review documentation for fixed asset acquisitions and disposals to determine whether the relevant acquisition and payment cycle accounts properly reflect the acquisitions and disposals.
Authorizations	**Audit Objective:** *Determine whether documented controls over authorizations are actually being employed in practice.* • Take a sample of transactions and examine evidence supporting that the controls are working. For example, review a document or a computer printout indicating proper approval (inspection of relevant documentation).
Reconciliations	**Audit Objective:** *Determine whether the organization conducts and implements controls whereby one individual reviews the work of another individual in the financial reporting process.* Also determine how the organization accomplishes this. • Take a sample of reconciliations to determine that (a) they were performed by an authorized person and that (b) they were performed properly (inspection of relevant documentation and reperformance of control).
Reviews for unusual transactions	**Audit Objective:** *Determine who is making top-side journal entries, when they are making them, and why they are making them to ensure that top management is not using top-side journal entries to fraudulently manipulate the financial position of the company.* • Review documentation of selected transactions to determine whether they were properly authorized and recorded in the correct time period (inspection of relevant documentation). • Take a sample of reports that management uses to identify unusual transactions. Review to determine (a) that they are used regularly and (b) that unusual items are identified and investigated further (inspection of relevant documentation).
Controls over adjusting entries	**Audit Objective:** *Determine whether there is documented evidence that there are controls over adjusting entries, including documentation that identifies (a) the reason and support for the adjustment and (b) the authorization of the adjustment.* • Take a sample of adjusting entries and review to determine that (a) there is supporting documentation for the entry, (b) the entry is appropriate, (c) the entry is made to the correct accounts, and (d) the entry was properly authorized (inspection of relevant documentation). • Give special attention to significant entries made near year-end (inquiry of management and inspection of relevant documentation).

Controls over accounting estimates	**Audit Objective:** *Determine whether there is documented evidence of the controls over the estimate. Further, the auditor should determine that controls are sufficient to ensure that (a) the estimate is made based on accurate data, (b) the process of making the estimate is performed consistently, and (c) the model is updated for changing economic or business conditions. For example, estimates of a healthcare liability should be updated for changes in the trend of healthcare costs and required employee deductibles and copays.*
	
	 • Review the process, noting that:
	   o All entries are properly authorized (inspection of relevant documentation).
	   o There are controls to ensure that estimates are updated for current market or economic conditions (inquiry of management and inspection of relevant documentation).
	   o There is evidence that data used to make the estimates come from reliable sources (inquiry of management and inspection of relevant documentation).

Example of Approaches to Testing the Operating Effectiveness of a Control Activity   As an example of alternative testing approaches, consider the following important control that exists in virtually all organizations:

> The organization requires a credit review and specific approval for all customers that are granted credit, and the amount of credit for any one company is limited by customer policy, which is based on financial health of the customer, past collection experience, and current credit rating of the customer.

The auditor might consider three approaches to testing the control:

1. Taking a sample of customer orders and trace the customer orders through the system to determine whether (a) there was proper review of credit and (b) credit authorization or denial was proper.
2. Taking a sample of recorded items (accounts receivable) and trace back to the credit approval process to determine that it was performed appropriately.
3. Using a computer audit program to read all accounts receivable and develop a printout of all account balances that exceed their credit authorization.

Different costs and advantages are associated with each of these three methods. The third method is dependent on proper input of the credit limits into the computer system. If there are no exceptions, the auditor could infer that the control is working even though the auditor did not directly test the control. This approach is cost effective, but it requires an inference about the control and covers only the operation of the controls related to the current account balances. The first method is the most effective because it not only requires that the auditor look at documentary evidence, but also requires that the auditor determines that the control did work effectively—it led to the correct conclusion, to either deny or provide credit. This method requires documentation of all credit applications and purchase orders and is based on audit sampling (not an examination of all transactions), whereas the third method was a 100% evaluation of each item currently recorded. The second method (sample from recorded items) can provide evidence on whether there was proper credit approval for all items that are presently recorded. However, it does not provide evidence as to whether other items should have been approved for credit, but had not been approved.

All three approaches provide relevant evidence of the operating effectiveness of controls related to credit approval. Which one is the most appropriate?

Auditors have to make decisions like this on every engagement. It seems trite to say "it depends," but the right choice does depend on the risk associated with the engagement, the auditor's experience with the credit level set by the organization (in other words, the credit approval level seems appropriate), the auditor's assessment of the control environment, the auditor's assessment of the quality of controls surrounding the computer applications, and the overall cost of the audit procedure. If other controls are effective and risk is low, the auditor will most likely use the third approach because (a) it is the least costly and (b) it tests 100% of the recorded population. The auditor might reason further that the major risk is overstatement of accounts receivable through bad credit. The auditor is not very concerned about customers who were turned down for credit; on the other hand, management, in its assessment, might prefer to test the control by sampling from all customer orders because they do not want valid customers to be turned down for credit.

While the auditor has various options when testing controls, an important point is that the auditor has to perform tests of controls if the auditor plans to rely on those controls for the financial statement audit.

Testing the Operating Effectiveness of the Control Environment, Risk Assessment, Information and Communication, and Monitoring Components   Auditors are often most comfortable testing control activities. However, similar to management's testing described in *Chapter 3*, the auditor tests the relevant principles of the other internal control components, including control environment, risk assessment, information and communication, and monitoring. For example, the auditor can test commitment to integrity and ethical values (Committee of Sponsoring Organizations (COSO) Principle 1) through first-hand knowledge of the client's attitude toward "pushing the accounting boundaries."

As part of testing the risk assessment component, the auditor might test COSO Principle 6 (The organization specifies objectives with sufficient clarity to enable the identification and assessment of risks relating to objectives.); testing can be done by reviewing documentation of the organization's objectives. In testing the information and communication component, the auditor might inquire of personnel and review relevant documentation indicating how the organization internally communicates information, including objectives and responsibilities for internal control (COSO Principle 14). An important principle of the monitoring component is that the organization communicates internal control deficiencies in a timely manner to those parties responsible for taking corrective action (COSO Principle 17). Reviewing appropriate documentation and inquiring of appropriate personnel could provide audit evidence on the extent to which this principle is operating effectively.

Considering the Results of Tests of Controls

The auditor considers the results of the tests of controls before finalizing decisions about substantive procedures. For the financial statement audit, there are two potential outcomes, with associated alternative courses of action:

1. If control deficiencies are identified, assess the severity of those deficiencies to determine whether and how the preliminary control risk assessment should be modified (should control risk be increased from low to high?), and document the implications for substantive procedures (should the substantive procedures be modified?).
2. If no control deficiencies are identified, assess whether the preliminary control risk assessment is still appropriate, determine the extent that controls can provide evidence on the accuracy of account balances, and determine planned substantive audit procedures. The substantive testing in this situation will be less than what is required in circumstances where deficiencies in internal control were identified.

The results of the tests of controls will allow the auditor to determine how much assurance about the reliability of account balances can be obtained from the effective operation of controls. Using the previous analogy of accumulating a box of evidence, the auditor needs to determine if evidence from tests of operating effectiveness of controls can be used to partially fill the evidence box. Organizations with strong internal controls should require less substantive testing of account balances since more assurance is being obtained from internal controls. Within any audit, that level of assurance will vary across accounts, disclosures, and assertions. Even if the auditor can fill a box with a lot of evidence from tests of controls, for most accounts, the auditor also needs to add some evidence from substantive procedures to the box.

Additional Considerations for an Integrated Audit   In an integrated audit, results of the tests of controls also have important implications for the auditor's opinion on internal control over financial reporting. The auditor evaluates the severity of each identified control deficiency to determine whether the deficiencies, individually or in combination, are material weaknesses. If any control deficiencies are severe enough to be material weaknesses, the auditor's report on internal control should describe the material weaknesses and include an opinion indicating that internal control over financial reporting is not effective.

The Need for Performing Tests of Controls and Considering the Results

Why It Matters

This feature makes the point that the auditor has to consider the results of tests of controls when designing substantive procedures.

The PCAOB performs periodic inspections of audit firms that conduct audits of public companies. Following are excerpts from an inspection report, indicating that either the appropriate tests of controls had not been performed or the implications of the tests of controls were not reflected in the substantive procedures performed.

> "The Firm failed to perform sufficient procedures to test the design and operating effectiveness of two important review controls on which it relied in evaluating internal controls over a number of significant accounts, including revenue, accounts receivable, inventory, and certain accruals."

"Further, for some Level 3 financial instruments, the Firm concluded that it did not need to change the nature, timing, and extent of its procedures, notwithstanding certain issues that came to the Firm's attention regarding controls related to the valuation of these instruments."

"The Firm failed to sufficiently test controls over the issuer's revenue recognition for certain revenue arrangements, as the Firm focused its testing on verifying that the control activity had occurred without evaluating its effectiveness, including its level of precision. Further, in certain instances, the Firm performed procedures related to the issuer's transaction processes but failed to test controls over those processes."

For Classroom Discussion

What Do You Think?

Review the three examples presented in the *Why It Matters* feature "The Need for Performing Tests of Controls and Considering the Results."

- What are the audit quality implications of not performing the procedures noted in that feature?
- Do you think that these deficiencies rise to the level of an 'audit failure,' i.e., issuing an unqualified audit opinion on financial statements that are materially misstated?

- Do you think that the auditors who were the subject of these inspections would necessarily agree with the PCAOB's assessments of these supposed audit failures? Why or why not?

Summary of Audit Decisions Prior to Determining Substantive Procedures

The activities in Phases II and III of the audit opinion formulation process are important to determining the substantive procedures that need to be performed as a basis for the audit opinion on the financial statements.

Exhibit 5.10 provides a summary of important audit activities and decisions leading up to the performance of substantive procedures. The process begins with identifying significant account balances and disclosures and their relevant assertions. For most organizations, the significant accounts and disclosures are obvious and include accounts such as revenue, cost of goods sold, inventory, receivables, and accounts payable.

As part of identifying significant accounts and disclosures and their relevant assertions, the auditor identifies the types of risk that could cause a material

Exhibit 5.10

Overview of Audit Decisions
Leading up to Decisions about
Substantive Procedures for
the Financial Statement Audit

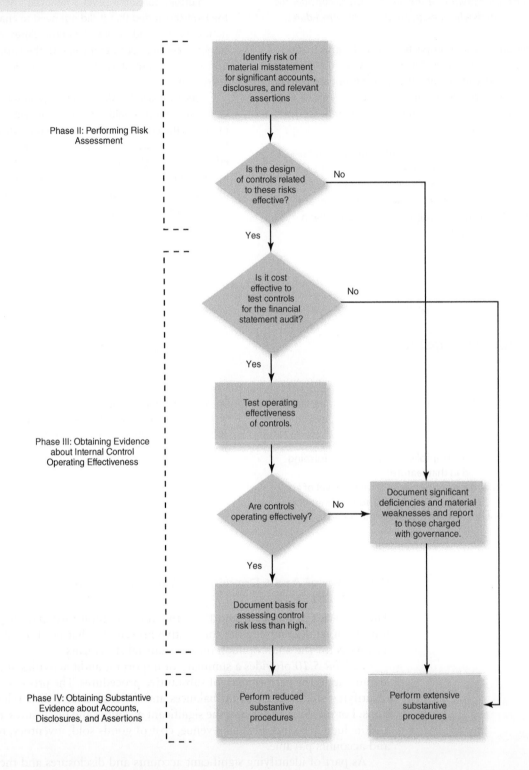

Phase II: Performing Risk
Assessment

Identify risk of
material misstatement
for significant accounts,
disclosures, and relevant
assertions

Is the design
of controls related
to these risks
effective? — No

Yes

Is it cost
effective to
test controls
for the financial
statement audit? — No

Yes

Phase III: Obtaining Evidence
about Internal Control
Operating Effectiveness

Test operating
effectiveness
of controls.

Are controls
operating effectively? — No

Document significant
deficiencies and material
weaknesses and report
to those charged
with governance.

Yes

Document basis for
assessing control
risk less than high.

Phase IV: Obtaining Substantive
Evidence about Accounts,
Disclosures, and Assertions

Perform reduced
substantive
procedures

Perform extensive
substantive
procedures

misstatement to occur. The auditor should understand the controls that the client has implemented to address those risks of material misstatement. If the auditor plans to rely on those controls, then the auditor should test their operating effectiveness. The results of these tests will influence the planned substantive procedures.

As an example, assume the auditor determines that a mid-sized public company has a heightened risk of material misstatement because the controller is not competent in addressing complex accounting issues. As a matter of policy, the company decided to mitigate the risks by: (a) not engaging in complex business transactions and (b) minimizing the percentage of management compensation that is directly attributed to reported profit. The auditor further reviews the revenue accounting process and determines that there are control activities designed to: (a) prevent unauthorized transactions, (b) assure that revenue is recorded only when earned, and (c) require that all unusual contracts be reviewed and approved by the chief executive officer (CEO). Further, because there is a risk of management override, the controller develops a list of unusual contracts to review with the chair of the audit committee and the lead director.

While there is a heightened risk of material misstatement due to the lack of competency of the controller, the organization has controls designed to mitigate the risks to the financial statements. If the auditor assesses the design of these controls as effective, the auditor should test their operating effectiveness. However, even if the controls are designed and operating effectively, the auditor may still have concerns about the residual risk of misstatement associated with revenue recognition because that process is prone to misstatement related to poor accounting judgments. The auditor may respond by planning and performing more, and more rigorous, substantive procedures for revenue and receivables. For example, the auditor might extensively review and follow-up on unusual transactions near year-end and might examine unusual sales contracts as part of the substantive tests of the account balance. The auditor may also choose to increase the sample size of confirmations sent to the client's customers.

Check Your Basic Knowledge

5-37 One valid approach to testing controls over credit review and approval for customers that are granted credit involves taking a sample of customer orders and tracing them through the system to determine whether: (a) there was proper review of credit and (b) credit authorization or denial was proper.   (T/F)

5-38 The results of the tests of controls allow the auditor to determine how much assurance about the reliability of account balances can be obtained from the effective operation of controls.   (T/F)

5-39 What actions should auditors take if they identify control deficiencies at their client?
   a. Assess the severity of those deficiencies.
   b. Determine whether and how the preliminary control risk assessment should be modified.

   c. Provide documentation about the effect of the control risk assessment on modifications to substantive procedures.
   d. Actions (a), (b), and (c) are all appropriate.
   e. Only (a) and (c) are appropriate.

5-40 In testing controls over adjusting journal entries, which of the following would the auditor likely review?
   a. Supporting documentation for the entry.
   b. Evidence proving that the entry is material.
   c. Evidence that the debits and credits are to appropriate accounts.
   d. All of the above.
   e. Only two of the above (a–c) are appropriate.

Phase IV—Obtaining Substantive Evidence About Accounts, Disclosures, and Assertions

Much of what most people think of as auditing—the testing of account balances—occurs in Phase IV. As illustrated in *Exhibit 5.10*, the information gathered in Phases II and III influences the substantive procedures the auditor will perform.

The auditor performs substantive procedures for the relevant assertions of each significant account and disclosure, regardless of the assessed level of control risk. These procedures can include both substantive analytical procedures and tests of details of account balances. Substantive analytical procedures are optional, whereas tests of details would be necessary for significant accounts and disclosures.

In determining appropriate substantive procedures, the auditor considers: (a) the source of potential misstatement and (b) the extent and type of potential misstatement. Consider the typical entries into accounts receivable, including the related allowance account, as follows:

Accounts Receivable

Previous balance	Cash receipts
Revenue	Write-offs
Adjustments	Adjustments

Allowance for Uncollectible Accounts

Write-offs	Previous balance
	Current provision

Note that multiple processes affect the account balances. Some of the processes contain subjectivity and are considered high risk—for example, determining how much of a receivable balance will ultimately be uncollectible, while others are less subjective and more routine, such as recording cash receipts.

- *Revenue*—The processing of routine transactions is usually computerized with controls built into the process. However, because of recurring evidence that companies that want to boost reported sales and/or earnings often do so by overriding controls related to the recording of revenue, the SEC has designated revenue recognition as high risk, requiring the auditor to do some direct tests of account balances, including receivables. These problematic overrides often occur in conjunction with special contracts or unusual shipments near the end of the year.
- *Cash receipts*—The processing of cash receipts is usually automated with implementation of controls. If an organization has effective segregation of duties, the likelihood of misstatement is relatively small.
- *Current provision for uncollectible accounts*—Most companies rely heavily on previous experience in making these estimates. Recent SEC cases indicate that the allowance is often subject to misstatements based on: (a) inaccurate or nonrelevant data fed into the model and (b) motivation of management to meet earnings goals and therefore allowing subjectivity and bias to enter into the estimate.
- *Write-offs*—The determination of when to write off account balances is subjective.
- *Adjustments*—Adjustments, other than those noted previously, should be rare. If there are significant adjustments, the auditor should test the process or the adjustments to determine the appropriate balance.

Similar analyses will be made for other related accounts and will incorporate the following concepts:

- Assertions affected by highly subjective estimates usually require direct tests of the account balances.
- Nonstandard and large adjusting entries should be reviewed and tested using appropriate substantive procedures.

Dual-Purpose Tests
Why It Matters

This feature notes that some audit efficiencies can result if the auditor performs substantive procedures at the same time as performing tests of controls.

In some situations, the auditor might perform a substantive procedure concurrently with a test of a control, if both are relevant to that assertion; this is called a **dual-purpose test**. The auditor should design dual-purpose tests to achieve the objectives of both the test of the control and the substantive procedure. Also, when performing a dual-purpose test, the auditor should evaluate the results of the test in forming conclusions about both the assertion and the effectiveness of the control being tested. Dual-purpose testing can be an efficient way to audit some assertions.

Not Performing Sufficient Appropriate Substantive Audit Procedures Leads to Low Audit Quality
Why It Matters

This feature makes the point that a failure to perform sufficient substantive procedures is indicative of a low-quality audit.

The PCAOB performs periodic inspections of audit firms that conduct audits of public companies. Following are excerpts from inspection reports indicating that sufficient appropriate substantive audit procedures had not been performed.

- "The Firm failed to perform sufficient substantive procedures to test a number of significant accounts, including revenue, accounts receivable, inventory, and certain accruals…."

- "The Firm failed to review contracts or perform other substantive procedures, beyond inquiry of management, to test the completeness of deferred sales and the completeness and accuracy of adjustments to revenue for promotional and rebate allowances."
- "The Firm failed to sufficiently test the valuation of accounts receivable and net revenue."
- "In this audit, the Firm failed to perform sufficient procedures to evaluate the reasonableness of a significant assumption management used to calculate the gain on the sale of a business."

It's Your Turn!
Prompt for Critical Thinking #3

Access the PCAOB's website and search for the 2016 inspection report for KPMG in the United States.

a. How many audit engagements did the PCAOB inspect? _____
b. How many audit deficiencies did the PCAOB identify? _____
c. List five deficiencies in audit planning, substantive testing, and/or documentation that the PCAOB has uncovered that you consider to be the most damaging to KPMG's reputation.

- _____
- _____
- _____
- _____
- _____

- The size of the account (materiality) influences, but does not totally dictate, the substantive procedures that should be performed.
- The extent and results of control testing performed by management, as well as the control testing performed by the auditor, will influence the substantive procedures of the account balance to be performed.
- The evidence the auditor has from risk assessment procedures and tests of controls influences the substantive procedures to be performed.
- The existence of other corroborating tests of the account balance, such as the knowledge gained from testing related accounts, affects substantive procedures to be performed.

Exhibit 5.11 contains a summary of the effects of some of these evidence factors on substantive procedures.

While performing substantive procedures, the auditor may identify misstatements—both material and immaterial—in the financial statements. The auditor accumulates a list of any identified misstatements for consideration prior to determining the appropriate audit opinion to issue.

Example: Effect of Nature of Misstatements on Audit Procedures

In determining appropriate audit procedures to perform, the auditor considers which account balances might be misstated and how they might be misstated. Assume the following scenario related to accounts receivable. Consistent with the relevant professional guidance, the auditor has assessed revenue to be high risk, even though management has concluded that internal controls over transactions processing are effective. A preliminary analytical review of the last quarter (conducted as part of the risk assessment procedures) led to the identification of a large number of sales with nonstandard contractual terms. After reading a sample of the sales contracts and testing controls, the auditor concludes that there is an unacceptable level of residual risk in the revenue account. The auditor identified a number of ways in which the account could be misstated. For example, sales might:

- Be recorded in the wrong period
- Contain unusual rights-of-return provisions that have not been accounted for correctly
- Contain terms more consistent with a consignment than a sale
- Be concentrated with few customers, many of whom are international customers and may have different credit risks than most other customers

Given the identified risks, the auditor decides to expand substantive audit procedures of the recorded transactions that have unusual sales terms and to focus on the existence and valuation assertions. The auditor has decided not to perform any substantive analytical procedures; the auditor will only perform substantive tests of details. In order to bring the residual risk to an acceptable level,

Exhibit 5.11

The Relationship Between Risk Assessment and Planned Substantive Procedures

Factor	If Auditor Assessment Is:	Effect on Extent/Nature of Substantive Procedures
Subjectivity of accounting process	High	More/more rigorous
Materiality of account balance	High	More/more rigorous
Effectiveness of internal control as assessed by management and the auditor	Internal controls are effective	Less/less rigorous

5-41 The auditor is expected to perform substantive procedures for each relevant assertion of each significant account and disclosure. (T/F)

5-42 Substantive procedures include substantive analytical procedures and tests of details. (T/F)

5-43 In performing substantive procedures, which of the following statements provides appropriate guidance to the auditor?

a. The auditor can perform both substantive analytical procedures and substantive tests of details.

b. The auditor should perform substantive procedures for all assertions of all financial statement accounts.

c. The auditor should perform more (or more rigorous) substantive procedures when control risk is low than when control risk is high.

d. All of the above statements provide appropriate guidance.

e. Only two of the above statements (a–c) provide appropriate guidance.

5-44 In which of the following scenarios is the auditor most likely to obtain more (or more rigorous) substantive evidence?

a. When subjectivity related to the assertion is low.

b. When controls are determined to be operating effectively.

c. When the account is immaterial.

d. When the design of controls is determined to be ineffective.

the auditor gathers substantive evidence on the revenue (and receivables) associated with the unusual contracts and identifies sales that have these special terms. In testing receivables, the auditor decides to concentrate accounts receivable tests on a combination of large accounts plus all of those that have unusual sales terms. Confirmations will be sent to both of those groups, with follow-up where confirmations are not returned, or where the auditor might suspect the validity of the contract, the customer, or the possibility of **side agreements** (an agreement made between the organization and its customer that includes agreements made outside of publicly known contracts) affecting the contracts.

Phase V—Completing the Audit and Making Reporting Decisions

In Phase V, the auditor: (a) completes various review and communication activities and (b) makes a decision about what type(s) of opinion(s) to issue. Examples of review and communication activities include assessing detected misstatements and identified control deficiencies; reviewing the adequacy of financial statement disclosures; performing final analytical review procedures; communicating with the audit committee and management about identified control deficiencies; and performing an engagement quality review.

After completing the required review and communication activities, the auditor decides on the appropriate opinion(s) to issue. In an integrated audit, the auditor issues an opinion on both the financial statements and internal control. The opinions can be issued in one report or in two separate reports. However, if separate reports are issued, each report must refer to the other. In *Chapter 1*, we presented Ford's combined audit report, which includes an unqualified opinion on the financial statements and an unqualified opinion on internal controls. If the auditor has reservations about the fair presentation of the financial statements, the audit opinion on the financial statements would be modified and expanded to explain the nature of the auditor's reservations.

If the auditor has reservations about the effectiveness of the client's internal controls, the auditor would issue an adverse opinion on internal controls. *Exhibit 5.12* provides an example of an audit report with an unqualified opinion on the

Exhibit 5.12
Example of Adverse Opinion on Internal Control and
Unqualified Opinion on the Financial Statements
(bold emphasis added in report)

Report of Independent Registered Public Accounting Firm

To the Board of Directors and Stockholders of Diamond Foods, Inc.

In our opinion, the accompanying consolidated balance sheet as of July 31, 2013 and the related consolidated statements of operations, comprehensive income (loss), stockholders' equity, and cash flows for the year then ended present fairly, in all material respects, the financial position of Diamond Foods, Inc. and its subsidiaries at July 31, 2013, and the results of their operations and their cash flows for the year then ended in conformity with accounting principles generally accepted in the United States of America. **Also in our opinion, the Company did not maintain, in all material respects, effective internal control over financial reporting as of July 31, 2013, based on criteria established in Internal Control—Integrated Frame work issued by the Committee of Sponsoring Organizations of the Treadway Commission (COSO) because material weaknesses in internal control over financial reporting related to the accounting for complex and non-routine transactions and due to certain key accounting personnel who have the ability to prepare and post journal entries without an independent review by someone without the ability to prepare and post journal entries existed as of that date.** A material weakness is a deficiency, or a combination of deficiencies, in internal control over financial reporting, such that there is a reasonable possibility that a material misstatement of the annual or interim financial statements will not be prevented or detected on a timely basis. The material weaknesses referred to above are described in Management's Report on Internal Control Over Financial Reporting appearing under Item 9A. **We considered these material weaknesses in determining the nature, timing, and extent of audit tests applied in our audit of the July 31, 2013 consolidated financial statements, and our opinion regarding the effectiveness of the Company's internal control over financial reporting does not affect our opinion on those consolidated financial statements.** The Company's management is responsible for these financial statements, for maintaining effective internal control over financial reporting and for its assessment of the effectiveness of internal control over financial reporting included in management's report referred to above. Our responsibility is to express opinions on these financial statements and on the Company's internal control over financial reporting based on our integrated audit.

We conducted our audit in accordance with the standards of the Public Company Accounting Oversight Board (United States). Those standards require that we plan and perform the audit to obtain reasonable assurance about whether the financial statements are free of material misstatement and whether effective internal control over financial reporting was maintained in all material respects. Our audit of the financial statements included examining, on a test basis, evidence supporting the amounts and disclosures in the financial statements, assessing the accounting principles used and significant estimates made by management, and evaluating the overall financial statement presentation. Our audit of internal control over financial reporting included obtaining an understanding of internal control over financial reporting, assessing the risk that a material weakness exists, and testing and evaluating the design and operating effectiveness of internal control based on the assessed risk. Our audit also included performing such other procedures as we considered necessary in the circumstances. We believe that our audit provides a reasonable basis for our opinions.

A company's internal control over financial reporting is a process designed to provide reasonable assurance regarding the reliability of financial reporting and the preparation of financial statements for external purposes in accordance with generally accepted accounting principles. A company's internal control over financial reporting includes those policies and procedures that (i) pertain to the maintenance of records that, in reasonable detail, accurately and fairly reflect the transactions and dispositions of the assets of the company; (ii) provide reasonable assurance that transactions are recorded as necessary to permit preparation of financial statements in accordance with generally accepted accounting principles, and that receipts and expenditures of the company are being made only in accordance with authorizations of management and directors of the company; and (iii) provide reasonable assurance regarding prevention or timely detection of unauthorized acquisition, use, or disposition of the company's assets that could have a material effect on the financial statements.

Because of its inherent limitations, internal control over financial reporting may not prevent or detect misstatements. Also, projections of any evaluation of effectiveness to future periods are subject to the risk that controls may become inadequate because of changes in conditions, or that the degree of compliance with the policies or procedures may deteriorate.

/s/ PricewaterhouseCoopers LLP

San Francisco, California
October 9, 2013

financial statements and an adverse opinion on internal control. Important aspects of *Exhibit 5.12* related to the opinion on internal control include:

- The report describes the material weaknesses but does not discuss any actions being taken by management to remediate the weaknesses.
- The report does not discuss whether the control weaknesses were first identified by management or by the auditor.
- The report recognizes the integrated nature of the audit in that the auditors considered the identified material weaknesses when planning the financial statement audit.

Check Your Basic Knowledge

5-45 Once the auditor completes the substantive procedures in Phase IV, the auditor is in a position to issue the audit opinion.   (T/F)

5-46 If the auditor issues an opinion on the client's internal controls and the client's financial statements, the auditor is required to issue two separate reports.   (T/F)

5-47 Which of the following procedures is <u>least</u> likely to be performed during Phase V of the audit opinion formulation process?

   a. Assessment of misstatements detected during the performance of substantive procedures and tests of controls.

   b. Performance of preliminary analytical review procedures.

   c. Performance of an engagement quality review.

   d. Determination of the appropriate audit opinion(s) to issue.

5-48 Which of the following statements is <u>true</u> regarding the auditor's report on a public company's internal control over financial reporting?

   a. The audit report will indicate whether it was the company or the auditor that initially identified the indicated material weakness.

   b. The auditor must explicitly reference the criteria for evaluating internal control using, for example, the COSO framework.

   c. The audit is performed in conjunction with the auditing standards promulgated by the AICPA's ASB.

   d. The auditor must report on whether management used the appropriate tools in its assessment of internal control over financial reporting.

LO 9

Apply the frameworks for professional decision making and ethical decision making for decisions made when conducting an audit.

Applying Decision-Making Frameworks

The following *End of Chapter* materials provide you an opportunity to apply the frameworks for professional decision making and ethical decision making for decisions made when conducting an audit: *5-42* and *5-44*.

Let's Review

- Auditors in the United States follow auditing guidance issued by the American Institute of Certified Public Accountants (AICPA), the Public Company Accounting Oversight Board (PCAOB), and the International Auditing and Assurance Standards Board (IAASB). The applicability of each of these alternative standards depends on the public trading status of the organization and the location of the exchange on which its securities trade. For example, the auditor of a private U.S. company will use AICPA standards, whereas the auditor of a public U.S. company will use PCAOB standards. (LO 1)

- The foundational principles underlying the auditing standards are stated somewhat differently depending on the standards setter, i.e., PCAOB, AICPA, or IAASB. But, the most fundamental tenant is that audits must be conducted in a quality manner. With respect to the PCAOB, the principles include exercising due professional care, obtaining reasonable assurance about the financial statements, maintaining an independent mental attitude, and having appropriate professional qualifications. The AICPA's principles articulate the purpose of the audit, the premise that management has responsibility over the financial statements while auditors are responsible for competence, ethics, and skepticism, and the performance and reporting standards by which auditors should adhere. The IAASB is a bit more general, focusing on obtaining reasonable assurance and reporting on the financial statements and communicating the auditor's findings. (LO 2)

- There are five phases of the audit opinion process: (I) making client acceptance and continuance decisions, (II) performing risk assessment, (III) obtaining evidence about internal control operating effectiveness, (IV) obtaining substantive evidence about accounts, disclosures, and assertions, and (V) completing the audit and making reporting decisions. (LO 3)

- Similar transactions that are linked by procedures and controls and that affect related accounts are often grouped together for analysis (and audit) purposes and are referred to as an accounting cycle (or process). The cycle concept provides a convenient way to break the audit up into manageable sections of related accounts. (LO 4)

- Managers make the following assertions when they present the unaudited statements to the auditor: existence or occurrence (e.g., that sales are valid, i.e., not overstated); completeness (that liabilities are actually recorded, i.e., not understated); valuation or allocation (i.e., that net accounts receivable after recording bad debt expense) is correct; rights and obligations (e.g., that the organization has valid title to a fixed asset); and presentation and disclosure (e.g., that long-term debt is accurately portrayed on the face of the financials and is completely discussed in the footnotes to the financial statements). (LO 5)

- Audit evidence is information obtained by the auditor to support the audit opinion. Most of the auditor's work in forming an opinion consists of obtaining and evaluating audit evidence through performing audit procedures. Audit procedures fall into three categories: risk assessment, tests of controls, and substantive procedures. (LO 6)

- The auditor prepares audit documentation to provide evidence that the audit was planned and performed in accordance with auditing standards. The terms *working papers* or *workpapers* are sometimes used to refer to audit documentation. The auditor should document the procedures performed, the audit evidence examined, and the conclusions reached with respect to relevant financial statement assertions to prove that they have obtained reasonable evidence to support their audit opinion, thereby yielding audit quality. (LO 7)

- Auditors complete the following activities when working to provide reasonable assurance about a client's financial statements: (1) they make client acceptance and continuance decisions as part of the audit firm's overall portfolio management strategy, (2) identifying and responding to risks of material misstatement, (3) evaluating the client's controls in terms of existence, appropriateness, and determining whether, in fact, the controls are being implemented by the client, (4) obtaining substantive evidence about accounts, disclosures, and assertions, and (5) completing the audit and making reporting decisions. (LO 8)

Significant Terms

Accounting cycle   Recording and processing transactions that affect a group of related accounts. The cycle begins when a transaction occurs and ends when it is recorded in the financial statements.

Audit documentation   The record of audit procedures performed, relevant audit evidence obtained, and conclusions the auditor reached (terms such as *working papers* or *workpapers* are also sometimes used).

Audit evidence   Information used by the auditor in arriving at the conclusions on which the auditor's opinion is based.

Audit procedures Procedures designed to obtain audit evidence to support the audit opinion(s). Three categories of procedures include risk assessment procedures, tests of controls, and substantive procedures (including substantive analytical procedures and tests of details).

Audit program An audit document that lists the audit procedures to be followed in gathering audit evidence and helps those in charge of the audit to monitor the progress and supervise the work.

Control risk The risk that a misstatement that could occur in an assertion about a class of transaction, account balance, or disclosure and that could be material, either individually or when aggregated with other misstatements, will not be prevented, or detected and corrected, on a timely basis by the organization's internal control. Control risk is a function of the effectiveness of the design and operation of internal control.

Controls reliance audit An audit that includes tests of controls and substantive procedures.

Dual-purpose test A substantive test and a related test of a relevant control that are performed concurrently, for example, a substantive test of sales transactions performed concurrently with a test of controls over those transactions.

Inherent risk The susceptibility of an assertion about a class of transaction, account balance, or disclosure to a misstatement that could be material, either individually or when aggregated with other misstatements, before consideration of any related controls.

Relevant assertion An assertion having a meaningful bearing on whether a financial statement account is fairly stated.

Risk assessment procedure A procedure performed by the auditor to obtain information for identifying and assessing the risks of material misstatement in the financial statements whether due to error or fraud. Risk assessment procedures by themselves do not provide sufficient, appropriate evidence on which to base an audit opinion but are used for purposes of planning the audit.

Side agreement An agreement made between the organization and its customer that includes agreements made outside of publicly known contracts.

Substantive audit An audit that includes substantive procedures and does not include tests of controls.

Substantive procedure An audit procedure designed to detect material misstatements at the assertion level. Substantive procedures comprise tests of details and substantive analytical procedures.

Sufficient appropriate audit evidence A measure of the quality of audit evidence (i.e., its adequacy, relevance, and reliability in providing support for the conclusions on which the auditor's opinion is based).

Test of controls An audit procedure designed to evaluate the operating effectiveness of controls in preventing, or detecting and correcting, material misstatements, typically at the assertion level.

Top-side journal entries Adjusting journal entries made by top management in the period-end financial reporting process.

Prompts for Critical Thinking

Prompt for Critical Thinking #1

- Revenue: accounts include sales, sales returns and allowances, sales discounts, account receivable, allowance for uncollectible accounts, warranty liabilities and expenses, bad debt expense, sales commission expense, cash
- Cash and Marketable Securities: various cash accounts (bank accounts, petty cash), marketable securities
- Capital Acquisitions and Repayments: notes payable, bonds payable, interest expense, accrued interest, capital stock, retained earnings, dividends payable

Prompt for Critical Thinking #2

- Audit programs
- Analyses prepared by the client or the auditor
- Memorandums
- Summaries of significant findings or issues
- Letters of confirmation and representation
- Checklists
- Correspondence (including email) concerning significant findings or issues

Prompt for Critical Thinking #3

a. 20
b. 11
c. There exists a plethora of specific deficiencies identified in the inspection report, and they exist in three broad categories:

Issue	Audits
Failure to sufficiency test the design and/or operating effectiveness of controls that the Firm selected for testing.	<u>14 Audits:</u> Issuers A, B, C, D, E, F, G, I, L, M, N, P, Q, and S
Failure to sufficiency test controls over, or sufficiency test, the accuracy and completeness of issuer-produced data or reports.	<u>8 Audits:</u> Issuers B, C, D, E, F, G, J, and O
Failure to perform substantive procedures to obtain sufficient evidence as a result of relying too heavily on controls (due to deficiencies in testing controls).	<u>7 Audits:</u> Issuers A, B, D, F, J, L, and O

Review Questions and Short Cases

INTERNATIONAL

NOTE: Completing *Review Questions and Short Cases does* not require the student to reference additional resources and materials.

NOTE: We make special note of problems addressing fraud, international issues, professional skepticism, and ethics.

5-1 **LO 1** Refer to *Exhibit 5.1.* Briefly describe the relevance of the following standard setters for auditors.
  a. AICPA
  b. PCAOB
  c. IAASB

5-2 **LO 1** The PCAOB has the authority to set auditing standards for all audits of public companies registered in the United States. The AICPA continues to set auditing standards for nonpublic companies through its Auditing Standards Board (ASB).
  a. What are the pros and cons of having the same audit standards for both public and nonpublic companies?
  b. In what ways might you expect auditing standards for audits of nonpublic companies to differ from the standards for public companies? Identify three ways and state your rationale.

5-3 **LO 2**
  a. Describe the guidance that the PCAOB provides within the General Auditing Standards about the responsibilities and functions of the independent auditor.
  b. Then think about the four additional requests that the PCAOB makes:
    • Exercise due professional care, including professional skepticism

- Obtain *reasonable assurance* about whether the financial statements are free of material misstatement, whether caused by error or fraud, or whether any material weaknesses exist as of the date of management's assessment
- Maintain an independence in mental attitude
- Have the appropriate professional qualifications

If you had to order these four requests, which would you order as most to least important? Explain your rationale.

5-4 `LO 2` Compare the PCAOB's General Standards with the AICPA's "Principles Governing an Audit in Accordance with Generally Accepted Auditing Standards."

5-5 `LO 3` Refer to *Exhibit 5.2*. What are the client responsibilities that are relevant to the auditor? How do those responsibilities affect the audit opinion formulation process?

5-6 `LO 3` Refer to *Exhibit 5.3*. List the phases of the audit opinion formulation process. What are the primary activities within each of the five phases?

5-7 `LO 4` Professional guidance indicates that the auditor should consider revenue recognition to be high risk in planning an audit of a company's financial statements.

   a. Identify the activities that affect the revenue cycle.
   b. Identify the financial statement accounts typically associated with the revenue cycle.

5-8 `LO 4` Identify the accounts associated with the acquisitions and payments for long-lived assets cycle.

5-9 `LO 5` Assume that an organization asserts that it has $35 million in net accounts receivable. Describe specifically what management is asserting with respect to net accounts receivable.

5-10 `LO 6` Describe how auditing standards affect the design of audit programs.

5-11 `LO 6` What is an audit program? What information should an auditor gather before developing an audit program?

5-12 `LO 7` Define the term *audit documentation* and provide examples.

5-13 `LO 8` List various procedures the auditor would perform in evaluating whether to accept a potential client.

5-14 `LO 8` List factors that might affect an audit firm's client portfolio.

5-15 `LO 8` How do the sources of risk of misstatement in *Exhibit 5.6* help the auditor plan the audit?

FRAUD

5-16 `LO 8` Refer to the *Focus on Fraud* feature "Controls to Address Fraud Risk." When assessing internal control design effectiveness, what types of controls would an auditor expect a client to have in place to address fraud risk? Why are these controls important?

5-17 `LO 8` Refer to the *Why It Matters* feature "Documenting the Auditor's Understanding of an Organization's Internal Controls." What should an auditor document regarding the design of controls? Why is this documentation important?

5-18 `LO 8` Explain how the auditor's preliminary assessment of control risk affects planned substantive audit procedures.

5-19 **LO 8** An important part of Phase II of the audit opinion formulation process is determining how to respond to identified risks of material misstatement. As indicated in *Exhibit 5.7*, the auditor might respond by modifying evidence decisions about the extent or nature of the substantive audit evidence to be collected. Using the box of evidence analogy, explain these responses to identified risks.

5-20 **LO 8** Segregation of duties is an important internal control. However, this control is often a challenge for smaller businesses because they do not have sufficient staff. Normally, a segregation of duties deficiency results in either a significant deficiency or a material weakness in internal control. For each segregation of duties deficiency identified as (1)–(6), complete the following three tasks:

a. Indicate the risk to financial reporting that is associated with the inadequacy of the segregation of duties.
b. Identify other controls that might mitigate the segregation of duties risks.
c. Identify possible tests of controls for the mitigating controls selected in (b).

The inadequate segregation of duty situations includes:
1. The same individual handles cash receipts, the bank reconciliation, and customer complaints.
2. The same person prepares billings to customers and also collects cash receipts and applies them to customer accounts.
3. The person who prepares billings to customers does not handle cash but does the monthly bank reconciliation, which, in turn, is reviewed by the controller.
4. The controller is responsible for making all accounting estimates and adjusting journal entries. The company does not have a chief financial officer (CFO) and has two clerks who report to the controller.
5. A start-up company has very few transactions, less than $1 million in revenue per year, and has only one accounting person. The company's transactions are not complex.
6. The company has one computer person who is responsible for running packaged software. The individual has access to the computer to update software and can also access records.

5-21 **LO 8** In a financial statement audit, what controls will an auditor test?

5-22 **LO 8** Refer to *Exhibit 5.8*. What controls might an auditor test related to the valuation assertion for the sales account?

5-23 **LO 8** A review of business failures as described in the financial press, such as the *Wall Street Journal*, suggests that the control environment is one of the major contributors to the failure. Often the tone at the top at the failed companies reflects a disdain for controls and an emphasis on accomplishing specific financial reporting objectives such as reporting increased profitability. How will the auditor's assessment of the operating effectiveness of the control environment affect the design and conduct of an audit? Consider both a positive and negative assessment.

5-24 **LO 8** Auditing standards indicate that if the preliminary control risk assessment is low, the auditor then gains assurance that the controls are operating effectively.

a. What is meant by testing the operating effectiveness of controls? How does an auditor decide which controls to test?
b. How is the auditor's assessment of control risk affected if a documented control procedure is not operating effectively? Explain the effect of such an assessment on substantive audit procedures.

ETHICS

5-25 **LO 8** An important principle of the control environment is the organization's commitment to ethics and integrity (COSO Principle 1). How might an auditor test the operating effectiveness of a client's commitment to ethics and integrity?

5-26 **LO 8** Is the auditor required to test the operating effectiveness of controls on every audit engagement? Explain.

5-27 **LO 8** What are the external auditor testing requirements of internal control over financial reporting for:

a. Large, publicly held companies?
b. Nonpublic companies and small, publicly held companies?

5-28 **LO 8** When the auditor determines that controls are not operating effectively, the auditor needs to consider the kind of misstatements that could occur, how they might occur, and how the auditor would adjust substantive audit procedures. Assume that the authorization process for ordering inventory contained a material weakness. Identify the accounts that could contain misstatements, how the misstatements might occur, and how the auditor would adjust substantive audit procedures because of the material weakness.

5-29 **LO 8** In analyzing the results of the tests of controls, there are two potential outcomes: (a) deficiencies are identified and (b) deficiencies are not identified. What are alternative courses of action for the financial statement audit associated with each of these alternative outcomes?

5-30 **LO 8** If a company's control risk is initially assessed as low, the auditor needs to gather evidence on the operating effectiveness of the controls. For each of the following control activities listed as (1)–(10), complete the following two tasks:

a. Describe the test of control that the auditor would use to determine the operating effectiveness of the control.
b. Briefly describe how substantive tests of account balances should be modified if the auditor finds that the control is not working as planned. In doing so, indicate: (a) what misstatement could occur because of the control deficiency, and (b) how the auditor's substantive tests should be expanded to test for the potential misstatement.

1. Credit approval by the credit department is required before salespersons accept any order of more than $15,000 and for all customers who have a past-due balance higher than $22,000.
2. All merchandise receipts are recorded on prenumbered receiving slips. The controller's department periodically accounts for the numerical sequence of the receiving slips.

3. Payments for goods received are made only by the accounts payable department on receipt of a vendor invoice, which is then matched for prices and quantities with approved purchase orders and receiving slips.

4. The accounts receivable bookkeeper is not allowed to issue credit memos or to approve the write-off of accounts.

5. Cash receipts are opened by a mail clerk, who prepares remittances to send to accounts receivable for recording. The clerk prepares a daily deposit slip, which is sent to the controller. Deposits are made daily by the controller.

6. Employees are added to the payroll master file by the payroll department only after receiving a written authorization from the personnel department.

7. The only individuals who have access to the payroll master file are the payroll department head and the payroll clerk responsible for maintaining the payroll file. Access to the file is controlled by computer passwords.

8. Edit tests built into the computerized payroll program prohibit the processing of weekly payroll hours in excess of 53 and prohibit the payment to an employee for more than three different job classifications during a one-week period.

9. Credit memos are issued to customers only on the receipt of merchandise or the approval of the sales department for adjustments.

10. A salesperson cannot approve a sales return or price adjustment that exceeds 6% of the cumulative sales for the year for any one customer. The divisional sales manager must approve any subsequent approvals of adjustments for such a customer.

ETHICS

5-31 **LO 8** The auditor of a public company client in the retailing industry is planning an integrated audit. The company has approximately 260 retail stores, primarily in the southeastern United States.

a. Explain why an assessment of the company's control environment is important to planning the integrated audit.

b. The company claims that it has a strong control environment, including a culture of high integrity and ethics (COSO Principle 1), a commitment to financial reporting competencies (COSO Principle 4), and an independent, active, and knowledgeable board of directors (COSO Principle 2). For each of these principles, develop an audit program to gather evidence that these principles are operating effectively. In developing your answer, indicate the type of audit procedures to use.

5-32 **LO 8** Refer to *Exhibit 5.9*. Assume that you are going to test computerized controls that your client has put in place. What is the important objective for you to consider when performing that testing? What are some possible tests of controls that you could perform? What are the audit implications if the controls are not working effectively?

5-33 **LO 8** Assume that you are planning to test a client's account reconciliation. You could test either by inspecting documentation of the reconciliation or by reperforming the reconciliation. Which procedure is more rigorous? What factors would cause you to choose reperformance instead of documentation inspection?

FRAUD

5-34 **LO 8** Assume that you want to test an entity-wide control related to the control environment. Specifically, you want to obtain evidence that the audit committee has periodic discussions about fraud. Recall that tests of controls include inquiry, observation, inspection of documentation, and reperformance of the control. Which approaches do you think you would use when testing this control relating to the control environment? Explain your answer.

5-35 **LO 8** Refer to *Exhibit 5.10*. What are some of the key decisions that influence the substantive testing that the auditor will perform?

5-36 **LO 8** Refer to the *Why It Matters* feature "Dual-Purpose Tests" What is a dual-purpose test, and why might an auditor choose to perform a dual-purpose test?

5-37 **LO 8** Refer to *Exhibit 5.11*. Explain how the factors in the first column affect the auditor's decision about substantive testing.

5-38 **LO 8** What substantive procedures could an auditor use to determine that all purchases debited to a fixed asset account in the current year are properly valued?

5-39 **LO 8** Audits of financial statements are designed to determine whether account balances are materially correct. Assume that your client is a construction company with the following assets on its balance sheet:
- Construction equipment: $1,278,000
- Accumulated depreciation: $386,000
- Leased construction equipment: $550,000
  a. Describe a substantive audit procedure that can be used to determine that all leased equipment that should have been capitalized during the year was actually capitalized (as opposed to being treated as a lease expense).
  b. The construction equipment account shows that the company purchased approximately $400,000 of new equipment this year. Identify a substantive audit procedure that will determine whether the equipment account was properly accounted for during the year.
  c. Assuming the auditor determines the debits to construction equipment were proper during the year, what other information does the auditor need to know to have reasonable assurance that the construction equipment—net of depreciation—is properly reflected on the balance sheet?
  d. How can an auditor determine that the client has assigned an appropriate useful life to the equipment and has depreciated it accurately?

5-40 **LO 8** The auditor provides an opinion on internal control over financial reporting for one of its public company clients.
  a. Is the auditor also required to audit the company's financial statements at the same time? Explain.
  b. Does an unqualified report on internal controls over financial reporting imply that the company does not have any significant deficiencies in controls? Explain.
  c. If the auditor did not detect any material misstatements in the financial statements, can the auditor conclude that there are no material weaknesses in internal control? Explain.

5-41 **LO 8** Review the external auditor's report on the integrated audit, presented in *Exhibit 5.12*. What are the important elements in that report related to internal control?

ETHICS

5-42 **LO 8, 9** The auditor is evaluating the internal control of a new client. Management has prepared its assessment of internal control and has concluded that it has some deficiencies, but no significant deficiencies and no material weaknesses. However, in reviewing the work performed by management, the auditor observes the following:

- Sample sizes taken were never more than ten transactions, and most of the tests of operating effectiveness were based on a sample of one, performed as part of a walkthrough of a transaction.
- Management has fired the former CFO and a new CFO has not been appointed, but management indicates that it is searching for a new CFO, and it currently has depth in the accounting area.
- The company has no formal whistle-blowing function because management has an open-door policy so that anyone with a problem can take it up the line.
- Management's approach to monitoring internal control is to compare budget with actual expenses and investigate differences.

In response to inquiries by the auditor, management responds that its procedures are sufficient to support its report on internal control.

The auditor's subsequent work yields the following:

- Many controls do not operate in the way described by management, and the procedures are not effective.
- There is no awareness of, or adherence to, the company's code of conduct.
- The accounting department does not have a depth of talent; moreover, although the department can handle most transactions, it is not capable of dealing with new contracts that the firm has entered into. The response of management is, "That is why we pay you auditors the big bucks—to help us make these decisions."

The auditor reaches a conclusion that there are material weaknesses in internal control, thus differing from management's assessment. Management points out that every issue where there is a disagreement is a subjective issue, and there is no one position that is better than the others. Management's position is that these are management's financial statements, and the auditor should accommodate management's view because there are no right answers.

a. The partner in charge of the job appears to be persuaded that the differences are indeed subjective and is proposing that an unqualified opinion on internal controls be issued. Recognize that this is a first-year client—and an important one to the office. Apply the ethical decision-making framework presented in *Chapter 1* to explore the actions the audit manager should take regarding: (1) whether to disagree with the partner and (2) if there is a disagreement, to what level it should be taken in the firm.

b. Given the deficiencies noted, does the information support the finding that there is a material weakness in internal control? What are the major factors that lead you to that conclusion?

c. Assume that the engagement team makes a decision that there is a material weakness in internal control. Write two or three paragraphs describing those weaknesses that could be included in the audit report.

Fraud Focus: Contemporary and Historical Cases

ETHICS

FRAUD

INTERNATIONAL

PROFESSIONAL SKEPTICISM

5-43 **ERNST & YOUNG UK (LO 1, 2, 6, 7, 8)**

Auditors who adhere to the professional auditing standards are viewed as conducting a quality audit. A lack of adherence to the professional auditing standards heightens the risk that the auditor will provide an unqualified audit opinion on financial statements that are materially misstated. This lesson is highlighted in the 2004–2006 audits of Thornton Precision Components, Limited (TPC) performed by Ernst & Young, LLP UK (E&Y UK).

TPC became a wholly owned U.K. subsidiary of Symmetry Medical, Inc. in 2003. Symmetry became a public company in 2004 and was listed on a U.S. stock exchange. Its consolidated financial statements included TPC's financial data. Beginning in 2003, Ernst & Young, LLP (E&Y US) became Symmetry's audit firm. In connection with the 2004–2006 audits of Symmetry, E&Y US engaged E&Y UK to perform audits of TPC, using PCAOB auditing standards. During the 2004–2006 audits, E&Y US relied on E&Y UK's audits to issue unqualified audit opinions for Symmetry.

From 1999 through September 2007, TPC's management participated in multiple schemes to increase TPC's revenues, net income, and other performance indicators. These schemes included booking fictitious revenues, understating costs of goods sold, creating fictitious inventories, and improperly capitalizing certain expenses. The fraud at TPC was not discovered by the auditors but only came to light in 2007 when a TPC employee alerted Symmetry's CEO to the fraud. In 2008, Symmetry restated its financial statements, which included, among other items, significant reductions in Symmetry's net income.

In 2012, the SEC concluded that E&Y UK (a firm registered with the PCAOB) had conducted its audits in such a way that the audits did not adhere to the relevant professional auditing standards. Deficiencies in E&Y UK's 2004–2006 audits of TPC included a failure to perform appropriate procedures to audit the accounts receivable balances; adequately review top-side journal entries; properly audit inventory; and a failure to plan, staff, and supervise the audits. During the audit, the audit partner and manager did not appropriately question management's representations, did not fully document the results of testing, did not appropriately consider the risks of misstatements due to fraud, and did not exercise due professional care and professional skepticism. The SEC prohibited both the audit manager and partner of TPC from auditing U.S. public companies for two years.

For further details, see Securities and Exchange Commission Accounting and Auditing Enforcement Release No. 3359 (January 2012).

a. What is the role of auditing standards and their underlying principles in promoting a quality audit?

b. What audit evidence is necessary for opining on a client's financial statements?

c. How does audit documentation provide evidence related to audit quality?

d. What audit activities are conducted during the audit opinion formulation process to provide reasonable assurance about a client's financial statements?

e. How does professional judgment and ethical decision making contribute to audit quality?

PROFESSIONAL SKEPTICISM

ETHICS **FRAUD**

INTERNATIONAL

5-44 **ERNST & YOUNG UK**
(LO 1, 2, 6, 7, 8, 9)

Refer to 5-43, which features details on the Ernst & Young-UK audits of Thornton Precision Components from 2004 to 2006. Use the ethical decision-making framework presented in *Chapter 1* to analyze the judgments made by the E&Y-UK audit partner responsible for the 2004–2006 audits of TPC.

FRAUD

5-45 **GENERAL MOTORS**
(LO 6, 8)

In March 2006, General Motors (GM) announced that it needed to restate its previous year's financial statements. Information from the *Wall Street Journal* describing the restatements includes:

- GM, which was already facing an SEC probe into its accounting practices, also disclosed that its 10-K report, when filed, will outline a series of accounting mistakes that will force the car maker to restate its earnings from 2000 to the first quarter of 2005. GM also said it was widening by $2 billion the loss it reported for 2005.

- Many of the other GM problems relate to rebates, or credits, from suppliers. Typically, suppliers offer an upfront payment in exchange for a promise by the customer to buy certain quantities of products over time. Under accounting rules, such rebates cannot be recorded until after the promised purchases are made.

- GM said that it concluded it had mistakenly recorded some of these payments prematurely. The biggest impact was in 2001, when the company said it overstated pretax income by $405 million as a result of prematurely recording supplier credits. Because the credits are being moved to later years, the impact in those years was less, and GM said it would have a deferred credit of $548 million that will help reduce costs in future periods. The issue of how to book rebates and other credits from suppliers is a thorny one that has tripped up other companies, ranging from the international supermarket chain Royal Ahold, N.V. to the U.S.-based Kmart Corporation.

- GM also said it had wrongly recorded a $27 million pretax gain from disposing of precious metals inventory in 2000, which it was obliged to buy back the following year.

- GM told investors not to rely on its previously reported results for the first quarter of 2005, saying it had underreported its loss by $149 million. GM said it had prematurely boosted the value it ascribed to cars it was leasing to rental-car companies, assuming they would be worth more after the car rental companies were done with them. GM previously had reported a loss of $1.1 billion, or $1.95 a share, for the first quarter (March 18, 2006).

You may assume all amounts are material.

a. Without determining whether the errors in accounting judgment were intentional or unintentional, discuss how the nature of the errors affects the auditor's judgment of the control environment and whether the auditor should conclude there are material weaknesses in internal control. What would your judgment be if the accounting treatment were deemed acceptable, but aggressive, by the company's CFO and CEO? How would those judgments affect the auditor's assessment of the control environment?

b. Describe the nature of the accounting judgment made by the company regarding the residual value of the cars it leases. What information and communication system should exist regarding the residual value of the cars returned from leasing? What controls should be in place? What evidence would the auditor need to evaluate the reasonableness of the change made by the company?

c. Explain the rebates, or upfront rebates, from the company's suppliers. Why would the suppliers pay the upfront credits? What is the proper accounting for the upfront credits? What controls should be in place to account for the upfront credits? How would the auditor test: (1) the controls over the accounting for the upfront credits and (2) the expense-offset account, or the liability account?

d. Do you believe that the material misstatements were the result of errors or fraud? Discuss the reasons for your opinion.

Application Activities

PROFESSIONAL SKEPTICISM

NOTE: Completing *Application Activities* requires students to reference additional resources and materials. Some *Application Activities* will require the student to reference relevant professional auditing standards. We make special note of these as *Auditing Standards Application Activities*.

5-46 PCAOB

(LO 1, 2, 6, 8) In April 2010, the PCAOB issued a disciplinary order instituting disciplinary proceedings, making findings, and imposing sanctions in the case of Robert T. Taylor, CPA (both the firm and the individual auditor). The order can be found in PCAOB Release No. 105-2010-006 at www.pcaobus.org. Obtain this release from the PCAOB website.

a. The order in the case of Robert T. Taylor recognizes that PCAOB standards require that an auditor exercise due professional care, exercise professional skepticism, and obtain sufficient evidence on which to base an opinion on the financial statements. Describe instances in which the respondents in the order did not adhere to these requirements.

b. Why is adhering to these professional requirements important for audit quality?

AUDITING STANDARDS APPLICATION ACTIVITY

5-47 PCAOB

(LO 7) Refer to the *Auditing Standards Exhibit* inside the front cover of this textbook. Identify the PCAOB AS that relates to audit documentation. Review that AS and describe the characteristics of good audit documentation that are noted in that standard.

5-48 LO 4, 7, 8 With your instructor's guidance, select a place where you have worked or an organization in which you have some acquaintance (relative or friend), and therefore have access. Choose one area of operations (cash receipts, sales, shipping, receiving, or payroll) for review. For the area selected:

a. Identify the major transactions processed.

b. Select a representative transaction and perform a walkthrough of the application to gain an understanding of processing and controls implemented to mitigate the risks of misstatements.

c. Document the important controls identified during the walkthrough.

d. Identify control procedures you would recommend to improve the organization's internal controls.

PROFESSIONAL SKEPTICISM

5-49 PCAOB
(LO 2, 3, 6, 7, 8) Two *Why It Matters* features in the chapter highlight audit deficiencies related to tests of controls and substantive procedures that were noted in PCAOB inspection reports. See "The Need for Performing Tests of Controls and Considering the Results " and "Not Performing Sufficient Appropriate Substantive Audit Procedures Leads to Low Audit Quality." Obtain a recent PCAOB inspection report of one of the Big 4 firms. Select several audit deficiencies identified in the report and determine which phase of the audit opinion formulation process the deficiency relates to. Discuss how the fundamental principle of professional skepticism might have been helpful in avoiding such deficiencies.

AUDITING STANDARDS
APPLICATION ACTIVITY

INTERNATIONAL

5-50 LO 5 Refer to the *Auditing Standards Exhibit* inside the front cover of this textbook. Identify the IAASB ISA that provides guidance on management assertions. List the management assertions identified in the IAASB ISA and compare and contrast the IAASB management assertions with those of the PCAOB.

AUDITING STANDARDS
APPLICATION ACTIVITY

INTERNATIONAL

5-51 Deloitte – Brazil
(LO 1, 2, 7)
Obtain the following PCAOB enforcement release: *https://pcaobus.org/Enforcement/Decisions/Documents/105-2016-031-Deloitte-Brazil.pdf*

a. What role did the audit engagement partner, Jose Domingos do Prado (hereafter, Prado), play in leading the Gol engagement and what role did he have in terms of interacting with the inspection team? How did he violate professional and ethical norms of behavior?

b. Describe the PCAOB rules and standards that are applicable to this case.

c. Locate AS 1215 on the PCAOB's website. Identify the paragraphs that are most relevant to the judgment errors that Prado made with respect to documentation requirements.

Academic Research Cases

NOTE: Completing the *Academic Research Cases* requires students to reference additional resources and materials.

SEARCH HINT

It is easy to locate academic research articles! Use a search engine such as Google Scholar or an electronic research platform such as ABI Inform, and search using the author names and part of the article title.

5-52 **LO 8** Locate and read the article listed below.

Franzel, J. M. (2014). A decade after Sarbanes-Oxley: The need for ongoing vigilance, monitoring, and research. *Accounting Horizons* 28(4): 917–930.

  a. What is the purpose of the study?
  b. Describe the design/method/approach used to conduct the study.
  c. What are the primary findings of the study?

5-53 **LO 7** Locate and read the article listed below.

Francis, J. R. (2011). A framework for understanding and researching audit quality. *Auditing: A Journal of Practice and Theory* 30(2): 125–152.

  a. What is the purpose of the study?
  b. Describe the design/method/approach used to conduct the study.
  c. What are the primary findings of the study?

The Audit Opinion Formulation Process

I. Making Client Acceptance and Continuance Decisions

Chapter 1

II. Performing Risk Assessment

Chapters 2, 3, 7, and 9–13

III. Obtaining Evidence About Internal Control Operating Effectiveness

Chapters 8–13

IV. Obtaining Substantive Evidence About Accounts, Disclosures, and Assertions

Chapters 8–13

V. Completing the Audit and Making Reporting Decisions

Chapters 14 and 15

Quality Auditing and the Need for Quality Auditor Judgments and Ethical Decisions

Chapter 1

Professional Liability

Chapter 4

The Audit Opinion Formulation Process and a Framework for Obtaining Audit Evidence

Chapters 5 and 6

Auditing requires gathering and evaluating sufficient appropriate evidence related to management assertions. As the auditor plans an audit, the auditor addresses basic evidence-related questions: *How much audit evidence is sufficient? What audit evidence is appropriate? What types of procedures should I perform? When should I obtain the evidence?* The auditor makes these evidence-related decisions in a way that will best address the risk of material misstatement in the financial statements or the risk that internal control over financial reporting contains material weaknesses.

Learning Objectives

LO 1 Identify factors affecting the sufficiency and appropriateness of audit evidence, and explain how these factors relate to the risk of material misstatement.

LO 2 Make professional judgments about the types and timing of audit procedures the auditor uses to obtain audit evidence.

LO 3 Discuss the use of, and apply, substantive analytical procedures.

LO 4 Describe the unique evidence requirements for accounts involving management estimates, accounts involving related-party transactions, and situations requiring the use of a specialist/expert.

LO 5 Describe the characteristics of quality audit documentation, including the role of audit programs.

LO 6 Apply the frameworks for professional decision making and ethical decision making to issues involving audit evidence.

Evidence-Related Findings in PCAOB Inspection Reports

Why It Matters

Following are excerpts from PCAOB annual inspection reports issued from 2011 through 2017. Each excerpt describes an audit deficiency related to evidence that is a failure by the firm to perform, or to perform sufficiently, certain necessary audit procedures and to obtain sufficient appropriate audit evidence.

PCAOB Release No. 104-2017-030

For one significant transaction, the Firm failed to identify and appropriately address what appeared to the inspection team to be an instance in which the financial statements were not presented fairly, in all material respects, in conformity with GAAP. Specifically, the Firm failed to identify that the issuer had incorrectly applied Financial Accounting Standards Board ("FASB") Accounting Standards Codification ("ASC") 605, *Revenue Recognition*, as the issuer recognized revenue for this transaction even though there was no persuasive evidence of an arrangement and collectibility was not reasonably assured.

PCAOB Release No. 104-2016-175

The Firm failed to sufficiently test the fair value of the acquired technology and vendor-relationship intangible assets for certain acquisitions. The Firm compared certain significant inputs and assumptions to financial information from another business combination the issuer consummated during the year or information disclosed by other companies. The Firm's procedures did not include evaluating the reasonableness of these inputs and assumptions underlying the valuation of these assets beyond such comparisons. In addition, the Firm failed to test the accuracy and completeness of certain data used in the valuation of these intangible assets.

PCAOB Release No. 104-2015-188

The Firm failed to perform sufficient substantive procedures to test the existence of loans. The Firm assessed control risk below the maximum for the existence of loans. Specifically, the Firm designed its substantive procedures to test the existence of loans—including its sample sizes—based on a level of control reliance that was not supported due to the deficiency in the Firm's testing of controls that is discussed below. As a result, the sample sizes that the Firm used to test the existence of loans were too small to provide sufficient evidence.

PCAOB Release No. 104-2014-196

The Firm vouched a sample of sales invoices issued during the first seven months of the year under audit to supporting evidence to substantiate the occurrence and valuation of revenue. In addition, the Firm confirmed with customers a sample of unpaid invoices at year end and tested revenue cut-off at year end by vouching a sample of sales invoices issued during the last 20 days of the year under audit to shipping documentation. The Firm failed to perform sufficient substantive procedures to test revenue during the last five months of the year under audit as the transactions encompassed by its procedures to test unpaid invoices and revenue cut-off at year end were not representative of the population of revenue transactions and only addressed a small portion of revenue during this period.

PCAOB Release No. 104-2013-242

The Firm failed to sufficiently evaluate the reasonableness of certain assumptions the issuer used in projecting future taxable income for the purposes of its analysis of the valuation of deferred tax assets. Specifically, there was no evidence in the audit documentation, and no persuasive other evidence, that the Firm had taken into account certain available information that appeared inconsistent with the issuer's assumptions relating to the forecasted level of acquisitions of accounts receivable portfolios and projected impairments of accounts receivable.

PCAOB Release No. 104-2012-095

The Firm failed to sufficiently test inventory. Specifically, the Firm failed to test the existence of a significant portion of inventory and failed to test the completeness and accuracy of the system-generated reports that it used in its substantive procedures related to the valuation of inventory. Further, the Firm failed to test the completeness of inventory.

PCAOB Release No. 104-2011-288

In this audit, the Firm failed to obtain sufficient appropriate audit evidence to support its opinion on the effectiveness of ICFR [internal control over financial reporting].

What You Will Learn

- What is sufficient appropriate evidence, and how does it differ across clients? (LO 1)
- What types of audit procedures should auditors perform to obtain sufficient appropriate evidence? (LO 2)
- How do substantive analytical procedures provide evidence on the accuracy of account balances? (LO 3)
- What are the unique evidence challenges for accounts based on management estimates, such as allowance for doubtful accounts? (LO 4)

- What are the unique evidence challenges for accounts that involve related-party transactions? (LO 4)
- What are the unique evidence challenges for accounts that require the use of a specialist/expert? (LO 4)
- What is quality audit documentation? (LO 5)
- What is an audit program and how does it contribute to quality audit documentation? (LO 5)

LO 1

Identify factors affecting the sufficiency and appropriateness of audit evidence, and explain how these factors relate to the risk of material misstatement.

Obtaining Sufficient Appropriate Audit Evidence

The auditor obtains evidence to reduce the risk of issuing an unqualified opinion on financial statements containing a material misstatement or on internal control that has a material weakness. AS 1105 defines audit evidence as:

> [A]ll the information, whether obtained from audit procedures or other sources, that is used by the auditor in arriving at the conclusions on which the auditor's opinion is based. Audit evidence consists of both information that supports and corroborates management's assertions regarding the financial statements or internal control over financial reporting and information that contradicts such assertions.

For Classroom Discussion

What Do You Think?

As you consider the need to obtain sufficient and appropriate evidence, why do you think that the auditors described in the *Why It Matters* feature "Evidence-Related Findings in PCAOB Inspection Reports" did not obtain sufficient appropriate evidence?

Do you think there could be valid disagreements between the PCAOB and audit firms on what constitutes sufficient appropriate evidence?

This definition is very similar to those used by the American Institute of Certified Public Accountants (AICPA) and the International Auditing and Assurance Standards Board (IAASB).

While the auditor needs sufficient appropriate evidence before issuing an opinion, determining what is "sufficient" and "appropriate" is not easy. The AICPA's AU-C 500 defines the sufficiency of audit evidence as "[t]he measure of the quantity of audit evidence. The quantity of the audit evidence needed is affected by the auditor's assessment of the risks of material misstatement and also by the quality of such audit evidence." That same standard defines the appropriateness of audit evidence as "[t]he measure of the quality of audit evidence (that is, its relevance and reliability in providing support for the conclusions on which the auditor's opinion is based)."

Exhibit 6.1 explains the relationship between the risk of material misstatement, evidence appropriateness, and evidence sufficiency.

Exhibit 6.1
Interrelationship of Risk of Material Misstatement, Evidence Appropriateness, and Evidence Sufficiency

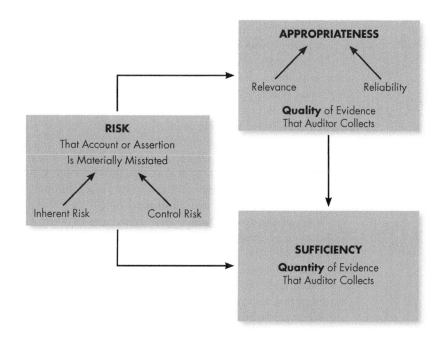

What is determined to be sufficient and appropriate is affected by the client's risk of material misstatement (in other words, its inherent and control risks) or risk of material weakness in internal control. Sufficiency and appropriateness will vary across accounts and assertions. Both the U.S. and international auditing standards encourage auditors to focus on accounts and assertions with the greatest likelihood of material misstatement. With that in mind, study the relationships in *Exhibit 6.1*. Consider an account where there is little risk of material misstatement, internal controls are effective, and the client has relatively noncomplex transactions. Here, the available audit evidence is relevant and reliable, and the quality of that evidence is high. In such a case, the auditor could likely perform less rigorous substantive procedures or only a minimal amount of substantive procedures, and the audit would therefore be less costly to conduct. Conversely, consider an account where there is high risk of material misstatement and internal controls over that account are not effective. Here, the available audit evidence from the client is of lower quality. Therefore, the auditor will have to find other high-quality evidence to corroborate evidence obtained from within the client's systems. Ultimately, these factors require the auditor to perform more, and more rigorous, substantive procedures. Therefore, obtaining such evidence will increase the cost to perform the audit.

Sufficiency of Audit Evidence

Sufficiency of evidence is the measure of the quantity of audit evidence (e.g., a sample size of documents that the auditor will review or the number of observations of a control activity). The quantity of audit evidence needed is affected by the auditor's assessment of the risks of material misstatement (the higher the assessed risks, the more audit evidence is likely to be required) and by the quality of such audit evidence (the higher the evidence quality, the less evidence may be required).

The amount of evidence must be of sufficient quantity to convince the audit team of the effectiveness of internal control or the accuracy of an account balance or assertion. Similarly, the evidence must stand on its own such that another unbiased professional would reach the same conclusion. However, how much evidence is enough? The answer to this question depends, in part, on experienced auditor professional judgment.

Sample Sizes

For many tests of controls and substantive tests of details, the auditor determines a sample size to use for testing. For example, assume that the auditor wants to send accounts receivable confirmations to a client's customers to obtain evidence related to the existence assertion. How many confirmations should the auditor send? Or, assume that the auditor wants to test the operating effectiveness of a control by inspecting purchase orders for the required approval. How many purchase orders should the auditor review? The auditor can determine the sample size by applying a statistically based formula or by using professional judgment. *Chapter 8* includes a discussion relating to sample sizes.

Substantive Tests   When determining sample sizes for a substantive test of details, such as confirmations, the auditor considers client factors such as the risk of material misstatement and the assurance obtained from other substantive procedures performed by the auditor.

Tests of Controls   When performing tests of controls, the extent of evidence necessary to persuade the auditor that the control is effective depends upon the risk associated with the control, that is, the risk that the control might not be effective and, if not effective, the risk that a material misstatement could occur. As the risk associated with the control being tested increases, the evidence that the auditor should obtain also increases.

When performing tests of controls, the amount of evidence the auditor needs to obtain depends on whether the client has tested controls as a basis for its assertion on the effectiveness of internal control. Furthermore, the type of control the

When an Auditor Fails to Collect Sufficient Appropriate Evidence: The Case at Ligand Pharmaceuticals

Focus on Fraud

This feature highlights the fact that no bright-line requirements tell auditors that they have collected enough evidence, yet if it is subsequently determined that they have not done so, severe ramifications can exist for what is deemed improper professional judgment.

James L. Fazio, age 46, was a CPA and partner in the San Diego office of Deloitte LLP. He was the partner-in-charge of the audit of Ligand Pharmaceuticals. At the time of the 2003 Ligand audit, Deloitte's audit policies required that each client's engagement risk be assessed annually as normal, greater than normal, or much greater than normal. In Ligand's case, the engagement team assessed engagement risk as "greater than normal" because of concerns regarding product sales and sales returns. Specifically, the engagement team documented concern in the audit workpapers that Ligand's estimates of sales returns and reserves were not sufficient to cover actual returns. Given the heightened risk, the written audit plan called for the engagement team to perform procedures to address the issue and to increase its professional skepticism regarding the returns issues.

However, the PCAOB found that James Fazio failed to obtain sufficient appropriate evidence to afford a reasonable basis for an opinion regarding the financial statements. Specifically, he failed to (1) adequately assess whether Ligand had gathered sufficient evidence to properly estimate future returns, (2) adequately evaluate the reasonableness of Ligand's estimates of returns, and (3) identify and address issues concerning Ligand's exclusion of certain returns from its estimates of returns.

The PCAOB concluded that Fazio's conduct met conditions warranting sanctions because of "intentional or knowing conduct, including reckless conduct." The PCAOB ordered that Fazio not be allowed to associate with a registered public accounting firm, but he could file a petition for PCAOB consent to have such an association after two years.

Ultimately, Ligand restated its financial statements for 2003 and other periods because its revenue recognition did not follow the applicable financial reporting framework. In its restatement, Ligand recognized about $59 million less in revenues (a 52% decrease from what was originally reported), and revealed a net loss that was more than 2.5 times the net loss originally reported. Thus, investors were misled by Ligand's misstated financial statements and by Fazio's failure to conduct sufficient audit tests in a manner that would have led to more accurate financial statements.

The audit partner was aware of factors that called into question the adequacy of Ligand's reserves for returns (e.g., lack of actual return history, limited visibility into distribution channels, and significant increases in or excess levels of inventory), but he did not adequately analyze whether those factors impaired Ligand's ability to make reasonable estimates of returns. Consequently, the PCAOB concluded that the auditor in this case did not have a sufficient basis to support the conclusion that Ligand's revenue recognition was appropriate.

For further details, see PCAOB Release No. 105-2007-006, December 10, 2007.

---

auditor is testing will affect the auditor's sample size. If the auditor is testing a manual control related to transaction processing, the auditor will base sample sizes on guidelines developed for attributes testing using statistical or nonstatistical sampling techniques. Generally, these sample sizes will vary between 30 and 100 transactions, although as we will learn in *Chapter 8*, when auditors use **data analytics tools**, they sometimes sample 100% of a population.

In contrast, as we discuss in *Chapter 3*, some controls related to transactions processing are automated controls built into computer applications. If the auditor has tested general computer controls, such as controls over program changes, and has concluded that those controls are effective, the tests of computerized application controls could be as small as one for each kind of control the auditor is testing. Another factor influencing sample sizes for tests of controls is the frequency with which a control is performed. For monthly controls, such as a bank reconciliation, the auditor could choose one month and perform a test of control, such as inspection of documentation or reperformance. In contrast, if a control is performed multiple times each day, such as controls over sales transactions, the auditor will use a larger sample.

Controls over adjusting entries require additional consideration as adjusting entries represent a high risk of material misstatement. The auditor's extent of tests of controls over adjusting entries will be inversely related to the control environment; in other words, the better the control environment, the smaller the sample size will be, and vice versa. The testing also varies directly with the materiality of the account balance and the auditor's assessment of risk that the account balance might be misstated. The auditor wants to review a sufficient number of transactions to determine that: (a) other controls are not being overridden by management; (b) there is support for the adjusting entries, for example, underlying data analyses; and (c) the entries are properly approved by the appropriate level of management. If the number of transactions is high, the auditor might use sampling. If the number of transactions is low, the auditor may choose to focus on the larger transactions.

Appropriateness of Audit Evidence

Appropriateness of audit evidence is a measure of evidence quality, including the relevance of the evidence. **Relevance of evidence** determines whether the evidence provides insight on the validity of the assertion the auditor is testing. Appropriateness of audit evidence also involves **reliability of evidence**, that is, whether the evidence is convincing.

Relevance of Audit Evidence

The relevance of evidence relates to the connection between the audit procedure being performed and the assertion being audited. Relevance is affected by many factors, including the purpose of the procedure being performed, the direction of testing, and the specific procedure or set of procedures being performed. Additionally, evidence can be directly or indirectly relevant to an assertion.

The auditor should guard against unwarranted inferences in gathering audit evidence. The following are examples of inappropriate inferences that auditors may make because they use evidence that is not entirely relevant to the assertion they are testing:

- The auditor tests the existence of the client's equipment by inspecting the asset and concludes that the asset exists and the client owns the equipment. However, evidence about the existence of the equipment that the auditor gains through inspecting the asset does not provide relevant evidence about who owns the asset.
- The auditor reviews documentation related to the largest accounts payable balances recorded in the client's financial statements and concludes that the accounts payable balance recorded in the financial statements is reasonable. Such evidence is relevant to the existence assertion (overstatements). For most liability accounts, the more relevant evidence would relate to the completeness assertion and *understatements*, not overstatements.

Why It Matters   The Need to Tailor the Evidence to the Identified Risks

A criticism of audits described in Public Company Accounting Oversight Board (PCAOB) inspection reports is that auditors often address high-risk audit areas by simply gathering more of the same type of evidence. This feature highlights that auditing standards indicate such an approach is not appropriate.

ISA 500 is very explicit in stating that gathering more of the same evidence will not meet either the sufficiency or appropriateness criteria. For example, if there is high risk regarding the valuation of accounts receivable, increasing the sample size for confirmations, which are focused on the existence assertion, would not be very useful. Rather, the auditor will need to expand procedures related to the allowance account. Auditors need to tailor the gathering of evidence—both the sufficiency and appropriateness—to identified risks for each disclosure, account, or assertion.

Purpose of an Audit Procedure   Recall from *Chapter 5* that audit procedures fall into three categories: risk assessment procedures, tests of controls, and substantive procedures. The purpose of an audit procedure determines whether it is a risk assessment procedure, a test of controls, or a substantive procedure.

The auditors use risk assessment procedures during audit planning to identify the risks of material misstatement. Tests of controls are relevant when the auditor wants to evaluate the operating effectiveness of controls in preventing, or detecting and correcting, material misstatements. Substantive procedures are relevant when the auditor wants to obtain direct evidence about material misstatements in the financial statements.

Direction of Testing   The relevance of evidence obtained through audit procedures may be affected by the direction of testing. **Directional testing** involves testing balances primarily for either overstatement or understatement (but not both). For example, if the auditor wants to test the existence assertion for accounts payable, the auditor is concerned as to whether all of the recorded accounts payable actually exist; that is, overstatement of accounts payable. In that case, the auditor's starting point for testing would be all of the recorded accounts payable, and the auditor would perform procedures to obtain evidence supporting the existence of the recorded accounts payable. For example, the auditor may look at supporting documentation such as vendor invoices. Conversely, if the auditor wants to test the completeness assertion for accounts payable, the auditor is concerned as to whether all of the accounts payable owed by the client are recorded; that is, understatement of accounts payable. In that case, obtaining evidence about the recorded accounts payable would not be relevant. Instead, the auditor would obtain evidence as to whether there were unrecorded accounts payable. Relevant evidence could include information such as subsequent disbursements, suppliers' statements, and unmatched receiving reports.

Exhibit 6.2 compares testing related to the existence and completeness assertions. Panel A illustrates the auditor's workflow when testing for existence. This process is referred to as **vouching**. Vouching involves taking a sample of recorded transactions and obtaining the original source documents supporting the recorded transaction. For example, for a sample of items recorded in the sales journal, the auditor will obtain the related shipping documents and customer orders. Vouching provides evidence on the assertion that recorded transactions are valid (existence/occurrence).

Exhibit 6.2

Illustration of Testing for Existence (Vouching) and Completeness (Tracing)

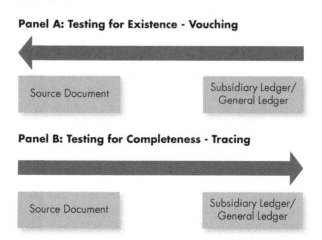

Panel A: Testing for Existence - Vouching

Source Document   Subsidiary Ledger/ General Ledger

Panel B: Testing for Completeness - Tracing

Source Document   Subsidiary Ledger/ General Ledger

Panel B of *Exhibit* 6.2 illustrates the auditor's workflow when testing for completeness. This process is referred to as **tracing**. Tracing involves taking a sample of original source documents and ensuring that the transactions related to the source documents have been recorded in the appropriate journal and general ledger. For example, the auditor might select a sample of receiving reports and trace them to the acquisitions journal and the general ledger.

Some assertions are directional by nature. The existence/occurrence assertion addresses overstatement; the completeness assertion addresses understatement. Therefore, the assertion the auditor is testing determines the direction of testing and what type of evidence is relevant. Assets and revenues are typically tested for overstatement because the usual presumption is that managers would prefer to show more assets and revenues. Testing an asset for overstatement also provides corollary evidence on the potential overstatement of revenue and liabilities or the potential understatement of other asset or expense accounts. For example, if accounts receivable are overstated, it is likely that revenue is overstated or cash is understated.

Liabilities and expenses are typically tested for understatement because the usual presumption is that managers would prefer to show fewer liabilities and expenses. Testing liabilities for understatement provides evidence on the potential understatement of expenses or assets, or the potential overstatement of revenue and other liabilities. For example, if there are unrecorded liabilities, such as a failure to accrue payroll expense, the related payroll expense is understated, and possibly inventory is understated if payroll costs are not properly allocated to inventory.

Type of Procedure A specific audit procedure may provide audit evidence that is relevant to certain assertions, but not others. For example, if the auditor were to walk through the client's warehouse to inspect inventory, the auditor would be obtaining evidence related to the existence of inventory. However, this procedure would not provide evidence relevant to the rights assertion. In some cases, a procedure may provide evidence relevant to multiple assertions. For example, if the auditor inspects documents related to the collection of accounts receivable after the year-end, this procedure will likely provide audit evidence relevant to both the existence and valuation of accounts receivable.

Direct and Indirect Evidence Some evidence is directly relevant to a specific assertion. For example, communicating (usually through a confirmation) with a client's customers about whether the customer owes payment for goods to the client provides **direct evidence** about the existence of an accounts receivable balance.

Indirect evidence can be relevant, but not as directly relevant, to an assertion. For example, tests of controls provide direct evidence about the operating effectiveness of controls and indirect evidence about accounts and assertions. If the auditor finds that controls over the existence of inventory are operating effectively, the auditor has direct evidence about the effectiveness of those controls. The auditor also has indirect evidence indicating a high likelihood that the inventory existence assertion is not materially misstated. The auditor will likely need to also obtain direct evidence related to inventory existence through substantive procedures.

Reliability of Audit Evidence

The reliability of audit evidence refers to its ability to provide convincing evidence related to the audit objective being evaluated. Factors affecting evidence reliability include its source, nature, and the circumstances under which the auditor obtains the evidence. In considering the reliability of audit evidence, ISA 500 (A31) notes the importance of considering the source of the evidence in assessing its reliability:

> The reliability of information to be used as audit evidence, and therefore of the audit evidence itself, is influenced by its source and its nature, and the circumstances under which it is obtained, including the controls over its preparation and maintenance where relevant. Therefore, generalizations about the reliability of various kinds of audit evidence are subject to important exceptions. Even when information to be used as audit evidence is obtained from sources

external to the entity, circumstances may exist that could affect its reliability. For example, information obtained from an independent external source may not be reliable if the source is not knowledgeable, or a management's expert may lack objectivity. (ISA 500, A31)

The IAASB, in ISA 500, has established the following generalizations about the reliability of audit evidence:

More Reliable Evidence	Less Reliable Evidence
Directly obtained evidence (e.g., observation of a control)	Indirectly obtained evidence (e.g., an inquiry about the working of a control)
Evidence derived from a well-controlled information system	Evidence derived from a poorly controlled system or easily overridden information system
Evidence from independent outside sources	Evidence from within the client's organization
Evidence that exists in documentary form	Evidence obtained through inquiry
Evidence from original documents	Evidence obtained from photocopies or facsimiles, or digitized data (would depend on the quality of controls over their preparation and maintenance)

Evidence reliability is influenced by multiple considerations. For example, if the auditor is testing warranty liabilities, most of the information likely resides internally—some in the client's accounting system and some in operational data. While internal documentation is generally less reliable than external documentation, internal documentation can be quite reliable when the underlying internal control system is effective and management cannot easily falsify the original documentation.

Internal Documentation   Internal documentation includes the following types of documents: legal, business, accounting, and planning and control. *Exhibit 6.3* provides examples of these types of internal documents. The reliability of internal documentation is influenced by:

- Effectiveness of internal controls over the documents
- Management motivation to misstate individual accounts (fraud potential)
- Formality of the documentation, such as acknowledgment of its validity by parties outside the organization or independent of the accounting function
- Independence of those preparing the documentation from those recording transactions

External Documentation   External documentation is generally highly reliable, but the reliability varies depending on whether the documentation: (a) was prepared by a knowledgeable and independent outside party and (b) is received directly by the auditor. Most external documentation, however, is received directly by the client. For example, a customer order that specifies prices and quantities is external documentation received by the client, not the auditor. Therefore, in high-risk situations the auditor should confirm the contents of the document with the pertinent outside party.

Exhibit 6.4 provides examples of external documentation. External documentation can range from business documents typically in the client's possession (vendor invoices and monthly statements), to confirmations received by the auditor directly from the client's legal counsel, banker, or customer, to trade and credit information.

One common business document in the client's possession is a vendor invoice. A vendor's invoice shows the purchase price (cost) of items in the client's inventory, dates of invoice and shipment, payment and ownership terms, shipping address

Exhibit 6.3
Examples of Internal Documents

Legal documents	Labor and fringe benefit agreements
	Sales contracts
	Lease agreements
	Royalty agreements
	Maintenance contracts
Business documents	Sales invoices
	Purchase orders
	Canceled checks
	Payment vouchers
	Electronic Data Interchange (EDI) agreements
Accounting documents	Estimated warranty liability schedules
	Depreciation and amortization schedules
	Standard cost computations and schedules
	Management exception reports
	Employee time cards
Other planning and control documents	Shipping and receiving reports
	Inventory movement documents such as scrap reports and transfer receipts
	Market research surveys
	Pending litigation reports
	Variance reports

(inventory location), purchase order reference, purchasing agent (evidence of authorization), and amount due (liability as well as asset valuation evidence). A vendor invoice is external documentation, but the auditor will typically obtain it from the client. Formal documents of this type are generally considered reliable except for situations in which the auditor questions management's integrity and has assessed the client and account balance being tested as high risk. Invoices often exist in electronic form. Thus, the auditor must assure that the data shown in an electronic invoice are safeguarded, well controlled in the client's computer system, and not easily manipulated.

Reliability and Relevance of Evidence from a Management's Specialist

Some of the evidence that auditors receive from a client has been prepared by a management's specialist hired by the client. AU-C 500 defines a **management's specialist** as "an individual or organization possessing expertise in a field other than accounting or auditing, whose work in that field is used by the entity to assist the entity in preparing the financial statements."

In preparing its financial statements, a client may require expertise in a field other than accounting or auditing, such as actuarial calculations, valuations, or engineering data. If the client does not have the expertise needed to prepare the financial statements, the client can use a management's specialist in these fields to obtain the needed expertise to provide the relevant data needed to prepare

Exhibit 6.4
Examples of External Documents

Business documents	Vendor invoices and monthly statements
	Customer orders
	Sales or purchase contracts
	Loan agreements
	Other contracts
Third-party documents	Confirmation letters from legal counsel
	Confirmation statements from banks
	Confirmation replies from customers
	Vendor statements requested by auditors
General business information	Industry trade statistics
	Credit-rating reports
	Data from computer service bureaus

the financial statements. Failure to hire such an expert when such expertise is necessary increases the risks of material misstatement and may be a significant deficiency or material weakness in internal control.

If a management's specialist prepares information that the auditor will use as audit evidence, the auditor should consider the following factors affecting the reliability and relevance of information produced by a management's specialist:

- Competence, capabilities, and objectivity of the specialist
- Work performed by the specialist
- Appropriateness of the specialist's work as audit evidence for the relevant assertion

Check Your Basic Knowledge

6-1 The appropriateness of audit evidence refers to its relevance and reliability.   (T/F)

6-2 The sufficiency of evidence is a measure of evidence quality.   (T/F)

6-3 An auditor determines that management integrity is high, the risk of material misstatement is low, and the client's internal controls are effective. Which of the following conclusions can be reached regarding the need to obtain direct evidence about the account balances?
   a. Direct evidence can be limited to material account balances, and the extent of testing should be sufficient to corroborate the auditor's assessment of low risk.
   b. Direct evidence of account balances is not needed.

   c. Direct evidence can be obtained solely through analytical procedures.
   d. Direct evidence should be obtained for all accounts, regardless of the auditor's assessment of control risk.

6-4 Which of the following statements is <u>true</u> regarding the sufficiency of evidence needed to test an account?
   a. Evidence sufficiency is a measure of evidence quality.
   b. Evidence sufficiency is affected by the quality of evidence.
   c. A relationship does not exist between evidence sufficiency and evidence quality.
   d. For a specific client, evidence sufficiency will be the same across all accounts.

LO 2
Make professional judgments
about the types and timing of
audit procedures the auditor
uses to obtain audit evidence.

Audit Procedures

Types of Audit Procedures

Audit procedures fall into three categories: risk assessment procedures, tests of controls, and substantive procedures. *Exhibit 6.5* identifies the types of audit procedures typically performed as tests of controls and substantive procedures, and includes relevant examples. We discuss risk assessment procedures in *Chapter 7*.

Inspection of Documentation Much of the audit process involves examining documentation, in either paper or electronic form. Important documentation

Exhibit 6.5
Types of Audit Procedures

Categories of Audit Procedures	Purpose	Types of Audit Procedures Typically Performed	Examples of Audit Procedures
Tests of controls	Evaluate the operating effectiveness of controls	Inspection of documentation	Review client-prepared internal control documentation
			Select purchase transactions and review documentation for required approval
		Observation	Observe whether controls designed to limit access to a secure area (e.g., ID card need to access storage room) are functioning
		Reperformance	Reperform a reconciliation performed by client personnel
		Inquiry	Inquire of management and supervisory personnel about their control-related responsibilities
Substantive procedures	Determine whether material misstatements exist in the financial statements	Inspection of documentation	Review shipping documents as evidence of a sale having occurred
		Inspection of assets	Tour the manufacturing facility and inspect client's equipment
		External confirmation	Obtain confirmations from client's customers regarding amount owed by the customer to the client
		Recalculation	Recalculate the total amount included on a sales invoice
		Analytical procedures	Estimate the expected amount of interest income to be recorded by the client and follow up on significant unexpected differences between expectation and client's recorded balance
		Scanning	Scan the sales journal to identify unusual transactions posted to the sales account and follow up on the transactions
		Inquiry	Inquire of client management as to its valuation of the allowance for doubtful accounts

that the auditor obtains generally includes the client's underlying **accounting records** such as:

- Evidence of internal controls over financial reporting, as well as supporting records such as checks, invoices, and contracts
- The general and subsidiary ledgers
- Journal entries
- Worksheets supporting cost allocations, computations, reconciliations, and disclosures

Common documents include invoices, payroll time cards, and bank statements. Auditors examine invoices from suppliers, for example, to establish the cost and ownership of inventory or various expenses. They also read contracts to help establish the potential existence of liabilities. Auditors should use original source documents rather than copies, because copies are easy for an unscrupulous management to falsify. Inspection of documents provides audit evidence of varying degrees of reliability. The reliability depends on the nature and source of the documentation and, in the case of internal records and documents, the effectiveness of controls over their production.

Inspection of Tangible Assets   Auditors will often inspect a client's assets, including inventory and long-lived assets (e.g., machinery or buildings). Inspection of tangible assets generally provides reliable evidence with respect to the existence of the asset, but not necessarily about the client's rights or completeness of the assets. For example, the inventory at a client location might be held on consignment from others and is therefore not owned by the audit client.

Observation   Observation involves looking at a client's process or procedure. For example, an auditor might choose to observe whether unauthorized client personnel are prohibited from entering secure areas. A common practice is also to observe the client's process of taking physical inventory to establish existence and valuation. Observation suffers from the following limitations:

- Observation of processing is rarely unobtrusive. Individuals who know they are being observed may act differently than when not observed.
- Observation of processing on one day does not necessarily indicate how the transactions were processed on a different day or over a relevant period.

External Confirmation   Confirmations consist of sending an inquiry to an outside party to corroborate information. The outside parties are asked to respond directly to the auditor as to whether they agree or disagree with the information, or to provide additional information that will assist the auditor in evaluating the correctness of an account balance. External confirmations include requests to legal counsel for an assessment of current litigation and the client's potential liability, letters to customers asking whether they owe the amount on the client's accounts receivable records, and letters to banks confirming bank balances and loans. In some cases, the auditor confirms the terms of sales agreements or other contracts.

Recalculation   Auditors often recalculate a number of client computations. *Exhibit 6.6* summarizes various types of recalculations.

Reperformance   **Reperformance** involves the auditor's independent execution of controls that the client originally performed as part of the client's internal control. For example, rather than only inspecting documents related to a bank reconciliation to determine whether the reconciliation was performed, the auditor may reperform bank reconciliations for selected months and compare them to the reconciliations prepared by the client. Depending on the risks, only inspecting bank reconciliation documents may not be sufficient evidence to test the bank reconciliation control.

Focus on Fraud   The Parmalat Confirmation Fraud

This feature notes that although confirmations can be a very reliable source of evidence, auditors must not improperly rely on them. When using confirmations with outside parties, the auditor must assure that the outside party:

- *Exists*
- *Is able to respond objectively and independently*
- *Is likely to respond conscientiously, appropriately, and in a timely fashion*
- *Is unbiased in responding*

The Parmalat fraud involved a large, family-held Italian company that produced dairy products around the world. The company's management perpetrated a fraud that involved taking cash from the business for family purposes but not recording the transactions in the books, thereby resulting in an overstatement of cash on the company's books. It also shifted monetary assets in and out of banks located in the Bahamas. The audit firm decided it should independently confirm the existence of Parmalat's

$3.2 billion account with the Bank of America in New York. Unfortunately, the audit senior was careless, and after preparing the confirmation, he put it in the client's mailroom where it was intercepted by management. Management was able to scan the signature of a Bank of America employee from another document and put it on a copy of the confirmation form. A Parmalat employee then flew to New York from Italy just to mail that confirmation to the auditors with the appropriate postmark. The auditors received the fraudulent confirmation and concluded that the cash balance existed. There is an important point here: there are no trivial tasks in an audit. Each procedure must be completed in a professional manner and with due care.

Professional auditing standards in the U.S. generally require that the auditor separately confirm accounts receivable. Confirmations must be sent independently of the client. The auditor often complements these types of confirmations with other sources of evidence, such as the customer's subsequent payment of the outstanding balance.

What Do You Think?   For Classroom Discussion

Do you think that confirmation fraud, similar to what occurred on the Parmalat audit, is a significant concern for auditors on many engagements? Should it be a significant concern?

Exhibit 6.6
Types of Recalculations Performed
by the Auditor

- **Footing** Adding a column of figures to verify the correctness of the client's totals.
- **Cross-footing** Checking the agreement of the cross-addition of a number of columns of figures that sum to a grand total. For example, the sum of net sales and sales discounts should equal total sales.
- **Tests of extensions** Recomputing items involving multiplication (e.g., multiplying unit cost by quantity on hand to arrive at extended cost).
- **Recalculating estimated amounts** Recomputing an amount that the client has already estimated, such as recomputing the allowance for doubtful accounts based on the client's formula related to the aging of accounts receivable ending balances.

Analytical Procedures **Analytical procedures** consist of evaluations of financial information through analyzing plausible relationships among both financial and nonfinancial data. Later in this chapter, we provide additional discussion on analytical procedures. **Scanning** is a type of analytical procedure involving the auditor's review of accounting data to identify significant or unusual items to test. Unusual individual items might include entries in transaction listings, subsidiary ledgers, general ledger control accounts, adjusting entries, reconciliations, or other detailed reports. For unusual or significant items, the auditor typically performs tests of details, such as client inquiry, inspection of documentation or assets, and, possibly, confirmations. While scanning can be conducted manually, data analytics tools may assist the auditor in identifying unusual items.

Inquiry The auditor uses inquiry of appropriate individuals extensively to gain an understanding of:

- The accounting system
- Management's plans for such things as marketable investments, new products, disposal of lines of business, and new investments
- Pending or actual litigation against the organization
- Changes in accounting procedures or accounting principles
- Management's approach and assumptions used in the valuation of key accounts (e.g., the collectibility of accounts receivable and saleability of inventory)
- Management's or the controller's assessment of complex financial matters

While inquiry is very helpful to understanding the client, evidence obtained through inquiry typically needs to be corroborated through other audit procedures. Inquiry alone ordinarily does not provide sufficient audit evidence of account balances and inquiry alone is insufficient to test the operating effectiveness of controls.

Application of Audit Procedures to Testing Management Financial Statement Assertions

The auditor selects audit procedures to provide evidence relevant to a particular assertion. *Exhibit 6.7* presents examples of procedures that address specific assertions regarding long-lived assets and contingencies. *Exhibit 6.7* organizes the procedures according to the assertion; however, some procedures cover more than one assertion.

Assessing the Consistency and Reliability of Evidence

AS 1105 provides guidance in determining the consistency and reliability of the evidence by stating:

> If audit evidence obtained from one source is inconsistent with that obtained from another, or if the auditor has doubts about the reliability of information to be used as audit evidence, the auditor should perform the audit procedures necessary to resolve the matter and should determine the effect, if any, on other aspects of the audit. (para. 29)

AS 1105 highlights that the auditor needs to consider all sources of evidence, as well as the consistency of the evidence, in determining whether the evidence clearly leads to a conclusion about the fairness of the financial statement presentation. In making this determination, the auditor should:

- Consider internal consistency of evidence gathered
- Consider the consistency of internal evidence generated with external evidence gathered that reflects economic conditions and client operations
- Expand evidence-gathering procedures for areas where results are inconsistent or where results raise questions on the correctness of account balances
- Document conclusions based on the evidence gathered such that someone knowledgeable in auditing can follow the reasoning process

Exhibit 6.7

Management Assertions and Examples of Relevant Audit Procedures

Assertions	Audit Procedures: Long-Lived Assets	Audit Procedures: Contingencies
Existence	• Inspect the assets • Select new assets that have been added to the subsidiary ledger or general journal and inspect supporting documentation (e.g., invoices)	• Inquire of management • Send confirmation request to legal counsel
Completeness	• Select source documents for repairs or maintenance expense to determine if a fixed asset was inappropriately expensed • Inquire regarding the process for determining whether an expenditure is an asset or an expense	• Inquire of management • Select source documents for legal expense and determine that the expenses were appropriately recorded
Rights/obligations	• Inspect documentation related to purchase contracts	• Inquire of management • Obtain confirmation from legal counsel • Inspect documentation of payments related to in-progress litigation
Valuation/allocation	• Inspect vendor's invoice to establish purchase price • Determine that estimated life and salvage value are consistent with similar purchases, company policies, expected future use, and past experience • Recalculate depreciation expense • Develop an expectation of total depreciation using analytical procedures	• Inquire of management • Obtain confirmation from legal counsel • Recalculate potential damages sought by plaintiff • Review court filings
Presentation/disclosure	• Review presentation within the financial statements to ensure completeness and conformance with the applicable financial reporting framework • Review disclosures to ensure that they are adequate and understandable	• Review presentation within financial statements to ensure completeness and conformance with the applicable financial reporting framework • Review disclosures to ensure that they are adequate and understandable

Cost–Benefit Considerations When Selecting Audit Procedures

When determining the audit procedures to perform, recognize that audit firms need to: (a) be profitable and (b) manage risk. Therefore, auditors must perform efficient and effective audits. For example, they should not perform unnecessary procedures, and they should select procedures that maximize effectiveness while minimizing cost.

Each of the audit procedures that an auditor performs takes time, effort, and ultimately money. Audit procedures that are more rigorous and that provide higher-quality evidence are generally more costly. *Exhibit 6.8* describes some generalizations about the cost–benefit trade-offs that auditors make when deciding on the appropriate mix of procedures. Consider an auditor testing the existence and valuation of inventory. The auditor may initially use substantive analytical procedures to gain a sense of the reasonableness of the ending inventory amount. The auditor will inspect the client's inventory to establish existence, and will inspect documents to determine that the client actually owns the inventory. The auditor may scan material inventory transactions around year-end to assess whether the client has made any unusual adjustments to the account. *Exhibit 6.8* highlights that each of these procedures has costs associated with it as well as differential evidence quality.

Exhibit 6.8
Cost of Audit Procedures
and Evidence Quality

Type of Substantive Procedure	Cost of Procedure	Evidence Quality
Inspection of documents (includes vouching and tracing)	Low to medium (depends on sample size)	Medium to high (assuming the documents are valid and unaltered, needs to consider source)
Inspection of physical assets	Low to high (depends on complexity, location of process, and expertise required)	High (existence); low to medium (valuation, ownership)
Observation	Low to high (depends on complexity, location of process, and expertise required)	Medium (because people may change behavior while being observed)
External confirmations	Low to medium (can be performed manually or electronically; depends on sample size)	Medium to high (assuming that there is no fraud in the confirmation process)
Recalculation	Low to medium (can be performed manually or electronically; depends on sample size)	Medium to high
Reperformance	Low to high (depends on sample size and complexity of process)	Medium to high
Analytical procedures	Low to medium (depends on the type of analytical procedure)	Medium to high (if the auditor who is conducting the test is competent and the data are reliable)
Scanning	Low to medium (can be performed manually or electronically; depends on the length of document)	Low to medium (will need to follow on significant or unusual items using other procedures)
Inquiry of knowledgeable persons	Low	Low (will also need corroborating evidence)

There are always exceptions to the generalizations in *Exhibit 6.8*. The important point is that the types of substantive procedures selected depend on the risk of material misstatement. For example, consider an account balance and related assertion with a low risk of misstatement. For this case, the auditor can obtain evidence using less rigorous and less costly procedures, such as inquiry, recalculation, and analytical procedures. In contrast, consider an account balance and related assertion with a high risk of misstatement, such as the valuation of receivables. For this case, the auditor needs to rely on relatively more rigorous and higher-cost procedures such as inquiry, confirmations, reperformance, and inspection of documentation.

For any particular account, assertion, or disclosure, the auditor may choose from the following options for substantive procedures:

- Performing only substantive analytical procedures (in practice, this approach would rarely be used)
- Performing only substantive tests of details
- Performing a combination of substantive analytical procedures and tests of details

Irrespective of the assessed risks of material misstatement, the auditor should perform substantive procedures for all relevant assertions related to each material account balance and disclosure.

Timing of Procedures

In addition to determining which types of procedures to perform, the auditor must determine when to perform them—at the balance sheet date, earlier than the balance sheet date (referred to as an **interim date**), or after the balance sheet date. The auditor determines the timing based on risk associated with the account, the effectiveness of internal controls, the nature of the account, and the availability of audit staff. Performing procedures after year-end may provide the most convincing evidence; for example, a cash collection of an accounts receivable after year-end is usually high-quality evidence regarding both the existence and valuation of the receivable.

Performing procedures prior to the balance sheet date allows earlier completion of the audit and might require less overtime of the audit staff. It might also meet management's desire to distribute the financial statements shortly after year-end. However, performing the procedures at an interim date increases the risk of material misstatements occurring between the interim date and the year-end. When an organization has effective internal control over financial reporting, the risk of misstatements occurring between the interim audit date and year-end decreases.

There are several accounts the auditor can effectively and efficiently test on an interim basis. For example, the auditor can test property, plant, and equipment additions and disposals during the year. The auditor can confirm accounts receivable balances prior to year-end. The auditor can use a similar approach for other noncurrent assets, long-term debt, and owners' equity. However, when performing procedures at an interim date, the auditor needs to perform additional audit procedures at or after year-end to make sure that no misstatements have occurred during the **roll-forward period** (the period between the interim date and the balance sheet date). These procedures could be substantive procedures, possibly combined with tests of controls for the intervening period. The auditor needs evidence that will provide a reasonable basis for extending the audit conclusions from the interim date to year-end.

Cutoff Tests

An important timing issue involves performing procedures during the cutoff period. The **cutoff period** is usually several days before and after the balance sheet date.

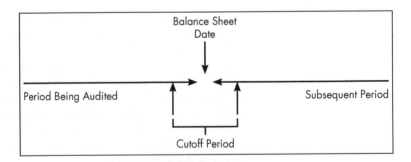

The greatest risk of recording transactions in the wrong period occurs during the cutoff period. For example, auditors are often concerned with whether the client has recorded sales, sales returns, and cash receipts transactions in the proper period. To make this determination, the auditor performs **cutoff tests**, and the extent of cutoff tests depends on the auditor's assessment of the effectiveness of the client's cutoff controls. If the client has effective controls to assure that transactions are recorded in the correct period, the auditor can minimize such testing. However, controls can be overridden and auditors have historically found a high degree of risk related to recording sales transactions in the correct period.

6-5   A procedure that involves only inspection of documentation is usually considered to be of lower quality than a procedure involving reperformance.   (T/F)

6-6   All audit procedures need to be performed at or after the client's balance sheet date.   (T/F)

6-7   The auditor is testing the completeness assertion. Which of the following statements is <u>true</u> regarding the auditor's work?

   a.   The auditor would take a sample of recorded transactions and obtain supporting documentation for those transactions.

   b.   The auditor would perform a process referred to as tracing.

   c.   The auditor would take a sample of source documents and obtain additional supporting documents for those transactions.

   d.   For a sample of items recorded in the sales journal, the auditor would obtain the related shipping documents and customer orders.

6-8   The auditor is gathering evidence to test the assertion that the client's capitalization of leased equipment assets is properly valued. Which of the following sources of evidence will the auditor generally find to be of the highest quality (most reliable and relevant)?

   a.   Inspection of the leased equipment.

   b.   Inspection of documents, including the lease contract and recalculation of capitalized amount and current amortization.

   c.   Confirmation of the current purchase price for similar equipment with vendors.

   d.   Confirmation of the original cost of the equipment with the lessor.

Substantive Analytical Procedures

LO 3

Discuss the use of, and apply, substantive analytical procedures.

Both U.S. and international auditing standards allow the auditor the option of performing substantive analytical procedures to test account balances; they are not required. A primary benefit of performing substantive analytical procedures is that they can reduce the need to perform additional, possibly more costly, substantive tests of details.

Exhibit 6.9 shows how the mix of tests may vary if the auditor performs substantive analytical procedures. In both Box A and Box B, the auditor uses a controls reliance approach for a specific account or assertion, with some of the audit evidence coming from tests of controls. In Box A, the auditor obtains the remainder of the audit evidence through substantive tests of details, which might include inspection of documentation, external confirmations, and recalculations. Conversely, in Box B, the auditor obtains the remainder of the audit evidence from both substantive analytical procedures and substantive tests of details. If the substantive analytical procedures suggest that the account is materially correct, then the auditor can reduce the evidence needed from tests of details. Note that the relative percentages are judgmental in nature; the examples are simply intended to give you a sense of how an auditor might select an appropriate mix of procedures.

In deciding to perform substantive analytical procedures, the auditor considers the following questions:

- *Does the organization have effective internal controls over the account?* The more effective a client's internal controls, the greater reliance an auditor can place on substantive analytical procedures. If an organization does not have effective internal controls, the auditor will rely more heavily on tests of details than on substantive analytical procedures, as the auditor will have concerns about the quality of information the auditor would be using in performing the analytical procedure.

Exhibit 6.9

Alternative Approaches to
Substantive Procedures

BOX A	BOX B
25% Tests of Controls	25% Tests of Controls
75% Substantive Procedures: Only tests of details	75% Substantive Procedures: Both tests of details and analytical procedures

- *Is the risk of material misstatement low enough that inferences from indirect evidence, such as substantive analytical procedures, are appropriate to make conclusions about an account?*
- *Are the underlying data used in evaluating an account both relevant and reliable?* External sources of data that the auditor might use to develop expectations include analyst reports and industry benchmarking data, while internal sources include budgets and forecasts, operational information for current and prior periods, and information from discussions with management.
- *Are the relationships among the data logical and justified by current economic conditions?* Plausible relationships among data may reasonably be expected to exist and continue in the absence of known conditions to the contrary. For example, a plausible relationship likely exists between store square footage and retail sales by store. Another example would be the comparison of linked account relationships, such as interest expense and interest-bearing debt.

Prompt for Critical Thinking #1   It's Your Turn!

Provide examples of relationships and sources of data that an auditor might use in performing analytical procedures.

- _____
- _____
- _____
- _____
- _____

Performing Analytical Procedures

The process for performing analytical procedures is the same regardless of whether the analytical procedures are performed during planning, as a substantive test, or during the final review. This chapter focuses on analytical procedures as a substantive test. *Chapter 7* provides discussion about using analytical procedures as a risk assessment procedure, while *Chapter 14* discusses using analytical procedures when completing the audit. We list the steps in the process here, along with a discussion of any differences due to when the analytical procedure is being performed:

1. Determine the suitability of a particular analytical procedure for given account(s)/assertion(s), considering the risks of material misstatement and tests of details planned.

2. Evaluate the reliability of data that the auditor is using to develop an expectation of account balances or ratios. In evaluating data reliability, the auditor should consider the source of the data, its comparability, the nature of information available about the data, and the controls over the preparation of the data.

3. Develop an expectation of recorded account balances or ratios, and evaluate whether that expectation is precise enough to accomplish the relevant objective. The expectation can be about an account balance, a ratio, or other expected relationship. For example, the auditor might develop an expectation about the client's revenue account, the gross profit margin, or the average payroll expenses per location. In developing an expectation, the auditor relies on information obtained during earlier activities in the audit opinion formulation process. Based on this information, the auditor, for example, may expect an account balance to increase or decrease from the prior period, the auditor may develop a range in which the account balance is expected to fall, or the auditor may develop a point estimate, depending on the objective of the procedure.

   Planning analytical procedures:
   Objective: Identify accounts with heightened risk of misstatement during audit planning to provide a basis for designing and implementing responses to the assessed risks
   Precision of expectation: Less precise

   Substantive analytical procedures:
   Objective: Obtain evidence regarding the accuracy of account balance/assertion
   Precision of expectation: More precise

   Review analytical procedures:
   Objective: Assist the auditor in forming an overall conclusion about whether the financial statements are consistent with the auditor's understanding of the entity
   Precision of expectation: Less precise

4. Define when the difference between the auditor's expectation and what the client has recorded would be considered significant. When the auditor develops an expectation, it is unlikely that the expectation will be the same as what the client has recorded. Before comparing the auditor's expectation with what the client has recorded, the auditor should define the difference amount that would be considered significant; this will require consideration of the auditor's assessed materiality level and the auditor's desired level of assurance. Typically, when the risk of material misstatement is higher, the amount of acceptable difference is lower.

5. Compare the client's recorded amounts with the auditor's expectation to determine any significant unexpected differences. This is a mechanical step that identifies any significant differences between the auditor's expectation and the client's recorded balance. For example, the auditor might have developed

an expectation that interest expense will be $1.5 million. If the client has a recorded balance of $1.75 million, the auditor will refer to the assessment made in Step 4 to determine whether this difference is significant. As another example, the auditor might have expected the gross profit margin to be 23%. If the client's recorded gross profit margin is 25.5%, the auditor will refer to the assessment made in Step 4 to determine if this difference is significant.

6. Investigate significant unexpected differences.

> *Planning analytical procedures*: Significant unexpected differences suggest that substantive procedures for the account/assertion will be increased.
>
> *Substantive analytical procedures*: The auditor should hypothesize as to the possible reasons for the difference, inquire of management as to possible reasons for the difference, and obtain evidence to quantify and corroborate these possible reasons. The auditor may need to increase the tests of details for the relevant account/assertion.
>
> *Review analytical procedures*: The auditor should perform additional procedures as necessary to form an overall conclusion about whether the financial statements are consistent with the auditor's understanding of the entity.

7. Ensure that the following have been appropriately documented: auditor's expectation from Step 3, including the factors that the auditor considered in developing the expectation, the results in Step 4, and the audit procedures conducted in Steps 5 and 6.

Why It Matters

Deficiencies in Substantive Analytical Procedures at KBA Group and PCAOB Practice Alert No. 12

This feature provides examples of the PCAOB's concerns regarding auditors' performance and documentation of substantive analytical procedures.

In its inspection of the audit firm KBA Group, the PCAOB noted that in one of KBA Group's audits, the audit team failed to perform and document adequate substantive analytical procedures relating to expenses. While substantive analytical procedures can provide important audit evidence related to income statement accounts, it is important for the audit team to appropriately document and adequately perform these procedures. Otherwise, reviewers of the workpapers, such as the PCAOB, might conclude that the audit team did not obtain sufficient appropriate evidence to support its audit opinion.

U.S. auditing standards require the auditor to document the process of substantive analytical procedures, including the expectation developed by the auditor, and follow up on unexpected differences between the auditor's expectation and the client's recorded account.

For further details, see PCAOB Release No. 104-2005-016.

PCAOB Staff Audit Practice Alert No. 12

The weaknesses in the application of substantive analytical procedures at KBA Group represent just one example of PCAOB concerns in this area. In its 2014 *Staff Audit Practice Alert No. 12*, the

PCAOB provides examples of other concerns related to appropriately performing substantive analytical procedures (p. 24):

Inspections staff observed instances in which auditors, when using substantive analytical procedures that were intended to achieve a high level of assurance;

- Failed to develop expectations that were sufficiently precise, for example, because the expectations did not appropriately disaggregate data to identify potential material misstatements;
- Did not determine that there was a plausible and predictable relationship among the data used in the substantive analytical procedure, which is necessary to develop suitable expectations of the recorded amount of revenue;
- Did not establish an amount of difference from the expectation that could be accepted without further investigation;
- Did not investigate significant differences from expectations;
- Failed to perform procedures to obtain evidence to corroborate management's responses regarding significant unexpected differences with other evidential matter; and
- Failed to test the completeness and accuracy of the information obtained from the company that was used in performing analytical procedures.

Source: PCAOB Staff Audit Practice Alert No. 12.

Improving the Effectiveness of Substantive Analytical Procedures

The effectiveness of a substantive analytical procedure depends on several factors, including: (a) the nature of the assertion being tested; (b) the plausibility and predictability of the relationships in the data; (c) the availability and reliability of the data used to develop the expectation; (d) the precision of the expectation that the auditor develops; and (e) the rigor of the analytical procedure employed. While the first three factors are relatively self-explanatory, we expand on the last two factors, precision and rigor.

Precision of Auditor Expectation In terms of expectation precision, the auditor can develop a very general expectation, for example, that interest income will increase over the prior year. This expectation is likely not precise enough for a substantive analytical procedure. To develop a more precise expectation, the auditor may use disaggregated data. **Disaggregation** involves breaking data down into their component parts, such as different periods, geographical locations, customer type, or product lines. For example, in the case of interest income, the auditor could disaggregate based on the type of investment, because interest rates will likely vary across investment types. The more you disaggregate the information, the more precise the expectation.

Rigor of Analytical Procedure In terms of the rigor of analytical procedure, there are various types of analytical procedures, and these types vary in rigor. Three types of analytical procedures that tend to be less rigorous include trend analysis, ratio analysis, and scanning. Trend analysis involves the analysis of changes over time, and its rigor can be improved by including more periods in the trend, using disaggregated data, and using relevant external benchmarks (e.g., industry averages). Ratio analysis involves the comparison of relationships between accounts or between an account and nonfinancial data. Similar to trend analysis, if the auditor uses ratio analysis as a substantive analytical procedure, it is important to improve its rigor by using disaggregated data and relevant external benchmarks. When performing scanning, the auditor looks at account balances, listings of transactions, journals, and so on, in an effort to detect any unusual or unexpected balances or transactions. As with all analytical procedures, the auditor who is performing scanning needs to have an idea of what is usual or expected. The expectation is based on the auditor's knowledge of the client, of accounting, and common sense. For example, the auditor would typically not expect to see several entries for round numbers in millions of dollars posted to the revenue journal at the end of each quarter. The auditor would consider such entries unusual and would follow up to investigate this unexpected finding. While scanning can be a substantive analytical procedure, its precision and rigor may not always be sufficient for the level required for substantive analytical procedures.

A more rigorous approach to substantive analytical procedures is a reasonableness test. In a **reasonableness test,** the auditor develops an expected value of an account by using data partly or wholly independent of the client's accounting information system. For example, the auditor may develop an expectation of a client's interest income, which is equal to the average amount of investments held by the client for the year multiplied by the average interest rate paid on investments as determined by a source external to the client. While such simple models may be sufficient, the auditor can improve the rigor of this analytic by disaggregating the data, possibly by investment type and time period (e.g., a separate expectation for each month or quarter). A reasonableness test for revenue may be more detailed. For example, an auditor could use a reasonable test for revenue based on the number of units sold, the unit price by product line, different pricing structures, and an understanding of industry trends.

One of the most rigorous approaches to analytical procedures is regression analysis. In performing regression analysis, the expected, or predicted, value is determined using a statistical technique where one or more factors are used to predict an account balance. For example, the auditor may develop a regression

What Do You Think? **For Classroom Discussion**

Although regression analysis is one of the most rigorous approaches to analytical procedures, auditors do not commonly use it on many audit engagements. Why do you think that might be the case?

model that predicts revenue for a client that has hundreds of retail stores. The factors used in the model might include store square footage, economic factors such as employment data, and geographical location.

Brief Application of Substantive Analytical Procedures

Substantive analytical procedures are not simple techniques; they are part of a difficult decision-making process designed to provide evidence about the correctness of an account balance and should be used when the procedures are: (a) reliable and (b) more cost effective than other substantive procedures.

For example, consider the audit of natural gas revenue at a utility company. Assume that the auditor has tested controls over revenue recognition, including the processes of reading gas meters and the proper pricing of gas sold to customer homes. The auditor has concluded that internal controls are designed and operating effectively. Further, the auditor has concluded that consumers tend to pay their bills and that consumers do not have independent knowledge of the amount they should have been billed. Given these data, the auditor develops a regression model based on:

- Previous year's gas billings
- Changes in housing developments
- Changes in pricing of natural gas for the year
- Changes in the efficiency of energy use (index of efficiency considering new furnaces, insulation, etc.)
- Economic growth in the area

Using these data, the auditor develops a regression model that predicts expected revenue within a tolerable range of error, with 95% accuracy. If the auditor finds that the recorded revenue is within that range, further substantive testing of the account balance may not be necessary. Note that this conclusion is based on the assessment that the risk of material misstatement is low. In areas where significant risks of material misstatement exist, it is unlikely that audit evidence obtained from substantive analytical procedures alone will be sufficient. In those situations, the auditor will likely also need to perform substantive tests of details. However, if substantive analytical procedures provide reliable evidence, the auditor may be able to alter the type, timing, or extent of substantive tests of details.

If a comparison of the auditor's expectation based on the regression analysis and the client's recorded revenue balance indicates a significant difference, the auditor will follow up on this difference. The auditor should consider possible explanations for the difference, even considering the possibility that the auditor's expectation is flawed in some way (e.g., the expectation did not incorporate important and recent economic events). Other causes for significant differences could be error or fraud in the client's accounting records. The auditor will also inquire of the client as to possible explanations. However, the auditor's follow-up needs to go beyond client inquiry; the follow-up needs to include quantification and corroboration. **Quantification** involves determining whether an explanation for the difference can account for the amount of the difference. If not, the auditor may

Analytical Procedures Are Not Client Estimates

This feature provides important advice about the distinction between the work of the auditor and the work of client management.

There is sometimes confusion about the use of analytical procedures because they often look like client estimates. For example, in smaller businesses, the auditor's working papers may have the most useful data on bad-debt write-offs, percentage of bad debts as a percentage of sales, changes in credit policies, and changes in the volume of sales. The auditor may use these data in testing an estimate of the allowance for uncollectible accounts prepared by the client. However—and this is important—management is responsible for estimating the allowance.

The auditor's work is to gather evidence on the accuracy of that estimate. The auditor's testing may come from gathering evidence to support the client's underlying assumptions and recomputing the estimate. Alternatively, the auditor's testing may come from a substantive analytical procedure—using accumulated data in the auditor's workpapers, plus additional economic data, to come up with an independent estimate of the proper account balance. That estimate, however, represents audit evidence that the auditor should use in determining whether the client's account balance is correct. Substantive analytical procedures provide independent evidence about account balances—they do not replace management's underlying estimation process.

6-9 Substantive analytical procedures are required on every audit. (T/F)

6-10 One of the most rigorous approaches to substantive analytical procedures is regression analysis. (T/F)

6-11 In which of the following scenarios are analytical procedures most appropriate as a substantive audit procedure?
   a. The auditor's primary objective is to reduce audit costs to a minimum.
   b. Internal control risk is high, and therefore it is not efficient to test controls.
   c. Planning analytical procedures indicate that misstatements are likely to occur in significant account balances.

   d. Substantive analytical procedures would not be appropriate in any of the above scenarios.

6-12 Which of the following statements is false regarding substantive analytical procedures?
   a. Substantive analytical procedures are not required to be performed on all audit engagements.
   b. If the results of substantive analytical procedures suggest that an account balance is materially correct, the auditor can reduce the evidence needed from tests of details.
   c. The auditor would perform substantive analytical procedures after tests of details.
   d. All of the above statements are true.

need to perform additional work. **Corroboration** involves obtaining sufficient evidence that the explanation is accurate. The auditor must not just accept the client's explanation without corroborating that explanation.

LO 4

Describe the unique evidence requirements for accounts involving management estimates, accounts involving related-party transactions, and situations requiring the use of a specialist/expert.

Additional Evidence Considerations

Auditing Management Estimates

Most significant measurements in the financial statements are subject to estimates, appraisals, or other management assumptions. Examples include warranty liabilities, allowance for doubtful accounts or loan loss reserves, pension costs

Focus on Fraud

Common Types of Earnings Management Techniques Involving Accounting Estimates

Accounting estimates have often been subject to earnings management. This feature highlights the importance of auditors taking special care to exercise appropriate professional skepticism in evaluating the reasonableness of management estimates so that the auditor can mitigate earnings management.

What types of earnings management related to estimates and other subjective assessments should auditors be prepared to detect and address? Examples of common types include:

- *Cookie jar reserves techniques*—This approach involves management over-accruing expenses in the current period to set up a reserve that is reversed back into income in a future period. Examples of areas where cookie jar reserves are often created include: accounts receivable allowance for doubtful accounts, sales returns and allowances, warranty allowances, and inventory allowance for valuation declines. This approach is typically used when management has already met its numbers and has extra cushion that can be saved for future periods that may not be as good.

- *Big bath techniques*—This approach is used when a company is already reporting bad news and involves charging as many potential future costs to expenses in the current bad year, so that those costs will not have to be recognized in the future. While the current year stock price will be negatively affected, management thinks that a little more bad news will not be noticed, and future years will look particularly good and the stock price will rebound accordingly. Auditors should watch for the application of big bath techniques when companies report asset impairments, dispose of a significant part of their operations, or restructure debt.

- *Amortization, depreciation, and depletion techniques*—When a company has long-lived assets, those assets are expensed through amortization, depreciation, or depletion. The auditor should watch for management to exercise judgment in making selective decisions about the type of write-off method used, the write-off period, and the estimate of salvage value that might indicate earnings management.

and liabilities, valuations of long-lived assets, fair market value assessments, and analysis of goodwill for possible impairment. The auditor must substantiate such estimates with independent, objective, and verifiable data.

Auditors need to understand the process used by management in developing management estimates, including: (a) controls over the process, (b) the reliability of underlying data in developing the estimate, (c) use of outside experts by management (e.g., how they were used and their expertise), and (d) how management reviews the results of the estimates for reasonableness.

The auditor should evaluate, based on the audit evidence, whether the accounting estimates in the financial statements are reasonable. The auditor should also obtain sufficient appropriate audit evidence about whether disclosures in the financial statements related to accounting estimates are appropriate. Options for obtaining evidence include:

- Determine whether events occurring up to the date of the auditor's report provide audit evidence regarding the accounting estimate (e.g., sale of a discontinued product shortly after the period end may provide audit evidence relating to the estimate of its net realizable value).
- Test how management made the accounting estimate and the data on which it is based. The auditor should evaluate whether the method of measurement used is appropriate, the assumptions used by management are reasonable, and the data on which the estimate is based are sufficiently reliable.
- Test the operating effectiveness of controls over the process management used to make the accounting estimate, together with appropriate substantive procedures.
- Develop a point estimate or range to evaluate management's point estimate.

Estimates based on industry-wide or economy-wide trends need to be independently evaluated. For example, earnings assumptions related to returns on pension funds should be based on how well stocks, as a whole, are doing within

PCAOB Considers Change in Standard for Auditing Management Estimates

Why It Matters

This feature outlines a proposed auditing standard that would strengthen the auditing of management estimates.

In 2017, the PCAOB proposed a new auditing standard for auditing accounting estimates, including fair value measurements. In response to the proposal, Board member, Steven Harris noted that "accounting estimates and fair value measurements are more prevalent and significant in today's financial statements than ever. These estimates often have a major impact on a company's reported financial position and results of operations. Because these estimates often involve subjective assumptions and measurement uncertainty, they are susceptible to management bias. Thus, these accounts usually comprise the areas of high risk in an audit." He goes on to state: "If auditors do not appropriately evaluate management's estimates . . . they may perform an insufficient audit, potentially harming investors."

The proposal emphasizes that auditors need to apply professional skepticism and devote greater attention to potential management bias when auditing accounting estimates. The proposal strengthens existing requirements by:

- Prompting auditors to devote greater attention to addressing potential management bias in accounting estimates, while reinforcing the need for professional skepticism;

- Extending certain key requirements in the existing standard on auditing fair value measurements—the newest and most comprehensive of the existing standards on auditing accounting estimates and fair value measurements—to all accounting estimates to reflect a uniform approach to substantive testing;

- Focusing auditors on estimates with greater risk of material misstatement;

- Providing specific requirements and direction to address certain aspects unique to auditing the fair value of financial instruments, including the use of information from pricing sources; and

- Making other updates to the requirements for auditing accounting estimates to address particular aspects of auditing estimates.

You may access the proposed standard at https://pcaobus.org/Rulemaking/Docket043/2017-002-auditing-accounting-estimates-proposed-rule.pdf

the economy and on long-run predicted growth within the economy. Other pension data include actuarial reports on life expectancies and benefits that rely on experts. The auditor should review such evidence for consistency with economic reports and actuarial reports, and compare with the assumptions used by other clients and other companies in the same industry.

Auditing Related-Party Transactions

Some client transactions are **related-party transactions**. These are transactions that a client has with other companies or individuals related to either the client or client's senior management. Related-party transactions can occur between:

- Parents and subsidiaries
- An entity and its owners
- An entity and other organizations in which it has part ownership, such as joint ventures
- An entity and an assortment of special-purpose entities (SPEs), such as those designed to keep debt off the balance sheet

Many related-party transactions are conducted in the normal course of business and have no higher risk of material misstatement than similar transactions with unrelated parties. However, the nature of related-party relationships and transactions may give rise to higher risks of material misstatement of the financial statements than transactions with unrelated parties. For example, related-party transactions may be motivated primarily to engage in fraudulent financial reporting or to conceal misappropriation of assets. In some cases, related-party transactions may not be conducted under normal market terms and conditions. These types of transactions present unique challenges for auditors.

Focus on Fraud   Red Flags of Related-Party Transactions

This feature identifies red flags that may indicate the presence of related-party frauds.

Loan Frauds
Interest-free loans
Loans to officers, board members, or employees
Purchasing Frauds
Purchases at bargain prices
Premium prices for generic products
Unusually large amounts of production scrap due to faulty materials
Sales Frauds
Unusual rights of return
Unusual extended repayment terms

When performing procedures for related-party transactions, the auditor should expect the client to have an information system, with effective internal controls, that can identify all related parties and account for all related-party transactions. The auditor should begin with an understanding of the information system developed by the client to identify such transactions. The auditor should be aware that, in some cases, the client might not want to have related-party transactions discovered. Still, the auditor will work to obtain a list of all related parties and develop a list of all transactions with those parties during the year.

Once the auditor has identified all related parties, the auditor can use data analytics tools (discussed in *Chapter 8*) to read the client files and list all transactions that occurred with these parties. The auditor then investigates the transactions to determine whether the client has properly recorded and disclosed them. *Exhibit 6.10* provides an overview of relevant audit procedures for related-party transactions.

Exhibit 6.10
Audit Procedures for Related-Party Transactions

AUDIT OBJECTIVE: Determine if related-party transactions occurred during the year and whether they are properly: (a) authorized, (b) recorded, and (c) disclosed in the financial statements.

a. Inquire of the client about processes used to identify related-party transactions and the client's approach to accounting for related-party transactions.
b. Ask the client to prepare a list of all related parties. Supplement that list with disclosures that have been made to the Securities and Exchange Commission (SEC) of top officers and directors in the company. For smaller businesses, supplement the list with a listing of known relatives who may be active in the business or related businesses.
c. Ask the client for a list of all related-party transactions, including those with SPEs or variable interest entities that occurred during the year.
d. Discuss the appropriate accounting for all identified related-party transactions with the client and develop an understanding of the appropriate disclosure for the financial statements.
e. Inquire of the client and its lawyers as to whether the client is under any investigation by regulatory agencies or law officials regarding related-party transactions.
f. Review the news media and SEC filings for any investigations of related-party transactions of the client.
g. Use generalized audit software to read the client's files and prepare a list of all transactions that occurred with related entities per the lists identified earlier. Compare the list to that developed by the client to help determine the quality of the client's information system.

(Continues)

(*Continued*)

h. Identify all unusual transactions using information specific to the client, including information on (a) unusually large sales occurring near the end of a period, (b) sales transactions with unusual terms, (c) purchase transactions that appear to be coming from customers, and (d) any other criteria the auditor might consider useful.

i. Review the transactions and investigate whether or not the transactions occurred with related entities. If related parties can be identified, determine the purpose of the transactions and consider the appropriate financial statement disclosure.

j. Determine whether any of the transactions were fraudulent or were prepared primarily to develop fraudulent financial statements. If there is intent to deceive, or if there is misuse of corporate funds, report the fraud or misuse to the board of directors. Follow up to determine if appropriate action is taken. If such action is not taken, consult with legal counsel.

k. Determine the appropriate accounting and footnote disclosure.

l. Prepare a memo on findings.

Throughout the audit, the auditor should remain alert for information that may indicate the existence of related-party relationships or transactions that management has not previously identified or disclosed to the auditor.

Using a Specialist/Expert to Assist with Obtaining Audit Evidence

When obtaining audit evidence, auditors may need to rely on work performed by an outside specialist/expert. (International auditing standards use the term *expert* rather than specialist; for simplicity, we use the term *specialist*.) For some accounts, expertise in a field other than accounting or auditing is necessary to obtain sufficient appropriate audit evidence. For example, using the work of and relying on the valuation opinions of outside specialists are particularly relevant in auditing natural resources and other long-lived assets in which subject-matter expertise is required. Another example where the auditor would likely rely on a specialist would be in estimating oil and gas reserves.

Auditing standards require the auditor to understand the role, knowledge, and objectivity of the specialist, and how the specialist's work affects important financial accounts.

When using the work of an **auditor's specialist**, the auditor needs to evaluate the professional qualifications of the individual. In making this evaluation, the auditor considers:

- The professional certification, license, or other recognition of the competence of the specialist in his or her field, as appropriate
- The reputation and standing of the specialist in the views of peers and others familiar with the specialist's capability or performance
- The specialist's experience in the type of work under consideration

Further, the auditor needs to understand the nature of the work performed by the specialist. The auditor will:

- Obtain an understanding of the methods and assumptions used by the specialist
- Make appropriate tests of data provided to the specialist, taking into account the auditor's assessment of control risk
- Evaluate whether the specialist's findings support the related assertions in the financial statements

It's Your Turn!   *Prompt for Critical Thinking #2*

Provide additional examples where the auditor would be likely to rely on the work of a specialist.

- _____

- _____

- _____

AU-C 620 notes that even when the auditor uses a specialist to obtain audit evidence, the auditor still has ultimate responsibility for the audit opinion.

The auditor has sole responsibility for the audit opinion expressed, and that responsibility is not reduced by the auditor's use of the work of an auditor's specialist. Nonetheless, if the auditor using the work of an auditor's specialist, having followed this section, concludes that the work of that specialist is adequate for the auditor's purposes, the auditor may accept that specialist's findings or conclusions in the specialist's field as appropriate audit evidence.

Why It Matters

PCAOB Considers New Standard on Using Specialists

This feature highlights an emerging issue related to auditors' use of specialists. Auditors need to be current on evolving standards.

In June 2017, the PCAOB proposed to amend its auditing standards to strengthen the requirements that apply when auditors use the work of specialists in an audit. Companies across many industries use specialists for many things including to assist in developing accounting estimates; to interpret laws, regulations, and contracts; or to evaluate the certain physical. Specialists include, among others, actuaries, appraisers, other valuation specialists, legal specialists, environmental engineers, and petroleum engineers. Auditors often use the work of these companies' specialists as audit evidence. Additionally, auditors might use the work of auditors' specialists to assist in their evaluation of significant accounts and disclosures, including accounting estimates in those accounts and disclosures.

The PCAOB has noted that there is substantial diversity in practice regarding the use of the work of specialists, such as how auditors use engaged specialists and what procedures auditors perform to evaluate the work of companies' specialists.

The goals of the proposed standard's amendments are to:

- Strengthen requirements for evaluating the work of a company's specialist
- Apply a risk-based approach to supervising and evaluating the work of both auditor-employed and auditor-engaged specialists.

You may access the proposed standard at https://pcaobus.org/ Rulemaking/Docket044/2017-003-specialists-proposed-rule.pdf

Check Your Basic Knowledge

6-13 When testing management estimates, the auditor should understand the process that management uses to develop estimates.   (T/F)

6-14 When the auditor uses the work of an auditor specialist, the auditor's responsibility for the audit opinion is reduced.   (T/F)

6-15 Which of the following transactions would be least likely to be a related-party transaction?

    a. A purchase transaction between an entity and its owners.

    b. A debt-related transaction between an entity and one of its SPEs.

    c. An exchange of property between an entity and a joint venture in which the entity has part ownership.

    d. Writing off obsolete inventory prior to year-end.

6-16 Which of the following procedures would an auditor typically perform first when assessing the reasonableness of management's estimate of its pension liability?

    a. Inspect documentation related to the pension transactions that the client has recorded.

    b. Develop an understanding of management's process for developing the estimate.

    c. Identify sensitive management assumptions.

    d. Review transactions occurring prior to the report release date to assess the reasonableness of management estimates.

LO 5

Describe the characteristics of quality audit documentation, including the role of audit programs.

Documenting Audit Evidence

Audit documentation is the record that forms the basis for the auditor's representations and conclusions. Audit documentation facilitates the planning, performance, and supervision of the audit and forms the basis of the review of the quality of the work performed. Documentation may be in paper or in electronic form.

Auditors would prefer that others never question their work; that is an unrealistic expectation. The documentation of audit work must stand on its own. The documentation should make it possible for an experienced auditor to evaluate the evidence independently of the individuals who performed the audit and reach the same conclusion. AS 1215 notes that the documentation provides the basis for conclusions reached on the audit, and document how the auditor reached significant conclusions. AS 1215 states, "Audit documentation should be prepared in sufficient detail to provide a clear understanding of its purpose, source, and the conclusions reached. Also, the documentation should be appropriately organized to provide a clear link to the significant findings or issues."

Audit documentation should include information about planning and risk assessment procedures (including the response to risk assessment procedures), audit work performed (including tests of controls and substantive procedures), conclusions reached, and significant issues identified and their resolution.

Documenting Risk Assessment Procedures

The auditor documents the risk assessment procedures, as they form the foundation for the audit. For example, the auditor should document the overall audit strategy and the audit plan. Further, the auditor should document the overall planned responses to the assessed risks of material misstatement, and the nature, timing, and extent of audit procedures to be performed, as well as the linkage of those procedures with the assessed risks at the relevant assertion level. The documentation serves an important planning function for the audit; it also serves as evidence that the auditors took their responsibilities seriously in evaluating potential problems or special circumstances related to the audit. *Exhibit 6.11* provides examples of information related to the risk assessment procedures that the auditor would typically document.

Exhibit 6.11

Examples of Information Documented from Risk Assessment Procedures

- Interviews with key executives, with implications clearly drawn for the conduct of the audit
- Business risk analysis, fraud risk analysis, and analytical procedures, with a clear identification of accounts and assertions requiring special audit attention
- The auditor's assessment of materiality, overall audit approach, and personnel needed
- Evidence of planning (including identification of and response to risks of material misstatement), including the audit program
- Audit approach and basic data utilized to identify risk, including fraud risk
- Updates on how significant issues from previous year's audits are addressed during the current audit
- An analysis of the auditor's assessment of internal control and a linkage of control deficiencies to expanded (or different) audit tests for accounts where high risk of material misstatements exists
- Memoranda that describe the auditor's conclusions regarding risk associated with acceptance or continuance of the client
- Extent of involvement of professionals with specialized skills

Documenting Tests of Controls and Substantive Procedures

After identifying risks of material misstatement and making a plan for responding to those risks, auditors execute that plan by performing audit procedures to obtain audit evidence. Documentation about audit procedures performed is critical in demonstrating that the auditor conducted the audit in a quality manner. The following are typical types of documentation used to demonstrate the auditor's work:

- The client's trial balance and any auditor-proposed adjustments to it
- Copies of selected internal and external documents
- Memos describing the auditor's approach to gathering evidence and the reasoning process in support of account balances
- Results of analytical procedures and tests of client records, the individuals responsible for performance, and subsequently, the review of the procedures performed
- Correspondence with specialists who provided evidence significant to the evaluation or accounting for assets or liabilities and the related revenue expense effects (e.g., valuation specialists), including an analysis of the independence and credentials of the specialists
- Auditor-generated analysis of account balances (e.g., audit software analysis of accounts and relationships)

As part of documenting the work performed, auditors assemble a **permanent file** that includes schedules, documents, and records that are relevant for the current and future audits. Items in the permanent file include the client's articles of incorporation, bylaws, bond covenant agreements, and loan agreements. The auditor also develops a **current file** that includes schedules, documents, and analyses that are relevant to the current-year audit. The current file includes findings from substantive tests and tests of controls. Examples of documents from outside parties retained in the current file include responses to the auditor's confirmation requests for accounts receivable, pending litigation, or bank loans. Auditor-generated documents, such as auditor memos, are also maintained in the current file.

Why It Matters

Auditor-Generated Memos as Audit Documentation

This feature discusses the importance of auditor-generated memos as audit documentation.

Auditors accumulate much evidence to reach an opinion as to whether a particular account balance is fairly stated. The auditor's reasoning process in assembling and analyzing evidence is important and should be documented via auditor-generated memos. At first you might think that documenting your own opinion is unnecessary. After all, you will have documented all the evidence underlying that opinion. However, the documentation must stand on its own; in other words, another auditor must be able to understand the reasoning process by which you evaluated that evidence and formulated your opinion. In order to gain that understanding, another auditor will not be able to rely on just talking to you. Over time you will likely forget important details about how you reached your opinions; therefore, documenting them for the audit file via an auditor-generated memo is essential.

Documenting Significant Findings and Their Resolution

Significant findings or issues are essential matters that are important to the analysis of the fair presentation of the financial statements. AS 1215 provides the following examples of significant finding or issues:

- Significant matters involving the selection, application, and consistency of accounting principles, including related disclosures. Significant matters include, but are not limited to, accounting for complex or unusual transactions, accounting estimates, and uncertainties, as well as related management assumptions.
- Evidence indicating a need for modifying planned auditing procedures.
- Results of auditing procedures signifying the existence of material misstatements, omissions in the financial statements, significant deficiencies, or material weaknesses in internal control over financial reporting.
- Evidence requiring audit adjustments. An **audit adjustment** is a correction of a misstatement of the financial statements that was or should have been proposed by the auditor, whether or not recorded by management, which could, either individually or when aggregated with other misstatements, have a material effect on the company's financial statements.

The PCAOB requires that the auditor document significant findings, as well as the actions taken to address them (including additional evidence obtained, where applicable). The following are factors the auditor will include in this documentation:

- Description of significant accounting issues that were identified during the course of audit and how they were resolved, including any correspondence with national office experts
- A clear articulation of the auditor's judgment and the reasoning process that led to the judgment on the fairness of the financial statements

Characteristics of Quality Audit Documentation

Audit documentation serves as the primary evidence of an audit. *Exhibit 6.12* provides an example of a workpaper related to an inventory price test. A review of *Exhibit 6.12* indicates that audit documentation should contain:

- A heading that includes the name of the audit client, an explanatory title, and the balance sheet date

---

It's Your Turn! *Prompt for Critical Thinking #3*

Provide examples of other significant findings that might occur in an audit. HINT: Reviewing AS 1215 will help you think of examples.

- _____
- _____
- _____
- _____

- The initials or electronic signature of the auditor performing the audit test and the date the test was completed
- The initials or electronic signature of the manager or partner who reviewed the documentation and the date the review was completed
- A unique workpaper page number (see C-1/2 in *Exhibit 6.12*; the page number is used to cross-reference to other workpapers)
- A description of the tests performed (including the items looked at) and the findings
- **Tick marks** and a tick mark legend indicating the nature of the work performed by the auditor († is an example of a tick mark used in *Exhibit 6.12*; the tick mark legend appears near the bottom of the workpaper)
- A conclusion as to whether the work performed indicates the possibility of material misstatement in an account
- A cross-reference to related documentation, when applicable (see references to other workpapers, including B-1 and B-2, in *Exhibit 6.12*)
- A section that identifies all significant issues that arose during the audit and how they were resolved
- A comprehensive memorandum that delineates the auditor's analysis of the consistency of audit evidence and the conclusions reached regarding the fairness of the financial presentation (see references to other work performed at B-1 and B-2 in *Exhibit 6.12*. A second page of this workpaper, C-2/2, would likely include a more comprehensive memo.)

Exhibit 6.12
Workpaper for Inventory Price Test

	C-1/2
Gordon's Bay Manufacturing	Prepared by: ACM
Inventory Price Test	Date: 1/21/19
Year Ended December 31, 2018	Reviewed by: KMJ
	Date: 1/30/19

Item No.	Item Name	Quantity	Cost per Unit	Extended Cost
4287	Advanced Microstamping machine	22*	$5,128†	112,816.00‡
5203	1/4 HP electric motor	10*	$39†	390.00‡
2208	Assembly kit for motor housing	25*	$12†	300.00‡
1513	Micro stamping machine, Model 25	200*	$2,100†	420,000.00‡
0068	Rack & Pinion component	300*	$42†	12,600.00‡
8890	Repair kits for stamping machines	1,000*	$48†	48,000.00‡
	Total value of items tested			594,106.00
	Items not tested			1,802,000.00
	Balance per general ledger			2,396,106.00§

Sampled items were selected utilizing a dollar unit sampling technique with materiality of $50,000, and internal control assessed as effective (B-1).

*Quantities agree with client physical inventory tested earlier.

†Traced to client's standard cost system that was independently tested (B-2). Amount agrees with client's standard cost.

‡Tested extension, no exceptions.

§Footed, no exceptions; agrees with trial balance.

Conclusion: No significant issues were noted. In my opinion, the pricing and clerical accuracy of inventory are proper.

Revisions to and Retention of Audit Documentation

Prior to the report release date, the auditor must have completed all necessary auditing procedures and obtained sufficient evidence to support the representations in the auditor's report. Audit documentation, which is the property of the auditor, should generally be completed and assembled within 45 to 60 days (depending on the type of client) following the audit report release date. After that date, the auditor must not delete or discard audit documentation before the end of the required retention period (generally seven years from the report release date).

Circumstances (discussed in *Chapter 14*) may require additions to audit documentation after the report release date. Any documentation that the auditor adds must indicate the date the documentation was added, the name of the person who prepared the additional documentation, and the reason for adding it.

Audit Programs

An audit program documents the procedures the auditor plans to perform in gathering audit evidence and records the successful completion of each audit step. The audit program provides an effective means of:

- Organizing and distributing audit work
- Monitoring the audit process and progress
- Recording the audit work performed and those responsible for performing the work
- Reviewing the completeness and persuasiveness of procedures performed

Most audit firms have standardized audit programs that auditors modify to fit a client's unique features, including risk factors. For example, the audit of accounts receivable might appear to be the same for most businesses. However, significant differences may exist in how each client processes receivables and the related controls, or their credit terms, or in the economic health of their industry that might cause an audit team to modify a standard audit program to fit the particular circumstances of the client.

Arthur Andersen's Shredding of Audit Firm Documentation

Why It Matters

This feature highlights the importance of retaining audit documentation.

As you may recall from our discussion of the downfall of Arthur Andersen in 2002, the final straw for Arthur Andersen was that when federal authorities began investigating the bankruptcy of Enron, the Houston office auditors on the Enron engagement (led by audit partner David Duncan) began aggressively destroying documentation and evidence related to their failed audit. Ultimately, the document destruction was what led to the downfall of Arthur Andersen. Federal investigators asked for documentation about the Enron audit and David Duncan, head partner of the Enron engagement team (who was ultimately the only person to plead guilty at the Arthur Andersen trial) ordered his team to destroy as many Enron-related documents as soon as possible. Almost comically, Duncan's secretary ultimately sent an email to the team stating: "Per Dave - No more shredding . . . We have been officially served for our documents."

What you may be surprised to learn is that the Supreme Court unanimously threw out the conviction of Arthur Andersen relating to document shredding. But, it was too late! Arthur Andersen had closed its doors, its clients had fled, and its 28,000 personnel had moved on, seeking employment elsewhere.

For further details, see https://www.legalzoom.com/articles/innocent-after-proven-guilty-supreme-court-throws-out-arthur-andersen-conviction

Exhibit 6.13 provides an excerpt of a typical audit program outlining some of the procedures that an auditor performed when auditing accounts, disclosures, and assertions in the revenue cycle, with a specific focus on procedures involving testing accounts receivables. *Exhibit 6.13* also highlights the primary assertion that the auditor is testing with each procedure.

Exhibit 6.13
Excerpt of Audit Program for Accounts Receivable

Procedure	Primary Assertion(s) Being Tested					Timing of Testing
	Existence	Completeness	Valuation or Allocation	Rights and Obligations	Presentation and Disclosure	
Obtain the accounts receivable information and agree it to the prior year and the ending general ledger		√				Year-end
Confirm accounts receivable (at the invoice level). For non-returned confirmations, vouch to provide evidence of (i) subsequent cash receipt and (ii) invoice or if not receipt, then (a) invoice and (b) evidence of delivery of service	√					End of third quarter
Confirm contract terms if there is a heightened risk of side agreements (e.g., software companies)	√		√	√		Year-end
Analytically review accounts receivable as a percentage of revenue at each of the three quarter ends (for this year and previous two years) and use this to predict accounts receivable at year-end	√	√				
Analytically review accounts receivable allowance, looking for abnormal swings in aging by size or quarter			√			Year-end
Inquire and review documentation to support the classification of receivables (i.e., short-term versus long-term classification; due from customers versus due from employees or officers; large credit balances that should be reclassified as a payable)					√	Year-end

6-17 The auditor should document significant issues that were identified and how they were resolved.   (T/F)

6-18 The auditor should use a standardized audit program, without any modifications, for all clients.   (T/F)

6-19 Which of the following statements is <u>true</u> regarding audit documentation?

   a. Auditors document only those significant issues that have not been resolved by the audit report date.

   b. Audit documentation provides the principal support for the audit opinion expressed by the auditor.

   c. Audit documentation would identify who reviewed the audit work but not who performed the audit work.

   d. Documentation must be in paper format.

6-20 Which of the following statements describes a purpose of an audit program?

   a. An audit program is used to specify the procedures to be performed in obtaining audit evidence.

   b. An audit program is used to record the completion of each audit step.

   c. An audit program is useful for monitoring the progress of the audit.

   d. All of the above statements describe the purpose of an audit program.

LO 6

Apply the frameworks for professional decision making and ethical decision making for decisions made when conducting an audit.

Applying Decision-Making Frameworks

The following *End of Chapter* materials provide you an opportunity to apply the frameworks for professional decision making and ethical decision making for decisions made when conducting an audit: *6-28, 6-29,* and *6-36.*

- The auditor's job is to obtain sufficient appropriate evidence to support the audit opinion. The sufficiency of audit evidence relates to the quantity of audit evidence. The appropriateness of audit evidence refers to the quality of audit evidence (i.e., its relevance and reliability). What is determined to be sufficient and appropriate is affected by the client's risk of material misstatement (in other words, its inherent and control risks) or risk of material weakness in internal control. Sufficiency and appropriateness will vary across accounts and assertions. Be sure you can explain the relationships in *Exhibit 6.1*. (LO 1)

- The two categories of audit procedures discussed in this chapter are tests of controls and substantive procedures. Be sure you can describe and provide examples of the types of the procedures outlined in *Exhibit 6.5*. (LO 2)

- Substantive analytical procedures consist of evaluations of financial information through analyzing plausible relationships among both financial and nonfinancial data. The objective of these procedures is to obtain evidence regarding the accuracy of account balance/assertion. In performing these procedures, the auditor hypothesizes as to possible reasons for a difference between the auditor estimate and the amount recorded by the client. The auditor will then inquire of management as to possible reasons for the difference, and obtain evidence to quantify and corroborate these possible reasons. (LO 3)

- The auditor must substantiate management estimates. Auditors need to understand the process used by management in developing management estimates, including: (a) controls over the process, (b) the reliability of underlying data in developing the estimate, (c) use of outside experts by management (e.g., how they were used and their expertise), and (d) how management reviews the results of the estimates for reasonableness. (LO 4)

- The nature of related-party relationships and transactions may give rise to higher risks of material misstatement of the financial statements than transactions with unrelated parties. The auditor focuses on identifying related-party transactions, and then investigates the transactions to determine whether the client has properly recorded and disclosed them. (LO 4)

- When auditing some accounts, auditors need to hire a specialist with expertise in a field other than accounting or auditing to obtain sufficient appropriate audit evidence. Auditing standards require the auditor to understand the role, knowledge, and objectivity of the specialist, and how the specialist's work affects important financial accounts. (LO 4)

- Audit documentation is the record that forms the basis for the auditor's representations and conclusions. Audit documentation facilitates the planning, performance, and supervision of the audit and forms the basis of the review of the quality of the work performed. (LO 5)

- An audit program documents the procedures the auditor plans to perform in gathering audit evidence and records the successful completion of each audit step. (LO 5)

Significant Terms

Accounting records The records of initial accounting entries and supporting records.

Analytical procedures Evaluations of financial information through analyzing plausible relationships among both financial and nonfinancial data.

Appropriateness of audit evidence A measure of the quality of audit evidence, and includes both the relevance and reliability of the evidence.

Audit adjustment Correction of a misstatement of financial statements that was, or should have been, proposed by the auditor, whether or not recorded by management, that could, either individually or when aggregated with other misstatements, have a material effect on the company's financial statements.

Audit documentation The written record that forms the basis for the auditor's conclusions.

Auditor's specialist An individual or organization possessing expertise in a field other than accounting or auditing, whose work in that field is used by the auditor to assist the auditor in obtaining sufficient appropriate audit evidence. An auditor's specialist may be either an auditor's internal specialist (who is a partner or staff, including temporary staff, of the auditor's firm or a network firm) or an auditor's external specialist.

Corroboration Obtaining sufficient evidence that management's explanation is accurate.

Cross-footing Checking the agreement of the cross-addition of a number of columns of figures that sum to a grand total.

Current file File that includes schedules, documents, and analyses that are relevant to the current-year audit.

Cutoff period A period of time usually covering several days before and after the client's balance sheet date.

Cutoff tests Procedures applied to transactions selected from those recorded during the cutoff period to provide evidence as to whether the transactions have been recorded in the proper period.

Data analytics tools Qualitative and quantitative techniques and processes that auditors use to enhance their productivity and effectiveness; auditors extract, categorize, identify and analyze patterns or trends in the data; data analytics tools vary according to organizational requirements.

Direct evidence Audit evidence that requires only one inference to reach a conclusion about the assertion being tested. Usually that inference is that the sample taken is representative of the population as a whole.

Directional testing An approach to testing account balances that considers the type of misstatement likely to occur in the account balance and the corresponding evidence provided by other accounts that have been tested. The auditor normally tests assets and expenses for overstatement, and liabilities and revenues for understatement, because: (1) the major risks of misstatements on those accounts are in those directions, or (2) tests of other accounts provide evidence of possible misstatements in the other direction.

Disaggregation Breaking data down into their component parts, such as different time periods, geographical locations, customer type, or product lines.

Electronic data interchange An agreement between two trading partners whereby they routinely exchange relevant data via the computer, e.g., for routine purchase orders.

Footing Adding a column of figures to verify the correctness of the client's totals.

Indirect evidence Audit evidence that requires a linkage of inferences to provide assurance about the assertion being tested, that is, one or more inferences are made. Examples include inferences made when using analytical procedures as audit evidence.

Interim date A date at which audit evidence is collected earlier than the balance sheet date.

Management's specialist An individual or organization possessing expertise in a field other than accounting or auditing, whose work in that field is used by the client to assist management in preparing the financial statements.

Permanent file File that includes schedules, documents, and records that are relevant for the current and future audits.

Quantification Determining whether management's explanation for observed differences can, in fact, account for the observed difference.

Reasonableness test The development of an expected value of an account by using data partly or wholly independent of the client's accounting information system.

Recalculating estimated amounts Recomputing an amount that the client has already estimated, such as recomputing the allowance for doubtful accounts based on a formula related to the aging of accounts receivable ending balances.

Related-party transactions Transactions that a client has with other companies or people who may be related to either the client or client's senior management.

Relevance of evidence Evidence that provides insight on the validity of the assertion being tested; that is, the evidence bears directly on the assertion being tested.

Reliability of evidence A measure of the quality of the underlying evidence. It is influenced by risk, potential management bias associated with the evidence, and the quality of the internal control system underlying the preparation of the evidence.

Reperformance The auditor's independent execution of controls that were originally performed as part of the entity's internal control.

Roll-forward period The period between the confirmation date and the balance sheet date.

Scanning A type of analytical procedure involving the auditor's review of accounting data to identify significant or unusual items to test.

Significant finding or issues Substantive matters that are important to the procedures performed, evidence obtained, or conclusions reached on an audit.

Sufficiency of evidence Measure of the quantity of audit evidence.

Tests of extensions Recomputing items involving multiplication.

Tick marks Abbreviations and symbols used by auditors to document the work they have performed and any issues identified during their work.

Tracing Taking a sample of original source documents and ensuring that the transactions related to the source documents have been recorded in the appropriate journal and general ledger.

Vouching Taking a sample of recorded transactions and obtaining the original source documents supporting the recorded transaction.

Prompts for Critical Thinking

Prompt for Critical Thinking #1

- Financial information for equivalent prior periods, such as comparing the trend of fourth-quarter sales for the past three years and analyzing dollar and percent changes from the prior year, with expectations as to how the current results are expected to compare with these prior periods
- Expected or planned results developed from budgets or other forecasts, such as comparing actual division performance with budgeted performance
- Ratios of financial information, such as examining the relationship between sales and cost of goods sold or developing and analyzing common-sized financial statements
- Company and industry trends, such as comparing gross margin percentages of product lines or inventory turnover with industry averages, with a prior expectation as to how similar the client is with the industry averages
- Analysis of relevant nonfinancial information, such as analyzing the relationship between the numbers of items shipped and royalty expense or the number of employees and payroll expense

Prompt for Critical Thinking #2

- The valuation of land and buildings, plant and machinery, jewelry, works of art, antiques, and intangible assets
- The interpretation of contracts, laws, and regulations
- The analysis of complex or unusual tax compliance issues

Prompt for Critical Thinking #3

- Disagreements among members of the engagement team or with others consulted on the engagement about final conclusions reached on significant accounting or auditing matters
- Circumstances that cause significant difficulty in applying auditing procedures
- Significant changes in the assessed level of audit risk for particular audit areas and the auditor's response to those changes
- Any matters that could result in the modification of the auditor's report

Review Questions and Short Cases

NOTE: Completing *Review Questions and Short Case* does not require the student to reference additional resources and materials.

NOTE: We make special note of problems addressing fraud, international issues, professional skepticism, and ethics.

6-1 **LO 1** Refer to *Exhibit 6.1*. Auditing standards require the auditor to gather sufficient appropriate evidence to provide a reasonable basis for an opinion regarding the financial statements. What are the characteristics of: (a) sufficient audit evidence and (b) appropriate audit evidence? How are sufficiency and appropriateness related?

6-2 **LO 1** Refer to *Exhibit 6.1*. Describe how the sufficiency and appropriateness of evidence for a specific account are influenced by the risk of material misstatement associated with that account. Contrast how sufficiency and appropriateness of evidence would differ for a high-risk and a low-risk assertion.

6-3 `LO 1` What two audit evidence characteristics determine the appropriateness of audit evidence? Define these characteristics and identify factors that affect these characteristics.

6-4 `LO 1` What is directional testing? How does directional testing relate to the appropriateness of audit evidence?

6-5 `LO 1` Refer to *Exhibit 6.2* and describe the differences between vouching and tracing.

6-6 `LO 1` Discuss the relative reliability of internal and external documentation. Provide two examples of each type of documentation.

6-7 `LO 1` Sufficiency is a measure of the quantity of evidence. Identify factors that affect evidence sufficiency.

6-8 `LO 1` An auditor typically selects samples when testing controls. What are some factors that affect the sample sizes used when testing controls?

6-9 `LO 2` Refer to *Exhibit 6.5* and identify the nine types of audit procedures. Assume you are planning the audit of the PageDoc Company's inventory. PageDoc manufactures a variety of office equipment. Describe how you could use each of the nine procedures when auditing of inventory. For each procedure, identify the related assertion(s) the procedure is designed to test.

6-10 `LO 2` Refer to *Exhibit 6.5* and identify the nine types of audit procedures used as part of the audit evidence-gathering process. Following is a list of audit procedures performed. For each procedure, listed as (a) through (p), classify the evidence gathered according to one (or more, if applicable) of the audit procedure types indicated in *Exhibit 6.5* and identify the primary assertion(s) being tested. Organize your answer as follows:

Procedure	Type of Procedure	Assertion Tested
a.		
b.		

a. Calculate the ratio of cost of goods sold to sales as a test of overall reasonableness of the balance for cost of goods sold.

b. Trace a sales transaction from the origination of an incoming sales order to the shipment of merchandise to an invoice and to the proper recording in the sales journal.

c. Test the accuracy of the sales invoice by multiplying the number of items shipped by the authorized price list to determine extended cost. Foot the total and reconcile it with the total invoiced.

d. Select recorded sales invoices and trace the corresponding shipping documents to verify the existence of goods shipped.

e. Examine canceled checks returned with the client's January bank statement as support of outstanding checks listed on the client's December year-end bank reconciliation.

f. Perform inspection and independently count a sample of the client's marketable securities held in a safe deposit box.

g. Tour the plant to determine that a major equipment acquisition was received and is in working condition.

h. Review a lease contract to determine the items it covers and its major provisions.

i. Request a statement from a major customer as to its agreement or disagreement with a year-end receivable balance shown to be due to the audit client.

j. Develop a spreadsheet to calculate an independent estimate of the client's warranty liability (reserve) based on production data and current warranty repair expenditures.

k. Meet with the client's internal legal department to determine its assessment of the potential outcome of pending litigation regarding a patent infringement suit against the company.

l. Review all major past-due accounts receivable with the credit manager to determine whether the client's allowance for doubtful accounts is adequate.

m. Make test counts of inventory items counted by client personnel.

n. Obtain information about the client's processing system and associated controls by asking the client's personnel to fill out a questionnaire.

o. Examine board of directors' minutes for the approval of a major bond issued during the year.

p. Have the client's outside law firm send a letter directly to the auditor providing a description of any differences between the lawyer's assessment of litigation and that of the client.

6-11 **LO 2** Assume that an automotive company discloses the following risk factors, listed as (1) through (7), that might affect the financial statements.

1. Continued decline in market share, and a market shift (or an increase in or acceleration of market shift) away from sales of trucks or sport utility vehicles, or from sales of other more profitable vehicles in the U.S.

2. Continued or increased price competition resulting from industry overcapacity, currency fluctuations, or other factors.

3. Lower than anticipated market acceptance of new or existing products.

4. Substantial pension and postretirement health care and life insurance liabilities impairing our liquidity or financial condition.

5. Worse than assumed economic and demographic experience for our postretirement benefit plans (e.g., discount rates, investment returns, and health care cost trends).

6. The discovery of defects in vehicles resulting in delays in new model launches, recall campaigns, or increased warranty costs.

7. Unusual or significant litigation or governmental investigations arising out of alleged defects in our products or otherwise.

For each risk factor, identify a related account balance that the risk might affect.

For each account balance identified, indicate how the risk will affect the audit evidence you will gather. Identify the specific assertion of primary concern to the auditor.

6-12 **LO 2** An auditor has to determine both the reliability and the relevance of potential audit evidence in order to determine that appropriate audit evidence is gathered.

a. Explain the difference between relevance and reliability.

b. How does an auditor determine the reliability of potential audit evidence?

c. For each of the following items, listed as (1) through (6), identify whether the auditor has made a judgment error, and if there is a judgment error, whether the error relates to evidence reliability or relevance. Organize your answer as follows:

Judgment Error	Nature of Error	Explanation
Yes or No	Relevance, Reliability, or Both	Description of error

1. The auditor receives only 20% of the confirmations that were sent to customers to verify their account balance. The auditor responds by taking another sample of receivables to send out in place of the first sample. The auditor is convinced the first sample is not representative of the population as a whole.
2. The auditor sent a confirmation to an independent warehouse to confirm the existence of inventory owned by the audit client. There was no response. The auditor decided to visit the warehouse to independently inspect the inventory on hand.
3. The auditor decides to test the completeness of accounts payable by taking a sample of recorded accounts payable and tracing to the source document evidencing receipt of the goods or services. No exceptions were noted so the auditor does not expand the audit work.
4. An auditor wishes to test the valuation of a marketable security and inquires about management's intent for using the securities. Management indicates that they are intending to hold the securities as a long-term investment. The auditor decides that no further evidence is needed and that the securities are properly valued at cost.
5. The auditor notes that there are some problems with segregation of duties over accounts receivable that could affect the existence assertion. The client is aware that the auditor normally sends out accounts receivable confirmations. The auditor decides to expand the audit work by sending additional confirmations.
6. During the observation of inventory, the auditor notes a number of items that look old and apparently not used. The auditor discusses each item with the marketing manager to determine whether or not the item is considered saleable at normal prices.

6-13 **LO 3** What are the basic assumptions that must hold for an auditor to justify using analytical procedures as a substantive audit procedure?

6-14 **LO 3** Refer to the *Why It Matters* feature "Analytical Procedures Are Not Client Estimates." What is the relationship between an auditor's analytical procedure and a client's estimate?

6-15 **LO 3** Assume that the auditor proposes to audit sales by examining the relationship of sales and cost of sales to that of the previous two years, as adjusted for an increase in gross domestic product. Further, the auditor has assessed the risk of material misstatement (inherent and control risk) for this account as high. Explain whether this would be an effective test of the sales account balance.

6-16 **LO 3** Indicate how the auditor could use substantive analytical procedures in testing the following accounts:
a. Interest expense related to bonds outstanding.
b. Natural gas expense for a public utility company.
c. Supplies expense for a factory.
d. Cost of goods sold for a fast-food franchisor (e.g., Wendy's or McDonald's). Note that cost of goods sold tends to average about 35% of sales in fast-food franchises.
e. Salary expense for an office (region) of a professional services firm.

PROFESSIONAL SKEPTICISM

FRAUD

6-17 **LO 3** Assume that you have finished your substantive analytical procedures in the area of revenue. You used trend analysis and a reasonableness test and conducted the procedures at a disaggregated level. You are very pleased that your expectation is almost identical to what the client has recorded. Specifically, revenue increased in line with prior period increases and with the industry increases. You let your senior know that you likely do not have any additional work to perform.

Your senior asks you to reconsider your conclusion. What is likely the concern of your senior?

6-18 **LO 3** Review *Exhibit 6.9* and describe how the two audit approaches differ. What factors would lead to such a difference?

PROFESSIONAL SKEPTICISM

FRAUD

6-19 **LO 4** Refer to the *Focus on Fraud* feature "Common Types of Earnings Management Techniques Involving Accounting Estimates." Why might it be difficult for auditors to disallow companies' preferences to decrease existing reserves? Explain the role of professional skepticism in the context of evaluating management's explanations for their accounting for reserves in this context.

6-20 **LO 4** When testing accounts based on management estimates, the auditor should understand the process management uses to develop those estimates. What aspects of the process should the auditor understand?

6-21 **LO 4** Why would an auditor need to use an outside specialist when performing an audit? Identify specific accounts or assertions where the auditor may rely on a specialist.

6-22 **LO 4** What factors should the auditor consider when evaluating the professional qualifications of a specialist?

6-23 **LO 4** What is a related-party transaction? Provide examples of related-party transactions.

6-24 **LO 4** Review *Exhibit 6.10* and identify audit procedures that an auditor might use for related-party transactions.

6-25 **LO 5** What is audit documentation? Refer to *Exhibit 6.12* and identify the key components that each audit workpaper should contain.

6-26 **LO 5** What is meant by the statement *audit documentation ought to stand on its own*? What is the importance of this concept?

6-27 **LO 5** What are the purposes of an audit program?

ETHICS

6-28 **LO 5, 6** Entry-level auditing staff often inspect client records and documentation supporting accounting transactions to obtain evidence about the appropriate application of the applicable financial reporting framework. One of these tasks involves comparing original client records of transactions to client reports that summarize those transactions. In this way, auditors gain assurance that the transactions used to construct the financial statements are complete and accurate. Next, we report a case, based on an actual situation, relating to this task. However, we have changed some names to achieve confidentiality concerning audit firm personnel issues.

Elizabeth Jenkins was a staff auditor assigned to a large insurance client engagement. She was working on the portion of the audit concerning the client's claims loss reserves (reserves for future claims submitted by those insured by the insurance company). This reserve is analogous to the allowance for doubtful accounts of a company in the manufacturing or service sector. Essentially, the audit firm wants to provide assurance that the client's estimate of the amount of future claims is correctly stated on the balance sheet, with the appropriate write-off appearing on the income statement. Elizabeth was asked by the senior accountant on the engagement (Brett Stein) to tie out (in other words to compare) the client's claim loss reserve estimate (summarized on a large Excel worksheet) with the client's system-generated reports that provided the underlying data for the reserve estimate. The calculation is complex and involves inputs from several sources. Therefore, the tie-out process was very detail oriented and rather repetitive, involving a significant amount of time and patience to complete accurately. To demonstrate that she had compared the amount on the claims loss reserve Excel spreadsheet with that on the system-generated reports, Elizabeth was instructed to put a tick mark in both documents that would enable her senior to review her work. Along with each tick mark, Elizabeth was to write a short note that described whether the two amounts did or did not agree. Elizabeth proceeded through the task, inserting tick marks where appropriate and noting agreement in all cases between the spreadsheet and the system-generated report. Because Elizabeth felt pressed for time and was exceedingly bored with her task, she skipped many of the comparisons and simply inserted tick marks indicating agreement even though she had not compared the numbers. She rationalized her actions by telling herself that this client had good internal controls and she had never found disagreements between source documents in other areas of the audit in which she was involved. In the audit profession, this action is known as *ghost tick marking*.

After Elizabeth had completed the task, she moved on to other parts of the audit as instructed by Brett. Subsequently, Brett reviewed Elizabeth's work. During that review, he recomputed amounts on both the Excel spreadsheet and the system-generated reports. To his surprise, there were instances in which Elizabeth had noted agreement between the two documents when in fact the numbers were not the same.

Brett met with Elizabeth and asked her about what had happened. She readily confessed to her actions. Brett counseled her that this behavior was unacceptable because it implies that audit work was done when in fact the work was not done. This puts the audit firm at risk because it provides inappropriate assurance that the client's records are accurate, when in fact they are not accurate. Elizabeth was embarrassed and remorseful and promised not to engage in ghost tick marking in the future. Brett fully documented the situation in Elizabeth's personnel records and notified the manager and partner on the engagement, along with relevant human resource personnel. During the course of the year, the supervisory audit firm personnel on all of Elizabeth's engagements were notified of her actions, and her work was subjected to a more thorough review. The firm noted no problems with the quality of Elizabeth's work during that time. During her annual review, Elizabeth's supervisor again coached her on the severity of her mistake. However, during the annual review process of all staff accountants, the firm did consider firing her based upon the mistake but ultimately decided that her confession, remorseful attitude, and subsequent high-quality work merited that she retain her employment.

a. Try to put yourself in Elizabeth's position for a moment. Have you ever been tempted to do a low-quality job on some task that you considered mundane? Have you ever thought that your low-quality work would remain undiscovered?

b. Why is Elizabeth's misrepresentation of her work important to the firm?

c. What did Elizabeth ultimately do right in this situation, once her misrepresentation was discovered?

d. Do you agree with the outcome? Do you think the firm was too lenient? Too harsh? What would you recommend the firm do in this situation? Use the framework for ethical decision making from *Chapter 1* to help you arrive at a conclusion.

Fraud Focus: Contemporary and Historical Cases

FRAUD

6-29 **PCAOB**
(LO 5, 6) The PCAOB *Staff Audit Practice Alert No. 14* (April 21, 2016) begins with comments about auditors' judgments and decisions around improper altering of audit documentation (p. 1):

> *The PCAOB staff has prepared this practice alert to emphasize that improperly altering audit documentation in connection with a PCAOB inspection or investigation violates PCAOB rules requiring cooperation with the Board's oversight activities and can result in disciplinary actions with severe consequences. Improperly altering audit documentation is also inconsistent with an auditor's professional duty to act with integrity and as a gatekeeper in the public securities markets. Evidence identified in connection with certain recent oversight activities has heightened the staff's concern about such misconduct.*

It is important to note that PCAOB standards around audit documentation acknowledge and allow for making additions to audit documentation after the audit report release date (AS 1215, paragraph 16):

> *Audit documentation must not be deleted or discarded after the documentation completion date, however, information may be added. Any documentation added must indicate the date the information was added, the name of the person who prepared the additional documentation, and the reason for adding it.*

Further, there exist rules about cooperating with PCAOB inspectors. For example, PCAOB Rule 4006 states that every firm and any associated employee of every accounting firm must cooperate with the Board as its inspectors work to complete their inspection processes. Unfortunately, what has happened repeatedly is that firms and personnel involved in interacting with PCAOB inspection teams have made poor judgments and decisions once they realize that a particular engagement has been chosen by the PCAOB for inspection.

In the simplest description, what sometimes happens is that the engagement team, upon learning of an impending inspection of a particular engagement, "freaks out!" and alters audit documentation to shore up any potential areas that the team believes might be subject to criticism by the PCAOB inspectors. When the PCAOB discovers instances of altered documentation, it has taken enforcement actions, including revoking the Firm's registration with the PCAOB and barring relevant firm personnel from being associated with the registered firms.

In *Staff Audit Practice Alert No. 14* (p. 4), the PCAOB reminds auditors about the implications of such actions:

> *Improper alteration of audit documentation in connection with an inspection undermines the integrity of the Board's inspection processes and, as a result, impedes the Board's efforts to improve audit quality and fulfill its mission to protect investors and further the public interest in the preparation of informative, accurate, and independent audit reports. Changes and additions to audit documentation, if any, following the documentation completion date must be made strictly in accordance with AS 1215.13. To reduce the risk of improper alteration of audit documentation in connection with a PCAOB inspection, it is important for registered firms to take actions to assure that (1) work papers are properly archived; (2) work papers, once archived, are not improperly altered; and*

(3) the documentation provided to PCAOB inspectors for an audit is the originally-archived documentation for that audit (supplemented, as appropriate, in accordance with AS 1215).

a. Speculate as to why altering audit documentation undermines the integrity of the Board's inspection processes. Why is it fraud to alter audit documentation inaccurately and in a manner designed to appear that the audit engagement team did a "better job" than it actually did?

b. Put yourself in the place of an audit engagement partner or manager who has just learned that his/her client engagement is going to be the subject of inspection by PCAOB inspectors. Do you think you might be a bit anxious and worried about the outcome of the inspection? Imagine and articulate the pressure that an individual in that position might feel.

c. Think about the professional and ethical decision-making frameworks presented in *Chapter 1*. Where in the process might an individual auditor "go wrong" when realizing that his/her engagement is going to be scrutinized by a PCAOB inspection team, thereby resulting in fraudulently altering audit documentation?

d. The PCAOB encourages auditors who become aware of improper alteration of audit documentation to inform them (*Staff Audit Practice Alert No. 14*, p. 6):

The staff urges registered firms or individuals that become aware of any improper alteration of audit documentation that has occurred in connection with a Board inspection or investigation to report that information to the Board. They can do so by directly contacting staff in the Division of Registration and Inspections or the Division of Enforcement and Investigations, or by contacting the PCAOB Tip and Referral Center, including anonymously.

Put yourself in the place of an audit staff or senior. What factors would influence your decision to inform the PCAOB of a situation in which you realize that your superiors have altered documentation in anticipation of a PCAOB inspection? What concerns might you have in doing so, i.e., what would be the risks to you? What motivation would you have to do as the PCAOB requests?

6-30 **PCAOB**

PROFESSIONAL SKEPTICISM

FRAUD

(LO 1, 2, 3, 4, 5) The *Why It Matters* feature "Evidence-Related Findings in PCAOB Inspection Reports" presented at the beginning of the chapter provides excerpts of various PCAOB inspection reports. Review the feature and consider the information you learned while reading this chapter.

a. What is sufficient appropriate evidence and how does it differ across clients? Can what is determined to be sufficient and appropriate differ across accounts within the same client?

b. What are substantive analytical procedures, and when is evidence from these procedures appropriate?

c. What are the unique evidence challenges for accounts such as allowance for doubtful accounts? How is professional skepticism helpful when testing this type of account?

d. How could the use of a standardized audit program lead to some of the problems identified in the PCAOB inspection reports?

e. If the audit clients in these settings were committing fraudulent financial reporting, what are the implications of the auditors' evidence-related decisions noted in these PCAOB reports?

6-31   **LONGTOP FINANCIAL TECHNOLOGIES LIMITED, DELOITTE TOUCHE TOHMATSU CPA LTD.**
(LO 1, 3)

In May 2011, Deloitte Touche Tohmatsu (DTT) resigned as the auditor for Longtop Financial Technologies Limited (Longtop). We provide excerpts from DTT's resignation letter here:

As part of the process for auditing the Company's financial statements for the year ended 31 March 2011, we determined that, in regard to bank confirmations, it was appropriate to perform follow up visits to certain banks. These audit steps were recently performed and identified a number of very serious defects, including statements by bank staff that their bank had no record of certain transactions; confirmation replies previously received were said to be false; significant differences in deposit balances reported by the bank staff compared with the amounts identified in previously received confirmations (and in the books and records of the Group); and significant bank borrowings reported by bank staff not identified in previously received confirmations (and not recorded in the books and records of the Group).

In the light of this, a formal second round of bank confirmation was initiated on 17 May. Within hours, however, as a result of intervention by the Company's officials including the chief operating officer, the confirmation process was stopped amid serious and troubling new developments including: calls to banks by the Company asserting that Deloitte was not their auditor; seizure by the Company's staff of second round bank confirmation documentation on bank premises; threats to stop our staff leaving the Company premises unless they allowed the Company to retain our audit files then on the premises; and then seizure by the Company of certain of our working papers.

Then on 20 May the Chairman of the Company, Mr. Jia Xiao Gong called our Eastern Region Managing Partner, Mr. Paul Sin, and informed him in the course of their conversation that "there were fake revenue in the past so there were fake cash recorded on the books." Mr. Jia did not answer when questioned as to the extent and duration of the discrepancies. When asked who was involved, Mr. Jia answered: "senior management."

a.   What audit evidence-related problems did DTT encounter during the audit of Longtop?

b.   *Exhibit 6.8* describes external confirmations as generally being a reliable, high quality type of evidence. When would that generality not be accurate? What assumptions should the auditor address concerning confirmations before concluding that using confirmations will result in reliable audit evidence?

c.   Explain the role of professional skepticism in the context of evaluating evidence obtained from confirmations.

6-32   **GATEWAY COMPUTERS**
(LO 1, 2, 4)

The SEC took action against Gateway Computers in 2001 because it believed that Gateway systematically understated the allowance for doubtful accounts to meet sales and earnings targets. This is essentially the way the alleged fraud took place:

• Gateway sold most of its computers over the Internet and had a strong credit department that approved sales.

• When sales dropped, management decided to go back to customers who had been rejected because of poor credit approval.

- During the first quarter, it went after the better of the previously rejected customers.
- As the need for more revenue and earnings remained, Gateway continued down the list to include everyone.
- However, Gateway did not change any of its estimates for the allowance for uncollectible accounts.

At the end of the process, the poor credit customers represented about 5% of total income, but the SEC alleged that Gateway understated the allowance account by over $35 million, which amounted to approximately $0.07 per share. In essence, Gateway wanted to show it was doing well when the rest of the industry was doing badly.

a. How does management determine the valuation of the allowance for doubtful accounts? Does this process differ from account balances based on recording transactions, such as cash transactions? Is more precision required for determining account balances that do or do not contain estimates?

b. What information should the company use to make the estimate of the allowance for uncollectible accounts?

c. What evidence should the auditor gather to determine whether the client's estimate of the allowance for uncollectible accounts is fairly stated?

d. How should Gateway's expansion of sales to customers who they had previously rejected for credit affect the estimate of the allowance for doubtful accounts?

e. How important are changes in economic conditions to making an estimate of the allowance for doubtful accounts? Explain.

FRAUD

PROFESSIONAL SKEPTICISM

6-33 **CENDANT CORPORATION**
(LO 1, 2, 3)

Cendant Corporation, a company that sold travel and health club memberships, was the subject of an intensive fraud investigation that culminated in 1998. The company's website revealed the following statements contained in a report given to the SEC:

- *Irregular charges against merger reserves*—Operating results at the former Cendant business units were artificially boosted by recording fictitious revenues through inappropriately reversing restructuring charges and liabilities to revenues. Many other irregularities were also generated by inappropriate use of these reserves.
- *False coding of services sold to customers*—Significant revenues from members purchasing long-term benefits were intentionally misclassified in accounting records as revenue from shorter-term products. The falsely recorded revenues generated higher levels of immediately recognized revenues and profits for Cendant.
- *Delayed recognition of canceled memberships and chargebacks (a chargeback is a rejection by a credit-card-issuing bank of a charge to a member's credit card account)*—In addition to overstating revenues, these delayed charges caused Cendant's cash and working capital accounts to be overstated.
- *Quarterly recording of fictitious revenues*—Large numbers of accounts receivable entries made in the first three quarters of the year were fabricated; they had no associated clients or customers and no associated sale of services. This practice also occurred in the prior two years.
- The company also had other accounting errors. Approximately 6–9 cents per share of the total estimated restatement of earnings resulted from the elimination of these errors. These accounting

errors include inappropriate useful lives for certain intangible assets, delayed recognition of insurance claims, and use of accounting policies that do not conform to the applicable financial reporting framework.

a. Identify audit procedures (and audit evidence) that could have detected the misstatement of revenues and intangible assets. Be specific about each of the four statements provided.

b. How would the auditor's assessment of management integrity and management motivation have affected the auditor's decision regarding the audit procedures to perform? Explain the role of professional skepticism in this context.

6-34 **MINISCRIBE**
(LO 1, 2)

FRAUD

As reported in the *Wall Street Journal* (September 11, 1989), MiniScribe, nc., inflated its reported profits and inventory through a number of schemes designed to fool the auditors. At that time, MiniScribe was one of the major producers of disk drives for personal computers. The newspaper article reported that MiniScribe used the following techniques to meet its profit objectives:

• An extra shipment of $9 million of disks was sent to a customer near year-end and booked as a sale. The customer had not ordered the goods and ultimately returned them, but the sale was not reversed in the year recorded.

• Shipments were made from a factory in Singapore, usually by air freight. Toward the end of the year, some of the goods were shipped by cargo ships. The purchase orders were changed to show that the customer took title when the goods were loaded on the ship. However, title did not pass to the customer until the goods were received in the U.S.

• Returned goods were recorded as usable inventory. Some were shipped without any repair work performed.

• MiniScribe developed a number of just-in-time warehouses and shipped goods to them from where they were delivered to customers. The shipments were billed as sales as soon as they reached the warehouse.

For each of the techniques described, identify the audit evidence that might have enabled the auditor to uncover the fraud.

Application Activities

AUDITING STANDARDS
APPLICATION ACTIVITY

NOTE: Completing *Application Activities* requires students to reference additional resources and materials. Some *Application Activities* will require the student to reference relevant professional auditing standards. We make special note of these as *Auditing Standards Application Activities*.

6-35 **PCAOB**
(LO 4)

Access the PCAOB's proposed rule on the use of specialists at *https://pcaobus.org/Rulemaking/Docket044/2017-003-specialists-proposed-rule.pdf*

a. How does the PCAOB define the term "specialist"?

b. Provide examples of activities that require the use of specialists.

c. Describe the four ways that auditors can use specialists. Your response should include both company's and auditor's specialist.

d. Explain the PCAOB's observations from audit inspections and enforcement cases that highlight weaknesses in the use of specialists.

ETHICS

6-36 | **PCAOB, ERNST & YOUNG**
(LO 5, 6)

In August 2011, the PCAOB barred two former Ernst & Young LLP (EY) employees from auditing public companies, alleging they provided misleading documents to PCAOB inspectors who were evaluating the audit firm's work. One partner was barred for three years, and a senior manager was barred for two years. The PCAOB said that shortly before its inspectors were to inspect an EY audit of an unidentified company, the two auditors created, backdated, and placed in the audit files a document concerning the valuation of one of the audit client's investments. One of the auditors allegedly authorized other members of the audit team to alter other working papers in advance of the inspection. The changes were not disclosed to the PCAOB. EY indicated that the conduct of the two auditors had no impact on the client's financial statements or on EY's audit conclusions. The two Disciplinary Orders, available at the PCAOB website, are PCAOB Release No. 105-2011-004 and PCAOB Release No. 105-2011-005.

a. What is audit documentation, and why is it important to a quality audit?

b. Given that the auditors' conduct did not affect the client's financial statements or EY's conclusions, why was this situation over audit documentation of concern to the PCAOB?

c. Suppose your superior asked you to add or alter an audit workpaper after completing an audit engagement. Use the framework for ethical decision making presented in *Chapter 1* to outline your actions in this situation.

PROFESSIONAL SKEPTICISM

6-37 | **PCAOB, DELOITTE & TOUCHE**
(LO 1, 2, 4, 5)

On May 4, 2010, the PCAOB issued its public inspection of Deloitte & Touche, LLP, covering their inspection of audits conducted during 2009. You can obtain the inspection report at the PCAOB website. In their summary comments, the PCAOB inspectors stated:

> In some cases, the conclusion that the Firm failed to perform a procedure may be based on the absence of documentation and the absence of persuasive other evidence, even if the Firm claims to have performed the procedure. PCAOB Auditing Standard No. 3, *Audit Documentation* ("AS No. 3") provides that, in various circumstances including PCAOB inspections, a firm that has not adequately documented that it performed a procedure, obtained evidence, or reached an appropriate conclusion must demonstrate with persuasive other evidence that it did so, and that oral assertions and explanations alone do not constitute persuasive other evidence. (p. 3)

The report went on to say:

> In some cases, the deficiencies identified were of such significance that it appeared to the inspection team that the Firm, at the time it issued its audit report, had not obtained sufficient competent evidential matter to support its opinion on the issuer's financial statements or internal control over financial reporting ("ICFR").

It is reasonable to ask: what is the nature of these deficiencies; could this criticism happen to me; why didn't the reviewing partners detect the deficiencies? In order to understand how to answer these questions, the following excerpts describe the nature of deficiencies found on individual audits:

> In this audit, the Firm failed in the following respects to obtain sufficient competent evidential matter to support its audit opinion—

- The Firm failed to perform adequate audit procedures to test the valuation of the issuer's inventory and investments in joint ventures (the primary assets of which were inventory). Specifically, the Firm:
  - o Failed to re-evaluate, in light of a significant downturn in the issuer's industry and the general deterioration in economic conditions, whether the issuer's assumption, which it had also used in prior years, that certain inventory required no review for impairment was still applicable in the year under audit;
  - o Excluded from its impairment testing a significant portion of the inventory that may have been impaired, because the Firm selected inventory items for testing from those for which the issuer already had recorded impairment charges;
  - o Failed to evaluate the reasonableness of certain of the significant assumptions that the issuer used in determining the fair value estimates of inventory and investments in joint ventures;
  - o Failed to obtain support for certain of the significant assumptions that the Firm used when developing an independent estimate of the fair value of one category of inventory; and
  - o Failed to test items in a significant category of inventory, which consisted of all items with book values per item below a Firm-specified amount that was over 70 percent of the Firm's planning materiality.
- The Firm failed to perform adequate audit procedures to evaluate the issuer's assertion that losses related to the issuer's guarantees of certain joint venture obligations were not probable, because the Firm's procedures were limited to inquiry of management.
  - a. What is the auditor's responsibility to consider information outside of the client's records and processing to develop sufficient and appropriate audit evidence?
  - b. Why did the PCAOB consider the identified items as critical mistakes in performing an audit? What is the critical error of omission by the audit firm? Why would the specific problem lead to a deficiency in sufficient appropriate evidence?
  - c. Why is inquiry of management not considered sufficient evidence by itself?
  - d. Assumptions are assumptions! What is the auditor's responsibility regarding the questioning of the assumptions used by the client? Keep in mind that the client will claim that assumptions are just assumptions; it is difficult to say that one assumption is more correct than another assumption.
  - e. What do the deficiencies identified by the PCAOB suggest about the level of professional skepticism on the audit engagements? What might be reasons for decreased professional skepticism?
  - f. How could a standardized audit program lead to some of the problems identified earlier, such as failing to test a category of inventory that had book value in excess of 70% of the firm's planning materiality, or limiting the testing of impairment to inventory that had already been assessed as impaired by management?

6-38 **LO 3** Using appropriate resources, obtain the financial statements of a company with which you are familiar. Identify specific account balances for which substantive analytical procedures would be appropriate and describe your reasoning for selecting the accounts.

**AUDITING STANDARDS
APPLICATION ACTIVITY**

6-39 **PCAOB**
(LO 1, 2)

Refer to the *Auditing Standards Exhibit* inside the front cover of this textbook and identify the PCAOB AS that addresses the topic of audit evidence. Obtain a copy of that AS.
  a. What are the three alternative means of selecting items for testing?
  b. For each alternative, describe situations in which the alternative would be appropriate.

**AUDITING STANDARDS
APPLICATION ACTIVITY**

6-40 **LO 1, 2**   Assume that you are auditing a nonpublic U.S. client. You have obtained evidence that appears to be inconsistent with other evidence documented in the audit workpapers. Refer to the *Auditing Standards Exhibit* inside the front cover of this textbook and identify the appropriate standard that will help you address this issue. What guidance does that standard give you?

PROFESSIONAL SKEPTICISM

FRAUD

6-41 **SEC**
(LO 1, 2)

Obtain a copy of Accounting and Auditing Enforcement Release (AAER) No. 3146, issued by the SEC on June 24, 2010.
  a. Identify the audit evidence deficiencies described in the release.
  b. In what ways did the auditor fail to exhibit professional skepticism?
  c. What sanction did the auditor receive? Does that sanction seem appropriate?

6-42 **PCAOB**
(LO 1, 2)

Obtain a copy of the PCAOB settled Disciplinary Order in the matter of Acquavella, Chiarelli, Shuster, Berkower & Co., LLP that was released by the PCAOB on November 21, 2013 (PCAOB Release No. 105-2013-010). The Order notes:

> *Throughout the relevant time period, ACSB failed to put policies and procedures in place to ensure that engagement personnel performed audit procedures necessary to comply with PCAOB standards. As a result, in certain instances described below, ACSB staff members failed to complete necessary audit work before the Firm released its audit reports for the Audits.*

Review the order and identify instances in which the auditor did not obtain sufficient appropriate evidence.

Academic Research Cases

FRAUD

NOTE: Completing *Academic Research Cases* requires students to reference additional resources and materials.

SEARCH HINT

It is easy to locate these academic research articles! Use a search engine such as Google Scholar or an electronic research platform such as ABI Inform, and search using the author names and part of the article title.

6-43 **LO 3**   Locate and read the article listed below.

Brazel, J. F., K. L. Jones, and D. F. Prawitt. (2014). "Auditors' reactions to inconsistencies between financial and nonfinancial measures: The interactive effects of fraud risk assessment and a decision prompt. *Behavioral Research in Accounting* 26(1): 131–156.

  a. What is the purpose of the study?
  b. Describe the design/method/approach used to conduct the study.
  c. What are the primary findings of the study?

FRAUD

6-44 **LO 1, 2, 4** Locate and read the article listed below.

Commerford, B. P., D. R. Hermanson, R. W. Houston, and M. F. Peters. (2016). Real earnings management: A threat to auditor comfort? *Auditing: A Journal of Practice and Theory* 35(4): 39–56.

a. What is the purpose of the study?
b. Describe the design/method/approach used to conduct the study.
c. What are the primary findings of the study?

Data Analytics Using ACL

FRAUD

NOTE: There is an *ACL Appendix* and tutorial at the end of the book that you may find helpful in completing this problem.

6-45 **LO 2, 5** You are auditing Pell grants provided to students at six state universities. The Pell grant program is a federal financial aid program for college students. The maximum grant a student can receive during a school year is $3,125, with a maximum of $1,041.67 per semester and summer session. The amount of a grant depends on financial need (need) and the number of credits taken (status). Students cannot receive a grant at two different schools during the same school term. You have obtained a file of grants for the current school year (downloaded from the Internet, labeled *pellA.XLS*) that contains the following information:

SSN	Social Security number
Last	Student's last name
First	Student's first name
Middle	Student's middle name or initial
School	School—coded 1 to 6
Term	Coded 1 to 3:
	• 1—Fall Semester
	• 2—Spring Semester
	• 3—Summer Semester
Need*	Financial need—coded 1 to 5:
	• 1—100% of allowable grant
	• 2—75%
	• 3—50%
	• 4—25%
	• 5—0%
Status*	Credits taken—coded 1 to 4:
	• 1—12 or more credits: 100%
	• 2—9 to 11 credits: 75%
	• 3—6 to 8 credits: 50%
	• 4—3 to 5 credits: 25%
Amount	Amount of grant for the term
	• Computation of grant: $3,125 / 3 * Need *Status
	• For a full-time student with maximum need: $3,125 / 3 * 100% * 100% = $1,041.67
	• For a student with a code 3 need taking 9 credits: $3,125 / 3 * 50% * 75% = $390.63

1. Develop an audit program to identify potential fraud using ACL.
2. Use ACL to perform the steps in your audit program.
3. Prepare the following:
    a. Your audit program referenced to the ACL printouts supporting each audit step.
    b. A report on your findings including additional steps you would take to determine if fraud actually occurred.
    c. Appropriate ACL printouts properly indexed with comments written on the printouts to explain the printout and its implications. *Do not print out the entire grant file*. Extract only the items of significance.

*Hint: To convert the NEED codes to the proper decimal value, use the expression $(1 - 0.25(NEED - 1))$. The same conversion can be used for STATUS codes.

7

Planning the Audit: Identifying, Assessing, and Responding to the Risk of Material Misstatement

The Audit Opinion Formulation Process

I. Making Client Acceptance and Continuance Decisions
Chapter 1

II. Performing Risk Assessment
Chapters 2, 3, 7, and 9–13

III. Obtaining Evidence About Internal Control Operating Effectiveness
Chapters 8–13

IV. Obtaining Substantive Evidence About Accounts, Disclosures, and Assertions
Chapters 8–13

V. Completing the Audit and Making Reporting Decisions
Chapters 14 and 15

Quality Auditing and the Need for Quality Auditor Judgments and Ethical Decisions
Chapter 1

Professional Liability
Chapter 4

The Audit Opinion Formulation Process and a Framework for Obtaining Audit Evidence
Chapter 5 and 6

The financial statements of all organizations are subject to the risk of material misstatement. During audit planning, the auditor identifies and assesses the risk of material misstatement, and then determines the audit procedures that will appropriately respond to that risk.

Learning Objectives

LO 1 Describe the concept of material misstatement and apply a process for making materiality judgments.

LO 2 Identify and assess the risk of material misstatement and describe how that risk relates to audit risk and detection risk.

LO 3 Respond to the assessed risk of material misstatement by planning the audit procedures that will appropriately address that risk.

LO 4 Apply the frameworks for professional decision making and ethical decision making to issues involving materiality, risk assessment, and risk responses.

The PCAOB Identifies Problems with Risk Assessment and Responses to Risk Assessment

This feature summarizes the objectives of the PCAOB risk assessment standards and highlights concerns of the PCAOB regarding the implementation of and compliance with these standards.

The PCAOB risk assessment standards related to planning the audit guide the auditor on obtaining the following objectives:

- Conduct the audit of the financial statements in a manner that reduces audit risk to an appropriately low level
- Plan the audit so that the audit is conducted effectively
- Supervise the audit engagement, including supervising the work of engagement team members, so that the work is performed as directed and supports the conclusions reached
- Apply the concept of materiality appropriately in planning and performing audit procedures
- Identify and appropriately assess the risks of material misstatement, thereby providing a basis for designing and implementing responses to the risks of material misstatement
- Address the risks of material misstatement through appropriate overall audit responses and audit procedures

Observations by the PCAOB based on inspections related to these objectives include firms:

- Not performing substantive procedures, including tests of details, that are responsive to fraud risks and other significant risks that audit teams identified
- Not performing sufficient testing of the design and operating effectiveness of controls to support their planned level of control reliance
- Using sample sizes that were too small to provide sufficient evidence
- Not performing sufficient procedures to extend audit conclusions from the date of interim procedures to the end of the year under audit
- Limiting inventory testing when fraud risk was identified to a selection of high-value inventory items that represented an insignificant portion of the total inventory balance at year end
- Not obtaining a sufficient understanding of the company, its environment, or its internal control over financial reporting
- Failing to identify fraud risks that are specific to the client

To obtain the relevant PCAOB report, see https://pcaobus.org/ Inspections/Documents/Risk-Assessment-Standards-Inspections.pdf

What You Will Learn

- What is materiality? (LO 1)
- What factors affect materiality judgments? (LO 1)
- How do auditors determine materiality? (LO 1)
- What factors affect the risk of material misstatement? (LO 2)

- How do auditors assess fraud risk? (LO 2)
- How do planning analytical procedures assist the auditor in determining the risk of material misstatement? (LO 2)
- How do auditors respond to the risk of material misstatement? (LO 3)

What Do You Think? For Classroom Discussion

In reviewing the PCAOB's concerns with risk assessment and responses to risk assessment in the *Why It Matters* feature "The PCAOB Identifies Problems with Risk Assessment and Responses to Risk Assessment" why do you think these deficiencies occurred? Did firm methodologies not comply with the standards? Did the auditors experience pressures to not comply with the standards? Were the firm tools and decision aids inadequate? Was there a lack of professional skepticism? Are there other explanations?

LO 1

Describe the concept of material misstatement and apply a process for making materiality judgments.

Materiality

The auditor designs and performs an audit that provides reasonable assurance that the audit will detect material misstatements. Materiality relates to the significance or importance of an item. A **misstatement** is an error, either intentional or unintentional, that exists in a transaction or financial statement account balance.

Materiality judgments: (1) are a matter of professional judgment, (2) depend on the needs of a reasonable person relying on the information (e.g., an investor, a potential investor, or other stakeholders), and (3) involve both quantitative and qualitative considerations. Materiality differs from one audit client to another; that is, what is material for one client may not be material for another client, and may change for the same client from one period to another. The auditor and management may even disagree about the level of materiality.

The purpose of making materiality judgments is to help the auditor gather sufficient appropriate evidence to obtain reasonable assurance about whether the financial statements are free of material misstatement. Auditors make materiality judgments for purposes of: (1) audit planning and (2) evidence evaluation after audit procedures are completed. Materiality judgments provide a basis for:

- Determining the nature and extent of risk assessment procedures
- Identifying and assessing the risks of material misstatement
- Determining the tests of controls and substantive audit procedures to perform

Definitions of Materiality

This feature outlines relevant guidance on how various standard setters and regulators define materiality. These definitions make it clear that materiality includes both the nature of the misstatement as well as the dollar amount of misstatement. Auditors should judge materiality in relation to the needs of the financial statement users.

In *Concepts Statement No. 2,* the Financial Accounting Standards Board (FASB) defines **materiality** as "the magnitude of an omission or misstatement of accounting information that, in light of surrounding circumstances, makes it *probable* that the judgment of a reasonable person relying on the information would have been changed or influenced by the omission or misstatement."

ISA 320, *Materiality in Planning and Performing an Audit,* makes the point that auditors should make materiality judgments based on a consideration of the information needs of users as an overall group.

The Supreme Court of the U.S. offers a somewhat different definition, stating that "a fact is material if there is a substantial likelihood that the ... fact would have been viewed by the reasonable investor as having significantly altered the 'total mix' of information made available" (see AS 2105).

Materiality Levels

Auditors consider materiality at multiple levels:

1. **overall materiality** (also known as **planning materiality**), which the auditor uses in determining whether the financial statements overall are materially correct
2. **performance materiality** (also known as **tolerable error**), which the auditor uses for determining significant accounts, significant locations, and audit procedures for those accounts and locations
3. **posting materiality**, which signifies the misstatements identified throughout the audit that will be considered at the end of the audit in determining whether the financial statements overall are materially correct.

In planning the audit, auditors consider planning materiality in terms of the smallest aggregate level of misstatements that could be material to any one of the financial statements. For example, if the auditor believes that misstatements aggregating approximately $100,000 would be material to the income statement, but misstatements aggregating approximately $200,000 would be material to the balance sheet, the auditor typically assesses overall materiality at $100,000 or less (not $200,000 or less).

Once the auditor determines planning materiality, the auditor then sets performance materiality to determine significant accounts and the audit procedures to perform. A common approach to determining performance materiality is to calculate 75% of planning materiality. Continuing the example of a client where planning materiality is set at $100,000, performance materiality would then be set at $75,000. While the auditor will commonly use 75% to set performance materiality, this percentage typically ranges from 50% to 75%. If performance materiality is set too high, the auditor might not perform sufficient procedures to detect material misstatements in the financial statements. If performance materiality is set too low, the auditor might perform more substantive procedures than necessary.

The auditor commonly sets posting materiality at 5% of planning materiality; however, this percentage typically ranges from 3% to 5%. Continuing with our example where planning materiality is set at $100,000, posting materiality

Why It Matters

Considering Materiality Throughout the Audit Opinion Formulation Process

This feature recognizes that materiality levels may change throughout the audit.

Sometimes auditors will revise their initial materiality judgments after more facts about the client and its circumstances become known. Situations potentially requiring a change in materiality judgments include:

- The auditor based initial materiality judgments on estimated or preliminary financial statement amounts that turn out to be different from the audited amounts.

- The financial statement amounts used in initially making the materiality judgments have changed significantly. For example, if during the course of the audit, the client

significantly adjusted its financial statements, then the auditor may need to revise initial materiality judgments accordingly.

- The auditor obtains information indicating that a member of top management or those charged with governance lack integrity.

If materiality judgments change during the audit, then auditors reassess decisions that relied upon these judgments. For example, if performance materiality turns out to have been set too high (such as $150,000 when it should have been $100,000), then the auditor might need to perform additional substantive audit procedures designed to detect misstatements at this lower level.

would then be set at $5,000. The auditor will accumulate all errors identified throughout the audit that are $5,000 or more, and at the end of the audit will consider all of these errors in determining whether the financial statements overall are materially correct.

Planning Materiality

The starting point to determining the various levels of materiality is planning materiality. How does an auditor determine planning material? Most audit firms provide firm-specific guidance and decision aids to assist auditors in making consistent materiality judgments. The guidelines usually involve applying a percentage to some benchmark, such as total assets, total revenue, or net income. In choosing a benchmark, the auditor considers the stability of the base from year to year, and the focus of the financial statement users.

Since many financial statement users of public companies focus on net income, a common approach for setting planning materiality for the financial statements is to use net income as the benchmark, and a percentage threshold of 5%. The auditor should use the result of the calculation as a starting point for planning materiality and then adjust as necessary for qualitative characteristics of the particular audit client. For example, if the client is planning a secondary stock offering, the auditor may want to set materiality at a lower level than suggested by the calculation, as the client may be very biased to make the company look particularly successful.

In *Staff Accounting Bulletin (SAB) No. 99*, the SEC expresses concern about auditors not considering qualitative factors in their materiality assessments:

> The use of a percentage as a numerical threshold, such as 5%, may provide the basis for a preliminary assumption that—without considering all relevant circumstances—a deviation of less than the specified percentage with respect to a particular item on the registrant's financial statements is unlikely to be material. The staff has no objection to such a "rule of thumb" as an initial step in assessing materiality. Quantifying, in percentage terms, the magnitude

It's Your Turn!

Prompt for Critical Thinking #1

Provide examples of other qualitative factors that may affect the level of materiality.

- _____
- _____
- _____
- _____

of a misstatement is only the beginning of an analysis of materiality; it cannot appropriately be used as a substitute for a full analysis of all relevant considerations.

The following quantitative benchmarks, percentage thresholds, and associated materiality judgments are typical:

Typical Materiality Judgments

Common Benchmarks	Likely Not Material	Likely Material	Likely Always Material
Net income	<5%	5% to 10%	>10%
Total assets	<1%	1% to 1.5%	>1.5%
Net sales	<1%	1% to 1.5%	>1.5%

While audit firms typically have policies related to setting materiality, professional judgment is very important. The auditor should consider the following items when setting materiality:

- Financial statement items on which users will focus their attention
- Nature of the client and industry
- Size of the client
- Manner in which the client is financed
- Volatility of the benchmark
- Intensity of the level of analyst following

Alternative Planning Materiality Benchmarks

Why It Matters

This feature illustrates how the type of organization and its characteristics can influence the appropriate benchmark.

While auditors commonly use net income, total assets, or net sales to set materiality, circumstances may indicate that other benchmarks are more appropriate. If an organization has significant and nonrecurring charges to nonoperating expenses, then income from continuing operations may be a more appropriate materiality benchmark than net income. If an organization's net income varies significantly from year to year, the auditor might consider using an average of net income from the prior three to five years to determine materiality. For non-profit organizations, appropriate benchmarks would include total expenses, total contributions, or total assets.

Prompt for Critical Thinking #2   It's Your Turn!

Consider the role that stock analysts may play in how **auditor-detected misstatements** get resolved. An auditor-detected misstatement occurs when, during the audit, the auditor comes to find that there exists an error in the recording of a particular transaction, regardless of whether it was intentional or unintentional. Managers and auditors will jointly determine how to proceed. They must decide whether the misstatement is material enough for management to correct it.

Let's use a real company and work through this complex set of circumstances. Below is a chart that shows you the consensus earnings forecast for a company you likely know, Target Corporation, which is a large, global retail company that sells items such as clothing, shoes, household items, and food. Below is a chart showing the number of analysts that follow Target, followed by a comparison between the actual earnings per share (EPS) for both yearly and quarterly results, along with the mean analyst EPS forecast for those related periods.

Analyst ratings

Glossary of financial terms

1-Strong Buy	2	Mean recommendation: **3.1**
2-Buy	1	▼
3-Hold	18	
4-Underperform	2	
5-Sell	3	Sell Strong buy

You can find the latest analyst ratings using the following link (and the companies that the analysts work for, e.g., Barclays, CITI, and Goldman Sachs): http://investors.target.com/phoenix.zhtml?c=65828&p=irol-estimates

What the results above show is that 26 analysts are following Target's stock and making EPS predictions. The last three years included the following number of analysts respectively, 12, 26, and 24; this implies that fewer analysts are following Target's stock now as compared to the last few years.

Now, let's find out what the analysts are predicting in terms of yearly and quarterly EPS, and compare that to Target's actual EPS. See the graph below for details.

Actuals

		Reported EPS	Mean Estimate	Surprise % Change
Annual	Jan 17	5.01	5.06	−1.00
Quarterly	Jul 16	1.23	1.12	9.71
Quarterly	Oct 16	1.04	0.83	25.37
Quarterly	Jan 17	1.45	1.51	−3.73
Quarterly	Apr 17	1.21	0.91	32.39
Annual	Jan 16	4.69	4.72	−0.58
Annual	Jan 15	4.27	3.96	7.71

Sometimes Target exceeds the mean analyst estimate, and sometimes they "miss" the estimate. Managers feel excessive pressure to at least "meet" or "beat" the mean analyst estimate, because missing the estimate yields negative stock market reactions when that happens. (If you are ambitious, you could prove that to yourself by looking at the daily stock market reaction for the latest EPS reported versus mean estimate).

Now, put yourself in the position of management at Target. Let's assume that the auditor (EY) detects a large *income-decreasing* misstatement in Target's revenue cycle and that on a per share basis, the journal entry necessary to correct that misstatement is as follows:

Dr. Revenue $0.07

  Cr. Accounts Receivable $0.07

Let's assume that this situation applies to the January 2017 data, whereby analysts' mean forecast is $5.06 per share. Managers know that their actual EPS is going to be $5.01 per share, and that's *if they don't correct* the detected misstatement. If they *do* correct the misstatement, the actual EPS will fall to $4.94 a share. So, instead of missing the analyst estimate by 1%, they will miss it by 2.4%.

Answer the following questions as you think about materiality in this situation.

1. Seven cents a share on a stock trading with an EPS of approximately $5/share is seemingly immaterial, $0.014. The quantitative benchmarks that we mention previously state that when using net earnings as a benchmark, anything less than 5% is immaterial. Based on this, is the misstatement material?
2. Do you think management will want to correct the detected misstatement? Why or why not?
3. Qualitative materiality relates to the fact that even a relatively small misstatement can influence the judgments and decisions of users. How does qualitative materiality relate to this situation?

Performance Materiality When Auditing Clients with Multiple Locations

Why It Matters

This feature notes that audit clients with multiple locations require special considerations when assessing performance materiality.

A difficulty that auditors face with some clients is how to identify significant locations and accounts when the client has:

- Many locations
- Some locations requiring separate reporting (regulatory reports) in addition to consolidated financial reports
- Significant segments and the importance of segments vary

In some cases, the auditor may aggregate the populations of various locations and perform testing, including the selection of audit samples, from the combined population, in the same manner as when there is one population. For example, if the underlying information system is centralized and separate reporting by location is not necessary, the auditor can treat multiple locations as one population and use performance materiality for testing (and sampling) a particular account balance across multiple locations. This may be the case for inventory observations conducted at multiple locations.

Alternatively, if the information systems across multiple locations are decentralized, or if separate reporting is required, or if certain locations or segments are especially important, the auditor faces additional testing considerations.

Individually important locations are those that are financially significant to the client's financial statements overall. A common quantitative approach to determining individually significant locations is to identify locations where the net income is greater than 10% of total consolidated net income or where the assets are greater than 10% of total consolidated assets. In practice, the percentage might range from 10% to 15%.

Auditors will also consider qualitative factors when determining individually significant locations. For example, does the location have specific risks that could create a material misstatement in the overall financial statements? One such risk might be the resignation of the location's top financial manager following allegations of ineffective controls or inappropriate reporting practices.

For Classroom Discussion

What Do You Think?

The auditor's report in the U.S. does not provide the user with details on the level of materiality that the auditor used during the audit. Do you think that the audit report should disclose materiality levels? Why might the user find such information useful? Why might auditors hesitate to publicly reveal the level of misstatement that they will accept as "immaterial"? Would management have a preference regarding the public disclosure of materiality?

Check Your Basic Knowledge

7-1 The auditor bases materiality solely on quantitative factors.   (T/F)

7-2 Performance materiality is an amount less than overall materiality and helps the auditor determine the extent of audit evidence needed.   (T/F)

7-3 Which of the following statements is <u>true</u> regarding materiality?

   a. Materiality is the magnitude of an omission or misstatement of accounting information that, in light of surrounding circumstances, makes it probable that the judgment of a reasonable person relying on the information would have been changed or influenced by the omission or misstatement.

   b. Materiality is the magnitude of an omission or misstatement of accounting information that, in light of surrounding circumstances, makes it possible that the judgment of a reasonable person relying on the information would have been changed or influenced by the omission or misstatement.

   c. A fact is material if there is a substantial likelihood that a reasonable investor would have viewed the fact as having significantly altered the total mix of information made available.

   d. Both (a) and (c) are correct.

   e. Both (b) and (c) are correct.

7-4 Which of the following statements is <u>true</u> concerning performance materiality?

   a. Performance materiality is set less than overall materiality and helps the auditor determine the extent of audit evidence to obtain.

   b. If performance materiality is set too low, the auditor might not perform sufficient procedures to detect material misstatements in the financial statements.

   c. If performance materiality is set too high, the auditor might perform more substantive procedures than necessary.

   d. Performance materiality is essentially the same as overall materiality.

LO 2

Identify and assess the risk of material misstatement and describe how that risk relates to audit risk and detection risk.

Identifying and Assessing the Risk of Material Misstatement

Client Business Risks

You cannot audit what you do not understand! When making client acceptance or continuance decision, the auditor obtains an initial understanding of the client and its business risks. The auditor continues to increase this understanding when planning the audit. **Client business risks** are risks affecting the business operations and potential outcomes of an organization's activities. These risks likely have pervasive effects across an organization and can potentially affect the risk of material misstatement for many accounts and assertions (the risk of material misstatement at the financial statement level).

When client business risk is high, the auditor is concerned that the organization might have difficulty operating effectively or profitably. The overall economic climate—whether favorable or unfavorable—can have a tremendous effect on the organization's ability to operate effectively and profitably. Economic downturns are often associated with the failure of otherwise successful organizations. Technological change also presents risk. For example, companies that were not previously in the phone business, such as Google and Apple, added communication products and greatly affected the phone business of Motorola and Nokia. Competitor actions, such as discounting prices or adding new product lines, also affect business risks. Finally, geographic locations of suppliers can represent a business risk. For example, sourcing products in China might offer a competitive advantage, but it might also expose the organization to business risk if the products contain lead. Management is responsible for managing its business risk. All organizations are subject to business risks; management reactions may worsen them or mitigate them.

Each organization has key processes that influence its competitive advantage. The auditor should gather sufficient information to understand these processes, the industry factors affecting key processes, how management monitors the processes and performance, and the potential operational and financial effects associated with key processes. The following factors are examples of factors that would lead the auditor to assess client business risk at a higher level:

- The company lacks personnel or expertise to deal with the changes in the industry
- New products and service offerings have uncertain likelihood of successful introduction and acceptance by the market
- The use of information technology is incompatible across systems and processes
- Expansion of the business for which the demand for the company's products or services has not been accurately estimated

It's Your Turn!

Prompt for Critical Thinking #3

Provide examples of other factors would lead the auditor to assess business risk at a higher level. *HINT*: You may want to review ISA 315.

- _____
- _____
- _____
- _____

Understanding the Client's Application of Accounting Principles when Assessing Client Business Risk

Why It Matters

This feature provides guidance to consider when assessing client business risk related to overall financial reporting.

One issue critical to understanding the client's financial reporting risks involves analyzing management's selection and application of accounting principles, including related disclosures. The auditor needs to determine whether management's decisions are appropriate for its business and are consistent with the applicable financial reporting framework for its industry.

For example, AS 2101 requires that the auditor obtain an understanding of the following types of matters relevant to understanding management's application of accounting principles and related disclosures:

- Significant changes in the company's accounting principles, financial reporting policies, or disclosures and the reasons for such changes

- The financial reporting competencies of personnel involved in selecting and applying significant new or complex accounting principles
- The accounts or disclosures for which judgment is used in the application of significant accounting principles, especially in determining management's estimates and assumptions
- The effect of significant accounting principles in controversial or emerging areas for which there is a lack of authoritative guidance or consensus
- The methods the company uses to account for significant and unusual transactions
- Financial reporting standards and laws and regulations that are new to the company, including when and how the company will adopt such requirements

- A new business strategy is incompletely or improperly implemented
- Financing is lost due to the company's inability to meet financing requirements
- Competence and integrity of financial and accounting management
- Potential incentives to misstate the financial statements

These factors suggest that client business risk is associated with recording transactions and presenting financial data in an organization's financial statements.

When this risk is high, the auditor is concerned that management has recorded transactions or presented financial data inaccurately. When assessing this risk, auditors consider all of the items on a company's financial statements that are subjective and based on judgment, such as asset impairments, mark-to-market accounting, warranties, returns, pensions, and estimates regarding the useful lives of assets, among others. While client business risk does not necessarily lead to material misstatements in the financial statements, the risk represents issues that could threaten the financial viability and financial reporting accuracy of the organization.

Exhibit 7.1 provides examples of auditor inquiries when assessing client business risk relating to financial reporting.

Exhibit 7.1

Questions to Ask When Assessing Financial Reporting Quality: Selected Excerpts from the NACD Blue Ribbon Commission on Audit Committees

- What are the significant judgment areas (reserves, contingencies, asset values, note disclosures) that affect the current-year financial statements? What considerations were involved in resolving these judgment matters? What is the range of potential impact on future reported financial results?
- What issues or concerns exist that could adversely affect the future operations and/or financial condition of the company? What is management's plan to deal with these future risks?
- What is the overall quality of the company's financial reporting, including the appropriateness of important accounting principles followed by the company?
- What is the range of acceptable accounting choices the company has available to it?
- Were there any significant changes in accounting policies, or in the application of accounting principles during the year? If yes, why were the changes made and what impact did the changes have on earnings per share (EPS) or other key financial measures?
- Were there any significant changes in accounting estimates, or models used in making accounting estimates during the year? If yes, why were the changes made and what impact did the changes have on earnings per share (EPS) or other key financial measures?
- Are there any instances where the company may be thought of as pushing the limits of revenue recognition? If so, what is the rationale for the treatment chosen?
- Have similar transactions and events been treated in a consistent manner across divisions of the company and across countries in which the company operates? If not, what are the exceptions and the reasons for them?
- Do the accounting choices made reflect the economic substance of transactions and the strategic management of the business? If not, where are the exceptions and why do they exist?
- To what extent are the financial reporting choices consistent with the manner in which the company measures its progress toward achieving its mission internally? If not, what are the differences?
- How do the significant accounting principles used by the company compare with leading companies in the industry, or with other companies that are considered leaders in financial disclosure? What is the rationale for any differences?
- Has there been any instance where short-run reporting objectives (e.g., achieving a profit objective or meeting bonus or stock option requirements) were allowed to influence accounting choices? If yes, what choices were made and why?

In 2008 and 2011, the PCAOB issued *Staff Audit Practice Alerts* to assist auditors in identifying economic factors that could affect an organization's risk of material misstatement. When you consider the current economic environment, what are some factors that might affect a client's business risk and the risk of material misstatement, and, therefore, require additional audit attention?

Risk Assessment Procedures for Assessing Client Business Risks

The auditor performs many procedures when obtaining an understanding of the client's business and associated business risks. These procedures include monitoring the financial press and SEC filings and broker analyses, developing a firm-specific and industry-based knowledge management system, and utilizing other online information sources about a company. The auditor also inquires of management, reviews internal risk management documentation, inquires of other knowledgeable individuals at the client, and reviews legal or regulatory proceedings against the company. Following are some resources an auditor can use to learn more about an organization's business risks:

- *Management inquiries*—The auditor should interview management to identify its strategic plans, its analysis of industry trends, the potential impact of actions it has taken or might take, and its management style.
- *Review of client's budget*—The budget, representing management's fiscal plan for the forthcoming year, provides insight into management's approach to operations and to risks the organization might face. The auditor looks for significant changes in plans and deviations from budgets, such as planned disposal of a line of business, significant research or promotion costs associated with a new product introduction, new financing or capital requirements, changes in compensation or product costs due to union agreements, and significant additions to property, plant, and equipment.
- *Tour of client's plant and operations*—A tour of the client's production and distribution facilities offers much insight into potential audit issues. The auditor can visualize cost centers, as well as shipping and receiving procedures, inventory controls, potentially obsolete inventory, and possible inefficiencies. The tour increases the auditor's awareness of company procedures and operations, providing direct experience into sites and situations that are otherwise encountered only in company documents or observations of client personnel.
- *Review relevant government regulations and client's legal obligations*—Few industries are unaffected by governmental regulation, and much of that regulation affects the audit. For example, auditors need to determine potential liabilities associated with cleanup costs defined by the Environmental Protection Agency. The auditor normally seeks information on litigation risks through an inquiry of management, but follows up that inquiry with an analysis of litigation prepared by the client's legal counsel.
- *Knowledge management systems*—Audit firms have developed these systems around industries, clients, and best practices. These systems also capture information about relevant accounting or regulatory requirements for the companies and can be used to develop risk alerts for the companies.
- *Online searches*—Internet search companies (such as Hoovers at www .hoovers.com) are an excellent source of information about companies. Other online searches can be conducted through other portals such as Google. Yahoo has two excellent sources of information: (1) a financial section that provides data about most companies and (2) a chat line that

contains current conversations about the company (much of which, of course, might be unreliable).

- *Review of SEC filings*—The auditor can search the SEC filings online through the EDGAR system. The filings include company annual and quarterly reports, proxy information, and registration statements for new security issues. These filings contain substantial information about the company and its affiliates, officers, and directors. The auditor can use this information to obtain an understanding of management's compensation arrangements, including incentive compensation that may provide important information about management incentives and bonus arrangements. Further, the auditor should monitor trading activity of the company's securities, along with the relevant holdings of top-level management and/or board members.
- *Company websites*—A company's web site can contain information that is useful in understanding its products and strategies. As companies provide more information online, auditors should review the information to keep informed of developments.
- *Economic statistics*—Most industry data, including regional data, can now be found online. The auditor can compare the results of a client with regional economic data. For example, the auditor would likely question why a company is growing at a rate of 50%, while the overall industry is growing at a significantly slower rate. That question arises only if the auditor has industry information.
- *Professional practice bulletins*—The American Institute of Certified Public Accountants (AICPA) publishes Audit Risk Alerts, and the SEC often issues practice bulletins to draw the profession's attention to important issues. Both

Why It Matters — Risk Assessment Procedures for Assessing Management Integrity

Evaluating management integrity is critical in assessing client business risk. However, making such an evaluation is difficult and subjective. This feature identifies information sources an auditor might use to evaluate management integrity.

- *Predecessor auditor*—Information obtained directly through inquiry of the predecessor auditor is required by professional auditing standards. The predecessor is required to respond to the auditor unless such data are under a court order or if the client will not approve communicating confidential information.
- *Other professionals in the business community*—Examples include lawyers and bankers with whom the auditor normally has good working relationships and of whom the auditor makes inquiries as part of the process of getting to know the client.
- *Other auditors within the audit firm*—Other auditors within the firm may have dealt with current management in connection with other engagements or with other clients.
- *News media and web searches*—Information about the company and its management might be available in financial journals, magazines, industry trade magazines, or on the web.
- *Public databases*—Computerized databases can be searched for public documents dealing with management

or any articles on the company. Similarly, public databases such as LEXIS can be searched for the existence of legal proceedings against the company or against key members of management.

- *Preliminary interviews with management*—These interviews can be helpful in understanding the amount, extent, and reasons for turnover in key positions. Personal interviews can also be helpful in analyzing the frankness or evasiveness of management in dealing with important company issues affecting the audit.
- *Audit committee members*—Members of the audit committee might have been involved in disputes between the previous auditors and management and might have additional insight.
- *Inquiries of federal regulatory agencies*—Although this is not a primary source of information, the auditor might want to make inquiries of specific regulatory agencies regarding pending actions against the company or the history of regulatory actions taken with respect to the company and its management.
- *Private investigation firms*—Use of such firms is rare, but is increasingly being done when the auditor becomes aware of issues that merit further inquiry about management integrity or management's involvement in potential illegal activities.

the Public Company Accounting Oversight Board (PCAOB) and the International Auditing and Assurance Standards Board (IAASB) have also published several Staff Audit Practice Alerts dealing with topics such as significant unusual transactions, fair value measurements, and the economic environment.

- *Stock analysts' reports*—Brokerage firms invest significant resources in conducting research about companies, their strategies, competitors, quality of management, and likelihood of success. Many of the major investment analysts have access to top management and are the beneficiaries of frequent analysts' meetings. These reports may contain a wealth of useful information about a client.
- *Company earnings calls*—The auditor can observe or read the transcripts of management's earnings calls in order to understand the most up-to-date issues that the company is facing, along with management's publicly disclosed plans.

The Audit Risk Model

Exhibit 7.2 provides an overview of the risks relevant to an audit and introduces the following risks included in the audit risk model:

- **Inherent Risk**—The susceptibility of an assertion about a class of transaction, account balance, or disclosure to a misstatement that could be material, either individually or when aggregated with other misstatements, before consideration of any related controls.
- **Control Risk**—The risk that a misstatement that could occur in an assertion about a class of transaction, account balance, or disclosure and that could be material, either individually or when aggregated with other misstatements, will not be prevented, or detected and corrected, on a timely basis by the entity's internal control.
- **Audit Risk**—The risk that the auditor expresses an inappropriate audit opinion when the financial statements are materially misstated.
- **Detection Risk**—The risk that the procedures performed by the auditor to reduce audit risk to an acceptably low level will not detect a misstatement that exists and that could be material, either individually or when aggregated with other misstatements.

The audit risk model is presented as *Audit Risk = Inherent Risk × Control Risk × Detection Risk*. This model provides a conceptual way to consider risks relevant to the audit.

The auditor begins by setting the appropriate level of acceptable audit risk, which the auditor bases on the audit firm's potential exposure or risk of being

Engagement Risk, Audit Risk, and Audit Pricing — *Why It Matters*

Auditors must evaluate engagement risk, because it affects both audit risk and audit pricing.

Auditors will consider **engagement risk** (also known as **auditor business risk**) when planning and pricing an audit. This risk is the potential for loss to the auditor because of being associated with the client. Factors increasing this risk include the engagement: being a publicly traded company, not being a profitable engagement, damaging the auditor's reputation, and/or resulting in litigation. Engagement risk is higher when the client

is issuing an initial public stock offering, or of likely interest to the PCAOB's inspection team.

If engagement risk is higher, the auditor will set audit risk at a low level, for example, 1%, whereas the auditor might be willing to set audit risk at a higher level, for example, 5% for a client with lower engagement risk. In addition to influencing audit risk, engagement risk also influences audit pricing because the audit firm will need to factor in current and potential future engagement costs in making sure it negotiates considering these costs. However, if engagement risk is too high, the audit firm may decide to not audit the organization.

associated with a client. For example, consider a public company client in a high-risk industry that has been the focus of PCAOB inspections. In this case, the auditor would set the audit risk they are willing to accept at a low level because of the higher potential risk to the audit firm. Contrast this example with a privately held company where the financial statements will not be widely distributed. In this case, the auditor would set the audit risk they are willing to accept at a higher level because the firm's potential risk due to association with this client is relatively low.

Once the auditor sets audit risk, the auditor assesses the **risk of material misstatement**, which represents the client's inherent and control risks. Client business risk is the risk of material misstatement at the financial statement level. AS 1101 recognizes that risk of material misstatement at the financial statement level relates pervasively to the financial statements as a whole and potentially affects multiple client assertions across multiple accounts. *Exhibit 7.2* illustrates that client business risk affects the inherent and control risks associated with the client.

Auditors will then assess the risk of material misstatement at the assertion level for significant accounts. That approach provides a basis for planning the audit. Risk of material misstatement (i.e., inherent risk and control risk) originate with the client, are controllable by the client, and relate to characteristics of the client (e.g., environment, internal control).

Having set audit risk and assessed risk of material misstatement, the auditor determines detection risk. Detection risk is under the control of the auditor, and the audit evidence that the auditor obtains depends on the level of detection risk. Detection risk relates to the substantive audit procedures that will achieve the desired overall audit risk.

When the risk of material misstatement is higher, detection risk is lower, in order to reduce audit risk to an acceptable level. The auditor reduces detection risk through the selection of substantive audit procedures. As detection risk decreases, evidence that the auditor obtains through substantive audit procedures should increase and/or be more appropriate (reliable and relevant). When the risk of material misstatement is lower, the auditor can accept a higher detection risk and still achieve an acceptable level of audit risk.

Exhibit 7.2
Risks Relevant to the Audit

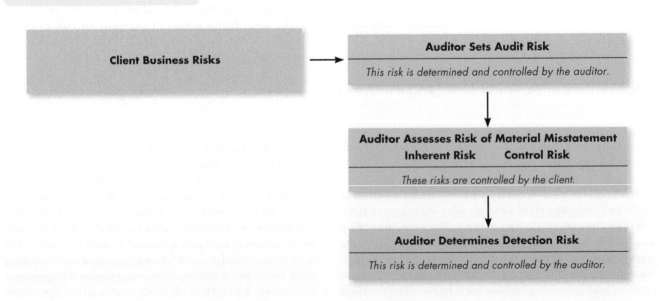

What Makes a Risk Significant?

Why It Matters

This feature outlines factors that the auditor considers in determining whether a particular identified risk is significant to the conduct of the audit.

According to AU-C 315, a **significant risk** is an identified and assessed risk of material misstatement that, in the auditor's professional judgment, requires special consideration. AU-C 315 provides guidance on factors that the auditor should consider when determining if a risk is significant. The standard states:

In exercising professional judgment about which risks are significant risks, the auditor should consider:

a. whether the risk is a risk of fraud;

b. whether the risk is related to recent significant economic, accounting, or other developments and, therefore, requires specific attention;

c. the complexity of transactions;

d. whether the risk involves significant transactions with related parties;

e. the degree of subjectivity in the measurement of financial information related to the risk, especially those measurements involving a wide range of measurement uncertainty; and

f. whether the risk involves significant transactions that are outside the normal course of business for the entity or that otherwise appear to be unusual.

Assessing Inherent Risk at the Assertion/Account Level

Inherent risk relates to the susceptibility of an account or assertion to a misstatement, due to either error or fraud, before considering any related controls. Most audit firms require that auditors assess inherent risk at the assertion level for all significant accounts. The level of inherent risk for an assertion is dependent on the account associated with the assertion. For example, since cash is more susceptible to theft than industrial equipment, the auditor will typically assess the existence assertion as having a higher level of inherent risk for cash than equipment. As another example, the auditor is likely to assess the valuation assertion as having a higher level of inherent risk for an account based on management estimates (e.g., pension liability) than for an account whose valuation is derived from routine, factual data (e.g., payroll expense).

The following factors should lead an auditor to assess assertion level inherent risk higher, as the auditor is concerned that there is an increased likelihood of a material misstatement:

- The account balance represents an asset that is relatively easily stolen, such as cash
- The account balance is made up of complex transactions
- The account balance requires a high level of judgment or estimation to value
- The account balance is subject to adjustments that are not in the ordinary processing routine, such as year-end adjustments
- The account balance is composed of a high volume of nonroutine transactions

Assessing Control Risk at the Assertion/Account Level

Control risk relates to the susceptibility that a misstatement, due to either error or fraud, will not be prevented or detected on a timely basis by the organization's internal control system. During audit planning, the auditor makes a preliminary assessment of control risk. Because control effectiveness can vary across accounts and assertions, most audit firms require that auditors assess control risk at the assertion level for all significant accounts.

When control risk is high, the auditor is concerned that a material misstatement may not be prevented or that if a material misstatement exists in the organization's financial statements that it will not be detected and corrected by management. Some level of control risk is always present because of the limitations in internal control.

The following factors can lead auditors to assess control risk at a higher level:

- Poor controls in specific countries or locations
- Difficulty gaining access to the organization or determining the individuals who own and/or control the organization
- Little interaction between senior management and operating staff
- Lack of supervision of accounting personnel

Prompt for Critical Thinking #4   It's Your Turn!

Provide additional examples of factors that could lead an auditor to assess control risk at a higher level.

- _____
- _____
- _____
- _____
- _____

Focus on Fraud   Lack of Oversight as a Control Weakness Leads to Embezzlement

This feature provides an example of how the lack of supervision of accounting personal can result in fraud. The implication for auditors is the need to be aware of weak internal controls and the negative consequences for a client's financial statements. A control risk assessment of high means that the auditor needs to perform additional substantive procedures. In contrast, when an auditor believes that controls are well designed and assesses control risk as low, the auditor needs to test those controls to see if they are operating effectively, and may need to modify the control risk assessment (to high) if they are not operating effectively.

Rita Crundwell was the comptroller for the city of Dixon, Illinois, from 1983 through early 2012. During that time, she stole millions of dollars from the city to fund her extravagant lifestyle related to breeding and showing quarter horses. While maintaining this lavish, high-profile lifestyle, Crundwell received an annual salary of $80,000 from the city. Apparently, the discrepancy between her salary and lifestyle went unnoticed by her supervisors or the city's auditors. Crundwell handled all of the city's finances, and it appears that she was left relatively unsupervised by the city's leadership. Most shocking is the magnitude of the theft—over $50 million—in

relation to the size of the community. Dixon, a small town about 100 miles southwest of Chicago, has a population of fewer than 16,000 people. It is difficult to understand how the leadership of a city so small could have not realized that the massive amount of funds was missing.

The fraud began late in 1990, when Crundwell opened a bank account in the joint name of the city of Dixon and an acronym, RSCDA. The account holder was listed as "RSCDA, c/o Rita Crundwell." RSCDA was purportedly the city's capital development fund. Crundwell transferred funds from Dixon's money market account to the RSCDA fund, as well as to various other city-held bank accounts. Crundwell then wrote checks from the RSCDA account to pay for her personal expenses, including expenses relating to her horse business. To conceal the fraud, Crundwell created fictitious invoices from the state of Illinois, made to look as though the funds she was fraudulently depositing into the RSCDA account were being used for a legitimate city purpose.

To give a sense of the magnitude of the fraud, Crundwell charged about $2.5 million to her American Express card between January 2007 and March 2012; this included charges of $339,000 on jewelry alone. Between September 2011 and March 2012, she wrote 19 checks worth $3,558,000 from a city account payable to "Treasurer"; she deposited these checks into the RSCDA account. She then took $3,311,860 from the RSCDA account by checks and online withdrawals, using only $74,274 for the city's actual operations. Crundwell used the remainder of those funds for personal and business expenses, including approximately $450,000 relating to her horse farming operations, $600,000 in online credit card payments, and $67,000 to purchase a 2012 Chevy Silverado pickup truck. After the fraud was discovered, the FBI seized, among other items, the following from Crundwell:

- 311 quarter horses
- 2009 Liberty Coach motor home: $2.1 million
- 2009 Kenworth T800 tractor truck: $146,000
- 2009 Freightliner truck: $140,000
- 2009 Chevrolet Silverado pickup truck: $56,646
- 2009 Featherlite horse trailer: $258,698

The fraud unraveled when Crundwell took a 12-week unpaid vacation during 2011. While she was away, a city employee who served as her replacement obtained bank statements from all of the city's bank accounts. After reviewing those statements, the employee contacted the city's mayor, Mayor Burke, to alert him that one particular account had unusual transactions within it. Specifically, the September 2011 statement for that account showed three deposits totaling $785,000, as well as 84 checks drawn totaling $360,493, and 40 withdrawals totaling $266,605. Burke was unaware that the account even existed, and it was apparent that the withdrawals had no legitimate purpose relating to the city's business. Crundwell was sentenced to nearly 20 years in prison after pleading guilty to a wire fraud count.

Risk Assessment Procedures for Assessing Control Risk   To have an appropriate level of understanding of the client's internal controls, the auditor needs to understand the controls management has designed and implemented to mitigate identified risks of material misstatement. For entity-wide controls, auditors will typically review relevant documentation prepared by management and interview appropriate individuals. As an example, consider the risk assessment procedures that auditors might perform related to one component of internal controls—management's risk assessment. To obtain this understanding, the auditor typically uses some or all of the following risk assessment procedures:

- Interview relevant parties to develop an understanding of the processes used by the board of directors and management to evaluate and manage risks
- Review the risk-based approach used by the internal audit function with the director of the internal audit function and with the audit committee
- Interview management about its risk approach, risk preferences, risk appetite, and the relationship of risk analysis to strategic planning
- Review outside regulatory reports, where applicable, that address the company's policies and procedures toward risk
- Review company policies and procedures for addressing risk
- Gain a knowledge of company compensation schemes to determine if they are consistent with the risk policies adopted by the company
- Review prior years' work to determine if current actions are consistent with risk approaches discussed with management
- Review risk management documents
- Determine how management and the board monitor risk; identify changes in risk; and react to mitigate, manage, or control the risk

Auditors also need to obtain an understanding of the controls designed and implemented at the process or transaction level. For process or transaction controls, auditors will typically review relevant documentation prepared by management and interview appropriate individuals with knowledge about these controls. Further, auditors will perform walkthroughs, following a transaction from origination to when it is reflected in the financial records to determine if the controls are effectively designed and have been implemented.

Prompt for Critical Thinking #5   It's Your Turn!

Let's think about two companies that are likely familiar, Ford Motor Company and one of its major suppliers, Goodyear Tires. PricewaterhouseCoopers (PwC) is the auditor for both companies.

What business, inherent and control risks do you think are present for the two companies? What engagement risks do you think that PwC might face in auditing these clients?

Ford Motor Company	Goodyear Tires
Company Business Risks	Company Business Risks
•	•
•	•
•	•
•	•
•	•
Company Inherent Risks	Company Inherent Risks
•	•
•	•
•	
•	
•	
Company Control Risks	Company Control Risks
•	•
•	•
•	•
•	
•	
PwC's Engagement Risks	PwC's Engagement Risks
•	•
•	•
•	•
•	•
•	

Assessing Fraud Risk

Although fraud risk is not explicitly included in *Exhibit 7.2*, auditing standards require the audit team to have a team discussion, often referred to as **brainstorming**. During brainstorming, auditors are to assess client risks relevant to the possible existence of fraud and should identify where fraud might likely occur. Brainstorming sessions occur predominantly during the planning phase of the audit, but the audit team will repeat these sessions if fraud is detected or at the end of the audit to ensure that all ideas generated during brainstorming have been addressed during the audit opinion formulation process. The entire audit team attends the brainstorming sessions, which the audit partner or manager often lead. These sessions are a way to transfer knowledge from top-level auditors to less senior members of the audit team via interactive and constructive group dialogue and idea exchange.

To encourage interactive and constructive group dialogue and idea exchange, the audit team typically follows important guidelines during the brainstorming session:

- *Suspension of criticism*—Participants are to refrain from criticizing or making value judgments during the session.
- *Freedom of expression*—Participants are encouraged to overcome their inhibitions about expressing creative ideas, and the audit team should note and accept every idea as a possibility.
- *Quantity of idea generation*—Participants are encouraged to provide more ideas rather than fewer, with the intent to generate a variety of possible risk assessment scenarios that the team can explore during the conduct of the audit.
- *Respectful communication*—Participants are encouraged to exchange ideas, further develop those ideas during the session, and to respect the opinions of others.

Brainstorming sessions normally include the following steps:

1. Review prior year client information
2. Consider client information, particularly with respect to the fraud triangle (incentive, opportunity, and rationalization)
3. Integrate information from Steps 1 and 2 into an assessment of the likelihood of fraud in the engagement
4. Identify audit responses to fraud risks

Most audit firms encourage participants in the brainstorming session to explicitly consider professional skepticism, both in general throughout the engagement and with respect to specific accounts with a higher risk of fraud. For example, audit firms encourage the brainstorming group to answer questions such as, "How could someone commit fraud at this client, or for a certain account balance?" Auditors should be skeptical about assurances that client personnel provide, verify the authenticity of documentation, and choose new and different audit procedures each year even if the results of brainstorming in the current year are similar to those in prior years. Brainstorming sessions usually last up to an hour, but occasionally may exceed two hours, depending on the complexity and risk profile of the client.

What is the Role of the Audit Partner in Promoting High-Quality Brainstorming?

Why It Matters

Young auditors may experience pressure to either "'speak up" in brainstorming, or "shut up," depending on the leadership style of the audit partner or manager leading the session, and resulting brainstorming can be either high or low quality. This feature identifies actions that can encourage high-quality brainstorming.

Features of high-quality brainstorming include:

- The audit partner is open to ideas that subordinates express
- The audit partner does not stifle discussion by indicating through tone and/or body language that s/he is not really interested in the contributions of less-senior members of the team

- Fraud and information technology specialists contribute to brainstorming
- Auditors conduct brainstorming early in audit planning, not as a "check the box" requirement that is relegated to late in the audit
- Auditors spend a lot of time engaging in meaningful discussions during brainstorming
- Auditors consciously think about how management might perpetrate fraud
- The extent of time during brainstorming about how the auditors should respond to the fraud risks that they identify during brainstorming

Using Planning Analytical Procedures to Assess the Risk of Material Misstatement

Planning analytical procedures used as a risk assessment procedure help auditors improve their understanding of the client's business. These procedures also help auditors identify risks of material misstatement in particular account balances and direct the auditor's attention to high-risk areas.

Recall from *Chapter 6* that a basic premise underlying analytical procedures is the existence of plausible relationships among data, and that the relationship continues over time in the absence of known conditions to the contrary. As initially described in *Chapter 6*, the steps that the auditor will take are:

1. Determine the suitability of a particular analytical procedure for given account(s)/assertion(s), considering the risks of material misstatement.
2. Evaluate the reliability of data that the auditor is using to develop an expectation of account balances or ratios.
3. Develop an expectation of recorded account balances or ratios, and evaluate whether that expectation is precise enough to accomplish the relevant objective. Recall that for planning analytical procedures the objective is to identify accounts with heightened risk of misstatement to provide a basis for designing and implementing responses to the assessed risks. Also recall that the precision of expectation tends to be less precise and based on more aggregated data. However, with highly aggregated data, this procedure will only provide broad indications of potential material misstatements.
4. Define when the difference between the auditor's expectation and what the client has recorded would be considered significant.
5. Compare the client's recorded amounts with the auditor's expectation to determine any significant unexpected differences.
6. Investigate significant unexpected differences. Recall that for planning analytical procedures, significant unexpected differences suggest that substantive procedures for the account/assertion will be increased.
7. Ensure that the following have been appropriately documented: auditor's expectation from Step 3, including the factors that the auditor considered in developing the expectation, the results in Step 4, and the audit procedures conducted relating to Steps 5 and 6.

As an example of a planning analytical procedure, the auditor may develop an expectation of revenue based on production capacity. Recorded revenue in excess of this expectation may indicate a heightened risk of misstatement in the revenue account—due to either fraud or error. In light of this heightened risk, the auditor will plan audit procedures to obtain sufficient appropriate evidence for the revenue account.

Types of Analytical Procedures   Two frequently used analytical procedures during risk assessment include trend analysis and ratio analysis. Most commonly, the auditor imports the client's unaudited data into a spreadsheet or software program to calculate trends and ratios and help pinpoint areas for further investigation. The auditor compares these trends and ratios with auditor expectations developed from knowledge obtained in previous years, industry trends, and current economic development in the geographic area served by the client.

Trend analysis includes simple year-to-year comparisons of account balances, graphic presentations, analysis of financial data, histograms of ratios, and projections of account balances based on the history of changes in the account. It is imperative for the auditor to develop expectations and to establish decision rules, or thresholds, in advance, in order to identify unexpected results for additional investigation. One potential decision rule, for example, is to investigate any change

Comparisons Used in Planning Analytical Procedures

Why It Matters

This feature describes common comparisons performed by auditors as part of planning analytical procedures.

Comparison with Industry Data

A comparison of client data with industry data may identify potential problems. For example, if the average collection period for accounts receivable in an industry is 43 days, but the client's average collection period is 65 days, this might indicate problems with product quality or credit risk. As another example, a bank's concentration of loans in a particular industry may indicate greater problems if that industry is encountering economic problems. One potential limitation to using industry data is that such data might not be directly comparable to the client's data. Companies may be quite different but still classified within one broad industry. Also, other companies in the industry may use accounting principles different from the client's (e.g., LIFO versus FIFO).

Comparison with Previous Years' Data

Simple ratio analysis comparing current and past data that is prepared as a routine part of planning an audit can highlight risks of misstatement. The auditor often develops ratios on asset turnover, liquidity, and product-line profitability to search for potential signals of risk. For example, an inventory turnover ratio might indicate that a particular product line had a turnover of four times for the past three years, but only three times this year. The change may indicate potential obsolescence problems or errors in the accounting records. Even when performing simple ratio analysis, it is important that the auditor go through each of the steps in the process, beginning with the development of expectations.

exceeding a specified percentage. Auditors often use a trend analysis over several years for significant accounts, as shown in the following example, in planning for the 2018 audit (2018 data are unaudited).

	2018	2017	2016	2015	2014
Gross sales ($000)	$29,500	$24,900	$24,369	$21,700	$17,600
Sales returns ($000)	600	400	300	250	200
Gross margin ($000)	8,093	6,700	6,869	6,450	5,000
Sales returns	150.0%	133.3%	120.0%	125.0%	104.6%
Percent of prior year: Sales	118.5%	102.2%	112.3%	123.3%	105.2%
Gross margin	132.8%	97.5%	106.5%	129.0%	100.0%
Sales as a percentage of 2014 sales	167.6%	141.5%	138.5%	123.3%	100.0%

In this example, the auditor's expectation might be that gross margin percentage and sales percentage would increase at about the same rate. Further, the auditor might have an expectation that sales returns would be relatively stable in comparison with that of the prior year. After setting a threshold and comparing the expectation to the client's data, the auditor, in this example, might conclude that the changes in gross margin and sales returns warrant further investigation. The auditor should gain an understanding about why gross margin is increasing more rapidly than sales and why sales returns are increasing. More importantly, the auditor should develop some potential hypotheses as to why gross margin increased along with the reason for the substantial increase in sales. Then, once the hypotheses are developed, the auditor should determine which set of hypotheses is most likely and then use those for prioritizing audit work. Potential hypotheses for the increase in gross margin include:

- The company has introduced a new product that is a huge market success (e.g., launches of the iMac Pro and the HomePod by Apple).
- The company has changed its product mix.
- The company has improved its operational efficiencies.
- The company has fictitious sales (and consequently no cost of goods associated with those sales).

Upon analysis, two of these hypotheses would best explain the unaudited changes in sales and gross margin for 2018: (a) a significant new product introduction that allows higher margins; or (b) fictitious sales. With this analysis, the auditor can prioritize which hypothesis to investigate first. For example, if the company has not introduced a new product and the company's sales growth and gross margin are significantly higher than the competition, then it is likely that the fictitious sales hypothesis is the most likely. Going through this process of performing planning analytical procedures helps the auditor identify areas where the risk of material misstatement is high and then allows the auditor to plan appropriate procedures to address those risks. Importantly, the auditor should determine potential hypotheses rather than just inquiring of management as to the reasons for the change.

As suggested previously, trend analysis can incorporate **ratio analysis**, which takes advantage of economic relationships between two or more accounts. It is widely used because of its power to identify unusual or unexpected changes in relationships. Ratio analysis is useful in identifying significant differences between the client results and a norm (such as industry ratios) or between auditor expectations and actual results. It is also useful in identifying potential audit problems when ratios change between years (such as inventory turnover).

Comparing ratio data over time for the client and its industry can yield useful insights. The auditor could rely on industry data to develop expectations for preliminary analytics. For example, if a particular industry ratio increased over time, the auditor should expect that the client's ratio would also increase over time. In the following example, the percentage of sales returns and allowances to net sales for the client does not vary significantly from the industry average for the current period, but comparing the trend over time yields an unexpected result.

Sales Returns as a % of Net Sales

	2018	2017	2016	2015	2014
Client	2.1%	2.6%	2.5%	2.7%	2.5%
Industry	2.3%	2.1%	2.2%	2.1%	2.0%

This comparison shows that even though the percentage of sales returns for 2018 is close to the industry average, the client's percentage declined significantly from 2017, while the industry's percentage increased. In addition, except for the current year, the client's percentages exceeded the industry average. The result is different from the auditor's expectation that the percentage would increase from the prior period—it likely exceeds the auditor's threshold, and, thus, the auditor should investigate the potential cause. Some possible explanations for the differences include:

- The client has improved its quality control.
- The client recorded fictitious sales in 2018.
- The client is not properly recording sales returns in 2018.

The auditor designs audit procedures to identify the cause of this difference to determine whether a material misstatement exists.

Exhibit 7.3 provides commonly used financial ratios that the auditor can use in performing planning analytical procedures. The first three ratios provide information on potential liquidity problems. The turnover and gross margin ratios are helpful in identifying fraudulent activity or items recorded more than once, such as fictitious sales or inventory. The leverage and capital turnover ratios help in evaluating going-concern problems or adherence to debt covenants. Although the auditor chooses the ratios deemed most useful for a particular client, auditors routinely calculate and analyze the ratios listed in *Exhibit 7.3* on a trend basis over time.

Some ratios are industry specific. In the banking industry, for example, auditors calculate ratios on percentages of nonperforming loans, operating margin, and average interest rates by loan categories. Auditors generally perform ratio and trend analysis through a comparison of client data with expectations:

- Based on industry data
- Based on similar prior-period data
- Developed from industry trends, client budgets, other account balances, or other bases of expectations

Exhibit 7.3
Commonly Used Ratios

Ratio	Common Formula
Short-term liquidity ratios	
Current ratio	Current Assets/Current Liabilities
Quick ratio	(Cash + Cash Equivalents + Net Receivables)/Current Liabilities
Current debt-to-assets ratio	Current Liabilities/Total Assets
Receivable ratios	
Accounts receivable turnover	Credit Sales/Accounts Receivable
Days' sales in accounts receivable	365/Turnover
Inventory ratios	
Inventory turnover	Cost of Sales/Ending Inventory
Days' sales in inventory	365/Turnover
Profitability measures	
Net profit margin	Net Income/Net Sales
Return on equity	Net Income/Stockholders' Equity
Financial leverage ratios	
Debt-to-equity ratio	Total Liabilities/Stockholders' Equity
Liabilities to assets	Total Liabilities/Total Assets
Capital turnover ratios	
Asset liquidity	Current Assets/Total Assets
Sales to assets	Net Sales/Total Assets
Net worth to sales	Stockholders' Equity/Net Sales

Prompt for Critical Thinking #6   It's Your Turn!

1. The following is an *actual assertion* from Goodyear Tires' management explaining why some of its sales revenue declined in one of its strategic business units:

   "Americas unit volume decreased 1.4 million units due to the impact of the deconsolidation of our Venezuelan subsidiary and 0.9 million units due to the dissolution of the global alliance with SRI." (FYE 2016 10-K, p. 31)

Below you will find disclosures about sales in Goodyear's strategic business units. After reviewing these disclosures, does this assertion seem reasonable?

2. The following is a *hypothetical assertion* from Goodyear Tires' management explaining why operating margins in Europe, the Middle East, and Africa are increasing:

   "Operating margins are increasing because our sales force has been able to implement per unit increases in sales of tire units."

Below you will find disclosures about sales in Goodyear's strategic business units. After reviewing these disclosures, does this assertion seem reasonable?

3. The following is a *hypothetical assertion* from Goodyear Tires' management explaining why net sales have increased from 2015 to 2016:

   "The increase in tire sales units has occurred because we have given price breaks in terms of prices that we charge per unit of sales."

Below you will find disclosures about sales in Goodyear's strategic business units. After reviewing these disclosures, does this assertion seem reasonable?

Disclosures about Sales in Goodyear's Strategic Business Units:

Americas

(In millions)	Year Ended December 31,		
	2016	**2015**	**2014**
Tire Units	74.1	79.1	78.5
Net Sales	$ 8,712	$ 9,370	$ 9,881
Operating Income	1,151	1,266	967
Operating Margin	14.1%	13.5%	9.8%

Europe, Middle East, and Africa

(In millions)	Year Ended December 31,		
	2016	**2015**	**2014**
Tire Units	61.1	61.1	60.5
Net Sales	$ 4,880	$ 5,115	$ 6,180
Operation Income	461	435	438
Operation Margin	9.4%	8.5%	7.1%

Asia Pacific

(In millions)	Year Ended December 31,		
	2016	**2015**	**2014**
Tire Units	30.9	26.0	23.0
Net Sales	$ 2,106	$ 1,958	$ 2,077
Operating Income	373	319	301
Operating Margin	17.7%	16.3%	14.5%

7-5 Detection risk is the susceptibility of an assertion to a material misstatement before consideration of related controls. (T/F)

7-6 Some level of control risk is always present in an organization because of the inherent limitations of internal control. (T/F)

7-7 Which of the following statements represents the appropriate directional relationships?
   a. As inherent risk increases, audit risk increases.
   b. As inherent risk increases, audit risk decreases.
   c. As control risk increases, detection risk decreases.
   d. As control risk increases, inherent risk decreases.

7-8 Which of the following statements is <u>false</u> regarding planning analytical procedures?
   a. The precision of the auditor's expectation tends to be less precise, and based on more aggregated data, for planning analytical procedures than for substantive analytical procedures.
   b. The objective for planning analytical procedures is to identify accounts with heightened risk of misstatement to provide a basis for designing and implementing responses to the assessed risks.
   c. For planning analytical procedures, significant unexpected differences suggest that the auditor will need to increase substantive procedures.
   d. A frequently used planning analytical procedure is regression analysis.

LO 3

Respond to the assessed risk of material misstatement by planning the audit procedures that will appropriately address that risk.

Responding to Identified Risk of Material Misstatement

Determining Evidence Needed in the Audit

By combining assessed inherent risk and control risk for each significant assertion/account, the auditor obtains the risk of material misstatement for each significant assertion/account. In practice, inherent risk and control risk are typically set at one of two levels: *high* or *low*. When the auditor combines these two risks into the risk of material misstatement, the risk of material misstatement will be at one of three levels: *high*, *moderate*, or *low*.

With the assessment of the risk of material misstatement, and consideration of the desired level of audit risk (usually 1% or 5%), the auditor determines detection risk. Detection risk provides guidance to the auditor on the substantive audit procedures needed to ensure that the audit achieves the desired audit risk. The sufficiency and appropriateness (relevance and reliability) of the evidence the auditor needs from substantive auditing procedures affect detection risk. Detection risk incorporates both types of substantive procedures—substantive analytical procedures and tests of details.

A high level of detection risk means that the audit firm is willing to take a higher risk of not detecting a material misstatement through its substantive procedures. In that case, the auditor is able to obtain less, and/or less appropriate, evidence from substantive procedures.

A low level of detection risk means that the audit firm is not willing to take as much of a risk of not detecting a material misstatement through its substantive procedures. In that case, the auditor needs to obtain more, and/or more appropriate, evidence from substantive procedures.

Exhibit 7.4 shows the directional relationships among the various risks, along with interpretations of their meanings. You can think of these concepts in terms of the components of the audit risk model:

Exhibit 7.4
Risks and Their Effects on Substantive Procedures

Desired Level of Audit Risk	Interpretation	Risk of Material Misstatement (Combines Inherent Risk and Control Risk)	Interpretation	Effect on Detection Risk	Interpretation	Effect on Sufficiency and Appropriateness of Substantive Procedures
1%	Auditor is willing to take only a 1% chance of expressing an audit opinion that the financial statements are fairly presented when they are materially misstated.	High	High likelihood that assertion/account contains a material misstatement.	Detection risk will be at a lower level.	Auditor is willing to take a lower risk that substantive procedures will not detect a material misstatement.	More, and/or more appropriate, evidence from substantive procedures.
5%	Auditor is willing to take a 5% chance of expressing an audit opinion that the financial statements are fairly presented when they are materially misstated.	Moderate	Moderate likelihood that assertion/account contains a material misstatement.	Detection risk will be at a moderate level.	Auditor is willing to take a moderate risk that substantive procedures will not detect a material misstatement.	Moderate, and/or moderately appropriate, evidence from substantive procedures.
5%	Auditor is willing to take a 5% chance of expressing an audit opinion that the financial statements are fairly presented when they are materially misstated.	Low	Low likelihood that the assertion/account contains a material misstatement.	Detection risk will be at a higher level.	Auditor is willing to take a higher risk that substantive audit procedures will not detect a material misstatement.	Less, and/or less appropriate evidence from substantive procedures.

Audit Risk = Inherent Risk × Control Risk × Detection Risk, where *Inherent Risk* and *Control Risk* combine to determine *Risk of Material Misstatement*.

After you are comfortable with the relationships in *Exhibit 7.4*, you can work through numerical applications of the audit risk model that we present next. In practice, audit firms do not typically assign numerical values to inherent risk, control risk, and detection risk. However, working through the applications will provide you with a better understanding of the relationships in the audit risk model.

Application of the Audit Risk Model: High Risk of Material Misstatement

Assume an account with many complex transactions and weak internal controls that heighten the risk of the existence assertion for this account. The auditor assesses both inherent risk and control risk at their maximum (100%) for the existence assertion for this account. This assessment implies that for the existence assertion for this account, the client does not have effective internal control and there is a high risk that transactions posted to this account would contain a material misstatement.

Further, assume that the auditor has set audit risk at 1%. This level implies that the auditor is willing to take only a 1% chance of expressing an audit opinion that the financial statements are fairly presented when they are materially misstated.

A numerical depiction of the relationship between inherent risk, control risk, detection risk, and audit risk is referred to as the **audit risk model**, and it is calculated as follows:

Audit Risk = Inherent Risk × Control Risk × Detection Risk

0.01 = 1.00 × 1.00 × Detection Risk

therefore:

Detection Risk = 0.1/(1.0 × 1.0) = 1%

This example yields an intuitive result: a high likelihood of material misstatement leads to more substantive audit work to achieve audit risk at an acceptable level.

Application of the Audit Risk Model: Low Risk of Material Misstatement

Assume an account with simple transactions, well-trained accounting personnel recording those transactions, no incentive to misstate the financial statements, and effective internal control over the account. The auditor's previous experience with the client and an understanding of the client's internal controls indicate a low risk of material misstatement for the existence assertion for this account. The auditor assesses inherent and control risk as low (at 50% and 20%, respectively). Audit risk has been set at 5%. This level implies that the auditor is willing to take a 5% chance of expressing an audit opinion that the financial statements are fairly presented when they are materially misstated. The auditor's determination of detection risk for this engagement is:

Audit Risk = Inherent Risk × Control Risk × Detection Risk

0.05 = 0.50 × 0.20 × Detection Risk

therefore:

Detection Risk = 0.05/(0.50 × 0.20) = 50%

In this example, the auditor could design substantive tests of the accounting records with a higher detection risk—in this case 50%. Because inherent and control risk are relatively low, the auditor is willing to accept a greater risk that substantive audit procedures will not detect a material misstatement. However, because the auditor is planning to rely on controls, the auditor will need to test the operating effectiveness of controls to support the lower control risk assessment. As in the prior illustration, this illustration yields an intuitive result: a low likelihood of material misstatement leads to less extensive substantive audit work to maintain audit risk at an acceptable level.

What Do You Think?   For Classroom Discussion

Do you find the audit risk model to be a useful conceptual tool for thinking about evidence-related decisions in the audit? In practice, why do you think that audit firms do not typically assign numerical values to inherent risk, control risk, and detection risk? Do you think there are trade-offs among the three risks, such that low levels of one or two would cause the auditor to minimize worry about the third?

Audit Procedures to Respond to the Assessed Risk of Material Misstatement

Recall from *Chapter 5* that for an integrated audit and for a financial statement audit where the auditor wants to rely on controls as part of the basis for the audit opinion, the auditor should design a controls reliance audit—an audit that includes tests of controls and substantive procedures. For some audits, the auditor might determine that it is not efficient or effective to rely on the client's controls. In those audits, the auditor designs a substantive audit—an audit that includes substantive procedures and does not include tests of controls.

When considering responses to the assessed risk of material misstatement, the auditor should:

1. Evaluate the reasons for the assessed risk of material misstatement
2. Estimate the likelihood of material misstatement due to the inherent risks of the client
3. Consider the role of internal controls, and determine whether control risk is relatively high or low, thereby determining whether the auditor should rely on controls (thereby necessitating tests of controls) or whether the auditor needs to conduct a substantive audit
4. Obtain more evidence and evidence that is of a higher level of rigor and relevance as the auditor's assessment of the risk of material misstatement increases

A practical analogy to conceptualize these steps is to compare an umbrella in a rainstorm to effective internal controls. Risks might result in material misstatement (rain); management is responsible for keeping the financial statements free of material misstatements (dry). The auditor's objective is to gather enough information to assess how well management is doing in keeping the financial statements free from material misstatement (dry). *Exhibit 7.5* shows that Client A has effective internal controls (the umbrella without holes) that prevent material misstatement (rain) from getting into the accounting records.

However, we know that umbrellas are not always perfect—they can spring leaks when least expected, or one of the supporting arms can fail, letting rain come through on one side. The auditor has to test the umbrella (controls) to see that it is working, but must do enough substantive testing of the account balance to determine that leaks (misstatements) had not occurred in an amount that would be noticeable (material misstatement).

Client B's umbrella has holes in it (weak internal controls), resulting in wet accounting records (they are likely to contain material misstatements). Because of the weak controls, it is unlikely that the auditor will perform any testing of

Exhibit 7.5
Effect of Risk Assessment on Risk Response

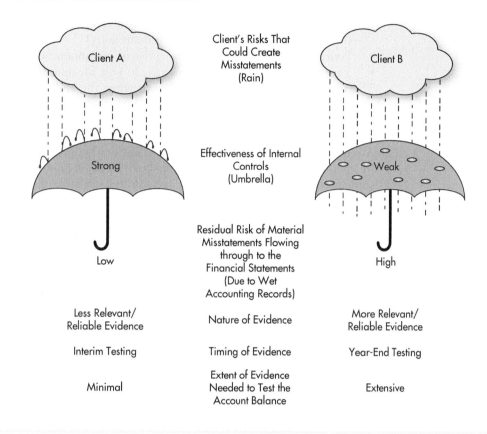

controls, and the use of substantive analytical procedures will probably be limited. Thus, the auditor must perform extensive direct tests of the account balances to identify any misstatements.

Nature, Timing, and Extent of Risk Responses

The nature, timing, and extent of the auditor's risk responses depend on the auditor's assessment of the risk of material misstatement. The **nature of risk response** includes the types of audit procedures the auditor will perform, with a focus on the appropriateness (relevance and reliability) of those procedures. For example, certain audit procedures may be more appropriate for some assertions than other assertions. The auditor can more effectively test the existence of inventory by inspecting the inventory, whereas the auditor can more effectively test the valuation of inventory by engaging a specialist.

The nature of risk response could occur at the engagement level such as assembling an audit team with more experienced auditors and auditors with specialized skills or including on the audit team outside specialists to address assessed risks. Other ways to address assessed risks at the engagement level include putting increased emphasis on professional skepticism or incorporating elements of unpredictability in the selection of audit procedures.

Some ways to introduce unpredictability include:

- Perform some audit procedures on accounts, disclosures, and assertions that would otherwise not receive audit attention because they are considered low risk
- Select items for testing that are outside the normal boundaries for testing (e.g., that are lower than prior-year materiality)
- Perform audit procedures on a surprise or unannounced basis
- Vary the locations or procedures year to year for multilocation audits

The **timing of risk response** refers to when the auditor conducts the audit procedures and whether the auditor conducts those procedures at announced or predictable times. When the risk of material misstatement is high, the auditor conducts the audit procedures closer to year-end and/or on an unannounced basis. Additionally, the auditor could include additional unpredictability in the timing by changing the timing of audit procedures from one audit to the next so that some procedures are performed on an interim basis and others are performed at year end.

Further, the auditor can only complete certain procedures at or after period end. These procedures include:

- Compare the financial statements to the accounting records
- Evaluate adjusting journal entries made by management in preparing the financial statements
- Conduct procedures to respond to risks that management may have engaged in improper transactions at period end

The **extent of risk response** refers to the sufficiency of evidence that is necessary given the risk of material misstatement and the level of acceptable audit risk. When the risk of material misstatement is high, the auditor increases the extent of audit procedures and obtains more evidence. An example of increasing the extent of risk response would be to increase the number of locations to be included in the scope of the audit (e.g., observing inventory counts at more warehouse locations).

Focus on Fraud

The City of Dixon, Illinois, Sues Its Auditor for $50 Million Related to the Rita Crundwell Embezzlement

This feature provides a reminder to auditors to accurately assess the risk of material misstatement and to respond accordingly. The message from this feature is clear—when auditors fail to assess and appropriately respond to the risk of material misstatement, there are severe consequences to all parties involved.

Recall from earlier in the chapter that Rita Crundwell embezzled about $50 million from the city of Dixon, Illinois. On June 8, 2012, the city sued the accountants that had conducted the city's audit for the past five years: Samuel Card CPA and Janis Card Company LLC. In addition, the lawsuit names former Dixon audit firm, CliftonLarsonAllen, as a respondent in discovery, which allows the city to request documents to determine whether to also sue the former audit firm. The lawsuit alleges professional negligence and negligent misrepresentation, and

it alleges certain deficiencies in how the auditors conducted the audit, including:

- Failing to identify inaccuracies in the city's financial statements and other financial documents
- Failing to properly perform audits and other financial services
- Failing to perform professional services and issue audits in conformance with nationally recognized standards and its own internal policies and procedures
- Failing to implement proper policies and procedures in order to perform the audits of the city
- Failing to properly train auditors and auditing staff to identify fraud, embezzlement, and criminal acts

In September 2013, CliftonLarsonAllen and Sam Card agreed to settle for a total of $40 million.

7-9   A high level of detection risk means that the audit firm is willing to accept a low risk of not detecting a material misstatement.   (T/F)

7-10   The nature of risk response refers to the sufficiency and appropriateness of evidence that is necessary given the risk of material misstatement and the level of acceptable audit risk.   (T/F)

7-11   Assume that the auditor sets audit risk at 1%. What is the appropriate interpretation of this level of audit risk?

   a.   The auditor is willing to take only a 1% chance that audit procedures will not detect a material misstatement.

   b.   The auditor is 99% confident that the audit procedures will detect a material misstatement.

   c.   The auditor is willing to take only a 1% chance of expressing an audit opinion that the financial statements are fairly presented when they are materially misstated.

   d.   The auditor is 99% confident that the audit opinion is correct.

7-12   Which of the following statements is <u>false</u> regarding the nature, timing, and extent of risk responses?

   a.   The nature of risk response refers to the types of audit procedures applied given the nature of the account balance and the most relevant assertions regarding that account balance.

   b.   The timing of risk response refers to when the auditor performs the audit procedures.

   c.   When the risk of material misstatement is low, the auditor conducts the audit procedures closer to year-end, on an unannounced basis, and includes more elements of unpredictability in the procedures.

   d.   The extent of risk response refers to the sufficiency of evidence that is necessary given the client's assessed risks, materiality, and the acceptable level of audit risk.

LO 4

Apply the frameworks for professional decision making and ethical decision making to issues involving materiality, risk assessment, and risk responses.

Applying Decision-Making Frameworks

The following *End of Chapter* materials provide you an opportunity to apply the frameworks for professional decision making and ethical decision making for decisions made when conducting an audit: *7-29* and *7-36*.

Let's Review

- Materiality relates to the significance or importance of an item. (LO 1)

- Materiality judgments: (1) are a matter of professional judgment, (2) depend on the needs of a reasonable person relying on the information (e.g., an investor, a potential investor, or other stakeholders), and (3) involve both quantitative and qualitative considerations. Materiality differs from one audit client to another; that is, what is material for one client may not be material for another client, and may change for the same client from one period to another. (LO 1)

- In planning the audit, auditors consider planning materiality in terms of the smallest aggregate level of misstatements that could be material to any one of the financial statements. Once the auditor determines planning materiality, the auditor then sets performance materiality to determine significant accounts and the audit procedures to perform. A common approach to determining performance materiality is to calculate 75% of planning materiality. The auditor commonly sets posting materiality at 5% of planning materiality. (LO 1)

- The risk of material misstatement includes inherent risk and control risk. Client business risk can be considered as the risk of material misstatement at the financial statement level. Some client business risks have direct relevant implications for multiple assertions and accounts. (LO 2)

- As part of assessing the risk of material misstatement, the audit team will have a team discussion, often referred to as brainstorming. During brainstorming, auditors assess the possible existence of fraud and where fraud might likely occur. (LO 2)

- Planning analytical procedures used as a risk assessment procedure help auditors improve their understanding of the client's business. These procedures also help auditors identify risks of material misstatement in particular account balances and direct the auditor's attention to high-risk areas. (LO 2)

- The nature, timing, and extent of the auditor's risk responses depend on the auditor's assessment of the risk of material misstatement. The nature of risk response includes the types of audit procedures the auditor will perform, with a focus on the appropriateness (relevance and reliability) of those procedures. The timing of risk response refers to when the auditor conducts the audit procedures and whether the auditor conducts those procedures at announced or predictable times. The extent of risk response refers to the sufficiency of evidence that is necessary given the risk of material misstatement and the level of acceptable audit risk. (LO 3)

Significant Terms

Audit risk The risk that the auditor expresses an inappropriate audit opinion when the financial statements are materially misstated.

Audit risk model A conceptual depiction of the relationship between inherent risk, control risk, detection risk, and audit risk.

Auditor business risk See engagement risk.

Auditor-detected misstatement Such a misstatement occurs when, during the audit, the auditor comes to find that there exists an error in the recording of a particular transaction, regardless of whether it was intentional or unintentional.

Brainstorming A group discussion designed to encourage auditors to creatively assess client risks, particularly those relevant to the possible existence of fraud in the organization.

Client business risk Risks affecting the business operations and potential outcomes of an organization's activities.

Control risk The risk that a misstatement that could occur in an assertion about a class of transaction, account balance, or disclosure and that could be material, either individually or when aggregated with other misstatements, will not be prevented, or detected and corrected, on a timely basis by the entity's internal control.

Detection risk The risk that the procedures performed by the auditor to reduce audit risk to an acceptably low level will not detect a misstatement that exists and that could be material, either individually or when aggregated with other misstatements.

Engagement risk (also known as auditor business risk) This risk reflects the potential for loss to the auditor that the client poses, including being a publicly traded client, not being a profitable engagement, damaging the auditor's reputation, and/or potential litigation relating to the engagement.

Extent of risk response The risk that the procedures performed by the auditor to reduce audit risk to an acceptably low level will not detect a misstatement that exists and that could be material, either individually or when aggregated with other misstatements.

Individually important locations Locations that are financially significant to the client's financial statements overall.

Inherent risk The susceptibility of an assertion about a class of transaction, account balance, or disclosure to a misstatement that could be material, either individually or when aggregated with other misstatements, before consideration of any related controls.

Materiality The magnitude of an omission or misstatement of accounting information that, in view of surrounding circumstances, makes it probable that the judgment of a reasonable person relying on the information would have been changed or influenced by the omission or misstatement.

Misstatement   An error, either intentional or unintentional, that exists in a transaction or financial statement account balance.

Nature of risk response   The types of audit procedures applied given the nature of the account balance and the most relevant assertions regarding that account balance.

Overall materiality (also known as planning materiality)   A materiality level that the auditor uses in determining whether the financial statements overall are materially correct

Performance materiality (also known as tolerable error)   A materiality level that the auditor uses for determining significant accounts, significant locations, and audit procedures for those accounts and locations

Planning materiality (also known as overall materiality)   A materiality level that the auditor uses in determining whether the financial statements overall are materially correct

Posting materiality   A materiality level that signifies the misstatements identified throughout the audit that will be considered at the end of the audit in determining whether the financial statements overall are materially correct.

Ratio analysis   An analytical technique that is useful in identifying significant differences between the client results and a norm (such as industry ratios) or between auditor expectations and actual results; ratio analysis is also useful in identifying potential audit problems that may be found in ratio changes between years.

Risk of material misstatement   Risk that exists at the overall financial statement level and at the assertion level, and within these levels risk can be categorized as involving inherent risk and control risk.

Significant risk   An identified and assessed risk of material misstatement that, in the auditor's professional judgment, requires special consideration.

Timing of risk response   Refers to when audit procedures are conducted and whether those procedures are conducted at announced or predictable times.

Tolerable error (also known as performance materiality)   A materiality level that the auditor uses for determining significant accounts, significant locations, and audit procedures for those accounts and locations.

Trend analysis   An analytical technique that includes simple year-to-year comparisons of account balances, graphic presentations, analysis of financial data, histograms of ratios, and projections of account balances based on the history of changes in the account.

Prompts for Critical Thinking

Prompt for Critical Thinking #1

- First year engagement
- Management turnover
- High market pressure
- Higher than normal risk of bankruptcy

Prompt for Critical Thinking #2

1. No, if we rely on the income as a benchmark (without considering any qualitative factors) the misstatement should not be material because it is less than the 5% cutoff.
2. No, because correcting the income-decreasing misstatement will make the actual EPS even lower than the analyst mean consensus forecast. Then again, since Target is going to miss the forecast anyway, maybe management will be happy correcting the misstatement.

3. This situation should make you realize that even small, seemingly immaterial misstatements in terms of quantitative benchmarks can have a big influence on users' judgments and decisions around valuing a company's stock. That puts pressure on managers as they interact with auditors, and incentives for correcting income-decreasing misstatements may put auditors and managers at odds.

Prompt for Critical Thinking #3

- New regulatory requirements increase legal exposure
- Alternative products, services, competitors, or providers pose a threat to current business
- There are significant supply chain risks
- The production and delivery processes are complex
- The industry is mature and declining
- The company lacks ability to control costs with the possibility of unforeseen costs
- The company produces products that have multiple substitutes
- Operations in regions that are economically unstable, such as countries with significant currency devaluation or highly inflationary economies
- Operations exposed to volatile markets, such as futures trading
- Operations that are subject to a high degree of complex regulation
- Going concern and liquidity issues, including loss of significant customers or constraints on the availability of capital or credit
- Offering new products or moving into new lines of business
- Changes in the entity, such as acquisitions or reorganizations
- Entities or business segments likely to be sold
- The existence of complex alliances and joint ventures
- Use of off-balance sheet financing, special-purpose entities, and other complex financing arrangements
- Significant transactions with related parties
- Lack of personnel with appropriate accounting and financial reporting skills
- Changes in key personnel, including departure of key executives
- Deficiencies in internal control, especially those not addressed by management
- Changes in the Information Technology (IT) system or environment and inconsistencies between the entity's IT strategy and its business strategies
- Inquiries into the organization's operations or financial results by regulatory bodies
- Past misstatements, history of errors, or significant adjustments at period end
- Significant amount of nonroutine or nonsystematic transactions, including intercompany transactions and large revenue transactions at period end
- Transactions that are recorded based on management's intent, such as debt refinancing, assets to be sold, and classification of marketable securities
- Accounting measurements that involve complex processes
- Pending litigation and contingent liabilities, such as sales warranties, financial guarantees, and environmental remediation

Prompt for Critical Thinking #4

- Weak tone at the top leading to a poor control environment
- Inadequate accounting staff or staff lacking requisite expertise
- Inadequate information systems
- Growth of the organization exceeds the accounting system infrastructure
- Disregard for regulations or controls designed to prevent illegal acts
- No internal audit function, a weak internal audit function, or lack of respect for the internal audit function by management
- Weak design, implementation, and monitoring of internal controls

Prompt for Critical Thinking #5

Ford Motor Company	**Goodyear Tires**

Company Business Risks

- Decline in sales volume due to financial crises, recessions, or geopolitical events in the U.S. and in the vast number of foreign countries in which Ford's supply chain exists, and where Ford's sales markets exist
- Market shifts away from more- to less-profitable vehicles based on changes in consumer preferences
- Continuing price competition
- Significant liabilities associated with post-retirement liabilities based on old labor union contracts
- The discovery of vehicle defects, and, therefore, unexpectedly high warranty costs

Company Inherent Risks

- Complexities of revenue recognition might yield inaccurate timing of recording revenue
- Inaccurate estimates of future interest rates or actuarial assumptions could yield inaccurate valuation of Ford's very significant postretirement benefit obligations
- Pressure to meet earnings targets might create an incentive for management to manipulate accounts to fictitiously meet their targets
- The Ford family members are still involved in the company, and there exist assorted related party transactions
- Ford's goodwill balances are substantial, and measures of fair value are subjective and subject to manipulation

Company Control Risks

- Failure to comply with required safety, emissions, and fuel economy regulations
- Cybersecurity risks to operational or security systems
- Foreign Corrupt Practices Act violations in foreign subsidiaries
- The large and complex supply chain could be subject to purchasing agent mismanagement of supplier relationships
- Weak controls over product quality standards might yield subsequent warranty claims or litigation related to safety problems

Company Business Risks

- Exposure to local economic conditions
- Restrictions on the withdrawal of foreign investment and earnings
- Spikes in raw material and energy costs may adversely affect profitability
- Fierce global competition
- Risk of unforeseen warranty expenditures should product quality or safety issues arise

Company Inherent Risks

- Adverse changes in the diplomatic relations of foreign countries with companies headquartered in the U.S.
- Hostility from local populations and insurrections
- Export and import restrictions
- Unfavorable tax policies and regulations
- Unfavorable labor regulations

Company Control Risks

- Sourcing products from foreign countries, some of which are prone to demanding bribes resulting in a risk that overseas employees might violate the Foreign Corrupt Practices Act
- Inadequate controls over currency exchanges
- Disruptions or failures in IT systems
- Far-flung operations and supply chains may be subject to control over-ride by local subsidiaries
- Because raw material supply quality is important, there exists a risk that controls over quality may fail

PwC's Engagement Risks for Both Engagements

- The audit might not be profitable
- Client management may perpetrate a fraud that the auditor will not detect, thereby yielding reputational loss and potential litigation
- By auditing both companies, PwC might be able to do a better audit of both companies because they understand the relationships between the purchaser (Ford) and the supplier (Goodyear)
- If one of the companies decides to switch to another auditor, the other company may abandon PwC as well

Note: For a complete listing of risks that Ford and Goodyear identify, obtain their respective 10-K filings at the SEC's website, and review Item 1A. Risk Factors.

Prompt for Critical Thinking #6

1. Management's assertion seems reasonable because tire units went from 79.1 million to 74.1 million from 2015 to 2016.
2. Management's assertion does not seem reasonable because sales of tire units remained stable at 61.1 million units and net sales *decreased* from 2015 to 2016, implying unit decreases in sales of tire units.
3. Management's assertion seems reasonable because tire unit sales have increased 18.8% from 2015 to 2016, while net sales have increased about 7.6%, implying that management used price breaks to enhance sales volumes.

Review Questions and Short Cases

NOTE: Completing *Review Questions and Short Cases* does not require the student to reference additional resources and materials.

NOTE: For the remaining problems, we make special note of those addressing fraud, international issues, professional skepticism, and ethics.

7-1 **LO 1** Define the term *misstatement* and describe characteristics that would make a misstatement material.

7-2 **LO 1** Some audit firms develop firm-specific quantitative guidelines relating planning materiality to sales or assets. Other audit firms leave the materiality judgments up to the individual partner or manager in charge of the audit. What are the major advantages and disadvantages of each approach? Which approach do you favor?

7-3 **LO 1** An auditor makes multiple materiality judgements.
   a. Define *planning materiality*. Explain how the auditor typically determines and uses it in the audit.
   b. Define *performance materiality*. Explain how the auditor typically determines and uses it in the audit.
   c. Define *posting materiality*. Explain how the auditor typically determines and uses it in the audit.
   d. Describe how qualitative factors can affect the quantitative materiality assessment.

7-4 **LO 1** The SEC is concerned about the need for auditors to recognize the qualitative aspect of materiality judgments. Explain what the qualitative aspect of materiality means. List some factors that would result in the auditor judging a quantitatively small misstatement as qualitatively material.

7-5 **LO 1** Panzero Bread is a major retailer of specialty sandwich items and baked goods. The following information represents the company's financial position as of December 31, 2018, and December 31, 2017.

	December 31, 2018 (unaudited)	December 31, 2017 (audited)
Total assets	$698,752,000	$542,609,000
Accounts receivable	$25,152,000	$19,041,000
Total sales	$1,066,691,000	$828,971,000
Cost of goods sold	$842,255,000	$628,534,000
Net income	$57,456,000	$58,849,000
Earnings per share	$1.81	$1.88

The auditors have detected misstatements in the accounts receivable in the past. The auditor knows that management is under considerable pressure to meet analyst expectations for earnings per share. Reducing earnings per share by even $0.01 would cause the trend in earnings to become even more negative than the unaudited financial numbers already reveal, and it would cause the company to miss analyst forecasts for earnings per share by just a small amount.

a. Use the three common benchmarks for making materiality judgments (net income, total assets, and net sales) to establish planning materiality for the financial statements overall.

b. What difficulties does the auditor face when the alternative benchmarks yield differing conclusions about planning materiality? What qualitative factors should the auditor consider in making the materiality judgment for this company?

c. Select the benchmark from those calculated in part (a) to use for planning materiality and provide your reasons.

PROFESSIONAL SKEPTICISM

7-6 **LO 1** Auditors make materiality judgments when planning the audit to be sure they ultimately gather sufficient appropriate evidence during the audit to provide reasonable assurance that the financial statements are free of material misstatements. Auditors often use quantitative benchmarks such as 1% of total assets or 5% of net income to determine whether misstatements materially affect the financial statements (planning materiality), but ultimately, it is an auditor's individual professional judgment as to the appropriate levels of materiality.

a. An auditor typically sets the initial amount of overall materiality using a quantitative approach. Then the auditor considers qualitative items, such as expectations relating to analysts' EPS forecasts, financial statement items on which users will focus their attention, nature of the client and industry, size of the client, the nature of the client's financing, and volatility of the benchmark. How might these qualitative factors influence the overall materiality that the auditor will use in planning the audit? Assume that Client A has a number of these qualitative factors noted above, while Client B does not (therefore, Client A is riskier than Client B). How might this information affect planning materiality?

b. Assume that Client A has a number of these qualitative factors noted above, while Client B does not (therefore, Client A is riskier than Client B). Assume that Client B is similar in size to Client A. After setting planning materiality for both clients, the auditor has determined that performance materiality for Client B is $5,000. Should the performance materiality threshold for Client A be the same for Client B? For which client will the auditor require more evidence?

c. How might an auditor's individual characteristics affect his or her professional judgments about materiality?

d. Assume that one auditor is more professionally skeptical than another auditor. Compare the possible alternative performance materiality thresholds that a more versus less skeptical auditor might make for Client A.

7-7 `LO 1` The audit report provides reasonable assurance that the financial statements are free from material misstatements. The auditor assesses materiality in planning the audit to ensure that sufficient appropriate audit work is performed to detect material misstatements. However, the auditor is in a difficult situation because materiality is defined from a user's viewpoint.

a. Define materiality as used in accounting and auditing, particularly emphasizing the differences that exist between the FASB and the U.S. Supreme Court materiality definitions.

b. Three major dimensions of materiality are: (1) the dollar magnitude of the item, (2) the nature of the item under consideration, and (3) the perspective of a particular user. Give an example of each.

c. Once the auditor develops an assessment of planning materiality, can it change during the course of the audit? Explain. If it does change, what is the implication of a change for audit work that the auditor has already completed?

7-8 `LO 2` Define the terms *client business risk, inherent risk, control risk, audit risk, detection risk, and engagement risk*. Explain how these risks relate to each other.

7-9 `LO 2` How does inherent risk relate to internal controls? Why is it important to assess inherent risks of material misstatement prior to evaluating the quality of an organization's internal controls?

7-10 `LO 2` What is the directional relationship between the risk of material misstatement (inherent and control risk) and both audit risk and detection risk? In other words, if the risk of material misstatement increases or decreases, how would those changes affect audit risk and detection risk?

7-11 `LO 1, 2` Explain how the concepts of audit risk, detection risk, and materiality are related.

7-12 `LO 2` Explain how engagement risk affects audit pricing.

7-13 `LO 2` List various risk assessment procedures that the auditor can perform to obtain evidence about inherent risk relating to the operations of a company.

FRAUD

PROFESSIONAL SKEPTICISM

ETHICS

7-14 `LO 2, 3` The auditor assesses management integrity as a potential indicator of inherent risk, particularly as it relates to the potential for fraud. Although the assessment of management integrity takes place on every audit engagement, it is a difficult and subjective task. This task requires that the auditor exhibit professional skepticism; this can be difficult because it is human nature to trust people we know!

a. Define management integrity and discuss how management integrity influences the auditor's decisions regarding the type of evidence to gather on an audit and the evaluation of the evidence.

b. What are possible sources of evidence that the auditor can use in assessing management integrity?

c. Is it ethical for upper level management to refuse to correct an income-decreasing detected misstatement because doing so would cause the company to miss its analysts' consensus earnings forecast?

d. For each of the following management scenarios: (1) indicate whether you believe the scenario reflects negatively on management integrity, and explain why; and (2) indicate how the assessment would affect the auditor's planning of the audit.

Management Scenarios

i. The owner/manager of a privately held company also owns three other companies. The individual companies could be run as one combined company, but they engage extensively in related-party transactions to minimize the overall tax burden for the owner/manager.

ii. The president of a publicly held company has a reputation for being stubborn and having a violent temper. He fired a divisional manager on the spot when the manager did not achieve profit goals.

iii. The financial vice president of a publicly held company has worked her way to the top by gaining a reputation as a great accounting manipulator. She has earned the reputation by being very creative in finding ways to circumvent FASB pronouncements to keep debt off the balance sheet and in manipulating accounting to achieve short-term earnings. After each short-term success, she has moved on to another company to utilize her skills.

iv. The president of a small publicly held company was indicted on tax evasion charges seven years ago. He settled with the Internal Revenue Service and served time doing community service. Since then, he has been considered a pillar of the community, making significant contributions to local charities. Inquiries of local bankers yield information that he is the partial or controlling owner of several companies that may serve as a "shell" company whose sole purpose is to assist the manager in moving income around to avoid taxes.

v. James J. James is the president of a privately held company that has been accused of illegally dumping waste and failing to meet government standards for worker safety. James responds that his attitude is to meet the minimum requirements of the law; if the government deems that he has not, he will clean up. "Besides," he asserts, "it is good business; it is less costly to clean up only when I have to, even if small fines are involved, than it is to take leadership positions and exceed government standards."

FRAUD

7-15 **LO 2** Brainstorming is a group discussion designed to encourage auditors to assess client risks, particularly those relevant to fraud.

a. When does brainstorming typically occur?

b. Who attends the brainstorming session? Who typically leads it?

c. Besides encouraging auditors to creatively assess client risks, what other purpose does brainstorming serve?

d. What are some guidelines that are helpful to maximizing the effectiveness of a brainstorming session?

e. What are the typical steps in the brainstorming process?

f. What are some features of high-quality brainstorming?

7-16 **LO 2** Assessing control risk is an important part of planning an audit.

a. List factors that would lead auditors to assess control risk at a higher level.

b. Discuss the auditor's risk assessment procedures for assessing control risk, and provide specific procedures related to understanding management's risk assessment component of internal control.

7-17 LO 2, 3 Explain how ratio analysis and industry comparisons (performed as part of planning analytical procedures) can be useful to the auditor in identifying potential risk of material misstatement on an audit engagement. How can such analysis also help the auditor plan the audit?

7-18 LO 2 Refer to *Exhibit 7.3*. What ratios would best indicate problems with potential inventory obsolescence or collectibility of receivables? How do you calculate those ratios?

PROFESSIONAL SKEPTICISM

7-19 LO 2, 3 The following information shows the past two annual periods of results for a fictional company, Jones Manufacturing, and a comparison with industry data for the same period.

ANALYTICAL DATA FOR JONES MANUFACTURING

	Prior Period (000 omitted)	Prior % of Sales	Current Period (000 omitted)	Current % of Sales	% Change	Industry Average as a % of Sales
Sales	$10,000	100	$11,000	100	10	100
Inventory	$2,000	20	$3,250	29.5	57.5	22.5
Cost of goods sold	$6,000	60	$6,050	55	0.83	59.5
Accounts payable	$1,200	12	$1,980	18	65	14.5
Sales commissions	$500	5	$550	5	10	NA
Inventory turnover	6.3	—	4.2	—	(33)	5.85
Average number of days to collect	39	—	48	—	23	36
Employee turnover	5%	—	8%	—	60	4
Return on investment	14%	—	14.3%	—	—	13.8
Debt/Equity	35%	—	60%	—	71	30

a. Assume that the auditor expects that the client's performance in the current year will be similar to its performance in the prior year. From the preceding data, identify potential risk areas and explain why they represent potential risk. Briefly indicate how the risk analysis should affect the planning of the audit engagement.

b. Identify any of the above data that should cause the auditor to increase the level of professional skepticism used on the audit.

7-20 LO 2, 3 The following table contains calculations of several key ratios for a fictional company, Indianola Pharmaceutical Company, a maker of proprietary and prescription drugs. Indianola Pharmaceutical Company is a small- to medium-sized publicly held pharmaceutical company. Approximately 80% of its sales has been in prescription drugs; the remaining 20% is in medical supplies normally found in a drugstore. The primary purpose of the auditor's calculations is to identify potential risk areas for the upcoming audit. The auditor recognizes that some of the data might signal the need to gather other industry- or company-specific data. A number of the company's drugs are patented. Its best-selling drug, Anecillin, which will come off patent in two years, has accounted for approximately 20% of the company's sales during the past five years. The auditor's expectation is that the company's own trends from the past few years should be relatively consistent with this year's trends, and that the company will not have significant deviations from industry norms.

INDIANOLA PHARMACEUTICAL RATIO ANALYSIS

Ratio	Current Year	One Year Previous	Two Years Previous	Three Years Previous	Current Industry
Current ratio	1.85	1.89	2.28	2.51	2.13
Quick ratio	0.85	0.93	1.32	1.76	1.40
Times interest earned	1.30	1.45	5.89	6.3	4.50
Days' sales in receivables	109	96	100	72	69
Inventory turnover	2.40	2.21	3.96	5.31	4.33
Days' sales in inventory	152	165	92	69	84
Research & development as % of sales	1.3	1.4	1.94	2.03	4.26
Cost of goods sold as % of sales	38.5	40.2	41.2	43.8	44.5
Debt/equity ratio	4.85	4.88	1.25	1.13	1.25
Earnings per share	$1.12	$2.50	$4.32	$4.26	NA
Sales/tangible assets	0.68	0.64	0.89	0.87	0.99
Sales/total assets	0.33	0.35	0.89	0.87	0.78
Sales growth over past year	3%	15%	2%	4%	6%

a. What major conclusions regarding financial reporting risk can you draw from this information? Be specific in identifying specific account balances that have a high risk of material misstatement. How will you use this risk analysis in planning the audit? Identify a minimum of four financial reporting risks that you will address during the audit and discuss how you will address those risks.

b. What other critical background information will you want to obtain when planning the audit? What information would you gather during the conduct of the audit? Briefly indicate the probable sources of that information.

c. What major actions did the company take during the immediately preceding year? Explain.

PROFESSIONAL SKEPTICISM

FRAUD

7-21 **LO 2, 3** The auditor for a fictional company, Johnston Wholesaling, has just begun planning analytical procedures as part of planning the audit for the coming year. Johnston Wholesaling is in a competitive industry, selling STP Brand products and Ortho Grow products to companies such as Walmart, Costco, and regional retail discount chains. The company is privately owned and has experienced financial difficulty this past year. The difficulty could lead to its major line of credit being pulled if the company does not make a profit in the current year. In performing the planning analytical procedures, the auditor notes the following changes in accounts related to accounts receivable:

	Current Year (000 omitted)	Previous Year (000 omitted)
Sales	$60,000	$59,000
Accounts receivable	$11,000	$7,200
Percent of accounts receivable current	72%	65%
No. of days' sales in accounts receivable	64	42
Gross margin	18.7%	15.9%
Industry gross margin	16.3%	16.3%
Increase in Nov–Dec sales over previous year	12%	3.1%

The auditor had expected the receivables balance to remain stable, but notes the large increase in receivables. After considering possible reasons for this increase, the auditor decides to make inquiries of management. Management explains that the change is due to two factors: (1) a new information system that has increased productivity, and (2) a new policy of rebilling items previously sold to customers, thereby extending the due dates from October to April. Management explains the rebilling as follows: Many of the clients' products are seasonal—for example, lawn care products.

To provide better service to Johnston's customers, management instituted a new policy whereby management negotiated with a customer to determine the approximate amount of seasonal goods on hand at the end of the selling season (October). If the customer would continue to purchase from the client, management would rebill the existing inventory, thereby extending the due date from October until the following April, essentially giving an interest-free loan to the customer. The customer, in turn, agreed to keep the existing goods and store them on its site for next year's retail sales.

The key to planning analytical procedures is to identify areas of heightened risk of misstatement and then plan the audit to determine whether potential explanations satisfy all the unexpected changes in account balances. Further, it is important to be professionally skeptical of management-provided explanations. For example, does the explanation of a new information system and the rebilling adequately explain all the changes? Whether the answer to that question is yes or no, are there other explanations that are equally viable?

The auditor must be able to answer these questions to properly apply the risk-based approach to auditing. There are several factors that would indicate to a skeptical auditor that the explanations offered by Johnston management might not hold:

- The company has a large increase in gross margin. This seems unlikely, because it is selling to large chains with considerable purchasing power. Further, other competitors are also likely to have effective computer systems.
- If the rebilling items are properly accounted for, there should not be a large increase in sales for the last two months of this year when the total sales for the previous year is practically the same as that of the preceding year.

- If the rebillings are for holding the inventory at customers' locations, the auditor should investigate to determine: (a) if the items were properly recorded as a sale in the first place or if they should still be recorded as inventory, (b) what the client's motivation is for extending credit to the customers indicated, and (c) whether it is a coincidence that all of the rebilled items were to large retailers who do not respond to accounts receivable confirmations received from auditors.

    a. What potential hypotheses would likely explain the changes in the financial data? Identify all that might explain the change in ratios, including those identified by management.
    b. Which hypothesis would best explain all the changes in the ratios and financial account balances? Explain the rationale for your answer.
    c. Given the most likely hypothesis identified, what specific audit procedures do you recommend as highest priority? Why?

7-22 **LO 2, 3**   A staff auditor was listening to a conversation between two senior auditors regarding the audit risk model. The following are some statements made in that conversation regarding the audit risk model. State whether you agree or disagree with each of the statements, and explain why.

    a. Audit risk should be set at zero for most audit engagements.
    b. Inherent risk may be very low for certain assertions for some accounts. One example might be the completeness assertion for payroll expenses at Walmart. In such cases, the auditor does not need to perform direct tests of the assertion/account balance if the auditor obtains assurance that the inherent risk is indeed that low and that internal controls, as designed, are effective, and are working appropriately.
    c. Control risk refers to both: (a) the design of controls, and (b) the operation of controls. To assess control risk as low, the auditor must gather evidence on both the design and operation of controls.
    d. Detection risk at 50% implies that the substantive tests have a 50% chance of not detecting a material misstatement and that the auditor is relying on client characteristics (inherent and control risk) to address the additional uncertainty regarding the possibility of a material misstatement.
    e. Audit risk should vary inversely with both inherent risk and control risk; the higher the risk of material misstatement, the lower should be the audit risk taken.
    f. In analyzing the audit risk model, it is important to understand that much of it is judgmental. For example, setting audit risk is judgmental, and assessing inherent and control risk is judgmental.

7-23 **LO 3**   Refer to *Exhibit 7.4* and consider the audit risk model, whereby *Audit Risk = Inherent Risk × Control Risk × Detection Risk*. Complete the boxes in the table below. Describe generalizations about the relationships among the components of the audit risk model that you gain from the completed table. In which case will the auditor perform the greatest amount of substantive audit work?

	Case 1	Case 2	Case 3	Case 4	Case 5	Case 6	Case 7	Case 8
Inherent Risk	30%	40%	50%	50%	70%	80%	90%	100%
Control Risk	50%	100%	60%	100%	70%	70%	80%	100%
Audit Risk	5%	5%	5%	5%	1%	1%	1%	1%
Detection Risk	?	?	?	?	?	?	?	?

7-24 **LO 3** Distinguish between a controls reliance audit and a substantive audit. Which approach should an auditor consider the most effective approach?

7-25 **LO 3** Provide examples of how an auditor might change the: (a) nature of risk response, (b) timing of risk response, and (c) extent of risk response.

7-26 **LO 3** How can an auditor introduce unpredictability into audit procedures?

7-27 **LO 3** What audit procedures can the auditor complete only at or after period end?

Fraud Focus: Contemporary and Historical Cases

PROFESSIONAL SKEPTICISM

FRAUD

ETHICS

7-28 **ContinuityX Solutions, Inc., EFP Rotenberg LLP (LO 2, 3)**

A. The Fraud

ContinuityX Solutions Inc. (hereafter ContX) was a company that *purported* to sell on-line IT management services. The company went public in late 2011, and reported $27.2 million revenues to the SEC for the period April 2011 to September 2012. In reality, 99% of those reported revenues were fictitious. Throughout the company's existence, top management (David Godwin: President, CEO, and Chairman of the Board, and Anthony Roth: Executive Vice President, CFO, Corporate Secretary, and board member; hereafter Godwin and Roth) entered into almost *no* legitimate business transactions.

In its 10-K for FYE June 30, 2012, the company had described its business strategy as follows (remember … all of this is a complete lie):

> By specializing in finance, health, manufacturing, large-scale distribution, and leveraging long-term leading relationships with companies, which we consider "Channel Partners" such as AT&T, Telx and XO Communications, we have been able to effectively market our company. Moreover, through anticipating the needs of our clients to connect and communicate more effectively with employees, customers, partners and suppliers, we and our Channel Partners have created a nationwide network of carrier and Cloud service companies which are strategically positioned to enable next-generation requirements that help manage, protect and optimize networked communications.

> Leveraging partnerships ensures a best-in-class redundancy service and equipment sourcing along with competitive pricing. We compete smartly with small teams combining technical certified experts with project implementation and management. This enables the Company to offer in-depth services at lower pricing.

> Our global growth strategy addresses the world-wide ever-growing need for the portability and consumption of data, conducting VoIP calls, reviewing analytics, backing-up servers and accessing video/social media services. The data-centric ecosystem has created a 24/7 appetite, fueled by lower cost smartphones and tablet devices now being adopted by all business sizes and classes. This data phenomenon transcends country borderlines and global time zones to present a type of Telco industry "gold rush" for talented companies to stake their claims vis-a'-vis the data implementation

and management pertaining to: government compliance issues, information recovery, voice and VoIP communications as well as public/private Cloud managed and hosted services. We expect to expand our footprint to include customers throughout North and South America, Europe, Middle and the Far East.

Godwin and Roth enticed investors to provide capital by engaging in *supposed* business contracts with AT&T and Hutchinson Telecommunications Hong Kong Holdings Limited; Godwin and Roth sought these contracts not because they were actually planning to do any legitimate business, but rather to make it seem to investors that they had well-known and high-quality companies as customers. Godwin and Roth claimed that they had earned sales commissions; before actually receiving the commission payments, ContX sold the accounts receivable to factoring firms, pocketing the cash. (*Note: factoring firms provide financing for companies by purchasing their accounts receivable at a discount in exchange for the right to collect the full payments due on those receivables at a later date*).

The SEC described how Godwin and Roth perpetrated various schemes to fraudulently record fictitious revenue (SEC Release 2015-224):

> *In one alleged scheme, Godwin and Roth approached companies to become a straw buyer of services from Internet providers, promising them they would not have to pay for the services and would receive a portion of the commissions paid to ContinuityX by the providers. ContinuityX allegedly reported the commissions from the sham sales as revenue in its quarterly and annual reports. In another scheme, Godwin is alleged to have fabricated service orders and to have caused ContinuityX to recognize revenue from these fake transactions.*

Timothy L. Warren, Associate Director of SEC's Chicago Regional Office had this to say about the scheme (SEC Release 2015-224):

> *We allege that Godwin and Roth cheated investors out of millions of dollars, depicting ContinuityX as a successful Internet service sales company, when in reality it was a sham from beginning to end, complete with phony customers and fake contracts.*

When the stock went public, the asking price was $0.05 per share for 300,000 shares, that is for a total possible IPO value of $150,000. The highest price that the company received was $0.04 per share, and the stock market chart below shows how the stock performed at the IPO up until the time the fraud was discovered in late 2015.

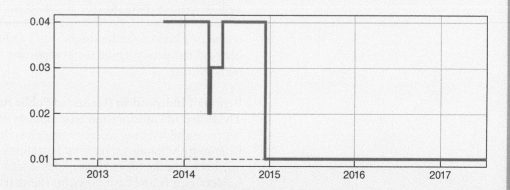

Godwin and Roth didn't raise a lot of money from the IPO; rather, they used the fraudulent SEC filings to advance their perceived legitimacy, thereafter raising millions of dollars from investors in connection with a private bond offering. Ultimately, the company sold $6.9 million in bonds to about 30 investors.

The company reported the following balance sheet and income statement for FYE 2011 and 2012 (source 10-K, FYE June 30, 2012), during the time in which they were trying to convince investors to purchase the private bond offering.

CONTINUITYX SOLUTIONS, INC. AND SUBSIDIARY
CONSOLIDATED STATEMENTS OF OPERATIONS

For the period March 25, 2011 (Inception) through June 30, 2011 and the Year Ended June 30, 2011

	2011	2012
Gross service revenues	$ 1,115,176	$ 18,586,466
Less; reseller commissions	–	1,031,691
Net service revenues	1,115,176	17,554,775
Costs of services	171,198	4,007,843
Gross profit	943,978	13,546,932
Other income and expenses:		
Selling and administrative expensive	811, 094	6,025,463
Interest expense	69,930	433,919
Other (income)	(24)	(2,306)
	880, 000	6,457,076
Income before income taxes	63,987	7,089,856
Provision for income taxes		
Current	11,325	–
Deferred	–	2,855,086
Net income	$ 52,653	$ 4,234,770
Earnings per share, basic and diluted:		
Basic net income per share	$ 0.00	$ 0.04
Weighted average number of common shares	97,330,900	117,239,334

Below is the *unqualified* audit report for the ContX audit that EFP Rotenberg performed, that is, a "clean" audit opinion whereby the auditor assures users that the financial statements present fairly, "in all material respects, the financial position of the company" (which, of course, we know with hindsight was a failed audit because EFP Rotenberg did not detect the financial reporting fraud that management was perpetrating).

Report of Independent Registered Public Accounting Firm
The Board of Directors and Shareholders of ContinuityX Solutions, Inc. We have audited the accompanying consolidated balance sheets of ContinuityX Solutions, Inc. and Subsidiary (the "Company") as of June 30, 2011 and the related consolidated statements of operations, shareholders' equity and cash flows for the years then ended. These financial statements are the responsibility of the Company's management.

Our responsibility is to express an opinion on these financial statements based on our audits.

We conducted our audits in accordance with auditing standards of the Public Company Accounting Oversight Board (United States). Those standards require that we plan and perform the audit to obtain reasonable assurance about whether the consolidated financial statements are free from material misstatement. An audit includes an examining, on a test basis, evidence supporting the amounts and disclosures of the financial statements. An audit also includes assessing the accounting principles used and significant estimates made by management, as well as evaluating the overfall financial statement presentation. We believe that our audits provide a reasonable basis for our opinion.

In our opinion, the consolidated financial statements referred to above present fairly, in all material respects, the financial position of ContinuityX Solutions, Inc. and Subsidiaries at June 30, 2012 and 2011, and the results of its operations and its cash flows for the years then ended, in conformity with accounting principles generally in the United States of America.

/s/ EFP Rotenberg, LLP

Rochester, New York
September 28, 2012

a. Identify likely risks associated with this company's business strategy, operations, and growth potential.

b. The net profit margin (i.e., net income divided by net revenue) for FYE 2011 and 2012 is 4.7% and 24.1%, respectively. Certainly, an auditor would be curious enough to question management as to how they achieved such a remarkable increase in profitability after just this one year. Management would logically anticipate that the auditor might question the increase. Assume for a moment that you are the fraudster managers at ContX, Godwin and Roth. What sort of explanations might you have "at the ready" if, and when, the auditor asks you to explain that remarkable accomplishment?

c. What types of planning analytical procedures might you consider applying to the income statement accounts? What insights might they provide to you? How would those insights shape your plans for conducting substantive procedures on this audit engagement?

d. Think about what you know about SOX 404 internal control assessment and reporting requirements. Why doesn't the audit opinion mention any assurance over internal controls? Why might an audit of internal controls in this case have been very informative in detecting the fraud?

e. Below is information contained in the Part II portion of PCAOB Release No. 104-2011-105A (and includes portions of Part II of the full report that were not included in PCAOB Release No. 104-2011-105, i.e., the Part I report). The PCAOB only issues Part II of the inspection report if the audit firm fails to remediate quality control concerns that the PCAOB previously warns them to correct. For more details, see the online report:

https://pcaobus.org/Inspections/Reports/Documents/2011_EFP_Rotenberg_LLP.pdf

Is there anything that makes you question if this is a high-quality audit firm? Why would a company like ContX decide to purchase audits from such an auditor?

PCAOB Inspection Results Part II:

* * * *

B. Issues Related to Quality Controls

The inspection of the Firm included Consideration of aspects of the Firm's system of quality control. Assessment of a firm's quality control rest both on a review of a firm's stated quality control policies and procedures and on interferences that can be drawn from respects in which a firm's system has failed to assure quality in the actual performance of engagements. On the basis of the information reported by the inspection team, the Board has the following concerns about aspect of the Firm's system of quality control.

* * * *

Monitoring and Addressing Identified Weakness

The Firm's system of quality control appears to lack a monitoring element sufficient to provide the Firm with reasonable assurance that the Firm's policies and procedures for engagement performance are suitably designed and effectively applied. The Firm's monitoring appears to have been deficient with respect to atleast one type of previously identified weakness. During an inspection of the Firm conducted in 2006, the PCAOB inspection team brought to the Firm's attention that the Firm's procedures appeared not to provide not sufficient assurance that the firm performed audit procedures to test journal entries and other adjustments for evidence of possible material misstatements due to fraud. An appropriate approach to monitoring would have resulted in the Firm avoiding this deficiency in audits performed after they were brought to the Firm's attention, yet the same deficiency was noted in this inspection.

B. The Failed Audit by EFP Rotenberg LLP

According to AAER 34-78393 (p. 2):

EFP Rotenberg willfully violated and Bottini willfully aided and abetted and caused EFP Rotenberg's violations of Section 10A(a) of the Exchange Act when it conducted the ContinuityX Audit without including procedures which were designed to:

1. provide reasonable assurance of detecting illegal acts; and
2. identify related party transactions.
3. Additionally, EFP Rotenberg and Bottini failed to comply with the standards of the Public Company Accounting Oversight Board (PCAOB).

EFP Rotenberg and Bottini repeatedly engaged in improper professional conduct that resulted in violations of professional standards and demonstrated a lack of competence to practice before the Commission. Specifically, during the ContinuityX Audit, EFP Rotenberg and Bottini failed to:

1. appropriately respond to risks of material misstatement;
2. identify related party transactions;
3. obtain sufficient audit evidence;

4. perform procedures to resolve and properly document inconsistencies;
5. investigate management representations that contradicted other audit evidence; and
6. exercise due professional care.

According to ContX's FYE 2012 10-K, EFP Rotenberg earned the following fees from its relationship with ContX:

Aggregate fees billed for professional services rendered for the Company by EFP Rotenberg, LLP through September 21, 2012 for the year ended June 30, 2012 and the period ended June 30, 2011 were:

Audit Fees. The aggregate fees billed by EFP Rotenberg, LLP for the year ended June 30, 2012 and the period ended June 30, 2011 were $13,930, which included the audits of the Company's annual financial statements, cost of the reviews of the Company's quarterly financial statements and other periodic reports for each respective period.

Audit-Related Fees. The aggregate fees billed by EFP Rotenberg, LLP for the year ended June 30, 2012 was $23,325, which represent consulting cost as well as Form 8-K filling and review.

Tax Fees. The aggregate fees billed by EFP Rotenberg, LLP for the year ended June 30, 2012 $1,200, which represent tax consulting costs.

f. Are you left shaking your head, asking "How could an audit go so wrong?" Reflect on the notion of professional skepticism and describe how Bottini's career was severely damaged, and how users' rights were violated, by his complete lack of professionalism on this audit.

PROFESSIONAL SKEPTICISM

INTERNATIONAL

ETHICS

FRAUD

7-29 **Kid Castle Educational Corporation, Brock, Schechter & Polakoff LLP, PCAOB**
(LO 2, 3, 4)

General Background. On May 22, 2012, the audit firm of Brock, Schechter & Polakoff LLP (hereafter BSP) was censured and fined $20,000 by the PCAOB in relation to its audits of public companies located in Taiwan and China. These public companies were listed on U.S. stock exchanges. James Waggoner, BSP's director of accounting and auditing, was the BSP auditor responsible for the audits. The charges against BSP and Waggoner include:

- BSP failed to develop policies and procedures to assure that the firm undertook only audit engagements that it could expect to conduct with professional competence. Prior to undertaking the audits of the Taiwan and Chinese companies, the firm had no experience auditing public companies in general or companies based in these locations. Further, BSP personnel lacked the ability to communicate in Chinese.
- BSP failed to develop policies and procedures to assure that the personnel assigned to the audits had the requisite technical training and proficiency.
- BSP failed to monitor the audits during its annual internal review process.
- BSP failed to comply with PCAOB standards on the planning, performance, and supervision of the audits.
- BSP failed to gather sufficient evidence, failed to use due care, and failed to exercise professional skepticism on the audits.
- BSP allowed two other audit firms, which were located in Taiwan and China, to plan and perform the audits. BSP had minimal contact with the foreign firms, and inadequately reviewed the working

papers of the foreign firms. BSP also failed to obtain and review engagement completion documentation from the foreign firms prior to issuing the audit reports.

- Waggoner failed to comply with professional auditing standards. Further, he failed to cooperate with PCAOB inspectors, and he falsified documentation relating to the audits.

The Kid Castle Audits. Kid Castle is a company located in Taiwan that provides English-language instruction to Chinese-speaking children. Kid Castle was traded on the OTC Bulletin Board and Pink Sheets. A Taiwanese audit firm approached BSP in June 2006 concerning the Kid Castle audit, and BSP was hired as the auditor on July 26, 2006. BSP expressed unqualified audit opinions on the company's 2006–2008 financial statements. In addition to the general criticisms detailed previously, the PCAOB enforcement release provides detailed information on audit quality deficiencies on the Kid Castle audits, including the following:

- BSP failed to consider the nature, extent, and timing of audit work necessary to audit Kid Castle. Instead, BSP relied completely upon the Taiwan firm to make these considerations and to develop the audit program.
- BSP failed to adequately supervise the auditors of the Taiwan firm, including:
  - o Failing to assess the technical competence of the Taiwan firm's auditors
  - o Failing to assign the Taiwan auditors to tasks according to their abilities
  - o Failing to instruct the Taiwan firm's auditors
  - o Failing to inform the Taiwan firm's auditors about their responsibilities and the objectives of the audit
  - o Failing to inform the Taiwan firm's auditors about matters that affected the nature, extent, and timing of audit procedures
  - o Failing to direct the Taiwan firm's auditors to bring to BSP's attention significant accounting/auditing issues encountered during the audits.
- BSP failed to adequately perform a review of the Taiwan firm's audit work, and such a review was the principal involvement required of BSP. In fact, Waggoner assigned the final responsibility for reviewing the audit to a BSP staff member.
- The reviewing staff member did find deficiencies in the audit procedures performed by the Taiwan auditor. Waggoner forwarded those deficiencies to the Taiwan firm's auditors, but they did not address those deficiencies or conduct additional audit work.
- For the 2007 audit, BSP did not receive or review any working papers from the Taiwan auditor, except for a set of worksheets showing consolidation work among Kid Castle's subsidiary accounts. For the 2008 audit, BSP did not receive or review any working papers.

Kid Castle Risk Factors and Financial Condition. In its December 31, 2008, Form 10-K, Kid Castle management disclosed the following risk factors relating to its business:

- There is a history of operating losses and difficulty maintaining profitability.

- Demand for products and services is unpredictable.
- The company's operating results are dependent upon the success of its franchises.
- Market competition from established competitors could negatively affect the business.
- International expansion plans may not be successful.
- There exist risks relating to the company's potential inability to defend and protect its intellectual property.
- The company relies on loans from shareholders and bank loans, which may adversely affect liquidity.
- Because the company's officers and directors are not U.S. persons and because subsidiaries are Taiwanese or Chinese, judgments under the U.S. securities laws may not be able to be enforced.
- Internal controls are not effective in accordance with the requirements of Sarbanes-Oxley Act of 2002 (SOX).
- The company's assets and operations in the People's Republic of China are subject to political, regulatory, and economic uncertainties.

In addition, BSP issued a going-concern audit report, which indicates concern about the company's ability to remain operational. The financial statements of Kid Castle are as follows:

KID CASTLE EDUCATIONAL CORPORATION CONSOLIDATED BALANCE SHEETS

(Expressed in U.S. dollars)	December 31, 2008	December 31, 2007
Current assets		
Cash and bank balances	1,985,818	1,238,212
Bank fixed deposits—pledged (Note 12)	2,847	363,562
Notes and accounts receivable, net (Notes 3 and 20)	2,171,768	2,453,868
Inventories, net (Note 4)	1,933,153	2,008,739
Other receivables (Notes 5 and 20)	396,003	88,139
Prepayments and other current assets (Note 6)	475,617	542,794
Pledged notes receivable (Note 12)	416,238	557,983
Deferred income tax assets (Note 7)	45,617	42,335
Total current assets	7,427,061	7,295,632
Deferred income tax assets (Note 7)	49,528	50,481
Interest in associates (Note 8)	68,336	58,625
Property and equipment, net (Note 9)	2,775,663	2,312,065
Intangible assets, net of amortization (Note 10)	371,056	572,005
Long-term notes receivable	356,901	420,636
Pledged notes receivable (Note 12)	283,469	183,453
Other assets	255,288	268,388
Total assets	$11,587,302	$11,161,285

LIABILITIES AND SHAREHOLDERS' EQUITY

Current liabilities

Bank borrowings—short-term and maturing within one year (Note 12)	242,879	1,212,534
Notes and accounts payable (Note 19)	1,017,552	389,639
Accrued expenses (Note 11)	1,617,717	985,764
Amounts due to officers (Note 19)	—	—
Other payables	270,458	573,237
Deposits received (Note 13)	751,151	912,535
Receipts in advance (Note 14)	2,305,980	2,372,403
Income tax payable (Note 7)	39,115	124,418
Total current liabilities	6,244,852	6,570,530
Bank borrowings maturing after one year (Note 12)	1,583,968	1,752,776
Receipts in advance (Note 14)	1,001,801	1,034,260
Deposits received (Note 13)	839,295	680,694
Deferred liability	41,775	38,787
Accrued pension liabilities (Note 15)	446,038	401,893
Total liabilities	10,157,729	10,478,940
Commitments and contingencies (Note 16		
Minority interest	216,754	162,343

Shareholders' equity

Common stock, no par share (Note 17):		
60,000,000 shares authorized; 25,000,000 shares issued and outstanding at December 31, 2008 and 2007, respectively.	8,592,138	8,592,138
Additional paid-in capital	194,021	194,021
Legal reserve	65,320	65,320
Accumulated deficit (Note 18)	(6,340,449)	(7,179,418)
Accumulated other comprehensive loss	(1,026,713)	(932,027)
Net loss not recognized as pension cost	(271,498)	(220,032)
Total shareholders' equity	1,212,819	520,002
Total liabilities and shareholders' equity	11,587,302	11,161,285

KID CASTLE EDUCATIONAL CORPORATION CONSOLIDATED STATEMENTS OF OPERATION

	Years Ended December 31		
	2008	**2007**	**2006**
	(Expressed in U.S. dollars)		
Operating revenue (Note 21)			
Sales of goods	7,905,949	7,671,392	6,774,260
Franchise income	2,380,930	2,205,668	2,080,551
Other operating revenue	2,558,232	1,359,552	856,772
Net operating revenue	12,845,111	11,236,612	9,711,583

	Years Ended December 31		
	2008	**2007**	**2006**
	(Expressed in U.S. dollars)		
Operating costs (Note 21)			
Cost of goods sold	(3,357,441)	(3,154,509)	(2,684,650)
Cost of franchising	(368,061)	(451,469)	(337,986)
Other operating costs	(1,777,862)	(491,869)	(616,102)
Total operating costs	(5,503,364)	(4,097,847)	(3,638,738)
Gross profit	7,341,747	7,138,765	6,072,845
Advertising costs	(22,735)	(29,241)	(21,833)
Other operating expenses	(6,272,753)	(5,342,216)	(5,526,318)
Profit from operations	1,046,259	1,767,308	524,694
Interest expense, net (Note 12)	(89,761)	(90,299)	(179,825)
Share of profit (loss) of investments	5,109	27,007	(39,489)
Other nonoperating income (loss), net	24,789	552,611	(153,803)
Profit before income taxes and minority interest income	986,396	2,256,627	151,577
Income taxes (expense) benefit (Note 7)	(106,215)	(278,191)	(173,325)
Income (loss) after income taxes	880,181	1,978,436	(21,748)
Minority interest income	(41,212)	(101,287)	(24,463)
Net income (loss)	838,969	1,877,149	(46,211)
Income (loss) per share—basic and diluted	0.034	0.075	(0.002)

During 2010, Kid Castle stock was no longer trading on any United States market. The PCAOB censured James Waggoner and prohibited him from practicing on any public company audits in the U.S. for at least three years.

a. Why would the inherent and control risks at Kid Castle be of concern to a potential auditor?

b. Review the financial statements and calculate the commonly used ratios from *Exhibit 7.3* for the years ending 2008 and 2007. Assume that the auditor expected the 2008 financial results to be in line with the 2007 financial results. Given this expectation, comment on the trends in the financial statements and ratios that would cause the auditor to assess a heightened risk of material misstatement. Would the auditor likely conclude that there was a heightened risk of fraud?

c. Based on your answers to (a) and (b), for what accounts would you recommend that the auditor plan to conduct more substantive audit procedures?

d. The 10-K discloses that BSP earned total audit fees in 2007 and 2008 of $121,026 and $150,000, respectively. Comment on the motivations of BSP and Waggoner to accept audit clients in international locations. How might those motivations have affected Waggoner's lack of ethics? Furthermore, how might those motivations might have affected his professional skepticism? Presumably, BSP had to pay the Taiwanese and Chinese audit firms a portion of the audit fee, and based on the allegations in the PCAOB enforcement release, BSP did virtually no audit work. Comment on your thoughts about the appropriateness of hiring a foreign audit firm to conduct the majority of audit work on an engagement and on BSP's actions (or lack thereof) in this regard.

e. Use the framework for making quality professional decisions from *Chapter 1* to identify those steps in the framework where Waggoner went wrong and describe what he should have done differently.

f. Describe the risks that an audit firm faces when it attempts to audit a company in an international location.

For additional details, see PCAOB Release Nos. 105-2012-002 and 105-2012-003.

FRAUD   **7-30**   **Lincoln Federal Savings and Loan (LO 2, 3)**

The following is a description of various factors that affected the operations of Lincoln Federal Savings and Loan, a California savings and loan (S&L). It was a subsidiary of American Continental Company, a real estate development company run by Charles Keating

Lincoln Federal Savings & Loan

Savings and Loan industry background—The S&L industry was developed in the early 20th century in response to a perceived need to provide low-cost financing to encourage home ownership. As such, legislation by Congress made the S&L industry the primary financial group allowed to make low-cost home ownership loans (mortgages).

For many years, the industry operated by accepting relatively long-term deposits from customers and making 25- to 30-year loans at fixed rates on home mortgages. The industry was generally considered to be safe. Most of the S&Ls (also known as *thrifts*) were small, federally chartered institutions with deposits insured by the FSLIC. The motto of many S&L managers seemed to be, "Get your deposits in, make loans, sit back, and earn your returns. Get to work by 9 a.m. and out to the golf course by noon."

Changing economic environment—During the 1970s, two major economic events hit the S&L industry. First, the rate of inflation had reached an all-time high. Prime interest rates had gone as high as 19.5%. Second, deposits were being drawn away from the S&Ls by new competitors that offered short-term variable rates substantially higher than current passbook savings rates. The S&Ls responded by increasing the rates on certificates of deposit to extraordinary levels (15–16%) while servicing mortgages with 20- to 30-year maturities made at old rates of 7–8%. The S&Ls attempted to mitigate the problem by offering variable-rate mortgages or by selling off some of their mortgages (at substantial losses) to other firms.

However, following regulatory accounting principles, the S&Ls were not required to recognize market values of loans that were not sold. Thus, even if loan values were substantially less than the book value, they would continue to be carried at book value as long as the mortgage holder was not in default.

Changing regulatory environment—In the early 1980s, Congress moved to deregulate the S&L industry. During the first half of 1982, the S&L industry lost a record $3.3 billion (even without marking loans down to real value). In August 1982, President Reagan signed the Garn-St. Germain Depository Institutions Act of 1982, hailing it as the most important legislation for financial institutions in 50 years. The bill had several key elements:

- S&Ls would be allowed to offer money market funds free from withdrawal penalties or interest rate regulation.
- S&Ls could invest up to 40% of their assets in nonresidential real estate lending. Commercial lending was much riskier than home lending, but the potential returns were greater. In addition, the regulators helped the deregulatory fever by removing a regulation that had required a savings and loan institution to have 400 stockholders with no one owning more than 25%—allowing a single shareholder to own a savings and loan institution.
- The bill made it easier for an entrepreneur to purchase a savings and loan. Regulators allowed buyers to start (capitalize) their thrift with land or other noncash assets rather than money.
- The bill allowed thrifts to stop requiring traditional down payments and to provide 100% financing, with the borrower not required to invest a dime of personal money in the deal.
- The bill permitted thrifts to make real estate loans anywhere. They had previously been required to make loans on property located only in their own geographic area.

Accounting—In addition to these revolutionary changes, owners of troubled thrifts began stretching already liberal accounting rules (with regulators' blessings) to squeeze their balance sheets into (regulatory) compliance. For example, goodwill, defined as customer loyalty, market share, and other intangibles, accounted for over 40% of the thrift industry's net worth by 1986.

Lincoln Federal S&L—American Continental Corporation, a land development company run by Charles Keating and headquartered in Phoenix, Arizona, purchased Lincoln Federal S&L in 1984. Immediately, Keating expanded the lending activity of Lincoln to assist in the development of American Continental projects, including the Phoenician Resort in Scottsdale.[1] Additionally, Keating sought higher returns by purchasing junk bonds marketed by Drexel Burnham and Michael Millken. Nine of Keating's relatives were on the Lincoln payroll at salaries ranging from over $500,000 to over $1 million.

Keating came up with novel ideas to raise capital. Rather than raising funds through deposits, he had commissioned agents working in the Lincoln offices who sold special bonds of American Continental Corporation. The investors were assured that their investments would be safe. Unfortunately, many elderly individuals put their life savings into these bonds, thinking they were backed by the FSLIC because they were sold at an S&L—but they were not. Keating continued investments in real estate deals, such as a planned megacommunity in the desert outside of Phoenix. He relied on appraisals, some obviously of dubious value, to serve as a basis for the loan valuation.

a. Discuss the risks identified that would be of concern to the auditor.
b. The auditor did review a few independent appraisals indicating the market value of the real estate for loans. How convincing are such appraisals? In other words, what attributes are necessary in order for the appraisals to constitute appropriate (relevant and reliable) evidence?

Application Activities

7-31 **Fraud at ContinuityX Solutions, Inc., EFP Rotenberg LLP (LO 2, 3)**

Review 7-28 above.

a. Access the FYE 2012 10-K of ContX on the SEC's website. Locate Item 1A. Based on that disclosure, what risks is the company facing? Knowing that the disclosures are completely fraudulent, which management statements do you find most surprising?

b. Below is a disclosure from the 10-K, which purports to provide information about the locations in which the company provides service, relating to its disclosure about strategic expansion planning. How could an auditor test the assertion that management is making with respect to these locations? Search Google Maps and focus on the three Los Angeles, California locations. What would a skeptical auditor ask the client about having three supposed locations within just blocks of one another?

Strategic Expansion planning

Interconnecting our network at key datacenter locations enables us to bridge services between various providers, data centers and even customers. Being an application centric, IP enabled, IT solutions-focused business with advanced networking technology, our offerings are more than just network services. Hence this enables us to continually look to expand our reach by leveraging strategic international partners that enable us to enter new markets with the lowest capital exposure and only take our network these as demand justifies. By establishing MPLS (Multi protocol label switching) Option A, B or C interconnects with other providers that meet our criteria for quality performance, we are able to not only deliver services on our private MPLS network but also to end-points on our partners' networks. These relationships are typically reciprocal enabling our partner to also reach location on our backbone and leverage our services as "white label" for their customers and offer new services such as Cloud computing.

We currently offer services in the following locations

- 36 North East 2nd Street, Miami, FL, USA
- 56 Marietta Street, Atlanta, GA, USA
- 60 Hudson Street, New York, NY, USA
- 111 Eighth Avenue, New York, NY, USA
- 113 N. Myers Street, Charlotte, NC, USA
- 120 East Van Buren Street, Phoenix, AZ, USA
- 200 Paul Avenue, San Francisco, CA, USA
- 300 Boulevard East, Weehawken, NJ, USA
- 600 South Federal Street, Chicago, IL, USA
- 600 West 7th Street, Los Angeles, CA, USA
- 1100 Space Park Drive, Santa Clara, CA, USA
- 2323 Bryan Street, Dallas, TX, USA
- 2820 Northwestern Parkway, Santa Clara, USA
- 50 NE 9th Street, Miami, FL, USA
- 530 West 6th Street, Los Angeles, CA, USA
- 624 South Grand Avenue, Los Angeles, CA, USA

- 650 South Grand Avenue, Los Angeles, CA, USA
- 800 South Hope Street, Los Angeles, CA, USA
- 3 Corporate Place, Piscataway, NJ, USA

c. Determine where ContX headquarters is located. Consider that the company was an early-stage company that went from approximately $1 million in sales to over $18 million in one year. Put on your 'skeptical auditor hat'. What questions would you ask management about their corporate headquarters, their very quick emergence into some extremely large city markets, and their amazing growth statistics coming out of the Great Recession of 2008?

d. Use online resources to determine the average net profit margin that a company in the telecommunications sector earns. Comment on that average, calculate the net profit margin for ContX, and develop some questions that you, as a skeptical auditor, would ask management about the pattern that emerges.

e. Use online resources to locate the Accounting and Auditing Enforcement Release that the SEC used to charge ContX auditors, AAER No. 3790 (July 22, 2016). What are the SEC's primary criticisms of the audit partner, Nicholas Bottini, and the failed audit of EFP Rotenberg LLP?

f. The following image is from EFP Rotenberg's 2011 PCAOB inspection of the quality of its audits.

PCAOB
Public Company Accounting Oversight Board

PCAOB Release No. 104-2011-105A
Inspection of EFP Rotenberg, LLP
March 31, 2001
Page 2

Part I
Inspection Procedures and certain Observations

Members of the Board's inspection staff ("the inspection team") conducted primary procedures for the inspection from August 25, 2008 to August 28, 2008. These procedures were tailored to the nature of the Firm, certain aspects of which the inspection team understood at the outset of the inspection to be as follows:

Number of offices	2 (Penn Yan and Rochester, New York)
Ownership structure	Limited liability partnership
Number of partners	11
Number of professional staff[4]	40
Number of issuer audit clients[5]	65

Use the PCAOB's online resource whereby audit partners sign their audit reports:
https://pcaobus.org/Pages/AuditorSearch.aspx
How many public company audits is EFP Rotenberg now conducting? What are your thoughts about what you find?

7-32 **LO 2** Important factors that auditors use in assessing inherent risk at the financial statement level related to analyst following include: a history of the client meeting analyst estimates exactly, analysts having high earnings growth expectations, and a situation in which the company is unable to meet its earnings estimates or is close to being unable to do so. It is important for auditors to understand issues relating to analyst following. Using an Internet source such as Yahoo

Finance (*http://finance.yahoo.com*), locate the analyst summary expectations (see analyst opinion and analyst estimates) for three companies in the same industry. For each company, answer the following questions:

a. How many analysts are following the company?

b. What is the average estimated sales growth for the year?

c. What is the earnings per share estimate?

d. What is the earnings per share actual?

e. What are the analysts' recommendations? For example, how many analysts are recommending buy versus hold, and so on?

f. What is your assessment of inherent risk relating to analyst following based on the data you have gathered? Use the terms *low* and *high* to make the risk assessment.

AUDITING STANDARDS APPLICATION ACTIVITY

7-33 **PCAOB (LO 2)** AS 2110 provides guidance regarding the auditor's responsibilities to understand management's application of accounting principles and related disclosures. Read through AS 2110 (you can find it on the PCAOB website) and summarize the risk assessment procedures addressed in the standard.

AUDITING STANDARDS APPLICATION ACTIVITY

7-34 **PCAOB (LO 2)** AS 2110 provides the following guidance regarding the auditor's need to obtain an understanding of the company's selection and application of accounting principle:

> As part of obtaining an understanding of the company's selection and application of accounting principles, including related disclosures, the auditor should evaluate whether the company's selection and application of accounting principles are appropriate for its business and consistent with the applicable financial reporting framework and accounting principles used in the relevant industry. Also, to identify and assess risks of material misstatement related to omitted, incomplete, or inaccurate disclosures, the auditor should develop expectations about the disclosures that are necessary for the company's financial statements to be presented fairly in conformity with the applicable financial reporting framework.

Read through AS 2110 (you can find it on the PCAOB website) and identify the specific issues that are relevant to the necessary understanding of the company's selection and application of accounting principles, including related disclosures.

7-35 **LO 3** *Exhibit 7.1* provides examples of questions that an auditor should ask when assessing financial reporting quality and risks that there are material misstatements in the financial statements. The first question asks, "What are the significant judgment areas (reserves, contingencies, asset values, note disclosures) that affect the current year financial statements?" Access the most recent financial statements for three companies in the same industry. For each company, locate the footnote disclosure that would answer the question about significant judgment areas (*often labeled as estimates and assumptions*). Briefly summarize the major judgment areas for these companies, and comment on any differences that you observe.

FRAUD

ETHICS

7-36 **Dixon, Illinois, Rita Crundwell (LO 2, 3, 4)** Refer to the *Focus on Fraud* feature "Lack of Oversight as a Control Weakness Leads to Embezzlement" and the *Focus on Fraud* feature "The City of Dixon, Illinois, Sues Its Auditor for $50 Million Related to the Rita Crundwell Embezzlement."

The situation described in these features relates to the fraud committed by Rita Crundwell in the city of Dixon, Illinois. Crundwell was sentenced to nearly 20 years in prison after pleading guilty to a wire fraud count. In September 2013, Dixon City auditors CliftonLarsonAllen and Sam Card agreed to settle for a total of $40 million.

a. Research this case and describe any recent developments.
b. Consider the framework in *Chapter 1* regarding ethical decision making. Comment on the parties at fault in this case and assess their relative level of fault.

FRAUD

AUDITING STANDARDS APPLICATION ACTIVITY

7-37 **LO 2, 3** You are helping to plan the audit for a client that is a U.S. public company. Your senior has indicated that it is important to modify the planned audit procedures to address assessed fraud risks. The senior also indicated that in responding to fraud risks, the plan should include should audit procedures that specifically address the risk of management override of controls. Your senior asks for your suggestions on how planned audit procedures should respond to assessed fraud risks. As you are not sure how to answer this question, you decide to obtain a copy of the auditing standard that would most likely provide relevant guidance. You may want to refer to the *Auditing Standards Exhibit* in the inside front cover of this textbook to determine the appropriate standard. What standard would be most appropriate? What guidance does the standard provide?

7-38 **LO 2** Companies disclose various risks in their 10-K filings. Regulators encourage companies to make these types of disclosures so that investors can estimate the uncertainties inherent in the organization. Select a company in the pharmaceutical industry; obtain its recent 10-K filing; and identify the risks the company included in its filing. Auditors need to be aware of these risks, as they could have misstatement implications for multiple financial statement accounts. What concerns should the auditor have about the risk of material misstatement in the financial statements for the company you selected?

Academic Research Cases

NOTE: Completing *Academic Research Cases* requires students to reference additional resources and materials

SEARCH HINT

It is easy to locate academic research articles! Use a search engine such as Google Scholar or an electronic research platform such as ABI Inform, and search using the author names and the article title.

7-39 **LO 2, 3** Locate and read the article listed below.

Mock, T. J., and H. Fukukawa. (2016). Auditors' risk assessments: The effects of elicitation approach and assertion framing. *Behavioral Research in Accounting* 28(2): 75–84.

a. What is the purpose of the study?
b. Describe the design/method/approach used to conduct the study.
c. What are the primary findings of the study?

7-40 **LO 2, 3** Locate and read the article listed below.

Dennis, S. A., and K. M. Johnstone. (2016). A field survey of contemporary brainstorming practices. *Accounting Horizons* 30(4): 449–472.

a. What is the purpose of the study?
b. Describe the design/method/approach used to conduct the study.
c. What are the primary findings of the study?

8

Specialized Audit Tools: Attributes Sampling, Monetary Unit Sampling, and Data Analytics Tools

The Audit Opinion Formulation Process

I. Making Client Acceptance and Continuance Decisions

Chapter 1

II. Performing Risk Assessment

Chapters 2, 3, 7, and 9–13

III. Obtaining Evidence About Internal Control Operating Effectiveness

Chapters 8–13

IV. Obtaining Substantive Evidence About Accounts, Disclosures, and Assertions

Chapters 8–13

V. Completing the Audit and Making Reporting Decisions

Chapters 14 and 15

Quality Auditing and the Need for Quality Auditor Judgments and Ethical Decisions

Chapter 1

Professional Liability

Chapter 4

The Audit Opinion Formulation Process and a Framework for Obtaining Audit Evidence

Chapters 5 and 6

Auditors use specialized tools to gather and evaluate evidence. These tools include sampling techniques, such as attributes sampling and monetary unit sampling. These tools also include techniques to analyze entire populations and sub-populations of client data, commonly known as data analytics tools. All of these tools are helpful to auditors in assessing the validity of management's assertions.

Learning Objectives

LO 1 Describe how auditors use sampling and data analytics tools to gather and evaluate sufficient appropriate audit evidence.

LO 2 Explain the objectives of sampling for testing controls and account balances, and describe the risks associated with sampling.

LO 3 Compare and contrast nonstatistical and statistical sampling and apply these sampling approaches.

LO 4 Describe attributes sampling and use it to test controls.

LO 5 Describe the basic steps in sampling for substantive tests of details and apply those steps in a nonstatistical sampling application.

LO 6 Describe monetary unit sampling and use it to test account balances and assertions.

LO 7 Describe how to use data analytics tools to obtain and evaluate client data.

LO 8 Apply the frameworks for professional decision making and ethical decision making to issues involving sampling and data analytics tools.

PCAOB Inspection Reports Regarding Audit Sampling: Continuing Deficiencies

This feature provides examples of audit sampling deficiencies noted by the PCAOB during its inspections of various audit firms.

Audit sampling is the application of an audit procedure to less than 100% of the items within an account balance or class of transactions for the purpose of evaluating some characteristic of the balance or class. Said another way, audit sampling allows the auditor to learn a lot about a population of items of interest without examining every one of those items individually. In 2008, the PCAOB issued its report on its 2004–2007 inspections of domestic annually inspected firms (PCAOB Release No. 2008–008). The report provides a summary of certain common issues related to sampling that were identified during those inspections:

The inspection teams identified deficiencies in firms' performance of audit sampling, including (a) using sample sizes that were too small to obtain enough evidence to form a conclusion about the account balance or class of

transactions being tested, (b) failing to appropriately project the effect of errors identified when testing the items selected to the entire population, (c) failing to select the sample in such a way that it could be expected to be representative of the underlying population, and (d) not appropriately testing all the items in the sample.

Since that time, the PCAOB has continued to criticize audit firms for weaknesses in sampling procedures. For example, in its 2015 inspection of Ernst & Young, the PCAOB stated (PCAOB Release No. 104-2016-142, p. 17):

The Firm selected key items to test whether the revenue recognition criteria were met. For the portion of revenue that was not covered by the Firm's testing of key items, which was multiple times the Firm's established level of materiality, the Firm failed to perform sufficient procedures. The Firm selected one contract from this portion of revenue to evaluate whether revenue was appropriately recognized and also tested revenue recognition for a sample of invoices. The Firm, however, had selected these invoices to support its accounts receivable cut-off testing; as a result, the sample was selected from only three months during the year and therefore was not representative of the revenue population. (Source: *https://pcaobus.org/Inspections/Reports/Documents/104-2016-142-EY.pdf.*)

Similarly, in its 2015 inspection of Deloitte (PCAOB Release No. 104-2016-141, p. 11), the PCAOB stated:

For a category of POC revenue that represented a significant portion of the issuer's total revenue, the Firm selected for testing two controls that involved reviews of the estimated costs to complete and the status of each project. The Firm, however, failed to identify and test any controls over the accuracy and completeness of certain important data that the control owners used in the operation of these controls. (Source: *https://pcaobus.org/Inspections/Reports/Documents/104-2016-141-Deloitte.pdf*)

Also along these same lines, the PCAOB stated the following in its 2015 inspection of KPMG (PCAOB Release No. 104-2016-175, p. 6):

For the locations at which substantive procedures were performed related to revenue and inventory, the Firm designed its substantive procedures – including sample sizes – based on a level of control reliance that was not supported due to the unsupported reduction in the number of locations selected for testing that is discussed above. As a result, the sample sizes the Firm used to test revenue and inventory were too small to provide sufficient evidence. (Source: *https://pcaobus.org/Inspections/Reports/Documents/104-2016-175-KPMG.pdf*)

Rounding out the Big 4, the PCAOB had this criticism of in its 2015 inspection of PwC (PCAOB Release No. 104-2016-140, p. 20):

For part of the sample that the Firm selected for dual-purpose testing, the Firm performed only the procedures that tested the control. For the remainder of the sample, it performed only substantive procedures. In addition, the Firm performed part of its testing as of an interim date and divided its sample between loans outstanding at the interim date and those outstanding at year end; the Firm, however, selected some of the same loans for testing at both dates. As a result, the Firm failed to perform both control and substantive testing for an appropriate sample of items based on the sample size for its dual-purpose test. (Source: *https://pcaobus.org/Inspections/Reports/Documents/104-2016-140-PwC.pdf*)

What Do You Think? For Classroom Discussion

The instances above are not the only criticisms that the PCAOB had for each of these firms with respect to their application of audit sampling; reading the PCAOB inspection reports yields further criticisms. Given that PCAOB inspection reports continue to identify these types of deficiencies, why do you think auditors have such difficulty satisfying the audit quality demands of the PCAOB? The PCAOB states that it uses a risk-based approach to selecting engagements to scrutinize; what does that imply about the generalizability of the criticisms to the firms' overall audit client portfolios?

What You Will Learn

- What is sampling, and what risks does the auditor face when using sampling? (LO 1, 2)
- What are data analytics tools and how do auditors use them to gather and evaluate audit evidence? (LO 1)
- In testing controls and account balances and assertions, what types of sampling are available for the auditors' use? (LO 3, 4, 5, 6)
- In testing controls and account balances and assertions, how many individual account items should the

auditor select, and which ones should the auditor select? (LO 4, 5, 6)
- If a sample contains an error, how does the auditor use that information to arrive at a conclusion regarding errors in the overall population? (LO 3, 4, 5, 6)
- How do auditors define data analytics? What are associated terms? How do auditors use data analytics to test management assertions? How do auditors use data in the audit? What are business intelligence platforms that support data analytics? (LO 7)

LO 1

Describe how auditors use sampling and data analytics tools to gather and evaluate sufficient appropriate audit evidence.

Using Sampling and Data Analytics Tools for Gathering and Evaluating Audit Evidence

This chapter describes two broad types of tools that auditors use to efficiently gather and evaluate evidence: (1) sampling for either testing the effectiveness of controls (attributes sampling) or direct tests of account balances and assertions (monetary unit sampling), and (2) data analytics tools that the auditor can use for obtaining, analyzing, visualizing, and evaluating client data.

Audit sampling involves looking at less than 100% of the transactions that occurred during the audit period. Sampling techniques would be appropriate when an auditor wants to perform procedures such as examining documents, reperforming calculations, or sending confirmations. Other types of audit procedures such as inquiry, observation, and analytical procedures would not involve sampling.

The auditor faces the challenge of gathering sufficient appropriate evidence as efficiently as possible. And, the auditor must reach conclusions about the accuracy of the underlying populations that make up an account balance, and generally must do so without examining 100% of the transactions during the audit period. Accordingly, audits involve sampling. Audit sampling is used to test the operation of controls and accuracy of account balances. Samples should be representative of the population if the auditor is going to minimize the risk of reaching an incorrect conclusion about the population. To increase the likelihood that samples will be representative, they must be of sufficient size and must be selected from the appropriate underlying population.

Data analytics tools include qualitative and quantitative techniques and processes that auditors use to enhance their productivity and effectiveness. For example, auditors use these tools to extract, categorize, identify, and analyze patterns or trends in the data. Data analytics tools are software programs that facilitate testing 100% of a population when appropriate and help focus the auditor's attention on specific risk areas or transactions, often involving sophisticated data visualization tools, e.g., https://www.tableau.com/. Data analytics tools also include platforms such as Excel, ACL, and IDEA; the landscape is changing dramatically and quickly in this space, so you should be prepared to be flexible and adaptive to change in utilizing data analytics tools as you complete audit (and other accounting) tasks.

Auditors use data analytics tools to import a client's data; then the auditor can employ these tools in various ways. For example, the auditor can scan the data,

For Classroom Discussion

What Do You Think?

Audit sampling requires that the auditor collect only a relatively small sub-sample of data, thereby resulting in detection risk, that is, the risk that, based on the sample the auditor takes, the auditor will fail to detect a material misstatement in the financial statements. Data analytics seems to present a panacea to that notion of risk because, by auditing 100% of the sample, detection risk can be lower.

- It seems like data analytics is the perfect answer to the audit risk problem. So, comment on a variety of reasons

that auditors might not be willing to rely on data analytics to drive audit risk down.

- Which do you think is costlier: sampling or data analytics? What are the different costs between sampling and data analytics?

- What role does cost-benefit play in the choice between employing statistical sampling versus data analytics?

sort and summarize it, stratify it, and transform it into visual representations. Auditors can also use data analytics tools to identify duplicate items (e.g., duplicate invoices), gaps in data (e.g., gap in a check sequence), and outliers in a population (e.g., invoices that exceed two times the average for a particular customer). You can think of data analytics tools as an enhanced Excel spreadsheet with easy-to-customize applications, often including advanced visualization tools.

Exhibit 8.1 outlines approaches to gathering and evaluating evidence about management assertions, includes examples of specific types of evidence that the auditor might gather, and provides an indication as to when sampling or data analytics tools would be appropriate.

Exhibit 8.1
Approaches to Gathering Audit Evidence About Assertions

Management Assertion	Using Sampling Tools to Gather Evidence	Using Data Analytics Tools to Gather Evidence
Existence or occurrence	Take a sample of recorded transactions (e.g., accounts receivable) and for selected items examine underlying evidence or send out confirmations.	Sort the file to identify the largest items, the smallest items, the last transactions during the year (for testing cutoff), or the most frequent items within the file; also useful in scanning for unusual transactions.
Completeness	Take a sample of subsequent cash disbursements to search for underrecorded liabilities.	Sort the file by vendor to identify the most commonly used vendors, or the least commonly used vendors; or compare the list of vendors from the prior year to the current year.
Rights or obligations	Perform in conjunction with existence testing, including examining source documents.	Sort the file and use data visualization to scan for unusual transactions.
Valuation or allocation	Select items (e.g., equipment) and trace back to source documents, such as purchase agreements or invoices.	Foot the file and test computations. Use data visualization to identify outliers.
Presentation and disclosure	Select items and verify estimates or other items for proper disclosure.	Use data visualization tools to evaluate whether disclosures about sales and profitability by region, product type, and industry segment are consistent with those asserted by management.

What Do You Think   For Classroom Discussion

Data analytics enables auditors to audit all transactions, rather than just a sample of transactions.

• Do you think that as the use of data analytics increases on audit engagements, the need for sampling will decrease?

• What role might the PCAOB or AICPA play in helping auditors determine when and how to incorporate data analytics into the audit?

8-1 Sampling can be used for both tests of controls and substantive tests of account balances and assertions. (T/F)

8-2 Auditors can use sampling for testing either the effectiveness of controls (attributes sampling) or direct tests of account balances and assertions (monetary unit sampling). (T/F)

8-3 For which of the following auditing procedures would sampling be most appropriate?
   a. Examining documents.
   b. Inquiring of management.

   c. Observing controls being completed.
   d. Conducting analytical procedures.

8-4 Which of the following activities would be most likely accomplished using sampling?
   a. Sorting a file to identify the largest items.
   b. Scanning for unusual transactions.
   c. Selecting items and tracing them back to source documents.
   d. Footing the file.

LO 2

Explain the objectives of sampling for testing controls and account balances, and describe the risks associated with sampling.

Objectives of Sampling and Risks Associated with Sampling

The objective of sampling when testing controls is to determine whether the controls are operating effectively. If they are not operating effectively, the auditor needs to consider this when deciding on the opinion for internal controls and when designing the substantive procedures. The objective of sampling when testing account balances is to estimate the amount of misstatement in an account balance. If there are large misstatements, the auditor wants to know about them so that the auditor can determine whether the account balance is materially misstated. However, sampling always contains some risk. For example, the auditor might not look at enough items (recall the examples from the *Why It Matters* feature at the beginning of the chapter), or the sample might not be representative of the population. Thus, auditors must consider how to obtain and evaluate samples that minimize the likelihood they will reach an incorrect conclusion.

Sampling units refer to the individual items making up the population. The **population** is a group of transactions or items for which the auditor wants to estimate some characteristic, such as the effectiveness of a control procedure or the extent of misstatement in an account. An example of sampling units might be the sales orders processed during the year that relate to the recognition of revenue. The auditor needs to answer four questions when sampling:

1. Which population and sampling unit should be tested, and what characteristics should be examined (*population*)?
2. How many items should be selected for audit testing (*sample size*)?
3. Which items should be included in the sample (*sample selection*)?
4. What inferences can be made about the overall population from the sample (*sample evaluation*)?

Nonsampling and Sampling Risks

When making inferences about a population from a sample, the auditor could make an error about the underlying population because either: (a) the auditor did not appropriately carry out the audit procedures or inappropriately diagnosed problems (nonsampling risk), or (b) the auditor used a sample that was not representative of the population (sampling risk). Fortunately, audit firms can control both of these risks through adequate planning and effective quality control.

Nonsampling Risk

Auditors should carefully examine all items in the sample and use appropriate procedures to test and evaluate the accuracy of an account balance or the effectiveness of an internal control. However, there may be cases when this does not occur. For example, the auditor may not have the appropriate knowledge to perform the test or may be fatigued or may be facing time pressure when performing the test. These examples illustrate the concept of **nonsampling risk,** that is, the risk that the auditor reaches an erroneous conclusion for any reason not related to sampling risk. The audit firm controls nonsampling risk through proper training and adequate supervision of the auditors, well-designed sampling programs, and carefully designed and executed audit programs.

Sampling Risk

There is always a risk that any inferences made from a sample might not be correct. There is uncertainty about the projected results because the sampling results are based on only a portion of the population. The smaller the sample, the more uncertainty; the larger the sample, the less uncertainty. **Sampling risk** is the risk that the auditor's conclusion based on a sample might be different from the conclusion that would be reached if the audit procedure were applied in the same way to the entire population.

Sampling Risks Related to Tests of Controls   In many audits, the auditor uses sampling to gather and evaluate evidence regarding the effectiveness of internal controls. The auditor wants an accurate estimate of control failures; for example, if a control does not operate effectively 4% of the time in the sample examined by the auditor, the auditor uses this information to reach a conclusion about the effectiveness of the control in the population. This conclusion will affect the extent of substantive testing to be performed or the opinion to issue on internal controls. Because sampling always involves some uncertainty, the auditor usually wants to control for the worst possible scenario that is, concluding that the control is effective, when it is actually ineffective. For example, the auditor may want to be 95% confident that the control does not fail more than 3% of the time. The auditor is always challenged to manage the risks of making incorrect inferences when using a sample.

 Exhibit 8.2 presents sampling risks relevant to tests of controls. The **risk of incorrect acceptance of internal control reliability** (also referred to as the **risk of assessing control risk too low** or the **risk of overreliance**) is the risk that the auditor will conclude that internal controls are effective (i.e., control risk is low) when internal controls are actually not effective.

 The **risk of incorrect rejection of internal control reliability** (also referred to as the **risk of assessing control risk too high** or the **risk of underreliance**) is the risk that the auditor will conclude that the internal controls are not effective (i.e., control risk is high) when internal controls are actually effective.

 The auditor's main concern when using sampling to test controls is the risk of incorrect acceptance. With incorrect acceptance, control failures in the population are more common than the sample indicates; the sample results lead the auditor to conclude that control risk is low when in fact it is high. Accordingly, the auditor will incorrectly conclude that the internal controls are effective and will not perform as much substantive testing as necessary or will issue an incorrect opinion on internal control effectiveness. Alternatively, if the auditor incorrectly concludes that the controls are ineffective, the auditor will not rely on internal controls and will perform more substantive testing than necessary.

Sampling Risks Related to Tests of Details of Account Balances   Auditors use sampling to estimate the amount of misstatement in an account balance. The auditor can, for example, select a sample of inventory items and perform a price test. If the sample contains pricing errors, the auditor projects these errors in the sample to the population to determine whether the population is materially

Exhibit 8.2
Sampling Risks Relevant to Tests of Controls

Auditor's Assessment of Control Risk Based on Sample Evidence	Actual State of Controls Based on the Entire Population	
	Effective	**Not Effective**
Low	Correct conclusion	*Risk of incorrect acceptance of internal control reliability.* Control failures in the population are higher than the sample indicates (also referred to as the *risk of assessing control risk too low* or the *risk of overreliance*). Leads to audit ineffectiveness.
High	*Risk of incorrect rejection of internal control reliability.* Control failures in the population are lower than the sample indicates (also referred to as the *risk of assessing control risk too high* or the *risk of underreliance*). Leads to audit inefficiency.	Correct conclusion

misstated because inventory is priced incorrectly. *Exhibit 8.3* presents sampling risks relevant to substantive tests of account balances. The **risk of incorrect acceptance of book value** is the risk that the auditor will conclude that the account balance does not contain a material misstatement when the account balance actually does contain a material misstatement. The **risk of incorrect rejection of book value** is the risk that the auditor will conclude that the account balance contains a material misstatement when the account balance actually does not contain a material misstatement.

The auditor's main concern when using sampling to perform substantive tests of details is the risk of incorrect acceptance of book value. With incorrect acceptance, the account balance contains a material misstatement, but the sample results lead the auditor to conclude the account does not contain a material misstatement. No additional audit work would be performed, and the financial statements will be issued with a material misstatement.

Alternatively, if the auditor incorrectly rejects a population that does not contain a material misstatement, the client will usually object and encourage the auditor to perform additional work. The additional audit work should lead to a correction of the inappropriate inference. The risk of incorrect rejection of book value thus affects the efficiency of the audit, but it should not affect the auditor's overall conclusion about the fairness of the financial statements.

Exhibit 8.3
Sampling Risks Relevant to Substantive Tests of Account Balances

Auditor's Conclusion Based on Sample Evidence	Actual Condition of Book Value Based on the Entire Population	
	Does Not Contain a Material Misstatement	**Contains a Material Misstatement**
Book value does not contain a material misstatement	Correct conclusion	*Risk of incorrect acceptance of book value.* Leads to audit ineffectiveness.
Book value likely contains a material misstatement	*Risk of incorrect rejection of book value.* Leads to audit inefficiency.	Correct conclusion

What Do You Think?   For Classroom Discussion

With respect to sampling risk regarding internal controls, which is worse: The risk of incorrect acceptance of internal control reliability or the risk of incorrect rejection of internal control reliability? Why?

With respect to sampling risk relating to tests of details of account balances, which is worse: Risk of incorrect acceptance of book value or the risk of incorrect rejection of book value? Why?

Check Your Basic Knowledge

8-5 Sampling risk is the risk that the auditor's conclusion based on a sample might be different from the conclusion that would be reached if the audit procedure were applied in the same way to the entire population.   (T/F)

8-6 The risk of incorrect acceptance of internal control reliability is the risk that the auditor will conclude that an internal control is not effective when the internal control is effective.   (T/F)

8-7 Which of the following questions would an auditor ask when sampling to perform tests of controls?
   a. Which population and sampling unit should be tested, and what characteristics should be examined?
   b. How many items should be selected for audit testing?
   c. Which items should be included in the sample?

   d. What inferences can be made about the overall population from the sample?
   e. All of the above.

8-8 Refer to *Exhibit 8.2* and determine which of the following terms matches this definition:
   The risk that the auditor will conclude that internal controls are effective when internal controls are actually not effective.
   a. The risk of incorrect acceptance of internal control reliability.
   b. The risk of incorrect acceptance of book value.
   c. The risk of incorrect rejection of internal control reliability.
   d. The risk of incorrect rejection of book value.
   e. None of the above.

LO 3

Compare and contrast nonstatistical and statistical sampling and apply these sampling approaches.

Nonstatistical and Statistical Sampling

Auditors use both nonstatistical and statistical sampling; however, the use of statistical sampling in practice is limited. When properly used, either sampling approach can be effective in providing sufficient appropriate audit evidence. Both sampling approaches require the exercise of auditor judgment during the planning, implementation, and evaluation of the sampling plan. The use of statistical methods does not eliminate the need for professional judgment. Furthermore, the audit procedures performed on the items in the sample will be the same, whether the auditor uses a statistical or nonstatistical approach.

Statistical sampling involves a probability sampling method, which provides an objective method of determining sample size and selected items. Statistical sampling also provides a means of quantitatively assessing sampling risk.

Nonstatistical sampling is the selection of sample items based on the auditor's judgment, rather than on a formal statistical method. If the auditor uses judgment to determine one of more of the following, the sampling approach is nonstatistical:

- Sample size
- Items selected for the sample
- Evaluation of the sample

Nonstatistical sampling does not allow the auditor to statistically measure sampling risk. *Exhibit 8.4* compares nonstatistical and statistical sampling on relevant dimensions.

Exhibit 8.4

Comparison of Nonstatistical and Statistical Sampling

	Nonstatistical Sampling	Statistical Sampling
Sample size	Sample size is determined by auditor professional judgment. Sample size should be similar to that obtained using statistical sampling.	Sample size is determined by probability sampling theory. The auditor uses tables or formulas to determine sample size.
Sample selection	Selection involves any method that the auditor believes will result in a sample representative of the population.	The sample must be randomly selected to give each unit in the population an equal chance to be included in the sample; there are several approaches to random selection including simple random sampling and systematic random sampling.
	Judgment sampling can also be directed at a portion of the population, for example, all transactions during the last five days of the year.	The population of interest can also be directed; for example, the transactions during the last 10 days of the year can be statistically selected.
Evaluation	Does not provide a quantitative measure of sampling risk when evaluating the sample results	Sampling risk can be quantified when evaluating the sample results.
Costs	Selection costs are lower because audit judgment is required only to determine an appropriate sample size and evaluate the results.	Training costs are higher because knowledge of statistical sampling methods and/or special computer sampling software is required.
	This type of sampling does not provide an objective way to measure sampling risk.	This type of sampling requires the auditor to define acceptable risk in advance.
Benefits	This method can be based on the auditor's prior expectations about errors in the account..	This method helps the auditor to design an efficient sample, measure the sufficiency of the evidence, and evaluate the results by providing an objective measure of sampling risk.
	This method may take less time to plan, select, and evaluate the sample.	This method helps the auditor to gain efficiencies through computerized selection and statistical evaluation and to defend sample inferences because they are based on statistical theory.
		This method helps the auditor to evaluate the sample by providing a quantitative measure of the most likely and the maximum failure rate of a control procedure that is being evaluated for three things: 1) effectiveness, 2) the most likely and maximum amount of misstatement in the recorded account balance or class of transactions, and 3) the risk that the auditor may judge incorrectly the state of controls or correctness of account balances.

For both sampling approaches, the auditor considers the nature of control deficiencies or misstatements detected in the sample, projects the sample findings to the population, and concludes on the overall population. In addition to evaluating the results of a sample quantitatively, the auditor should consider the qualitative aspects of control failures and misstatements. Are the sample results caused by errors, or do they indicate the possibility of fraud, and how do the control deficiencies affect other phases of the audit?

What Do You Think? For Classroom Discussion

Imagine that you conducted an audit, and now have been accused by the client of negligence because you failed to detect an ongoing and highly material fraud in the acquisition and payment cycle involving the theft of inventory.

You used nonstatistical sampling in conducting the audit of inventory. Auditors commonly employ nonstatistical sampling, yet statistical sampling is more "defensible" in court. In fact, combining statistical sampling with audit judgment generally produces a higher quality audit conclusion than using audit judgment alone. In addition, statistical sampling may help to avoid second guessing by regulators or jurors, should those parties question the quality of the sampling method used.

Why do you think auditors use nonstatistical sampling when statistical sampling may be more defensible?

Check Your Basic Knowledge

8-9 A benefit of nonstatistical sampling as compared to statistical sampling is that the sample size can be significantly smaller, thereby making the audit more efficient. (T/F)

8-10 A benefit of statistical sampling as compared to nonstatistical sampling is that less auditor judgment is required because the auditor can leverage the power of probability theory. (T/F)

8-11 Refer to *Exhibit 8.4* and determine which of the following statements is <u>true</u>.
   a. In nonstatistical sampling, sample size is determined by auditor judgment.
   b. In statistical sampling, the sample must be randomly selected to give each unit in the population an equal chance to be included in the sample.
   c. In nonstatistical sampling, evaluation is based on auditor judgment and projections are based on sample results.
   d. In statistical sampling, the auditor is required to define acceptable risk in advance.
   e. All of the above are true.

8-12 Which of the following statements is <u>false</u>?
   a. When properly used, either nonstatistical or statistical sampling can be effective in providing sufficient appropriate audit evidence.
   b. Statistical sampling allows the auditor to measure the risk of making an incorrect inference about the population from which the sample is taken, whereas nonstatistical sampling does not allow for such measurement.
   c. Nonstatistical sampling may help avoid second guessing by regulators or jurors should those parties question the quality of the sampling method used.
   d. Combining statistical sampling with audit judgment generally produces a higher quality audit conclusion than using audit judgment alone.
   e. All of the above are false.

LO 4

Describe attributes sampling and use it to test controls.

Attributes Sampling for Tests of Controls

The auditor tests the operating effectiveness of important controls over financial reporting. The auditor will only perform such tests if the auditor has determined that the design and implementation of the controls are effective in minimizing the likelihood of material misstatements in the account balances. Control testing provides the auditor with evidence necessary to issue an opinion on internal control effectiveness and to assess the client's control risk. The assessment of control effectiveness may be based on:

- A sample to test the effectiveness of controls in operation
- The auditor's observation of the controls within significant business processes
- Tests of controls built into the client's computer system
- Inquiry of relevant employees
- Review of monitoring reports

Sampling techniques are not used for all tests of controls. For example, when effective general computer controls are present, tests of automated application controls are generally performed with just one or a few items. Sampling generally is not applicable for determining the appropriate segregation of duties and may not apply to tests of operating effectiveness of the control environment.

When sampling is appropriate, the auditor uses a sample to infer whether the control in the population is operating effectively. The most commonly used statistical sampling approach for tests of controls is attributes sampling. **Attributes sampling** is a statistical sampling method used to estimate the rate of control procedure failures based on selecting a sample and performing the appropriate audit procedure.

An **attribute** is a characteristic of the population of interest to the auditor. Typically, the attribute the auditor wishes to examine is the effective operation of a control, for example, evidence that the client has matched vendor invoice details with the purchase order and receiving report before payment approval, and noting that they match before authorizing a payment for the goods received.

Steps in Attributes Sampling

Attributes sampling is used to test the operating effectiveness of controls. It is used to gather evidence to answer questions such as "Was credit properly approved?" or "Was the customer's order shipped before it was billed?" or "Were the expenses

It's Your Turn!   *Prompt for Critical Thinking #1*

Provide examples of control attributes that an auditor might test.

- _____
- _____
- _____
- _____

claimed by the CEO consistent with company policies?" The steps to implement an attributes sampling plan include:

1. Define the attributes of interest and what constitutes failure(s).
2. Define the population from which the auditor takes the sample.
3. Determine the sample size.
4. Determine the method of selecting the sample.
5. Select the sample items and perform the test of control.
6. Evaluate the sample results and consider the effect on planned substantive procedures and the opinion on internal control effectiveness.
7. Document all phases of the sampling process.

Step 1. Define the Attributes of Interest and What Constitutes Failure(s)

A number of attributes could be tested, but the auditor tests only important controls. Control failures should be precisely defined to make sure that the auditor clearly understands what to look for, thereby reducing nonsampling risk. For example, a failure to seek credit approval for a new account, when such approval is required by company policy, would be considered a control failure.

A control failure does not mean that a misstatement has occurred. For example, most companies require a credit approval process before issuing credit. When pressed for time, a marketing manager may approve a sale without obtaining proper credit approval. The control requiring credit approval has failed, but it is not known whether the: (a) credit would have been granted if the process had been completed, or (b) customer is less likely to pay. Finally, the failure of this control does not affect the proper recording of the initial transaction. It may, however, affect the valuation of receivables at year-end.

Step 2. Define the Population from Which the Auditor Takes the Sample

In defining the population, the auditor considers:

- The period to be covered by the test; for example, the audit year, or an interim period
- The sampling unit; for example, monthly bank reconciliations
- The completeness of the population; data analytical tools are useful for this purpose

Period Covered by the Test   In most instances, the period covered by the test is the time period covered by the audited financial statements. As a practical matter, tests of controls are often performed prior to the balance sheet date and may cover the first 10 or 11 months of the year. If the controls are found to be effective, the auditor should take additional steps to assure that the controls continue to be effective during the remainder of the year. The additional steps may include making inquiries, further testing of the controls, or gathering evidence of control effectiveness as part of dual purpose tests performed later in the audit. If the auditor is issuing an opinion on internal controls over financial reporting, the auditor needs reasonable assurance that the controls are effective as of the client's balance sheet date.

Sampling Unit   The sampling unit is the item identified in the population as the basis for testing. It could be a document, an entry in the computer system, or a line item on a document. One company may require supervisory approval with initials to authorize payment of several invoices; the sampling unit would be the document authorizing the invoices. Another company may require written authorization for each invoice; the sampling unit would be the individual invoices processed for payment.

Completeness of Population The auditor should take steps to help assure that the population sampled is the total population of interest. The auditor normally performs some procedures, such as footing the file and reconciling the balance to the general ledger or reviewing the completeness of prenumbered documents, to assure that the population is complete.

Step 3. Determine the Sample Size

An optimal sample size minimizes sampling risk and promotes audit efficiency. The following audit judgments affect sample size: (1) sampling risk, (2) the tolerable rate of deviation, and (3) the expected population deviation rate.

- *Sampling risk*—Sampling risk is often set at 5% or 10%, as shown in *Exhibit 8.5*. This risk is sometimes referred to as the allowable risk of overreliance.

Exhibit 8.5
Attributes Sample Size Tables

Table 1 Statistical Sample Sizes for Tests of Controls—5 Percent Risk of Overreliance (with number of expected errors in parentheses)

Expected Deviation Rate	Tolerable Deviation Rate										
	2%	3%	4%	5%	6%	7%	8%	9%	10%	15%	20%
0.00%	149 (0)	99 (0)	74 (0)	59 (0)	49 (0)	42 (0)	36 (0)	32 (0)	29 (0)	19 (0)	14 (0)
0.25%	236 (1)	157 (1)	117 (1)	93 (1)	78 (1)	66 (1)	58 (1)	51 (1)	46 (1)	30 (1)	22 (1)
0.50%	313 (2)	157 (1)	117 (1)	93 (1)	78 (1)	66 (1)	58 (1)	51 (1)	46 (1)	30 (1)	22 (1)
0.75%	386 (3)	208 (2)	117 (1)	93 (1)	78 (1)	66 (1)	58 (1)	51 (1)	46 (1)	30 (1)	22 (1)
1.00%	590 (6)	257 (3)	156 (2)	93 (1)	78 (1)	66 (1)	58 (1)	51 (1)	46 (1)	30 (1)	22 (1)
1.25%	1,030 (13)	303 (4)	156 (2)	124 (2)	78 (1)	66 (1)	58 (1)	51 (1)	46 (1)	30 (1)	22 (1)
1.50%		392 (6)	192 (3)	124 (2)	103 (2)	66 (1)	58 (1)	51 (1)	46 (1)	30 (1)	22 (1)
1.75%		562 (10)	227 (4)	153 (3)	103 (2)	88 (2)	77 (2)	51 (1)	46 (1)	30 (1)	22 (1)
2.00%		846 (17)	294 (6)	181 (4)	127 (3)	88 (2)	77 (2)	68 (2)	46 (1)	30 (1)	22 (1)
2.25%		1,466 (33)	390 (9)	208 (5)	127 (3)	88 (2)	77 (2)	68 (2)	61 (2)	30 (1)	22 (1)
2.50%			513 (13)	234 (6)	150 (4)	109 (3)	77 (2)	68 (2)	61 (2)	30 (1)	22 (1)
2.75%			722 (20)	286 (8)	173 (5)	109 (3)	95 (3)	68 (2)	61 (2)	30 (1)	22 (1)
3.00%			1,098 (33)	361 (11)	195 (6)	129 (4)	95 (3)	84 (3)	61 (2)	30 (1)	22 (1)
3.25%			1,936 (63)	458 (15)	238 (8)	148 (5)	112 (4)	84 (3)	61 (2)	30 (1)	22 (1)
3.50%				624 (22)	280 (10)	167 (6)	112 (4)	84 (3)	76 (3)	40 (2)	22 (1)
3.75%				877 (33)	341 (13)	185 (7)	129 (5)	100 (4)	76 (3)	40 (2)	22 (1)
4.00%				1,348 (54)	421 (17)	221 (9)	146 (6)	100 (4)	89 (4)	40 (2)	22 (1)
5.00%					1,580 (79)	478 (24)	240 (12)	158 (8)	116 (6)	40 (2)	30 (2)
6.00%						1,832 (110)	532 (32)	266 (16)	179 (11)	50 (3)	30 (2)
7.00%							585 (41)	298 (21)	68 (5)	37 (3)	
8.00%								649 (52)	85 (7)	37 (3)	
9.00%									110 (10)	44 (4)	
10.00%									150 (15)	50 (5)	
12.50%									576 (72)	88 (11)	
15.00%										193 (29)	
17.50%										720 (126)	

(Continues)

Exhibit 8.5 *Continued*

Table 2 Statistical Sample Sizes for Tests of Controls—10 Percent Risk of Overreliance (with number of expected errors in parentheses)

Expected Deviation Rate	Tolerable Deviation Rate										
	2%	3%	4%	5%	6%	7%	8%	9%	10%	15%	20%
0.00%	114 (0)	76 (0)	57 (0)	45 (0)	38 (0)	32 (0)	28 (0)	25 (0)	22 (0)	15 (0)	11 (0)
0.25%	194 (1)	129 (1)	96 (1)	77 (1)	64 (1)	55 (1)	48 (1)	42 (1)	38 (1)	25 (1)	18 (1)
0.50%	194 (1)	129 (1)	96 (1)	77 (1)	64 (1)	55 (1)	48 (1)	42 (1)	38 (1)	25 (1)	18 (1)
0.75%	265 (2)	129 (1)	96 (1)	77 (1)	64 (1)	55 (1)	48 (1)	42 (1)	38 (1)	25 (1)	18 (1)
1.00%	398 (4)	176 (2)	96 (1)	77 (1)	64 (1)	55 (1)	48 (1)	42 (1)	38 (1)	25 (1)	18 (1)
1.25%	708 (9)	221 (3)	132 (2)	77 (1)	64 (1)	55 (1)	48 (1)	42 (1)	38 (1)	25 (1)	18 (1)
1.50%	1,463 (22)	265 (4)	132 (2)	105 (2)	64 (1)	55 (1)	48 (1)	42 (1)	38 (1)	25 (1)	18 (1)
1.75%		390 (7)	166 (3)	105 (2)	88 (2)	55 (1)	48 (1)	42 (1)	38 (1)	25 (1)	18 (1)
2.00%		590 (12)	198 (4)	132 (3)	88 (2)	75 (2)	48 (1)	42 (1)	38 (1)	25 (1)	18 (1)
2.25%		974 (22)	262 (6)	132 (3)	88 (2)	75 (2)	65 (2)	42 (1)	38 (1)	25 (1)	18 (1)
2.50%			353 (9)	158 (4)	110 (3)	75 (2)	65 (2)	58 (2)	38 (1)	25 (1)	18 (1)
2.75%			471 (13)	209 (6)	132 (4)	94 (3)	65 (2)	58 (2)	52 (2)	25 (1)	18 (1)
3.00%			730 (22)	258 (8)	132 (4)	94 (3)	65 (2)	58 (2)	52 (2)	25 (1)	18 (1)
3.25%			1,258 (41)	306 (10)	153 (5)	113 (4)	82 (3)	58 (2)	52 (2)	25 (1)	18 (1)
3.50%				400 (14)	194 (7)	113 (4)	82 (3)	73 (3)	52 (2)	25 (1)	18 (1)
3.75%				583 (22)	235 (9)	131 (5)	98 (4)	73 (3)	52 (2)	25 (1)	18 (1)
4.00%				873 (35)	274 (11)	149 (6)	98 (4)	73 (3)	65 (3)	25 (1)	18 (1)
5.00%					1,019 (51)	318 (16)	160 (8)	115 (6)	78 (4)	34 (2)	18 (1)
6.00%						1,150 (69)	349 (21)	182 (11)	116 (7)	43 (3)	25 (2)
7.00%							1,300 (91)	385 (27)	199 (14)	52 (4)	25 (2)
8.00%								1,437 (115)	424 (34)	60 (5)	25 (2)
9.00%									1,577 (142)	77 (7)	32 (3)
10.00%										100 (10)	38 (4)
12.50%										368 (46)	63 (8)
15.00%											126 (19)
17.50%											457 (80)

Note: Sample sizes over 2,000 items not shown. These tables assume a large population.

Source: *Audit Sampling* (New York: AICPA, 2012), 145–146. AICPA audit and accounting guides by American Institute of Certified Public Accountants. Copyright © 2012 Reproduced with permission of American Institute of Certified Public Accountants in the format Textbook via Copyright Clearance Center.

- *Tolerable rate of deviation*—The AICPA's 2012 *Audit Sampling* formally defines the **tolerable rate of deviation** as a rate of deviation set by the auditor in respect of which the auditor seeks to obtain an appropriate level of assurance that the rate of deviation set by the auditor is not exceeded by the actual rate of deviation in the population. This term is sometimes referred to as the **tolerable failure rate**. In more practical terms, the auditor's tolerable rate of deviation is the level at which the control's failure to operate would cause the auditor to conclude that the control is not effective and would likely change the auditor's planned assessment of control risk in performing tests of account balances.

- *Expected population deviation rate*—The **expected population deviation rate** is an anticipation of the deviation rate in the entire population. This term is sometimes referred to as the **expected failure rate**. Failures occur when personnel are in a hurry or careless, are not competent, or are not properly trained. The auditor likely has evidence on the rate at which a particular control fails, based on past experience as modified by any changes in the system or personnel. The expected failure rate should be less than the tolerable failure rate; otherwise the auditor should not test controls.

In general, the number of items in the population has relatively little effect on the sample size, unless the population is very small. The tables in *Exhibit 8.5* assume large populations and give sample sizes for several combinations of these factors and for both 5% and 10% levels of sampling risk. Using these tables for small populations is a conservative approach because the sample size will be overstated.

The determination of sample size using the tables is straightforward. The auditor:

1. Selects the allowable sampling risk (risk of overreliance of 5% or 10%) based on factors such as audit risk, and whether the auditor will be issuing a separate opinion on internal control (Note: we use the term *risk of overreliance* because that is the term used in the AICPA's sample size tables. Recall that the terms *risk of incorrect acceptance of internal control reliability or risk of assessing control risk too low* are also used to refer to the same concept.)
2. Determines the tolerable rate of deviation. The tolerable rate of deviation would be lower for more important controls, such as controls over more significant accounts and for controls over accounts that are more susceptible to misstatement.
3. Uses past knowledge to determine the expected population deviation rate.
4. Determines sample size by looking at the intersection of the expected population deviation rate and the tolerable rate of deviation in the appropriate table.

Example 1: (More Important Control, Integrated Audit): The auditor sets the risk of overreliance at 5% (implying that the auditor is willing to accept a 5% chance that inferences from the sample will be incorrect), sets the tolerable rate of deviation at 5%, and anticipates that the expected population deviation rate will be 1%. The auditor refers to *Table 1* in *Exhibit 8.5* and finds a sample size of 93.

It's Your Turn!

Prompt for Critical Thinking #2

Respond to these scenarios, which provide you with the opportunity to use *Exhibit 8.5*.

Scenario 1. If you were auditing a riskier audit, e.g., a publicly traded company, which panel of *Exhibit 8.5* would you be more likely to use, i.e., what risk of overreliance are you willing to take?

Scenario 2. The auditor sets the risk of overreliance at 5% (implying that the auditor is willing to accept a 5% chance that inferences from the sample will be incorrect), sets the tolerable rate of deviation at 5%, and anticipates that the expected population deviation rate will be 1%. What is the sample size?

Scenario 3. The auditor sets the risk of overreliance at 10%, sets the tolerable rate of deviation at 10%, and anticipates that the expected population deviation rate is 1%. What is the sample size?

Scenario 4. Would you be more confident in your conclusions about the efficacy of controls in Scenario 2 or 3?

Example 2: (Less Important Control, No Separate Opinion on Internal Control): The auditor sets the risk of overreliance at 10% (implying that the auditor is willing to accept more risk than in Example 1), sets the tolerable rate of deviation at 10% (suggesting that the control is less important than in Example 1), and anticipates that the expected population deviation rate is 1%. The auditor uses *Table 2* in *Exhibit 8.5* and finds a sample size of 38. Also note that the number in parentheses after each sample size represents the number of errors the auditor can find without concluding that the control is not working correctly (1 in a sample of 93 for the more important control, and 1 in a sample of 38 for the less important control).

Check Your Basic Knowledge

8-13 Attributes sampling is a statistical sampling method used to estimate the rate of control procedure failures based on selecting a sample and performing the appropriate audit procedure. (T/F)

8-14 In attributes sampling, the attribute of interest is an individual dollar amount in the population. (T/F)

8-15 Use *Exhibit 8.5* to determine which of the following statements is <u>false</u>.
   a. As the tolerable deviation rate rises, the sample size decreases.
   b. As the expected deviation rises, the sample size decreases.
   c. If the auditor accepts a 5% risk of overreliance, a 7% tolerable deviation rate, and expects a deviation rate of 2.5%, the sample size will equal 109.
   d. If the auditor accepts a 10% risk of overreliance, a 7% tolerable deviation rate, and expects a deviation rate of 2.5%, the sample size will be a number less than 109.
   e. All of the above are false.

8-16 In attributes sampling, which of the following will <u>not</u> affect the sample size?
   a. The risk of incorrect rejection of book value.
   b. Sampling risk.
   c. The tolerable rate of deviation.
   d. The expected population deviation rate.

Why It Matters   Understanding the Assumptions for Obtaining a Sample Size

This feature provides examples to help you understand the assumptions that must be made to justify a certain sample size, e.g., 30 items. A sample size of 30 requires the auditor to tolerate a fairly high rate of deviation in the sample, a choice that ultimately yields greater audit risk for the audit firm.

Example 1: Consider an example from *Table 1* of *Exhibit 8.5*, for risk of overreliance of 5%. The auditor can only get to a sample size of 29 by assuming a tolerable rate of deviation of 10% and an expected population deviation rate of 0. The auditor could get

to a sample size of 30 using a tolerable rate of deviation of 15% and allowing the expected population deviation rate to increase. However, it is difficult to justify a tolerable deviation rate of 15% for an important control.

Example 2: Consider an example from *Table 2* of *Exhibit 8.5*, for risk of overreliance of 10%. The auditor can get to a sample size of 28 by assuming a tolerable deviation rate of 8% and an expected population deviation rate of 0. Other combinations work similarly by moving the tolerable rate of deviation up to 15% and allowing the expected population deviation rate to go as high as 4%.

Testing Multiple Attributes   Auditors frequently test several controls or attributes using the same source documents. When doing so, the auditor should use the same sampling risk for all the tests. However, the tolerable rates of deviation and expected population deviation rates for these attributes are likely to be different, resulting in different sample sizes.

For example, the auditor may want to test whether sales transactions are classified correctly, whether they have been recorded accurately, and whether there was proper review and approval for credit using tolerable deviation rates of 5%, 3%, and 3%, respectively, and expected population deviation rates of 2%, 1%, and 0%, respectively. If the auditor sets the risk of overreliance at 10%, the sample sizes range from a high of 176 for Attribute 2 to a low of 76 for Attribute 3:

Attribute	Tolerable Rate	Expected Rate	Sample Size
1. Evidence of independent review of account distribution	5%	2%	132
2. Evidence of comparison of description, quantity, and price between the customer's order and sales invoice	3%	1%	176
3. Evidence of proper review and approval for credit	3%	0%	76

There are three reasonable approaches to selecting the items for these tests:

- The auditor could select 176 sales transactions (the largest sample size) and audit all of them for Attribute 2, three of four for Attribute 1, and every other one for Attribute 3. This process, however, is quite cumbersome.
- The auditor could examine the first 76 randomly selected documents for all three attributes and documents, sample items 77–132 for Attributes 1 and 2, and the remainder only for Attribute 2. This process is also quite cumbersome.
- Often the most efficient approach is to test the 176 items for all three attributes. Attributes 1 and 3 will be in some sense over audited, but the over auditing may take less time than keeping track of which sample items should be tested for which attribute. Testing for Attributes 1 and 3 does not take very long once the auditor has selected the documents in the sample. The auditor's evaluation of the control is based on the 176 items examined and improves the accuracy of the control risk assessment.

Step 4. Determine the Method of Selecting the Sample

Once the sample size has been determined, the auditor selects sample items so the sample will be representative of the population and thus the results can be projected to the population. Common sampling approaches included simple random sampling, systematic sampling, haphazard sampling, or block sampling.

Simple Random Sampling   A **simple random sample** is chosen in such a way that every item in the population has an equal chance of being selected for the sample. It is appropriate for both nonstatistical and statistical sampling applications. An auditor using this approach will use a random number generator such as the one included in Excel. The random number generator uses information on population size and sample size to generate random numbers. Assume that the population is 500 invoices (numbered 1 to 500) and the sample size is 50. The application will generate 50 random numbers between 1 and 500. The random numbers represent the document numbers on the invoices that you will select for your sample.

Systematic Sampling **Systematic sampling** is a statistical sampling method that involves dividing the number of physical units in the population by the sample size to determine a uniform interval; a random starting point is selected in the first interval, and one item is selected throughout the population at each of the uniform intervals after the starting point. This interval, called the **sampling interval**, is calculated by dividing the population size by the desired sample size. In order to use systematic selection, the auditor must be sure that there is not a systematic pattern in the population.

For example, assume that the population consists of payroll transactions in a payroll journal that are listed in employee number order. These numbers are not in sequence because of employee turnover. There are 1,300 payroll transactions, and the auditor has determined a sample size of 26. Every 50th transaction $(1,300 / 26 = 50)$ should be selected for testing. To randomize the selection process, a random number from 1 to 50 should be used to identify the first sample item. This could be done, for example, by using the last two digits of a serial number on a dollar bill. If those digits were 87, subtract 50, leaving 37 as the first sample item. Every 50th transaction thereafter would also be included in the sample. When the first item is selected randomly from the interval, this sampling technique is called **systematic random sampling**.

The validity of a systematic sampling is based on the assumption that the items in the population are randomly distributed. The auditor must be knowledgeable about the nature of the population to be sure that no repeating or coinciding pattern in the population would cause the sample to not be representative. Many auditors try to increase the chances that the systematically selected samples are representative of the population by using multiple random starts.

Haphazard Sampling **Haphazard sampling** is a nonstatistical sample selection method that attempts to approximate a random selection. The word *haphazard* is not intended to convey that that the sampled items are selected in a careless manner. Rather, the auditor chooses the sample items, trying to select items that are representative of the population. However, it does not usually work, because of **selection bias**: knowingly or unknowingly creating unrepresentative samples. In order to create a true random selection, it is more appropriate to use random selection method, such as simple random sampling.

Block Sampling **Block sampling** is a nonstatistical sampling selection method that involves selecting a sample that consists of contiguous population items, such as selecting transactions by day or week. This is an efficient approach, but the risk is that the way the transactions were processed on these days or weeks may not be representative of how they were processed the other 364 days or 51 weeks. This judgmental decision is subject to second guessing that such a sample could not be representative. Block sampling is most appropriate for performing year-end cutoff tests.

Step 5. Select the Sample Items and Perform the Test of Control

When selecting the sample, the auditor decides how to handle inapplicable, voided, or unused documents. An example of an inapplicable document would be a telephone bill when testing for an error defined as "cash disbursement transactions not supported by a receiving report." If the inapplicable document does not represent the control being tested, it should be replaced by another randomly selected item.

When selected items cannot be located, and the auditor is not able to perform appropriate alternative procedures for those items, the auditor should consider the reasons for this limitation, and should ordinarily consider those selected items to be control deviations for the purpose of evaluating the sample.

Step 6. Evaluate the Sample Results and Consider the Effect on Planned Substantive Procedures and the Opinion on Internal Control Effectiveness

Evaluation of sample results requires the auditor to project the sample results to the population before drawing a conclusion about the population.

Quantitative Evaluation The auditor needs to determine whether the upper limit of the possible deviation rate exceeds the tolerable deviation rate. To make this assessment, the auditor should use a statistical evaluation approach. Tables such as those in *Exhibit 8.6* help the auditor determine the upper limit of the possible deviation rate. If the upper limit of the possible deviation rate exceeds the tolerable deviation rate, the auditor should: (1) test a different control designed to mitigate the same risk, or (2) adjust the nature, timing, and/or extent of the related substantive testing of the accounts affected by the control. The change in substantive testing will be necessary because the auditor will need to increase the assessed level of control risk and, thus, decrease the level of detection risk.

Exhibit 8.6

Attributes Sampling Evaluation Tables

Table 1: Statistical Sampling Results Evaluation Table for Tests of Controls—Upper Limits at 5 Percent Risk of Overreliance

Sample Size	Actual Number of Deviations Found										
	0	**1**	**2**	**3**	**4**	**5**	**6**	**7**	**8**	**9**	**10**
20	14.0	21.7	28.3	34.4	40.2	45.6	50.8	55.9	60.7	65.4	69.9
25	11.3	17.7	23.2	28.2	33.0	37.6	42.0	46.3	50.4	54.4	58.4
30	9.6	14.9	19.6	23.9	28.0	31.9	35.8	39.4	43.0	46.6	50.0
35	8.3	12.9	17.0	20.7	24.3	27.8	31.1	34.4	37.5	40.6	43.7
40	7.3	11.4	15.0	18.3	21.5	24.6	27.5	30.4	33.3	36.0	38.8
45	6.5	10.2	13.4	16.4	19.2	22.0	24.7	27.3	29.8	32.4	34.8
50	5.9	9.2	12.1	14.8	17.4	19.9	22.4	24.7	27.1	29.4	31.6
55	5.4	8.4	11.1	13.5	15.9	18.2	20.5	22.6	24.8	26.9	28.9
60	4.9	7.7	10.2	12.5	14.7	16.8	18.8	20.8	22.8	24.8	26.7
65	4.6	7.1	9.4	11.5	13.6	15.5	17.5	19.3	21.2	23.0	24.7
70	4.2	6.6	8.8	10.8	12.7	14.5	16.3	18.0	19.7	21.4	23.1
75	4.0	6.2	8.2	10.1	11.8	13.6	15.2	16.9	18.5	20.1	21.6
80	3.7	5.8	7.7	9.5	11.1	12.7	14.3	15.9	17.4	18.9	20.3
90	3.3	5.2	6.9	8.4	9.9	11.4	12.8	14.2	15.5	16.9	18.2
100	3.0	4.7	6.2	7.6	9.0	10.3	11.5	12.8	14.0	15.2	16.4
125	2.4	3.8	5.0	6.1	7.2	8.3	9.3	10.3	11.3	12.3	13.2
150	2.0	3.2	4.2	5.1	6.0	6.9	7.8	8.6	9.5	10.3	11.1
200	1.5	2.4	3.2	3.9	4.6	5.2	5.9	6.5	7.2	7.8	8.4
300	1.0	1.6	2.1	2.6	3.1	3.5	4.0	4.4	4.8	5.2	5.6
400	0.8	1.2	1.6	2.0	2.3	2.7	3.0	3.3	3.6	3.9	4.3
500	0.6	1.0	1.3	1.6	1.9	2.1	2.4	2.7	2.9	3.2	3.4

(Continues)

Exhibit 8.6 *Continued*

Table 2 Statistical Sampling Results Evaluation Table for Tests of Controls—Upper Limits at 10 Percent Risk of Overreliance

Sample Size	Actual Number of Deviations Found										
	0	1	2	3	4	5	6	7	8	9	10
20	10.9	18.1	24.5	30.5	36.1	41.5	46.8	51.9	56.8	61.6	66.2
25	8.8	14.7	20.0	24.9	29.5	34.0	38.4	42.6	46.8	50.8	54.8
30	7.4	12.4	16.8	21.0	24.9	28.8	32.5	36.2	39.7	43.2	46.7
35	6.4	10.7	14.5	18.2	21.6	24.9	28.2	31.4	34.5	37.6	40.6
40	5.6	9.4	12.8	16.0	19.0	22.0	24.9	27.7	30.5	33.2	35.9
45	5.0	8.4	11.4	14.3	17.0	19.7	22.3	24.8	27.3	29.8	32.2
50	4.6	7.6	10.3	12.9	15.4	17.8	20.2	22.5	24.7	27.0	29.2
55	4.2	6.9	9.4	11.8	14.1	16.3	18.4	20.5	22.6	24.6	26.7
60	3.8	6.4	8.7	10.8	12.9	15.0	16.9	18.9	20.8	22.7	24.6
65	3.5	5.9	8.0	10.0	12.0	13.9	15.7	17.5	19.3	21.0	22.8
70	3.3	5.5	7.5	9.3	11.1	12.9	14.6	16.3	18.0	19.6	21.2
75	3.1	5.1	7.0	8.7	10.4	12.1	13.7	15.2	16.8	18.3	19.8
80	2.9	4.8	6.6	8.2	9.8	11.3	12.8	14.3	15.8	17.2	18.7
90	2.6	4.3	5.9	7.3	8.7	10.1	11.5	12.8	14.1	15.4	16.7
100	2.3	3.9	5.3	6.6	7.9	9.1	10.3	11.5	12.7	13.9	15.0
125	1.9	3.1	4.3	5.3	6.3	7.3	8.3	9.3	10.2	11.2	12.1
150	1.6	2.6	3.6	4.4	5.3	6.1	7.0	7.8	8.6	9.4	10.1
200	1.2	2.0	2.7	3.4	4.0	4.6	5.3	5.9	6.5	7.1	7.6
300	0.8	1.3	1.8	2.3	2.7	3.1	3.5	3.9	4.3	4.7	5.1
400	0.6	1.0	1.4	1.7	2.0	2.4	2.7	3.0	3.3	3.6	3.9
500	0.5	0.8	1.1	1.4	1.6	1.9	2.1	2.4	2.6	2.9	3.1

Note: These tables present upper limits (body of table) as percentages. These tables assume a large population.

Source: *Audit Sampling* (New York: AICPA, 2012), 148–149. AICPA audit and accounting guides by American Institute of Certified Public Accountants. Copyright © 2012 Reproduced with permission of American Institute of Certified Public Accountants in the format Textbook via Copyright Clearance Center.

If the auditor is performing an integrated audit, the auditor will need to consider whether the results will affect the opinion on internal control effectiveness.

In determining what changes to make in substantive audit procedures, the auditor should consider the nature of control deviation (pattern of errors) and determine the effect of such deviations on potential material misstatements in the financial statements. When the upper limit of the possible deviation rate exceeds the tolerable deviation rate, the auditor has to decide whether the control failure, in conjunction with other control failures, leads to a conclusion that there are either significant deficiencies or material weaknesses regarding internal control over financial reporting.

Sample Evaluation—An Illustration   To illustrate the use of the tables in *Exhibit 8.6*, assume that the auditor tested the controls designed to make sure that sales were not billed until shipped, using a 5% risk of overreliance, a tolerable population deviation rate of 6%, and an expected population deviation rate of 1%. Recall what these judgments mean:

- A 5% risk of overreliance means the auditor wants to limit the risk to 5% that the actual deviation rate in the population will not exceed the tolerable population deviation rate of 6%. This is equivalent to using a 95% confidence level.

8-17 Block sampling involves selecting a sample that consists of contiguous population items, such as selecting transactions by day or week. (T/F)

8-18 Haphazard sampling is a statistical sample selection method that attempts to approximate a random selection by selecting sampling units without any conscious bias, or special reason for including or omitting certain items from the sample. (T/F)

8-19 Refer to *Exhibit 8.6*. Assume a 5% risk of overreliance, a tolerable deviation rate of 8%, a sample size of 100, and that the number of deviations is five. What is the upper limit of the possible deviation rate, and what does it mean?

   a. 10.3%. The auditor is 95% confident that the real error rate in the population is no greater than 10.3%.

   b. 10.3%. The auditor is 95% confident that the real error rate in the population is no greater than 5%.

   c. 5%. The auditor is 92% confident that the real error rate in the population is no greater than 10.3%.

   d. 5%. The auditor is 92% confident that the real error rate in the population is no greater than 5%.

8-20 Consider the case whereby the risk of overreliance is 5%, the sample size is 20, and the auditor detects no deviations in the operation of the control. What can the auditor conclude?

   a. This is good news; no deviations were found, so we conclude that the control is working effectively.

   b. The upper limit of deviations is 14%, so we conclude that the control is not working effectively.

   c. If we doubled the sample size, the upper limit of deviations would decrease by about half.

   d. One of the above a-c.

   e. Two of the above a-c.

- The tolerable deviation rate is 6%; if there is more than a 5% chance that the actual deviation rate is greater than 6%, the auditor must conclude that the control is not operating at an acceptable level.
- The auditor did not expect many errors; the auditor expects the control to not be operating effectively only about 1% of the time; this expectation is based on good past experience with the control and the client's careful monitoring practices.
- If the upper limit of the possible deviation rate in the appropriate table exceeds the tolerable deviation rate set by the auditor, then the auditor's tests of controls do not support the original control assessment, and control risk must be increased. The remainder of the audit needs to be adjusted accordingly.

Assume that the auditor selects a sample of 80 from a population of 100,000 sales transactions and detects three control deviations (a deviation rate of 3.75%, calculated as 3/80). The auditor might conclude that 3.75% is less than 6%, and so the control is working effectively. But this conclusion is incorrect. Remember, the auditor's decision is whether there is more than a 5% risk (95% confidence level) that the control deviation rate could be more than 6% in the population—not just in the sample. To make the correct evaluation, the auditor uses *Table 1* of *Exhibit 8.6*, moves down the first column to find 80 as the sample size, and moves to the right under the column of three failures, and finds a figure of 9.5. What does that 9.5 mean? It means that the auditor is 95% confident that the upper limit of the real deviation rate in the population does not exceed 9.5%. Stated another way, there is a 5% chance that the real deviation rate exceeds 9.5%. The auditor had set an upper limit of 6%, and this 9.5% clearly exceeds that limit. The control testing does not support a conclusion that the control is operating effectively. The auditor needs to assess control risk as higher than was originally set and, further, must perform a qualitative evaluation of the deviations detected.

One point to notice when examining *Exhibit 8.6* is that the upper limit of deviations is greater than zero even when no deviations are detected in the sample. For example, consider the case where risk of overreliance is 5%, sample size is 20, and no deviations are detected. In this case, the upper limit of deviations from *Exhibit 8.6* is 14%. The reason for this result is that the sample size is very low, so there is a strong possibility that even though the auditor detected no deviations in the sample of 20 items, deviations exist that the auditor failed to detect. Taking this case a bit further, assume the same facts, but move down *Exhibit 8.6* to the row where sample size is doubled to 40. In this case, notice that the upper limit of deviations when no deviations are detected falls dramatically to just 7.3%.

Qualitative Evaluation   When the auditor finds control deviations, the auditor should analyze them *qualitatively* as well as *quantitatively*. The auditor should try to determine whether the failures: (1) were intentional or unintentional, (2) were random or systematic, (3) had a direct dollar effect on the account balance, or (4) were of such magnitude that a material misstatement could occur and not be detected.

The auditor is much more concerned if the control failures appear to be *intentional*, which might indicate fraud. If the failures are *systematic*, the auditor should be cautious in deciding to isolate the problem and reducing substantive testing. For example, if all of the failures were related to pricing errors—and all were connected to one sales associate—the auditor may expand audit testing to review all of the transactions related to that one sales associate. However, the auditor should not typically reduce substantive testing in other areas because the identified errors appear to be isolated to the one sales associate. The sampling evidence may be signalling that there are other isolated failures that did not happen to appear in the sample.

Often, a failure in a control does not lead directly to dollar misstatements in the accounting records. Lack of proper approval for payment of a vendor's invoice, for example, does not necessarily mean that the invoice should not have been paid. While it may have been an appropriate invoice, it might also have been a fictitious invoice.

Linkage of Test of Controls to Substantive Procedures   In addition to being the basis of a report on internal controls, the tests of controls are used to determine whether the nature, timing, or extent of the planned substantive procedures needs to be modified. For example, if the tests of controls indicate that the client is not careful about assuring that shipment has taken place before billing and recording a sale, the auditor may need to increase sales cutoff testing and/or concentrate on sales recorded just before the balance sheet date. If credit approvals are not working correctly, the auditor will have to take more time to determine whether the allowance for doubtful accounts is reasonable. Additional testing of subsequent collections and follow-up on old, uncollected balances may be needed. In general, if controls are not operating effectively, the auditor will increase the assessment of control risk and will likely choose to rely less on substantive analytical procedures and more on tests of details for those accounts related to identified control failures.

When the auditor concludes that a control is not operating effectively based on attributes sampling, the auditor can pursue the following alternative courses of action:

- A compensating control could be identified and tested. The decision to test the compensating control will depend on the perceived effectiveness of the control and the additional cost to test the control procedure.
- A larger sample could be taken, but this is not likely to be cost-beneficial unless the auditor has reason to believe the original sample was not representative.
- The assessment of control risk can be set higher than originally planned and the nature, timing, and/or the extent of the related substantive tests can be modified. If the upper limit of the possible deviation rate does not exceed the tolerable failure rate by very much, this modification could be very slight. For example, if the upper limit was 5.4% and the tolerable rate was 5%, very little modification is needed.
- The auditor will analyze the nature of the control deviations and determine the implications on the type of misstatements, or causes of misstatements, that might occur in the financial statements and adjust the nature, timing, and/or extent of the planned substantive testing.

Step 7. Document All Phases of the Sampling Process

All of the preceding steps and related decisions regarding the sampling process should be documented to allow for appropriate supervision and provide adequate support for the conclusions reached.

Nonstatistical Sampling Approach to Testing Controls

Why It Matters

This feature provides guidance to the auditor who chooses to use a nonstatistical sampling approach when testing controls.

If the auditor chooses to use nonstatistical sampling procedures to test the operating effectiveness of controls, the auditor may not quantify the planning factors. Instead, the auditor addresses deviation rates through the more global concepts of none, few, and many. Sampling risk is often set as low, moderate, or high. The effect of these factors on sample size follows:

	Condition Leading to	
Factor	**Smaller Sample**	**Larger Sample**
Tolerable deviation rate	High	Low
Expected population deviation rate	Low	High
Sampling risk (risk of overreliance)	High	Low
Population size	Little effect	Little effect

With these subjective judgments, the auditor cannot quantitatively assess the risk of making an incorrect inference based on the sample results. For this reason, many auditors who use nonstatistical sampling should review the factors and select a sample size consistent with a statistically determined sample.

Check Your Basic Knowledge

8-21 When the auditor detects control deviations, it is best to evaluate them quantitatively rather than qualitatively.　(T/F)

8-22 When using nonstatistical sampling, the auditor cannot quantitatively assess the risk of making an incorrect inference based on the sample results.　(T/F)

8-23 Which of the following relationships is inaccurate?

8-24 The auditor should <u>not</u> pursue which of the following options when a control is ineffective?
   a. Identify a compensating control.
   b. Take a larger sample.
   c. Assess control risk as lower than originally planned and change the audit approach accordingly.
   d. Analyze the nature of the control deviations and identify implications.

	Condition Leading to	
Factor	**Smaller Sample**	**Larger Sample**
a. Tolerable deviation rate	High	Low
b. Expected population deviation rate	Low	High
c. Sampling risk (risk of overreliance)	Low	High
d. Population size	Little effect	Little effect

LO 5

Describe the basic steps in sampling for substantive tests of details and apply those steps in a nonstatistical sampling application.

Basic Steps in Sampling Account Balances and Assertions: A Nonstatisical Sampling Application

Basic Steps in Sampling Account Balances and Assertions

The basic steps in sampling for substantive tests of details are the same for both nonstatistical and statistical sampling approaches:

1. Specify the audit objective of the test and define a misstatement.
2. Define the population from which the auditor takes the sample.
3. Choose an appropriate sampling method.
4. Determine the sample size.
5. Select sample items and perform the substantive procedure.
6. Evaluate the sample results.
7. Document all phases of the sampling process.

Step 1. Specify the Audit Objective of the Test and Define a Misstatement

The auditor designs a sampling plan for tests of details to provide assurance regarding one or more financial statement assertions (e.g., existence of accounts receivable). Specifying the audit objective determines the population to test. For example, if the objective is to determine the existence of customer balances, the sample should be selected from the recorded balances. If the objective is to determine the completeness of accounts payable, the sample should be selected from a complementary population, such as cash disbursements made after the balance sheet date. The auditor looks for payments for goods and services received by the balance sheet date that should be payable at year-end, but were not recorded until after year-end. Populations involving the testing of the existence assertion are generally easy to define because they include all recorded transactions. On the other hand, populations involving the completeness assertion are more difficult to define because some of those transactions may not yet be recorded.

The auditor should define misstatements before beginning the sampling application to preclude the client or auditor from rationalizing away misstatements as isolated events and provide guidance to the audit team. A **misstatement** is a dollar amount of misstatement, either intentional or unintentional, that exists in a transaction or financial statement account balance. When sampling for substantive tests of details, a misstatement involves differences between recorded values and audited values. For example, if a cash payment were posted to the wrong customer's subsidiary account, the overall account balance would still be correct and should not be considered a misstatement. Even so, the auditor should carefully follow up on this finding to be sure it is not evidence of a cover-up of an employee's misappropriation of cash. If, however, the client inappropriately billed a customer before the end of the period, the premature billing would be considered a misstatement because the overall receivable balance would be overstated at the end of the period.

Misstatements are categorized as factual misstatements or projected misstatements. **Factual misstatements** are those that have been specifically identified and about which there is no doubt, such as a difference identified in a sample item or an item in a population examined 100%. Factual misstatements are also referred to as **known misstatements**.

Projected misstatements are developed by extrapolation from the factual misstatements in sample items to the population. **Projected misstatements** are those that are the auditor's best estimate of the misstatements in a given population based on the sample results. Projected misstatements are also referred to as **likely misstatements**. The total factual and projected misstatement (can be referred to as total estimated misstatement) is compared with the tolerable misstatement when evaluating the sample results.

Auditors also need to define tolerable misstatement and expected misstatement. The AICPA's 2012 *Audit Sampling* formally defines a **tolerable misstatement** as a monetary amount set by the auditor in respect of which the auditor seeks to obtain an appropriate level of assurance that the monetary amount set by the auditor is not exceeded by the actual misstatement in the population. In more practical terms, a tolerable misstatement is the maximum amount of misstatement the auditor can accept in the population without requiring an audit adjustment or a qualified audit opinion.

When planning a sample for a test of details, the auditor should identify the maximum monetary misstatement in the account balance that, when combined with misstatements found in other tests, would cause the financial statements to be materially misstated. As discussed in *Chapter 7*, tolerable misstatement is based on planning materiality. An **expected misstatement** is the level of misstatement that the auditor expects to detect, and it is based on projected misstatements in prior-year audits, results of other substantive tests, professional judgment, and knowledge of changes in personnel and the accounting system. It is usually desirable to be conservative and use a slightly larger expected misstatement than is actually anticipated. This conservative approach may marginally increase the sample size, but it minimizes sampling risk. If expected misstatement is greater than tolerable misstatement, sampling is not appropriate unless it is used to estimate the size of the required adjustment to the account balance.

Step 2. Define the Population from Which the Auditor Takes the Sample

The population is that group of items in an account balance that the auditor wants to test. The population, as defined for sampling purposes, does not include any items that the auditor has decided to examine 100% or items that will be tested separately. Because sample results can be projected to only that group of items from which the sample is selected, it is important to properly define the population. For example, a sample selected from the inventory at one location can be used to estimate the amount of misstatement only at that location, not at other locations.

Define the Sampling Unit   Sampling units are the individual auditable items and often are made up of individual account balances. However, a sampling unit for confirming accounts receivable could be the individual customer's balance, individual unpaid invoices, or a combination of these two. The choice depends on effectiveness and efficiency of the process and the manner in which the client has recorded the individual items. Some customers are more likely to return a confirmation when asked to confirm one unpaid invoice rather than verify the correctness of an entire account balance. If a customer does not return a positive confirmation, alternative procedures must be performed, including identifying subsequent payments and/or vouching the sales transactions to supporting documents. If customers typically pay by invoice, it will be more efficient to perform alternative procedures on individual invoices than on total balances.

Completeness of the Population   A sample is selected from a physical representation of the population, such as a list of customer balances or a computer file. The auditor needs assurance that the list accurately represents the population. A common procedure is to foot the list and reconcile it with the general ledger. The auditor can use data analytics tools to complete this procedure.

Identify Individually Significant Items   Many account balances are composed of a few relatively large items and many smaller items. A significant portion of the total value of many accounting populations is concentrated in a relatively few large-dollar items. Because of this, the auditor often will examine all the large-dollar items. These large-dollar items are often referred to as the top stratum. **Top-stratum** items are population items whose book values exceed the sampling interval and are therefore included in the sample. Because the auditor knows the amount of errors in the top stratum (all items were evaluated), no estimate or projection of errors is required. The remaining items are then sampled using an appropriate sampling method. **Lower-stratum** items are those that are not in the top stratum. The audit results reflect the sum of top-stratum misstatements and the projected misstatement based on lower-stratum items.

The auditor often uses judgment to determine the cutoff point for top-stratum items. The division of the population into two or more subgroups is referred to as **stratification**. Stratification of the population into several homogeneous subpopulations generally creates audit efficiency. The stratification process can be enhanced with the use of data analytics tools that have the capability of creating a profile of the population of book values, e.g., sorted by dollar value, size of customer, and customer credit rating.

Step 3. Choose an Appropriate Sampling Method

Once the auditor has decided to use audit sampling, either nonstatistical or statistical sampling is appropriate for substantive tests of details. The most common statistical approaches for substantive testing are classical variables sampling (beyond the scope of this text) and monetary unit sampling (MUS). MUS, which is discussed in the next section, is a subset of a broader class of procedures, sometimes referred to as **probability proportional to size (PPS) sampling**. The term *PPS* describes a method of sample selection where the probability of an item's selection for the sample is proportional to its recorded amount; *MUS* is a specific method of PPS that has been developed for auditors. As is common, we use the terms *MUS* and *PPS* interchangeably.

Steps 4, 5, and 6. Determine the Sample Size, Select the Sample Items, Perform the Substantive Procedure, and Evaluate the Sample Results

Determining the sample size, the method of selecting the sample, and the approach to evaluating the sample results depend on the sampling method used. Whatever sampling method is chosen, the auditor must consider the risk of misstatement in the account, sampling risk, and the auditor's assessment of tolerable and expected misstatement. If the auditor uses a statistical sampling method, the sample must be selected randomly to give each item in the population an equal chance to be included in the sample.

Unacceptable Sample Results   When the total estimated misstatement (the sum of the total factual and projected misstatement) exceeds the tolerable misstatement, the auditor has several possible courses of action. The auditor can:

- *Ask the client to correct the factual misstatements*—If this is done, the total estimated misstatement can be adjusted for those corrections, but not for the projection of misstatements associated with those items. In some cases, simply correcting the factual misstatement can bring the total estimated misstatement below the auditor's tolerable misstatement level.
- *Analyze the detected misstatements for common problem(s)*—When misstatements are discovered, the auditor should look beyond the quantitative aspects of the misstatements to understand the nature and cause of the misstatements—especially to determine if there is a systematic pattern to the misstatements. If a systematic pattern is found, the client can be asked to investigate and make an estimate of the correction needed. The auditor can review and test this estimate. Further, the auditor can recommend improvements to prevent such errors in the future. For example, assume several

confirmation replies indicate that merchandise was returned prior to year-end but credit was not recorded until the subsequent year. A careful review of receiving reports related to merchandise returned prior to year-end and of credits recorded in the subsequent year will provide evidence regarding the extent of the needed correction. The auditor should also consider the relationship of the misstatements to other phases of the audit; problems in recording receivables may also reveal problems in the accuracy of recorded sales.

- *Design an alternative audit strategy*—Discovering more misstatements than expected in the risk assessment phase of the audit suggests that the planning assumptions may have been incorrect and that internal controls were not as effective as originally assessed. In such cases, the auditor should plan the rest of the audit accordingly. For public companies, significant problems with internal control will cause the auditor to consider whether it is necessary to express an adverse opinion on the effectiveness of the client's internal controls over financial reporting.

- *Expand the sample*—The auditor can calculate the additional sample size needed by substituting the most likely misstatement from the sample evaluation for the original expected misstatement in the sample interval formula and determine a new interval and total sample size based on the new expectations. The number of additional sample items can then be determined by subtracting the original sample size from the new sample size. The new sampling interval can be used for selection of items not already included in the sample.

- *Change the audit objective to estimating the correct value*—In cases where material misstatements are likely, it may be necessary to change from an objective of testing details to an objective of estimating the correct population value. A lower detection risk and a smaller tolerable misstatement should be used because the auditor is no longer testing the balance but is estimating the correct population value from the sample. The auditor will expect the client to adjust the book value to the estimated value. A larger sample size will normally be required.

Step 7. Document All Phases of the Sampling Process

All of the preceding steps and related decisions regarding the sampling process should be documented to allow for appropriate supervision and provide adequate support for the conclusions reached.

Nonstatistical Sampling for Substantive Tests of Account Balances and Assertions

In determining sample size, all significant items should be tested. The auditor should select all items over a specific dollar amount, and then, depending on audit objectives, select items with other characteristics, such as sales billed in the last week or billed to specific parties. The sample size of the other items to be tested should be based on the same factors used in statistical sampling. In terms of selecting the sample, the auditor should take steps to increase the likelihood that the sample is representative of the population. The auditor may obtain a representative sample using a random-based sampling method.

In terms of evaluating the sample results, the auditor projects misstatements found in the sample to the population. There is no way to mathematically measure sampling risk in a nonstatistical sample; the auditor can project only the detected misstatements and make a professional judgment as to whether the account is likely to be materially misstated and then decide whether more audit work is needed.

For example, assume the auditor is using nonstatistical sampling to confirm accounts receivable to test the existence assertion. The auditor confirmed

Prompt for Critical Thinking #3   It's Your Turn!

There is a common ethical dilemma that early-career auditors sometimes encounter with their supervisors in performing sampling. The ethical dilemma plays out as follows:

Staff: "I've completed sending confirmations for Accounts Receivable, and I've received 4 in which the client's Accounts Receivable balance was materially overstated. What should I do?"

Senior: "Darn! That's a problem. Here's what I want you to do. Throw away those 4 and collect 4 additional confirmations."

Staff: "Hmmm….that doesn't sound right…"

Senior: "I know what I'm doing. Just do what I'm telling you to do and it will save us all a lot of time and hassle."

Staff: "Ok."

Think about the situation and answer the following questions:

1. What does throwing away the 4 'bad' confirmations and replacing them with new, and hopefully 'good' confirmations, i.e., those showing no exceptions, do to audit risk, i.e., the risk that the audit firm issues a clean opinion on materially misstated financial statements?

_____

_____

_____

2. What ethical mistake is the senior making in directing the subordinate team member?

_____

_____

_____

3. What mistake is the staff auditor making? If he or she further questions the senior, it is clear that the senior auditor will be angry; yet, if he or she goes up the chain of command and dutifully reports the inappropriate judgment and decision of the senior to the manager, the senior might be even angrier. How would you suggest that the staff auditor resolve the situation properly?

_____

_____

_____

all twenty-one customer balances equal to or greater than $50,000. These items comprise the top stratum. The auditor confirmed a random sample of the lower stratum of 190 balances less than $50,000. The details are presented in the following table:

	Population		Sample		
	Number	**Amount**	**Number**	**Amount**	**Factual Misstatement**
>=$50,000	21	$2,000,000	21	$2,000,000	$1,500
<$50,000	190	$2,500,000	19	$310,000	$900
Total	211	$4,500,000	40	$2,310,000	$2,400

The factual misstatement of $1,500 in the top stratum needs no projection to the population because all of these items in the stratum were tested. However, the auditor would project factual misstatements in the lower stratum to the rest of the lower stratum as follows: $900 / $310,000 × 2,2500,00 = $7,258

Therefore, the total factual and projected misstatement is estimated to be $8,758 ($1,500 + $7,258). The $8,758 is the auditor's best estimate, but of course there is some probability that the actual amount may be higher. Assume tolerable misstatement is $150,000. Because $8,758 is so much smaller than the tolerable misstatement, there is an ample cushion between the tolerable misstatement and the factual and projected misstatement. Therefore, the auditor would be reasonable in concluding that there is a low risk of material misstatement related to the existence of accounts receivable.

Check Your Basic Knowledge

8-25 Top-stratum items are population items whose book values exceed the sampling interval and are therefore excluded from the sample   (T/F)

8-26 The division of a population into two or more subgroups is referred to as *stratification*.   (T/F)

8-27 Which of the following definitions is <u>true</u>?

a. *Factual misstatement*—A misstatement that has been specifically identified and about which there is no doubt.

b. *Projected misstatement*—The auditor's best estimate of the misstatement in a given population based on projecting the sample results to the population.

c. *Tolerable misstatement*—A monetary amount set by the auditor in respect of which the auditor seeks to obtain an appropriate level of assurance that the monetary amount set by the auditor is not exceeded by the actual misstatement in the population.

d. *Expected misstatement*—The level of misstatement that the auditor expects to detect.

e. All of the above are true.

8-28 Which of the following statements is <u>false</u>?

a. Top-stratum items are population items whose book values exceed the sampling interval and are therefore all included in the sample.

b. Because the auditor knows the amount of errors in the top stratum (all items were evaluated), no estimate of errors is required for the top stratum.

c. Stratification of the population into several subpopulations generally reduces audit efficiency.

d. Sampling evaluation reflects the sum of top-stratum misstatements and the projected misstatement derived from lower-stratum items.

e. None of the above are false.

LO 6

Describe monetary unit sampling and use it to test account balances and assertions.

Statistical Sampling for Substantive Tests of Account Balances and Assertions: Monetary Unit Sampling (MUS)

Monetary unit sampling (MUS) is a sampling method based on attributes sampling, but involving dollar misstatements rather than control failure rates. MUS is a widely used statistical sampling method because it results in an efficient sample size and concentrates on the dollar value of the account balances. It has been developed especially for use in auditing and has been given various names, including dollar-unit sampling, PPS, and combined attributes-variables sampling. MUS was designed to be especially effective in testing for overstatements in situations when few or no misstatements are expected.

Summary of MUS Strengths and Weaknesses

As an auditor considers whether to use MUS as the sampling approach for substantive tests of details, it is helpful to review its strengths and weaknesses. Strengths of MUS include:

- MUS is generally easier to apply than other statistical sampling approaches.
- MUS automatically selects a sample in proportion to an item's dollar amount, thus providing automatic stratification of the sample.
- If the auditor expects (and finds) no misstatements, MUS usually results in a highly efficient sample size.

Examples of the circumstances in which MUS might be used include:

- Accounts receivable confirmations (when credit balances are not significant)
- Loans receivable confirmations (e.g., real-estate mortgage loans, commercial loans, and installment loans)

- Inventory price tests in which the auditor anticipates relatively few misstatements and the population is not expected to contain a significant number of large understatements
- Fixed-asset additions tests where existence is the relevant assertion

The auditor should also be aware of difficulties in using MUS:

- MUS is not designed to test for the understatement of a population.
- If an auditor identifies understatements in a MUS sample, evaluation of the sample requires special considerations.
- Selection of zero or negative balances requires special design considerations.

Some circumstances in which MUS might not be the most appropriate approach include:

- Accounts receivable confirmations in which a large number of credit balances exist
- Inventory test counts and price tests for which the auditor anticipates a significant number of misstatements that can be both understatements and overstatements

Designing and Selecting a MUS Sample

The population for MUS is defined as the number of dollars in the population being tested. Each dollar in the population has an equal chance of being chosen, but each dollar chosen is associated with a tangible item such as a customer's balance or an inventory item, so items with more dollars have a greater likelihood of being selected.

The sample size in a MUS sample depends on the: (1) risk of incorrect acceptance, (2) ratio of expected misstatement to tolerable misstatement, and (3) ratio of tolerable misstatement to the total population value. *Exhibit 8.7* provides a table that auditors can use to determine the appropriate sample size for MUS. Note that the AICPA's 2012 *Audit Sampling* also presents other alternative methods of sample selection; we use one method for simplicity.

To illustrate the use of *Exhibit 8.7*, consider a setting where the risk of incorrect acceptance is 10%, tolerable misstatement is 5% of population dollars, and expected misstatement is 20% of tolerable misstatement (in other words, 1% of the population dollars), the auditor identifies a sample size of 69 units.

One complexity that you will encounter when using *Exhibit 8.7* is that sometimes the ratio of expected to tolerable misstatement or tolerable misstatement as a percentage of the population will not be even numbers that appear in the table. For example, the ratio of expected to tolerable misstatement may be 24.5%, and the ratio of tolerable misstatement to the population may be 3.5%. To address this complexity, you can round the numbers in either case to ensure that an adequate sample size is obtained. For the ratio of expected to tolerable misstatement, you can round up to 30% because that will yield a larger sample size than if you had rounded down to 20%. For the tolerable misstatement as a percentage of the population, you can round down to 3% because that will yield a larger sample size than if you had rounded up to 4%.

Once the auditor has determined the appropriate sample size, a sampling interval is calculated by dividing the population size by the sample size.

Thus,

Sampling Interval = Population Size ÷ Sample Size

So, in our example,

Sampling Interval = $807,906 ÷ 69; thereby yielding a sampling interval of $11,708.

The sample is then selected using the fixed-interval approach—every *n*th dollar is selected after choosing a random start, which is required to give every dollar

Exhibit 8.7
Monetary Unit Sample Size Determination Table

		Tolerable Misstatement as a Percentage of Population											
Risk of Incorrect Acceptance	Ratio of Expected to Tolerable Misstatement	50%	30%	10%	8%	6%	5%	4%	3%	2%	1%	0.50%	Expected Sum of Taints
5%	—	6	10	30	38	50	60	75	100	150	300	600	—
5%	0.10	8	13	37	46	62	74	92	123	184	368	736	0.37
5%	0.20	10	16	47	58	78	93	116	155	232	463	925	0.93
5%	0.30	12	20	60	75	100	120	150	200	300	600	1,199	1.80
5%	0.40	17	27	81	102	135	162	203	270	405	809	1,618	3.24
5%	0.50	24	39	116	145	193	231	289	385	577	1,154	2,308	5.77
10%	—	5	8	24	29	39	47	58	77	116	231	461	—
10%	0.20	7	12	35	43	57	69	86	114	171	341	682	0.69
10%	0.30	9	15	44	55	73	87	109	145	217	433	866	1.30
10%	0.40	12	20	58	72	96	115	143	191	286	572	1,144	2.29
10%	0.50	16	27	80	100	134	160	200	267	400	799	1,597	4.00
15%	—	4	7	19	24	32	38	48	64	95	190	380	—
15%	0.20	6	10	28	35	46	55	69	91	137	273	545	0.55
15%	0.30	7	12	35	43	57	69	86	114	171	341	681	1.03
15%	0.40	9	15	45	56	74	89	111	148	221	442	883	1.77
15%	0.50	13	21	61	76	101	121	151	202	302	604	1,208	3.02
20%	—	4	6	17	21	27	33	41	54	81	161	322	—
20%	0.20	5	8	23	29	38	46	57	76	113	226	451	0.46
20%	0.30	6	10	28	35	47	56	70	93	139	277	554	0.84
20%	0.40	8	12	36	45	59	71	89	118	177	354	707	1.42
20%	0.50	10	16	48	60	80	95	119	159	238	475	949	2.38
25%	—	3	5	14	18	24	28	35	47	70	139	278	—
25%	0.20	4	7	19	24	32	38	48	64	95	190	380	0.38
25%	0.30	5	8	23	29	39	46	58	77	115	230	460	0.69
25%	0.40	6	10	29	37	49	58	73	97	145	289	578	1.16
25%	0.50	8	13	38	48	64	76	95	127	190	380	760	1.90
30%	—	3	5	13	16	21	25	31	41	61	121	241	—
30%	0.20	4	6	17	21	27	33	41	54	81	162	323	0.33
30%	0.40	5	8	24	30	40	48	60	80	120	239	477	0.96
30%	0.60	9	15	43	54	71	85	107	142	213	425	850	2.55
35%	—	3	4	11	14	18	21	27	35	53	105	210	—
35%	0.20	3	5	14	18	23	28	35	46	69	138	276	0.28
35%	0.40	4	7	20	25	34	40	50	67	100	199	397	0.80
35%	0.60	7	12	34	43	57	68	85	113	169	338	676	2.03
50%	—	2	3	7	9	12	14	18	24	35	70	139	—
50%	0.20	2	3	9	11	15	18	22	29	44	87	173	0.18
50%	0.40	3	4	12	15	19	23	29	38	57	114	228	0.46
50%	0.60	4	6	17	22	29	34	43	57	85	170	340	1.02

Source: *Audit Sampling* (New York: AICPA, 2012), 152–154. Reprinted with permission from AICPA; copyright © 2012 by American Institute of Certified Public Accountants.

in the population an equal chance of being included in the sample. Each selected dollar acts as a hook for the entire physical unit in which it occurs, such as a customer's account balance or the extended cost of an inventory item.

Again, in our example the sampling interval is $11,708. If the sample is to be selected manually, it will be easier if a rounded interval is used, such as $11,000. Rounding the interval down (rather than up) assures that the sample size will be adequate. The random start should be between 1 and the sampling interval (1 to 11,000 in our example). This random start number can be obtained from a variety of sources, including the serial number of a dollar bill, a random number table, or a computer-generated random number. To illustrate using a dollar bill, the auditor could use the image below as evidence of a random start at $9,263.

The auditor can use a calculator or data analytics tool to select the sample. If you are using a calculator, clear the calculator, enter the random start, add each customer book value, and subtotal after each entry, giving a cumulative total for each item. We illustrate this process in *Exhibit 8.8* using a random start of 9,263. The first sample item is the one that first causes the cumulative total to equal or exceed the sampling interval of $11,000. (Customer 3 in *Exhibit 8.8*). Successive sample items are those first causing the cumulative total to equal or exceed multiples of the intervals ($22,000, $33,000, $44,000, and so forth).

As we noted previously, the probability of selecting any particular item is proportional to the number of dollars in it. For example, if the sampling interval is $11,000, a customer's balance of $220 would have a 2% chance (220/11,000) of being included in the sample. A customer with a book value of $2,200 has a 20% chance of being selected. There is a 100% chance of including the balance of a customer whose book value is $11,000 or greater.

All items with a book value equal to or greater than the interval will be selected for auditor evaluation. As we previously note, these items are referred to as top-stratum items. The balance for Customer 7 has four selection points, but it will be examined only once. Thus, the number of **logical units** (customer balances) will be less than the sample size of dollar units. The population has effectively been divided into two groups: the top-stratum items and the lower-stratum items. The sample selection process uses dollar-based stratification and focuses the auditor on large-dollar coverage with relatively small sample sizes.

This selection method also tests the mathematical accuracy of the population. Note in *Exhibit 8.8* that the last cumulative amount is $817,169. This represents the population total of $807,906 plus the random start of $9,263.

Exhibit 8.8
Fixed Interval Sample Selection

Customer	Book Value ($)	Cumulative Book	Cumulative Book Plus Random Start ($)	Included in Sample?	Selection Amount ($)
	Random start	0	9,263	No	
1	220	220	9,483	No	
2	2,200	2,420	11,683	Yes	11,000
3	22,000	24,420	33,683	Yes	22,000 & 33,000
4	880	25,300	34,563	No	
5	6,128	31,428	40,691	No	
6	2,800	34,228	43,491	No	
7	45,023	79,251	88,514	Yes	44,000 &55,000 & 66,000 & 77,000, & 88,000
8	10	79,261	88,524	No	
9	8,231	87,492	96,755	No	
10	16,894	104,386	113,649	Yes	99,000 & 110,000
.	.	.	.		.
.	.	.	.		.
.	.	.	.		.
450	1,900	807,906	807,906 + 9,263 = $817,169		.

It's Your Turn!

Prompt for Critical Thinking #4

- Pull out your own dollar bill. What number between 0 and $11,000 can you use to obtain a random start number?
- Re-work the numbers in *Exhibit 8.8* using your new random start.

- Did you get selection amounts that were different than those in *Exhibit 8.8*? Why do you think this might be the case?

Zero and Negative Balances   Population items with zero balances have no chance of being selected using PPS sampling. If evaluation of sampling units with zero balances is necessary to achieve the audit objective of the test, they should be segregated and audited as a different population. Population items with negative balances require special consideration. For example, credit balances in customer accounts represent liabilities; the client owes money, merchandise, or service. An approach to dealing with negative items is to exclude them from the selection process and test them as a separate population; this should be done when a significant number of such items are included in the population. Another approach is to change the sign of the negative items and add them to the population before selection. This approach is generally used only when there are few negative items and few or no misstatements are expected.

Check Your Basic Knowledge

8-29 One strength of MUS is that it automatically selects a sample in proportion to an item's dollar amount, thus providing automatic stratification of the sample. (T/F)

8-30 The population for MUS is defined as the number of dollars in the population being tested. Each dollar in the population has an equal chance of being chosen, but each dollar chosen is associated with a tangible item such as a customer's balance or an inventory item, so items with more dollars have a greater likelihood of being selected. (T/F)

8-31 Refer to *Exhibit 8.7*. Assume that the risk of incorrect acceptance is 10%, tolerable misstatement is 5% of population dollars, and expected misstatement is 30%

of tolerable misstatement (in other words, 1.5% of the population dollars). What is the minimum sample size that the auditor should use?

a. 28
b. 87
c. 120
d. 162

8-32 Which of the following represents the calculation of the sampling interval?

a. Tolerable error ÷ Risk of incorrect acceptance.
b. Sample size ÷ Population size.
c. Tolerable error × Risk of incorrect acceptance.
d. Population size ÷ Sample size.

Evaluating a MUS Sample

PPS sampling is designed to determine the likelihood that the account balance may exceed tolerable misstatement. In other words, if the auditor designs the sample with a 10% risk of incorrect acceptance and a tolerable misstatement of 5% of population dollars ($807,906), thereby yielding $40,395 (and round down to $40,000), the auditor is testing the hypothesis that there is no more than a 10% probability that misstatements related to the assertion being tested can cause the account balance to be overstated by more than $40,000.

Recall that our example's assumptions are:

- the risk of incorrect acceptance is 10%
- tolerable misstatement is 5% of population dollars, rounded down to $40,000
- and expected misstatement is 20% of tolerable misstatement, yielding $8,000.

When evaluating the MUS sample results, the auditor calculates the total estimated misstatement in the account balance based on the sampling process. This total includes the following four components:

- *Factual misstatement for items in the top stratum*
- **Basic precision**—The amount of uncertainty associated with testing only a part of the population (sampling risk). Basic precision is the amount of error you are confident of not exceeding if no errors are detected in the sample. Basic precision is calculated as the sampling interval multiplied by a confidence factor. See *Exhibit 8.9* for the confidence factors.
- *Projected misstatement for items in the lower stratum*—The best estimate of the actual amount of dollar misstatements in the population based on projecting the sample results to the population. The projected misstatement is calculated as the sampling interval multiplied by the tainting percentage. The terms *likely misstatement* or **most likely misstatement** are also used to refer to projected misstatement.

Exhibit 8.9
Confidence Factors for Sample Evaluation

Number of Overstatement Misstatements	Risk of Incorrect Acceptance								
	5%	10%	15%	20%	25%	30%	35%	37%	50%
0	3.00	2.31	1.90	1.61	1.39	1.21	1.05	1.00	0.70
1	4.75	3.89	3.38	3.00	2.70	2.44	2.22	2.14	1.68
2	6.30	5.33	4.73	4.28	3.93	3.62	3.35	3.25	2.68
3	7.76	6.69	6.02	5.52	5.11	4.77	4.46	4.35	3.68
4	9.16	8.00	7.27	6.73	6.28	5.90	5.55	5.43	4.68
5	10.52	9.28	8.50	7.91	7.43	7.01	6.64	6.50	5.68
6	11.85	10.54	9.71	9.08	8.56	8.12	7.72	7.57	6.67
7	13.15	11.78	10.90	10.24	9.69	9.21	8.79	8.63	7.67
8	14.44	13.00	12.08	11.38	10.81	10.31	9.85	9.68	8.67
9	15.71	14.21	13.25	12.52	11.92	11.39	10.92	10.74	9.67
10	16.97	15.41	14.42	13.66	13.02	12.47	11.98	11.79	10.67
11	18.21	16.60	15.57	14.78	14.13	13.55	13.04	12.84	11.67
12	19.45	17.79	16.72	15.90	15.22	14.63	14.09	13.89	12.67
13	20.67	18.96	17.86	17.02	16.32	15.70	15.14	14.93	13.67
14	21.89	20.13	19.00	18.13	17.40	16.77	16.20	15.98	14.67
15	23.10	21.30	20.13	19.24	18.49	17.84	17.25	17.02	15.67
16	24.31	22.46	21.26	20.34	19.58	18.90	18.29	18.06	16.67
17	25.50	23.61	22.39	21.44	20.66	19.97	19.34	19.10	17.67
18	26.70	24.76	23.51	22.54	21.74	21.03	20.38	20.14	18.67
19	27.88	25.91	24.63	23.64	22.81	22.09	21.43	21.18	19.67
20	29.07	27.05	25.74	24.73	23.89	23.15	22.47	22.22	20.67

Source: *Audit Sampling* (New York: AICPA, 2012), 155–156. AICPA audit and accounting guides by AMERICAN INSTITUTE OF CERTIFIED PUBLIC ACCOUNTANTS. Copyright © 2012 Reproduced with permission of AMERICAN INSTITUTE OF CERTIFIED PUBLIC ACCOUNTANTS in the format Textbook via Copyright Clearance Center.

- **Incremental allowance for sampling risk**—An increase in the total estimated misstatement caused by the statistical properties of misstatements detected in the lower stratum.

The calculation of the total estimated misstatement will differ depending on whether misstatements are detected, as depicted in *Exhibit 8.10*.

No Misstatements in the Sample   If the auditor finds no misstatements in the sample, the misstatement projection is zero dollars, and the total estimated misstatement will equal basic precision. The basic precision is the amount of error you are confident of not exceeding if no errors are reported for the sample. It is determined by multiplying the sampling interval by the confidence factor for the specified risk of incorrect acceptance (assuming no errors).

For example, if the auditor specified a 10% risk of incorrect acceptance, used a $11,000 sampling interval, and detected no misstatements, the total estimated misstatement equals $25,410 (2.31 × $11,000). Note that "2.31" is the confidence factor obtained from *Exhibit 8.9* and can be found at the intersection of

Exhibit 8.10

Total Estimated Misstatement Calculation Summary

	If No Misstatements Detected	If Misstatements Detected
Factual misstatement in top-stratum	0	Amount of factual misstatement
Basic precision	Interval × confidence factor	Interval × confidence factor
+ Projected misstatement in lower stratum	0	Calculate
+ Incremental allowance for sampling risk in lower stratum	0	Calculate
= Total estimated misstatement	= Basic precision	Sum of the four

Number of Overstatement Misstatements Overstatement Misstatements = 0 and Risk of Incorrect Acceptance = 10%. If no misstatements are found, the auditor will conclude that the recorded value of the population is not overstated by more than the tolerable misstatement at the specified risk of incorrect acceptance.

Overstatements in the Sample When the auditor detects misstatements, the evaluation process is more involved because in addition to calculating basic precision, the auditor must also calculate the projected misstatement and the incremental allowance for sampling risk. When evaluating the MUS sample where overstatements have been detected, the auditor begins by identifying the percentage that the book value of each misstated sample item is overstated or understated (referred to as the *tainting percentage*).

The **tainting percentage** is the percentage of misstatement present in a logical unit, such as the sample item's book value. The tainting percentage equals the amount of misstatement in the item divided by the item's recorded amount (in other words, the book value). A tainting percentage is calculated for all sample items with misstatement in the lower stratum. The auditor multiplies the tainting percentage by the sampling interval to calculate the projected misstatement for each misstated item.

Illustration with Overstatements in the Sample Using the example in *Exhibit 8.8* with a sampling interval of $11,000 and the risk of incorrect acceptance of 10%, assume the auditor detects the following misstatements:

Book Value	Audit Value	Misstatement	Tainting Percentage
$45,023	$44,340	$683	NA
$2,000	$1,940	$ 60	3%
$8,300	$8,217	$ 83	1%

There was only one top-stratum misstatement. An item with a book value of $45,023 had an audited value of $44,340—resulting in a $683 top-stratum overstatement. For the top-stratum item, there is no need to obtain a tainting percentage or to project the misstatement because all of the items in the top stratum were audited.

The lower stratum contained two misstatements. The first lower-stratum misstatement was the result of a book value of $2,000 that had an audited value of $1,940, thus yielding an overstatement of $60. The tainting percentage is $60 divided by $2,000 or 3%. Because this item was selected from an interval of $11,000, it is projected that the overstatement is 3% or $330. Similarly, the second misstatement was $83 (book value of $8,300; audit value of $8,217), resulting in a 1% tainting or a projected amount of $110 for the interval. The sum of the projected lower-stratum misstatements is therefore $440. This same result can be obtained by multiplying the sampling interval by the sum of the tainting percentages $11,00 \times 4\% = \$440$. *Exhibit 8.11* summarizes the sample evaluation calculations.

Next, the auditor calculates incremental allowance for sampling risk for the lower-stratum items by completing the following steps, which are summarized in *Exhibit 8.12*.

First, list the dollar value of the projected misstatements in descending order and calculate their sum.

Second, calculate incremental changes in the confidence factors for each misstatement at the relevant risk of incorrect acceptance. Recall that *Exhibit 8.9* contains the confidence factors. To calculate the incremental changes, subtract the value related to overstatement 0 (in our example, 1.90) from the value related to overstatement 1 (in our example, 3.38), and so on, depending on the number of misstatements detected.

Exhibit 8.11
Example of Calculation of Total Estimated Misstatement When Overstatements Are Detected

	Confidence Factor*	Tainting Percentage	Sampling Interval	Conclusion
Factual misstatement in top stratum				683
Basic precision	2.31×		11,000=	25,410
Projected misstatement in lower stratum:				
First largest tainting %		3%		
First largest tainting %		1%		
		4% ×	11,000=	440
Incremental allowance for sampling risk in lower stratum		239**		
Total estimated misstatement:	***683 + 25,410 + 440 + 239 = 26,772***			

*Confidence factors come from the 15% column in *Exhibit 8.9*.
**See *Exhibit 8.12* and the following discussion for the calculation of this value.

Exhibit 8.12
Illustration of Calculating the Incremental Allowance for Sampling Risk

Projected Misstatement	Incremental Changes in Confidence Factor (Step 2)	Projected Misstatement × Factor (Step 3)
330 +	3.89 − 2.31 = 1.58	521 +
110	5.33 − 3.89 = 1.44	158
440 **(Step 1)**		679 **(Step 4)**
Incremental allowance for sampling risk:		***679 − 400 = 239 (Step 5)***

Third, multiply the projected misstatements by the incremental change in the confidence.

Fourth, sum these values.

Fifth, subtract the total projected misstatement from the total value of projected misstatement multiplied by the incremental change in confidence factor.

Adding all four components together (see *Exhibit 8.11*), we see that the total estimated misstatement equals $26,772. The statistical conclusion is that the auditor is 90% confident that this population is not overstated by more than $26,772. Because the total estimated misstatement is less than the tolerable misstatement ($40,000), the auditor can conclude that, at the desired level of risk of incorrect acceptance, the population does not contain a material amount of overstatement. If the total estimated misstatement had exceeded the tolerable misstatement, additional audit analysis would have been required (see Unacceptable Sample Results, earlier in this section). In addition to evaluating the quantitative amounts of monetary misstatements, the auditor should consider the qualitative aspects of these misstatements.

Understatements in the Sample The preceding example assumes that only overstatements were found in the audit sample. However, the auditor may encounter situations in which the account balance may be understated. For example, in addition to the two overstatement misstatements, the auditor might discover that an accounts receivable balance may be understated because the client did not include a freight charge on the invoice. Assume, for example, that an account balance of $500 had omitted a $50 freight charge, yielding a 10% understatement tainting.

When an understatement is encountered, the auditor has two possible courses of action. First, the understatement can be ignored for purposes of this sample valuation and if there are other audit tests for understatements, this understatement can be included as part of other tests. Alternatively, the auditor can perform a separate analysis specifically for understatements. Although the auditor may use this evaluation approach when there are both over and understatements, the auditor should use caution in drawing any definitive conclusions regarding the amount of understatement in the account. MUS is not designed to test for the understatement of a population. If the auditor has concerns about the understatement of an account, an alternative approach, such as classical variables approach, may be more appropriate.

Check Your Basic Knowledge

8-33 The projected misstatement for items in the upper stratum is calculated as the sampling interval multiplied by the tainting percentage.   (T/F)

8-34 Projected errors for items in the top stratum equal basic precision multiplied by a confidence factor.   (T/F)

8-35 Which of the following statements is <u>false</u> with respect to basic precision?

    a. Basic precision represents the increase in the total estimated misstatement caused by the statistical properties of misstatements detected in the lower stratum.

    b. Basic precision is the amount of uncertainty associated with testing only a part of the population (sampling risk).

    c. Basic precision is the amount of error you are confident of not exceeding if no errors are detected in the sample.

    d. Basic precision is calculated as the sampling interval multiplied by a confidence factor.

8-36 In a MUS sample, the total estimated misstatement calculation includes which of the following amounts?

    a. The factual misstatement in the top-stratum.

    b. Basic precision.

    c. The projected misstatement in the lower stratum.

    d. An incremental allowance for sampling risk in the lower stratum.

    e. All of the above.

LO 7

Describe how to use data analytics tools to obtain and evaluate client data.

Using Data Analytics Tools to Obtain and Evaluate Evidence

Today, auditors use many data analytics tools, and you can expect this trend to increase during your time in the profession. We note that any one particular data analytics tool is not necessarily superior to others, and these tools are evolving rapidly. The implication is that it is not necessarily a specific tool that is critical for students to learn; rather, it is an understanding of the existence, application, and flexible use of such tools that matters in terms of achieving audit quality and efficiency.

Defining Data Analytics and Associated Terms

Data analytics is a broad construct referring to both qualitative and quantitative analysis tools that enable a decision maker to extract data, categorize it, identify patterns within it, and use it to enhance efficiency and effectiveness in decision making. Users of data analytics are increasingly using **big data**, which includes extremely large and complex datasets that users can analyze to reveal patterns and associations. Big data is often so large that users cannot efficiently analyze it using tools such as Excel because the data overloads the tool. Software companies are aggressively developing and marketing **business intelligence platforms** that enable organizations to use data analytics and big data by providing online analytical processing, information transformation (e.g., dashboards that display key performance indicators), and data management and security.

A **key performance indicator (KPI)** is an individual unit in an overall performance measurement system that organizations use. Organizations define success in achieving performance goals relating to business strategy. Organizations must develop and employ appropriate KPIs to effectively use them. KPIs will differ based upon the area in the organization that deploys them. For example, KPIs relating to implementing the sales strategy will differ from those relating to supply chain management. Managers often use KPIs in performance enhancement initiatives.

An organization's KPIs are relevant to auditors because they can evaluate them in data analytics as they engage in more general analytical procedures; KPIs serve as a reasonable benchmark against which the auditor can compare expected to actual results. Further, auditors might construct their own KPIs about the client. In other words, auditors are not limited to evaluating a given client's KPIs; they can go beyond them to make more sophisticated, predictive KPIs and then compare them against the actual performance assertions that management makes. One way that auditors who specialize in a particular industry accomplish this is by transferring their knowledge about KPIs for one client to KPIs for another client in the same industry; differences might yield interesting inferences.

Auditors are increasing their use of **data mining**, which is the process of sorting through large data sets to identify patterns, measure and predict trends, and establish relationships to solve problems through data analytics. As we note in *Exhibit 8.13*, the processes involved in data mining include data capture and cleaning, data exploration, data modeling, and deploying models.

Data capture involves activities that users complete to retrieve data, for example, bar coding. **Data cleaning** includes activities that users complete to correct or remove erroneous data, for example, contradictory data, input keying mistakes, duplicate data, missing information, and inappropriate changes to the data.

Data exploration involves gaining an understanding of the data by using techniques such as path analysis, classification, and visualization. **Path analysis** involves looking for instances in which one construct or measure predicts one that follows another. **Classification analyses** include investigating new patterns in

Why It Matters **Common KPIs and Practical Examples in Revenue Cycle Accounts**

This feature provides examples of KPIs that client organizations may use, auditors may assess, or that auditors may develop independently to assess management's assertions.

The following are common categorical indicators of KPIs:

- Quantitative (numbers-based)
- Qualitative (visual or narrative
- Leading (predictive)
- Lagging (backward looking or after the fact)
- Input-based (measures of resources that the organization uses)
- Process-based (measures of efficiency or productivity)
- Output-based (measures of organizational outcomes)
- Directional (measures that reveal whether the organization is moving toward its strategic goals)

- Financial (measures that relate to the ongoing and future financial viability of the organization

The following are KPIs that might be applicable to revenue cycle activities in an organization:

- Number of new customers
- Credit history profile of new customers
- Demographics of new, continuing, and past customers
- Reasons for customer attrition
- Revenue by segments or geographic regions
- Accounts receivable balances and trends over time
- Bad debt expenses and trends over time
- Credit term policies and changes therein
- Profitability and trends over time

Exhibit 8.13
The Phases of Data Mining

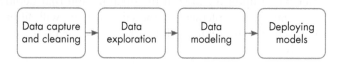

data that might change the way that the organization organizes and uses its data. **Visualization** includes the process of understanding the significance of and patterns in data by placing it in a visual context. By using visualization, users can detect patterns, trends, and inter-relationships that might otherwise remain undetected. Today's data visualization tools go far beyond typical charts and graphs that software such as Excel produces. The visualizations also include interactive capabilities that enable users to drill down further into interesting features of the data that they observe.

What Do You Think? **For Classroom Discussion**

There exists a famous quote by Professor John W. Tukey in his 1977 book *Exploratory Data Analysis*. The quote reads:

The greatest value of a picture is when it forces us to notice what we never expected to see.

What does this quote mean to you in the context of data analytics in auditing? How might you use visualization to add value to your audit clients?

Other Terms Relating to Data Analytics

This feature highlights various terms that you might encounter when using data analytics tools during an audit.

Data architecture includes organizational procedures that articulate how users collect, store, organize, and use data.

A **data bank** is a repository for data that enables users to categorize and store any type of data.

A **data center** is an organization that manages hardware, software, air conditioning, backup systems, communication, and security equipment for multiple organizations; data centers allow organizations to store data "off-site" to prevent misuse, manipulation, or destruction.

A **data dictionary** helps users understand the structure and content of a database, including the name of the data, its description, relationships among various related data, and access rights.

A **data driven attack** is electronic in nature and involves the perpetrator embedding seemingly valid data that enables malicious computer codes to exploit weaknesses in the computer system.

Data science is an inter-disciplinary field about scientific methods, processes, and information systems that aims to help users gain insights from complex, and often unstructured data.

The Powerful Images that Tableau.com Produces

This feature provides a link introducing you to Tableau, and provides illustrations to reveal the powerful images that Tableau produces; think about these images in the context of the quote we contemplated previously: "The greatest value of a picture is when it forces us to novice what we never expected to see."

We recommend that you watch the following video, which introduces you to one data analytics tool, Tableau:

https://www.tableau.com/#hero-video

The image that we reproduce below is taken from Tableau's training video using its Global Superstore database. Notice that the image helps you understand sales by market, country, and geographic region. If you go to the mapping training video at the following link you can learn how to use the various mapping functionalities of Tableau:

https://www.tableau.com/learn/tutorials/on-demand/maps-tableau

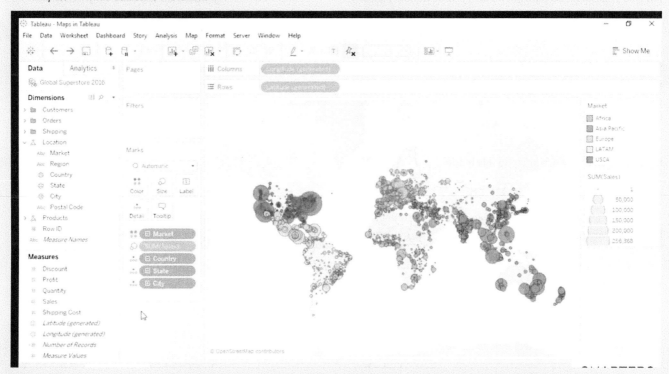

Source: Tableau.com

What Do You Think?   For Classroom Discussion

To discover the amazing insights that you can gain by using data visualization, see an early TED talk video on youtube.com. The video relates to the relationship between political change and public health. While the topical content of the video is not related to auditing, it provides insight about just how powerful a storyteller can be when using dynamic data visualization tools. To watch this well-known video, access this link:

https://www.youtube.com/watch?v5hVimVzgtD6w

What did you learn by watching the video? How might you be able to educate your client about perspectives on their financial statements and business risks using a data visualization tool?

Data modeling is a process by which data scientists define and analyze data requirements that they need to support the business processes through data-producing information systems within organizations. Data modeling involves documenting a complex software system in a visual diagram, using text and symbols to express the logical underpinnings of how the data flow through the system.

Why It Matters   The Power of Data from Social Media

This feature provides a link to a humorously titled consumer-based website designed as an outlet for disgruntled Ford Motor Company customers to complain; it also illustrates how an auditor might use this type of social media data in estimating Ford's warranty liability assertions.

Imagine that you are an auditor for a client who sells a retail product that includes a warranty, for example, Ford Motor Company. You are attempting to evaluate management's assertion that the accrued warranty liability is materially correct. Data, coupled with analytics, can improve the auditor's predictive capabilities. By evaluating social media data about the client, for example,

customer complaints, the auditor can more skeptically evaluate management's assertions about the valuation of its accrued warranty liability.

For an interesting read, visit the following website where consumers of Ford Motor Company products complain about the vehicles that they have purchased:

https://ford.pissedconsumer.com/

Here is an example that highlights certain types of defects for a particular model of vehicle; the auditor could use patterns in these customer social media posts to validate or challenge management's assertions.

Ford - Very poor service and cheaply made

July 20

0 comments

Bought a 2015 ford Explorer within a year the door panel on the passenger side started buckling, they replaced that, but 3 months later the drivers side did the same.Of course now it's out of warranty and they want over 300 dollars to replace and the door panels are on back order.

The service rep said they are having a problem with the panels. Also took it in for noise coming from the dash when going 50mph or higher the dealer said it was coming from the glove department, what a joke. 2 months later the trim molding on the windshield broke off. Air was getting underneath and it finally snapped.

over 400 dollars to fix and not covered under warranty.Never will buy a Ford product again.

Review about: 2015 Ford Explorer Car.

Reason of review: Damaged or defective.

Deploying models includes integrating the data and models to solve problems or make decisions. For example, the data modeling might produce a model that decision makers use to predict sales volume and profitability for the organization's portfolio of products. Then, users can also employ a model to predict and track bad debt expense by various categories.

Using Data Analytics Tools in the Audit

Auditors can use data analytics tools to assist in testing internal controls and virtually every assertion related to financial statement account balances—as well as supporting testing of assertions through other means, such as selecting samples to send confirmations on accounts receivable balances.

Analyze a File

Before performing tests of details, the auditor often wants to gain an understanding of the composition of items making up a population. For example, the auditor might want a graphical analysis of the dollar amounts of individual account balances, such as those that are above or below a certain dollar amount. Alternatively, the auditor might want to develop a graph of the account balance by deciles. In many cases, the auditor wants to know some combination, such as the number of items past due profiled by dollar amount.

Using Data Analytics Tools to Test Financial Account Assertions—Revenue Cycle Accounts

Why It Matters

This feature illustrates the breadth of data analytics applications that the auditor can use; really, auditors are only limited by their own creativity now to design unique and powerful tests using advanced data analytics tools.

(illustrative examples—not a comprehensive listing)

Assertion	Examples of Using Data Analytics Tools
Existence/occurrence	Compare sales invoices with shipping documents. Compare sales invoices with sales contracts. Analyze data around year-end to ensure that sales are recorded in the correct period.
Completeness	Analyze data to assess the proper operation of sales cutoff tests around year-end. Compare shipping documents with invoices to determine if billed in the proper period.
Rights or obligations	Review sales contracts and compare them to sales revenue to test for any exceptions.
Valuation	Build an estimation model of uncollectible accounts based on historical data. Make projections of sales by region or product type and compare to recorded amounts. Age accounts receivable. Foot the file. Create a file of current-year write-offs to compare with previous years.
Presentation and disclosure	Use data visualization tools to evaluate whether disclosures about sales and profitability by region, product type, and industry segment are consistent with those asserted by management.

What Do You Think? For Classroom Discussion

Organizations face risks relating to cybersecurity attacks. And they take great efforts to prevent such attacks. The following are organizational risks associated with cybersecurity attacks:

- Damage to the organization's reputation
- A loss of intellectual property
- A disruption of the organization's operations as remediation efforts commence
- Harm to the organization's customers
- Potential litigation costs

Organizational stakeholders demand information about how managers are addressing these risks. For example, the board of directors inquire about the cybersecurity risk management program that managers are charged with implementing. Analysts and investors want to know about how the organization perceives its vulnerability to cybersecurity attacks and the nature and extent of any potential adverse effect on the organization's value and accompanying stock price.

As an auditor, you will need to assess the risk associated with cybersecurity attacks and the implications for the financial statements. You will need to consider how managers are implementing controls to prevent these attacks.

Sophisticated and well-controlled companies know that they face cybersecurity attacks; other companies may choose to 'look the other way' and hope that they will not face such attacks.

Do you agree with the prominent sentiment that "It's Not If, But When" in terms of cybersecurity attacks? How do organizational controls relate to the answer to this question? What types of procedures might auditors use to assess the risk of a cybersecurity attack at their client? How might these risks affect the financial statements?

Select Transactions Based on Logical Identifiers

Auditors often need to review transactions or the details that make up account balances and may be interested in those that meet specific criteria. For example, the auditor may want to confirm all customer balances above a specific dollar limit and all those that are past due by a specific period of time. Data analytics tools can easily accomplish these types of tasks, even including visual representations of items near important thresholds and any outliers.

Analyze Overall File Validity

Data analytics tools contain edit controls to detect and prevent transactions from being erroneously recorded. Although the auditor can test the correct functioning of these controls by other means, audit software can assist in evaluating the effectiveness of the controls by reading the computer file and comparing individual items with control parameters to determine whether edit controls were overridden. For example, assume the auditor has tested a control procedure that limits credit to individual customers in accordance with the credit department's rating of the customer. The credit department rates each customer on a 1-to-5 scale, with a 5 representing the least credit risk. A rating of 1 might indicate that shipments can be made only on a prepayment basis, and a rating of 2 might indicate that the total credit cannot exceed $5,000. The auditor data analytics tools to compare customers' account balances with the maximum specified by the credit policy and generates a printout of each account balance that exceeds the specified credit limit.

Perform Numerical Analyses

One of the more interesting features of data analytics tools is the ability of these tools to perform complex statistical analyses. A mathematician named Benford studied the nature of numerical patterns and observed that the patterns of numbers across many different applications are consistent. For example, if sales invoices or payroll checks have five-digit numbers, Benford's Law would predict the first digit to be the number 1 about 30% of the time. His analysis also predicts the expected frequency of specific numbers occurring as the second number, and so forth, in a five-digit number. The predictive ability of Benford's Law is extremely high.

Interestingly, most people committing fraud go to great lengths in perpetrating and covering up the fraud. However, they usually have to assign numbers to documents and, not surprisingly, those numbers often do not follow the patterns

Blockchain: A Revolution in Auditing

Why It Matters

This feature introduces you to a very quickly evolving financial phenomenon with respect to digital currency and the online verification of transactions among multiple parties using a technology known as blockchain.

What is blockchain? It is a digital accounting ledger of transactions that can be programmed to record financial transactions among multiple parties. We traditionally think of recording transactions using double-entry accounting. So, each transaction is recorded twice, for example, a debit to Cash and a credit to Revenue. Blockchain extends this to triple-entry accounting, whereby the debit and credit still occur, but they are accompanied by a cryptographic signature verifying that the transaction did, indeed, occur at the recorded amount.

The figure below visually aids in understanding the various concepts involved in blockchain and digital currency.

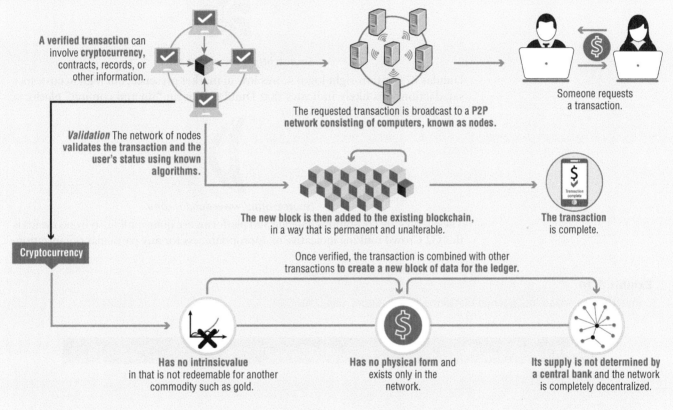

A verified transaction can involve **cryptocurrency**, contracts, records, or other information.

Validation The network of nodes validates the transaction and the user's status using known algorithms.

The requested transaction is broadcast to a **P2P** network consisting of computers, known as nodes.

Someone requests a transaction.

The new block is then added to the existing blockchain, in a way that is permanent and unalterable.

The transaction is complete.

Cryptocurrency

Once verified, the transaction is combined with other transactions **to create a new block of data for the ledger.**

Has no intrinsicvalue in that is not redeemable for another commodity such as gold.

Has no physical form and exists only in the network.

Its supply is not determined by a central bank and the network is completely decentralized.

See *https://blockgeeks.com/guides/what-is-blockchain-technology/*

Why might blockchain lead to a revolution in auditing? Because auditors currently perform a verification role; now that role in evaluating assertions about a particular transaction can occur electronically through the blockchain and its triple-entry accounting functionality.

of numbers naturally occurring in practice. It is not surprising, because the person who is perpetrating the fraud makes up the numbers, and it is extremely difficult to anticipate the occurrence of every digit in a five-, eight-, or even ten-digit number. Data analytics tools can help auditors find such non-routine patterns.

Business Intelligence Platforms

The powerful computer platforms that decision makers rely on to conduct data analytics are known as **business intelligence (BI) platforms**. Auditors will be using these platforms more and more as the technology advances. BI platforms enable organizations to bring together data analytics tools across three categories: (1) online analytical processing, (2) information delivery, e.g., dashboards, and (3) platform integration that allows for the management of big data.

Exhibit 8.14 provides an example of various business intelligence platforms that currently exist . . . but these platforms are very rapidly emerging and changing, so this is just a snapshot. G2 Crowd Enterprise Grid[SM] for Business Intelligence Platforms provides these rankings, and they are helpful in identifying useful business intelligence platforms based upon an organization's specific needs. For example, Tableau Desktop (top-right logo) scores high in terms of market presence and customer satisfaction, yielding a "Leaders" G2 Score.

Source: *https://www.tableau.com/*

In contrast, Birst (bottom-left logo) scores low in satisfaction and market presence, yielding a "Niche" G2 Score.

Source: *https://www.birst.com/*

Dundas BI (bottom-right logo) scores low in market presence, but high in customer satisfaction; this likely indicates that Dundas BI is an "up and coming" platform that might become more popular.

Source: *http://www.dundas.com/*

These scores are constantly changing and platforms are quite nimble, so by no means is this G2 Crowd ranking indicative of appropriateness for any particular organization.

Exhibit 8.14

Comparing Business Intelligence Platforms that Auditors Can Use

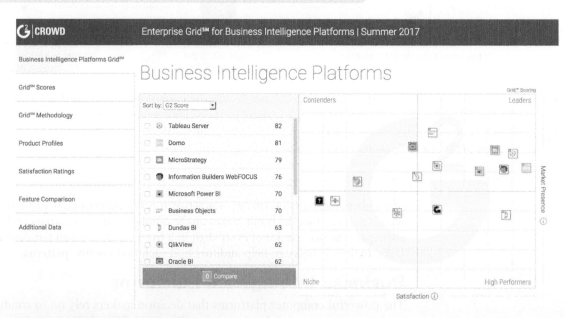

Source: Business Intelligence Platforms

For further details about these rankings, see *https://www.g2crowd.com/grid_report/documents/business-intelligence-platforms-summer-2016-report?gated_consumer_a9831a72-fbc5-4b5c-ad22-89d5c0e5b865&utm_campaign_gate-743050*

It's Your Turn!

Go to the website containing the BI platforms in *Exhibit 8.14*. Evaluate the information that you learn about each of the platforms. For each of the four quadrants of *Exhibit 8.14* (i.e., contenders, leaders, niche, and high performers) identify which of the platforms you would choose. Explain your rationale.

8-37 Benford's Law helps predict frequency patterns of deviations of controls. (T/F)

8-38 Data analytics is a broad construct referring to both qualitative and quantitative analysis tools that enable a decision maker to extract data, categorize it, identify patterns within it, and use it to enhance efficiency and effectiveness in decision making. (T/F)

8-39 The acronym KPI relates to which of the following phrases?
a. Key Profitability Indicator
b. Key Performance Indicator
c. Known Performance Increment
d. Known Profitability Increment

8-40 To test the existence assertion for sales, which of the following data analytics tools might you use?
a. Compare sales invoices with shipping documents.
b. Compare sales invoices with sales contracts.
c. Analyze data around year-end to ensure that sales are recorded in the correct period.
d. Two of the above (a-c).
e. All of the above (a-c).

LO 8

Apply the frameworks for professional decision making and ethical decision making for decisions made when conducting an audit.

Applying Decision-Making Frameworks

The following *End of Chapter* materials provide you an opportunity to apply the frameworks for professional decision making and ethical decision making for decisions made when conducting an audit: *8-33*.

- Audit sampling includes the application of an audit procedure to less than 100% of the items within an account balance or class of transactions for the purpose of evaluating some characteristic of the balance or class. Risks associated with sampling include concluding that:
  o controls are effective when they actually are not effective (risk of incorrect acceptance of internal control reliability)
  o controls are ineffective when they are actually effective (risk of incorrect rejection of internal control reliability)
  o an account balance is correct when it is actually not correct (risk of incorrect acceptance of book value); and
  o an account balance is incorrect when it is actually correct (risk of incorrect rejection of book value). (LO 1, 2)

- Data analytics tools include qualitative and quantitative techniques and processes that auditors use to enhance their productivity and effectiveness. Data analytics tools are software programs that facilitate testing 100% of a population when appropriate and help focus the auditor's attention on specific risk areas or transactions, often involving sophisticated data visualization tools. Auditors use data analytics tools to import a client's data; then the auditor can employ the software in various ways. For example, the auditor can scan the data, sort and summarize it, stratify it, and transform it into visual representations. Auditors can also use data analytics tools to identify duplicate items (e.g., duplicate invoices), gaps in data (e.g., gap in a check sequence), and outliers in a population (e.g., invoices that exceed two times the average for a particular customer) (LO 1)

- Auditors have available to them: (1) attributes sampling, i.e., answering the question, "Are controls effective or not?" and (2) monetary unit sampling, i.e., answering the question, "Is the balance of a particular account accurate?" Depending on the method, the auditor will select an appropriate number of controls to test and account balances to evaluate. The auditor will also use that evaluation to arrive at a conclusion as to errors in the overall population. (LO 3, 4, 5, 6)

- Data analytics is a broad construct referring to both qualitative and quantitative analysis tools that enable a decision maker to extract data, categorize it, identify patterns within it, and use it to enhance efficiency and effectiveness in decision making. Users of data analytics are increasingly using big data, which includes extremely large and complex datasets that users can analyze to reveal patterns and associations; big data is often so large that users cannot efficiently analyze it using tools such as Excel because the data overloads the system. To accomplish these tasks, software companies are aggressively developing and marketing business intelligence platforms that enable organizations use data analytics and big data by providing online analytical processing, information transformation (e.g., dashboards that display key performance indicators), and data management and security. (LO 7)

Significant Terms

Attribute   A characteristic of the population of interest to the auditor.

Attributes sampling   A statistical sampling method used to estimate the rate of control procedure failures based on selecting one sample and performing the appropriate audit procedure.

Audit sampling   The application of an audit procedure to less than 100% of the items within an account balance or class of transactions for the purpose of evaluating some characteristic of the balance or class.

Basic precision   The amount of uncertainty associated with testing only a part of the population (sampling risk). Basic precision is calculated as the sampling interval multiplied by a confidence factor.

Big data   A term that describes extremely large and complex datasets that users can analyze to reveal patterns and associations; big data is often so large that users cannot efficiently analyze it using tools such as Excel because the data overloads the system.

Block sampling   A sampling technique that involves selecting a sample that consists of contiguous population items, such as selecting transactions by day or week.

Business intelligence platforms   Electronic computer programs software companies are developing and marketing that enable organizations use data analytics and big data by providing online analytical processing, information transformation (e.g., dashboards that display key performance indicators), and data management and security.

Classification analyses   A process that includes investigating new patterns in data that might change the way that the organization organizes and uses its data.

Data analytics A broad construct referring to both qualitative and quantitative analysis tools that enable a decision maker to extract data, categorize it, identify patterns within it, and use it to enhance efficiency and effectiveness in decision making.

Data analytics tools Qualitative and quantitative techniques and processes that auditors use to enhance their productivity and effectiveness; auditors extract, categorize, identify and analyze patterns or trends in the data; data analytics tools vary according to organizational requirements.

Data architecture Organizational procedures that articulate how users collect, store, organize, and use data.

Data bank A repository for data that enables users to categorize and store any type of data.

Data capture Activities that users complete to retrieve data, e.g., bar coding.

Data center An organization that manages hardware, software, air conditioning, backup systems, and communication and security equipment for multiple organizations; data centers allow organizations to store data "off-site" to prevent misuse, manipulation, or destruction.

Data cleaning Activities that users complete to correct or remove erroneous data, e.g., contradictory data, input keying mistakes, duplicate data, missing information, and inappropriate changes to the data.

Data dictionary Helps users understand the structure and content of a database, including the name of the data, its description, relationships among various related data, and access rights.

Data driven attack An electronic exploitation that involves the perpetrator embedding seemingly valid data that enables malicious computer codes to exploit weaknesses in the computer system.

Data exploration Gaining an understanding of the data by using techniques such as path analysis, classification, and visualization.

Data mining The process of sorting through large data sets to identify patterns, measure and predict trends, and establish relationships to solve problems through data analytics. When conducting data mining, users create and analyze data.

Data modeling A process by which data scientists define and analyze data requirements that they need to support the business processes through data-producing information systems within organizations.

Data science An inter-disciplinary field about scientific methods, processes, and information systems that aims to help users gain insights from complex, and often unstructured data.

Deploying models Integrating data and models to solve problems or make decisions in an organization.

Expected failure rate See *expected population deviation rate*.

Expected misstatement The level of misstatement that the auditor expects to detect, and it is based on projected misstatements in prior-year audits, results of other substantive tests, professional judgment, and knowledge of changes in personnel and the accounting system.

Expected population deviation rate An anticipation of the deviation rate in the entire population. Also referred to as the *expected failure rate*.

Factual misstatements Misstatements that have been specifically identified and about which there is no doubt. Also referred to as *known misstatements*.

Haphazard sampling A nonstatistical sample selection method that attempts to approximate a random selection by selecting sampling units without any conscious bias, or special reason for including or omitting certain items from the sample.

Incremental allowance for sampling risk An increase in the total estimated misstatement caused by the statistical properties of misstatements detected in the lower stratum.

Key performance indicator (KPI) An individual unit in an overall performance measurement system; KPIs will differ based upon the area in the organization that deploys them.

Known misstatements See *factual misstatements.*

Likely misstatement See *projected misstatement.*

Logical unit The balance or transaction that includes the selected dollar in a monetary unit sample.

Lower stratum Items that are not in the top stratum.

Misstatement An error, either intentional or unintentional, that exists in a transaction or financial statement account balance. For substantive sampling purposes, a misstatement involves differences between recorded values and audited values.

Monetary unit sampling (MUS) A sampling method based on attributes estimation sampling but involving dollar misstatements rather than failure rates. MUS is often referred to as *probability proportional to size (PPS) sampling.*

Most likely misstatement See *projected misstatement.*

Nonsampling risk The risk that the auditor reaches an erroneous conclusion for any reason not related to sampling risk.

Nonstatistical sampling The application of auditor judgment and experience in a sample application to assist the auditor in determining an appropriate sample size and in evaluating the sample results.

Path analysis A process that involves looking for instances in which one construct or measure predicts one that follows another.

Population A group of transactions or the items that make up an account balance for which the auditor wants to estimate some characteristic, such as the effectiveness of a control procedure or estimate the extent of misstatement in an account.

Probability proportional to size (PPS) sampling A sampling selection method in which each item in the population has a probability of being included in the sample proportionate to the dollar value of the item. Monetary unit sampling uses this method to select a sample and is considered a subset of PPS sampling.

Projected misstatement The best estimate of the actual amount of dollar misstatements in the population based on projecting the sample results to the population. The projected misstatement is calculated as the sampling interval multiplied by the tainting percentage. Also see likely misstatement or most likely misstatement.

Risk of assessing control risk too high See *risk of incorrect rejection of internal control reliability.*

Risk of assessing control risk too low See *risk of incorrect acceptance of internal control reliability.*

Risk of incorrect acceptance of internal control reliability The risk that the auditor will conclude that the state of internal controls is effective when internal controls are actually not effective (also referred to as the *risk of assessing control risk too low*).

Risk of incorrect acceptance of book value The risk that the auditor will conclude that the account balance contains a material misstatement when the account balance actually does not contain a material misstatement.

Risk of incorrect rejection of internal control reliability The risk that the auditor will conclude that the state of internal controls is not effective when internal controls are actually effective (also referred to as the *risk of assessing control risk too high*).

Risk of incorrect rejection of book value   The risk that the auditor will conclude that the account balance contains a material misstatement when the account balance actually does not contain a material misstatement.

Risk of overreliance   See *risk of incorrect acceptance of internal control reliability*.

Risk of underreliance   See *risk of incorrect rejection of internal control reliability*.

Sampling interval   Calculated by dividing the population size by the desired sample size.

Sampling risk   The risk that the auditor's conclusion based on a sample might be different from the conclusion he or she would reach if the test were applied in the same way to the entire population.

Sampling units   The individual items to be tested.

Selection bias   Results in knowingly or unknowingly creating unrepresentative samples.

Simple random sampling   Selecting a random sample by matching random numbers generated by a computer or selected from a random-number table with, for example, document numbers such as an invoice or a purchase order.

Statistical sampling   The application of probability theory and statistical inference, along with auditor judgment and experience, in a sample application to assist the auditor in determining an appropriate sample size and in evaluating the sample results.

Stratification   Dividing the population into two or more subgroups.

Systematic random sampling   This sampling technique involves systematic sampling in which the first item is selected randomly from the interval.

Systematic sampling   This sampling technique involves dividing the number of physical units in the population by the sample size to determine a uniform interval; a random starting point is selected in the first interval and one item is selected throughout the population at each of the uniform intervals after the starting point.

Tainting percentage   The percentage of misstatement present in a logical unit, such as the sample item's book value. The tainting percentage equals the amount of misstatement in the item divided by the item's recorded amount.

Tolerable failure rate   See *tolerable rate of deviation*.

Tolerable misstatement   A monetary amount set by the auditor in respect of which the auditor seeks to obtain an appropriate level of assurance that the monetary amount set by the auditor is not exceeded by the actual misstatement in the population. In practical terms, a tolerable misstatement is the maximum amount of misstatement the auditor can accept in the population without requiring an audit adjustment or a qualified audit opinion.

Tolerable rate of deviation   A rate of deviation set by the auditor in respect of which the auditor seeks to obtain an appropriate level of assurance that the rate of deviation set by the auditor is not exceeded by the actual rate of deviation in the population. Also referred to as the *tolerable failure rate*.

Top stratum   Population items whose book values exceed the sampling interval and are therefore all included in the sample. The top stratum consists of all account balances exceeding a specific dollar amount.

Visualization   A process that includes the process of understanding the significance of and patterns in data by placing it in a visual context.

Prompts for Critical Thinking

Prompt for Critical Thinking #1

With respect to answering this question, the authors went back to *Chapter 3* to get a listing of control activities by COSO category. Answers to the prompt with respect to COSO Principle 10, "the organization selects and develops control activities," yields the following possible attributes (note that they are all yes/no, i.e., dichotomous questions).

Controls over adjusting, closing, and any unusual entries are in place:

- There exists documented support for all entries. __Yes __No
- The audit committee is made aware of any material adjustments for which management and the auditor disagree. __Yes __No
- There exists a reference to underlying supporting data with a well-developed transaction trail. __Yes __No
- There exists a review by the CFO or controller for all unusual entries. __Y __N

Prompt for Critical Thinking #2

Scenario 1. Panel A because you are taking less of a chance of not detecting a control weakness.

Scenario 2. 93

Scenario 3. 38

Scenario 4. Scenario 2, because you are accepting less risk and are collecting more evidence upon which to base your evaluation about the efficacy of internal controls.

Prompt for Critical Thinking #3

1. Throwing away "bad" confirmations in which the auditor detects an error, particularly a material error, heightens audit risk by understating the estimated total misstatement in the account; the audit team is therefore more likely to issue an unqualified opinion on materially misstated financial statements.

2. The staff auditor's mistake lies in acquiescing to the senior's inappropriate directive.

3. This situation puts the staff auditor in a really tough spot in which it seems he or she cannot win with the senior. Students will vary in ways that the staff auditor might proceed.

Prompt for Critical Thinking #4

Because of the random nature of the number selection process, the numbers in the text will differ by student. The selection amounts will usually not be particularly different from the example in the textbook because of the top-stratum item selections.

Prompt for Critical Thinking #5

Answers will vary by student; discussing the various rationales in class provides for a very interesting discussion.

Review Questions and Short Cases

8-1 **LO 1** Describe how auditors use sampling and data analytics tools for obtaining and evaluating audit evidence.

8-2 **LO 1** Refer to *Exhibit 8.1*. Describe at least one auditing procedure that might be applicable to each financial statement assertion for sampling and data analytics tools.

8-3 **LO 2** Define the terms *sampling units* and *population*, and describe how these two concepts relate to each other.

8-4 **LO 2** What four questions must the auditor answer when sampling?

8-5 **LO 2** Distinguish between the terms *sampling risk* and *nonsampling risk*.

8-6 **LO 2** Refer to *Exhibit 8.2* and *Exhibit 8.3*.

a. Define the following risks:
   - Risk of incorrect acceptance of internal control reliability
   - Risk of incorrect rejection of internal control reliability
   - Risk of incorrect acceptance of book value
   - Risk of incorrect rejection of book value
b. Explain which of these risks should concern the auditor the most.

8-7 **LO 3** Refer to *Exhibit 8.4* and compare and contrast statistical sampling and nonstatistical sampling on the following dimensions: sample size determination, sample selection, evaluation, costs, and benefits.

8-8 **LO 4** Define the terms *attributes sampling* and *attribute*. Give an example of an attribute of interest to an auditor. Give an example of a control failure.

8-9 **LO 4** List the factors that the auditor should address when defining the population for attributes sampling.

8-10 **LO 4** Define the term *tolerable rate of deviation* in formal terms (in other words, in the manner in which the AICPA's 2012 *Audit Sampling* formally defines it) and in more practical terms.

8-11 **LO 4** Practice calculating the sample size and the number of expected errors in attributes sampling by using the tables in *Exhibit 8.5* and the following combinations of inputs:

	Risk of Overreliance	Tolerable Rate of Deviation	Expected Population Deviation Rate	Sample Size (with Expected Errors in Parentheses)
a.	5%	2%	1%	
b.	5%	6%	5%	
c.	5%	10%	8%	
d.	10%	2%	1%	
e.	10%	6%	5%	
f.	10%	10%	8%	

8-12 **LO 4** Using the tables in *Exhibit 8.5*, explain at least one set of assumptions that the auditor would have to make to justify the following sample sizes:

	Risk of Overreliance	Tolerable Rate of Deviation	Expected Population Deviation Rate	Sample Size
a.				11
b.				14
c.				22
d.				29
e.				38
f.				52

g. Explain what these assumptions and associated sample sizes imply.

8-13 **LO 4** What is the effect of increasing each of the following on an attribute sample size?
a. Sampling risk (or risk of overreliance).
b. The tolerable rate of deviation.
c. The expected population deviation rate.
d. Population size.

8-14 **LO 4** Define the following terms: (a) *simple random sampling*, (b) *systematic sampling*, (c) *systematic random sampling*, (d) *haphazard sampling*, and (e) *block sampling*.

8-15 **LO 4** Practice evaluating the results of attributes sampling by using the tables in *Exhibit 8.6* and the following combinations of inputs. Assume the tolerable deviation rate is 12%. For each item labeled (a) through (f), state your interpretation of the result, including the appropriate conclusion about whether the control is operating effectively. For those situations when no deviations are detected in the sample, comment on why the upper limit of deviations is greater than zero.

	Risk of Overreliance	Sample Size	Number of Deviations	Upper Limit of Deviations
a.	5%	20	0	
b.	5%	75	5	
c.	5%	150	10	
d.	10%	20	0	
e.	10%	75	5	
f.	10%	150	10	

8-16 **LO 4** When evaluating an attributes sample, why is the focus on the upper limit of deviations in the sample? If the upper limit of deviation exceeds the tolerable deviation rate in attributes sampling, what alternative courses of action are available to the auditor?

8-17 **LO 4** Assume that you are using attributes sampling to test the controls over revenue recognition of the Packet Corporation, a public company. You will use the results as part of the evidence on which to base your opinion on internal controls and to determine what substantive auditing procedures you should performed on revenue and accounts receivable. You have decided to test the following controls and have set the risk of overreliance at 5%, the tolerable deviation rate at 5%, and the expected deviation rate at 1%. A sample size of 100 is used. (Note that this sample size is just rounded up from the sample size of 93 that would have been obtained from the appropriate table.) The results of your testing are as indicated here.

Control	Results
1. All sales over $10,000 must be approved by the sales manager by initialing the customer's order.	1. There were only twenty-five sales over $10,000 in the sample. So, the auditor randomly collects an additional seventy-five sales transactions that were over $10,000. All were approved by the sales manager.
2. Credit must be approved by the credit department prior to shipment and noted on the customer's order.	2. Three sales were recorded without evidence of credit approval. The sales manager said she had approved the sales. No customer order could be found for two of the other sampled items.
3. Sales are recorded only when a shipping document is forwarded to the billing department.	3. No shipping document could be found for three of the sampled items.
4. The date of recording the sale must correspond to the date on the shipping document.	4. Four sales were recorded prior to the date of shipment. Your follow-up indicates that a temporary employee worked for the last two months of the fiscal year and was unaware of this requirement.
5. All prices are obtained from the current price list that is periodically updated by the sales manager.	5. All prices agreed with the appropriate price list.
6. The shipping department is not to ship products without first receiving an approved customer's order.	6. No customer order could be found for two sample items as indicated in Step 2.
7. The billing department compares the quantity billed with the customer's order.	7. Four billed quantities were for more than the customer order. Three of these took place near year-end. In addition, there was no customer order for the two items indicated in Step 2.

a. Determine the upper limit of deviation for each of the controls.
b. What impact do these results have on the type of opinion to be given on the client's internal controls?
c. Indicate the potential misstatements that could result from the control deviations.
d. Determine what substantive audit procedures should be performed in response to each of the identified control deviations.

8-18 **LO 5** Define the following terms: (a) *misstatement*, (b) *factual misstatement*, (c) *projected misstatement*, (d) *tolerable misstatement*, and (e) *expected misstatement*.

8-19 **LO 5** What is the sampling unit when gathering evidence about misstatements in account balances and associated assertions? Provide examples of sampling units in the context of accounts receivable.

8-20 **LO 5** What is stratification? Distinguish between top-stratum items and lower-stratum items.

8-21 **LO 5** When using nonstatistical sampling to test an account balance, how does the auditor perform the following?

a. Determine the sample size.
b. Select the sample.
c. Evaluate the sample results.

8-22 **LO 5** The following information relates to a nonstatistical sample used for a price test of inventory:

	Population		Sample		
	Number	**Amount**	**Number**	**Amount**	**Misstatement**
>$30,000	20	$1,600,000	20	$1,600,000	$1,000
<$30,000	200	$1,500,000	20	$185,000	$600
Total	220	$3,100,000	40	$2,785,000	$1,600

a. What is the best estimate of the total misstatement?
b. Are these results acceptable, assuming tolerable misstatement is $25,000? Explain.
c. Assume that the results are not acceptable. What possible courses of action can the auditor take?

8-23 **LO 6** What are the strengths of MUS? Provide at least three examples in which MUS might be used.

8-24 **LO 6** What are the difficulties that the auditor may experience in using MUS?

8-25 **LO 6** The sample size in a MUS sample is a function of what three factors?

8-26 **LO 6** Practice calculating the sample size in a MUS sample using *Exhibit 8.7*, with the following combinations of inputs.

	Risk of Incorrect Acceptance	**Ratio of Expected to Tolerable Misstatement**	**Ratio of Tolerable Misstatement to Population (%)**	**Sample Size**
a.	5%	0.20	50%	
b.	10%	0.20	30%	
c.	15%	0.30	8%	
d.	20%	0.30	5%	
e.	25%	0.40	4%	
f.	30%	0.40	3%	
g.	35%	0.50	2%	
h.	50%	0.50	1%	

8-27 **LO 6** Calculate the sampling interval for cases (a) through (h) in *8-26*, assuming a population size of $8,500,000. Recall that *sampling interval = population size ÷ sample size*. Round the value of the interval down to the nearest $1,000 or $10,000 to ensure that the sample size is adequate and is easy for the auditor to select the sample.

8-28 **LO 6** Assume you are planning the confirmation of accounts receivable. There are 2,000 customer accounts with a total book value of $5,643,200. Tolerable misstatement is set at $200,000, and expected misstatement is $40,000. The risk of incorrect acceptance is 30%. The ratio of expected to tolerable misstatement is 20%, and the ratio of tolerable misstatement to the population is 3.5% (round down to 3% for use in *Exhibit 8.7*).

a. What is the sample size?
b. What is the sampling interval?
c. What is the largest value you can use for a random start?
d. Using the following list of the first fifteen items in your population, a random start of $25,000, and a rounded sample interval of $100,000, identify the items to be included in your sample.

Item	Book Value	Cumulative Book	Cumulative Book Plus Random Start	Included in Sample?	Selection Amount ($)
Random Start					
1	3,900				
2	26,000				
3	5,000				
4	130,000				
5	2,000				
6	260,000				
7	100				
8	25,000				
9	19,000				
10	10,000				
11	9,000				
12	2,500				
13	65,000				
14	110,000				
15	6,992				

e. What is the probability of selecting each of the following population items, assuming a $100,000 sampling interval?

Item	Book Value	Probability of Selection
1	3,900	
2	26,000	
4	130,000	
6	360,000	

f. Why might the final sample size include fewer logical units than the computed sample size?

8-29 **LO 6** Based on the information in *Problem 8-28*, assume that your sampling interval is $100,000.

a. What is your statistical conclusion if no misstatements are found in the sample? Is the account balance acceptable? Explain.

b. Calculate the total estimated misstatement assuming the following misstatements are found in the sample:

Misstatement Number	Book Value	Audit Value
1	$210,000	$208,000
2	9,000	8,910
3	15,000	14,250

c. Do these results indicate that the account balance, as stated, is acceptable? Explain.

d. If the results are not acceptable, what courses of action are available to the auditor?

8-30 **LO 6** Assume that you are auditing the inventory of Husky Manu-facturing Company for the year ended December 31, 2018, and you are using MUS. The book value is $8,124,998.66. The risk of incorrect acceptance is 10% (90% confidence level). The tolerable misstatement is $275,000, and expected misstatement is $80,000, so the ratio of expected misstatement to tolerable misstatement is 29%. The ratio of tolerable misstatement to the population book value is 4.3%.

a. Calculate the sample size and the sampling interval.
b. Calculate the total estimated misstatement assuming the following misstatements were found in the sample:

Book Value	Audit Value
$41,906.45	$36,906.45
$335,643.28	$333,643.28

c. What conclusion do you reach based upon your calculation?

8-31 **LO 6** Assume that the auditor is auditing accounts receivable for a long-time client. The auditor has assessed the risk of incorrect acceptance at 10%. The client's book value in accounts receivable is $8,425,000. Tolerable misstatement is $200,000, and expected misstatement is $40,000. Therefore, the ratio of expected to toler-able misstatement is 20%. The ratio of tolerable misstatement to the population book value is 2.4%.

a. Calculate the sample size and sampling interval.
b. Analyze each difference detected (1. through 5. below) during the audit to determine if it is a misstatement.
c. Calculate the total estimated misstatement assuming the misstate-ments detailed in the following table were found in the sample. Identify the top-stratum items, the lower-stratum items, and taint-ing percentages, where applicable. What conclusion do you reach based upon your calculation?
d. Discuss the audit implications, that is, whether the audit work supports book value or whether additional auditing procedures should be recommended, and, if so, describe the nature of the recommended auditing procedures.

	Book Value	Audited Value	Nature of Difference
1.	$25,000	$15,000	$10,000 was billed to Jason Company, but it should have been billed to Johnson Company. Subsequent follow-up work confirmed that it should be billed to Johnson, and Johnson acknowledged the $10,000 debt.
2.	$40,000	$20,000	Merchandise was returned before year-end, but credit was not recorded until the next period.
3.	$325,000	$250,000	Major dispute on cost overrun charges. Subsequent review supports customer position.
4.	$105,000	$100,000	Another dispute on cost overrun. Again customer position is correct.
5.	$122	$0	A credit memo was supposed to have been issued for defective merchandise, but was not.

8-32 **LO 6** What courses of action should the auditor consider pursuing when the results of the MUS sample are unacceptable, in other words, when the total estimated misstatement exceeds the tolerable misstatement?

8-33 **LO 6, 8** Respond to the ethical judgments required based on the following scenarios.

Scenario 1. Assume you have collected a sample using MUS and that you have evaluated that sample to calculate a total estimated misstatement of $213,500. Prior to sampling, you set tolerable misstatement at $215,000. What is the implication of the fact that estimated total misstatement is very close to the tolerable misstatement threshold? What does the closeness of these dollar amounts imply with regard to whether the accounts receivable amount requires downward adjustment? Using the ethical decision-making framework from *Chapter 1*, develop an appropriate course of action to take, assuming the following possibilities:

a. You think that the accounts receivable balance is fairly stated because the misstatement is below the tolerable misstatement amount, but you are not entirely convinced of the soundness of your judgment given how close the estimate is to the tolerable misstatement.

b. You collect a larger sample size. You send out ten more accounts receivable confirmations and find two more overstatements, totaling $88,000. Your senior tells you that the client has agreed to write down those two specific accounts receivable. He says that because of this agreement, you should disregard these overstatements for purposes of making a conclusion about the accounts receivable balance in total.

Scenario 2. Assume the same facts as in Scenario 1, but now assume that your senior tells you he has decided to increase the tolerable misstatement amount to $250,000. His rationale for this change is that the client is in good financial health and has relatively strong internal controls. What is the implication of the change in tolerable misstatement amount with regard to whether the accounts receivable amount requires downward adjustment? Using the ethical decision-making framework from *Chapter 1*, develop an appropriate course of action to address this situation.

Scenario 3. Assume that the pattern of errors that you have detected in the sample is the same as that was uncovered in *Problem 8-31*, in other words, five audit differences. Notice that for nearly all of those cases, the book value was greater than the audited value. What is management's incentive with regard to potential misreporting associated with accounts receivable (or other assets)? Assume that this pattern of overstatements has become routine on this engagement during the past several years. What does this trend potentially reveal about management? What are the ethical implications of this trend? What should you do?

8-34 **LO 7** Define the term *key performance indicator*. The text provides you with examples of KPIs applicable to revenue cycle activities. Extend that line of thinking and identify at least five possible KPIs relating to inventory accounts.

8-35 `LO 7` Define the term *data center*. Do you think that Arthur Andersen might still be in existence today if the firm had employed a secure data center, whereby employees of the Houston office of the Enron audit engagement could not have engaged in document shredding?

8-36 `LO 7` Explain the four phases of data mining.

8-37 `LO 7` Articulate organizational risks associated with cybersecurity attacks.

8-38 `LO 7` Explain the concepts of blockchain and triple-entry accounting.

Application Activities

NOTE: Completing *Application Activities* requires students to reference additional resources and materials.

8-39 `LO 7` Tableau is a powerful tool that has emerged and that is very useful in analyzing "big data" as you engage in data analytics. It is like Excel (i.e., rows and columns), but it is much more powerful and versatile. But that comes with a cost! While incredibly useful, you will have to make an investment in time and effort to master some of its many functionalities. Below are the videos that the authors found most useful in helping to guide you toward this powerful data analytics tool.

In this chapter and through this end-of-chapter problem, you will learn about the basics of Tableau. Then in subsequent chapters that address the various transaction cycles, you will have the opportunity to practice your Tableau skills as you work to enhance your ability to effectively leverage data analytics in conducting a quality audit.

Step 1. Obtain the software and download it to your computer.
Step 2. Watch the following training videos (at a minimum).

Tableau Desktop

Do you have data and Tableau Desktop? These videos are for you! Learn how to connect, explore, analyze, present, and share your data.

3 VIDEOS Getting Started		34 MIN
⊙ Getting Started	●	25 MIN
⊙ The Tableau Interface	●	4 MIN
⊙ Distributing and Publishing	●	4 MIN
11 VIDEOS Connecting to Data		62 MIN
21 VIDEOS Visual Analytics		115 MIN
7 VIDEOS Dashboards and Stories		36 MIN
10 VIDEOS Mapping		40 MIN
16 VIDEOS Calculations		65 MIN

Source: Tableau.com

Data Analytics: Spreadsheet Modelling and Database Querying

8-40 **LO 7** Download and complete the following case, which relates to data analytics around purchasing card transactions:

> Dow, K. E., M. W. Watson, and V. J. Shea. (2013). Understanding the links between audit risks and audit steps: The case of procurement cards. *Issues in Accounting Education* 28(4): 913–927.

Academic Research Cases

NOTE: Completing *Academic Research Cases* requires students to reference additional resources and materials.

SEARCH HINT

It is easy to locate these academic research articles! Use a search engine such as Google Scholar or an electronic research platform such as ABI Inform, and search using the author names and the article title.

8-41 **LO 1, 7** Locate and read the article listed below.

Cao, M., R. Chychyla, and T. Stewart. (2015). Big data analytics in financial statement audits. *Accounting Horizons* 29(2): 423–429.

a. What is the purpose of the study?
b. Describe the design/method/approach used to conduct the study.
c. What are the primary findings of the study?

8-42 **LO 1, 2, 3, 4, 5, 6** Locate and read the article listed below.

Christensen, B. E., R. J. Elder, and S. M. Glover. (2015). Behind the numbers: Insights into large audit firm sampling policies. *Accounting Horizons* 29(1): 61–81.

a. What is the purpose of the study?
b. Describe the design/method/approach used to conduct the study.
c. What are the primary findings of the study?

The Audit Opinion Formulation Process

I. Making Client Acceptance and Continuance Decisions
Chapter 1

II. Performing Risk Assessment
Chapters 2, 3, 7, and 9–13

III. Obtaining Evidence About Internal Control Operating Effectiveness
Chapters 8–13

IV. Obtaining Substantive Evidence About Accounts, Disclosures, and Assertions
Chapters 8–13

V. Completing the Audit and Making Reporting Decisions
Chapters 14 and 15

Quality Auditing and the Need for Quality Auditor Judgments and Ethical Decisions
Chapter 1

Professional Liability
Chapter 4

The Audit Opinion Formulation Process and a Framework for Obtaining Audit Evidence
Chapters 5 and 6

Auditors consider accounts in the revenue cycle as high risk because these accounts are highly susceptible to misstatement—due to either error or fraud. Recording revenue can be very complex and subject to error. In some cases,

management is motivated to report revenue at a certain level, and might use various methods to improperly inflate revenue. Auditors need an appropriate level of professional skepticism when auditing the accounts in the revenue cycle.

Learning Objectives

LO 1 Identify the significant accounts, disclosures, and relevant assertions in the revenue cycle.

LO 2 Identify and assess inherent risks of material misstatement in the revenue cycle.

LO 3 Identify and assess fraud risks of material misstatement in the revenue cycle.

LO 4 Identify and assess control risks of material misstatement in the revenue cycle.

LO 5 Describe how to use planning analytical procedures to identify possible material misstatements for revenue cycle accounts, disclosures, and assertions.

LO 6 Determine appropriate responses to identified risks of material misstatement for revenue cycle accounts, disclosures, and assertions.

LO 7 Determine appropriate tests of controls and consider the results of tests of controls for revenue cycle accounts, disclosures, and assertions.

LO 8 Determine and apply sufficient appropriate substantive audit procedures for testing revenue cycle accounts, disclosures, and assertions.

LO 9 Apply the frameworks for professional decision making and ethical decision making to issues involving the audit of revenue cycle accounts, disclosures, and assertions.

How to Account for Virtual Sales at Zynga

This feature highlights some unique revenue recognition issues.

Have you ever purchased a piece of virtual farm equipment while playing Zynga's popular game FarmVille? You can see the game at the following website if you are not already familiar with it: *https://www.zynga.com/games/farmville-2*

The company reports that its revenue depends on its ability to publish games on mobile platforms on iOS and Android, and on social networking sites, primarily Facebook. In 2016, the company derived 46% of its revenue from Apple, 30% from Google, and 20% from Facebook.

Maybe you have purchased a tractor that allows you to plow multiple plots of land at one time. You might have used FarmVille currency to make these purchases. Alternatively, you could have converted real dollars from a credit card or PayPal account into the FarmVille currency and then used that currency to buy a virtual tractor or other piece of equipment. For example, you could purchase a hot rod tractor for 55 in Farm Cash, which translates into $10 in real U.S. money.

How do the involved companies account for these sales? Consider, for example, that you buy and hold Facebook credits (used to buy virtual goods in games on Facebook). Facebook treats the purchase of these credits as deferred revenue. This approach works in the same way as a retailer would record the sale of a gift card. Now assume that you buy a FarmVille hot rod tractor. To make this purchase, you could use your Facebook credits or charge $10 (which buys 100 Facebook credits that are converted to 55 in Farm Cash). Facebook sends $7 to Zynga and keeps $3—30%—as a processing fee. At this point, Facebook moves that $3 from deferred revenue into current revenue.

Now the relevant question is: When does Zynga get to recognize its $7 in revenues? In general, revenue should not be recognized until it is realized or is realizable and earned. So even if a company has cash in hand, it cannot be counted as current revenue until the company has delivered the product or service it is being paid for. However, neither the Financial Accounting Standards Board (FASB) nor the Securities and Exchange Commission (SEC) has issued rules for sales of virtual harvesters or any other virtual products. However,

Zynga's audit firm, Ernst & Young (EY), has published a document that provides revenue recognition guidance in this area.

EY's guidance outlines three different revenue approaches: game-based, in which revenue is recognized very slowly, over the life of the game; user-based, a faster approach that lasts over the time a typical user sticks with the game; and speedy item-based, based on the properties of the individual virtual goods. Using the last method, Zynga recognizes revenues from consumable virtual items, like energy, immediately and revenues from durable ones, like tractors, over the time a player is projected to stick with a game. In many ways, these suggestions seem reasonable. The difficult part is that all of the methods are dependent on management estimates of the life of a game, a customer, or a virtual item. The estimates can make a big difference in Zynga's net income. As Zynga management notes in its FYE 2016 10-K:

> … *we recognize revenue from the sale of our virtual goods in accordance with U.S. GAAP, which is complex and based on our assumptions and historical data with respect to the sale and use of various types of virtual goods. In the event that such assumptions are revised based on new data or there are changes in the historical mix of virtual goods sold due to new game introductions, reduced virtual good sales in existing games or other factors or there are changes in our estimates of average playing periods and player life, the amount of revenue that we recognize in any particular period may fluctuate significantly. In addition, changes in the policies of Facebook, Apple, Google or other third party platforms or accounting policies promulgated by the SEC and national accounting standards bodies affecting software and virtual goods revenue recognition could further significantly affect the way we report revenue related to our products. Such changes could have an adverse effect on our reported revenue, net income and earnings per share under U.S. GAAP.*

What Do You Think?   For Classroom Discussion

Zynga's 2016 Def 14-A (proxy statement) reveals that Zynga paid EY approximately $4.6 million in audit and audit-related fees. Think about this very challenging revenue recognition situation, while simultaneously considering the audit firm portfolio management discussion that we presented in *Chapters 1* and *5*.

Why do you think that EY is willing to take the risk of providing an unqualified opinion on financial statements for which revenue recognition is such a unique and challenging undertaking? What auditing procedures over revenue recognition might enable EY to gain comfort that revenue, is indeed, properly valued? Speculate on EY's decision to publish revenue recognition guidance in this particular valuation space.

What You Will Learn

- What are the significant accounts, disclosures, and relevant assertions in the revenue cycle? (LO 1)
- What are the inherent risks associated with revenue transactions? (LO 2)
- What are fraud risks associated with revenue transactions? (LO 3)
- What controls should management have in place to mitigate the risks associated with revenue transactions? (LO 4)
- How can auditors use planning analytical procedures to identify any potential concerns related to revenue? (LO 5)
- What is sufficient appropriate evidence when auditing revenue transactions and related accounts? (LO 6, 7, 8)

LO 1

Identify the significant accounts, disclosures, and relevant assertions in the revenue cycle.

Significant Accounts, Disclosures, and Relevant Assertions

The **revenue cycle** involves receiving a customer's order, approving credit for a sale, determining whether the goods are available for shipment, shipping the goods, billing the customer, collecting cash, and recognizing the effect of this process on revenue and other related accounts such as accounts receivable, inventory, and sales commission expense. In the revenue cycle, the most significant accounts include revenue and accounts receivable. The auditor will likely obtain evidence related to each of the financial statement assertions discussed in *Chapter 5* for both accounts. However, for specific accounts and specific clients, some assertions are more relevant than other assertions. For many clients, the existence assertion related to revenue may be one of the more relevant assertions, especially if the client has incentives to overstate revenues. For accounts receivable, the more relevant assertions are usually existence and valuation. The assertions that are determined to be more relevant are those for which the risk of material misstatement is higher and for which the auditor will need more, and/or more appropriate, evidence.

The cycle approach recognizes the interrelationship of accounts. Audit evidence addressing the existence and valuation of accounts receivable also provides evidence on the existence and valuation of recorded revenue, and vice versa. When examining sales transactions and internal controls over revenue processing, the auditor also gathers evidence on credit authorization and valuation of the recorded transactions. Sales transactions often serve as a basis for computing commissions for sales staff. Sales information is used for strategic long-term decision-making and marketing analysis. Therefore, the accuracy of recording transactions in the revenue cycle is important for management decisions, as well as for the preparation of financial statements. *Exhibit 9.1* depicts the accounts typically affected by sales transactions.

Exhibit 9.1
Revenue Cycle Accounts

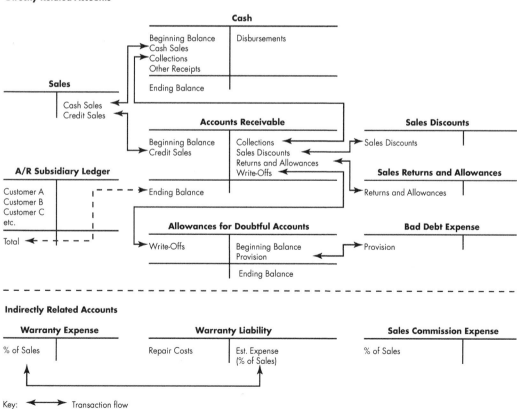

Processing Revenue Transactions

The revenue process differs with each client, and each client may have more than one revenue process. For example, a sales transaction for a shirt in a department store differs from a sale of construction equipment, and both of these differ from a book sale on a website. The website sale and the retail sale most likely require a credit card or cash for payment. The construction equipment sale most likely involves an account receivable or a loan with a third party. Some sales transactions involve long-term contractual arrangements that affect when and how the client will record revenue. Notwithstanding these differences, most sales transactions include the procedures and related documents shown in *Exhibit 9.2* and discussed next.

Exhibit 9.2
Overview of the Sales Process

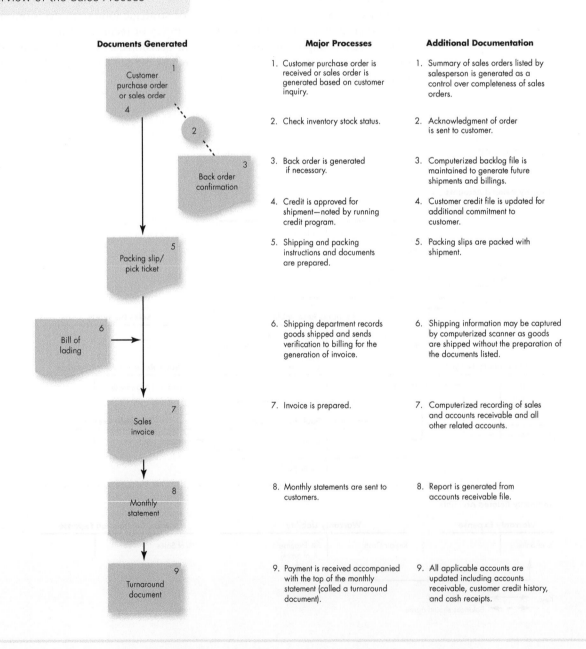

Documents Generated

1 Customer purchase order or sales order
4

2

3 Back order confirmation

5 Packing slip/ pick ticket

6 Bill of lading

7 Sales invoice

8 Monthly statement

9 Turnaround document

Major Processes

1. Customer purchase order is received or sales order is generated based on customer inquiry.

2. Check inventory stock status.

3. Back order is generated if necessary.

4. Credit is approved for shipment—noted by running credit program.

5. Shipping and packing instructions and documents are prepared.

6. Shipping department records goods shipped and sends verification to billing for the generation of invoice.

7. Invoice is prepared.

8. Monthly statements are sent to customers.

9. Payment is received accompanied with the top of the monthly statement (called a turnaround document).

Additional Documentation

1. Summary of sales orders listed by salesperson is generated as a control over completeness of sales orders.

2. Acknowledgment of order is sent to customer.

3. Computerized backlog file is maintained to generate future shipments and billings.

4. Customer credit file is updated for additional commitment to customer.

5. Packing slips are packed with shipment.

6. Shipping information may be captured by computerized scanner as goods are shipped without the preparation of the documents listed.

7. Computerized recording of sales and accounts receivable and all other related accounts.

8. Report is generated from accounts receivable file.

9. All applicable accounts are updated including accounts receivable, customer credit history, and cash receipts.

1. Receive a Customer Purchase Order The revenue cycle begins with the receipt of a purchase order from a customer or the preparation of a sales order by a salesperson. The order might be taken by: (1) a clerk at a checkout counter, (2) a salesperson making a call on a client, (3) a customer service agent of a catalog sales company answering a toll-free call, (4) a computer receiving purchase order information electronically from the customer's computer, or (5) the sales department directly receiving the purchase order. For example, consider a customer service agent for a catalog merchandiser taking an order over the phone. The agent keys the information into a computer file, and uniquely identifies each transaction. The computer file (often referred to as a *log of transactions*) contains all the information for sales orders taken over a period and is used for control and reconciliation purposes.

2. Check Inventory Stock Status Many organizations have computer systems capable of informing a customer of current inventory status and likely delivery date. The customer is informed of potential back-ordered items, as well as an expected delivery date.

3. Generate Back Order If an item is to be back-ordered for later shipment to the customer, a confirmation of the back order is prepared and sent to the customer. If the back order is not filled within a specified time, the customer is often given the option of cancelling the order. The clients maintain an accurate list of back-ordered items to meet current customer demand and future inventory needs. Appending a separate field to the individual inventory records to show back-ordered items usually accomplishes this.

4. Obtain Credit Approval Organizations implement formal credit approval policies to minimize credit losses. Some organizations eliminate credit risk by requiring payment through a credit card. Others require that a check accompany the order, and the company may delay the shipment until the check clears to assure that the payment is collectible.

Many organizations issue credit to their customers because it is a more convenient way to transact business. However, the organization making the sale accepts some risk that it ultimately will not receive payment from the customer. Many reasons can exist for nonpayment, ranging from: (a) dissatisfaction with, or return of, the goods received, to (b) inability to make payments because of financial constraints. Therefore, organizations need to have a credit approval process that: (a) evaluates the creditworthiness of new customers, and (b) updates the creditworthiness (including timelines of payments) of existing customers. The credit approval might include a review of sales orders and customer credit information by a computer program that contains current account balance information and credit scoring information to determine whether the organization should extend credit to the customer. Most organizations set credit limits for customers and develop controls to assure that a pending sale will not push the customer over the credit limit.

5. Prepare Shipping and Packing Documents Many organizations have computerized the distribution process for shipping items from a warehouse. Pick tickets (documents that tell the warehouse personnel the most efficient sequence in which to pick items for shipment) are generated from the sales order or from the customer's purchase order. Separate packing slips are prepared to insert with the shipment and to verify that all items have been shipped. Some organizations put a bar code on the shipping container that identifies the contents. The customer can scan the bar code to record receipt of the order.

6. Ship and Verify Shipment of Goods   Most goods are shipped to customers via common carriers such as independent trucking lines, railroads, or airfreight companies. The shipper prepares a bill of lading that describes the packages to be conveyed by the common carrier to the customer, the shipping terms, and the delivery address. The **bill of lading** is a formal legal document that conveys responsibility to the shipper. A representative of the common carrier signs the bill of lading, acknowledging receipt of the goods. The shipping department confirms the shipment by: (1) completing the packing slip and returning it to the billing department, (2) electronically recording everything shipped and transmitting the shipping information to the billing department, or (3) preparing independent shipping documents, a copy of which is sent to the billing department.

7. Prepare and Send the Invoice   Invoices are normally prepared when the organization receives notice that goods were shipped. The invoice should include items such as the terms of sale, payment terms, and prices for merchandise shipped. The invoice will serve as an important document in terms of audit evidence.

8. Send Monthly Statements to Customers   Many organizations prepare monthly statements of open items and mail these statements to customers. The monthly statement provides a detailed list of the customer's activity for the previous month and a statement of all open items.

9. Receive Payments   The proper recording of all revenue receipts is crucial to the ultimate valuation of both cash and accounts receivable. This part of the revenue process is typically considered part of the cash transaction cycle and is discussed in *Chapter 10*.

An Overview of the Audit Opinion Formulation Process in the Revenue Cycle

In auditing the revenue cycle, the auditor will perform risk assessment procedures, tests of controls, and substantive procedures—Phases II, III, and IV of the audit opinion formulation process.

As part of performing risk assessment procedures, the auditor obtains information to assess the risk of material misstatement. This includes information about inherent risks at the financial statement level (e.g., client's business and operational risks, financial reporting risks) and at the account and assertion levels, fraud risks including feedback from the audit team's brainstorming sessions, strengths and weaknesses in internal control, and results from planning analytical procedures.

Once the risks of material misstatement have been identified, the auditor then determines how best to respond to them. For an integrated audit and for a financial statement audit where the auditor wants to rely on controls as part of the basis for the audit opinion, the auditor will perform tests of controls and consider the effect of those tests on the substantive evidence to obtain. In other audits, the auditor will rely only on substantive tests to obtain evidence about the accuracy of the financial statements.

9-1 The revenue cycle involves receiving a customer's order, approving credit for a sale, determining whether the goods are available for shipment, shipping the goods, billing the customer, collecting cash, and recognizing the effect of this process on revenue and other related accounts such as accounts receivable, inventory, and sales commission expense.   (T/F)

9-2 In the revenue cycle, the most significant accounts typically include revenue and accounts receivable.   (T/F)

9-3 Which of the following statements is <u>true</u> regarding assertions in the revenue cycle?
   a. It is typical that all five assertions for revenue are equally important.
   b. If a client has an incentive to overstate revenues, the existence assertion would be more relevant than the completeness assertion.

   c. Audit evidence about the existence of revenues is also the most appropriate evidence about the valuation of receivables.
   d. The allowance for doubtful accounts has important implications for the ownership assertion of accounts receivable.

9-4 Which of the following statements is <u>true</u> regarding the processing and recording of revenue transactions?
   a. The accurate recording of revenue transactions is important for preparing financial statements, but not important for the client's management decisions.
   b. Invoices should be prepared once the client determines that the goods ordered by a customer are available.
   c. A bill of lading provides documentation that the customer has received the goods.
   d. Sales transactions typically begin with the receipt of a purchase order from a customer.

LO 2

Identify and assess inherent risks of material misstatement in the revenue cycle.

Identifying Inherent Risks

Inherent Risks: Revenue

An important inherent risk related to revenue transactions is the timing of revenue recognition. Complex sales transactions often make it difficult to determine when a sale has actually taken place. For example, the client might structure a transaction so that title passes only when some contingent situations are met, or the customer may have an extended period to return the goods. To audit the revenue cycle, the auditor must understand:

- The organization's principal business, that is, what is the organization in the business of selling?
- The earnings process and the nature of the obligations that extend beyond the normal shipment of goods. For example, after goods are shipped, does the seller have any ongoing service requirements to the purchaser?
- The impact of unusual terms, and when title has passed to the customer.
- The right of the customer to return a product, a well as the returns history.
- Contracts that are combinations of leases and sales.
- The proper treatment of sales transactions made with recourse or that have an abnormal or unpredictable amount of returns.

Criteria for Revenue Recognition

When to recognize revenue and how much revenue to recognize are often difficult decisions. Accounting guidelines (ASC 606) effective for reporting periods beginning after December 15, 2017 (2018 for non-public companies), require organizations to go through a five-step process to recognize revenue:

1. *Identify the contract with the customer*
   All of these criteria need to have been met for a contract to exist:
   - The parties have approved it
   - The goods and/or services involved are clearly identified

Why It Matters   Possible PCAOB Implementation Guidance

This feature notes that the PCAOB is considering issuing implementation guidance for auditors who must assess management assertions using the new revenue recognition standards.

At the May 25, 2017, Standing Advisory Group (SAG) meeting, PCAOB Chief Auditor Martin Baumann said that the PCAOB has a project to update Staff Audit Practice Alert (APA) No. 12, *Matters*

Related to Auditing Revenue in an Audit of Financial Statements, to reflect changes that have been made in the new revenue standard. Some SAG members recommended a joint roundtable discussion between the SEC and the PCAOB; they also recommended that the PCAOB develop a brief for audit committee members so they understand potential implications of the new standard, and any related risks that may arise.

- The payment terms are spelled out.
- There is commercial value to the contract–money is involved
- It is probable that the client will collect the payment

Risks relating to this step include recognizing revenue when a contract does not exist, or not recognizing revenue when a contract does exist, and side agreements of which accounting personnel are unaware. Controls relevant to addressing these risks include identifying contracts for which the criteria in the new standard apply, ensuring that payment terms are proper, assessing the criteria for collectibility, and evaluating any contract modifications that occur over time.

2. *Identify the performance obligations*   A performance obligation (also called a deliverable) is a promise within the contract to transfer a good or service to your customer. The client can bundle distinct goods or services together within the contract, or the goods or services could be in series, as long as they are substantially similar and delivered in the same way.

 A risk relating to this step includes not properly identifying performance obligations. Controls relevant to addressing this risk include identifying implied promises, evaluating whether management should treat a number of goods or services as a single performance obligation, and evaluating whether any warranties are performance obligations.

3. *Determine the transaction price*   This step seems easy! The contract states a price the customer will pay for the products and services you will provide. However, things can get challenging when you factor in work performed on a time and material basis, financing considerations, performance bonuses, penalties, rebates, and more.

 A risk relating to this step is that management estimates may be inaccurate because they have applied an inappropriate revenue recognition method, or made inappropriate assumptions to a significant part of the contract. Controls relevant to addressing this risk include re-evaluating the accuracy of judgmental assumptions used in determining fair value for non-cash consideration and determining any significant financing components.

4. *Allocate the transaction price to the deliverables*   If the contract stipulates more than one deliverable, the client must allocate a separate price to each deliverable. The accounting standards detail how to determine a transaction price, and how to handle complicating factors such as discounts and change orders.

 A risk relating to this step is that management's estimates might possibly be inaccurate if they used an inappropriate method or made inappropriate assumptions about allocating separate prices to different deliverables. Controls relevant to addressing this risk include determining the appropriate transaction price allocation, estimating the stand-along selling price for the deliverables, and having management maximize using observable data.

5. ***Recognize revenue when (or as) you satisfy performance obligations*** The client recognizes revenue when they satisfy a performance obligation by transferring the promised goods or services to the customer. Determining when a service is transferred, however, is not always a straightforward task, especially if the services are performed over time. The accounting standards detail how to complete this step. However, this step may ultimately prove the most challenging step for companies to get right.

A risk relating to this step is that management may recognize revenue before the organization satisfies the performance obligations. Controls relevant to addressing this risk include carefully determining whether/when the organization satisfies performance obligations and accurately measuring progress toward satisfaction of various performance obligations.

These criteria help to ensure that recognized revenue represents the transfer of promised goods or services to customers in an amount that reflects the consideration which the entity expects in exchange for those goods or services. These criteria are not as straightforward as they might seem. Consider a situation in which the client has delivered a product to a customer and the customer has physical possession of the asset. When evaluating whether to recognize revenue, the client needs to consider any agreement to repurchase the asset. If such an agreement exists, delivery of the asset may not coincide with revenue recognition.

As part of this process, the client needs to assess the collectibility of cash or the receivable related to the revenue. **Collectibility** refers to the risk that the seller will be unable to collect the entitled contractual consideration from the customer. One of the required criteria in ASC 606 is that it be probable that the client will collect substantially all of the payment to which it will be entitled in exchange for the goods or services that will be transferred to the customer to be considered a contract with a customer. Revenue will be recognized based on the amount to which the seller expects to be entitled, without considering the risks associated with collectibility. If collectibility is in significant doubt, a contract may be determined to not exist and any impairment losses are to be presented as a separate line item adjacent to revenue.

Some revenue recognition areas require special consideration. The following is a sample of issues that have emerged in recent years:

- How much should be recognized as revenue when a company sells another company's product but does not take title until it is sold? For example, should Priceline.com (a travel website) record the full sales price of airline tickets it sells or the net amount it earns on the sale (the sales commission)?
- Should shipment of magazines by a magazine distributor to retail stores result in revenue when delivered or await the sale to the ultimate consumers? What if the arrangement with convenience stores, such as 7–11, is that all magazines not sold can be returned to the distributor when the racks are filled with the next month's magazines?
- Should revenue be recognized in barter advertising in which two websites exchange advertising space?

Preadoption Disclosures

Why It Matters

This feature outlines what the auditor expects to see from clients who have not yet adopted the new guidance in ASC 606.

Prior to adopting the revenue recognition guidance in ASC 606, companies are required to make appropriate disclosures in compliance with *Staff Accounting Bulletin* (SAB) No. 74 (codified in SAB Topic 11.M). Those disclosures should discuss the impact the new standard will have on future financial statements when the company adopts the new standard in the future. The disclosures should be both quantitative and qualitative.

For further details, see https://www.sec.gov/interps/account/sabcod et11.htm#M

- At what point in time should revenue be recognized when:
    - o The right of return exists.
    - o The product is being held awaiting the customer's instructions to ship (bill and hold).
    - o A bundled product is sold. For example, assume that a software company sells software bundled with installation and service for a total of $5,000. Should the total revenue be $5,000, or should the service element be separately estimated and recognized along with an attendant liability to perform the service work? What if the software entitles the user to free updates for a period of three years?

Inherent Risks: Accounts Receivable

The primary inherent risk associated with receivables is that the net amount is not valid because the receivables recorded do not exist or they are not collectible from the customer. If a valid sales transaction does not exist, a valid receivable does not exist. Alternatively, if the company has been shipping poor-quality goods, there is a high risk of return. Finally, some companies, in an attempt to increase sales, may have chosen to sell to new customers who have questionable credit-paying ability. The most relevant financial statement assertions for receivables are usually existence and valuation. Another important risk relates to ownership of the receivables. For example, a company may desperately need cash and decide to sell its receivables to a bank, but the bank may have a right to seek assets from the company if the receivables are not collected.

Some inherent risks affecting receivables include:

- Receivables are pledged as collateral against specific loans with restricted use (disclosures of such restrictions are required).
- Receivables are incorrectly classified as current when the likelihood of collection during the next year is low.

Focus on Fraud

Channel Stuffing at ArthroCare—The Importance of Professional Skepticism

This feature highlights the importance of professional skepticism when auditing the revenue account. The ArthroCare case illustrates the material misstatements that can occur if a client chooses to improperly record revenue and the auditor fails to detect the misstatement.

ArthroCare is a manufacturer of medical devices, based in Austin, Texas, whose shares are traded on NASDAQ. From 2006 through the first quarter of 2008, two company sales executives, John Raffle and David Applegate, were alleged to have engaged in a channel stuffing scheme that improperly inflated company revenue and earnings. Specifically, the two salesmen shipped certain products to distributors even though the distributors often did not need them or have the ability to pay for them. Chief executive officer (CEO) Michael Baker and chief financial officer (CFO) Michael Gluk were also implicated in the scheme. As a result, for 2006, 2007, and the first quarter of 2008, revenues were overstated by, respectively, 7.9%, 14.1%, and 17.4%, totaling almost $72.3 million. For the same period, net income was overstated by 14.5% in

2006, 8,694% for 2007, and 315% for just the first quarter of 2008, totaling about $53.7 million. The company eventually restated its financial statements.

In 2014, former executives John Raffle and David Applegate pled guilty to conspiracy to commit securities and wire fraud. ArthroCare agreed to pay a $30 million fine to resolve the investigation. In 2014, the PCAOB settled a disciplinary order against Randall Stone, a former PwC auditor, for violating PCAOB rules and standards in PwC's 2007 audit of ArthroCare. Stone was the partner in charge of the 2007 audit and was barred from associating with a registered public accounting firm and faced a monetary penalty and censure. His violations included not properly addressing numerous indicator of improperly recognized revenue.

For further information, refer to ArthroCare Corp. Securities Litigation, case number 1:08-cv-00574 in the U.S. District Court for the Western District of Texas. For further details on the PCAOB disciplinary order against Randall Stone, see PCAOB Release No. 105-2014-007.

9-5 Channel stuffing is a fraud in the revenue cycle that involves recording revenue after a customer has requested to purchase the inventory.   (T/F)

9-6 If the contract stipulates more than one deliverable, the client must allocate a separate price to each deliverable.   (T/F)

9-7 Under the FASB's guidance on revenue recognition, which of the following is <u>not</u> a criteria that must be met in order for a contract to exist?
   a. The parties have approved it.
   b. The auditor has ensured that the contract's valuation is reasonable in all material respects.
   c. The goods and/or services involved are clearly identified.

   d. The payment terms are spelled out.
   e. There is commercial value to the contract.

9-8 Which of the following statements is <u>false</u> regarding the fraud at ArthroCare?
   a. Two of ArthroCare's sales executives overstated ending inventory that improperly inflated company revenue and earnings.
   b. PricewaterhouseCoopers' audit was deficient for ArthroCare, thereby enabling the fraud to go undetected for a period of time.
   c. ArthroCare agreed to pay a $30 million fine to resolve the investigation.
   d. ArthroCare is a manufacturer of medical devices, based in Austin, Texas, whose shares are traded on NASDAQ.

- Collection of a receivable is contingent on specific events that cannot currently be estimated.
- Payment is not required until the purchaser sells the product to its end customers.
- Accounts receivable are aged incorrectly, and potentially uncollectible amounts are not recognized.
- Orders are accepted from customers with poor credit, but the allowance for doubtful accounts is not increased accordingly.

LO 3

Identify and assess fraud risks of material misstatement in the revenue cycle.

Identifying Fraud Risks

Research indicates that over 60% of frauds involve inappropriate revenue recognition. Virtually every client has revenue, so identifying fraud risks relating to revenue recognition is critical. Auditing standards state that auditors should ordinarily presume there is a risk of material misstatement caused by fraud relating to revenue recognition.

How do Fraudsters Perpetrate their Schemes?

Fraud investigations by the SEC and the PCAOB note many creative methods companies use to misstate accounts in the revenue cycle, including:

- Recognizing revenue on shipments that never occurred or that occurred after the end of the period
- Utilizing hidden **side letters**, which are agreements containing contract terms that are not part of the formal contract (often involving rights of return), thereby increasing audit risk because they enable key contract terms affecting revenue recognition to be hidden from the auditor as part of a revenue recognition fraud
- Recording consignment sales as final sales
- Shipping unfinished products, those that the customer never ordered, or before the customers agreed to delivery
- Creating fictitious invoices
- Recording shipments to the company's own warehouse as outside sales

- Shipping goods that had been returned and recording the reshipment as a sale of new goods before issuing credit for the returned sale
- Incorrect aging accounts receivable and not recording write-downs of potentially uncollectible amounts
- Recording purchase orders as completed sales

Another fraudulent scheme in the revenue cycle is **lapping**, which is a technique used to cover up the embezzlement, that is, outright theft of cash. This technique causes individual customer accounts receivable balances to be misstated. Lapping is most likely to occur when duties are inadequately segregated—the fraudster has access to cash or incoming checks *and* (most importantly) to the accounting records of the customer's accounts receivable balance.

To accomplish lapping, the fraudster first steals a payment from a customer by pocketing the customer's cash or cashing the customer's check. The fraudster does not give that customer credit for the payment. If no other action is taken, that customer will detect the absence of the credit for payment on the next monthly statement and will likely object or otherwise alert the organization.

To prevent detection, the fraudster then covers up the fraud by posting another customer's payment to the first customer. Then, the second customer's account is missing the recording of a legitimate payment, which the fraudster then covers up with a subsequent collection from a third customer (hence, the term *lapping*). At no time will any customer's account be very far behind in the posting of the credit to their account. Perpetrating a lapping scheme takes a great deal of time by the fraudster. Signs of lapping include an employee working excessively long hours and refusing to take vacations.

Of course, there will always be at least one customer whose balance is overstated, unless the fraudster repays the stolen cash. Lapping can occur even if all incoming receipts are in the form of checks. The employee can either restrictively endorse a check to another company or go to another bank and establish an

Why It Matters   A Recent Example of Lapping in a Governmental Setting

This feature describes an interesting lapping case and highlights that individuals who engage in lapping are always just one customer payment away from being discovered.

Nancy Tonkin employed a lapping scheme to defraud the Township of South Whitehall, which occupies a portion of Lehigh County, Pennsylvania. She managed to steal $844,000 during her 32-year career as the township's utility manager. She oversaw taxpayer payments for their water, sewer, trash, and recycling bills. According to the grand jury report, Tonkin was able to successfully execute the scheme for a very long time "due to the obvious incompetence of her immediate supervisor, Linda Perry, who served as the finance director for the last 17 years."

Tonkin retired in 2012, and was arrested in April 2014 after a grand jury investigation. It seems that following Perry's retirement in 2012, the Township's finance department found indications of the fraud and initiated an investigation, thereby leading to the ultimate discovery of the money that she stole.

Tonkin used the money to gamble at a variety of nearby casinos. There is some hint that Tonkin's husband, a former local police officer,

had knowledge of the scheme. Nancy Tonkin agreed to abandon any chance for appeal of her sentence, and the couple had to forfeit their Township retirement savings plans and most of their pensions. In return, the judge instituted a penalty against Tonkin's husband whereby he has to make a $600 restitution payment each month, which equates to about one-third of his pension. If he fails to make a single payment, the judge can reinstate the charges against him.

The Township has now implemented new accounting controls, including segregation of duties among four employees who collect cash and checks, and requiring that all checks that the township writes for expenses have two signatures.

Tonkin received a two- to seven-year prison sentence. She had this to say as an explanation for her actions: "I can't say 'sorry' enough. They trusted me and I betrayed them all," she said. "I have no excuse. I was raised by good parents who taught me right from wrong."

For further details, case, see http://www.mcall.com/news/breaking/mc-tonkins-plead-guilty-south-whitehall-embezzlement-20150408-story.html

Imagine that you are the fraudster in this case of lapping at the Township of South Whitehall. You will have to constantly shift purported payments from one customer to the other, always staying just one-step away from a given customer complaining and thereby revealing your fraudulent actions. Think back to our discussion of fraud in *Chapter 2* about the fraud triangle.

The incentive here is clear: to steal cash for personal use with respect to gambling. The opportunity exists because of a system of weak internal controls.

- How might the fraudster rationalize his or her actions?
- How might the fraudster make things right again, or is that even possible?
- Is the Township of South Whitehall in any way to blame for the lapping scheme being so large and lasting for such a long time?

account with a similar name. Usually, very few accounts will be misstated at any one time, resulting in difficulty in uncovering such a scheme.

Exhibit 9.3 provides examples of the wide range of methods that organizations have used to inflate revenue in high-profile fraud cases. Notice that while some of these companies have gone out of business or have been acquired and renamed (e.g., WorldCom), many are still thriving financially and have successfully moved on from the fraud (e.g., Coca-Cola).

Identifying Fraud Risk Factors

There are many motivations to overstate revenue. For example, bankruptcy may be imminent because of operating losses, technology changes in the industry are causing the company's products to become obsolete, or a general decline in the industry is negatively affecting revenue. Management bonuses or stock options may be dependent on reaching a certain earnings goal. A merger may be pending, and management may want to negotiate the highest price possible. In other cases, management might make optimistic public announcements of the company's revenues, net income, and earnings per share before the auditor's work is completed. These earnings expectations put enormous pressure on management not to disappoint the market.

The examples in *Exhibit 9.3* are only a few of the revenue schemes to which auditors should be alert. Identifying these revenue schemes and related risk factors involves the auditor:

- Assessing motivation to enhance revenue because of either internal or external pressures
- Reviewing the financial statements through planning analytical procedures to identify account balances that differ from expectations or general trends in the economy
- Recognizing that not all of the fraud will be instigated by management; for example, a CFO or accounting staff person may engage in misappropriating assets for his or her own use
- Becoming aware of representations made by management to analysts and the potential effect of those expectations on stock prices which determines whether the company's performance is significantly different from that of the rest of the industry or the economy
- Determining whether the company's accounting is being investigated by organizations such as the SEC
- Considering management compensation schemes, especially those that rely on stock options and therefore current stock prices
- Determining whether accounting functions are centralized, and if not centralized, assessing if the decentralization is appropriate

Exhibit 9.3
Examples of Revenue Recognition and Accounts Receivable Fraud Schemes

Coca-Cola was charged with coercing its largest distributors to accept delivery of more syrup than they needed at the end of each quarter, thus inflating sales by about $10 million a year.

WorldCom's CEO, Bernard Ebbers, pressured the chief operating officer (COO) to find and record one-time revenue transactions that were fictitious and were hidden from the auditors by altering key documents and denying auditor access to the appropriate database. As of 2016, WorldCom's bankruptcy is the largest in U.S. history.

HealthSouth understated its allowance for doubtful accounts when it was clear certain receivables would not be collected.

Gateway recorded revenue for each free subscription to AOL services that was given with each computer sale, thus overstating pre tax income by over $450 million.

Royal Ahold (a Dutch company that was the world's second-biggest operator of grocery stores) booked higher promotional allowances, provided by suppliers to promote their goods, than they received in payment.

Kmart improperly included as revenue a $42.3 million payment from American Greetings Corp. that was subject to repayment under certain circumstances and therefore should not have been fully recognized by Kmart in that quarter.

Xerox improperly accelerated $6 billion of revenue from long-term leases of office equipment.

Qwest immediately recognized long-term contract revenue rather than over the eighteen-month to two-year period of the contract, inflating revenue by $144 million.

Bristol-Myers inflated revenue by as much as $1 billion, using sales incentives to wholesalers who then packed their warehouses with extra inventory.

Lucent Technologies improperly booked $679 million in revenue. The bulk of this revenue, $452 million, reflected products sent to its distribution partners that were never actually sold to end customers.

Charter Communications, a cable company, added $17 million to revenue and cash flow in one year through a phony ad sales deal with an unnamed set-top decoder maker. They persuaded the set-top maker to add $20 onto the invoice price of each box. Charter held the cash and recorded it as an ad sale. Net income was not affected, but revenue was increased.

Nortel Networks, a telecommunications equipment company, fraudulently manipulated reserve accounts across two years to initially *decrease* profitability (so as to *not* return to profitability faster than analyst expectations) and to then increase profitability (so as to meet analyst expectations about the timing of a return to profitability and also to enable key executives to receive early return to profitability bonuses worth tens of millions of dollars). Nortel's board fired key executives, and the company restated its financial statements four times in four years and remediated a key internal control material weakness associated with the fraud.

Diebold, Inc., an Ohio-based maker of ATMs, bank security systems, and electronic voting machines, agreed to pay $25 million to settle SEC charges related to accounting fraud. The alleged schemes included fraudulent use of bill-and-hold accounting and improper recognition of lease-agreement revenue. When company reports showed that the company was about to miss its analysts' earnings estimate, Diebold finance executives allegedly used these schemes to meet the earnings estimate.

General Electric (GE) paid $50 million to settle accounting fraud charges with the SEC for revenue recognition schemes. GE improperly booked revenues of $223 million and $158 million for six locomotives reportedly sold to financial institutions, "with the understanding that the financial institutions would resell the locomotives to GE's railroad customers in the first quarters of the subsequent fiscal years." The problem is that the six transactions were not true sales and therefore did not qualify for revenue recognition under U.S. generally accepted accounting principles (GAAP). Most important, GE did not give up ownership of the trains to the financial institutions.

Motorola booked $275 million of earnings by keeping its third quarter books open after the quarter ended so that it could record the revenue, which represented 28% of the net income Motorola reported for that quarter.

For Classroom Discussion

What Do You Think?

In thinking about overcoming the negative publicity and securities fraud fines related to revenue fraud, some companies succeed and move on, while others fail following the fraud. What forces might influence corporate "survivability" in the face of financial reporting fraud related to revenue?

The Incentive for Managers to Commit Fraud in the Revenue Cycle: The Role of Stock Analysts and Consensus Earnings Calculations

Why It Matters

This feature provides insight into the role that stock analyst following and consensus analyst earnings per share calculations play in affecting managements' incentives to commit fraud.

Stock analysts follow companies and issue earnings per share and revenue forecasts they anticipate for the companies they follow. To understand this concept better, see the analysts' forecast report for Ford Motor Company as of June 2017, which we reproduce below.

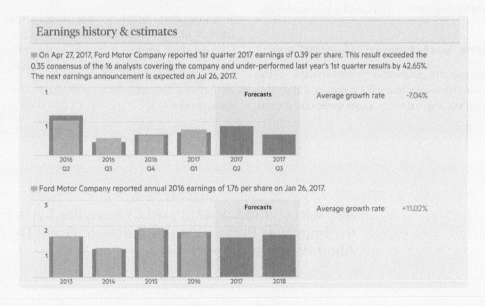

This report shows that 16 analysts together, that is, by consensus, predict Q1 2017 earnings per share of $0.35 per share, and that the actual results were better than that at $0.39 per share. It also shows that the annual earnings per share for 2016 was $1.76; analysts make predictions about both quarterly and annual earnings per share. Managers do not want to "disappoint" the market by having their earnings results come in "under forecast," which creates the incentive for earnings manipulation.

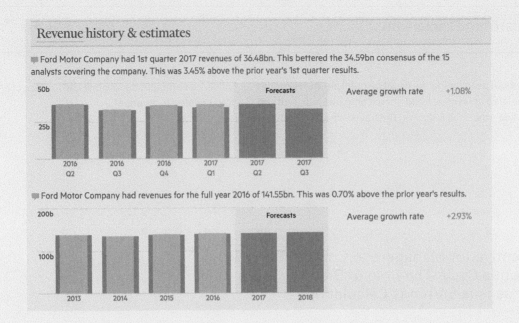

This report shows that 15 analysts together, that is, by consensus, predict Q1 2017 revenues at $34.59 billion, while the actual revenue that Ford reported exceeded that estimate, coming in at $36.48 billion. Managers do not want to "disappoint" the market by having their revenue results come in "under forecast," which creates the incentive for fraudulently overstated revenue amounts.

What does the term *"analyst consensus forecast"* mean?

It means the average earnings per share or revenue based on all the analysts that are following the company. If a company is at or near its consensus forecast and the auditor proposes a material, income decreasing audit adjustment, client management may resist because they do not want to report a negative earnings surprise.

What is a negative earnings surprise or a negative revenue surprise?

It is a negative departure from the consensus analyst earnings forecast or the revenue forecast; for example, lower actual earnings per share amount compared to the consensus or lower revenue compared to the consensus expectation.

For further details, see https://markets.ft.com/data/equities/tearsheet/forecasts?s=F:NYQ

Focus on Fraud

Assisted Living Concepts (ALC) Revenue Cycle Fraud and the Improper Professional Conduct of Grant Thornton's Audit Partners

This feature summarizes a case that presents a striking example of corporate governance and audit oversight gone terribly wrong.

Alternative Living Concepts (ALC) was a publicly traded company that operated more than 200 senior living residences in the United States, constituting about 9,000 individual units. During the period of the fraud (2008–2012), ALC leased units from Ventas, Inc. The Ventas lease contained certain financial covenants, requiring ALC to maintain strict occupancy rate percentages.

Beginning in 2008, and shortly after ALC entered into the lease agreement with Ventas, occupancy rates declined sharply. ALC's CEO and CFO fraudulently overstated the number of units that it claimed were occupied. To meet the lease covenant requirements, the CEO and CFO reported that occupants of the facilities included various ALC employees (which was fictitious).

Grant Thornton was ALC's auditor, and the firm and its partners were aware of various fraud risks related to ALC's lease covenant calculations. The partner on the ALC engagement was

Melissa Koeppel, Grant Thornton's managing partner of the Wisconsin practice. *(Note that Koeppel was also the audit partner on the failed Koss Corporation audit that we discussed in Chapter 2, so she is definitely a repeat offender in terms of low audit quality.)*

During the course of the audit, Koeppel repeatedly violated professional standards while ignoring various fraud risks that allowed ALC to file numerous reports with the SEC that were materially false and misleading. In defining improper professional conduct, the SEC explains what it means by negligence:

1. A single instance of highly unreasonable conduct that results in a violation of applicable professional standards in circumstances in which an accountant knows, or should know, that heightened scrutiny is warranted.

2. Repeated instances of unreasonable conduct, each resulting in a violation of applicable professional standards, that indicate a lack of competence to practice before the Commission.

Koeppel engaged in repeated instances of unreasonable conduct, leading to a failed audit whereby Grant Thornton issued unqualified audit opinions on materially falsified financial statements. She relied on the results of weak auditing procedures completed by very junior audit staff members and essentially ignored the fraud risks. It is important to interpret the failed audits in light of the fact that the ALC audit was one of Grant Thornton's largest audit clients in the state of Wisconsin, which provided Koeppel an incentive to ignore the financial problems at ALC.

As an example of poor professional judgment, the Grant Thornton engagement team planned to conduct site visits to five Ventas facilities in Georgia and one in South Carolina to, among other things, verify facility occupancy figures, physically inspect the houses and the assets therein, make fraud inquiries with facility employees and review documentation maintained at the facilities. However, ALC requested that the engagement team choose other site visit locations in lieu of the Georgia facilities, and Koeppel acquiesced to ALC's request, thereby essentially giving control to ALC management about the conduct of the audit.

Excerpts of the SEC's Accounting and Auditing Enforcement Release (AAER) are particularly poignant in terms of articulating the disturbing course of events with respect to Grant Thornton's recognition that Audit Partner Koeppel was a significant audit quality risk (paragraphs 40-43 of the AAER):

40. By the time Grant Thornton was conducting field work for the third quarter 2010 review, Grant Thornton national professional standards and risk management personnel had become aware of negative quality indicators with respect to Koeppel, who was placed on a November 2010

monitoring list for partners with such negative indicators. Grant Thornton placed Koeppel on this list because, among other things, her audit clients had restated their financial statements or interim financial information four times in the preceding two years. The Public Company Accounting Oversight Board ("PCAOB"), in its 2008 inspection report, had also found deficiencies on one of Koeppel's engagements because Grant Thornton had failed to gather sufficient audit evidence.

41. One of the restatements that led to Koeppel's inclusion on the partner monitoring list involved Grant Thornton's audit client, Koss Corporation (Koss). In June 2010, Koss restated its financial statements for the preceding two fiscal years because one of its vice presidents had embezzled $31.5 million from 2005 through 2009 and would plead guilty to criminal charges based on the misconduct. Koeppel was the engagement partner for the Koss audit for three of the four years of the embezzlement. In July 2012, Grant Thornton, without admitting any liability, paid $8.5 million to settle a malpractice case filed by Koss.

42. By November of 2010, Grant Thornton's National Professional Practice Director for the Midwest region (NPPD) became aware of negative audit quality indicators with respect to Koeppel as a result of an ongoing PCAOB inspection. Although the NPPD did not know that Koeppel had been placed on the partner monitoring list, he was informed by others in the firm that Koeppel had a number of negative audit quality indicators. The NPPD also became aware of observations by other Grant Thornton partners that the Wisconsin practice, for which Koeppel was the managing partner, had "gotten off the tracks from a methodology perspective."

43. By the fall of 2010, Grant Thornton had removed Koeppel from all of her other public company engagements, but decided to allow her to continue as the engagement partner for the 2010 ALC audit.

44. Following the completion of the second quarter 2010 review, the audit manager assigned to the ALC engagement team resigned.

Of particular interest, as of June 2017, Koeppel was still listed as a partner of Grant Thornton on her LinkedIn profile.

ALC is no longer a publicly traded company. They were bought out by private equity investors and have changed the company name to Enlivant. For information about the new organization, see its website at *http://www.enlivant.com/*

For further details, see the SEC's AAER No. 3718 (December 2, 2015).

How would you feel entrusting the care of your elderly relative to a company that was previously involved in fraudulent financial reporting? Would you be able to trust that company to care for your relative? Do you think that the company has moved on and is now a reliable caregiver that you could trust?

Check Your Basic Knowledge

9-9 Research indicates that a majority of financial statement frauds involve inappropriate recording of revenue.   (T/F)

9-10 When assessing fraud risks, the auditor should consider the client's motivation to increase revenue due to both internal and external pressures.   (T/F)

9-11 Which of the following factors is <u>not</u> a motivation for clients to fraudulently misstate revenue?
  a. Bankruptcy may be imminent.
  b. Management bonuses are contingent on a certain revenue goal.
  c. Controls over revenue process are ineffective.
  d. Management wants to meet publicly announced earnings expectations.

9-12 Which of the following explanations best describes the purpose of lapping?
  a. Lapping is a technique used by client personnel to cover up the embezzlement of cash.
  b. Lapping is an approach used by client personnel to eliminate differences between a customer's records and the client's records reported on confirmations.
  c. Lapping is a procedure used by the auditor to obtain evidence the client's customer does return a positive confirmation.
  d. Lapping is an agreement containing contract terms that are not part of a formal sales contract.

Identifying Control Risks

LO 4

Identify and assess control risks of material misstatement in the revenue cycle.

Once the auditor has obtained an understanding of the inherent and fraud risks of material misstatement in the revenue and accounts receivable accounts, the auditor needs to understand the controls that the client has designed and implemented to address those risks. Remember, the auditor is required to gain an understanding of internal controls for both integrated audits and financial statement only audits. The auditor typically obtains this understanding by means of a walkthrough of the process, inquiry, observation, and review of the client's documentation. The auditor considers both entity-wide controls and transaction controls at the account and assertion levels. This understanding provides the auditor with a basis for making an initial control risk assessment for each relevant account and assertion.

At the entity-wide level, the auditor considers the control environment, including such principles as commitment to financial accounting competencies and the independence of the board of directors. The auditor will also consider the remaining components of internal control that are typically entity-wide—risk assessment, information and communication, and monitoring controls. Although the auditor needs to understand all the components of internal control, the auditor typically finds it useful to focus on significant control activities in the revenue cycle. As part of this understanding, the auditor focuses on the relevant assertions for each account and identifies the controls that relate to risks for these assertions. In an integrated audit or in a financial statement only audit where the auditor relies on controls, the auditor uses this understanding to identify important controls that need to be tested.

Preadoption Disclosure Controls Relating to the New Revenue Recognition Standard (ASC 606)

This feature highlights that as a resulting of adopting ASC 606, companies might face new financial reporting risks that require new processes and new internal controls. Auditors should be alert to these issues as they audit revenue.

The SEC has been providing guidance to preparers and auditors about the impending shift in rules surrounding revenue recognition. According to a publication by Deloitte (p. 2):

> *In light of the SEC's guidance and recent comments from the SEC staff, such disclosures should address the impact the new revenue standard is expected to have on the financial statements and should include:*
>
> - *A comparison of the company's current accounting policies (which, to the extent available, could include*

tabular information or ranges comparing historical revenue patterns) with the expected accounting under the new standard.

- *The transition method (full retrospective or modified retrospective) elected.*
- *The status of the implementation process.*
- *The nature of any significant implementation matters that have not yet been addressed.*

For further details, see https://www2.deloitte.com/content/dam/ Deloitte/us/Documents/audit/ASC/HU/2017/us-aers-headsup- internal-control-considerations-related-to-adoption-of-the-new- revenue-recognition-standard-050917.pdf

Controls Related to Existence/Occurrence

Controls for existence should provide reasonable assurance that a sale and accounts receivable are recorded only when revenue has been earned and the company has received cash or a collectible receivable. A control to mitigate the risk that unearned revenues are recorded is to distribute monthly statements to customers. However, the control should be such that someone independent of the department who initially processed the transaction should prepare and mail these statements. Further, customer inquiries about their balances should be channeled to a department or individual that is independent of the original recording of the transactions.

Unusual transactions, because of their size, complexity, or special terms, should require a high level of management review, with management review serving as a control. Upper levels of management—and maybe even the board—should be involved in approving highly complex and large transactions. For typical transactions, authorization should be part of an audit trail and should not be performed by the same person who records the transactions.

AmTrust Financial: Internal Control Material Weaknesses Lead to a Restatement

This feature provides an example of ineffective internal controls result- ing in a material misstatement of revenue and the need for competent accounting personnel so that the company gets the accounting right.

AmTrust management had the following to say as they announced the restatement:

> As previously disclosed, on March 14, 2017, the Audit Committee of our Board of Directors, in consultation with management and our current and former independent

registered public accounting firms, concluded that our previously issued Consolidated Financial Statements for fiscal years 2015 and 2014, along with each of the four quarters included in fiscal year 2015 as well as the first three quarters of fiscal year 2016, needed to be restated.

Accordingly, within this report, we have included restated audited results as of and for the years ended December 31, 2015 and 2014, as well as restated unau- dited quarterly financial data for fiscal year 2015 and the first three quarters of 2016, which we refer to as the "Restatement." Our consolidated financial statements as of and for the years ended December 31, 2015 and 2014 included in this report have been restated from the consolidated financial statements included in our Annual Report on Form 10-K for the year ended December 31, 2015. In Note 3. "Restatement of Previously Issued Consolidated Financial Statements," we have included information regarding the Restatement and specific changes to our previously issued financial statements. Additionally, in Note 29. "Quarterly Financial Data (Unaudited)," we have included restated unaudited interim financial data for the four quarters included in fiscal year ended 2015 and the first three quarters of 2016. In each case, we have also provided details of the adjustments to the previously issued financial information as a result of the Restatement.

Background of the Restatement

The restatement of our financial statements and related disclosures primarily relates to the correction of two errors reported in our historical consolidated financial statements. In accordance with accounting guidance presented in ASC 250-10 and SEC Staff Accounting Bulletin No. 99, *Materiality*, management assessed the materiality of these errors and concluded that they were material to the Company's previously issued financial statements. The two primary errors relate to: (1) **upfront recognition of the portion of warranty contract revenue associated with administration services, instead of recognizing the revenue over the life of the contract**, and (2) bonuses that were expensed in the year paid but that should have been accrued as earned based on ASC 270, *Interim Reporting* and ASC 450, *Contingencies*. We also identified other adjustments described in Note 3. "Restatement of Previously Issued Consolidated Financial Statements" that we have corrected as part of this Restatement.

The impact of the Restatement on the Consolidated Statements of Income primarily resulted in **decreased service and fee income, increased acquisition costs and other underwriting expenses, and decreased interest expense, which ultimately resulted in decreases to net income**. The impact of the Restatement on the Consolidated Balance Sheets primarily resulted in an increase of premiums receivable and other assets, a reduction of deferred policy acquisition costs and property plant and equipment, an increase in accrued expenses and other liabilities, and a decrease in shareholders' equity. The impact of the Restatement adjustments on the Consolidated Statements of Cash Flows resulted in an increase of net cash provided by operating activities in both 2015 and 2014, an increase of net cash provided by investing activities in 2015 and 2014, and a decrease in net cash provided by financing activities in 2015 and 2014.

Because of the restatement, AmTrust announced a significant investment in hiring accounting function professionals. The company's Chairman and CEO had this to say:

"With AmTrust's strategic growth in product scope and geographic reach, working to ensure our accounting and finance systems, expertise and skills are aligned to support our size and scale," said Barry Zyskind, Chairman and Chief Executive Officer, AmTrust. "We are pleased to welcome several new highly experienced senior finance and treasury professionals to the AmTrust team and to promote and recognize several other current executives in our finance and accounting organization. Through these enhancements to our senior financial leadership team, we are further strengthening our internal controls, analysis and reporting environment, in support of our commitment to sound and transparent financial disclosure."

For further details, see http://ir.amtrustgroup.com/releasedetail.cfm?releaseid=1020727

Prompt for Critical Thinking #1   It's Your Turn!

Research the restatement of AmTrust to learn how the internal control material weaknesses were discovered, and the dramatic nature of the process by which the restatement took place. Use the terms "AmTrust," "BDO," and "whistleblower."

Explain at least three insights that you learned from your search.

1. _____

2. _____

3. _____

Conduct additional research to learn about further developments in this case.

Diageo plc and the Foreign Corrupt Practices Act — *Why It Matters*

This feature highlights that companies who make bribes in a possible effort to generate revenue may face large financial fines.

Diageo is one of the world's largest producers of premium alcoholic beverages. The SEC's AAER states that, through its subsidiaries, and over a period of six years (approximately 2003 to 2009), Diageo made improper cash payments to government officials in India ($792,310 and $186,299), employees of India's Canteen Stores Department and Label Registration and Excise Officials ($530,955), a government official in Thailand ($599,322), and a reward payment to a South Korean Customs Official ($86,339 and $51,802).

The AAER states that Diageo failed to accurately account for these payments in its books, records, and financial statements. In addition, Diageo management exercised lax oversight and failed to devise, maintain, or monitor internal controls that would be sufficient to detect and prevent the payments.

Why would Diageo management engage in this behavior, which is clearly in direct violation of the Foreign Corrupt Practices Act? In part, management simply had difficulty implementing internal controls over a variety of acquisitions that it made in foreign subsidiaries in India, Thailand, and South Korea. Diageo's subsidiaries in these countries disguised the improper payments as legitimate vendor expenses or under other misleading account titles (e.g., factory expenses, telephone expenses, and sales support). The other reason management likely ignored this behavior on the part of its subsidiaries was simply to ensure continuity of business and the generation of sales revenues.

Diageo was required to pay a penalty of $11,306,081 to the U.S. Treasury, along with interest of $2,067,739.

For further details, see AAER No. 3307, July 27, 2011.

Controls Related to Completeness

Controls related to completeness are intended to provide reasonable assurance that all valid sales transactions are recorded. For example, transactions may not be recorded because of sloppy procedures. In some cases, companies may choose to omit transactions because they want to minimize taxable income. Thus, the auditor needs to consider controls over completeness, which might include:

- Use of prenumbered shipping documents and sales invoices and the subsequent accounting for all numbers
- Immediate online entry into the computer system and immediate assignment of unique identification number by the computer application
- Reconciliation of shipping records with billing records
- Supervisory review, such as review of transactions at a fast-food franchise
- Reconciliation of inventory with sales, such as the reconciliation of liquor at a bar at the end of the night with recorded sales

Controls Related to Valuation

Implementing controls related to proper valuation of routine sales transactions should be relatively straightforward. Sales should be made from authorized price lists—for example, the price read by a scanner at Wal Mart or the price accessed by a salesperson from a database maintained on a laptop. In these situations, the control procedures should provide reasonable assurance of the correct input of authorized price changes into the computer files and limit access to those files, including:

- Limiting access to the files to authorized individuals
- Printing a list of changed prices for review by the department that authorized the changes
- Reconciling input with printed output reports to assure that all changes were made and no unauthorized ones were added
- Limiting authorization privileges to those individuals with the responsibility for pricing

Valuation issues most often arise in connection with unusual or uncertain sales terms. Examples include sales where the customer has recourse to the selling company, franchise sales, bundled sales, cost-plus contracts, or other contracts covering long periods with provisions for partial payments. If these complex transactions are common, the company should have established policies and processes for handling them, and the auditor should understand these policies and processes.

Another issue affecting the valuation of sales is returns and allowances. Abnormal returns or allowances may be the first sign that a company has inappropriately recorded revenue.

Two examples of controls that the client should implement for identifying and promptly recording returned goods include formal policies and procedures for:

- Clearly articulating contractual return provisions in the sales contract
- Approving acceptance of returns

Valuation of accounts receivable also has important risks that the client needs to mitigate with appropriate controls. Formal credit policies should provide reasonable assurance of the realization of the accounts receivable into cash. Companies should use the following procedures to address credit risk:

- A formal credit policy, which may be automated for most transactions but requires special approval for large and/or unusual transactions
- A periodic review of the credit policy by key executives to determine whether changes are dictated either by current economic events or by deterioration of the receivables

Prompt for Critical Thinking #2   It's Your Turn!

Identify other potential controls related to properly recording returned goods.

- _____
- _____
- _____
- _____

Why It Matters   Risks Associated with Sales Returns: The Case of Medicis and Ernst & Young

This feature notes the problems that can arise if controls related to returns and allowances are not designed and operating effectively, and the auditor does not appropriately respond to this control risk.

In 2012, the PCAOB settled a disciplinary order censuring Ernst & Young (EY), imposing a $2 million penalty against the firm and sanctioning four of its current and former partners. In the audits of Medicis' December 31, 2005, 2006, and 2007 financial statements, the PCAOB found that EY and its partners failed to properly evaluate a material component of the company's financial statements—its sales returns reserve. EY did not properly evaluate Medicis' practice of reserving for most of its estimated product returns at replacement cost, instead of

at gross sales price. It appears that EY accepted the company's basis for reserving at replacement cost, when the auditors should have known that this approach would not be supported by the audit evidence. By using replacement cost for the reserve, rather than gross sales price, Medicis' reported sales returns reserve were materially understated and its reported revenue was materially overstated.

Ultimately, EY concluded that Medicis' practice of reserving for its sales returns was not in conformity with GAAP. The company corrected its accounting for its sales returns reserve and had to file restated financial statements with the U.S. SEC.

For further details, see PCAOB Release No. 105-2012-001.

- Continuous monitoring of receivables for evidence of increased risk, such as increases in the number of days past due or an unusually high concentration in a few key customers whose financial prospects are declining
- Adequate segregation of duties in the credit department, with specific authorization to write off receivables segregated from individuals who handle cash transactions with the customer

An additional aspect of the valuation of net receivables is management's process for estimating the allowance account. Management should have a well-controlled process in place to develop a reasonable and supportable estimate for this allowance account.

Documenting Controls

Auditors need to document their understanding of internal controls for both integrated audits and financial statement only audits. *Exhibit 9.4* provides an example of an internal control questionnaire for sales and accounts receivable. The first part documents the auditor's understanding of the process; in the second part of the questionnaire, each negative (*no*) answer represents a potential internal control deficiency. Given a negative answer, the auditor should consider the effect of the response on the initial assessment of control risk. For example, a negative response to the question regarding segregation of duties between those receiving cash and those authorizing write-offs or adjustments of accounts indicates that a risk exists that an individual could take cash receipts and cover up the fraud by writing off a customer's balance. Unless another control compensates for this deficiency, the auditor will likely have a control risk assessment of high in this area.

Exhibit 9.4
Control Risk Assessment Questionnaire: Sales and Receivables

SALES ORDERS

Sales authorized by: (Describe the source and scope of authority, and the documentation or other means of indicating authorizations. Include explicitly the authorization of prices for customers.)

_____

_____

Sales orders prepared by, or entered into the system by:

_____

_____

Individuals authorized to change price tables: (Indicate specific individuals and their authority to change prices on the system and the methods used to verify the correctness of changes.)

_____

_____

Existence of major contracts with customers that might merit special attention during the course of the audit: (Describe any major contracts and their terms.)

_____

_____

Restrictions on access to computer files for entering or changing orders: (Describe access control systems and indicate whether we have tested them in conjunction with our review of data processing general controls.)

_____

_____

continues

Exhibit 9.4 *Continued*

	Check (x) one:	
	Yes	No
1. Are orders entered by individuals who do not have access to the goods being shipped?	_____	_____
2. Are orders authorized by individuals who do not have access to the goods being shipped?	_____	_____
3. Are batch and edit controls used effectively on this application? If so, describe the controls.	_____	_____
4. Are sales invoices prenumbered? Is the sequence of prenumbered documents independently accounted for?	_____	_____
5. Are control totals and reconciliations used effectively to ensure that all items are recorded and that subsidiary files are updated at the same time invoices are generated? If so, describe.	_____	_____
6. Do procedures exist to ensure that the current credit status of a customer is checked before an order is shipped? If so, describe.	_____	_____
7. Are price lists stored in the computer independently reconciled to authorized prices by the marketing manager or someone in the marketing manager's office?	_____	_____
8. Are duties segregated such that the personnel receiving cash differ from the personnel authorized to make account write-offs or adjustments of accounts?	_____	_____

Auditors can also document their understanding of controls in control matrices, flowcharts, and documented walkthroughs of processes. *Exhibit 9.5* presents a partially completed control matrix for contract revenue that links the risk of misstatement to the client's control and provides a means for the auditor to document the testing approach and testing results.

Exhibit 9.5
Partially Completed Controls Matrix for Contract Revenue

Control Description	Risk of Misstatement— Relevant Assertion(s)	Testing Approach (Nature of Testing)	Timing of Testing	Extent of Testing	Testing Results (Including Deficiencies)
A revenue recognition review is performed by the revenue accountant before revenue is recorded.	The risks are that revenue will be recorded before the criteria for recognizing revenue have been met or that revenue will be recorded at the incorrect amount. • Valuation • Existence	Reperformance of analyses performed by the revenue accountant.	Year-end		

Note: The matrix is a partial illustration. The matrix would typically link to a supporting flowchart that would detail the key controls related to contract review, and all key controls would be included in the matrix.

9-13   It is not possible for internal controls to mitigate risks associated with the valuation of accounts receivable.   (T/F)

9-14   Diageo made improper cash payments to government officials in Mexico, Brazil, and Argentina during the period 2003–2009, which violated provisions of the Foreign Corrupt Practices Act.   (T/F)

9-15   Which of the following procedures can organizations use to address credit risk most effectively?

a.   An informal credit policy, which may be automated for most transactions, but requires special approval for large and/or unusual transactions.

b.   A periodic review of the credit policy by key executives to determine whether changes are dictated either by current economic events or by deterioration of the receivables.

c.   Periodic monitoring of receivables for evidence of increased risk, such as increases in the number of days past due or an unusually high concentration in a few key customers whose financial prospects are declining

d.   Adequate segregation of duties over fixed assets, with specific authorization to write off fixed assets that have been fully depreciated.

9-16   Which of the following statements about the Medicis fraud is <u>false</u>?

a.   In 2012, the PCAOB settled a disciplinary order censuring Ernst & Young (EY), imposing a $2 million penalty against the firm and sanctioning four of its current and former partners.

b.   The PCAOB found that EY and its partners failed to properly evaluate a material component of the company's financial statements—its allowance for doubtful accounts.

c.   EY did not properly evaluate Medicis' practice of reserving for most of its estimated product returns at replacement cost, instead of at gross sales price. It appears that EY accepted the company's basis for reserving at replacement cost, when the auditors should have known that this approach would not be supported by the audit evidence.

d.   The PCAOB investigation revealed that by using replacement cost for the reserve, rather than gross sales price, Medicis' reported sales returns reserve were materially understated and its reported revenue was materially overstated.

e.   All of the above are true.

LO 5

Describe how to use planning analytical procedures to identify possible material misstatements for revenue cycle accounts, disclosures, and assertions.

Performing Planning Analytical Procedures

Planning analytical procedures help auditors identify areas of potential material misstatements. The objective of planning analytical procedures is to identify accounts with heightened risk of misstatement during audit planning to provide a basis for designing and implementing responses to the assessed risks. Planning analytical procedures can be relatively imprecise.

As initially described in *Chapter 6*, the steps that the auditor will take are as follows:

1. Determine the suitability of a particular analytical procedure for given account(s)/assertion(s), considering the risks of material misstatement and tests of details planned.
2. Evaluate the reliability of data that the auditor is using to develop an expectation of account balances or ratios. In evaluating data reliability, the auditor should consider the source of the data, its comparability, the nature of information available about the data, and the controls over the preparation of the data.
3. Develop an expectation of recorded account balances or ratios and evaluate whether that expectation is precise enough to accomplish the relevant objective.

4. Define when the difference between the auditor's expectation and what the client has recorded would be considered significant.

5. Compare the client's recorded amounts with the auditor's expectation to determine any significant unexpected differences.

6. Investigate significant unexpected differences. Significant unexpected differences suggest that substantive procedures for the account/assertion will be increased.

7. Ensure that the following have been appropriately documented: auditor's expectation from Step 3, including the factors that the auditor considered in developing the expectation, the results in Step 4, and the audit procedures conducted relating to Steps 5 and 6.

Step 1: Identify Suitable Analytical Procedures

Exhibit 9.6 contains examples of planning analytical procedures that the auditor might consider relevant for assessing risk of material misstatement in revenue cycle accounts.

Step 2: Evaluate Reliability of Data Used to Develop Expectations

Various factors can influence reliability of data in revenue cycle accounts during planning analytical procedures. One is the source of information that is available. Information is more reliable when it is obtained from independent sources outside the company. For example, outside evidence of gross margin in the company's industry is more reliable than simply using a historical trend of the company's own gross margin, without regard to industry considerations. Another factor influencing reliability of data is comparability. The auditor should consider whether the company's data may differ in an expected way from the overall industry. For example, bad debt expense as a percentage of sales may not be comparable to the overall industry if the company has a significantly different client base or credit policy than the industry (e.g., much more stringent or much less stringent credit terms).

EXHIBIT 9.6

Planning Analytical Procedures in the
Revenue Cycle

Some basic ratios used in planning analytical procedures include:

- Gross margin analysis
- Turnover of receivables (ratio of credit sales to average net receivables) or the number of days' sales in accounts receivable
- Average receivables balance per customer
- Receivables as a percentage of current assets and/or total assets
- Aging of receivables
- Allowance for uncollectible accounts as a percentage of accounts receivable
- Bad debt expense as a percentage of net credit sales
- Sales in the last month (or quarter) to total sales
- Sales discounts to credit sales
- Returns and allowances as a percentage of sales

Some basic trend analyses in planning analytical procedures include:

- Monthly sales analysis compared with past years and budgets
- Identification of spikes in sales at the end of quarters or the end of the year
- Trends in discounts allowed to customers that exceed both past experience and the industry average

Step 3: Develop Expectations

Developing expectations about relationships in the data is important to identifying accounts with heightened risk of material misstatement during audit planning. Possible expected relationships in the revenue cycle include:

- There is no unusual year-end sales activity.
- Accounts receivable growth is consistent with revenue growth.
- Revenue growth, receivables growth, and gross margin are consistent with the activity in the industry.
- There is no unusual concentration of sales made to customers (in comparison with the prior year).
- The accounts receivable turnover is not significantly different from the prior year.
- The ratio of the allowance for doubtful accounts to total receivables or to credit sales is similar to the prior year.

Step 4 and Step 5: Define and Identify Significant Unexpected Differences

Step 4 requires the auditor to define the difference amount (between the auditor's expectation and what the client has recorded) that would be considered significant; this will require consideration of the auditor's assessed materiality level and the auditor's desired level of assurance. Typically, when the risk of material misstatement is higher, the amount of acceptable difference is lower.

In Step 5, the auditor compares the client's recorded amounts with the auditor's expectation. Once this mechanical step is completed, the auditor will have identified any significant differences between the auditor's expectation and the amount the client has recorded.

If planning analytical procedures do not identify any unexpected relationships, the auditor may conclude that a heightened risk of material misstatements does not exist in these accounts. If there are unusual or unexpected relationships, the planned substantive audit procedures would be adjusted to address the potential material misstatements. The auditor should be aware that if a revenue fraud is taking place, the financial statements usually will contain departures from industry norms but may not differ from the expectations set by management. Thus, the auditor should compare the unaudited financial statements with both past results and industry trends. The following unexpected relationships might suggest a heightened risk of fraud:

- Revenue is increasing even though there is strong competition and a major competitor has introduced a new product.
- Revenue increases are not consistent with the industry or the economy.
- Gross margins are higher than average, or there is an unexpected change in gross margins.
- Large increases in revenue occur near the end of the quarter or year.
- Revenue has grown and net income has increased, but there is negative cash flow from operations.

Step 6 and Step 7: Investigate Significant Unexpected Differences and Ensure Proper Documentation

Significant unexpected differences suggest that evidence sufficiency and/or evidence appropriateness for the account/assertion will need to be increased. The auditor will develop a plan for how to address the identified risks. As the auditor proceeds through planning analytical procedures, the auditor will document the analytical procedures used, the auditor's expectations, how the level of significant difference was determined, the identification of significant unexpected differences, and the planned follow-up to address significant unexpected differences.

Prompt for Critical Thinking #3   It's Your Turn!

The following example demonstrates how planning analytical procedures may be helpful to the auditor. The company is a wholesaler selling to major retail chains in a competitive industry. The auditor notes the following changes in ratios:

- The number of days' sales in accounts receivable increased in one year from 44 to 65.
- The gross margin increased from 16.7% to 18.3% (industry average was 16.3%).
- The amount of accounts receivable increased 35% from $9 million to $12 million, while sales remained virtually unchanged.

All of these ratios are substantially greater than the industry averages; the auditor's expectations were that the company should be somewhat similar to the industry averages. An auditor comparing the client's ratios with the auditor's expectations should carefully consider reasons for the changes.

1. What alternatives could potentially explain these changes?
2. What corroborating evidence is available for potential explanations?

Check Your Basic Knowledge

9-17 The auditor might conclude that a heightened risk of fraud exists if the planning analytical procedures indicate increases in revenue and net income, but negative cash flow from operations.   (T/F)

9-18 When performing planning analytical procedures, the auditor could perform trend analysis with ratios, but not with account balances.   (T/F)

9-19 Which of the following statements is false regarding planning analytical procedures in the revenue cycle?

   a. As revenue is typically regarded as a high-risk account, planning analytical procedures related to revenue are not required.
   b. The first step in planning analytical procedures includes developing an expectation of recorded amounts or ratios, and evaluating whether that expectation is precise enough to accomplish the relevant objective.
   c. Trend analysis would not be appropriate as a planning analytical procedure in the revenue cycle.
   d. All of the above statements are false.

9-20 Assume that an auditor expected that the client's activities related to sales and accounts receivable would be similar to industry averages. Which of the following relationships detected as part of planning analytical procedures would not suggest a heightened risk of material misstatement in the revenue cycle?

   a. The number of days' sales in accounts receivable decreased from 65 days in the prior year to 47 days in the current year. The industry average increased from 45 to 47 days.
   b. The gross margin increased from 16.7% to 18.3%, while the industry average changed from 16.7% to 16.3%.
   c. Accounts receivable increased 35% over the prior year, while sales stayed relatively stable.
   d. All of the above relationships are suggestive of a heightened risk of fraud.

LO 6

Determine appropriate responses to identified risks of material misstatement for revenue cycle accounts, disclosures, and assertions.

Responding to Identified Risks of Material Misstatement

Once the auditor understands the risks of material misstatement, the auditor is in a position to determine the appropriate audit procedures to perform. Audit procedures should be proportional to the assessed risks, with areas of higher risk requiring more evidence and/or evidence that is more appropriate. Responding to identified risks typically involves developing an audit approach that contains substantive procedures (e.g., tests of details and, when appropriate, substantive analytical procedures) and tests of controls, when applicable. The sufficiency and appropriateness of selected procedures will vary to achieve the desired level of assurance for each relevant assertion. While audit firms may have a standardized audit program for the revenue cycle, the auditor should customize the audit program based on the assessment of risk of material misstatement.

Consider a client where the auditor has assessed the risk of material misstatement related to the completeness of revenue at high. This client has incentives to understate revenue in an effort to smooth earnings and the auditor believes the client has implemented somewhat effective controls in this area. The auditor may develop an audit program that consists of first performing limited tests of operating effectiveness of controls, then performing limited substantive analytical procedures, and finally performing substantive tests of details. Because of the high risk, the auditor will want to obtain a great deal of evidence directly from tests of details.

In contrast, consider a client where the auditor has assessed the risk of material misstatement related to the completeness of revenues as low, and believes that the client has implemented effective controls in this area. For this client, the auditor can likely perform tests of controls, gain a high level of assurance from substantive analytical procedures such as a reasonableness test, and then complete the substantive procedures by performing tests of details at a limited level.

Panel A of *Exhibit 9.7* makes the point that because of differences in risk, the box of evidence to be filled for testing the completeness of revenue at the low-risk is smaller than the box of evidence to be filled at the high-risk client. Panel B makes the point that because of the higher risk associated with the completeness of revenue at Client B, the auditor will want to design the audit so that more of the assurance or evidence is coming from direct tests of account balances. Note that the relative percentages are judgmental in nature; the examples are simply intended to illustrate how an auditor might select an appropriate mix of procedures.

Check Your Basic Knowledge

9-21 Responding to identified risks in the revenue cycle rarely involves developing an audit approach that contains substantive procedures (e.g., tests of details and, when appropriate, substantive analytical procedures). (T/F)

9-22 While audit firms may have a standardized audit program for the revenue cycle, the auditor should customize the audit program based on the assessment of risk of material misstatement. (T/F)

9-23 After identifying the risks of material misstatement, the auditor develops an audit plan in response to those risks. Which of the following plans for testing revenue would be most likely when the auditor believes that control risk is high?

   a. The only evidence the auditor plans to obtain is from tests of details.
   b. The auditor plans to obtain 40% of the necessary audit evidence from tests of controls, and the remaining 60% from substantive analytical procedures.

   c. The auditor plans to obtain the majority of the necessary audit evidence from tests of controls.
   d. Any of the above would be an appropriate audit plan if the auditor believes that control risk is high.

9-24 Responding to identified risks involves developing an audit approach that addresses those risks. Which of the following statements about the planned audit approach is <u>true</u> for the revenue cycle?

   a. The audit approach needs to include tests of controls, substantive analytical procedures, and tests of details.
   b. The audit approach will typically require more evidence for higher risk assertions than lower risk areas.
   c. The audit approach should follow the audit firm's standardized audit program.
   d. The sufficiency and appropriateness of selected procedures will not vary across assertions.

Exhibit 9.7

Panel A: Sufficiency of Evidence for Completeness of Revenue

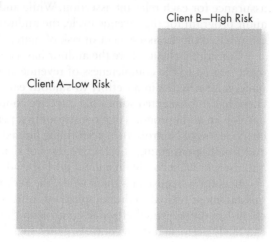

Panel B: Approaches to Obtaining Audit Evidence for Completeness of Revenue

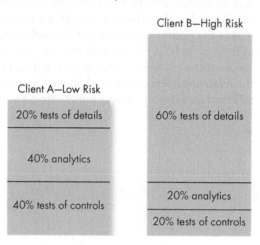

LO 7

Determine appropriate tests of controls and consider the results of tests of controls for revenue cycle accounts, disclosures, and assertions.

Obtaining Evidence About Internal Control Operating Effectiveness in the Revenue Cycle

For integrated audits, the auditor will test the operating effectiveness of important controls throughout the year, with a heightened focus on controls as of the client's year-end. If the auditor wants to rely on controls for the financial statement audit, the auditor will test the operating effectiveness of those controls throughout the year.

Returning to the Case of AmTrust Financial: Internal Control Material Weaknesses Leads to a Restatement

Why It Matters

This feature provides excerpts from the AmTrust FYE 12/31/2016 10-K that articulate the internal control weaknesses that ultimately resulted in the company's restatement of its previously issued financial statements.

Internal Control Considerations

As previously disclosed, in assessing the effectiveness of our internal control over financial reporting as of December 31, 2016, management identified certain material weaknesses. Specifically, management concluded that we did not maintain effective internal control over financial reporting as of December 31, 2016 due to ineffective assessment of the risks of material misstatement in financial reporting and insufficient resources in our corporate accounting and corporate financial reporting groups. The foregoing control deficiencies contributed to the restatement of our consolidated financial statements for fiscal years 2015 and 2014, and our unaudited quarterly financial information for each of the four quarters in fiscal year 2015 and for the first three quarters in fiscal year 2016. As a result of these deficiencies, we now believe our internal control over financial reporting was not effective as of December 31, 2015. For a description of the material weaknesses identified by management and management's plan to remediate such material weaknesses, see Part II, Item 9A. "Controls and Procedures."

Item 9A

Ineffective assessment of the risks of material misstatement in financial reporting

We did not effectively assess the risk of material misstatement in certain processes and change the internal control over financial reporting as a result of the significant increase in the size and complexity of the Company that was, in part, due to numerous acquisitions undertaken by the Company. A significant portion of these processes were managed and controlled by a centralized group within the Company and the material weakness affected: the design, implementation and operation of controls over the preparation, analysis and review of significant balances and closing adjustments necessary to achieve appropriately stated consolidated account balances and disclosures. Specifically, management did not appropriately assess

the risks associated with the financial reporting of foreign exchange, deferred acquisition costs, goodwill impairment, warranty administration services revenue, capitalized costs, period-end expense accruals and the statements of cash flows and other comprehensive income. As a result, we did not design, implement and operate process level controls to effectively address the complexity of the underlying financial reporting.

Insufficient resources in the Corporate Accounting and Corporate Financial Reporting Groups

We did not have a sufficient complement of personnel, in certain geographic locations, with an appropriate level of knowledge and experience to help ensure proper selection and application of U.S. GAAP in the accounting for the areas stated above. In addition, we were not able to effectively design and execute our process level controls around the consolidation process and preparation of financial statements, specifically subsidiary close and consolidation adjustments, segregation of duties related to the creation and posting of a discrete number of journal entries, foreign exchange, deferred acquisition costs, goodwill impairment, warranty administration services revenue, capitalized costs, period-end expense accruals and the statements of cash flows and other comprehensive income, and associated disclosures.

These material weaknesses contributed to material misstatements related to warranty services revenue and accrual of bonuses that were corrected prior to the issuance of the financial statements. Additionally, these material weaknesses contributed to other misstatements to foreign exchange adjustments, deferred acquisition costs, and period-end accruals. If these material weaknesses are not effectively remediated, a reasonable possibility exists that material misstatements of the annual or interim financial statements will not be prevented or detected on a timely basis…

… The effectiveness of our internal control over financial reporting as of December 31, 2016 has been audited by KPMG LLP, an independent registered public accounting firm, as stated in its report that appears in this Annual Report on Form 10-K. This adverse report states that internal control over financial reporting was not effective.

To help you understand the stock market implications of AmTrust's restatement, consider the following graph, which reveals a sharp decline in the company's market capitalization that resulted: (if you search the stock market history of AmTrust, you will see that the stock continued to decline in value into the time period of early 2018).

Source: sec.gov

For further details, see https://www.sec.gov/Archives/edgar/data/1365555/000136555517000059/afsi1231201610k-2016annual.htm

Selecting Controls to Test and Performing Tests of Controls

The auditor selects controls that are important to the auditor's conclusion about whether the organization's controls adequately address the assessed risk of material misstatement in the revenue cycle. The auditor will select both entity-wide and transaction controls for testing. Typical tests of transaction controls include inquiry of personnel performing the control, observation of the control being performed, inspection of documentation confirming that the control has been performed, and reperformance of the control by the auditor testing the control.

For example, a control may include reconciliation between the sales sub ledger and the general ledger. The approaches to testing the reconciliation control could involve one or more of the following:

- *Inquiry*—Talk with the personnel who perform the control about the procedures and processes involved in the reconciliation.
- *Observation*—Observe the entity personnel performing the reconciliation.
- *Inspection*—Review the documentation supporting completion of the reconciliation.
- *Reperformance*—Perform the reconciliation and agree to the reconciliation completed by the entity personnel.

The auditor uses professional judgment to determine the appropriate tests of controls to perform. However, inquiry alone is generally not sufficient evidence; the auditor would need to supplement inquiry with observation, examination, and/or reperformance.

Exhibit 9.8 presents an overview of various transaction controls that the client might use to mitigate risks in the revenue cycle and how the auditor might test

Exhibit 9.8
Control Examples and Tests of Controls

Objective	Examples of Controls	How Control Would Be Tested	Implications if Control Is Not Working
1. Recorded transactions are authorized and actually occurred.	a. Sales recorded only with valid customer order and shipping document. b. Credit is approved before shipment.	a. Sample recorded sales transactions and vouch back to source documents. Use generalized audit software to match sales with electronic shipping document or customer order. b. Use ACL to determine each customer's balance and compare with its credit limit.	a. Recorded sales may not have occurred. Extend accounts receivable confirmation work and review of subsequent collections. b. Receivables may not be collectible. Expand confirmation work and review of subsequent collections.
2. Sales are recorded in the correct accounting period.	a. Computer records sale upon entry of customer order and shipping information. Transactions entered, but not yet processed, are identified for an exception report and followed up. b. Monthly statements are sent to customers. A group independent of those recording the transactions receives and follows up complaints.	a. Review monitoring controls (e.g., management's review of transactions entered into the system and not shipped and billed). b. Review nature of complaints received. Investigate to determine if there is a pattern.	a. Company may have unrecorded sales transactions. Discuss with management to determine if it has plans to bill the sales. b. Sales may be recorded in the wrong year. Expand sales cutoff testing.
3. All sales are recorded.	a. Prenumbered shipping documents and invoices which are periodically accounted for. b. Online input of transactions and independent logging are done. c. Monitoring: Transactions are reviewed and compared with budgets and differences are investigated.	a. Review reconciliations to determine that control is working. b. Use generalized audit software to verify transaction trails. c. Review management reports and evidence of actions taken.	a–c. Expand cutoff tests at year-end to determine that all transactions are recorded in the correct period.
4. Sales are accurately recorded.	a. Sales price comes from authorized sales price list maintained on the computer.	a. Test access controls. Take a sample of recorded sales invoices and trace price back to authorized list.	a. Accounts receivable may be overstated or understated due to pricing errors. Expand confirmation and subsequent collection procedures.
5. Sales are correctly classified.	a. Chart of accounts is up to date and used. b. Computer program is tested before implementation	a. Take a sample of transactions and trace to general ledger to see if they are properly classified. b. When testing general controls, determine that controls over program changes are working.	a. Expand test of sales and receivables to determine that all items represent bona fide contracts and not consignment sales or sale of operating assets. b. Expand confirmations to customers.

those controls. Note that the tests of controls include selecting samples of transactions and obtaining supporting documents, reviewing monitoring controls, testing computer access controls, using data analytics tools to match documents and look for gaps or duplicate document numbers, reviewing customer complaints, reviewing documents such as reconciliations and management reports noting timely action taken, and reviewing sales contracts.

Considering the Results of Tests of Controls

The auditor analyzes the results of the tests of controls to determine additional appropriate procedures. There are two potential outcomes:

1. If the auditor identifies control deficiencies, the auditor will assess those deficiencies to determine their severity. (Are they significant deficiencies or material weaknesses?) The auditor would then modify the preliminary control risk assessment (possibly from low to high) and document the implications of the control deficiencies. The last column in *Exhibit 9.8* provides examples of implications of control deficiencies for substantive testing. The auditor will determine appropriate modifications to planned substantive audit procedures based on the types of misstatements that are most likely to occur because of the control deficiency.

2. If the auditor does not identify any control deficiencies, the auditor will likely determine that the preliminary assessment of control risk as low is still appropriate. The auditor then determines the extent that controls can provide evidence on the accuracy of account balances and determines planned substantive audit procedures. Substantive testing in this situation will be less than what is required in circumstances where the auditor identified internal control deficiencies. From the audit risk model, we know for companies with effective internal controls, the auditor will perform less substantive testing.

Check Your Basic Knowledge

9-25 In testing controls over whether sales are properly valued, the auditor could take a sample of recorded sales invoices and agree the price on the invoice to an authorized price list.   (T/F)

9-26 Surprisingly, AmTrust's restatement was followed by a stock price increase, likely because investors inferred that by revealing the restatement the company could move forward with confidence.   (T/F)

9-27 When auditing a nonpublic company, the auditor would generally make a decision not to test the operating effectiveness of controls in which of the following situations?

a.   The preliminary assessment of control risk is high.

b.   It is more cost efficient to directly test ending account balances than to test controls.

c.   The auditor believes that controls are designed effectively but are not operating as described.

d.   All of the above are situations when the auditor would likely not test the operating effectiveness of controls.

9-28 An auditor performs tests of controls in the revenue cycle. First, the auditor makes inquiries of company personnel about credit-granting policies. The auditor then selects a sample of sales transactions recorded in the general ledger and examines documentary evidence of credit approval. Which of the financial statement assertion(s) does this test of controls most likely support?

Completeness	Valuation or Allocation
a. Yes	Yes
b. No	Yes
c. Yes	No
d. No	No

LO 8

Determine and apply sufficient appropriate substantive audit procedures for testing revenue cycle accounts, disclosures, and assertions.

Obtaining Substantive Evidence About Accounts, Disclosures, and Assertions in the Revenue Cycle

In performing substantive procedures, the auditor wants reasonable assurance that the client's revenue recognition policies are appropriate and that revenue transactions are in accordance with GAAP. Substantive procedures (substantive analytical procedures, tests of details, or both) should be performed for all relevant assertions related to significant revenue cycle accounts and disclosures. Even if the auditor has evidence indicating that controls are operating effectively, the auditor cannot rely solely on control testing to provide evidence on the reliability of these accounts and assertions. Substantive tests in the revenue cycle typically provide evidence that:

- Sales transactions exist and are properly valued.
- Accounts receivable exist.
- The balance in the allowance account is reasonable.
- Fraudulent transactions are not included in the financial statements.

Exhibit 9.9 details typical substantive procedures for sales and accounts receivable. The extent to which the auditor performs substantive analytical procedures and tests of details depends on the risk of material misstatement.

Exhibit 9.9

Management Assertions and Substantive Procedures in the Revenue Cycle

Management Assertion	Substantive Procedure
Existence/occurrence—Recorded sales and accounts receivable are valid.	1. Perform substantive analytical procedures. 2. Trace sales invoices to customer orders and bills of lading. 3. Confirm balances or unpaid invoices with customers. 4. Examine subsequent collections as evidence that the sale existed. 5. Scan sales journal for duplicate entries.
Completeness—All sales are recorded.	1. Perform substantive analytical procedures. 2. Trace bills of lading to sales invoice and sales journal. 3. Account for sequence of sales invoices in sales journal.
Rights and obligations—The accounts receivable are owned by the organization (e.g., none have been sold).	1. Inquire of management. 2. Review minutes of board meetings.
Valuation or allocation—Sales and accounts receivable are properly valued and recorded in the correct period. Revenue has been recognized in accordance with GAAP.	1. Verify clerical accuracy of sales invoices and agreement of sales invoices with supporting documents. 2. Trace sales invoices to sales journal and customer's ledger. 3. Confirm balances or unpaid invoices with customers. 4. Foot sales journal and accounts receivable trial balance and reconcile accounts receivable trial balance with control account. 5. Review adequacy of the allowance for doubtful accounts. 6. Perform sales cutoff test.
Presentation and disclosure—Credit balance and related-party accounts receivable are properly disclosed. Revenue recognition policies have been properly disclosed.	1. Obtain confirmations from banks and other financial institutions. 2. Inquire of management. 3. Review work performed in other audit areas. 4. Review revenue recognition policies for appropriateness and consistency.

Why It Matters: An International Perspective

Performing Appropriate Substantive Audit Procedures in the Revenue Cycle: The Case of Kyoto Audit Corporation

This feature highlights the importance of performing and documenting sufficient appropriate substantive procedures in the revenue cycle.

In February 2012, the PCAOB released its first inspection report on Kyoto Audit Corporation (Kyoto), a Japanese affiliate of the Big 4 audit firm PricewaterhouseCoopers (PwC). PwC describes Kyoto as a cooperating firm. While Kyoto is not a full member of PwC's global network, it appears that Kyoto has the right to use PwC's audit methodology and has access to the expertise of the PwC network.

In December 2010 and January 2011, the PCAOB's staff reviewed Kyoto's audits for two companies and found audit deficiencies in both audits. The deficiencies they found included "the failure, in both audits, to perform adequate substantive analytical audit procedures to test revenue." The report also cited Kyoto's failures to perform sufficient procedures "to test the allowance for doubtful accounts." It appears that the audit firm had not gathered sufficient appropriate evidence to determine whether recorded revenue was accurate or whether customers could pay their bills.

While most audits are quality audits, this inspection report serves to illustrate the importance of complying with professional standards in performing and documenting sufficient appropriate substantive procedures in the revenue cycle. Kyoto ultimately performed additional audit procedures in response to the PCAOB inspection report, but did not change the audit reports issued. The companies with the audit deficiencies did not change their financial statements. Therefore, it appears that while the procedures performed by Kyoto were insufficient, the underlying financial accounts and assertions were not materially misstated.

For further details, see PCAOB Release No. 104-2012-053.

What Do You Think?

For Classroom Discussion

A May 3, 2017, *Wall Street Journal* article reports that the SEC is cracking down on several solar energy system companies, including San Francisco-based Sunrun, Inc. and San Mateo-based SolarCity Corp. The SEC alleges that these companies are not adequately disclosing an important metric that investors use to value their stock. The disclosure metric includes information about customer cancellations on orders for energy systems.

What appears to be happening is that salespeople at these companies are very aggressive in their approach, and the systems are quite expensive. As a result, customers have become increasingly likely to back out of the deals prior to installation. According to the *WSJ*: "Some customers say they were strong-armed into buying solar-energy systems by sales representatives who threatened to sue them if they didn't proceed with a project or to place a so-called mechanic's lien on their homes—a measure used to force a homeowner to pay for a home-improvement project... Others say they didn't realize they had actually signed contracts. Many said they believed they were just giving permission for a consultation."

These types of solar-energy companies have revealed in both their public filings and earnings calls that they are experiencing increased customer cancellations. However, the SEC contends that such companies have not provided enough details about the number of cancellations, and the effect of such cancellations on revenue cycle accounts and related effects on profitability.

SolarCity, for example, defends their disclosure policies as follows according to the *WSJ*: SolarCity ... "has remained focused on reporting the quality of our installed assets, not pre install cancellation rates. Our growth projections have always been based on actual deployments."

Both Sunrun and SolarCity prominently disclose the risks associated with customer cancellations of sales revenue in their respective Management Discussion & Analysis. However, neither provides monetary values or numbers with respect to how they get to their revenue, net of cancellations.

Put yourself in the perspective of these companies. Why can you empathize with their reluctance to provide detailed disclosure on cancellations?

Now put yourself in the perspective of the SEC and investors. Why would detailed information about cancellations be useful?

For further details, see the following two WSJ articles: https:// www.wsj.com/articles/sec-probes-solar-companies-over-disclosure- of-customer-cancellations-1493803801

https://www.wsj.com/articles/solar-company-sunrun-was- manipulating-sales-data-say-former-managers-1495445402

Revenue and Accounts Receivable: Performing Substantive Analytical Procedures

The process for conducting substantive analytical procedures in the revenue cycle is similar to that used for planning analytical procedures and follows the same seven-step process.

Step 1: Identify Suitable Analytical Procedures The relevant analytical procedures for conducting substantive analytics are not necessarily different from those for planning analytical procedures as depicted in *Exhibit 9.6*. Rather, the auditor conducts the procedures at a more precise level, often using disaggregated data. For example, the auditor can perform ratios and trend analyses by product line, geographic region, or business unit. Further, ratios and trends can be compared to industry averages and to relevant prior periods (e.g., monthly, quarterly, or yearly).

When performing substantive analytical procedures, the auditor is most likely to conduct a reasonableness test. An example of a reasonableness test would be estimating room revenue for a hotel using the number of rooms, the average room rate, and average occupancy rate. Alternatively, the auditor could estimate revenue from an electrical utility company by considering revenue rates approved by a Public Service Commission (where applicable) and demographic information about growth in households and industry in the service area the company serves.

Step 2: Evaluate Reliability of Data Used to Develop Expectations In evaluating reliability of data used to develop expectations in substantive analytical procedures, the auditor may test the operating effectiveness of controls over the preparation of information used in those analytics. When the auditor considers these controls effective, the auditor will have greater confidence in the reliability of the information. Further, the auditor may use data from independent external sources (e.g., industry ratios), as that data are generally considered reliable.

Step 3: Develop Expectations Expectations that the auditor develops for substantive analytical procedures will be more precise than those developed during planning analytical procedures. An increase in precision occurs by using more disaggregated data. The appropriate level of disaggregation depends on the nature of the organization, its size, and its complexity. As an example, consider the reasonableness test related to hotel revenue presented earlier. The auditor could develop an expectation of overall room revenue by using the number of rooms across the hotel chain, the average room rate across the chain, and the average occupancy rate across the chain. This approach would not result in a very precise estimate. However, if the auditor disaggregated the analysis based on types of hotels within the chain (luxury, resort, or economy), the auditor could improve the precision of the estimate. Usually, the more detailed the information, the more precise the expectation.

Step 4 and Step 5: Define and Identify Significant Unexpected Differences At this point, the auditor is trying to answer the question of whether the auditor's expectation is significantly different from what the client has recorded. The amount of difference that the auditor considers significant is influenced by materiality, desired level of assurance, and assessed risk of material misstatement. As the auditor's assessed risk of material misstatement increases, the amount of the unexpected difference that would be considered significant declines.

The auditor then compares the client's recorded amount with the auditor's expectation. Once this mechanical step is completed, the auditor will have identified any significant differences between the auditor's expectation and the amount the client has recorded.

Step 6 and Step 7: Investigate Significant Unexpected Differences and Ensure Proper Documentation Materiality and the desired level of assurance aid the auditor in determining how to investigate significant unexpected differences. The auditor investigates these differences through substantive tests of details, as described next. In general, if substantive analytical procedures do not result in unresolved issues, the auditor can reduce direct testing of account balances. However, in the revenue cycle, it is unlikely that audit evidence obtained from substantive analytical procedures alone will be sufficient evidence for the auditor.

Finally, as with planning analytical procedures, the auditor will document evidence gathered and judgments reached during substantive analytical procedures.

Revenue: Substantive Tests of Details

Substantive tests of details for revenue transactions primarily involve inspection of relevant client documentation. These tests focus on the existence and valuation assertions, although the auditor might also perform tests of details related to completeness.

Revenue: Existence and Valuation Assertions

The existence and valuation assertions are usually the most relevant for revenue accounts. Vouching a sample of recorded sales transactions back to customer orders and shipping documents provides support for the existence assertion. The auditor compares the quantities billed and shipped with customer orders and verifies the clerical accuracy of the sales invoices to provide assurance on valuation. These procedures also provide evidence on the existence and valuation of accounts receivable.

As we discuss in *Chapter 8*, data analytics tools can also be useful. These tools can identify duplicate sales and select a sample of recorded sales transactions for vouching. Furthermore, these tools may be able to compare the transactions detail with the supporting electronic documents. They can also verify the clerical accuracy of the invoices and foot the sales journal.

Revenue: Completeness Assertion

In testing the completeness assertion, the auditor expects the client to have used prenumbered shipping and billing documents. The auditor selects a sample of shipping documents and trace them into the sales journal to obtain evidence on whether the client has recorded all shipments as sales transactions in accordance with the revenue recognition accounting standards. The auditor can use audit software to look for gaps in the recorded sales invoice numbers and verify that the missing numbers are appropriate and do not represent unrecorded sales. For example, the gaps may be voided documents or the client may have used different numbers at different locations.

Revenue: Cutoff Issues

Additional audit attention should be given to sales transactions recorded just before and after year-end. A specific concern related to existence is whether a recorded revenue transaction actually occurred before the end of the accounting period. For an example, refer back to *Exhibit 9.3*, which contains a description of the situation in which Motorola kept its third quarter books open after the quarter ended so that it could record additional revenues. The auditor is also concerned with whether transactions recorded in the subsequent year actually relate to the current year audit. Performing cutoff tests with sales transactions recorded several days before and after year-end is important to assuring both the existence and completeness of the revenue transactions.

The auditor can examine the following items to determine whether the client has achieved a proper cutoff of sales and sales returns:

Cutoff Test	Items to Examine
Sales	Shipping documents and related recorded sales
Sales returns	Receiving reports and related credits to customer accounts

The auditor can test sales cutoff in alternative ways. For example, the auditor can select a sample of sales transactions from the cutoff period to determine when the transaction occurred. The auditor will look at the shipping terms and shipment dates to determine whether there was an appropriate cutoff. The auditor may also want to inspect the sales contracts for terms indicating that the client should delay recording of the sale. For example, the customer's right of return (and a high probability of return), the existence of additional performance by the seller, the probability of collection based on some future event (contingency), or the existence of an unusually low probability of collection might indicate that the client should not recognize revenue in the current audit year.

As a second approach to cutoff testing, if reliable shipping dates are stored electronically, the auditor can use data analytics tools to identify any sales recorded in the wrong period.

Accounts Receivable: Substantive Procedures

A starting point for accounts receivable substantive procedures is obtaining a detailed aged accounts receivable trial balance from the client, manually preparing an aged trial balance, or using data analytics tools to develop aging information. *Exhibit 9.10* provides an example of an aged trial balance. A detailed trial balance lists each customer's balance or unpaid invoices, with columns to show those that are current, 30 days overdue, 60 days, and so on.

If the client prepared the aged trial balance, the auditor should recalculate the mathematical and aging accuracy, and agree it to the general ledger. The auditor will also identify credit balances, if significant, ask the client to reclassify those as liabilities. The auditor uses the aged trial balance to:

- Agree the detail to the balance in the control account
- Select customer balances for confirmation
- Identify amounts due from officers, employees, or other related parties or any nontrade receivables that need to be separately disclosed in the financial statements
- Help determine the reasonableness of the allowance for doubtful accounts by identifying past-due balances

Accounts Receivable: Substantive Tests of Details—Confirmations

A widely used auditing procedure is to ask the client's customers to confirm the existence and the amount they owe to the client. Existence is necessary for correct valuation. However, existence does not necessarily assure correct valuation; for example, a customer might acknowledge the existence of the debt, but might not have sufficient resources to pay it. Confirmations generally provide quality evidence about the existence of receivables and the completeness of collections, sales discounts, and sales returns and allowances. For example, if a customer had made a payment, but the client has not recorded the payment, or the client has sent an invoice but no shipment occurred, the customer would likely report the discrepancy on the confirmation. A confirmation can be very effective in addressing the existence of fictitious sales. The presumption is that if the client records fictitious

Exhibit 9.10

Accounts Receivable Aging

Name	Balance	Current	30–60	61–90	91–120	Over 120
Alvies	154,931	154,931				
Basch	71,812		71,812			
Carlson	115,539	115,539				
Draper	106,682	106,682				
Ernst	60,003			60,003		
Faust	90,907	90,907				
Gerber	241,129	211,643	29,486			
Hal	51,516	51,516				
Harv	237,881	237,881				
Kaas	18,504				18,504	
Kruze	44,765	44,765				
Lere	28,937	28,937				
Misty	210,334	210,334				
Mooney	216,961	216,961				
Otto	273,913	273,913				
Paggen	209,638	209,638				
Quast	88,038					88,038
Rauch	279,937	279,937				
Sundby	97,898	97,898				
Towler	96,408	85,908		10,500		
Zook	31,886	31,886				
	...	...				
Zough	245,927	245,927				
Totals	2,973,546	2,695,203	101,298	70,503	18,504	88,038

sales to the account of a valid customer, the customer will note that some of the recorded sales are not correct.

Auditing standards in the U.S. generally require the use of confirmations unless one of the following conditions exists:

- Accounts receivable are not material.
- The use of confirmations would be ineffective. An auditor might determine that confirmations are ineffective if customers have previously refused to confirm balances or customers do not have a good basis on which to respond to the confirmation.
- The auditor's assessment of the risk of material misstatement is low and that assessment, in conjunction with the evidence provided by other substantive tests, is sufficient.

When the auditor sends confirmation, the auditor can use two types of accounts receivable confirmations: positive confirmations and negative confirmations.

Positive Confirmations

Positive confirmations are correspondence (paper or electronic) sent to a sample of customers, asking them to review the current balance or unpaid invoice(s) due to the client and return the letters directly to the auditor indicating whether they agree with the balance. If the customer does not return a signed confirmation, the auditor needs to use follow-up audit procedures to verify the existence of the customer's balance. *Exhibit 9.11* contains an example of a positive confirmation. Notice that it is printed on the client's letterhead, is addressed to the customer, is signed by the client, indicates the balance or unpaid invoice amount as of a particular date—referred to as the confirmation date—and tells the customer to respond directly to the auditor in an enclosed self-addressed, postage-paid envelope.

Auditors may choose to confirm the terms of unusual or complex agreements or transactions in conjunction with or separately from the confirmation of account balances. The confirmation may need to be addressed to customer personnel who would be familiar with the details rather than to their accounts payable personnel. Auditors should also specifically inquire during the confirmation process about the possibility of bill-and-hold transactions (such as transactions in which the seller recognizes the sale and bills the customer but does not actually deliver the goods or services), extended payment terms or nonstandard installment receivables, or an unusual volume of sales to distributors or retailers (possible channel stuffing).

Furthermore, the auditor should confirm not only the terms of the transactions but also the potential existence and content of side letters. Recall that a side letter is an agreement containing contract terms that are not part of the formal contract (often involving rights of return), thereby increasing audit risk because it enables key contract terms affecting revenue recognition to be hidden from the auditor as part of a revenue recognition fraud. Side letters are often associated with material revenue misstatements.

Exhibit 9.11
Positive Confirmation

Gordon's Bay Manufacturing Company

14 Kidman Street
Austin, TX 73301
January 10, 2019

Alexander Industrial Supplies
1265 Lombardi Avenue
Green Bay, WI 54304

Our auditors, Johnstone, & Gramling, CPAs, are making an annual audit of our financial statements. Please confirm the balance due our company as of December 31, 2018, which is shown in our records as $32,012.38.

Please indicate in the space provided below if the amount is in agreement with your records. If there are differences, please provide any information that will assist our auditors in reconciling the difference.

Please mail your reply directly to Johnstone, & Gramling, CPAs, 975 University Avenue, Madison, WI 53706, in the enclosed return envelope. PLEASE DO NOT MAIL PAYMENTS ON THIS BALANCE TO OUR AUDITORS.

Very truly yours,

Meg Christianson

Meg Christianson
Controller
Gordon's Bay Manufacturing Company
To: Johnstone, & Gramling, CPAs
The balance due Gordon's Bay Manufacturing Company of $32,012.38 as of 12/31/18 is correct with the following exceptions, (if any):

Signature: _____
Title: _____
Date: _____

Negative Confirmations

A **negative confirmation** asks the customer to review the balance owed to the client, but requests the customer to respond directly to the auditor only if the customer disagrees with the indicated balance. *Exhibit 9.12* provides an example of a negative confirmation. A negative confirmation is less expensive to administer than a positive confirmation because it does not require follow-up procedures when a customer does not return the confirmation. The auditor assumes that a nonresponse means that the customer agrees with the stated balance.

Today, in practice, negative confirmations are rarely used. Historically, the auditor would use negative confirmations if the following conditions existed:

- There are a large number of relatively small customer balances.
- The assessed level of the risk of material misstatement for receivables and related revenue transactions is low.
- The auditor has a reason to believe that the customers are likely to give proper attention to the requests; for example, the customers have independent records from which to make an evaluation, will take the time to do so, and will return the confirmation to the auditor if significant discrepancies exist.

Comparing Positive and Negative Confirmations

Positive confirmations provide higher quality evidence than negative confirmations because they result in the: (1) receipt of a response from the customer, or (2) use of alternative procedures by the auditor to verify the existence of the receivable.

Exhibit 9.12
Negative Confirmation

Gordon's Bay Manufacturing Company

14 Kidman Street
Austin, TX 73301
January 10, 2019

Alexander Industrial Supplies
1265 Lombardi Avenue
Green Bay, WI 54304

Our auditors, Johnstone, & Gramling, CPAs, are making an annual audit of our financial statements. Please confirm the balance due our company as of December 31, 2018, which is shown in our records as $32,012.38. If the amount is not correct, please report any differences directly to our auditors using the space below and the enclosed return envelope. NO REPLY IS NECESSARY IF THIS AMOUNT AGREES WITH YOUR RECORDS. PLEASE DO NOT MAIL PAYMENTS ON ACCOUNT TO OUR AUDITORS.

Very truly yours,

Meg Christianson

Meg Christianson
Controller
Gordon's Bay Manufacturing Company
To: Johnstone, & Gramling, CPAs
The balance due Gordon's Bay Manufacturing Company of $32,012.38 as of 12/31/18 does not agree with our records because (No reply is necessary if your records agree.)

Signature: _____
Title: _____
Date: _____

PCAOB Enforcement Actions Related to Confirming Accounts Receivable

Why It Matters

This feature highlights some problems auditors have had related to adhering to the professional standards related to accounts receivable confirmations.

Regulatory enforcement actions provide many examples of auditors not adhering to professional standards related to confirming accounts receivable. Two enforcement actions that illustrate this point are summarized here.

In a PCAOB enforcement action against Moore & Associates, the PCAOB notes that the audit firm's staff often did not do any work to confirm either the existence or the valuation of clients' receivables. At one client, the audit team documented that confirmation procedures were not applicable without documenting how they came to that unusual conclusion. Further, for another client, the firm's staff considered confirmation responses from client management as acceptable, when in fact confirmations should have come directly to the auditors from the clients' customers.

In a PCAOB enforcement action involving the audits of Satyam, the PCAOB notes the failure of the auditors to audit Satyam's accounts receivable balances in accordance with PCAOB standards. Specifically, the enforcement action indicates that the engagement team relied on Satyam's management to send confirmation requests associated with accounts receivable balances.

Further, the auditors received no responses to these confirmation requests and made no attempt to follow up on the nonresponses with second confirmation requests.

Even more recently, the PCAOB censured Wander Rodrigues Teles, a former partner of PwC-Brazil, relating to the audit of Sara Lee Cafes do Brasil. The PCAOB criticized Teles because he and his team failed to exercise professional skepticism with respect to management's assertions that the accounts receivable aging schedule was realistic and reliable. Teles knew that there existed many customer disputes relating to accounts receivable, and that Sara Lee management had not accrued reserves to offset disputed accounts receivable amounts. In Sara Lee's restatement of its financial statements relating to this case, we learn that accounts receivable was overstated by 246% in FYE 2010 and by 263% in FYE 2011, which are clearly highly material discrepancies.

Thus, while U.S. professional auditing standards are quite clear on the need to confirm accounts receivable, there exist examples in which auditors inexplicably do not adhere to those standards. While most audits are performed in a quality manner, these examples serve to illustrate that problems do occur and that you should be aware of such a possibility as you enter the profession.

For further details, see PCAOB Release No. 105-2009-006, PCAOB Release No. 105-2011-002 and PCAOB Release No. 105-2017-007.

Regardless of the type of confirmation, the auditor needs to take care that the confirmation process adheres to professional auditing standards.

The Confirmation Process

The auditor may use electronic-based or paper-based confirmations. The auditor should assure that the information in each confirmation is correct and should control the dissemination of the confirmation requests so that the client cannot modify them. For paper-based confirmations, customers are to return confirmations directly to the auditor's office in an enclosed self-addressed, postage-paid envelope. Similarly, the mailing should show the auditor's address as the return address if the confirmation is not deliverable. Undeliverable confirmations should raise the auditor's suspicion regarding the existence of the recorded receivable. To avoid receiving confirmation responses for fictitious receivables, the auditor must take care to assure that the confirmation is not delivered to a location where the client can act as a surrogate and confirm an inappropriate receivable.

When using an electronic confirmation process, the auditor needs to be sure that the:

- Process is secure and properly controlled,
- Information obtained is a direct communication to the auditor in response to the auditor's request, and
- Information is obtained from a third party (in the case of accounts receivable, that party is the organization that owes money to the audit client) who is the intended respondent.

Why It Matters Electronic Confirmations at Confirmation.com

This feature provides information about electronic confirmations.

Confirmation.com is a leading provider of all types of electronic confirmations, including accounts receivable confirmations. Electronic confirmations are equally as acceptable as audit evidence as paper-based confirmations. Electronic confirmations have reliability benefits because of the controls built into the software system, whereby management cannot intercept or alter the confirmations, as is potentially the case with paper-based confirmations.

They also have efficiency benefits because a third-party vendor automates and controls the process, thereby saving the auditor time. Usually the electronic confirmation responses are available within two days, whereas customers may not return paper-based confirmations for several weeks. Of course, there is a cost to the auditor in using the services of a company like Confirmation.com, but audit firms and their clients often consider this service a good investment. The figure below presents pricing information for this service as of July 2017.

Confirmation.com Pricing

Source: Confirmation.com

	Confirmation.com™	Confirmation.com Consolidated Form	Confirmation.com Email™	Confirmation.com Mail™
AR/AP	$23 per confirmation	N/A	Free	$2.95 in US, $4.95 outside US
Bank	$23 per account, per client, per responder, & per As-of-Date. Capped at 5 ($115)	$99 per group, per bank	Free	$2.95 in US, $4.95 outside US
EBP	N/A	N/A	Free	$2.95 in US, $4.95 outside US
Legal	$30 per confirmation	N/A	N/A	N/A

To find out your savings go to www.cpa.com/audit-confirmations#calculator

Confirmation.com

Sample Selection The auditor can use several approaches to select the specific receivables to confirm, and each of these is applicable to either paper-based or electronic-based confirmations. The auditor can confirm all of the large balances and randomly or haphazardly select some of the smaller balances using either non-statistical or monetary unit sampling (MUS). The auditor may decide to include in the sample those accounts that have credit balances, are significant and past due, and/or have unusual customer names that are unfamiliar to the auditor.

Sampling Unit The sampling unit can be a customer's entire account balance, or one or more of the unpaid invoices making up that balance. When a balance is composed of several unpaid invoices, it will help the customer if the confirmation includes a list of those invoices.

Undeliverable Confirmations If some confirmations are returned as undeliverable, the auditor should determine why this occurred. If the wrong address was used, the correct address should be obtained and another request should be sent.

False Confirmations

Focus on Fraud

This feature provides an example of fraudulent activity in the accounts receivable confirmation process.

A **false confirmation** is one in which the respondent (in this case, the client's customer) responds inaccurately to the audit firm with respect to the information on the confirmation. In a classic example, Just for Feet (an athletic shoe retailer) executives pressured the director of sales at Adidas to respond inaccurately to the auditor's accounts receivable information. Adidas' director of apparel sales confirmed that the company owed Just for Feet $2.2 million, when in fact Adidas only owed $40,000. The sales director's motive for agreeing to respond inaccurately was because of threats from Just for Feet to terminate the relationship with Adidas.

The following notable examples of false confirmation schemes illustrate the high-profile nature of the company providing the false confirmation and the senior positions held by the individuals providing the false confirmations:

Company with Accounts Receivable Confirmation Fraud	Company That Provided False Confirmation	Title of Individual That Provided the False Confirmation
Kmart	Eastman Kodak	Vice president of sales
	Pepsi-Cola	National director of sales
	Frito-Lay	Director of sales and national account manager
Just for Feet	Adidas	Director of apparel sales
	Fila	President and CEO
	Converse	Vice president of U.S. sales
Royal Ahold	Sara Lee Foods	Sales manager
	Conagra Foods	Account manager
	Heritage Bag	CEO

False confirmations are problematic for auditors in terms of evidence reliability expectations. Auditors usually expect that externally provided evidence is reliable because it is from a third party. In the case of false confirmations, this expectation is invalid. In recent years, the SEC has actively pursued enforcement actions against individuals that have provided false confirmations to auditors.

It is also possible that the customer does not exist. The auditor should make every effort to determine the customer's existence. For example, the customer's name and address could be located in the telephone directory, in the publication of a credit-rating service, or on the Internet. If a valid address cannot be located, the auditor should presume that the account does not exist or might be fictitious.

Follow-Up to Nonresponses for Positive Confirmations The auditor is required to perform follow-up procedures for positive confirmations that are not returned within a reasonable time after being mailed, such as two weeks. Second, and sometimes third, requests are mailed. If the amount being confirmed is relatively large, the auditor may consider calling the customer to encourage a written reply. When customers do not respond to the positive confirmation requests, the auditor should perform other procedures, referred to as **alternative procedures**, to verify the existence of the receivable. Remember that mailed confirmations represent only a sample of the many account balances shown in the client's records. The results of the sample represent the total population; therefore, it is important that the auditor develop sufficient follow-up procedures to gain satisfaction about each of the balances selected for confirmation. Alternative procedures that the auditor can perform include:

- *Subsequent cash receipts after year-end*—Care should be taken to assure that these subsequent receipts relate to the balance as of the confirmation date, not to subsequent sales. Evidence obtained from testing subsequent collections can be a stronger indicator of the validity of the customer's balance than that obtained from confirmations. If the client normally collects a significant amount of the year-end receivables balance before the end of the audit, the auditor may choose to emphasize tests of subsequent collections and minimize confirmation work. Testing subsequent collections provides strong evidence about both the existence and valuation of the related receivables.

- *Examination of supporting documents*—If all, or a portion, of the balance has not been collected at the time alternative procedures are being performed, the auditor should examine documents supporting the uncollected invoices. These documents include customer orders, sales orders, bills of lading or internal shipping documents, and sales invoices. The auditor must consider that evidence obtained from internal copies of customer orders, internal shipping documents, and sales invoices is not as persuasive as that obtained from subsequent cash receipts. Bills of lading are usually external and provide independent verification of shipments.

Follow-Up Procedures for Exceptions Noted on Positive Confirmations

Customers are to provide details of any differences (referred to as **exceptions**) between their records and the amount shown on the confirmation. The auditor investigates exceptions to determine whether the difference is a customer error, an item in dispute, a client misstatement, or a timing difference. **Timing differences** are due to transactions that are in process at the confirmation date, such as in-transit shipments or payments. If the auditor can determine that the timing difference did not result in recording the receivable in the wrong period, the differences do not represent misstatements in the account balance. Examples of exceptions include:

- *Payment has already been made*—The customer has made a payment before the confirmation date, but the client has not received the payment before the confirmation date.

- *Merchandise has not been received*—The client records the sale at the date of shipment and the customer records the purchase when the goods are received. The time the goods are in transit is typically the cause of this type of exception.

- *The goods have been returned*—The client's failure to record a credit memo. Such a failure could result from timing differences or from the improper recording of sales returns and allowances.

- *Clerical errors and disputed amounts exist*—The customer states that there is an error in the price charged for the goods, the goods are damaged, the proper quantity of goods was not received, or there is some other type of customer issue. These exceptions should be investigated to determine whether the client's records are in error and, if so, the amount of the error. Such differences might have implications for the valuation of the receivables account. However, what may initially appear to be a timing difference may actually be the result of lapping, discussed earlier in the chapter.

Because the auditor selects only a sample of accounts receivable for confirmation purposes, investigation of all exceptions and determination of the cause for any exceptions, rather than rationalizing the exception away as an isolated instance, are important. As discussed in *Chapter 8*, the auditor projects misstatements to the entire population of receivables to determine whether there is a material misstatement in the account balance. If the projected amount of misstatement appears to have a material effect on the financial statements, the auditor will discuss with the client the magnitude and cause of such misstatement to decide the appropriate response. If subsequent work supports the conclusion of a material misstatement, a client adjustment will be required.

Follow-Up Procedures for Negative Confirmations   The basic premise underlying negative confirmations is that if the auditor does not receive a response, the auditor assumes that the customer agrees with the balance. This assumption is not always the correct assumption. The customer may not respond even though the balance is wrong because: (1) the confirmation was lost, misplaced, or sent to the wrong address; (2) the customer did not understand the request; or (3) the request was simply ignored and thrown away. The auditor must have some assurance that these factors do not comprise the reliability of the negative confirmation process. The auditor does not expect that many customers will return negative confirmations. However, when the auditor receives a returned negative confirmation, responses from the customer might indicate that:

- the customer did not understand the request
- the customer confirms an incorrect amount because payments or shipments are in transit
- the amount recorded by the client is in error or is fraudulent.

The auditor must perform follow-up work to determine whether the confirmed amount represents a misstatement. The auditor might look at subsequent cash receipts or vouch back to the customer's order and evidence of shipment to help make this assessment. If the auditor detects errors, the auditor should use expanded procedures to: (1) find the underlying cause of the errors, and (2) estimate the amount of misstatement in the account balance.

Additional Procedures When Confirmations are Sent at an Interim Date   If the auditor confirms receivables at an interim date, the auditor must gather additional evidence during the roll-forward period. Roll-forward procedures in the revenue cycle include:

- Comparing individual customer balances at the interim confirmation date with year-end balances and confirming any that have substantially increased
- Comparing monthly sales, collections, sales discounts, and sales returns and allowances during the roll-forward period with those for prior months and prior years to see whether they appear out of line; if they do, obtaining an explanation from management and acquiring corroborative evidence to determine whether that explanation is valid
- Reconciling receivable subsidiary records to the general ledger at both the confirmation date and year-end
- Testing the cutoff of sales, cash collections, and credit memos for returns and allowances at year-end
- Scanning journals to identify receivables postings from unusual sources and investigate unusual items
- Computing the number of days' sales in receivables at both the confirmation date and year-end and comparing these data and data from prior periods
- Computing the gross profit percentage during the roll-forward period and comparing that to the percentage for the year and for prior periods

Accounts Receivable: Substantive Procedures for the Allowance Account

Substantive procedures related to the allowance account are relevant to the valuation of accounts receivable. Tests of details for the revenue account provide evidence as to whether the client initially recorded receivables transactions at their correct value (gross value). However, the auditor is also concerned as to whether it is likely that the client will collect the outstanding receivables (net realizable value). This concern relates to determining the reasonableness of the client's allowance for doubtful accounts. Accounts receivable should be valued at its net realizable value; that is, the gross amount customers owe less the allowance for doubtful accounts.

Determining the reasonableness of the client's estimate of the allowance for doubtful accounts is one of the more difficult audit judgments because, at the time of the audit, a single correct answer is not available. Recording the allowance for doubtful accounts and determining bad-debt expense for the year is the result of an accounting estimate. The allowance should reflect management's best estimate of accounts receivable that the company will not collect. The client's estimate must reflect the economic status of the client's customers, current economic conditions, and an informed expectation about potential default on payment. For many companies, determining the allowance will have a substantial effect on the company's profitability.

After reviewing and testing the process used by management, including the controls over the process, auditors generally use one or a combination of the following approaches to obtain evidence about the reasonableness of the client's estimate:

- Inquire of management about the collectibility of customer balances, particularly those that are large and long overdue
- Develop an independent model to estimate the accounts
- Review credit reports from outside credit bureaus, such as Dun & Bradstreet (*http://www.dnb.com/*), to help determine the likelihood of the collection of specific accounts
- Review customer correspondence files to gain additional insight into the collectibility of specific accounts
- For accounts that are unusually large or past due, review the customer's latest financial statements to perform an independent analysis of collectibility
- Inquire about the client's procedures for deciding when to write off an account

Accounts Receivable: Other Substantive Procedures

Accounts Receivable: Rights and Obligations

Some companies sell their receivables to banks or other financial institutions but may retain responsibility for collecting the receivables and may be liable if the percentage of collection falls below a specified minimum. Substantive audit procedures that would reveal these ownership and related disclosure issues include:

- Reviewing all such arrangements and obtaining confirmations from the client's banks about any contingent liabilities
- Inquiring of management about any activities related to the receivables
- Scanning the cash receipts journal for relatively large inflows of cash that are posted from unusual sources
- Obtaining bank confirmations, which includes information on obligations to the bank and loan collateral
- Reviewing the board of directors' minutes, which generally contain approval for these items

Accounts Receivable: Presentation and Disclosure

Accounting standards require that trade accounts receivable be presented separately from other receivables. For example, material receivables from related parties, including officers, directors, stockholders, and employees, should be shown separately in the financial statements, with appropriate disclosures being provided. Audit procedures directed toward identifying related-party transactions such as these include:

- Reviewing SEC filings
- Reviewing the accounts receivable trial balance
- Inquiring of management and the audit committee about receivables from related parties

The client should reclassify:

- Material debit balances in accounts payable for amounts due from vendors as accounts receivable,
- Material credit balances in accounts receivable as accounts payable, and
- Receivables not due within the normal operating cycle or one year as non-current assets.

Audit procedures to identify misclassified receivables include making inquiries of management, reviewing the aged trial balance for large or old outstanding balances, reading the board of directors' minutes, and scanning the subsidiary ledger to identify unusually large receivable balances (particularly those that resulted from a single transaction or that are from an unusual source).

The client should disclose receivables that the client has sold with recourse, discounted, or pledged as collateral on loans in the notes to the financial statements.

Performing Substantive Fraud-Related Procedures

Substantive procedures need to address specific fraud risk factors that are present. Potential fraud risks in the revenue cycle include:

- Excessive credit memos or other credit adjustments to accounts receivable after the end of the fiscal year
- Customer complaints and discrepancies in accounts receivable confirmations (e.g., disputes over terms, prices, or amounts)
- Unusual entries to the accounts receivable subsidiary ledger or sales journal
- Missing or altered source documents or the inability of the client to produce original documents in a reasonable period of time
- A lack of cash flow from operating activities when income from operating activities has been reported
- Unusual reconciling differences between the accounts receivable subsidiary ledger and control account
- Sales to customers in the last month of the fiscal period at terms more favorable than previous months
- Predated or postdated transactions
- Large or unusual adjustments to sales accounts just prior to or just after the fiscal year-end

The auditor might use the following fraud-related audit procedures to respond to these fraud risks:

- Perform a thorough review of original source documents, including invoices, shipping documents, customer purchase orders, cash receipts, and written correspondence between the client and the customer.
- Analyze and review credit memos and other accounts receivable adjustments for the period subsequent to the balance sheet date.
- Analyze all large or unusual sales made near year-end and vouch to original source documents.

Prompt for Critical Thinking #4 It's Your Turn!

Provide examples of other fraud-related audit procedures that the auditor might perform in the revenue cycle.

- _____
- _____
- _____

Why It Matters Using Data Analytics in the Revenue Cycle in the Healthcare Sector

This feature provides insights on big data and data analytics in the healthcare sector, identifies incentives to use these analytics, and discusses how healthcare organizations can use these analytics to their decision-making advantage.

One sector of the economy, the healthcare sector, reports a dramatic rise in exploiting the power of data analytics. This sector benefits tremendously because it is inherently complex, employs massive amounts of data-related transactions, that is, high volume that relates to relatively predictable categories of revenue cycle-related transactions; for example, billing and payments.

Why do healthcare organizations use data analytics, i.e., what are the incentives?

Hospitals typically lose 1–4% of their net revenue to **revenue attrition**, which equals beginning period reoccurring revenue minus end-of-period reoccurring revenue, less any new revenue gained, divided by beginning period revenue. In simpler terms, revenue attrition helps organizations determine the relative extent to which they are losing versus gaining customers. If an organization experiences revenue attrition, it means that instead of holding steady or improving, revenue starts to decline, for example, due to customers

who move away or who switch to another supplier, for example, because they are unhappy with customer service. Data analytics help healthcare organizations prevent or reverse revenue attrition.

Data analytics also enable these organizations to respond to changes in the sector, for example, their revenue is currently based upon negative healthcare episodes, but will be moving toward rewards for healthy behavior changes are occurring in the reimbursement process whereby these organizations receive payments not from individuals, but from a group of bundled payments; payments and penalties will become the norm relating to negative healthcare episodes; and there exists a dramatic increase in the extent of patient responsibility arising from significant increases in high-deductible health plans.

Further, data analytics enables hospitals to very closely monitor their revenues and expenses as they struggle to address cost pressure, Obamacare, and restrictions on and reductions in the reimbursements that they receive. In other words, data analytics helps companies grow their revenue, while addressing systematic changes in the underlying revenue and cost structure in the market in which they operate.

A key concept motivating the move toward data analytics is as follows (with a catchy phrase at the end to illustrate the point):

Key Concept:

"A central, dedicated enterprise data warehouse for use by your primary Revenue Cycle Workflow Application with integrated Business Intelligence and analytic query systems will yield much better results and allow for significantly greater flexibility and capacity than trying to analyze a distributed set of separate, independent data silos (**Excel hell**)."

http://www.gaffeyhealth.com/images/Big-Data.pdf

The Gaffey Health whitepaper (p. 2) that we reference above defines **big data** as follows: "high volume, high velocity, and/or high variety information assets that require new forms of processing to enable enhanced decision making, insight discovery and process optimization." The simplest way to think about big data is that it encompasses lots of information, from lots of

sources, that when combined and integrated, enables better decision making, thereby helping to assure long-term organizational sustainability and **business intelligence**, which *"is the process of transforming all of the raw data that companies (providers) collect from their various operations into actionable information"* (Gaffey Health, p. 3).

How do healthcare organizations employ data analytics?

In this sector, there exists the following types of big data: clinical healthcare outcomes and assessments, operating expenses, fixed asset expenses, property, plant and equipment management, patient billing, insurance company interfaces, Federal and State-level requirements and associated revenue structures, customer service and physician practice data, underpayments, denials of payments, and uncollectible payments.

The challenge that healthcare organization managers face is bringing all this data, that is, key performance indicators, together to make good decisions. Managers can use this plethora of financial and operating data to measure current performance quality and profitability, discover improvement opportunities, and remediate underperforming personnel or processes.

To employ data analytics, organizations need to visualize the data quickly and efficiently (e.g., using Tableau), move away from manual report creation via silos of Excel files, and move toward a variety of financial applications that support the management of big data. For an example of six metrics in the healthcare sector, explore the following link:

(*https://www.healthcatalyst.com/wp-content/uploads/2015/01/Figure-1-Sample-Revenue-Cycle-Explorer-executive-dashboard.png*)

In addition, consider the associated big data dashboard, which focuses on analyzing data across six categories of **key performance indicators**. These indicators are quantifiable measures that decision-makers can use to evaluate the success of an organization, unit, employee, or account as they seek to meet performance objectives.

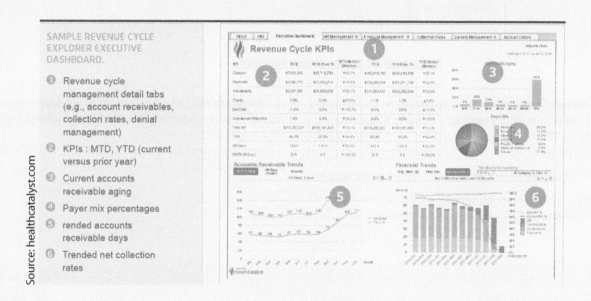

SAMPLE REVENUE CYCLE EXPLORER EXECUTIVE DASHBOARD.

① Revenue cycle management detail tabs (e.g., account receivables, collection rates, denial management)

② KPIs : MTD, YTD (current versus prior year)

③ Current accounts receivable aging

④ Payer mix percentages

⑤ rended accounts receivable days

⑥ Trended net collection rates

Source: healthcatalyst.com

As an additional series of examples, see the key performance indicators (KPIs) that the Maryland Healthcare Financial Management Association identifies, tracks, and uses:

KPIs by Functional Area

PATIENT ACCESS	REVENUE INTEGRITY	CLAIMS MANAGMENT	REIMBURSEMENT	OTHER MANAGEMENT
• Pre-Registration Rate	• Days Gross Revenue in Discharged-Not-Final-Billed (DNFB)	• Final-Billed-Not-Submitted (FBNS)	• Initial Zero Paid Denial Rate	• Cash Collections as % of Net Revenue
• Point-of-Service Collections Rate	• Discharged-Not-Submitted to Payer (DNSP)	• Clean Claim Submission Rate	• Initial Partial Paid Denial Rate	• Days Cash on Hand
• Uninsured Patient Conversion Rate	• Late Charges as % of Total Charges	• Net days in A/R	• Total Denial Write-Off as a % of Net Revenue	• Case Mix Index
• Insurance Verification Rate		• A/R Aging Distribution	• Overturned Denial Rate	• Bad Debt Write-offs as % of Gross Revenue
• Insurance Authorization Rate		• Billed A/R >90 Days • 3rd Party >90 Days • Self Pay > 90 Days		• Charity Care Write-offs as % of Gross Revenue
• Charity Care to Uncompensated Care		• Days Gross Revenue Held in Credit Balances		• Cost-to-Collect

If these were your KPIs, what would you do?

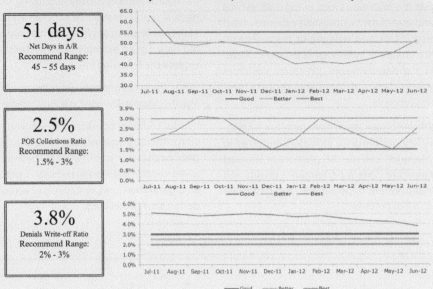

These examples provide a unique perspective on exploiting big data for decision-making advantage. Of course, KPIs will vary by industry, but these examples can get you started on thinking about the power of these types of data analytics tools.

For further details, and an exploration of this literature, see the following:

http://health-system-management.advanceweb.com/how-to-use-data-analytics-to-optimize-the-revenue-cycle/

https://www.healthcatalyst.com/success_stories/healthcare-revenue-cycle-management-timely-data http://www.gaffeyhealth.com/images/Big-Data.pdf

http://hfmamd.org/downloads/REGION_IV_2015/12:pnc_presentation.pdf

Prompt for Critical Thinking #5

After reading the preceding discussion about how organizations in the healthcare sector are using data analytics, think about and then answer the following question:

How might these findings apply to other sectors of our economy?

• _____

• _____

• _____

Documenting Substantive Procedures

The auditor documents a number of important items for the revenue cycle. Documentation of confirmation procedures should detail the extent of dollars and items confirmed, the confirmation response rate, the number and dollar amount of exceptions that were not misstatements, the number and amount of exceptions that were misstatements (cross-referenced to the working paper B-4 that includes an explanation and conclusion), and a projection of the sample misstatements to the population. The following is an example of such a summary:

	Items	Amount
Population	3,810	5,643,200.00
Positive confirmations	29	193,038.71
Percent confirmed	0.76%	3.42%
Responses	27	180,100.11
Percent responding	93.1%	93.3%
Exceptions	5	32,061.50
Cleared	4	19,105.82
Misstatements—B-4	1	971.68
Projected to the population		30,446.31

Other documentation requirements for accounts receivable might include:

- Tests of the adequacy of the allowance for doubtful accounts
- Details on inquires made regarding whether receivables are sold, pledged, or assigned
- Cutoff tests
- Evidence of roll-forward procedures if confirmations were sent at an interim date

Documentation related to the revenue substantive procedures would typically include:

- Substantive analytical procedures performed
- Unusual sales transactions
- Information indicating an understanding of the client's revenue recognition policies
- Identification of specific items tested (e.g., all sales transactions in excess of $100,000)
- Relevant information on tests of details

Check Your Basic Knowledge

9-29 Auditors in practice commonly use negative confirmations. (T/F)

9-30 A substantive audit procedure that would reveal ownership and related disclosure issues includes scanning the cash receipts journal for relatively large inflows of cash that from unusual sources. (T/F)

9-31 To test the completeness of sales, the auditor would select a sample of transactions from which of the following populations?
a. Customer order file.
b. Open invoice file.
c. Bill of lading file.
d. Sales invoice file.

9-32 The auditor is concerned that the client has recorded fictitious sales. Which of the following procedures would be the best audit procedure to identify fictitious sales?
a. Select a sample of recorded sales invoices and trace to shipping documents (bills of lading and packing slips) to verify shipment of goods.
b. Select a sample of shipping documents (bills of lading) and trace to the sales invoice to determine whether the invoice was properly recorded.
c. Select a sample of customer purchase orders and trace through to the generation of a sales invoice.
d. Select a sample of customer purchase orders to determine whether a valid customer actually exists.

Applying Decision-Making Frameworks

The following *End of Chapter* materials provide you an opportunity to apply the frameworks for professional decision making and ethical decision making for decisions made when conducting an audit: *9-47* and *9-48*.

Let's Review

- The most significant accounts in the revenue cycle include revenue and accounts receivable. Disclosures should include a breakdown of revenue by type, along with information to enable users to estimate receivables net of any allowance for doubtful accounts. The existence and valuation assertions are usually the most relevant to revenue and accounts receivable. (LO 1)

- An important inherent risk related to revenue transactions is the timing of revenue recognition. Complex sales transactions often make it difficult to determine when a sale has actually taken place. (LO 2)

- The fraud risks most associated with the revenue cycle transactions relate to the existence and valuation assertions, with a concern about the overstatement of revenue and accounts receivable and a corresponding understatement of bad debt. (LO 3)

- At the entity-wide level, the auditor will consider the control environment, including such principles as commitment to financial accounting competencies and the independence of the board of directors. The auditor will also consider the remaining components of internal control that are typically entity-wide—risk assessment, information and communication, and monitoring controls. Although all the auditor needs to understand all components of internal control, the auditor typically finds it useful to focus on significant control activities in the revenue cycle. As part of this understanding, the auditor focuses on the relevant

assertions for each account and identifies the controls that relate to risks for these assertions. (LO 4)

- Planning analytical procedures help auditors identify areas of potential material misstatements. The objective of planning analytical procedures is to identify accounts with heightened risk of misstatement during audit planning to provide a basis for designing and implementing responses to the assessed risks. Planning analytical procedures can be relatively imprecise. (LO 5)

- The auditor obtains sufficient appropriate evidence for revenue transactions and related accounts through the following types of procedures:
  o Vouching sales transactions back to customer orders
  o Selecting a sample of shipping documents and tracing them into the sales journal
  o Performing cutoff tests for revenue
  o Checking a sample of receiving reports to credits in Accounts Receivable
  o Reviewing the aged trial balance for Accounts Receivable
  o Sending and evaluating confirmations, considering the alternative costs and benefits of negative and positive confirmations
  o Examining the valuation of the Allowance for Doubtful Accounts
  o Reviewing documents to test for rights and obligations
  o Evaluating the financial statements and associated footnotes for presentation and disclosure (LO 6, 7, and 8)

Significant Terms

Alternative procedures Procedures used to obtain evidence about the existence and valuation of accounts receivable when a positive confirmation is not returned, including examining cash collected after the confirmation date and vouching unpaid invoices to customers' orders, sales orders, shipping documents, and sales invoices.

Big data High volume, high velocity, and/or high variety information assets that require new forms of processing to enable enhanced decision making, insight discovery, and process optimization.

Bill of lading A shipping document that describes items being shipped, the shipping terms, and delivery address; a formal legal document that conveys responsibility for the safety and shipment of items to the shipper.

Business intelligence The process of transforming all of the raw data that companies (providers) collect from their various operations into actionable information.

Collectibility The risk that the seller will be unable to collect the entitled contractual consideration from the customer.

Exceptions Differences between a customer's records and the client's records reported on positive or negative confirmations.

False confirmation A situation in which the respondent to a confirmation request (in this chapter, an accounts receivable confirmation) responds inaccurately to the audit firm with respect to the information on the confirmation.

Key performance indicators Quantifiable measures that decision makers can use to evaluate the success of an organization, unit, employee, or account as they seek to meet performance objectives.

Lapping A technique used to cover up the embezzlement of cash whereby a cash collection from one customer is stolen by an employee who takes another customer's payment and credits the first customer. This process continues, and at any point in time at least one customer's account is overstated.

Negative confirmation A request to customers asking them to respond directly to the auditor only if they disagree with the indicated balance.

Positive confirmation A request to customers asking them to respond directly to the auditor if they agree or disagree with the indicated balance.

Revenue attrition Equals beginning period reoccurring revenue minus end-of-period reoccurring revenue, less any new revenue gained, divided by beginning period revenue. In simpler terms, revenue attrition helps organization determine the relative extent to which they are losing versus gaining customers.

Revenue cycle The process of receiving a customer's order, approving credit for a sale, determining whether the goods are available for shipment, shipping the goods, billing the customers, collecting cash, and recognizing the effect of this process on other related accounts.

Side letter An agreement containing contract terms that are not part of the formal contract (often involving rights of return). Side letters increase audit risk because they enable key contract terms affecting revenue recognition to be hidden from the auditor as part of a revenue recognition fraud.

Timing differences Confirmation exceptions caused by transactions that are in process at the confirmation date, such as in-transit shipments or payments. These are not misstatements.

Prompts for Critical Thinking

Prompt for Critical Thinking #1

A search using the terms "AmTrust," "BDO," and "whistleblower" will lead students to websites such as: *http://www.investopedia.com/news/amtrust-plunges-19-report-whistleblower-afsi/*

and *http://www.businessinsurance.com/article/20170411/NEWS08/912312874/AmTrust-denies-federal-investigation-after-whistleblower-reportedly-surfaces*

In terms of future developments on this case, we will have to see what the future holds.

Prompt for Critical Thinking #2

- Recording goods returned on prenumbered documents that are accounted for, to be sure they are all recorded promptly
- Identifying whether credit should be given or whether the goods will be reworked according to warranty provisions and returned to the customer
- Determining the potential obsolescence or defects in the goods
- Assuring proper classification of the goods and determining that the goods are not reshipped as if they were new goods
- Developing and implementing a sales returns reserve methodology, requiring reasonable and supportable assumptions

Prompt for Critical Thinking #3

1. Given the facts presented in this prompt, the auditor should develop a potential set of alternative explanations that could account for the changes in all three ratios and design audit procedures to gather independent corroborating evidence that either supports or contradicts that explanation. In this example, the company was engaged in a complicated scheme of recording fictitious sales. Management offered other explanations—increased efficiency, a new computer system, better customer service, and so forth.

    However, only fictitious sales could account for the change in the gross margin, the increase in the number of days' sales in accounts receivable, and the increase in the total balance of accounts receivable that occurred when sales were not increasing. The auditor would address this conclusion through substantive audit procedures.

2. In other words, there are two parts to this problem

    - Proof of increased efficiency
    - An explanation of how the new computer system led to increased efficiency
    - Evidence about the customer service experience
    - Accounts receivable aging schedule
    - Evidence about sales by month, quarter, and year compared to last year and this year's budget

Prompt for Critical Thinking #4

- Confirm terms of the transaction directly with the customer, such as the absence of side agreements, acceptance criteria, delivery and payment terms, the right to return the product, and refund policies.
- Compare the number of weeks of inventory in distribution channels with prior periods for unusual changes that may indicate channel stuffing.
- Scan the general ledger, accounts receivable subsidiary ledger, and sales journal for unusual activity.
- Perform analytical reviews of credit memo and write-off activity by comparing to prior periods. Look for unusual trends or patterns, such as large numbers of credit memos pertaining to one customer or salesperson, or those processed shortly after the close of the accounting period.
- Analyze recoveries of written-off accounts.
- Inquire of the company's nonaccounting personnel (e.g., sales and marketing personnel or even in-house legal counsel) about sales or shipments near year-end and whether they are aware of any unusual terms or conditions in connection with these sales.

Prompt for Critical Thinking #5

All companies face tremendous pressures in achieving success in the revenue cycle. The findings in the healthcare sector with respect to big data and data analytics can apply to other sectors of the economy in the following ways:

- Revenue trends, at the organizational level and with respect to budget-to-actual and industry comparisons, and by location or type of service
- Understanding drivers of late payments, or underpayments by client type or payer type (i.e., by different types of insurance companies, or the Federal or State government)
- Understanding drivers of differential service provider quality, through customer satisfaction surveys that are linked to data about the underlying services that the customer purchased

Review Questions and Short Cases

NOTE: Completing *Review Questions and Short Cases* does not require the student to reference additional resources and materials.

NOTE: For the remaining problems, we make special note of those addressing fraud, international issues, professional skepticism, and ethics.

9-1 **LO 1** Refer to *Exhibit 9.1.* Which accounts are relevant in the revenue cycle? Identify the relationships among them.

9-2 **LO 1** For accounts receivable, what are the more relevant assertions? Why should an auditor identify which assertions are more relevant?

9-3 **LO 1** Refer to *Exhibit 9.2.* What are the major activities involved in generating and recording a sales transaction? What are the major documents generated as a part of each activity?

9-4 **LO 2** An important task in the audit of the revenue cycle is determining whether a client has appropriately recognized revenue.
   a. What is the five-step process that companies should use in recognizing revenue? Why might the auditor need to do additional research and consider additional criteria on revenue recognition?
   b. The following are situations in which the auditor will make decisions about the amount of revenue to be recognized. For each of the following scenarios, labeled (1) through (6):

- Identify the key issues to address in determining whether or not revenue should be recognized.
- Identify additional information the auditor may want to gather in making a decision on revenue recognition.
- Based only on the information presented, develop a rationale for either the recognition or nonrecognition of revenue.

1. AOL sells software that is unique as a provider of Internet services. The software contract includes a service fee of $19.95 for up to 500 hours of Internet service each month. The minimum requirement is a one-year contract. The company proposes to immediately recognize 30% of the first-year's contract as revenue from the sale of software and 70% as Internet services on a monthly basis as fees are collected from the customer.

2. Modis Manufacturing builds specialty packaging machinery for other manufacturers. All of the products are high end and range in sales price from $5 million to $25 million. A major customer is rebuilding one of its factories and has ordered three machines with total revenue for Modis of

$45 million. The contracted date to complete the production was November, and the company met the contract date. The customer acknowledges the contract and confirms the amount. However, because the factory is not yet complete, it has asked Modis to hold the products in the warehouse as a courtesy until its building is complete.

3. Standish Stoneware has developed a new low-end line of baking products that will be sold directly to consumers and to low-end discount retailers. The company had previously sold high-end silverware products to specialty stores and has a track record of returned items for the high-end stores. The new products tend to have more defects, but the defects are not necessarily recognizable in production. For example, they are more likely to crack when first used in baking. The company does not have a history of returns from these products, but because the products are new, it grants each customer the right to return the merchandise for a full refund or replacement within one year of purchase.

4. Omer Technologies is a high-growth company that sells electronic products to the custom copying business. It is an industry with high innovation, but Omer's technology is basic. In order to achieve growth, management has empowered the sales staff to make special deals to increase sales in the fourth quarter of the year. The sales deals include a price break and an increased salesperson commission but not an extension of either the product warranty or the customer's right to return the product.

5. Electric City is a new company that has the exclusive right to a new technology that saves municipalities a substantial amount of energy for large-scale lighting purposes (e.g., for ball fields, parking lots, and shopping centers). The technology has been shown to be very cost effective in Europe. In order to get new customers to try the product, the sales force allows customers to try the product for up to six months to prove the amount of energy savings they will realize. The company is so confident that customers will buy the product that it allows this pilot-testing period. Revenue is recognized at the time the product is installed at the customer location, with a small provision made for potential returns.

6. Jackson Products decided to quit manufacturing a line of its products and outsourced the production. However, much of its manufacturing equipment could be used by other companies. In addition, it had over $5 million of new manufacturing equipment on order in a noncancelable deal. The company decided to become a sales representative to sell the new equipment ordered and its existing equipment. All of the sales were recorded as revenue.

9-5 **LO 2** Refer to *Exhibit 9.3*. What are some examples of sales transactions involving product delivery that might have a high level of inherent risk?

9-6 **LO 3** Why should auditors ordinarily consider revenue recognition to be a fraud risk factor? What are some reasons that management might want to fraudulently overstate revenue?

9-7 **LO 3** Refer to *Exhibit 9.3* and to the *Focus on Fraud* features "Channel Stuffing at ArthroCare—The Importance of Professional Skepticism" and "Assisted Living Concepts (ALC) Revenue Cycle Fraud and the Improper Professional Conduct of Grant Thornton's Audit Partners." What methods do companies use to fraudulently inflate revenue? How can auditors use professional skepticism to help identify these fraud schemes?

FRAUD

PROFESSIONAL SKEPTICISM

FRAUD

FRAUD

9-8 **LO 3** What steps should an auditor take identify fraud risks in the revenue cycle?

9-9 **LO 4** Refer to *Exhibit 9.4* and *Exhibit 9.5*. What are a control risk assessment questionnaire and a controls matrix? How does an auditor use these documents?

9-10 **LO 4** Why are monthly customer statements considered a control? Why is it important to separate the duties of responding to customer complaints from the accounts receivable and cash collection functions?

9-11 **LO 4** Refer to the *Why It Matters* feature "Risks Associated with Sales Returns: The Case of Medicis and Ernst & Young." What problems can occur if controls related to sales returns and allowances are not designed and operating effectively?

9-12 **LO 4**

a. Explain the two main reasons for AmTrust's restatement. Why do you think that management judged these issues material, and therefore deemed it necessary to issue the restatements?

b. The restatement led to corrections of the company's three prior years, as well as the first three quarters of results for 2016. What does a restatement imply about financial reporting quality? What does a restatement imply about audit quality?

9-13 **LO 5** Refer to *Exhibit 9.6*. Identify planning analytical procedures that can help auditors identify areas of potential material misstatements in the revenue cycle.

FRAUD

9-14 **LO 5** What factors influence the reliability of data used in planning analytical procedures in the revenue cycle?

PROFESSIONAL SKEPTICISM

9-15 **LO 5** Consider an audit client that manufactures fishing boats and sells them all over the country to dealers who finance their purchases with their banks. The banks usually pay your client within two weeks of shipment. The company's profits have been increasing over the past several years. To perform planning analytical procedures you have obtained the following information related to your 2018 audit ($ in millions):

	2018**	2017*	2016*	2015*	2014*	Major Competitor (2018)
Accounts receivable	6.8	3.3	2.3	1.8	1.7	4.2
Inventory	16.0	10.0	7.2	5.5	5.1	13.9
Accounts payable	3.1	2.6	1.9	1.5	1.4	3.2
Sales	84.7	77.9	56.8	43.6	39.8	110.3
Gross profit (%)	19	17	18	17	18	21
Number of days' sales in receivables	29	16	15	16	16	14
Number of days' sales in ending inventory	69	47	46	46	47	46

*Audited
** Unaudited

a. Assume that you had expected that your client's performance would be similar to that of the client's major competitor. Based on these expectations, identify potential risk areas and explain why they represent potential risks.

b. Suggest possible explanations for any unexpected results.

c. What inquiries and follow-up audit procedures would you perform to determine the accuracy of the client's data?

d. As part of the brainstorming session, be prepared to discuss how the CFO might use accounts receivable and inventory to conceal the embezzlement of cash.

e. Discuss the importance of professional skepticism when performing planning analytical procedures.

FRAUD

PROFESSIONAL SKEPTICISM

9-16 **LO 5** Stainless Steel Specialties (SSS) is a manufacturer of hot water–based heating systems for homes and commercial businesses. The company has grown about 10% in each of the past five years. The company has not made any acquisitions. Following are some statistics for the company:

Overview of Operational Data Stainless Steel Specialties (SSS)
(Sales and Net Income Reported in $ Millions)

	2014	2015	2016	2017	2018 (unaudited)
Sales	$800	$880	$950	$1,050	$1,300
Net income	$28	$38	$42	$52	$68
Stock price	$17	$24	$19	$28	$47
Economic growth in areas served (index with 1.00 for 20 × 1)	1.00	1.04	1.09	1.13	1.14
Percent of heating market by SSS	8.9	9.4	9.6	10.8	14.0
Accounts receivable	$180	$170	$196	$210	$297
Percent of sales made in last quarter	38	36	40	38	43
Gross margin (%)	28.0	28.3	28.8	29.2	33.6

Additional information available to the auditor includes:

- The company has touted its new and improved technology for the increase both in sales and in gross margin.
- The company claims to have decreased administrative expenses, thus increasing net profits.
- The company has reorganized its sales process to a more centralized approach and has empowered individual sales managers to negotiate better prices to drive sales as long as the amounts are within corporate guidelines.
- The company has changed its salesperson compensation by increasing the commission on sales to new customers.
- Sales commissions are no longer affected by returned goods if the goods are returned more than 90 days after sale and/or by not collecting the receivables. SSS has justified the changes in sales commissions on the following grounds:
  o The salesperson is not responsible for quality issues—the main reason that customers return products.
  o The salesperson is not responsible for approving credit; rather credit approval is under the direction of the global sales manager.

a. What is the importance of the information about salesperson compensation to the audit of receivables and revenue? Explain how the auditor would use this information in planning analytical procedures.

b. Perform planning analytical procedures using the data included in the table and the information about the change in performance. For each year, you will most likely want to focus on the % change of the various statistics over the prior year. Focus on Steps 3, 4, and 5 of the planning analytical procedures process. What are the important insights that the auditor should gain from performing such procedures?

c. Why should the auditor be interested in a company's stock price when performing an audit, as stock price is dependent, at least in part, on audited financial reports?

d. What information about SSS might the auditor consider as fraud risk factors?

e. Identify specific substantive audit procedures that should be performed as a result of the planning analytical procedures performed by the auditor (Step 6 of the planning analytical procedures process).

9-17 LO 6 How do auditors use their knowledge about the risk of material misstatement in developing an audit approach? Comment on extensiveness of testing, types of audit procedures, and the rigor of audit procedures in higher versus lower risk settings (e.g., for an assertion with a higher risk of material misstatement versus an assertion with a lower risk of material misstatement).

9-18 LO 6 Refer to *Exhibit* 9.7. Describe the differences in the planned audit approaches for Clients A and B and the reasons for such differences.

9-19 LO 6 Read the following description of Drea Tech Company and identify the elements of inherent risk associated with the revenue cycle. Determine the appropriate audit response (audit procedure) to address the risks.

Drea Tech Company has been growing rapidly and has recently engaged your firm as its auditor. It is actively traded over the counter and management believes it has outgrown the service capabilities of its previous auditor. However, on contacting the previous auditor, you learn that a dispute led to the firm's dismissal. The client wanted to recognize income on contracts for items produced but not shipped. The client believed the contracts were firm and that they had performed all the principal revenue-producing activities. The change in accounting principle would have increased net income by 33% during the last year.

Drea is 32% owned by Anthony Dreason, who has a reputation as a turnaround artist. He bought out the previous owner of Drea Tech three years ago. The company's primary products are in the materials handling business, such as automated conveyors for warehouses and production lines. Dreason has increased profits by slashing operating expenses, most notably personnel and research and development. In addition, he has outsourced a significant portion of component part production. Approximately 10% of the company's product is now obtained from Materials Movement, Inc., a privately held company 50% owned by Dreason and his brother.

A brief analysis of previous financial statements shows that sales have been increasing by approximately 20% per year since Dreason assumed control. Profitability has increased even more. However, a tour of the plant gives the impression that the client has not kept it up to date. Additionally, a large amount of inventory is sitting near the receiving dock awaiting final disposition.

9-20 LO 7 What is the effect on the substantive tests of accounts receivable when the auditor assesses the risk of material misstatement as low rather than high because a client has effective internal controls? Provide specific examples.

9-21 **LO 7** When testing whether the controls are operating effectively, does the auditor need to reperform the control? For example, if client personnel check the correctness of computations on an invoice and initial the bottom of a document to indicate that the control has been performed, does the auditor need to reperform the procedure? Explain the rationale for your response.

9-22 **LO 7** The following is a list of controls, numbered (1) through (7), typically implemented in the revenue cycle.
   a. For each control listed, briefly indicate the financial misstatement that could occur if the control is not operating effectively.
   b. Identify a test of control that the auditor can perform to determine the operating effectiveness of the control.
   1. All transactions under $10,000 may be approved by the computer authorization program. The credit manager must approve all transactions over $10,000.
   2. All invoices are priced according to the authorized price list maintained on the computer. Either the regional or divisional sales manager must approve any exceptions.
   3. All shipping documents are prenumbered and periodically accounted for. Shipping document references are noted on all sales invoices.
   4. Customer complaints regarding receipt of goods are routed to a customer service representative. Any discrepancies are immediately evaluated to determine the cause of the discrepancy.
   5. All merchandise returns must be received by the receiving department and recorded on prenumbered documents for receipts. A document is created for each item (or batches of like items). Returns are sent to quality control for testing, and a recommendation for ultimate disposition is made (scrap, rework and sell as a second, or close out as is), noted, and sent to accounting for proper inventorying.
   6. The quantity of items invoiced is reconciled with the packing document developed on receipt of the order and the shipping notice by a computer program as the goods are marked for shipment. If discrepancies appear, the shipping document prevails. A discrepancy report is prepared daily and sent to the warehouse manager for follow-up.
   7. The company pays all freight charges, but the customer is charged a freight fee based on a minimum amount and a sliding scale as a percentage of the total invoice. The policy is documented, and the computer automatically adds the charge.

9-23 **LO 7** Most accounting systems have the ability to generate exception reports identifying control procedure failures or transactions that are out of the norm so that management can determine whether it needs to take any special action.
   a. Identify how the auditor might use each of the following four types of exception reports, labeled (1) through (4), in assessing the effectiveness of controls.
   b. For each type of exception report, address the following question. If the exceptions are properly evaluated and corrected, would the fact that many exceptions occurred affect the auditor's judgment of the effectiveness of controls and the auditor's assessment of control risk? Explain.
   1. A list of all invoices over $5,000 for which credit was not preauthorized by the credit manager (the computer program is

designed so that if the authorization is not provided within 24 hours of the original notice to the credit manager, the shipment is made as if it were authorized). This exception report goes to the credit manager.

2. A report of any sales volume to one customer exceeding $2 million in a month sent to the sales manager with a copy to the credit manager.

3. A report of exceptions for which shipping documents and packing slips did not reconcile.

4. A report noting that goods ordered were not shipped (or back-ordered) within five days of receipt of the order as is required per company policy.

9-24 **LO 7** The auditor has provided a preliminary assessment of control risk of low in the revenue cycle accounts of Acco, Inc. for each of the relevant assertions. The auditor selected a sample of sales transactions for control testing. Each of the following types of control or transaction-processing deficiencies uncovered in the sample was significant enough to cause the auditor to increase control risk assessment from low to moderate. For each deficiency, labeled as (a) though (i), discuss the type of financial statement misstatement that may result, the assertion(s) affected, and the effect on the nature, timing, and/or extent of related substantive tests. Consider each deficiency independently from the others.

a. No evidence that price and quantity on the invoice were compared with the supporting documents

b. Failure to approve customer credit before shipping the merchandise on open account

c. Recording sales before they were shipped

d. Recording sales several days after they should have been recorded

e. Recording sales several days before and several days after they should have been recorded

f. Lack of customer orders; items were shipped

g. Lack of shipping documents; customer order was found

h. Incorrect invoice price

i. Quantity shipped differed from the quantity billed

9-25 **LO 7** Assume the auditor plans to test controls over the shipment and recording of sales transactions. Identify the controls that the auditor would expect to find to achieve the objective that all transactions are recorded correctly, and in the correct period. For each control identified, indicate how the auditor would test whether the control operated effectively.

9-26 **LO 8** Refer to the *Why It Matters* feature "Performing Appropriate Substantive Procedures in the Revenue Cycle: The Case of Kyoto Audit Corporation." What substantive procedures did Kyoto not perform appropriately? If an auditor does not perform these procedures appropriately, will the client's financial statements necessarily be misstated? Explain your answer.

9-27 **LO 5, 8** The third step in performing analytical procedures involves developing expectations of recorded amounts or ratios, and evaluating whether the expectations are precise enough to accomplish the relevant objective. How do expectations differ between planning analytical procedures and substantive analytical procedures? What factors influence the precision of expectations?

9-28 **LO 8** When might it be advisable to send the confirmation to the customer's personnel who are familiar with the details of sales contracts rather than to the accounts payable department?

9-29 **LO 8** Refer to *Exhibit 9.9*.
a. What are typical substantive procedures in the revenue cycle, and how do these procedures relate to management assertions?
b. For the following procedures, labeled (1) through (6), indicate the assertion that is being tested.
1. Take a block of shipping orders and account for the invoicing of all items in the block and account for the prenumbering of the documents.
2. Review the general access controls to the computer application and the authorized ability to make changes to computer price files.
3. Recompute the invoice total and individual line items on a sample of sales invoices.
4. Review client documentation to determine policy for credit authorization.
5. Select a sample of shipping notices and trace to invoices.
6. Randomly sample entries into the sales journal and trace back to sales orders and shipping documents.

9-30 **LO 8** Refer to *Exhibit 9.10*. What is an aged trial balance of accounts receivable? How does an auditor use it? How does an auditor determine that the aging is correct?

9-31 **LO 8** Refer to *Exhibit 9.11* and *Exhibit 9.12*. Distinguish between the positive and negative forms of accounts receivable confirmations. Which confirmation type, positive or negative, is considered more reliable? Why?

9-32 **LO 8** If a customer does not return a confirmation, what follow-up work should the auditor perform for: (a) positive confirmations and (b) negative confirmations?

FRAUD **9-33** **LO 8** Identify potential fraud risks in the revenue cycle. What substantive audit procedures can the auditor use to determine if fraud has occurred in the revenue cycle?

FRAUD **9-34** **LO 8** What is a false confirmation? Why are false confirmations problematic for auditors in terms of evidence reliability expectations?

9-35 **LO 8** Address the following questions about the confirmation of customers' accounts receivable.
a. Why do confirmations not typically provide reliable evidence about the completeness assertion?
b. What is a confirmation exception, and why is it important to investigate a confirmation exception?
c. When should an auditor perform alternative procedures to substantiate the existence of accounts receivable?
d. Under what condition would substantive testing of accounts receivable before the balance sheet date be appropriate?

9-36 **LO 8** During a discussion, one auditor noted that her approach to testing sales transactions was to select a random sample of recorded sales and trace back through the system to supporting documents, noting that all items billed were shipped and were invoiced at correct prices. She stated that she then had high confidence about the correctness of the sales account, and, therefore, having performed a dual-purpose test, the remaining work on sales (assuming the procedures also evidenced the working of control procedures) could be limited.

A second auditor disagreed. Her approach was to select evidence of shipments, such as prenumbered shipping documents, and then trace forward through the system to the actual invoice, noting the existence of control procedures and the correctness of the invoice processing. If no exceptions were noted, however, she agreed with the first auditor that the remaining audit work on the sales account could be limited.

a. Which auditor is right; or are both right? Explain.
b. What assertion is the second auditor testing?
c. What is a dual-purpose test? Explain whether the tests performed by both of the auditors are dual-purpose tests.

9-37 **LO 8** Bert Finney, CPA, was engaged to conduct an audit of the financial statements of Clayton Realty Corporation for the month ending January 31, 2018. Examining documentation of the monthly rent reconciliation is an important part of the audit engagement.

The controller of Clayton Realty Corporation prepared the following rent reconciliation and presented it to Finney, who subjected it to various audit procedures:

Clayton Realty Corporation
Rent Reconciliation
For the Month Ended January 31, 2018

Gross apartment rents (Schedule A)	$1,600,800†
Less vacancies (Schedule B)	20,500†
Net apartment rentals	1,580,300
Less unpaid January rents (Schedule C)	7,800†
Total	1,572,500
Add prepaid rent collected (Apartment 116)	500†
Total cash collected	$1,573,000†

Schedules A, B, and C are available to Finney, but not presented here. Finney evaluated and tested internal controls and found that they could be relied on to produce reliable accounting information. The client deposits cash receipts from rental operations in a special bank account.

What substantive audit procedures should Finney use during the audit to obtain evidence of each of the dollar amounts marked by the dagger (†) tick mark?

9-38 **LO 8** You are auditing the revenue from membership fees of your local chapter of the Institute of Management Accountants, of which you are not a member. The local chapter receives an allocation of national dues. The remainder of the dues comes from chapter members. The chapter maintains a detailed list of membership. Describe substantive analytical procedures you could use to obtain assurance that fee revenue is fairly stated.

9-39 **LO 8** As part of the audit of KC Enterprises, the auditor assessed control risk for the existence and valuation assertions related to accounts receivable at the maximum level. Katie, the staff person assigned to the engagement, sent positive confirmation requests to a sample of the company customers based on their balances as of December 31, 2018. For each of the three customers described here, review the relevant confirmation letter and Katie's comments at the bottom of each. Select the procedure that the auditor should use to clear the exception, if one exists. Choose only one procedure per confirmation. A procedure may be used once, more than once, or not at all.

February 1, 2019

Meehan Marine Sales, Inc.
1284 River Road
Louisville, Kentucky 40059

Re: Balance at December 31, 2018—$267,000

As of December 31, 2018, our records indicate your balance with our company as the amount listed above. Please complete and sign the bottom portion of this letter and return the entire letter to our auditors, GJ LLP, P.O. Box 100, Orlando, Florida 32806.

A stamped, self-addressed envelope is enclosed for your convenience.

Sincerely,

_____

KC Enterprises

....

The above balance is   Correct

                    X   Incorrect (show amount)   _$325,000_

If incorrect, please provide information that could help to reconcile your account.

Response: We placed an order for $58,000 on December 26, 2018.

Signature:_____
Title:_____
Date:_____

_____

Katie's note to file:
Per discussion with the controller and review of relevant documentation, the order for $58,000 was shipped FOB shipping point on December 30, 2018, and was received by the customer on January 3, 2019. Therefore, the client has made no entry to record the sale in 2018.

February 1, 2019

West Coast Ski Center, Inc.
163 Tide Avenue
Monterey, California 93940

Re: Balance at December 31, 2018—$414,000

As of December 31, 2018, our records indicate your balance with our company as the amount listed above. Please complete and sign the bottom portion of this letter and return the entire letter to our auditors, GJ LLP, P.O. Box 100, Orlando, Florida 32806.

A stamped, self-addressed envelope is enclosed for your convenience.

Sincerely,

_____

KC Enterprises

....

The above balance is   Correct

                              X   Incorrect (show amount)   _$320,000_

If incorrect, please provide information that could help to reconcile your account.
Response: We made a payment of $94,000 on December 12, 2018.

Signature:_____

Title:_____

Date:_____

_____

Katie's note to file:
   Per discussion with the controller and review of relevant documentation, the company received the payment of $94,000 on December 15, 2018, and posted it to "Other Income."

February 1, 2019

Fish & Ski World, Inc.
5660 Ocean Blvd
Port Arkansas, Texas 78373

Re: Balance at December 31, 2018—$72,000

As of December 31, 2018, our records indicate your balance with our company as the amount listed above. Please complete and sign the bottom portion of this letter and return the entire letter to our auditors, GJ LLP, P.O. Box 100, Orlando, Florida 32806.

(continued)

A stamped, self-addressed envelope is enclosed for your convenience.

Sincerely,

_____

KC Enterprises

....

The above balance is   Correct

                                    X   Incorrect (show amount)   *$163,000*

If incorrect, please provide information that could help to reconcile your account.

Response: Per our records, the following invoices are outstanding:
Invoice #4212 $72,000
Invoice #4593 $66,000
Invoice #4738 $25,000

Signature:_____

Title:_____

Date:_____

_____

Katie's note to file:
   Per review of the A/R aging report, invoices #4593 and 4738 are not on the A/R aging report at December 31, 2018.

Possible procedures:
1. Not an exception, no adjustment necessary. Determine the sufficiency of allowance for doubtful accounts.
2. Exception noted; propose adjustment and request that the controller post it to the accounting records.
3. Verify by examining subsequent cash collections and/or shipping documents.
4. Review appropriate documentation to verify that additional invoices noted on confirmation pertain to the subsequent year.

FRAUD

9-40 **LO 8** Read the following scenario about Strang Corporation and identify the substantive procedures that the CPA (Elaine Stanley) should perform to determine whether lapping exists. Do not discuss deficiencies in the system of internal control.

During the year, Strang Corporation began to encounter cash flow difficulties, and a cursory review by management revealed receivable collection problems. Strang's management engaged Elaine Stanley, CPA, to perform a special investigation. Stanley studied the billing and collection cycle and noted the following:

The accounting department employs one bookkeeper who receives and opens all incoming mail. This bookkeeper is also responsible for depositing receipts, filing daily remittance advices, recording receipts in the cash receipts journal, and posting receipts in the individual customer accounts and the general ledger accounts. There are no cash sales. The bookkeeper prepares and controls the mailing of monthly statements to customers. The concentration of functions and the receivable collection problems caused Stanley to suspect that a systematic theft of customers' payments through a delayed posting of remittances (lapping of accounts receivable) is present.

9-41 **LO 8** Your audit client, Madison, Inc., has an automated accounts receivable system. There are two master files, a customer data file and an unpaid invoice file. The customer data file contains the customer's name, billing address, shipping address, identification number, phone number, purchase and cash payment history, and credit limit. For each unpaid invoice, the second file contains the customer's identification number, invoice number and date, date of shipment, method of shipment, credit terms, and gross invoice amount. Discuss how data analytics tools could be used to aid in the audit of Madison's accounts receivable.

PROFESSIONAL SKEPTICISM

FRAUD

9-42 **LO 8** You have sent confirmations to 40 customers of Berg-Shovick Express, a long-time audit client experiencing some financial difficulty. The company sells specialized high-technology goods. You have received confirmations from 32 of the 40 positive confirmations sent. A few minor errors were noted on these accounts, but the projected amount of errors on the confirmations returned is just below tolerable error. The following information is available to you:

Book value of receivables	$7,782,292
Book value of items selected for confirmations	$3,100,110
Book value of items confirmed	$1,464,000
Audit value of items confirmed	$1,335,000

Summary of the selected confirmations not returned:

Name	Outstanding Amount	Management Comments on Account Balance
Yunkel Specialty Mfg.	$432,000	Regular sales, but extended credit terms were given on $200,000 of goods. Yunkel has responded that it does not respond to confirmations.
Hi-Tech Companies	$300,000	No response to either confirmation request. Management indicates the sale was a special-term sale, and the goods are being held for the convenience of this company. The company is located in Albuquerque, New Mexico, and recently had a fire in its main production plant but expects to resume production early next month. The goods will be shipped as soon as production begins, but the sale has legally been completed.

(Continued)

Name	Outstanding Amount	Management Comments on Account Balance
Beaver Dam Electronics	$275,000	Account balance represents sales of specialty products made in late December. The president of Berg-Shovick has orally confirmed the receivable because Beaver Dam Electronics is 50% owned by him.
California Hi-Fi	$200,000	Regular sales, but company has renegotiated its account balance due because of defective merchandise. Management has indicated it has issued a credit to the company, but because management had inspected the goods on the customer's property, it did not require the return of the merchandise. It expects the company to pay the $200,000.
Brenner Specialties	$175,000	Regular sales. This is a new company. Most of the sales ($100,000) were made in December.
Sprague Electronics	$100,000	Regular sales. Customer is negotiating a potential return of defective items.
Williams Pipeline	$100,000	Williams is a large company. Prior experience indicates that it does not respond to confirmations.
Long Tom Towers	$54,110	Customer is new this year and is located in Medicine Hat, Saskatchewan.

a. Identify the specific alternative audit procedures that the auditor should perform.
b. Assuming that the auditor cannot clear all items to the auditor's satisfaction, identify the audit procedures that the auditor should perform to finish auditing the valuation and existence assertions for accounts receivable.

Fraud Focus: Contemporary and Historical Cases

FRAUD

9-43 **ZYNGA**
(LO 2, 3, 4, 5, 6, 8)

Refer to the *Why It Matters* feature "How to Account for Virtual Sales at Zynga."
a. What are the inherent risks associated with the revenue transactions at Zynga?
b. What are management's incentives to fraudulently misstate revenue transactions?
c. What controls should Zynga management have in place to mitigate the risks associated with revenue transactions?
d. How might auditors use planning analytical procedures to identify any potential concerns with Zynga's revenue?
e. What might be considered sufficient appropriate evidence when auditing Zynga's revenue transactions?

FRAUD

INTERNATIONAL

ETHICS

9-44 **CHINESE COMPANIES LISTED ON U.S. AND HONG KONG STOCK EXCHANGES**
(LO 1, 2, 3, 6, 8)

There has been a shocking number of frauds perpetrated by Chinese companies listed on both the U.S. and Hong Kong stock exchanges. Fraudulent financial reporting is a serious problem for companies doing business in China. These frauds tend to be very bold and simplistic, involving blatant and flagrant overstatements of cash and revenue. Consider the following bogus journal entry, recording fictitious revenue:
Dr. Cash
　　Cr. Revenue

What could be better? The company gets the best of two worlds: its balance sheet looks better because cash is fraudulently overstated, and its income statement looks better because revenue is fraudulently overstated. Below we briefly outline a number of these frauds:

- **China Media Express Holdings, Inc.** (see https://www.sec.gov/litigation/complaints/2013/comp-pr2013-115.pdf)

  The company fraudulently asserted that it operated a television advertising network on buses operating in China. However, those operations did not actually exist. The company overstated its cash balances by a range from 400% to 4,000%, for example, purporting to have cash on hand of $57 million when it actually only had cash on hand of $141,000. The company also claimed that it had as clients two multinational corporations, when in fact those claims were fraudulent. China Media's audit firm was Deloitte. View the results of the company's stock performance; as of mid-2017 it is delisted.

CCME:US

Ticker Delisted

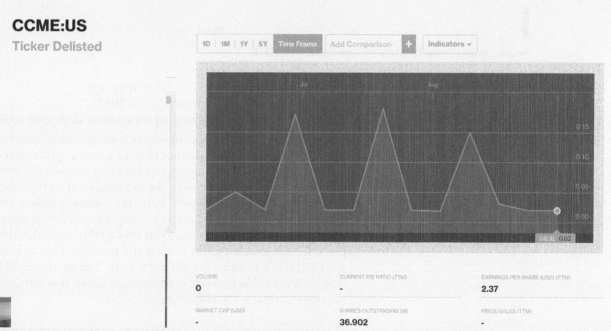

Source: https://www.bloomberg.com/quote/CCME:US

- **AgFeed Industries, Inc.** (see https://www.sec.gov/divisions/enforce/claims/agfeed.htm) and (http://www.feednavigator.com/Regulation/US-firm-AgFeed-moves-to-settle-with-SEC-in-239m-fraud-case)

  AgFeed Industries Inc. executives fraudulently overstated revenue for three years, from 2008 to 2011. They created fake invoices for the supposed sale of pigs that did not exist (they later fraudulently claimed that those pigs had died!) and animal feed, and also increased the purported weight of the pigs that were real and actually sold, resulting in overstated revenues of approximately $240 million. Management and the audit committee chair colluded to thwart the SEC's investigation. View the results of the company's stock performance. It has since been delisted, but notice that before the fraud was revealed, the stock enjoyed large increases in trading volume, although never at particularly high per share prices. AgFeed's audit firm was Goldman Parks Kurland Mohidin, LLP (see http://www.gkmcpas.com/contact.php).

Source: https://www.bloomberg.com/quote/FEEDQ:US

- **China Public Procurement** (see http://www.scmp.
  com/business/china-business/article/1079065/
  audit-says-no-proof-china-public-procurement-deals-ever-took)

  This company engages in commodities trading, energy management
  contracting, and the operation of electronic public procurement
  platforms, including developing software and providing software-
  related services to its customers. As an example of its fraudulent
  financial reporting, in February 2010, the company announced that
  it had won a $48 billion contract to supply construction materi-
  als and equipment, when in fact this was a fabrication. Unlike the
  previous two examples, this stock is still trading, albeit at very
  marginal levels of value per share. Its audit firm as of mid-2017
  is ShineWing CPAs (to review information about this firm, see
  http://www.shinewing.hk/background.aspx)

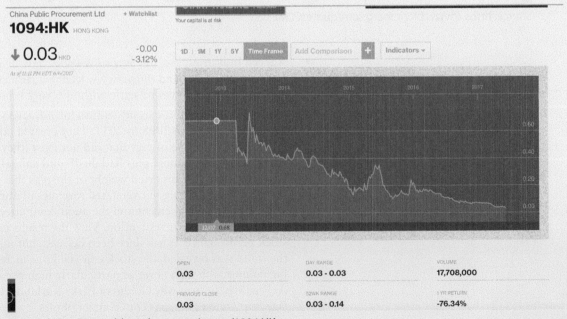

Source: https://www.bloomberg.com/quote/1094:HK

- **China Biotics** (see *https://www.sec.gov/litigation/opinions/2013/34-70800.pdf*)

  China Biotics engages in R&D, production, marketing, and distribution of probiotics supplements in China. This company engaged in a fraudulent scheme to fictitiously report its cash and revenues. The audit firm (BDO) attempted to perform a cash confirmation test with the company's banks, only to experience obstruction from top management and a fictitious bank website supposedly representing a bank to which management claimed it had deposits, but of course did not. As of mid-2017, the company's stock is delisted.

Source: https://www.bloomberg.com/quote/CHBT:US

a. Why do you think investors were willing to contribute capital to these companies in the first place?

b. Now that you see the negative stock market implications of fraudulent financial reporting, how do you feel about investing in the stock market?

c. Consider the audit firm of the four companies profiled above. Two companies were audited by either a Big 4 (Deloitte) or other large audit firm (BDO). Regional firms with no national or international reputation audited the other two companies. Think about the audit firm portfolio management strategies discussed in *Chapters 1* and *5*. How does the fact that each of these audit firms was willing to perform audit services for what turned out to be some very disreputable companies imply about the types of clients that each of these firms is willing to accept into its portfolio?

d. Imagine that you were one of the investors in any of these four companies. You rely on financial regulators and auditors to ensure that the information you use to make your investment decisions is accurate. What is your recourse (if any) in the face of massive stock market capitalization losses resulting from these frauds and the subsequent stock market collapses for these investments?

e. How might an audit team's fraud brainstorming judgments and decisions differ if a client had operations in the United States as compared to a client operating in China?

FRAUD   **9-45**   **MONSANTO COMPANY**
(LO 1, 2, 3, 6, 8)

Monsanto Company is an agricultural seed and chemical company that manufactures an herbicide under the trade name "Roundup."

You can learn more about the company and this product by visiting the following website: http://www.monsanto.com/pages/default.aspx

According to SEC AAER #3741 (February 9, 2016), it seems that during 2009–2011, Monsanto improperly accounted for rebates offered to Roundup distributors to incentivize them to purchase more Roundup. Monsanto improperly accounted for rebate payments by misallocating them to SG&A expenses rather than as rebates in an effort to fraudulently overstate its gross margins. Complicating matters (and thereby enabling management to commit the financial reporting fraud), Monsanto did not have sufficient internal controls around rebate calculations and reporting. Collectively, all of these factors helped the company materially overstate its revenues and earnings, thereby enabling the company to meet its consensus earnings per share analyst estimates for 2009.

In thinking about the fraud triangle, Monsanto management experienced the incentive to commit fraud because the patent for Roundup (historically its most profitable products) expired in 2000, and by 2009, Roundup experienced significant price competition from generic brands. The opportunity element existed because of weak internal controls.

During this period, Deloitte audited the financial statements and internal controls of Monsanto, issuing unqualified opinions about both.

According to the New York Times (https://www.nytimes.com/2016/09/11/business/for-monsanto-whistle-blower-a-22-million-award-that-fell-short.html?mcubz=2), the whistleblower who alerted the SEC to the company's wrongdoings was dissatisfied with the penalties issued by the SEC against top management at Monsanto (despite earning a $22 million whistle-blower award):

> *"It was frustrating, the whistle-blower said, that the S.E.C. took no action against others at Monsanto who, he said, knew about the improprieties. 'It's really difficult when your company is doing something you know is wrong but you've got everybody around you saying it's perfectly fine,' the former employee recalled. 'The Monsanto culture is very tightknit. Everybody has stock options and everyone is financially at risk. So, they go with the flow.'*

a. What do you think might have been management's rationalization for committing the fraud?

b. Does the AAER against Monsanto and some of its accountants imply that Deloitte's integrated audit was faulty? Explain your rationale. What do you make of the fact that the SEC did *not* pursue charges against Deloitte?

c. Think about the whistleblower's comments. What do they imply about corporate governance and tone at the top for Monsanto? Usually we think of giving employees stock options as a way to align the interests of managers and shareholders. How did managers' professional judgments and decisions go wrong in this case?

For further details, see https://www.sec.gov/litigation/ admin/2016/33-10037.pdf (AAER No. 3741, February 9, 2016).

FRAUD

INTERNATIONAL

PROFESSIONAL SKEPTICISM

9-46 **UTSTARCOM, INC.**
(LO 2, 3, 4, 5, 6, 8)

UTStarcom is a global leader in the manufacture, integration, and support of networking and telecommunications systems. The company sells broadband wireless products and a line of handset equipment to operators in emerging and established telecommunications markets worldwide. The following excerpt was obtained from the 2004 10-K of UTStarcom, Inc., which reported material weaknesses in the company's internal controls. In describing the company's remediation efforts, the company stated that "planned remediation measures are intended to address material weaknesses related to revenue and deferred revenue accounts and associated cost of sales."

These material weaknesses were evidenced by the identification of six separate transactions aggregating approximately $5 million in which revenue was initially included in the company's fourth-quarter 2004 financial statements before all criteria for revenue recognition were met. In addition, there were other transactions for which there was insufficient initial documentation for revenue recognition purposes but which did not result in any adjustments to the company's fourth-quarter 2004 financial statements. If unremediated, these material weaknesses have the potential of misstating revenue in future financial periods. The company's planned remediation measures include the following:

- "The Company plans to design a contract review process in China requiring financial and legal staff to provide input during the contract negotiation process to ensure timely identification and accurate accounting treatment of nonstandard contracts."
- "In March 2005, the Company conducted a training seminar regarding revenue recognition, including identification of nonstandard contracts, in the United States and, in April 2005, the Company conducted a similar seminar in China. Starting in May 2005, the Company plans to conduct additional training seminars in various international locations regarding revenue recognition and the identification of nonstandard contracts."
- "At the end of 2004, the Company began requiring centralized retention of documentation evidencing proof of delivery and final acceptance for revenue recognition purposes."

a. What features of this case should have indicated to the auditor a potentially heightened risk of fraudulent financial reporting?

b. Using the previous disclosures as a starting point, identify challenges regarding internal controls that a company may face in doing business internationally.

c. The company had disclosed its planned remediation efforts for 2004. How might the auditor have used that information in planning the 2005 audit?

d. Considering potential analytical procedures relevant to the revenue cycle, identify analytics that the auditor might use in 2005 to provide evidence that the problems detected in 2004 have been remedied.

e. Considering potential substantive tests of revenue, identify procedures that might be applied in 2005 to provide evidence that the problems detected in 2004 have been remedied.

FRAUD

ETHICS

PROFESSIONAL SKEPTICISM

9-47

HBOC, ARTHUR ANDERSEN LLP
(LO 6, 7, 8, 9)

Robert A. Putnam, an engagement partner for Arthur Andersen LLP, was in charge of the audit for HBOC, an Atlanta-based maker of software for the health-care industry, during the period 1996–1999. HBOC had a fantastic earnings track record. In fact, HBOC's management was so confident of the strength of its financial statements that it made public announcements of the company's revenues, net income, and earnings per share before Andersen's audits or reviews were completed, a practice of which Putnam was aware. However, these financial results reflected the fact that senior officers of HBOC were fraudulently recognizing revenue on transactions that failed to comply with GAAP.

Early in 1997, Putnam learned that HBOC's management was inappropriately recognizing revenue on contracts where a sale was contingent on later approval by a customer's board of directors (such a situation is referred to as a *board contingency*). Putnam discussed the issue with Jay Gilbertson, the CFO, who claimed that the board contingencies were perfunctory and contained no real risk of cancellation. Gilbertson agreed to provide documentation supporting his claim, but he never did so. Putnam had additional reason to be skeptical concerning HBOC's accounting practices. During the prior year's audit, the auditors identified an instance where HBOC used side letters in its contract negotiations with customers. Auditors were aware of the risks associated with side letters, and Andersen had warned its audit staff that such side letters often are the cause of material revenue misstatements, especially in the software industry. Putnam also had reason to be skeptical about the integrity of HBOC's management. During 1997, Gilbertson represented to Andersen that HBOC had complied with the latest draft of SOP 97–2, the new software revenue recognition guidelines prohibiting revenue recognition if any board contingency existed. Despite the new standard, HBOC continued to enter into some contracts with board contingencies.

Despite these issues, Putnam failed to expand the scope of the audit to address the increased risk of fraud. In January 1999, McKesson Corporation acquired HBOC. On April 28, 1999, McKesson announced that it "had determined that software sales transactions aggregating $26.2 million in the company's fourth quarter ended March 31, 1999, and $16.0 million in the prior quarters of the fiscal year, were improperly recorded because they were subject to contingencies, and have been reversed. The audit process is ongoing and there is a possibility that additional contingent sales may be identified." After the announcement, the company's share price tumbled from approximately $65 to $34 a share (a loss of about $9 billion in market value).

Ultimately, the SEC determined that Putnam failed to exercise due professional care, to adequately plan and supervise the audits, and to obtain sufficient appropriate evidence to afford a reasonable basis for an opinion regarding the financial statements. The SEC issued a cease-and-desist order against Putnam, and denied him the privilege of appearing or practicing before the commission as an accountant for at least five years. In addition, fraud charges were brought against the management of HBOC.

Summarizing the facts from the SEC's Administrative Proceeding against Putnam dated April 28, 2008, we know the following about the quarterly and year-end audits that led to the problems for Arthur Andersen LLP on the HBOC engagement:

- **Andersen's Review of HBOC's financial statements—First Quarter 1997** HBOC reported $68 million of software revenue during Q1, and the engagement team tested the account balance and found that $14 million was improperly recorded, which overstated pre-tax income by 9.4%. Most of the improperly recognized revenue related to board contingencies, and the remainder related to revenue recognized on a contract signed after quarter-end. HBOC management refused to eliminate the improperly recorded revenue, and Putnam did not insist that it does so. Putnam approved an unqualified quarterly review report.

- **Andersen's Review of HBOC's financial statements—Second Quarter 1997** The engagement team learned that HBOC continued to improperly recognize revenue on contracts containing board contingencies and that the company was improperly recording revenue on sales subject to side letter contingencies that allowed for contract cancellation. Further, the engagement team learned that at least one such contract that had been recorded as revenue in Q1 had been canceled during Q2. The engagement team also learned that HBOC had again recognized revenue on a contract signed after quarter-end. Putnam recommended to HBOC's management that the revenue from these contracts be reversed, but Gilbertson (the CFO) refused to do so. The errors overstated pre tax income by 7%. Despite these facts, Putnam approved an unqualified quarterly review report.

- **Andersen's Review of HBOC's financial statements—Third Quarter 1997** The engagement team continued to experience the same difficulties as they had noted in Q2; Putnam continued to do nothing about the problems and continued to approve an unqualified quarterly review report.

- **Andersen's Audit of HBOC's financial statements—1997** Year-End Andersen's year-end audit included testing of HBOC's revenue recognition and accounts receivable. The engagement team used confirmations as their primary substantive evidence on these accounts. The team sent eight confirmation requests (11 fewer than they had sent during the 1996 audit). The confirmations requested customers to confirm amounts owed to HBOC and to confirm that no revenue contingencies existed on software purchased from HBOC. Only three customers responded, and two of those noted contingencies included in side letters. Putman did not direct the team to send any additional confirmations or to perform any additional audit procedures. In addition, the engagement team learned that HBOC was recognizing too much revenue on maintenance contracts and that material amounts should have been deferred to later periods. Putnam asked Gilbertson to increase deferred revenue, but Gilbertson refused, promising to do so in later periods. In addition, HBOC acquired other companies during 1997 and recorded acquisition reserves of $95.3 million associated with the expenses of the acquisition. Putnam proposed that HBOC reverse $16 million of the reserves because they were excessive, overstating expenses by 20% (in other words, a cookie jar reserve). Gilbertson refused to make the proposed adjustment. Despite all these problems, Putnam approved an unqualified audit report and disclosed none of the issues to the audit committee.

- **Andersen's Review of HBOC's financial statements—First Quarter 1998** During the review, Putnam discovered that HBOC was misusing the acquisition reserve to offset current period operating expenses, which is in violation of GAAP and had the effect of overstating HBOC's net income. The engagement team also identified another instance of improper revenue recognition associated with a contract involving a side letter. Once again, Putnam proposed an adjusting entry to correct the problems, but Gilbertson refused to make the entry. Putnam again approved an unqualified quarterly review report.

By April 1998, the engagement manager (Putnam's subordinate) expressed concerns about the earnings management issues occurring at HBOC to Putnam, and Putnam shared the same concerns despite doing nothing to address them. In May 1998, Putnam and the engagement team called a special meeting with Gilbertson and others at HBOC to discuss the issues, and Gilbertson expressed promises to begin properly recording the various transactions.

- **Andersen's Review of HBOC's financial statements—Second Quarter 1998** During the quarterly review, the engagement team again noted a variety of errors. These included inappropriate application of acquisition reserves to reduce current period expenses, recognition of excessive revenue from software maintenance agreements, and an understatement of the allowance for doubtful accounts. Putnam informed Gilbertson that if HBOC did not reverse the application of the acquisition reserves, Andersen would not issue its review report. After a heated discussion, Gilbertson reversed the entry related to acquisition reserves but did not correct any of the other errors. Putnam approved the issuance of the quarterly review report.

- **Andersen's Review of HBOC's financial statements—Third Quarter 1998** The engagement team again discovered the same types of earnings management issues as in prior quarters, but Putnam did not require HBOC to make corrections. Further, Putnam approved an unusual transaction in which HBOC simultaneously sold to and purchased a product from another company. Putnam advised Gilbertson that the accounting for the transaction would be correct only if the sale and purchase were not linked and if there was a defined end user for the HBOC software. Neither of these conditions was true, and Putnam was aware of this fact (and this transaction ultimately led to a restatement of $30 million about a year later). However, Putnam still approved the issuance of the quarterly review report.

- At the November 1998 meeting of HBOC's audit committee, the CEO informed the audit committee that Gilbertson was resigning as CFO, which was an unexpected event. The CEO asked Putnam if he "had a Cendant on his hands," referring to a widely reported financial fraud case at the time. Putnam responded that he knew of no problems or disagreements with Gilbertson.
  In October 1998, McKesson and HBOC announced their merger. Putnam approved the use of Andersen's reports in related filings and made no mention of the associated accounting errors.

- **Andersen's Audit of McKesson's financial statements—1998 Year-End** McKesson hired Andersen to complete the audits, and Putnam and the engagement team continued to discover various accounting errors. Still, Putnam did not require the team to expand the scope of audit testing. Putnam again approved the issuance of an unqualified audit report.

During the spring of 1999, McKesson initially disclosed some of the revenue recognition issues, and by the summer of 1999, McKesson reported restatements of the 1997 and 1998 financial statements. Ultimately, six members of upper management of HBOC were charged with securities fraud. The SEC issued a cease-and-desist order against Putman and denied him the privilege of appearing or practicing before the commission as an accountant for at least five years.

In many instances of fraudulent financial reporting, the auditor is completely unaware of the fraud until it ultimately unravels. That is certainly *not* the case for the HBOC fraud. Rather, it is very clear that Putnam and his Andersen engagement team were well aware of the fraud and possessed detailed knowledge of precisely how it was accomplished. Yet, they did virtually nothing to address the situation.

Source: *Adapted from information contained in the following sources: (1) Securities Act of 1933 Release No. 8912, April 28, 2008; (2) Securities Exchange Act of 1934 Release No. 57725, April 28, 2008; (3) Accounting and Auditing Enforcement Release No. 2815, April 28, 2008; and (4) Administrative Proceeding File No. 3-10998.*

a. What was Putnam's critical mistake in the review of Q1 1997? How did that critical mistake affect his willingness to take action to address the problems in the HBOC audit in later periods?

b. What do you think could have motivated Putnam to act as he did? Why do you think that after all the problems that he encountered, he was still willing to acquiesce to the obviously inappropriate sale/purchase transaction in Q3 1998?

c. What other elements of corporate governance failed in the HBOC situation?

d. The confirmation process in the 1997 year-end audit was clearly flawed. What did the engagement team and Putnam do wrong?

e. The McKesson acquisition of HBOC provided an opportunity for Putnam to deal with what he knew. Obviously, McKesson management would have been eager to know about the earnings management issues at HBOC prior to acquiring the company. Instead, Putnam did not reveal the problems he had been encountering, even when asked directly by the CEO and the audit committee. Use the professional decision-making framework introduced in *Chapter 1* to make a recommendation about a course of action that would have enabled Putnam to do the right thing during the acquisition process and alert the other parties involved in corporate governance of HBOC and McKesson about the problematic behaviors he had been encountering. Recall that the framework is as follows:

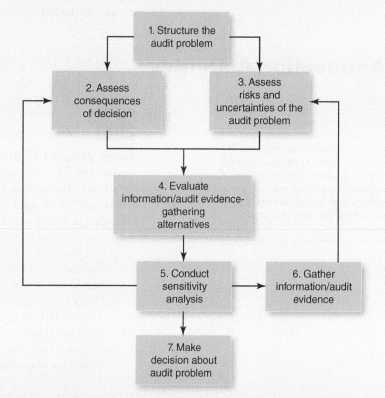

Source: Adapted from Judgment and Choice, by Robin Hogarth.

FRAUD

ETHICS

9-48 | **HBOC, ARTHUR ANDERSEN LLP**
(LO 6, 7, 8, 9)

For this case, use the same facts as presented in *Problem 9-47*, where we focused on the inappropriate actions of Robert A. Putnam, the engagement partner on the HBOC audit. In this case, we expand on the problems detected in the audit and ultimately ask that you decide on an appropriate, alternative course of action for the manager of the HBOC audit, that is, Putman's subordinate. In the actual case, the audit manager questioned Putnam's actions but never took proactive action (other than talking to Putnam) to correct the known audit deficiencies.

In his book, *The Courageous Follower: Standing up to and for Our Leaders* (1995), Ira Chaleff describes five characteristics of individuals who stand up to their organizational leaders. These characteristics include the courage to: (1) assume responsibility for themselves and their organization, (2) serve the organization in a responsible manner, (3) challenge the behaviors or policies of the leader, (4) participate in transforming an organization or dealing with the difficulties associated with change, and (5) take moral action, including refusing to obey direct orders, appealing to the next level of authority, or resigning.

Consider the ideas outlined by Chaleff, and use the ethical decision-making framework from *Chapter 1* to make a recommendation about an alternative, appropriate course of action that the audit manager on the HBOC audit could have taken.

Recall that the seven steps in the framework are: (1) identify the ethical issue; (2) determine who are the affected parties and identify their rights; (3) determine the most important rights; (4) develop alternative courses of action; (5) determine the likely consequences of each proposed course of action; (6) assess the possible consequences, including an estimation of the greatest good for the greatest number; and (7) decide on the appropriate course of action.

Application Activities

NOTE: Completing *Application Activities* requires students to reference additional resources and materials. Some *Application Activities* will require the student to reference relevant professional auditing standards. We make special note of these as *Auditing Standards Application Activities*.

9-49 | **ZYNGA**
(LO 1)

Locate Zynga's FYE 2016 10-K and its 2017 Proxy Statement to answer the following questions:

a. Use online resources to help you define the term "non-GAAP measures." Why do companies use non-GAAP measures?

b. Zynga uses a non-GAAP measure, "bookings," to assist readers in understanding the company's financial statements and associated disclosure. Define how Zynga uses the non-GAAP measure, bookings. Read management's description of this non-GAAP measure. What do the results of it imply for the financial viability of Zynga?

c. How do bookings compare to GAAP-based revenue?

d. What are limitations to the non-GAAP measure, bookings? As an investor, could you live with those limitations, or would you avoid relying on bookings?

9-50 **AMTRUST FINANCIAL**
(LO 7)

In March 2017, AmTrust Financial revealed that it had a variety of internal control material weaknesses, one of which led to a material misstatement in the revenue cycle.

a. Obtain the 10-K of AmTrust Financial Services. Describe the types of services that the company provides. You can find it using the following link:
https://www.sec.gov/Archives/edgar/data/1365555/000136555517000059/0001365555-17-000059-index.htm

b. What is the nature of the errors and why was it critical for the company to remedy those errors?

c. The subsequently restated 2014 and 2015 financial statements were audited by BDO LLP. The Company switched auditors to KPMG LLP for the FYE2016 financial statements, and KPMG's audit resulted in the detection of the internal control material weaknesses and the subsequent restatements of the financial statements. Why might a new auditor discover an internal control material weakness that the prior auditor did not discover?

d. What does the auditor switch and subsequent revelation of the internal control material weakness imply about the quality of BDO's audits of the 2014 and 2015 financial statements?

e. As it turns out, a former BDO auditor was actually the one who alerted the Federal Bureau of Investigation of the financial woes of AmTrust. S(he) became a whistleblower, carrying around a tiny recording device disguised as a Starbucks gift card. Given this information, revisit your answer to part c. of this question.

f. Search the internet to determine the decline in AmTrust's stock price on the day that the whistleblower allegations became public.

9-51 **GOL INTELLIGENT AIRLINES**
(LO 1, 2, 3, 4, 5, 6, 7, 8)

Obtain the following PCAOB enforcement release:
https://pcaobus.org/Enforcement/Decisions/Documents/105-2016-031-Deloitte-Brazil.pdf

Also, review the client's website relating to this case (Gol Intelligent Airlines) so that you are familiar with its general business model, operations, and financial condition: *https://www.voegol.com.br/en/gol/about-gol*

Finally, read a summary of the case and associated personnel below.

Fact Sheet—Deloitte Brazil Enforcement Orders

The PCAOB announced a settlement with Brazil-based Deloitte Touche Tohmatsu Auditores Independentes that included the largest civil penalty ever imposed by the PCAOB.

Details of the Case

The charges stem largely from Deloitte Brazil's audit of the 2010 financial statements and internal control over financial reporting of its client - a Brazilian airline (the "Issuer").

During the 2010 audit, Deloitte Brazil violated securities laws and PCAOB standards by:

• *Improperly acquiescing to the Issuer's accounting of its maintenance deposit assets*
• *Failing to obtain sufficient evidence of the Issuer's reported advance ticket sales and passenger revenue*

- *Issuing materially false and unqualified audit reports on the Issuer's 2010 financial statements and ICFR, in violation of Exchange Act Section 10(b), Exchange Act Rule 10b-5, and PCAOB standards.*

On May 10, 2011, the Issuer announced an adjustment to revenue as a result of its advance ticket sales accounting issues.

After the 2010 audit was completed, Deloitte Brazil violated PCAOB rules and standards by:

- *Improperly altering work papers in advance of a 2012 PCAOB inspection which included the 2010 audit and providing those papers to inspectors*
- *Failing to cooperate with a subsequent PCAOB investigation by providing the altered work papers, and other misleading information, to PCAOB enforcement staff*

Deloitte Brazil admitted to noncooperation with a PCAOB inspection and investigation. The PCAOB found that, in light of the violations listed above, Deloitte Brazil violated PCAOB quality control standards in numerous ways.

Deloitte Brazil admitted that it failed to maintain a quality control system that provided reasonable assurance that its personnel would act with integrity.

Sanctions Imposed on Deloitte Brazil

The firm has agreed to the following sanctions:

- An $8 million civil penalty, the largest ever imposed by the PCAOB
- Censure
- Significant changes to the firm's system of quality control
- Appointment of an independent monitor to review and assess the firm's progress toward achieving remedial benchmarks
- Immediate practice limitations, including a prohibition on accepting certain new audit work until the monitor confirms the firm's progress in achieving its remedial benchmarks
- Additional professional education and training for the firm's audit staff

Individuals Named in Separate Orders

The following individuals also were sanctioned. None is currently associated with Deloitte Brazil. Their roles at the firm and sanctions are listed below.

- **José Domingos do Prado,** 2010 audit engagement partner, firm audit practice leader—Censure and permanent bar on associating with a PCAOB-registered accounting firm
- **Maurício Pires de Andrade Resende,** firm risk and reputation leader, ethics partner, and policy committee member—Censure and bar on associating with a PCAOB-registered accounting firm for five years (sanctions reduced for cooperation)
- **Wanderley Olivetti,** firm national professional practice director—Censure and bar on associating with a PCAOB-registered accounting firm for five years (sanctions reduced for cooperation)
- **André Ricardo Aguillar Paulon,** 2010 audit senior manager, partner—Censure and restriction on serving as an engagement partner or engagement quality reviewer for one year (sanctions reduced for cooperation)

- **James Roderick Talbot Oram,** 2010 audit engagement quality reviewer—Censure and suspension from associating with a PCAOB-registered accounting firm for one year
- **Joao Rafael Belo de Araujo Filho,** senior manager, partner— Censure, $10,000 civil penalty, and bar on associating with a PCAOB-registered accounting firm for one year
- **Leonardo Fonseca de Freitas Maia,** senior manager, partner— Censure, $10,000 civil penalty, and bar on associating with a PCAOB-registered accounting firm for one year
- **José Fernando Alves,** audit partner for IT—Censure, $20,000 civil penalty, and bar on associating with a PCAOB-registered accounting firm for one year
- **Renata Coelho de Sousa Castelli,** audit manager for IT—Censure and bar on associating with a PCAOB-registered accounting firm for three years
- **Marco Aurelio Paulino Neves,** partner—Censure, $20,000 civil penalty, and bar on associating with a PCAOB-registered accounting firm for three years
- **Simone Pacheco Lemos do Amaral,** senior manager—Censure and bar on associating with a PCAOB-registered accounting firm for one year
- **Walter Vinicius Barreto Brito Silva,** manager—Censure and bar on associating with a PCAOB-registered accounting firm for one year
- **Michael John Morrell,** Chairman of Deloitte Brazil's policy committee, governing body of Deloitte entities in Brazil—Censure, $35,000 civil penalty, and bar on associating with a PCAOB-registered accounting firm for five years
- **Juarez Lopes de Araújo,** CEO and managing partner of Deloitte Brazil—Censure and permanent bar on associating with a PCAOB-registered accounting firm
  a. Briefly describe in your own words the nature of the underlying potential misstatements and associated weaknesses in internal control at Gol. For each, articulate how the auditors failed in their duties.
  b. What role did the audit engagement partner, Jose Domingos do Prado (hereafter, Prado) play in leading the Gol engagement and what role did he have in terms of interacting with the inspection team?
  c. Describe the PCAOB rules and standards that the auditors had violated.
  d. Locate AS 3 (using the new numbering convention, this is now AS 1215) on the PCAOB's website. Identify the paragraphs that are most relevant to the judgment errors that Prado made with respect to documentation requirements.
  e. Go to the following website to learn about what stock analysts are saying about Gol: http://www.nasdaq.com/symbol/gol/analyst-research

    1. Why might the client, Gol, have resisted making the proposed audit adjustment?
    2. What is the current analyst consensus earnings for Gol today?
    3. What does the term "analyst consensus forecast" mean?
    4. What is a negative earnings surprise?

f. Use online resources to determine the stock market reaction to the PCAOB enforcement filings on December 5, 2016.

g. The Gol audit was conducted in Brazil, a country very different from the one in which the regulator (the PCAOB) resides.

1. Use online resources to locate tips for conducting business in Brazil. Also, investigate how culture may play a role in understanding the behavior of Prado.

2. Locate Sao Paulo, Brazil on a map. Next, research Brazil's corruption index and interpret it by comparing it to the United States' corruption index. Consider the implications of these differences.

3. Define the term "corruption." Comment on how it relates to this case.

h. Ultimately, one of the managers on the engagement (André Ricardo Aguillar Paulon), who was involved in the audit-related misconduct and the improper document alteration became a whistleblower, secretly recording a senior partner (Mauricio Pires de Andrade Resende) on a cellphone as evidence. Using this evidence, he sought credit for and was granted consideration for extraordinary cooperation with the PCAOB, unlike many other members of the team who were involved in the cover-up.

1. What is a whistleblower? What risks do they face? Do you think that the cost/benefit to the whistleblower in the Deloitte case was worth taking that risk?

2. Why should audit firms set up internal whistleblower hotlines?

3. Locate Deloitte's whistleblower hotline and provide the link to it. What are your impressions of the information contained on the website?

4. Review the PCAOB's policy on cooperation at the following website:
https://pcaobus.org/News/Releases/Pages/04242013_PolicyStatement.aspx
Identify what actions the PCAOB considers to be extraordinary cooperation and how the PCAOB will give credit reflecting such cooperation. Do you think the whistleblower would have come forward without such incentive?

5. How might you garner the courage to be a whistleblower? Under what conditions would you find that whistleblowing was to your benefit (including the protections that the PCAOB provides for cooperation), despite the risks that it may pose to you?

6. Finally, it is important to know that Paulon, along with two others involved in the cover-up, were promoted to audit partner during or shortly after the activities outlined in the enforcement actions took place. Reflect in your team about the implications evident in Deloitte's corporate culture with respect to these promotions.

AUDITING STANDARDS
APPLICATION ACTIVITY

INTERNATIONAL

9-52 **LO 8** Refer to the *Auditing Standards Exhibit* inside the front cover of this textbook. Identify the relevant auditing standards (PCAOB, AICPA, and IAASB) relating to external confirmations. Locate the standards on each organization's website.

a. What generalizations are applicable to audit evidence with respect to confirmations?

b. What do the standards direct the auditor to do if management refuses to allow the auditor to send a confirmation request?

c. Comment on similarities or substantive differences between the standards for each standard-setting body.

AUDITING STANDARDS APPLICATION ACTIVITY

INTERNATIONAL

9-53 **LO 5, 8** Refer to the *Auditing Standards Exhibit* inside the front cover of this textbook. Identify the relevant auditing standards (PCAOB, AICPA, and IAASB) concerning using analytical procedures as a substantive test. Locate the standards on each organization's website.

a. What is a basic premise underlying analytical procedures that this guidance notes?

b. What types of documentation are appropriate for substantive analytical procedures?

c. Why might using substantive analytical procedures help auditors achieve efficiencies? Why might others criticize auditors for using substantive analytical procedures rather than substantive tests of details?

Data Analytics Using Excel: A Case in the Context of the Pharmaceutical Industry

NOTE: In this and select cycle chapters, we present a case set in the pharmaceutical industry. The case enables students to practice developing and conducting planning and substantive analytical procedures. The case was developed using the published financial statements of three prominent companies in this industry, with adaptations to make the case suitable for classroom use. The fictional company names are: PharmaCorp, Novartell, and AstraZoro. You will access an Excel file on the text's website at *https://login.cengage.com/cb/*. The Excel file contains financial data and information from footnote disclosures substantive analytical procedures using data analytics in Excel. The primary analytical procedures tasks will focus on PharmaCorp. You will use Novartell and AstraZoro as industry comparison companies. Access and download the file, then complete the requirements in 9-54.

9-54 **LO 5, 8** This case will enable you to practice conducting planning and substantive analytical procedures for accounts in the revenue cycle. When analyzing the financial data, you may assume that the 2015 information is unaudited, while prior year data is audited.

As you complete this case, consider the following features of and trends in the pharmaceutical industry and for PharmaCorp specifically:

- After a long period of industry dominance by companies in the United States, the United Kingdom, and Europe, these companies are facing increasing competition from companies domiciled in emerging economies, such as Brazil, India, and China.

- There exists significant uncertainty in the market because of recent regulation covering health-care and government payouts for certain procedures and related pharmaceuticals.

- Health-care policy makers and the government are increasingly mandating what physicians can prescribe to patients.

- Health-care policy makers and the government are increasingly focusing on prevention regimes rather than treatment regimes, thereby leading to shifts in the demand for various pharmaceuticals.

- The global pharmaceutical market is anticipated to grow by 5% to 7% in 2016 compared with a 4% to 5% growth rate in 2015, according to a leading industry analyst publication.

- Beginning in 2014, PharmaCorp initiated and executed a significant company-wide cost reduction initiative aimed at improving manufacturing efficiency, cutting back on research and development expenses, and eliminating unnecessary corporate overhead.

- PharmaCorp's policies for extending credit to customers has remained stable over the last three years. PharmaCorp's credit-granting policies are considered stringent within the industry, and analysts have sometimes criticized the company for this, contending that such policies have hindered the company's revenue growth relative to industry peers.

- PharmaCorp's policies for extending credit to customers have remained stable over the last three years. PharmaCorp's credit granting policies are considered stringent within the industry, and analysts have sometimes criticized the company for this, contending that such policies have hindered the company's revenue growth relative to industry peers.

- Two of PharmaCorp's popular pharmaceuticals, Selebrax and Vyvox, came off patent during the fourth quarter of FYE 2015. These pharmaceuticals now face competition in the generic drug portion of the overall industry market.

Part I: Planning Analytical Procedures

a. *Step 1: Identify Suitable Analytical Procedures.* Your audit senior has suggested that you should use the following ratios (on an overall financial statement level) for planning analytical procedures in the revenue cycle at PharmaCorp:
   - Gross margin: (revenues-cost of sales)/revenues
   - Turnover of receivables: (revenues/average accounts receivable); for ease of computation simply use ending accounts receivable
   - Receivables as a percentage of current assets and as a percentage of total assets: (accounts receivable/total current assets) and (accounts receivable/total assets)
   - Allowance for uncollectible accounts as a percentage of accounts receivable: (allowance/accounts receivable)

     As part of Step 1, identify any other relevant relationships or trend analyses that would be useful to consider as part of planning analytics. Explain your reasoning.

b. *Step 2: Evaluate Reliability of Data Used to Develop Expectations.* The audit team has determined that the data you will be using to develop expectations in the revenue cycle are reliable. Indicate the factors that the audit team likely considered in making that determination.

c. *Step 3: Develop Expectations.* Complete Step 3 of planning analytical procedures by developing expectations for relevant accounts in the revenue cycle and for the ratios from Part (a). Develop expectations by considering both historical trends of PharmaCorp, and also by considering features of and historical trends in the industry. Given that this is a planning analytical procedure, the expectations are not expected to have a high level of precision. You might indicate that you expect a ratio to increase, decrease, or stay the same, and possibly indicate the size of any expected increases or decreases, or the range of the expected ratio. PharmaCorp's financial information is on first tab of the Excel file, while the financial information for Novartell and AstraZoro is provided on the last two tabs of the Excel file.

d. *Step 4 and Step 5: Define and Identify Significant Unexpected Differences.* Refer to the guidance in *Chapter 7* on overall materiality, performance materiality, and posting materiality. Apply those materiality guidelines to Step 4 of planning analytical procedures in the revenue cycle for PharmaCorp, to define what is meant by a significant difference. Explain your reasoning. Also, comment on qualitative materiality considerations in this context. Now that you have determined what amount of difference would be considered significant, calculate the ratios identified in Step 1 (and any additional ratios or trend analyses that you suggested), based on PharmaCorp's recorded financial statement amounts. Identify those ratios where there is a significant unexpected difference.

e. *Step 6 and Step 7: Investigate Significant Unexpected Differences and Ensure Proper Documentation.* Complete Step 6 of planning analytical procedures by describing accounts or relationships that you would investigate further through substantive audit procedures. Explain your reasoning. To complete Step 7, describe what information should be included in the auditor's workpapers.

Part II: Substantive Analytical Procedures

f. At the Excel file, you will see three tabs that you should review: *PharmaCorp Segment Information, PharmaCorp Geographic Information,* and *PharmaCorp Other Revenue Info.* These tabs provide excerpts from PharmaCorp's footnote disclosures regarding segment, geographic, and other revenue information. Read these disclosures and describe the various operating segments and geographic regions in which the company operates.

g. Which operating segments are most important to the company in terms of revenue generation? Which geographic regions are most important to the company? What are the three most important products produced by PharmaCorp? Comment on trends that you notice in revenue in each of these categories.

h. Explain the types of ratio analysis that you could conduct in substantive analytical procedures using the data provided in the segment, geographic, and other revenue information, for example, R&D expenses/revenues. How would the substantive analytics differ from the planning analytics? Comment on the trends and relationships that you believe are most relevant, and implications for further substantive testing.

Data Analytics Using ACL

NOTE: There is an ACL Appendix at the end of the text that you may find helpful in completing this problem.

9-55 `LO 5, 8`   You are auditing FloorMart, a retailer with 200 stores around the country. It has two basic sizes of stores—minimarts with 3,000 square feet and maximarts with 7,500 square feet. Both types of stores carry the same types of products. The client has provided an Excel file with the square feet, sales, and inventory at each store. Access the book's resources on the Cengage website. The file is labeled "FloorMart Data."

a. Using either Excel or ACL, identify the stores for which sales appear to be out of line with the other stores and require additional evidence.

b. What procedures would the auditor use to gather the additional evidence?

9-56 `LO 7, 8`   You are auditing Accounts Receivable of HUSKY Corp. as of December 31, 2013. The Accounts Receivable general ledger balance is $4,263,919.52. Access the textbook's resources on the Cengage website. The files are labeled "HUSKY Unpaid Invoices 2013" (the 12/31/2013, unpaid invoices), "HUSKY Shipping File 2013" (contains the shipment numbers and shipment dates for those invoices), and "HUSKY Credit Limit 2013" (contains each customer's credit limit). Sales are made FOB shipping point. The auditor has verified that the last shipment in 2013 is numbered 62050 and that shipping numbers have been used in proper sequence.

• Foot the file of unpaid invoices using the menu option **Analyze**, then **Statistical**, then **Statistics** and agree to the general ledger. Print the statistics for the audit documentation and note the other statistics provided.

- Identify customers with balances over their credit limit and print out the results. (*Hint*: Before combining files, be sure the matching fields, such as CUSTNUM or INVNUM, have been changed in each table from a number format to ASCII format using the menu item **Edit** then **Table Layout**. Double click on the field you want to change).
- Perform a sales cutoff test to identify any invoices for which sales were recorded in 2013 but shipment was not made until 2014 and print out the results, including the total of those invoices.
- Age the unpaid invoices as of December 31, 2013, print the aging and graph of the aging, extract (by double-clicking on the over 45 days aging indicator) and print out a list of invoices over 45 days old that also shows the total of those invoices.

Summarize your results and describe what procedures should be performed based on those results. Use ACL to stratify the population of customer balances, print the results, and describe how this information could be used to help determine which balances to confirm.

Data Analytics Using Tableau

Note: We have slightly modified the database in certain ways to achieve our learning objectives. So, do NOT use the database version that is on Tableau's website.

9-57 LO 1, 2, 5, 6, 7, 8 Refer to *https://www.tableau.com/resource/desktop-welcome/interface*

Access the Superstore Sales database on the Cengage website. *https://login.cengage.com/cb/*

a. Sort the file from largest to smallest Sales revenue. Determine a lower bound for the upper stratum. Defend your choice.

b. Assume that Superstore Sales' FYE is 12/31/12. Check for appropriate sales cutoff. Identify any potential errors in Sales revenue.

c. Use Tableau to determine the market segment of sales by product category and consumer market region. What category of product has the highest sales volume? What category has the lowest sales volume? What are the top two regions in the world for sales volume of consumer office supplies? Which market region is an emerging market for Superstore Sales?

d. What month is the highest in terms of sales value? What is the year with the highest sales so far for Superstore Sales?

e. Use the "Show Me" feature to determine which category of furniture sales yields the lowest profit, regardless of geographic location.

f. Learn about how to create a forecast in Tableau using the following link (and associated webinar):

https://www.tableau.com/learn/webinars/forecasting-tableau

Assume that you wish to develop an expectation to compare likely sales levels by month across the three product categories, that is, furniture, office, and technology. What is your forecast of sales for FYE 2013 for each of these categories? How would you use these forecasts as compared to actual FYE 2013 amounts as asserted by management?

Academic Research Cases

9-58 `LO 1, 2, 3, 6, 7, 8` Locate and read the article listed below.

Perols, Johan L., R. M. Bowen, C. Zimmermann, and B. Samba. (2017). Finding needles in a haystack: Using data analytics to improve fraud prediction. *The Accounting Review* 92(2): 221–245.

    a. What is the purpose of the study?
    b. Describe the design/method/approach used to conduct the study.
    c. What are the primary findings of the study?

9-59 `LO 1` Locate and read the article listed below.

Rasmussen, S. J. (2013). Revenue recognition, earnings management, and earnings informativeness in the semiconductor industry. *Accounting Horizons* 27(1): 91–112.

    a. What is the purpose of the study?
    b. Describe the design/method/approach used to conduct the study.
    c. What are the primary findings of the study?

Auditing Cash, Marketable Securities, and Complex Financial Instruments

The Audit Opinion Formulation Process

I. Making Client Acceptance and Continuance Decisions

Chapter 1

II. Performing Risk Assessment

Chapters 2, 3, 7, and 9–13

III. Obtaining Evidence About Internal Control Operating Effectiveness

Chapters 8–13

IV. Obtaining Substantive Evidence About Accounts, Disclosures, and Assertions

Chapters 8–13

V. Completing the Audit and Making Reporting Decisions

Chapters 14 and 15

Quality Auditing and the Need for Quality Auditor Judgments and Ethical Decisions

Chapter 1

Professional Liability

Chapter 4

The Audit Opinion Formulation Process and a Framework for Obtaining Audit Evidence
Chapters 5 and 6

Cash is the focal point of many accounting entries, with a high volume of transactions flowing through cash accounts. Cash, both on deposit in banks and petty cash, are subject to misappropriation through many different schemes. The majority of asset misappropriation schemes involve cash. There are many examples of fraudulent financial reporting involving cash. Because of these risks, organizations and auditors usually emphasize controls over cash transactions. However, it is common for smaller organizations to have a number of control deficiencies over cash activities. Marketable securities and complex financial instruments are also relevant accounts in this transaction cycle. Auditors should understand the specific risks of material misstatement of cash accounts at a client and perform audit procedures accordingly.

Learning Objectives

LO 1 Identify the significant accounts, disclosures, and relevant assertions in auditing cash accounts.

LO 2 Identify and assess inherent risks of material misstatement in cash accounts.

LO 3 Identify and assess fraud risks of material misstatement in cash accounts.

LO 4 Identify and assess control risks of material misstatement in cash accounts.

LO 5 Describe how to use planning analytical procedures to identify possible material misstatements for cash accounts, disclosures, and assertions.

LO 6 Determine appropriate responses to identified risks of material misstatement for cash accounts, disclosures, and assertions.

LO 7 Determine appropriate tests of controls and consider the results of tests of controls for cash accounts, disclosures, and assertions.

LO 8 Determine and apply sufficient appropriate substantive audit procedures for testing cash accounts, disclosures, and assertions.

LO 9 Identify types of marketable securities, articulate the risks and controls typically associated with these accounts, and outline an audit approach for testing these accounts.

LO 10 Describe audit considerations for complex financial instruments.

LO 11 Apply the frameworks for professional decision making and ethical decision making to issues involving the audit of cash accounts, disclosures, and assertions.

Fraudulent Petty Cash Transactions at Koss Corporation and the Embezzlement Fraud at Peregrine Financial Group, Inc.

Why It Matters

This feature provides details on two high-profile frauds involving cash.

The first fraud involves Sue Sachdeva, former vice president of finance for Koss Corporation. Sachdeva orchestrated a $31 million embezzlement at Koss Corporation. In addition to expenditures at upscale clothing retailers, she used Koss funds on various luxury items such as a personal trainer, limousine rides, vacations, and items for her home. Astonishingly, federal authorities took more than 22,000 items—some with price tags still attached—in connection with the investigation. The seized items included fur coats, designer clothing, jewelry, art items, and hundreds of pairs of shoes. As part of the embezzlement scheme, Sachdeva took more than $145,000 from petty cash, in increments ranging from $482 to $9,049. While that is many disbursements coming out of petty cash, it is often true that petty cash doesn't get a lot of attention. Following this embezzlement, Koss took various remediation actions, which included eliminating the petty cash fund so that all reimbursements are processed through standard controlled accounts payable processes. The former executive was convicted in 2010 of six felonies and began serving her sentence in February 2011. The U.S. Bureau of Prisons initially predicted that she would be released in August 2020, but she was released in April 2017 after serving just six years in prison. According to news reports, Sachdeva spent the preceding year in an Oakland, CA halfway house, and she will be under supervision for the three following years. Federal authorities gave her a 15% reduction of her sentence for good behavior, which is a common discount. In addition, the authorities gave her another 25% reduction for aiding them in prosecuting two former cohorts that stole some of the items that Sachdeva had purchased with Koss funds.

The second fraud involves Russell Wasendorf Sr., who attempted to commit suicide after embezzling over $200 million from Peregrine Financial Group's (PFG) brokerage clients over a twenty-year period. His son, Russell Wasendorf Jr., ran the operations of PFG and was the president and chief operating officer of the company but did not have detailed access to important financial records of the company. Instead, Russell Wasendorf Sr. had sole control of the company's bank accounts. Wasendorf Sr. left a detailed suicide note in which he explained his actions and described how he committed the fraud.

One part of the suicide note reads as follows:

"I was able to conceal my crime of forgery by being the sole individual with access to the U.S. Bank accounts held by PFG. No one else in the company ever saw an actual U.S. Bank statement. I made counterfeit statements within a few hours of receiving the actual statements and gave the forgeries to the accounting department."

He also stated:

"With careful concealment and blunt authority, I was able to hide my fraud from others at PFG. If anyone questioned my authority I would simply point out that I was the sole shareholder. I ordered that US Bank statements were to be delivered directly to me unopened, to make sure no one was able to examine an actual US Bank Statement. On US Bank side, I told representatives at the Bank that I was the only person they should interface with at PFG."

The December 31, 2011, financial statements showed that PFG had over $220 million in its bank account, but in reality the bank account contained only about $6 million. What likely prompted the timing of Wasendorf's attempted suicide was the fact that the National Futures Association (NFA) had just implemented a change to its online system whereby bank statement information would be sent electronically from the banks directly to the NFA (see www.confirmation.com). The NFA started receiving confirmations through that system one day before Wasendorf's attempted suicide. PFG filed for bankruptcy almost immediately after Wasendorf's attempted suicide and subsequent arrest.

What Do You Think?   For Classroom Discussion

As you read about the flagrant and ultimately humiliating detection of fraud in the cases of both Sachdeva and Wasendorf, you might ask yourself: Why would someone do something like that? How could they live with themselves? How does someone go from being a trustworthy accountant to a fraudster?

An insightful psychological phenomenon that helps to shed light on these types of behaviours is termed escalation of commitment. **Escalation of commitment** refers to a phenomenon in which individuals continue with their previous, inappropriate or unfortunate, course of action even when they face increasingly negative risks and outcomes should others become aware of their escalation. In everyday terms, one can think of escalation of commitment as going down a "slippery slope," whereby once you are on that course you find it very difficult to get back to the right place.

Do you think Sachdeva and Wasendorf experienced this phenomenon? Why is it difficult to change course once you have made one, or more, bad decisions?

What You Will Learn

- What are the significant accounts, disclosures, and relevant assertions related to cash? (LO 1)

- What are the inherent risks associated with cash transactions? (LO 2)

- What are fraud risks associated with cash transactions? (LO 3)

- What controls should management have in place to mitigate the risks associated with cash transactions? (LO 4)

- How might auditors use planning analytical procedures to identify any potential concerns related to cash? (LO 5)

- What is sufficient appropriate evidence when auditing cash transactions and related accounts? (LO 6, 7, 8)

- What are the various types of marketable securities; what are the risks and controls associated with those accounts; and what would be an appropriate audit approach for testing these accounts? (LO 9)

- What are complex financial instruments, and what audit considerations are relevant for such instruments? (LO 10)

LO 1

Identify the significant accounts, disclosures, and relevant assertions in auditing cash accounts.

Significant Accounts, Disclosures, and Relevant Assertions

An organization may have many different kinds of cash accounts including checking accounts, cash management accounts, and petty cash.

Common Cash Accounts: Checking, Cash Management, and Petty Cash Accounts

Organizations use a general checking account to process most cash transactions, including regular cash receipts and disbursements. In some cases, the organization's bank receives receipts directly through a **lockbox** or electronic funds transfer (EFT), and then directly deposits the receipts into the client's account.

Almost all organizations use one or more petty cash accounts to disburse funds to employees who are authorized to make various purchases on behalf of the organization. The petty cash fund should have a sufficient amount of money to pay for routine expenses. While most petty cash funds involve only a small amount of money, a risk of fraud is associated with this fund, as illustrated in the *Why It Matters* feature at the beginning of the chapter (see the first fraud in the feature). As that example illustrates, the cumulative disbursements made through petty cash funds can become significant.

Good cash management requires the organization to effectively balance returns and risks on idle cash balances. Most organizations have developed relationships with their financial institutions to move excess cash into and out of short-term savings accounts to generate extra returns.

Exhibit 10.1 depicts the accounts typically affected by cash transactions.

Exhibit 10.1
Cash Cycle Accounts

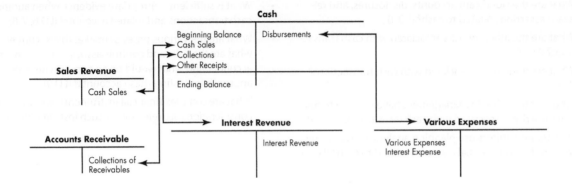

Relevant Financial Statement Assertions

The five management assertions relevant to cash are:

1. *Existence/occurrence*—Cash balances exist at the balance sheet date.
2. *Completeness*—Cash balances include all cash transactions that have taken place during the period.
3. *Rights and obligations*—The company has title to the cash accounts as of the balance sheet date. For example, cash might be pledged as collateral; if this is the case, the company must disclose relevant information about the collateral arrangement. In most cases, risk related to ownership of cash is low.
4. *Valuation or allocation*—The recorded balances reflect the true underlying economic value of those assets. This assertion usually has a low level of inherent risk, unless the client has cash holdings in foreign currency in a country experiencing political instability.
5. *Presentation and disclosure*—Cash is properly classified on the balance sheet and disclosed in the notes to the financial statements. For example, restricted cash might need to be reported in the noncurrent asset section of the balance sheet. Further, the auditor will want to determine the accuracy of the classifications on the cash flow statement.

Because of the high level of inherent risk often associated with cash, the auditor primarily focuses on the existence/occurrence and completeness assertions. The auditor typically focuses on whether the cash does, in fact, actually exist, and whether the client records all cash transactions.

Disclosures for Cash Accounts

Disclosures for cash (and marketable equity securities) include ending balances on the face of the Balance Sheet, and descriptive statements from management in the footnotes. Next are examples depicting these disclosures from Ford Motor Company's 2016 Annual Report.

Assets	December 31, 2016			
	Automotive	Financial Services	All Other, Special Items, & Adjustments	Consolidated
Cash and cash equivalents	$ 7,820	$ 8,077	$ 8	$ 15,905
Marketable securities	19,642	3,280	—	22,922

Cash and Cash Equivalents. Included in *Cash and cash equivalents* are highly liquid investments that are readily convertible to known amounts of cash and are subject to an insignificant risk of change in value due to interest rate, quoted price, or penalty on withdrawal. A debt security is classified as a cash equivalent if it meets criteria and if it has a remaining time to maturity of three months or less from the date of acquisition. Amounts on deposit and available upon demand, or negotiated to provide for daily liquidity without penalty, are classified as *Cash and cash equivalents.* Time deposits, certificates of deposit, and money market accounts that meet the above criteria are reported at par value on our balance sheet.

Marketable Securities. Investments in securities with a maturity date greater than three months at the date of purchase and other securities for which there is more than an insignificant risk of change in value due to interest rate, quoted price, or penalty on withdrawal are classified as *Marketable securities.* We generally measure fair value using prices obtained from pricing services. Pricing methods and inputs to valuation models used by the pricing services depend on the security type (i,e., asset class). Where possible, fair values are generated using market inputs including quoted prices (the closing price in an exchange market), bid prices (the price at which a buyer stands ready to purchase), and other market information. For fixed income securities that are not actively traded, the pricing services use alternative methods to determine fair value for the securities, including quotes for similar fixed-income securities, matrix pricing, discounted cash flow using benchmark curves, or other factors. in certain cases, when market data are not available, we may use broker quotes to determine fair value.

Challenging the Cash Existence Assertion at China Huishan Dairy Holdings Co. Ltd: Muddy Waters Shorts the Company's Stock

Why It Matters: An International Perspective

This feature highlights the significant consequences related to material misstatement of cash.

Muddy Waters Capital, LLC describes its business model as follows:

> Muddy Waters, LLC is a pioneer in on-the-ground, freely published investment research. Muddy Waters peels back the layers, often built up by seemingly respected but sycophantic law firms, auditors, and venal managements. We pride ourselves on assessing a company's true worth, and being able to see through the opacity and hype that some managements create. Our research approach is to combine diverse talents, including forensic accountants, trained investigators, valuation experts and entrepreneurs, many of whom have hands-on experience running businesses in the U.S. and emerging markets. For more information on Muddy Waters, see *http://www.muddywatersresearch.com/about/*

In December 2016, Muddy Waters issued a statement alerting investors that it had taken a significant short selling position (i.e., in China Huishan Dairy Holdings (hereafter 'Huishan'), asserting that the company's operations were a complete fraud and that its shares were worthless. Muddy Waters asserted that the company's Chairman, CEO, and founder, Mr. Kai Yang, had stolen at least 150 RMB of assets from the company. A few days after Muddy Waters' allegations, Huishan launched a campaign of damage control, publicly asserting that Muddy Waters' were groundless, misrepresentative, malicious, and false.

Huishan traded on the Hong Kong Stock Exchange and had been widely considered a stable and reliable investment. On March 24, 2017, trading of Huishan's shares was halted as the market learned that Ms. Kun Ge, the company's Senior Vice President and Executive Director (and the wife of Chairman

Yang) went missing on March 21, 2017. Following her disappearance, Huishan reported that it could not locate the vast majority of its cash balances.

The figure below reveals the significant loss of market capitalization that investors suffered as a result of the underlying financial reporting fraud and theft of its cash. The decline in market capitalization happened in just one hour; the loss of market capitalization is estimated to be approximately $4 billion.

In addition to the outright theft of cash by its Senior Vice President (who had control over sales and branding, human resources and government affairs, and treasury operations and banking relationships), Huishan also had a **fake cash problem**. A fake cash problem means that the organization has recorded fictitious additions to cash to validate fictitious additions to revenues; thus, the existence assertion is violated for both cash and revenue accounts.

The fictitious entry would appear as follows:

Dr. Cash

    Cr. Revenue

Because the revenue is fictitious, the cash is as well. Huishan maintained its operations during the last several years by borrowing heavily. The figure below reveals a significant increase in the company's debt-to-equity ratio.

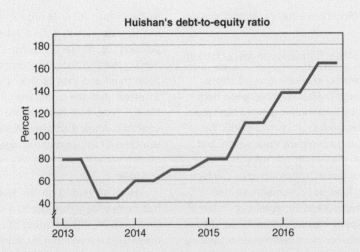

As of mid-2017, the Chinese government was injecting cash into the company to save it from financial collapse because the company produces a significant amount of dairy products necessary for the country's citizens.

For more details, see https://qz.com/943491/china-is-desperately-trying-to-save-a-huishan-dairy-holdings-6863hk-a-company-that-turns-out-is-too-big-to-fail/

It's Your Turn!   *Prompt for Critical Thinking #1*

Think about the role that Muddy Waters played in warning investors about the impending fraudulent financial reporting and outright theft of cash at Huishan.

1. What is short selling?

2. Why is short selling an important component of investment markets?

3. Why do you think that investors did *not* initially react to Muddy Waters' allegations of fraud, e.g., it took the market about three additional months to devalue the company's securities?

4. Use online resources to learn about the fallout of this fraud and the current state of Huishan Dairy Holdings.

An Overview of the Audit Opinion Formulation Process for Cash Accounts

In auditing the cash accounts, the auditor will perform risk assessment procedures, tests of controls, and substantive procedures—Phases II, III, and IV of the audit opinion formulation process.

As part of performing risk assessment procedures, the auditor obtains information that to assess the risk of material misstatement. This includes information about inherent risks at the financial statement level (e.g., client's business and operational risks, financial reporting risks) and at the account and assertion levels, fraud risks including feedback from the audit team's brainstorming sessions, strengths and weaknesses in internal control, and results from planning analytical procedures.

Once the risks of material misstatement have been identified, the auditor then determines how best to respond to them. For an integrated audit and for a financial statement audit where the auditor wants to rely on controls as part of the basis for the audit opinion, the auditor will perform tests of controls and consider the effect of those tests on the substantive evidence to obtain. In other audits, the auditor will rely only on substantive tests to obtain evidence about the accuracy of the financial statements.

Check Your Basic Knowledge

10-1 A fake cash problem relates to management's cash valuation assertion.   (T/F)

10-2 Short selling enables managers to get away with perpetrating fraud undetected and undeterred.   (T/F)

10-3 Which of the following assertions is relevant to whether the company owns the cash accounts as of the balance sheet date?
   a. Existence/occurrence.
   b. Completeness.
   c. Rights and obligations.

   d. Valuation or allocation.
   e. All of the above.

10-4 Which of the following assertions is relevant to whether the cash balances reflect the true underlying economic value of those assets?
   a. Existence/occurrence.
   b. Completeness.
   c. Rights and obligations.
   d. Valuation or allocation.
   e. All of the above.

LO 2

Identify and assess inherent risks of material misstatement in cash accounts.

Identifying Inherent Risks

Cash transactions are generally routine, and the accounting for these transactions involves minimal judgment and subjectivity. However, cash is an inherently risky asset because it may be used for unauthorized purposes, posted to the wrong customer's account, or not recorded on a timely basis. Why is this the case?

- *Volume of activity*—The volume of transactions flowing through the account during the year makes the account susceptible to error.
- *Liquidity*—The cash account is susceptible to theft because cash is liquid and easily transferable.
- *Automated systems*—The electronic transfer of cash and the automated controls over cash are such that if errors are built into computer programs, they will be repeated on a large volume of transactions.
- *Debt covenants*—Debt covenants are often tied to cash balances or to maintaining minimum levels of working capital. Debt covenants specify restrictions on the organization to protect the lender. Typical covenants restrict cash balances, specify the maintenance of minimum working capital, and may restrict the company's ability to pay dividends.
- *Misrepresentation and outright theft*—As we learn through discussions of cash-related frauds at Koss Corporation, Peregrine Financial Group, and China Huishan Dairy Holdings, cash can be stolen by an individual with power over the account balances if there exists a lack of oversight.

The following are examples of questions that auditors might ask in assessing inherent risk in cash accounts:

- Does the company have significant cash flow problems in meeting its current obligations on a timely basis?
- Does the company use cash budgeting techniques? How effective are the company's cash budgeting techniques?
- Does the company use the cash management services offered by its financial institutions? What is the nature of these arrangements?
- Has the company made significant changes in its cash processing during the past year? Have any major changes taken place in the company's computerized cash management applications during the year?
- Does the company have loan or bond covenants that influence the use of cash or the maintenance of working-capital ratios?
- Is there any reason to suspect that management may have a motivation to misstate the cash balance?

Prompt for Critical Thinking #2   It's Your Turn!

Meeting debt covenants is an important inherent risk for an auditor to consider. The debt-to-equity ratio is a calculation that individuals use to evaluate the relative proportion of a company's debt level; minimum acceptable debt-to-equity ratios tend to be in the range of 1.5 to 2.0.

Review the debt-to-equity ratio of Huishan Dairy presented in the previous *Why It Matters* feature.

1. What does it imply with respect to the financial condition of the company over the period 2014–2017?

2. Given that investors could have seen through publicly available financial reporting that the company's debt-to-equity ratio was growing alarmingly high, and the fact that Muddy Waters alerted investors to its short selling position, do you feel sorry for the investors? Do you believe that the investors should be compensated for their loss of market capitalization?

10-5 The volume of activity in cash accounts makes cash accounts less susceptible to error than most other accounts.　(T/F)

10-6 The electronic transfer of cash and the automated controls over cash are such that if errors are built into computer programs, they could be repeated on a large volume of transactions.　(T/F)

10-7 Inherent risk for cash is usually assessed as high for which of the following reasons?
   a. The volume of transactions flowing through cash accounts throughout the year makes the account more susceptible to error.
   b. The cash account is more susceptible to fraud because cash is liquid and easily transferable.
   c. The electronic transfer of cash and the automated controls over cash are such that if errors are built into

computer programs, they will be repeated on a large volume of transactions.
   d. Cash can be easily manipulated.
   e. All of the above.

10-8 Which of the following questions would be relevant for an inherent risk analysis related to cash?
   a. Does the company have significant cash flow problems in meeting its current obligations on a timely basis?
   b. Are cash transactions properly authorized?
   c. Are bank reconciliations performed on a timely basis by personnel independent of processing?
   d. Does the internal audit department conduct timely reviews of the cash management and cash-handling process?
   e. All of the above.

LO 3

Identify and assess fraud risks of material misstatement in cash accounts.

Identifying Fraud Risks

In assessing fraud risk, auditors engage in brainstorming to consider incentives, opportunities to commit fraud, and rationalization relating to cash. Fraud risks relating to cash relate most primarily to misrepresentation and theft.

In terms of incentives, auditors might consider whether an individual with access to cash or its recording is experiencing financial or personal distress, whether the company might be close to violating its debt covenants, and whether the company has sufficient cash flow to support continuing operations.

In terms of opportunities to commit fraud relating to cash, the auditor might consider the following questions:

- Does the company conduct background checks and credit checks on employees with access to cash? Are these checks completed on a routine basis thereafter?
- Can employees easily convert the company's assets to their own use?
- Is cash physically available to employees?
- Is there insufficient segregation of duties related to cash?
- Are the company's records for cash inadequate?
- Is there lack of oversight and review of cash or cash-related transactions?
- Does the company have an anonymous way for employees to report on suspicions of fraud related to cash?
- Does the company have a policy of job or assignment rotation for employees with access to cash?

The following is a list of common schemes relating to cash:

- The employee purchases merchandise and records the sale at an unauthorized discounted amount.
- The employee steals cash and conceals it by recording a fictitious discount.
- The employee writes a check to a fictitious vendor and deposits the check into an account that he or she controls that has been set up in the name of the fictitious vendor.

Prompt for Critical Thinking #3   It's Your Turn!

Identify at least three rationalizations that individuals might employ to help them cope with the fact that they have committed fraud related to cash.

- _____

- _____

- _____

Focus on Fraud   Common Fraud Schemes Relating to Cash Receipts

This feature provides a list of common schemes involving cash receipts.

- The employee makes a sale but does not record it and steals the cash. This type of conduct is known as **skimming**.

- An employee receives a check and deposits it, but does not record the sale; then the employee writes a check out to himself and does not record the disbursement.

- The employee collects a customer payment, steals the cash, and writes off the accounts receivable as uncollectible.

- The employee steals a payment from Customer X. To cover the theft, the employee applies a payment from Customer Y to Customer X's account. Before Customer Y has time to notice that its account has not been appropriately credited, the employee applies a payment from Customer Z to Customer Y's account. This type of conduct is known as **lapping**, which we discussed in *Chapter 9*.

What Do You Think?   For Classroom Discussion

Consider the preceding list of common schemes relating to cash. How would a skeptical auditor answer the following questions?

- How would an employee go about purchasing merchandise and recording the sale at an unauthorized discounted amount?

- How would an employee record a fictitious discount to cover up their theft of cash?

- What actions would an employee have to take to write a check to a fictitious vendor and deposit the check into an account that he or she controls that has been set up in the name of the fictitious vendor?

10-9 Skimming occurs when an employee purchases merchandise and records the sale at an unauthorized discounted price.   (T/F)

10-10 In assessing fraud risk related to cash, auditors engage in brainstorming to consider incentives, opportunities to commit fraud, and rationalization about risks relating to cash.   (T/F)

10-11 Which of the following terms best defines the following scenario?

> The employee steals a payment from Customer X. To cover the theft, the employee applies a payment from Customer Y to Customer X's account. Before Customer Y has time to notice that its account has not been appropriately credited, the employee applies a payment from Customer Z to Customer Y's account.

   a. Skimming.
   b. Kiting.
   c. Collateralizing.
   d. Lapping.

10-12 Affirmative answers to which of the following questions would lead the auditor to assess fraud risk at a higher level for cash?

   a. Is an individual with access to cash or its recording experiencing financial or personal distress?
   b. Is an individual with access to cash or its recording being compensated at an amount that he or she might consider low?
   c. Is the company in potential violation of its debt covenants?
   d. Two of the above (a-c)
   e. All of the above (a-c).

LO 4

Identify and assess control risks of material misstatement in cash accounts.

Identifying Control Risks

Once the auditor has obtained an understanding of the inherent and fraud risks of material misstatement in cash accounts, the auditor needs to understand the controls that the client has designed and implemented to address those risks. Remember, the auditor is required to gain an understanding of internal controls for both integrated audits and financial statement only audits. The auditor typically obtains this understanding by a walkthrough of the process, inquiry, observation, and review of the client's documentation. The auditor considers both entity-wide controls and transaction controls at the account and assertion levels. This understanding provides the auditor with a basis for making an initial control risk assessment for each relevant account and assertion.

At the entity-wide level, the auditor considers the control environment, including such principles as commitment to financial accounting competencies and the independence of the board of directors. The auditor will also consider the remaining components of internal control that are typically entity-wide—risk assessment, information and communication, and monitoring controls. Although the auditor needs to understand all the components of internal control, the auditor typically finds it useful to focus on significant control activities related to cash accounts. As part of this understanding, the auditor focuses on the relevant assertions for each account and identifies the controls that relate to risks for these assertions. In an integrated audit or in a financial statement only audit where the auditor relies on controls, the auditor uses this understanding to identify important controls that need to be tested.

Exhibit 10.2 provides examples of questions used in assessing control risk in cash accounts.

Exhibit 10.2

Control Risk Questionnaire: Cash

1. Have cash management service arrangements been reviewed by management and the board of directors? Are the arrangements monitored on a current basis?

2. Do management and the board periodically review the cash management process? Does the cash management organization provide for effective segregation of duties, review, and supervision?

3. Are cash transactions, including electronic cash transfers, properly authorized? What authorization is required to make electronic cash transfers?

4. Are bank reconciliations performed on a timely basis by personnel independent of processing? Is follow-up action taken promptly on all reconciling items?

5. Does the internal audit department conduct timely reviews of the cash management and cash-handling process? If yes, review recent internal audit reports.

6. Does the company use a lockbox to collect cash receipts? What is the agreement with the financial institution? What are the company's controls associated with the lockbox agreement?

7. Who is authorized to make cash transfers, including EFTs, and what are the procedures by which that authorization is verified before the transfers take place? What procedures does management use to assure that the authorization process is monitored?

8. Are there any restrictions in getting access to cash? For example, does the company have cash in sweep accounts, or other accounts with financial institutions that may be in trouble, and that may restrict access to cash?

Typical Controls Over Cash

The following are common controls over cash:

- Segregation of duties
- Restrictive endorsements of customer checks
- Independent bank reconciliations by employees who do not handle cash
- Computerized control totals and edit checks
- Authorization of transactions
- Prenumbered documents and turnaround documents
- Periodic internal audits
- Competent and well-trained employees

Segregation of Duties

The general concept of segregation of duties does not change as processing systems become more automated and integrated. Automation can enhance control, yet there is still a risk of errors or fraud occurring on a larger scale. An assigned employee should be responsible for recording customer cash and check receipts, while other individuals should be responsible for the subsequent processing of these receipts. Postings to accounts receivable should be reconciled to the postings to cash and checks received. Segregation of duties is further enhanced if inquiries by customers concerning their account balances are referred to an independent group, such as a customer relations department, for investigation. Finally, the individuals who reconcile the bank accounts should not handle cash or record cash transactions.

Restrictive Endorsements

Customers should make their checks payable to the client and restrictively endorsed for deposit by the client when received. The restrictive endorsement helps prevent modifications and theft of customer payments.

It's Your Turn!   *Prompt for Critical Thinking #4*

The preceding list of common controls over cash seems exhaustive, i.e., it includes eight common controls. Think about your own work experiences, and identify two controls over cash that you have encountered. Explain those controls, how they worked at your employer's organization, and any deficiencies that you perceived about those controls.

Explain two controls that you have experienced:

- _____
- _____

Explain how those controls worked and their objectives:

- _____
- _____

Explain any deficiencies that you perceived about those controls:

- _____
- _____

Embezzlement at a Casket and Burial Product Company: A Case of Inadequate Segregation of Duties

Focus on Fraud

This feature provides a discussion of a fraud that made headlines in Pennsylvania with respect to a large-scale, long-lasting embezzlement by Cynthia Mills, who was a cashier and treasury specialist at Matthews International, a company that makes caskets and other burial products.

Mills embezzled $13 million over 16 years. She pleaded guilty in March 2017 and is expected to serve approximately seven years in federal prison; her husband was indicted on federal tax evasion charges related to his wife's embezzlement, and reports are that he cut a deal with prosecutors in exchange for providing them information about his wife's activities.

Similar to the case of Sue Sachdeva at Koss Corporation presented at the beginning of the chapter, Mills had a passion for purchasing luxury items such as fur coats, jewellery, and designer handbags. In addition, she and her husband enjoyed gambling, and purchasing expensive boats, cars, a rental property, and a vacation home.

How did she accomplish the embezzlement? For the first 14 years of the embezzlement, she converted checks that customers had written to the company into cash, falsifying bank statements to cover the thefts. In 2013, she changed the scheme by creating a fake company, Designs by Cindy. She initiated wire transfers from Matthews International, and continued to falsify the bank statements. Note that she was a relatively low-level employee, but as Kelly Paxton, a fraud investigator who runs the website "pinkcollarcrime.com," indicated this type of embezzlement is common for women in such roles, stating that "They're down in the weeds . . .

they know where the holes are" (Pittsburgh Post-Gazette July 22, 2017). **Pink collar crimes** are those that involve women who commit financial crimes. In this case, Mills was able to exploit the fact that she had the power to both execute and record transactions.

Given that Matthews International is a publicly traded company that has been in operation since 1850 (see http://matw.com/), one might think that its internal controls were good. In fact, in its 2016 audit report, Ernst & Young LLP issued an unqualified opinion on internal controls. The prior year, PricewaterhouseCoopers LLP issued an unqualified opinion on internal controls. Of note, on December 23, 2015, Matthews International management reported in an 8-K filing reporting that the audit committee dismissed PricewaterhouseCoopers and appointed Ernst & Young.

How could both PricewaterhouseCoopers and Ernst & Young issue unqualified opinions on the company's internal controls? Likely it was because the dollar value of the embezzlement was $13 million (an admittedly large amount), but in relation to the company's assets and sales, each less than one-tenth of one percent, the auditors likely deemed the internal control failures leading to the fraud as immaterial

For further details, see http://www.post-gazette.com/local/region/2017/07/23/cynthia-mills-matthews-international-pittsburgh-embezzlement-13-million/stories/201707230077 and https://www.sec.gov/Archives/edgar/data/63296/000006329615000109/form8kaccountant.htm

To complete an *Application Activity* relating to this fraud, see Problem 10-45.

Independent Bank Reconciliations

The client should perform two types of reconciliations related to cash:

1. *Reconciliation of items received with items recorded (control totals)*—Reconciliation is more effective when control procedures exist to establish the initial integrity of the population. In an electronic environment, the client may have a procedure by which the bank sends details of each remittance directly to the client for posting to cash and accounts receivable. These control totals should be reconciled daily with the amount shown as direct deposits by the bank.

2. *Periodic reconciliation of the bank accounts*—Independent reconciliation of the balance on the bank statement with the balance on the books should identify misstatements and unusual banking activity that may have occurred. From a financial reporting risk perspective, this is the single most important control over the existence of cash.

Computerized Control Totals and Edit Tests

Computerized controls should assure that all items are uniquely identified and that an adequate audit trail exists for transactions. Such controls include:

- *A unique identifier assigned to each item*—The unique identifier establishes the integrity of the total population and provides a basis for assuring that no items are added to or dropped from the population.
- *Control totals to assure the completeness of processing*—Control totals should be established and reconciled with the computer-generated totals. A control total would also be established to reconcile the debits to cash and the credits to accounts receivable.
- *Edit tests to identify unusual or incorrect items*—Standard edit tests such as reasonableness tests, field checks, self-checking digits on account numbers, and alphanumeric tests should be implemented as deemed practical for the particular application.

Authorization of Transactions

Individuals with proper authorization are able to electronically transfer very material sums of money each day. As a result, opportunities for abuse abound. The following authorization and authentication controls should be implemented:

- Authorization privileges should be assigned to individuals based on unique activities associated with the individual and position. Authorization should follow the principles of *need to know* and *right to know*. Authorizations should be reviewed periodically by senior management.
- Authentication procedures should assure that only authorized personnel execute transactions. The authentication process may be implemented through electronic verification by using elements such as passwords, physical characteristics, cards, encryption, or terminals that are hardwired to the computer. In a manual system, the authorization controls may involve limiting access to the area where checks are signed and to the prenumbered checks.
- Any changes to existing bank accounts or the opening of a new bank account must be authorized and reviewed by senior management.
- Monitoring should be established so that a detailed daily review of transactions occurs and is compared with cash budgets, authorization limits by individuals, and riskiness of transactions.

Prenumbered Documents and Turnaround Documents

Prenumbered documents are important in establishing the completeness of a population. The numbering may occur after the receipt where each payment is assigned a unique identifier when the payment is received by the company. Another option

Think about the above bulleted item regarding control authorization that reads "Any changes to existing bank accounts or the opening of a new bank account must be authorized and reviewed by senior management."

1. Why should senior management review these types of activities related to bank accounts?

2. What could go wrong if senior management did not review these activities?

3. Provide one example of a situation where things went terribly wrong because of a lack of this control.

is to use **turnaround documents** that customers return with their cash payment. A clerk can quickly review the turnaround document and compare the amount indicated paid with the actual cash remittance. The turnaround document contains other information useful for further processing, such as account number, invoice number, date billed, and date received (entered by clerk). Of course, turnaround documents are unnecessary in an electronic payment environment.

Periodic Internal Audits

Internal audit departments are effective deterrents when they periodically conduct detailed audits of cash controls and cash management. Internal auditors may also review the development of new systems to determine whether adequate controls have been built into the new systems.

Competent, Well-Trained Employees

To better ensure that cash is handled appropriately, the organization should have competent, well-trained employees. Such employees are in a better position to carry out their assigned responsibilities, including their control-related responsibilities.

Implications of Ineffective Controls

Controls related to the existence assertion should provide reasonable assurance that the cash balances included on the financial statements exist; that is, cash is not materially overstated.

Controls related to completeness provide reasonable assurance that all valid cash transactions (receipts and disbursements) are recorded; controls might

How can an organization's internal controls prevent the following common schemes relating to cash payments?

*   The employee purchases merchandise and records the sale at an unauthorized discounted amount.

*   The employee steals cash and conceals it by recording a fictitious discount.

*   The employee writes a check to a fictitious vendor and deposits the check into an account that he or she controls that has been set up in the name of the fictitious vendor.

Focus on Fraud: An International Perspective

The Parmalat Fraud and Its Many Victims: The Existence Assertion

This feature provides an example in which the company included a material amount of fictitious cash on its financial statements, thereby violating the existence assertion.

Parmalat is an international company based in Italy that produces milk, dairy, and fruit-based beverages. The financial fraud involving Parmalat evolved over a ten-year period and ultimately included the invention of over $11 billion in fictitious cash in offshore front companies to offset liabilities at the parent company. The fraud was led by Chairman Calisto Tanzi and his son, Stefano Tanzi, and was orchestrated by the company's CFO Fausto Tonna. In one of the telling moments of the unraveling of the fraud, representatives of a New York–based private equity firm raised questions about Parmalat's financial statements during meetings regarding a possible leveraged buyout of the company. During the meeting, the representative commented on liquidity problems at Parmalat, which contrasted with Parmalat's issued financial statements showing that the company had a large amount of cash. Stefano Tanzi admitted that the cash was not accounted for and that Parmalat actually had only about 500 million euros in cash.

Approximately 35,000 shareholders lost money due to the Parmalat fraud, and shareholders were not the only ones affected. Alessandro Bassi, a 32-year-old accountant who worked in the financial director's office at Parmalat, killed himself by jumping off a bridge near the company's Italian headquarters. Mr. Bassi worked for the company's CFO and had been questioned by a prosecutor in the case earlier on the day of his suicide. Ultimately, Mr. Tanzi admitted to moving over $630 million from the company to family-owned related entities. One of the most shocking features of the fraud was that it involved a large number of individuals acting collusively in various ways. In the end, 29 former Parmalat executives, along with bankers, auditors, and various financial institutions, were implicated in the fraud.

Focus on Fraud

Skimming and the Completeness Assertion

This feature provides an example of fraud involving theft of cash where the employee does not record a transaction, and then steals the cash.

In the restaurant and bar business, shrinkage due to thefts of inventory and thefts of cash are a significant source of losses. Industry estimates show that about 2% to 4% of sales are lost to such shrinkage at the overall restaurant level and that about 20% is lost to shrinkage in terms of liquor and draft beer. So, how do bartenders accomplish this type of fraud? Consider the elements of the fraud triangle:

- They are usually compensated with a low hourly wage and, therefore, depend upon cash tips as their primary source of income. This provides bartenders with an incentive to steal cash from their employer and a rationalization afterward.

- They operate in an environment where they are typically unsupervised and have weak or nonexistent physical controls. This provides an opportunity for theft.

To accomplish the theft of inventory, the bartender can simply give out free drinks. To accomplish the theft of cash, the bartender engages in skimming. Skimming is accomplished in the following manner:

- The customer orders a drink for $4 and gives the bartender $20 in cash.

- The bartender hits the No Sale button on the cash register to open the drawer. The bartender deposits the $20 and gives the customer the correct change of $16. The customer is satisfied. However, the bartender did not record the sale, thereby violating the completeness assertion. An important and necessary control implied in this part of the example is that the cash register should have controls to ensure that it opens only upon the recording of a sale.

- The cash register now has $4 in it that should not be there according to the accounting records. The bartender somehow has to get the $4 out of the register without detection.

- The next customer orders a drink for $7 and gives the bartender $20 in cash. This time, the bartender records the sale, thereby opening the register. The bartender deposits the $20 and gives the customer the correct change of $13, but the bartender also takes $4 out and puts it in his or her tip jar. Theft accomplished! And there is no record of it in the accounting records, making it very difficult to detect via the audit. An important and necessary control implied in this part of the example is that video camera surveillance of the cash register area, and the bar in general, should occur.

This example is a simplification. Usually, bartenders accomplishing fraud of this type keep track of the extra money in the cash register and do not remove it until it reaches a threshold, for example, $100. Therefore, surprise counts of cash registers are a method used to detect this type of behavior. If the surprise count reveals more cash than has been recorded, there is evidence consistent with fraud.

Sophisticated restaurant and bar owners have controls in place to prevent and detect such fraud. If they do not, they will likely be victims of a skimming fraud.

While this example is from the restaurant and bar business, it applies to any business where customers pay cash directly to an employee, thus providing an opportunity for skimming. When a transaction is not immediately recorded, the completeness assertion is violated.

include prenumbered cash receipts documents, as well as competent and well-trained employees. The main concern related to the completeness assertion for cash accounts is that an employee who should be recording a cash receipt simply does not record the transaction. If a cash receipt is not recorded, the financial statements do not reflect the fact that cash was received; therefore, a sale or decrease in accounts receivable may not be recorded.

Controls for Petty Cash

Companies should have policies and procedures related to petty cash funds. These controls could include limiting access to petty cash, requiring receipts for petty cash disbursements, reconciling the fund before replenishing it, and having internal audit conduct periodic surprise audits of petty cash funds.

Controls for Cash Management Techniques

Cash management techniques require controls specific to the risks associated with those techniques.

Electronic Funds Transfers

The client should have EFT agreements with suppliers, customers, and banks that have adequate controls built into the process. For example, the client should be notified of any receipts from customers or disbursements to suppliers. There should exist automated or manual reconciliation procedures between the client and the bank, and the client should maintain an audit trail to enable subsequent oversight regarding any assertions with respect to cash transactions, e.g., existence and completeness.

Cash Management Agreements with Financial Institutions

The client needs to take care regarding the amount of control given to the financial institution regarding the investment of cash. For example, if the client invests most of its cash in high-risk securities or nonliquid securities, the client should have a risk assessment process in place related to understanding the risks associated with the investments.

Documenting Controls

Auditors need to document their understanding of internal controls for both integrated audits and financial statement only audits. A questionnaire, such as the one shown in *Exhibit 10.3*, can guide auditors in documenting their understanding of internal controls. The questionnaire captures information about specific controls. A negative answer in the questionnaire represents a potential internal control deficiency. Given a negative answer, the auditor should consider the effect of the response on the initial assessment of control risk. Unless another control

Exhibit 10.3
Control Activities Questionnaire:
Cash Receipts (Partial Example)

	Yes	No	N/A

OBJECTIVE OF CONTROLS: Are all payments received deposited intact on a timely basis? Consider:

Procedures for Cash Remittances Received In-House

1. Key control activities

   a. A list of incoming receipts is prepared by the person who opens the remittances and who delivers the list to a person independent of the deposit function.

   b. A duplicate deposit slip is prepared by someone other than the person opening the mail.

   c. Deposits are made daily.

   d. An authorized person compares the deposit slip with the listing prepared in Step 1(a), noting agreement and completeness of deposit.

2. Documented evidence of performance

   a. The listing prepared in Step 1(a) is initialed by its preparer.

   b. The listing is attached to the deposit slip and is initialed by the person in Step 1(d).

   c. Bank accounts are independently reconciled.

Procedures for Cash Remittances Received Electronically by Bank on Behalf of Client

1. Key control activities

   a. An agreement exists between the bank and the company on cash-handling activities, including when the remittances are added to the client's account.

   b. Procedures and responsibilities exist for forwarding detailed remittance advices to client on a daily basis.

   c. An independent reconciliation of cash received is reported by bank, with remittance advices forwarded to company and posted to accounts receivable.

   d. Management monitors controls to follow up on discrepancies in accounts receivable postings reported by customers.

   e. Access to cash is limited through computerized access controls, including passwords and biometrics to those individuals with a need to know or to engage in transactions.

2. Documented evidence of performance

   a. Reports of daily reconciliations and follow-up are done by treasury personnel.

   b. Periodic reviews by internal audit or the treasury function are conducted.

   c. A periodic comparison is made by the treasury function to contrast cash budgets with projections.

(Continues)

(*Continued*)

	Yes	No	N/A

OBJECTIVE OF CONTROLS: Are payments received completely credited to the correct customer accounts? Consider:

Procedures to Ensure Integrity of Within-Organization Posting Process

1. Key control activities

    a. When the posting process is a function of a computerized application, assurance is gained by the following ways:

        (1) Prenumbered batch control tickets include control totals of number of remittances to be processed and total dollars to be applied.

        (2) Edit reports or online edit routines are used to identify invalid customer numbers, invoice numbers, and invoice amounts.

        (3) Online entry includes the input of a control total and/or **hash total** for each payment.

2. Documented evidence of performance

    a. Edit reports and/or processing transmittals exist, which are saved and signed by the person clearing the exceptions.

    b. The person performing the independent check initials the remittance, noting agreement of the posting operation.

    c. Online entry control totals and/or hash totals are noted on the face of the appropriate documents.

    d. Batch control tickets are agreed to the edit reports and initialed to indicate agreement.

Conclusion

Controls appear adequate to justify a preliminary control risk assessment as:

_____ Low control risk

_____ High control risk

Check Your Basic Knowledge

10-13 Controls for completeness of cash are important because they help to provide reasonable assurance that the cash exists. (T/F)

10-14 Because a primary concern is that cash will be stolen and thus understated, the auditor is <u>not</u> usually concerned about overstatements of cash. (T/F)

10-15 Skimming most likely results in a violation of which of the following management assertions?

    a. Existence

    b. Completeness

    c. Rights and obligations

    d. Valuation

    e. All of the above

10-16 Which of the following is <u>not</u> a type of common control over cash?

    a. Segregation of duties

    b. Restrictive endorsements of customer checks

    c. Bank reconciliations by employees who handle cash

    d. Prenumbered cash receipt documents and turn-around documents

    e. Two of the above (a-d)

compensates for this deficiency, the auditor will likely have a control risk assessment of high in this area. Usually, the questionnaire identifies the specific individual responsible for performing each procedure, which assists the auditor in evaluating the segregation of duties. As you review *Exhibit 10.3*, note the emphasis on management reports indicating a departure from a required procedure and the need for follow-up action.

LO 5

Describe how to use planning analytical procedures to identify possible material misstatements for cash accounts, disclosures, and assertions.

Performing Planning Analytical Procedures

Planning analytical procedures help auditors identify areas of potential material misstatements. The objective of planning analytical procedures is to identify accounts with heightened risk of misstatement during audit planning to provide a basis for designing and implementing responses to the assessed risks. Planning analytical procedures can be relatively imprecise.

Analytical procedures for cash balances are not very effective because of the absence of a stable relationship with past cash levels and the fact that cash is a managed account. However, auditors may use management's budgeted cash balance as an expectation, and can compare that expectation to the balance that the client has recorded at year-end. Trend analysis of account balances and ratios are planning analytical procedures that are routinely used on cash accounts. The auditor should consider the observed trends in relation to the auditor's expectations. *Exhibit 10.4* provides examples of trend analysis of accounts and ratios the auditor might consider for cash accounts.

Further, auditors should be aware of the importance of cash balances to debt covenants. For example, the auditor can read the debt covenants, determine the relevant thresholds for cash or other liquid assets contained in those covenants, and then track how close the company is to violating those covenants over time.

Exhibit 10.4

Using Trend Analysis of Account Balances and Ratios in Planning Analytical Procedures for Cash Accounts

- Compare monthly cash balances with past years and budgets

- Identify unexpected spikes or lows in cash during the year

- Compute trends in interest returns on investments

- Analyze cash balances, and changes therein, in relation to new or retiring debt obligations

- Compare cash ending account balances with those of preceding years, possibly on a month-by-month basis if there are anticipated collection patterns

- Compute typical short-term liquidity ratios, including the current ratio (current assets/current liabilities) and the quick ratio (cash + cash equivalents + net receivables/current liabilities)

- Compare cash flow to sales (operating cash flow/sales) and profitability (operating cash flow/net income)

The following are examples of reasonable expected relationships for cash accounts:

- No unusual large cash transactions
- Operating cash flow consistent with sales and net income
- Operating cash flow not significantly different from the prior year
- Investment income consistent with the level of and returns expected from the investments

If planning analytical procedures do not identify any unexpected relationships, the auditor would conclude that there is not a heightened risk of material misstatements in these accounts. If planning analytical procedures do identify unusual or unexpected relationships, the auditor would adjust the planned substantive audit procedures to address the potential material misstatements. The auditor should compare the unaudited financial statements with both past results and industry trends. The following relationships might suggest a heightened risk of fraud in cash:

- Consistent profits over several years, but cash inflows are declining
- Unexpected reductions in accounts receivable collections, or the timeliness of collections
- Unexpected declines in the petty cash account

Using Data Analytics to Detect Money Laundering

Why It Matters

This feature highlights the risks associated with financial institutions' obligations to detect money laundering and the related potential application of data analytics in the cash cycle.

As the sophistication and widespread use of data analytics increases, the potential for analytics to aid auditing effectiveness and efficiency is becoming more evident. As an interesting example, it is now possible to analyze a full population of cash transactions to ensure a financial institution's compliance with money laundering regulations. **Money laundering** involves creating the *appearance* that large amounts of cash that an organization obtains from criminal activity such as drug trafficking or terrorist activities originate from a legitimate, noncriminal business source. The first step in money laundering involves placement, introducing "dirty" money into a financial system in some way. The second step involves layering, which means concealing the source of the "dirty" money through a series of complex transactions. The final step includes integration, which refers to the act of obtaining the money through purportedly legitimate means.

Financial institutions are required by law to be watchful for money laundering. They must engage in activities that enable them to know their customer's identities through due diligence and transaction monitoring, and they must submit a Suspicious Activity Report (SAR) to the Financial Crimes Enforcement Network (FinCEN) within 60 days when they suspect an incident of

money laundering; SARs are mandated under the United States Bank Secrecy Act of 1970.

Currency transaction reporting is mandatory for all transactions above $10,000, so money launderers strategically report transactions just *under* $10,000, a tactic known as **smurfing**, or by dividing the amount into multiple transactions, a tactic known as **split payments**.

To avoid costly fines and comply with the requirements of the FinCEN, financial institutions must merge data from publicly available sanctions lists (that reveal specially designated nationals or politically exposed persons), client and legal entity data, financial transaction data, personal communications, and website and data application logs designed to understand the activity of customers on financial institution websites.

Companies are beginning to specialize in helping financial institutions merge these various data using data analytics software, seeking to capitalize on the demand for exposing money laundering schemes. One leader in this business space is Datameer, which purports to provide a "self-service platform…that… allows compliance or auditing analysts to perform the entire analytic process – from integration to visualization – thereby reducing analytic cycles from months to days. It does all this while providing the enterprise-level governance needed to maintain the security, privacy, and access control that banks require."

For further details, see https://www.datameer.com/wp -content/uploads/pdf/solution_brief/Anti-Money-Laundering.pdf

Check Your Basic Knowledge

10-17 Planning analytical procedures for cash balances are highly effective because of the generally stable relationship with past cash levels and the fact that cash is a managed account.   (T/F)

10-18 If the auditor observes that the company reports consistent profits over several years while cash inflows are decreasing, the auditor should likely assess a heightened risk of fraud in cash.   (T/F)

10-19 The first step in performing planning analytical procedures is to develop an expectation of the account balance. Which of the following does not typically represent a likely expected relationship for cash accounts?

    a. The company reports consistent profits over several years, but operating cash flows are declining.

    b. No unusual large cash or other liquid asset transactions are found.

    c. Operating cash flow is not significantly different from that of the prior year.

    d. Investment income is consistent with the level of and returns expected from the investments.

    e. All of the above represent likely expected relationships.

10-20 Which of the following is a common example of trend analysis of accounts and ratios that the auditor might consider for cash accounts?

    a. Compare monthly cash balances with past years and budgets.

    b. Identify unexpected spikes or lows in cash during the year.

    c. Compute trends in interest returns on investments.

    d. Two of the above (a-c).

    e. All of the above (a-c).

LO 6

Determine appropriate responses to identified risks of material misstatement for cash accounts, disclosures, and assertions.

Responding to Identified Risks of Material Misstatement

Once the auditor understands the risks of material misstatement, the auditor is in a position to determine the appropriate audit procedures to perform. Audit procedures should be proportional to the assessed risks, with areas of higher risk receiving more audit attention and effort. Responding to identified risks typically involves developing an audit approach that contains substantive procedures (e.g., tests of details and, when appropriate, substantive analytical procedures) and tests of controls, when applicable.

The sufficiency and appropriateness of selected procedures will vary to achieve the desired level of assurance for each relevant assertion. While audit firms may have a standardized audit program for cash accounts, the auditor should customize the audit program based on the assessment of risk of material misstatement.

Consider a client where the auditor has assessed the risk of material misstatement related to the existence and completeness of cash at high. This client has incentives to overstate cash in order to meet debt covenants. Further, the client has relatively weak controls to prevent theft of cash, with a few controls being somewhat effective. The auditor may develop an audit program that consists of first performing limited tests of operating effectiveness of controls, then performing limited substantive analytical procedures, and finally performing significant substantive tests of details. Because of the high risk, the auditor will want to obtain a great deal of evidence directly from tests of details.

In contrast, consider a client where the auditor has assessed the risk of material misstatement related to the existence and completeness of cash as low, and believes that the client has implemented effective controls in this area. Because substantive analytical procedures are relatively ineffective for cash accounts, the auditor will still perform only limited substantive analytical procedures. The auditor will likely perform tests of controls and then complete the substantive procedures by performing tests of details at a more limited level.

Panel A of *Exhibit 10.5* makes the point that because of differences in risk, the box of evidence to be filled for testing the existence and completeness of cash at the low-risk client is smaller than that at a high-risk client. Panel B of *Exhibit 10.5* illustrates the different levels of assurance that the auditor will obtain from tests of controls and substantive procedures for the two clients. Panel B makes the point that because of the higher risk associated with the existence and completeness of cash at Client B, the auditor will want to design the audit so that more of the assurance is coming from direct tests of account balances. Note that the relative percentages are judgmental in nature; the examples are simply intended to give you a sense of how an auditor might select an appropriate mix of procedures.

Exhibit 10.5

Panel A: Sufficiency of Evidence for Existence and Completeness of Cash

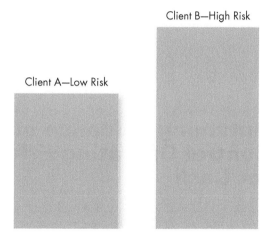

Panel B: Approaches to Obtaining Audit Evidence for Existence and Completeness of Cash

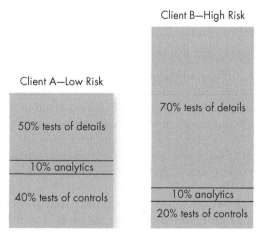

Check Your Basic Knowledge

10-21 The relative percentage of substantive analytics that an auditor will use as evidence in the audit of cash will be somewhat limited regardless of the riskiness of the client.   (T/F)

10-22 When auditing cash, the auditor will perform a relatively larger percentage of tests of details for a high-risk client compared to a low-risk client.   (T/F)

10-23 Which mix of evidence would be most appropriate for the following scenario?

This is a client where the auditor has assessed the risk of material misstatement related to the existence and completeness of cash at high. This client has incentives to overstate cash in order to meet debt covenants. Further, the client has relatively weak controls to prevent theft of cash.

  a. 100% tests of details.

  b. 70% tests of details, 10% analytics, 20% tests of controls.

  c. 50% tests of details, 10% analytics, 40% tests of controls.

  d. 20% tests of details, 40% analytics, 40% tests of controls.

10-24 Which mix of evidence would be most appropriate for the following scenario?

This is a client where the auditor has assessed the risk of material misstatement related to the existence and completeness of cash as low, and believes that the client has implemented effective controls in this area.

  a. 100% tests of details.

  b. 70% tests of details, 10% analytics, 20% tests of controls.

  c. 50% tests of details, 10% analytics, 40% tests of controls.

  d. 20% tests of details, 40% analytics, 40% tests of controls.

LO 7

Determine appropriate tests of controls and consider the results of tests of controls for cash accounts, disclosures, and assertions.

Obtaining Evidence about Internal Control Operating Effectiveness for Cash

For integrated audits, the auditor will test the operating effectiveness of important controls throughout the year, with a heightened focus on controls as of the client's year-end. If the auditor wants to rely on controls for the financial statement audit, the auditor will test the operating effectiveness of those controls throughout the year.

Selecting Controls to Test and Performing Tests of Controls

The auditor selects controls that are important to the auditor's conclusion about whether the organization's controls adequately address the assessed risk of material misstatement in the cash accounts. The auditor will select both entity-wide and transaction controls for testing. Typical tests of transaction controls include inquiry of personnel performing the control, observation of the control being performed, inspection of documentation confirming that the control has been performed, and reperformance of the control by the individual testing the control.

Exhibit 10.6 presents an overview of various controls that the client might use to mitigate risks in the cash cycle and how the auditor might test those controls.

Exhibit 10.6
Control Examples and Tests of Controls

Objective	Examples of Controls	How Control Would Be Tested	Implications if Control is Not Working
1. Cash accounts are accurate.	Client management reviews monthly bank reconciliations completed by employees.	Review evidence of management reviews and determine if evidence is persuasive that the reviews are effective (e.g., review the frequency of control; determine its effectiveness through reviews of reports; and evaluate descriptions of corrective actions taken).	There might be unusual cash transactions caused by fraud or errors. The auditor will prepare a year-end bank reconciliation using the client's cash records and a bank cutoff statement. Expand confirmations.
2. Cash receipts are appropriately recorded.	a. There is segregation of duties between those handling cash and those recording cash transactions. b. Remittance advices are prepared for cash receipts.	a. Perform a walkthrough of the processing of cash collections. Review documentation providing evidence of segregation of duties. b. Same as (a).	a. If there exists inadequate segregation of duties between cash received and cash deposited, employees can steal cash and covering it up with a lapping scheme. The auditor will expand confirmations with customers, select a sample of daily deposits and trace to accounts receivable credits for payments. b. Same as (a).
3. Limit access for individuals who can initiate electronic transfers of cash.	Appropriate procedures exist for authorizing passwords or other access codes related to initiating electronic transfers of cash.	Review procedures for passwords and access codes and obtain related documentation.	If there exists lack oversight in this regard, a fraudster could inappropriately access cash. The auditor will review a list of individuals who have access to initiating electronic transfers of cash. The auditor may elect to perform background checks on some of these individuals on a random basis, alerting all such individuals to this fact (as a deterrent).

Considering the Results of Tests of Controls

The auditor analyzes the results of the tests of controls to determine additional appropriate procedures. There are two potential outcomes:

1. If the auditor identifies control deficiencies, the auditor will assess those deficiencies to determine their severity. (Are they significant deficiencies or

Check Your Basic Knowledge

10-25 An example of a monitoring control in cash would include a review of cash budgets and a comparison of them with actual cash balances, with appropriate follow-up. (T/F)

10-26 Because of the level of inherent risk associated with cash accounts, auditors are required to test the controls over cash accounts. (T/F)

10-27 Refer to *Exhibit 10.6*. Which of the following represents a reasonable test of controls for cash receipts?

   a. Document internal controls over cash by completing the internal control questionnaire or by flowcharting the process.

   b. Segregation of duties between those handling cash and those recording cash transactions.

   c. Obtain a bank confirmation.

   d. Obtain a bank cutoff statement.

   e. All of the above.

10-28 Which of the following represents a control related to cash that an auditor might test?

   a. Reviews of reconciliations of reported cash receipts with remittances prepared by independent parties.

   b. Reviews of cash budgets and comparison of them with actual cash balances.

   c. Reviews of discrepancies in cash balances.

   d. Two of the above (a-c).

   e. All of the above (a-c).

material weaknesses?) The auditor would then modify the preliminary control risk assessment (possibly from low to high) and document the implications of the control deficiencies. The last column in *Exhibit 10.6* provides examples of implications of control deficiencies for substantive testing. The auditor will determine appropriate modifications to planned substantive audit procedures based on the types of misstatements that are most likely to occur because of the control deficiency.

2. If the auditor does not identify any control deficiencies, the auditor will likely determine that the preliminary assessment of control risk as low is still appropriate. The auditor then determines the extent that controls can provide evidence on the accuracy of account balances and determines planned substantive audit procedures. Substantive testing in this situation will be less than what is required in circumstances where the auditor identified internal control deficiencies. From the audit risk model, we know for companies with effective internal controls, the auditor will perform less substantive testing.

LO 8

Determine and apply sufficient appropriate substantive audit procedures for testing cash accounts, disclosures, and assertions.

Obtaining Substantive Evidence about Cash Accounts, Disclosures, and Assertions

In performing substantive procedures, the auditor wants reasonable assurance that the client's cash transactions are in accordance with generally accepted accounting principles (GAAP). Substantive procedures (substantive analytical procedures, tests of details, or possibly both) should be performed for all relevant assertions related to significant cash accounts, disclosures, and assertions. Even if the auditor has evidence indicating that controls are operating effectively, the auditor cannot rely solely on control testing to provide evidence on the reliability of these accounts and assertions.

Weaknesses in Substantive Procedures Related to Cash: Evidence from PCAOB Disciplinary Proceedings

Why It Matters

This feature provides evidence from PCAOB disciplinary proceedings against audit firms about the types of substantive audit procedures related to cash that auditors should perform, and illustrates examples where auditors did not perform such procedures.

In the first example, the auditor failed to sufficiently test whether cash existed, was owned by the client, and was properly valued; thereby the auditor failed to examine the existence, rights and obligations, and valuation assertions. The PCAOB enforcement action notes the materiality of the cash balances to the client:

> In its 2012 and 2013 financial statements, ColorStars reported cash and equivalents from its Taiwanese subsidiary of approximately $289,000 and $112,000, respectively. These asset balances represented 13% and 7% of the total assets for ColorStars at the end of each of the respective years. Respondents failed to perform sufficient appropriate procedures over cash and cash equivalents balances of the Taiwanese subsidiary.
>
> *For further details, see PCAOB Release No. 105-2016-018.*

The second example involves Jaspers + Hall PC (hereafter J + H) and its two audit partners. In one audit, they failed to perform sufficient procedures to verify the existence of approximately $155 million of cash, which represented 57% of the client's assets. J + H's workpapers included copies of the client's bank statements, accounting for approximately two-thirds of the reported cash, but when J + H received no reply to a confirmation request sent to the bank, the auditors failed to perform alternative procedures to verify that the client actually had the cash. They also failed to perform any procedures or obtain any audit evidence concerning the other one-third of the reported cash.

For further details, see PCAOB Release No. 105-2008-002.

The third example involves Armando C. Ibarra, P.C., and its two audit partners. In one of their audits, they failed to audit a client's cash balance of $687,971, which represented approximately 95% of total assets. Essentially, they failed to test the highly material cash balance.

For further details, see PCAOB Release No. 105-2006-001.

For Classroom Discussion

What Do You Think?

Consider the disciplinary proceedings we describe above related to the audits of ColorStars (PCAOB Release 105-2016-018).

The PCAOB's description of the audit failures reads as follows:

"Paragraph 14. In its 2012 and 2013 financial statements, ColorStars reported cash and equivalents from its Taiwanese subsidiary of approximately $289,000 and $112,000, respectively. These asset balances represented 13% and 7% of the total assets for ColorStars at the end of each of the respective years. Respondents failed to perform sufficient appropriate procedures over cash and cash equivalents balances of the Taiwanese subsidiary. Other than obtaining management representations, inspecting certain bank statements, recalculating cash and cash equivalent schedules and tracing the total cash balances from those schedules to the consolidated trial balance, Respondents failed to perform any other procedures related to cash and cash equivalents

during the 2012 and 2013 audits. As a result, Respondents failed to sufficiently test whether cash and cash equivalents existed, were owned by ColorStars, and were appropriately valued."

- Do you think that the cash balance was material for ColorStars? Explain your rationale.

- The Enforcement Release notes that the auditors *did* do some audit work. In other words, this was not a sham audit whereby the auditors completely failed their professional obligations. Rather, the auditors did not do *enough* work, and failed to be professionally skeptical with respect to the evidence that they collected. What other audit evidence do you think that the auditors should have collected and skeptically evaluated?

For further details, see https://pcaobus.org/Enforcement /Decisions/Documents/105-2016-018-Albanese.pdf

The auditor needs to consider the types of substantive procedures for cash accounts that should be performed and then make sure that the engagement team does perform these procedures. This is especially true when the cash balance represents a significant portion of the client's assets.

Cash Accounts: Performing Substantive Analytical Procedures

Substantive analytics for cash accounts are typically not very effective. Rather, the auditor tends to focus on substantive tests of details. The minimal substantive analytics that an auditor might perform include identifying significant differences between management's cash budget, which is prepared at the beginning of the year and the recorded year-end balance.

Cash Accounts: Performing Substantive Tests of Details

Exhibit 10.7 contains an example of various substantive tests of detail applicable to cash accounts, along with their relationship to relevant assertions.

Typical substantive tests of details for cash accounts include:

- Inspecting or reperforming bank reconciliations
- Obtaining bank confirmations
- Obtaining bank cutoff statements
- Preparing interbank transfer schedules

Exhibit 10.7

Management Assertions and Substantive Procedures for Cash Accounts

Assertion	Substantive Tests of Details
Existence/occurrence	1. Request bank confirmations to ensure that the reported cash balance actually exists.
	2. Inspect and re-perform the client's bank reconciliations to ensure that the year-end cash balance is correct.
	3. Use online resources to ensure that the bank reported by the client is a real bank, i.e., overstating cash by creating fictitious bank account statements.
Completeness	4. Obtain bank cutoff statements to ensure that the client has not mailed checks to vendors but neglected to record the cash disbursements in the current period (i.e., overstating cash and understated liabilities).
Rights	5. Examine bank statements and ensure that reported bank balances are actually owned by the client.
Valuation/allocation	6. Obtain bank cutoff statements to ensure that the client has not held open the cash receipts book to record the next period's sales collections as current-period revenue and cash received (i.e., overstating cash and revenue).
Presentation and disclosure	7. Determine that any restrictions to cash are appropriately disclosed in the notes to the financial statements.

U.S. Companies Continue to Use Paper Checks

Why It Matters

This features notes that auditors should expect their clients to continue using paper checks, even in an increasingly digital economy. In testing bank reconciliations, auditors should expect that their clients would use both electronic transfers and paper checks.

Why is this the case? Checks contain more information than electronic payments (because it is easy to attach invoices to paper checks), making it more convenient to match cash payments with cost of goods sold. Paying by check enables the payee more time to pay because of the time it takes to process paper checks,

thereby aiding liquidity. And there is simply momentum that is difficult to change in terms of willingness to switch from one payment medium to another. However, with advances in technology, this situation is likely to change sooner rather than later.

With the increase in electronic commerce, auditors might expect that their clients would have stopped using paper checks. Even in this world of online banking, 97 percent of the companies responding to a recent survey said they still cut paper checks to their business vendors and still receive paper checks from their business customers.

Inspecting or Reperforming Bank Reconciliations

The auditor's inspection or reperformance of a reconciliation of the client's bank accounts provides evidence as to the accuracy of the year-end cash balance. The process reconciles the balance per the bank statements with the balance that the client has recorded. Testing the bank reconciliation is effective in detecting misstatements, such as those that might be covered up by omitting or underfooting outstanding checks. The auditor will want to determine that all outstanding checks have been listed on the bank reconciliation. The auditor will obtain information on the last checks issued by the fiscal year-end, such as the last check number, and will then examine canceled checks returned with the bank statement to determine that the checks dated prior to year-end were included as outstanding checks on the reconciliation.

As part of testing the bank reconciliation, the auditor may want to obtain information on the client's last cash receipts. The auditor usually notes the last few receipts as a basis for determining the recording in the correct period. The auditor traces this information to the company's bank reconciliation and bank accounts to determine if items were recorded in the proper period. The auditor can also trace deposits in transit into the statement to determine if the client deposited in a timely fashion.

When testing the client's bank reconciliation, the auditor should independently verify all material items such as the balance per the bank statement, deposits in transit, outstanding checks, and other adjustments. The auditor should also foot all totals. *Exhibit 10.8* presents an example of a bank reconciliation performed by the auditor.

Obtaining Bank Confirmations

The auditor usually sends a standard **bank confirmation** to each bank with which the company has transacted business during the year. This procedure is most relevant to the existence assertion. The paper-based process auditors use to confirm the client's account balances with a bank is a manual process that can be inefficient and open to confirmation fraud.

Exhibit 10.8
Tests of Client's Bank Reconciliation

	Gordon's Bay Manufacturing December 2018 Bank Reconciliation Year Ended December 31, 2018	Prepared by _KMJ_ Reviewed by _____ Date _____

Balance per bank statement		$1,073,852.65*
Add: Deposits in transit:		
12/28 Deposit	$287,000,001†	
12/31 Deposit	300,000,001†	587,000.00 F
Less: Outstanding checks:		
2809	$ 435.56#	
3678	67,892.09#	
3679	75,000.00#	
3899	700.00**	
3901	12,500.00#	
3903	50,000.00#	(206,527.65) F
Adjusted balance		$1,454,325.00 F
Balance per books		**$1,481,350.00 TB**
Bank charges not recorded		(25.00)‡
NSF checks:		
Bailey's Main	$12,000.00§	
Silver Dollar's	15,000.00!	(27,000.00) F
Adjusted balance		$1,454,325.00 F

Note: Legend of Audit Work Performed:

*Confirmed per bank. See WP reference C-1.

†Traced to deposits shown on bank statement on 1 /3 and 1 /4 contained in bank cutoff statement. The 12/31 deposit was traced to bank transfer WP C-12 and was listed as an outstanding check on the subsidiary account.

‡Traced to bank cutoff statement. Charge was for service fees, which should have been recorded by the client. Amount is not material, and no adjustment is proposed.

§NSF check was returned with 12/31 bank statement. Examined support showing client redeposited the checks. Traced to deposit in cutoff bank statement and determined that it had not been returned in subsequent statement.

!Examined NSF check returned with 12/31 bank statement. Silver Dollar's is a retail company that has gone bankrupt. The likelihood of ultimate collection is low. Based on discussion with the client, the amount should be written off. See AJE 35.

#Outstanding checks were traced to checks returned on 1/20/19 bank cutoff statements. Checks were examined, and all were dated 12/31 or earlier and were canceled by the bank subsequent to 12/31.

**Check had not cleared as of 1/20/19. Examined supporting document for the check. All appeared proper, and no exceptions were noted.

TB Traced to general ledger.

F Footed, no exceptions noted.

Electronic Bank Confirmations through Confirmation.com

Why It Matters

This feature notes that auditors have the option of sending bank confirmations in electronic format through a third-party vendor.

Confirmation.com is a leading provider of all types of electronic confirmations, including bank confirmations. Over 11,000 accounting firms, 70,000 auditors, and thousands of responding organizations around the globe use Confirmation.com for their audit confirmation needs.

Electronic confirmations are as acceptable as audit evidence as paper-based confirmations. Electronic confirmations have reliability benefits because of the controls built into the software system, whereby management cannot intercept or alter the confirmation, as is potentially the case with paper-based confirmations. Auditors will typically experience quicker responses, improved response rates, and decreased errors when compared to paper confirmations.

When using an electronic confirmation process, the auditor needs to be sure that the:

- process is secure and properly controlled
- information obtained is a direct communication to the auditor in response to the auditor's request, and
- auditor obtains information from a third party (in the case of cash accounts, that party is the organization that has the client's bank accounts) who is the intended respondent

The process that Confirmation.com uses ensures that all parties are validated so requests are sent to the correct recipient. This control eliminates clients intercepting confirmations and modifying information and the technology ensures that auditors maintain control of the confirmation process.

The confirmation, whether paper or electronic, has two parts. The first part, shown in *Exhibit 10.9*, seeks information on the client's deposit balances, the existence of loans, due dates of the loans, interest rates, dates through which interest has been paid, and **collateral** for all loans outstanding with the bank at year-end.

The second part of the bank confirmation, shown in *Exhibit 10.10*, seeks information about any loan guarantees. If loans are outstanding, the auditor usually asks for copies of the loan agreements to identify restrictions on the ability of the organization to pay dividends or to determine whether the organization will have to maintain specific working capital or debt ratios. These requirements are generally referred to as *covenants*, a violation of which will make the loans immediately due and payable unless the financial institution temporarily waives the violation. If covenants are violated and the financial institution will not waive them, the auditor will have to consider whether the client will be able to continue to operate as a going concern and, if it is a long-term debt, reclassify it as a current liability. Additionally, the auditor typically inquiries about the existence of cash management or other programs that the client has with the financial institution.

Obtaining Cutoff Bank Statements

In many instances of fraud, management has either held open the cash receipts book to record the next period's sales collections as part of the current period or has mailed checks to vendors but did not record the cash disbursements until the subsequent period. Sometimes these problems occur because a company is in financial difficulty and needs an improved balance sheet to avoid violation of loan covenants. If the auditor assesses the risk of such misstatements to be high, the auditor will request a **cutoff bank statement** directly from the bank. This statement will list the activity for a period of seven to ten days after year-end. For example, if the client's year-end is December 31, the auditor may request a cutoff bank statement as of January 10.

The auditor should be alert for groups of checks that do not clear for an unusually long time after year-end. The delay in clearing the bank may indicate

Exhibit 10.9
Standard Bank Confirmation—Account Balances

Financial   [   ]
Institution's
Name and
Address   [   ]

CUSTOMER NAME

We have provided to our accountants the following information as of the close of business on —, 20—, regarding our deposit and loan balances. Please confirm the accuracy of the information, noting any exceptions to the information provided. If the balances have been left blank, please complete this form by furnishing the balance in the appropriate space below. Although we do not request nor expect you to conduct a comprehensive, detailed search of your records, if during the process of completing this confirmation additional information about other deposit and loan accounts we may have with you comes to your attention, please include such information below. Please use the enclosed envelope to return the form directly to our accountants.

1. At the close of business on the date listed above, our records indicated the following deposit balance(s):

ACCOUNT NAME	ACCOUNT NO.	INTEREST RATE	BALANCE*

2. We were directly liable to the financial institution for loans at the close of business on the date listed above as follows:

ACCOUNT NO./ DESCRIPTION	BALANCE**	DATE DUE	INTEREST RATE	DATE THROUGH WHICH INTEREST IS PAID	DESCRIPTION OF COLLATERAL

_____   _____
(Customer's Authorized Signature)   (Date)

The information presented above by the customer is in agreement with our records. Although we have not conducted a comprehensive, detailed search of our records, no other deposit or loan accounts have come to our attention except as noted below.

_____   _____
(Financial Institution Authorized Signature)   (Date)

_____
(Title)

EXCEPTIONS AND/OR COMMENTS

Please return this form directly to our accountants:

*Ordinarily, balances are intentionally left blank if they are not available at the time the form is prepared.

Approved 1 990 by American Bankers Association, American Institute of Certified Public Accountants, and Bank Administration Institute. Additional forms available from: AICPA—Order Department, P.O. Box 1003, NY, NY 10108-1003. D 451 5851

Exhibit 10.10

Standard Bank Confirmation—Loan Guarantees

(*Date*)

Financial Institution Official*

First United Bank

Any town, USA

Dear Financial Institution Official:

In connection with an audit of the financial statements of (name of customer) as of (balance-sheet date) and for the (period) then ended, we have advised our independent auditors of the information listed below, which we believe is a complete and accurate description of our contingent liabilities, including oral and written guarantees, with your financial institution. Although we do not request nor expect you to conduct a comprehensive, detailed search of your records, if during the process of completing this confirmation, additional information about other contingent liabilities, including oral and written guarantees, between (name of customer) and your financial institution comes to your attention, please include such information below.

Name of Maker	Date of Note	Due Date	Current Balance	Interest Rate	Date Through Which Interest is Paid	Description of Collateral	Description of Purpose of Note

Information related to oral and written guarantees is as follows:

_____

_____

_____

_____

Please confirm whether the information about contingent liabilities presented above is correct by signing below and returning this directly to our independent auditors (name and address of auditing firm).

Sincerely,

(*Name of Customer*)

_____

By: _____

(*Authorized Signature*)

Dear Auditing Firm:

The above information listing contingent liabilities, including oral and written guarantees, agrees with the records of this financial institution. ** Although we have not conducted a comprehensive, detailed search of our records, no information about other contingent liabilities, including oral and written guarantees, came to our attention. (Note exceptions below or in an attached letter.)

_____

_____

_____

_____

                                                          _____

                                                           (*Name of Financial Institution*)

                                                           _____

                                                     (*Officer and Title*)   (*Date*)

*This letter should be addressed to a financial institution official who is responsible for the financial institution's relationship with the client or is knowledgeable about the transactions or arrangements. Some financial institutions centralize this function by assigning responsibility for responding to confirmation requests to a separate function. Independent auditors should ascertain the appropriate recipient.

**If applicable, comments similar to the following may be added to the confirmation reply by the financial institution. This confirmation does not relate to arrangements, if any, with other branches or affiliates of this financial institution. Information should be sought separately from such branches or affiliates with which any such arrangements might exist.

the recording of checks, but not mailing them until after year-end. By considering the number of checks returned listed on the cutoff statement, the auditor may obtain evidence that the client is writing checks to pay current liabilities but is not mailing the checks until after year-end. A client may use this approach to improve its current ratio.

Preparing an Interbank Transfer Schedule

A company with many divisions frequently transfers cash from one division to another. The auditor should be alert to the fact that companies wanting to overstate cash may use a technique called **kiting** to record the same cash twice. Kiting is done by making transfers near year-end from one bank account to another bank account, recording the deposit in the second division's account, but not recording the disbursement on the first division's account until the next fiscal period. For example, a December 31 transfer would show the receipt on one account but not the disbursement on the other, resulting in the recording of the transferred amount twice. *Exhibit 10.11* shows the elements of a classic kiting scheme.

An effective and efficient way to test for the existence of kiting is to prepare an **interbank transfer schedule** like the one shown in *Exhibit 10.12*. The bank transfer schedule lists all transfers between the company's bank accounts for a short period before and after year-end. All transfers are accounted for to determine that they are recorded in the correct period and the client is not overstating the year-end cash account. Note the transfer of check number 8702, recorded as a deposit on December 30—an example of kiting. The check was recorded as a deposit in the Cleveland account on December 31 but was not recorded as a disbursement in the Rockford account until after year-end.

Performing Substantive Fraud-Related Procedures for Cash Accounts

Substantive procedures need to address specific fraud risk factors that are present. The auditor might use the following fraud-related audit procedures to respond to fraud risks:

- Confirm with financial institutions those individuals that are authorized to access cash accounts, along with those authorized to start a new account or eliminate an existing account
- Scrutinize checks that are payable to cash
- Scrutinize checks with unusual vendor names

Exhibit 10.11
Example of Kiting—All Within One Company

Division A	Division B
• Transfers $1,000,000 to Division B near the end of the year but records the transaction in the following year.	• Receives $1,000,000 before year-end and records the deposit in the current year.
• Transfer does not clear the bank in the current year.	• Deposit may or may not be deposited by year-end. If not, the deposit will be shown as a deposit in transit in the division's bank reconciliation.
• Transfer does not decrease the year-end cash balance because it has not been recorded in the current year.	• Transfer increases the year-end cash balance by the amount of the transfer. The net effect is to overstate cash on the consolidated financial statements by the amount of the transfer.

Note: Cash is recorded in both divisions at year-end, resulting in the double counting.

Exhibit 10.12
Bank Transfer Schedule

Gordon's Bay Manufacturing

Bank Transfer Schedule
Year Ended December 31, 2018

Transferred from Branch	Check Number	Amount	DATE DEPOSITED		DATE WITHDRAWN	
			Per Books	Per Bank	Per Branch Books	Per Bank
Cleveland	15910	$ 45,000	12/26[1]	12/27[2]	12/26[1]	12/30[2]
Cleveland	15980	100,000	12/28[1]	12/29[2]	12/27[1]	12/31[2]
Rockford	8702	87,000	12/30[1]	12/31[2]	1/2[3]	1/3[2]
Cleveland	16110	25,000	1/3[1]	1/4[2]	1/2[1]	1/5[2]
Rockford	8725	65,000	1/5[1]	1/7[1]	1/4[1]	1/8[2]

[1]Traced to cash receipts/disbursements records.
[2]Traced to bank statement.
[3]Withdrawal recorded in wrong period. See AJE C–11.

It's Your Turn!

Prompt for Critical Thinking #6

Identify at least three additional potential substantive procedures for cash accounts that might address the risk of fraud.

- _____
- _____
- _____

Documenting Substantive Procedures

The auditor documents a number of important items related to cash accounts. Documentation requirements for cash accounts might include:

- Copies of bank reconciliations inspected or reperformed
- Copies of bank confirmations
- Documentation of oral confirmations, if applicable
- Copies of bank cutoff statements
- Copies of bank transfer schedules
- Evidence of any restrictions on the use of cash balances or bank compensating balances

Check Your Basic Knowledge

10-29 Because cash balances are usually relatively low at year-end, auditing standards encourage auditors to send bank confirmations on a sample basis. (T/F)

10-30 A typical bank statement prepared at an interim agreed-upon date and sent directly to the auditor is a *bank transfer statement.* (T/F)

10-31 Which of the following statements regarding reperformance of bank reconciliations is <u>true</u>?

   a. The auditor's reperformance of a reconciliation of the client's bank accounts provides evidence as to the accuracy of the year-end cash balance.

   b. The process reconciles the balance per the bank statements with the balance per the books.

   c. Reperformance of the bank reconciliation is ineffective in detecting major errors, such as those that might be covered up by omitting or underfooting outstanding checks.

   d. Two of the above (a-c) are true.

   e. All of the above (a-c) are true.

10-32 A bank confirmation contains which of the following two parts?

   1. A part that seeks information on the client's deposit balances, the existence of loans, due dates of the loans, interest rates, dates through which interest has been paid, and collateral for loans outstanding.

   2. A part that contains a listing of the last checks issued near year-end.

   3. A part that seeks information about any loan guarantees.

   4. A part that lists all transfers between the company's bank accounts for a short period of time before and after year-end.

   a. 1 & 2.

   b. 1 & 3.

   c. 2 & 3.

   d. 2 & 4.

   e. 3 & 4.

LO 9

Identify types of marketable securities, articulate the risks and controls typically associated with these accounts, and outline an audit approach for testing these accounts.

Auditing Marketable Securities

Significant Accounts, Disclosures, and Relevant Assertions

A **marketable security** can be either an equity or debt security that is held as a temporary investment. Marketable securities also include short-term cash management securities, such as U.S. Treasury bills and certificates of deposit (CDs). In addition, marketable securities can include **commercial paper**, which include short-term unsecured promissory notes issued by companies at rates close to **prime lending rates** (i.e., the interest rate that commercial banks charge their most credit-worthy customers).

Two points about marketable securities directly affect the proper accounting for those securities. First, there is an obvious implication about whether the security is, indeed, marketable; that is, it is able to be purchased and/or sold in a functioning market. Second, securities may carry various levels of risk, including the risk that they may not be tradable at all if the market turns down. Ultimately, the auditor needs to understand the economic purpose of major marketable securities transactions in relation to the risk undertaken by management in making the investment.

The investments in securities are classified as:

1. Held-to-maturity securities
2. Trading securities
3. Available-for-sale securities

There are important financial reporting and audit implications for the classification chosen by the company. The held-to-maturity securities are valued at amortized cost, subject to an impairment test. Both the trading securities and the available-for-sale securities are carried at fair market value. Thus, the auditor has a major judgmental challenge in:

- Corroborating management's intent in classifying the assets, including gathering information about management's trades in the investments, the importance of market value to management compensation
- Determining fair market value

The market value of regularly-traded securities (e.g., stocks listed on the NYSE or NASDAQ) is easy to assess because trading data are regularly available. However, for more thinly traded securities, the market does not have many participants and a financial crisis can cause the market to dry up. In such cases, the financial institutions that hold many of the securities have been very reluctant to mark the values to fair market value.

The five management assertions relevant to marketable securities are:

1. *Existence/occurrence*—The marketable securities exist at the balance sheet date.
2. *Completeness*—The marketable securities balances include all securities transactions that have taken place during the period.
3. *Rights and obligations*—The company has title to marketable securities accounts as of the balance sheet date.
4. *Valuation or allocation*—The recorded balances reflect the true underlying economic value of those assets and are reported in accordance with the applicable reporting framework.
5. *Presentation and disclosure*—Marketable securities are properly classified on the balance sheet and disclosed in the notes to the financial statements.

The valuation assertion is usually the most relevant for auditing marketable securities because of the difficulties sometimes experienced when securities are thinly traded and management reluctance in writing down the value of securities.

Determining Whether a Decline in Security Value Is Other than Temporary

Why It Matters

This feature identifies a number of factors that an auditor considers in determining whether a decline in market value of a security is other than temporary. Fundamentally, these requirements are not much different from the understanding that an auditor must have to properly evaluate accounts such as the allowance for doubtful accounts, loan loss reserves, or the market value of distressed inventory.

Auditing standards describe factors that indicate an other-than-temporary impairment of a security's value has occurred. These factors include:

- The length of time and extent to which the market value has been less than cost
- The financial condition and near-term prospects of the issuer, including specific events that may affect the issuer's operations or future earnings, such as changes in technology or the discontinuance of a segment of the business
- The intent and ability of the holder to retain its investment in the issuer for a period sufficient to allow for any anticipated recovery in market value
- Whether a decline in fair value is attributable to adverse conditions specifically related to the security or specific conditions in an industry or geographic area
- The investee's credit rating and whether the security has been downgraded by a rating agency
- Whether dividends have been reduced or eliminated, or scheduled interest payments have not been made
- The cash position of the investee

An Overview of the Audit Opinion Formulation Process for Marketable Securities

In auditing marketable securities, the auditor will perform risk assessment procedures, tests of controls, and substantive procedures—Phases II, III, and IV of the audit opinion formulation process.

As part of performing risk assessment procedures, the auditor obtains information to assess the risk of material misstatement including information about inherent risks at the financial statement level (e.g., client's business and operational risks, financial reporting risks). At the account and assertion levels, fraud risks including feedback from the audit team's brainstorming sessions, strengths and weaknesses in internal control, and results from planning analytical procedures are assessed.

Once the risks of material misstatement have been identified, the auditor then determines how best to respond to them. For an integrated audit and for a financial statement audit where the auditor wants to rely on controls as part of the basis for the audit opinion, the auditor will perform tests of controls and consider the effect of those tests on the substantive evidence to obtain. In other audits, the auditor will rely only on substantive tests to obtain evidence about the accuracy of the financial statements.

Identifying Inherent, Fraud, and Control Risks Relevant to Marketable Securities

A company may invest in many types of marketable securities. Some are more marketable than others, and some carry promises of greater return (but at much greater risk) than others. Traditional marketable securities are straightforward and do not present much in the way of inherent risk. Traditional marketable securities are readily traded, and management usually intends to hold them for a short period. Because they are held for trading, or available for sale, they are valued at market value. In normal market situations, these short-term investments turn over and are not complex to audit. However, some risks of material misstatement relating to marketable securities still exist. Inherent and fraud risks related to marketable securities include:

- Risk of sudden market declines, which would adversely affect the valuation of securities
- Management manipulation of the classification of securities to achieve preferable valuation treatment, that is, market value versus amortized cost
- Management manipulation of the valuation of fair market value if the securities are thinly traded

Control risks related to marketable securities include:

- Risk of theft of securities if they are not physically controlled, or if authorization and monitoring over their purchase or sale is not effective
- Lack of policies over purchase or sale of securities
- Lack of monitoring of changes in securities balances
- Lack of policies over valuation or classification of securities
- Lack of segregation of duties between individuals responsible for making investment decisions and those responsible for the custody of securities
- Lack of involvement or oversight by internal audit in relation to securities

It's Your Turn!   *Prompt for Critical Thinking #7*

The Case of Genie Energy and Its Israeli Subsidiary Afek Oil and Gas

Investor Robert Murdoch owns a significant minority interest in Genie Energy's stock (hereafter, Genie). He explained the rationale for his investment as follows:

> "I believe Genie Energy's technologies and vast shale oil licenses have real potential to spur a global, geo-political paradigm shift by moving a major portion of new oil production to America, Israel, and other western-oriented democracies," said Murdoch, explaining his reasons for investing in the firm.

> "Covering and distributing news has been my life's work," responded Murdoch, whose holdings include Fox Entertainment, *The Wall Street Journal*, the *New York Post*, HarperCollins and significant other media assets on six continents.

> "If Genie's effort to develop shale oil is successful, as I believe it will be, then the news we'll report in the coming decades will reflect a more prosperous, more democratic, and more secure world."

Genie Energy is traded on the NYSE at around $7–$8 per share.

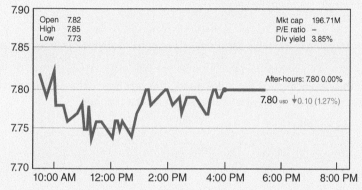

Genie Energy Ltd Class B
NYSE: GNE – 19 Jun., 5:24 pm GMT-4

Open	7.82		Mkt cap	196.71M
High	7.85		P/E ratio	–
Low	7.73		Div yield	3.85%

After-hours: 7.80 0.00%

7.80 uso ▼0.10 (1.27%)

To illustrate the volatile environment in which Genie operates, consider the following quote

(Source: *https://en.wikipedia.org/wiki/Genie_Energy*).

To illustrate the volatile environment in which Genie operates, consider the following facts about the geo-political environment in which Genie and Afek operate. Genie conducts oil exploration in the Golan Heights, the western two-thirds of which is controlled by Israel, and the eastern one-third of which is controlled by Syria. Syria is in the midst of a deadly civil war, with lawlessness and terror running rampant. Israel's border in the Golan Heights is therefore subject to extreme geo-political uncertainty. Some individuals, organizations, and governments in the international community reject Israeli claims to the Golan Heights, and view the region as sovereign Syrian territory.

Murdoch is of the opposite view, firmly in support of the State of Israeli.

In early 2013, the Israel government awarded Afek a 36-month petroleum exploration license applicable to a 150-squre-mile portion of the Golan Heights, in an area that the United Nations recognizes as Syrian territory. In 2015, Afek discovered a large reserve of oil and gas in this region, and has since drilled three exploratory wells to begin to exploit the discovery. Given the divisiveness of politics in the region, different parties with differing incentives and agendas are each laying claim to this vast supply of oil and gas commodities, and the political situation is unstable in the extreme.

Think about the political situation in Israel and the Middle East in general.

- What are some inherent risks in owning stock in Genie?
- What are some inherent risks in valuing an investment in marketable equity securities for companies that do business in highly unstable environments?

For further details, see https://www.fastcompany.com/1704559 /boogeymen-trifecta-murdoch-allies-oil-company -cheney and https://www.counterpunch.org/2015/03/27 /rupert-murdoch-and-the-israeli-genie/

Auditors can document risks relating to marketable securities by completing questionnaires. *Exhibit 10.13* provides an example of an inherent risk questionnaire and *Exhibit 10.14* provides an example of a control risk questionnaire.

Exhibit 10.13
Inherent Risk Analysis Questionnaire: Marketable Securities

1. Does the company regularly invest in marketable securities? How material are the balances in marketable securities accounts?

2. Has management changed the classification of securities during the year from either trading securities or available-for-sale securities to held-to-maturity securities? If yes, what is the reason for the change?

3. Is there a ready market for the securities?

Exhibit 10.14
Control Risk Analysis Questionnaire: Marketable Securities

1. Does the company have written policies and guidelines regarding investments in marketable securities? Are the policies approved by the board of directors? What process is used to authorize investments in marketable securities?

2. Does the company have a clear policy as to whether marketable securities are properly classified as trading securities, available-for-sale securities, or held-to-maturity securities? Is there evidence that the company follows the policy?

3. If management has changed the classification of securities during the year from either trading securities or available-for-sale securities to held-to-maturity securities, are the amounts significant? Were they reviewed by the audit committee? Do the audit committee and the board concur with the change?

4. If a liquid market does not exist for the marketable securities, how does management estimate the value of the securities that need to be marked to current market value?

5. Does the company provide for effective segregation of duties among individuals responsible for making investment decisions and those responsible for the custody of securities?

6. Does the internal audit department conduct regular audits of the controls over marketable securities? If yes, review recent reports.

This feature provides examples of common fraud schemes relating to investments.

- Securities are purchased, but those purchases are not authorized.
- Securities are purchased, but are not recorded as purchased. Or securities are recorded as purchased, but they are not actually purchased.

- Securities are sold, but are not recorded as sold. Or securities are recorded as sold, but they are not actually sold.
- Investment income (e.g., dividends or interest) is stolen.
- Investments are purposely valued inaccurately, that is, by making inaccurate fair value judgments.
- Investment classifications are purposely inaccurate.

Performing Planning Analytical Procedures for Marketable Securities

Planning analytical procedures help auditors identify areas of potential material misstatements. The objective of planning analytical procedures is to identify accounts with heightened risk of misstatement during audit planning to provide a basis for designing and implementing responses to the assessed risks. Planning analytical procedures can be relatively imprecise.

The following are examples of common planning analytical procedures that auditors may use for marketable securities accounts:

- Develop expectations about the level of amounts in ending balances of marketable securities accounts based on purchase or sales activity reported by management during the year
- Develop expectations about the relationship between the balances in marketable securities accounts, the rates anticipated to be earned on those accounts, and any changes therein, and associated interest and dividend revenues
- Review changes in the balances, risk composition, and classification types of marketable securities in relation to stated investment policies and plans

Responding to Identified Risks of Material Misstatement

Once the auditor understands the risks of material misstatement, the auditor is in a position to determine the appropriate audit procedures to perform. Audit procedures should be proportional to the assessed risks, with areas of higher risk receiving more evidence and/or more appropriate evidence. Responding to identified risks typically involves developing an audit approach that contains substantive procedures (e.g., tests of details and, when appropriate, substantive analytical procedures) and tests of controls, when applicable. The sufficiency and appropriateness of selected procedures will vary to achieve the desired level of assurance for each relevant assertion. While audit firms may have a standardized audit program for marketable securities, the auditor should customize the audit program based on the assessment of risk of material misstatement.

Obtaining Evidence about Internal Control Operating Effectiveness for Marketable Securities

The following are common tests of controls for marketable securities:

- Review policies for authorization to purchase, sell, and manage marketable securities
- Inquire of the board of directors about the board's oversight of the marketable securities process and examine related documentation
- Examine documentation of authorization for selected purchases and sales of marketable securities during the year
- Review the minutes of the board meetings for reference to investment policies and associated oversight
- Examine evidence of authorization controls for changes in classification of marketable securities
- Inquire of management about its process for establishing valuation of marketable securities and review related documentation
- Inquire of management about their process for reclassifications and review related documentation
- Examine documentation for selected marketable securities transactions to determine whether segregation of duties is maintained
- Review reports of internal audit in relation to their activities involving monitoring of marketable securities

Considering the Results of Tests of Controls

The auditor analyzes the results of the tests of controls to determine additional appropriate procedures. There are two potential outcomes:

1. If the auditor identifies control deficiencies, the auditor will assess those deficiencies to determine their severity. (Are they significant deficiencies or material weaknesses?) The auditor would then modify the preliminary control risk assessment (possibly from low to high) and document the implications of the control deficiencies. The auditor will determine appropriate modifications to planned substantive audit procedures based on the types of misstatements that are most likely to occur because of the control deficiency.
2. If the auditor does not identify any control deficiencies, the auditor will likely determine that the preliminary assessment of control risk as low is still appropriate. The auditor then determines the extent that controls can provide evidence on the accuracy of account balances and determines planned substantive audit procedures. Substantive testing in this situation will be less than what is required in circumstances where the auditor identified internal control deficiencies. From the audit risk model, we know for companies with effective internal controls, the auditor will perform less substantive testing.

Obtaining Substantive Evidence about Marketable Securities

The planning analytical procedures discussed previously as part of risk assessment procedures would also be appropriate as a substantive analytical procedure, if conducted using the appropriate level of precision.

However, it is likely that the auditor will focus more audit effort on substantive tests of details. *Exhibit 10.15* shows typical substantive tests of details applicable to marketable securities, along with their relationship to relevant assertions.

Exhibit 10.15
Assertions and Related Substantive Tests of Details:
Marketable Securities

Assertion	Substantive Tests of Details
Existence/occurrence	1. Request that the client prepare a schedule of all marketable securities held by the company at year-end. Verify the existence of securities by either (a) counting and examining selected securities or (b) confirming the existence with trustees holding them. Reconcile the amounts with the general ledger.
Completeness	2. Foot the schedule of marketable securities and examine the securities (Step 1). Examine selected transactions and brokers' advices near year-end to determine that the transactions are recorded in the correct period.
Rights	3. Examine selected documents to determine if there are any restrictions on the marketability of securities. Inquire of management as to existence of any restrictions.
Valuation/allocation	4. Determine current market value through reference to a financial reporting service or a similar electronic source.
	5. Recompute interest and determine that accrued interest is properly recorded at year-end.
	6. Determine that unrealized gains and losses are properly accounted for.
Presentation and disclosure	7. Determine management's intent to hold securities and review classification. Document that intention in a management representation letter.
	8. Determine whether the securities are properly classified and that any restrictions on their use are appropriately disclosed in the notes to the financial statements.

Exhibit 10.16 contains an example of an audit workpaper used to document the audit work related to testing marketable securities.

You should note the following about the audit workpaper in *Exhibit 10.16*:

1. The client prepares a schedule of all marketable securities it owns at year-end. The schedule includes the accrued interest and dividends associated with each security for the period of time held. The auditor is testing both the balance sheet and the related income accounts at the same time.
2. If the risk of material misstatement is low, the auditor will test only a small sample of the items. If risk is high, the auditor may verify all the material items on the worksheet.
3. The document shows three items related to the value of the security: cost, year-end market value, and carrying value for debt.
4. Disposals and resulting gains/losses are shown for all accounts during the year.
5. The auditor verifies the cost or sales price of the assets by examining broker's advices evidencing either the purchase or sale of the security. If control risk is low, the verification can be performed on a sample of the transactions.
6. The schedule is an abbreviated worksheet. For most audits, the auditor will have to determine whether securities are properly classified either as intent to hold to maturity or trading. That determination must be corroborated by, and consistent with, management's actions. The appropriate classification determines the accounting valuation.
7. For most investments, the auditor determines market value by referring to the year-end closing price in the *Wall Street Journal* or by collecting this data electronically on the audit firm's own database.
8. The auditor recomputes income on a selected basis for interest, dividends, and realized and unrealized gains and losses.

Exhibit 10.16
Gordon's Bay Manufacturing Summary of Marketable Securities Year Ended December 31, 2018

Gordon's Bay Manufacturing

Summary of Marketable Securities
Year Ended December 31, 2018

Prepared by __AMI__
Date __1/28/19__
Reviewed by _____
Date _____

Marketable Investments	Beginning Balance	PURCHASES Date	PURCHASES Amount	DISPOSALS Date	DISPOSALS Amount	Gain/Loss Disposal	Ending Balance	Market Value (12/31)	INCOME ACCOUNTS Interest	Dividends	Total
Gen. Motors 8% comm. paper	$45,000.00	10/31/16		4/30/16	$45,000.00*	$0.00	$0.00		$1,800.00R		$1,800.00
Ford Motor 8.25% comm. paper	100,000.00	12/1/17					100,000.00C	$100,000.00†	8,937.50R		8,937.50
1000 Sh Sears' common stk	22,367.00	10/31/17					22,367.00C	16,375.00†		$1,000.00R	1,000.00
1000 Sh AMOCO	8,375.00	12/31/14		7/13/16	62,375.00*	14,000.00R	0.00	0.00		1,000.00R	1,000.00
1000 Sh Consolidated paper	0.00	7/31/16	$41,250.00*				41,250.00C	44,500.00†		500.00‡	500.00
Bank America Zero Cpn Bond	1,378.00	6/30/17					1,378.00C	1,587.00†	209.00R		209.00
Totals	$217,120.00		$41,250.00		$107,375.00	$14,000.00	$164,995.00	$162,462.00	$10,946.50	$2,500.00	$13,446.50
	T/B		F		F	F	CF	F	F	F	F

Market value $162,462.00
Excess cost >
Mkt. Value $2,533.00§ F

*Correct, per examination of broker's invoice.
CSecurities held in broker's account, confirmed with broker.
RRecomputed, no exceptions.
†Per December 31 stock transaction listing in the Wall Street Journal.
‡Amount should be $1,000. Company failed to accrue dividend declared.
T/BPer December 31, 2017 trial balance and 12/31/17 working papers, schedule M-2.

FFooted.
CFCross-footed.
§Loss not recorded. Trace to AJE 31.
‖Traced to year-end trial balance.
#Interest and dividend payments verified through examination of Dividend and Interest Digest for year-end December 31, 2018.

Audit Procedures Used to Address Risk Related to Common Fraud Schemes for Investments

This feature provides examples of substantive procedures that auditors may perform as necessary given the assessed level of fraud risk.

- Employ a specialist to assist in fair value measurements
- Conduct background checks on and credit ratings of employees who have access to investment accounts, or the authorization to purchase or sell securities
- Require that the client produce original documentation of securities, not copies or faxes
- Trace dividend payments, interest payments, and sales of securities to cash deposits recorded on the bank statement
- Trace purchases of securities to cash disbursements on the bank statement
- Review any unusual journal entries in investment accounts

---

9. The auditor foots the schedule to determine the mechanical accuracy and the correct valuation of the account.
10. The audit tests address all of the audit assertions except presentation and disclosure. That assertion is verified directly with management and documented separately.
11. Document the conclusion regarding the fairness of presentation of the account balance as adjusted.

Documenting Substantive Procedures

The auditor will include the following types of documentation related to substantive procedures for marketable securities:

- Schedule of marketable securities as prepared by the client and as reviewed by the auditor, including purchases, sales, dates, market values, interest income, and gains or losses on sale
- Documentation of any confirmation of securities
- Documentation of marketable securities transactions that were scrutinized, for example, those exceeding a certain dollar value

---

10-33 The following is an inherent risk that is particularly applicable to owning stock in a company like Genie Energy: *Risk of sudden market declines, which would adversely affect the valuation of securities.* (T/F)

10-34 The following is a reasonable test of control over marketable securities: *Inquire of management about its process for establishing valuation of marketable securities and review related documentation.* (T/F)

10-35 Refer to *Exhibit 10.15*. Which of the following assertions is relevant to whether the marketable securities balances include all securities transactions that have taken place during the period?
  a. Existence/occurrence.
  b. Completeness.
  c. Rights and obligations.
  d. Valuation or allocation.
  e. All of the above.

10-36 Refer to *Exhibit 10.15*. Which of the following assertions is relevant to the audit procedure for marketable securities that requires the auditor to examine selected documents to identify any restrictions on the securities?
  a. Existence/occurrence.
  b. Completeness.
  c. Rights and obligations.
  d. Valuation or allocation.
  e. All of the above.

- Memo containing rationalization for judgments made about management's classification of securities
- Memo containing rationalization for judgments made about management's valuation of securities
- Reports of any outside valuation experts
- Documentation of calculation of any potential impairments

LO 10

Describe audit considerations for complex financial instruments.

Auditing Complex Financial Instruments

Overview of Complex Financial Instruments

Many clients have complex **financial instruments**. Financial professionals create such instruments to take advantage of short-term market anomalies, such as differences in interest rates between short- and long-term securities. They have developed others for the explicit purpose of removing liabilities from an organization's balance sheet. Given these complexities, specialized auditor expertise is required to skeptically evaluate the fair market values of these instruments.

Exhibit 10.17 contains selected examples of these instruments. As you review *Exhibit 10.17*, note the following:

- Some instruments do not provide recourse to other specific resources in the event of default but try to make the deal more attractive by providing other terms, such as higher interest rates, to entice users to invest in the securities. For example, most debt securities may be collateralized or provide preference in liquidation. However, many of these securities do not carry such privileges.
- Although many of the instruments are described as marketable securities, the market is often very thin. Therefore, market quotations may not be an accurate assessment of what the marketable value of the specific securities might be at the balance sheet date.
- Some of the instruments defer the payment of cash to the future, often in the hope that the instrument will be replaced by another one at that time and therefore will not constitute a significant cash-flow burden on the issuer.
- Some of the instruments have specific options, such as the put option that allows the investor to put (sell) the instrument back to the original issuer on the occurrence of a specific event. It would seem that the market value of such instruments would be near par, but remember that the instrument holder's ability to realize par value depends on the original issuer's ability to pay at the time of the triggering event.

Audit Considerations for Complex Financial Instruments

When there is a ready market for financial instruments, and risks can be calculated and controlled, the valuation and disclosure issues for financial instruments are straightforward. However, this is not necessarily the case for complex financial instruments. The auditor must understand the extent that risks affect the valuation of financial instruments, and the client needs to reflect those risks in the financial

Call Option

A call option is a financial contract between two parties, the buyer and the seller, in which the buyer has the right (but not the obligation) to buy an agreed quantity of a particular commodity or financial instrument (the underlying asset) from the seller of the option at a certain time (the expiration date) for a certain price (the strike price). The seller (or writer) is obligated to sell the commodity or financial instrument if the buyer exercises the option. The buyer pays a fee (a premium) for this right.

Put Option

A put option is a financial contract between two parties, the buyer and the seller, in which the buyer has the right (but not the obligation) to sell an agreed quantity of a particular commodity or financial instrument (the underlying instrument) to the seller of the option at a certain time for a certain price. The seller of the option is obligated to purchase the underlying asset at that strike price, if the buyer exercises the option.

Collateralized Debt Obligation

A collateralized debt obligation (CDO) is a financial instrument that is essentially a bet on whether an underlying obligation, most often underlying mortgages on homes, will fail or not fail. The holder can be on either side of the bet. Most financial institutions hold the underlying instrument and sell the bet that the instrument will fail.

Event-Risk Protected Debt

An event-risk debt covenant is associated with bonds and is intended to protect the bondholder in case of a credit downgrading of the bond, such as might happen in the case of a leveraged buyout (LBO). The covenants generally allow the investors to resell the debt to the original issuer at par if a stipulated event (such as a change in ownership) were to occur.

Hedges

- Hedges are an instrument that allows an organization to hedge against a change in some underlying economic event that may affect the organization. Three common hedges include the following: Foreign currency hedge—to protect against a change of the dollar in relation to some other currency

- Fuel hedge—to protect against future changes in fuel prices, for example, Southwest Airlines hedging against future changes in aviation fuel costs

- Commodity hedge—to protect against (or take advantage of) future changes in commodity prices

Floating Rate Note

A floating rate note is a debt instrument with a variable interest rate. Interest rate adjustments are made periodically, often every six months, and are tied to a money market index such as the Treasury bill rate or London InterBank Organizational Rate (LIBOR).

Junk Bond

Junk bonds are high-yielding bonds issued by a borrower with a lower- than-investment-grade credit rating. Many of these bonds were issued in connection with LBOs, while others were issued by companies without long records of sales and earnings.

Interest Rate Swaps

An interest rate swap is an instrument that allows an organization to hedge against future changes in interest rates by either swapping financial instruments, usually a fixed-term investment, for a variable-rate investment, or vice versa. Companies usually do not swap the actual instruments, but they make a notational swap with a financial institution that arranges an equal swap in the other direction.

Zero-Coupon Bond

With no periodic interest payments, these bonds are sold at a deep discount from face value. The holder of the bond receives gradual appreciation in the carrying value of the bond, which is redeemed at face value at maturity. The appreciation in value represents interest income.

Continues

Exhibit 10.17 *Continued*

Securities Sold with a Put Option

Marketable securities can be sold by an investor (not the original issuer) together with a put option that entitles the purchaser to sell the securities back to the investors who sold the securities at a fixed price in the future. These securities often carry low yields.

Collateralized Mortgage Obligation

A collateralized mortgage obligation (CMO) is a debt obligation issued as a special-purpose instrument that is collateralized by a pool of mortgages. The financial instrument is handled as a purchase of a group of mortgages using the proceeds of an offering of bonds collateralized by the mortgages. The financial instrument uses the underlying cash flows of the collateral to fund the debt service on the bonds. The bonds are priced based on their own maturity and rate of return rather than that of the underlying mortgages. CMOs have created secondary markets in the mortgage industry and have assisted the industry in attaining greater levels of liquidity. However, they are subject to the default risk of the underlying mortgages. For an amusing summary of the risks associated with Collateralized Mortgage Obligations, watch the move titled "The Big Short": https://en.wikipedia.org/wiki/The_Big_Short_(film)

Securitized Receivables

Securitized receivables have been converted into a form that can be sold to investors (similar in concept to CMOs). The issuer of the special financial instrument uses the cash flows of the receivables to fund debt service on the securities. In most cases, investors have no recourse to the sponsor or originator of the financial instrument if the underlying loans go into default.

statements. *Exhibit 10.18* includes a list of risks that are commonly associated with complex financial instruments securities.

In conjunction with understanding the risks associated with complex financial instruments, the auditor should understand the controls that a client has implemented to minimize these risks, which we highlight in *Exhibit 10.19*.

Exhibit 10.18
Risks Associated with Complex Financial Instruments

Auditors need to understand the following types of risks that are associated with complex financial instruments, which include the following:

- Management may have inappropriate objectives in entering into these transactions may relate to the potential for material misstatements.
- Management may not seek proper oversight in approving employing such instruments from those charged with governance.
- Complex financial instruments that do not involve an initial cash exchange are subject to heightened risk that they will not be identified for valuation at fair value.
- If management and/or those charged with governance lack experience with complex financial instruments, they may find it difficult to skeptically understand and challenge an outside party's valuation of a complex financial instruments.

Exhibit 10.19
Controlling Risks Associated with Complex Financial Instruments

Auditors should expect clients to have the following controls if the client uses financial instruments, particularly derivatives:

1. *Identify the risk management objectives*—Investments in financial instruments should follow a well-developed management strategy for controlling risks.
2. *Understand the product*—Analyzing the economic effect of a transaction on each party is crucial for gaining insight into potential risk. Transactions are becoming more complex, with a single instrument often divided into a dozen or more instruments with differing yields and maturities.
3. *Understand the accounting and tax ramifications*—The FASB has worked on a comprehensive document to clarify the accounting for financial instruments based on risks and obligations. Although the FASB cannot anticipate every kind of instrument that may evolve in the next decade, general concepts in the guide serve to lead the client and management to proper accounting. The potential for tax savings has motivated many of the instruments; therefore, potential tax law changes may affect the economics of the instruments.
4. *Develop corporate policies and procedures*—Companies should have explicit policies, preferably in writing, defining the objectives for entering into the new forms of financial transactions. Management should clearly define the nature, risk, and economics of each authorized instrument or type of transaction. The policies should also set limits for investments in specific types of instruments. The board of directors should approve the overall corporate policy.
5. *Monitor and evaluate results*—Procedures should be established to monitor the transaction (instrument) on a regular basis to determine whether the expected benefits fall within the assumed risk levels. If the risk was initially hedged or collateral was obtained, the value of the hedge or collateral should be remeasured. Procedures should be in place to react to risk that has grown greater than the entity wishes to bear.
6. *Understand the credit risk*—Investors should make sure that proper protection exists against default by counterparties. A mechanism is needed for continued monitoring of the counterparty's economic health. Formal credit-monitoring procedures—similar to credit policies for accounts receivable—need to be considered (even for counterparties with prominent names).
7. *Control collateral when risk is not acceptable*—Sometimes credit risk becomes higher than anticipated, but the investor allows the counterparty to keep the collateral. In such cases, investors should implement procedures to assure that they have possession of the collateral.

Check Your Basic Knowledge

10-37 When there is a ready market for financial instruments, the audit procedures related to valuation and disclosures are more straightforward than when the instrument is not readily marketable.   (T/F)

10-38 Auditor expertise is critically important in evaluating the validity of the valuation of complex financial instruments.   (T/F)

10-39 An audit client has invested heavily in new equity and debt securities. Which of the following would not constitute an appropriate role for the organization's board of directors or others charged with governance?

    a. Receive and review periodic reports by the internal audit function on compliance with the organization's investment policies and procedures.

    b. Approve all new investments prior to reviewing their risks.

    c. Review and approve written policies and guidelines for investments in marketable securities.

    d. Periodically review the risks inherent in the portfolio of marketable securities to determine whether the risk is within parameters deemed acceptable by the board.

10-40 Which of the following is a risk associated with complex financial instruments?

    a. Management's objective for entering into such transactions may relate to misstating the financial statements.

    b. Most of these financial instruments have a high volume of activity and relate to deep capital markets.

    c. Most management teams today have the necessary sophistication to invest in complex financial instruments with relatively little downside risk.

    d. All of the above are risks.

LO 11

Apply the frameworks for professional decision making and ethical decision making to issues involving the audit of cash accounts, disclosures, and assertions.

Applying Decision-Making Frameworks

The following *End of Chapter* materials provide you an opportunity to apply the frameworks for professional decision making and ethical decision making for decisions in this transaction cycle: *10-26, 10-34, 10-36,* and *10-37.*

Let's Review

- The significant accounts in the cash cycle include general checking accounts, cash management accounts, and petty cash. Disclosures for cash include ending balances on the face of the balance sheet, and descriptive statements from management in the footnotes. Because of the high level of inherent risk often associated with cash, the auditor primarily focuses on the existence/occurrence and completeness assertions. The auditor typically focuses on whether the cash does, in fact, exist, and whether the client has recorded all cash transactions. (LO 1)

- Inherent risks relating to cash include the fact that cash has a high volume of transactions, is liquid and easily transferable, is subject to large errors if automated systems around it fail, is subject to manipulation by management relating to debt covenants, and is always threatened by misrepresentation and outright theft. (LO 2)

- Fraud risks relating to cash relate primarily to misrepresentation and theft. (LO 3)

- Control risks relating to cash include potential failures in addressing inherent and fraud risk. Typical controls over cash include segregation of duties, restrictive endorsements, bank reconciliations, computerized control totals and edit tests, authorizations, prenumbered documents, period internal audits, and competent, well-trained employees. (LO 4)

- Planning analytical procedures for cash balances are not very effective because of the absence of a stable relationship with past cash levels and the fact that cash is a managed account. However, auditors may use management's budget as an expectation that can be compared to the balance that the client has recorded at year-end. Trend analysis of account balances and ratios are planning analytical procedures that are routinely used on cash accounts. The auditor should consider the observed trends in relation to the auditor's expectations. (LO 5)

- Because substantive analytical procedures are relatively ineffective for cash accounts, the auditor will still perform only limited substantive analytical procedures. The auditor will likely perform tests of controls and then complete the substantive procedures by performing tests of details at a more limited level. (LO 6)

- Appropriate tests of control over cash accounts include inquiring of management, reviewing the company risk analysis, documenting internal controls, reviewing monitoring controls, reviewing the frequency of use and effectiveness of monitoring activities, performing walkthroughs of cash collections processes, and testing specific controls over receipts and payments). (LO 7)

- Substantive audit procedures for testing cash accounts include: substantive analytics, inspecting or reperforming bank reconciliations, obtaining bank confirmations and bank cutoff statements, and preparing interbank transfer schedules. (LO 8).

- Marketable securities include temporary marketable equity and debt securities, Treasury bills, certificates of deposits, and commercial paper. Risks relating to marketable securities include sudden market declines and management manipulation of the classification of securities to achieve preferable valuation treatment, and risk of theft of securities. Controls to mitigate those risks include policies for authorization to purchase, sell, and manage marketable securities and board oversight of the marketable securities process. Auditors will examine documentation related to these policies and procedures, documentation of authorization for selected purchases and sales of marketable securities during the year, and documentation of the minutes of the board meetings for reference to investment policies and associated oversight. (LO 9)

- Complex financial instruments include financial instruments, usually including debt securities, but also equity or hedges, that represent financial agreements between a party (usually an issuer) and a counterparty (usually an investor) based on either underlying assets or agreements to incur financial obligations or make payments; instruments range in complexity from a simple bond to complicated agreements containing puts or options. Audit considerations relevant to such instruments include assessing risks, understanding the various financial instrument products, and evaluating the client's controls around these risks. (LO 10)

Significant Terms

Bank confirmation A standard confirmation sent to all banks with which the client had business during the year to obtain information about the year-end cash balance and additional information about loans outstanding.

Collateral An asset or a claim on an asset usually held by a borrower or an issuer of a debt instrument to serve as a guarantee for the value of a loan or security. If the borrower fails to pay interest or principal, the collateral is available to the lender as a basis to recover the principal amount of the loan or debt instrument.

Commercial paper Notes issued by major corporations, usually for short periods of time and at rates approximating prime lending rates, usually with high credit rating; their quality may change if the financial strength of the issuer declines.

Cutoff bank statement A bank statement for a period of time after year-end (usually seven to ten days); sent directly to the auditor, who uses it to verify reconciling items on the client's year-end bank reconciliation.

Escalation of commitment A phenomenon in which an individual (or group) continues on with their previous, inappropriate, course of action even when faced with increasingly negative risks and outcomes should their escalation become known or understood by others.

Fake cash problem This issue exists when a company creates fictitious additions to its cash account in order to validate fictitious additions to revenues; thereby violating the existence assertion for both revenue and cash accounts.

Financial instruments A broad class of instruments—usually debt securities, but also equity or hedges—that represents financial agreements between a party (usually an issuer) and a counterparty (usually an investor) based on either underlying assets or agreements to incur financial obligations or make payments; instruments range in complexity from a simple bond to complicated agreements containing puts or options.

Hash total A method by which organizations attempt to ensure accuracy when using processed data. A hash total includes a summation of numerous data fields from a file, including those not necessarily related to calculations (for example, an account number). Over the course of processing, the hash total is recalculated and any discrepancies with the original value signal an error to be investigated.

Interbank transfer schedule An audit document that lists all transfers between client bank accounts starting a short period before year-end and continuing for a short period after year-end; its purpose is to assure that cash in transit is not recorded twice.

Kiting A fraudulent cash scheme to overstate cash assets at year-end by showing the same cash in two different bank accounts using an interbank transfer.

Lapping This type of fraud occurs when an employee steals a payment from one customer, and covers it up by using payments from another customer to disguise the theft. For example, the employee steals a payment from Customer X. To cover the theft, the employee applies a payment from Customer Y to Customer X's account. Before Customer Y has time to notice that its account has not been appropriately credited, the employee applies a payment from Customer Z to Customer Y's account.

Lockbox A cash management arrangement with a bank whereby an organization's customers send payments directly to a post office box number accessible to the client's bank; the bank opens the cash remittances and directly deposits the money in the client's account.

Marketable security A security that is readily marketable and held by the company as an investment.

Money laundering This activity involves creating the *appearance* that large amounts of cash that an organization obtains from criminal activity such as drug trafficking or terrorist activities originate from a legitimate, non-criminal business source.

Pink collar crimes Financial crimes committed by women.

Prime lending rate The interest rate that commercial banks charge their most credit-worthy customers.

Skimming This type of fraud occurs when an employee makes a sale but does not record it, and steals the cash.

Smurfing A tactic by which money launderers strategically report transactions just under the $10,000 mandatory reporting requirement to financial institutions.

Split payments A tactic by which money launderers strategically divide payments into multiple small transactions to avoid detection by financial institutions

Turnaround document A document sent to the customer to be returned with the customer's remittance; may be machine-readable and may contain information to improve the efficiency of receipt processing.

Prompts for Critical Thinking

Prompt #1

1. Short selling is essentially betting that an investment will decline in value. As an example, imagine that you took the advice of Muddy Waters and shorted 1,000 shares of stock of Huishan at $4 per share. You are betting that the price of the stock will fall in the future. After time (and if you are lucky/smart), the share price falls to $1 per share. Your profit (before considering brokerage fees) is calculated as follows:

   ($4 − $1) × 1,000 = $3,000.

   To learn more about short selling, visit the following website: *http://www.investopedia.com/university/shortselling/shortselling1 .asp#ixzz4kPPAe4pI*

2. Short selling is an important component of investment markets because it allows an investor to "bet against" a company when said investor believes that the financial position of the company, as asserted by management, is false; short-selling helps markets achieve efficiency and effectiveness in terms of the allocation of capital.

3. Likely, investors did not believe the assertions of Muddy Waters. Investment media reports reveal that investors believed very strongly in the quality of financial reporting and profitability by Huishan. Clearly, that belief was inaccurate. Further, investors know that it is in Muddy Waters' financial interest to have the stock price go down, so investors are skeptical of short sellers' motives.

4. There is no telling exactly what will happen, so enjoy your research and learning experience.

Prompt #2

1. The debt-to-equity ratio implies that the company was becoming dangerously over-leveraged, thereby threatening its ability to pay its liabilities.

2. Students will vary in their sympathy for investors and their extent of willingness to believe that they should be compensated.

Prompt #3

- I'm being paid too low of an amount. I deserve more!
- Top management is setting a poor tone by taking cash without recording those transactions, so why can't I?
- Top management engages in ostentatious with displays of wealth (thereby inciting jealousy in its employees); what about me?
- Top management has ignored past instances of misappropriations of cash; maybe I can get away with it too.

Prompt #4

Answers to this prompt will differ by student. An example answer appears below.

Explain two controls that you have experienced:

- Restrictive endorsements
- Pre-numbered documents

Explain how those controls worked and their objective:

- At a grocery store where I worked, the cash register automatically endorsed customers' checks when I recorded the sale. This prevented anyone from endorsing the check to themselves.
- At a restaurant where I worked, the waitstaff use paper tickets to record customer orders. The cook staff uses the paper tickets to determine what to prepare. The waitstaff use the paper tickets to give the bill to each customer. The tickets are pre-numbered and are not returned to the customer (they hand them in at the register). The control that happens at the end of the day is to ensure that the total fees charged to customers have been completely recorded and that they add up to the number that sums the day's receipts.

Explain any deficiencies that you perceived about those controls:

- I never encountered any deficiencies in this particular control because it was part of the overall cash recording process, which was handled electronically.
- One problem that we encountered is that sometimes customers forget to pay their bill, or walk out intentionally not paying their bill. So, sometimes a customer comes in the next day and then we can figure out which bill was not paid. Otherwise, we assume that we have been ripped off on that transaction.

Prompt #5

1. If these reviews do not take place, individual employees might set up a bank account and funnel money into that account without the organization realizing what has happened.
2. What can happen is that a fraudster sets up a bank account that sounds like it is legitimately for the entity or for an entity that has a name very similar to an existing vendor, when in fact it is the fraudster's own bank account that the organization doesn't know about. The fraudster might be a purchasing agent, writing checks supposedly to a vendor, who is actually the fraudster him or herself. Senior management needs to make sure that checks are being cut only to valid, registered suppliers.
3. Provide one example of a situation from practice where things went terribly wrong because of a lack of this control. A good example is one that we introduced to you in *Chapter 7*: Rita Crundwell and the City of Dixon, IL. In that case, **the fraud began late in 1990, when Crundwell opened a bank account in the joint name of the city of Dixon and an acronym, RSCDA. The account holder was listed as "RSCDA, c/o Rita Crundwell."** RSCDA was purportedly the city's capital development fund. Crundwell transferred funds from Dixon's money market account to the RSCDA fund, as well as to various other city-held bank accounts. Crundwell then wrote checks from the RSCDA account to pay for her personal expenses, including expenses relating to her horse business. To conceal the fraud, Crundwell created fictitious invoices from the state of Illinois, made to look as though the funds she was fraudulently depositing into the RSCDA account were being used for a legitimate city purpose.

Prompt #6

- Scrutinize checks made out to employees outside of the normal payroll processing system
- Compare the timing of deposits into bank accounts with the timing of cash receipts, noting any unusual time lags
- Compare time lags between the date a check was issued for payment and the date that it clears the bank, noting any unusual time lags
- Investigate voided checks and analyze voided transactions

Prompt #7

Potential risks include:

- Oil production assets might be subject to terrorism and destruction
- The ability to execute contractual obligations may be impeded by political unrest
- It may be difficult to collect cash based upon oil production
- Genie Energy's employees may be subject to physical harm
- What are some inherent risks in valuing an investment in marketable equity securities for companies that do business in highly unstable environments?

Read Genie Energy's own discussion of Risk Factors relating to its business model at:

https://www.sec.gov/Archives/edgar/data/1528356/000121390017002459 /f10k2016_genieenergy.htm

Some of the most impactful risks include:

- Unfair business practices may adversely affect the company
- Regulatory conditions can affect the amount of taxes and fees the company is required to pay, resulting in pricing disadvantages

Further examples are as follows from Genie's FYE 2016 10K:

Risks Related to Genie Oil and Gas

We have no current production of oil and gas and we may never have any. We do not have any current production of oil and gas. We cannot assure you that we will produce or market oil or gas at all or in commercially profitable quantities. Our ability to produce and market oil and gas may depend upon our ability to develop and operate our planned projects and facilities, which may be affected by events or conditions that impact the advancement, operation, cost or results of such projects or facilities, including:

- Energy commodity prices relative to production costs;
- The occurence of unforeseen technical difficulties;
- The outcome of negotiations with potential partners, governmental agencies, regulatory bodies, suppliers, customers or others;
- Changes to existing legislation or regulation governing our current or planned operations;
- Our ability to obtain all the necessary permits to operate our facilities;
- Changes in operating conditions and costs, including costs of third-party equipment or services such as drilling and processing and access to power sources; and
- Security concerns or acts of terrorism that threaten or disrupt the safe operation of our facilities.

Operating hazards and uninsured risks will respect to the oil and gas operations may have material adverse effects on our operations.

Review Questions and Short Cases

INTERNATIONAL

FRAUD

10-1 **LO 1** Describe the following types of cash accounts: (a) general checking accounts, (b) cash management accounts, and (c) petty cash accounts.

10-2 **LO 1** Explain the two ways China Huishan Dairy Holdings Co. Ltd. management violated the existence assertion.

10-3 **LO 1** Match the following assertions with their associated description: (a) existence/occurrence, (b) completeness, (c) rights and obligations, (d) valuation or allocation, (e) presentation and disclosure.

1. Cash accounts are properly classified on the balance sheet and disclosed in the notes to the financial statements.
2. Cash balances exist at the balance sheet date.
3. The recorded balances reflect the true underlying economic value of those assets.
4. The company has title to the cash accounts as of the balance sheet date.
5. Cash balances include all cash transactions that have taken place during the period.

10-4 **LO 2** Refer to the *Why It Matters* feature at the beginning of the chapter.

a. Why does cash have a high risk of material misstatement, and why was the petty cash account at Koss Corporation inherently risky?
b. What three things surprised you most about the Peregrine Financial Group embezzlement by Russell Wasendorf Sr.?

10-5 **LO 2** Evaluate the following statement made by a third-year auditor: "In comparison with other accounts, such as accounts receivable or property, plant, and equipment, it is my assessment that cash contains less inherent risk. There are no significant valuation problems with cash." Do you agree or disagree with the auditor's assessment of inherent risk? Explain.

10-6 **LO 2, 4** The following are items relating to inherent risk (Category A) or control risk (Category B) in the cash cycle. Categorize each item as relating to A or B.

1. Does the company have significant cash flow problems in meeting its current obligations on a timely basis?
2. Are there any restrictions in getting access to cash? For example, does the company have cash in sweep accounts, or other accounts with financial institutions that may be in trouble, and that may restrict access to cash?
3. Does the internal audit department conduct timely reviews of the cash management and cash handling process? If yes, review recent internal audit reports.
4. Does the company use cash budgeting techniques? How effective are the company's cash management budgeting techniques?
5. Are bank reconciliations performed on a timely basis by personnel independent of processing? Is follow-up action taken promptly on all reconciling items?
6. Does the company use the cash management services offered by its banker? What is the nature of these arrangements?
7. Has the company made significant changes in its cash processing during the past year? Have any major changes taken place in the

company's computerized cash management applications during the year?

8. Have cash management service arrangements been reviewed by management and the board of directors? Are the arrangements monitored on a current basis?

9. Does the company have loan or bond covenants that influence the use of cash or the maintenance of working-capital ratios?

10. Are cash transactions, including electronic cash transfers, properly authorized? What authorization is required to make electronic cash transfers?

11. Does the company use a lockbox to collect cash receipts? What is the agreement with the financial institution? What are the company's controls associated with the lockbox agreement?

12. Is there any reason to suspect that management may desire to misstate the cash balance?

13. Do management and the board periodically review the cash management process? Does the cash management organization provide for effective segregation of duties, review, and supervision?

14. Who is authorized to make cash transfers, including EFTs, and what are the procedures by which that authorization is verified before the transfers take place? What procedures does management use to assure that the authorization process is monitored?

FRAUD   **10-7** **LO 3** Refer to the *Focus on Fraud* feature "Common Fraud Schemes Relating to Cash" and describe three schemes. Prepare a brief summary of a fraud scheme that you have learned about in your local community.

FRAUD   **10-8** **LO 3** Describe: (a) lapping and (b) skimming.

FRAUD   **10-9** **LO 4** Fraud related to cash often happens in nonprofit organizations because they tend to lack segregation of duties. Explain how an individual could steal cash from a nonprofit if the individual has responsibility for collecting cash, depositing cash, and recording journal entries.

10-10 **LO 4** List three common controls for petty cash.

10-11 **LO 4** Refer to *Exhibit 10.3*. Match each of the following objectives to the relevant control activities.

Objectives That Cash Receipts Controls Are Trying to Achieve

a. Payments received are deposited intact on a timely basis.
b. Payments received are completely credited to the correct customer accounts.

Control Activities

1. A list of incoming receipts is prepared by the person who opens the remittances and who delivers the list to a person independent of the deposit function.
2. Online entry that includes the input of a control total and/or hash total is used for each payment.
3. A duplicate deposit slip is prepared by someone other than the person opening the mail.
4. Deposits are made daily.
5. Prenumbered batch control tickets include control totals of the number of remittances to be processed and total dollars to be applied.

6. An agreement exists between the bank and the company on cash-handling activities, including when the remittances are added to the company's account.
7. Management monitors controls to follow up on discrepancies in accounts receivable postings.

INTERNATIONAL   **10-12** `LO 4, 7, 8` This problem is designed to get you to think about controls that would be effective in a real-world setting. The Canada Border Services Agency (CBSA) receives cash payments for services, fees, and taxes (e.g., customs duties, excise taxes, taxes on goods and services) at various ports of entry around Canada. Cash includes payments made in liquid cash, by debit or credit cards, and by checks.

   a. What types of controls should the CBSA have over its cash receipts?
   b. Given the controls that you identified in part (a), what types of tests of controls or substantive audit procedures should an auditor perform?

FRAUD   **10-13** `LO 5` Categorize each of the following trends or relationships as suggesting either: (a) a normal trend or relationship, or (b) a trend or relationship suggesting a heightened risk of material misstatement, from error or fraud:

1. The company reports consistent profits over several years, but cash flows are declining.
2. Operating cash flow is consistent with sales and net income.
3. The timeliness of accounts receivable collections declines, but credit policies are unchanged.
4. Operating cash flow is not significantly different from that of the prior year, and operations have been consistent across the two years.
5. Investment income is consistent with the level of and returns expected from investments.
6. There are unexpected declines in the petty cash account.

10-14 `LO 7` Refer to *Exhibit 10.6*. Describe one control objective, one associated example of that control, how the auditor would test the control, and the implications if that control is not working.

PROFESSIONAL SKEPTICISM   **10-15** `LO 8` Independent periodic reconciliations of cash accounts represent an important control activity.

   a. What is the impact on the audit if the client does not perform independent periodic reconciliations of its cash accounts?
   b. What substantive audit procedures would the auditor perform because of the lack of the client's independent reconciliations?
   c. How would the fact that the client does not perform this important control affect the auditor's professional skepticism?

10-16 `LO 8` Explain the purpose of the following audit procedures:

   a. Sending a bank confirmation to all the banks with which the company does business.
   b. Obtaining a bank cutoff statement.
   c. Preparing an interbank transfer statement.

FRAUD   **10-17** `LO 8` In auditing cash, auditors may need to be alert for kiting.

   a. Define and illustrate *kiting*.
   b. What controls should the client institute to prevent it?
   c. What audit procedures should the auditor use to detect kiting?

FRAUD

10-18 **LO 8** The following information is from the bank transfer schedule prepared during the audit of Fox Co.'s financial statements for the year ended December 31, 2018. Assume all checks were dated and issued on December 30, 2018.

	Bank Accounts		Disbursement Date		Receipt Date	
Check No.	From	To	Per Books	Per Bank	Per Books	Per Bank
101	National	Federal	Dec. 30	Jan. 4	Dec. 30	Jan. 3
202	County	State	Jan. 3	Jan. 2	Dec. 30	Dec. 31
303	Federal	State	Dec. 31	Jan. 3	Jan. 2	Jan. 2
404	State	County	Jan. 2	Jan. 2	Jan. 2	Dec. 31

a. Which of the checks might indicate kiting?
b. Which of the checks illustrates deposits/transfers in transit on December 31, 2018?

FRAUD

10-19 **LO 8** The following items were discovered during the audit of a cash account. For each item identified, indicate the substantive audit procedure that most likely would have led to the discovery of the misstatement.

1. The company had overstated cash by transferring funds at year-end to another account but failed to record the withdrawal until after year-end.
2. On occasion, customers with smaller balances send in checks without specific identification of the customer except the name printed on the check. The client has an automated cash receipts process, but the employee opening the envelopes pocketed the cash and destroyed other supporting documentation.
3. Same as finding (2), but the employee prepared a turnaround document that showed either an additional discount for the customer or a credit to the customer's account.
4. The controller was temporarily taking cash for personal purposes but intended to repay the company (although the repayment never occurred). The cover-up was executed by understating outstanding checks in the monthly bank reconciliation.
5. The company had temporary investments in six-month CDs at the bank. The CDs were supposed to yield an annual interest rate of 12% but apparently are yielding only 6%.
6. Cash remittances are not deposited in a timely fashion and are sometimes lost.
7. Substantial bank service charges have not been recorded by the client prior to year-end.
8. A loan has been negotiated with the bank to provide funds for a subsidiary company. The loan was negotiated by the controller of the division, who apparently was not authorized to negotiate the loan.
9. A check written to a vendor had been recorded twice in the cash disbursements journal to cover a cash shortage.

FRAUD

10-20 **LO 8** Pembrook Company had poor internal control over its cash transactions. The following are facts about its cash position on November 30:

- The company's books showed a balance of $18,901.62, which included undeposited receipts.
- A credit of $100 on the bank statement did not appear on the company's books.

- The balance, according to the bank statement, was $15,550.
- Outstanding checks were:
  - No. 62 for $116.25
  - No. 183 for $150.00
  - No. 284 for $253.25
  - No. 8621 for $190.71
  - No. 8623 for $206.80
  - No. 8632 for $145.28.
- The only deposit was for $3,794.41 on December 7. The cashier handles all incoming cash and makes the bank deposits personally. He also reconciles the monthly bank statement. His November 30 reconciliation follows:

Balance, per books, November 30		$18,901.62
Add: Outstanding checks:		
8621	$190.71	
8623	206.80	
8632	45.28	442.79
		$19,344.41
Less: Undeposited receipts		3,794.41
Balance per bank, November 30		$15,550.00
Deduct: Unrecorded credit		100.00
True cash, November 30		$15,450.00

a. You suspect that the cashier may have misappropriated some money and are concerned specifically that some of the undeposited receipts of $3,794.41 may have been taken. Prepare a schedule showing your estimate of the loss.

b. How did the cashier attempt to conceal the theft?

c. On the basis of this information only, name two specific features of internal control that were apparently missing.

d. If the cashier's October 31 reconciliation is known to be proper and you start your audit on December 10, what specific substantive audit procedures would help you discover the theft?

10-21 **LO 8** Assume that you are testing the client's bank reconciliation at year-end. Following is a list of items on the reconciliation. For each item listed as (a) through (e), identify one or more procedures that the auditor would perform to gather sufficient appropriate evidence regarding that item.

a. Balance per bank
b. Balance per books
c. Deposits in transit
d. Customer note collected by bank
e. Outstanding checks

10-22 **LO 8** The AICPA has developed a standard bank confirmation form for consistent communication with the banking community.

a. Is the auditor required to send a bank confirmation to banks from which the client receives a bank cutoff statement shortly after year-end? Explain.

b. What additional information does the auditor obtain through a bank confirmation? Explain how the auditor uses this other information.

c.   For each scenario below, listed as (1) through (3), recommend a substantive audit procedure or additional audit work that should be performed:

1.   The client has one major bank account located in a distant city, and the auditor is not familiar with the bank. The auditor has assessed control risk as high for the cash accounts on this engagement. The mailing address of the bank is simply a post office box number, but such a number is not considered unusual.

2.   The client has three accounts with its major bank. For two of the three accounts, the confirmation returned by the bank shows different balances from what the client shows. The balance per the client for one of the accounts is the same as the bank shows in the cutoff statement received from the bank shortly after year-end. The auditor did not request a cutoff statement on the other account for which the confirmation differs.

3.   The returned confirmation shows a loan that the client does not list as a liability.

10-23 LO 8 Kautz, CPA is examining the following client-prepared bank reconciliation during the audit of Concrete Products, Inc.

Concrete Products, Inc.
Bank Reconciliation
December 31, 2018

Balance per bank (a)		$18,375.91
Deposits in transit (b):		
December 30	1,471.10	
December 31	2,840.69	4,311.79
Outstanding checks (c):		
837	6,000.00	
1941	671.80	
1966	320.00	
1984	1,855.42	
1985	3,621.22	
1986	2,576.89	
1991	4,420.88	(19,466.21)
Subtotal		3,221.49
NSF check returned Dec. 29 (d)		200.00
Bank charges		5.50
Error check no. 1932		148.10
Customer note collected by the bank		
($2,750 plus $275 interest) (e)		(3,025.00)
Balance per books (f)		$ 550.09

Identify one or more substantive audit procedures that Kautz should perform in gathering evidence in support of each of the items (a) through (f) in this bank reconciliation.

10-24 **LO 8** Pacific River Plastics Company has a major branch located in Phoenix. The branch deposits cash receipts daily and periodically transfers the receipts to the company's home office in Pacific River. The transfers are accounted for as intercompany entries into the home office and branch office accounts. All accounting, however, is performed at the home office under the direction of the assistant controller. The assistant controller is also responsible for the transfers. The controller, however, independently reconciles the bank account each month or assigns the reconciliation to someone in the department (in some cases, could be the assistant controller). The company is relatively small; therefore, the controller is also the financial planner and treasurer for the company. As part of the year-end audit, you performing procedures related to bank transfers. As part of the process, you prepared the following schedule of transfers.

Information per Client's Records			Information per Bank Statements	
			Date Cleared	
Date per Branch	Date per Amount	Date Deposited Home Office	Per Home Bank	Per Branch Bank
12/27	$23,000	12/31	12/31	1/3
12/29	$40,000	12/31	12/31	1/7
12/31	$45,000	1/2	1/3	1/8
1/2	$14,000	12/31	12/31	1/5
1/5	$28,000	1/3	1/7	1/12
1/3	$10,000	1/3	12/31	1/5

    a.   Identify the substantive audit procedures that you would use to test the correctness of the client's interbank transfers.

    b.   Identify any adjusting journal entries that would be needed on either the home or branch office accounting records as a result of the preceding transactions.

PROFESSIONAL SKEPTICISM

10-25 **LO 8** The following are deficiencies in internal controls over cash. For each deficiency indicate what substantive audit procedure(s) should be performed to determine whether any material misstatements exist. Consider each deficiency independently of the others. While each deficiency poses potential problems, identify two that would heighten your professional skepticism the most and explain your rationale.

    a.   The person who opens the mail prepares the deposit when the cashier is not available.

    b.   If a customer does not submit a remittance advice with a payment, the mail clerk sometimes does not prepare one for the accounts receivable department.

    c.   Occasionally, the treasurer's department does not cancel the supporting documents for cash disbursements.

    d.   Customer correspondence concerning monthly statements is handled by the person who makes the bank deposits.

    e.   Bank reconciliations are not prepared on a timely basis. When prepared, they are prepared by the person who handles incoming mail.

10-26 **LO 8, 11** One of the procedures that you are performing on the audit of Reengage Corporation is sending bank confirmations. Your audit firm has a policy of sending confirmations to all financial institutions where a banking relationship exists, although the policy acknowledges that various instances may not require sending confirmations (e.g., accounts with no activity for the period under audit, petty cash accounts at branch locations). You note several accounts in which the cash balances are relatively small. You believe that sending confirmations to the financial institutions where Reengage Corporation has an account with a small balance will not be necessary.

a. What type of evidence will you obtain from the bank confirmations?
b. Use the framework for professional decision making from *Chapter 1* to determine which financial institutions you will send a confirmation. Recall that the framework is:

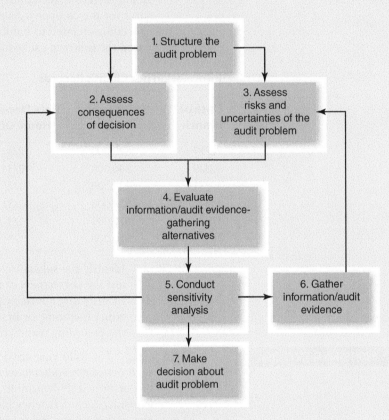

Source: Adapted from Judgment and Choice, by Robin Hogarth.

10-27 LO 9 As a staff auditor, you may find yourself auditing marketable securities.

a. What are the three major categories of marketable securities?
b. What is the GAAP classification for such securities?
c. What judgmental challenges do auditors face in auditing marketable securities?

10-28 LO 9 Match the following assertions related to marketable securities with their associated description: (a) existence/occurrence, (b) completeness, (c) rights and obligations, (d) valuation or allocation, (e) presentation and disclosure.

1. The marketable securities balances include all securities transactions that have taken place during the period.
2. The company has title to marketable securities accounts as of the balance sheet date.

3. The recorded balances reflect the true underlying economic value of those assets.
4. Marketable securities are properly classified on the balance sheet and disclosed in the notes to the financial statements.
5. Marketable securities exist at the balance sheet date.

FRAUD

10-29 **LO 9** The following are risks relating to marketable securities. Categorize each risk as relating to either: (a) inherent or fraud risk, or (b) control risk.

1. Management manipulation of the classification of securities to achieve preferable valuation treatment, for example, market value versus amortized cost.
2. Lack of policies over valuation or classification of securities.
3. Management manipulation of the valuation of market value if the securities are thinly traded.
4. Lack of policies over purchase or sale of securities.
5. Lack of monitoring of changes in securities balances.
6. Lack of segregation of duties between individuals responsible for making investment decisions and those responsible for the custody of securities.
7. Risk of theft of securities if they are not physically controlled, or if authorization and monitoring over their purchase or sale is not adequate.
8. Risk of sudden market declines, which would adversely affect the valuation of securities.
9. Lack of involvement or oversight by internal audit in relation to securities.

10-30 **LO 9** Refer to *Exhibit 10.13* and *Exhibit 10.14*. Categorize each of the following questions relating to marketable securities as being appropriate for use in: (a) an inherent risk questionnaire or (b) a control risk questionnaire.

1. Does the internal audit department conduct regular audits of the controls over marketable securities?
2. If management has changed the classification of securities during the year from either trading securities or available-for-sale securities to held-to-maturity securities, are the amounts significant? Were they reviewed by the audit committee? Do the audit committee and the board concur with the change?
3. Does the company regularly invest in marketable securities? How material are the balances in marketable securities accounts?
4. Does the company have written policies and guidelines regarding investments in marketable securities? Are the policies approved by the board of directors? What process is used to authorize investments in marketable securities?
5. Does the company have a clear policy as to properly classifying marketable securities as trading securities, available-for-sale securities, or held-to-maturity securities? Is there evidence that the company follows the policy?
6. Has management changed the classification of securities during the year from either trading securities or available-for-sale securities to held-to-maturity securities? If yes, what is the reason for the change?
7. If a liquid market does not exist for marketable securities, how does management estimate the value of the securities that need to be marked to current market value?

8. Does the company provide for effective segregation of duties among individuals responsible for making investment decisions and those responsible for the custody of securities?

9. Is there a ready market for the securities?

10-31 **LO 9** Refer to the *Prompt for Critical Thinking #7.*

a. What is your reaction to the following comments made by Robert Murdoch, which explain some of his motivation for investing in marketable equity securities of Genie, an oil and gas exploration company:

> "If Genie's effort to develop shale oil is successful, as I believe it will be, then the news we'll report in the coming decades will reflect a more prosperous, more democratic, and more secure world."

b. Writers in The Free Thought Project (*http://thefreethoughtproject.com/about-us/*) had this to say about Genie's oil exploration in the Golan Heights Region:

For more details, see http://thefreethoughtproject.com/cheney-murdoch-rothschild-drill-oil-reserves-syrian-occupied-territory-violate-international-law/

While Syria is torn apart by the warring of U.S. imperialists and Islamic fundamentalists–**leaving its children to die of starvation**–another country plans to take advantage of the chaos by stealing resources from Syria's southern region. The theft will be carried out by the most notorious pushers of military hegemony, and they don't care that it violates international law.

Genie Energy is an American-based oil and gas company with major investors and advisors comprising a who's who list of war profiteers–Dick Cheney, Rupert Murdoch, Lord Jacob Rothschild, and James Woosley. The president of their Israeli subsidiary is Efraim "Effi" Eitam, an Israeli military commander who **called for expelling the "cancer" of Arabs from Israel.**

Together, these warmongers and would-be ethnic cleansers will **soon be drilling** into a vast oil and gas reserve located in Syrian territory occupied by Israel since 1967, known as Golan Heights. The move would be in clear violation of international law, specifically the **Annex to the Fourth Geneva Convention.**

Israeli authorities granted Genie Energy's subsdiary, Afek Oil and Gas, exclusive petroleum exploration rights in a 153-square-mile region in Golan Heights. In 2015, above-ground geophysical tests discovered the presence of oil and natural gas reserves that could make Israel energy Israel energy self-sufficient. Afek has already drilled three exploratory wells.

Do you agree with the views of The Free Thought Project? Explain your rationale.

c. Given our previous discussion about audit firm portfolio management in *Chapter 1* and *Chapter 4*, what do you think about BDO's decision to include Genie as one of its audit clients? Is there room for politics in audit firm portfolio management? Defend your thoughts.

10-32 **LO 9** A client prepared the following worksheet listing all activities in the marketable securities accounts for the year under audit. For the purpose of this question, assume there are no unusual securities. Assume also that the audit team assessed control risk as high and that the auditor will use substantive tests of details for the account balance. The account balances at the beginning and end of the year per the company's trial balance are:

	Beginning Balance	Ending Balance
Investment in marketable securities	$400,000	$675,000
Allowance to reduce securities to market	$ 35,000	$ 35,000
Subtotal	365,000	640,000
Balance per general ledger		
Interest income		$ 25,000
Dividend income		$ 18,000
Net gain on the disposal of securities		$ 32,000

Identify the audit procedures needed to complete the audit of marketable securities. Assume that the same audit firm audited the client last year. Be sure to cover the steps the auditor would use to determine that the securities are properly classified.

10-33 LO 10 In what ways do complex financial instruments differ from more traditional financial instruments? What additional risks are associated with such instruments?

ETHICS

10-34 LO 10, 11 The advent of sophisticated financial instruments has dramatically changed the nature of investing during the past decade. Many financial instruments offer potentially greater returns for the investor but at higher levels of risk.

a. Review the FASB's discussion on financial instruments, or a finance book, to identify various types of financial instruments. Select five instruments that you consider interesting and prepare a report addressing: (1) the nature of the instrument, (2) its underlying business purpose, (3) risks associated with the instrument, and (4) special audit procedures that should be applied during the audit of a client with a significant investment in the instrument.

b. Now assume that one of your audit clients has a large investment in a particularly risky financial instrument. This financial instrument exposes the client to significant economic loss in the event that the marketability of the instrument declines. You do not feel that the client's footnote disclosures adequately reveal the true risk profile of the instrument. What is your ethical obligation to the shareholders of the client with regard to your knowledge of the riskiness of this investment?

c. Use the framework for ethical decision making outlined in *Chapter 1* to formulate your answer. Recall that the steps in that framework are: (1) identify the ethical issue(s); (2) determine who are the affected parties and identify their rights; (3) determine the most important rights; (4) develop alternative courses of action; (5) determine the likely consequences of each proposed course of action; (6) assess the possible consequences, including an estimation of the greatest good for the greatest number, and determine whether the rights framework would cause any course of action to be eliminated; and (7) decide on the appropriate course of action.

Fraud Focus: Contemporary and Historical Cases

FRAUD

INTERNATIONAL

10-35 | **Agricultural Bank of China**
(LO 3, 4, 9)

The Agricultural Bank of China (AgBank) was the victim of an interesting 3.8 billion yuan ($578 million) embezzlement scheme. In early 2015, China's stock market was rallying, with share prices increasing dramatically. Two employees of AgBank saw an opportunity to embezzle and make money off the stock market. They replaced the AgBank's acceptance bills (a type of liability that is issued and exchanged in paper format), with newspaper clippings. They then cashed the acceptance bills at another Chinese bank, and invested the funds in the stock market, expecting to make a quick profit. They planned to cover up their embezzlement by paying back the other Chinese bank, re-obtaining the acceptance bills, and then replacing them in the vault at AgBank.

The problem was that instead of continuing to rally, the Chinese stock market bubble burst in the summer of 2015, leaving the fraudsters with no ability to exit their scheme in the manner in which they had intended.

Chinese banks have been plagued with accusations of corruption. For example, a former Vice President of AgBank was sentenced to life in prison in 2015 for accepting bribes. Stock markets globally are devaluing bank stocks due to very low (or sometimes even negative) interest rates; but the situation in China is even worse because of the endemic bribery, fraud, and embezzlements that have been revealed in recent years.

The effect of the revelation of the embezzlement and the stock market pressures is evident in the following chart showing AgBank's share price:

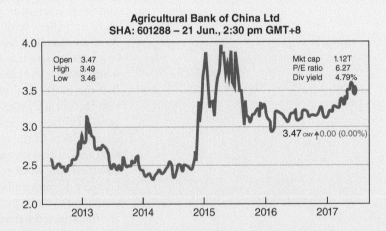

Agricultural Bank of China Ltd
SHA: 601288 – 21 Jun., 2:30 pm GMT+8

a. Think about the fraud triangle. What was the incentive for the fraudsters in this case? What was the opportunity? Speculate on potential rationalizations that these individuals might have had as they perpetrated this fraud.

b. What implications do you draw from the stock market reaction to the AgBank embezzlement?

c. There are four state-owned commercial banks in China:

- Industrial and Commercial Bank of China.
- Bank of China.
- China Construction Bank.
- Agricultural Bank of China

These are among the largest banks in the entire world. One might expect that these banks would have very sophisticated internal controls around the physical protection of acceptance bills. PricewaterhouseCoopers (PwC) is the external auditor of AgBank. In fact, AgChina's 2015 Annual Report stated that PwC had issued an unqualified report on the company's internal controls over financial reporting. What responsibility do you think that PwC has in this case, if any?

FRAUD

ETHICS

PROFESSIONAL SKEPTICISM

10-36 **Peregrine Financial Group (PFG), Inc. and Russell Wasendorf Sr. (LO 2, 3, 4, 8, 11)** Refer to the Why It Matters feature at the beginning of the chapter. On July 14, 2012, Russell Wasendorf Sr. attempted to commit suicide inside his vehicle in the parking lot of Peregrine Financial Group, Inc.'s (PFG) corporate offices, leaving a remarkable suicide note in his vehicle detailing a fraud scheme in which he embezzled over $200 million from PFG's brokerage clients over a 20-year period. Wasendorf led a very interesting and affluent lifestyle and ran the business in some unusual ways. Examples include:

- In addition to owning PFG, he also owned an Italian restaurant, My Verona, in Cedar Rapids, Iowa, along with publishing companies (SFO Magazine and W&A Publishing/Trader's Press) and a real estate operation in Bucharest, Romania.
- He married his fiancée, who works at My Verona, in the Bellagio Hotel in Las Vegas on June 30, 2012.
- His son, Russell Wasendorf Jr. ran the operations of PFG and was the president and chief operating officer of the company, but did not have detailed access to important financial records of the company. Instead, Russell Wasendorf Sr. had sole control of the company's bank accounts.
- He flew his private jet to Chicago often for business, but was also known to take the jet all around the world to attend Lady Gaga concerts.
- He recently pledged a $2 million donation to the Athletic Department at the University of Northern Iowa.
- He attempted, but failed, to commit suicide by hooking up a tube to his car's tailpipe when suspicions of the fraud were revealed. An empty bottle of vodka was next to his body. He was subsequently hospitalized at the University of Iowa Hospitals and Clinics in Iowa City, and was removed from his hospital bed by FBI agents while simultaneously speaking to his Chicago-based lawyer, Thomas Breen. Later that day, he appeared in federal court related to charges of lying to federal regulators and was considered a flight risk.

Following are quotes from Wasendorf's suicide note:

"I have committed fraud. For this I feel constant and intense guilt. I am remorseful that my greatest transgressions have been to my fellow man. Through a scheme of using false bank statements I have been able to embezzle millions of dollars from customer accounts at Peregrine Financial Group, Inc. The forgeries started nearly twenty years ago and have gone undetected until now. I was able to conceal my crime of forgery by being the sole individual with access to the US Bank accounts held by PFG. No one else in the company ever saw an actual US Bank statement. The Bank statements were always delivered directly to me when they arrived in the mail. I made counterfeit statements within a few hours of receiving the actual statements and gave the forgeries to the accounting department.

I had no access to additional capital and I was forced into a difficult decision: Should I go out of business or cheat? I guess my ego was too big to admit failure. So I cheated, I falsified the very core of the financial documents of PFG, the Bank Statements. At first I had to make forgeries of both the Firstar Bank Statements and the Harris Bank Statements. When I chose to close the Harris Account I only had to falsify the Firstar statements. [Note: Firstar eventually became U.S. Bank.] I also made forgeries of official letters and correspondence from the bank, as well as transaction confirmation statements.

Using a combination of PhotoShop, Excel, scanners, and both laser and ink jet printers I was able to make very convincing forgeries of nearly every document that came from the Bank. I could create forgeries very quickly so no one suspected that my forgeries were not the real thing that had just arrived in the mail.

With careful concealment and blunt authority I was able to hide my fraud from others at PFG. PFG grew out of a one man shop, a business I started in the basement of my home. As I added people to the company everyone knew I was the guy in charge. If anyone questioned my authority I would simply point out that I was the sole shareholder. I established rules and procedures as each new situation arose. I ordered that US Bank statements were to be delivered directly to me unopened, to make sure no one was able to examine an actual US Bank Statement. I was also the only person with online access to PFG's account using US Bank's online portal. On US Bank side, I told representatives at the Bank that I was the only person they should interface with at PFG.

When it became common practice for Certified Auditors and the Field Auditors of the Regulators to mail Balance Confirmation Forms to Banks and other entities holding customer funds I opened a post office box. The box was originally in the name of Firstar Bank but was eventually changed to US Bank. I put the address "PO Box 706, Cedar Falls, IA 50613–0030" on the counterfeit Bank Statements. When the auditors mailed the Confirmation Forms to the Bank's false address, I would intercept the Form, type in the amount I needed to show, forge a Bank Officer's signature and mail it back to the Regulator or Certified Auditor. When online Banking became prevalent I learned how to falsify online Bank Statements and the Regulators accepted them without question."

At about the same time that emergency officials responded to the 911 call in the parking lot of PFG's offices, Russell Wasendorf Jr. arrived at his office inside the building and found an exact copy of the suicide note. Immediately thereafter, he contacted U.S. Bank and obtained a bank statement with an ending balance as of December 31, 2011, equaling $6,337,628.14. The ending balance reported by his father on the falsified bank statement was $221,770,946.18.

PFG is a futures trading firm. Futures trading firms match buyers and sellers of contracts for commodities like wheat, oil, and aluminum and charge a commission for the service. Companies use futures contracts to protect themselves from price fluctuations. PFG is a privately held entity, so it is not subject to oversight by the SEC or PCAOB. Instead, the U.S. Commodities Futures Trading Commission (CFTC) is the regulatory agency responsible for the oversight of the industry, and the NFA is the industry association that operates under the supervision of the CFTC. The NFA is responsible for monitoring and auditing PFG for compliance with financial reporting requirements of the domestic exchanges, of which PFG was a member. The NFA never required electronic verification of PFG's bank statements.

In 2004, a PFG client complained to the NFA that PFG was misusing customer funds. In 2009, an anonymous complaint was filed with the NFA asking for a review of PFG's bank account information. What, if anything, the NFA did about the complaint was not known. Interestingly, Wasendorf Sr., serves on an advisory committee of the NFA. Veraja-Snelling Co. is PFG's audit firm. The firm is operated out of a home in Glendale Heights, Illinois. Jeannie Veraja-Snelling is the sole practitioner and has never performed any public company audits, even though she did register her audit firm with the PCAOB in 2010. On the December 31, 2010, financial statements, Veraja-Snelling certified that PFG was in compliance with federal commodities regulations governing the segregation of customer money.

What likely prompted the timing of Wasendorf's attempted suicide was the fact that the NFA had just implemented a change to its online system whereby bank statement information was directed electronically from the banks directly to the NFA (the system can be viewed at *www.confirmation.com*). The NFA started receiving confirmations through that system one day before Wasendorf's attempted suicide.

PFG filed for bankruptcy almost immediately after Wasendorf's attempted suicide and subsequent arrest. In addition, all the other businesses that Wasendorf ran immediately ceased operations, firing all employees. These businesses began the process of immediate liquidation. All customer accounts at PFG have been frozen, so investors have no access to their assets. Because PFG is a futures trading firm, not a traditional brokerage firm, investors do not have access to the protections normally provided by the Securities Investor Protection Corporation, which returns assets held in accounts of traditional brokerage firms that fail.

a. Describe any inherent, fraud, or control risks that are evident from the facts in the case.

b. Comment on your perceptions of the quality of the NFA's oversight of PFG.

c. Do you think it is ethically problematic that Wasendorf served on an advisory committee of the NFA? Why might NFA have wanted Wasendorf to serve on its advisory committee? What conflict might that have caused?

d. Comment on your perceptions of the quality of Veraja-Snelling's certification of PFG's compliance status. Is a sole practitioner likely capable of sufficiently overseeing a large, complex entity like PFG? Was it acceptable for Veraja-Snelling to accept a paper copy of the bank confirmation, which she would have believed came directly from U.S. Bank? Why might Veraja-Snelling have lacked professional skepticism for this engagement?

e. Having the CEO personally involved in receiving bank statements and in limiting the bank's access to other individuals within the company would be very unusual for a large company such as PFG. U.S. Bank should have expected to receive an auditor's confirmation request annually, but did not because Wasendorf circumvented the process. Using the ethical decision making framework from *Chapter 1*, comment on whether you think that U.S. Bank is responsible in any way for this fraud. Explain. Recall that the steps are: (1) identify the ethical issue, (2) determine the affected parties and identify their rights, (3) determine the most important rights for each affected party, (4) develop alternative courses of action, (5) determine the likely consequences of each proposed course of action on each affected party, (6) assess the possible consequences, and (7) decide on an appropriate course of action.

FRAUD

ETHICS

PROFESSIONAL SKEPTICISM

INTERNATIONAL

10-37 **PCAOB, SEC, Satyam Computer Services, Ramalinga Raju (LO 1, 2, 3, 4, 7, 8, 11)** In the late 1990s, Satyam Computer Services (Satyam) was a relatively unknown, family-owned information technology (IT) company located in Hyderabad, India. All that changed when Satyam received a contract to establish IT architecture at the World Bank. The selection of Satyam was, at the time, quite surprising given Satyam's relative size and obscure reputation. However, the company's business continued to thrive as demand grew for IT outsourcing from Indian companies like Satyam. At the height of its success, Satyam employed about 50,000 employees and operated in 67 countries around the world. As it turns out, the reason for selecting Satyam for the World Bank contract was that Mohamed Muhsin, the chief information officer for the World Bank, was financially involved in Satyam. After suspicions of this became known in 2006, Muhsin retired and was subsequently banned from any further relationship with the World Bank. According to World Bank officials, they alerted the U.S. Department of Justice that Satyam top management engaged in fraudulent and corrupt business practices.

In October 2008, the World Bank fired Satyam, accusing the company of installing spy systems on its computers and of stealing assets from the World Bank. Also during October 2008, a stock analyst questioned Satyam's large cash balances during an earnings conference call. The stock analyst's questions were largely ignored, and the company's stock price continued to rise. Satyam continued to report record profits despite the worldwide economic downturn. In December 2008, Satyam's board of directors approved the purchase of two companies owned by Raju's family, Maytas Properties and Maytas Infrastructure. Investors were outraged by the proposed transaction because of the relationship between Raju and the two companies. As a result of the outcry, the transaction was not finalized. However, the resulting bad press coverage caused analysts to put sell recommendations on

Satyam's stock, sending share prices down 10% and resulting in four of five independent board members resigning.

Responding to the resulting pressure, on January 7, 2009, Raju made a shocking revelation admitting to a massive fraud, in a letter addressed to Satyam's remaining board members. Portions of the letter are reproduced here (*note that original typos are retained for accuracy*):

"It is with deep regret, and tremendous burden that I am carrying on my conscience, that I would like to bring the following facts to your notice:

1. The Balance Sheet carries as of September 30 2008
    1. Inflated (non-existent) cash and bank balances of Rs. 5,040 crore (as against Rs. 5361 crore reflected in the books)
    2. An accrued interest of Rs. 376 crore which is non-existent
    3. An understated liability of Rs. 1,230 crore on account of funds arranged by me
    4. An over stated debtors position of Rs. 490 crore (as against Rs. 2,651 in the books)
2. For the September quarter (Q2) we reported a revenue of Rs. 2,700 crore and an operating margin of Rs. 649 crore (24% Of revenues) as against the actual revenues of Rs. 2,112 crore and an actual operating margin of Rs. 61 Crore (3% of revenues). This has resulted in artificial cash and bank balances going up by Rs. 588 crore in Q2 alone

This gap in the Balance Sheet has arisen on account of inflated profits over a period of last several years (limited only to Satyam stand-alone, books of subsidiaries reflecting true performance). What started as a marginal gap between actual operating profit and the one reflected in the books of accounts continued to grow over the years. It has attained unmanageable proportions as the size of company operations grew significantly…. Every attempt made to eliminate the gap failed. As the promoters held a small percentage of equity, the concern was that poor performance would result in a takeover, thereby exposing the gap. *It was like riding a tiger, not knowing how to get off without being eaten. (emphasis added)*

Under the circumstances, I am tendering my resignation as the chairman of Satyam and shall continue in this position only till such time the current board is expanded. My continuance is just to ensure enhancement of the board over the next several days or as early as possible. I am now prepared to subject myself to the laws of the land and face consequences thereof.

(B. Ramalinga Raju)
Copies marked to:

1. Chairman SEBI
2. Stock Exchanges"

Ultimately, it was revealed that assets on Satyam's balance sheet were overstated by about $1.5 billion and that over $1 billion in bank loans and cash that the company claimed to own were nonexistent. The fictitious assets accounted for 50% of the company's total assets. To accomplish the fraud, Raju and other individuals in top management (including the CFO, the head of internal audit, and Raju's brother) took the following actions:

• Created fictitious bank statements to inflate cash
• Reported fictitious interest income from the fictitious bank accounts

- Created 6,000 fake salary accounts and stole the money after Satyam deposited it
- Created fictitious customer identities and generated fictitious invoices against their names to inflate revenue
- Forged board of director resolutions to obtain loans for Satyam

PricewaterhouseCoopers (PwC) was Satyam's auditor from 2000 to the time the fraud was revealed. PwC was criticized for failing to exercise professional skepticism regarding the $1.04 billion cash balance of non-interest-bearing deposits. Normally, companies would either invest that money in an interest-bearing account or disburse the money through dividends to shareholders. As such, the large amount of cash should have been a red flag to the auditors that verification of the account balances was necessary. It was later revealed that PwC did not independently confirm the cash accounts with the banks in which Satyam claimed to have accounts. Subsequent PCAOB and SEC investigations revealed that PwC allowed their audit clients to control the cash confirmation process and did not challenge management regarding the validity of confirmations. In fact, some banks sent PwC confirmations directly, and those confirmations contradicted the statements that management had provided. For example, one bank told PwC that the Satyam account had a balance of $11.2 million, but management reported a balance of $108.6 million. Another bank reported $330,172 in the Satyam account, but management reported a balance of $152.9 million. Further complicating matters, the PwC network firm partner reviewed the working papers for the 2008 audit one month before the audit report was issued. During the review, the partner noted the deficiencies in the confirmation process and advised the engagement team not to rely on confirmations that were not received directly from the banks. The engagement team ignored the review comment, taking no actions to address the confirmation process weaknesses. It is unclear whether the reviewing partner knew that the comments were left unaddressed, but in any case, the partner should have followed up to make sure that the audit opinion was not issued until the confirmation process weaknesses were resolved.

Raju, his brother, the former managing director of the board, the head of internal audit, and the CFO were all arrested by Indian officials on charges of fraud. Indian officials also arrested two of the PwC auditors on charges of fraud. On April 5, 2011, the SEC settled a civil action with Satyam Computer Services, in which the company paid a penalty of $10 million (see Accounting and Auditing Enforcement Release No. 3258). On May 6, 2011, PwC and its Indian affiliates agreed to a $25.5 million settlement in a class action lawsuit. On October 12, 2011, the two PwC auditors were granted bail and left jail.

a. Aside from the shocking disclosure of the fraud and its magnitude, one of the most interesting comments in Raju's statement to the board of directors was "It was like riding a tiger, not knowing how to get off without being eaten." Speculate on why he may have stated that.
b. Describe why PwC's cash confirmation process was flawed. Comment on why PwC may have had an incentive to not exercise professional skepticism in this situation.
c. Which management assertion did Raju's fraud violate?
d. Based on the facts in this case, what internal controls over cash appear to have been missing or not operating effectively?

e. Consider the situation of the PwC network firm partner. That individual correctly reviewed the workpapers and suggested that the engagement team should not have relied on the cash confirmations from management. Using the ethical decision making framework from *Chapter 1*, determine what next steps the audit partner should have taken upon making the review suggestions. Recall that the steps are: (1) identify the ethical issue; in this case the ethical issue is how to properly ensure that the review comments are taken seriously and addressed; (2) determine the affected parties and identify their rights; (3) determine the most important rights for each affected party; (4) develop alternative courses of action; (5) determine the likely consequences of each proposed course of action on each affected party; (6) assess the possible consequences; and (7) decide on an appropriate course of action.

FRAUD

PROFESSIONAL SKEPTICISM

INTERNATIONAL

10-38 **Parmalat (LO 8)** As an example of difficulties that auditors experience in collecting confirmations of cash balances, consider the Parmalat fraud that was exposed in 2003. In that case, the company overstated cash by about $5 billion, which reflected a fictitious amount in a Bank of America account in the Cayman Islands. The Italian segment of the audit firm, Grant Thornton, received a cash confirmation that noted no exceptions to the confirmation the audit firm had sent. Parmalat accomplished the deception, in part, by providing the audit firm with a fictitious bank mailing address.

a. What role does the concept of materiality play in the substantive testing of cash balances?

b. How might online resources and associated electronic confirmation processes help to avoid fraud associated with cash confirmations?

c. What are two or three key factors the auditor might consider that could have indicated that the cash account was a high-risk account for this client and would require more skeptical audit work?

Application Activities

FRAUD

NOTE: Completing *Application Activities* requires students to reference additional resources and materials. Some *Application Activities* will require the student to reference relevant professional auditing standards. We make special note of these as *Auditing Standards Application Activities*.

INTERNATIONAL

10-39 **LO 2, 3, 4** Refer to the *Focus on Fraud* feature "Skimming and the Completeness Assertion." Using appropriate resources, find an example of a skimming fraud and describe the fraud. Your description should indicate who committed the fraud, how they committed the fraud (e.g., controls that were absent), and how much money was stolen (if disclosed or estimated).

10-40 **LO 2, 3, 4, 9** In *10-35*, we noted that there are four state-owned commercial banks in China:

- Industrial and Commercial Bank of China
- Bank of China
- China Construction Bank
- Agricultural Bank of China

Use appropriate online resources and obtain the stock price charts for each of these marketable equity securities for the **past five** years.

a. What is the approximate price per share for each of these banks' marketable equity securities? What is the market capitalization (in

Chinese currency, CNY or RNB (see Wait, What's The Difference Between "Yuan" And "Renminbi" at *http://www.npr.org/sections /money/2010/03/wait_whats_the_difference_betw.html*), and $USD) for each of these banks today? During what period in the last five years was the stock valuation for these banks the highest? To what do you attribute those high prices?

b. Locate the names of the auditor(s) of each of these banks.

c. Read the article at the following website with respect to audit firm rotation and audit fees:

http://www.chinaaccountingblog.com/weblog/the-big-four-and -the-big.html

What happened to audit fees upon audit firm rotation for these banks? How do you interpret that with respect to potential implications for audit quality? Translate the audit fees from Chinese RNB into USD for each of the four largest banks.

> Note: *You can locate audit fee disclosure data in Chinese banks' annual reports by searching for the term: "auditors' remuneration." You can determine how to translate currencies from RNB to USD by searching online using the terms "rmb to usd."*

d. Determine the audit firm and audit fee for the Bank of America, a prominent U.S. bank. Determine the approximate price per share of its marketable equity securities over the **past five** years. Compare this information to the information you have gleaned for the top Chinese banks. Speculate on why there exists differences in marketable equity securities pricing, along with audit fees between these various banks.

e. Considering the issues in part d of this question, articulate the notion of competitive market behavior and its implications for the allocation of capital around the globe. What does an investor gain by investing in Bank of America stock as compared to Bank of China stock? What are the risk-reward tradeoffs?

FRAUD

ETHICS

10-41 **PFG, Wasendorf (LO 3, 8)** Read about the massive fraud committed by Russell Wasendorf Sr. at PFG that we present in *10-36*. Use appropriate resources to document the latest developments in the case against Wasendorf. Describe developments relating to Wasendorf Sr., Wasendorf Jr. and the auditor, Jeannie Veraja-Snelling.

FRAUD

ETHICS

10-42 **Parmalat (LO 8)** Refer to the *Focus on Fraud* feature "The Parmalat Fraud and Its Many Victims." Use appropriate resources to answer the following questions.

a. Which two audit firms did Parmalat sue after the company's bankruptcy?

b. What was the amount that Parmalat sought to recover?

c. What was the ultimate resolution of the case?

10-43 **LO 5, 8** Access the two most recent financial statements of two companies in the same industry. For example, you might look at Yahoo and Google or Coca-Cola and PepsiCo. Perform ratio analysis using relevant ratios for both companies, and compare the following between the two companies:

a. Analyze trends in the ending cash balance over time.

b. Compute trends in interest returns on investments.

    c. Analyze cash balances, and changes therein, in relation to new or retiring debt obligations.

    d. Compute the current ratio (current assets/current liabilities).

    e. Compute the quick ratio (cash + cash equivalents + net receivables)/current liabilities.

    f. Compare cash flow to sales (operating cash flow/sales) and profitability (operating cash flow/net income).

FRAUD   **10-44**   `LO 3`   Refer to the *Focus on Fraud* feature "Common Fraud Schemes Relating to Cash." Access appropriate resources and search for recent fraud schemes related to cash. Describe one of the schemes you found. Your description should indicate who committed the fraud, how they committed the fraud (e.g., controls that were absent), and how much money was stolen (if disclosed or estimated).

FRAUD   **10-45**   **Matthews International (LO 3, 4)**   Refer to the *Focus on Fraud* feature "Embezzlement at a Casket and Burial Product Company: A Case of Inadequate Segregation of Duties."

    a. Access the following link to find a description and pictures of the over 250 assets that the federal government seized from Cynthia and Gary Mills *http://www.post-gazette.com/local/west/2017/01/25/Feds-charge-Robinson-woman-with-stealing-9-5-million-from-Matthews-International-pittsburgh/stories/201701250171* What is your reaction to seeing these items?

    b. Visit the website *www.pinkcollarcrime.com*. Since 1990, what has been the rate of increase in embezzlement by men as compared to women? Read the section of the website titled "The Ladies of PCC." Explain one of the cases that the author describes; explain what is funny about the situation, and what is sad.

    c. Obtain the June 30, 2015, 8-K filing of Matthews International. Read the filing, particularly the Other Events section. What does this 8-K reveal?

    d. The amended 10-K for FYE 2014, filed on August 7, 2015, had this to say about the discovery of the embezzlement, the company's evaluation of the materiality of the embezzlement, and the state of its internal controls:

> In addition, as disclosed in a Current Report on Form 8-K dated July 30, 2015, the Company identified a theft of funds from the Company by an employee that had occurred over a multi-year period through May 2015 which had not been recorded in the Company's financial statements. Pursuant to the guidance of Staff Accounting Bulletin ("SAB") No. 99, "Materiality", the Company evaluated the materiality of these amounts quantitatively and qualitatively and has concluded that the amounts described above were not material to any of its annual or quarterly prior period financial statements or trends of financial results. However, because of the significance of the cumulative out-of-period adjustment to the fiscal 2015 third quarter, the financial statements for years prior to fiscal 2015 have been revised in accordance with SAB No. 108, "Considering the Effects of Prior Year Misstatements when Quantifying Misstatements in Current Year Financial Statements". As a result of this matter, a reassessment was conducted on the internal controls in the Company's treasury process. Specifically, the design of the internal controls over segregation of duties within the treasury process has been determined to

constitute a "material weakness" (as defined in Rule 12b-2 of the Securities Exchange Act of 1934, as amended) in internal control over financial reporting and disclosure controls and procedures at September 30, 2014, as discussed in Part II, Item 9A "Controls and Procedures" of this Amendment. In response to this matter, the Company has taken immediate action and implemented changes in the design of this internal control to ensure appropriate segregation of duties within the Company's treasury process.

Do you agree that the embezzlement was immaterial? Explain your rationale.

e. Obtain the December 23, 2015, 8-K filing of Matthews International. Read the filing. How do you feel about the transparency of the disclosures made about possible reasons for the change of auditors? It seems that the audit committee decided to change auditors from PricewaterhouseCoopers to Ernst & Young because of the detection of the theft. However, it was the company itself that had weak controls that led to the theft. Comment on your views about the fairness of this situation to the various parties involved.

10-46 **FASB**
(LO 1) As of mid-2017, the FASB was conducting early stage research about developing an accounting standard for digital currency. With the use of digital currency increasing, proponents argue that inconsistent accounting practices are becoming a problem. As the digital currency Bitcoin becomes more of a household name, the FASB is considering whether it needs to develop accounting guidance for digital currencies. Bitcoin is the biggest name in the digital currency business, but there are other competitors in the market such as Ethererum and Ripple. Companies such as Microsoft Corp., Dell Inc., and Overstock.com are accepting digital currency as payment. In addition to a form of payment, digital currency also is held as an asset by businesses, which can sell the currency when its value goes up. Using appropriate resources identify any progress that FASB has made on this topic. Consider the auditing challenges with any new guidance provided by the FASB.

AUDITING STANDARDS APPLICATION ACTIVITY

INTERNATIONAL

10-47 **IAASB**
(LO 8) Refer to the *Auditing Standards Appendix* inside the front cover of this textbook. Determine the relevant International Standard on Auditing (ISA) for external confirmations, and locate the standard on the IAASB's website.

a. What is the number of the standard?
b. Define the following key terms noted in the standard: (1) exception, (2) external confirmation, (3) negative confirmation request, (4) nonresponse, and (5) positive confirmation request.
c. What does the standard advise the auditor to do if management refuses to allow the auditor to perform external confirmation procedures?
d. What does the standard advise the auditor to do if the auditor identifies factors that give rise to doubts about the reliability of the response to a confirmation request? What factors would cause such doubt?
e. What does the standard advise the auditor to do if a confirmation request is not reliable?
f. What factors does the standard urge auditors to consider when designing confirmation requests?

FRAUD

10-48 **LO 9** Refer to the *Focus on Fraud* feature "Common Fraud Schemes Relating to Investments." Access appropriate resources and search for recent fraud schemes related to investments.

Describe one of the schemes you found. Your description should indicate who committed the fraud, how they committed the fraud (e.g., controls that were absent), and the possible incentives and rationalizations of the fraudster(s).

Data Analytics: Spreadsheet Modelling and Database Querying

10-49 **LO 5, 8** Download and complete the following case, which relates to cash accounts.

Borthick, A. F., G. P. Schneider, and T. R. Viscelli. (2017). Analyzing data for decision making: Integrating spreadsheet modelling and database querying. *Issues in Accounting Education* 32(1): 25–41.

Auditing Inventory, Goods and Services, and Accounts Payable: The Acquisition and Payment Cycle

The Audit Opinion Formulation Process

I. Making Client Acceptance and Continuance Decisions

Chapter 1

II. Performing Risk Assessment

Chapters 3, 7, and 9–13

III. Obtaining Evidence About Internal Control Operating Effectiveness

Chapters 8–13

IV. Obtaining Substantive Evidence About Accounts, Disclosures and Assertions

Chapters 8–13

V. Completing the Audit and Making Reporting Decisions

Chapters 14 and 15

Quality Auditing and the Need for Quality Auditor Judgments and Ethical Decisions

Chapter 1

Professional Liability

Chapter 4

The Audit Opinion Formulation Process and a Framework for Obtaining Audit Evidence

Chapters 5 and 6

The acquisition and payment cycle includes processes for identifying goods and services to acquire, purchasing goods and services, receiving the goods and services, approving payments, and paying for goods and services received. Audit deficiencies related to inventory, cost of sales, and other activities in the acquisition and payment cycle are frequently included in PCAOB inspection reports. The numerous financial reporting frauds that have occurred in the acquisition and payment cycle should cause auditors to ensure an appropriate level of professional skepticism when auditing accounts in this cycle.

Learning Objectives

LO 1 Identify the significant accounts, disclosures, and relevant assertions in the acquisition and payment cycle.

LO 2 Identify and assess inherent risks of material misstatement in the acquisition and payment cycle.

LO 3 Identify and assess fraud risks of material misstatement in the acquisition and payment cycle.

LO 4 Identify and assess control risks of material misstatement in the acquisition and payment cycle.

LO 5 Describe how to use planning analytical procedures to identify possible material misstatements in acquisition and payment cycle accounts, disclosures, and assertions.

LO 6 Determine appropriate responses to identified risks of material misstatement for acquisition and payment cycle accounts, disclosures, and assertions.

LO 7 Determine appropriate tests of controls and consider the results of tests of controls for acquisition and payment cycle accounts, disclosures, and assertions.

LO 8 Determine and apply sufficient appropriate substantive audit procedures for testing acquisition and payment cycle accounts, disclosures, and assertions.

LO 9 Apply the frameworks for professional decision making and ethical decision making to issues involving conducting the audit of acquisition and payment cycle accounts, disclosures, and assertions.

General Cable Corporation: Inventory Theft and a Cover-up

Why It Matters: An International Perspective

This feature provides an interesting example of inventory theft and collusion among top management.

General Cable Corporation (GCC) is a manufacturer of copper, aluminium, and fiber optic wire based in Highland Heights, Kentucky. It has operations worldwide (the company's stock ticker is BGC on the New York Stock Exchange). An SEC Accounting and Auditing Enforcement Release (AAER) reveals that from 2008 to 2012, GCC's financial statements were materially inaccurate because of improper inventory accounting at one of its recently acquired subsidiaries in Brazil.

The accountants in Brazil exploited weaknesses in GCC's internal controls to make fictitious journal entries to hide the fact that significant copper inventory was missing from the company's manufacturing plants. The internal controls were manual and decentralized, enabling the accountants to manually calculate inventory in a spreadsheet and then enter those values into the general ledger. The physical controls to protect inventory were inadequate, thereby enabling the thefts. There was also a lack of segregation of duties for making, approving, and reviewing manual journal entries. The accountants overstated inventory by $46.7 million, thereby overstating net income by 21.6%, 11.3%, and 29.8% for the years ending 2011, 2010, and 2009, respectively.

During the period from February through September 2012, the Brazil segment's CEO and CFO concealed the inaccurate financial reporting from GCC's executive management in the US. To accomplish the concealment, they took the following actions:

- directed their subordinates to destroy all records relating to the missing inventory

- submitted false certifications about the accuracy of the segment's financial statements

- instructed the segment finance managers to not disclose the inaccuracies in inventory accounting to GCC's Internal Audit

- failed to reveal the inventory overstatement in reports to GCC executive management

GCC ultimately restated its financial statements for the periods 2008–2014. Stock market participants reacted to the restatements via downgrades in valuation, depicted as follows:

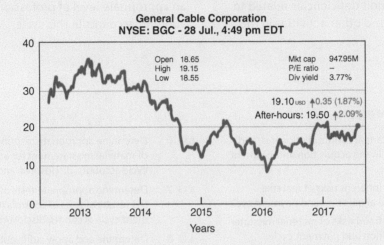

To track the company's stock, see *https://www.google.com/search?q=general+cable+corporation+stock+ticker&ie=utf-8&oe=utf-8*

GCC ultimately had to pay about $75 million to resolve investigations by both the SEC and the U.S. Department of Justice relating to its violations of the Foreign Corrupt Practices Act (FCPA); the company also had to pay another $6.5 million penalty to the SEC to settle accounting violations.

Deloitte has been the external auditor for GCC throughout the entire period. By FYE 2016, things seem to have turned around. Deloitte issued unqualified opinions on both the financial statements and the company's internal control.

For further details, see SEC AAER No. 3840 (December 29, 2016).

What Do You Think?   For Classroom Discussion

Review the *Why It Matters* feature at the beginning of the chapter. Copper theft is very common, both in the U.S. and abroad. Given that its value has more than quadrupled over the last decade—and it is a commodity that is hard to trace—it is a desirable target for thieves. There exist two main types of fraud in the acquisition and payment cycle with respect to inventory: (a) outright theft, and (2) financial reporting fraud, whereby managers seek to overstate net income by overstating ending inventory (and thus understating cost of goods sold).

Consider the control environment of the COSO Framework; which of these two types of fraud is worse from a shareholder's perspective?

Consider the control activities and monitoring components of the COSO Framework; what significant difficulties did top management at GCC encounter with respect to controlling the operations and financial reporting at the Brazilian subsidiary?

What are your thoughts about the stock valuation history of GCC? Notice that the share prices during the fraud period are quite a bit higher than the prices currently reported. Also, notice the stock market reaction to the revelation of the frauds, and consider the implications for shareholders.

What You Will Learn

- What are the significant accounts, disclosures, and relevant assertions in the acquisition and payment cycle? (LO 1)
- What are the inherent risks associated with transactions in the acquisition and payment cycle? (LO 2)
- What are fraud risks associated with the acquisition and payment cycle? (LO 3)

- What controls should management have in place to mitigate the risks associated with the acquisition and payment cycle? (LO 4)
- How might auditors use planning analytical procedures to identify any potential concerns related to the acquisition and payment cycle? (LO 5)
- What is sufficient appropriate evidence when auditing the acquisition and payment cycle? (LO 6, 7, 8)

LO 1

Identify the significant accounts, disclosures, and relevant assertions in the acquisition and payment cycle.

Significant Accounts, Disclosures, and Relevant Assertions

The significant accounts in the acquisition and payment cycle are inventory, cost of goods sold, accounts payable, and other related expense accounts. *Exhibit 11.1* contains an overview of the significant accounts typically included in this cycle.

Accounting for inventories is a major consideration for many organizations because of its significance to both the balance sheet and the income statement. **Inventories** are items of tangible property that are: (1) held for sale in the ordinary course of business, (2) in the process of production for such sale, or (3) to be used in the production of goods or services to be available for sale. For example, inventory includes such items as steel held for future production of an automobile, electronic goods in a retail store, drugs on shelves in a hospital or in a pharmaceutical company, and petroleum products at an oil-refining company. While the focus of this chapter concerns the purchase of inventory, organizations also purchase a variety of services (e.g., consulting and legal) and other goods (e.g., supplies).

Exhibit 11.1

Significant Accounts in the Acquisition and Payment Cycle

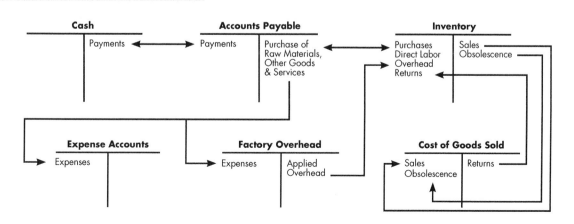

A major component of accounts payable relates to inventory purchases. When shipments of raw materials and finished goods are received and placed in inventory, this results in an account payable until payment is made. Accounts payable is also comprised of amounts owed to other suppliers (such as suppliers of electricity or other goods and services not used in production or resale).

Processing Transactions in the Acquisition and Payment Cycle

The acquisition and payment cycle consists of five distinct activities.

1. Requisition (request) for goods or services
2. Purchase of goods and services
3. Receipt of goods and services
4. Approval of items for payment
5. Cash disbursements

The acquisition process begins with a **requisition** (formal request) for goods and services. An approved requisition will result in a purchase. The receipt of goods or services should cause the recognition of accounts payable with debits to an expense account (e.g., legal expense) or an inventory account. Most companies have specific procedures for approving the payments for these purchases. When the company makes an approved payment for goods or services received, the payment is reflected as a cash disbursement.

For many companies, the acquisition and payment cycle is an automated process integrated with **supply chain management**. Supply chain management is the management and control of materials in the logistics process from the acquisition of raw materials to the delivery of finished products to the end user (customer). An **automated purchasing system** includes a networked software system linking to vendors whose offerings and prices supply chain management personnel have preapproved. The technology enables purchasers to negotiate favorable prices with vendors while streamlining the purchasing process. Best practice for an automated system consolidates the acquisition and

---

Why It Matters

Purchasing Cards as an Alternative to the Traditional Purchasing Process

This feature notes that some organizations use a purchasing card (P-card) that allows employees to make purchases without using the traditional purchasing process. If a client has significant purchasing activities with P-Cards, auditors should understand the client's risks and controls related to P-Cards.

The traditional purchasing process can be labor-intensive, costly, and lengthy. The average administrative cost for a purchase order is over $90, while the average time to complete a purchase transaction is over 30 days. The purchasing card (P-card) is a form of company charge card that is an alternative to the traditional purchasing process. Organizations issue P-cards to employees so that the employees can easily purchase low-dollar goods and services, thereby eliminating the need for various activities in the traditional purchasing process, including purchase requisitions, purchase

orders, and vendor invoices. Organizations using P-cards should implement a variety of controls, including dollar limits, merchant category code restrictions, and periodic reviews of P-card activity; employees receiving P-cards are expected to follow the organization's policies and procedures.

While P-cards provide benefits to organizations, their use is not without risks. The primary risk is intentional unauthorized use by employees, which is considered fraud. As an example, Georgia Institute of Technology issued a report about inappropriate use of P-cards by its employees, including employees using P-Cards to buy a jet ski, football tickets, a diamond ring, and wedding catering services.

For further details, see https://www.casewareanalytics.com /blog/state-georgia-under-fire-further-p-card-misuse

payment activities, assuring timely and accurate orders. An automated purchasing system will perform the following tasks:

- Apply preloaded specifications and materials lists to the system to start the process
- Automatically flag invoices that do not reconcile with purchase orders
- Create change orders and analyze variances from purchase orders

Assertions Relevant to Inventory

The five management assertions relevant to inventory are:

1. *Existence/occurrence*—Inventory balances exist at the balance sheet date.
2. *Completeness*—Inventory balances include all inventory transactions that have taken place during the period.
3. *Rights and obligations*—The organization has title to the inventory as of the balance sheet date.
4. *Valuation or allocation*—The recorded balances reflect the true underlying economic value of those assets.
5. *Presentation and disclosure*—Inventory is properly classified on the balance sheet and disclosed in the notes to the financial statements.

Thor Industries, Inc. and Mark Schwartzhoff: Fraudulent Reductions in Cost of Goods Sold Through Manipulation of Inventory

Focus on Fraud

This feature provides an interesting example of using inventory and cost of sales to fraudulently overstate net income.

On May 13, 2011, the Securities and Exchange Commission (SEC) filed settled enforcement actions against Thor Industries, Inc. and Mark Schwartzhoff, the former vice president of finance at Thor's Dutchmen Manufacturing subsidiary. Thor produces and sells recreational vehicles, and Dutchmen is one of Thor's 15 subsidiaries. During the period of the fraud, Schwartzhoff served as an internal auditor, controller, and ultimately vice president of finance, which was Dutchmen's most senior financial officer position.

From 2002 to January 2007, Schwartzhoff engaged in a fraudulent accounting scheme to understate Dutchmen's cost of goods sold in order to avoid recognizing rising inventory costs during the period. Schwartzhoff had access to all of Dutchmen's accounting systems and could make manual journal entries without authorization or meaningful review by anyone at either Dutchmen or Thor headquarters. Schwartzhoff perpetrated the fraud by making fictitious journal entries understating the cost of inventory purchases, thereby achieving lower cost of goods sold and higher net income. Schwartzhoff credited inventory purchases accounts and made offsetting debits to increase other assets or decrease liabilities. To hide the fraud, Schwartzhoff created fictitious documentation and reconciliations and submitted them to Thor's external auditor. He falsified inventory records to make it appear that ending inventory had increased when, in fact, it had not. Schwartzhoff also concealed the fraud by delaying the recruiting and hiring of the controller position at Dutchmen, and he assigned the duties of his subordinates so that he would retain the ability to continue perpetrating the fraud without detection. Thor headquarters did not supervise Schwartzhoff and did not conduct internal audits of Dutchmen.

The magnitude of the fraud grew from less than $1 million in 2003 to $14 million by 2006. Throughout the period of the fraud, pre-tax income was overstated by about $27 million. Despite this manipulation, Thor's auditor, Deloitte, issued unqualified audit opinions and agreed with management's assessment that internal controls were effective. Schwartzhoff perpetrated the fraud because it resulted in increased bonuses from his incentive compensation plan. His bonus was a percentage of pre-tax income, so by understating cost of goods sold he was able to show higher income, and thereby earn a larger bonus. Ultimately, he earned about $300,000 in excess, fraudulently derived, bonus compensation. Once the fraud was uncovered, Thor fired Schwartzhoff and restated its financial statements from 2004 to 2007. Following the discovery of the fraud, Thor also reported a material weakness in its internal controls relating to the conduct of Schwartzhoff.

Thor was fined $1 million. Schwartzhoff was permanently barred from serving as an officer or director of a public company and was fined $394,830 by the SEC. He was also convicted of one count of wire fraud and had to pay restitution to the U.S. Attorney's Office for the Northern District of Indiana for $1.9 million.

For further details, see SEC Litigation Release No. 21966 (May 13, 2011).

What Do You Think? **For Classroom Discussion**

Consider the elements of the fraud triangle from the perspective of Schwartzhoff's activities described in the *Focus on Fraud* feature above. What were Schwartzhoff's likely incentives, opportunities, and rationalizations?

Are you surprised that despite the accounting manipulation, Thor's auditor, Deloitte, issued an unqualified audit opinion and agreed with management's assessment that internal controls were effective? Should investors have expected Deloitte to detect this misstatement?

The existence and valuation assertions are usually the most relevant for inventory. Existence is a concern because, as the Thor Industries, Inc. and Schwartzhoff example from the *Focus on Fraud* feature illustrates, managers can manipulate the inventory account to manipulate cost of goods sold and net income. Valuation of inventory is a concern because inventory may fluctuate in value, and there may be complexities in assessing an accurate value. Rights and obligations can also be a concern; even though a company possesses inventory, that does not necessarily imply the company owns it.

We do not separately discuss assertions for cost of goods sold. Recall that cost of goods sold is simply the result of the following calculation: *beginning inventory + purchases − ending inventory = cost of goods sold*. The most common concerns for inventory are that purchases are understated or ending inventory is overstated, which will result in both lower cost of goods sold and higher net income. The diagram below illustrates how the overstatement of ending inventory yields fraudulently overstated gross margin and net income.

	Fraudulent	**Truthful**	
Revenue	100	100	
− Cost of Goods Sold:			
Beginning Inventory	50	50	
+ Purchases	20	20	
−Ending Inventory	**40**	**20** ◄——— The fraud
= COGS	30	50	
Revenue − COGS = Gross Margin	**70**	**50** ◄——— The result
− Operating Expenses	10	10	
= Net income	**60**	**40** ◄——— The result

Assertions Relevant to Accounts Payable

The five management assertions relevant to accounts payable are:

1. *Existence/occurrence*—Accounts payable balances exist at the balance sheet date.
2. *Completeness*—Accounts payable balances include all accounts payable transactions that have taken place during the period.
3. *Rights and obligations*—The organization actually owes a liability for the accounts payable as of the balance sheet date.
4. *Valuation or allocation*—The recorded balances reflect the true underlying economic value of those liabilities.
5. *Presentation and disclosure*—Accounts payable is properly classified on the balance sheet and disclosed in the notes to the financial statements.

11-1 The existence and presentation/disclosure assertions are usually the most relevant for inventory.   (T/F)

11-2 The most common concerns for inventory are that purchases are understated or ending inventory is overstated, both of which will result in lower cost of goods sold and higher net income.   (T/F)

11-3 Which of the following activities is <u>not</u> an activity associated with the acquisition and payment cycle?
   a.   Receive a customer purchase order.
   b.   Purchase of goods and services.
   c.   Receipt of goods and services.
   d.   Approval of items for payment.

11-4 Which of the following tasks will an automated purchasing system perform?
   a.   Apply preloaded specifications and materials lists to the system to start the process.
   b.   Automatically flag invoices that do not reconcile with purchase orders.
   c.   Create change orders and analyze variances from purchase orders.
   d.   All of the above.

Completeness is usually the most relevant assertion for accounts payable. The primary concern is that the account is understated; managers may not record accounts payable transactions because they do not want to record the associated liability and expense.

An Overview of the Audit Opinion Formulation Process in the Acquisition and Payment Cycle

In auditing the acquisition and payment cycle, the auditor will perform risk assessment procedures, tests of controls, and substantive procedures—Phases II, III, and IV of the audit opinion formulation process.

As part of performing risk assessment procedures, the auditor obtains information to assess the risk of material misstatement. This includes information about inherent risks at the financial statement level (e.g., client's business and operational risks, financial reporting risks) and at the account and assertion levels, fraud risks including feedback from the audit team's brainstorming sessions, strengths and weaknesses in internal control, and results from planning analytical procedures.

Once the risks of material misstatement have been identified, the auditor then determines how best to respond to them. For an integrated audit and for a financial statement audit where the auditor wants to rely on controls as part of the basis for the audit opinion, the auditor will perform tests of controls and consider the effect of those tests on the substantive evidence to obtain. In other audits, the auditor will rely only on substantive tests to obtain evidence about the accuracy of the financial statements.

LO 2

Identify and assess inherent risks of material misstatement in the acquisition and payment cycle.

Identifying Inherent Risks

Inventory is usually material, complex, and subject to manipulation, because of the following factors:

- A great variety (diversity) of items exists in inventory.
- Inventory accounts typically experience a high volume of activity.
- Inventory accounts may be valued according to various alternative accounting valuation methods.

- Identifying obsolete inventory and applying the lower of cost or market principle to determine valuation are difficult tasks.
- Inventory is easily transportable.
- Inventory often exists at multiple locations, with some locations being remote from the company's headquarters.

In terms of accounts payable and related expense accounts, the auditor should consider the inherent risk that management is more likely to: (1) understate, rather than overstate, expenses and payables, and (2) classify expense items as assets.

Prompt for Critical Thinking #1　　　　It's Your Turn!

Provide examples of other factors that could lead to a high level of inherent risk related to inventory.

- _____
- _____
- _____
- _____
- _____

Check Your Basic Knowledge

11-5　The audit of inventory can be complex because inventory is easily transportable, exists at multiple locations, may become obsolete, and may be difficult to value.　(T/F)

11-6　Two important complexities in auditing inventory arise because inventory accounts experience a high volume of activity and are valued according to various inventory valuation methods.　(T/F)

11-7　Which of the following is a common inherent risk relating to accounts payable and related expenses?

a. Management would generally prefer to record assets as expenses.

b. Because of debt covenants requiring that the client maintain a certain level of the current ratio, management may prefer to understate accounts payable.

c. Ending inventory balances may be valued according to various accounting valuation methods.

d. Because of the lower of cost or market requirements, it may be difficult to value accounts payable.

11-8　Which of the following is not an inherent risk relating to inventory?

a. Sales contracts may contain unusual terms, and revenue recognition is often complex.

b. Inventory accounts typically experience a high volume of activity.

c. Inventory accounts may be valued according to various accounting valuation methods.

d. Identifying obsolete inventory and applying the lower of cost or market principle to determine valuation are difficult.

LO 3

Identify and assess fraud risks of material misstatement in the acquisition and payment cycle.

Identifying Fraud Risks

Because of the significant number of inherent risks noted previously, the acquisition and payment cycle is often the subject of fraud. Financial reporting frauds in this cycle often involve overstatement of inventory or assets and understatement of expenses. Asset misappropriation frauds in this cycle often involve fictitious purchases or kickbacks to suppliers. Examples of fraud in the acquisition and payment cycle include:

- Theft of inventory by the employee
- **Inventory shrinkage,** which is a reduction in inventory presumed to be due to physical loss or theft
- Employee schemes involving **vendor fraud,** which include schemes involving improper payments to real or fictitious vendors; vendor fraud can occur through an internal employee or employees (i.e., collusion), through an outside vendor, or through collusion between an outside vendor and an internal employee(s)
- Employees recording fictitious inventory or inappropriately recording higher values for existing inventory by creating false records for items that do not exist (e.g., inflated inventory count sheets and bogus receiving reports or purchase orders)
- Large manual adjustments to inventory accounts
- Schemes to classify expenses as assets (e.g., inappropriately capitalizing items that are truly current-period expenses)
- Executives misusing travel and entertainment accounts and charging them as company expenses

Exhibit 11.2 identifies some of the possible fraudulent financial reporting methods used in manipulating inventory and cost of goods sold.

Exhibit 11.2

Methods of Fraudulent Financial Reporting in Inventory and Cost of Goods Sold

Event	Affected Accounts	Possible Manipulations
1. Purchase inventory	Inventory, accounts payable	Under-record purchases Record purchases in a later period Fail to record purchases
2. Return inventory to supplier	Accounts payable, inventory	Overstate returns Record returns in an earlier period
3. Inventory is sold	Cost of goods sold, inventory	Record at too low an amount Not record cost of goods sold nor reduce inventory
4. Inventory becomes obsolete	Loss on write-down of inventory, inventory	Fail to write off or write down obsolete inventory
5. Periodic count of inventory quantities	Inventory shrinkage, inventory	Overcount inventory (double counting, etc.)

Focus on Fraud

Financial Reporting Fraud in the Acquisition and Payment Cycle at WorldCom and Phar-Mor

This feature provides details on two well-known frauds in the acquisition and payment cycle.

WorldCom

WorldCom management recorded billions of line rental expenses as fixed assets. In other words, managers inappropriately debited fixed assets rather than debiting expenses, thereby bolstering current-period income. Managers were motivated to engage in the fraud to meet earnings expectations and to show that they were able to manage their line expenses better than the rest of the industry. Because the expenses were consistent with previous years, their relatively low level did not raise auditor suspicion. In this case, the auditors should have been skeptical that WorldCom was able to achieve what other companies in its industry could not.

Phar-Mor

Phar-Mor, a major discount retailer, had over 300 stores in the 1990s with great operating results and a concept that captured the imagination of Wall Street. Typical of many frauds, the company was dominated by an officer who viewed the company as his own and diverted more than $10 million to support a now failed minor league basketball team. To cover up this misuse of company money, the officers directed the managers of each store to inflate their inventory costs. For example, if a carton of Coca-Cola cost $1.99, they were to value it at $2.99. Company management was emboldened to commit the fraud because they knew that the auditor would not visit all 300 stores to test inventory valuation.

Check Your Basic Knowledge

11-9 One of the common ways that managers have committed fraud in the acquisition and payment cycle involves inappropriately classifying assets (e.g., inventory) as expenses. (T/F)

11-10 The following are possible manipulations that may occur when employees perpetrate fraud during the purchase of inventory: under-recording purchases, recording purchases in a later period, and not recording purchases. (T/F)

11-11 Which of the following is an example of fraud in the acquisition and payment cycle?
a. Theft of inventory by an employee.
b. Employee schemes involving fictitious vendors as means to transfer payments to themselves.

c. Executives recording fictitious inventory or inappropriately recording higher values for existing inventory.
d. All of the above.

11-12 Refer to *Exhibit 11.2* to identify the possible inventory or cost of goods sold manipulation that might occur when inventory is sold.
a. Overstate returns.
b. Overcount inventory.
c. Not record cost of goods sold nor reduce inventory.
d. Under-record purchases

LO 4

Identify and assess control risks of material misstatement in the acquisition and payment cycle.

Identifying Control Risks

Once the auditor has obtained an understanding of the inherent and fraud risks of material misstatement in the acquisition and payment cycle, the auditor needs to understand the controls that the client has designed and implemented to address those risks. Remember, the auditor is required to gain an understanding of internal controls for both integrated audits and financial statement only audits. The auditor typically obtains this understanding by means of a walkthrough of the process, inquiry, observation, and review of the client's documentation. The auditor considers both entity-wide controls and transaction controls at the account and assertion levels. This understanding provides the auditor with a basis for making an initial control risk assessment for each relevant account and assertion.

At the entity-wide level, the auditor considers the control environment, including such principles as commitment to financial accounting competencies and the independence of the board of directors. The auditor will also consider the remaining components of internal control that are typically entity-wide—risk assessment, information and communication, and monitoring controls. Although the auditor needs to understand all the components of internal control, the auditor typically finds it useful to focus on significant control activities in the acquisition and payment cycle. As part of this understanding, the auditor focuses on the relevant assertions for each account and identifies the controls that relate to risks for these assertions. In an integrated audit or in a financial statement only audit where the auditor relies on controls, the auditor uses this understanding to identify important controls that need to be tested.

Overview of Internal Controls in the Acquisition and Payment Cycle

The auditor usually begins by developing an understanding of the cost components of inventory and by considering how current market prices affect inventory valuation. We focus on the inventories of a manufacturing client. A well-conceived inventory control system should provide reasonable assurance that:

- All purchases are authorized.
- There exists a timely, accurate, and complete recording of inventory transactions.
- Receipt of inventory is properly accounted for and independently tested to verify quality in adherence to company standards.
- The cost accounting system is up-to-date; costs are properly identified and assigned to products; and variances are analyzed, investigated, and properly allocated to inventory and cost of goods sold.

Management may use two types of inventory systems for reporting purposes and for assisting in inventory management:

- A **periodic inventory system** is a system of inventory recordkeeping in which management does not keep a continuous record of changes in inventory (receipts, uses, sales of inventory items). At the end of an accounting period, management determines the ending inventory by a physical count of every item, and computes its value using a suitable method.
- A **perpetual inventory system** is a system of inventory recordkeeping where book inventory is continuously in agreement with inventory on hand within specified time periods. In some systems, book inventory and inventory on hand may be reconciled with each transaction; in other systems, these two numbers may be reconciled less often. This process is useful in keeping track of availability of goods and determining the correct time to reorder from suppliers. **Cycle counts** are part of a perpetual inventory system. Cycle counts involve periodic testing of the accuracy of the perpetual inventory record by counting all inventories on a cyclical, or periodic, basis.

Other controls in this cycle include:

- Assigned employees systematically review all products for obsolescence, and follow up with appropriate accounting action.
- Management periodically reviews inventory, takes action on excessive inventory, and manages inventory to minimize losses caused by technological obsolescence.

- Market studies and quality-control tests are performed before new products are introduced.
- Assigned employees closely monitor long-term contracts and excess purchase requirements, and follow up with appropriate accounting action (e.g., recognize potential losses).

The specific controls implemented by the client will vary with the extent of automation of the process. The following discussion highlights typical controls for each of the five activities in the acquisition and payment cycle.

1. Requisition (Request) for Goods and Services The acquisition process for inventory begins with the company's production or sales plan. Some companies will have long-term production plans. For example, in the automotive industry a manufacturer might schedule production for a month in advance and notify its suppliers of the production plan. The auditor must thoroughly understand the company's relationships with its suppliers and should examine major contracts that specify delivery, quantity, timing, and quality conditions. The traditional acquisition process begins with recognizing the need for the purchase—either by an individual or by an automated process that monitors inventory or production.

Embedded in the requisition process are controls to provide assurance that appropriate employees have properly approved all purchases. Typically, a department supervisor prepares a requisition request and obtains approval for the request. A requisition request is an internal document requesting the purchase of goods or services. An employee in the accounting area often serves as the approver. Some departments may have authority for individual purchases up to a specific dollar limit.

The purchase of supplies will go through a similar process as inventory purchases. Purchases of services, such as legal or consulting services, rely on ongoing approved contractual arrangements with the service providers.

2. Purchase of Goods and Services Approved requisitions are sent to the individual or department responsible for making purchases. Once the purchasing department has received an approved requisition, it issues a purchase order to the vendor. A **purchase order** is a legally binding document between a supplier and a buyer. It details the items the buyer agrees to purchase at a certain price point. It also outlines the delivery date and terms of payment for the buyer. Purchase orders are typically created using electronic purchasing systems, which enable businesses to track purchase orders and submit them electronically. Prenumbered purchase orders are used to establish the uniqueness of each order and the completeness of the purchase order population. The receiving department uses the purchase order to determine whether to accept a shipment of goods. The accounting department uses the purchase order to verify that a purchase was authorized and that the vendor's invoice is correct.

Requisitions and purchase orders are important controls in the acquisition and payment cycle. An efficient approach is an electronic system that integrates easily with other financial systems. Organizations that use electronic systems instead of relying on Excel and email to create, share, and track these documents often see a reduction in costs, greater control over company expenditures, and more streamlined processes.

Organizations face several risks related to purchasing. A significant risk is that purchasing agents may enter into kickback arrangements with vendors. Controls to mitigate this risk include requiring competitive bids for large purchases and rotating purchasing agents across product lines. Perhaps the most important control is an authorized vendor database. Company employees cannot purchase from vendors other than those in the database, thereby making it difficult to set up fictitious vendors.

Other important purchasing controls include approval supplier contracts, restricted access to the relevant computer programs, a bidding process for large

Exhibit 11.3
Overview of Common Controls in the Requisition
and Purchasing Processes

Inventory Purchases: Manufacturing Organization

- Written requisitions are made for specific products by the production manager or stockroom manager.
- Computer-generated requisitions are generated based on current inventory levels and production plans.

Inventory Purchases: Retail Organization

- Overall authorization to purchase product lines is delegated to individual buyers by the marketing manager. The authorization is built into the computer as a control. The limits for individual goods can be exceeded only on specific approval by the marketing manager.
- Store managers may be granted authority to purchase a limited number of goods. The store manager's ability to issue a purchase order may be subject to overall corporate limits, usually specified in dollars.
- The supplier may have access to the retailer's inventory database and, by contract, ship replacement merchandise based on sales activity and reorder points.

Inventory Purchases: Just-in-Time Manufacturing Process

- An agreement is signed with the supplier whereby the supplier agrees to ship merchandise (just in time) according to the production schedule set by the manufacturer. A long-term supply contract is negotiated specifying price, quality of products, estimated quantities, penalties for product shortages or quality problems, and so forth. Specific purchase orders are not issued; rather, the production plan is communicated to the supplier with the specified delivery dates. The production plan serves as the requisition.

Supplies Purchases

- Requisitions are issued by individual departments and sent to the appropriate department manager for approval.
- Each department may be given a budget for supplies and may have the ability to issue purchase orders directly for the needed items or may be able to purchase a limited number of items without a purchase order.

---

purchases, and monitoring of inventory and purchase levels by management. Some services, such as auditing services, will have additional controls, including review and approval by the audit committee.

Exhibit 11.3 provides an overview of controls over the requisition and purchasing processes at different types of organizations and for different types of purchases.

In some automated purchasing systems, the organization digitally communicates the purchase order to the vendor, according to pre-existing contracts with no additional review by the purchasing department. For example, General Motors (GM) collaborated with Eaton Corporation who furnished already-assembled subassemblies that GM loaded directly into the production line. This kind of relationship requires close coordination and may never involve a requisition request or purchase order. It may involve only the development of a long-term contract and the sharing of production schedules with the supplier. In the GM case, GM receives the goods and moves them directly into production. GM pays Eaton Corporation upon the production of an automobile.

With its automated process, GM will likely have implemented automated controls, such as: (1) a maximum quantity that can be ordered within a given time period, (2) a minimum amount of previous usage during a specified time period, and (3) a required review by a purchasing agent for some accounts or for high-dollar levels.

Focus on Fraud

Weak Internal Controls, Unethical Decisions, and a Fictitious Vendor at Baird Products

This feature provides an example in which weak controls led to a fraud at a company that manufactures metal parts for the automotive parts products industry.

Baird Products manufactures metal parts for the automotive parts products industry. Robert Grant was the manager in charge of the metal-casting department, and he reported to Linda Thompson, the facility manager. Thompson trusted Grant and relied on his judgment and honesty. However, Grant developed a lavish lifestyle that included gambling; he also had three college-age children to support.

The purchasing process and controls at Baird were uncomplicated. All purchase requests were to be approved by the department manager and then sent to the accounting department for issuance of the purchase order. The accounting department would then determine whether the purchase was within the budget and whether the vendor was on an approved list. Although the accounting department required that approved vendors provide a company name, address, telephone number, and principal contact, it did no actual verification of the vendors, a control weakness that Grant learned about and ultimately exploited.

Grant's fraud began with suppliers for products in his department. He began requiring vendors to provide him with money and gifts in order to maintain their sales volume at Baird; vendors that refused risked being shut out of business with Baird. Later, the fraud grew larger when he required all the vendors that he dealt with to pay him a commission on their sales to Baird that

essentially amounted to a bribe. Vendors feared losing sales if they did not comply, so they did not report this practice to Thompson or other members of management. The fraud grew still larger when Grant set up a fictitious vendor (RGWB, Inc.), and embezzled nearly $200,000 over about 18 months. The fraud was finally discovered when Grant became ill and another employee took over his job during his absence. Baird fired Grant and brought criminal charges against him, but Grant fled and never faced justice. Baird learned the following lessons from this fraud:

- Even though controls are in place, they are sometimes not followed or they are followed incompletely; if employees understand this control weakness, they may exploit it.

- Companies need to have fraud hotlines where employees, vendors, and third parties can report inappropriate activity without fear of retaliation.

- Controls must be strong in the purchasing area, and there should be adequate segregation of duties of individuals who place orders versus individuals who select vendors, compare prices, and make the orders. Further, adequate supervision and knowledge of vendors is a vital job for top management.

- For ongoing frauds to remain undetected, it is often necessary for the employee(s) involved to be in a position to continue the fraud on a daily basis. Mandating vacations for all employees can be a useful control in trying to prevent and detect fraud.

What Do You Think?

For Classroom Discussion

Consider the *Focus on Fraud* feature "Weak Internal Controls, Unethical Decisions, and a Fictitious Vendor at Baird Products." Grant's supervisor trusted Grant and relied on his judgment and honesty. Many frauds occur because of a trusting relationship, coupled with a lack of effective controls.

Employees who seem honest and trustworthy sometimes violate that trust. Anyone in a position with control over monetary

resources needs to be treated with professional skepticism, both by the company and by its auditors.

Why might it be difficult to maintain your professional skepticism when you have worked with a client employee for many years and you have grown to trust that person? What actions or perspectives could you take to guard against trusting an employee too much?

A variation of the system-generated purchase order is the electronic consignment system used by some retailers. For example, Wal-Mart encourages its partners to monitor store activities, inventory levels, and current trends in sales and authorizes the vendor to ship additional goods to stores when inventory levels decrease. However, the trade-off is that the partner—for example, Levi Strauss—maintains ownership of its product until a consumer purchases it. When the consumer brings the jeans to the checkout counter, the ownership transfers to Wal-Mart and then immediately to the consumer. The accounting system captures the sales information by recording the sale, as well as the cost of goods sold and a payable to Levi Strauss. The contract between the trading partners also specifies controls to assure that Wal-Mart acknowledges receipt of goods and takes steps to assure that the goods are not subject to damage, theft, or loss.

3. Receipt of Goods and Services Receiving departments should make sure that: (1) the department accepts only authorized goods, (2) the goods meet order specifications, (3) an accurate count of the goods received is taken, and (4) accountability is established to assure that all receipts are recorded. Methods of recording the receipt of goods include:

- The receiving department prepares prenumbered receiving documents to record all receipts.
- The receiving department electronically scans bar codes on the goods received to record quantity and vendor and then visually inspects the goods for quality. The information system prepares a sequentially numbered receiving record for goods scanned in.
- Departments may receive goods directly, such as office supplies, and must approve payment for the merchandise.
- Goods are received directly into the production process. The vendor is paid according to the long-term contract based on the purchaser's actual production, and the vendor is penalized for production delays that are due to failures to deliver the goods.

The traditional receiving process creates a prenumbered receiving document based on a count of the merchandise received. A copy of the purchase order (usually with quantities blanked out to help assure an independent count of the goods received) is reviewed to determine whether a shipment is authorized. Prenumbered receiving documents establish the completeness of the population and are useful in determining that all goods are recorded in the correct period.

Automated scanning can improve both control and efficiency of the receiving process. Products shipped with bar codes can be directly scanned into the system. Actual receipts can be automatically matched with purchase orders to determine if the shipment contains errors. Goods received into production must match the production process. If they do not, then there is a potential problem of the production line either shutting down or producing the wrong subcomponents. For example, if Eaton fails to deliver the correct subassembly to GM, the production line will shut down and GM will know the cause. Although this is not a traditional accounting control, it is very effective because any failure immediately gets the attention of management and the vendor. Therefore, there is strong motivation to avoid any mistakes.

As auditors increasingly encounter these integrated order, delivery, and payment supply chain management systems, they have to consider the types of controls that should be present. *Exhibit 11.4* provides an overview of controls in traditional receiving systems and in more automated systems. Regardless of the approach taken in the receiving function, the auditor must gain reasonable assurance that management has effective controls related to receiving.

Exhibit 11.4
Comparison of Controls in Traditional and Automated Systems

Traditional Receiving System	Automated Integrated Receiving System
Purchase orders are prepared and sent to vendors.	Long-term contract is signed with vendor specifying: • Quality • Shipping and delivery requirements • Payment terms • Penalties for performance failures • Reconciliations between trading partners for goods shipped/received
Purchase orders are based on projected sales or production, or current inventory levels.	Quantities are based on production plans or sales programs. Quantities and delivery times are updated monthly or more frequently depending on scheduling and shipping constraints.
Price is either negotiated or competitively bid among a number of vendors.	Price is locked in with a preferred vendor.
Independent receiving function exists.	Goods are delivered to production line.
Independent, sequentially numbered receiving documents are prepared to provide evidence that the goods are received.	Disruptions of production provide evidence that goods were not delivered.
Accounts payable department matches purchase order, receiving document, and invoice and accrues accounts payable.	Accruals are set up based on contract (production, sales of goods, etc.).
Payments are made via check or by electronic transfer once or twice a month.	Payments are electronically transferred to vendor based on contractual terms.
Differences between goods received and goods ordered are identified before payments are made.	Processes are described in the contract to resolve difference between goods received and goods that were shipped by vendor.

4. Approval of Items for Payment Approval for payment typically involves a **three-way match** among the vendor invoice, the purchase order, and the receiving report to determine whether the vendor's invoice is correct and should be paid. This process can be automated or manual. If all items on the three documents properly match, the vendor's invoice is set up as an account payable with a scheduled payment date. The purchasing agent reviews all discrepancies. The supporting documentation and authorization are then presented to the accounts payable department for payment. Internal controls should assure that all items are recorded in a timely manner, that the authorization process includes a review of documents, and that supporting documentation is cancelled on payment to avoid duplicate payments.

The manual matching approach is labor-intensive and error prone. The automated matching approach can be more efficient. Purchase orders are entered into a purchase order database that is accessed by the receiving department to determine whether an incoming shipment of goods should be accepted. The receiving department electronically records the receipt of goods through scanning the bar code or other means and cross-references the receipt to the purchase order. The computerized application matches the three documents (purchase order, receiving document, and vendor invoice), and if the three-way match is within a prespecified tolerance limit, the invoice is approved for payment. A payment date is scheduled, and a check is automatically generated on the scheduled date and is signed using an authorized signature plate. The complete payment process occurs without any apparent human intervention. There is no authorized reviewer, no physical matching, and no individual physically signing the checks. In some systems, the payment may be transferred electronically to the vendor.

The lack of human intervention is compensated for by control procedures and authorization concepts built into the automated system such as:

- *Authorized vendors*—Purchases can be made only from authorized vendors.
- *Restricted access*—Access is restricted to databases, in particular to the vendor database and the purchasing database. Anyone with the ability to add a vendor or make unauthorized purchase orders is in a position to set up fictitious vendors and purchases. Therefore, someone outside the purchasing department should maintain the vendor database (a list of authorized vendors).
- *Automatic processes*—Although the receiving department has access to the purchase order (read-only), the use of automatic scanners and other counting devices decreases counting and identification errors.
- *Reconciliations inherent in the process*—Most retailers mark retail prices on the goods at the distribution center when they are received. The retail price tickets for an order can be generated from the purchase order. The actual number of tickets used should be reconciled with the goods received, and any leftover tickets should be an adjustment made to the receiving report.
- *Automation of error-prone activities*—Vendor invoices are traditionally entered into the system by accounts payable personnel, thereby segregating this process from the other two functions. An alternative is to receive invoices electronically. It is still important that purchasing and receiving not have the ability to enter vendor invoice data or access the vendor invoice file.
- *Restricted access to transferring funds*—Access to physical checks, or authorization of electronic cash transfers, is limited to the appropriate, designated individuals.
- *Monitoring*—Activity reports are prepared on a regular basis for management review.

Because most of the control procedures are developed during the system design process, it is important that users and internal auditors actively participate in reviewing the effectiveness of controls designed into the computer application.

5. Cash Disbursements

In a manual system, an authorized employee reviews the completeness of the documentation supporting a request for cash disbursement and signs a check for payment of goods or services. In most automated systems, the checks, or electronic transfers, are generated automatically according to the scheduled payment date, and the supporting documents are cancelled when the invoice is set up for payment.

Important controls in these systems are: (1) review of transactions, by which someone reviews the expenditures and compares them to other key data (e.g., production, budgets, other measures of volume) and (2) review of vendor disputes by someone outside the process.

Focus on Fraud   Controls to Prevent and Detect Vendor Fraud

This feature discusses vendor fraud, including how organizations can prevent and detect it.

What is a vendor? A vendor (also known as a supplier) is an organization that sells goods or services to another party. Vendor fraud includes schemes involving improper payments to real or fictitious vendors; vendor fraud can occur through an internal employee or employees (i.e., collusion), through an outside vendor, or through collusion between an outside vendor and an internal employee.

The AICPA provides the following guidelines to organizations about how to prevent and detect vendor fraud (see AICPA *Forensic and Valuation Services Quarterly Report on Fraud Trends and Topics*, Spring 2017, Issue 3). The auditor should ensure that clients are following these guidelines; the auditor might apply data analytics tools when testing these controls.

1. Perform appropriate due diligence when selecting new vendors.

   - Compare a vendor's address to the employee address master file.
   - Check the vendor's address to ensure that it actually exists.
   - Ensure that the vendor's address makes sense (i.e., an actual business location versus a simple post office box).
   - Verify the vendor's business registration, tax identification, website, and phone numbers.
   - Conduct a search of the existing vendor database to ensure that the vendor really is a new vendor and not a variation of an existing vendor.

2. Ensure segregation of duties.

   - Different employees should approve a new vendor and input the new vendor to the master list; failing to do so yields the risk of fictitious vendors.

   - Different employees should process invoices from and payments to vendors.
   - Different employees should process vendor payments and reconcile bank statements.
   - If a company is too small to enact these controls, the manager should carefully review and monitor these duties, and make it clear to the subordinate that he or she is doing so in a timely and repetitive manner.

3. Use data analytics to your advantage.

   - Run queries and reports on vendor invoices received, vendor payments made, vendor information changes (e.g., changes in address), and watch for duplicate invoices paid on the same day or to the same vendor, and/or the use of the same purchase order on multiple payments.
   - Test contract terms against invoices, e.g., ensure that total payments made to a vendor do not exceed a contractual limit.
   - Test for duplicate payments.
   - Test for orders placed or payments made outside of normal business hours (e.g., in the middle of the night, during holidays, or on weekends).

4. Provide training to all employees with respect to vendor fraud, and the organization's commitment to prevent and detect it; this serves as a warning to potential fraudsters.

5. Establish a fraud hotline. Doing so enables employees to report suspicious activity, and enables vendors who are being coerced by purchasing agents to report their situation to the organization.

Documenting Controls

Auditors need to document their understanding of internal controls for both integrated audits and financial statement only audits. *Exhibit 11.5* provides an example of a partial internal control questionnaire for the acquisition and payment cycle. Each negative *(no)* answer in the questionnaire represents a potential internal control deficiency. Given a negative answer, the auditor should consider

Exhibit 11.5
Control Risk Assessment Questionnaire: Acquisition and Payment Cycle

	Check (x) one:	
	Yes	No
1. Are purchases of inventory approved at the proper level?	_____	_____
2. Is there adequate documentation of approvals?	_____	_____
3. Are purchase orders prenumbered and accounted for?	_____	_____
4. Are purchases of inventory made from an approved vendor list?	_____	_____
5. Are changes to the approved vendor list approved at the proper level?	_____	_____
6. Does the company have a formal policy and appropriate oversight about the nature of appropriate vendor relationships and gifts?	_____	_____
7. Are controls over the process of handling returned goods adequate?	_____	_____
8. Is the recording of purchases made in a timely manner?	_____	_____
9. Is the recording of returns made in a timely manner?	_____	_____

Check Your Basic Knowledge

11-13 A well-conceived inventory control system should provide reasonable assurance that all purchases are authorized and that inventory transactions are recorded accurately, completely, and in a timely manner.   (T/F)

11-14 Because a purchase order is an external document, its level of reliability is generally higher than that of a requisition, which is an internal document.   (T/F)

11-15 Refer to *Exhibit 11.3* to identify which of the following is a typical control associated with the requisition process for inventory purchases in a just-in-time manufacturing process.

a. The store manager's ability to issue a purchase order may be subject to overall corporate limits, usually specified in dollars.

b. An agreement is signed with the supplier whereby the supplier agrees to ship merchandise according to the production schedule set by the manufacturer.

c. Overall authorization to purchase product lines is delegated to individual buyers by the marketing manager.

d. The limits for individual goods can be exceeded only on specific approval by the marketing manager.

11-16 Which of the following controls is related to the payment of inventory purchases?

a. Cycle counts.

b. A disclosure committee.

c. A three-way match.

d. Both a. and c.

the effect of the response on the initial assessment of control risk. Unless another control compensates for a control deficiency, the auditor will likely have a control risk assessment of high in this area and, therefore, have to rely more on substantive audit procedures.

Performing Planning Analytical Procedures

LO 5

Describe how to use planning analytical procedures to identify possible material misstatements in acquisition and payment cycle accounts, disclosures, and assertions.

Planning analytical procedures help auditors identify areas of potential material misstatements. The objective of planning analytical procedures is to identify accounts with heightened risk of misstatement during audit planning to provide a basis for designing and implementing responses to the assessed risks. Planning analytical procedures can be relatively imprecise.

As initially described in *Chapter 6*, the steps that the auditor will take are as follows:

1. Determine the suitability of a particular analytical procedure for given account(s)/assertion(s), considering the risks of material misstatement and tests of details planned.
2. Evaluate the reliability of data that the auditor is using to develop an expectation of account balances or ratios. In evaluating data reliability, the auditor should consider the source of the data, its comparability, the nature of information available about the data, and the controls over the preparation of the data.
3. Develop an expectation of recorded account balances or ratios and evaluate whether that expectation is precise enough to accomplish the relevant objective.
4. Define when the difference between the auditor's expectation and what the client has recorded would be considered significant.
5. Compare the client's recorded amounts with the auditor's expectation to determine any significant unexpected differences.
6. Investigate significant unexpected differences. Significant unexpected differences suggest that substantive procedures for the account/assertion will be increased.
7. Ensure that the following have been appropriately documented: auditor's expectation from *Step 3*, including the factors that the auditor considered in developing the expectation, the results in *Step 4*, and the audit procedures conducted relating to *Steps 5* and *6*.

Step 1: Identify Suitable Analytical Procedures

In this transaction cycle, auditors will calculate and analyze the dollar and percent change in inventory, cost of goods sold, and expense account balances relative to both past performance and industry performance. The auditor can disaggregate this analysis by product line or location. A common-sized income statement can help identify cost of goods sold or expense accounts that are out of line with the auditor's expectations. The auditor will base expectation on prior years, industry information, and the auditor's knowledge of the business. *Exhibit 11.6* presents examples of additional planning analytical procedures that the auditor might consider relevant for acquisition and payment cycle accounts.

Step 2: Evaluate Reliability of Data Used to Develop Expectations

Various factors can influence reliability of data in acquisition and payment cycle accounts during planning analytical procedures. One is the source of information that is available. Information is generally more reliable when it is obtained from independent sources outside the company. For example, obtaining outside evidence of the number of days' sales in inventory in the company's industry would be considered more reliable data than simply using a historical trend of

Exhibit 11.6

Using Ratios and Trends Analyses in Planning Analytical
Procedures in the Acquisition and Payment Cycle

Inventory Ratios

- Gross margin analysis
- Inventory turnover (cost of goods sold/ending inventory)
- Number of days' sales in inventory (365/inventory turnover)
- Shrinkage ratio (inventory write-down/ending inventory)
- Inventory per square foot of retail space (for retail clients; and comparisons should be made across locations in stores of comparable size and product mix to test for unexpected differences)
- Inventory overhead application. Analyze the relationship between materials, labor, and overhead to total product costing; compare over time and across product categories.
- Consider trends in the above ratios.

Accounts Payable Ratios

- Accounts payable turnover (purchases/average accounts payable)
- Days outstanding in accounts payable (365/accounts payable turnover)
- Accounts payable/current liabilities
- Purchase returns and allowances/purchases
- Consider trends in the above ratios

the company's own day's sales data, without regard to industry considerations. Another factor influencing reliability of data is comparability. The auditor should consider whether the company's data may differ in an expected way from the overall industry. For example, the company's shrinkage ratio may not be comparable to the overall industry if the company has a particularly stable type of inventory that is not likely subject to theft.

Step 3: Develop Expectations

Developing expectations about relationships in the data is important to identifying accounts with heightened risk of material misstatement during audit planning. Expectations are based on the auditor's knowledge of the client and the industry. Assume that the client's production and pricing strategies have remained the same during the past year. In this case, the auditor would expect gross margin to be stable and consistent with the industry average.

Step 4 and Step 5: Define and Identify Significant Unexpected Differences

Step 4 requires the auditor to define the difference (between the auditor's expectation and what the client has recorded) that would be considered significant; this will require consideration of the auditor's assessed materiality level and the auditor's desired level of assurance. Typically, when the risk of material misstatement is higher, the amount of acceptable difference is lower.

In Step 5, the auditor compares the client's recorded amounts with the auditor's expectation. Once this mechanical step is completed, the auditor will have

Prompt for Critical Thinking #2   It's Your Turn!

Expand on your thinking with respect to Step 3: Develop Expectations. Specifically, provide two additional relationships that an auditor might expect in the acquisition and payment cycle. Be sure to identify what you have assumed about your client and the industry.

• Assumption: _____

• Expectation: _____

• Assumption: _____

• Expectation: _____

identified any significant differences between the auditor's expectation and the amount the client has recorded.

If planning analytical procedures do not identify any unexpected relationships, the auditor would conclude that there is not a heightened risk of material misstatement in these accounts. If unusual or unexpected relationships exist, the auditor would adjust planned audit procedures (tests of controls, substantive procedures) to address the potential material misstatements. The auditor should be aware that if a fraud is taking place in the acquisition and payment cycle, the financial statements usually will contain departures from industry norms but may not differ from the expectations set by management. Therefore, the auditor should compare the unaudited financial statements with both past results and industry trends. The following relationships might suggest a heightened risk of misstatement:

• Unexpected increases in gross margin
• Inventory that is growing at a rate greater than sales
• Expenses that are either significantly above or below industry norms
• Unexpected increases in the number of suppliers
• Capital assets that seem to be growing faster than the business and for which there are no strategic plans
• Expense accounts that have significant credit entries
• Travel and entertainment expense accounts, but no documentation or approval of expenditures
• Inadequate follow-up to the auditor's recommendations on needed controls

Step 6 and Step 7: Investigate Significant Unexpected Differences and Ensure Proper Documentation

Significant unexpected differences suggest that evidence sufficiency and/or evidence appropriateness for the account/assertion will need to be increased. The auditor will develop a plan to address the identified risks. As the auditor proceeds through planning analytical procedures, the auditor will document the analytical procedures used, the auditor's expectations, how the level of significant difference was determined, the identification of significant unexpected differences, and the planned follow-up to address significant unexpected differences.

Using Data Analytics to Identify Employees' Fraudulent Travel and Expense Reimbursement Claims

This feature discusses the prevalence of travel and entertainment (T&E) fraud, and how organizations can use data analytics to detect it. If the organization does not employ these types of data analytics, the auditor can add significant value by employing them and reporting the results to management. Even if no T&E reimbursement fraud is found, management would find value in the assurance that no fraud is occurring.

T&E fraud often happens when employees use their organizations' purchasing cards (P-cards) to pay for personal expenditures; there exists a heightened threat when employees realize that their purchases are not subject to review and approval.

The following are data analytics that an organization or the auditor can employ to test for fraudulent T&E reimbursement claims:

- Analyze complete populations of data to identify various types of anomalies, e.g., duplicate expense report charges whereby one is filed through a manual reimbursement and the other is filed through the P-card.

- Compare T&E records with human resources records to see if there exist instances whereby an employee uses their P-card while on vacation.

- Compare employee descriptions of expenses with data from credit card companies in terms of merchant codes and categories of expenses.

- Checking for instances in which a P-card limit is increased, e.g., from $1,000 to $20,000 for just a few hours, and any p-card charges during those hours.

- Identify transactions in which a larger purchase is paid for in sub-amounts, which include values just below review or approval thresholds.

- Watch for P-card holders whose expense reimbursements are particularly high compared to others holding a similar role.

Inventory Restatement at Barnes & Noble

This feature provides an example of how planning analytical procedures can provide the auditor with insight regarding possible material misstatements in the financial statements.

Barnes & Noble is a retailer of books and digital media, including the Nook e-book reader and associated accessories. On January 13, 2014, a class-action lawsuit was filed against the company. The relevant period for the class-action lawsuit was for individuals that purchased the company's stock between February 25, 2013, and December 5, 2013. The Nook e-book market had not performed up to expectations over the prior years. Sales in that niche have suffered as a result, with build-ups of relevant inventory. Among other things, the lawsuit alleges that Barnes & Noble: (1) materially overstated its inventory related to Nook products by $133 million, (2) was unable to timely file its FYE 2013 financial results, and (3) might be forced to restate previously reported financial results.

This lawsuit comes on the heels of the SEC's announcement on October 16, 2013, that the Commission had launched an investigation of the company's previously submitted financial statements for FYEs 2011 and 2012. Barnes & Noble had previously restated three prior-year financial statements during the summer of 2013 relating to an internal control material weakness unrelated to the acquisition and payment cycle accounts, replacing its prior auditor (BDO) with Ernst & Young (EY).

What types of planning analytical procedures might have been helpful to the auditors in evaluating the valuation of inventory, particularly that relating to the troubled Nook segment? Some possibilities include:

- Tracking quarterly and yearly trends in Nook sales. For example, for the third quarter ending in January 2014, Nook sales were down to about $419 million, compared to $668 million in the same quarter the year prior. This indicates a slowdown in sales, so the auditor will expect potential reduction in inventory valuation given the need to potentially measure to lower of cost or market, and slower inventory turnover.

- Capital expenditures on the Nook segment were down for the third quarter ending in January 2014 to about $22 million, compared to $49 million in the same quarter the year prior. This significant reduction indicates that management is moving away from supporting this segment, so the auditor will expect that the declining trends in inventory valuation and turnover to continue into the future, likely with an increasing rate of decline.

- Given these valuation and turnover concerns, the auditor will track Nook sales and inventory turnover by quarter or month and by geographic segment until the uncertainty with respect to this segment is resolved. Further, the auditor may consider engaging an inventory valuation specialist in responding to identified risks of material misstatement in inventory.

Check Your Basic Knowledge

11-17 In terms of planning analytical procedures, assume that the client has introduced a new product with a low price point and significant customer demand. The auditor would expect inventory turnover to increase and days' sales in inventory to also increase. (T/F)

11-18 A planning analytical procedure in the acquisition and payment cycle that might indicate fraud is that inventory is growing at a rate greater than sales. (T/F)

11-19 Which of the following expected relationships is reasonable in terms of performing planning analytical procedures in the acquisition and payment cycle?

 a. Assume that the company's production and pricing strategies have remained the same during the past year. Gross margin is expected to improve because of the stability.

 b. Assume that the company has introduced a new product with a low price point and significant customer demand. Inventory turnover is expected to increase and days' sales in inventory is expected to decrease.

 c. Assume that the company has invested in a new manufacturing process resulting in significantly less waste and overall increases in efficiency during the production process. Cost of goods sold is expected to increase, and gross margin is expected to decrease.

 d. All of the above are reasonable expected relationships.

11-20 Which of the following planning analytical relationships is most typically suggestive of a heightened risk of fraud in the acquisition and payment cycle?

 a. Unexpected increases in gross margin.

 b. Unexpected decreases in gross margin.

 c. Inventory that is growing at a rate slower than sales.

 d. Expense accounts that have significant debit entries.

LO 6

Determine appropriate responses to identified risks of material misstatement for acquisition and payment cycle accounts, disclosures, and assertions.

Responding to Identified Risks of Material Misstatement

Once the auditor understands the risks of material misstatement, the auditor determines the appropriate audit procedures to perform. Audit procedures should be proportional to the assessed risks, with areas of higher risk requiring more evidence and/or evidence that is more appropriate. Responding to identified risks typically involves developing an audit approach that contains substantive procedures (e.g., tests of details and, when appropriate, substantive analytical procedures) and tests of controls, when applicable. The sufficiency and appropriateness of selected procedures will vary to achieve the desired level of assurance for each relevant assertion. While audit firms may have a standardized audit program for the acquisition and payment cycle, the auditor should customize the audit program based on the assessment of risk of material misstatement.

Consider a client where the auditor has assessed the risk of material misstatement related to the existence of inventory as high. Similar to the Thor Industries, Inc. and Schwartzhoff example from the *Focus on Fraud* feature, assume incentives exist to overstate income to achieve profit targets that affect management bonuses. Assume further that oversight of the vice president of finance is relatively weak because of a lack of supervision by top management. The auditor may develop an audit program that consists of first performing limited tests of operating effectiveness of controls, then performing limited to moderate substantive analytical procedures, and finally performing extensive substantive tests of details. Because of the high risk, the auditor will want to obtain a great deal of evidence directly from tests of details.

In contrast, consider a client where the auditor has assessed the risk of material misstatement related to the existence of inventory as low and believes that the client has implemented effective controls in this area. For this client, the auditor will likely perform tests of controls, gain a high level of assurance from substantive analytical procedures such as a reasonableness test, and then complete the substantive procedures by performing tests of details at a limited level.

Panel A of *Exhibit 11.7* makes the point that because of differences in risk, the box of evidence to be filled for testing the existence of inventory at the low-risk client is smaller than that at a high-risk client. Panel B of *Exhibit 11.7* illustrates the different levels of assurance that the auditor will obtain from tests of controls and substantive procedures for the assertion at the two different clients. Panel B makes the point that because of the higher risk associated with the existence of inventory at Client B, the auditor will want to design the audit so that more of the assurance is coming from tests of details. Note that the relative percentages are judgmental in nature; the examples are simply intended to give you a sense of how an auditor might select an appropriate mix of procedures.

Exhibit 11.7
Panel A: Sufficiency of Evidence for Existence of Inventory

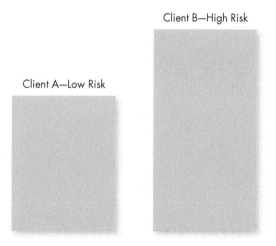

Panel B: Approaches to Obtaining Audit Evidence for Existence of Inventory

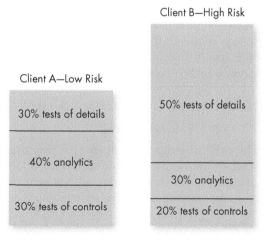

Check Your Basic Knowledge

11-21   When conducting the audit of the acquisition and payment cycle for a client with a high risk of material misstatement in its inventory accounts, the following mix of evidence would be appropriate: significant tests of internal control, significant reliance on substantive analytical procedures, and limited tests of details.   (T/F)

11-22   When considering the appropriate mix of evidence, the sufficiency and appropriateness of selected procedures vary across inventory assertions to achieve the desired level of assurance for each relevant assertion.   (T/F)

11-23   Which mix of evidence would be most appropriate for the following scenario?

Assume a client where the auditor has assessed the risk of material misstatement related to the existence of inventory as high. This client has incentives to overstate income to achieve profit targets that affect management bonuses. Oversight of the vice president of finance is relatively weak because of a lack of supervision by top management. Other controls are effectively designed.

a.   100% tests of details.
b.   50% tests of details, 30% analytics, 20% tests of controls.

c.   30% tests of details, 40% analytics, 30% tests of controls.
d.   20% tests of details, 40% analytics, 40% tests of controls.

11-24   Which mix of evidence would be most appropriate for the following scenario?

Assume a client where the auditor has assessed the risk of material misstatement related to the existence of inventory as low. Top management appears to have a high level of integrity. Management has spent the resources necessary to ensure effective design, implementation, and operation of controls.

a.   100% tests of details.
b.   70% tests of details, 10% substantive analytics, 20% tests of controls.
c.   50% tests of details, 10% substantive analytics, 40% tests of controls.
d.   20% tests of details, 40% substantive analytics, 40% tests of controls.

LO 7

Determine appropriate tests of controls and consider the results of tests of controls for acquisition and payment cycle accounts, disclosures, and assertions.

Obtaining Evidence About Internal Control Operating Effectiveness in the Acquisition and Payment Cycle

For integrated audits, the auditor will test the operating effectiveness of important controls throughout the year, with a heightened focus on controls as of the client's year-end. If the auditor wants to rely on controls for the financial statement audit, the auditor will test the operating effectiveness of those controls throughout the year.

Selecting Controls to Test and Performing Tests of Controls

The auditor selects controls that are important to the auditor's conclusion about whether the client's controls adequately address the assessed risk of material misstatement in the acquisition and payment cycle. The auditor selects both entity-wide and transaction controls for testing. The auditor tests those internal controls that are designed to provide reasonable assurance that: (1) all purchases are authorized, (2) all payments are for goods received, (3) payments are made at the appropriate amount and in the correct period, and (4) payments are paid only once to the authorized vendor.

Typical tests of controls include inquiry of relevant personnel, observation of the control being performed, examination of documentation corroborating that the control has been performed, and reperformance of the control by the auditor testing the control. *Exhibit 11.8* provides examples of various controls that a client might use to mitigate the risk of material misstatement in the acquisition and payment cycle.

An important control in this cycle is a three-way match. This control may be manual or automated. For a manual three-way match control, the auditor may test whether the control was operating effectively by taking a sample of payments and tracing them to the documentation corroborating that the control was performed. Attributes sampling, discussed in *Chapter 8*, would likely be used to determine and select the sample. In addition, the auditor might take a sample of receiving reports and trace them through the system to test controls related to the completeness assertion for inventory and accounts payable. Significant lags in recording the liability indicate potential problems that the auditor should address during substantive testing of accounts payable at year-end.

Evidence of proper authorization should be available for each purchase and payment. Paper-based systems provide evidence of authorization through signatures. To test these types of controls, the auditor usually checks for signatures on the appropriate documentation. For any exceptions, the auditor follows up with responsible personnel. Computerized systems are controlled through access controls and exception reports that are tested by the auditor using computerized audit techniques, as well as inquiry and examination of documentation.

Considering the Results of Tests of Controls

The auditor analyzes the results of the tests of controls to determine additional appropriate procedures. There are two potential outcomes:

1. If the auditor identifies control deficiencies, the auditor will assess those deficiencies to determine their severity. (Are they significant deficiencies or material weaknesses?) The auditor would then modify the preliminary control risk assessment (possibly from low to high) and document the implications of the control deficiencies. *Exhibit 11.8* provides examples of implications for control deficiencies for substantive testing. The auditor will determine appropriate modifications to planned substantive audit procedures based on the types of misstatements that are most likely to occur because of the control deficiency.

2. If the auditor does not identify any control deficiencies, the auditor will likely determine that the preliminary assessment of control risk as low is still appropriate. The auditor then determines the extent that controls can provide evidence on the accuracy of account balances and determines planned substantive audit procedures. Substantive testing in this situation will be less than what is required in circumstances where the auditor identified internal control deficiencies. From the audit risk model, we know for companies with effective internal controls, the auditor will perform less substantive testing.

Exhibit 11.8
Control Examples and Tests

Objective	Control Example	How Control Would be Tested	Implications if Control is Not Working
Recorded inventory exists.	Near year-end, the client takes a complete physical count of inventory.	The auditor attends the inventory count and observes whether the client follows the appropriate procedures.	Recorded inventory may not exist. The auditor may need to increase test counts and cutoff tests.
All completed purchases are recorded.	The client employs prenumbered receiving reports to provide evidence that the goods are received.	For a sample of purchases, the auditor will review receiving reports and trace them through the system to the recording of the purchase.	Not all purchases may have been recorded in the correct period. The auditor will expand cutoff tests at year-end to determine that all purchases during the audit year have been recorded in the correct period.
Accounts payable are only recorded for approved purchases and goods or services received.	The accounts payable department matches the purchase order, receiving document, and invoice to record accounts payable.	For a sample of recorded accounts payable, the auditor will obtain and review supporting documentation, including the purchase order, receiving document, and invoice.	Payments may be made in the wrong amount, for the wrong quantity ordered, or for instances when goods have not been received. The auditor may want to send confirmations to vendors and suppliers to confirm transactions the client has recorded. The auditor may vouch recorded payables balances to suppliers' statements for an expanded sample of transactions.
Inventory disclosures provided in the financial statements comply with the relevant accounting literature.	A **disclosure committee** reviews the client's financial statements and footnotes; a disclosure committee is a sub-committee of the Board of Directors, and is charged with ensuring that the organization's MD&A and footnotes to the financial statements comply with financial accounting standards.	The auditor can review documentation of the disclosure committee's review.	Inventory disclosures may not be accurate or complete or comply with the relevant accounting literature. The auditor will need to expand the review of these disclosures.

Inventory Controls at Flow International Corporation

Why It Matters: An International Perspective

The effectiveness of a client's internal controls can significantly influence the audit of the accounts and assertions affected by those controls. This feature highlights a situation where the auditor will likely rely heavily on substantive tests of details to obtain sufficient appropriate evidence related to inventory.

Flow International Corporation is a company that produces high-pressure water pumps. These pumps cut materials, remove coatings, and prepare surfaces for coating. The following is an excerpt from Flow International's *Management Report*

on Internal Controls Over Financial Reporting for the Year Ended April 30, 2013.

Brazil Control Environment. Management determined that we had a material weakness in the control environment within our Brazilian operations, and in our related monitoring of these operations, that resulted in design and operating control deficiencies, including those related to the physical quantities and valuation of inventory and the preparation and review of income taxes for our subsidiary in Brazil.

Check Your Basic Knowledge

11-25 When selecting controls to test and performing tests of controls in the acquisition and payment cycle, the auditor might reasonably take a sample of receiving reports and trace them through the system to test controls related to the completeness assertion for inventory and accounts payable. (T/F)

11-26 When conducting the audit of acquisition and payment cycle accounts, the auditor will likely conduct less substantive tests for companies with effective internal controls than for companies with ineffective internal controls. (T/F)

11-27 Which of the following statements is <u>false</u> regarding obtaining evidence about internal control operating effectiveness in the acquisition and payment cycle?

    a. For integrated audits, the auditor will test the operating effectiveness of important controls as of the client's year-end.

    b. The auditor will select controls to test that are important to the auditor's conclusion about whether the client's controls adequately address the

assessed risk of material misstatement in the acquisition and payment cycle.

    c. Evidence of proper payment is not necessary for each purchase and payment, but is only necessary for those that are material.

    d. The auditor will take a sample of receiving reports and review whether independent counts were made of the goods received.

11-28 Refer to the *Why It Matters* feature "Inventory Controls at Flow International Corporation." Which of the following represents an implication of weaknesses in the company's controls over inventory?

    a. The company could not adequately process and account for the valuation of inventory.

    b. The board of directors fired the CEO because of the internal control deficiencies.

    c. The company developed a plan to remediate its material weaknesses related to inventory.

    d. Both a. and c.

    e. Both a. and b.

LO 8

Determine and apply sufficient appropriate substantive audit procedures for testing acquisition and payment cycle accounts, disclosures, and assertions.

Obtaining Substantive Evidence About Accounts, Disclosures, and Assertions in the Acquisition and Payment Cycle

Substantive Tests of Inventory and Cost of Goods Sold

In performing substantive procedures for inventory and cost of goods sold, the auditor wants reasonable assurance that inventory exists, that it is owned by the company, and that the value of inventory is accurate. Substantive procedures (substantive analytical procedures, tests of details, or both) should be performed for all relevant assertions related to significant acquisition and payment cycle accounts and disclosures. Even if the auditor has evidence indicating that controls are operating effectively, the auditor cannot rely solely on control testing to provide evidence on the reliability of these accounts and assertions. *Exhibit 11.9* details typical substantive procedures for inventory and cost of goods sold. The extent to which the auditor performs substantive analytical procedures and tests of details depends on the risk of material misstatement.

Exhibit 11.9

Management Assertions and Substantive Procedures for Inventory and Cost of Goods Sold

Assertion	Substantive Audit Procedures
Existence/occurrence	1. Review the client's proposed physical inventory procedures to determine whether they are likely to result in a complete and correct physical inventory.
	2. Observe the client's count of the annual physical inventory. Randomly select items from the client's perpetual inventory record and observe (count) the items on hand. Sample should emphasize high-dollar-value items.
Completeness	1. Perform year-end cutoff tests by noting the last shipping and receiving document numbers used before physical inventory is taken. Review the purchase and sales journal for a period of time shortly before and after year-end, noting the shipping and receiving document numbers to determine whether the goods are recorded in the proper time period.
	2. Make inquiries of the client regarding the potential existence of goods on consignment or located in outside warehouses. For material items, either visit the locations or send a confirmation to the outside warehouse management.
	3. Make inquiries of the client regarding allowances made for expected returns. Determine client policy for accounting for returned items. Review receipt of transactions for a selected period of time to determine whether significant returns are received and appropriately accounted for.
Rights and obligations	1. Review vendor invoices when testing disbursements to determine that proper title is conveyed.
	2. Review purchase contracts to assess rights to return merchandise.

(Continues)

Exhibit 11.9 *Continued*

Assertion	Substantive Audit Procedures
Valuation/allocation	1. Determine whether the valuation method is appropriate for the client.
	2. Inquire of production and warehouse personnel about the existence of obsolete inventory.
	3. Note potentially obsolete inventory while observing the physical inventory counts. Trace the potentially obsolete items to the client's inventory compilation and determine whether they are properly labeled as obsolete items.
	4. Test inventory cost by taking a sample of recorded inventory and trace to source documents, including:
	• Tracing raw material purchases to vendor invoices
	• Testing standard costs as built up through the standard cost system
	5. Test for the possibility of obsolete inventory that should be written down to market value:
	• Review trade journals for changes in product technology.
	• Follow up potentially obsolete items noted during the observation of the client's physical inventory counts.
	• Use audit software to read the inventory file and age the inventory items and compute inventory turnover. Investigate products with unusually low turnover or items that have not been used or sold for an extended period of time.
	• Inquire of the client about sales adjustments (markdowns) that have been offered to sell any products.
	• Verify sales price by reviewing recent invoices to determine whether the sales price is the same as that included on the computer file. Use generalized audit software (GAS) to compute net realizable value for inventory items, and prepare an inventory printout for all items where net realizable value is less than cost.
	• Analyze sales by product line, noting any significant decreases in product-line sales.
	• Review purchase commitments for potential loss exposures. Determine whether contingent losses are properly disclosed or recorded.
	• Use audit software to test extensions and prepare a printout of differences.
	• Use audit software to foot the inventory compilation. Trace the total to the trial balance.
Presentation and disclosure	1. Review client's financial statement disclosure of:
	• Inventory valuation methods used
	• FIFO cost figures and LIFO liquidation effects if LIFO is used
	• The percentage of inventory valued by each different valuation method
	• The classification of inventory as raw material, work in process, and finished goods
	• The existence of contingent losses associated with long-term contracts or purchase commitments
	• Inventory policy regarding returns and allowances, if expected to be material, for merchandise expected to be returned

Inventory and Cost of Goods Sold: Performing Substantive Analytical Procedures

Before performing tests of details, the auditor may perform substantive analytical procedures, such as a reasonableness test. An example of a reasonableness test would be to estimate the account balance and to determine whether that amount is close to what the client has recorded. For example, if purchases and sales volume are relatively stable from year to year, the auditor might compare ending inventory balances by location to prior-year balances. If the auditor's expectations are significantly different from what the client has recorded, the auditor needs to follow up with sufficient appropriate tests of details. If the auditor's expectations are not significantly different from what the client has recorded, the auditor may be able reduce tests of details. The auditor should apply analytical procedures to cost of goods sold to determine if any unexpected significant variations—either overall or by product line—occur. Unexpected significant variations in cost of goods sold might indicate a need for further inventory work.

Furthermore, in the acquisition and payment cycle it is unlikely that audit evidence obtained from substantive analytical procedures alone will be sufficient appropriate evidence.

Inventory and Cost of Goods Sold: Substantive Tests of Details for the Existence/Occurrence Assertion

Auditing standards require auditors to observe the client taking physical inventory in order to obtain assurance about the existence of inventory. The auditor may perform this observation in its entirety at year-end or on a cycle basis throughout the year. Note that the audit of cost of goods sold relates directly to the audit of inventories. If the auditor has verified beginning and ending inventory and tested acquisitions, the auditor can calculate cost of goods sold. This calculation of cost of goods sold relates to the completeness assertion; in other words, if inventory exists then the recording of cost of goods sold is complete.

Year-End Physical Inventory   Standard procedure for some organizations is to shut down operations at year-end or near year-end to take a complete physical count of inventory (often referred to as the *physical*). The client adjusted its book

---

Why It Matters

Weaknesses in Auditing Inventory: Grant Thornton's PCAOB Inspection Report

This feature provides an example of various audit deficiencies regarding the audit of inventory as identified in a PCAOB inspection report. Because of these deficiencies, the audit firm did not obtain sufficient appropriate audit evidence to support its audit opinions on the financial statements and on the effectiveness of ICFR.

The audit firm failed to perform sufficient procedures related to inventory. Specifically:

• A significant portion of the issuer's inventory was subject to cycle counts, and the issuer used system-generated reports that specified which items to count each day. The Firm's procedures to test the existence of, and controls over the existence of, this inventory were insufficient. Specifically, although the Firm tested ITGCs over the inventory system that produced the reports, in determining that the cycle-count procedures that the issuer used for this inventory were

sufficiently reliable, the Firm failed to determine the extent of the inventory items counted and the frequency of the counts that were specified in the system-generated reports.

• The Firm failed to sufficiently test the issuer's allowance for excess and obsolete inventory. Specifically, the Firm's procedures were limited to inquiring of management regarding the methodology used to estimate the allowance; testing the mathematical accuracy of the issuer's calculations; and, for one subsidiary, comparing the current-year allowance to the prior-year allowance, noting that the balance did not change significantly. The Firm, however, failed to evaluate the reasonableness of the significant assumptions that the issuer used in determining its allowance for excess and obsolete inventory.

For further details, see PCAOB Release Number 104–2017-027.

inventory to this physical inventory (often referred to as the *book to physical adjustment*). Organizations that use these procedures are typically small organizations using a periodic inventory system, where the perpetual records are not sufficiently reliable, or where fraud risk indicators exist.

If the client performs a year-end physical inventory count, the auditor should:

- Review the client's procedures for the count
- Observe the client personnel taking inventory to determine if the personnel are following the procedures
- Make selected test counts for subsequent tracing into the client's inventory compilation
- Test the client's inventory compilation by tracing test counts to the compilation and independently test the client's computation of extended cost
- Look for evidence of slow-moving, obsolete, or damaged inventory that the client may need to write down to lower of cost or market
- Walk through the inventory areas, documenting the first and last tag numbers used as well as the tag numbers not used
- Observe the handling of scrap and other material
- Observe whether any physical movement of goods occurs during the counting of inventory
- Record all high-dollar-value items for subsequent tracing into the accounting records.

After the clients completes the inventory count, the auditor's observations and test counts provide an independent source of evidence on the accuracy of the client's inventory compilation. Noting the unused tag numbers prohibits the insertion of additional inventory items.

Exhibit 11.10 outlines the procedures an auditor should perform when observing the count of physical inventory. The process assumes that client personnel systematically arranges the inventory for ease of counting and attaches prenumbered tags (paper or electronic) to each group of products. Supervisory personnel (usually from the accounting department) and the auditors review the counts. The client uses the count tags to compile the year-end physical inventory. During the counting process, the client's supervisory personnel arrange not to ship or receive goods. Alternatively, the client can segregate all goods received during the process and label the goods as *after inventory*.

An auditor can use data analytics tools to obtain the following types of evidence related to inventory accounts:

- The mathematical accuracy of inventory records
- Reports of recent shipments to be used for cutoff testing
- Items to be counted during the physical inventory observation
- Evaluations of gross margin amounts by product line

It's Your Turn! *Prompt For Critical Thinking #3*

Identify reasons that the auditor will note and evaluate all high-dollar value items during the physical inventory count.

- _____
- _____

Prompt for Critical Thinking #4　　　　It's Your Turn!

Provide examples of other types of evidence related to inventory accounts that an auditor can obtain through using data analytics tools.

• _____

• _____

• _____

Exhibit 11.10
Procedures for Observing a Physical Inventory Count

1. Meet with client personnel to discuss the procedures, timing, location, and personnel involved in taking the annual physical inventory.
2. Review plans for counting and tagging inventory items.
3. Review the inventory-taking procedures with all audit firm personnel. Familiarize them with the nature of the client's inventory, potential problems with the inventory, and any other information that will ensure that both the client and audit personnel will properly recognize inventory items, high-dollar-value items, and obsolete items, and understand potential problems that might occur in counting the inventory.
4. Determine whether specialists are needed to test or assist in correctly identifying inventory items.
5. Upon arriving at each site:
   a. Meet with client personnel, obtain a map of the area, and obtain a schedule of inventory counts to be made for each area.
   b. Obtain a list of sequential tag numbers to be used in each area.
   c. Observe the procedures that client supervisory personnel have implemented to shut down movement of goods.
   d. Observe that the client has shut down production.
   e. Obtain document numbers for the last shipment and receipt of goods before the physical inventory is taken. Use the information to perform cutoff tests.
6. Observe the counting of inventory and note the following on inventory count working papers:
   a. The first and last tag number used in the section.
   b. All tag numbers and the disposition of all tag numbers in the sequence.
   c. The product identification, product description, units of measure, and number of items on a count sheet.
   d. Items that appear to be obsolete or of questionable value.
   e. All high-dollar-value items included in inventory.
   f. Movement of goods into or out of the company during the process of inventory taking. Determine if goods are properly counted or excluded from inventory.
7. Document conclusion as to the quality of the client's inventory-taking process, noting any problems that could be of audit significance. Determine whether a sufficient inventory count has been taken to properly reflect the goods on hand at year-end.

Many organizations that take an annual physical inventory find that year-end is not a convenient time to do it. For example, the organization may have a natural model changeover and shut down operations during that time, or it may want to take the physical inventory shortly before or after year-end to expedite

Using Technology and Data Analytics When Auditing Inventory

Why It Matters

This feature highlights how technology and data analytics have begun to change the audit process.

In the near future, the auditing profession may undergo a transformation by exploiting the use of drone technology. One audit area where this disruption has begun is in auditing inventory.

Today, drones are used for photography, surveillance, observations, and recording in many industries. With cameras and sensors attached, drones can perform many activities. For example, recordings and videos taken by the drone can be fed into software applications for understanding through data analytics. Such use of drone technology could easily be applied to inventory valuation, observation, and counts.

In June 2017, EY announced that it would begin testing the use of drones when auditing inventory. Audit teams could use the drones to count units in an automotive manufacturing plant, or to conduct an automated inventory count in a warehouse. The firm's expectation is that the technology will improve the accuracy and frequency of inventory counts.

To watch a video of Eyesee, an inventory-taking drone technology, see the following video: *https://www.youtube.com /watch?v5R1qtwoPde0U*

Additional Audit Risks When Clients Have Inventory at Multiple Locations

Why It Matters

This feature highlights procedures that auditors might take when clients have inventory at multiple locations.

Many organizations have multiple locations, therefore making it difficult to take an annual inventory. For example, one major company that perpetrated a famous fraud was Phar-Mor, Inc. The company had more than 300 stores across the country. The auditors insisted that the client take a year-end physical count, but notified client management that they would observe the taking of inventory at only a few select locations. To expedite the observation of inventory, the auditor worked with management to identify the locations that they auditor would observe. Although there was a massive overstatement of inventory by Phar-Mor, Inc., the auditors did not discover the misstatement because the company made sure that no material misstatements occurred at the locations visited by the auditors.

When multiple locations contain inventory, the auditor should review a variety of locations to determine that they are comparable and should use analytical procedures to see if the locations not visited seem to have inventory levels that are significantly different from those observed. If there are significant differences, the auditor may need to observe more locations, or at least follow up with other procedures. The auditor may also want to plan to visit some locations on an unannounced or surprise basis to avoid the type of fraudulent activity that occurred at Phar-Mor.

the preparation of year-end financial statements. It is acceptable to have the client take the physical inventory before year-end provided that:

- Internal control is effective.
- There are no red flags indicating both opportunity and motivation to misstate inventory.
- The auditor can effectively test the year-end balance through a combination of analytical procedures and selective testing of transactions between the physical count and year-end.
- The auditor reviews transactions in the roll-forward period for evidence of any manipulation or unusual activity.

What Do You Think?   For Classroom Discussion

Depending on the industries you audit, you may find yourself performing inventory counts of some interesting inventories!

Some organizations, such as the American Red Cross, have inventories of blood and blood components, which they often keep in freezers. What blood inventory management controls would you expect your client to have? How comfortable would you be with counting this inventory?

As another example, consider a client who is a poultry producer. This client will likely have a farm with chicken houses containing thousands of birds. While counting this inventory, you will have to comply with prescribed health standards, which may include showering each time you enter a different sector of the farm. Would you want to be involved in this inventory count?

For a large steakhouse chain, one auditor reported to us that he spent six hours in a large freezer counting steaks. As he reported to one of the authors, "I had to use pencil to write my counts because the ink in my pen froze solid."

Other fun examples include counting diamonds at a jeweler, pills at a pharmacy, and frozen waffles!

What other "quirky" inventory experiences do you think auditors might encounter?

As organizations move toward innovative partnerships with their suppliers and customers, more agreements will take place where a supplier's goods will be at a retailer such as Walmart, but title will not change until the retailer makes sale to the customer. In these situations, the auditor needs to determine that the client has an effective process for determining the amount of inventory that is physically stored at a trading partner's location. Many times, the client will have monitoring controls which its uses to examine existing inventory at the trading partners' locations and to compare the inventory to the perpetual records. If such controls do not exist, the auditor will need to consider complementary testing methodologies, which might include: (a) confirming inventory amounts with the trading partner, (b) examining subsequent payments from the trading partner, or (c) visiting selected trading partners to inspect inventory.

It is not sufficient for a client to assert that its trading partners hold the client's inventory. To corroborate this assertion, the auditor will examine the contract, determine the existence and effectiveness of controls, and examine documentation of reconciliations between trading partners, cash remittances, and client accounting records. If red flags are present, the auditor must go beyond these procedures and confirm with the trading partner information on the amount of the client's inventory the trading partner shows on hand. Finally, the auditor needs assurance that the trading partner is a real company.

There may be cases in which it is difficult or impractical for the auditor to attend the physical inventory count. For example, the nature and location of the inventory may pose safety threats for the auditor. In these situations, the auditor conducts alternative audit procedures. Such procedures include inspecting documents related to the subsequent sale of specific inventory items to validate their existence and valuation as of the balance sheet date.

If it is simply inconvenient for the auditor to attend the physical inventory count, then the auditor has an obligation to find a way to be present. If it is truly impossible for the auditor to attend the physical inventory count, and the auditor is unable to conduct alternative procedures, then the auditor's report would be modified because of this scope limitation (assuming that inventory is a material amount to the financial statements as a whole).

Inventory and Cost of Goods Sold: Substantive Tests of Details for the Completeness Assertion

The auditor typically performs a cutoff test of receipts and shipments of inventory at year-end to determine whether all items are recorded in the correct period. Cutoff tests provide evidence related to both the existence and completeness assertions.

The auditor typically performs the cutoff test by obtaining information on the last items shipped and received at year-end and examining samples of transactions recorded in the sales and purchases journals near year-end. In addition, the auditor can use GAS to match shipping dates and billing dates if the files containing that information have been tested for accuracy. The auditor should also inquire about any inventory on consignment or stored in a public warehouse and consider confirming its existence.

> **Cutoff example**—A sale of $100 is recorded on December 30 for a product costing $80 that is not shipped until the next month. If a physical count of inventory is taken on December 31, this product will be included in the physical count, which will exceed the quantity shown in the perpetual records. The perpetual inventory record is always adjusted to the actual count (in this case by debiting inventory and crediting cost of goods sold). Unless corrected, sales, gross profit, and pre-tax income are overstated by the full $100. The client can correct this misstatement by reversing the sales entry, including the entry to accounts receivable. Because the perpetual inventory is adjusted to the physical count, that part of the original entry (debiting inventory, crediting cost of goods sold) is already made.

Allowance for Returns Expected returns will vary depending on the client's business. Some organizations (e.g., mail-order companies like Lands' End or L.L. Bean) provide return guarantees and expect significant returns—especially after year-end holiday sales. They use previous experience, updated for current economic conditions, to develop estimates of returns. When such returns are material to the overall financial presentation, the client should establish an allowance for returns, in effect reversing the recorded gross profit on the original sale. The auditor should consider the allowance account for any organization experiencing a large volume of returns. As with other accounting estimates, the auditor needs to understand management's process for determining the estimate and then test the reasonable of that process.

Inventory and Cost of Goods Sold: Substantive Tests of Details for Rights and Obligations Assertion

The auditor performs much of the audit work regarding rights to and ownership of inventory the auditor's test of the initial recording of purchases. The auditor should also review long-term contracts to determine obligations to take delivery of merchandise, customer rights to return merchandise, or buy-back obligations. The auditor should inquire about and gain an understanding of any inventory held on consignment.

Inventory and Cost of Goods Sold: Substantive Tests of Details for Valuation/Allocation Assertion

Valuation is the most complex assertion related to inventory because of the volume of transactions, diversity of products, variety of costing methods, and difficulty in estimating net realizable value of products. The auditor will likely use a combination of tests of details and substantive analytical procedures to determine inventory valuation. The auditor should verify the correct cost of inventory and then test for lower of cost or market valuation. Usually, the auditor tests the cost part of the valuation assertion by examining underlying invoices and/or supporting cost records. The auditor usually evaluates current market data and other information that might indicate a drop in sales price or potential inventory obsolescence.

Direct Tests of Product Costs   The auditor can use sampling techniques, as discussed in *Chapter 8*, to select items for testing. Then, the auditor should examine underlying supporting documentation—for example, invoices—to determine that the client has recorded the cost correctly. As an example, assume that the auditor selected product YG350 to test the cost of inventory recorded on the FIFO basis as part of a perpetual inventory system:

Product YG350

	Total		Balance	
Transaction	Quantity	Cost	Quantity	Dollars
Beginning balance			100	$1,000
3/1 Purchase	50	550	150	1,550
6/1 Purchase	100	1,200	250	2,750
6/1 Sale	150	1,550	100	1,200
9/1 Purchase	50	500	150	1,700
10/1 Sale	25	275	125	1,425
12/1 Sale	50	600	75	825
12/1 Purchase	75	975	150	1,800

The auditor would examine vendor invoices for the purchases of the last 150 items (12/1, 9/1, and 6/1) to determine whether $1,800 was the correct cost. (Note: You should verify that the recorded cost should have been $1,775. The calculation is as follows: 12/1 is $975, 9/1 is $500, and the remaining 25 units are from 6/1 at a cost of $25 × $12/unit, for a total of $1,775.)

The auditor will identify differences between vendor invoices and recorded amounts as errors and will project the sample error to the population as a whole to determine whether the misstatement might be material. The auditor will perform similar tests if the company uses other valuation methods, such as average cost or LIFO. If the company uses a standard cost system, the auditor will verify the costs by testing the cost system and by tracing the selected items to standard costs. Significant variances should be allocated between cost of goods sold and inventory.

Testing for Obsolete Inventory (Net Realizable Value Tests)   Determining the amount of inventory that the client should write off because of obsolescence is a difficult and challenging audit task. The challenges include the fact that: (1) the client will usually state that most of the goods are still saleable at current selling prices, and (2) net realizable value is only an estimate, which may be subject to management bias. The auditor should understand management's process for determining the value of its inventory and gather evidence on potential inventory obsolescence from a number of corroborating sources, including:

- Noting potential obsolete inventory when observing the physical inventory count
- Calculating inventory turnover, number of days' sales in inventory, date of last sale or purchase, and other similar analytic techniques to identify potential obsolescence

- Calculating net realizable value for products by referring to current selling prices, cost of disposal, and sales commissions
- Monitoring trade journals and the Internet for information regarding the introduction of competitive products
- Inquiring of management about its approach to identifying and classifying obsolete items
- Monitoring turnover or age of products individually or by product lines and comparing the turnover with past performance and expectations for the current period

It's Your Turn!

Prompt for Critical Thinking #5

Identify other sources of corroborating evidence related to potential inventory obsolescence.

- _____
- _____
- _____
- _____
- _____

Inventory Valuation at MagnaChip Leads to Desired Increase in Gross Margins

Focus on Fraud: An International Perspective

This feature describes an SEC Accounting and Auditing Enforcement Release related to inventory valuation at MagnaChip Semiconductor Corporation, a company that violated several provisions of the federal securities laws. Inventory valuation should be a focus area for auditors.

MagnaChip is a South-Korea-based semiconductor company that has been publicly traded in the United States since its Initial Public Offering ("IPO") in 2011. Shortly after its IPO, MagnaChip began engaging in a variety of practices to inappropriately inflate its revenues and meet the gross margin targets it previously had announced to the public. In several instances, the improper accounting practices involved employees throughout the company, including some employees directed and overseen by MagnaChip's former Chief Financial Officer. Most of MagnaChip's employees and management, including the CFO, were based in Korea.

While MagnaChip engaged in many inappropriate transactions, one type of transaction relates to inventory and the company's efforts to manipulate its gross margins. Company employees delayed scrapping inventory for obsolete inventory by several months or years. The delayed scrapping violated GAAP requirements, as MagnaChip was required to record the scrap as an expense when the inventory became aged or obsolete. By failing to do so, MagnaChip improperly inflated its gross margin and its financial statements did not accurately reflect inventory values.

To settle the SEC's charges, MagnaChip agreed to pay a $3 million penalty and its CFO agreed to pay a $135,000 penalty. Over the period of the fraud, MagnaChip's stock price increased by approximately 70%.

To view the stock price performance of MagnaChip during and after the fraud, and its current market value, see the diagram below. Notice the initial public offering price, the subsequent decline (which likely led to the motivation to commit the fraud), the steady increase in share prices from 2012–2015, and then the dramatic decline in 2015 when the fraud was discovered.

For further details, see SEC Accounting and Auditing Enforcement Release No. 3869 / May 1, 2017, at https://www.sec.gov/litigation/admin /2017/33-10352.pdf

For stock ticker details, see https://www.google.com/search?q=magnachip+semiconductor+stock+ticker&ie=utf-8&oe=utf-8

Testing a Standard Costing System Most manufacturing organizations use standard cost systems to control costs, streamline accounting, and cost inventory. Ending inventory valuation is directly related to the quality of the client's cost system. The auditor, who should be conversant with activity-based costing systems, will inquire of client management about:

- The method for developing standard costs
- How recently the standards have been updated
- The method for identifying components of overhead and of allocating overhead to products
- The methods for identifying variances, following up on their causes, and allocating them to inventory and cost of goods sold
- The procedures for assigning raw material costs to products or cost centers

Exhibit 11.11 contains an audit program to test a standard cost system. The program outlines the steps the auditor should use to determine the accuracy and reliability of the standard cost system as a basis for valuing a client's year-end inventory. The audit program assumes a standard cost system, but the concepts implicit in the program could be modified for other systems, such as a job cost system. The program requires the auditor to understand the client's business process as well as its standard cost system (including methods of estimating costs). The program also requires analyses of both variances and individual cost assignments.

Exhibit 11.11
Audit Program for Standard Cost System

AUDIT OF STANDARD COST SYSTEM

Prepared by _____

Reviewed by _____

	Performed by:	**W/P Ref:**

1. Review prior-year audit documentation for a description of the standard cost system. Inquire about any major changes made in the system during the current year.

2. Tour the production facilities and make note of cost centers, general layout of the plant, storage of inventory, functioning of the quality control department, and process for identifying and accounting for scrap or defective items.

3. Examine prior-year audit documentation and current-year variance accounts as a basis for determining the amount of variances identified by the standard cost accounting system. Determine whether the variances imply the need for significant revisions in the standard cost system.

4. Inquire of the process used to update standard costs. Determine the extent to which revisions have been made during the current year.

5. Inquire whether significant changes have been made in the production process during the current year, whether major manufacturing renovations have taken place, and whether new products have been added.

6. Randomly select X number of standard cost buildups for products, and for each product buildup selected:

   • Review engineering studies on the cost buildup, noting the items used, amount of product used, and standard cost of the product used.

   • Test the reasonableness of the client's costs by randomly sampling components of product cost and tracing back to purchases or contracts with suppliers.

   • Review payroll records to determine that labor costs are specifically identified by product or cost center and used in calculating variances.

   • Review the reasonableness of the method for allocating overhead to products. Determine whether any significant changes have been made in the method of allocation.

7. Select a representative sample of products requisitioned into work in process, and determine that all entries are properly recorded.

8. Review the method for identifying overhead costs. Select a representative sample of expenditure charged to overhead, and trace to underlying support to determine that the costs are properly classified.

9. Review variance reports. Determine the extent to which the client has investigated and determined the causes of the variances. Determine whether the causes of the variances signal a need to revise the standard cost system.

10. Inquire about the method used by the client to allocate variances to inventory and cost of goods sold at year-end. Determine the reasonableness of the method and its consistency with prior years.

11. Document your conclusion on the accuracy and completeness of the standard cost system used by the client. Indicate whether the standard costs can be relied on in assigning costs to year-end inventory.

Testing a Perpetual Inventory System   Many organizations use a perpetual inventory system to manage inventory. If there is a low risk that the perpetual inventory records are inaccurate, the client may save the time and cost associated with a complete year-end count of inventory. The auditor will typically test perpetual inventory records to determine that: (1) authorized receipts and sales of inventory are recorded accurately and promptly, and (2) only authorized receipts and sales of inventory have been recorded. The auditor selects transactions from the perpetual records and traces them back to source documents to determine that only authorized transactions have been recorded and that unit costs are accurate. The auditor also selects items from the source documents and traces them to the perpetual records to determine that all receipts and sales are recorded accurately and on a timely basis. Finally, the auditor examines support for any material adjustments made to the perpetual records based on physical counts.

Using the Work of a Specialist or Expert When Auditing Inventory   The nature of inventory at some clients may require the auditor to rely on the work of a specialist in determining quantities and valuation of inventory. For example, the auditor might use a specialist to determine the physical characteristics relating to inventory on hand or condition of minerals, mineral reserves, or materials stored in stockpiles.

Inventory and Cost of Goods Sold: Substantive Tests of Details for the Presentation and Disclosure Assertion

The auditor reviews the client's proposed disclosure for compliance with the relevant accounting literature. The auditor will review the client's inventory footnote for completeness and accuracy. *Exhibit 11.12* contains an example of an inventory disclosure for Ford Motor Company.

In addition to the typical inventory disclosures, the auditor must identify any unusual circumstances regarding sales or purchase contracts that would merit additional disclosure. A number of financial disclosures are required for inventory:

- Inventory valuation method used (FIFO, LIFO, moving average) and the percentage of inventory valued under each method
- Changes made in the method of valuing inventory
- FIFO or current cost if the inventory is valued using LIFO
- Composition of inventory as to raw materials, work-in-process, and finished goods
- Purchase commitments that could have an adverse effect on future financial results

What Do You Think?   For Classroom Discussion

In January 2017, the FASB issued a proposed accounting standard update to change inventory disclosures in the footnotes of financial statements. A key provision in the update would require companies to disclose nonroutine reasons for changes in inventory other than the routine buying, selling, and manufacturing of goods. An example of a nonroutine change might be the acquisition of a company that has a large supply of inventory. Another nonroutine change might stem from write-downs of the value of inventory.

Further, companies that report on operating segments would have to disclose the segments' inventory components—for example, how much of it consists of raw materials, work in process, finished goods, and supplies.

Do you think that this proposed disclosure change would benefit financial statement users? What audit challenges, if any, do you think might result from this change?

Exhibit 11.12
Ford Motor Company Inventory Footnote
From the 2016 Annual Report

NOTE 9. INVENTORIES

All inventories are stated at the lower of cost and net realizable value. Cost for a substantial portion of U.S. inventories is determined on a last-in, first-out ("LIFO") basis. LIFO was used for 27% and 30% of total inventories at December 31, 2015 and 2016, respectively. Cost of other inventories is determined by costing methods that approximate a first-in, first-out ("FIFO") basis.

Inventories at December 31 were as follows (in millions):

	2015	2016
Raw materials, work in process, and supplies	$ 4,005	$ 3,843
Finished products	5,254	5,943
Total inventories under FIFO	9,259	9,786
LIFO adjustment	(940)	(888)
Total inventories	$ 8,319	$ 8,898

Performing Substantive Fraud-Related Procedures for Inventory and Cost of Goods Sold

In audits with a heightened risk of fraud related to inventory and cost of goods sold, the auditor will want to consider performing the following procedures or, if the procedures are already being performed, altering the timing and extent of the procedures:

- Observe all inventory locations simultaneously
- Confirm inventories at locations that are outside the entity
- Compare carrying inventory amounts to recent sales amounts
- Examine consignment agreements and determine that consignments are properly accounted for
- Send confirmations to vendors confirming invoices and unusual terms
- Determine if there are bulk sales at steep discounts, as these sales could indicate decreasing values for the company's products

Substantive Tests of Accounts Payable and Related Expense Accounts

In performing substantive procedures for accounts payable and related expense accounts, the auditor focuses on obtaining reasonable assurance that these accounts are complete. The auditor should consider that management is more likely to: (1) understate, rather than overstate, expenses, and (2) classify expense items as assets. However, it is important for the auditor to understand client motivations. For example, client management may be motivated to minimize income taxes and thus would want to overstate expenses and understate income. In such cases, the auditor should concentrate on items classified as expenses that should be recorded as an asset.

Substantive procedures (either substantive analytical procedures, tests of details, or both) should be performed for all relevant assertions related to significant accounts payable accounts, related expense accounts, and disclosures. *Exhibit 11.13* details typical substantive procedures for accounts payable. The extent to

Focus on Fraud   Examples of Fraud in Inventory

This feature outlines common inventory-related frauds provided in AICPA Practice Alert No. 94–2, "Auditing Inventories—Physical Observations."

- Empty boxes or hollow squares in stacked goods
- Mislabeled boxes containing scrap, obsolete items, or lower-value materials
- Consigned inventory, inventory that is rented, or traded-in items for which credits have not been issued
- Inventory diluted so it is less valuable (e.g., adding water to liquid substances)
- Altering the inventory counts for those items the auditor did not test count
- Programming the computer to produce fraudulent physical quantity tabulations or priced inventory listings
- Manipulating the inventory counts/compilations for locations not visited by the auditor
- Double-counting inventory in transit between locations
- Physically moving inventory and counting it at two locations
- Including in inventory merchandise recorded as sold but not yet shipped to a customer (bill and hold sales)

- Arranging for false confirmations of inventory held by others
- Including inventory receipts for which corresponding payables had not been recorded
- Overstating the stage of completion of work in process
- Reconciling physical inventory amounts to falsified amounts in the general ledger
- Manipulating the roll-forward of an inventory taken before the financial statement date

How can the auditor detect these types of inventory frauds? The answer lies in analyzing the data. The following trends are indicative of fraud relating to the overstatement of inventory:

- Ending inventory increasing faster than sales trends
- Unexplained reductions in inventory turnover (cost of goods sold ÷ ending inventory)
- Shipping expenses that are decreasing as a percentage of inventory.
- Inventory levels rising faster than increases in total assets.
- Cost of goods sold for financial reporting purposes not agreeing with cost of goods sold for income tax purposes.

which the auditor performs substantive analytical procedures and tests of details depends on the risk of material misstatement.

If there is a low risk of material misstatement, testing might be limited to substantive analytical procedures, such as a comparison of underlying expenses with that of the prior year and related tests of the underlying asset or liability account. Alternatively, the auditor could compare ending accounts payable balances by major vendor to prior-year balances, or to the volume of activity during the year. The auditor expects high-volume vendors to have relatively large accounts payable balances. In addition, if there is no balance for a vendor that in previous years was significant, the auditor would want to consider why that would be the case.

Accounts Payable and Related Expense Accounts: Performing Substantive Analytical Procedures

When the auditor concludes that control risk is low for expense accounts, the primary substantive tests may be substantive analytical procedures. In conducting analytical procedures, the auditor should recognize that many account balances directly relate to the client's volume of activity. The auditor would typically expect stable relationships between specific accounts (e.g., cost of goods sold and sales) and would investigate unusual discrepancies. Examples of expenses that should vary directly with sales include warranty expense, sales commissions, and supplies expense. The auditor could develop expectations for account balances using a statistical model with either audited data or independently generated data.

If the expense account falls within expected ranges, the auditor can be comfortable in concluding that it is not materially misstated. If the account balance is

Exhibit 11.13
Management Assertions and Substantive
Procedures for Accounts Payable

Assertions	Substantive Audit Procedures
Existence/occurrence	1. Perform a cutoff test of purchases and cash disbursements
Completeness	1. Request vendors' monthly statements or send confirmations to major vendors requesting a statement of open account items
	2. Agree monthly statements and confirmations from major vendors with accounts payable list
	3. Examine a sample of cash disbursements made after the end of the year to determine whether the disbursements are for goods and services applicable to the previous year
	4. Perform analytical review of related expense accounts, such as travel and entertainment or legal expenses
Rights and obligations	1. Review long-term purchase commitments and determine whether a loss needs to be accrued
Valuation/allocation	1. Use data analytics tools to verify mathematical accuracy of accounts payable, and agree to general ledger
Presentation and disclosure	1. Review management's financial statement disclosure of: • Accounts payable • Expense accounts such as travel and entertainment

not within the expected range, the auditor develops hypotheses as to why it may differ and systematically investigates the situation through tests of details. The investigation should include inquiries of client personnel and the examination of corroborating evidence (including a detailed examination of the expense accounts, where merited).

As an example, sales commissions may have averaged 3% of sales over the past five years, and the auditor may expect that trend to continue. If that ratio drops to 1% this year, the auditor should examine the cause of the change. If the auditor obtains sufficient appropriate evidence through substantive analytical procedures, the auditor may decrease the extent of substantive tests of details.

Understatement of Liabilities and Expenses at Advanced Marketing Services

Focus on Fraud

This feature provides an example of an expense-related fraud that might have been detected earlier using substantive analytics.

Advanced Marketing Services (AMS) is a San Diego, California–based wholesaler of general-interest books that provides other services, including promotional and advertising services. A scheme to fraudulently overstate earnings at AMS involved not informing retailers of credits that AMS owed them for advertising and promotional services that the retailers provided. Instead of contacting the retailers and reconciling amounts, AMS improperly reversed the liability for these credits and thereby decreased expenses and increased income. An executive at AMS profited from her participation in the fraudulent schemes through her receipt of annual bonuses and sales of AMS stock.

An analytical comparison of expenses with the previous years and with sales volumes would have been a good indicator that something was wrong.

For further details, see SEC Accounting and Auditing Enforcement Release (AAER) No. 2312.

Accounts Payable and Related Expense Accounts: Substantive Test of Details for the Existence/Occurrence Assertion

While the existence assertion is not typically a very relevant assertion for accounts payable and related expenses, depending on the specific client risks including the results of substantive analytical procedures, auditors may perform tests of details related to this area. Although not a common procedure, one test of details is to send confirmations to vendors and suppliers to confirm transactions the client has recorded. As an alternative to confirmations, auditors may vouch recorded payables balances to suppliers' statements. This test of details is more effective when recorded accounts payable are reconciled to monthly statements received from suppliers.

Accounts Payable and Related Expense Accounts: Substantive Test of Details for the Completeness Assertion

Testing Subsequent Disbursements   The auditor examines a sample of cash disbursements the client made after year-end (**subsequent disbursements**) to determine whether the disbursements are for goods and services applicable to the previous year—and, if so, whether the client recorded the liability in the previous year. If control risk is high or there are fraud-related red flags, the auditor may review 100% of the larger subsequent disbursements. The auditor will also examine vendor invoices and receiving reports to determine whether goods or services received in the previous year were properly set up as a payable.

Reconciling Vendor Statements or Confirmations with Recorded Payables   The auditor may request vendors' monthly statements or send confirmations to major vendors requesting a statement of open account items. The auditor reconciles the vendor's statement or confirmation with the client's accounts payable trial balance. The method generates reliable evidence, but is costly (in auditor time spent reconciling the amounts) and is used when there is a high risk that the company does not pay vendors on a timely basis.

Related Expense Accounts   Some expense accounts in the acquisition and payment cycle are of intrinsic interest to the auditor simply because of the nature of the account, even though they are likely not as material as inventory, cost of goods sold, or accounts payable. These accounts include legal expense, travel and entertainment expense, repairs and maintenance expense, and income tax expense. The auditor will examine legal expenses as a possible indicator of litigation that may require recording and/or disclosure. The auditor will examine travel and entertainment expenses for questionable or non-business-related items. The auditor will review repairs and maintenance expense, together with fixed-asset additions, to assure a proper distinction between expenditures that should be expensed and those that should be capitalized. The auditor, or the auditor's tax specialist, will review income tax expense and related liability(s) to assure that tax laws and regulations have been followed. In each of these areas, the auditor will review underlying documentation to determine the nature of the expenditure, its appropriate business use, and the accuracy of the recorded item.

The approach auditors often use to perform substantive tests of details for expenses is to either:

- have the client create a schedule of all larger items making up the expense account (usually done for smaller clients), or
- use data analytical tools to examine randomly selected items from the expense account using sampling and to generate a list of all credits to the expense items for further review.

Expenses at Rite Aid

Focus on Fraud

This feature provides an example of a fraud related to expenses in the acquisition and payment cycle.

Executive management at Rite Aid conducted a wide-ranging accounting fraud resulting in the significant inflation of Rite Aid's income. When the fraud was ultimately discovered, Rite Aid was forced to restate its pre-tax income by $2.3 billion and net income by $1.6 billion, the largest restatement ever recorded at the time.

One aspect of the fraud involved reversals of actual expenses. Rite Aid's accounting staff reversed amounts that had been recorded for various expenses incurred and already paid (debiting accounts payable and crediting expenses). These reversals were unjustified and, in each instance, were put back on the books in the subsequent quarter. The effect was to overstate Rite Aid's income during the period in which the expenses were incurred. Specifically, entries of this nature caused Rite Aid's pre-tax income for one quarter to be overstated by $9 million. This example makes an important point: *Sometimes executive management wants to misstate only a particular quarter to keep their stock price high, with the intent that they can fix problems before year-end.*

For further details, see SEC AAER No. 1581 and No. 2023.

Accounts Payable and Related Expense Accounts: Substantive Test of Details for the Rights and Obligations Assertion

Organizations are increasingly entering into long-term contracts to purchase inventory at fixed prices or at a fixed price plus inflation adjustments. These contracts can extend over a period of years, and there is always some risk that economic circumstances can change and the contracts may no longer be economically viable. The auditor should examine these contracts to determine penalties associated with default, and the auditor should gain sufficient knowledge to assess the client's estimate of the probability of contract default or losses.

Accounts Payable and Related Expense Accounts: Substantive Test of Details for the Valuation/Allocation Assertion

Substantive tests of accounts payable and related expense accounts for valuation usually involve simply verifying the mathematical accuracy of the accounts and agreeing them to general ledger and supporting documentation.

Accounts Payable and Related Expense Accounts: Substantive Test of Details for the Presentation and Disclosure Assertion

Companies disclose very little about accounts payable and related expense accounts. These accounts and related amounts typically only appear on the face of the financial statements.

Review of Unusual Entries to Expense Accounts

The vast majority of transactions to expense accounts should be debits accompanied by purchases of goods or services that the auditor can validate through independent receipts and independent vendor invoices. The exceptions to this rule are expense accounts that represent estimates or accounts that are based on a relationship with specific asset or liability accounts such as fixed assets (depreciation expense) or bonds (interest expense).

Focus on Fraud   **WorldCom and Unusual Adjusting Entries**

This feature provides an example of a fraud perpetrated through unusual adjusting entries to an expense account.

Management at WorldCom wanted to keep line expenses at 42% of total costs because: (a) line expense was a key ratio followed by Wall Street analysts, and (b) it helped to keep reported profits high. One of the processes used was to credit line expense by reducing restructuring reserves. The reserve account would be debited for a round amount, such as:

Dr. Restructuring Reserve	$450,000
Cr. Line Expense	$450,000

The auditor's examination of the credits in the expense account would have provided insight into this highly unusual accounting transaction.

Performing Substantive Fraud-Related Procedures for Accounts Payable and Related Expenses

In audits with a heightened risk of fraud related to accounts payable and other related expenses, the auditor will want to consider performing the following procedures or, if the procedures are already being performed, altering the timing and extent of the procedures:

- Send blank confirmations or electronic confirmations via confirmation. com to vendors that ask them to furnish information about all outstanding invoices, payment terms, payment histories, and so forth. The auditor can expand this procedure to include new vendors and accounts with small or zero balances.
- Scan journals for unusual or large year-end transactions and adjustments, for example, transactions that are not typical, approvals not going through standard processes, or not having the usual supporting documentation.
- Review client's vendor files for unusual items. Unusual items might include nonstandard forms, different delivery addresses, or vendors that have multiple addresses.
- Obtain and examine documentation for payments of invoices that are for amounts just under the limit that typically requires some level of approval.

Documenting Substantive Procedures

The auditor would typically include the following types of documentation related to the substantive procedures for accounts in the acquisition and payment cycle:

- Substantive analytical procedures (including fraud-related procedures) conducted, conclusions reached, and related actions that were taken
- Evidence about physical inventory observations for all material amounts:
  - Include information about locations observed, counts that were made and recorded, controls over inventory observation that were used, and specific test counts taken

Using Data Analytics to Identify Payroll Fraud

Focus on Fraud

This feature discusses the prevalence of payroll fraud, and how organizations and auditors can use data analytics to detect it.

The three primary types of **payroll fraud** include:

1. **Timesheet fraud**: paying employees incorrectly for the hours they work. Employees accomplish this type of fraud by falsifying their timesheets, having another employee clock in for them when they are not actually at work, or having a payroll clerk increase the rate of pay.

2. **Ghost employee fraud**: a ghost employee is a fake employee who has never worked for the organization, or a former employee who was never terminated from the payroll system and is still receiving paychecks.

3. **Worker misclassification fraud**: the organization fraudulently classifies employees as independent contractors (i.e., 1099 employees) when these employees are actually full-time employees (i.e., W-2 employees) to avoid having to pay payroll taxes, healthcare premiums, and pension benefits.

How can organizations and auditors identify payroll fraud using data analytics? Below is a list of analytics that can help to identify payroll fraud:

- Search for duplicate payroll checks.
- Identify instances in which an employee receives more than one paycheck during a given pay period.
- Search for instances in which tax deductions are not removed from the employee's paycheck.
- Search the payroll database for duplicate names, addresses, or bank account numbers.
- Search for employees who are receiving no benefit payments, but are employed full-time.
- Extract a list of terminated employees, and match that list to current payroll payments.
- Search the payroll database for duplicate Social Security numbers.
- Understand controls around changes in hourly rates and salary amounts.
- Search for excessive overtime by department or individual employees.

- Include information about the dollar amount (e.g., $50,000) above which inventory items would have been specifically tested
- If the physical inventory counts were taken at an interim date, the workpapers should include evidence about the procedures that were performed between the interim date and the balance sheet date
- Evidence about product costing, such as the audit program for auditing the standard costing system and related evidence that was obtained
- Evidence pertaining to net realizable valuable calculations
- Evidence from inventory specialists
- Summaries of evidence obtained and conclusions reached about material amounts of inventory on consignment
- Evidence from evaluating subsequent disbursements for accounts payable
- Vendor statements
- Confirmations with vendors regarding accounts payable
- Evidence regarding conducting a review of unusual entries, including documentation of such entries and the explanations for them

Check Your Basic Knowledge

11-29 A substantive procedure appropriate for testing the existence of inventory would be to perform year-end cutoff tests by noting the last shipping and receiving document numbers used before the physical inventory count is taken. (T/F)

11-30 A substantive procedure appropriate for testing rights and obligations associated with inventory would be to review vendor invoices when testing disbursements to determine that proper title is conveyed. (T/F)

11-31 Which of the following audit procedures would an auditor use to test the existence assertion for inventory?

   a. Perform year-end cutoff tests by noting the last shipping and receiving document numbers used before the client takes physical inventory.

   b. Make inquiries of the client regarding the segregation of duties between the purchasing department and the receiving department.

   c. Review the client's proposed physical inventory procedures to determine whether they are likely to result in a complete and correct physical inventory.

   d. Make inquiries of the client regarding allowances made for expected returns.

11-32 Which of the following audit procedures would an auditor use to test the valuation or allocation assertion for inventory?

   a. Inquire of production and warehouse personnel about the existence of obsolete inventory.

   b. Test inventory cost by taking a sample of recorded inventory, and trace to source documents indicating cost of inventory.

   c. Review trade journals for changes in product technology.

   d. Inquire of the client about sales adjustments (markdowns) that have been offered to sell any products.

   e. All of the above.

LO 9

Apply the frameworks for professional decision making and ethical decision making for decisions made when conducting an audit.

Applying Decision-Making Frameworks

The following *End of Chapter* materials provide you an opportunity to apply the frameworks for professional decision making and ethical decision making for decisions made when conducting an audit: *11-41, 11-45,* and *11-47.*

Let's Review

- The significant accounts in the acquisition and payment cycle are inventory, cost of goods sold, accounts payable, and other related expense accounts. You should be familiar with the information in *Exhibit 11.1.* Other related expenses such as legal expenses as well as travel and entertainment expenses are important because, while likely not as material as inventory, cost of goods sold, or accounts payable, these accounts may be a possible indicator of litigation or may contain questionable or non-business-related expenditures. (LO 1)

- Inventory existence and valuation are the assertions of primary concern in the acquisition and payment cycle because by overstating ending inventory, cost of goods sold is understated and net income is overstated. In terms of accounts payable and related expense accounts, the auditor is most concerned with completeness assertion because management may have incentives to not record all transactions relating to these accounts. (LO 1)

- Inventory is usually material, and subject to a high level of inherent risk due to its complexity and its being subject to manipulation. In terms of accounts payable and related expense accounts, the auditor should consider the inherent risk that management is more likely to: (1) understate, rather than overstate, expenses, and (2) classify expense items as assets. (LO 2)

- Financial reporting frauds in this cycle often involve overstatement of inventory or assets and understatement of expenses. Asset misappropriation frauds in this cycle often involve fictitious purchases or kickbacks to supply chain management personnel. You should be familiar with the information in *Exhibit 11.2*. (LO 3)

- Controls over inventory should provide reasonable assurance that: (a) all purchases are authorized; (2) there exists a timely, accurate, and complete recording of inventory transactions; (3) receipt of inventory is properly accounted for and independently tested to verify quality in adherence to company standards; and (4) the cost accounting system is up-to-date; costs are properly identified and assigned to products; and variances are analyzed, investigated, and properly allocated to inventory and cost of goods sold. (LO 4)

- Before performing tests of details, the auditor may perform substantive analytical procedures, such as a reasonableness test. For example, if purchases and sales volume are relatively stable from year to year, the auditor might compare ending inventory balances by location to prior-year balances. The auditor should apply analytical procedures to cost of goods sold to determine if any unexpected significant variations—either overall or by product line—occur.

- For inventory accounts, it is unlikely that audit evidence obtained from substantive analytical procedures alone will be sufficient appropriate evidence. For accounts payable and related expenses accounts, if there is a low risk of material misstatement, testing might be limited to substantive analytical procedures, such as a comparison of underlying expenses with that of the prior year and related tests of the underlying asset or liability account. (LO 5)

- Responding to identified risks typically involves developing an audit approach that contains substantive procedures (e.g., tests of details and, when appropriate, substantive analytical procedures) and tests of controls, when applicable. (LO 6)

- Typical tests of controls include inquiry of relevant personnel, observation of the control being performed, examination of documentation corroborating that the control has been performed, and reperformance of the control by the auditor testing the control. Evidence of proper authorization should be available for each purchase and payment. Paper-based systems provide evidence of authorization through signatures. To test these types of controls, the auditor usually checks for signatures on the appropriate documentation. (LO 7)

- Typical substantive tests of inventory include physical observation, test counts, net realizable valuation tests, tests of costing systems, and consultation with inventory valuation experts. Typical substantive tests of accounts payable and related expenses include review of subsequent cash payments, contracts, and unusual entries to expense accounts. (LO 8)

Significant Terms

Automated purchasing system A networked software system that links a company's website to other vendors whose offerings and prices have been preapproved by appropriate management.

Cycle count Periodic testing of the accuracy of the perpetual inventory record by counting all inventories on a cyclical basis.

Disclosure committee A disclosure committee reviews the client's financial statements and footnotes; a disclosure committee is a sub-committee of the Board of Directors, and is charged with ensuring that the organization's MD&A and footnotes to the financial statements comply with financial accounting standards.

Ghost employee fraud A ghost employee is a fake employee who has never worked for the organization, or a former employee who was never terminated from the payroll system and is still being paid.

Inventories Items of tangible personal property that are held for sale in the ordinary course of business, that are in the process of production for such sale, or that are to be currently consumed in the production of goods or services to be available for sale.

Inventory shrinkage Reduction in inventory presumed to be due to physical loss or theft.

Payroll fraud A general category of fraud that includes timesheet, ghost employee, and worker misclassification frauds.

Periodic inventory system A system of inventory recordkeeping in which no continuous record of changes in inventory (receipts and issues of inventory items) is kept. At the end of an accounting period, the ending inventory is determined by an actual physical count of every item, and its cost is computed using a suitable method.

Perpetual inventory system A system of inventory recordkeeping where book inventory is continuously in agreement with inventory on hand within specified time periods. In some cases, book inventory and stock on hand may be reconciled with each transaction; in other systems, these two numbers may be reconciled less often. This process is useful in keeping track of the actual availability of goods and determining what the correct time to reorder from suppliers might be.

Purchase order A legally binding document between a supplier and a buyer for the purchase of goods or services.

Requisition A request for the purchase of goods or services by an authorized department or function within the organization; may be documented on paper or in a computer system.

Subsequent disbursements Cash disbursements made by the client after year-end.

Supply chain management The management and control of materials in the logistics process from the acquisition of raw materials to the delivery of finished products to the end user (customer).

Three-way match A control in which a purchase order, receiving information, and a vendor invoice are matched to determine whether the vendor's invoice is correct and should be paid. This control can be automated or manual.

Timesheet fraud Paying employees incorrectly for the hours they work. Employees accomplish this type of fraud by falsifying their timesheets, having another employee clock in for them when they are not actually at work, or having a payroll clerk increase the rate of pay.

Vendor fraud These fraud schemes involve improper payments to real or fictitious vendors; vendor fraud can occur through an internal employee or employees (i.e., collusion), through an outside vendor, or through collusion between an outside vendor and an internal employee.

Worker misclassification fraud The organization fraudulently classifies employees as independent contractors (i.e., 1099 employees) when these employees are actually full-time employees (i.e., W-2 employees) to avoid having to pay payroll taxes, healthcare premiums, and pension benefits.

Prompts for Critical Thinking

Prompt for Critical Thinking #1

- Inventory may become obsolete because of technological advances even though there are no visible signs of wear.
- Customers often return inventory; the client must be careful to separately identify returned merchandise, check it for quality, and record it at net realizable value.
- Because inventory often includes a variety of types of products, the auditor must possess and apply significant knowledge about the business in order to address obsolescence and valuation questions.
- Individuals involved with the purchase of inventory may have incentives to exploit weaknesses in the control system to their economic advantage.

Prompt for Critical Thinking #2

- Assume that the client has introduced a new product with a low price point and significant customer demand. The auditor expects inventory turnover to increase, and days' sales in inventory to decrease.
- Assume that the client has invested in a new manufacturing process resulting in significantly less waste and overall increases in efficiency during the production process. The auditor expects cost of goods sold to decline, and gross margin to increase.

Prompt for Critical Thinking #3

- The notation of high-dollar-value items is a check against potential client manipulation of inventory by adding new items or adjusting the cost or quantities of existing items after the physical inventory is completed.
- Because high-dollar-value items are noted, the auditor can systematically review documentary support for major items included on the final inventory compilation that were not noted during the physical inventory observation.

Prompt for Critical Thinking #4

- Analyses of inventory whose cost exceeds the market value
- Comparisons of inventory quantities to budgetary plans
- Lists of inventory items with unusual prices, units, or descriptions

Prompt for Critical Thinking #5

- Comparing current sales with budgeted sales
- Periodically reviewing, by product line, the number of days of sales currently in inventory
- Adjusting for poor condition of inventory, reported as part of periodic cycle counts
- Monitoring sales for amount of product markdown and periodic comparison of net realizable value with inventoried costs
- Reviewing current inventory in light of planned new product introductions
- Reviewing sales subsequent to year-end and discussing future sales prospects with management for items that appear to be obsolete

Review Questions and Short Cases

NOTE: Completing *Review Questions and Short Cases* does not require the student to reference additional resources and materials.

NOTE: For the remaining problems, we make special note of those addressing fraud, international issues, professional skepticism, and ethics.

11-1 `LO 1` List the five primary activities in the acquisition and payment cycle.

11-2 `LO 1` What is an automated purchasing system? Describe the tasks that an automated purchasing system can perform.

11-3 `LO 1` Match the following assertions with their associated description: (a) existence/occurrence, (b) completeness, (c) rights and obligations, (d) valuation or allocation, (e) presentation and disclosure.

1. The company has title to the inventory as of the balance sheet date.
2. Inventory balances exist at the balance sheet date.

3. Inventory is properly classified on the balance sheet and disclosed in the notes to the financial statements.
4. Inventory balances include all inventory transactions that have taken place during the period.
5. The recorded inventory balances reflect the true underlying economic value of the inventory assets.

11-4 `LO 1` Match the following assertions with their associated description: (a) existence/occurrence, (b) completeness, (c) rights and obligations, (d) valuation or allocation, (e) presentation and disclosure.
1. The recorded accounts payable balance reflects the true underlying economic value of those liabilities.
2. Accounts payable balances include all accounts payable transactions that have taken place during the period.
3. The company actually owes a liability for the accounts payable as of the balance sheet date.
4. Accounts payable is properly classified on the balance sheet and disclosed in the notes to the financial statements.
5. Accounts payable balances exist at the balance sheet date.

11-5 `LO 2` List at least five reasons that inventory is a complex accounting and auditing area.

FRAUD

11-6 `LO 3` List at least five common fraud schemes in the acquisition and payment cycle.

FRAUD

11-7 `LO 3` Refer to the *Focus on Fraud* feature "Fraud in the Acquisition and Payment Cycle at WorldCom and Phar-Mor." Compare and contrast: (a) the nature of these two frauds; (b) motivations underlying the frauds; and (c) how management perpetrated these frauds.

FRAUD

11-8 `LO 3, 4, 8`

PROFESSIONAL SKEPTICISM

Each year Susan Riley, president of Bargon Construction, Inc., takes a three-week vacation to Hawaii and signs several blank checks to pay major bills during the period in which she is absent. Riley's vacation often occurs near the end of Bargon's fiscal reporting period because it is a slack time for the construction business. Jack Morgan, head bookkeeper for the company, uses this practice to his advantage. He makes out a check to himself for the amount of a large vendor's invoice and records it as a payment to the vendor for the purchase of supplies. He holds the check for several weeks to make sure the auditors will not examine the canceled check. Shortly after the first of the year, Morgan resubmits the invoice to Riley for payment approval and records the check in the cash disbursements journal. At that point, he marks the invoice as paid and files it with all other paid invoices. Morgan has been following this practice successfully for several years and feels confident that he has developed a foolproof fraud.
a. What is the auditor's responsibility for discovering this type of fraud?
b. What deficiencies exist in the client's internal controls?
c. What substantive audit procedures are likely to uncover the fraud?

11-9 `LO 4` Following is a list of controls in the acquisition and payment cycle for inventory and cost of goods sold. Match each control with the following activities in this cycle: (1) requisition for goods and services,

(2) purchase of goods and services, (3) receipt of goods and services, (4) approval of items for payment, and (5) cash disbursements.

a. The receiving department electronically scans bar codes on the goods received to record quantity and visually inspects for quality.
b. Computer-generated purchase orders are reviewed by the purchasing department.
c. Management approves contracts with suppliers.
d. Management reviews payments and compares them to data such as production budgets.
e. Management requires competitive bids for large purchases.
f. An individual in a position of authority reviews the completeness of supporting documentation prior to signing a check for payment.
g. A policy exists and is enforced whereby purchasing agents are rotated across product lines.
h. A requisition form is forwarded to the purchasing department by a supervisor.
i. A policy exists and is enforced whereby employees cannot purchase from vendors outside an authorized vendor database.
j. Controls exist to ensure that only authorized goods are received.
k. Controls exist to ensure that goods meet order specifications.
l. The receiving department prepares prenumbered receiving documents to record all receipts.
m. A three-way match is made between the invoice, the purchase order, and the receiving report.
n. Limits on the purchase of inventory can be exceeded only on specific approval by a manager.
o. Supporting documentation is canceled on payment to avoid duplicate payments.
p. Management monitors inventory and purchase levels.
q. Vendor disputes about payments are handled by individuals outside the purchasing department.
r. An agreement exists with the supplier whereby the supplier agrees to ship merchandise (just in time) according to the production schedule set by the manufacturer.

PROFESSIONAL SKEPTICISM

11-10 **LO 4, 6, 8** Consider a manufacturing company that includes the following departments: purchasing, receiving, inspecting, warehousing, and controllership. You are assigned to audit the receiving department. During audit planning, you determine the following information:

1. A copy of each purchase order is routinely sent to the receiving department by the purchasing department via intracompany email. This is followed by the physical copy via regular intracompany mail. Each purchase order is filed by purchase order number. In response to a job enrichment program, everyone in the receiving department is authorized to file the purchase orders. Whoever happens to be available is expected to file any purchase orders received.

2. When a shipment of goods is delivered to the receiving dock, the shipper's invoice is signed and forwarded to the controller's office, the vendor's packing slip is filed in receiving by vendor name, and the goods are stored in the warehouse by receiving personnel. In response to a job enrichment program, all persons in the receiving department have been trained to perform all three activities independently. Whoever happens to be available when a shipment

arrives is expected to perform all three of the activities associated with that shipment.

    a. What are the major deficiencies and inefficiencies in the process?

    b. How could the process be improved?

    c. Why is it important to have segregation between the purchasing, receiving, and payment functions? How is that segregation maintained when all three functions are automated?

    d. Assume that the purchasing and receiving functions operate as described. What would be your preliminary assessment of control risk? What are the implications for substantive testing of the related account balances? Describe the substantive procedures the auditor should consider for inventory, expenses, payables, and other related accounts.

11-11   **LO 5**   How can cross-sectional analysis performed as a planning analytical procedure help the auditor identify potential inventory misstatements for a multi-location retail client?

11-12   **LO 5**   How might an auditor effectively use planning analytical procedures in the audit of various expense accounts? Provide an example.

11-13   **LO 6**   Refer to *Exhibit 11.7*. Describe the differences in the planned audit approaches for Clients A and B and the reasons for such differences.

11-14   **LO 7**   When assessing whether controls are operating effectively, does the auditor need to reperform the control? For example, consider a client with a control that includes reconciling recorded accounts payable to monthly statements received from suppliers. Would the auditor review the reconciliation or reperform the reconciliation? Explain the rationale for your response.

11-15   **LO 7**   What is the effect on substantive tests of accounts payable and related expenses when the auditor assesses the risk of material misstatement as low because the client has effective internal controls?

11-16   **LO 7, 8**   Refer to the *Why It Matters* feature "Weaknesses in Auditing Inventory: Grant Thornton's PCAOB Inspection Report." Describe the audit deficiencies in the procedures the auditors performed for inventory. Explain the potential implications of their errors.

11-17   **LO 8**   The following are the procedures that an auditor should complete when observing a client's physical inventory. Refer to *Exhibit 11.10* to list these procedures in the order in which they would be completed, from Step 1 to Step 7.

Steps to Take When Observing a Client's Physical Inventory

_____Upon arriving at each site:

    a. Meet with client personnel, obtain a map of the area, and obtain a schedule of inventory counts to be made for each area.

    b. Obtain a list of sequential tag numbers to be used in each area.

    c. Observe the procedures the client supervisory personnel have implemented to shut down movement of goods.

    d. Observe that the client has shut down production.

    e. Obtain document numbers for the last shipment and receipt of goods before the physical inventory is taken. Use the information to perform cutoff tests.

_____Meet with the client to discuss the procedures, timing, location, and personnel involved in taking the annual physical inventory.

_____Review the inventory-taking procedures with all audit firm personnel. Familiarize them with the nature of the client's inventory; potential problems with the inventory; and any other information that will ensure that the client and audit personnel will properly recognize inventory items, high-dollar-value items, and obsolete items; and understand potential problems that might occur in counting the inventory.

_____Document conclusion as to the quality of the client's inventory-taking process, noting any problems that could be of audit significance. Determine whether a sufficient inventory count has been taken to properly reflect the goods on hand at year-end.

_____Determine whether specialists are needed to test or assist in correctly identifying inventory items.

_____Observe the counting of inventory and note the following on inventory count working papers:

a. The first and last tag number used in the section.

b. All tag numbers and the disposition of all tag numbers in the sequence.

c. The product identification, product description, units of measure, and number of items on a count sheet.

d. Items that appear to be obsolete or of questionable value.

e. All high-dollar-value items included in inventory.

f. Movement of goods into or out of the company during the process of inventory taking. Determine if goods are properly counted or excluded from inventory.

_____Review the plans for counting and tagging inventory items.

11-18 **LO 8** The auditor completes the following procedures while observing the physical inventory count. For each task, state which assertion(s) is being primarily tested by the procedure: (1) existence/occurrence, (2) completeness, (3) rights and obligations, (4) valuation or allocation, or (5) presentation and disclosure.

a. The auditor makes test counts of selected items and records the test counts for subsequent tracing into the client's inventory compilation.

b. The auditor takes notations of all items that appear to be obsolete or that are in questionable condition; the auditor follows up on these items with inquiries of client personnel and retains the data to determine how they are accounted for in the inventory compilation.

c. The auditor observes the handling of scrap and other material.

d. The auditor observes whether any physical movement of goods occurs during the counting of inventory.

e. The auditor records all high-dollar-value items for subsequent tracing into the client's records.

11-19 **LO 8** Describe the conditions under which it is acceptable to have the client take a physical count of inventory before year-end.

11-20 **LO 8** Determining the amount of inventory that should be written off because of obsolescence is difficult and challenging because: (1) the client will usually state that most of the goods are still saleable at current selling prices; and (2) net realizable value is only an estimate (in other words, there is no specific, correct price at which inventory should be valued). Because of this, the auditor usually gathers corroborating evidence to provide evidence on valuation and, relatedly, obsolescence. Identify at least five sources of such corroborating evidence.

FRAUD

11-21 **LO 8** In those audits where a heightened risk of fraud exists related to inventory ad cost of goods sold, the auditor will want to consider performing certain fraud-related substantive procedures. List at least five such procedures.

FRAUD

PROFESSIONAL SKEPTICISM

11-22 **LO 8** The *Focus on Fraud* feature "Examples of Fraud in Inventory" provides examples of how clients may fraudulently manipulate inventory amounts. List at least five such examples. Explain why even a professionally skeptical auditor might fall victim to a client that is perpetrating such a fraud.

11-23 **LO 8** Refer to *Exhibit 11.13*, which describes assertions and related audit procedures for accounts payable. Match the following assertions with their associated auditing procedure: (a) existence/occurrence, (b) completeness, (c) rights and obligations, (d) valuation or allocation, (e) presentation and disclosure.

1. Request vendors' monthly statements or send confirmations to major vendors requesting a statement of open account items.
2. Review the client's financial statement disclosures of accounts payable and expense accounts such as travel and entertainment.
3. Use GAS to verify mathematical accuracy of accounts payable, or agree to the general ledger.
4. Examine a sample of cash disbursements made after the end of the year to determine whether the disbursements are for goods and services applicable to the previous year.
5. Perform a cutoff test of purchases and cash disbursements made after year-end.
6. Perform analytical review of related expense accounts; for example, travel and entertainment, or legal expenses.
7. Review long-term purchase commitments, and determine whether a loss needs to be accrued.
8. Reconcile monthly statements and confirmations from major vendors with the accounts payable list.

11-24 **LO 8** Explain why examining a sample of cash disbursements made after the end of the year is useful in determining the completeness of recorded accounts payable at year-end.

FRAUD

PROFESSIONAL SKEPTICISM

11-25 **LO 8** Refer to the *Focus on Fraud* feature "WorldCom and Unusual Adjusting Entries," which explains how WorldCom executives used unusual journal entries to perpetrate their fraud.

a. What is unusual about the journal entry in this *Focus on Fraud* feature?
b. If confronted, do you think that management at WorldCom would have some reasonable, or at least plausible, explanation for the entry? Explain.
c. Imagine yourself as an early career auditor who discovers this unusual entry and inquires about it with someone at the client. What factors might cause you to lack professional skepticism in evaluating the client's explanation?

11-26 **LO 8** During observation of a client's year-end inventory, the auditor notes that shipping document 8702 was the last shipment for the year and that receiving report 10163 was the last receiving report for the year. Explain how the auditor would use this information in performing an inventory cutoff test.

11-27 `LO 8` The Northwoods Manufacturing Company has automated its production facilities dramatically during the last five years, to the extent that the number of direct-labor hours has remained steady, while production has increased fivefold. Automated equipment, such as robots and drones, has helped increase productivity. Overhead, previously applied at the rate of $7.50 per direct-labor hour, is now applied at the rate of $23.50 per direct-labor hour. Explain how an auditor might evaluate the reasonableness of the application of factory overhead to year-end inventory and cost of goods sold.

FRAUD

PROFESSIONAL SKEPTICISM

11-28 `LO 8` The auditor has always received cooperation from a particular client and has no reason to question management's integrity. The controller has requested that the auditor inform her about which warehouse locations that the auditor will visit during the upcoming inventory count. In addition, the controller has requested copies of the auditor's observations on the physical inventory because she wants to make sure that a good inventory was taken. Should the auditor comply with these requests? State your rationale, including a discussion of professional skepticism.

11-29 `LO 8` You have been assigned to the audit of Marathon Oil Company and will observe the testing of inventory at a major storage area in Ohio. The company has approximately 15 different types of fuel oils stored in various tanks. The value of the fuel varies dramatically according to its grade. Explain how you might use a specialist in auditing the inventory.

11-30 `LO 8` The auditor should be concerned as to whether slow-moving or potentially obsolete inventory is included in inventory, and whether the client should reduce inventory to a lower market value. Identify five substantive audit procedures the auditor might use to determine any obsolete goods or goods whose market value is less than cost.

11-31 `LO 8` Explain how an auditor could use data analytical tools to identify potentially obsolete inventory.

11-32 `LO 8` Explain the purpose of test counts and other inventory observations that the auditor notes while the client is performing a physical inventory.

11-33 `LO 8` Review *Exhibit 11.12*. What financial statement disclosures are required for inventory? How does the auditor determine the adequacy of the client's financial statement disclosures?

11-34 `LO 8` Identify two substantive audit procedures that an auditor might use to gain assurance about the correctness of perpetual inventory records.

11-35 `LO 8` The following audit procedures, labeled (1) through (8), are found in audit programs addressing the acquisition and payment cycle. For each audit procedure:

a. Identify the objective of the procedure or the management assertion being tested.
b. Classify the procedure as primarily a substantive test, a test of controls, or both.

1. The auditor examines payments to vendors following year-end and then reviews any open accounts payable files.
2. The auditor reviews computer-center records on changes to passwords and the client's procedures to monitor unusual amounts of access by password type. The auditor makes inquiries of purchasing agents about how often passwords are changed and whether assistants are allowed to access computer files in their absence in order to efficiently handle inquiries or process standing orders.
3. The auditor reviews a report of all accounts payable items that were not matched by the automated matching system but had been paid upon authorization of the accounts payable department. A sample of selected items is taken and traced to the vendor payment and supporting documentation.
4. The auditor uses GAS to prepare a report of all debits to accounts payable other than payments to vendors. A sample of the debits is selected and examined for support.
5. The auditor uses GAS to access all recorded receipts of merchandise that have not been matched to an open purchase order.
6. The client prepares a report from a database showing inventory write-downs by product line and by purchasing agent. The auditor reviews the report and analyzes the data in relation to sales volume by product.
7. The auditor creates a spreadsheet showing the amount of scrap generated monthly, by product line.
8. The auditor downloads client data to create a report showing monthly sales and inventory levels, by product line.

11-36 **LO 8** Auditing standards require the auditor to observe the client's physical inventory. That requirement could be met by observing the client's annual physical count of inventory and, in some circumstances, by observing inventory in connection with tests of the accuracy of the client's perpetual inventory.

a. What major purpose is served by requiring the auditor to observe the client's physical inventory count? What are the primary assertions for which the auditor gains evidence during the inventory observation?
b. Identify at least five items related to inventory that the auditor should be looking for and should document during the observation of the client's inventory.
c. How does the observation process differ when the client takes a complete physical count at or near year-end versus when the client takes physical counts throughout the year to test the accuracy of the perpetual records?

PROFESSIONAL SKEPTICISM

11-37 **LO 8** You have been assigned to audit the accounts payable of an audit client where there is a high risk of material misstatement related to accounts payable. Control risk is high, management integrity is marginal, and the company is near violation of important loan covenants, particularly one that requires the maintenance of a minimum working-capital ratio. Explain how you would approach the year-end audit of accounts payable, including a discussion of specific substantive audit procedures and the importance of professional skepticism.

11-38 **LO 8** Paul Mincin, CPA, is the auditor of Raleigh Corporation. Mincin is considering the audit work to perform in the accounts payable area for the current-year engagement. The prior-year documentation shows that confirmation requests were mailed to 100 of Raleigh's 1,000 suppliers. The selected suppliers were based on Mincin's sample that was designed to select accounts with large dollar balances. Mincin and Raleigh staff spent a substantial number of hours resolving relatively minor differences between the confirmation replies and Raleigh's accounting records. The auditors used alternative audit procedures for those suppliers who did not respond to the confirmation requests.

a. Identify the accounts payable management assertions that Mincin must consider in determining the audit procedures to perform.
b. Identify situations in which Mincin should use accounts payable confirmations, and discuss whether he is required to use them.
c. Discuss why using large dollar balances as the basis for selecting accounts payable for confirmation might not be the most effective approach and indicate what more effective procedures could be followed when selecting accounts payable for confirmation.

11-39 **LO 8** The auditor often examines some expense accounts, such as legal expenses, in detail even if the account balance is not material. Explain why.

11-40 **LO 8** Why does the auditor examine travel and entertainment expenses? What would poor controls regarding executive reimbursements say about the tone at the top for purposes of evaluating and reporting on internal control?

PROFESSIONAL SKEPTICISM

11-41 PCAOB, Grant Thornton (LO 1, 6, 8, 9) On October 4, 2008, the PCAOB issued its annual inspection report of Grant Thornton LLP (PCAOB Release No. 104-2008-046). In conducting its inspections, the PCAOB focuses on audit engagements that it considers particularly risky or prone to error.

In its inspection report of Grant Thornton, the PCAOB noted the following problems in testing the inventory valuation assertion for a Grant Thornton client.

- There was no evidence in the audit documentation, and no persuasive other evidence, that the firm had performed sufficient substantive procedures to test the raw materials and/or labor and overhead components of inventory at certain of its manufacturing locations. Analytical procedures, consisting of various high-level comparisons, including average cost, inventory balances, gross profit margins, and inventory turnover, were the firm's primary tests, but these procedures failed to meet the requirements for substantive analytical procedures. Specifically, the firm failed to develop expectations that were precise enough to provide the desired level of assurance that differences that may be potential material misstatements, individually or in the aggregate, would be identified, and failed to obtain corroboration of management's explanations of significant unexpected differences.
- The firm failed to evaluate the assumptions that management had used to determine the reserve for obsolete inventory.

a. The PCAOB inspection report summarized a problem with Grant Thornton's testing of a client's inventory valuation assertion. Discuss why you believe the PCAOB was dissatisfied with the firm's performance. Indicate how the inspection report would suggest a lack of professional skepticism.

b. Use the framework for professional decision making from *Chapter 1* to determine the appropriate steps that the firm could have taken that would have ultimately been acceptable to the PCAOB. Recall that the framework is as follows:

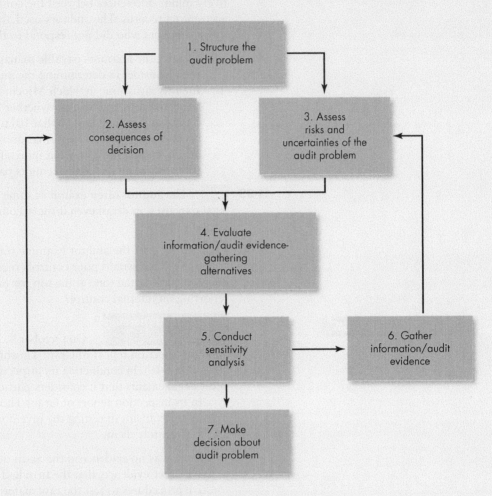

Source: Adapted from Judgment and Choice, by Robin Hogarth

Fraud Focus: Contemporary and Historical Cases

FRAUD

PROFESSIONAL SKEPTICISM

11-42 **Thor Industries, Inc., Mark Schwartzhoff, Deloitte (LO 2, 3, 4, 6, 8)**

Refer to the *Focus on Fraud* feature "Thor Industries, Inc. and Mark Schwartzhoff: Fraudulent Reductions in Cost of Goods Sold Through Manipulation of Inventory Accounts."

a. List the incentives and opportunities that enabled Schwartzhoff to commit the fraud. Speculate on his possible rationalizations.

b. What do the control deficiencies imply about the approach Deloitte should have used to audit the inventory-related accounts and assertions on the Thor and Dutchmen audits? Discuss your answer in terms of the relative mix of evidence in the form of tests of details, substantive analytics, and tests of controls. Why might Deloitte auditors have lacked professional skepticism regarding the financial results of Dutchmen?

c. What substantive audit procedures (both tests of details and analytical procedures) could have potentially detected this type of fraud earlier?

FRAUD

PROFESSIONAL SKEPTICISM

11-43 **Ace Hardware, KPMG**
(LO 2, 3, 4)

Ace Hardware is a retailer-owned cooperative, with 4,600 hardware, home center, and building materials stores. At the time of this case, Ace was a private company that was planning to go public. In September 2007, Ace Hardware said it discovered a $154 million accounting discrepancy between its general ledger and its actual inventory. The accounting error was discovered during an internal review of financial reports. The company explained that it had found a difference between the company's 2006 general ledger balance—the company's primary method for recording financial transactions—and its actual inventory records, referred to as its *perpetual inventory balance.* .

Ace hired a law firm and a consulting firm to investigate. The investigation cost about $10 million. As a result of the investigation, in January 2008, Ace Hardware reported that a mid-level employee in the finance department caused a $152 million accounting discrepancy between the general ledger and the actual inventory. The former finance worker made journal entries of a sizeable amount that masked a difference in numbers between the two ledger books. The ledgers looked as though they were reconciled, but were not. About one-quarter of the error dated to 1995, and the rest took place from 2002 through 2006. In its 10-K filing, the company reported that gross margins had increased by about 2% in the five years leading up to fiscal year-end 2002, rising from 7.7% to 9.4%. Home Depot, in contrast, maintained a very stable gross margin over that period, which was consistently about 30%. KPMG issued unqualified audit opinions on the company's financial statements during the period of the inventory misstatements.

Company officials stressed that the employee did not commit fraud and that no inventory or money was missing. Rather, the company suggested that the finance person was not properly trained or equipped to do the job. The company further suggested that the situation was Ace's fault, in that the finance person was not appropriately trained and that oversight and checks and balances were not in place. Company officials also blamed the error partly on the increasingly complex and competitive retail hardware industry. Specifically, systems in place were not adequate for addressing complications that arose from Ace's recent increase in product imports from Asia. Since that time, Ace has implemented a modern, point-of-sale inventory management system that has significantly improved internal controls and inventory pricing at individual retailer locations.

As a result of the discovery of the inventory problem, Ace had to put on hold its plans to issue a public offering of stock. While we often think of inventory misstatements as due to fraud, this case illustrates that such misstatements can also be caused by errors.

a. List the inherent, control, and fraud risk factors relevant to this case.
b. State plausible reasons that KPMG audit personnel may have lacked professional skepticism in their audits of Ace Hardware.

FRAUD

PROFESSIONAL SKEPTICISM

11-44 **VeriFone Holdings, Inc.**
(LO 2, 3, 4, 5, 6, 8)

In 2009, the SEC charged VeriFone Holdings, Inc., a technology company, with falsifying the company's financial statement to improve gross margins and income. VeriFone relied on gross margin as an indicator of its financial results and provided forecasts of its quarterly gross margins to investment analysts.

In early February 2007, during the quarterly closing process for the fiscal year ending January 31, 2007, preliminary financial results revealed a gross margin of 42.8%, which was about 4 percentage points below internal forecasts that had been communicated to analysts. Paul Periolat was a mid-level controller at VeriFone, and his responsibilities included forecasting gross margins and making final inventory-related valuation adjustments relating to royalties, warranty reserves, and inventory obsolescence. When the CEO and CFO learned of the unexpectedly low gross margins in the preliminary financial results, they sent emails calling the issue an "unmitigated disaster" and instructed VeriFone managers beneath them to "figure it [and related low results] out."

Periolat determined that the problem in gross margin was due to incorrect accounting by a foreign subsidiary. He made a manual adjusting entry to record an increase to ending inventory of $7 million, thereby decreasing cost of goods sold and increasing gross margin. He failed to confirm the adjustments with the foreign subsidiary's controller and knew that the adjustments were incorrect. Periolat continued to make large manual quarterly adjustments to inventory balances for which there was no reasonable basis over the next two quarters. These adjustments allowed the company to continue to meet its internal forecasts and its earnings guidance made to analysts. Periolat was able to make his unwarranted adjustments, in part, because VeriFone had few internal controls to prevent them. Neither the employee's supervisor nor any other senior manager reviewed the employee's work. Further, effective controls were not in place to prevent the person responsible for forecasting financial results from making adjustments that allowed the company to meet the forecasts.

Ultimately, when the misstatements were revealed and VeriFone restated its financial statements, the company's operating income fell from $65.6 million to $28.6 million, a reduction of 129%. When the misrepresentations were revealed in December 2007, VeriFone's stock price dropped 46%, which represented a one-day drop in market capitalization of $1.8 billion. With this much at stake, auditors need to remember to be professionally skeptical about manual entries and to require that appropriate documentation supporting the entries be available for their review. Further, in areas where internal controls are not effective, the auditor should implement appropriate substantive procedures due to the heightened risk of misstatement.

For further information, see SEC AAER No. 3044, September 1, 2009.

a. List the inherent, control, and fraud risk factors relevant to this case.
b. What substantive audit procedures would have detected the fraud? Would planning or substantive analytics have been helpful in detecting the fraud?

FRAUD

PROFESSIONAL SKEPTICISM

11-45 **Cenco Medical Health Supply Corporation**
(LO 2, 3, 4, 6, 7, 8, 9)

Cenco Medical/Health Supply Corporation (CMH) was an SEC-registered company that went bankrupt after it had materially misstated its financial statements for a number of years. It inflated the reporting of its physical inventory by 50% during two years prior to its bankruptcy. The fraud was perpetrated by "(1) altering the quantities recorded on the prenumbered, two-part inventory tags used in counting the inventory; (2) altering documents reflected on a computer list prepared to record the physical count of inventory; and (3) creating inventory tags to record quantities of nonexistent inventory."

The SEC asserted that the auditors should have detected the fictitious inventory but did not because the audit firm "left the extent of various observation testing to the discretion of auditors, not all of whom were aware of significant audit planning that should have related directly to the extent of such testing. Observation of inventory counts at year end was confined to six locations (representing about 40% of the total CMH inventory) as opposed to nine in the preceding year. The field auditors did not adequately control the inventory tags and the auditor did not detect the creation of bogus inventory tags which were inserted in the final inventory computations." The SEC was also critical of the audit firm for assigning interns to a significant portion of the inventory observation without training them in the nature of the client's inventory or its counting procedures. This is an example of a situation in which auditors' lack of professional skepticism led to low audit quality and a subsequent audit failure.

Source: R. W. V. Dickenson, "Why the Fraud Went Undetected," *CA Magazine* April 1977, pp. 67–69.

The SEC alleged that many deficiencies occurred during the audit of CMH, including:

1. The audit firm "left the extent of various observation testing to the discretion of auditors, not all of whom were aware of significant audit conclusions which related directly to the extent of such testing. Observations of inventory counts at year end were confined to six locations (representing about 40% of the total CMH inventory) as opposed to nine in the preceding year. The field auditors did not adequately control the inventory tags and Seidman & Seidman [the auditor] did not detect the creation of bogus inventory tags which were inserted in the final inventory computations."

2. The comparison of recorded test counts to the computer lists in the nine warehouse locations in which the inventory count was observed indicated error rates ranging from 0.9% to 38.3% of the test counts, with error rates in excess of 10% in several locations. Management attributed the differences to errors made by a key-punch operator. When the auditors asked to see the inventory tags, the CMH official stated that they had been destroyed.

3. The Seidman & Seidman auditor who performed the price testing of the CMH inventory determined that, as in previous years, in numerous instances CMH was unable to produce sufficient vendor invoices to support the purchase by CMH of the quantities being tested. This was true even though Seidman & Seidman ultimately accepted vendor invoices reflecting the purchase of the item by any CMH branch, regardless of the location of the inventory actually being price tested.

4. A schedule of comparative inventory balances reflected significant increases from the prior year. A CMH financial officer wrote on this schedule management's explanations for the increases in inventory accounts.

5. CMH did not use prenumbered purchase orders and shipping documents.

6. Several differences exist between the tags reflected on the computer list for the Miami warehouse and the observation of the same tag numbers by Seidman & Seidman auditors. The computer list contained a series of almost 1,000 tags, covering about 20% of the tags purportedly used and more than 50% of the total reported value of the Miami inventory, which were reported as being unused on the tag control document obtained by Seidman & Seidman during its observation work.

7. Because CMH management did not provide sufficient invoices as requested, the auditors relied primarily on vendor catalogs, price lists, and vendor invoices to test the accuracy of the CMH inventory pricing representations.

   a. For each of the deficiencies identified, indicate the appropriate action that the auditor should have taken.

   b. What inventory information should be communicated to an auditor who is not regularly assigned to the audit of a particular client prior to the observation of a physical inventory count?

   c. How do questions of management integrity affect the approach that the auditor should take in planning the observation of a client's inventory-counting procedures?

   d. Identify instances in which the auditors in this case did not exercise appropriate professional skepticism. For each of those instances, describe an alternative way that the auditor should have handled this situation.

   e. The individual auditors conducting the audit inventory tests were lacking the appropriate training or knowledge to conduct their jobs. Assume that you and your classmates were assigned to an audit client and you find yourselves in a similar situation when you arrive to conduct an inventory observation. In particular, you are asked to observe inventory counts of products for which you are unsure of the appropriate measurement technique and are lacking in knowledge of the product itself. The client quickly describes the measurement process and offers to help you identify the different products. You are still somewhat unsure of your abilities to conduct this inventory observation. Use the framework for professional decision making from *Chapter 1* to determine the appropriate steps to take.

Application Activities

11-46 **MagnaChip** **(LO 2, 3, 4)**

Refer to the *Focus on Fraud* feature "Inventory Valuation at MagnaChip Leads to Desired Increase in Gross Margins." Obtain a copy of the SEC's AAER for this case.

a. The *Focus on Fraud* feature describes one approach that MagnaChip used to manipulate gross margin. Identify another approach MagnaChip used to manipulate gross margin through inventory accounts.

b. Identify internal control deficiencies that may have allowed this fraud to occur.

c. When MagnaChip restated its financial statements in early 2015, what happened to its stock price? Has the stock price recovered?

d. What role did MagnaChip's external auditors play in identifying the fraud? Were the auditors professionally skeptical?

FRAUD

ETHICS

PROFESSIONAL SKEPTICISM

11-47 **WorldCom**
(LO 2, 3, 4, 9)

The Focus on Fraud feature "Fraud in the Acquisition and Payment Cycle at WorldCom and Phar-Mor" introduced you to the basic facts underlying the WorldCom fraud. Use appropriate sources to answer the following questions:

a. Identify the names of the following individuals at the company, describe their role in the fraud, and describe the penalties that they ultimately faced (if any): the CEO, CFO, controller, and the director of internal audit.

b. What appears to have been the incentives and opportunities to commit the fraud?

c. Review the framework for ethical decision making presented in *Chapter 1*. Comment on the likely ethical dilemma that Cynthia Cooper faced when she initially uncovered the fraud. What action did Cynthia Cooper take related to this dilemma?

d. Which audit firm conducted the external audit on WorldCom's financial statements in the years prior to the discovery of the fraud? Why might the auditors have lacked the necessary professional skepticism to uncover the fraud?

FRAUD

11-48 **Baird Products**
(LO 2, 3, 4)

The *Focus on Fraud* feature "Weak Internal Controls, Unethical Decisions, and a Fictitious Vendor at Baird Products" introduced you to an example of a purchasing manager who used a fictitious vendor to accomplish a fraud in the acquisition and payment cycle. Using appropriate sources, locate an example of another such case. If you perform an electronic search, you might want to use the search terms *fraud* and *fictitious vendor*. Answer the following questions:

a. What was the company involved, and who was the fraudster?
b. How did the fraudster perpetrate the fraud?
c. What was the dollar value of the loss?
d. What was the resolution of the case; for example, did the fraudster get fined or jailed?

11-49 **LO 4, 5, 6**

Refer to *Exhibit 11.6* and access the three most recent SEC filings (10K) for three companies in the same industry.

a. Calculate the following ratios from *Exhibit 11.6* for each of the companies:
   - Gross margin %
   - Inventory turnover
   - Days' sales in inventory
   - Accounts payable/current liabilities

b. Compare and contrast your results across companies, and note any areas of audit attention that are evident.

c. Summarize management's disclosures about internal control for each company for the most recent fiscal year. Comment on audit implications, including the relative proportion of evidence that you would gather from tests of details, substantive analytics, and tests of controls.

PROFESSIONAL SKEPTICISM

ETHICS

11-50 **PCAOB, Ibarra**
(LO 8)

The PCAOB disciplined the Ibarra audit firm because the auditors failed to identify and address a departure from GAAP relating to their client's valuation of inventory. GAAP requires inventory to be valued at the lower of cost or market value. The PCAOB's inspection report notes that the client's consolidated balance sheet reported inventory of $356,973, or approximately 95% of total assets. However, based on cost of goods actually sold during that fiscal year, the client's inventory balance represented approximately 22 years' worth of sales. This fact alone should have increased the auditors' skepticism about the inventory's stated value. Instead, the auditors relied solely on management's representation regarding the valuation of inventory and mechanical tests of inventory costs, and they missed the big picture.

Obtain a copy of PCAOB Release No. 2006–009 which describes this case.

a. Identify the pervasive problems that were detected by the PCAOB in its inspections of Ibarra.
b. Comment on the nature of punishments that were imposed. Were the punishments appropriate?
c. What conduct of Ibarra strikes you as the most unethical in this situation?

FRAUD

11-51 | LO 3, 5, 8

Refer to the *Focus on Fraud* feature "Examples of Fraud in Inventory." The AICPA's *Practice Alert* described in the feature provides examples of many types of inventory frauds that have occurred. Access and read the following article that describes how to detect these types of frauds: *http://www.journalofaccountancy.com/Issues/2001/Jun GhostGoodsHowToSpotPhantomInventory.htm*

a. What are the four techniques that companies use to commit inventory fraud?
b. What analytical procedures may indicate inventory fraud?
c. Who are the most common perpetrators of inventory fraud?
d. List at least five indicators of heightened risk for inventory fraud.

AUDITING STANDARDS APPLICATION ACTIVITY

11-52 | AICPA (LO 8)

Refer to the *Auditing Standards Exhibit* inside the front cover of this textbook.

Locate the AICPA standard relating to audit evidence-specific considerations for selected items (inventory), then obtain the standard on the AICPA's website.

a. What is the number of the standard?
b. What does the standard require the auditor to do to obtain sufficient appropriate audit evidence regarding the existence and condition of inventory?
c. What does the standard require the auditor to do if physical inventory count is conducted at a date other than the date of the financial statements?

11-53 | Grant Thornton, PCAOB (LO 7, 8)

In February 2017, the PCAOB issued an inspection report of Grant Thornton. The report is PCAOB Release No. 104-2017-027. Obtain a copy of this Release from the PCAOB website.

a. Identify the audit deficiencies related to inventory.
b. Indicate the auditing standards related to the deficiencies you identified in a.
c. Why do you think that these inventory-related deficiencies occurred?

11-54 PCAOB
(LO 6, 7, 8)

In May 2017, the PCAOB issued PCAOB Release No. 105-2017-027, which is a settled disciplinary order. Obtain a copy of this Release from the PCAOB website.

a. This disciplinary order notes that the firm and the auditor violated PCAOB rules and standards in connection with the firm's audits of two issuer clients. Specifically, there was a failure to exercise due professional care, including professional skepticism, and a failure to perform audit procedures to obtain sufficient appropriate audit evidence. Describe the failures that relate to auditing inventory accounts.

b. What audit procedures related to inventory should the auditor have performed?

c. Why do you think that these inventory-related deficiencies occurred?

Data Analytics Using Excel: A Case in the Context of the Pharmaceutical Industry

NOTE: In this and select cycle chapters, we present a case set in the pharmaceutical industry. The case enables students to practice developing and conducting planning and substantive analytical procedures. The case was developed using the published financial statements of three prominent companies in this industry, with adaptations to make the case suitable for classroom use. The fictional company names are as follows: PharmaCorp, Novartell, and AstraZoro. You will access an Excel file on the textbook's website at *https://login.cengage.com/cb/*. The Excel file contains financial data and information from footnote disclosures. The primary analytical procedures tasks will focus on PharmaCorp. You will use Novartell and AstraZoro as industry comparison companies. Access and download the file, then complete the requirements in *11-55*.

11-55 LO 5, 8   This case will enable you to practice conducting planning and substantive analytical procedures for accounts in the acquisition and payment cycle. When analyzing the financial data, you may assume that the 2015 information is *unaudited*, while prior-year data is audited.

As you complete this case, consider the following features of and trends in the pharmaceutical industry and for PharmaCorp specifically:

- After a long period of industry dominance by companies in the United States, the United Kingdom, and Europe, these companies are facing increasing competition from companies domiciled in emerging economies, such as Brazil, India, and China.
- There exists significant uncertainty in the market because of recent regulation covering health-care and government payouts for certain procedures and related pharmaceuticals.
- Health-care policy makers and the government are increasingly mandating what physicians can prescribe to patients.
- Health-care policy makers and the government are increasingly focusing on prevention regimes rather than treatment regimes, thereby leading to shifts in the demand for various pharmaceuticals.
- The global pharmaceutical market is anticipated to grow by 5% to 7% in 2016 compared with a 4% to 5% growth rate in 2015, according to a leading industry analyst publication.
- Beginning in 2014, PharmaCorp initiated and executed a significant company-wide cost reduction initiative aimed at improving manufacturing efficiency, cutting back on research and development expenses, and eliminating unnecessary corporate overhead.
- PharmaCorp's policies for extending credit to customers have remained stable over the last three years. PharmaCorp's credit-granting policies are considered stringent within the industry, and analysts have sometimes criticized the company for this, contending that such policies have hindered the company's revenue growth relative to industry peers.

- Two of PharmaCorp's popular pharmaceuticals, Selebrax and Vyvox, came off patent during the fourth quarter of FYE 2015. These pharmaceuticals now face competition in the generic drug portion of the overall industry market.

Information specific to the Acquisition and Payment Cycle

- Raw materials inventory required in the businesses are purchased from numerous suppliers. No serious shortages or delays of raw materials inventory were encountered in 2015, and none are expected in 2016. PharmaCorp has successfully secured the raw materials inventory necessary to meet its requirements where there have been short-term imbalances between supply and demand, but generally at higher prices than those historically paid.
- A risk that companies in this industry face with respect to the acquisition and payment cycle is that there is a possibility of failing to maintain the integrity of supply chains, possibly resulting in intentional and criminal acts such as product diversion, product theft, and counterfeit raw materials inventory.
- In response to pricing pressure, several major suppliers changed their policy with respect to discounts for early payment of amounts due on credit sales. In response, PharmaCorp changed its policy of paying within two weeks to paying within four weeks since it is no longer monetarily beneficial to do so from a cash management perspective.

Part I: Planning Analytical Procedures

a. *Step 1: Identify Suitable Analytical Procedures.* Your audit senior has suggested that the following ratios (on an overall financial statement level) will be used for planning analytical procedures in the acquisition and payment cycle at PharmaCorp:

Inventory Ratios

- Gross margin analysis (revenues-cost of sales)/revenues
- Changes in cost of goods sold on a percentage basis, yearly comparisons
- Inventory turnover (cost of goods sold/ending inventory)
- Number of days' sales in inventory (365/inventory turnover)

Accounts Payable Ratios

- Accounts payable turnover (purchases/average accounts payable)
- Days outstanding in accounts payable (365/accounts payable turnover)
- Accounts payable/current liabilities

As part of Step 1, identify any other relevant relationships or trend analyses that would be useful to consider as part of planning analytics. Explain your reasoning.

b. *Step 2: Evaluate Reliability of Data Used to Develop Expectations.* The audit team has determined that the data you will be using to develop expectations in the acquisition and payment cycle are reliable. Indicate the factors that the audit team likely considered in making that determination.

c. *Step 3: Develop Expectations.* Complete Step 3 of planning analytical procedures by developing expectations for relevant accounts in the acquisition cycle and for the ratios from Part (a). Develop expectations by considering both historical trends of PharmaCorp, and also by considering features of and historical trends in the industry. Given that this is a planning analytical procedure, the expectations are not expected to have a high level of precision. You might indicate that you expect a ratio to increase, decrease, or stay the same, and possibly indicate the size of any expected increases or decreases, or the range of the expected ratio. PharmaCorp's financial information is on first tab of the Excel file, while the financial information for Novartell and AstraZoro is provided on the last two tabs of the Excel file.

d. *Step 4 and Step 5: Define and Identify Significant Unexpected Differences.* Refer to the guidance in *Chapter 7* on performance materiality, tolerable misstatement, and clearly trivial amounts. Apply those materiality guidelines to Step 4 of planning analytical procedures in the acquisition and payment cycle for PharmaCorp to define what is meant by a significant difference. Explain your reasoning. Also comment on qualitative materiality considerations in this context. Now that you have determined what amount of difference would be considered significant, calculate the ratios identified in Step 1 (and any additional ratios or trend analyses that you suggested), based on PharmaCorp's recorded financial statement amounts. Identify those ratios where there is a significant unexpected difference.

e. *Step 6 and Step 7: Investigate Significant Unexpected Differences and Ensure Proper Documentation.* Complete Step 6 of planning analytical procedures by describing accounts or relationships that you would investigate further through substantive audit procedures. Explain your reasoning. To complete Step 7, describe what information should be included in the auditor's workpapers.

Part II: Substantive Analytical Procedures

f. Management has explained the decline in cost of goods sold as involving:

- Lower purchase accounting charges, primarily reflecting fair value adjustments relating to acquired inventory that was subsequently sold
- Lower costs related to new cost reduction and productivity initiatives, as well as savings generated from ongoing productivity initiatives to streamline the supply chain network
- Reduced manufacturing volumes related to products that lost exclusivity in various markets
- The impact of favorable foreign exchange rates of 3%.
- Explain the types of ratio analysis that you could conduct in substantive analytical procedures to test the validity of management's explanations. Comment on the trends and relationships that you believe are most relevant, and implications for further substantive testing.

Academic Research Cases

NOTE: Completing *Academic Research Cases* requires students to reference additional resources and materials.

SEARCH HINT

It is easy to locate these academic research articles! Use a search engine such as Google Scholar or an electronic research platform such as ABI Inform, and search using the author names and part of the article title.

FRAUD

11-56 LO 4, 7   Locate and read the article listed below.

Feng, M., C. Li, S. E. McVay, & H. Skaife. (2015). Does ineffective internal control over financial reporting affect a firm's operations? Evidence from firms' inventory management. *The Accounting Review* 90(2): 529–557.

a. What is the purpose of the study?
b. Describe the design/method/approach used to conduct the study.
c. What are the primary findings of the study?

11-57 LO 2, 8   Locate and read the article listed below.

Bhattacharjee, S., K. K. Moreno, & T. Riley. (2012). The interplay of interpersonal affect and source reliability in auditors' inventory judgments. *Contemporary Accounting Research* 29(4): 1087–1108.

a. What is the purpose of the study?
b. Describe the design/method/approach used to conduct the study.
c. What are the primary findings of the study?

ACL

NOTE: There is an ACL Appendix at the end of the textbook that you may find helpful in completing this problem.

11-58 **HuskyCorporation**
(LO 5, 8)

Assume that you are auditing inventory of HUSKY Corp. as of December 31, 2013. The inventory general ledger balance is $8,124,998.66. HUSKY manufactures lawn and garden tractors, snow-mobiles, and supplies. Download the data file labeled "HUSKY Inventory 2013" from the book's website under Student Resources. This file contains the following information:

SNUMB	Stock number (The first letter is F—finished goods, W—work in progress, R—raw material.)
LASTSALE	Date of last sale (finished goods) or use (raw material)
NUMSOLD	Number sold (finished goods) or used (raw materials) year-to-date
UNITCOST	Unit cost
INVQTY	Quantity on hand
EXTCOST	Unit cost × Quantity on hand
SELPRICE	Current selling price (finished goods only)
REPLCOST	Current replacement cost (raw material only)

Also, note that salespersons receive a 10% commission based on selling price.

a. Using the menu option **Analyze**, choose **Statistical** then **Statistics** on the amount field, print the statistics, and agree the total inventory to the general ledger.

b. Extract and print out all inventory items that have not been used or sold in six months. Include in the printout the total extended cost of those items.

c. Extract the finished goods into a separate file (Hint: Use the expression SNUMB = "F"):

   i. Extract those items that have a net realizable value less than cost. Add a column and calculate the amount each of those items that should be written down, and print a report that includes those items and the total of the write-down.

   ii. Add a field and calculate inventory turnover for each item in inventory. Extract and print a report of those items with a turnover less than 2. The report should include the total extended cost of those items.

d. Extract the raw materials into a separate file (see hint in Part c, but replace "F" with "R"):

   i. Extract those items that have a replacement cost less than cost, add a column and calculate the amount each of those items that should be written down, and print a report that includes those items and the total of the write-down.

   ii. Add a column and calculate inventory turnover for each item. Extract and print a report of those items with a turnover less than 2. The report should include the total extended cost of those items.

e. Prepare a report of the audit implications of your findings, indicating any additional procedures that should be performed.

12

Auditing Long-Lived Assets and Merger and Acquisition Activity

The Audit Opinion Formulation Process

I. Making Client Acceptance and Continuance Decisions
Chapter 1

II. Performing Risk Assessment
Chapters 2, 3, 7, and 9–13

III. Obtaining Evidence About Internal Control Operating Effectiveness
Chapters 8–13

IV. Obtaining Substantive Evidence About Accounts, Disclosures, and Assertions
Chapters 8–13

V. Completing the Audit and Making Reporting Decisions
Chapters 14 and 15

Quality Auditing and the Need for Quality Auditor Judgments and Ethical Decisions
Chapter 1

Professional Liability
Chapter 4

The Audit Opinion Formulation Process and a Framework for Obtaining Audit Evidence
Chapters 5 and 6

Auditing long-lived assets is usually straightforward—perform tests of changes in account balances during the year. However, the auditor should be skeptical and alert to the possibility that management is managing earnings with biased estimates without justification or by capitalizing costs that it should be expensing. The major challenge related to long-lived assets is determining asset impairment and assessing whether the recorded depreciation/amortization/depletion is appropriate.

Merger and acquisition transactions also present significant challenges related to long-lived assets. These challenges include: (a) valuing the assets and associated liabilities upon acquisition, (b) measuring restructuring charges and recognition of the liability, and (c) determining goodwill impairment.

Learning Objectives

LO 1   Identify the significant accounts, disclosures, and relevant assertions in auditing long-lived assets.

LO 2   Identify and assess inherent risks of material misstatement associated with long-lived assets.

LO 3   Identify and assess fraud risks of material misstatement associated with long-lived assets.

LO 4   Identify and assess control risks of material misstatement associated with long-lived assets.

LO 5   Describe how to use planning analytical procedures to identify possible material misstatements associated with long-lived assets.

LO 6   Determine appropriate responses to identified risks of material misstatement in auditing long-lived assets.

LO 7   Determine appropriate tests of controls and consider the results of tests of controls in auditing long-lived assets.

LO 8   Determine and apply sufficient appropriate substantive audit procedures in auditing long-lived assets.

LO 9   Describe audit considerations for merger and acquisition activities, including related management estimates.

LO 10   Apply the frameworks for professional decision making and ethical decision making to issues involving the audit of long-lived assets.

PCAOB Disciplinary Order Questions Land Valuation

Why It Matters: An International Perspective

This feature highlights the importance of reporting transactions in accordance with their substance. The auditor should consider whether the substance of transactions differs materially from their form.

The PCAOB Disciplinary Order discussed in this feature includes two respondents: (1) KCC & Associates, which was a sole proprietorship in Los Angeles, California, and (2) Chun Cho Kwok, a certified public accountant who was the sole proprietor of KCC. The order concerns the 2013 and 2014 audits of San Lotus Holding, Inc. Kwok served as the engagement partner for those two audits. For both audits, San Lotus received an unqualified audit opinion on its financial statements.

In 2013, San Lotus entered into three land transactions. The assets recorded from these transactions ($11.7 million)

represented 94% of total assets at year-end 2013. When planning the 2013 audit, the auditor identified the land transactions as significant, equity-based transactions, outside of the normal course of business with related parties. The sellers included San Lotus directors and officers, and/or business entities in which San Lotus shareholders held an ownership interest. San Lotus issued shares to the land sellers to pay for the land.

Kwok identified a risk of material misstatement due to fraud related to the valuation of the land assets acquired. The values were based on appraisals that contained language indicating that they were only to be used as a reference for certain Taiwanese urban renewal-related purposes and could not be used as a reference for other appraisal purposes.

643

While it appears that Kwok's planning risk assessments were appropriate, the auditor failed to appropriately respond to those risks. The auditor failed to:

- perform sufficient appropriate procedures to evaluate the business rationale of the land transactions

- plan and perform audit procedures that were specifically responsive to the assessed fraud risks of the land transaction

- consider whether management may have been placing more emphasis on the need for a particular accounting treatment for the land transactions than on the underlying economics of the transactions.

- perform any procedures to evaluate whether it was appropriate to record assets from the land transactions at appraised values.

Source: https://pcaobus.org/Enforcement/Decisions/Documents/105-2016-026-KCC-Kwok.pdf

Between October 2014 and January 2015, San Lotus was in correspondence with the SEC regarding the SEC's concern whether the recorded land assets should be valued at historical cost. On March 6, 2015, San Lotus disclosed that its previously filed 2013 financial statements should no longer be relied on. Among other things, San Lotus stated that the 2013 financial statements "fail[ed] to properly reflect the value of each land purchased in 2013 . . . at its historical carrying value."

In the 2014 financial statements, San Lotus continued to record the value of those land assets based on the third-party appraisals conducted in 2013. When planning the audit of the 2013 (restated) financial statements and the 2014 financial statements, the auditor again identified the land transactions as significant, equity-based transactions, outside of the normal course of business, with related parties. The auditor also again identified a risk of material misstatement due to fraud related to the valuation of the land assets acquired in the foregoing land transactions. Again, Kwok failed to plan and to perform appropriate procedures to evaluate the business rationale of the land transactions, or to plan and perform audit procedures that were specifically responsive to the risks of fraud associated with those transactions. Instead, Kwok continued to accept management's valuations of the land assets based on the appraisals, and failed to perform sufficient appropriate procedures to test those values.

These deficiencies indicate the auditor failed to exercise due professional care, including professional skepticism, during the audit, and failed to obtain sufficient appropriate evidence to support the audit opinions issued in connection with San Lotus's 2013, 2013 (restated), and 2014 financial statements.

For more details, see PCAOB Release No. 105-2016-026.

The Def-14A proxy statements for the FYEs 2013, 2014, 2015, and 2016 reveal the following auditors and their respective audit fees:

2013: $50,300 KCC & Associates
2014: $20,000 KCC & Associates
2015: $60,000 WLCC Accountancy Corporation
2016: $230,000 Davidson & Company LLP

What Do You Think?   For Classroom Discussion

Put yourself in Kwok's shoes. Why do you think he failed to change his audit approach for the 2013 (restated) and 2014 audits? What do you think would be the appropriate sanctions for Kwok and his firm? Compare the audit fees for KCC & Associates to those of Davidson & Company LLP. What inferences can you draw about the relationship between audit fees and audit quality?

What You Will Learn

- What are the significant accounts, disclosures, and relevant assertions related to long-lived assets? (LO 1)

- What are the inherent risks associated with transactions related to long-lived assets? (LO 2)

- What are fraud risks associated with long-lived assets? (LO 3)

- What controls should management have in place to mitigate the risks associated with long-lived assets? (LO 4)

- How might auditors use planning analytical procedures to identify any potential concerns related to long-lived assets? (LO 5)

- What is sufficient appropriate evidence when auditing accounts related to long-lived assets? (LO 6, 7, 8)

- What audit considerations are relevant for merger and acquisition activities, including goodwill estimates? (LO 9)

LO 1

Identify the significant accounts, disclosures, and relevant assertions in auditing long-lived assets.

Significant Accounts, Disclosures, and Relevant Assertions

Long-lived assets often represent the largest single asset category of many organizations. Long-lived assets are noncurrent assets that organizations use over multiple operating cycles and include **tangible assets** of land, buildings, fixtures, and equipment. Some organizations also have natural resources, such as timber tracts, oil wells, and mineral deposits. Long-lived assets also include **intangible assets**. For example, drug companies like Pfizer have patent costs that they capitalized as intangible assets, and companies like Coca-Cola have franchise licenses that make up a significant portion of the company's total assets. Many organizations also have goodwill as a significant intangible asset. *Exhibit 12.1* contains an overview of the accounts typically associated with long-lived assets.

The asset account (equipment, buildings, or similarly titled assets) represents the culmination of additions and disposals. Other accounts associated with long-lived assets include the related depreciation or impairment expense, any related gains from disposals, any related losses from disposals or impairments, and the accumulated depreciation account. For natural resources, the related expense account is **depletion expense** (the expense associated with the extraction of natural resources). For intangible assets with a definite life, the related expense account is **amortization expense**.

Organizations acquire some assets through capital leases; these organizations need to consider whether the relevant criteria for capitalizing the leases have been met and whether the off-balance sheet disclosures are appropriate.

Activities in the Long-Lived Asset Acquisition and Payment Cycle

The purchase of long-lived assets includes the same activities in the acquisition and payment cycle that we discussed in *Chapter 11*: (a) an employee will request to purchase a long-lived asset, (b) for approved requests, the organization will purchase the asset, (c) the organization will receive the asset, (d) appropriate personnel will approve payment, and (e) the organization will pay for the asset. An important difference is that the acquisition of long-lived assets is based on an organization's

Exhibit 12.1
Long-Lived Assets: Account Interrelationships

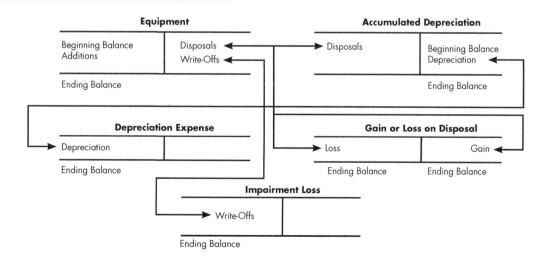

planning for long-term productive capacity, and approval for these purchases may need to be obtained from the organization's board of directors.

Once the organization acquires an asset, the organization will allocate a portion of the asset's cost as an expense—depreciation, amortization, or depletion, depending on the type of asset—in each reporting period. The organization will also review its long-lived tangible and intangible assets for possible asset impairment and, when appropriate, will recognize an impairment loss and write down the asset to its fair value. When an organization disposes of its long-lived assets, it will determine and record the gain or loss on the asset disposal.

Relevant Financial Statement Assertions

The five management assertions relevant to long-lived assets are:

1. *Existence/occurrence*—The long-lived assets exist at the balance sheet date. The focus is typically on additions during the year.
2. *Completeness*—Long-lived asset account balances include all relevant transactions that have taken place during the period.
3. *Rights and obligations*—The organization has ownership rights for the long-lived assets as of the balance sheet date.
4. *Valuation or allocation*—The recorded balances reflect the balances in accordance with generally accepted accounting principles (GAAP) (includes appropriate cost allocations and impairments).
5. *Presentation and disclosure*—The long-lived asset balance is reflected on the balance sheet in the noncurrent section. The disclosures for depreciation methods and capital lease terms are adequate.

The existence and valuation assertions related to long-lived assets are usually the most relevant assertions. Organizations may have incentives to overstate their long-lived assets and may do so by including fictitious long-lived assets on the financial statements. Alternatively, organizations may capitalize some costs, such as repairs and maintenance costs, which they should expense. When capitalizing costs that should be expensed, organizations still have to recognize the expense, but they can spread that amount over a longer period, thereby boosting current-period income. Concerns regarding valuation include whether the organization properly and completely recorded depreciation and any asset impairments. The valuation issues typically involve management estimates that may be subject to management bias.

An Overview of the Audit Opinion Formulation Process in the Long-Lived Asset Acquisition and Payment Cycle

In auditing long-lived assets, the auditor will perform risk assessment procedures, tests of controls, and substantive procedures—Phases II, III, and IV of the audit opinion formulation process.

As part of performing risk assessment procedures, the auditor obtains information to assess the risk of material misstatement. This includes information about inherent risks at the financial statement level (e.g., client's business and operational risks, financial reporting risks) and at the account and assertion levels, fraud risks including feedback from the audit team's brainstorming sessions, strengths and weaknesses in internal control, and results from planning analytical procedures.

Once the risks of material misstatement have been identified, the auditor then determines how best to respond to them. For an integrated audit and for a financial statement audit where the auditor wants to rely on controls as part of the basis for the audit opinion, the auditor will perform tests of controls and consider the effect of those tests on the substantive evidence to obtain. In other audits, the auditor will rely only on substantive tests to obtain evidence about the accuracy of the financial statements.

12-1 Long-lived assets are typically immaterial for most manufacturing organizations.   (T/F)

12-2 Patents are an example of long-lived assets.   (T/F)

12-3 Which of the following is a long-lived asset?
   a. Tangible assets such as equipment.
   b. Intangible assets such as patents.
   c. Natural resources.
   d. All of the above.

12-4 Which of the following statements is <u>true</u>?
   a. Existence and valuation assertions related to long-lived assets are usually the most relevant assertions.
   b. A concern regarding the existence of long-lived assets relates to whether management has properly recorded depreciation.
   c. Depletion expense is not an account that would be included when auditing long-lived assets.
   d. All of the above statements are true.

LO 2

Identify and assess inherent risks of material misstatement associated with long-lived assets.

Identifying Inherent Risks

Much of the inherent risk associated with long-lived assets relates to management estimates, such as estimating useful lives and residual values and determining whether asset impairment has occurred. Inherent risk related to **asset impairment** stems from the following factors:

- Normally, management does not have incentives to identify and write down assets.
- Sometimes, management wants to write down every potentially impaired asset to a minimum realizable value (although this will cause a one-time reduction to current earnings, it will lead to higher reported earnings in the future; this earnings management technique is called a "big bath").

Other inherent risks associated with long-lived assets and related expenses include incomplete recording of asset disposals and amortization or depreciation schedules that do not reflect economic impairment or use of the asset.

It's Your Turn!

Prompt for Critical Thinking #1

Provide examples of other inherent risk factors related to asset impairment.

- _____
- _____
- _____

Why It Matters   Auditing of Long-Lived Assets Does Present Risks

This feature makes the point that the audit of long-lived assets may not always be a low-risk audit area.

Many early career auditors just returning from an internship believe that the audit of long-lived assets is primarily mechanical, for example, recalculating depreciation, tracing amounts to accumulated depreciation, and vouching fixed-asset additions. In some organizations, that may be the case. As with all other aspects of the audit, the auditor must understand the client's business strategy, current economic conditions, and potential changes in the economic value of the assets. Auditors can make serious mistakes if they perform the audit as if long-lived assets are always a low-risk audit area.

The auditor will become aware of these risks through:

- Knowledge of the client's business, including industry trends and technological advances
- Review of various documents, including:
  - The business plan for major acquisitions or changes in the way the company conducts its business
  - Major contracts regarding capital investments or joint ventures with other companies
  - The minutes of board of directors' meetings
  - Company filings with the Securities and Exchange Commission (SEC) describing company actions, risks, and strategies

Inherent Risks Associated with Natural Resources   Natural resources present unique inherent risks. First, it is often difficult to identify the costs associated with the discovery of the natural resource. Second, once the natural resource has been discovered, it is often difficult to estimate the amount of commercially available resources to be used in determining a depletion rate. Third, the client may be responsible for restoring the property to its original condition (reclamation) after the resources are removed. Reclamation costs may be difficult to estimate.

Inherent Risks Associated with Intangible Assets   Organizations should initially record intangible assets at cost. However, the determination of cost for intangible assets is not as straightforward as it is for tangible assets, such as equipment. A particularly difficult area is the cost of a patent. For example, research and development costs related to new products, such as drugs or software, should be expensed as incurred up until the point that there is a viable product and a plan to bring the product to market. Legal costs for obtaining and defending a patent are capital expenditures if the defense is successful. If it is not successful, the patent has no value and any related costs should be expensed. Patents purchased from another company are capital costs. The cost of patents should be amortized over the lesser of their legal life or their estimated useful life. Minor changes to the patented item have been made by drug companies to extend the life of some patented drugs. As with tangible long-lived assets, management needs to determine if the values of patents and other intangible assets have been impaired.

12-5 The pervasiveness of management estimates is a factor that heightens the inherent risk associated with long-lived assets. (T/F)

12-6 An inherent risk associated with intangible long-lived assets is the difficulty in determining the cost of the asset. (T/F)

12-7 Which of the following is not an inherent risk related to long-lived asset accounts?

   a. Failing to record asset disposals.

   b. Capitalizing repairs and maintenance expense.

   c. Changing depreciation estimates to manage earnings.

   d. All of the above are inherent risks related to long-lived asset accounts.

12-8 Which of the following risks is an inherent risk related to asset impairment?

   a. Determination of asset impairment requires management judgment.

   b. It is difficult to identify the costs associated with the discovery of natural resources.

   c. Management might have incentives to not record all asset disposals.

   d. All of the above are inherent risks related to asset impairment.

LO 3

Identify and assess fraud risks of material misstatement associated with long-lived assets.

Identifying Fraud Risks

Some common techniques that managers may use to fraudulently misstate financial statements in this transaction cycle include overvaluing existing assets, recording fictitious assets, or capitalizing expenses. The WorldCom fraud case is a classic example illustrating some of the fraud risks relating to long-lived asset accounts. One element of the WorldCom fraud involved management reducing the accumulated depreciation account by debiting that account and crediting depreciation expense. WorldCom employees recorded these entries on a regular basis, and, the auditors did not view them as unusual or otherwise worthy of separate investigation. Management also misstated assets by routinely capitalizing their line expense (in other words, cash paid to other carriers when WorldCom used their lines to transmit calls). Finally, upon making new acquisitions, management boosted the value of the assets, and established reserves for plant closings and related expenses. When the actual expenses were less, management debited the liability and credited the expense, thereby increasing net income in subsequent periods.

Other potential fraud schemes relating to long-lived assets include:

- Not recording the sales of assets, and misappropriating the proceeds.
- Failing to remove assets from the books when the items have been sold.
- Inappropriately assigning residual values or lives to the assets, resulting in miscalculation of depreciation.
- Purposely miscalculating amortization of intangible assets.

It's Your Turn!

Prompt for Critical Thinking #2

Identify other potential fraud schemes relating to long-lived assets.

- _____

- _____

- _____

Focus on Fraud Fraud Involving Outright Theft of Long-Lived Assets

This feature describes risks related to the theft of long-lived assets.

The U.S. Department of Defense has a long history of falling victim to the outright theft of long-lived assets. For example, a major undercover sting operation in 2007–2008 revealed that stolen equipment, including fighter jet parts, nuclear protective gear, and body armour was readily available for sale to the highest bidder on Craigslist and eBay. Other organizations, both large and small, face a similar challenge: employees stealing fixed assets and selling them for cash, which they then fraudulently keep for themselves.

Most external audits include procedures around additions and sales of fixed assets; but many audits do not include an audit of existing fixed assets that the organization owned at the beginning of the year. By failing to audit the existence assertion by conducting a complete physical inventory of beginning-of-year fixed assets and during-the-year fixed-asset transactions, the auditor and the organization face the possibility that material long-lived assets were stolen.

To prevent fraud involving outright theft of long-term assets, organizations should have controls in place. Control examples include performing physical counts, assigning responsibility for long-lived assets to specific individuals to ensure accountability, and monitoring for theft of items that fall below a capitalization threshold (i.e., that are expensed immediately).

Check Your Basic Knowledge

12-9 Some common techniques that managers may use to fraudulently misstate financial statements related to long-lived assets include overvaluing existing assets, recording fictitious assets, or capitalizing expenses.   (T/F)

12-10 A fraud scheme that WorldCom top-management employed involved capitalizing items that should have been expensed.   (T/F)

12-11 Which of the following statements is <u>false</u> regarding fraud risk related to long-lived assets?

 a. A potential fraud scheme involves not removing sold assets from the books.

 b. Because long-lived assets are typically an audit area of low risk, auditors do not need to perform brainstorming activities related to long-lived assets.

 c. Management might use unreasonably long depreciable lives in an effort to reduce current-period expenses.

 d. None of the above statements is false.

12-12 Which of the following techniques can managers use to prevent the outright theft of long-lived assets?

 a. Assign accountability for long-lived assets to specific individuals.

 b. Conduct physical counts of existing and new long-lived assets purchased during the year.

 c. Capitalize transactions that they should expense.

 d. All of the above.

 e. Two of the above.

LO 4

Identify and assess control risks of material misstatement associated with long-lived assets.

Identifying Control Risks

Once the auditor has obtained an understanding of the inherent and fraud risks of material misstatement related to long-lived assets, the auditor needs to understand the controls that the client has designed and implemented to address those risks. Remember, the auditor is required to gain an overall understanding of internal controls for both integrated audits and financial statement only audits. The auditor normally gains this understanding by performing a walkthrough of the process, inquiry, observation, and review of the client's documentation. The auditor considers both entity-wide controls and transaction controls at the account and assertion levels. This understanding provides the auditor with a basis for making an initial control risk assessment.

At the entity-wide level, the auditor considers the control environment, risk assessment, information and communication, and monitoring controls.

Although the auditor needs to understand all the components of internal control, the auditor typically finds it useful to focus on important control activities related to the long-lived asset accounts. As part of this understanding, the auditor focuses on the relevant assertions for each account and identifies the controls that relate to risks for these assertions. In an integrated audit or in a financial statement only audit where the auditor relies on controls, the auditor uses this understanding to identify important controls that need to be tested.

WorldCom and Waste Management: Two Historical Examples of Asset Misstatement

Focus on Fraud

The weaknesses in the control environment at these two companies provided opportunities for management to override existing controls and to commit historically significant frauds.

WorldCom

The WorldCom bankruptcy was one of the largest in U.S. history. From the first quarter of 1999 through the first quarter of 2002, WorldCom's management improperly released approximately $984 million in depreciation reserves to increase pre-tax earnings by decreasing depreciation expense or increasing miscellaneous income. The depreciation reserves were created in the following ways:

- The cost of equipment returned to vendors for credit after being placed in service was credited to the reserve (accumulated depreciation), rather than the asset itself.
- Unsupported additions to an asset account were recorded with a corresponding increase in the reserve.
- After the end of each fiscal quarter, management in general accounting would direct property accounting personnel to release large balances from this reserve account (debit to the accumulated depreciation account), usually to reduce depreciation expense. If it was too late in the quarterly closing process to record depreciation expense as a standard adjusting entry, property accounting personnel were

directed to prepare a draft journal entry so that general accounting could make the adjustment. WorldCom also inappropriately capitalized line expense (amounts paid to other carriers such as AT&T to use their lines) as fixed assets.

Source: *Report of Investigation* by the Special Investigative Committee of the Board of Directors of WorldCom, Inc., March 31, 2003.

Waste Management

Waste Management, Inc. is the nation's largest waste disposal company. The company grew though extensive acquisitions—seemingly all dependent on ever-increasing sales and net income that fueled higher stock prices. Waste Management's previous management recognized the importance of stock prices to pay for more acquisitions, but the company was losing its profitability.

Management struck on a new way to increase reported net income—simply increase the estimated useful lives of all the depreciable assets. The auditors never questioned the change even though the change accounted for virtually all of Waste Management's increase in earnings over a period of years. Finally, the SEC stepped in and pointed out these estimated useful lives simply were not realistic. Waste Management had misstated earnings by a whopping $3.5 billion. Arthur Andersen paid fines of $220 million, and the SEC fined the individual auditors on the engagement.

For Classroom Discussion

What Do You Think?

After reading the *Focus on Fraud* feature related to WorldCom's and Waste Management's asset misstatements, do you think that similar control environment weaknesses are present at many organizations today?

What would you do if you found yourself auditing a manufacturing client, and the client had decided to extend the useful

lives of its manufacturing equipment? What evidence would you want for assurance that the increase in useful lives was appropriate? How would the effectiveness of the control environment influence your decision?

Internal Controls for Long-lived Assets

To provide reasonable assurance that the existence and valuation assertions for tangible long-lived assets are materially correct, controls should be in place to:

- Identify existing assets, inventory them, and reconcile the physical asset inventory with the property ledger on a periodic basis (existence). Many organizations face a challenge in tracking the location, quantity, condition, maintenance, and deprecation status of their fixed assets. One approach to dealing with this challenge is to use serial numbered asset tags, often with bar codes. Then periodically, the organization takes inventory, utilizing a bar-code reader.
- Provide reasonable assurance that all purchases are authorized and properly valued (valuation)
- Provide reasonable assurance that additions to tangible assets include all repairs and maintenance costs that should be capitalized (completeness)
- Appropriately classify new equipment according to its expected use and estimated useful life (valuation)
- Periodically reassess the appropriateness of depreciation categories (valuation)
- Identify obsolete or scrapped equipment and write the equipment down to scrap value (valuation)
- Review management strategy and systematically assess the impairment of assets (valuation)
- Inquire of management about the controls related to asset impairment judgments, and review related documentation (valuation)

The client should have controls that include:

- A systematic process to identify assets that are not currently in use
- Projections of future cash flows, by reporting unit, that are based on management's strategic plans and economic conditions
- Systematic monitoring of current market values of similar assets

Typical control activities affecting multiple assertions for long-lived assets include:

- A formal budgeting process with appropriate follow-up variance analysis
- Written policies for acquisition and disposals of long-lived assets, including required approvals
- Limited physical access to assets, where appropriate
- Periodic comparison of physical assets to subsidiary records
- Periodic reconciliations of subsidiary records with the general ledger

Controls Over Natural Resources   Most established natural resource companies have developed procedures and associated internal controls for identifying costs associated with natural resources. These organizations typically use geologists to establish an estimate of the reserves contained in a new discovery. They will periodically reassess the amount of reserves as more information becomes available during the course of mining, harvesting, or extracting resources.

Controls Over Intangible Assets   For intangible assets, the client should have controls designed to:

- Provide reasonable assurance that decisions are appropriately made to capitalize (completeness of assets) or expense (existence of assets) research and development expenditures
- Develop amortization schedules that reflect the remaining useful life of intangible assets such as patents or copyrights (valuation)
- Identify and account for intangible-asset impairments (valuation)

Exhibit 12.2

Examples of Controls Over Intangible Long-Lived Assets

- Management authorizations are required for intangible asset transactions.
- Documentation regarding intangible assets should be maintained, and such documentation should include:
  - Manner of acquisition (e.g., purchased, developed internally)
  - Basis for the capitalized amount
  - Expected period of benefit
  - Amortization method
- Required approval and review of amortization periods and calculations by appropriate personnel.

Management should have a monitoring process in place to review valuation of intangible assets. For example, a pharmaceutical company should have fairly sophisticated models to predict the success of newly developed drugs and monitor actual performance against expected performance to determine whether a drug is likely to achieve expected revenue and profit goals. Similarly, a software company should have controls in place to determine whether capitalized software development costs will be realized. *Exhibit 12.2* identifies examples of other controls over intangible long-lived assets that clients may design and implement.

Documenting Controls

Auditors need to document their understanding of internal controls for both integrated audits and financial statement only audits. Similar to other audit areas, the auditor can provide this documentation in various formats, including a control matrix, a control risk assessment questionnaire, and/or a memo. The documentation should include the auditor's preliminary control risk assessments at the account or assertion level.

Check Your Basic Knowledge

12-13 Auditors should expect clients to have written policies for the acquisition and disposal of long-lived assets. (T/F)

12-14 A formal budgeting process tied to the acquisition of long-lived assets is a management activity, but is <u>not</u> a control over long-lived assets. (T/F)

12-15 Which of the following controls would be most useful in providing reasonable assurance about the valuation of tangible long-lived assets?
   a. A policy requiring the reconciliation of the physical asset count with the property ledger.
   b. A policy requiring that deprecation categories and lives be periodically assessed.

   c. A formal budgeting process.
   d. Written policies requiring authorization for the acquisition of long-lived assets.

12-16 Which of the following controls should management have in place to provide reasonable assurance about asset impairment judgments?
   a. A policy requiring the reconciliation of the physical asset count with the property ledger.
   b. Limits to physical access of long-lived assets.
   c. A systematic process to identify assets that are not currently in use.
   d. A formal budgeting process.

LO 5

Describe how to use planning analytical procedures to identify possible material misstatements associated with long-lived assets.

Performing Planning Analytical Procedures

Planning analytical procedures help auditors identify areas of potential material misstatements. The objective of planning analytical procedures is to identify accounts with heightened risk of misstatement during audit planning to provide a basis for designing and implementing responses to the assessed risks. Planning analytical procedures can be relatively imprecise. We provide an outline of the analytical procedure steps in *Chapter 6*.

To perform meaningful planning analytical procedures for long-lived assets, auditors must understand the business and economics of the client's business. Consider a simple example. A local company is in the business of picking up and hauling garbage. Shouldn't the auditors have a good idea of approximately how long the trucks will last? They know the mileage; they know the beating the trucks take every day; they know something about the company's policy for cleaning and repairing the trucks. What if management comes in and makes a decision to extend the depreciable life from five to twelve years when the rest of the industry is at about six years? Does this make sense? Although the auditor cannot always make a decision as to whether five years is better than six years, the auditor needs to be in a position to understand whether five years is closer to economic reality than twelve years.

Ratio and Trend Analyses   Planning analytical procedures for long-lived assets can include:

- Review and analyze gains or losses on disposals of equipment (gains indicate that depreciation lives are too short; losses indicate the opposite).
- Compare depreciable lives used by the client for various asset categories with those of the industry, with a typical expectation that the client's depreciable lives would be consistent with those in the industry. Large differences may indicate earnings management.
- Compare the asset and related expense account balances in the current period to similar items in the prior audit and determine whether the amounts appear reasonable in relation to other information you know about the client, such as changes in operations.

Focus on Fraud   Performing Planning Analytical Procedures

This feature highlights that planning analytical procedures can be useful in identifying management fraud related to long-lived assets.

The auditor should be aware that if a fraud exists in long-lived asset accounts, the financial statements usually will contain departures from industry norms, but may not differ from the expectations set by management (e.g., through budgets) or expectations that the auditor may have based on prior financial reporting results for the organization.

If the auditor relies solely on consistency with budgets or prior financial results, but those figures already reflect an ongoing fraud, evaluating them will not yield differences from expectations, that is, will not raise any "red flags". Therefore, the auditor should compare the unaudited financial statements with budgeted amounts, past financial results, and industry trends, and should be particularly skeptical if analytical procedures reveal any anomalies between those three sources.

Ratios that the auditor should plan to review, after developing independent expectations, include:

- *Ratio of depreciation expense to total depreciable long-lived tangible assets*— This ratio should be predictable and comparable over time unless there is a change in depreciation method or asset lives. The auditor should plan to analyze any unexpected deviations and assess whether any changes are reasonable.
- *Ratio of repairs and maintenance expense to total depreciable long-lived tangible assets*—This ratio may fluctuate because of changes in management's policies (e.g., maintenance expenses can be postponed without immediate breakdowns or loss of productivity). The auditor should plan to analyze any unexpected deviation with this consideration in mind.

It's Your Turn!   *Prompt for Critical Thinking #3*

Provide three other planning analytical procedures that an auditor can perform for long-lived assets.

- _____
- _____
- _____

Check Your Basic Knowledge

12-17   The auditor needs to understand the client's business to perform meaningful planning analytical procedures.   (T/F)

12-18   When performing planning analytical procedures, the auditor should <u>not</u> typically expect the client to use depreciable lives similar to organizations in the same industry.   (T/F)

12-19   An auditor performing planning analytical procedures scans the repairs and maintenance expense accounts. Which of the following statements is likely to be consistent with the auditor's focus?
- a.   Expenditures for long-lived assets have not been charged to expense.
- b.   Expenditures for long-lived assets have been properly approved.

c.   Expenditures for long-lived assets have been recorded in the correct period.
d.   The auditor would not be performing scanning as a planning analytical procedure.

12-20   Which of the following analyses might an auditor perform as part of planning analytical procedures for long-lived assets?
- a.   Develop an overall estimate of depreciation expense.
- b.   Compare capital expenditures with the client's capital budget.
- c.   Perform a trend analysis of the ratio of depreciation expense to total depreciable long-lived tangible assets.
- d.   All of the above could be performed as part of planning analytical procedures.

If planning analytical procedures do not identify any unexpected relationships, the auditor would conclude that there is not a heightened risk of material misstatements in these accounts. If unusual or unexpected relationships exist, the planned audit procedures (tests of controls, substantive procedures) would be adjusted to address the potential material misstatements.

LO 6

Determine appropriate responses to identified risks of material misstatement in auditing long-lived assets.

Responding to Identified Risks of Material Misstatement

Once the auditor understands the risks of material misstatement, the auditor is in a position to determine the appropriate audit procedures to perform. Audit procedures should be proportional to the assessed risks, with areas of higher risk requiring more evidence and/or evidence that is more appropriate. Responding to identified risks typically involves developing an audit approach that contains substantive procedures (e.g., tests of details and, when appropriate, substantive analytical procedures) and tests of controls, when applicable. The sufficiency and appropriateness of selected procedures will vary to achieve the desired level of assurance for each relevant assertion. While audit firms may have a standardized audit program for the acquisition and payment cycle, the auditor should customize the audit program based on the assessment of risk of material misstatement.

Consider a client where the auditor has assessed the risks of material misstatement related to the existence of equipment at high. Furthermore, assume that incentives exist to overstate income to achieve profit targets that affect management bonuses, and oversight is relatively weak because of a lack of supervision by top management. Therefore, there is a heightened risk of management capitalizing items that it should expense. The auditor may develop an audit program that consists of first performing limited tests of operating effectiveness of controls, then performing limited substantive analytical procedures, and finally performing extensive substantive tests of details. Because of the high risk, the auditor will want to obtain a great deal of evidence directly from tests of details.

In contrast, consider a client where the auditor has assessed the risks of material misstatement related to the existence of equipment as low, and believes that the client has designed and implemented effective controls in this area. For this client, the auditor will likely perform tests of controls, gain a high level of assurance from substantive analytical procedures such as a reasonableness test, and then complete the substantive procedures by performing tests of details at a limited level.

Panel A of *Exhibit 12.3* shows that because of differences in risk, the box of evidence to be filled for testing the existence of equipment at the low-risk client is smaller than that at a high-risk client. Panel B of *Exhibit 12.3* illustrates the different levels of assurance that the auditor will obtain from tests of controls and substantive procedures for the two types of clients. Panel B makes the point that because of the higher risk associated with the existence of equipment (in part, due to less effective controls) at Client B, the auditor will want to design the audit so that more of the assurance is coming from tests of details. Note that the relative percentages are judgmental in nature; the examples are simply intended to give you a sense of how an auditor might select an appropriate mix of procedures.

Exhibit 12.3

Panel A: Sufficiency of Evidence for Existence of Equipment

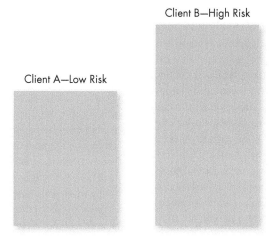

Panel B: Approaches to Obtaining Audit Evidence for Existence of Equipment

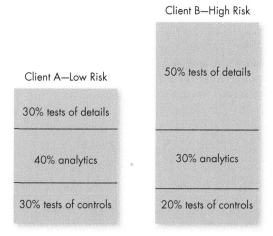

Client-Specific Considerations When Responding to Risks of Material Misstatement: The Case of Schneider National, Inc.

Why It Matters

This feature emphasizes that the auditor should always consider the unique circumstances of the client when making decisions about how to respond to identified risks of material misstatement. We use the example of a high capital-intensive business that provides disclosures about its long-lived assets, depreciation, and potential impairments.

For many organizations, long-lived assets involve only a few assets of relatively high value. For these clients, the time and effort needed to perform tests of controls to reduce substantive testing may exceed the time required to simply perform the substantive tests. Therefore, the most efficient approach would be a substantive approach, using tests of details, for obtaining evidence. However, if an organization has a high volume of long-lived asset transactions, it may be more efficient to perform tests of controls to support an assessment of low control risk, and reduce substantive testing.

As an example of the latter, consider Schneider National, Inc. (Schneider) which issued a form S-1 with the SEC in late 2016 to provide investors with data about its upcoming initial public offering of stock. As this disclosure reveals, Schneider has 12,000 trucks and over 38,000 trailers alone! Take a moment and consider how well-controlled the company would need to be to keep track of all that valuable equipment.

"Iconic large-scale diversified North American truck-load provider with a modern fleet

Over the past 80 years, we have become one of North America's largest and most trusted providers of truckload services, including specialty equipment services. We have established a leading position through our commitment to provide an outstanding level of customer service. In 2016 alone, we have received 17 awards from customers and the media in recognition of our exceptional service and reliability. We operate one of North America's largest truckload fleets with approximately 12,000 trucks and 38,100 trailers used in our truckload business. Given our large scale, we offer both network density and broad geographic coverage to meet our customers' transportation needs across North America. Our scale and strong balance sheet provides us with access to capital necessary to consistently invest in our capacity, technology and people to drive performance and growth, and to comply with regulations. Our scale also gives us significant purchasing benefits in third-party capacity, fuel, equipment and MRO (maintenance, repair and operations), lowering our costs compared to smaller competitors."

With respect to depreciation and potential impairments, Schneider's disclosures reveal the following:

"We operate a significant number of trucks, trailers, containers, chassis and other equipment in connection with our business and must select estimated useful lives and salvage values for calculating depreciation. Property and equipment is stated at cost less accumulated depreciation. It is depreciated to an estimated salvage value using the straight-line method over the asset's estimated useful life. Depreciable lives of revenue equipment range from 4 to 20 years and are based on historical experience, as well as future expectations regarding the period we expect to benefit from the assets and company policies around maintenance and asset replacement. Estimates of salvage value at the expected date of sale are based on the expected market values of equipment at the expected time of disposal. We consider our experience with similar assets, conditions in the used revenue equipment market and operational information such as average annual miles. We periodically review the reasonableness of our estimates regarding useful lives and salvage values of our revenue equipment and adjust these assumptions appropriately when warranted. We review our property and equipment whenever events or circumstances indicate the carrying amount of the asset may not be recoverable. An impairment loss equal to the excess of carrying amount over fair value would be recognized if the carrying amount of the asset is not recoverable."

To illustrate the materiality of Schneider's property and equipment, notice that it is the largest line item on the balance sheet.

Schneider National, Inc., and Subsidiaries Consolidated Balance Sheets as of December 31, 2015 and 2014 (in thousands, except share and per share information)

	2015	2014
ASSETS		
CURRENT ASSETS:		
Cash and cash equivalents	$ 160,676	$ 149,885
Marketable securities	50,318	47,739
Receivables:		
Trade—net of allowance	400,399	410,030
Managed freight	6,881	3,677
Other	64,645	44,122
Current portion of lease receivables—net of allowance	118,183	87,636
Inventories	68,466	44,944
Prepaid expenses and other assets	43,430	40,295
Total current assets	912,998	828,328
PROPERTY AND EQUIPMENT		
Transportation equipment-net	1,409,445	1,194,411
Land, buildings, and improvements-net	64,578	63,623
Other—net	29,934	18,168
Net property and equipment	1,503,957	1,276,202
LEASE RECEIVABLES	106,344	89,213
CAPITALIZED SOFTWARE AND OTHER NONCURRENT ASSETS	71,932	92,746
GOODWILL	26,706	33,722
TOTAL	$ 2,621,937	$ 2,320,211

In its Form S-1, Schneider had this to say in terms of risks relating to its internal controls:

"Our internal controls over financial reporting may not be effective and our independent registered public accounting firm may not be able to certify as to their effectiveness, which could have a significant and adverse effect on our business, reputation and stock price.

We are not currently required to comply with SEC rules that implement Section 404 of the Sarbanes-Oxley Act, or Section 404, and are therefore not required to make a formal assessment of the effectiveness of our internal controls over financial reporting for that purpose. The process of designing and implementing effective internal controls is a continuous effort that requires us to anticipate and react to changes in our business and the economic and regulatory environments and to expend significant resources to maintain a system of internal controls that is adequate to satisfy our reporting obligations as a public company. If we are unable to establish or maintain appropriate internal financial reporting controls and procedures, it could cause us to fail to meet our reporting obligations on a timely basis, result in material misstatements in our consolidated financial statements and harm our operating results. As a public company, we will be required, pursuant to Section 404, to furnish a report by management on, among other things, the effectiveness of our internal control over financial reporting for the first fiscal year beginning after the effective date of this offering.

When evaluating our internal controls over financial reporting, we may identify material weaknesses that we may not be able to remediate in time to meet the applicable deadline imposed upon us for compliance with the requirements of Section 404. In addition, if we fail to achieve and maintain the adequacy of our internal controls, as such standards are modified, supplemented or amended from time to time, we may not be able to ensure that we can conclude, on an ongoing basis, that we have effective internal controls over financial reporting in accordance with Section 404. We cannot be certain as to the timing of completion of our evaluation, testing and any remediation actions or the impact of the same on our operations. If we are not able to implement the requirements of Section 404 in a timely manner or with adequate compliance, we may be subject to sanctions or investigation by regulatory authorities, such as the SEC. If either we are unable to conclude that we have effective internal control over financial reporting or our independent registered public accounting firm is unable to provide us with an unqualified report, investors could lose confidence in our reported financial information, which could have a material adverse effect on the trading price of our Class B common stock."

On April 5, 2017, Schneider raised $550 million in its IPO. You might consider downloading Schneider's first available 10-K following its IPO, (the company has a FYE September year-end date); it will be interesting to see what Deloitte finds when it conducts the SOX 404 internal control audit. As of the writing of this textbook, the 10-K was not yet available. Challenge yourself and locate the 10-K at *www.sec.gov*.

Check Your Basic Knowledge

12-21 If a client's long-lived assets involve only a few assets of relatively high value, it might be most efficient to test long-lived assets by using only substantive tests of details.   (T/F)

12-22 Assume a client setting where there are weak controls and client incentives to capitalize items that it should expense. In such a setting, the auditor likely obtains most of the audit evidence through tests of controls.   (T/F)

12-23 Assume that the auditor decides to only perform substantive tests of details when auditing the equipment account. Which of the following statements best describes the account being audited?

   a. The client does not have effective controls over equipment.

   b. The equipment account involves only a few assets of relatively high value.

   c. Either (a) or (b) could be descriptive the account being audited.

   d. Neither (a) nor (b) would be descriptive of the account being audited.

12-24 Assume that a client's controls over recording retirements of long-lived tangible assets are <u>not</u> well designed. Which of the following procedures would the auditor plan to perform as a way of responding to the heightened risk of material misstatement?

   a. Select long-lived tangible assets recorded in the property ledger and locate them for inspection.

   b. Inspect long-lived tangible assets located at the client location and trace those assets to the property ledger.

   c. Review the tangible long-lived asset property ledger to see if depreciation was recorded on each tangible long-lived asset.

   d. The auditor would perform all of the above procedures to respond to the heightened risk of material misstatement due to poor client controls over recording retirements.

LO 7

Determine appropriate tests of controls and consider the results of tests of controls in auditing long-lived assets.

Obtaining Evidence About Internal Control Operating Effectiveness for Long-Lived Asset Accounts and Related Expenses

For integrated audits, the auditor will test the operating effectiveness of important controls throughout the year, with a heightened focus on controls as of the client's year-end. If the auditor wants to rely on controls for the financial statement audit, the auditor will test the operating effectiveness of those controls throughout the year.

Selecting Controls to Test and Performing Tests of Controls

The auditor selects and tests controls that are important to the auditor's conclusion about whether the organization's controls adequately address the assessed risk of material misstatement for the long-lived asset accounts. The auditor selects both entity-wide and transaction controls for testing.

Typical tests of transaction controls include inquiry of personnel performing the control, observation of the control being performed, inspection of documentation confirming that the control has been performed, and reperformance of the control by the auditor testing the control. For example, assume that a client implements a policy requiring the establishment and enforcement of property management training for all personnel involved in the use, stewardship, and management of equipment. The auditor can test this control (the policy and its implementation) in various ways, including:

- *Inquiry*
- *Observation*
- *Inspection of documentation*

Exhibit 12.4 provides examples of various controls that a client might use to mitigate the risk of material misstatement in the acquisition and payment cycle.

Prompt for Critical Thinking #4　　　　It's Your Turn!

Provide a specific example for each of the three approaches identified to test the control whereby a client implements a policy requiring the establishment and enforcement of property management training for all personnel involved in the use, stewardship, and management of equipment.

• INQUIRY

_____

• OBSERVATION

_____

• INSPECTION OF DOCUMENTATION

_____

Exhibit 12.4
Control Examples and Tests

Objective	Control Example	How Control Would be Tested	Implications if Control is Not Working
Capitalized property additions should not be expensed (as repairs and maintenance or other expense).	A capitalization policy to ensure that long-lived assets are treated consistently. For example, a company might require capitalization of any long-lived asset purchases over $5,000. Purchases under $5,000 would be classified as expenses in the period when they are bought.	The auditor would select a sample of long-lived asset purchases and review documentation to determine whether the organization's capitalization policy had been adhered to.	Expenses will be understated and long-lived assets will be overstated. The auditor may need to increase tests of current period purchases. For the extended sample, the auditor will determine whether the purchase should have been capitalized or expensed.
All recorded long-lived tangible asset purchases are approved.	A policy for asset purchase authorization by the board for high-dollar purchases.	The auditor might take a sample of recorded asset purchases and obtain documentation showing board approval.	Fraud and/or bad purchasing decisions could result. The auditor will extend testing of current period asset purchases. For the extended sample, the auditor will obtain documentary support.
Long-lived assets exist.	A procedure whereby company personnel perform periodic asset counts/evaluations to verify that all plant assets on the books still exist and note their location.	The auditor may review selected documentation of these asset counts/evaluations or reperform a recent count/evaluation.	Long-lived assets may be overstated. The auditor will extend the inspection of tangible assets.
Long-lived assets and related expenses are appropriately presented in the financial statements.	A disclosure committee reviews the client's financial statements and footnotes.	The auditor can review documentation of the disclosures committee's review.	Long-lived asset disclosures may not be accurate or complete or comply with the relevant accounting literature. The auditor will need to expand the review of these disclosures.

Considering the Results of Tests of Controls

The auditor analyzes the results of the tests of controls to determine additional appropriate procedures. There are two potential outcomes:

1. If the auditor identifies control deficiencies, the auditor will assess those deficiencies to determine their severity. (Are they significant deficiencies or material weaknesses?) The auditor would then modify the preliminary control risk assessment (possibly from low to high) and document the implications of the control deficiencies. *Exhibit 12.4* provides examples of implications for control deficiencies for substantive testing. The auditor will determine appropriate modifications to planned substantive audit procedures based on the types of misstatements that are most likely to occur because of the control deficiency.

2. If the auditor does not identify any control deficiencies, the auditor will likely determine that the preliminary assessment of control risk as low is still appropriate. The auditor then determines the extent that controls can provide evidence on the accuracy of account balances and determines planned substantive audit procedures. Substantive testing in this situation will be less than what is required in circumstances where the auditor identified internal control deficiencies. From the audit risk model, we know for companies with effective internal controls, the auditor will perform less substantive testing.

Why It Matters

How Your Clients Can Use Data Analytics Tools to Control, Manage, and Report Fixed Asset Accounts

This feature notes opportunities for audit clients to improve the management, and accordingly, internal controls, of their fixed assets. An important message is that data analytics tools are not just for auditors; they are for clients, too!

While most areas of accounting are highly automated, many organizations have not fully applied such automation to fixed assets management. Fixed asset management continues to be a time-consuming and resource-intensive process at many organizations. Research shows that organizations still rely on high-effort, high-risk, manual processes to manage their fixed assets tax data, calculate federal and state depreciation, reconcile depreciation with the general ledger, manage repair expenses, and report on fixed assets. The massive amounts of data require an inordinate amount of time to manage. The manual nature of the process is error prone and often somewhat lacking in internal controls.

In *Chapter 8*, we identify many data analytics tools and business intelligence platforms available to auditors. Your clients can use many of these tools as well, as the tools can be particularly helpful in maintaining good records and controls over fixed assets.

One such tool that, if your client uses it, would provide you comfort with regard to control risks relating to fixed assets is the Oracle Business Intelligence platform developed by KPI Partners.

This pre-packaged tool will enable your clients to manage accounting functions relating to acquiring, maintaining, depreciating, and ultimately disposing of an asset over its lifespan. The tool includes pre-built dashboards for monitoring, and pre-built reports for evaluating the status of fixed asset accounts. This tool includes the following functionalities:

- Reporting on acquisitions and adjustments to fixed assets
- Fixed asset sales and retirements
- Depreciation analyses
- Asset transaction history
- Drill-down from the general ledger to the fixed asset details
- Reconciliations between fixed-asset acquisitions and accounts payable history.

For further details, see http://www.kpipartners.com/solutions /application-extensions/fixed-asset-analytics-for-oracle-ebs

Check Your Basic Knowledge

12-25 When testing a control that requires training for all employees involved in equipment management, the auditor would typically reperform the control.   (T/F)

12-26 Auditors who are aware of control deficiencies that could result in the material misstatement of lease accounts need to modify their substantive testing in response to those deficiencies.   (T/F)

12-27 Which of the following situations would lead an auditor to test controls over long-lived assets?
   a. Substantive analytical procedures suggested that controls over long-lived assets were not effective.
   b. Risk assessment procedures indicated that controls were effectively designed.
   c. Tests of details identified many errors in recording long-lived asset transactions.

   d. The auditor has decided that the additional effort to test controls would not exceed the potential reduction in substantive procedures.

12-28 Which of the following procedures could the auditor perform to test the effectiveness of controls over asset impairment?
   a. Perform substantive analytical procedures.
   b. Send confirmations to the management specialist who performed work related to the impairment.
   c. Inquire of management as to its process for determining assessment impairment, and follow up as appropriate.
   d. Inspect the asset for potential impairment.

LO 8

Determine and apply sufficient appropriate substantive audit procedures in auditing long-lived assets.

Obtaining Substantive Evidence About Accounts, Disclosures, and Assertions for Long-Lived Asset Accounts and Related Expenses

In performing substantive procedures, the auditor wants reasonable assurance that:

- Long-lived assets reflected in the balance sheet physically exist.
- The organization has rights of ownership to recorded long-lived assets.
- Long-lived assets include all relevant items, including those that are purchased, contributed, constructed in-house or by third parties, and leases meeting the criteria for capital leases.
- Retirements, trade-ins, and unused property and equipment are identified and recorded correctly.
- Long-lived assets and related expenses, such as depreciation, amortization, or depletion, are appropriately presented in the financial statements with adequate disclosures.
- Fraudulent transactions are not included in the financial statements.

Exhibit 12.5 details typical substantive procedures for long-lived assets. The extent to which the auditor performs substantive analytical procedures and tests of details depends on the risk of material misstatement.

Exhibit 12.5

Management Assertions and Substantive Procedures for Long-Lived Assets and Related Expenses

Assertions	Substantive Audit Procedures
Existence/occurrence—Recorded long-lived assets exist.	1. Perform substantive analytical procedures. 2. Inspect tangible assets. 3. Vouch additions to supporting documentation. 4. Review account activity for the year and vouch significant items.
Completeness—All long-lived assets have been recorded.	1. Perform substantive analytical procedures. 2. Review capitalization policy to assure that all significant capital expenditures are properly capitalized. 3. Review entries to repair and maintenance expense to determine whether some items should have been capitalized.
Rights/obligations—The organization has legal title or similar rights of ownership to recorded long-lived assets.	1. Inquire of management as to whether long-lived assets have been pledged as collateral. 2. Inspect documents of title. 3. Inspect insurance policies. 4. Inspect property tax records.
Valuation/allocation—Long-lived assets are properly valued.	1. Review depreciation policy and test depreciation calculations. 2. Inquire of management about assets that are idle. 3. Test amortization expense. 4. Assess the reasonableness of carrying amounts and unamortized balances. 5. Inquire of management as to whether there has been any permanent impairment of assets. 6. Assess management's impairment estimates.
Presentation/disclosure—Long-lived assets and related expenses, such as depreciation, amortization, or depletion, are appropriately presented in the financial statements with adequate disclosures.	1. Review presentation and disclosure in the financial statements and determine whether they are in accordance with GAAP. 2. Inquire of management about disclosures and other reporting issues.

Prompt for Critical Thinking #5   It's Your Turn!

Identify three other objectives for which auditors will want reasonable assurance regarding long-lived assets.

- _____
- _____
- _____

What Do You Think?   For Classroom Discussion

Numerous sources have provided examples of the auditor identifying a specific risk related to long-lived assets, and then not responding to that risk. For example, a PCAOB inspection report notes that an auditor identified a significant risk related to management's assessment of goodwill. But, the firm failed to sufficiently evaluate the reasonableness of certain significant assumptions, including revenue projections, growth rate, and related assumptions that appeared contradictory to recent historical results used by the issuer in its analysis, as the firm's procedures were limited to inquiring of management.

As another example, a PCAOB Disciplinary Order describes a case where the auditor identified a risk of material misstatement due to fraud related to the valuation of the land assets acquired. While it appears that the auditor's planning risk assessments were appropriate, the auditor failed to appropriately respond to those risks. The auditor failed to:

- perform sufficient appropriate procedures to evaluate the business rationale of the land transactions
- plan and perform audit procedures that were specifically responsive to the assessed fraud risks of the land transaction
- consider whether management may have been placing more emphasis on the need for a particular accounting treatment for the land transactions than on the underlying economics of the transactions
- perform any procedures to evaluate whether it was appropriate to record assets from the land transactions at appraised values

Why do you think that these situations occur? Is it a lack of professional skepticism? A desire to please the client? Time constraints? Other reasons? Could these examples be situations where the auditor performed the required procedures but did not document them?

Performing Substantive Analytical Procedures

Before performing tests of details, the auditor may perform substantive analytical procedures, such as a reasonableness test. The use of substantive analytical procedures will likely be most appropriate when the risk of material misstatement is low.

Step 1: Identify Suitable Analytical Procedures The relevant analytical procedures for conducting substantive analytics are not necessarily different from those for planning analytical procedures. However, when performing substantive analytical procedures, the auditor is more likely to conduct a reasonableness test. For example, the auditor can use a reasonableness test to estimate depreciation expense. The analytical procedures could also incorporate a number of ratios including:

- *Current depreciation expense as a percentage of the previous-year depreciation expense.*
- *Fixed assets (by class) as a percentage of previous-year assets*—The relative increase in this percentage can be compared with the relative increase in depreciation as a test of overall reasonableness.

- *Depreciation expense (by asset class) as a percentage of assets each year—* This ratio can indicate changes in the age of equipment or in depreciation policy.
- *Accumulated depreciation (by class) as a percentage of gross assets each year—*This ratio provides information on the overall reasonableness of the account and may indicate problems of accounting for fully depreciated equipment.
- *Average age of assets (by class)—*This ratio provides additional insight on the age of assets and may be useful in modifying depreciation estimates.

Step 2: Evaluate Reliability of Data Used to Develop Expectations   In evaluating reliability of data used to develop expectations in substantive analytical procedures, the auditor may test the operating effectiveness of controls over the preparation of information used in those analytics. If the client's controls related to long-lived assets are effective, then the auditor can rely more extensively on substantive analytical procedures to obtain evidence on account balances. When such controls are effective, the auditor will have greater confidence in the reliability of the information. Furthermore, the auditor may use data from independent external sources (e.g., industry ratios), as that data are generally considered reliable.

Step 3: Develop Expectations   Expectations for substantive analytical procedures will be more precise than those considered during planning analytical procedures. The auditor can increase precision by using more disaggregated data. The appropriate level of disaggregation depends on the nature of the organization, its size, and its complexity. To develop an expectation for deprecation, the auditor can use the client's long-lived asset ledger, which should uniquely identify each asset and provide details about: the cost of the asset; its acquisition date; the depreciation method the client uses, its estimated life, its estimated scrap value (if any); and accumulated depreciation to date. The auditor will develop expectations for each asset or each category of assets to compare with what the company has recorded.

Step 4 and Step 5: Define and Identify Significant Unexpected Differences
At this point, the auditor is trying to answer the question of whether the auditor's expectation is significantly different from what the client has recorded. The amount of difference that the auditor considers significant is influenced by materiality, desired level of assurance, and assessed risk of material misstatement. As the auditor's assessed risk of material misstatement increases, the amount of the unexpected difference that would be considered significant declines.

The auditor then compares the client's recorded amounts with the auditor's expectation. Once this mechanical step is completed, the auditor will have identified any significant differences between the auditor's expectation and the amount recorded by client.

Step 6 and Step 7: Investigate Significant Unexpected Differences and Ensure Proper Documentation   Materiality and the desired level of assurance aid the auditor in determining how to proceed with investigating significant unexpected differences. The auditor will investigate significant unexpected differences through substantive tests of details. In general, if substantive analytical procedures do not result in unresolved issues, the auditor can reduce direct testing of account balances.

Finally, as with planning analytical procedures, the auditor will accumulate documentation with respect to evidence gathered and judgments reached during substantive analytical procedures.

Substantive Tests of Details for Tangible Assets
Current-Period Additions

The proper recording of current-period additions is important due to the long-term effect these assets have on the financial statements. Because most organizations typically have relatively few long-lived asset transactions, the auditor often examines supporting documentation of individual transactions. One approach is to examine a schedule of additions (usually prepared by the client). After the auditor agrees the schedule to the general ledger, the auditor should select items for testing. For example, auditors obtain documentary support (such as invoices or contracts) for additions above a certain amount or physically inspect a sample of additions made during the audit period. The auditor also wants to determine that capitalized additions were appropriate and that none of them should have been expensed as repairs and maintenance or other costs.

Organizations often make judgments as to whether a particular expenditure should be capitalized or expensed as a repair. Most organizations have policies, usually based on materiality, as to whether expenditures under a certain amount are expenses—even if they appear to be of a capital nature. Usually, the auditor starts by determining if such a policy is reasonable. Furthermore, the auditor considers whether management might attempt to not comply with the policy because of an incentive to manipulate reported earnings; for example, decrease reported earnings in a good period and vice versa in a poor period. If the auditor perceives that such risks are present at a client, the auditor will adjust the substantive procedures, usually by requesting that the client prepare a schedule of both fixed-asset additions and repair and maintenance expense transactions. The auditor can vouch selected transactions from both schedules to vendor invoices, work orders, or other supporting evidence to determine their proper classification.

When conducting these procedures, the auditor can usually test existence, rights, and valuation assertions at the same time. *Exhibit 12.6* presents an example of typical audit documentation for testing fixed-asset additions. Even though the total fixed-asset account balance may be large, the audit work can be efficient if the auditor concentrates on the additions and then adjusts the estimates of depreciation expense and accumulated depreciation for changes made during the year.

Focus on Fraud

Improper Capitalization of Operating Expenses: The Case of Safety-Kleen Corporation

This feature provides a well-known example of a company that capitalized, rather than expensed, certain costs.

Safety-Kleen Corporation (SK) was one of the leading providers of industrial waste collection and disposal services. In the late 1990s, SK merged with another company, and SK's management made promises to investors and analysts that the merger would result in annual savings of $100 to $160 million. Unfortunately, those savings never materialized, and the company's CFO, controller, and vice president of accounting orchestrated an accounting fraud to overstate SK's revenue and earnings. One element of the fraud involved the improper capitalization and deferral of operating expenses. For example, at the end of the third quarter of 1999, they improperly capitalized $4.6 million of payroll expenses. At the end of the fourth quarter of 1999, they improperly capitalized $1.8 million of salaries and wages. Also during the fourth quarter of 1999, they recorded $7.3 million of fraudulent adjustments to capitalize the tires on the company's trucks and the fuel in the tanks. Safety-Kleen ultimately filed for bankruptcy, and the SEC pursued the company and the individuals involved.

For further details, see SEC Complaint No. 17891 (December 12, 2002).

Exhibit 12.6

Schedule of Long-Lived Asset Additions and Disposals

Gordon's Bay Manufacturing
Schedule of Long-Lived Asset Additions and Disposals
12/31/2018

PBC
Work Performed by *KJ*
Date 1/28/2019

Description	Date Purchased	Cost				Accumulated Depreciation			
		Beginning Balance	Additions	Disposals	Ending Balance	Beginning Balance	Depreciation Expense	Disposals	Ending Balance
Beginning balance	Various	124,350			124,350	33,429	12,435*		45,864
Additions:									
40" lathe	10/30/18	–0–	9,852†		9,852	–0–	1,250‡		1,250
1040 press	3/25/18	–0–	18,956†		18,956	–0–	1,895‡		1,895
60" lathe	5/29/18	–0–	13,903†		13,903	–0–	950‡		950
Disposals:									
Fork lift	6/2/15			7,881§	(7,881)			3,753	(3,753)
Computer	7/2/16			3,300§	(3,300)			2,625	(2,625)
Totals		124,350@	42,711**	11,181**	155,880**††	33,429@	16,530**	6,378**	43,581**††

* Estimated from prior year; includes one-half year depreciation for assets disposed of during the year. See Working Paper PPE-4 for calculation of the estimate.

† Examined invoice or other supporting document, noting cost and appropriate categorization for depreciation purposes.

‡ Recalculated, noting that depreciation is in accordance with company policy and asset classification- estimated economic life.

§ Traced to asset ledger and verified that equipment had been removed. Examined sales document or scrap disposal document for the disposal of the asset.

@ Agreed to December 31, 2017, audit documentation.

** Footed/cross footed.

†† Traced to trial balance.

Current-Period Disposals

Exhibit 12.6 includes two disposals that occurred during the year. Similar to testing additions, the auditor typically obtains a schedule from the client of all sales or other disposals made during the year. The auditor should trace the original cost of the item and its accumulated depreciation to the supporting documentation. The auditor should trace proceeds from the disposal, if material, to the cash receipts journal and the bank deposit. The auditor should also recompute any gain or loss to determine whether it the client accounted for in conformity with GAAP.

The auditor should also perform procedures to search for any unrecorded disposals. First, the auditor may make inquiries of appropriate client personnel about disposals. The auditor could obtain evidence of unrecorded retirements by examining the cash receipts journal, property tax records, insurance records, or scrap sales accounts. Another approach is to use data analytical tools to prepare a printout of fully depreciated (or nearly fully depreciated) assets and then attempt to locate them for physical examination. Alternatively, the auditor can trace trade-ins noted during the audit of asset additions to the removal of the old equipment from the books.

Depreciation Expense and Accumulated Depreciation

The procedures used by the auditor to test depreciation of tangible assets depend on the risk of material misstatement. The auditor's primary objective in testing depreciation is to determine whether the client is following a consistent depreciation policy and whether the client's calculations are accurate. The auditor should make sure that the depreciation methods used are consistent with the prior year unless the client has reasonable justification for changing methods. The auditor should carefully read the notes to the financial statements to be sure that the client discloses all relevant information about such changes. The auditor should determine whether management's estimates, such as estimated useful lives and salvage values, are reasonable. As described earlier, the auditor may perform primarily substantive analytical procedures to test these accounts, especially when the risk of material misstatement is low.

In situations where controls are not effective, that is, there is a high risk of material misstatement, the auditor needs to perform more extensive detailed tests of depreciation. The auditor would start with the long-lived asset ledger, which should uniquely identify each asset and provide details about: (a) the cost of the asset, (b) its acquisition date, (c) the depreciation method the client uses, (d) its estimated life, (e) its estimated scrap value (if any), and (f) accumulated depreciation to date.

The auditor would use data analytical tools to foot the ledger, agree it to the general ledger, and take a sample of items contained in the detailed ledger. For the selected items, the auditor will recalculate depreciation. The auditor can also use data analytical tools to identify all unusual entries posted to the depreciation and accumulated depreciation accounts.

Substantive Tests of Details for Natural Resources and the Related Expense Accounts

For natural resource accounts, the auditor's focus is on the costs and the estimate of reserves contained in a new discovery. The auditor typically has experience with the quality of the client's estimates and would want to evaluate the credentials of the individual making the estimates—whether it is a member of management or a specialist hired by management. The auditor may also decide to use an auditor specialist to perform additional analysis, including reviewing the client's analysis.

The audit procedures for determining the cost of natural resources are similar to those for other fixed assets. The auditor should test the capitalization of all new natural resources and verify the costs by examining documents, including the client's documentation of the exploration and drilling costs.

| Auditing a Forestry Company Results in a Class-Action Lawsuit | *Focus on Fraud: An International Perspective* |

This feature highlights the need for sufficient appropriate audit procedures when auditing natural resources.

In 2011, the Chinese forestry company, Sino-Forest Corp., which once traded on the Toronto Stock Exchange and was worth $6 billion, collapsed following fraud allegations. In December 2012, the Ontario Securities Commission (OSC) accused Ernst & Young LLP of failing to conduct a proper audit of Sino-Forest Corp. The OSC alleged that Ernst & Young failed to perform sufficient audit work to verify the ownership and existence of Sino-Forest's most significant assets and failed to undertake its audit work "with a sufficient level of professional skepticism." The SEC said Ernst & Young failed to adequately review and question documentation related to the ownership and existence of standing timber reserves the company held in China. The commission said Ernst & Young did "very limited" site visits to inspect the firm's purported assets, which were widely scattered throughout China. In 2013, an Ontario judge approved Ernst & Young LLP's $117-million settlement of a shareholder class-action lawsuit tied to the collapse of Sino-Forest Corp. The $117-million settlement is the largest payment ever made by an auditor in Canada to settle a class-action suit.

In 2015, the financial institutions that helped Sino-Forest raise funds agreed to pay investors $32.5 million, in what may have been Canada's largest securities class-action settlement to date reached with investment bank underwriters.

The client determines depletion expense based on the items extracted during the year, using the units of production method. The client should have production records of daily extractions. In addition, the auditor will substantiate the amount of items sold during the year. Furthermore, the client should have procedures to estimate any changes in reserves in order to update the depletion procedures.

Substantive Tests of Details for Intangible Assets and the Related Expense Accounts

Auditors commonly use the following substantive procedures when testing intangible assets:

- Determine that the intangible assets exist by reviewing appropriate documentation, for example, legal documentation (in the case of a license or patent).
- Determine that the client owns the intangible assets by inspecting relevant documentation, such as the purchase agreement or sales agreement.
- Test management's calculation of any gain or loss on the disposal of intangible assets and determine whether the client has properly reduced carrying amounts.
- For amortizable intangibles with finite lives, determine whether amortization expense is accurate and whether the amortization policy and useful lives are reasonable and consistent with prior years.
- Inquire of management about whether circumstances indicate that the carrying amounts of intangibles (which are subject to amortization) may not be recoverable. Where such circumstances exist, evaluate management's impairment testing and conclusion regarding the write-off.

Substantive Procedures Related to Asset Impairment

Even though determining the potential impairment of long-lived assets is difficult, the accumulated knowledge of industry product trends, changes in client product lines, and technological changes will assist the auditor in making necessary judgments. An asset may be impaired if it does not generate as much cash flow in future years as it has in the past. A tour of the plant may provide hints that the client is not using some assets, indicating a potential impairment in value. Indicators suggesting that impairment of an asset might have occurred include:

- A change in circumstances, such as the legal environment or business climate, that could affect the asset's value or cause an adverse action by a regulator
- An accumulation of costs that are significantly in excess of the amount originally expected to be needed to acquire or construct the asset
- Losses or projections indicating continuing losses associated with an asset used to generate revenue
- A current expectation that, more likely than not, an asset will be sold or otherwise disposed of significantly before the end of its previously estimated useful life.

The auditor needs reasonable assurance that the long-lived assets are valued at their economic benefit to the organization and that, when the value has been impaired, the organization has written down the asset reflecting the decline in its economic benefit. If there is evidence that an asset has been impaired, the auditor needs to address the valuation issue. In most situations, the auditor needs to understand management's process for assessing impairment and needs to evaluate the reasonableness of management's assumptions.

Why It Matters   Asset Impairments Can Be Highly Material!

This feature provides examples of the significance of asset impairments recorded by various organizations. A challenging aspect of these impairment valuations is their subjective nature and the process managers and the external auditor use to estimate the amounts with a reasonable level of precision. When testing potential impairment of assets, the auditor may need to rely on work performed by a specialist/expert.

- When Deluxe Corporation, a leader in providing small businesses and financial institutions with various products and services revenue, announced its financial results for the second quarter ended June 30, 2017, it announced an impairment charge. Specifically, GAAP diluted EPS included aggregate charges of $0.07 per share for an asset impairment charge, restructuring and transaction-related costs. The asset impairment charge related to a small business distributor that Deluxe sold during the quarter.

- In 2016, SABMiller recorded $721 million in one-time charges principally relating to the impairment of its investments in Angola and strife-torn South Sudan.

- PepsiCo had a $373 million impairment charge in 2016 in its Chinese beverage joint venture.

- In 2015, General Mills reported that fourth-quarter profits fell 53% to $186.8 million, or 30 cents a share, largely because of a $260 million asset impairment charge from its struggling Green Giant frozen and canned produce line.

- In fiscal year 2015, Microsoft recorded impairment charges of $2.2 billion related to its Phone Hardware intangible assets.

- Duff & Phelps reports that fifty-six percent of energy companies recorded an impairment in 2015, leading to a grand total of over $18 billion. In contrast, the same industry reported about $6 billion in impairments in the prior year. Duff & Phelps attributes the impairments to the decline in oil prices, which has had a significant, negative impact on the oil industry. National Oilwell Varco, Hess, and Crestwood Equity Partners were the biggest losers, each averaging about $1.5 billion.

- In the third quarter of 2014, Sprint recorded $1.9 billion and $233 million of impairment losses on the Sprint trade name in its Wireless Segment and property, plant, and equipment in its Wireline Segment, as operating expenses respectively, due to estimated fair values that were less than the carrying amounts.

- At June 30, 2013, Pan American Silver Corporation determined that the carrying value related to its Dolores mine of approximately $1,061 million, including goodwill and net of associated deferred tax liabilities, was greater than its recoverable amount of $872.5 million. Pan American Silver recorded an impairment charge related to the Dolores mine of $187.5 million, net of tax ($188.6 million before tax) comprised of goodwill of $184.7 million and non current assets of $3.9 million.

For Classroom Discussion

What Do You Think?

Some experts argue that unless there is a material change in earnings, cash flow and leverage, the impact of impairment on an organization's valuation may be negligible. They further argue that there is no reliable way to forecast the stock movement after an organization decides to take an impairment hit.

Do you think these experts are right? Remember that impairments do affect some ratios used to value organizations and, thus, potentially how the market perceives the organization in question. You might want to research the stock market reactions to the impairment announcements presented in the *Why It Matters* feature "Asset Impairments Can Be Big Dollars!"

In addition, think about the variation in the level of precision of these estimates. For example, consider SABMiller's $721 million impairment charge. What do you think the likelihood is that number is *exactly* right? Consider the graphs below, which represent alternatively precise estimates of the likelihood that $721 is the "right" number, one with a broader distribution of possible values, and the other with a narrower distribution:

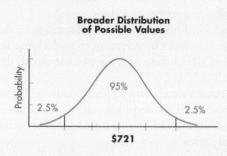

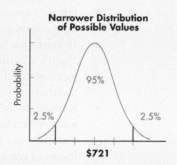

If you were a user of the financial statements and this type of distribution was available to you, which distribution provides you with greater confidence in the "right" value of the impairment charge?

PCAOB Identifies Audit Deficiencies Related to Asset Impairment Issues

Why It Matters

This feature provides findings from PCAOB inspection reports issued from 2015 to 2017. These findings highlight that auditors continue to have challenges related to auditing asset impairments.

The Firm's procedures to test the valuation of property and equipment were insufficient. The issuer performed an annual analysis of the possible impairment of the property and equipment at its stores, using cash-flow data for the individual stores for three preceding years. The issuer also used the cash-flow data in the operation of a control over the valuation of property and equipment that the Firm tested, and the Firm used the cashflow data in its substantive testing. The Firm, however, failed to identify and test any controls over the cash-flow data and failed to substantively test the data, other than by comparing the data to a report that it had not tested.

For more details, see PCAOB Release No. 104-2015-189.

The Firm identified an impairment indicator related to property and equipment. The Firm's procedures related to the possible impairment of property and equipment were insufficient. Specifically:

- The Firm failed to test any controls over the issuer's process for assessing property and equipment for possible impairment.

- The Firm failed to perform any procedures to evaluate the reasonableness of two important assumptions used in the issuer's analysis to support the issuer's conclusion that there were no events or circumstances that would require an assessment of property and equipment for possible impairment.

    For more details, see PCAOB Release No. 104-2016-129.

This inspection report noted the failure of the firm to perform sufficient procedures to evaluate whether intangible assets were impaired.

For more details, see PCAOB Release No. 104-2017-090

Substantive Procedures Related to Leases

When auditing leases, the auditor needs to determine that all leases are recorded with appropriate classifications, expenses related to leases (depreciation, interest expense, rent expense) have been calculated and reported properly in the income statement, and the disclosure of lease obligations is adequate and in compliance with disclosure requirements.

The auditing procedures consist primarily of examining (and understanding!) the lease documents to determine the substance of the transaction and the proper accounting treatment. Specific substantive procedures for leases include:

- Obtain copies of lease agreements, read the agreements, and develop a schedule of leases.
- Review the relevant expense accounts, select entries to those accounts, and determine if there are entries related to the client leases. Determine if the client has properly accounted for the expenses.
- For all capital leases, determine that the client has recorded assets and lease obligations at their appropriate values.
- Develop a schedule of all future lease obligations or determine whether the client's schedule is correct by referring to underlying lease agreements.
- Review the client's disclosure of lease obligations to determine that it is in accordance with GAAP.
- Review the relevant criteria from FASB's codified standards (ASC) to determine which leases meet the requirement of capital leases. Under guidance issued by the FASB in 2016, organizations will account for virtually all leases as capital leases.

Substantially all leases will be on the balance sheet under the standard issued by FASB in 2016. Under the previous lease accounting rules, FASB ASC 840, organizations only have to record lease obligations on their balance sheets when the arrangements are basically financing transactions, such as rent-to-own contracts for buildings or vehicles. Few leases were recorded under these rules because of "bright lines" in GAAP that let organizations arrange some deals as simple rentals.

To comply with the new standard, organizations should start with existing lease agreements. However, the process is more involved. For example, many organizations have equipment leases, and the data collection related to those can be a time-consuming process. Consider a retailer like Home Depot or Lowe's. Such organizations may need to sort through rental agreements for thousands of leased forklifts and, separately, the rented batteries for each forklift. Some organizations will likely identify unexpected leases. For example, many retail stores pipe in music for customers when they shop. The rental for speakers or satellite receivers can represent a leased asset and corresponding liability that organizations may need to record on the balance sheet.

Furthermore, leases may be embedded within other contracts, such as service agreements. Organizations will also need to evaluate embedded leases, which are often time-consuming to identify, for lease accounting implications. The requirement to identify embedded leases is not new, but in the past, leases embedded in service agreements were often operating leases and would have been off-balance sheet.

Organizations will need to update processes, systems and controls, and will also need to design and test controls over the implementation process when implementing this standard.

Changes in Lease Accounting: Implications for Auditors and Clients

Why It Matters

This feature highlights the importance of auditors staying current on changing financial accounting standards.

On February 25, 2016, after working on the topic for almost a decade, the FASB issued ASU 2016-02, its standard on accounting for leases. Under this standard, a lessee is required to recognize most leases on its balance sheet, which is a significant change from the previous accounting requirements. In general, this new standard requires organizations to move leased assets and related liabilities out of footnote disclosures and onto the face of their balance sheets.

The new standard defines a lease as a contract, or part of a contract, that conveys the right to control the use of identified property, plant, or equipment (an identified asset) for a period of time, in exchange for consideration. An organization needs to determine the classification of a lease at lease commencement. The classification criteria under the new standard apply to both lessees and lessors. The evaluation focuses on whether control of the underlying asset is effectively transferred to the lessee (e.g., substantially all of the risks and rewards related to ownership of the underlying asset are transferred to the lessee). Therefore, a lease would be classified as a finance lease (from the standpoint of a lessee) or a sales-type lease (from the standpoint of a lessor) if any of the following criteria are met:

- "The lease transfers ownership of the underlying asset to the lessee by the end of the lease term.
- The lease grants the lessee an option to purchase the underlying asset that the lessee is reasonably certain to exercise.
- The lease term is for the major part of the remaining economic life of the underlying asset.
- The present value of the sum of the lease payments and any residual value guaranteed by the lessee . . . equals or exceeds substantially all of the fair value of the underlying asset.
- The underlying asset is of such a specialized nature that it is expected to have no alternative use to the lessor at the end of the lease term."

The lease standard is effective for public business entities for periods beginning after December 15, 2018 (i.e., calendar 2019). Nonpublic entities will have an additional year to adopt (i.e., periods beginning after December 15, 2019).

Performing Substantive Fraud-Related Procedures

Auditors can use the following fraud-related audit procedures to respond to fraud risks that the auditor identified while performing risk assessment:

- Physically inspect tangible assets, including major additions, and agree serial numbers with invoices or other supporting documents.
- Request that the client perform a complete inventory of long-lived assets at year-end.
- Carefully scrutinize appraisals and other specialist reports that seem out of line with reasonable expectations, and challenge the underlying assumptions.
- Use the work of a specialist for asset valuations, including impairments.
- When vouching long-lived asset additions, accept only original invoices, purchase orders, receiving reports, or similar supporting documentation.
- Confirm the terms of significant additions of property or intangibles with other parties involved in the transaction.

If these procedures were part of the original audit program, the auditor should consider expanding the extent of testing or in some way modifying the timing or nature of testing to respond to significant fraud risk factors.

Check Your Basic Knowledge

12-29 One procedure that the auditor can use to test management's assertion that tangible long-lived assets exist would be to inspect the tangible asset. (T/F)

12-30 When testing potential impairment of assets, the auditor may need to rely on work performed by a specialist/expert. (T/F)

12-31 When auditing intangible assets, the auditor would likely recompute amortization and determine whether management's recorded amount is reasonable. When performing this procedure, which assertion is the auditor focusing on?
   a. Completeness.
   b. Existence.
   c. Valuation.
   d. Rights and obligations.

12-32 As part of auditing equipment, the auditor will inspect new equipment additions selected from the client's property ledger. When performing this procedure, which assertion is the auditor focusing on?
   a. Completeness.
   b. Existence.
   c. Valuation.
   d. Rights and obligations.

Documenting Substantive Procedures

For tangible assets such as property, the auditor's documentation of substantive procedures should include:

- A summary schedule showing beginning balances, additions, deletions, and ending balances for the asset account and for accumulated depreciation (see *Exhibit 12.6*)
- Identification of the specific items tested (e.g., all additions greater than $100,000)

For intangible assets, the documentation should include evidence supporting the evaluation and review of the reasonableness of the valuation assertion.

LO 9

Describe audit considerations for merger and acquisition activities, including related management estimates.

Auditing Merger and Acquisition Activities

Merger and acquisition transactions commonly occur. These transactions typically involve one organization acquiring either an entire organization or an individual operating division. For example, in 2017, British American Tobacco bought the remaining stake in Reynolds American that it did not already own in a $49 billion deal. In 2016, Microsoft finalized its $26 billion acquisition of LinkedIn. In 2014, Facebook purchased WhatsApp for $19 billion.

These transactions present significant challenges related to valuation issues, including:

- Valuing the assets and associated liabilities of an acquisition
- Measuring restructuring charges and recognition of the liability
- Determining goodwill impairment

Valuing the Assets and Liabilities of an Acquisition

It may seem straightforward to determine the cost of an acquisition—it is the amount paid to make the acquisition. However, a number of issues complicate the cost determination. These include acquisitions:

- Made via stock rather than cash
- In which the final price is contingent upon the value of the assets received (post audit)
- In which the final price is contingent on the future performance of the acquired organization or division

An acquisition made via stock is usually straightforward, but is dependent on the marketability of the stock issued. Some contracts simply specify the number of shares issued, while others require the organization to transfer shares equal to a specified market value at a given date.

Most purchase transactions have a good-faith clause in which the purchaser has the right to offset against the purchase price the value of assets that were represented to exist but do not exist. For example, an acquired organization might assert that $1.3 million in accounts receivable exists. However, after 180 days, the organization has collected only $600,000, and supporting documentation for the remaining $700,000 cannot be located. In some instances, the contract allows the offset of the $700,000 against the purchase price, but in other instances, it may not. The auditor needs to examine the specifics of the contract and the procedures the organization uses to resolve disputes on the existence of assets in order to reach a final purchase price.

In many acquisitions, the acquiring organization may want the management of the acquired organization to continue running the business. The managers know the business, they have contacts with the customers, and their cooperation may be crucial to the effective integration of the two organizations. Often, in these situations, the organizations reach an agreed-upon price with significant contingency payments based upon the newly acquired organization reaching specified performance objectives. The auditor and the client must assess the likelihood of the acquired organization meeting those performance objectives and determine when to recognize the contingency payments as part of the cost of the acquired organization. If it is highly likely that the organization will meet the objectives, the full cost should be recognized at the time of acquisition.

The acquiring organization needs to bring all the specifically identifiable tangible and intangible assets and liabilities onto its books at their fair market values at the time of acquisition. Fair market values of the assets may differ significantly from the book value of those assets. Usually, the organization hires an independent appraiser to value the tangible assets—for example, property, machinery, and office equipment. The intangible assets—for example, patents or copyrights—may be more difficult to value. These assets should typically be valued at the net present value of future (net) cash flows associated with the asset. For example, the copyright to a book might be valued at the net present value of future positive cash flows associated with sales of the book minus the cash outflows to produce and market the book. These estimates may be more difficult to obtain, but can often be estimated based on the organization's history with similar books.

Focus on Fraud: An International Perspective

Caterpillar Books an Impairment Relating to a Chinese Manufacturing Acquisition

This feature provides an example of an acquisition based on inaccurate reported financial results, thereby resulting in an impairment charge.

In November 2011, Caterpillar acquired a Chinese manufacturer of mining machines, subsequently renamed ERA Mining Machinery, for $866 million. During the process of integrating the organization, Caterpillar management uncovered a deliberate plan and associated actions to inaccurately portray the financial health of the organization by fraudulently inflating reported revenue amounts.

In 2013, Caterpillar booked an impairment charge of $580 million relating to the declining value associated with the acquisition. Deloitte and Ernst & Young were the two audit firms that conducted due diligence on the acquisition transaction. In February 2012, the Chinese government issued new rules restricting access to corporate information, which may have hindered the auditors in conducting their due diligence. Both the international nature of the transaction, and the underlying fraudulent representations made by management, illustrate the risks that organizations and their auditors face relating to acquisition transactions.

Fair Value Estimates

Acquisitions require management to make fair value estimates. Fair value is the amount for which an asset could be exchanged, or a liability settled, between knowledgeable, willing parties in an arm's length transaction. When auditing a **fair value estimate**, the auditor is not auditing transactions that have taken place. Rather, the auditor is evaluating outside market values, industry data on sales and trends, and models of future cash flows.

The concept of fair value implies an orderly market and may not be applicable to certain distressed assets where no market exists. In such situations, the asset may be required to be valued at the lower of cost or market. To guide management and auditors, the FASB recognizes that the persuasiveness of information in making an estimate may differ—and there may be many different sources of relevant information. Therefore, FASB has set the following hierarchy when assessing fair value:

- *Level 1*—quoted prices for identical items in active, liquid, and visible markets such as stock exchanges. An example would be a recent trade on the NYSE of a stock or a bond.
- *Level 2*—observable information for similar items in active or inactive markets, such as two similarly situated buildings in a downtown real estate market.
- *Level 3*—unobservable inputs to be used in situations where markets do not exist or are illiquid. This is often referred to as *mark to model* because it is dependent on management's estimates of future cash flows associated with the asset or liability to be valued. Level 3 valuations are generally viewed as highly subjective.

The client should have: (a) a systematic process to identify each asset that is subject to fair value estimation, (b) a process to identify relevant market values, (c) an analysis of whether the organization has the ability to hold the asset to maturity and whether the decline in value is other than temporary, and (d) a realistic process to estimate future cash flows to discount back to a present value.

Audit Considerations for Valuing Identifiable Assets and Liabilities

When auditing the valuation of identifiable assets obtained in an acquisition, the auditor cannot simply accept an appraisal and management's assessment of the FMV of the assets. Rather, the auditor must gather sufficient appropriate evidence to determine whether the assessed values are appropriate. When auditing long-lived assets and the related liabilities obtained through an acquisition, the following types of situations often require the auditor to rely on an auditor's specialist to obtain sufficient appropriate evidence:

- Assets acquired and liabilities assumed in business combinations and assets that may have been impaired
- The valuation of environmental liabilities, and site clean-up costs
- The actuarial calculation of liabilities associated with insurance contracts or employee benefit plans

In relying on evidence from a specialist, the auditor should:

- Evaluate the qualifications of any management specialists, ascertaining whether the individuals are certified, experienced, and reputable
- Determine if the specialists hired by management are sufficiently independent of management that they will not be influenced by management's objectives
- Review the methodologies used by the specialists to determine whether they are sound, such as determining if specialists identify sales prices for comparable land or property, or reconstruction costs for buildings

Exhibit 12.7 contains an overview of audit considerations concerning fair value estimates. You will note the specific audit challenges relevant to each level of fair value estimation.

Exhibit 12.7
Overview of Audit Considerations for Fair Value Estimates

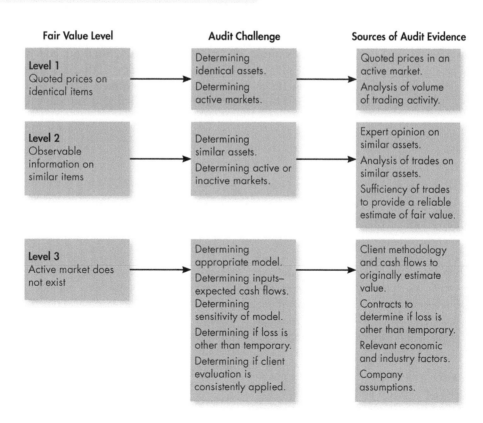

Fair Value Level	Audit Challenge	Sources of Audit Evidence
Level 1 Quoted prices on identical items	Determining identical assets. Determining active markets.	Quoted prices in an active market. Analysis of volume of trading activity.
Level 2 Observable information on similar items	Determining similar assets. Determining active or inactive markets.	Expert opinion on similar assets. Analysis of trades on similar assets. Sufficiency of trades to provide a reliable estimate of fair value.
Level 3 Active market does not exist	Determining appropriate model. Determining inputs—expected cash flows. Determining sensitivity of model. Determining if loss is other than temporary. Determining if client evaluation is consistently applied.	Client methodology and cash flows to originally estimate value. Contracts to determine if loss is other than temporary. Relevant economic and industry factors. Company assumptions.

Level 1 does not represent unusual challenges for the auditor. However, Levels 2 and 3 represent significant challenges—including determining whether or not an active market exists. Level 2 is broad and applies to financial instruments, property, or lower of cost or market considerations for inventory, loans, or receivables. The audit approach for Level 2 requires the auditor to review and assess:

- The correspondence of the client's assets to similar assets in an active market
- Whether an active market exists for similar assets
- The client's systematic process for estimating fair value
- Characteristics of any outside appraisers, including whether the appraiser is independent, objective, competent, and has used comparable items in estimating value
- The data used by the organization in estimating future cash flows, including whether the data consider economic conditions and changes in the market-place and use an appropriate discount rate to determine net present value

Audits of Level 3 balances present the most difficulty because they do not involve an observable, active market. The approach—often criticized—is referred to as *marking to model* because the client is expected to estimate fair value based on a model of the future cash flows associated with the instrument or the asset. For example, many distressed financial instruments do not have a current market value. Furthermore, there is a reluctance to trade such instruments because the value is difficult to ascertain. Therefore, auditors and clients use comparisons of distressed sales in the market place. Obviously, there is considerable lack of precision in these estimates.

Audit Considerations for Restructuring Charges Related to an Acquisition

Organizations restructure their operations continuously, and typically reflect those costs in current operating earnings. However, following an acquisition, an organization often makes a decision to restructure operations and develops a restructuring plan. As part of the restructuring, management often promises great cost savings. For example, in 2016, Royal Dutch Shell merged with BG Group Plc. Following the merger, Shell management reported that it had cut thousands of jobs and eliminated much duplication. They announced that expected synergies would result in $4.5 billion in savings by 2018. Shell also announced planned asset sales over 18 months of $30 billion.

Focus on Fraud   The Case of WorldCom's Restructuring Reserves

This feature describes how WorldCom used restructuring charges and reserves to fraudulently inflate reported earnings. When auditing restructuring charges, the auditor cannot rely on conservatism as a reason to let a client overestimate its reserve for restructuring. The subsequent reversal of the overestimated liability will affect future income.

WorldCom grew from a small telephone company that emphasized data transmissions to a company that acquired MCI, then the country's second-largest long distance telephone carrier—a

company that was significantly larger than WorldCom. World-Com grew through numerous acquisitions that were used to fuel growth and stock market value. In practically every acquisition, WorldCom would set up a restructuring reserve for the expected future costs associated with the integration of the operations into WorldCom and used the offsetting debit to increase goodwill rather than expenses.

As was its common practice, WorldCom always estimated the restructuring costs to be significantly higher than truly expected, thus creating a large amount of restructuring reserves on the balance sheet. The subsequent expenses associated with the restructuring were significantly less than the reserve that was established.

The Bankruptcy Trustee report on WorldCom indicated that WorldCom would systematically release (debit) these reserve (liability) accounts and credit expenses, thereby increasing reported earnings for the period. Clearly, the entries crediting expenses were fraudulent. However, the audit firm never questioned the amounts of reserves established in the first place because of an attitude that creating a liability is conservative. It did not consider the effect on future income when the company would choose to take the liability off the balance sheet. It is important to note that conservative accounting in one period creates a base for aggressive accounting in a future period. The audit implication is that conservatism is not necessarily the accounting objective. Rather, the objective is the accurate measurement of the economics and condition of the company and acquisition transaction.

Audit procedures for restructuring charges include:

- Review current and proposed financial accounting standards to determine if changes have occurred in accounting for restructuring.
- Review the detail developed by the client in determining its estimate; this should include the identification of specific assets to be disposed of, number of people to be terminated, union contracts on termination, and planned severance pay.
- Review specific steps taken to date that would indicate that management has moved beyond a plan to terminate to the identification of specific parties or operations that will be affected by the plan. Specific parties or operations must be identified before a liability can be recognized.
- Review and independently test the estimates by reviewing (a) contracts, (b) appraisals for property or estimates from investment bankers, and (c) severance contracts.
- Mathematically test the estimates.
- Develop an overall conclusion on the reasonableness of the liability and the appropriateness of the accounting used by the client.

Audit Considerations for Valuing Goodwill

An acquisition will typically result with the acquiring organization bringing goodwill onto its books. **Goodwill** is the excess of the purchase price over the fair market values of the acquired organization's tangible assets, identifiable intangible assets, and liabilities. Management has primary responsibility for recording and periodically valuing goodwill; the auditor has responsibility for determining the reasonableness of management's processes and valuations.

FASB Updates Guidance on Goodwill Impairment

Why It Matters

This feature provides details on an updated accounting standard for goodwill impairment tests.

On January 27, 2017, the FASB issued an accounting standards update doing away with the two-step goodwill impairment test organizations have been using. While the required adoption date is not until 2019, auditors should know that clients are permitted early adoption for interim or annual goodwill impairment tests performed on testing dates after January 1, 2017.

Public companies that file their financials with the SEC should adopt the new standard for annual or any interim goodwill impairment tests in fiscal years beginning after December 15, 2019. For other public companies, the date is December 15, 2020. For private companies and not-for-profits, the date is December 15, 2021.

Once the organization records goodwill, the organization then tests goodwill for impairment. FASB guidance states that organizations should perform goodwill impairment tests annually, as well as on an interim basis at the time events and circumstances warrant. When performing an impairment test, the organization needs to determine the reporting unit, which is usually an operating segment (or part of an operating segment) that: (a) provides separate accounting; (b) is managed as a separate segment; or (c) could be easily separated from the organization, such as by a sale of the segment.

The impairment test involves a quantitative comparison of the carrying value with the fair value of the reporting units. Under accounting guidance issued in 2017, **goodwill impairment loss** is measured as the excess of a reporting unit's carrying amount over its fair value (not to exceed the total goodwill allocated to that reporting unit). For example, when the fair value of the reporting unit is less than its carrying value, there will be a goodwill impairment charge under the new test, even if the difference is attributable to the fair value of other assets in the reporting unit (such as loan receivables or fixed assets) being less than their respective carrying values.

The concern for the auditor in auditing the goodwill amount originally recorded is management's determination of the fair market value of the acquired organization or reporting units. In auditing any potential impairment losses, the auditor will evaluate management's conclusions and will obtain supporting documentation.

Why It Matters

The PCAOB Identifies Audit Deficiencies Related to Goodwill Impairment

This feature provides findings from PCAOB inspection reports issued in 2015 and 2017. These findings highlight that auditors continue to have challenges related to auditing goodwill impairment.

The Firm failed to obtain sufficient appropriate audit evidence to support its audit opinion on the financial statements, as its procedures to test the valuation of goodwill for one of the issuer's reporting units were insufficient. The issuer performed an annual analysis of the possible impairment of goodwill. The Firm identified a significant risk related to management's assessment of goodwill. The Firm failed to sufficiently evaluate the reasonableness of certain significant assumptions, including revenue projections, growth rate, and related assumptions that appeared contradictory to recent historical results used by the issuer in its analysis, as the Firm's procedures were limited to inquiring of management.

For more details, see PCAOB Release No. 104-2015-178.

The issuer performed its annual analysis of the possible impairment of goodwill as of an interim date and recorded a goodwill impairment charge for one of its reporting units. During the period between the annual impairment test date and year end, the issuer's share price decreased significantly. The Firm failed to evaluate whether the decrease in share price represented a sustained decrease that, under generally accepted accounting principles ("GAAP"), required further analysis of possible goodwill impairment, as the Firm's procedures were limited to noting that the issuer's shares were thinly traded and that certain analysts projected a significant increase in the issuer's share price.

For more details, see PCAOB Release No. 104-2017-027.

12-33　Goodwill is the excess of the purchase price over the fair market value of the acquired organization's tangible assets, identifiable intangible assets, and liabilities.　(T/F)

12-34　Because of conservatism considerations, auditors should require a client to overestimate its reserve for restructuring.　(T/F)

12-35　Which of the following valuation issues are associated with merger and acquisition activity?

    a.　Valuing assets of the acquired organization at their FMV at the time of acquisition.

    b.　Measuring restructuring charges associated with the acquisition.

    c.　Valuing liabilities of the acquired organization at their FMV at the time of acquisition.

    d.　All of the above.

12-36　Which of the following evidence items would an auditor most likely <u>not</u> consider when evaluating the potential impairment of goodwill?

    a.　The acquisition made by a competitor of an organization that is not a direct competitor of the client.

    b.　The current market capitalization of the organization in comparison with its net book value.

    c.　The cash flows and operating data of the reporting unit since acquisition compared with estimates made at the time of acquisition.

    d.　The growth or decline in market share of the reporting unit since acquisition.

LO 10

Apply the frameworks for professional decision making and ethical decision making for decisions made when conducting an audit.

Applying Decision-Making Frameworks

The following *End of Chapter* materials provide you an opportunity to apply the frameworks for professional decision making and ethical decision making for decisions made when conducting an audit: *12-27* and *12-28*.

- Long-lived assets are noncurrent assets that organization use over multiple operating cycles and include tangible assets of land, buildings, fixtures, and equipment. Some organizations also have natural resources, such as timber tracts, oil wells, and mineral deposits. Long-lived assets also include intangible assets such as patents, franchise licenses, and goodwill. (LO 1)

- Inherent risks associated with transactions related to long-lived assets include incomplete recording of asset disposals, obsolescence of assets, incorrect recording of assets due to complex ownership structures, and amortization or depreciation schedules not reflecting economic impairment or use of the asset. Furthermore, management does not typically have incentives to identify and write down

assets. However, in some situations management wants to write down every potentially impaired asset to a minimum realizable value (although this will cause a one-time reduction to current earnings, it will lead to higher reported earnings in the future). (LO 2)

- Natural resources present unique inherent risks. It is often difficult to identify the costs associated with the discovery of the natural resource. Furthermore, once the natural resource has been discovered, it is often difficult to estimate the amount of commercially available resources to be used in determining a depletion rate. (LO 2)

- Inherent risk for intangible assets focuses on determining the cost of such assets, which is not as straightforward as it is for tangible assets, such as equipment. (LO 2)

- One of the more common techniques used to fraudulently misstate financial statements involves the overstatement of assets through overvaluing existing assets, including fictitious assets, or capitalizing expenses. Other potential fraud schemes relating to long-lived assets include not recording asset sales and misappropriating the proceeds, selling assets but not removing them from the books, assigning inappropriate residual values or lives to the assets, and "miscalculating" amortization of intangible assets. (LO 3)

- Typical controls over long-lived assets include a formal budgeting process with appropriate follow-up variance analysis, written policies for acquisition and disposals of long-lived assets, limited physical access to assets, periodic comparison of physical assets to subsidiary records, and periodic reconciliations of subsidiary records with the general ledger. (LO 4)

- Planning analytical procedures help auditors identify areas of potential material misstatements. The objective of planning analytical procedures is to identify accounts with heightened risk of misstatement during audit planning to provide a basis for designing and implementing responses to the assessed risks. Auditors will typically use trend and ratio analysis when performing planning analytical procedures related to long-lived assets. (LO 5)

- Responding to identified risks typically involves developing an audit approach that contains substantive procedures (e.g., tests of details and, when appropriate, substantive analytical procedures) and tests of controls, when applicable. (LO 6)

- Typical tests of transaction controls include inquiry of personnel performing the control, observation of the control being performed, inspection of documentation confirming that the control has been performed, and reperformance of the control by the auditor testing the control. For example, assume that a client implements a policy requiring the establishment and enforcement of property management training for all personnel involved in the use, stewardship, and management of equipment. The auditor can test this control (the policy and its implementation) in various ways, including inquiry, observation, and inspection of documentation. (LO 7)

- Examples of substantive tests related to long-lived assets include reviewing documentary support (such as invoices or contracts) for additions above a certain amount, physically inspecting a sample of additions made during the audit period, tracing asset disposals to the original cost of the item and its accumulated depreciation to the supporting documentation, and performing substantive analytical procedures to test depreciation related accounts. (LO 8)

- Merger and acquisition transactions present significant challenges related to valuation issues, including valuing the assets and associated liabilities upon acquisition, measuring restructuring charges and recognition of the liability, and determining goodwill impairment. (LO 9)

Significant Terms

Amortization expense A process of expensing the acquisition cost minus the residual value of intangible assets over their estimated useful economic life.

Asset impairment A term used to describe management's recognition that a significant portion of fixed assets is no longer as productive as had originally been expected. When assets are so impaired, the assets should be written down to their expected economic value.

Depletion expense Expense associated with the extraction of natural resources.

Escalation of commitment A human behavior pattern in which an individual or group—when faced with increasingly negative outcomes from some decision, action, or investment—continues the same behavior rather than alter course.

Fair value estimate The price that would be received to sell an asset or paid to transfer a liability in an orderly transaction between market participants at the measurement date

Goodwill The excess of the purchase price over the fair market values of the acquired organization's tangible assets, identifiable intangible assets, and liabilities.

Goodwill impairment loss The excess of a reporting unit's carrying amount over its fair value (not to exceed the total goodwill allocated to that reporting unit).

Intangible Assets Nonphysical assets, such as patents, trademarks, copyrights, and brand recognition.

Long-lived assets Noncurrent assets that organizations use over multiple operating cycles and include tangible assets of land, buildings, fixtures, and equipment. Long-lived assets also include intangible assets.

Tangible assets Assets that have a physical form, such as machinery, buildings, and land.

Prompts for Critical Thinking

Prompt for Critical Thinking #1

- Obsolescence of assets
- Incorrect recording of assets, due to complex ownership structures
- Determining asset impairment, especially for intangible assets, requires a good information system, a systematic process, effective controls, and professional judgment

Prompt for Critical Thinking #2

- Costs that should have been expensed are improperly capitalized.
- Impairment losses on long-lived assets are not recognized.
- Fair value estimates are unreasonable or unsupportable.

Prompt for Critical Thinking #3

- Develop an overall estimate of depreciation expense.
- Compare capital expenditures with the client's capital budget, with an expectation that capital expenditures would be consistent with the capital budget.
- Ratio of long-lived assets to total assets—This ratio will fluctuate in relation to acquisitions, disposals, and depreciation.

Prompt for Critical Thinking #4

- *Inquiry*—Select a sample of personnel required to complete such training and talk with them about whether they have completed the training and the nature of that training.
- *Observation*—Observe a training session in process or observe property management actions in process.
- *Inspection of documentation*—Review the training materials and, for a sample of personnel, review documentation showing completion of the training.

Prompt for Critical Thinking #5

- Long-lived asset additions are recorded correctly.
- Items to be capitalized are identified and distinguished from repairs and maintenance expense items.
- Depreciation/amortization/depletion calculations are made and based on appropriate estimated useful lives and methods.

Review Questions and Short Cases

NOTE: Completing *Review Questions and Short Cases* does not require the student to reference additional resources and materials.

NOTE: For the remaining problems, we make special note of those addressing fraud, international issues, professional skepticism, and ethics.

FRAUD

FRAUD

PROFESSIONAL SKEPTICISM

FRAUD

12-1 **LO 1** Refer to *Exhibit 12.1*. One of the significant accounts in this cycle is equipment. For this account, what would typically be the more relevant assertions for the auditor to consider? Why is it important for the auditor to identify the more relevant assertions?

12-2 **LO 1** Refer to *Exhibit 12.1*. Depreciation expense is included in the exhibit. How is depreciation expense similar to depletion expense and amortization expense?

12-3 **LO 1** Identify the five management assertions and describe how they are relevant to long-lived assets.

12-4 **LO 2** What is asset impairment, and what inherent risk factors are associated with asset impairment?

12-5 **LO 2** What are some inherent risks of material misstatement associated with natural resources?

12-6 **LO 2** What are some inherent risks of material misstatement associated with intangible assets?

12-7 **LO 3** Ways in which long-lived assets can be fraudulently overstated include:
- Fictitious assets on the books
- Improper and incomplete depreciation
- Failure to record impairment of assets, especially goodwill
- Expired or worthless assets left on a company's books
- Assets overvalued upon acquisition, especially in the purchase of a company
  a. What incentives might motivate management to overstate fixed assets?
  b. What other factors should the auditor consider when assessing fraud risk related to long-lived assets?

12-8 **LO 3** Explain what a skeptical auditor might consider when trying to understand management's potential for adjusting earnings through manipulation of long-lived asset accounts.

12-9 **LO 3** Identify potential fraud schemes related to long-lived assets.

12-10 **LO 4** Consider the risks typically associated with tangible long-lived assets and identify the internal controls over these assets that you would expect a client to have implemented.

12-11 **LO 4** Consider the risks typically associated with intangible long-lived assets and identify the internal controls over these assets that you would expect a client to have implemented.

12-12 **LO 5** Identify planning analytical procedures related to depreciation expense that may be effective in identifying potential material misstatements.

12-13 **LO 5** Identify ratios and expected relationships that an auditor might use when performing planning analytical procedures related to long-lived assets.

12-14 **LO 6** Refer to *Exhibit 12.3*. Describe the differences in the planned audit approaches for Clients A and B and the reasons for such differences.

12-15 `LO 6` Explain why in some audit settings with long-lived assets, auditors choose to perform only substantive tests of details, even though controls are designed effectively.

12-16 `LO 6` The following questions might be addressed when an auditor is completing an internal control questionnaire. For each question, labeled as 1 through 8:

a. Indicate the purpose of the control.

b. Indicate the impact on the planned substantive audit procedures if the answer to the question indicates weak controls.

   1. Does the client periodically take a physical inventory of property and reconcile to the property ledger?

   2. Does the client have a policy manual to classify property and assign an estimated life for depreciation purposes to the class of assets?

   3. Does the client have a policy on minimum expenditures before an item is capitalized? If yes, what is the minimum amount?

   4. Does the client have a mechanism to identify pieces of equipment that have been designated for scrap? If yes, is it effective?

   5. Does the client have an acceptable mechanism to differentiate major renovations from repair and maintenance? If yes, is it effective?

   6. Does the client regularly self-construct its own assets? If yes, does the client have an effective procedure to appropriately identify and classify all construction costs?

   7. Does the client systematically review major classes of assets for potential impairment?

   8. Does management periodically review asset disposal or the scrapping of assets as a basis for reviewing the assignment of estimated life for depreciation purposes?

12-17 `LO 7` Based on the following description, determine appropriate tests of controls for the company's controls over tangible long-lived assets.

A corporation operates a highly automated flexible manufacturing facility. The capital-intensive nature of the corporation's operations makes internal control over the acquisition and use of tangible long-lived assets important management objectives.

The corporation establishes a tangible long-lived assets budget indicating planned capital expenditures by department at the beginning of each year. Department managers request capital expenditures by completing a tangible long-lived assets requisition form, which senior management reviews for approval. The corporation has a written policy that establishes whether a budget request is a capital expenditure or a routine maintenance expenditure.

A management committee meets each month to review budget reports that compare actual expenditures made by managers to their budgeted amounts and to authorize any additional expenditures that may be necessary. The committee also reviews and approves, as necessary, any departmental request for sale, retirement, or scrapping of tangible long-lived assets. Copies of vouchers used to document department requests for sale, retirement, or scrapping of fixed assets are forwarded to the accounting department to initiate removal of the asset from the tangible long-lived assets ledger.

The accounting department is responsible for maintaining a detailed ledger of tangible long-lived assets. When the corporation acquires a tangible long-lived asset, the asset is tagged for identification. The identification number as well as the cost, location, and other information necessary for depreciation calculations are entered into the tangible long-lived assets ledger. Depreciation calculations are made each quarter and are posted to the general ledger. Periodic physical inventories of tangible long-lived assets are taken for purposes of reconciliation to the tangible long-lived assets ledger as well as appraisal for insurance purposes.

12-18 **LO 7** Refer to *Exhibit 12.2*. Identify tests of controls that an auditor could use to test the controls included in *Exhibit 12.2*.

FRAUD

12-19 **LO 8** Long-lived assets can be fraudulently overstated in many ways, including:
- Fictitious assets on the books
- Improper and incomplete depreciation
- Failure to record impairment of assets, especially goodwill
- Expired or worthless assets left on a company's books
- Assets overvalued upon acquisition, especially in the purchase of a company

What substantive audit procedures might detect each of these types of frauds?

12-20 **LO 8** The audit senior has asked you to perform analytical procedures to obtain substantive evidence on the reasonableness of recorded depreciation expense of the delivery equipment of a client. Changes in the account occurred pretty evenly during the year. The estimated useful life is six years. Estimated salvage value is 10% of original cost. Straight-line depreciation is used. Additional information includes:

Delivery Equipment (per General Ledger)	
Beginning balance	$380,500
Additions	154,000
Disposals	(95,600)
Ending balance	$438,900

Current year depreciation expense per books = $60,500

a. Based on this information, develop an expectation of the amount of depreciation expense for the year as part of a reasonableness test.
b. Does the recorded depreciation expense seem acceptable? What additional information might you need to make this determination? Explain.
c. What is the impact of the result of this analytical procedure on other substantive procedures that the auditor may perform?

12-21 **LO 8** What audit procedures might an auditor use to identify fully depreciated equipment? How might the auditor determine that such equipment is properly valued?

12-22 **LO 8** A client has a policy manual that categorizes equipment by type and assigns a depreciation life based on the categorization. The client depreciates all equipment in a category using the same depreciation method. How does the auditor determine the reasonableness of the client's approach?

12-23 **LO 8** What evidence might an auditor obtain to determine the proper valuation of an impaired asset?

12-24 `LO 8` Assume that a company obtains an appraisal for equipment that may be impaired. Does the auditor need to test the appraisal? What work should the auditor perform to determine whether the auditor should rely on the appraisal as an estimate of the value of the assets?

12-25 `LO 8` Describe the basic approach to auditing leases.

12-26 `LO 8` You are performing the year-end audit of Halvorson Fine Foods, Inc. for December 31, 2018. The client has prepared the following schedule for the fixed assets and related allowance for depreciation accounts.

Description	Final Balance December 31, 2017	Additions	Retirements	Per Books, December 31, 2018
Assets:				
Land	$22,500	$5,000		$27,500
Buildings	120,000	17,500		137,500
Machinery and equipment	385,000	40,400	$26,000	399,400
	$527,500	$62,900	$26,000	$564,400
Allowance for depreciation:				
Building	$60,000	$5,150		$65,150
Machinery and equipment	173,200	39,220		212,470
	$233,250	$44,370		$277,620

You have compared the opening balances with your prior-year audit working papers. You find the following information, labeled as 1 through 6, during your current-year audit. Review this information and indicate how you might have found each of the described items, labeled as 1 through 6, during the audit (other than through client inquiry).

1. All equipment is depreciated on a straight-line basis (no salvage value taken into consideration) based on the following estimated lives: buildings, 25 years; all other items, 10 years. The company's policy is to take one-half year's depreciation on all asset acquisitions and disposals occurring during the year.

2. On April 1 of the current year, the company entered into a ten-year lease contract for a die-casting machine with annual rentals of $5,000, payable in advance every April 1. The lease is cancelable by either party (60 days' written notice is required), and there is no option to renew the lease or buy the equipment at the end of the lease. The estimated useful life of the machine is ten years with no salvage value. The company recorded the die-casting machine in the machinery and equipment account at $40,400, the present value at the date of the lease, and $2,020, applicable to the machine, has been included in depreciation expense for the year.

3. The company completed the construction of a wing on the plant building on June 30 of the current year. The useful life of the building was not extended by this addition. The lowest construction bid received was $17,500, the amount recorded in the buildings account. Company personnel were used to construct the addition at a cost of $16,000 (materials, $7,500; labor, $5,500; and overhead, $3,000).

4. On August 18, Halvorson paid $5,000 for paving and fencing a portion of land owned by the company for use as a parking lot for employees. The expenditure was charged to the land account.

5. The amount shown in the retirements column for the machinery and equipment asset represents cash received on September 5, on disposal of a machine purchased in July 2004 for $48,000. The bookkeeper recorded a depreciation expense of $3,500 on this machine in 2018.

6. Crux City donated land and building appraised at $10,000 and $40,000, respectively, to Halvorson for a plant. On September 1, the company began operating the plant. Because no costs were involved, the bookkeeper made no entry for the foregoing transaction.

ETHICS

12-27 `LO 8, 10` Your audit firm has audited Cowan Industries for many years. The company manufactures a wide range of lawn care products and typically sells to major retailers. In recent years, the company has expanded into ancillary products, such as recreation equipment, that use some of the same technology. The newer lines of business, while successful, have not been particularly profitable. The company's stock price has languished, and top management has recently been replaced.

The new management team announces that it will close two factories and will phase out one of the newer lines of business. It plans to expand existing products and increase marketing efforts. Even though there is no technological obsolescence of existing products, the new management does not believe the company has a competitive advantage. It wants to take a one-time hit to the balance sheet and income statement of $15.3 million (about one-third of total assets) as a reserve for the shutdown of the plants and the disposal of a line of business. It also plans on severance pay for employees at the two plants.

a. Define the term *impairment of assets*. Identify indicators suggesting that impairment of an asset might have occurred.

b. Is management typically motivated to understate or overstate the write-down because of asset impairment? Explain.

c. Assume in this situation that the auditor believes management is overestimating the impairment charge and thus the improvement in future earnings because of reduced depreciation charges in subsequent periods. Furthermore, assume that the auditor has gathered and evaluated evidence that convincingly reveals the impairment charge should more reasonably fall in a range from $8 to $10 million, rather than management's estimate of about $15 million. Finally, assume the auditor has discussed the issue with management and management refuses to change its original estimate. Management has stated that its assumptions and evidence are just as convincing as the auditor's. Use the seven-step framework for ethical decision making from *Chapter 1* to make a recommendation about the course of action the auditor should take. Recall that the steps are as follows: (1) identify the ethical issue; in this case the ethical issue is how to properly ensure that the review comments are taken seriously and addressed; (2) determine the affected parties and identify their rights; (3) determine the most important rights for each affected party; (4) develop alternative courses of action; (5) determine the likely consequences of each proposed course of action on each affected party; (6) assess the possible consequences; and (7) decide on an appropriate course of action.

12-28 `LO 8, 10` Novelis, Inc. is the world's leading rolled-aluminum products producer. Items 1 through 3 below provide descriptions of issues involving asset impairments derived from the company's footnote disclosures.

1. In connection with the decision to close and sell our plant in Borgofranco, Italy, we recognized an impairment charge of $5 million to reduce the net book value of the plant's fixed assets

to zero. We based our estimate on third-party offers and negotiations to sell the business.

2. We recorded an impairment charge of $65 million to reduce the carrying value of the production equipment at two facilities in Italy to their fair value of $56 million. We determined the fair value of the impaired assets based on the discounted future cash flows of these facilities using a 7% discount rate.

3. We announced that we would cease operations in Falkirk, Scotland. We designated certain production equipment with a nominal carrying value for transfer to our Rogerstone facility. We reduced the carrying value of the remaining fixed assets to zero, which resulted in an $8 million impairment charge.

Complete the first four steps of the seven-step framework for professional decision making introduced in *Chapter 1* by answering the following questions:

a. What difficulties will the auditor of Novelis face when deciding whether the impairment charges that Novelis incurred are reasonable?

b. What are the consequences of the auditor's decisions in evaluating impairments?

c. What are the risks and uncertainties associated with Novelis' estimation?

d. What types of evidence should the auditor gather to evaluate the reasonableness of management's estimates?

Recall that the framework is:

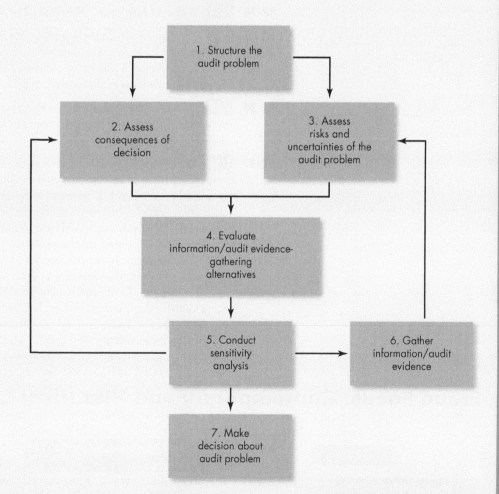

12-29 **LO 9** What are some sources of inherent risk in mergers and acquisitions?

12-30 **LO 9** Explain how WorldCom used restructuring reserves (liabilities) to fraudulently manipulate reported earnings.

12-31 **LO 9** Organizations have a number of issues to address when acquiring another organization. How does an organization measure the acquisition of another organization? What factors often complicate the determination of these measurements? Explain how each factor complicates the calculation of cost and the steps the auditor has to take to reach a conclusion about the cost of the acquisition.

12-32 **LO 9** An acquisition will typically result with the acquiring organization bringing goodwill onto its books.
a. How is the amount of goodwill determined at the time of acquisition?
b. When should an organization consider whether goodwill has been impaired? How is goodwill impairment determined?
c. What are the auditor's concerns related to goodwill?

12-33 **LO 9** Organizations will often hire a specialist to determine the value of the tangible and intangible assets obtained in an acquisition. Does the auditor always need to engage his or her own specialist to test the work of the specialist hired by the organization? Explain, incorporating the idea of the importance of auditor professional skepticism into your response.

12-34 **LO 9** What is fair value? When are fair value concepts applied?

12-35 **LO 9** Fair value guidance suggests that there may be three levels of evidence available to assess fair value. Explain the nature of Level 1, Level 2, and Level 3 fair value estimates and the type of information the auditor needs to evaluate each type.

12-36 **LO 9** What factors might signal the likelihood that goodwill may be impaired? Explain and indicate how the auditor would be aware of each of these factors.

12-37 **LO 9** Assume that in 2018, Nelson Communications purchased a controlling interest in Telnetco that resulted in goodwill in the 2018 consolidated financial statements of $4,500,000. Goodwill is the only intangible assets. Telnetco continues to be listed on NASDAQ. Near the end of 2019, Nelson estimated that the fair market value of Telnetco was $50,500,000 based on the present value of its future cash flows. Using the assistance of a professional appraisal firm, the fair market value of its net tangible assets was determined to be $46,900,000, resulting in a goodwill impairment of $900,000.
a. Describe the inherent risks related to recording this impairment.
b. Describe the audit evidence needed to evaluate the appropriateness of this impairment.
c. How might an auditor use a specialist to assist?

Fraud Focus: Contemporary and Historical Cases

12-38 **Miller Energy Resources, Inc., KPMG LLP**
(LO 3, 6, 8, 9) Miller Energy, Incorporated (hereafter, Miller) was a thinly traded, penny stock, oil and gas company headquartered in Knoxville, Tennessee. Miller won a competitive bid to purchase assets of a company filing for bankruptcy for

$2.25 million in cash, along with assuming liabilities of about $2 million. A California-based energy company in the process of legally abandoning those assets. The assets consisted of leases covering 602,000 acres of land in Alaska that contained mostly unproven exploratory oil and gas reserves. The assets also included five oil and gas wells, two production facilities, and an offshore oil platform, hereafter the "Alaska Assets."

This case highlights both financial reporting fraud by Miller, as well as audit failures on the part of its auditor, KPMG, and the audit engagement partner, John Riordan. Ultimately, the SEC fined Miller $5,000,000, KPMG $1,000,000, and Riordan $25,000.

KPMG issued unqualified audit opinions on the financial statements throughout the fraudulent period, and remained Miller's auditor even after the fraud was discovered. On March 12, 2015, Miller submitted a NT-10-K, which is a notification of its ability to file its 10-K in a timely fashion. KPMG issued an adverse opinion on the company's internal controls, and the company was trying to remediate those by hiring more internal accounting staff. Ultimately, the SEC delisted the company's stock and on March 29, 2016, its series registration was terminated. KPMG's audit fees during 2011 through 2014 were:

FYE 2014: $1,214,000
FYE 2013: $890,000
FYE 2012: $578,000
FYE 2011: $451,005

The Financial Reporting Fraud

To access Miller's 2011 10-K, see:
https://www.sec.gov/Archives/edgar/data/785968
/000094344011000519/mill_10ka.htm

Miller reported the assets that it had purchased at an overstated value of $480 million, and recognized a bargain purchase gain of $277 million. To justify this fraudulent valuation, the CFO used a fair value reserve report that a petroleum-engineering firm produced. Shortly after the purchase, Miller filed its 10-Q for its fiscal third quarter year ending January 31, 2010. That report asserted that the company's fixed assets were comprised of $368 million of oil and gas properties, and $110 million of long-lived assets. Of particular interest, the SEC AAER states that the following occurred with respect to fraud relating to long-lived assets:

"In a February 8, 2010 email, the CFO informed the Alaska CEO that he needed an amount to use as fair value for the fixed assets obtained as part of the Alaska acquisition. He noted that, ideally, the value should be what a willing buyer would pay for the assets, but "[i]n the absence of that, replacement values or something similar would probably work." Two days later, the CFO was sent an "asset replacement cost study" purportedly provided by an independent insurance broker, which appeared to list the replacement cost for the assets as $110 million. The "study" was dated September 5, 2008, but "revised" on February 9, 2010. Without any additional analysis, the CFO recorded the amount in the revised insurance study on Miller Energy's balance sheet. The recording of assets at a value of $110 million was improper for several reasons. Miller Energy's use of the values in the insurance study resulted in counting the value of the fixed assets twice, thereby overstating the value of such assets. The reserve report Miller Energy relied on to value the acquired oil and gas properties used a discounted cash flow model. Valuation specialists use such models to estimate the value of an enterprise's "operating assets" – i.e., the assets employed to generate future cash flows – by converting future benefit streams into a net present value. In Miller Energy's case, the fixed assets in the insurance study were the very same operating assets that were expected to generate the future cash flows in the reserve report. Accordingly, they should not have been separately valued." (Source AAER 3731, para. 42–45.)

Miller also reported a bargain purchase gain of $277 million, which was a material improvement over its prior fiscal year end loss of $556,097. Because of this fraudulent reporting, Miller's stock rose from $0.61 per share to $6.60 per share. After achieving that fraudulent performance, Miller's stock started trading on the NASDAQ, and then on the NYSE a year later; the all-time high price of the stock occurred on December 9, 2013 at a value of $8.83 per share! How could Miller management gotten away with this fraudulent scheme?

The Audit Failures

AAER No. 3888 details the following failures by KPMG and the engagement partner:

With regard to client acceptance:

The engagement partner, John Riordan, had no experience in the oil and gas industry. Only one of two senior managers on the engagement had such experience; KPMG assigned her to the engagement specifically because of that experience. The AAER (paragraph 23) states the following:

> KPMG's client acceptance procedures also failed to adequately address the audit team's lack of industry experience. Although a client acceptance evaluation form completed by Riordan noted that the assigned engagement partner and senior manager had no prior experience with oil and gas companies like Miller Energy, it stated that there were no concerns regarding the overall skills and experience of the engagement team. Consequently, KPMG assigned to the engagement team personnel who had insufficient expertise to appropriately address the risks presented by Miller Energy. Riordan lacked the necessary experience to serve as the partner-in-charge of the engagement, resulting in departures from professional standards.

With regard to lack of planning, supervision, due care, and professional skepticism, the SEC had this to say about KPMG's audit quality (AAER, paragraphs 2 and 3):

> KPMG and Riordan failed to obtain sufficient competent evidence regarding the impact of the opening balances on the current-year financial statements, despite knowing that no proper fair value assessment had been performed by management in the prior year. Although KPMG and Riordan did undertake some audit procedures relating to the opening balances, these procedures failed to appropriately consider the facts leading to Miller Energy's acquisition of the Alaska Assets, including the multiple offers received for those assets and the "abandonment" of the assets by the prior owner. In applying these procedures, KPMG and Riordan also failed to sufficiently review certain forecasted costs associated with the estimation of the fair value of the Alaska Assets, which were understated, and to detect that certain fixed assets were double counted in the company's valuation.

KPMG and Riordan failed to properly assess the risks associated with accepting Miller Energy as a client and to properly staff the audit. KPMG and Riordan also overlooked evidence that indicated a possible overvaluation of the Alaska Assets and failed to exercise the requisite degree of due professional care and skepticism. And while KPMG management and national office personnel became aware of the unusual and highly material prior-year transaction, the firm did not take sufficient action to determine that an appropriate response was taken by the engagement team regarding the risk of overvaluation of the Alaska Assets.

With regard to weaknesses in the audit procedures relating to the $110 million of fixed assets, the SEC levied the following criticisms (AAER, paragraphs 51, 52, and 53):

KPMG and Riordan agreed with Miller Energy's accounting treatment for the fixed assets without performing sufficient procedures to obtain the necessary evidence to properly assess the reasonableness of that accounting treatment. Although EVS (*author's note: EVS stands for KPMG's internal valuation specialists, Economic and Valuation Services*) was aware of potential double-counting and made inquiries of the core engagement team about the relationship between the fixed assets and the reserve report's cash flows, the discussion and the resolution of this issue were not documented in KPMG's workpapers.

There was also insufficient competent evidence to support the $110 million valuation of the fixed assets. Despite workpapers that state the opposite, KPMG and Riordan knew that the insurance broker was not a valuation specialist and that the insurance report was not sufficient evidential matter to support the value of the fixed assets (*see, supra,* paragraph 34).

To corroborate the $110 million number listed in the insurance report, Miller Energy, at KPMG's request, created a second estimate in 2011, without the assistance of any valuation professionals. In preparing this analysis, Miller Energy adjusted its original estimates of the replacement costs for the various fixed assets – increasing the values for some assets and reducing the value of others – and made further adjustments to these replacement costs for depreciation and for functional obsolescence. KPMG and Riordan accepted the new replacement cost values from this analysis as reasonable without obtaining adequate corroboration, and they did so even though the values were based on management's own internal cost estimates and included miles of additional pipelines (representing a 175% increase in pipeline mileage from the original report). Based mostly on this additional analysis, EVS determined that the overall replacement cost estimate in the insurance report was a "reasonable proxy" for fair value.

a. What is a penny stock? Why does the SEC care about such a small and thinly traded stock? Do you think that the fact that this was a relatively small company within minimal stock capitalization might have played into the engagement partner's relative lack of skepticism regarding management's assertions? Explain your reasoning.

b. What audit procedures *should* KPMG have conducted with regard to the valuation of the oil and gas reserves?

c. This is clearly not a case where the audit partner and his team purposely failed in their duties. They did perform some reasonable tests, just not enough and with too little skepticism. The beginning of the revelations about the fraud and KPMG's low quality audit began to become known on July 28, 2011. On that date, *TheStreetSweeper*, a financial blog dedicated to exposing corporate fraud, published the results of its assessment of the validity of the financial statements for Miller.

They challenged the valuation of the Alaska Assets, providing numerous links to public sources that called that valuation into question. Riordan and KPMG learned of *TheStreetSweeper* report on the date it became public, and reached out to KPMG's national office Department of Professional Practice (DPP). The SEC's AAER reports that DPP and the engagement team did not react with sufficient diligence in responding to *TheStreetSweeper's* allegations, and discounted the information contained in the allegations, and then proceeded to issue an unqualified audit opinion on Miller's FYE 2011 financial statements.

In addition to all these red flags, on July 29, 2011, Miller management filed its 10-K before KPMG had completed the audit and issued its independent accountants' report, or its consent to the use of their report filed. On August 29, 2011, KPMG issued an unqualified audit opinion.

Why do you think that the KPMG professionals convinced themselves that there were *not* problems with the audit? In answering this question consider professional skepticism and the role of the psychological phenomenon known as **escalation of commitment**, which "refers to a human behavior pattern in which an individual or group—when faced with increasingly negative outcomes from some decision, action, or investment—continues the same behavior rather than alter course" (see *https://www.google.com/search?q=escalation+of+commitment&ie=utf-8&oe=utf-8*).

d. Evaluate the pattern of audit fees that KPMG earned on the Miller audits. Discuss how auditor independence may be at issue in this case.

e. Comment on the relative fairness of the fines levied on Miller, KPMG, and Riordan, respectively.

For more details, see: AAER Release No. 3731 (January 12, 2016) and AAER Release No. 3888 (August 15, 2017).

Also, we present a follow-up Application Activity in 12-42.

FRAUD   **12-39** **Ignite Restaurant Group**
(LO 1, 2, 3, 4, 6, 8)   Ignite Restaurant Group (IRG), the owner of various restaurants including Joe's Crab Shack, went public in May 2012. Just two months later, the company announced that it needed to restate its financial statements to correct errors related to the treatment of certain leases. The announcement resulted in a single day stock price decline of 22%. The lease errors began in 2006 (the year of the company's origination) and continued through the first quarter of 2012. The restatement related to the leases was estimated to be between $3.4 and $3.8 million. As a result of this situation, IRG planned a fixed-asset accounting review to assess historical asset additions, dispositions, useful lives, and depreciation from 2006 through the first quarter of 2012. At the time of the announcement in July 2012, IRG anticipated additional restatements of at least $1.2 million related to the accounting for its other fixed assets and related depreciation expense.

In October 2012, IRG announced that it had completed its internal review of this situation. The aggregate impact of the restatement adjustments and related tax effects (from the company's inception in 2006 through the first quarter of 2012) reduced net income by a total of $6.4 million over the five-year plus period. In connection with the restatement, management identified material weaknesses in its internal control over financial reporting related to lack of sufficient qualified accounting and tax personnel; lack of adequate supervision and monitoring of accounting operations; inadequate lease accounting controls; and lack of effective controls related to the existence, completeness, and accuracy of fixed assets and related depreciation and amortization expense.

a. What long-lived asset accounts at Ignite Restaurant Group (IRG) were misstated?

b. The situation was described in the press as a minor, but embarrassing, accounting issue. Notwithstanding this description, assume for purposes of this question that the accounting issue was the result of fraudulent financial reporting by management. If that had been the case, what might have motivated management to materially misstate the assets you identified in part (a)?

c. What controls should be in place at IRG to mitigate the misstatements that needed to be corrected?

d. What procedures should the auditor have performed when auditing the assets you identified in part (a)?

FRAUD

PROFESSIONAL SKEPTICISM

12-40 **WorldCom**
(LO 2, 3, 8) The WorldCom bankruptcy was one of the largest in U.S. economic history at the time it occurred. Much of the fraud involved capitalizing operating expenses, such as payments to other companies for line rental, as fixed assets. Adjusting journal entries were made at the company's headquarters in Mississippi, even though property accounting records were located in Dallas, Texas.

a. Would it be unusual to find debits to fixed assets coming from an adjusting journal entry source rather than a purchase journal? Explain.

b. Would it be unusual to find entries to accumulated depreciation and depreciation expense to come from an adjusting journal entry source rather than another source?

c. Assume you were auditing WorldCom, and in your sample of debits to fixed assets, you find an entry for $500,000 with the following notation: "Capitalization of line capacity per CFO, amounts were originally incorrectly recorded as an expense." Explain what you would do to complete the audit of this item. How might the professionally skeptical auditor respond? What evidence would you need to corroborate the entry?

FRAUD

12-41 **Safety-Kleen, PricewaterhouseCoopers**
(LO 2, 3, 4, 6, 8) Refer to the *Focus on Fraud* feature "Improper Capitalization of Operating Expenses: The Case of Safety-Kleen Corporation." In addition to the information provided in the feature, consider the following information.

At the close of each quarter, Safety-Kleen executives met to discuss the results of operations. Typically, they discussed the targeted earnings amount, and then they discussed potential accounting adjustments to help them achieve the target. Although the company had always made legitimate quarterly adjusting entries in preparing its financial statements, the magnitude and nature of the adjustments changed dramatically during fiscal year 1999. Over time, the discrepancy between the company's projected results and the actual results increased, and management made several improper adjustments each quarter to reach the earnings targets. As the following table indicates, Safety-Kleen's quarterly earnings were materially increased as a result of the accounting adjustments (in other words, the legitimate adjustments and the improper adjustments combined). In some reporting periods, the company's reported earnings were increased by more than 100%.

As an example of inappropriate entries, at the end of the third quarter of fiscal year 1999, they improperly capitalized approximately $4.6 million of payroll expenses relating to certain marketing and start-up activities. At the close of the fourth quarter of fiscal year 1999, they improperly capitalized $1.8 million of salaries and wages incurred in connection with the development and implementation of various software systems. Not only did this adjusting entry fail to comply with GAAP, it ultimately was recorded twice.

Name	Earnings Before Adjustments (in Millions)	Earnings as Reported After Adjustments (in Millions)	Total Adjustments (in Millions)	%
First Quarter FY 1999	$90.9	$127.5	$36.6	40.3
Second Quarter FY 1999	$76.7	$107.6	$30.9	40.3
Third Quarter FY 1999	$47.9	$123.4	$75.5	157.6
Fourth Quarter FY 1999	$57.3	$110.4	$53.1	92.7
First Quarter FY 2000	$47.0	$116.8	$69.8	148.5
Total	$319.8	$585.7	$265.9	83.1

On March 6, 2000, after Safety-Kleen's board of directors had received information concerning possible accounting irregularities, the company announced that it had initiated an internal investigation of its previously reported financial results and certain of its accounting policies. On March 10, 2000, Safety-Kleen filed a Form 8-K stating that the company's independent accounting firm, PricewaterhouseCoopers LLP, had withdrawn its audit reports on the financial statements for fiscal years 1997, 1998, and 1999.

In 2005, a lawsuit brought by a group of institutional investors against former officers of Safety-Kleen Corporation ended with a $200 million judgment against two former officers and more than $84 million in settlements against the company's former auditor and directors. PricewaterhouseCoopers, Safety-Kleen's former auditors, agreed to settle and pay $48 million, and the directors agreed to pay $36 million.

a. What were likely factors contributing to the fraud?

b. What audit procedures might have identified the inappropriate adjustments?

Application Activities

NOTE: Completing *Application Activities* requires students to reference additional resources and materials. Some *Application Activities* will require the student to reference relevant professional auditing standards. We make special note of these as *Auditing Standards Application Activities*.

12-42 **Miller Energy Resources, Inc., KPMG LLP (LO 2, 3, 9)**   This *Application Activity* relates to the fraud case in *12-38*, involving Miller Resources Group, and KPMG LLP. These activities will help you to appreciate Miller managers' compensation incentives, and the losses that investors incurred.

a. Use online resources at the SEC's website to locate Miller's yearly Def-14A (proxy) statements for the years 2011–2014 *(https://www.sec.gov/cgi-bin/browse-edgar?action=getcompany &CIK=0000785968&type=def+14A&dateb=&owner=exclude &count=40)*

Filings	Format	Description	Filing Date	File/Film Number
DEF 14A	Documents	Other definitive proxy statements Acc-no: 0000785968-14-000147 (34 Act) Size: 1 MB	2014-08-28	001-34732 141072425
DEF 14A	Documents	Other definitive proxy statements Acc-no: 0000785968-14-000047 (34 Act) Size: 1 MB	2014-03-31	001-34732 14727847
DEF 14A	Documents	Other definitive proxy statements Acc-no: 0001354488-13-000301 (34 Act) Size: 972 KB	2013-01-24	001-34732 13546156
DEF 14A	Documents	Other definitive proxy statements Acc-no: 0001354488-12-000853 (34 Act) Size: 935 KB	2012-02-24	001-34732 12635012
DEF 14A	Documents	Other definitive proxy statements Acc-no: 0001354488-11-000295 (34 Act) Size: 847 KB	2011-01-28	001-34732 11556723

Calculate the Total Direct Compensation for Fiscal Year Performance for each of the following individuals, by year and in total. Articulate your thoughts about what you learn.

Name	Title	FYE 2011	FYE 2012	FYE 2013	FYE 2014	TOTAL
Deloy Miller	Chairman of the Board					
Scott Boruff	CEO					
Paul Boyd	CFO					
TOTAL						

b. Use online resources to track the stock price history of Miller. Comment on the estimated economic loss that shareholders would have experienced by accessing the company's FYE 10-K (use the search term "aggregate market value"). Think about the fact that managers engaged in fraud, auditors failed to do their job, and investors paid the price. Recall the $5,000,000 fine that the SEC imposed; was that fine sufficient?

c. Comment on the trend in the stock, along with trends in associated trading volume.

12-43 **LO 2, 8, 9**   Conduct research to identify a company that has recently recorded impairment charges in its financial statements. You may want to refer to the *Why It Matters* feature "Asset Impairments Can Be Big Dollars!" to identify a company. For the selected company, indicate:

a. The company name and its principal line of business.

b. The nature of financial difficulties the company is facing.

c. The nature of the company's long-lived assets that were impaired.

d. The nature of the impairment charges and their magnitude as a percentage of total assets, total sales, and net income.

e. What judgments did management at the company make that may affect the ability of the external auditor to assess the reasonableness of the impairment charges? Discuss the importance of auditor professional skepticism related to these management judgments.

f. The stock market reaction to the revelation of the impairment charge.

PROFESSIONAL SKEPTICISM

FRAUD

12-44 HP

(LO 2, 3, 6, 8, 9)   In 2012, HP announced an impairment charge of $8.8 billion related to its 2011 acquisition of Autonomy. More than $5 billion of the impairment charge related to accounting improprieties, misrepresentation, and disclosure failures discovered by an internal investigation by HP, and a forensic review into Autonomy's accounting practices prior to its acquisition by HP. Research this case so that you can answer the following questions:

a. What are some examples of the accounting improprieties and misrepresentations made by Autonomy?

b. Consider the fraud triangle. Which factor was most likely the most relevant to the financial statement fraud?

c. For the 10 quarters prior to the acquisition, compare Autonomy's reported revenues with analyst expectations. How might a skeptical auditor respond to these comparisons?

PROFESSIONAL SKEPTICISM

12-45 PCAOB

(LO 2, 4, 6, 7, 8)   Obtain a copy of PCAOB Release No. 104-2017-033.

a. What is this PCAOB Release?

b. Identify the audit deficiency related to long-lived assets.

c. How could that deficiency negatively affect the quality of the audit?

d. Discuss how professional skepticism might relate to that deficiency.

PROFESSIONAL SKEPTICISM

12-46 PCAOB

(LO 2, 4, 6, 7, 8)   Obtain a copy of PCAOB Release No. 104-2016-142.

a. What is this PCAOB Release?

b. How many issuer audits did the PCAOB review?

c. How many issuer audits with audit deficiencies are included in the inspection report?

d. Which issuer audits included deficiencies related to business combinations?

e. Which issuer audits included deficiencies related to impairment of goodwill and other intangible audits?

f. Which issuer audits included deficiencies related to other long-lived assets?

g. Identify the audit deficiencies related to long-lived assets for Issuers A and D.

h. Discuss how professional skepticism might relate to the deficiencies that you reviewed for Issuers A and B.

AUDITING STANDARDS APPLICATION ACTIVITY

FRAUD

12-47 LO 8   Assume you are helping to plan the audit for a client that is a U.S. nonpublic company (non-issuer). The client is a forestry company and your senior is familiar with the Sino-Forest Corp. case discussed in the *Focus on Fraud* feature "Auditing a Forestry Company Results in Class-Action Lawsuit." Because of her concerns based on this case, your senior has indicated that she would like to use an auditor specialist to help obtain evidence related to this client's timber reserves. Your senior asks you for guidance on what responsibilities the auditor has regarding the qualifications of such a specialist. Furthermore, the senior wonders if the audit report should mention that the audit team included a specialist. As you are not sure of the answers to these questions, you decide to obtain a copy of the auditing standard that would most likely provide relevant guidance. You may want to refer to the *Auditing Standards Exhibit* inside the front cover of this textbook to determine the appropriate standard. What standard would be most appropriate and what guidance does it provide that can help you answer your senior's questions?

AUDITING STANDARDS APPLICATION ACTIVITY

12-48 **LO 8** Assume you are working on the audit of a client that is a U.S. nonpublic company (non-issuer) and you are focusing on long-lived assets. The senior on the audit team has noted that this audit area has a number of estimates including management judgments and decisions such as depreciation methods and useful lives. Your senior warns you to be alert to indicators of possible management bias in these judgments and decisions. As you are not sure what such indicators might be, you consult the relevant auditing standard. You may want to refer to the *Auditing Standards Exhibit* inside the front cover of this textbook to determine the appropriate standard. What standard would be most appropriate; what guidance does it provide?

Academic Research Cases

NOTE: Completing *Academic Research Cases* requires students to reference additional resources and materials.

12-49 **LO 1** Locate and read the article listed below.

Peytcheva, M. and P. R. Gillett. (2011). How partners' views influence auditor judgment. *Auditing: A Journal of Practice & Theory* 30(4): 285–301.

a. What is the purpose of the study?
b. Describe the design/method/approach used to conduct the study.
c. What are the primary findings of the study?

FRAUD

12-50 **LO 9** Locate and read the article listed below.

Lobo, G.J., L. Paugam, D. Zhang, and J. Francois Casta. (2017). The effect of joint auditor pair composition on audit quality: Evidence from impairment tests. *Contemporary Accounting Research* 34(1): 118–153.

SEARCH HINT

It is easy to locate these academic research articles! Use a search engine such as Google Scholar or an electronic research platform such as ABI Inform, and search using the author names and part of the article title.

a. What is the purpose of the study?
b. Describe the design/method/approach used to conduct the study.
c. What are the primary findings of the study?

13 Auditing Debt, Equity, and Long-Term Liabilities Requiring Management Estimates

The Audit Opinion Formulation Process

I. Making Client Acceptance and Continuance Decisions
Chapter 1

II. Performing Risk Assessment
Chapters 2, 3, 7, and 9–13

III. Obtaining Evidence About Internal Control Operating Effectiveness
Chapters 8–13

IV. Obtaining Substantive Evidence About Accounts, Disclosures, and Assertions
Chapters 8–13

V. Completing the Audit and Making Reporting Decisions
Chapters 14 and 15

Quality Auditing and the Need for Quality Auditor Judgments and Ethical Decisions
Chapter 1

Professional Liability
Chapter 4

The Audit Opinion Formulation Process and a Framework for Obtaining Audit Evidence
Chapters 5 and 6

Auditing debt and equity transactions includes a variety of challenges. With respect to debt, these challenges relate to the potential violation of debt covenants, management's desire to omit debt from the balance sheet, and management's incentive to improperly classify debt as long term or short term depending on their financial reporting preferences. Challenges in auditing equity relate to management valuing stock issuances improperly, recording inappropriate transactions directly to retained earnings (rather than through the income statement), and issuing stock in violation of covenants. To manage audit risk, the auditor must therefore employ sufficient professional skepticism when auditing debt and equity.

In addition, a number of long-term liabilities require judgment-based management estimates. Auditors should be alert to management bias in these estimates that managers may use to manipulate earnings. Complex estimates, such as pensions, are difficult to understand and, thus, auditors often rely on specialists when auditing these estimates.

Learning Objectives

LO 1 Identify the significant accounts, disclosures, and relevant assertions related to debt and equity.

LO 2 Identify and assess inherent risks of material misstatement in debt and equity accounts.

LO 3 Identify and assess fraud risks of material misstatement in debt and equity accounts.

LO 4 Identify and assess control risks of material misstatement in debt and equity accounts.

LO 5 Describe how to use planning analytical procedures to identify possible material misstatements in debt and equity accounts, disclosures, and assertions.

LO 6 Determine appropriate responses to identified risks of material misstatement in debt and equity accounts, disclosures, and assertions.

LO 7 Determine appropriate tests of controls and consider the results of tests of controls for debt and equity accounts, disclosures, and assertions.

LO 8 Determine and apply sufficient appropriate substantive audit procedures for testing debt and equity accounts, disclosures, and assertions.

LO 9 Describe audit considerations for long-term liabilities requiring management estimates.

LO 10 Apply the frameworks for professional decision making and ethical decision making for decisions made when conducting an audit.

Improper Accounting for Debt and Equity

This feature provides an example of a company that improperly accounted for one of its debt-related transactions and an example of an individual who fraudulently accounted for stock options. Auditors need to consider potential fraud risks related to debt and equity.

Debt: Swisher Hygiene

Swisher Hygiene, Inc. is a Delaware corporation headquartered in Charlotte, North Carolina. During 2011, Swisher acquired 63 franchises and independent businesses.

In March 2011, Swisher paid off a $39.2 million debt of one of the companies that it acquired. In paying off the debt, Swisher incurred a prepayment penalty of $1.5 million. Swisher accounted for the prepayment penalty as part of the purchase price, resulting in an increase in recorded goodwill for the first quarter of 2011. A senior Swisher officer told the company's outside auditor that the debt could not be assumed and had to be paid off contractually. That information was not accurate. In fact, the debt was legally assumable by Swisher and, thus, Swisher should have expensed the prepayment penalty and not included it as a part of the purchase price (and therefore recording it as an asset, goodwill).

Swisher's improper accounting for the prepayment penalty resulted in a $1.5 million increase in income in the company's original Form 10-Q for the first quarter of 2011.

For more details, see SEC AAER No. 3775 / May 24, 2016.

Equity: Vitesse Semiconductor Corporation

Eugene F. Hovanec served as Vice President of Finance and Chief Financial Officer at Vitesse Semiconductor Corporation from December 1993 through April 2005. In April 2005, after his promotion to Executive Vice President, he relinquished his role as CFO. Vitesse is a major producer of high-performance integrated circuits for use primarily by systems manufacturers in the storage and communications industries.

The SEC's AAER against Hovanec alleged, that from 1995 to 2006, Hovanec participated in a scheme to backdate stock option grant dates for his personal benefit and the benefit of other Vitesse executives and employees. Hovanec also failed to ensure that Vitesse properly recorded compensation expense for backdated stock option grants.

For more details, see SEC AAER No. 3591 / October 23, 2014.

What Do You Think?

For Classroom Discussion

Review the *Why It Matters* feature "Improper Accounting for Debt and Equity."

Do you think it is difficult for auditors to detect these types of misstatements? How might a fraud brainstorming session help auditors in these types of situations?

With respect to the timeliness of the SEC's enforcement process, comment on why you think it might take, e.g., eight years in the case of Vitesse, from the time of the fraud to the SEC's issuance of the AAER.

What You Will Learn

- What are the significant accounts, disclosures, and relevant assertions related to debt and equity? (LO 1)
- What are the inherent risks associated with debt and equity? (LO 2)
- What are fraud risks associated with debt and equity? (LO 3)
- What controls should management have in place to mitigate the risks associated with debt and equity? (LO 4)

- How might auditors use planning analytical procedures to identify any potential concerns related to debt and equity? (LO 5)
- What is sufficient appropriate evidence when auditing the acquisition and payment cycle? (LO 6, 7, 8)
- What are the important audit considerations for long-term liabilities requiring management estimates? (LO 9)

LO 1

Identify the significant accounts, disclosures, and relevant assertions related to debt and equity.

Significant Accounts, Disclosures, and Relevant Assertions

Organizations use two common approaches to meet their long-term financing needs: issuing debt or equity.

Debt

Organizations issue bonds to finance major expansions or to refinance existing debt. Organizations can also obtain debt financing through notes or mortgages. Furthermore, organizations may acquire debt when they engage in merger and acquisition activities. An organization typically has only a few debt transactions during the audit period, but each transaction is usually highly material to the financial statements. Relevant accounts when auditing debt include:

- Bonds payable
- Bond premium/discount
- Interest expense
- Gains or losses on refinancing debt
- Notes payable
- Mortgages payable

The overall objective when auditing debt is to determine whether the client has recorded all obligations and properly classified and disclosed them. The auditor is primarily concerned with understatement and, therefore, focuses on the completeness assertion. Other relevant assertions in auditing bonds or other long-term debt include:

- Proper valuation of premium or discount (includes amortization)
- Valuation of gains or losses on refinancing debt
- Proper presentation and disclosure, including important restrictions contained in the debt obligations or violations of debt restrictions

Activities Related to Debt

Bond Issuance and Amortization Schedules   Organizations typically market bonds through an underwriter, with the proceeds going to the issuer after deducting the underwriter's commission. The authorization to issue a bond is usually limited to the board of directors. A bond premium/discount amortization spreadsheet helps assure that the bond is appropriately valued and disclosed in the financial statements. A **bond indenture** provides important information regarding the bond, including the period before repayment, amount of interest paid, if the bond is convertible (and if so, at what price or what ratio), if the bond is callable, and the amount of money that is to be repaid.

Periodic Payments and Interest Expense   Most organizations have agreements with bond trustees to handle the registration of current bondholders and to make the periodic interest payments. The organization issuing the bond makes interest payments to the trustee, plus a fee for the trustee's service, and the trustee disburses the individual payments to the bondholders.

Debt Covenants   **Debt covenants** are written restrictions designed to protect bondholders against possible financial decline of the issuer or against the subordination of the value of the debt by the issuance of other debt. Common restrictions include:

- Maintaining a minimum level of retained earnings before dividends can be paid
- Maintaining a minimum working-capital ratio
- Specifying a maximum debt-equity ratio
- Articulating contractual provisions that identify procedures for calling and retiring debt at prespecified prices and dates

Equity

Relevant accounts when auditing equity include:

- Stock accounts (common, preferred, and treasury)
- Additional paid-in capital
- Dividend accounts
- Retained earnings

In auditing equity accounts, the auditor primarily focuses on whether the securities are accurately valued (valuation assertion) and are properly classified and appropriately presented and disclosed (presentation and disclosure assertions).

Stock issuances generally do not present valuation problems because most stock is issued for cash. However, when stock is not issued for cash, valuation difficulties can occur in determining: (1) whether the market value of the stock issued or the market value of the asset acquired is a better representation of value, and (2) the proper accounting for an exchange of stock to acquire another business.

Furthermore, stock is also issued in the form of stock options and the exercise of those options. The stock option is an expense that is measured at the fair value of the option—usually measured by the Black-Scholes method. Companies then purchase stock on the open market to fulfill the exercise of those options.

Disclosure includes a proper description of: (1) each class of stock outstanding and the number of shares authorized, issued, and outstanding and special rights associated with each class, (2) stock options outstanding, (3) convertible features, and (4) existence of stock warrants. Any restrictions or appropriations of retained earnings should be disclosed, as well as prior-period adjustments and other comprehensive income adjustments.

Exhibit 13.1 provides Ford Motor Company's balance sheet disclosure related to equity. Note that the balance sheet disclosure includes information related to common stock, the amount of capital in excess of par value, accumulated other comprehensive income/(loss), retained earnings, and treasury stock.

Activities Related to Equity

Common transactions affecting equity include:

- Issuing new stock
- Purchasing treasury stock
- Declaring and paying dividends
- Granting stock options and warrants
- Exercising and accounting for the expiration of stock options and warrants
- Transferring net income to retained earnings
- Recording of prior-period adjustments to retained earnings

Exhibit 13.1
Example of Balance Sheet Disclosure of Equity

FORD MOTOR COMPANY AND SUBSIDIARIES CONSOLIDATED BALANCE SHEET
(in millions)

EQUITY

Capital stock (Note 22)	December 31, 2015	December 31, 2016
Common Stock, par value $.01 per share (3,976 million shares issued of 6 billion authorized)	40	40
Class B Stock, par value $.01 per share (71 million shares issued of 530 million authorized)	1	1
Capital in excess of par value of stock	21,421	21,630
Retained earnings	14,414	15,634
Accumulated other comprehensive income/(loss) (Note 18)	(6,257)	(7,013)
Treasury stock	(977)	(1,122)
Total equity attributable to Ford Motor Company	28,642	29,170
Equity attributable to noncontrolling interests	15	17
Total equity	$28,657	$29,187

An Overview of the Audit Opinion Formulation Process for Debt and Equity

In auditing debt and equity, the auditor will perform risk assessment procedures, tests of controls, and substantive procedures—Phases II, III, and IV of the audit opinion formulation process.

As part of performing risk assessment procedures, the auditor obtains information to assess the risk of material misstatement. This includes information about inherent risks at the financial statement level (e.g., the client's business and operational risks, along with financial reporting risks) and at the account and assertion levels, fraud risks including feedback from the audit team's brainstorming sessions, strengths and weaknesses in internal control, and results from planning analytical procedures.

Once the auditor identifies the risks of material misstatement, the auditor then determines how best to respond to them. For an integrated audit and for a financial statement audit where the auditor wants to rely on controls as part of the basis for the audit opinion, the auditor will perform tests of controls and consider the effect of those tests on the substantive evidence to obtain. In other audits, the auditor will rely only on substantive tests to obtain evidence about the accuracy of the financial statements.

Check Your Basic Knowledge

13-1 An organization typically has many debt transactions during the year, with each individual transaction being immaterial.   (T/F)

13-2 Typically, the most relevant assertion related to debt is completeness.   (T/F)

13-3 Which of the following can organizations use to obtain financing?
   a. Notes.
   b. Mortgages.
   c. Bonds.
   d. All of the above.

13-4 Which of the following accounts would not typically be included in the audit of debt?
   a. Interest income.
   b. Interest expense.
   c. Bonds payable.
   d. Notes payable.

LO 2

Identify and assess inherent risks of material misstatement in debt and equity accounts.

Identifying Inherent Risks

Inherent Risks—Debt

Inherent risks related to debt concern authorization of debt, receipt of funds, recording of debt transactions, and compliance with debt covenants. For authorization, inherent risks include incurring debt that is not properly authorized or reviewed. Similarly, there are risks that new debt, debt extinguishments, or debt payment transactions are not properly authorized.

In terms of recording debt transactions, risks include the potential that management may not properly record interest expense or may not classify and record debt in accordance with generally accepted accounting principles (GAAP).

Regarding debt covenant compliance issues, inherent risks relate to whether management accurately calculates debt covenants and whether compliance with debt covenants is appropriately reviewed and disclosed.

Inherent Risks—Equity

Exhibit 13.2 outlines common inherent risks associated with each management assertion related to equity.

EXHIBIT 13.2
Inherent Risks Associated with Stockholders'
Equity

Stock Sale and Issuance

Assertion	Inherent Risk
Existence	Issuances or sales are not authorized in accordance with organization's bylaws. Proceeds are not received. Stock issuances or sales are recorded in the wrong period.
Valuation	Stock issued in exchange for goods or services is not properly valued.
Presentation and disclosure	Equity activities are not properly disclosed in accordance with GAAP.

Purchase of Treasury Stock

Assertion	Inherent Risk
Completeness	All stock repurchased is not recorded as treasury stock. Treasury stock transactions are recorded in the wrong period.
Valuation	The cost of treasury stock that is subsequently retired is not properly allocated among the appropriate accounts.

Dividend Declaration and Payment

Assertion	Inherent Risk
Existence	Dividends may be recorded and paid before being declared. Dividends may not be properly approved before being declared. Dividends are recorded in the wrong period.

Stock Option sand Warrants

Assertion	Inherent Risk
Existence	Options/warrants are granted without being properly approved. Inadequate records as to options/warrants issued but not exercised.
Rights/obligations	Options exercised or expired remain on the organization's books.
Valuation	Option/warrant grants are not properly valued due to inappropriate assumptions or models. Inappropriate amortization methods are used. Inaccurate period of service is used.

Check Your Basic Knowledge

13-5 Recording the purchase of treasury stock is straightforward and therefore does <u>not</u> pose any inherent risk of material misstatement.   (T/F)

13-6 An inherent risk associated with debt is that management might try to avoid complete and accurate disclosure of debt covenants and potential violations.   (T/F)

13-7 Which of the following is an inherent risk typically related to debt?
a. Debt is not properly authorized.
b. Interest expense is not properly accrued.
c. Debt covenants are not properly disclosed.
d. Debt is not appropriately classified as short or long term.
e. All of the above are inherent risks related to debt.

13-8 Which of the following is <u>not</u> an inherent risk typically associated with dividends?
a. Dividends are recorded before being declared.
b. Dividends are not properly amortized.
c. Dividends have not been approved before being declared.
d. Dividends are recorded in the wrong period.

LO 3
Identify and assess fraud risks of material misstatement in debt and equity accounts.

Identifying Fraud Risks

Auditing standards require the auditor to identify and assess the risks of material misstatement due to fraud at the financial statement level and at the assertion level. As part of brainstorming activities, the auditor should identify possible frauds that could occur.

Some potential frauds that management may perpetrate related to debt include:

- Not appropriately seeking authorization of debt obligations.
- Misclassifying long-term or short-term debt.
- Not properly recording prepayment penalties.

Some potential frauds that management may perpetrate related to equity include:

- Not appropriately seeking authorization of stock sales or issuances.
- Violating debt covenants through stock sales or issuances.
- Not recording stock sales or issuances properly.
- Enabling the exercise of stock options that are not properly authorized or that are not in accordance with the terms of options granted.

Fraud Risks Related to Debt and Equity: Insights from SEC Accounting and Auditing Enforcement Releases

Focus on Fraud

This feature provides examples of frauds related to debt and equity.

Debt: Federico Quinto Jr., CPA

The client involved in this case, Soyo Group, acted fraudulently by not accurately disclosing violations of its debt covenants.

In August 2012, the SEC issued an Accounting and Auditing Enforcement Release in the matter of Federico Quinto Jr., CPA. Quinto was an audit engagement partner for Soyo Group, Inc., in 2007. During 2007 and the first three quarters of 2008, Soyo booked over $47 million in fictitious revenues. At the same time, Soyo was financing its business with debt from United Commercial Bank (UCB). As of December 31, 2007, Soyo's debt with UCB was approximately $27.8 million, which represented 63% of Soyo's total liabilities. Because of Soyo's struggling business, the company often found itself in violation of its debt covenants with UCB.

Quinto's audit team conducted an analysis that identified that Soyo was not in compliance with three of its six debt covenants with UCB as of December 31, 2007. Because of the debt covenant violations, UCB could take action that would force Soyo into bankruptcy, as Soyo needed the financing to fund its business operations. The audit team did not follow up on the identified debt covenant violations and did not obtain any evidence indicating whether a waiver had been granted by UCB. The audit workpapers did not provide any evidence that the audit team considered whether these violations could impact the going concern status of Soyo. Further, the audit report for 2007 included an unqualified opinion, although Soyo did not make the required disclosures regarding noncompliance with its debt covenants.

Source: Securities and Exchange Commission, Accounting and Auditing Enforcement Release No. 3403, August 31, 2012, available at http://www.sec.gov/litigation/admin/2012/34-67767.pdf

Equity: Delphi Corporation

In this case, members of Delphi's management and staff acted fraudulently by charging expenses directly to retained earnings rather than to the appropriate expense accounts.

In 2006, the SEC outlined its case of allegations involving Delphi Corporation and certain of its senior officers, accounting staff, and treasury staff. The allegations involve a pattern of violations of federal securities laws from 2000 through 2004. One of the alleged violations related to Delphi improperly accounting for an increase in warranty reserves related to warranty claims made by its former parent company.

Delphi recorded the reserve increase as a direct adjustment to retained earnings rather than as an expense. There was no basis for Delphi to record the reserve adjustment as an adjustment to retained earnings. The SEC further alleged that Delphi disclosed the adjustment in an intentionally and materially misleading way. Specifically, the disclosure suggested, falsely, that the adjustment primarily related to certain pension and other postemployment benefit (OPEB) matters and Delphi failed to disclose highly material information concerning the reserve increase and the former parent company's warranty claim.

The misclassification of the reserve increase as a direct adjustment to retained earnings, rather than as an expense item, resulted in Delphi materially overstating its net income for 2000 by $69 million. Given that either way, Delphi management was recording this transaction, why would it care about charging it to retained earnings as compared to net income? Some reasons include meeting or beating analysts forecasted earnings expectations, and attempting to focus users' attention on net income, a very common benchmark in terms of users' assessments of profitability. In this case, appropriate classification among the financial statement accounts was very important, and management was misleading in its allocation choices.

Source: SEC Accounting and Auditing Enforcement Release No. 2504, October 30, 2006. A related SEC complaint in this matter is available at http://www.sec.gov/litigation/complaints/2006/comp19891.pdf

Prompt for Critical Thinking #1   It's Your Turn!

Provide examples of other potential frauds related to debt and equity. *Hint: Use a search engine with the following types of phrases to find actual examples of frauds relating to debt and/or equity: "how to detect financial reporting fraud relating to debt".*

Debt:

_____

_____

Equity:

_____

_____

_____

Check Your Basic Knowledge

13-9   A potential fraud risk associated with debt is the intentional misclassification of short-term debt as long-term debt.   (T/F)

13-10   Charging expenses directly to retained earnings rather than to the appropriate expense account is a potential fraud risk associated with equity.   (T/F)

13-11   Which of the following most accurately describes the nature of fraud related to debt described in the case of Federico Quinto Jr., CPA, presented in the *Focus on Fraud* feature?

    a.   Interest expense was recorded in the wrong period.

    b.   Entire loan payments were charged to principal.

    c.   Debt covenants and potential violations were not appropriately presented and disclosed.

    d.   Long-term debt was misclassified as short-term debt.

13-12   Which of the following most accurately describes the nature of fraud related to equity described in the case of Delphi Corporation presented in the *Focus on Fraud* feature?

    a.   Stock options were backdated.

    b.   Stock sales were not authorized.

    c.   Proceeds from stock sales were misappropriated.

    d.   Expenses were charged directly to retained earnings, rather than to the appropriate expense accounts.

LO 4

Identify and assess control risks of material misstatement in debt and equity accounts.

Identifying Control Risks

Once the auditor has obtaining an understanding of the inherent and fraud risks of material misstatement associated with debt and equity, the auditor needs to understand the controls that the client has designed and implemented to address those risks. Remember, the auditor is required to gain an overall understanding of internal controls for both integrated audits and financial statement only audits. The auditor typically obtains this understanding by means of a walkthrough of the process, inquiry, observation, and review of the client's documentation. The auditor considers both entity-wide controls and transaction controls at the account and assertion levels. This understanding provides the auditor with a basis for making an initial control risk assessment.

At the entity-wide level, the auditor considers the control environment, including such principles as a commitment to financial accounting competencies and the independence of the board of directors. The auditor also considers the remaining components of internal control that are typically entity wide—risk assessment, information and communication, and monitoring controls. Although the auditor needs to understand all the components of internal control, the auditor typically finds it useful to focus on significant control activities. As part of this understanding, the auditor focuses on the relevant assertions for each account and identifies the controls that relate to risks for these assertions. In an integrated audit or in a financial statement only audit where the auditor relies on controls, the auditor uses this understanding to identify important controls that need to be tested.

Important controls for both debt and equity would include policies, procedures, and reviews related to providing assurance that all appropriate disclosures have been made.

Controls—Debt

Given the typical inherent and fraud risks for debt, the auditor would expect an organization to have implemented the following controls:

* The board of directors approves all new debt.
* Debt and interest accounts are updated and reconciled to the general ledger on a monthly basis.
* Top management and the board of directors review draft financial statements prior to issuance for proper disclosure of debt obligations.
* A debt amortization schedule is prepared for each new debt obligation, updated as appropriate, and is reviewed by appropriate personnel.

Controls—Equity

Given the typical inherent and fraud risks for equity, the auditor would expect an organization to have implemented the following controls:

* The board of directors approves all stock transactions (including options and warrants).
* The CEO and CFO authorize all stock transactions (including options and warrants) approved by the board of directors.
* Stockholders' equity accounts are updated and reconciled to the general ledger on a timely basis.
* Top management and the board of directors review draft financial statements prior to issuance for proper disclosure of equity accounts.
* An outside party, such as an attorney, maintains details of shares issued, repurchased, and cancelled.
* The organization's accountant researches and analyzes proper accounting for stock option grants, and the organization's legal counsel and CFO review and approve the analysis.

Documenting Controls

Auditors need to document their understanding of internal controls for both integrated audits and financial statement only audits. Similar to other audit areas, the auditor can provide this documentation in various formats, including a control matrix, a control risk assessment questionnaire, and/or a memo.

Check Your Basic Knowledge

13-13 If the auditor is not testing controls related to equity, he or she does not need to have an understanding of controls over equity.   (T/F)

13-14 A reconciliation of debt and interest accounts to the general ledger is a control designed to mitigate the risks of material misstatement associated with debt.   (T/F)

13-15 Which of the following would an auditor typically <u>not</u> perform as part of gaining an understanding of the client's controls related to debt?
  a. Review the client's documentation of controls.
  b. Recalculate interest expense.
  c. Inquire of management about the process for reviewing compliance with debt covenants.
  d. Review policies related to approval required for new debt.

13-16 Which of the following is a control the auditor would expect a client to have implemented related to equity?
  a. A policy requiring approval by the board of directors for all stock transactions.
  b. Reconciliation of equity accounts to the general ledger.
  c. CFO and CEO authorization of all stock transactions approved by the board of directors.
  d. The auditor would typically expect all of the above controls to be in place.

LO 5

Describe how to use planning analytical procedures to identify possible material misstatements in debt and equity accounts, disclosures, and assertions.

Performing Planning Analytical Procedures

Planning analytical procedures help auditors identify areas of potential material misstatements. *Chapter 6* outlines the steps that the auditor will take in performing planning analytical procedures.

The following are examples of typical analytical procedures related to debt:

- Perform a trend analysis of the balances in notes payable and accrued interest with prior periods, considering known client activities related to debt.
- Estimate overall interest expense based on average interest rates and average debt outstanding.
- Calculate debt-to-equity ratios and perform a trend analysis with prior periods, considering known client activities related to debt and equity.
- Calculate the times interest earned ratio and perform a trend analysis with prior periods.

The primary planning analytical procedure for equity is a comparison of current-year account balances with prior-year account balances. The auditor should have an expectation as to the nature and magnitude of any account balance changes.

If planning analytical procedures do not identify any unexpected relationships, the auditor would conclude that a heightened risk of material misstatement

13-17 The primary planning analytical procedure for equity is a comparison of current-year account balances with prior-year account balances, after considering the auditor's expectations based on knowledge of client activities.   (T/F)

13-18 An auditor would typically <u>not</u> use trend analyses as a planning analytical procedure when auditing debt.   (T/F)

13-19 Which of the following statements is <u>true</u> regarding planning analytical procedures for debt and equity?
   a. Because there are typically only a few stockholders' equity transactions, the auditor is not required to perform planning analytical procedures for stockholders' equity accounts.
   b. The auditor would not typically perform trend analysis for debt.

   c. The auditor could consider the long-term debt-to-equity ratio as part of the planning analytical procedures.
   d. All of the above statements are true.

13-20 Which of the following are typical planning analytical procedures related to debt?
   a. Estimate interest expense based on average interest rates and average debt outstanding.
   b. Calculate the total debt-to-equity ratio and perform a trend analysis with prior periods.
   c. Calculate the long-term debt-to-equity ratio and perform a trend analysis with prior periods.
   d. Calculate the times interest earned ratio and perform a trend analysis with prior periods.
   e. The auditor could perform all of the above planning analytical procedures related to debt.

does not exist in these accounts. If unusual or unexpected relationships exist, the auditor would adjust the planned audit procedures (tests of controls, substantive procedures) to address the potential material misstatements.

LO 6

Determine appropriate responses to identified risks of material misstatement in debt and equity accounts, disclosures, and assertions.

Responding to Identified Risks of Material Misstatement

Once the auditor has developed an understanding of the risks of material misstatement, the auditor is in a position to determine the appropriate audit procedures to perform. Audit procedures should be proportional to the assessed risks, with areas of higher risk requiring more evidence and/or evidence that is more appropriate. Responding to identified risks typically involves developing an audit approach that contains substantive procedures (e.g., tests of details and, when appropriate, substantive analytical procedures) and tests of controls, when applicable. The sufficiency and appropriateness of selected procedures will vary to achieve the desired level of assurance for each relevant assertion.

Typically, the auditor tests debt, including interest transactions, using only substantive procedures. This approach is often appropriate because the number of transactions is relatively small and the dollar amounts involved are usually quite material.

Similarly, when auditing equity, the auditor commonly uses a substantive approach. This approach is often appropriate because the number of equity transactions with outside parties is usually small. In fact, a substantive approach using only tests of details is most commonly used to audit equity accounts.

For both debt and equity, the boxes of evidence would typically be filled only with evidence obtained through substantive procedures.

Check Your Basic Knowledge

13-21 When responding to identified risks of material misstatement associated with equity, the auditor often decides to rely heavily on tests of controls. (T/F)

13-22 When testing debt, the auditor typically uses a substantive audit approach. (T/F)

13-23 How does an auditor typically respond to identified risks of material misstatement associated with debt?

    a. The auditor will typically plan to perform a controls reliance approach to the audit.

    b. The auditor will typically plan an approach that uses only substantive procedures.

    c. The auditor does not need to respond to identified fraud risks since the risk of fraud related to debt is typically minimal.

    d. Because of the low level of risk of material misstatement, the auditor would only rely on planning analytical procedures.

13-24 How does an auditor typically respond to identified risks of material misstatement associated with equity?

    a. The auditor will typically plan to perform a controls reliance approach to the audit.

    b. The auditor will typically plan an approach that uses only substantive procedures.

    c. The auditor does not need to respond to identified fraud risks since the risk of fraud related to stockholders' equity accounts is typically minimal.

    d. Because of the low level of risk of material misstatement, the auditor would only rely on preliminary analytical procedures.

LO 7

Determine appropriate tests of controls and consider the results of tests of controls for debt and equity accounts, disclosures, and assertions.

Obtaining Evidence about Internal Control Operating Effectiveness for Debt and Equity

For integrated audits, the auditor will test the operating effectiveness of important controls throughout the year, with a heightened focus on controls as of the client's year-end. If the auditor wants to rely on controls for the financial statement audit, the auditor will test the operating effectiveness of those controls throughout the year.

Selecting Controls to Test and Performing Tests of Controls

The auditor selects controls that are important to the auditor's conclusion about whether the client's controls adequately address the assessed risk of material misstatement for the debt and equity accounts. The auditor selects both entity-wide and transaction controls for testing. Typical tests of transaction controls include inquiry of personnel performing the control, observation of the control being performed, inspection of documentation confirming that the control has been performed, and reperformance of the control by the auditor testing the control.

If control testing results in identified control deficiencies, the auditor assesses those deficiencies to determine their severity (are they significant deficiencies or material weaknesses?) and their impact on the audit.

However, for financial statement audit purposes, when auditing debt and equity, the auditor most likely performs a substantive audit and therefore does not perform tests of controls for purposes of the audit.

13-25 When auditing debt, the auditor will test controls for the audit opinion on internal controls, but choose <u>not</u> to test controls for the financial statement audit. (T/F)

13-26 When auditing equity, the auditor will test controls for the audit opinion on internal controls, but choose <u>not</u> to test controls for the financial statement audit. (T/F)

13-27 Which of the following statements best describes the auditor's typical approach to testing controls related to debt?

  a. The auditor would test controls for integrated audit purposes, but not for financial statement audit purposes.

  b. The auditor would test controls for financial statement audit purposes, but not for integrated audit purposes.

  c. The auditor would test controls for both the integrated audit and financial statement audit.

  d. The auditor would not test controls for either the integrated audit or financial statement audit.

13-28 Which of the following statements best describes the auditor's typical approach to testing controls related to stockholders' equity accounts?

  a. The auditor would test controls for integrated audit purposes, but not for financial statement audit purposes.

  b. The auditor would test controls for financial statement audit purposes, but not for integrated audit purposes.

  c. The auditor would test controls for both the integrated audit and financial statement audit.

  d. The auditor would not test controls for either the integrated audit or financial statement audit.

LO 8

Determine and apply sufficient appropriate substantive audit procedures for testing debt and equity accounts, disclosures, and assertions.

Obtaining Substantive Evidence About Accounts, Disclosures, and Assertions for Debt and Equity

The audits of debt and equity typically involve only substantive procedures. The auditor can test debt accounts with both substantive analytical procedures and tests of details. In contrast, auditors typically only use tests of details to audit equity accounts. Furthermore, the transactions in the equity accounts are typically tested 100% because they are usually so few, and yet they are highly material.

Substantive Analytical Procedures—Debt

When auditing debt, the primary substantive analytical procedure involves the auditor developing an independent expectation of interest expense. The auditor bases this expectation on average debt outstanding and average interest rates. When performing this analysis as a substantive procedure, the auditor will use disaggregated data—likely disaggregated by type of debt. If the auditor's expectation is similar to what the client has recorded, additional substantive testing of interest expense and accrued interest will not be necessary. *Exhibit 13.3*—Panel A notes that in this situation the box of evidence that the auditor will obtain includes evidence only from substantive analytical procedures.

If there is a significant difference between the auditor's expectation and the amount recorded by the client, the auditor needs to perform additional substantive tests of details to determine the reason for the difference. For example, if the client records interest expense at an amount that is significantly lower than the auditor's expectation, it may mean that the client has not properly recorded interest. *Exhibit 13.3*—Panel B notes that in this situation, the box of evidence that the auditor obtains will likely include evidence from substantive analytical procedures

EXHIBIT 13.3

Alternative Approaches for Auditing Debt

Panel A: Substantive Analytical Procedures Approach to Obtaining Audit Evidence
for Completeness of Interest Expense

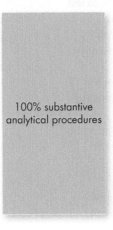

100% substantive
analytical procedures

Panel B: Substantive Analytical Procedures and Tests of Details Approach to Obtaining
Audit Evidence for Completeness of Interest Expense

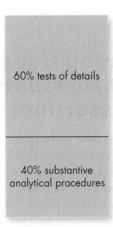

60% tests of details

40% substantive
analytical procedures

Why It Matters   Tests of Controls Might Not Be Performed

This feature describes instances in which the auditor may not test a client's controls prior to performing substantive analytical procedures.

When performing substantive analytical procedures, the auditor typically performs these procedures after testing the relevant controls. However, when performing substantive analytical procedures related to interest expense, the auditor will likely not test controls.

The primary reason is that the information that the auditor uses to perform the analytical procedure (debt amounts and interest rates) is typically confirmed with an independent outside party. Therefore, the effectiveness of the client's controls is not as important as in other areas where the information being used for the substantive analytical procedures is not subject to external independent confirmation.

and tests of details. Note that the relative percentages are judgmental in nature; the examples that we provide are simply intended to give you a sense of how an auditor might select an appropriate mix of procedures.

Substantive Tests of Details—Debt

Typical substantive procedures include:

- Reading new loan agreements (may be performed during planning/risk assessment procedures)
- Determining what changes, if any, have been made to prior loan agreements (may be performed during planning/risk assessment procedures)
- Confirming with relevant outside parties any significant factors and the transactions that have occurred

As a starting point for these procedures, the auditor will have the client provide a schedule of debt obligations and interest. The client should also have a bond premium/discount amortization schedule that the auditor can review in assessing whether bonds are appropriately valued and disclosed in the financial statements.

For additions to debt, the auditor traces the proceeds into the cash receipts records and the bank statement. The auditor might also examine the debt instrument and obtain assurance regarding board approval of the debt through review of board meeting minutes.

For debt reductions, the auditor examines payments through the cash disbursements records, possibly including cancelled checks. For notes or mortgages that have been paid in full, the auditor should examine the cancelled notes.

Exhibit 13.4 provides typical substantive procedures for relevant assertions related to debt.

EXHIBIT 13.4

Relevant Management Assertions and Substantive Procedures for Debt

Management Assertion	Substantive Procedure
Completeness—Recorded debt obligations include all debt obligations.	1. Perform substantive analytical procedures.
	2. Confirm debt obligations.
	3. Vouch additions and deletions to debt obligations.
Completeness—All interest expense is recorded.	1. Perform substantive analytical procedures to analyze interest expense and recalculate accrued interest.
Presentation/disclosure—Debt obligations are properly classified in the balance sheet between current and noncurrent liabilities, and adequate disclosures are made in accordance with GAAP requirements.	1. Review debt agreements for the restrictive covenants and consider their effect on disclosures in the financial statements.
	2. Inquire of management.
	3. Examine balance sheet for proper disclosure of current and noncurrent portions, related parties, and restrictions resulting from debt.
	4. Read all disclosures for appropriateness, consistency, and clarity. Important considerations include:
	• Should the outstanding debt be classified as current or noncurrent?
	• Is there appropriate disclosure for instances when a violation of debt covenants has been waived?

Why It Matters   Understanding Debt Covenants

This feature describes the importance of the auditor obtaining an understanding of the procedures management uses to determine whether the company is in compliance with its debt covenants.

The auditor should independently determine if a client is in compliance with its debt covenants. Consider a covenant that requires the client to maintain a current ratio that does not fall below a specified level. If the auditor determines that the client's current ratio is below that level, the auditor should assess the effects of the violation.

If the creditor waives the debt covenant (that is, there is not a violation due to the waiver), the client must disclose the amount of the obligation and the period of the waiver. The auditor will want to assess the accuracy of the client's disclosure regarding the waiver.

If the creditor does not waive the violation and the loan is in **default** (i.e., in violation of the debt covenant requirements resulting in a failure to fulfill the obligation to repay the loan), the creditor may declare the outstanding balance immediately due and payable. In that case, the auditor generally would assume that the client would need to reclassify the debt as short-term debt. In addition, the auditor must consider what financial statement disclosures will be required and how the events of default will affect the audit opinion. For example, could the default suggest going-concern issues that the auditor would need to identify in the audit opinion?

Substantive Tests of Details—Equity

The auditor begins testing equity accounts by reviewing the client's articles of incorporation. This document provides relevant information with respect to each class of stock. The auditor then agrees that information to the disclosures included in the client's financial statements. The auditor prepares, or asks the client to prepare, an analysis of all **capital stock** transactions during the audit period, which includes the amount of **contributed capital**. This analysis should include documentation of the client's record keeping of stock transactions. The client or **transfer agent** may maintain this documentation. Review of this documentation provides the auditor with evidence related to the existence and completeness of capital.

To obtain evidence related to the valuation of stock, the auditor reviews the minutes of the board of directors' meetings and examines the stock records books (or confirms with the transfer agent) to determine issuance and repurchase of stock. The auditor would typically obtain evidence for all stock transactions.

If the organization sells stock, the auditor traces the proceeds to the cash receipts journal and reviews documentation indicating that the client recorded the proper amount in the stock and paid-in capital accounts. The auditor may also have clients who issued capital stock in a nonmonetary transaction. For those clients, the auditor needs to determine that the client has properly recorded the issuance in accordance with GAAP.

For clients with **treasury stock,** the auditor examines documentation supporting changes in the number of shares since the prior year. This documentation might include confirmation from the stock transfer agent and tracing the transaction through the cash journal.

Dividends   The auditor examines the minutes of the board of directors' meetings for authorization of the dividend per share amount and the dividend record date. For those clients who maintain their own records and pay the dividends, the auditor recalculates the amount of the dividends and agrees that amount to the cash disbursements journal. If a client uses a transfer agent, the auditor traces the payment to a cash disbursement made by the client to the agent. The auditor may also confirm the amount with the agent.

Stock Buybacks Can Be Material for Many Companies

Why It Matters

This feature highlights the increase in companies buying back their stock over the last decade.

Since 2008, U.S. companies have used nearly $4 trillion of their cash in buying back their stock. For example, in the first three months of 2017, Apple spent $7.2 billion on stock buybacks. In 2017, Citigroup announced a whopping $15.6 billion stock buyback.

In the three-year period ending in 2012, 449 companies in the S&P 500 index used 54% of their earnings, or $2.4 trillion, buying back their own stock. In 2016, 66% of corporate earnings went to buybacks.

Why do companies buy back their own stock? One important reason is that management believes that the stock is undervalued, so it may view the purchase as a "bargain." Another reason is that by purchasing the shares, the denominator in the earnings per share (EPS) calculation declines, thereby yielding a higher EPS.

The auditor will also obtain evidence as to whether the payment was made to the stockholders who owned the stock as of the dividend record date. The auditor can trace the payee's name on the cancelled check to the dividend records to make sure the payee was, indeed, supposed to have received the dividend.

Retained Earnings   The auditor typically examines all transactions recorded in the retained earnings account during the audit period. The common entries include net income or loss. The auditor tests these amounts through substantive audit procedures related to revenues and expenses. The other common entry includes dividends. If there are additional entries, the auditor examines documentation supporting the entries. For example, if there is a correction of an error from a prior period, the auditor determines that the correction is made in accordance with relevant accounting standards.

Disclosure of Dividend Payment Restrictions

Why It Matters

This feature highlights important considerations for the auditor in determining whether the client has appropriately disclosed relevant dividend payment restrictions in its financial statements.

The SEC has disclosure requirements related to restrictions imposed on a company's ability to pay dividends. Typically, these restrictions arise when loan agreements prohibit the company from paying cash dividends without the consent of a third party, such as a lender. A public company must disclose the nature of any restrictions on the ability of the company or any of its subsidiaries to pay dividends and the amounts subject to such restrictions. The auditor will review these disclosures for accuracy.

As an example of one such disclosure, consider Tenaris' description of its dividend restriction policy:

> … the Company's ability to pay dividends to shareholders is subject to legal and other requirements and restrictions in effect at the holding company level. For example, the Company may only pay dividends out of net profits, distributable retained earnings and distributable reserves and premiums.

For further details on this disclosure and Tenaris in general, see http://www.wikinvest.com/stock/Tenaris_S.A

Performing Substantive Fraud-Related Procedures for Debt and Equity

If the auditor identifies a fraud risk of material misstatement related to debt or equity, the auditor needs to determine the appropriate responses, potentially including changing the nature, timing, and extent of planned audit procedures.

Fraud-Related Substantive Procedures for Debt

In audits with a heightened risk of fraud related to debt, the auditor should consider performing the following procedures or, if the procedures are already being performed, altering the timing and extent of the procedures:

- Search public records to identify debt obligations
- Vouch and trace loan proceeds and debt payments
- Send confirmations to lenders and creditors, including confirmation of compliance with any debt covenants
- Require original supporting documents rather than copies
- Agree, i.e., to double check by comparing, the detail of debt terms to appropriate authorizations that management should have documented in the minutes of board of director meetings

Fraud-Related Substantive Procedures for Equity

In audits with a heightened risk of fraud related to equity, the auditor should consider performing the following procedures or, if the procedures are already being performed as a routine part of the audit plan, altering the timing and extent of the procedures so that they contain an element of unpredictability:

- Confirm terms of equity arrangements and shares held directly with shareholders
- Confirm with shareholders whether there are any side agreements
- Employ an appropriate level of professional skepticism and carefully analyze transactions to determine whether the terms and substance of the transactions indicate that the proceeds should be recorded as debt or as equity
- Confirm with the transfer agent information on issued stock
- Account for and vouch all proceeds from stock issues

Documenting Substantive Procedures

The auditor should document important items related to substantive procedures for debt and equity. For debt, the auditor's documentation should include:

- Copies of the debt agreements
- Identification of the specific items tested
- Confirmations or documentation of alternative procedures performed

For equity, the auditor's documentation should include:

- A summary of changes in equity accounts
- Verification of authorization with respect to any changes in capitalization or declaration of dividends

Prompt for Critical Thinking #2   It's Your Turn!

Provide examples of other audit documentation related to debt and equity.

Debt:

- _____
- _____

Equity:

- _____
- _____

13-29 Auditors can use confirmations as a substantive procedure to obtain evidence on the completeness of debt. (T/F)

13-30 If there is a heightened risk of fraud related to the completeness of debt, the auditor may choose to search public records to identify debt obligations. (T/F)

13-31 Which of the following substantive procedures should be included in the audit program for long-term debt?
   a. Verification of the existence of the bondholders.
   b. Review of debt loan agreements.
   c. Inspection of the accounts payable master file.

   d. Review of supporting documentation for credit entries to the bond interest income account.

13-32 When a client does <u>not</u> maintain its own stock records, the auditor should obtain written confirmation from the stock transfer agent concerning which of the following?
   a. Restrictions on the payment of dividends.
   b. The number of shares issued and outstanding.
   c. Guarantees of preferred stock liquidation value.
   d. The number of shares subject to agreements to repurchase.

LO 9

Describe audit considerations for long-term liabilities requiring management estimates.

Long-Term Liabilities Requiring Management Estimates

Much of the accounting for long-term liabilities is straightforward. For example, bonds are disclosed at unamortized issue price and are not adjusted to market unless the organization is calling the bonds or is in the process of converting the bonds to equity. However, a number of long-term liabilities require multi-faceted subjective judgments by the client and the auditor. Long-term liability accounts with a high risk of material misstatement include accounts such as warranty reserves, pension obligations, and **other postemployment benefits (OPEB)**.

Warranty Reserves

The warranty reserve or liability represents the expected future cost related to the sales of an organization's product. The cost of the future warranty claims, including the expense and liability, is estimated and recorded at the time the product is sold. For example, every time Ford sells a new vehicle, it estimates the costs it expects to incur in meeting its warranty promised at the time of sale. Costs incurred to satisfy the warranty claims are charged against the liability. The client should monitor warranty claims to determine whether an unanticipated change exists in the number or dollar amounts associated with the claims. If the amounts are significantly different than expected, the client should adjust the warranty liability.

For Classroom Discussion

What Do You Think?

In January 2015, Beazer Homes announced an unexpected warranty charge of $13.6 million stemming from stucco installation issues in some of its Florida homes that resulted in water damage.

How did Beazer likely arrive at that estimate? What is the auditor's responsibility related to this type of estimate? Do you think that estimates like this could result in differences of opinion between the audit firm and the audit client? How would the auditor handle these differences?

Audit Considerations for Warranty Reserves

The auditor's objective is to assess whether management's estimate for warranty reserves is reasonable. The warranty reserves should incorporate the prior warranty experience of the organization, and should consider current-year changes in:

- The product, including manufacturing that either enhances or decreases the quality of the product
- The nature of the warranty
- Sales volume, for example, if more sales were made during the last quarter this year than in previous years
- The average cost of repairing products under warranty

The auditor can audit the warranty account by first testing the internal controls. For the control testing, the auditor should inquire about and test the effectiveness of the information system used to track warranty items. A proper control allows a company to take effective action to prevent a potential problem with its products.

Next, the auditor can perform substantive analytical procedures that involve developing an independent warrant estimate based on relevant factors. For example, the auditor might conduct a trend analysis of the number of claims and analyze the defects causing the claims. The auditor might also consider the reasonableness of dollar amounts to fix each claim and similar variables to estimate the warranty liability.

Focus on Fraud   Warranty Accrual Accounting

This feature highlights a company that knowingly understated its warranty liability. While auditors inquire of management about such issues, company management in this case simply failed to inform the external auditors about its warranty cost issues. It is not clear why the auditors did not detect the warranty errors during their audits.

Logitech International S.A. (LOGI) is incorporated in Switzerland and has substantial operations in the United States. LOGI is primarily involved in manufacturing and selling peripherals for computers and electronic devices.

LOGI offered warranties on its products sold throughout the world. Depending upon the particular country and type of product, the warranties ranged from one to five years. In FY09, after its independent auditor raised the need to accrue for its warranty liability, LOGI began recording a liability.

In the latter part of FY09, LOGI accountants developed a warranty accrual model based on the assumption that, if a product failed, it would fail quickly and be returned within one quarter. The Company did not have a basis for this assumption, nor did it have sufficient data to evaluate such an assumption. The warranty model also did not consider when the warranty liability began (i.e., when products were purchased by end users) or when the liability ended (i.e., one, two, or five years after purchase of a product by the end user).

An internal employee discovered that if LOGI were to change its warranty terms (e.g., increase the length of the warranty from one year to three years), the model's required accrual would not change. In other words, the model calculated the same warranty accrual regardless of whether products carried a three-month warranty or a 10-year warranty. The company's warranty accrual model did not comply with GAAP.

From FY08 through FY11, the deficiencies of LOGI's model—and the need for a more robust method—were known within LOGI's finance and accounting groups. During FY10, LOGI's then-controller noted that the company's warranty model was "not good" because it was not based on the total number of products under warranty in the hands of consumers. However, LOGI continued to use the model to record the warranty liability.

In Q3 12, a LOGI accountant developed a new, more robust model, which indicated that LOGI was under-reserved by several million dollars. By February 2013, LOGI employees estimated that an additional $4.2 million in warranty liability existed. There were two options for transitioning to the new model: a one-time switch in methodology or a gradual change to existing approach. The first option would result in an immediate charge to LOGI's financial results. The second option would change the current model gradually to increase reserves before switching the model. LOGI chose to implement the second option, even though this option was not GAAP-compliant.

On May 30, 2013, LOGI filed its Form 10-K for FY13, which contained material misstatements and omissions about the company's product warranty accruals. On August 7, 2013, LOGI filed an amended Form 10-K for FY13, disclosing and correcting the warranty accrual (and other errors), and revising its financial statements for FY09 through FY13.

For additional details, see SEC AAER No. 3765 / April 19, 2016.

For Classroom Discussion

What Do You Think?

Consider the *Focus on Fraud* feature "Warranty Accrual Accounting." The AAER notes that LOGI shared its warranty accrual model with its independent auditors.

What procedures should the audit firm have performed related to warranties? How could the auditors have used LOGI's model as part of their audit procedures? Why do you think that the auditors did not identify the warranty errors during their audit?

Pension Obligations and Other Postemployment Benefits

Pension obligations are based on a combination of many items that are difficult to estimate, including:

- Projected lifetime of former employees who will receive a pension
- Nature of the pension plan, for example, a defined benefit or a defined contribution plan
- Future earnings of employees prior to retiring for defined benefit plans
- Earnings rate on invested pension assets, including an assessment of the safety of the invested assets
- Long- term interest rates to discount future costs back to present value
- Changes in pension plans
- Changes in health insurance rates or plans
- Agreements with insurance companies about life and/or disability insurance premiums
- Agreements with law firms about potential services that the organization will reimburse for its retirees

The client usually engages an actuarial firm to help management make these specialized estimates. These specialists work for management, not for the auditor.

Pension Costs

Why It Matters

This feature provides a disclosure from Ford's 2016 Annual Report (Note 13) and gives you a sense of the importance and materiality of the amounts related to pension costs.

Pension Plan Contributions

Our policy for funded pension plans is to contribute annually, at a minimum, amounts required by applicable laws and regulations. We may make contributions beyond those legally required.

In 2016, we contributed $1.2 billion to our worldwide funded pension plans (most of which were mandatory contributions) and made about $300 million of benefit payments to participants in unfunded plans. During 2017, we expect to contribute about $1 billion from cash and cash equivalents to our worldwide funded pension plans (most of which are mandatory) and to make about $300 million of benefit

payments to participants in unfunded plans, for a total of about $1.3 billion.

These enormous costs have taken a toll on U.S. corporations' ability to compete globally, because the pension payments cause companies to fund those pensions rather than investing in profitable business ventures that relate directly to the company's forward-looking business model. As a result, the vast majority of organizations, including companies, governmental units, and non profit entities now provide their employees with **defined contribution pension plans**, i.e., whereby the uncertainty of retirement savings is placed on the employee rather than the employer, as opposed to the historically popular **defined benefit pension plans**, whereby the uncertainty of paying for former employees' retirement is placed on the organizations.

https://corporate.ford.com/microsites/sustainability-report-2016-17/doc/sr16-annual-report-2016.pdf.

Many companies also furnish medical insurance coverage as part of their postemployment benefits. The cost of future medical services is difficult to estimate, and includes estimates of changes in medical expenses, changes in coverage, changes in average life expectancies, and the nature of illnesses to be considered. The client needs an information system to gather and analyze such information in order to make an informed estimate.

Audit Considerations for Pension Obligations and Other Postemployment Benefits

The auditor's objective is to assess whether management's estimates are reasonable. The auditor will determine whether the actuarial firm hired by management is independent, capable, and objective so that the actuarial firm's work provides sufficient appropriate information to assist management in developing the liability estimates. The auditor also evaluates the appropriateness of the actuarial firm's work as audit evidence. The auditor may hire actuarial specialists to assist the audit team in auditing pension obligations. Such individuals work for the auditor, not for management.

Why It Matters

The Importance of Professional Skepticism When Auditing Pension Obligations

This feature reminds the auditor of the importance of exercising professional skepticism in areas requiring management estimates.

Companies have used pension obligations to smooth earnings by changing the assumed long-term discount rate or the earnings rate. The potential for this behavior heightens the need for the auditor to exercise appropriate professional skepticism and skeptically question significant assumptions. For example, some companies have used assumptions that their pension assets will grow at a rate of 9.5% for the future, when historical growth rates have been around 6% (and even less); this approach results in possibly overstating pension assets, and understating the net liability. Other assumptions made by actuaries also need to be examined for reasonableness, for example, average life span; a retired coal miner is not likely to have a retired life expectancy as long as a retired office worker.

Check Your Basic Knowledge

13-33 Auditors can test the client's warranty reserves using primarily tests of controls and substantive analytical procedures. (T/F)

13-34 When auditing pension obligations, the auditor likely uses a specialist to assist the audit team. (T/F)

13-35 Which of the following would the auditor <u>not</u> try to determine about a client's warranty estimate?
  a. Whether the estimate is reasonable in the circumstance.
  b. Whether management based the estimate on verifiable, objective assumptions.
  c. How management developed the estimate.

  d. Whether the factors and assumptions used by management deviate from historical patterns.

13-36 Which of the following procedures would an auditor most likely perform when auditing management estimates of long-term liabilities?
  a. Inquire of management about related party transactions.
  b. Confirm inventories held at outside warehouses.
  c. Review past experience of the client related to warranty claims.
  d. Send confirmations to client vendors.

LO 10

Apply the frameworks for professional decision making and ethical
decision making for decisions
made when conducting an audit.

Applying Decision-Making Frameworks

The following *End of Chapter* material provides you an opportunity to apply
the frameworks for professional decision making and ethical decision making for
decisions made when conducting an audit: *13-33*.

Let's Review

- Relevant accounts when auditing debt include bonds payable, bond premium/discount, interest expense, gains or
losses on refinancing debt, notes payable, and mortgages
payable. The overall objective when auditing debt is to
determine whether the client has recorded all obligation
and properly classified and disclosed them. The auditor is
primarily concerned with understatement and, therefore,
focuses on the completeness assertion. (LO 1)

- Relevant accounts when auditing equity include stock
accounts (common, preferred, and treasury), additional
paid-in capital, dividend accounts, and retained earnings.
In auditing equity accounts, the auditor primarily focuses
on whether the securities are accurately valued (valuation
assertion) and are properly classified and appropriately
presented and disclosed (presentation and disclosure
assertion). (LO 1)

- Inherent risks related to debt focus on the authorization
of debt, receipt of funds, recording of debt transactions,
and compliance with any debt covenants. Similarly,
inherent risks related to equity include proper authorization, proper recording of transactions, and proper
disclosure. (LO 2)

- Potential frauds related to debt include debt obligations
are not properly authorized, long-term or short-term debt
is misclassified, and prepayment penalties are not properly
recorded. Potential frauds related to equity include stock
sales or issuances are not authorized, stock sales or issuances violate debt covenants, stock sales or issuances are
not recorded, and stock options exercised are not authorized or are not in accordance with the terms of options
granted. (LO 3)

- Important controls for both debt and equity include
policies, procedures, and reviews related to providing
assurance that all appropriate disclosures have been
made. (LO 4)

- Planning analytical procedures help auditors identify
areas of potential material misstatements. The objective of
planning analytical procedures is to identify accounts with
heightened risk of misstatement during audit planning to

provide a basis for designing and implementing responses
to the assessed risks. Typical planning analytical procedures
for debt would include trend analysis and reasonableness
tests. The primary planning analytical procedure for equity
is a comparison of current-year account balances with
prior-year account balances. (LO 5)

- Responding to identified risks typically involves developing
an audit approach that contains substantive procedures
(e.g., tests of details and, when appropriate, substantive
analytical procedures) and tests of controls, when applicable. When auditing debt and equity, the auditor commonly
uses a substantive approach. (LO 6)

- Typical tests of transaction controls include inquiry of
personnel performing the control, observation of the
control being performed, inspection of documentation
confirming that the control has been performed, and reperformance of the control by the auditor testing the control.
However, for financial statement audit purposes, when
auditing debt and equity, the auditor most likely performs
a substantive audit and therefore does not perform tests of
controls for purposes of the audit. (LO 7)

- The audits of debt and equity typically involve only substantive procedures. The auditor can test debt accounts
with both substantive analytical procedures and tests
of details. In contrast, auditors typically only use tests
of details to audit equity accounts. Further, the transactions in the equity accounts are typically tested 100%
because they are usually so few, and yet they are highly
material. (LO 8)

- Much of the accounting for long-term liabilities is straightforward. For example, bonds are disclosed at unamortized
issue price and are not adjusted to market unless the
organization is calling the bonds or is in the process of
converting the bonds to equity. However, a number of
long-term liabilities require multi-faceted subjective judgments by the client and the auditor. Long-term liability
accounts with a high risk of material misstatement include
accounts such as warranty reserves, pension obligations,
and other postemployment benefits. (LO 9)

Significant Terms

Bond indenture A contract between an issuer of bonds and the bondholder stating the time period before repayment, amount of interest paid, if the bond is convertible (and if so, at what price or what ratio), if the bond is callable, and the amount of money that is to be repaid.

Capital stock The combination of a corporation's common stock and preferred stock (if any).

Contributed capital The amount a company received when it issued its shares of stock; includes par value of preferred stock, par value of common stock, and contributed capital in excess of par value.

Debt covenants Restrictions in debt agreements aimed at protecting the lender (creditor, debt holder, or investor) by restricting the activities of the borrower (debtor).

Default The results of a violation of debt covenant requirements resulting in a failure to fulfill the obligation to repay the loan.

Defined benefit pension plan A retirement plan in which the company calculates the former employee's pension benefits based upon the length of their service and the salary that they earned while employed; these types of retirement plans are becoming increasingly rare.

Defined contribution pension plan A retirement plan in which the company puts a specific amount of money into a fund each year, for the eventual withdrawal by retired employees; the benefits that the retired employees ultimately receive depends on how well, or how poorly, the fund performs between the time the company deposits the money and the employee withdraws it; these types of retirement plans are becoming increasingly common.

Other postemployment benefits (OPEB) Benefits (other than pensions) that organizations provide to their retired employees, e.g., healthcare benefits, life and/or disability insurance, and legal services.

Transfer agent An entity such as a trust company, bank, or other financial institution that is used by an organization to maintain records of investors and account balances and transactions, to cancel and issue certificates, and to process investor mailings.

Treasury stock The portion of shares that a company keeps in its own treasury. Treasury stock may have come from a repurchase or buyback from shareholders, or it may have never been issued to the public in the first place.

Prompts for Critical Thinking

Prompt for Critical Thinking #1

Debt:
- Interest expense is recorded in the wrong period, at the wrong amount, is not recorded at all, or is misclassified.
- Entire loan payments (consisting of both interest and principal) are charged to either only principal or interest.

Equity:
- Stock options are backdated.
- Dividends are paid in violation of restrictive covenants.
- Dividends are paid to wrong parties or at incorrect amounts.
- Proceeds from stock sales are misappropriated.

Prompt for Critical Thinking #2

Debt:
- Schedule of debt obligations and interest
- A summary of the calculations supporting compliance with debt covenants

Equity:
- Client's articles of incorporation
- Confirmations with transfer agent or shareholders

Review Questions and Short Cases

NOTE: Completing *Review Questions and Short Cases* does not require the student to reference additional resources and materials.

NOTE: For the remaining problems, we make special note of those addressing fraud, international issues, professional skepticism, and ethics.

FRAUD

FRAUD

FRAUD

FRAUD

13-1 `LO 1` What are the relevant accounts when auditing debt, and what is the auditor's primary objective?

13-2 `LO 1` What are the relevant accounts related to equity, and what is the auditor's primary objective?

13-3 `LO 1` Identify common transactions affecting equity accounts.

13-4 `LO 1` Review *Exhibit 13.1*. Describe the balance sheet presentation related to equity provided by Ford Motor Company.

13-5 `LO 2` Identify common inherent risks associated with debt.

13-6 `LO 2` Review *Exhibit 13.2* and identify inherent risks associated with typical stockholders' equity transactions.

13-7 `LO 3` Identify fraud risks associated with debt.

13-8 `LO 3` Identify fraud risks associated with equity.

13-9 `LO 4` Given typical inherent and fraud risks related to material misstatement of debt, identify controls that an auditor would expect a client to have implemented.

13-10 `LO 4` Given typical inherent and fraud risks related to material misstatement of equity, identify controls that an auditor would expect a client to have implemented.

13-11 `LO 5` What are typical planning analytical procedures related to debt?

13-12 `LO 5` What are typical planning analytical procedures related to equity?

13-13 `LO 6` What type of audit approach does the auditor typically plan for debt? Why is this typically the most appropriate approach?

13-14 `LO 6` What type of audit approach does the auditor typically plan for equity? Why is this typically the most appropriate approach?

13-15 `LO 6` An audit firm is engaged to audit the financial statements of Zeitlow Corporation for the current year. Zeitlow Corporation's financial statements and records have never been audited. The stockholders' equity section of Zeitlow Corporation's balance sheet at year end follows.

Stockholders' Equity

Capital stock—10,000 shares of $10 par value authorized:	
5,000 shares issued and outstanding	$50,000
Capital contributed in excess of par value of capital stock	58,800
Retained earnings	105,000
Total stockholders' equity	$213,800

Founded eight years ago, Zeitlow Corporation has 10 stockholders and serves as its own transfer agent. Prepare the detailed audit program for the examination of the three accounts composing the stockholders' equity section of Zeitlow Corporation's balance sheet. Do not include procedures related to the verification of the results of the current-year operations.

13-16 **LO 7** Describe the evidence typically obtained from tests of controls when auditing debt or equity.

13-17 **LO 8** Review the two panels in *Exhibit 13.3*. Describe the two alternative approaches to auditing interest expense and the reason for the difference in approaches.

13-18 **LO 8** Refer to *Exhibit 13.4* and identify typical substantive procedures for relevant assertions related to debt.

13-19 **LO 8** Identify substantive procedures that the auditor should perform related to dividends.

13-20 **LO 8** Retained earnings is a component of stockholders' equity. What substantive procedures will the auditor typically perform related to retained earnings?

13-21 **LO 8** What important items should the auditor document related to substantive procedures for debt and equity?

13-22 **LO 8** What information should the auditor note when reading a bond indenture? How will the auditor use this information in the audit?

13-23 **LO 8** After the auditor completes auditing all other account balances on the balance sheet, it might appear that the retained earnings figure is a balancing figure and requires no further audit procedures. Why would an auditor still audit retained earnings?

13-24 **LO 8** Assume your audit client declared a 5% stock dividend. Identify the evidence you would examine to determine whether the client appropriately accounted for the stock dividend.

13-25 **LO 8** Explain how the auditor might use a bond amortization spreadsheet when auditing interest expense over the life of a bond.

13-26 **LO 8** The auditor should review a bond indenture at the time a bond is issued and anytime subsequent changes are made to it.

a. Briefly identify the information the auditor would expect to obtain from a bond indenture. List at least five specific pieces of information that would be relevant to the audit.

b. Because auditors are especially concerned with the potential understatement of liabilities, should they confirm the existence of the liability with individual bondholders? State your rationale.

c. Assume that a company issued bonds at a discount. Explain how to compute the amount of the discount and how the auditor could determine whether the amount is properly amortized each year.

    d. Explain how the auditor could verify that semi-annual interest payments are made on the bond each year.

    e. Assume a company has a 15-year, $20 million loan that is due on September 30 of next year. It is the company's intent to refinance the bond before it is due, but it is waiting for the best time to issue new debt. Because its intent is to issue the bond next year, the company believes that the existing $20 million bond need not be classified as a current liability. What evidence should the auditor gather to determine the appropriate classification of the bond?

13-27 `LO 8` The following covenants, labeled as a. through d. below, are from a bond indenture. The indenture provides that failure to comply with its terms in any respect automatically advances the due date of the loan to the date of noncompliance (the maturity date is 20 years hence). Identify the audit steps that the auditor should take in connection with each one of the following independent scenarios.

    a. The debtor company shall maintain a working capital ratio of 2 to 1 at all times, and, in any fiscal year following a failure to maintain the said ratio, the company shall restrict compensation of the CEO and executive officers to a total of no more than $500,000. Executive officers for this purpose shall include the chair of the board of directors, the president, all vice presidents, the secretary, and the treasurer.

    b. The debtor company shall insure all property that serves as security for this debt against loss by fire for 100% of its value. The company will provide insurance policies securing this protection to the trustee.

    c. The debtor company shall pay all taxes legally assessed against the property that serves as security for this debt. The company should make payment within the time provided by law without penalty and shall deposit receipted tax bills or equally acceptable evidence of payment of the same with the trustee.

    d. The debtor company shall deposit a sinking fund with the trustee of semi-annual payments of $300,000. The trustee shall use this fund, at his or her discretion, to purchase bonds of this issue.

13-28 `LO 8` The following long-term debt documentation (indexed K-1), and presented on the next page, was prepared by client personnel and audited by AA, an audit assistant, during the calendar year 2018 audit of American Widgets, Inc., a continuing audit client. The engagement supervisor is reviewing the workpapers. Note any deficiencies in the audit workpapers (shown on the next page) that the engagement supervisor should identify.

13-29 `LO 9` An often contentious area of discussion between the auditor and the client is the precision needed for an estimate, for example, an estimate of the warranty liability of an automotive manufacturer.

    a. Scenario: Your client argues that because an estimate is subjective, materiality should be larger than it would be for a less subjective account. How would you respond to the client?

    b. Regarding the precision of the estimate, respond to the following quote from an ex–audit partner: "The preciseness of the estimate is dependent on the soundness of the underlying prediction model. If the auditor determines that the inputs are correct and agrees on the model, there is no need for audit judgment."

      i. Indicate the extent to which you agree or disagree with the statement.

13-28 `CONTINUED`

December 31, 2018   K-1   Initials AA
Prepared by
Reviewed by   Date 2/10/2019

Lender	Interest Rate	Payment Terms	Collateral	Balance December 31, 2017	2018 Borrowings	2018 Reductions	Balance December 31, 2018	Interest Paid to	Accrued Interest Payable December 31, 2018	Comments
First Commercial Bank*	4.2%	Interest only on 25th of month, principal due in full 1/1/22, no prepayment penalty	Inventories	$50,000††	$300,000‡ 1/31/18	$100,000*** 6/30/18	$250,000‖	12/25/18		Dividend of $80,000 paid 9/2/18 (W/P N-3) violates a provision of the debt agreement, which thereby permits lender to demand immediate payment; lender has refused to waive this violation
Lender's Capital Corp.*	Prime plus 1	Interest only on last day of month, principal due in full 3/5/22	Second mortgage on Park St. building	100,000††	50,000‡ 2/29/18	—	200,000†	12/31/18		Prime rate was 3% to 4% during the year
Gigantic Building & Loan Association*	3.7%	$5,000 principal plus interest due on 5th of month, due in full 12/31/19	First mortgage on Park St. building	720,000††	—	60,000***	660,000†	12/5/18		Reclassification entry for current portion proposed (See RJE-3)
J. Lott, majority stockholder*	0%	Due in full 12/31/20	Unsecured	300,000††	—	100,000‖‖	200,000†	—		
				$1,170,000† †††	$350,000 †††	$260,000 †††	$1,310,000 †††			

††† Footed without exception
† Confirmed without exception, W/PK-2
‖ Confirmed with exception
‡ Agreed to loan agreement, validated bank deposit ticket, and board of directors' authorization, W/PW-7
*** Agreed to canceled checks and lender's monthly statements
‖‖ Agreed to cash disbursements journal and canceled check dated 12/31/18, clearing 1/8/19
†† Agreed to 12/31/17 work papers
* Agreed interest rate, terms, and collateral to copy of note and loan agreement

Overall Conclusions
Long-term debt, accrued interest payable, and interest expense are correct and complete at December 31, 2018.

ii. How might an auditor verify that the model is sound?

iii. If there is a precise estimate, should the auditor overrule the estimate with a judgment that contains subjectivity? If you believe the answer is yes, identify the factors that should lead the auditor to override the judgment. If you believe the answer is no, state your rationale.

13-30 **LO 9** Describe the information that auditors would consider when auditing the estimates for each of the following liability accounts.

a. Warranty reserves
b. Pension obligations
c. Postemployment benefit liabilities other than pensions

13-31 **LO 9** Explain how auditors might use outside specialists when auditing pension obligations.

13-32 **LO 9** You are on the audit of Oshkosh Truck Corporation. The organization is the leading manufacturer of fire trucks and heavy-duty army trucks. The company warranties all of the basic components for 100,000 miles or four years, whichever comes first. The one exception is for trucks used in desert lands; those warranties are for 40,000 miles or 18 months, whichever comes first. Most of their sales have historically been for trucks not used in desert lands.

a. Identify the components of an information system that Oshkosh Truck should establish to develop an estimate of the warranty liability and warranty expense.
b. Assume the organization established an information system to your specifications described in part (a). Write an audit program to audit the accuracy of the process that would provide audit evidence on the reasonableness of the warranty expense and warranty liability account.
c. Assume that last year, there was an increase in trucks sold to the army and used in the desert lands. Recall that these trucks carried only the 40,000 miles or 18-month warranty. Explain how this change would affect the recognition of the warranty expense and liability account.
d. Assume that the warranty liability has been growing over the past few years because actual warranty expenditures have been significantly less than estimated. Assume there has been no significant decline in the quality of the vehicles produced. What information would the auditor gather to determine whether the liability might be materially overstated?

Fraud Focus: Contemporary and Historical Cases

FRAUD

PROFESSIONAL SKEPTICISM

ETHICS

13-33 **Federico Quinto Jr., CPA, Soyo Group (LO 1, 2, 3, 4, 6, 8, 10)** Refer to the *Focus on Fraud* feature "Fraud Risks Related to Debt and Equity: Insights from SEC Accounting and Auditing Enforcement Releases." Review the panel related to Federico Quinto Jr., CPA.

a. What risks of material misstatement were present in the case?
b. What are the auditor's responsibilities related to debt covenants? What would you consider the most relevant assertion(s) related to debt covenants, and what substantive procedures should the auditor have performed?

    c. Identify ways in which the audit team appeared to have a lack of appropriate professional skepticism.

    d. Assume that you were part of the audit team for the Soyo 2007 audit, and knew that the client had not provided the appropriate disclosures related to debt covenants in the financial statements. Use the framework for ethical decision making presented in *Chapter 1* to determine the actions you should take. Recall that the steps are as follows: (1) identify the ethical issue, (2) determine the affected parties and identify their rights, (3) determine the most important rights, (4) develop alternative courses of action, (5) determine the likely consequences of each proposed course of action, (6) assess the possible consequences, and (7) decide on an appropriate course of action.

FRAUD

PROFESSIONAL SKEPTICISM

13-34 **Delphi Corporation**
(LO 1, 2, 3, 4, 6, 8, 9)   Refer to the *Focus on Fraud* feature "Fraud Risks Related to Debt and Equity: Insights from SEC Accounting and Auditing Enforcement Releases." Review the panel related to Delphi Corporation.

    a. What risks of material misstatement were present in the case?

    b. What are the auditor's responsibilities related to auditing retained earnings? What procedures should the auditor have performed?

    c. Identify ways in which the audit team appeared to have a lack of appropriate professional skepticism.

Application Activities

FRAUD

NOTE: Completing *Application Activities* requires students to reference additional resources and materials. Some *Application Activities* will require the student to reference relevant professional auditing standards. We make special note of these as *Auditing Standards Application Activities*.

13-35 **Deloitte & Touche LLP, Adelphia**
(LO 2, 3, 4, 8)   In April 2005, the SEC announced that Deloitte & Touche had agreed to pay $50 million to settle charges stemming from its audit of Adelphia Communications Corporation's fiscal year 2000 financial statements. After performing appropriate research, address the following questions:

    a. Once the auditor identifies risks of material misstatement, the auditor is to determine the audit approach that best addresses those risks. In what ways did Deloitte & Touche fail to do this?

    b. What was the nature of the fraud at Adelphi as it related to debt and equity?

    c. In addition to paying the $50 million settlement, what other actions did Deloitte & Touche agree to? Do you believe these actions will lead to improved audit quality at Deloitte & Touche?

FRAUD

PROFESSIONAL SKEPTICISM

13-36 **Federico Quinto Jr., CPA, Soyo Group**
(LO 8)   Refer to the *Focus on Fraud* feature "Fraud Risks Related to Debt and Equity: Insights from SEC Accounting and Auditing Enforcement Releases." Review the panel related to Federico Quinto Jr., CPA. Obtain a copy of the SEC Auditing and Enforcement Release related to this case (AAER 3403, August 31, 2012).

    a. How does the AAER describe Quinto's failure to act with due professional care and failure to maintain an attitude of appropriate professional skepticism?

    b. What sanctions did the SEC impose on Quinto; do these sanctions seem appropriate?

13-37 Logitech (LO 9)   Refer to the *Focus on Fraud* feature "Warranty Accrual Accounting." Obtain a copy of the related SEC AAER (*SEC AAER No. 3765 / April 19, 2016*) and other relevant news articles.

a. Why did Logitech's management choose not to follow GAAP? Consider the fraud triangle in answering this question.

b. Does the AAER provide any insight as to whether the warranty "problem" was material?

c. Do you think that the Logitech auditors exhibited an appropriate level of professional skepticism?

13-38 IAASB, ASB (LO 9)   Auditors are often concerned with accounts requiring management estimates because of the possibility of management bias.

a. Review ISA 540 and AU-C 540, and for each identify indicators of possible management bias.

b. Does the presence of an indicator of management bias mean that there is a material misstatement? Explain.

Data Analytics Using Excel: A Case in the Context of the Pharmaceutical Industry

NOTE: In this and select cycle chapters, we present a case set in the pharmaceutical industry. The case enables students to practice developing and conducting planning and substantive analytical procedures using data analytics in Excel. The case was developed using the published financial statements of three prominent companies in this industry, with adaptations to make the case suitable for classroom use. The fictional company names are as follows: PharmaCorp, Novartell, and AstraZoro. You will access an Excel file on the textbook's website at *https://login. cengage.com/cb/*. The Excel file contains financial data and information from footnote disclosures. The primary analytical procedures tasks will focus on PharmaCorp. You will use Novartell and AstraZoro as industry comparison companies. Access and download the file, then complete the requirements in *13-39*.

13-39 LO 5, 8   This case will enable you to practice conducting planning and substantive analytical procedures for accounts in the acquisition and payment cycle. When analyzing the financial data, you may assume that the 2015 information is *unaudited*, while prior-year data are audited.

As you complete this case, consider the following features of and trends in the pharmaceutical industry and for PharmaCorp specifically:

- After a long period of industry dominance by companies in the United States, the United Kingdom, and Europe, these companies are facing increasing competition from companies domiciled in emerging economies, such as Brazil, India, and China.
- There exists significant uncertainty in the market because of recent regulation covering health care and government payouts for certain procedures and related pharmaceuticals.
- Health care policy makers and the government are increasingly mandating what physicians can prescribe to patients.
- Health care policy makers and the government are increasingly focusing on prevention regimes rather than treatment regimes, thereby leading to shifts in the demand for various pharmaceuticals.
- The global pharmaceutical market is anticipated to grow by 5–7% in 2016 compared with a 4–5% growth rate in 2015, according to a leading industry analyst publication.
- Beginning in 2014, PharmaCorp initiated and executed a significant company-wide cost reduction initiative aimed at improving manufacturing efficiency, cutting back on research and development expenses, and eliminating unnecessary corporate overhead.
- PharmaCorp's policies for extending credit to customers have remained stable over the last three years. PharmaCorp's credit granting policies are considered stringent within the industry, and analysts have sometimes criticized the company for this,

contending that such policies have hindered the company's revenue growth relative to industry peers.

- Two of PharmaCorp's popular pharmaceuticals, Selebrax and Vyvox, came off patent during the fourth quarter of FYE 2015. These pharmaceuticals now face competition in the generic drug portion of the overall industry market.

Information specific to the PharmaCorp's debt activities:

- Long-term debt balances (in the millions) for 2015 (unaudited) and 2014 (audited) were $31,036 and $34,926, respectively.
- The primary financing activity related to debt was net repayments of just over $1,500,000.
- Approximately $2,500,000 of long-term debt was reclassified as current in 2015.
- The average interest rate on the long-term debt (based on the high and low rates of PharmaCorp's debt instruments) was 5.34%.
- Interest expense in 2014 (audited) was approximately $2,000,000.

Part I: Planning Analytical Procedures

a. *Step 1: Identify Suitable Analytical Procedures.* Your audit senior has suggested that the following ratio (on an overall financial statement level) will be used for planning analytical procedures related to debt activities at PharmaCorp:
    - Estimate interest expense (related to long-term debt) based on average long-term debt interest rates and average long-term debt outstanding. As part of Step 1, identify any other relevant relationships or trend analyses that would be useful to consider as part of planning analytics. Explain your reasoning.

b. *Step 2: Evaluate Reliability of Data Used to Develop Expectations.* The audit team has determined that the data you will be using to develop expectations in relation to long-term interest expense is reliable. Indicate the factors that the audit team likely considered in making that determination.

c. *Step 3: Develop Expectation.* Complete Step 3 of planning analytical procedures by developing an expectation for interest expense for long-term debt. Even before you develop a point estimate, what is the nature of the change of the interest expense account that you expect (from the prior year)? Using only the information provided here, what is your point estimate of interest expense?

d. *Step 4 and Step 5: Define and Identify Significant Unexpected Differences.* Refer to the guidance in Chapter 7 on performance materiality, tolerable misstatement, and clearly trivial amounts. Apply those materiality guidelines to Step 4 of planning analytical procedures to define what is meant by a significant difference. Explain your reasoning. Also comment on qualitative materiality considerations in this context. Now that you have determined what amount of difference would be considered significant, indicate whether there was a significant unexpected difference, assuming that the client recorded $1,800,000 of interest expense related to long-term debt.

e. *Step 6 and Step 7: Investigate Significant Unexpected Differences and Ensure Proper Documentation.* Complete Step 6 of planning analytical procedures by describing how your results will affect your substantive audit procedures. Explain your reasoning. To complete Step 7, describe what information should be included in the auditor's workpapers.

Part II: Substantive Analytical Procedures

f. As you talk with your audit senior, you realize that your estimate during planning was not very precise because it was based on data that were highly aggregated. While this approach would be appropriate for planning analytics, it is likely not appropriate for substantive analytics. How could you improve the precision of your estimate so that it would be precise enough to constitute evidence as a substantive analytical procedure?

g. Access the PharmaCorp Excel file at the text website. Refer to the worksheet labeled "PharmaCorp Long Term Debt." Use that information to develop a more precise estimate for interest expense for long-term debt. Given the estimate that you developed, what is your conclusion regarding the client's asserted amount of interest expense for long-term debt?

Academic Research Case

NOTE: Completing the *Academic Research Case* requires students to reference additional resources and materials.

SEARCH HINT

It is easy to locate these academic research articles! Use a search engine such as Google Scholar or an electronic research platform such as ABI Inform, and search using the author names and part of the article title.

13-40 **LO 2, 8** Locate and read the article listed below.

Bhaskar, L. S., G. V. Krishnan, and W. Yu. (2017). Debt covenant violations, firm financial distress, and auditor actions. *Contemporary Accounting Research* 34(1): 186–215.

a. What is the purpose of the study?
b. Describe the design/method/approach used to conduct the study.
c. What are the primary findings of the study?

The Audit Opinion Formulation Process

I. Making Client Acceptance and Continuance Decisions

Chapter 1

II. Performing Risk Assessment

Chapters 2, 3, 7, and 9–13

III. Obtaining Evidence About Internal Control Operating Effectiveness

Chapters 8–13

IV. Obtaining Substantive Evidence About Accounts, Disclosures, and Assertions

Chapters 8–13

V. Completing the Audit and Making Reporting Decisions

Chapters 14 and 15

Quality Auditing and the Need for Quality Auditor Judgments and Ethical Decisions

Chapter 1

Professional Liability

Chapter 4

The Audit Opinion Formulation Process and a Framework for Obtaining Audit Evidence

Chapters 5 and 6

Auditors must perform additional tasks prior to completing the audit, each designed to help provide reasonable assurance that the audit team conducted the audit in a quality manner and that the ultimate audit opinion is appropriate. These activities include obtaining remaining audit evidence, writing both a management representation letter and a management letter (and knowing the difference between the two), performing an engagement quality review, and identifying issues to communicate with the audit committee. After completing these activities, the auditor will be ready to issue the audit report!

Learning Objectives

LO 1 Obtain remaining audit evidence on:
- Detected misstatements
- Loss contingencies
- Adequacy of disclosures
- Noncompliance with laws and regulations
- Review analytical procedures
- The going-concern assumption
- Subsequent events

LO 2 Distinguish between a management representation letter and a management letter.

LO 3 Identify the procedures to perform when conducting an engagement quality review.

LO 4 Identify issues to communicate to the audit committee.

What You Will Learn

- What are the auditor's responsibilities with respect to detected misstatements? (LO 1)

- What activities does the auditor perform when reviewing and assessing the appropriateness the client's contingencies? (LO 1)

- What activities does the auditor perform when reviewing and assessing the adequacy of disclosures? (LO 1)

- What activities does the auditor perform in reviewing and assessing noncompliance with laws and regulations? (LO 1)

- Why and how does the auditor perform review analytical procedures? (LO 1)

- What activities does the auditor perform when reviewing and assessing the going-concern assumption? (LO 1)

- What are subsequent events and what is the auditor's responsibility with respect to them? (LO 1)

- What is the purpose and content of a management representation letter and a management letter? (LO 2)

- What activities does the auditor perform when performing an engagement quality review? (LO 3)

- What issues should the auditor communicate to the audit committee? (LO 4)

Why It Matters   The Implications of Busy Season

About 65% of publicly traded companies in the United States have a FYE of December 31, and they have 60 to 90 days (depending on size) afterward to file their form 10K. Accordingly, this period is the busiest for auditors. This intensive period is known as **busy season***, that is, the time of the year during which the auditor faces the greatest deadline pressure and work volume (most auditors work 60–80 hours per week during busy season). This feature provides suggestions on how audit firms should prepare for busy season.*

As Benjamin Franklin is quoted as saying, "By failing to prepare, you are preparing to fail." How can audit teams prepare for the rigor of busy season, as teams attempt to accomplish many complex tasks in a relatively short time. Think about LO 1, for example, how can an audit team complete all those tasks in the last weeks of the audit?

According to an article in *The CPA Journal (http://www.cpajournal.com/2016/12/23/5-steps-prepare-audit-season/)*, every firm should take the following five steps to prepare for busy season:

1. Evaluate last year's busy season
    Engagement team leaders should objectively evaluate the difficulties that teams encountered the prior year on each specific client. Leaders and their teams should consider what went well, what went poorly (and why), and what the team can do to avoid any prior pitfalls. One way to accomplish this is to evaluate the prior year's audit workpapers to identify areas where there were time and cost overruns; then teams can plan ahead to avoid those difficulties going forward.

2. Assess current authoritative literature
    Engagement team leaders should determine whether any new financial accounting standards or auditing standards have emerged in the past year that will affect the audit. The firm should develop a staff and education plan that will help teams adapt to any new requirements.

3. Consider recent peer review and inspection findings
    Firms that perform audits must have a peer audit firm review a sample of their engagements every three years. For example, EY might review KPMG, and KPMG might review Deloitte. Engagement team leaders should consider the results of peer reviews and other inspection findings to identify areas of busy season–related audit quality detriments, and initiate corrective actions well in advance of the next busy season. In addition, the AICPA and PCAOB also provide insights as to what they see "going wrong" in audits, and by reviewing those lists, audit teams can work to avoid problem areas. For additional details, see *http://www.aicpa.org/InterestAreas/PeerReview/Community/PeerReviewers/DownloadableDocuments/Matters-in-PR.pdf* and *https://pcaobus.org/Inspections/Pages/PublicReports.aspx*

4. Communicate early with clients
    The engagement team should have a list of appropriate client contacts, and individual members of the team should reach out well in advance of the audit to alert client personnel of their plans, intended timing of various procedures, and schedules and information that they will require.

5. Prepare staff and invest time in planning
    Engagement teams should work to avoid having disparities between their risk assessments and their audit planning responses; if the team identifies a risk, it needs to follow up. Teams should focus on efficiency, coordination, time management, stress management, and teamwork to successfully navigate all the work that has to be conducted during the end of audits.

What Do You Think?   For Classroom Discussion

In reviewing LO 1 above, the audit team has to complete many activities at the very end of the audit.

*   What kind of stress do you think that creates?
*   What risks regarding audit quality might result?

*   Why don't audit firms just hire more professionals to cover the demands of busy season?
*   How do you personally plan to cope with the inevitable demands of busy season?

Obtain Remaining Audit Evidence

Detected Misstatements

The auditor summarizes the misstatements detected during the audit to determine whether they are material and whether the client needs to correct them. A misstatement may be a difference between the amount the client reports in the financial statements versus what the client should report under generally accepted accounting principles (GAAP), or the omission of an amount that should be disclosed in accordance with GAAP.

Misstatements fall into three categories: known misstatements, projected misstatements, and judgmental misstatements. **Known misstatements** are those that the auditor has specifically identified and about which there is no doubt; known misstatements are also referred to as **factual misstatements**. **Projected misstatements** are the auditor's best estimate of the total misstatements in a given population, based on the misstatements detected in an audit sample of that population. **Judgmental misstatements** are those that arise from material differences in judgments of the auditor and client management concerning accounting estimates or the application of account principles.

Most audit firms use a schedule, often referred to as **summary of unadjusted audit differences** (SUAD), to accumulate the known and projected misstatements and the carryover effects of prior-year uncorrected misstatements. *Exhibit 14.1* provides an example of a summary of misstatements. At the end of the audit, management and the auditor discuss which misstatements the client will correct in the financial statements, and which the client will waive, that is leave uncorrected. The client can only waive immaterial misstatements.

In *Exhibit 14.1*, the first adjustment reflects a pricing error detected by confirming a sample of receivables. The known misstatement is $972, as shown in the first section of the schedule. However, the projected misstatement for the unknown (and unexamined) part of the population is $13,493, as shown in the second section of the schedule. If these were corrected, both sales and accounts receivable would be reduced by $14,465 ($972 + $13,493), resulting in a reduction of pretax earnings and current assets.

The second adjustment involves an unrecorded check for $1,500. The third adjustment involves the carryover effects of understating last year's accrued salaries and salary expense ($6,900). Because the carryover effect is to overstate this year's salary expense, the correction is a reduction in the current year's salary expense, thereby resulting in an increase in pretax earnings and a reduction in the beginning balance of retained earnings.

The income tax effects are included in the schedule to show the total effects of correcting these misstatements. Near the end of the audit, the auditor will review these possible adjustments in the aggregate to determine whether the combined effect is material. The auditor compares the total misstatements (the sum of known and projected misstatements) to each significant segment of the financial statements, such as total current assets, total noncurrent assets, total current liabilities, total noncurrent liabilities, owners' equity, and pretax income. The auditor determines if these are, in aggregate, material to the financial statements. The total misstatement as a percentage of these segments is clearly immaterial, and the auditor notes that conclusion in the workpaper.

The materiality of a misstatement includes consideration of the quantitative amount of the misstatement, and any qualitative features that could make it material. For example, if the misstatement reflects negatively on management, or if correcting the misstatement would have the effect of changing a positive earnings trend to a negative earnings trend. As another example, consider a misstatement that is immaterial, but the auditor determines is intentional. Even if immaterial, an intentional misstatement could result in additional challenges. The intentional misstatement may be fraudulent or in violation of applicable laws.

Exhibit 14.1
Summary of Possible Adjustments to Correct Misstatements

| | Debit (Credit) | | | | | |
| | Assets | | Liabilities | | | |
W/P Account Description	Current	Noncurrent	Current	Noncurrent	Retained Earnings	Net Earnings
Uncorrected Known Misstatements						
Sales						972
Accounts receivable	(972)					
Misstatement from A/R confirmations ($972 known misstatement and $13,493 additional projected misstatement)						
Accounts payable			1,500			
Cash	(1,500)					
Unrecorded check # 14,389						
Projected Misstatements						
Sales						
Accounts receivable	(13,493)					13,493
Projected pricing misstatements from sample						
Carryover Effect of Prior-Year Misstatements						
Retained earnings					6,900	
Salary expense						(6,900)
Under accrual of prior year's salaries						
Subtotal: Income Before Taxes						7,565
Tax Adjustment						
Income taxes payable ((13,493 + 972) × 0.34)			4,918			
Income tax expense (7,565 × 0.34)						(2,572)
Retained earnings (6,900 × 0.34)					(2,346)	
Total Misstatements	(15,965)	0	6,418	0	4,554	4,993
Balance from trial balance	19,073,000	1,997,000	(3,346,000)	(13,048,000)	(4,676,000)	1,678,000
Total misstatement as % of balance	0.08%	0.0%	0.19%	0.0%	0.1%	0.3%

Conclusion: In my opinion, the total likely misstatements are not material to the financial statements taken as a whole. The projected misstatements are quantitatively immaterial and do not reflect material weaknesses in internal control. Therefore, no adjustments are required, nor is any additional audit work needed for these account balances.

Marginal tax rate: 34%

PREPARED BY: _____KMJ_____ DATE ___2-17-19___

REVIEWED BY: _____AAG_____ DATE ___2-21-19___

If the client is publicly traded, Section 10A(b) of the Exchange Act requires auditors to take action upon discovery of an illegal act even if it does not have a material effect on the financial statements, including alerting management and the audit committee.

When auditors detect an intentional misstatement, they: (1) reconsider the level of audit risk for the client, (2) consider revising the nature, timing, and extent of audit procedures, and (3) evaluate whether to resign from the audit engagement. Further, the detection of an intentional misstatement likely signals the existence of an internal control material weakness and certainly speaks to control environment deficiencies, such as the tone from management.

Incentives offered to management may bias management's willingness to correct material detected misstatements. For example, some detected misstatements are material, and if management wishes to show higher net income, it may argue with the auditor against correcting an income-reducing misstatement. In such a situation, the auditor might feel some pressure to acquiesce to management's demands in order to preserve a harmonious working relationship. It is in these situations in which audit firm culture, an important driver of audit quality, is important. It is critical that the auditor is confident that the audit firm will support a decision insisting that management correct a misstatement, even if management does not want to do so.

Thus, audit firm culture that emphasizes doing the right thing encourages auditors to take sufficient time to deal with difficult issues. A culture that emphasizes the audit firm's long-term reputation over the immediate satisfaction of client preferences encourages quality actions by its auditors. Likewise, a culture that encourages auditors to seek consultation with other members of the audit firm helps provide reasonable assurance that the auditor does not feel isolated in making difficult decisions; this support is critical when the auditor is pressured by inappropriate or aggressive client behavior regarding detected misstatements.

Prior Period and Current Period Misstatements

When the auditor evaluates the misstatements posted to the SUAD, the auditor needs to recognize that misstatements from prior periods may have been uncorrected because they were judged immaterial in the prior period. However, those misstatements may materially affect the current period's financial results. To illustrate, assume $100,000 materiality level for the warranty liability account. Further assume that the warranty liability misstatement is the only misstatement the auditor needs to consider. In the first year, the auditor's evidence supports a conclusion that the amount recorded by the client is overstated by $75,000. In the second year, the auditor's evidence supports a conclusion that the amount recorded by this client understates the liability by $85,000. The misstatement in each individual year is under the $100,000 materiality threshold. The effect for each of the two years is as follows:

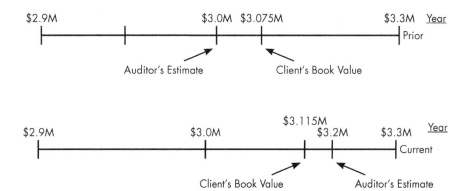

In each year, the client's estimate of the warranty liability does not differ from the auditor's estimate by a material amount. What is the effect of the client *not* correcting the immaterial misstatements? You likely recognize that the balance sheet is materially correct. However, the client's book value is higher than the auditor's estimate in the prior year and lower than the auditor's estimate in the current year, resulting in a swing of $160,000. Looking at the income statement effect only, not correcting the immaterial amount in the prior year and not correcting the immaterial amount in the current year causes income to be overstated by a total of $160,000 in the current year—an amount exceeding the materiality threshold. Clearly, the direction of the misstatement makes a difference when the effect on the income statement is considered. This example illustrates a client using the warranty liability account to build a cookie jar reserve in the previous year (overestimating the account balance) and then using the account balance to smooth reported earnings in the subsequent year.

The SEC's *Staff Accounting Bulletin* (SAB) 108 addresses the approach auditors should use in assessing both current-year and prior-year misstatements. SAB 108 mandates what is termed a **dual approach** to uncorrected misstatements. The dual approach requires the simultaneous application of *both* the **rollover method** and the **iron curtain method**. If a misstatement is material under *either* method, the client must correct the misstatement in the current period. Essentially, the rollover method focuses on the materiality of current-year misstatements and the reversing effect of prior-year misstatements on the income statement. This method may allow misstatements to accumulate on the balance sheet. The iron curtain method focuses on assuring that the year-end balance sheet is correct and does not consider the impact of prior-year uncorrected misstatements reversing in later years.

Subjective Differences between the Auditor and the Client

Auditors may have difficulties with clients regarding misstatements in accounts such as warranties where there is not necessarily a correct account balance, but only an estimate of a reasonable amount for the account balance. In the example dealing with the warranty estimate, the client may conclude that the estimate is subjective and that there is no way to determine the correct balance until a time in the future when all claims are made. Therefore, the client maintains that its estimate is as good as the auditor's estimate. Similarly, a client may claim that its subjective estimate of the allowance for uncollectible accounts is as good as the auditor's estimate—and therefore, there is not misstatement in the account balance.

Why It Matters   Aggregating and Netting Misstatements

This feature notes the importance of considering misstatements individually and in the aggregate.

Should the auditor consider each detected misstatement individually or should the auditor aggregate the misstatements to consider their combined effect? The answer is that the auditor should evaluate each misstatement individually *and* the auditor should consider the aggregate effect of all misstatements.

Further, if an individual misstatement causes the financial statements as a whole to be materially misstated, that effect cannot be eliminated by other misstatements that have a different directional effect on the financial statements. For example, if an organization's revenues are materially *overstated*, the auditor cannot conclude that the effect is immaterial if there is an equal and offsetting *overstatement* of expenses. Rather, the auditor would conclude that the financial statements *taken as a whole* are materially misstated. One rationale is that the trend in revenue growth may be just as important to a user as the effect on net income.

What should the auditor's response be to the client's claim that its estimate is as good as the auditor's estimate? The answer should be simple: the auditor should have gathered sufficient appropriate evidence that incorporates relevant information about the correctness of the account balance and should be able to defend the accuracy of that estimate. Remember, the auditor usually reaches a conclusion about accounting estimates by: (a) testing the client's methodology for reaching the estimate (when the auditor believes the client's process is strong and incorporates all relevant variables), or (b) developing the auditor's own model to come up with the estimate and then comparing that estimate to the amount recorded by the client (when the client does not have a robust estimation methodology). In either case, the auditor should not fall victim to an argument that no one can determine the right amount, so the client's estimate is as good as the auditor's estimate.

It's Your Turn!

Prompt for Critical Thinking #1

What transpires if a material misstatement exists in the financial statements and the auditor *fails* to detect it, or *fails* to require the client to correct it prior to year end? Management will have to issue a **restatement**, which occurs when and if the misstatement is ultimately discovered; at that point, management will have to issue revised financial statements with the misstatement corrected.

Restatements generally, but not always, result in negative stock market reactions. Of two evils, detecting and correcting a misstatement prior to the balance sheet date would be preferable to having to subsequently restatement the financials, thereby illustrating the importance of considering individual, aggregate, and net misstatements that the auditor detects during and at the end of the audit. The following example provides some context around these ideas.

In March 2017, Chelsea Logistics Holdings Corporation (CLC) purchased a significant interest in 2GO Group. New management and the board of directors decided to critically evaluate 2GO Group's financial reporting, which resulted in a restatement of 2GO Group's financial statements for the periods ending December 31, 2016, and March 31, 2017.

Chairman Uy made the following statement:
It is only prudent to … release the restated financials; it is being transparent… The restatement… reflects the commitment … to raise … governance standards.

Chairman Uy noted that the restated items concern non-cash amounts and they are non-recurring, so 2GO's financial prospects remain strong. The company has tried to reassure users about the restatement, discussing positive indications from both retail and institutional investors with respect to the company's future.

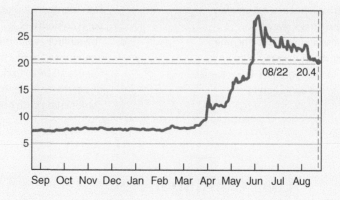

In this case, the stock market reaction to the restatement on July 11 was minimal. Think about the restatement, management's disclosure, and be prepared to explain why that might be the case.

For further details, see https://philbizwatcher.wordpress.com/2017/07/10/dennis-uys-statement-on-restatement-of-2go-financial-statement-inquirerbiz/

Source: *https://markets.ft.com/data/equities/tearsheet/charts?s=2GO:PHS*

Why It Matters

Misstatements in the Statement of Cash Flows

This feature highlights the importance of considering misstatements in the statement of cash flows.

Because of the importance of cash flows to investment decisions, the statement of cash flows is important to many financial statement users. Auditors should consider whether the statement of cash flows is materially correct, with a focus on assuring appropriate presentation and classification.

When the auditor identifies a misstatement in cash flow classification, the auditor should assess the materiality of the misstatement to determine whether a reclassification is necessary to assure that the statement of cash flows is materially correct.

The assessment as to whether the misstatement in classification is material should go beyond the income statement perspective. The auditor should look to factors that are unique to cash flows. For example, cash flow associated with operating activities is often an important measure for investors.

Check Your Basic Knowledge

14-1 Known misstatements are those that the auditor has specifically identified and about which there is no doubt; they are also known as factual misstatements.   (T/F)

14-2 Even if immaterial, an intentional misstatement may cause serious difficulties in the audit, and for the client.   (T/F)

14-3 The auditor discovers various errors in the client's financial statements during the audit. At the end of the audit, the auditor analyzes these misstatements to determine if the client needs to correct them. In which of the following situations could management and the auditor decide <u>not</u> to correct the misstatement?
   a. If, by correcting the misstatements, net income would increase rather than decrease.
   b. If, by correcting the misstatements, net income would decrease rather than increase.
   c. If the misstatements, in the aggregate, are material.
   d. If the misstatements, in the aggregate, are immaterial.

14-4 Which of the following statements is <u>false</u>?
   a. Management's incentives may bias their willingness to book, or correct, detected misstatements.
   b. Known misstatements are those that arise from differences in judgments of management concerning accounting estimates that the auditor considers unreasonable, or the selection or application of accounting policies that the auditor considers inappropriate.
   c. Section 10A(b) of the Exchange Act requires auditors to take action upon discovery of an illegal act even if it does not have a material effect on the financial statements, including alerting management and the audit committee.
   d. The auditor evaluates the misstatements that have been posted to the summary of unadjusted audit differences (SUAD) to determine whether uncorrected misstatements are material—either individually or in combination with other misstatements.

Loss Contingencies

Management is responsible for designing and maintaining policies and procedures to identify, evaluate, and account for loss contingencies. Auditors are responsible for determining that the client has properly identified, accounted for, and disclosed material loss contingencies.

In Accounting Standards Codification (ASC) 450, the Financial Accounting Standards Board (FASB) provides the standard for accruing and disclosing loss contingencies that can be reasonably estimated. The categories of contingencies are organized around probability of outcomes that reflect the contingent (not known for sure) nature of the loss. These categories include: (1) probable, (2) reasonably possible, and (3) remote.

ASC 450 requires the accrual and disclosure of contingent losses that are reasonably estimated and probable. It also requires that the client disclose a contingent loss if there is at least a reasonable possibility that a loss may occur and either an accrual has not been made or an exposure exists that is greater than the amount accrued. Examples of loss contingencies include:

- Threat of expropriation of assets in a foreign country
- Litigation, claims, and assessments
- Guarantees of debts of others
- Obligations of banks under standby letters of credit
- Agreements to repurchase receivables that have been sold
- Purchase and sale commitments

It's Your Turn!

Prompt for Critical Thinking #2

The following is an excerpt from the U.S. Department of State that articulates just how hostile the business environment is in South Sudan, relating to both physical safety as well as the threat of expropriation of assets.

"The government of the Republic of South Sudan (RSS) officially encourages foreign direct investment, and has made some progress in recent years to open the market to foreign companies. The U.S. government's long-standing sanctions against the Sudan were officially removed from applicability to newly independent South Sudan in December 2011, and senior RSS officials participated in a high-level international engagement conference in Washington, D.C., to help connect foreign investors with the RSS and South Sudanese private sector representatives. Until January 2012, oil production accounted for 98 percent of the government's revenues. The shutdown of oil production in late January 2012, due to a dispute with Sudan through which oil exports were transported by pipeline, radically reduced government revenue; tax and customs revenues, through better collection, have since increased to around 12 percent of the current government budget. The government is now looking to increase investment in non-oil sectors, including agriculture, mining, and teak wood exports.

The RSS enacted several major pieces of legislation governing investment since its independence from Sudan on July 9, 2011, and continues to use legislation passed during the country's semi-autonomous period, as part of Sudan, from January 9, 2005- July 8, 2011. Relevant key pieces of legislation penned since 2005 include the 2009 Investment Promotion Act, the 2011 Insolvency Act, the 2012 Imports and Exports Act, and the 2012 Companies Act. Under the 2009 Investment Promotion Act, foreign investors may own or control business organizations in any sector; however, South Sudan's Investment Authority Board of Directors is authorized to publish periodically a list limiting the sectors in which non-South Sudanese nationals are permitted to invest. There is a widespread misconception that non-South Sudanese nationals attempting to incorporate new businesses in South Sudan are required by law to have 31 percent South Sudanese ownership; this requirement does not appear in the Companies or Investment Promotion Acts. Under the 2012 Companies Act medium and large companies must have 31 percent South Sudanese ownership; small companies are "to be the domain of South Sudanese nationals only." "

Despite RSS efforts to attract foreign investment, investors face an extremely challenging investment climate. According to the World Bank's 2011 *Doing Business* report, the economy of Juba, South Sudan's capital is ranked 159 among 183 economies on its "ease of doing business" scale. The legal framework governing investment and private enterprises remains underdeveloped. A new labor law, public procurement bill, and several pieces of legislation related to land ownership are either in the drafting stage or awaiting approval by the National Legislative Assembly. Existing laws and regulations are not always enforced and are not well-publicized. Domestic and foreign investors often have an incomplete understanding of existing laws.

Although the RSS is committed to judicial reform, the existing legal system is ineffective, underfunded, overburdened, and subject to executive interference. High-level government and military officials are often immune from prosecution in practice, and frequently interfere with court decisions. Parties in contract disputes are sometimes arrested and imprisoned until the party agrees to pay a certain sum of money, often without ever going to court and sometimes without being formally charged.

Other factors inhibiting investment in South Sudan include limited physical infrastructure and a lack of both skilled and unskilled labor. South Sudan, roughly the size of France, has fewer than 400 kilometers of paved roads, and large parts of the country are inaccessible during the rainy season (April through October). Despite the existence of three power plants, none of which are working at full capacity, the country is almost completely reliant on diesel-run generators for electricity. According to the 2008 census, 94 percent of young persons enter the labor market with no qualifications. The majority of South Sudanese work in non-wage jobs, often in the agricultural sector. The country's literacy rate is just 27 percent.

The RSS has been operating under austerity measures (i.e., low levels of government spending) since April 2012, following the January 2012 shutdown of oil production, which previously accounted for 98 percent of government revenue. The loss of oil revenue has taken a toll on the economy: the market value of the South Sudanese Pound sank as low as 5.8 South Sudanese Pound (SSP) to 1 USD from the official rate of 2.96 SSP to 1 USD; that low has since rebounded to 4.2 SSP to 1 USD as of January 2013. Annual inflation stood at 25 percent in December 2012. RSS domestic and foreign currency reserves are running very low and the RSS, due to severe budgetary cuts, has ceased paying many basic operating costs. Failure by the government to pay for services is commonplace. Some private companies claim the government has reneged on or delayed payment for contracts in which work was undertaken. Government benefits, which account for up to 50 percent of employees' take-home pay, were drastically reduced in July 2012. The distribution of hard currency is tightly controlled by the government and limited to supporting the importation of food, medicine, fuel, and limited building materials. Many companies cite access to hard currency and convertibility of profits as major problems."

Surprisingly, companies are still willing to invest in the South Sudan because of its vast potential oil reserves, even though there is obviously a threat of expropriation of assets, or worse in terms of the safety of employees.

For example, oilprice.com reports the following: *(http://oilprice.com/Energy/Crude-Oil/Oil-Companies-Exploiting-Famine-And-Financial-Ruin-In-South-Sudan.html)*

> "Toward the end of last year, Suiss Finance Luxembourg AG announced a $10.5 billion deal that could rise to $105 billion in value when joint ventures in infrastructure and transportation are taken into account. While some may view this as a large stepping stone toward bringing back its oil revenues, Kiir's critics were quick to attack the leader over the deal once news broke, referring to what they called "shadowy" businessmen from Kampala who had brokered the contract.

Another recent deal involves Oranto Petroleum, which has committed to a $500 million:

> *"comprehensive exploration campaign, starting immediately"* to evaluate oil prospects in the 25,150 kilometers that make up Block B3. Juba approved the block a couple of weeks ago, giving Oranto a 90 percent share, while keeping only 10 percent for the government's Nile Petroleum (Nilepet). Oranto is a subsidiary of Nigeria's Atlas Petroleum International Ltd ("Atlas").

> The East African said the deal with Oranto has drawn harsh criticism due to a report from technical officials in the Ministry of Petroleum in which claims were made that the company lacked the technical expertise and financial capacity to manage the Block B3 project."

If you review the stock chart history of Suiss Finance, you will see the market optimism associated with the significant investment opportunity:

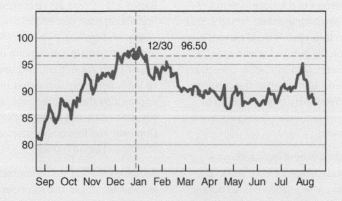

Assume you have an audit client with investments in Suiss Finance. Do you think these investments are a wise choice for your client? What do you think the risks are with respect to such an investment? What might be the upside potential, because clearly the market is valuing that potential (despite the risks, including the risk of expropriation of tangible assets and an overwhelming amount of overall uncertainty)? What loss contingency disclosures, if any, would you expect this client to have?

For further details, see (https://www.state.gov/e/eb/rls/othr/ics/2013/204855.htm)

Source: https://www.bloomberg.com/quote/

Contingent Liabilities at Alphabet Inc.

Why It Matters: An International Perspective

This feature provides an example of a disclosure of a material contingent liability totaling over $2.7 billion.

In July 2017, Alphabet Inc. announced its financial results for the quarter ended June 30, 2107. In the notes to its financial statements in its SEC filing (*https://www.sec.gov/cgi-bin/viewer ?action5view&cik51652044&accession_number50001652044 -17-000026&xbrl_type5v#; see Notes-Contingencies*), the company provides the following discussion:

On November 30, 2010, the European Commission's (EC) Directorate General for Competition opened an investigation into various antitrust-related complaints against us.

On April 15, 2015, the EC issued a Statement of Objections (SO) regarding the display and ranking of shopping search results and ads, to which we responded on August 27, 2015. On July 14, 2016, the EC issued a Supplementary SO regarding shopping search results and ads. On June 27, 2017, the EC announced its decision that certain actions taken by Google regarding its display and ranking of shopping search results and ads infringed European competition law. The EC decision imposes a €2.42 billion (approximately $2.74 billion) fine and directs the termination of the conduct at issue. We are in the process of reviewing the EC's decision in detail as we consider an appeal. We are also evaluating the impact of potential remedies we may implement to address the EC's findings. We accrued the fine in the second quarter of 2017, resulting in a charge of approximately $2.74 billion. The fine is included in accrued expenses and other current liabilities on our Consolidated Balance Sheet.

For Classroom Discussion

What Do You Think?

In July 2010, British Petroleum (BP) released its second quarter 2010 earnings report. The report discussed the risks associated with the ongoing events and cleanup effort in the Gulf of Mexico due to the oil spill associated with BP. It also included an income statement with a $32 billion pre-tax charge and a notation that "second quarter and first half 2010 include a charge of $32,192 million in production and manufacturing expenses, and a credit of $10,003 million in taxation in relation to the Gulf of Mexico oil spill."

In conducting the annual audit, BP's auditors would have obtained assurance that the client accurately reported and disclosed the contingency in connection with the oil spill.

In its FYE 2013 Form 20-F, BP disclosed that the total charge since the incident had risen to $42.7 billion and that the company had put an additional $20 billion into the Deepwater Horizons Oil Spill trust to fund future expenditures relating to the oil spill.

There is a movie about British Petroleum's oil spill in the Gulf of Mexico, *Deepwater Horizon*, which documents the failures in oversight and internal controls, and poor decision making that led to the disaster. If your instructor asks, or you are just curious, watch the movie and consider the following questions:

- Who was most at fault in causing the disaster?
- Who were the heroes and what did they do right?
- What types of internal controls and governance might have prevented the disaster?
- Why didn't one of the people on the oil rig cut off the well sooner?
- What role did BP's corporate culture play in the disaster?
- What types of evidence do you think the auditors would have obtained to assess the appropriateness of the disclosure?

Sources of Audit Evidence

An important primary source of evidence concerning loss contingencies is client management. The auditor should obtain the following from management:

- A description and evaluation of contingencies that existed at the balance sheet date or that arose prior to the end of the fieldwork and for which matters were referred to legal counsel, including correspondence and invoices from lawyers
- Assurance that the accounting and disclosure requirements concerning contingent liabilities have been met

- Information about major contracts in which contingencies may be present, such as the sale of receivables
- Documentation of communication with internal and external legal counsel of the client
- Documentation of contingent liabilities contained in corporate minutes, correspondence from governmental agencies, and bank confirmations

Letter of Audit Inquiry The primary source of corroborative evidence concerning litigation, claims, and assessments is the client's legal counsel. The auditor should ask the client to send a **letter of audit inquiry** to its legal counsel asking counsel to confirm information about asserted claims and those claims that are probable of assertion. Attorneys are hesitant to provide much information to auditors because their communications with clients are usually privileged. As a result, the American Bar Association and the American Institute of Certified Public Accountants (AICPA) have agreed that the letter of audit inquiry should include:

- Identification of the company, its subsidiaries, and the date of the audit
- Management's list (or a request by management that the lawyer prepare a list) that describes and evaluates the contingencies to which the lawyer has devoted substantial attention
- A request that the lawyer furnish the auditor with:
  1. A comment on the completeness of management's list and evaluations
  2. For each contingency:
     a. A description of the nature of the matter, the progress to date, and the action the company intends to take
     b. An evaluation of the likelihood of an unfavorable outcome and an estimate of the potential loss or range of loss
  3. Any limitations on the lawyer's response, such as not devoting substantial attention to the item or that the amounts are not material

The client should instruct legal counsel to respond directly to the auditors. The auditor and client should agree on what is material for this purpose. If a lawyer refuses to furnish the requested information, it is considered a scope limitation and the auditor would not be able to issue an unqualified audit opinion (see discussion on this issue in *Chapter 15*).

Check Your Basic Knowledge

14-5 The auditor is responsible for designing and maintaining policies and procedures to identify, evaluate, and account for loss contingencies; management is responsible for determining that the auditor has properly identified, accounted for, and disclosed material loss contingencies. (T/F)

14-6 One important primary source of evidence concerning loss contingencies is the client's management; a primary source of corroborative evidence concerning contingencies is the client's legal counsel, which provides the management representation letter. (T/F)

14-7 In obtaining evidence about loss contingencies, which of the following are sources of evidence that the auditor should obtain from management?

a. A description and evaluation of contingencies that existed at the balance sheet date.

b. Assurance that the accounting and disclosure requirements concerning contingent liabilities have been met.

c. Documentation of communication with internal and external legal counsel of the client.

d. All of the above.

14-8 In completing the audit, the auditor obtains a letter of audit inquiry. Which of the following is an accurate description of a letter of audit inquiry?

a. A letter that is the primary source of corroborative evidence concerning litigation, claims, and assessments, which is received from the client's legal counsel.

b. A letter that is the primary source of corroborative evidence concerning cash valuation, which is received from the client's bank.

c. A letter that is the primary source of corroborative evidence concerning accounts receivable valuation, which is received from the client's customer.

d. A letter that is the primary source of corroborative evidence concerning inventory valuation, which is received from the client's supplier.

Adequacy of Disclosures

The auditor's report covers the basic financial statements, which include the balance sheet, income statement, statement of cash flows, a statement of changes in stockholders' equity or retained earnings, and the related notes. If the auditor determines that disclosures are not reasonably adequate, the auditor must identify that fact in the auditor's report. Disclosures can be made on the face of the financial statements (in the form of classifications or parenthetical notations), or they can be made in the notes to the statements.

When assessing the adequacy of disclosures, the auditor should have reasonable assurance that:

- Disclosed events and transactions have occurred and pertain to the organization.
- All disclosures that should have been included are included.
- The disclosures are understandable to users.
- The information is accurately disclosed and at appropriate amounts.

To review and assess the adequacy of disclosures, the auditor will complete the following types of activities:

- Read the client's disclosures for each financial statement line item and associated discussion in the footnotes
- Obtain evidence to determine whether the disclosures are adequate in light of required GAAP, e.g., by completing a disclosure checklist
- Consider alternative or enhanced disclosures that may be helpful to users

Evaluating the Accuracy of Management's Disclosure Assertion: The Role of Disclosure Checklists

Engagement teams use audit firm disclosure checklists to help ensure a quality audit so that auditors do not forget important disclosures. A **disclosure checklist** serves as a cue to guiding audit planning around management's assertions in various disclosures. These disclosure checklists are often industry-specific, e.g., disclosures for a bank (e.g., Wells Fargo) are very different from those of a retailer (e.g., Target). Disclosure checklists can also be specific to a certain set of financial reporting standards (e.g., U.S. GAAP versus IFRS).

In addition to aiding audit quality, disclosure checklists are a convenient documentation format for evidence that the auditor adequately evaluated management's assertions about the adequacy of its disclosures. Of course, there may be items that should be disclosed but that are not covered by the audit firm's checklist. The auditor, therefore, should not blindly follow a checklist, but use good audit judgment when there are unusual circumstances of which the users should be aware.

Why It Matters: An International Perspective   Related Party Disclosures at OAO Gazprom

This feature provides an example of related party disclosures in a client's footnotes and the problems that its auditor experienced in conducting an audit of that client.

OAO Gazprom produces natural gas and as of 2010 was the largest company in Russia. The company's 2010 International Financial Reporting Standards (IFRS)-based disclosures to the financial statements state the following with respect to related parties:

> "For the purpose of these consolidated financial statements, parties are considered to be related if one party has the ability to control the other party or exercise significant influence over the other party in making financial and operational decisions as defined in IAS 24 'Related Party Disclosures'. Related parties may enter into transactions which unrelated parties might not, and transactions between related parties may not be effected on the same terms, conditions, and amounts as transactions between unrelated parties."

The disclosures go on to state that:

> "The Government of the Russian Federation is the ultimate controlling party of OAO Gazprom and has a controlling interest (including both direct and indirect ownership) of over 50% in OAO Gazprom" and that "As a condition of privatization in 1992, the Government imposed an obligation on the Group to provide an uninterrupted supply of gas to customers in the Russian Federation at government controlled prices."

Of interest, however, is the relative lack of detail in terms of specific related parties or specific related party transactions that are contained in the notes to the financial statements. This is in contrast to related party disclosures at companies such as Ford Motor Company, which describe individual Ford family members, their relationships with the company, and the exact nature of their related party transactions with the company.

PwC found out just how difficult it can be to conduct an audit of a company in the Russian Federation, particularly because of the complex nature of related party transactions and high-level interrelationships between executives in companies operating in the Federation. Of particular importance, top members of management at OAO Gazprom have friends or relatives that transact in a related party context with the company. For example, in one transaction, Gazprom sold natural gas to a related company at $2 per cubic meter, and then the related company sold the gas to European customers for more than $40 per cubic meter. In doing so, the related company (and its management owners) essentially siphoned profits out of Gazprom and into their personal accounts. Gazprom entered into a very significant number of such transactions, but PwC did not require the company to disclose them in its audited financial statements.

Minority shareholders of Gazprom were very outspoken in their objections to these types of transactions and to PwC's audits of the company. Ultimately, the political pressure on PwC led to Gazprom putting the audit engagement up for bid. In addition, Hermitage Capital filed multiple lawsuits against PwC in 2002 related to the firm's audits of Gazprom. Those lawsuits were ultimately dismissed, and the company reinstated PwC as its auditor. PwC was still Gazprom's auditor through FYE 2014, so the firm appears to have weathered the political storm of the early 2000s. Since FYE 2015, the audit firm OOO FBK has been auditing Gazprom.

Note: This company is quite interesting and important because it is a global energy company that holds the world's largest natural gas reserves. If you are interested, follow the company at *http://www.gazprom.com/about/*

See the End of Chapter problem 14-43 for an application activity relating to subsequent stock price movements of OAO Gazprom.

Exhibit 14.2 contains an excerpt from an international GAAP disclosure checklist, with Panel A containing the General portion of the disclosure checklist, and Panel B containing the comparative information portion of the disclosure checklist. You will notice that the checklist provides a link to the relevant International Accounting Standard (IAS), a description of the disclosure, a visual box for the auditor to indicate whether the disclosure is made (or is not applicable), along with room for comments.

Exhibit 14.2
Excerpts from EY's International GAAP Disclosure Checklist

Panel A. General Disclosures

			Disclosure made			
			Yes	No	N/A	Comments

General

Identification and components of financial statements

1 *IAS 1.49*   Are the financial statements identified clearly (using an unambiguous title) and distinguished from other information in the same published document   ☐ ☐ ☐

2 *IAS 1.10*   Does the entity present a complete set of financial statements which comprises:

    a. A statement of financial position as at the end of the period   ☐ ☐ ☐

    b. A statement of profit or loss and other comprehensive income for the period   ☐ ☐ ☐

    c. A statement of changes in equity for the period   ☐ ☐ ☐

    d. A statement of cash flows for the period   ☐ ☐ ☐

    e. Notes, comprising significant accounting policies and other explanatory information   ☐ ☐ ☐

    f. Comparative information in respect of the preceding period as specified in IAS 1.38 and 38A   ☐ ☐ ☐

IAS 1.10A   An entity may present a single statement of profit or loss and other comprehensive income, with profit or loss and other comprehensive income presented in two sections. The sections shall be presented together, with the profit or loss section presented first followed directly by the other comprehensive income section.

IAS1.139P   *The Disclosure Initiative (Amendments to IAS 1)* was released in December 2014 and amended paragraphs 10, 31, 54, 55, 82A, 85,113–114, 117, 119 and 122, added paragraphs 30A, 55A and 85A-85B and deleted paragraphs 115 and 120. Entitles are not required to disclose the information required by paragraphs 28–30 of IAS 8 in relation to these amendments.

3 *IAS 1.51*   Does the entity prominently display the following at least once in the financial statements:

    a. The name of the reporting entity or other means of identification, and any change in that information from the end of the preceding reporting period   ☐ ☐ ☐

    b. Whether the financial statements cover the individual entity or a group of entities   ☐ ☐ ☐

    c. The date of the end of the reporting period or the period covered by the financial statements or notes   ☐ ☐ ☐

IAS 21.8   d. The presentation currency, as defined in IAS 21.8   ☐ ☐ ☐

    e. The level of rounding used in the presentation of amounts in the financial statements   ☐ ☐ ☐

Corporate information

4 *IAS 1.138*   If not disclosed elsewhere in information published with the financial statements, does the entity disclose the following:

    a. The domicile of the entity   ☐ ☐ ☐

    b. The legal form of the entity   ☐ ☐ ☐

    c. The entity's country of incorporation   ☐ ☐ ☐

    d. The address of the registered office (or principal place of business, if different from the registered office)   ☐ ☐ ☐

    e. The nature of the entity's operations and its principal activities   ☐ ☐ ☐

    f. The name of the parent   ☐ ☐ ☐

    g. The name of the ultimate parent of the group   ☐ ☐ ☐

    h. If the entity is a limited life entity, information regarding the length of its life   ☐ ☐ ☐

(Continues)

Exhibit 14.2 *Continued*

Panel B. Comparative Information Disclosures

Comparative information

13	*IAS 1.38*	Does the entity present comparative information for the previous period for all amounts reported in the current period's financial statements, unless an IFRS permits or requires otherwise	☐	☐	☐
14	*IAS 1.38*	Does the entity include comparative information for narrative and descriptive information, if it is relevant to an understanding of the current reporting period's financial statements	☐	☐	☐
15	*IAS 1.41*	If the presentation or classification of items in the financial statements is amended and comparative amounts are reclassified (unless the reclassification cannot be applied after making every reasonable effort to do so), does the entity disclose:			
		a. The nature of the reclassification	☐	☐	☐
		b. The amount of each item or class of items that is reclassified	☐	☐	☐
		c. The reason for the reclassification	☐	☐	☐
16	*IAS 1.42*	If the entity cannot reclassify comparative amounts after making every reasonable effort to do so, does the entity disclose:			
		a. The reason for not reclassifying the amounts	☐	☐	☐
		b. The nature of the adjustments that would have been made if the amounts were reclassified	☐	☐	☐
17	*IAS 1.38A*	Does the entity present, as a minimum, two statements of financial position, two statements of profit or loss and other comprehensive income, two separate statements of profit or loss (if presented), two statements of cash flows and two statements of changes in equity, and related notes	☐	☐	☐

IAS 1.38B | In some cases, narrative information provided in the financial statements for the preceding period(s) continues to be relevant in the current period.

For further details, see http://www.ey.com/Publication/vwLUAssets/CTools-DCL-September2016/$FILE/CTools-DCL -September2016.pdf

Why It Matters: An International Perspective

SEC Focuses on Disclosure Rules: Complaint against Keyuan Petrochemicals Related to Disclosure and Accounting Violations

This feature highlights that appropriate disclosures are important from both public policy and regulatory perspectives.

On February 28, 2013, the SEC charged Keyuan Petrochemicals and its former chief financial officer (CFO), Aichun Li, with violations of U.S. financial accounting and disclosure rules. The SEC complaint states that Keyuan failed to disclose related party transactions between the company and its chief executive officer (CEO) and controlling shareholders, entities controlled by or affiliated with these individuals, and entities controlled by Keyuan's management or their close family members.

The CFO's job was to ensure that Keyuan's financial statements complied with U.S. financial accounting and disclosure

rules. She discovered information indicating that the company was not identifying or reporting related party transactions relating to raw materials purchases, short-term financing arrangements, and loan guarantees. The company used an off-balance sheet cash account to pay for top management's cash bonuses, travel, and entertainment expenses, and gifts to Chinese government officials. Due to the use of the off-balance sheet account, there existed misstatements in the company's financial statements related to cash, receivables, construction-in-progress, interest income, other income, and general and administrative expenses. Despite knowledge of the problems, the CFO failed to take action to remedy them or to reveal them to the external audit firm or audit committee, despite the fact that those parties expressly questioned her about potential related party transactions.

As an example of the related party transactions, in the first 18 months of its operations, 17% to 24% of the company's sales were to a related company whose majority shareholder was the CEO's mother. In October 2011, Keyuan restated its financial statements. The company and the CFO ultimately were ordered to pay penalties for their actions in the amounts of $1 million and $25,000, respectively.

In December 2013, the SEC issued a report to Congress regarding disclosure rules for U.S. public companies. The SEC's Division of Corporate Finance is currently reviewing disclosure requirements and is actively reviewing financial disclosure requirements in Forms 10-K, 10-Q, and 8-K. In addition, on April 7, 2014, the FASB issued a Disclosure Framework project, the objective of which is to improve the effectiveness of disclosures in financial statement footnotes. As of mid-2017, the project is in process.

For further details, see the SEC's Litigation Release No. 22627, February 28, 2013 at https://www.sec.gov/litigation/litreleases/litrelarchive/litarchive2013.shtml

For Classroom Discussion

What Do You Think?

You should know that the auditor's report does **not** provide assurance over the statements that management makes in the Management Discussion and Analysis (MD&A) section of the annual report. Management's disclosures in the MD&A are considered *voluntary* disclosures, not mandatory disclosures such as those on the face of the financial statements or in the notes. Auditors routinely examine the MD&A to check that it does not contain information that is factually inaccurate or inconsistent with the audited portion of the financial statements and accompanying footnotes.

Do you think that users might assume that auditors **do** provide assurance over the statements that managers make in the MD&A? Do you think that auditors should provide such assurance?

Check Your Basic Knowledge

14-9 Management can provide disclosures on the face of the financial statements, or in the notes to the financial statements. (T/F)

14-10 OAO Gazprom is a natural gas producer in Russia; top management used their power to siphon profits out of Gazprom and into their own pockets. In its filings, the company did <u>not</u> disclose many specific details about its related party transactions. (T/F)

14-11 In completing the audit, the auditor should review the adequacy of the disclosures in the financial statements. When assessing the disclosures, the auditor should have reasonable assurance about which of the following?
   a. The disclosed events and transactions have occurred and pertain to the entity.
   b. All the disclosures that should have been included are included.

   c. The disclosures are understandable to users.
   d. All of the above.

14-12 Which of the following statements is <u>false</u>?
   a. Disclosure checklists are a convenient documentation format for evidence that the auditor adequately evaluated management's assertions about the adequacy of its disclosures.
   b. The auditor's report, and assurance therein, covers mandatory disclosures in the basic financial statements and the related notes, along with voluntary disclosures in the MD&A.
   c. When assessing the adequacy of disclosures, the auditor should have reasonable assurance that the disclosures are understandable to users.
   d. Disclosure checklists tend to be industry-specific.
   e. All of the above are false.

Noncompliance with Laws and Regulations

Management must be sure that its operations and financial reporting are conducted in accordance with laws and regulations. **Noncompliance** involves "acts of omission or commission by the entity, either intentional or unintentional, which are contrary to the prevailing laws or regulations" (AU-C 250). Auditors are responsible for obtaining reasonable assurance that the financial statements are free from material misstatements, including material misstatements relating to a client's compliance with laws and regulations. However, auditing standards recognize that there are inherent limitations in an auditor's ability to detect material misstatements relating to the client's compliance with laws and regulations. These limitations include:

- Laws and regulations often relate to operational issues within the client that do not necessarily relate to the financial statements, so the information systems relating to financial reporting may not capture noncompliance.
- Management may act to conceal noncompliance, or may override controls, or may intentionally misrepresent facts to the auditor.
- The legal implications of noncompliance are ultimately a matter for legal authorities to resolve, and are not a matter the auditor can resolve.

In reviewing for potential noncompliance, the auditor should first obtain an understanding of internal controls the client has implemented to achieve proper compliance with laws and regulations. If management does not demonstrate a commitment to internal control over noncompliance, then the auditor should expend additional effort reviewing for instances of noncompliance. Furthermore, if an auditor becomes aware of violations of law, the auditor should notify the audit committee about the violations, their circumstances, and the effect on the financial statements. The auditor should also consider whether risk assessments made prior to knowledge of identified violations are still appropriate. Second, the auditor should obtain the knowledge necessary to understand applicable laws and regulations relevant to the client's business, both nationally and internationally. Third, the auditor should search for indications of noncompliance, e.g., tips to whistleblower hotlines, and/or unusual payments to vendors in countries

---

Why It Matters

Compliance with the Foreign Corrupt Practices Act (FCPA) of 1977

This feature highlights an important law that many companies have failed to comply with.

The FCPA was written to respond to SEC investigations in the 1970s revealing that over 400 companies had made questionable or illegal payments of over $300 million to foreign officials, politicians, and political parties. The payments involved bribery of foreign officials to facilitate business operations in their respective foreign countries. The main provisions of the FCPA include:

- No U.S. person or company that has securities listed on U.S. markets may make a payment to a foreign official for the

purpose of obtaining or retaining business. This provision is commonly called the anti-bribery provision of the FCPA.

- Companies that have securities listed on U.S. markets must make and keep financial records that accurately and fairly reflect the transactions of the company and must design and maintain an adequate system of internal accounting controls.
- Certain payments to foreign officials are acceptable. These include grease payments, which are payments made to an official to expedite the performance of the duties that the official would already be bound to perform.

with high corruption indices. In 1995, Transparency International developed a **corruption perception index,** which is a ranking of countries according to the extent to which people believe corruption exists. Transparency International ranks about 200 countries on a scale from 0 (highly corrupt) to 100 (very clean).

Prompt for Critical Thinking #3

Before reading this text, had you heard of the Transparency International corruption perception index? Think critically about what you know about the political and economic structure of the following countries. In the spaces below: (1) rank the six countries from most corrupt to least corrupt just from what you know, and (2) guess what their ranking is on a scale from 0–100 on the corruption perception index from 0 (highly corrupt) to 100 (very clean):

Country (in alphabetical order)	Rank (1 = most to 6 = least corrupt among this list)	Estimated Corruption Perception Index (0 – 100)
Belgium		
Brazil		
New Zealand		
Somalia		
South Korea		
United States of America		

After ranking the countries, visit Transparency International and compare your answers and estimates against theirs: *https://www.transparency.org/news/feature/corruption_perceptions_index_2016#table*

What are your reactions to what you have learned? What rankings surprised you? How accurate were your rankings?

Triton Energy and Noncompliance with Laws and Regulations

Focus on Fraud

This feature describes a historically important case involving noncompliance with the Foreign Corrupt Practices Act (FCPA) of 1977.

Triton Energy engages in the exploration and production of crude oil and natural gas in many areas around the world. Triton has traditionally operated in relatively high-risk, politically unstable areas where larger and better-known producers do not operate. Top Triton Indonesia officials (President, CFO, Commercial Manager, and Controller) were investigated by the SEC for violations of the Foreign Corrupt Practices Act. These violations included:

- Improper payments were made to a middleman who used the funds to reduce Triton Indonesia's tax liability.
- Improper payments were made to a middleman who used the funds to ensure a favorable governmental audit.

- Improper payments were made to a middleman who used the funds to obtain corporate tax refunds from government officials.
- The recording of false journal entries by Triton Indonesia's Commercial Manager and Controller were made to cover up the improper payments. These improper payments and false journal entries were facilitated because Triton's CEO, Bill Lee, was an aggressive top manager who provided weak tone at the top in terms of his failure to encourage compliance with applicable laws and regulations, failure to discourage improper payments, and failure to implement internal controls to deter improper payments. Triton was ultimately fined $300,000 related to the scandal.

For further details, see the SEC's Securities Exchange Act of 1934 Release No. 38343 and Accounting and Auditing Enforcement Release No. 889, February 27, 1997.

What Do You Think?

For Classroom Discussion

The FCPA of 1977 was enacted a LONG time ago!

1. Do you think it is still relevant today? Why or why not?

2. Review the following SEC website:

https://www.sec.gov/spotlight/fcpa/fcpa-cases.shtml What are your impressions? What surprises you? What companies on this list are well-known? Focus on one of the enforcement actions (perhaps at the discretion of your instructor) and explain how the company violated the FCPA.

Check Your Basic Knowledge

14-13 Auditing standards recognize that there are inherent limitations in an auditor's ability to detect material misstatements relating to an organization's compliance with laws and regulations. (T/F)

14-14 The legal implications of a client's noncompliance with laws and regulations are ultimately a matter for the auditor to resolve before the auditor can issue the audit opinion. (T/F)

14-15 The auditor has responsibility regarding a client's noncompliance with laws and regulations. Management may try to hide acts involving noncompliance, which limits the auditor's ability to detect such acts. Which of the following are inherent limitations that affect the auditor's ability to detect acts involving noncompliance?

a. Laws and regulations often relate to operational issues within the entity that do not necessarily relate to the financial statements, so the information systems relating to financial reporting may not capture noncompliance.

b. Management may act to conceal noncompliance, or override controls, or intentionally misrepresent facts to the auditor.

c. The legal implications of noncompliance are ultimately a matter for legal authorities to resolve and are not a matter about which the auditor can resolve.

d. All of the above.

14-16 Which of the following is an important provision of the Foreign Corrupt Practices Act?

a. Auditors of clients operating in foreign countries must hire a joint auditor in the foreign country to provide assurance that laws and regulations have been followed by the client.

b. Auditors of clients operating in foreign countries must provide reasonable assurance that any inventory observations that occur in the foreign country are observed by at least some audit personnel from the U.S.; this requirement is in place because fraud often occurs in inventory accounts.

c. Companies that have securities listed on U.S. markets must make and keep financial records that accurately and fairly reflect the transactions of the company and must design and maintain an adequate system of internal accounting controls.

d. Companies that have securities listed on U.S. markets must adhere to the internal control requirements of both the U.S. and the applicable foreign country.

Review Analytical Procedures

The objective of review analytical procedures is to help the auditor form an overall conclusion about whether the financial statements are consistent with the auditor's understanding of the entity. The auditor's expectation when performing review analytical procedures will be less precise than if the auditor were performing substantive analytical procedures.

Review analytical procedures indicate whether certain relationships make sense in light of the knowledge obtained during the audit. Ratio analysis, common-size analysis, and analysis of the dollar and percentage changes in each income statement item over the previous year are useful for this purpose. The auditor should have accumulated sufficient appropriate evidence during the audit to explain any unusual changes, such as changes when none are expected, no changes when they are expected, or changes that are not of the expected size or direction. For example, if the client paid more attention to quality control and order processing during the current year, then sales returns and allowances should have decreased as a percentage of sales.

As another example, if a client increased its market share by substantially reducing prices for the last three months of the year and undertaking a massive advertising campaign, the auditor would expect a decrease in the gross profit margin. If these expected changes are not reflected in the accounting records, the audit documentation should contain adequate evidence, supplementing the explanations of management to corroborate those explanations. Otherwise, the auditor should investigate to determine the reason for the discrepancies in the data, as they could represent account balances that are misstated.

Ultimately, review analytical procedures should corroborate conclusions formed during the audit. If review analytical procedures identify a previously unrecognized risk of material misstatement, the auditor must go back, revise the original risk assessment, and conduct additional audit procedures to address the risk. The need for additional audit procedures is particularly relevant when management is unable to provide an explanation for the previously unrecognized risk identified through the analytical procedures.

See *Exhibit 14.3* for an example of the financial data and some relevant ratios for Koss Corporation, including concerns that seem relevant in terms of analytical review of the financial position of the company.

Exhibit 14.3

Identifying Risks at Koss Corporation Using Analytical Procedures

The fraud at Koss Corporation perpetrated by the company's CFO, Sue Sachdeva, occurred during the period 2005–2009. Following are the audited financial statements of Koss during that period (prior to restatement). Put yourself in the position of the auditor conducting review analytical procedures for the 2009 audit. After analyzing the financial results and ratios and using your knowledge of analytical review procedures, consider the following patterns in the data:

- Cash balances have declined to their lowest level since FYE 2004.
- Sales increased over the period, but have returned to about FYE 2004 levels.
- Cost of goods sold as a percentage of sales has risen sharply over the period, with a particularly significant increase from FYE 2008 to 2009.
- Relatedly, gross profit has decreased sharply over the period, with a particularly significant decrease from FYE 2008 to 2009.
- SG&A as a percentage of sales has risen sharply over the period, with a particularly significant increase from FYE 2008 to 2009.
- Net income as a percentage of sales has decreased sharply over the period, with a particularly significant decrease from FYE 2008 to 2009.

(Continues)

Exhibit 14.3 *Continued*

- Accounts receivable as a percentage of sales has remained relatively stable over the period, so there do not appear to be problems in billing or collections.
- Current liabilities as a percentage of sales has remained relatively stable over the period, so there do not appear to be problems in the purchasing cycle.

Account ($ millions)	FYE 2009	FYE 2008	FYE 2007	FYE 2006	FYE 2005	FYE 2004
Net sales	38,185	46,943	46,202	50,892	40,287	40,493
Cost of goods sold	24,917	29,152	28,285	31,095	25,217	24,531
Gross profit	13,267	17,792	17,917	19,796	15,070	15,962
SG&A	10,653	10,792	10,066	10,064	8,544	8,090
Net income	1,977	4,494	5,157	6,222	4,494	5,448
Cash	1,664	3,323	4,188	6,147	5,219	2,111
Accounts receivable	8,680	10,149	7,939	6,820	8,764	9,340
Inventory	9,763	9,374	9,924	10,522	7,596	7,315
Net PP&E	4,076	2,746	2,567	3,038	2,994	2,697
Current liabilities	3,619	5,587	4,130	9,149	6,034	3,480
Ratios:						
COGS/Sales	65%	62%	61%	61%	63%	61%
Gross profit %	35%	38%	39%	39%	37%	39%
SG&A/Sales	28%	23%	22%	20%	21%	20%
Net income/Sales	5%	10%	11%	12%	11%	13%
Accts. receivable/Sales	23%	22%	17%	13%	22%	23%
Inventory/Sales	26%	20%	21%	21%	19%	18%
Current liability/Sales	9%	12%	9%	18%	15%	9%

Taken together, these financial data and ratios signal a very significant shift in performance from FYE 2008 to 2009. We assume that the auditor did not include an expectation for this type of shift. Concerns related to the analytical procedures that the auditor should investigate include:

- Why is cash showing such a decline? What are controls over cash?
- Are costs being inappropriately allocated to cost of goods sold or SG&A? Who has oversight over allocations and journal entries to these accounts? Is that individual adequately supervised?
- Gross margins are usually relatively stable; what is management's explanation for the significant change?
- While sales seem to be slowing, perhaps due to the recession, profitability has declined even more substantially. What is the explanation for this unexpected relationship?

Of course, hindsight makes these trends appear consistent with the fraud that was ultimately discovered. It is unclear why the audit team and engagement partner did not exercise professional skepticism to better understand these puzzling analytics.

Ultimately, the fraud was exposed when American Express employees recognized that Sachdeva was paying her credit card bills with large wire transfers from a Koss bank account. They alerted Koss CEO, Michael Koss, and at that point, the FBI confronted Sachdeva. Therefore, no individual charged with governance at Koss appears to have ever seriously challenged the declining and unusual financial results at Koss. In fact, because of situations like this, the PCAOB issued *Staff Audit Practice Alert No. 10*: "Maintaining and Applying Professional Skepticism in Audits" on December 4, 2012, urging auditors to be vigilant in exercising appropriate professional skepticism.

14-17 Review analytics should corroborate conclusions formed during the audit, thereby enabling the auditor to draw conclusions upon which to base the audit opinion. (T/F)

14-18 The auditor's expectations when performing review analytical review can be less precise than those for substantive analytics. (T/F)

14-19 Which of the following statements concerning review analytical procedures is <u>false</u>?

    a. Review analytical procedures help auditors assess the overall presentation of the financial statements.

    b. The auditor's expectations in review analytical procedures should be more precise than those for substantive analytics.

    c. Auditing standards require the use of review analytical procedures to assist in identifying ending account relationships that are unusual.

    d. Ratio analysis, common-size analysis, and analysis of the dollar and percentage changes in each income statement item over the previous year are useful for performing review analytical procedures.

14-20 The analytical procedures of the financial statements of Koss Corporation that are depicted in *Exhibit 14.3* reveal which of the following indicators of the fraud?

    a. Cash balances had declined to their lowest level since FYE 2004.

    b. Cost of goods sold as a percentage of sales had risen sharply over the period, with a particularly significant increase from FYE 2008 to 2009.

    c. Net income as a percentage of sales had decreased sharply over the period, with a particularly significant decrease from FYE 2008 to 2009.

    d. All of the above.

    e. Two of the above (a–c).

The Going-Concern Assumption

Business failures result from a variety of causes, including inadequate financing, cash-flow problems, poor management, product obsolescence, natural disasters, loss of a major customer or supplier, and competition. Investors and creditors become upset when a business fails, particularly when it happens shortly after the auditor has issued an unqualified opinion indicating that the financial statements are fairly stated. However, an audit opinion is not a guarantee that the business is a going concern; rather auditors issue an opinion based on a **going-concern assumption**. As part of this assumption, auditors are required to evaluate the likelihood of each client continuing as a going concern for a **reasonable period of time**. *Exhibit 14.4* highlights the process that the auditor follows in making a going-concern assessment.

The auditor's assessment of the going-concern assumption is based on information obtained from typical audit procedures performed to test management assertions. The auditor does not need to perform separate procedures, unless the auditor believes that there is substantial doubt about the client's ability to continue as a going concern.

If there is substantial doubt about the ability of the client to remain a going concern, the auditor identifies and assesses management's plans to overcome the problems. If, after reviewing management's plans, the auditor concludes that substantial doubt about the entity's ability to continue as a going concern has been alleviated, the auditor considers the disclosure of the conditions or events that initially caused the auditor to believe there was substantial doubt. The auditor should consider the possible effects of such conditions or events, and any mitigating factors, including management's plans. Alternatively, if the auditor concludes

Exhibit 14.4
Going-Concern Process

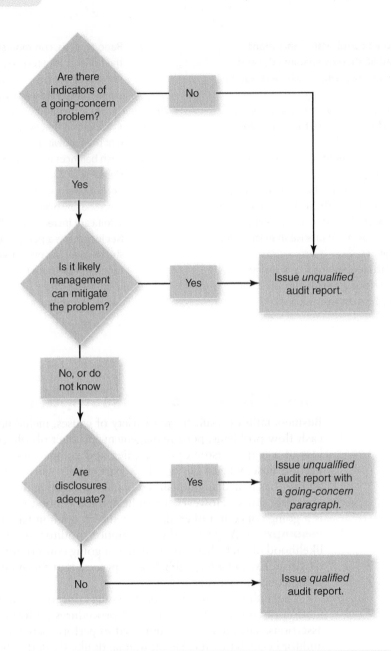

that substantial doubt about the entity's ability to continue as a going concern for a reasonable period of time remains, the auditor should modify the audit report to include an emphasis-of-matter paragraph that reflects that conclusion (see discussion on this issue in *Chapter 15*).

Management often resists a going-concern modification, making the argument that such a qualification will cause investors, lenders, and customers to lose faith in the business and thus cause it to fail. Auditors also may be reluctant to issue a going-concern audit opinion because it can be a self-fulfilling prophecy that the company will go bankrupt. In other words, if an audit firm issues a report stating that the going-concern assumption is not valid, lenders and customers may become worried, and stop lending money or doing business with the company, thereby hastening its demise. In addition, auditors may be reluctant to issue a going-concern opinion because it is simply very difficult to know beforehand whether a financially distressed client will actually cease operations or will somehow pull itself away from that outcome.

Indicators of Potential Going-Concern Problems

Auditors must carefully analyze all the factors that indicate a going-concern problem and determine if management has a viable plan to address the problems. Potential indicators of going-concern problems include:

- Negative trends, such as recurring losses, working-capital deficiencies, negative cash flows from operating activities, and adverse key financial ratios
- Internal matters, such as loss of key personnel, employee strikes, outdated facilities and products, and uneconomic long-term commitments
- External matters, such as new legislation, pending litigation, loss of a key franchise or patent, loss of a principal customer or supplier, and uninsured or underinsured casualty loss
- Other miscellaneous matters, such as default on a loan, inability to pay dividends, restructuring of debt, violation of laws and regulations, and inability to buy from suppliers on credit
- Significant changes in the competitive market and the competitiveness of the client's products

Bankruptcy Prediction Models Audit firms may use bankruptcy prediction models in analyzing whether the going-concern assumption is valid for a particular client. Numerous studies have shown that certain combinations of ratios can indicate the likelihood of bankruptcy. Two **Altman Z-scores**—a five-ratio model for publicly owned manufacturing companies and a four-ratio model for privately owned non-manufacturing companies—are available for auditor use, with newer models available representing variations of these original models.[1]

Z-scores calculations are shown in *Exhibit 14.5*. Z-scores falling below 1.81 in the five-ratio model or below 1.1 in the four-ratio model indicate high potential for bankruptcy. Scores above 2.99 in the five-ratio model or above 2.6 in the

Exhibit 14.5
Altman Z-Score Models

Weight	Z-Score for Publicly Owned Manufacturing Companies — Ratio	Weight	Z-Score for Private Non-Manufacturing Companies — Ratio
1.2 ×	Working capital to total assets	6.56 ×	Working capital to total assets
+ 1.4 ×	Retained earnings to total assets	+ 3.26 ×	Retained earnings to total assets
3.3 ×	Return on total assets	+ 6.72 ×	Earnings before interest and taxes to total assets
+ 0.99 ×	Sales to total assets		
+ 0.6 ×	Market value of equity to total debt	+ 1.05 ×	Net worth to total liabilities
	Interpretation of Z-Score		
< 1.81	High potential for bankruptcy	< 1.1	High potential for bankruptcy
> 2.99	Little potential for bankruptcy	> 2.6	Little potential for bankruptcy

four-ratio model indicate very little potential for bankruptcy. For example, using the four-ratio model, a company that has a strong working-capital position, has accumulated significant retained earnings, and is profitable would score above the 2.6 threshold and be unlikely to have a going-concern problem. Although a low Z-score (or a similar score using a different bankruptcy prediction model) does not indicate that the company will fail, it does provide evidence that the going-concern assumption may not be valid.

Mitigating Factors

If the auditor concludes that the going-concern assumption may not be valid for a client, the auditor should assess management's plans to overcome this problem. Management may plan to sell nonessential assets, borrow money or restructure existing debt, reduce or delay unnecessary expenditures, and/or increase owner investments. The auditor should identify those factors that are most likely to resolve the problem and gather independent evidence to determine the likely success of such plans. For example, if financial projections are an integral part of the solution, the auditor should ask management to provide that information and the underlying assumptions. The auditor should then consider, and independently test, the adequacy of support for the major assumptions. As another example, if management indicates that their major financial institution is willing to renegotiate the terms of an outstanding loan to provide more favorable terms, the auditor should consider this when evaluating management's recovery plans. Of course, the auditor should confirm the new terms with the bank, through obtaining corroborating evidence directly from the bank rather than relying on management's verbal representations. The auditor should also evaluate the reasonableness of other assumptions made by management, including:

- Management's assumption about increasing prices or market share should be analyzed in relation to current industry developments.
- Management's assumptions about cost savings related to a reduction in workforce should be recomputed and evaluated to determine if there are hidden costs (such as pension obligations) that were overlooked by management.
- Management's assumptions about selling off assets—either a division or specifically identified assets—should be evaluated in relation to current market prices.

After considering these factors, the auditor will assess whether management can mitigate the going-concern problem, and audit reporting decisions will follow based upon that assessment and possible disclosures that may be necessary.

AICPA Guidance on Going Concern Issues

The AICPA issued an updated standard on going-concern, SAS No. 132, *The Auditor's Consideration of an Entity's Ability to Continue as a Going Concern,* which is effective for organizations whose year-end is on or after December 15, 2017.

The AICPA's updated standard includes the following subtle clarifications and enhancements that the auditor should consider. SAS No. 132:

- Clarifies that the auditor is supposed to make separate determinations regarding: (1) the use of the going-concern basis of accounting, when relevant, in the preparation of the financial statements, and (2) based on the audit evidence obtained whether substantial doubt exists about an entity's ability to continue as a going concern for a reasonable period of time.
- Requires that when the entity's management asserts that they will be able to remain a going concern because they have received promises of financial support by third parties or the entity's owner-manager (e.g., the owner-manager has financed a loan to which the entity has access), the auditor

cannot simply accept such an assertion at face value. Rather, the auditor must obtain the following sufficient appropriate audit evidence:

- o Written evidence of such intent directly from the supporting parties who are planning to provide necessary financial support
- o Convincing evidence that the supporting parties have the ability to provide the necessary financial support; this can include written evidence from management of the commitment of necessary financial support (a **support letter**), or confirmation directly with the supporting parties, e.g., if management only has oral evidence of financial support.

- Makes specific reference to the possibility that the auditor may be required to evaluate the entity's ability to continue as a going concern as the auditor prepares interim financial information, i.e., not just year-end financial reporting. Specifically, the standard requires that the auditor perform procedures relating to:
  - o Whether the going-concern basis of accounting is appropriate
  - o Management's evaluation of the events raising substantial doubt about the entity's ability to remain a going concern
  - o Management's plans to mitigate the events causing difficulty
  - o Evaluating management's related disclosures in the interim financial information, e.g., quarterly reports.

If you would like to learn more about the specfici details, you can read the standard at *http://www.aicpa.org/Research/Standards/AuditAttest/DownloadableDocuments /SAS_132.pdf*

The PCAOB has not responded in terms of definitive action to for a standards updates in this area. Rather, the Standard-Setting Update of the Office of the Chief Auditor (September 30, 2017) notes that issues relating to going concern are the subject of current outreach, monitoring, and research. For further details, you may read the Update at *https://pcaobus.org/Standards/Documents/Q42017-standard -setting-update.pdf*

FASB Guidance on Going-Concern Disclosures: Sears and Deloitte Reach Differing Conclusions

Why It Matters

This feature provides an interesting example of a company and its auditor reaching different decisions on whether the company is a going concern.

The FASB's Accounting Standards Update "Presentation of Financial Statements—Going Concern (Subtopic 205-40)" directs that substantial doubt about an entity's ability to continue as a going concern exists when it is probable that the entity will be unable to meet its obligations as they become due within one year after the date that the financial statements are issued. You will note that this definition differs somewhat from the definition used by auditors.

The evaluation requires management to perform two steps. Management must first evaluate whether there are conditions and events that raise substantial doubt about the entity's ability to continue as a going concern (step 1). If management concludes that substantial doubt exists, management also is required to consider whether its plans alleviate that doubt (step 2). Disclosures in the notes to the financial statements are required if management

concludes that substantial doubt exists or that its plans alleviate substantial doubt that was raised.

Footnote 1 to Sears' FYE 2016 financial statements, under a section captioned "Uses and Sources of Liquidity," discusses a series of actions that management has undertaken to mitigate doubt about the entity's ability to continue as a going concern, including financing arrangements, restructuring programs, and the sale of the Craftsman brand.

For further details, see https://www.sec.gov/Archives/edgar /data/1310067/000131006717000005/shld201610k.htm#s1EA3666 A1332564793B6D04734C91678

What has attracted the most attention in the media is that Sears' auditors reached a different conclusion; they did **not** issue an audit report alerting users to concerns about the company's going-concern issues. Deloitte's audit opinion is as follows:

"In our opinion, the consolidated financial statements referred to above present fairly, in all material respects, the financial position of Sears Holdings Corporation and subsidiaries as of January 28, 2017, and January 30, 2016, and the results of their operations and their cash flows for each of the three fiscal years in the period ended January 28, 2017, in conformity with accounting principles generally accepted in the United States of America. Also, in our opinion, such financial statement schedule, when considered in relation to the basic consolidated financial statements taken as a whole, present fairly, in all material respects, the information set forth therein. Also, in our opinion, the Company maintained, in all material respects, effective internal control over financial reporting as of January 28, 2017, based on the criteria established in Internal

Control - Integrated Framework (2013) issued by the Committee of Sponsoring Organizations of the Treadway Commission."

Why do company management and its auditors reach different conclusions? It seems that management deems it appropriate to disclose the risk, while the auditor deems that mitigating actions that management plans will be successful in mitigating that risk. In any case, the disclosures by management about going-concern risks are informative. Because of the going-concern disclosure, the company's shares closed down more than 12 %, falling below $8, after Sears management expressed doubt about its future as a retailer.

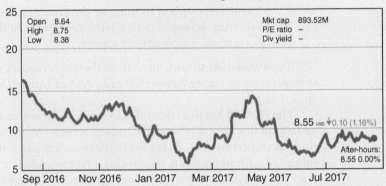

Sears Holdings Corp
NASDAQ: SHLD – 21 Aug., 4:14 pm EDT

Open 8.64	Mkt cap 893.52M
High 8.75	P/E ratio –
Low 8.38	Div yield –

8.55 USD ↓0.10 (1.16%)

After-hours: 8.55 0.00%

Source: *https://www.google.co.in/search?rlz=1C1WZPD_enIN744IN744&q=NASDAQ: SHLD&stick=H4sIAAAAAAAAAONgecRoyi3w8sc9YSmdSWtOXmNU4-IKzsgvd80rySyp FJLgYoOy-KR4uLj0c_UNzKtysowqeABzk0DZOgAAAA&sa=X&ved=0ahUKEwj6yNyaq9TWA hXLQo8KHY75DflQsRUIxAEwGg&biw=1280&bih=617*

Other examples of management applying ASC 205-40 and auditors reacting in a variety of ways include:

ImmunoGen, Inc. *(https://www.sec.gov/Archives/edgar /data/855654/000155837017001331/imgn-20161231x10k.htm)*

Omeros Corporation *(https://www.sec.gov/Archives /edgar/data/1285819/000128581917000004/omer-20161231x 10k.htm), and*

Hooper Holmes *(https://www.sec.gov/Archives/edgar /data/741815/000074181517000004/hh1231201610-k.htm)*

Prompt for Critical Thinking #4   It's Your Turn!

Research the comments that the auditors of ImmunoGen, Inc., Omeros Corporation, and Hooper Holmes make about the going-concern disclosures of their respective clients.

Document the disclosures that each of the auditors makes with respect to going-concern issues at their clients:

1. ImmunoGen, Inc.: Ernst & Young _____

2. Omeros Corporation: Ernst & Young _____

3. Hooper Holmes: KPMG _____

14-21 The going-concern evaluation is based on information obtained from typical audit procedures performed to test management's assertions; no separate procedures are required, unless the auditor believes that there is substantial doubt about the client's ability to continue as a going concern.   (T/F)

14-22 Auditors should <u>not</u> issue a going-concern audit opinion if it would be a self-fulfilling prophecy that the company will, indeed, go bankrupt.   (T/F)

14-23 In evaluating whether the client is a going concern, which of the following questions should the auditor ask?
   a. Are there indicators of going-concern problems?
   b. Is it likely that management can mitigate any identified going-concern problems?

   c. Are disclosures about the going-concern problems adequate?
   d. All of the above.

14-24 The Altman Z-Score is a model used to help assess the likelihood that a company will go bankrupt. Which of the following ratios is included in the model?
   a. Working capital to total assets.
   b. Working capital to total sales.
   c. Sales to total debt.
   d. Sales to total accounts receivable.

Subsequent Events

Auditors have responsibility for some events occurring after the client's balance sheet date. The timeline in *Exhibit 14.6* illustrates the relevant time periods. Every audit includes procedures to review for subsequent events and transactions that occur in the period between the balance sheet date and the audit report date (Period A). The auditor has no responsibilities to continue obtaining audit evidence after the audit report date: Period B and Period C. However, the auditor may become aware of relevant information during Period B and Period C and will have to assess appropriate actions to take.

Review of Subsequent Events (Period A)

Two types of events occurring in Period A in *Exhibit 14.6* have been identified as subsequent events that may require dollar adjustments to the financial statements and/or disclosure: Type I subsequent events and Type II subsequent events. **Subsequent events** are events occurring between the date of the financial statements and the date of the auditor's report. A **subsequent events review**

Exhibit 14.6

Subsequent Periods

is the auditor's review of events occurring in the period between the balance sheet date and the audit report date to determine their possible effect on the financial statements.

Some of the procedures discussed in previous chapters relate to subsequent events, such as cutoff tests, review of subsequent collections of receivables, and the search for unrecorded liabilities. Additional procedures related to subsequent events include:

- Read the minutes of the meetings of the board of directors, stockholders, and other authoritative groups. The auditor should obtain written assurance that minutes of all such meetings, through the audit report date, have been made available. This can be included in the management representation letter described earlier in this chapter.
- Read interim financial statements and compare them to the audited financial statements, noting and investigating significant changes.
- Inquire of management concerning:
  o Any significant changes noted in the interim statements
  o The existence of significant contingent liabilities or commitments at the balance sheet date or date of inquiry, which should be near the audit report date
  o Any significant changes in working capital, long-term debt, or owners' equity
  o The status of items for which tentative conclusions were drawn earlier in the audit
  o Any unusual adjustments made to the accounting records after the balance sheet date

Type I Subsequent Events   **Type I subsequent events** provide evidence about conditions that existed at the balance sheet date. The financial statement numbers should be adjusted to reflect these events. Footnote disclosure may also be necessary to provide additional information. The following are examples of Type I subsequent events:

- A major customer files for bankruptcy during the subsequent period because of a deteriorating financial condition, which the client and auditor were unaware of until learning about the bankruptcy filing. The auditor should consider this information in establishing an appropriate amount for the allowance for doubtful accounts and in asking the client to make an adjustment if the allowance is not sufficient to cover this potential loss.
- The client settles a lawsuit for a different amount than was accrued.
- The client should disclose a stock dividend or split that takes place during the subsequent period. In addition, the client should adjust earnings-per-share figures to show the retroactive effect of the stock dividend or split.
- A sale of inventory below carrying value provides evidence that the net realizable value was less than cost at year-end.
- Information becomes available that provides evidence about the valuation of an estimate or reserve that had been accrued at year-end.

Type II Subsequent Events   **Type II subsequent events** indicate conditions that did not exist at the balance sheet date, but that may require disclosure. The events that the auditor should consider for disclosure are financial in nature and material. The following are examples of Type II subsequent events:

- An uninsured casualty loss that occurred after the balance sheet date causes a customer's bankruptcy during the subsequent period. Because the inability of the customer to pay did not exist as of the balance sheet date, the allowance for doubtful accounts should not be adjusted, but the information should be disclosed.

- A customer initiates a significant lawsuit relating to an incident that occurred after the balance sheet date.
- Because of a natural disaster such as fire, earthquake, or flood, a company loses a major facility after the balance sheet date.
- The client makes a major decision during the subsequent period, such as to merge, discontinue a line of business, or issue new securities.
- A material change occurs in the value of investment securities.

The client should not adjust the financial statement account balances, but should consider the possibility of disclosure.

Dual Dating (Period B)

When the auditor becomes aware of an event that occurs after the audit report date, but before the **report release date** (Period B in *Exhibit 14.6*), and the event is disclosed in the footnotes, the auditor has two options for dating the audit report:

1. Use the date of this event as the date of the audit report.
2. Dual-date the report, using the dates of the original audit report and the date of the event, to disclose the work done only on that event after the original audit report date.

As an example, consider a situation in which the original audit report date is February 27, 2019, and a fire destroyed the client's main manufacturing plant and warehouse on March 2, 2019. The client discloses this event in Note 14 to the financial statements. The audit report release date was March 5, 2019. The auditor may date the report March 2, 2019, or dual-date it as "February 27, 2019, except for Note 14, as to which the date is March 2, 2019."

The auditor assumes less responsibility by dual-dating the report. The only event occurring after the original audit report date for which the auditor is taking responsibility is disclosed in Note 14. If the report were dated March 2, 2019, the auditor would be taking responsibility for all events occurring during Period B. In that case, the auditor should perform audit procedures to identify other significant subsequent events that occurred between February 27 and March 2.

Subsequently Discovered Facts That Become Known to the Auditor after the Report Release Date (Period C)

Facts may come to the auditor's attention after the report release date (Period C in *Exhibit 14.6*) that may have affected the financial statements and auditor's report, if the auditor had known the facts at the report release date. Such facts may come to the auditor's attention through reading news reports, performing another service for the client or other business contacts, or performing a subsequent audit. If the auditor had known such facts at the report date, and therefore would have investigated those facts during the audit, the auditor should determine:

- The reliability of the new information
- Whether the development or event had occurred by the report date, as issuance of revised financial statements and an audit report is not required when the development or event occurs after the report date
- Whether users are likely to still be relying on the financial statements
- Whether the audit report would have been affected had the facts been known to the auditor at the report date

If the auditor decides that steps should be taken to prevent further reliance on the financial statements and audit report, the client is advised to make appropriate and timely disclosure of these new facts. The key action is to notify users as soon as possible so they do not continue to rely on information that is now incorrect. The appropriate action depends on the circumstances:

- If the revised financial statements and audit report can be quickly prepared and distributed, the reasons for the revision should be described in a footnote and referred to in the auditor's report.
- Revision and explanation can be made in the subsequent-period audited financial statements if their distribution is imminent.
- If it will take an extended amount of time to develop revised financial statements, the client should immediately notify the users that they should no longer rely on the previously distributed financial statements and auditor's report, and that revised statements and report will be issued as soon as possible.

The auditor should make sure the client takes the appropriate action. If the client will not cooperate, the auditor should notify:

- the client and any regulatory agency having jurisdiction over it, such as the SEC, that the audit report should no longer be associated with the client's financial statements.
- users known to the auditor that the users should no longer rely on the audit report. Auditors typically do not know all the users who receive the report. Therefore, the appropriate regulatory agency should be requested to take whatever steps are needed to disclose this situation.

Check Your Basic Knowledge

14-25 Type I subsequent events provide evidence about conditions that existed at the balance sheet date, while Type II subsequent events provide evidence about conditions that did <u>not</u> exist at the balance sheet date, but that may require disclosure. (T/F)

14-26 An example of a Type I subsequent event would be when a significant lawsuit is initiated relating to an incident that occurred after the balance sheet date. (T/F)

14-27 Which of the following is an example of a Type II subsequent event?
a. The client settles a lawsuit for a different amount than was accrued at the balance sheet date.
b. A sale of inventory below carrying value provides evidence that the net realizable value was less than cost at year-end.
c. Information becomes available that provides evidence about the valuation of an estimate or reserve that had been accrued at year-end.
d. None of the above.

14-28 After the report release date, the auditor may become aware of facts that may have affected the financial statements and auditor's report, had the auditor known the facts at the time of issuance. With regard to this situation, which of the following statements is <u>true</u>?
a. Because such facts become known after the report release date, the auditor cannot reasonably be held accountable for these issues; no action is required on the part of the auditor.
b. If the auditor decides that steps should be taken to prevent further reliance on the financial statements and audit report, the client is advised to make appropriate and timely disclosure of these new facts.
c. If such facts would have been investigated had they been known at the report date, the auditor should determine whether engagement personnel are competent and qualified to perform audits; action is required on the part of the auditor to assess whether engagement personnel should be retained to work on the engagement in the subsequent year.
d. If the auditor decides that steps should be taken to prevent further reliance on the financial statements and audit report, the auditor should notify the audit committee immediately; no action beyond this is required on the part of the auditor because of confidentiality concerns.

LO 2

Distinguish between a management representation letter and a management letter.

Management Representation Letter versus a Management Letter

Management Representation Letter

Auditors should obtain a **management representation letter** at the end of each audit. The letter is not a substitute for audit procedures performed during the audit. Rather, the purposes of the letter include:

- Reminding management of its responsibility for the financial statements
- Confirming oral responses obtained by the auditor earlier in the audit and the continuing appropriateness of those responses
- Reducing the possibility of misunderstanding concerning the matters that are the subject of the representations

Exhibit 14.7 contains a management representation letter example from AU-C 580. The letter is prepared on the client's letterhead, addressed to the auditor, and signed by the CEO and the CFO. The auditor usually prepares the letter for the client to read and sign. The contents depend on the circumstances of the audit and the nature and basis of presentation of the financial statements. It may be limited to matters considered material to the financial statements and should include representations about known fraud involving management or employees. If management refuses to sign the representation letter, it means that they are not willing to stand by their verbal representations when asked to do so in writing; in short, it would imply that management was being untruthful in representations.

Exhibit 14.7

Management Representation Letter Example from AU-C 580 "Management Representations"

(Entity Letterhead)

(To Auditor) (Date)

This representation letter is provided in connection with your audit of the financial statements of ABC Company, which comprise the balance sheet as of December 31, 20XX, and the related statements of income, changes in stockholders' equity, and cash flows for the year then ended, and the related notes to the financial statements, for the purpose of expressing an opinion on whether the financial statements are presented fairly, in all material respects, in accordance with accounting principles generally accepted in the United States (U.S. GAAP).

Certain representations in this letter are described as being limited to matters that are material. Items are considered material, regardless of size, if they involve an omission or misstatement of accounting information that, in the light of surrounding circumstances, makes it probable that the judgment of a reasonable person relying on the information would be changed or influenced by the omission or misstatement.

Except where otherwise stated below, immaterial matters less than $[*insert amount*] collectively are not considered to be exceptions that require disclosure for the purpose of the following representations. This amount is not necessarily indicative of amounts that would require adjustment to or disclosure in the financial statements.

(Continues)

Exhibit 14.7 *Continued*

We confirm that to the best of our knowledge and belief, having made such inquiries as we considered necessary for the purpose of appropriately informing ourselves [as of (date of auditor's report),]:

Financial Statements

- We have fulfilled our responsibilities, as set out in the terms of the audit engagement dated [*insert date*], for the preparation and fair presentation of the financial statements in accordance with U.S. GAAP.
- We acknowledge our responsibility for the design, implementation, and maintenance of internal control relevant to the preparation and fair presentation of financial statements that are free from material misstatement, whether due to fraud or error.
- We acknowledge our responsibility for the design, implementation, and maintenance of internal control to prevent and detect fraud.
- Significant assumptions used by us in making accounting estimates, including those measured at fair value, are reasonable.
- Related party relationships and transactions have been appropriately accounted for and disclosed in accordance with the requirements of U.S. GAAP.
- All events subsequent to the date of the financial statements and for which U.S. GAAP requires adjustment or disclosure have been adjusted or disclosed.
- The effects of uncorrected misstatements are immaterial, both individually and in the aggregate, to the financial statements as a whole. A list of the uncorrected misstatements is attached to the representation letter.
- The effects of all known actual or possible litigation and claims have been accounted for and disclosed in accordance with U.S. GAAP.

Information Provided

We have provided you with:

- Access to all information, of which we are aware that is relevant to the preparation and fair presentation of the financial statements such as records, documentation and other matters;
- Additional information that you have requested from us for the purpose of the audit; and
- Unrestricted access to persons within the entity from whom you determined it necessary to obtain audit evidence.
- All transactions have been recorded in the accounting records and are reflected in the financial statements.
- We have disclosed to you the results of our assessment of the risk that the financial statements may be materially misstated as a result of fraud.
- We have [*no knowledge of any*][*disclosed to you all information that we are aware of regarding*] fraud or suspected fraud that affects the entity and involves:
  - Management;
  - Employees who have significant roles in internal control; or
  - Others when the fraud could have a material effect on the financial statements
- We have [*no knowledge of any*][*disclosed to you all information that we are aware of regarding*] allegations of fraud, or suspected fraud, affecting the entity's financial statements communicated by employees, former employees, analysts, regulators or others.
- We have disclosed to you all known instances of noncompliance or suspected noncompliance with laws and regulations whose effects should be considered when preparing financial statements.
- We [*have disclosed to you all known actual or possible*][*are not aware of any pending or threatened*] litigation and claims whose effects should be considered when preparing the financial statements [*and we have not consulted legal counsel concerning litigation or claims*]
- We have disclosed to you the identity of the entity's related parties and all the related party relationships and transactions of which we are aware.

[*Name of Chief Executive Officer and Title*]

[*Name of Chief Financial Officer and Title*]

Management's refusal to sign the management representation letter is a scope limitation sufficient to preclude the auditor from issuing an unqualified opinion (see discussion on this issue in *Chapter 15*).

Management Letter

Throughout an audit, auditors often notice opportunities for recommendations to management. The auditor generally reports these observations in a **management letter**. Such a letter is different from a management representation letter. The management letter is not required; the auditor uses it to make significant operational or control recommendations to the client. The letter helps to provide management comfort that the auditor has done a quality job and that the auditor knows and understands the client's business. Many audit firms consider management's inattention to addressing comments in the letter to be an important risk factor in subsequent-year audits. See *Exhibit 14.8* for an example of the contents and structure of a typical management letter.

Exhibit 14.8
An Example Management Letter to a College Foundation

Below, we provide an example management letter from the audit firm of Johnstone & Gramling LLP related to the June 30, 2018, audit of the Bucky Badger College Foundation. You should note the following features of the letter:

- It contains the auditor's observations and recommendations to management.
- It contains management's response.

It addresses the issue of whether/how management responded to the management letter related to the prior year's audit.

Bucky Badger College Foundation

Addendum A

Financial System Reporting

Observation

Currently, the financial reporting system used by the college and the foundation produces various reports that must be printed and manually reclassified to properly report amounts in the financial statements. Efficiencies could be gained by accounting personnel if the financial reporting system were updated.

Recommendation

We recommend that management work with Information Technology at the college to develop an updated financial reporting system.

Management's Response

We agree with the recommendation. The current system will be updated, and adequate funds are available to accomplish the update.

Allowance for Doubtful Accounts

Observation

Currently the foundation reviews the pledge accounts receivables from promised gifts by donors to determine the appropriateness of the allowance for doubtful accounts. This process has produced reasonable estimates in the past. The foundation is beginning a new capital campaign to donors, which should result in increased pledges over the next several years. These pledges and associated receivables should be carefully and separately tracked from those amounts arising from prior capital campaigns.

(Continues)

Exhibit 14.8 *Continued*

Recommendation

We recommend that management develop a process to estimate and track the collectability of campaign pledge receivables from the new campaign. Management should also allocate sufficient staffing resources to do so.

Management's Response

We agree with the recommendation. A multipledge campaign evaluation process will be developed and implemented for future financial reporting.

Disposition of Prior-Year Comments

In our management letter for the year ended June 30, 2017, we made several comments and recommendations intended to improve the Foundation's internal controls. During our current-year audit, we reviewed these comments to determine if the recommendations were implemented.

Pledge Receivable

Observation

During our audit, it became apparent that the Foundation recorded as a pledge receivable the death benefit of an insurance policy in which it was named the beneficiary. However, accounting rules state that it does not meet the criteria to be recorded as a pledge receivable because the Foundation was only a named beneficiary.

Recommendation

We recommend that management review similar insurance policies to determine if the accounting is proper for these accounts.

Management's Response

We agree with the recommendation. We have initiated an internal review process to track and properly record pledge receivables.

Investment Income

Observation

During our audit, it came to our attention that unrealized gains and losses are allocated to individual fund balances yearly rather than semi-annually, resulting in potential inaccuracies during the year.

Recommendation

We recommend that unrealized gains and losses be posted to individual fund balances on a semi-annual basis, or quarterly if possible.

Management's Response

We agree with the recommendation. Unrealized gains or losses will be posted for each fund on a semi-annual basis beginning with the period ending December 31, 2018.

In Summary

The comments relating to the prior year's audit have been adequately addressed.

14-29 The management letter confirms management responses obtained by the auditor earlier in the audit and the continuing appropriateness of those responses.   (T/F)

14-30 The management letter is not required, but auditors use it to make significant operational or control recommendations to the client.   (T/F)

14-31 In completing the audit, the auditor communicates with management via the management letter. Which of the following statements is <u>false</u> about management letters?

   a. The management letter is used to make significant operational or control recommendations to management.

   b. Many audit firms consider management's inattention to addressing comments in the letter to be an important risk factor in subsequent-year audits.

   c. The management letter is required for publicly traded companies in the United States, but not privately held companies.

   d. All of the above are false.

14-32 In *Exhibit 14-8* which of the following items is <u>not</u> present in the management letter?

   a. The auditor's observations and recommendations to management.

   b. Management's response.

   c. The issue of whether or how management responded to the management letter related to the prior year's audit.

   d. What actions the auditor will take in the subsequent-year audit to help management address the identified weaknesses.

LO 3

Identify the procedures to perform when conducting an engagement quality review.

Engagement Quality Review

As part of a quality audit for public companies, the audit firm has policies and procedures for conducting an engagement quality review of each audit before issuing the audit opinion. Auditors of privately held companies generally perform these reviews, even though they are not explicitly required. An experienced reviewer who was not a part of the audit team, but who has appropriate competence, independence, integrity, and objectivity, should perform this independent review, referred to as an **engagement quality review** or **concurring partner review**. The purpose of these reviews is to provide reasonable assurance that the audit and audit documentation are complete and support the audit opinion on the financial statements and, for integrated audits, on the client's internal controls.

The engagement quality review is a risk-based review, where the reviewer evaluates the significant judgments and conclusions made by the engagement team. Some of the procedures the reviewer should perform include:

- Discussing with the audit team any significant matters related to the financial statements and internal controls, including the audit team's identification of material weaknesses and audit procedures to address significant risks
- Evaluating judgments about materiality and the disposition of corrected and uncorrected identified misstatements
- Reviewing the engagement team's evaluation of the firm's independence in relation to the engagement
- Reviewing the related audit documentation to determine its sufficiency
- Reading the financial statements, management's report on internal control, and auditor's report
- Confirming with the lead audit partner that there are no significant unresolved matters

- Determining if appropriate consultations have taken place on difficult or contentious matters
- Evaluating whether the auditor documentation supports the conclusions reached by the engagement team with respect to the matters reviewed
- Assessing whether appropriate matters have been communicated to audit committee members, management, and other appropriate parties
- Evaluating whether appropriate levels of supervision and reviews of individual audit tasks were completed adequately during the audit

---

Why It Matters

The PCAOB's Evaluation of Audit Firm Performance in Conducting Engagement Quality Reviews

This feature provides examples of difficulties firms have encountered in performing engagement quality reviews.

The Public Company Accounting Oversight Board (PCAOB)'s AS 1220, *Engagement Quality Review*, provides guidance on engagement quality reviews. On December 6, 2013, the PCAOB issued a report, *Observations Related to the Implementation of the Auditing Standard on Engagement Quality Review*. This report provides a summary of deficiencies related to engagement quality reviews that PCAOB audit firm inspection teams identified. The report covers inspection reports completed in 2011 and 2012. The report states that in about 39% of 111 audits in which PCAOB inspection staff concluded that the audit opinion was insufficiently supported, the staff concluded that the underlying audit deficiency should have been detected by the engagement quality review (but it was not).

The following are examples of deficiencies in engagement quality review included in the report:

- "The engagement quality reviewer failed to identify that the engagement team had neither designated an audit as higher-risk during the engagement planning nor identified any specific risks associated with the engagement even though the issuer had various risks including, for example, that it was a development stage entity engaged in developing activities in a foreign location.

- The engagement quality reviewer failed to identify that the engagement team had not sufficiently planned, reviewed or supervised the audit work performed by a foreign affiliated firm even though audit considerations for multi-location engagements was part of the scope of work reviewed by the engagement quality reviewer.

- The engagement quality reviewer identified that additional audit procedures were required to test revenue in response to the risk of material misstatement due to fraud. The engagement quality reviewer, however, did not determine that the additional procedures were performed.

- The engagement team identified control deficiencies affecting the same account or disclosure, but failed to evaluate whether, in combination, these deficiencies resulted in material weaknesses. The engagement quality reviewer

failed to identify that the engagement team had not made this assessment.

- The engagement quality reviewer assessed the audit work performed related to estimates but failed to identify that the engagement team had limited to inquiry its testing of the assumptions underlying the issuer's calculation of a significant estimate."

The PCAOB investigated potential root causes of noncompliance, and noted the following items:

- "The engagement completion document did not include all of the information necessary for understanding certain significant findings or issues (or cross references to available supporting audit documentation). This document, along with any documents cross-referenced should collectively be as specific as necessary in the circumstances for a reviewer to gain a thorough understanding of the significant findings or issues. Failing to include the information necessary to understand the findings or issues in the engagement completion document does not provide the engagement quality reviewer with an opportunity to identify audit deficiencies;

- Engagement quality reviewers over-relied on the engagement team's responses to firm engagement quality review checklists and on discussions with the engagement team, without reviewing the work papers supporting significant judgments made by the engagement team;

- Engagement quality reviewers did not devote sufficient time to the engagement quality reviews, or did not conduct their reviews in a timely fashion, which may have been due to competing priorities. For example, in an audit engagement in which Inspections staff determined that the firm failed to support its audit opinion, the engagement quality reviewer did not review the engagement planning until the fourth quarter, which gave the engagement team less time to alter its planned audit procedures in response to any concerns raised by the engagement quality reviewer;

- And Firms failed to consider known concerns about the quality of work of certain partners who were appointed to perform engagement quality reviews."

Source: *https://pcaobus.org/Standards/Auditing/pages/au337aspx*

For Classroom Discussion

According to the PCAOB's AS 1220, *Engagement Quality Review*, the engagement quality review partner must document the procedures that they conducted and the judgments that they made:

Documentation of an Engagement Quality Review

.19 Documentation of an engagement quality review should contain sufficient information to enable an experienced auditor, having no previous connection with the engagement, to understand the procedures performed by the engagement quality reviewer, and others who assisted the reviewer, to comply with the provisions of this standard, including information that identifies:

a. The engagement quality reviewer, and others who assisted the reviewer,

b. The documents reviewed by the engagement quality reviewer, and others who assisted the reviewer,

c. The date the engagement quality reviewer provided concurring approval of issuance or, if no concurring approval of issuance was provided, the reasons for not providing the approval.

.20 Documentation of an engagement quality review should be included in the engagement documentation.

In thinking about these documentation requirements and the criticisms that the PCAOB has levied on auditors conducting engagement quality reviews, which of the criticisms might be explained by the engagement quality reviewer simply not adequately documenting their procedures and judgments?

14-33 The terms *engagement quality review* and *concurring partner review* are synonymous. (T/F)

14-34 An engagement quality review is required for publicly traded companies, and is optional for privately held company audits. (T/F)

14-35 Which of the following statements is <u>false</u> concerning engagement quality reviews?
   a. The purpose of the engagement quality review is to provide reasonable assurance that the audit and audit documentation are complete and that they support the audit opinion on the financial statements.
   b. The engagement quality review must be documented, and the documentation should include who performed the review, which documents were reviewed, and the date the engagement quality reviewer provided approval of the issuance of the audit opinion.
   c. Engagement quality reviews are required for both publicly traded companies and private companies in the United States.

   d. One of the procedures that would be performed during the engagement quality review is to determine if appropriate consultations have taken place on difficult or contentious matters.

14-36 Which of the following is <u>not</u> a procedure that an engagement quality reviewer would perform?
   a. Evaluating whether or not to continue providing audit services to the client in the subsequent year, based on information gained during the current-period audit.
   b. Discussing significant matters related to the financial statements and internal controls.
   c. Evaluating judgments about materiality and the disposition of corrected and uncorrected identified misstatements.
   d. Reviewing the engagement team's evaluation of the firm's independence in relation to the engagement.

LO 4

Identify issues to communicate to the audit committee.

Audit Committee Communications

It is important that the auditor have a constructive and detailed dialogue with the audit committee. This communication is important because the audit committee serves as an independent subcommittee of the board of directors. The audit committee can also assist the auditor should a disagreement occur between the auditor and management. The audit committee must be assured that the auditor is free of any restrictions and has not been inappropriately influenced by management during the course of the audit. The following are typical communications between the auditor and the audit committee:

- *Auditor's Responsibilities.* The auditor must clearly communicate the audit firm's responsibility to perform the audit according to relevant auditing standards and independently assess the fairness of the financial statements, to assess the quality of the entity's internal controls over financial reporting, and to design the audit to detect material misstatements. The auditor should communicate that the audit of the financial statements does not relieve management of its financial reporting responsibilities.

- *Overview and Planned Scope of the Audit.* The auditor needs to communicate the planned scope of the audit engagement to the audit committee and have a discussion with it on the adequacy of the planned scope.

- *Independence.* The auditor should affirm that the engagement team and others in the audit firm have complied with relevant independence requirements.

- *Significant Accounting Policies.* The auditor should inform the audit committee about the initial selection of, and changes in, significant accounting policies or their application, and discuss the quality of accounting principles used. SOX requires that the auditor communicate all alternative treatments of financial information within GAAP that have been discussed with management, ramifications of using alternative treatments or disclosures, and the treatment that the audit firm prefers.

- *Management Judgments and Accounting Estimates.* Many corporate failures have involved manipulation of accounting estimates such as loan loss reserves. The auditor should inform the audit committee of the processes used by management in making sensitive accounting estimates and should convey the auditor's assessment of those processes and accompanying estimates.

- *Significant Audit Adjustments.* Significant audit adjustments may reflect on the stewardship and accountability of management. The audit committee should be made aware of such adjustments, even if management readily agrees to make them. Significant adjustments, by definition, suggest that there have been internal control failures that must be communicated to management and to the audit committee. The auditor should also communicate about any uncorrected misstatements.

- *Judgments About the Quality of the Company's Accounting Principles.* The auditor needs to discuss with the audit committee the quality of the company's financial statements and provide reasonable assurance that they are acceptable under GAAP. Auditors should be prepared to have a frank discussion about differences in assessments of the quality of the financial statements. In other words, the auditor should be prepared to discuss the quality, not just the acceptability, of significant accounting policies.

- *Other Information in Annual Reports.* The auditor should briefly describe his or her responsibility to review other information contained in an annual report and whether such information is consistent with the audited financial statements.

- *Disagreements with Management.* All major accounting disagreements with management, even if eventually resolved, should be discussed with the audit committee. This requirement is intended to insulate the auditors from management pressure to change or bend accounting treatments to suit management and should remove any hints that the audit firm may be replaced because it disagrees with management's proposed accounting treatments.

- *Major Issues Discussed with Management Before Retention.* During the proposal and hiring stages of the engagement, management and the auditor discuss issues related to accounting principles and audit standards. These issues should be discussed with the audit committee.

- *Internal Control over Financial Reporting.* The auditor should discuss the quality of internal controls and any deficiencies therein (including material weaknesses, significant deficiencies, and those deficiencies that are less severe than significant deficiencies), even if they were remediated, prior to year-end. The audit committee needs to understand these issues in order to help assess the elements of the Committee of Sponsoring Organizations of the Treadway Commission (COSO) framework and to engage in remediation discussions. For integrated audit clients, the auditor must provide these communications in writing to management and the audit committee prior to issuing the auditor's report on internal control over financial reporting.

Guidance on Assessing the Quality, Not Just the Acceptability, of Significant Accounting Policies

Why It Matters

This feature provides guidance on issues for auditors to consider when evaluating the quality of a client's accounting policies.

Objective criteria for evaluating the quality of the client's accounting policies is not available, so assessing the quality, not just the acceptability of significant accounting policies is a matter of professional judgment. Auditors might consider the following questions in making this judgment:

- What is the consistency of the organization's accounting principles and their application?
- What is the clarity of the financial statements and related disclosures?
- What is the completeness of the financial statements and related disclosures?

- Are there any items that have a significant impact on the representational faithfulness, verifiability, and neutrality of the accounting information included in the financial statements? For example, are there:
- Selection of new accounting policies or changes to current ones
- Estimates, judgments, and uncertainties
- Unusual transactions
- Accounting policies relating to significant financial statement items, including the timing of transactions and the period in which they are recorded
- Is the organization using accounting practices that are not specifically addressed in the accounting literature, such as industry-specific practices?

Check Your Basic Knowledge

14-37 Objective criteria for evaluating the quality of the client's accounting policies is not available; assessing the quality, not just the acceptability of the significant accounting policies is a matter or professional judgment.   (T/F)

14-38 One of the issues that the auditor is required to communicate to the audit committee is the competence, training, and industry specialization of each of the highest ranking members of the engagement team (the partner, manager, and audit senior).   (T/F)

14-39 Which of the following is <u>not</u> a typical communication between the auditor and the audit committee at the end of an audit engagement?
   a. Discussion of the auditor's responsibility.
   b. Discussion of the client continuance decision.
   c. Discussion about auditor independence.
   d. Discussion about management judgments and accounting estimates.

14-40 With regard to discussing significant audit adjustments with the audit committee, which of the following statements is <u>false</u>?
   a. Significant audit adjustments reflect a lack of independence between the auditor and client management.
   b. Significant audit adjustments may reflect on the stewardship and accountability of management.
   c. The audit committee should be made aware of significant audit adjustments, even if management readily agrees to make them.
   d. Significant adjustments, by definition, suggest that there have been internal control failures that must be communicated to the audit committee.
   e. Two of the above (a–d).

Let's Review

- The auditor's responsibilities with respect to detected misstatements include accumulating the known and projected misstatements, assessing the carryover effects of prior-year misstatements, discussing these with management, jointly deciding which misstatements the client will correct and which the client will leave uncorrected. Sometimes resolving detected misstatements is difficult because legitimate, subjective differences exist between the judgments of management and the auditor. (LO 1)

- Loss contingencies include the threat of expropriation of assets in a foreign country, litigation, claims, and assessments, among others. The auditor performs a variety of procedures to review and assess the appropriateness of loss contingencies. The auditor gathers evidence from management about e.g., a description of the contingencies, information about contracts in which contingencies may exist, along with appropriate documentation of management's assertions. This documentation will include a letter of audit inquiry to legal counsel, which includes management's list of contingencies, to which the attorney will comment on its completeness, the nature of the contingencies and their likely outcome, and any limitations to the attorney's response. (LO 1)

- The auditor reviews and assesses the adequacy of disclosures by reading the client's disclosures for each financial statement line item and associated discussion in the footnotes, obtaining evidence to determine whether the disclosures are adequate in light of required GAAP, e.g., by completing a disclosure checklist, and considering alternative or enhanced disclosures that may be helpful to users. (LO 1)

- The auditor performs various activities in reviewing and assessing potential noncompliance with laws and regulations. Noncompliance involves acts by the entity that are contrary to prevailing laws. Activities that auditors perform to review and assess potential noncompliance include: (1) obtaining an understanding of internal controls the client has implemented to achieve proper compliance with laws and regulations, (2) obtaining the knowledge necessary to understand applicable laws and regulations relevant to the client's business, both nationally and internationally, and (3) searching for indications of noncompliance, e.g., tips to whistleblower hotlines, and/or unusual payments to vendors in countries with high corruption indices. (LO 1)

- The auditor performs review analytical procedures because they help the auditor form an overall conclusion about whether the financial statements are consistent with the auditor's understanding of the entity based upon the findings in the audit. The auditor conducts review analytical procedures in a manner similar to other analytical procedures, but this analysis comes at the end of the audit and the expectations will be less precise than if the auditor were performing substantive analytical procedures. (LO 1)

- The auditor performs the following activities when reviewing and assessing the going-concern assumption: (1) determining whether there are indications of a going-concern problem, (2) estimating the likelihood that management can mitigate any problems causing doubt about going-concern status, (3) deciding whether to issue an unqualified audit report or an unqualified audit report with a going-concern paragraph, and (4) assessing whether management has provided adequate disclosures about any potential going-concern problems. (LO 1)

- Subsequent events are events occurring between the date of the financial statements and the date of the auditor's report. A subsequent events review is the auditor's review of events occurring in the period between the balance sheet date and the audit report date to determine their possible effect on the financial statements. The auditor's responsibility with respect to subsequent events includes the following types of tests: performing cutoff tests, reviewing collections of receivables, searching for unrecorded liabilities, reading minutes of the board of directors, reading interim financial statements and comparing them to audited financial statements, and inquiring of management concerning any issues relating to potential subsequent events. (LO 1)

- The purpose of a management representation letter is to remind management of its responsibility for the financial statements, confirm oral responses that the auditor obtained earlier in the audit and the continuing appropriateness of those responses, and reduce the possibility of misunderstanding concerning the matters that are the subject of the representations. In contrast, the purpose of a management letter is to provide the auditor the opportunity to communicate with management regarding business, operational, or control improvement opportunities. The management representation letter is required; the management letter is optional, but serves as a way for the auditors to prove their "value-added" to the client. (LO 2)

- An engagement quality review is conducted by an experienced reviewer who was not part of the audit team; this individual performs an independent review intended to provide reasonable assurance that the audit and audit documentation are complete and support the audit opinion on the financial statements. The engagement quality reviewer will perform the following types of tasks: discussing with the audit team any significant matters related to the financial statements and internal controls, including the audit team's identification of material weaknesses and audit procedures to address significant risks, evaluating judgments about materiality and the disposition of corrected and uncorrected identified misstatements, and reviewing the engagement team's evaluation of the firm's independence in relation to the engagement, among others. (LO 3)

- The auditor should communicate important issues to the audit committee as part of completing the audit. These communications might include the auditor's responsibilities, an overview of the scope of the audit, a discussion of the auditor's independence, an explanation of the client's significant accounting policies, and areas in which management made significant judgments around accounting estimates, among others. Auditor communications with the audit committee are an integral part of completing the audit because they bring these two elements of the corporate governance mosaic together in one room, at one time, to discuss the client. (LO 4)

Significant Terms

Altman Z-score   A series of ratios that have predictive power in indicating the likelihood of bankruptcy. This score is named for the person who first introduced the concept and associated measurement.

Busy season   An intensive time of the year during which the auditor faces the greatest deadline pressure and work volume based upon the need to provide assurance over the client's financial reports.

Concurring partner review   See *engagement quality review.*

Corruption perception index   A ranking put forth by Transparency International that ranks countries according to the extent to which people believe corruption exists; the ranking includes about 200 countries and ranks them on a scale from 0 to 10 (0 = high corruption; 10 = low corruption).

Disclosure checklist   A decision aid that the auditor uses to serve as a cue to guiding audit planning around management's assertions in various disclosures.

Dual approach   An approach to considering uncorrected misstatements that requires the simultaneous application of *both* the rollover method and the iron curtain method.

Engagement quality review   A review at the end of each audit conducted by an experienced auditor, usually a partner, who was not a part of the audit team, but who has appropriate competence, independence, integrity, and objectivity. The purpose of this review is to help make sure that the audit and audit documentation are complete and support the audit opinion on the financial statements and, for public companies, on the client's internal controls.

Factual misstatement   See *known misstatement*; a misstatement about which there is no doubt.

Going-concern assumption   An accounting guideline which assumes that the company will continue on long enough to carry out its objectives and commitments. In other words, there is belief that the company will not liquidate in the near future.

Iron curtain method   A method of misstatement correction that focuses on assuring that the year-end balance sheet is correct; this method does not consider the impact of prior-year uncorrected misstatements reversing in later years.

Judgmental misstatement   A misstatement that arises from differences in judgments of management concerning accounting estimates that the auditor considers unreasonable, or the selection or application of accounting policies that the auditor considers inappropriate.

Known misstatement   A misstatement that has been specifically identified; known misstatements are also referred to as *factual misstatements.*

Letter of audit inquiry   A letter that the auditor asks the client to send to its legal counsel to gather corroborative evidence concerning litigation, claims, and assessments.

Management letter   A letter from the auditor to the client identifying any problems and suggested solutions that may help management improve its effectiveness or efficiency.

Management representation letter A letter to the auditors that the client's chief executive and chief financial officers are required to sign that specifies management's responsibility for the financial statements and confirms oral responses given to the auditor during the audit.

Noncompliance This involves acts of omission or commission by the entity, either intentional or unintentional, which are contrary to the prevailing laws or regulations.

Projected misstatement A misstatement that is the auditor's best estimate of the misstatement in a given population, and that is a projection of the misstatement identified in an audit sample to the entire population from which the sample was drawn.

Reasonable period of time A period of time not to exceed one year beyond the date of the financial statements being audited.

Report release date The date the auditor grants the entity permission to use the auditor's report in connection with the financial statements.

Restatement A financial reporting disclosure that occurs when and if a material misstatement is ultimately discovered; at that point, management will have to issue revised financial statements with the misstatement corrected.

Rollover method A method of misstatement correction that focuses on the materiality of the current-year misstatements and the reversing effect of prior-year misstatements on the income statement, thereby allowing misstatements to accumulate on the balance sheet.

Subsequent events Events occurring between the date of the financial statements and the date of the auditor's report.

Subsequent events review A review of events occurring in the period between the balance sheet date and the audit report date to determine their possible effect on the financial statements.

Summary of unadjusted audit differences A summary of unadjusted audit differences that is communicated to the audit committee is described in the management representation letter, and that is evaluated individually and in the aggregate for determining whether the financial statements are materially correct.

Support letter Written evidence from management to the auditor providing assurance that the entity has received a commitment of necessary financial support to ensure that the entity remains a going concern.

Type I subsequent events Events that existed at the balance sheet date.

Type II subsequent events Events that did not exist at the balance sheet date, but that may require disclosure.

Prompts for Critical Thinking

Prompt for Critical Thinking #1

Students will likely have varying reactions to the fact that there really wasn't much of a negative stock price reaction to the revelation of the restatement. Likely, the lack of market reaction was due to the change in leadership, and their forthright disclosure of the facts, coupled with very reassuring language in the press release.

Prompt for Critical Thinking #2

Students will likely have varying reactions with respect to whether the client should invest in Suiss Finance. The risks they may discuss include:

• Physical security
• A weak market for oil and associated by-products

- Lack of infrastructure
- Governmental transitions
- Threat of expropriation of significant fixed assets required to conduct business in the oil and gas industry

With regard to upside potential, and the fact that the market is clearly valuing that potential students will likely express surprise and curiosity that investors are willing to put money into South Sudan.

Prompt for Critical Thinking #3

Students will likely vary in the ranking that they perceive prior to investigating the actual ranking of various countries on Transparency.com.

The actual rankings for each of the countries listed is as follows, based on the link in the prompt:

Country (in alphabetical order)	ACTUAL Rank (1 = most to 6 = least corrupt among this list)	ACTUAL Corruption Perception Index 0–100
Belgium	5	77
Brazil	2	40
New Zealand	6	90
Somalia	1	10
South Korea	3	53
United States of America	4	74

Prompt for Critical Thinking #4

1. With respect to ImmunoGen and Ernst & Young, LLP:

   "The accompanying consolidated financial statements have been prepared assuming that the Company will continue as a going concern. As discussed in Note A to the consolidated financial statements, the Company has recurring losses from operations and insufficient cash resources that raise substantial doubt about its ability to continue as a going concern. Management's plans in regard to these matters are also described in Note A. The consolidated financial statements do not include any adjustments that might result from the outcome of this uncertainty."

2. With respect to Omeros Corporation, Ernst & Young provides no alerts relating to going-concern risks.

3. With respect to Hooper Holmes, KPMG provides the following alert to users relating to going-concern risks:

   "The accompanying consolidated financial statements have been prepared assuming the Company will continue as a going concern. As discussed in Note 2 to the consolidated financial statements, the Company has suffered recurring losses from operations, negative cash flows from operations and other related liquidity concerns, which raises substantial doubt about the Company's ability to continue as a going concern. Management's plans in regard to these matters are also described in Note 2. The consolidated financial statements and financial statement schedule do not include any adjustments that might result from the outcome of this uncertainty."

Review Questions and Short Cases

14-1 **LO 1** What is an adjustment, and why is the resolution of adjustments important to audit quality? What role should professional skepticism play when management disagrees with the auditor about making an audit adjustment to correct a misstatement? What types of management bias might be revealed in this type of setting?

14-2 **LO 1** How does a summary of unadjusted audit differences help the auditor determine whether the financial statements are materially correct? What information might it contain? How might an analysis of the summary affect the auditor's internal control report on a public company?

14-3 **LO 1** Why is audit firm culture important in ensuring that individual audit engagement partners resolve adjustments in a quality manner?

14-4 **LO 1** During the audit of Nature Sporting Goods, the auditor discovered the following:

- The accounts receivable confirmation work revealed one pricing misstatement. The book value of $12,955.68 should be $11,984.00. The total misstatement based on this difference is $14,465, which includes a $972 known misstatement and an unknown projected misstatement of $13,493.
- Nature Sporting Goods had understated the accrued vacation pay by $13,000. A review of the prior-year documentation indicates the following uncorrected misstatements:
  o Accrued vacation pay was understated by $9,000.
  o Sales and accounts receivable were overstated by an estimated $60,000 because of cutoff errors.

Prepare a summary of unadjusted audit differences and draw your conclusion about whether the aggregate effect of these misstatements is material. Use the trial balance numbers shown in *Exhibit 14.1*, but ignore the misstatements shown in the exhibit. The income tax rate is 40% for the current and prior year. (*Note*: Consider materiality in developing your answer.)

14-5 **LO 1** Consider loss contingencies.

a. What is the primary source of information about litigation, claims, and assessments? What is the primary source of corroborative evidence in this regard?

b. Why might client lawyers be hesitant to disclose information to auditors?

c. Who sends the letter of audit inquiry to the client's lawyers? To whom should the lawyer send the response to that letter?

d. What is the effect on the auditor's report of a lawyer's refusal to furnish the information requested in the letter of audit inquiry?

14-6 **LO 1** Each of the following, labeled a - c, is an independent situation related to a loss contingency. Describe what the auditor should do in each situation.

a. The lawyer refused to furnish the requested information.

b. The lawyer was unable to form an opinion on the probability or amount of a pending lawsuit, but the auditor believes that the amount could be material.

c. The client stated that it had not consulted lawyers during the past year.

14-7 **LO 1** An audit client is being sued for $500,000 for discriminatory hiring practices. Indicate the appropriate action the auditor should take for each of the following independent responses to the letter of audit inquiry:

    a. The lawyer stated that there is only a remote chance that the client will lose. The client did not accrue any contingent loss or disclose this situation.

    b. The lawyer stated that the client will probably lose, and the amount of loss could be anywhere between $250,000 and $500,000, with no amount within that range being more likely. The client disclosed this situation, but did not accrue a loss.

    c. The lawyer stated that there is a reasonable possibility that the client will lose. The client disclosed this situation, but did not accrue a loss.

    d. The lawyer stated that the client will probably lose between $250,000 and $500,000, but most likely will lose $400,000. The client accrued a $250,000 contingent loss and disclosed the situation.

14-8 **LO 1** How is a disclosure checklist helpful? What precautions should the auditor take when using such a checklist?

14-9 **LO 1** When assessing disclosures, about what matters regarding disclosures should the auditor have reasonable assurance?

INTERNATIONAL

14-10 **LO 1** Refer to the *Why It Matters* feature "Related Party Disclosures at OAO Gazprom." What risks do the related party transactions with the Russian government pose for PwC in its audits of the company? Why might companies without such government ownership be less sensitive about their related party disclosures?

14-11 **LO 1** What are the inherent limitations in an auditor's ability to detect material misstatements relating to the client's compliance with laws and regulations?

FRAUD

14-12 **LO 1** What are the main provisions of the Foreign Corrupt Practices Act?

ETHICS

FRAUD

14-13 **LO 1** Refer to the *Focus on Fraud* feature "Triton Energy and Noncompliance with Laws and Regulations."

    a. What provisions of the Foreign Corrupt Practices Act did Triton Energy violate?

    b. What are the auditors' responsibilities when they become aware of violations of law at their client?

14-14 **LO 1** What is the purpose of performing review analytical procedures?

14-15 **LO 1** The audit of Golf Day Company, a manufacturer of bicycle racks and golf carts, is almost finished. Krista Heiss is the most experienced auditor on this engagement and is in charge of performing review analytical procedures. The company ships most of its products to a combination of distributors and retailers. The business is entirely within the United States and is seasonal.

    a. Why is it important that review analytical procedures be performed by experienced auditors?

    b. What are some analytical procedures that Heiss might perform?

    c. How can these procedures be useful at this stage of the audit to help provide reasonable assurance with respect to audit quality?

FRAUD

PROFESSIONAL SKEPTICISM

14-16 **LO 1** Refer to *Exhibit 14.3* and review the analytical procedure results and trends. Presumably, Sue Sachdeva knew that the auditors might ask pointed questions about the financial results and odd analytics apparent in the data from FYE 2004 to FYE 2009. For each of the trends listed here, describe how you think Sachdeva might have tried to explain away the issue (because, of course, she would not admit to the fraud). Indicate how a professionally skeptical auditor might have responded to her explanations.

Financial Trend	CFO's Likely Explanation
Cash balances have declined to their lowest level since FYE 2004.	
Sales increased over the period, but have returned to about FYE 2004 levels.	
Cost of goods sold as a percentage of sales has risen sharply over the period, with a particularly significant increase from FYE 2008 to 2009.	
Relatedly, gross profit has decreased sharply over the period, with a particularly significant decrease from FYE 2008 to 2009.	
SG&A as a percentage of sales has risen sharply over the period, with a particularly significant increase from FYE 2008 to 2009.	
Net income as a percentage of sales has decreased sharply over the period, with a particularly significant decrease from FYE 2008 to 2009.	
Accounts receivable as a percentage of sales has remained relatively stable over the period, so there do not appear to be problems in billing or collections.	
Current liabilities as a percentage of sales has remained relatively stable over the period, so there do not appear to be problems in the purchasing cycle.	

14-17 LO 1 What are the types of subsequent events the auditor should identify and evaluate as part of performing an audit? Give an example of each type of subsequent event. How should the client treat each type in the financial statements?

14-18 LO 1 What audit procedures should the auditor perform to search for subsequent events?

14-19 LO 1 Explain the auditor's responsibilities when the auditor discovers that facts existed at the date of the audit report that were not known to the auditor until after the report release date.

14-20 LO 1 Assume that the auditor discovers a material subsequent event requiring management to take action to notify users. What steps should the auditor take if the client refuses to take the appropriate action?

14-21 LO 1 What is dual dating in terms of the audit report? Assume the following facts: The original audit report is dated March 18, 2019. The company entered into a definitive agreement to discontinue a material line of business on March 22, 2019. This event is disclosed in Note 22 to the financial statements. The report release date was March 25, 2019. On which dates may the auditor date the report? Which dating convention yields the least responsibility for the auditor?

14-22 LO 1 The auditor is auditing financial statements for the year ended December 31, 2018, and is completing the audit in early March 2019. The following situations, labeled a - f, have come to the auditor's attention. Indicate and explain whether the financial statements should be adjusted only, adjusted and disclosed, disclosed only, or neither adjusted nor disclosed.

a. On February 12, 2019, the client agreed to an out-of-court settlement of a property damage suit resulting from an accident caused by one of its delivery trucks. The accident occurred on November 20, 2018. The client accrued an estimated loss of $30,000 in the 2018 financial statements. The settlement was for $50,000.

b. Same facts as in Part 1, except the accident occurred January 1, 2019, and the client did not accrue a loss.

c. The client is a bank. A major commercial loan customer filed for bankruptcy on February 26, 2019. The bankruptcy was caused by an adverse court decision on February 15, 2019, involving a product liability lawsuit initiated in 2018 arising from products sold in 2018.

d. The client purchased raw materials that it received just before year-end. The client recorded the purchase based on its estimated value. The invoice was received January 31, 2019, and the cost was substantially different than was estimated.

e. On February 2, 2019, the board of directors took the following actions:
  1. Approved officers' salaries for 2019.
  2. Approved the sale of a significant bond issue.
  3. Approved a new union contract containing increased wages and fringe benefits for most of the employees. The employees had been on strike since January 2, 2019.

f. A major customer was killed in a boating accident on January 25, 2019. The customer had pledged his boat as collateral against a loan that he took out in 2018. The boat, which was destroyed in the accident, was not insured. The allowance for doubtful accounts is not adequate to cover the anticipated loss.

14-23 LO 1 Are auditors required to evaluate the likelihood of a client remaining a going concern as a part of each audit? What types of conditions and factors should auditors consider when making this evaluation?

14-24 LO 1 An Altman Z-score indicates the possibility that a client will go bankrupt. What effect could this score have on the audit report? Explain.

14-25 LO 1 List various factors suggesting that a client may not remain a going concern. For each, indicate the degree of subjectivity and judgment that would be required in determining if the indicator would, in fact, result in the company going bankrupt (use the following categories: high, medium, low).

14-26 LO 1 This is the third-year audit of Green Lawns. The company has carved out a new market niche online for the delivery of lawn and garden supplies, including links with local companies that provide lawn services. The company issued stock two years ago and raised sufficient capital to continue operations through this year. The company is currently trading at five times revenue. The company showed no profits in its first three years. Revenue growth has been 100%, 65%, and 30%, respectively, over each of the last three years. The current-year revenue is at $220 million. The auditor has audited current cash flow and has serious reservations about the ability of the company to remain a going concern without either some profitability or an infusion of cash. The company has responded with the following management plan:

- Another public offering of stock to raise $200 million in capital, which will be equal to 30% of the existing stock outstanding
- Sign an agreement with at least 50 more local distributors during the year
- Improve warehousing and distribution to cut at least 20% off the distribution costs
- Increase sales by 50% through more advertising, coupons, and better marketing to existing customers
- Improve profit margins by using its purchase power to sign more attractive purchase agreements with vendors but stay away from major-brand vendors such as Scott's, Ortho products, and so forth

   a. What is the auditor's responsibility to evaluate the effectiveness of management's plan? What action should the auditor take if he or she does not believe that management's plan will be effective?

   b. Assume that the auditor's report contains language indicating concern about the ability of the client to continue as a going concern. What does this action say to the users of the financial statements about confidence in management's ability to remain a going concern?

   c. What is the required disclosure regarding management's plans?

   d. For each element in management's plan, indicate the auditor's responsibility to assess the element. Indicate procedures the auditor should performed to assess each part of management's plan.

14-27 **LO 2** What is a management representation letter? Who prepares it? Who should sign it? When should it be dated?

14-28 **LO 2** What are the implications if management refuses to sign a management representation letter? If management signs a management representation letter, is that a good indication that all of management's statements described in the letter are true? What is the importance of professional skepticism in assessing the management representation letter as audit evidence?

14-29 **LO 2** Refer to *Exhibit 14.7*. What role does materiality play in the contents of the management representation letter? Is the same level of materiality applied to the audited financial statements as to the management representation letter?

14-30 **LO 2**

   a. Describe the purpose of a management letter, and distinguish it from a management representation letter.

   b. Refer to *Exhibit 14-8*. What observations does the auditor provide? What is the tone of management's responses? How does management plan to address the observations, and what does this say about management's commitment to financial reporting quality?

14-31 **LO 3** What are the purposes of the engagement quality review (concurring partner review)? What procedures should the reviewer perform as part of the review?

14-32 **LO 3** Consistent quality in the performance of an audit is one of the major goals of audit firms. However, internal inspections by audit firms themselves, along with external inspections by peer review teams and the PCAOB, point out that although effective audit policies and procedures are generally in place, audit teams do not always follow these policies and procedures. The result is that audit quality may sometimes be compromised, yet audit firm management is unaware of which particular audits are of low quality.

a. What audit documentation should engagement quality review partners retain to provide evidence that they have properly evaluated the consistent quality of the audit work performed?
b. Assume that a senior auditor concludes that management's assumptions regarding warranties are appropriate. What documentation would an engagement quality review partner expect to see to support such a conclusion?

14-33 `LO 3` What criticisms has the PCAOB levied against auditors in performing engagement quality reviews?

14-34 `LO 3` Describe the documentation requirements relating to the PCAOB's AS 1220, *Engagement Quality Review*.

14-35 `LO 4` Each of the following are typical communications between the auditor and the audit committee. Explain why each is important.

- Auditor's responsibility
- Overview and planned scope of the audit
- Auditor independence
- Significant accounting policies
- Management judgments and accounting estimates
- Significant audit adjustments
- Judgments about the quality of the company's accounting principles
- Other information in annual reports
- Disagreements with management
- Major issues discussed with management before retention
- Internal control over financial reporting

14-36 `LO 4` Refer to the *Why It Matters* feature "Guidance on Assessing the Quality, Not Just the Acceptability, of Significant Accounting Policies." Assessing the quality of accounting policies is a matter of professional judgment. What considerations are relevant in making this judgment?

Fraud Focus: Contemporary and Historical Cases

FRAUD

PROFESSIONAL SKEPTICISM

14-37 **Dell, Inc.**
(LO 1, 3)   In July 2010, the SEC issued a complaint against senior management at Dell, Inc., including the company's chairman, CEO, and CFO. The complaint includes allegations that Dell engaged in fraud during the period 2002–2006 by failing to disclose a significant relationship with its major vendor (Intel) that led to Intel's making payments back to Dell. According to the complaint, Intel agreed to make cash payments to Dell in exchange for Dell's promise that it would not purchase microprocessors from Intel's archrival, Advanced Micro Devices (AMD). The cash payments were very large, ranging from 10% to 76% of operating income over the period of the fraud. In March 2006, Dell announced that it would begin using AMD as a vendor, and Intel immediately retaliated by ceasing to make its usual cash payments to Dell, thereby resulting in a 36% drop in Dell's quarterly income. In the quarterly earnings conference call, Michael Dell attributed the drop to pricing pressures in the face of slowing demand and to component costs that declined less than expected; of course, these statements were false.

Consider the difficulty that this scheme posed for Dell's auditors, PwC. The most senior members of the management team were actively involved in this deception and not intending to make full and fair disclosures to investors or the auditors. However, should the auditors have otherwise known of the payments? This question is at the heart of a continuing debate about auditing versus forensic accounting (looking for fraud). The auditors, heretofore, had not seen any reason to question management's integrity, but economic situations and motivations change. Further, instituting a standard audit procedure in which audit software is used to search for cash receipts from major vendors (where only cash disbursements are expected) would have likely uncovered the cash received from Intel. Should such procedures—even when fraud is not expected—be performed on every audit, simply because such fraud can occur? Perhaps so, but this would also mean that audit firms would have to systematically think about a host of situations that may occur with all clients and add the standard software analysis to the audits—thereby driving up audit costs (maybe without an increase in audit fees).

This example illustrates the difficulty that auditors sometimes face in their obligation to review the adequacy of disclosures—when faced with fraud, intentional concealment, and collusion among the perpetrators, it is very difficult for the auditors to reach an accurate conclusion regarding their audit work. Critics of PwC might say that PwC conducted the audit in a low-quality manner, thereby resulting in a failure to detect the fraud.

a. Why were Dell's recording and disclosure of the payments from Intel materially false and misleading?
b. What changes in the economic environment, or in the management culture of Dell, might have led PwC to become more skeptical of the company and therefore to expand audit procedures?
c. Should using data analytical tools to identify significant cash receipts from vendors be a required part of every audit engagement? Explain your rationale and consider such things as audit cost and user expectations.
d. Assume that instead of negotiating payments from Intel, Dell would have negotiated a long-term supply contract with Intel that resulted in lower prices for Intel chips as long as Dell agreed not to use a competitor's chips in its products. Should the amount of the price reduction be disclosed as a separate item in the financial statements under GAAP? Why or why not?
e. Assume the company negotiated lower prices with Intel as described in Part d. How would the auditor become aware of the lower prices? Consider that, especially in tougher economic times, many companies were negotiating lower prices from their suppliers.
f. Assume the role of the engagement quality review partner. What reviews and analyses might have alerted you to the size and nature of the Intel payments?
g. Considering this case and the many ways in which the payments (or price reductions) from Intel could have occurred, how would you decide when the judgments and decisions made by management moves from aggressive accounting to outright fraud?

FRAUD

ETHICS

PROFESSIONAL SKEPTICISM

14-38 **MCA Financial (LO 1, 3)** This case involves a fraud perpetrated by MCA Financial Corporation, which was incorporated in 1989 as a holding company for four wholly owned subsidiaries, with 45 branch offices in seven states. MCA primarily was involved in the residential mortgage banking business. MCA's fraudulent scheme was accomplished through related party transactions and involved the following steps.

1.   MCA purchased distressed rental properties in the city of Detroit, sold them to the Related Limited Partnerships at inflated prices, advanced the Related Limited Partnerships small down payments (usually 10% or 20%), and accepted executed mortgages or land contracts for the remainder of the purchase prices.

2.   MCA established the prices at which it sold the rental properties to the Related Limited Partnerships by calculating the value each property would have after substantial rehabilitation, even though rehabilitation work had not been completed or even begun. MCA then recognized the entire gain on each sale as revenue, even though MCA knew that the Related Limited Partnerships could not afford to pay for the properties because of the inflated sales prices and the prevailing rental rates. In fact, the Related Limited Partnerships failed to make most of the required loan payments to MCA for the properties.

3.   MCA recorded the money owing from the Related Limited Partnerships as a result of advancing the down payments on the asset side of its balance sheet under the heading of Accounts Receivable-Related Parties. MCA carried those receivables without any valuation allowance, despite the Related Limited Partnerships' inability to repay the receivables.

4.   MCA fraudulently sold some related party mortgages and land contracts to the pools and carried the remainder at cost or with an inadequate allowance for loan losses under the headings of Mortgages Held for Resale or Land Contracts Held for Resale, despite the Related Limited Partnerships' inability to repay and the inadequate collateral. The collateral for these mortgages and land contracts was the real estate that MCA had sold to the Related Limited Partnerships at inflated prices. As a result, MCA knew that foreclosing on the collateral would not result in MCA receiving the full principal amount of the loans. MCA did not disclose in its financial statements that a material amount of its mortgages and land contracts held for resale were related party mortgages and land contracts.

The Auditors Grant Thornton LLP was one of two firms that jointly provided audit services to MCA and jointly signed reports containing unqualified opinions on MCA's annual financial statements from 1993 through 1998. Doeren Mayhew & Co. P.C., a Michigan accounting firm, was the other firm that jointly provided audit services to MCA and jointly signed reports containing unqualified opinions on MCA's annual financial statements from 1993 through 1998.

Peter Behrens is a CPA who served as an engagement partner for Grant Thornton's joint audits of MCA. Marvin Morris is a CPA who served as an engagement partner for Doeren Mayhew's joint audits of MCA. Benedict Rybicki is a CPA who served as the engagement manager for Doeren Mayhew's joint audits of MCA. Morris obtained personal mortgages through MCA in July 1994 for approximately $344,000 and in July 1995 for approximately $200,000. The 1994 mortgage was discharged when the 1995 mortgage was executed. Morris did not review the auditors' workpapers for several key portions of the 1998 MCA audit, including the workpapers for mortgages and land contracts held for resale and gains on sale of real estate. As late as 2001, Morris stated that he had only ever read the first 13 of the approximately 150 Statements of Financial Accounting Standards. Reading the Statements of Financial Accounting Standards was not "what [Morris did] for a living." Rather, he considered himself a "salesperson."

As the engagement manager, Rybicki signed a workpaper in connection with the 1998 MCA audit (a) confirming that the entire MCA engagement had been performed in accordance with professional standards; (b) confirming that related parties or unusual transactions and relationships were properly disclosed and documented in MCA's financial statements; and (c) agreeing with the issuance of the report containing an unqualified opinion. Rybicki socialized with Alexander Ajemian, MCA's controller, during the time that Doeren Mayhew acted as one of MCA's auditors. Rybicki first met Ajemian in approximately 1987, when both were staff accountants at the Detroit office of Pannell Kerr & Forster. Rybicki and Ajemian both played on Pannell Kerr's softball team. They continued playing on the same team even after each had left Pannell Kerr, including while Ajemian was MCA's controller and Rybicki was the engagement manager for the MCA audits. Rybicki, Ajemian, and the remainder of the softball team often ate and drank together after the games. Between 1993 and 1998, Rybicki and Ajemian occasionally spent weekends in Petosky, Michigan, where they stayed at a lakefront condominium owned by MCA. During the same time period, Rybicki and Ajemian spoke socially on the telephone, ate together, water-skied, and traveled to the Kentucky Derby. After MCA filed for bankruptcy in 1999 and Ajemian pled guilty in 2001 to federal criminal charges in connection with his conduct at MCA, Rybicki and Ajemian continued socializing. They dined together, attended sporting events, played on the same softball team, and traveled together.

While acting as MCA's auditors, Doeren Mayhew and Grant Thornton personnel, including Behrens, Morris, and Rybicki, sometimes attended a party, known as the "Bean Counters Bash," held by Ajemian annually at his home and paid for by MCA. This party was held to celebrate the completion of the annual audit. MCA executives provided Doeren Mayhew and Grant Thornton auditors with free tickets to Detroit Red Wings hockey games and University of Michigan football games. MCA executives also invited the auditors to tailgate parties paid for by MCA at the football games. Rybicki obtained a personal mortgage through MCA for approximately $59,000 to purchase his house in the early 1990s.

During the 1998 MCA audit, Behrens, Morris, and Rybicki knew that millions of dollars of the mortgages and land contracts held for resale reported in MCA's 1998 annual financial statements consisted of related party mortgages and land contracts. Behrens, Morris, and Rybicki obtained this knowledge through their preparation of the 1998 MCA audit plan, their review of the 1998 audit workpapers and other materials, their performance of audit procedures during the 1998 audit, their communications with MCA executives, and/or their knowledge of MCA's business from prior audits.

Specifically, with respect to the workpapers, Behrens and Rybicki reviewed them as part of the 1998 MCA audit, which showed that MCA sold approximately $10.8 million in real estate to the Related Limited Partnerships in fiscal year 1998. Those workpapers also showed that MCA advanced the Related Limited Partnerships a small down payment for the real estate and accepted an executed mortgage or land contract for the remaining portion of the purchase price. Those workpapers further calculated that approximately $4.9 million of those related party mortgages and land contracts had not been sold as of MCA's balance sheet date and thus were included in the total mortgages or land contracts held for resale as reported in MCA's 1998 annual financial statements. Rybicki prepared, and Behrens and Morris reviewed, a workpaper in connection with the 1998 MCA audit entitled "Audit Planning." In this workpaper, Rybicki assessed the audit risk on the MCA engagement as high. Later in the workpaper, Rybicki noted that the reasons for the high-risk assessment were that MCA had "significant and/or frequent difficult-to-audit transactions or balances" and "material, related-party transactions on a recurring basis." Behrens and Rybicki also reviewed workpapers as part of the 1998 MCA audit that contained balance sheets for the Related Limited Partnerships reflecting approximately $57.3 million in liabilities under the heading of Mortgages and Land Contracts Payable. Behrens and Rybicki additionally reviewed workpapers as part of the 1998 MCA audit that showed approximately $4 million of MCA's land contracts held for resale, those that had been pledged as collateral for one of MCA's debenture offerings, were related party land contracts.

During the 1998 MCA audit, Behrens, Morris, and Rybicki read MCA's 1998 annual financial statements. Those financial statements did not disclose any related party mortgages or land contracts held for resale or state the total amount of such mortgages and land contracts held for resale. Grant Thornton and Doeren Mayhew issued a report, dated April 28, 1998, containing an unqualified opinion on MCA's 1998 annual financial statements, even though Behrens, Morris, and Rybicki knew that MCA had failed to disclose material, related party mortgages, and land contracts.

a. Summarize the nature of the fraud perpetrated by MCA involving related party transactions, and describe the problems with the lack of disclosure and engagement quality review.
b. Summarize the nature of the inappropriate relationships between MCA and its auditors.
c. Discuss how the concepts of auditor independence, ethics, and professional skepticism are related, with an emphasis on the facts in this case. Discuss the issue of what personal relationships are or are not acceptable between an audit firm and the client.
d. Recommend changes that these audit firms should make to improve their quality-control procedures.

Application Activities

INTERNATIONAL

NOTE: Completing *Application Activities* requires students to reference additional resources and materials. Some *Application Activities* will require the student to reference relevant professional auditing standards. We make special note of these as *Auditing Standards Application Activities*.

14-39 Siemens (LO 1)   Access the most recently available annual report of Siemens (*www.siemens.com/investor/en/financials/annual_reports.htm*). Locate and read the MD&A section of the report. Comment on why the audit report does not provide assurance regarding the MD&A.

14-40 Northwest Airlines, Ernst & Young (LO 1)   On February 25, 2005, Ernst & Young LLP issued the following opinion about the financial statements of Northwest Airlines:

> "We also have audited, in accordance with the standards of the Public Company Accounting Oversight Board (U.S.), the consolidated balance sheets of Northwest Airlines Corporation as of December 31, 2004, and 2003, and the related consolidated statements of operations, stockholders' equity (deficit), and cash flows for each of the three years in the period ended December 31, 2004. Our report dated February 25, 2005 expressed an unqualified opinion thereon."

On September 14, 2005, Northwest Airlines filed for bankruptcy. On March 13, 2006, Ernst & Young LLP issued the following opinion about the financial statements of Northwest Airlines:

"We also have audited, in accordance with the standards of the Public Company Accounting Oversight Board (U.S.) the consolidated balance sheets of Northwest Airlines Corporation (Debtor-in-Possession) as of December 31, 2005, and 2004, and the related consolidated statements of operations, stockholders' equity (deficit), and cash flows for each of the three years in the period ended December 31, 2004. Our report dated March 13, 2006 expressed an unqualified opinion thereon and included explanatory paragraphs related to (i) the Company's reorganization under Chapter 11 of the U.S. Bankruptcy Code, (ii) the Company's ability to continue as a going concern, and (iii) the change in method of recognizing certain pension plan administrative expenses associated with the Company's defined benefit pension plans."

Surely, Ernst & Young realized that Northwest was in serious financial difficulty as of early 2005.

a. Do you think that Ernst & Young provided adequate warning to users of Northwest's financial statements as of February 25, 2005?

b. Whose responsibility is it to recognize and report problems regarding the going-concern status of a company? Review *Exhibit 14.3* and briefly describe the main steps the auditor should follow when assessing the going-concern status of a company.

c. Auditors cannot predict the future. Given this, what responsibility should the auditors have to determine whether a company is likely to remain in operation as a going concern?

d. Why might Ernst & Young have been reluctant to issue an audit report highlighting problems regarding the going-concern status of Northwest Airlines in early 2005?

ETHICS

INTERNATIONAL

14-41 **IRIDEX (LO 1)**   Access the following publicly available disclosures made by IRIDEX Corporation on the SEC's website (www.sec.gov)

- 8-K filed 8–29–2007
- 10-K filed 3–30–2007
- 10-K filed 4–10–2008
- Def 14A (proxy) filed 4–28–2008
- Def 14A (proxy) filed 5–4–2009

a. Review the disclosures in the 10-K filed March 30, 2007. Imagine that you are on PwC's engagement team for the December 31, 2006 year-end audit of IRIDEX. Describe the key business that IRIDEX engages in and list its three most important strategies for success. What risk characteristics of the company indicate that it may have difficulties remaining a going concern?

b. Review the disclosures in the 8-K filed August 29, 2007. What is the purpose of the 8-K filing? What does it reveal about PwC's ongoing relationship with IRIDEX? Based on the disclosures made in the filing, what risk factors were likely most relevant to PwC in making their client continuance decision about IRIDEX?

c. Review the disclosures in the 10-K filed April 10, 2008. Which audit firm accepted IRIDEX as a new client following PwC's resignation? In what important ways does that audit firm differ from PwC? Considering the concept of audit firm portfolio management discussed in *Chapter 1* and *Chapter 5*, discuss why it is reasonable for one audit firm to resign from a client like IRIDEX, and another audit firm to accept it as a new client immediately thereafter.

d. Review the audit fee and total fee disclosures in the Def 14A proxy statements filed April 28, 2008 and May 4, 2009. Use that information to compare and contrast the audit fees and total fees that IRIDEX paid to its auditors for the fiscal years ending December 31, 2006, 2007, and 2008. What inferences do you draw from that comparison?

e. Describe the ethical decisions that an auditor must make during portfolio management decisions, such as client acceptance and client continuance decisions. What is the relationship between ethics and audit quality?

14-42 **LO 4** Refer to the *Auditing Standards Exhibit* inside the front cover of this textbook. Identify the relevant auditing standards (PCAOB, AICPA, and IAASB) relating to communicating with audit committees. Locate the standards on each organization's website.

a. Compare the scope of communication intended in the PCAOB standard versus that of the harmonized AICPA/IAASB standards.

b. How do the AICPA/IAASB standards define "those charged with governance"?

c. The PCAOB standard notes that the prior auditing standard relating to this topic, AU 380 (1989), indicated that audit committee communications are incidental to the audit. The new PCAOB standard takes quite a different approach, articulating the critical importance of audit committee/auditor communication throughout the year, and certainly before the issuance of the audit report. Comment on why you think the profession has shifted its focus in this regard so significantly.

d. According to the PCAOB standard, what are the four objectives of the auditor in communicating with the audit committee?

14-43 **OAO Gazprom (LO 1)** The *Why It Matters* feature on OAO Gazprom speaks to issues of lack of disclosure quality at the company in and around 2009. Below is a stock price chart that shows the market's reaction to those weak disclosures. Use online resources to determine other reasons that OAO Gazprom stock was suffering at the time. In addition, search for information about OAO's audit firm in FYE 2015; do you think its quality is on par with that of PwC? What does your answer to the preceding question imply?

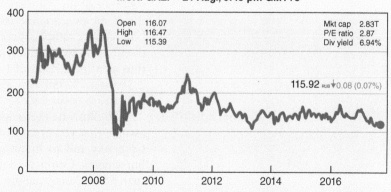

Gazprom PAO
MCX: GAZP - 21 Aug., 6:49 pm GMT+3

Open	116.07
High	116.47
Low	115.39

Mkt cap	2.83T
P/E ratio	2.87
Div yield	6.94%

115.92 RUB ▼0.08 (0.07%)

Source: https://www.google.co.in/search?rlz=1C1WZPD_enIN744IN744&q=MCX:GAZP&stick=H4sIAAAAAAAAAONgecRozi3w8sc9YSm9SWtOXmPU4OIKzsgvd80rySypFJLiYoOyBKT4uHj00_UNDY0qUwqr0gt4ANcvxQo8AAAA&sa=X&ved=0ahUKEwiJ97rOq9TWAhVEuo8KHY6xD78QsRUIzAEwGg&biw=1280&bih=617

Using ACL to Perform Benford Analysis

FRAUD

NOTE: There is an ACL Appendix at the end of the textbook that you may find helpful in completing this problem.

14-44 **LO 7** Dr. Frank Benford, a physicist at General Electric in the 1920s, found that the first and second digits of many populations of numbers occur with a fairly consistent frequency. This has been found true, for example, of census numbers and certain accounting populations, such as accounts payable. Benford developed a model that predicted the frequency of each digit occurring in a particular location depending on the length of a number. For example, he finds that the digit #1 occurs as the first digit in about 30% of all populations, while the digit #2 occurs as the first digit in about 17.5% of all populations. On the other hand, the digit #9 occurs as the first digit only about 4.5% of the time. Therefore, digits such as 990 do not occur as often as digits such as 124. Many others have empirically verified the Benford predictions.

Auditors have found that as individuals commit fraud or make up fraudulent transactions, their intuition in developing numbers for the fake documents often does not follow Benford's Law. Therefore, auditors have come to use Benford's Law to identify a wide variety of unusual transactions, including fraud, double payments, and other fictitious accounts. Audit software, such as ACL, comes with modules that allow auditors to apply Benford's Law to search for unusual patterns in populations by identifying numbering patterns that differ significantly from that predicted by Benford's Law.

Benford Analysis can be found by clicking **Analysis | Perform Benford Analysis**. You will be instructed to select a field on which to perform the analysis. You then make a choice to perform an analysis on the leading digit only, or you can perform an analysis on the two leading digits.

You can choose the type of output you want for the analysis by clicking the **Output** tab at the top of the window. The **GRAPH** option provides a bar graph with the predicted and actual frequencies of each leading digit or the two leading digits. The **SCREEN** and **FILE** options create a report containing the following:

- The actual count of the leading digit (or two leading digits)
- The expected count of the digit(s)
- A Zstat statistic

The Zstat statistic is derived from the probability of the deviation between the actual count and the expected count of the digit. The significance of the Zstat statistic is determined by comparing it with the Z statistic used to describe normal distributions in most statistical textbooks. For example, there is a 95% chance that most samples from a distribution would fall within 1.96 standard deviations from the mean, thus creating a Zstat of 1.96 for a 5% tail end of a distribution and 2.58 for a 1% tail. Any Zstat statistic greater than 2.58 would indicate a very rare occurrence.

To illustrate the power of Benford's Law in an auditing context, assume that you are the internal auditor for Knot Manufacturing Company and are auditing the travel, entertainment, and meal reimbursements. Company policy requires receipts for expenses greater than $25. Management must separately approve all reimbursements over $5,000. Download the file *Expense Reimbursements* from the "Student Resources" section of the textbook website. Analyze expense reimbursements using Benford's Law and ACL. Import the *Expense Reimbursements* file, which contains the reimbursement document numbers, employee numbers, and the amount of each reimbursement. Click **Analysis | Perform Benford Analysis** for the **AMOUNT** of the reimbursement.

1. Analyze on the leading digit. Choose **Output** to **Screen** and again to **Graph**. Print both outputs.
2. Analyze on the leading two digits. Choose **Output** to **Screen** and again to **Graph**. Print both outputs.
3. Summarize the number and amount of reimbursements between $24 and $25 by employee number. Do the same for amounts between $4,900 and $5,000. (*Hint:* Create filters for each of these dollar ranges.) Print the results.
4. Analyze the results and provide possible explanations for the results. Identify reimbursements for certain employees that may need further investigation.

Academic Research Cases

NOTE: Completing the *Academic Research Cases* requires students to reference additional resources and materials.

SEARCH HINT

It Is Easy to Locate Academic Research Articles! Use a Search Engine Such as Google Scholar or an Electronic Research Platform Such as Abi Inform, and Search Using the Author Names and Part of the Article Title.

14-45 `LO 4` Locate and read the article listed below.

Cohen, J., L. M. Gaynor, G. Krishnamoorthy, and A. M. Wright. (2007). Auditor communications with the audit committee and the board of directors: Policy recommendations and opportunities for future research. *Accounting Horizons* 21(2): 165–187.

a. What is the purpose of the study?
b. Describe the design/method/approach used to conduct the study.
c. What are the primary findings of the study?

14-46 `LO 1` Locate and read the article listed below.

Ruhnke, K., and M. Schmidt. (2014). Misstatements in financial statements: The relationship between inherent and control risk factors and audit adjustments. *Auditing: A Journal of Practice and Theory* 33(4): 247–269.

a. What is the purpose of the study?
b. Describe the design/method/approach used to conduct the study.
c. What are the primary findings of the study?

The Audit Opinion Formulation Process

I. Making Client Acceptance and Continuance Decisions **Chapter 1**	II. Performing Risk Assessment **Chapters 2, 3, 7, and 9–13**	III. Obtaining Evidence About Internal Control Operating Effectiveness **Chapters 8–13**	IV. Obtaining Substantive Evidence About Accounts, Disclosures, and Assertions **Chapters 8–13**	V. Completing the Audit and Making Reporting Decisions **Chapters 14 and 15**

Quality Auditing and the Need for Quality Auditor Judgments and Ethical Decisions

Chapter 1

Professional Liability

Chapter 4

The Audit Opinion Formulation Process and a Framework for Obtaining Audit Evidence

Chapters 5 and 6

You have now gathered sufficient appropriate audit evidence and are ready to issue the audit report! What type of audit report should you issue? Answering this question is critically important, as the audit report is the primary means that the auditor has of communicating the results of the audit to the users of the financial statements. While the expectation is for the auditor to issue an unqualified opinion on the financial statements and internal control, this chapter describes situations in which other opinions or modifications to the audit report would be expected.

Learning Objectives

LO 1 Describe the principles related to audit reporting on financial statements.

LO 2 Describe the format of an unqualified/unmodified audit report on financial statements and list the requirements for issuing this type of report.

LO 3 Describe financial statement audits resulting in an unqualified/unmodified audit opinion with report modifications, and identify the appropriate audit report modifications.

LO 4 Describe financial statement audits resulting in a qualified opinion, an adverse opinion, or a disclaimer of opinion, and identify the appropriate audit report modifications.

LO 5 Describe critical audit matters and key audit matters included in the auditor's report.

LO 6 For U.S. public companies, describe the information included in an auditor's report on internal control over financial reporting.

LO 7 Respond to situations in which omitted procedures come to the auditor's attention after the audit report has been issued.

LO 8 Apply the frameworks for professional decision making and ethical decision making to audit reporting situations.

A Move Toward Enhanced Disclosures in Audit Reports

This feature provides some insight into auditor reporting requirements in various countries and investor preferences related to auditor's reports.

Audit reports differ around the world. An interesting example is in the U.K. where auditors have adopted the concept of extended audit reports, which include an overview of:

- Risks of material misstatement that the auditor identified, and an explanation about which of these had the greatest impact on audit strategy, required resources, and work of the audit team
- How the auditor applied the concept of materiality
- The scope of the audit, including how the auditor responded to the risks of material misstatement

The UK reporting requirements are set at a high, conceptual level to encourage auditors to be innovative in their approach to reporting. These requirements represent a move away from boilerplate reporting with a pass/fail opinion (i.e., unqualified audit opinion or not), and move toward recognizing the importance of exercising professional judgment in determining the appropriate audit opinion.

Only a small number of countries, including the Netherlands and Australia, have implemented similar reporting requirements. More recently, the standards of the IAASB and the PCAOB require auditors to report important audit matters, which might be broadly equivalent to the assessed risks of material misstatement and associated reporting that the U.K. requires.

A recent review of the audit reports of the largest U.K. listed companies and related discussions with investors provide some interesting findings.

- Investors seek additional transparency, including more complete information about the sensitivity ranges applicable to audit testing, how the auditor's assessment of the quality of an entity's internal controls informed their risk assessment, the auditor's view on the appropriateness of management estimates, and assumptions that management made and benchmarks that the auditor used in decision making.

- Investors favor audit reports that are structured with the user in mind and that provide clear, concise, and transparent disclosures about risk, **audit scope** (the range of accounts and transactions that the auditor evaluates, along with the amount of evidence that they gather, assessments

of which accounts and transactions are material), as well as the critical areas where the auditor employed significant assumptions and made associated professional judgments.

- Many investors are disappointed with the widespread absence of explanations that auditors provide about any changes in their audit approach, their assessments about what is or is not material, and the risks that they assess from one year to the next.

- Users welcome and appreciate information that the auditor voluntarily provides, i.e., disclosures that go above and beyond the requirements in auditing standards about the auditor's findings and associated risks of material misstatement.

Source: *https://www.frc.org.uk/getattachment/76641d68-c739-45ac-a251-cabbfd2397e0/Report-on-the-Second-Year-Experience-of-Extended-Auditors-Reports-Jan-2016.pdf*

What You Will Learn

- What are the principles related to audit reporting? (LO 1)
- What information is included in an unqualified/unmodified audit report? (LO 2)
- What are the requirements for issuing an unqualified/unmodified audit report? (LO 2)
- What circumstances require a deviation from an unqualified audit report? (LO 3, 4)

- What are critical audit matters and key audit matters? (LO 5)
- What are the components of an audit report on internal control over financial reporting? (LO 6)
- What should an auditor do when learning, after issuing the audit report, that some important audit procedures were not performed? (LO 7)

LO 1

Describe the principles related to audit reporting on financial statements.

Audit Reporting Principles

Professional auditing standards provide guidance for auditors making reporting decisions, and there are some differences in audit report requirements across the standards of the AICPA, PCAOB, and IAASB. In general, auditing standards require auditors to provide **positive assurance**—that is, an explicit statement as to whether the financial statements are presented fairly and, for larger U.S. public companies, whether internal control over financial reporting is effective.

With respect to the financial statements, the expectation of both the auditor and the client is usually that the report includes an **unqualified opinion** (also referred to as an **unmodified opinion**); that is, the auditor has no reservations about the fairness of presentation.

The auditor forms an opinion on the financial statements based on an evaluation of the audit evidence obtained, and expresses that opinion in a written report. The AICPA describes the basic principles related to audit reporting as follows:

The purpose of an audit is to enhance the degree of confidence that users can place in the financial statement. This purpose is achieved when an auditor expresses an opinion on the financial statements.

The auditor expresses an opinion as to whether the financial statements are free of material misstatement or states that an opinion cannot be expressed.

The PCAOB provides similar guidance:

> The objective of the ordinary audit of financial statements by the independent auditor is the expression of an opinion on the fairness with which they present, in all material respects, financial position, results of operations, and its cash flows in conformity with generally accepted accounting principles. The auditor's report is the medium through which he expresses his opinion or, if circumstances require, disclaims an opinion.[1]

The IAASB notes that the objectives of the auditor are:

a. To form an opinion on the financial statements based on an evaluation of the conclusions drawn from the audit evidence obtained; and

b. To express clearly that opinion through a written report.

Recall that the objective of an audit is to obtain reasonable assurance about whether the financial statements are free from material misstatement, and to provide an opinion about the financial statements for the benefit of users. The principles, guidance, and objectives of AICPA, PCAOB, and IAASB vary somewhat in terminology, but all support this objective. Auditors' assurances about the financial statements that they provide in the audit report enhance the credibility of management's financial statement assertions.

For Classroom Discussion

What Do You Think?

A well-known, simple characterization that gets at the very essence of the purpose of auditing includes the following phrase:

Auditing is the difference between management telling the truth, and users believing it.

What does this phrase mean to you? Have you ever told the truth and had someone refuse to believe it? How does this phrase relate to the usefulness of the auditor report?

Check Your Basic Knowledge

15-1 The auditor should provide an audit report on the financial statements only if the audit opinion indicates that the financial statements are fairly stated in all material respects.   (T/F)

15-2 The auditor should provide the audit opinion in a written report.   (T/F)

15-3 Which of the following statements is <u>false</u> regarding audit reporting?

  a. Auditing standards require auditors to provide positive assurance—that is, an explicit statement as to whether the financial statements are presented fairly.

  b. The auditor should provide an opinion in accordance with the auditor's findings or state that an opinion cannot be expressed.

  c. The auditor's opinion should state whether the financial statements are presented fairly, in all material respects, in accordance with the applicable financial reporting framework.

  d. None of the above statements are false.

15-4 Which of the following statements is <u>true</u> regarding the auditor's responsibilities related to reporting?

  a. Auditors should obtain sufficient appropriate evidence to provide a reasonable basis for the opinion regarding the financial statements under audit.

  b. The audit opinion relates only to the client's financial statements, and does not relate to the required footnote disclosures.

  c. If the auditor has reservations about the fairness of presentation of the financial statements, the auditor does not need to provide the reason for this reservation, but needs to only state that the financial statements are not fairly presented.

  d. All of the above statements are true.

LO 2

Describe the format of an unqualified/unmodified audit report on financial statements and list the requirements for issuing this type of report.

Unqualified/Unmodified Audit Reports on Financial Statements

An auditor will issue an unqualified/unmodified report when all of the following conditions are present:

- there are no material violations of generally accepted accounting principles (GAAP)
- disclosures are adequate
- the auditor was able to perform all of the necessary procedures
- there was no change in accounting principles that had a material effect on the financial statements
- the auditor does not have significant doubt about the client remaining a going concern
- the auditor is independent

When these conditions are not present, the auditor will modify the unqualified report in one of the following ways, each of which we discuss later in the chapter:

- Issue an unqualified opinion, with report modifications
- Qualify the audit opinion
- Issue an adverse opinion
- Issue a disclaimer of opinion

The timeliness of the audit report matters. The Security and Exchange Commission (SEC) wants organizations—and their auditors—to provide timely financial information to investors, while allowing for enough time to gather sufficient appropriate audit evidence. The SEC also recognizes that smaller companies may not have the same resources to enable them to report as quickly compared to larger companies. *Exhibit 15.1* shows how timeliness requirements vary by the size of the organization.

Exhibit 15.1
SEC Reporting Deadlines

Size of Filer	Form 10-K (Annual Report)
Large accelerated filer—Market capitalization greater than $700 million	60 days after year end
Accelerated filer—Market capitalization greater than $75 million, but less than $700 million	75 days after year end
Nonaccelerated filer—Market capitalization less than $75 million	90 days after year end

What Do You Think?   For Classroom Discussion

Exhibit 15.1 reveals differences in reporting deadlines for U.S. public companies. For example, nonaccelerated filers have an entire month longer than large accelerated filers to provide information to users.

Does this difference seem fair to you from a user perspective? What reasons do you think that the SEC has for allowing nonaccelerated filers to have more time to provide these disclosures? All else held equal, would you prefer to invest in a company that provides disclosures after 60 days, or one that provides disclosures after 90 days?

Unqualified Audit Reports: U.S. Public Companies

Effective for fiscal years ending on or after December 15, 2017, auditors following PCAOB standards will issue audit reports that include the following basic elements, as illustrated in *Exhibit 15.2, Panel A*:

- *Title* "Report of Independent Registered Public Accounting Firm," and the *addressee(s)*
- *Opinion on the Financial Statements*
- *Basis for Opinion* section that follows the *Opinion*
- *Signature, Tenure, Location,* and *Date*

This format became effective with the adoption of the new reporting standard AS 3101 in 2017. The audit firm is also required to report the name of the engagement partner and information about the involvement of other accounting firms participating in the audit on PCAOB Form AP, "Auditor Reporting of Certain Audit Participants." The auditor may include this information in the auditor's report for an individual engagement, but is not required to do so.

As you will see when comparing *Exhibit 15.2, Panels A and B*, the new reporting standard retains the pass/fail opinion, which has been in existence for many decades. The new reporting standard also includes the following changes in the report (which we highlight in bold in *Exhibit 15.2, Panel A*):

- Specific mention of comprehensive income and the notes to the financial statements
- An affirmative statement the audit firm is registered with the Public Company Accounting Oversight Board
- An affirmative statement regarding the requirement for the auditor to be independent with respect to the company
- Amended language that adds the phrase *whether due to error or fraud* when describing the auditor's responsibility to plan and perform the audit to obtain reasonable assurance about whether the financial statements are free of material misstatements
- A new disclosure, which includes the year in which the auditor began serving consecutively as the company's auditor

Exhibit 15.2
Differences Between the "New" Audit Report and "Old" Audit Report Under PCAOB Standards

Panel A: The "New" Audit Report

NOTE: The format of the audit report depends on the auditing standards the auditor is following.

This Panel provides the unqualified audit report format for U.S. public companies subsequent to the adoption of the new reporting standard AS 3101 in 2017. **Bold** *text highlights important differences between the "new" and "old" audit reports.*

Report of Independent Registered Public Accounting Firm

To the shareholders and the board of directors of X Company

Opinion on the Financial Statements

We have audited the accompanying balance sheets of X Company (the "Company") as of December 31, 20X2 and 20X1, the related statements of [titles of the financial statements, e.g., income, **comprehensive income**, stockholders' equity, and cash flows], for each of the three years in the period ended December 31, 20X2, **and the related notes [and schedules]** (collectively referred to as the "financial statements"). In our opinion, the financial statements present fairly, in all material respects,

(Continues)

Exhibit 15.2 *Continued*

the financial position of the Company as of [at] December 31, 20X2 and 20X1, and the results of its operations and its cash flows for each of the three years in the period ended December 31, 20X2, in conformity with [the applicable financial reporting framework].

Basis for Opinion

These financial statements are the responsibility of the Company's management. Our responsibility is to express an opinion on the Company's financial statements based on our audits. **We are a public accounting firm registered with the Public Company Accounting Oversight Board (United States) ("PCAOB") and are required to be independent with respect to the Company in accordance with the U.S. federal securities laws and the applicable rules and regulations of the Securities and Exchange Commission and the PCAOB.**

We conducted our audits in accordance with the standards of the PCAOB. Those standards require that we plan and perform the audit to obtain reasonable assurance about whether the financial statements are free of material misstatement, **whether due to error or fraud. Our audits included performing procedures to assess the risks of material misstatement of the financial statements, whether due to error or fraud, and performing procedures that respond to those risks.** Such procedures included examining, on a test basis, evidence regarding the amounts and disclosures in the financial statements. Our audits also included evaluating the accounting principles used and significant estimates made by management, as well as evaluating the overall presentation of the financial statements. We believe that our audits provide a reasonable basis for our opinion.

[*Signature of the AUDIT FIRM; note that the identity of the engagement partner may also be provided here, but at a minimum it must be provided by the issuer in PCAOB Form AP*]

We have served as the Company's auditor since [*year*].

[*City and State or Country*]

[*Date*]

Source: *PCAOB Release No. 2017-001, June 1, 2017*

Panel B. The "Old" Audit Report for U.S. Public Companies

NOTE: This Panel provides the unqualified audit report format for U.S. public companies prior to the adoption of the new reporting standard AS 3101 in 2017.

Report of Independent Registered Public Accounting Firm

To the shareholders and the board of directors of X Company

We have audited the accompanying balance sheets of X Company as of December 31, 20X2 and 20X1, and the related statements of income, retained earnings, and cash flows for the years then ended. These financial statements are the responsibility of the Company's management. Our responsibility is to express an opinion on these financial statements based on our audits.

We conducted our audits in accordance with the standards of the Public Company Accounting Oversight Board (United States). Those standards require that we plan and perform the audit to obtain reasonable assurance about whether the financial statements are free of material misstatement. An audit includes examining, on a test basis, evidence supporting the amounts and disclosures in the financial statements. An audit also includes assessing the accounting principles used and significant estimates made by management, as well as evaluating the overall financial statement presentation. We believe that our audits provide a reasonable basis for our opinion.

In our opinion, the financial statements referred to above present fairly, in all material respects, the financial position of X Company as of [at] December 31, 20X2 and 20X1, and the results of its operations and its cash flows for the years then ended in conformity with accounting principles generally accepted in the United States of America.

[*Signature of the AUDIT FIRM*]

[*City and State or Country*]

[*Date*]

Source: *PCAOB, AS 3101: Reports on Audited Financial Statements*

For Classroom Discussion

What Do You Think?

Compare the two versions of the auditor's report in *Exhibit 15.2, Panels A* and *B.*

- What features of the new audit report do you find helpful/informative? You may find it helpful to review *Staff Guidance* issued by the PCAOB in December 2017 related to changes in the auditor's report. The guidance is available at *https://pcaobus.org/Standards/Documents/2017-12-04-Auditors-Report-Staff-Guidance.pdf*
- Do you think these new features benefit users?
- Do you think that there is room for further improvement in the auditor's report for U.S. companies?
- Are there other features that you think an investor might find helpful?

Some additional features discussed in the profession include the auditor's assessment of management's estimates and judgments, unusual transactions, restatements and other changes, and the auditor's assessment of the quality of the issuer's accounting policies and practices.

- Would you support including such features in the audit report?
- What information would you suggest be included in the auditor's report?
- Speculate on the political forces in play in terms of auditors' willingness to provide assurance over these types of additional features.

Unmodified Audit Reports: U.S. Nonpublic Companies

The components of the audit report for U.S. nonpublic companies include:

- *Title* and *Addressee*
- What was audited (*introductory paragraph*)
- Responsibilities of client management (*management's responsibility paragraph*; should include the heading "Management's Responsibility for the Financial Statements")
- Responsibilities of the auditor and the nature of the audit process (*auditor's responsibility paragraph*; should include the heading "Auditor's Responsibility")
- The auditor's opinion on the fairness of the financial statements (*opinion paragraph*; should include the heading "Auditor's Opinion")
- *Signature of the auditor*
- *Auditor's Address*
- *Date of the Auditor's Report*

The language contained in the management's responsibility paragraph is:

> Management is responsible for the preparation and fair presentation of these consolidated financial statements in accordance with accounting principles generally accepted in the United States of America; this includes the design, implementation, and maintenance of internal control relevant to the preparation and fair presentation of consolidated financial statements that are free from material misstatement, whether due to fraud or error. (AICPA, AU-C 700, Appendix A)

The language contained in the auditor's responsibility paragraph is:

> Our responsibility is to express an opinion on these consolidated financial statements based on our audits. We conducted our audits in accordance with auditing standards generally accepted in the United States of America. Those standards require that we plan and perform the audit to obtain reasonable assurance about whether the consolidated financial statements are free from material misstatement.
>
> An audit involves performing procedures to obtain audit evidence about the amounts and disclosures in the consolidated financial statements. The procedures selected depend on the auditor's judgment, including the assessment of the risks of material misstatement of the consolidated financial statements, whether

due to fraud or error. In making those risk assessments, the auditor considers internal control relevant to the entity's preparation and fair presentation of the consolidated financial statements in order to design audit procedures that are appropriate in the circumstances, but not for the purpose of expressing an opinion on the effectiveness of the entity's internal control. Accordingly, we express no such opinion. An audit also includes evaluating the appropriateness of accounting policies used and the reasonableness of significant accounting estimates made by management, as well as evaluating the overall presentation of the consolidated financial statements.

We believe that the audit evidence we have obtained is sufficient and appropriate to provide a basis for our audit opinion. (AICPA, AU-C 700, Appendix A)

Unmodified Audit Reports: Non-U.S. Companies

Auditors following the ISAs would refer to ISA 700 for relevant guidance on audit reports. The format of an ISA audit report is similar to the PCAOB's report format under the reporting standard, AS 3101, adopted in 2017 (see *Exhibit 15.2, Panel A*).

One difference between the ISA and AS guidance involves terminology. ISA 700 allows for the description in the audit report to indicate that the financial statements *present fairly, in all material respects* or *give a true and fair view of*. U.S. auditing standards do not include any references to *true and fair view* because

Why It Matters

Auditing Standards Board Considers Proposed Changes to Expand the Auditor's Report

This feature illustrates the Auditing Standards Board's (ASB) continuing effort to align its standards with those of the IAASB, this time in the area of auditor reporting. Auditors need to be alert to changing guidance.

In July 2017, the AICPA's ASB voted to issue an exposure draft that would improve the auditor's report by aligning its guidance with standards the IAASB issued in 2015. At some future time, the audit report of U.S. nonpublic organizations may look very similar to the audit reports issued under ISAs.

Why It Matters

Using Multiple Sets of Auditing Standards

This feature provides guidance for auditors on language to use when conducting an audit in accordance with more than one set of auditing standards in their entirety.

As an example, consider an auditor who uses audit standards generally accepted in the United States of America (GAAS) and the International Standards on Auditing (ISA). For those engagements, AU-C 700 states that the auditor's responsibility section should include the following language:

We conducted our audits in accordance with auditing standards generally accepted in the United States of America and in accordance with International Standards on Auditing. (Source: *AICPA, AU-C 700, Appendix A*)

Guidance from the PCAOB (AS 3101) requires that the auditor indicate in the auditor's report that the audit was conducted in accordance with the standards of the PCAOB; it does not prohibit the auditor from indicating that the audit also was conducted in accordance with another set of auditing standards. If the audit was also conducted in accordance with the International Standards on Auditing, in their entirety, the auditor may so indicate in the auditor's report. Following is acceptable language to reflect this situation:

We conducted our audit in accordance with the standards of the PCAOB and in accordance with International Standards on Auditing. (Source: *PCAOB Release No. 2017-001, June 1, 2017*)

such wording has not historically been used in the U.S.; these standards continue to require the use of *present fairly, in all material respects* in the audit report.

Another difference is that the engagement partner's name must be included in the ISA audit report, while for U.S. public company audits, it is optional to include that information in the audit report (but it is required in the PCAOB's Form AP). A third difference is that the ISA report does not include information on audit firm tenure with the client.

A major current difference in audit reports between non-U.S. companies and U.S. companies is the inclusion of important audit matters in the audit report. These are issues the auditor viewed as most significant during the audit. ISA 701, *Communicating Key Audit Matters in the Independent Auditor's Report*, requires that such matters be included in the audit report. In July 2017, the ASB voted to consider aligning it guidance with ISA 701, and require auditors to include in the auditor's report key audit matters.

Under AS 3101 (approved in 2017), audit reports for large U.S. public companies will include important audit matters, known as critical audit matters, for fiscal years ending on or after June 30, 2019. Audit reports for smaller U.S. public companies will include these matters for fiscal years ending on or after December 15, 2020. We discuss important audit matters as part of *LO 5*.

Dating the Auditor's Report: Guidance from the Standards

Why It Matters

This feature summarizes guidance on the date of the auditor's report.

The date of the auditor's report informs the users of the auditor's report that the auditor has considered the effect of events and transactions of which the auditor became aware and that occurred up to that date. Auditing standards of the AICPA, PCAOB, and IAASB provide similar guidance on the date of the auditor's report. The auditor's report should be dated no earlier than the date on which the auditor has obtained sufficient appropriate audit evidence on which to base the auditor's opinion on the financial statements.

Check Your Basic Knowledge

15-5 If an auditor conducts an audit in accordance with multiple auditing standards in their entirety, the auditor can only mention one set of standards in the audit report.   (T/F)

15-6 Under guidance issued by the PCAOB in 2017, the audit report should include a statement indicating how long the audit firm has served as the company's auditor.   (T/F)

15-7 In which of the following situations would an auditor ordinarily issue an unqualified audit opinion without any report modifications?

a. The auditor wishes to emphasize that the client had significant related party transactions.

b. The auditor complies with only one set of auditing standards.

c. The client issues financial statements that present financial position and results of operations, but omits the statement of cash flows.

d. The auditor has substantial doubt about the client's ability to continue as a going concern, and the circumstances are fully disclosed in the financial statements.

15-8 Which of the following would require other than an unqualified opinion?

a. The client has prepared its financial statements using IFRS as the financial reporting framework.

b. The auditor has complied with the auditing standards of both the AICPA and the IAASB.

c. The auditor is not independent.

d. The auditor believes that the client will remain a going concern for a reasonable period of time.

LO 3

Describe financial statement audits resulting in an unqualified/ unmodified audit opinion with report modifications, and identify the appropriate audit report modifications.

Unqualified/Unmodified Audit Opinions with Report Modifications

The following are common situations when the auditor would issue an unqualified/unmodified audit opinion with report modifications:

- The auditor chooses to emphasize some matter in the financial statements
- The auditor opts to include information about audit participants in the audit report (applicable only for PCAOB audits)
- The auditor decides to refer to other auditors as the basis, in part, for the auditor's own report
- There is a lack of consistency in the financial statements
- There is a justified departure from GAAP
- Substantial doubt about the client being a going concern exists
- The client had a material misstatement in previously issued financial statements that it has corrected

Emphasis-of-Matter

Auditors have the option of including a paragraph with an unqualified opinion to emphasize a matter regarding the financial statements. The *choice* to emphasize a matter (other than those *required* to be emphasized) is strictly one of auditor judgment. Including an emphasis-of-matter paragraph does not affect the auditor's opinion. If the auditor includes an emphasis paragraph in the auditor's report, the auditor should use an appropriate section title. Following are examples of when the auditor may choose to include an emphasis-of-matter paragraph:

- An uncertainty relating to the future outcome of unusually important litigation or regulatory action
- A major catastrophe that has had, or continues to have, a significant effect on the entity's financial position
- Significant transactions with related parties
- Unusually important subsequent events

The following is example language that auditors use to emphasize a matter related to the financial statements in the auditor's report:

> We draw attention to Note X of the financial statements, which describes the effects of hurricane-related damage in the Company's production facilities and headquarters offices.

Distinguishing Between Emphasis-of-Matter and Other-Matter

There is a difference between the terms *emphasis-of-matter* and *other-matter*. According to AU-C 706, an **emphasis-of-matter paragraph** is one that is "included in the auditor's report that is required by auditing standards, or is included at the auditor's discretion, and that refers to a matter appropriately presented or disclosed in the financial statements that, in the auditor's professional judgment, is of such importance that it is fundamental to users' understanding of the financial statements."

In contrast, an **other-matter paragraph** is one that is included in the auditor's report that is required by the auditing standards, or is included at the auditor's discretion, and that refers to a matter other than those presented or disclosed in the financial statements that, in the auditor's professional judgment, is relevant to users' understanding of the audit, the auditor's responsibilities, or the auditor's report. For example, an other-matter paragraph may be relevant to users' understanding of the audit in the rare situation when the auditor is unable to withdraw from an engagement even though the possible effect of an inability to obtain sufficient appropriate audit evidence due to a limitation on the scope of the audit imposed by management is pervasive. The auditor may consider it necessary to include an other-matter paragraph in the auditor's report to explain why it is not possible for the auditor to withdraw from the engagement.

Information about Certain Audit Participants

For U.S. public companies, the auditor may include in the auditor's report information regarding the engagement partner and/or other accounting firms participating in the audit that is required to be reported on PCAOB Form AP. If the auditor decides to provide this information in the audit report, the auditor must disclose:

a. *Engagement partner*—the engagement partner's full name as required on Form AP;

and/or

b. *Other accounting firms participating in the audit*—specific information as outlined in Appendix A to PCAOB Release No. 2017-001

If the auditor decides to include information regarding certain audit participants in the auditor's report, the auditor should use an appropriate section title. Furthermore, the auditor should include a statement indicating that the auditor is responsible for the audits or audit procedures performed by the other public accounting firms and has supervised or performed procedures to assume responsibility for their work in accordance with PCAOB standards.

For Classroom Discussion

What Do You Think?

Listen (at *https://www.youtube.com/watch?v=78LKXWVt4oA*) to the PCAOB's then- Chairman, James Doty, explain the Board's rationale for requiring public disclosure of the audit partner, and any other audit firms that have completed important parts of the audit (but who are not signing the opinion). "AP" is an abbreviation for the term "Audit Participants," not "Audit Partner."

Do you think that auditors will choose to include information regarding the engagement partner and/or other participating accounting firms *voluntarily in the auditor's report*? Or will they only report this information *in the PCAOB Form AP*? Which approach do you think investors would prefer?

It's Your Turn!

Prompt for Critical Thinking #1

Access AuditorSearch at *https://pcaobus.org/Pages/AuditorSearch.aspx*. This is a public database of engagement partners and audit firms participating in audits of U.S. public companies. The database summarizes required disclosures from Form AP.

What are some important facts that a user can obtain and critically analyze in thinking about a particular issuer client, audit firm, or engagement partner? Let's walk through a few examples in the database to answer this question.

Example 1.

(Analysis purpose: How many and what types of clients does an audit partner of a large retailer audit?)

Hint: for (a) search on Target Corporation for "Issuer"; for (b) search on Partner name X to obtain the other clients for that partner; for (c) review the names of the companies and search online for data on them to determine their relative business models and industries.

a. Who is the audit partner of Target Corporation? _____
b. On what other public companies is he the engagement partner? _____

c.   How similar or different are those companies as compared to Target? What might you infer from the similarities/differences in this audit partner's portfolio of audit clients? _____

Example 2.

(Analysis purpose: How many publicly traded clients do audit firms of various sizes audit in the U.S.?)

Hint: Search on United States for "Firm Country"; then search by Firm for "Deloitte", then "KPMG", and then "Baker Tilly", noting the sample size of hits that you obtain for each firm.

a.   How many publicly traded clients does Deloitte audit? _____

b.   How many publicly traded clients does KPMG audit? _____

c.   How many publicly traded clients does Baker Tilly audit? _____

What can a critical user learn about relative market share by conducting these analyses?

Example 3.

Analysis purpose: For an audit firm that had a PCAOB enforcement action in a particular country, how many audits (and who are the clients) is that firm doing this year? In this example, we will focus on Deloitte because of PCAOB Enforcement Action 105-2016-031 relating to its audit of Gol Intelligent Airlines.

Hint: Search on Brazil for "Firm Country"; then sort by Firm Name (A–Z).

_____

_____

_____

Reference to Other Auditors

For some clients, part of the audit will be performed by other independent auditors, or by another legal entity within the firm's network (e.g., KPMG US, and KPMG AG — Switzerland). For example, an auditor may involve another auditor to observe the inventory count or inspect long-term assets at a remote location. If the principal auditor is satisfied as to the independence and professional reputation of the other auditor, and takes steps to ensure that the audit work performed by the other auditor is satisfactory, the principal auditor may decide to express an opinion on the financial statements taken as a whole without making reference in his report to the audit of the other auditor.

When the principal auditor decides to make reference to the audit of the other auditor, the audit report should clearly indicate the division of responsibility between that portion of the financial statements covered by the principal auditor and that covered by the other auditor. The report should disclose the magnitude of the portion of the financial statements audited by the other auditor. This may be done by stating the dollar amounts or percentages of one or more of the following: total assets, total revenues, or other appropriate criteria, whichever most clearly reveals the portion of the financial statements audited by the other auditor. *Exhibit 15.3* provides example audit report language for this situation. The basis for opinion for the situation in *Exhibit 15.3* would include a statement indicating, "We believe that our audit and the report of the other auditors provide a reasonable basis for our opinion." The other auditor may be named, but only with that auditor's express permission and provided that the other auditor's report is presented together with that of the principal auditor.

Exhibit 15.3

Example of an Excerpt from an Unqualified Audit Report with Explanatory Language Indicating the Division of Responsibility and Making a Reference to the Other Auditors: PCAOB Audit

NOTE: The format of the audit report depends on the auditing standards the auditor is following.

Opinion on the Financial Statements

We have audited the accompanying consolidated balance sheet of X Company (the "Company") and subsidiaries as of December 31, 20. . . ., and the related consolidated statements of [*titles of the financial statements, e.g., income, comprehensive income, stockholders' equity, and cash flows*] for the year then ended, and the related notes [*and schedules*] (collectively referred to as the "consolidated financial statements"). In our opinion, based on our audit and the report of the other auditors, the consolidated financial statements present fairly, in all material respects, the financial position of the Company as of [at] December 31, 20. . . ., and the results of its operations and its cash flows for the year then ended in conformity with accounting principles generally accepted in the United States of America.

We did not audit the financial statements of B Company, a wholly-owned subsidiary, which statements reflect total assets and revenues constituting 20 percent and 22 percent, respectively, of the related consolidated totals. Those statements were audited by other auditors whose report has been furnished to us, and our opinion, insofar as it relates to the amounts included for B Company, is based solely on the report of the other auditors.

Source: PCAOB Release No. 2017-001, June 1, 2017

Differing Guidance on Referring to Other Auditors for Group Audits

Why It Matters

This feature notes that auditing standards differ in their guidance on referring to other auditors in the audit report.

Similar to the PCAOB standards (see *Exhibit 15.3*), AU-C 600 allows the auditor's report to include a reference to another auditor. In contrast, ISA 600 does not permit the auditor's report to make reference to another auditor, unless required by law or regulation.

The relevant terminology in the auditing standards refers to a **group audit** in which a **group audit opinion** is issued. The term **group** refers to all the components whose financial information is included in the group financial statements. A group always has more than one component. A **component** is an entity or business activity for which group or component management prepares financial information that is required by the applicable financial reporting framework to be included in the group financial statements.

If the **group engagement partner** decides to assume responsibility for work of a **component auditor**, no reference should be made to the component auditor in the auditor's report on the **group financial statements**.

It's Your Turn!

Prompt for Critical Thinking #2

Access AuditorSearch at *https://pcaobus.org/Pages/Auditor Search.aspx*. This is a public database of engagement partners and audit firms participating in audits of U.S. public companies. The database summarizes required disclosures from Form AP.

For this Prompt, search the database to find an audit under the oversight of the PCAOB, which was conducted in Australia.

Hint: Search on "Firm Country", and indicate Australia. Note: Answers are based on accessing the database on September 19, 2017.

Look for an entry that contains a notation of "other participating firms," such as that depicted below for the audit of BHP Billiton Limited:

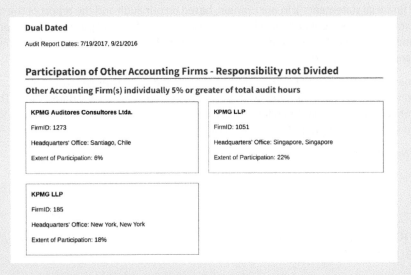

| Aug. 22, 2017 | Anthony W Young | BHP Billiton Limited (BHP \| 0000811809) | KPMG (1020) ❂ other participating firms | 2016 |

https://pcaobus.org/form-ap-filings/11163/11163

Click on the "other participating firms" icon and select the Form AP filing (in this case at *https://pcaobus.org/form-ap-filings/11163/11163*). You will then be presented with the relative split of engagement effort across various participating firms (or worldwide affiliates that share the same name):

Dual Dated

Audit Report Dates: 7/19/2017, 9/21/2016

Participation of Other Accounting Firms - Responsibility not Divided

Other Accounting Firm(s) individually 5% or greater of total audit hours

KPMG Auditores Consultores Ltda.
FirmID: 1273
Headquarters' Office: Santiago, Chile
Extent of Participation: 6%

KPMG LLP
FirmID: 1051
Headquarters' Office: Singapore, Singapore
Extent of Participation: 22%

KPMG LLP
FirmID: 185
Headquarters' Office: New York, New York
Extent of Participation: 18%

https://pcaobus.org/form-ap-filings/11163/11163

In this particular case, we see that three affiliated KPMG firms conducted the audit, with the majority in Australia, but with a total of 46% conducted with the help of offices in Chile, Singapore, and the U.S.

- What inferences do you draw based upon the fact that multiple offices participated in the audit?
- What benefits might having multiple offices participate in the audit yield?
- What disadvantages might occur by having multiple offices participate in the audit?

Inconsistent Application of GAAP

A change in accounting principle that has a material effect on the financial statements should be recognized in the audit report. A change in accounting principles includes a change from one GAAP to another, such as from FIFO to LIFO. A change from non-GAAP to GAAP—such as from the cash basis to the accrual basis—is accounted for as a correction of an error, but is treated by the auditor as a change in accounting principle requiring an additional paragraph.

Both changes require the auditor to add a paragraph to the audit report. If there is a change in reporting entity that is not due to a transaction or event, for example, a change to present consolidated statements rather than the statements of an individual company, the auditor would address this change by adding an additional paragraph. However, if the change in reporting entity arises from a transaction or event such as an acquisition, the auditor would not add an explanatory paragraph.

If the client has changed an accounting principle, has reasonable justification for the change, and has followed GAAP in accounting for and disclosing this change, the explanatory paragraph serves as a flag directing the user's attention to the relevant footnote disclosure. This flag can be very useful. For example, consider a company that reported a 22% increase in net income and highlighted the increase several times in its annual report to shareholders. Only by noting the additional paragraph in the auditor's report and carefully reading the financial statements and footnotes would the user have seen that the increase in net income would have been only 6% had there not been a change in an accounting principle.

The following is an example of language describing a change in accounting principle resulting from the adoption of a new accounting pronouncement:

> As discussed in Note X to the financial statements, the Company has changed its method of accounting for [*describe accounting method changes*] in [*year(s) of financial statements that reflect the accounting method change*] due to the adoption of [*name of accounting pronouncement*]. (Source: *PCAOB Release No. 2017-001, June 1, 2017*)

If the change in accounting principle is not justified or accounted for correctly, or there is inadequate disclosure, the auditor is dealing with a departure from GAAP. As we note later, a GAAP departure leads either to a qualified opinion or, in some cases, an adverse opinion.

Justified Departure from GAAP

The "Accounting Principles Rule" (of the AICPA Code of Professional Conduct) states (italics added for emphasis):

> A member shall not (1) express an opinion or state affirmatively that the financial statements or other financial data of any entity are presented in conformity with generally accepted accounting principles or (2) state that he or she is not aware of any material modifications that should be made to such statements or data in order for them to be in conformity with generally accepted accounting principles, if such statements or data contain any departure from an accounting principle promulgated by bodies designated by Council to establish such principles that has a material effect on the statements or data taken as a whole.
>
> *If, however, the statements or data contain such a departure and the member can demonstrate that due to unusual circumstances the financial statements or data would otherwise have been misleading, the member can comply with the rule by describing the departure, its approximate effects, if practicable, and the reasons why compliance with the principle would result in a misleading statement.*

Following is possible audit report language an auditor could use to describe a justified departure from GAAP:

> As described in Note 3, in May, the company exchanged shares of its common stock for $5,060,000 of its outstanding public debt. The fair value of the common stock issued exceeded the carrying amount of the debt by $466,000, which has been shown as an extraordinary loss in the statement of operations. Because a portion of the debt exchanged was convertible debt, a literal application of FASB ASC Topic 470 "Debt" would have resulted in a further reduction in net income of $3,611,000, which would have been offset by a corresponding $3,611,000 credit to additional paid-in capital; accordingly, there would have been no net effect on stockholders' investments. In the opinion of company management, with which we agree, a literal application of accounting literature would have resulted in misleading financial statements that do not properly portray the economic consequences of the exchange.

Substantial Doubt about the Client Being a Going Concern

As we discuss in *Chapter 14*, the auditor has a responsibility to evaluate whether there is substantial doubt about the client's ability to continue as a going concern for a reasonable period of time. If, after considering identified conditions and events and management's plans, the auditor concludes that substantial doubt about the entity's ability to continue as a going concern for a reasonable period of time remains, the audit report should include an additional paragraph, including an appropriate title to reflect that conclusion.

Why It Matters   The Drama of Survival: The Case of ImmunoGen

This feature explains a series of inter related events concerning a struggling pharmaceutical company, its auditor, and another company that is pulling ImmunoGen away from the brink of bankruptcy. This feature also highlights the drama that companies encounter in their bid to survive, along with the stock market reaction and associated analysts' predictions and recommendations.

Ernst & Young had this to say about its assessment of Immuno-Gen's going-concern status (March 3, 2017) (emphasis added):

> The accompanying consolidated financial statements have been prepared assuming that the Company will continue as a going concern. **As discussed in Note A to the consolidated financial statements, the Company has recurring losses from operations and insufficient cash resources that raise substantial doubt about its ability to continue as a going concern. Management's plans in regard to these matters are also described in Note A. The consolidated financial statements do not include any adjustments that might result from the outcome of this uncertainty.**

ImmunoGen's Management had this to say about its assessment of the company's going-concern status (FYE 2016, 10-K, Note A p. 66) (emphasis added):

> The Company has incurred operating losses and negative cash flows from operations since inception, incurred a net loss of approximately $78.9 million during the six months ended December 31, 2016, and has an accumulated deficit of approximately $932.6 million as of December 31, 2016... To date, **the Company has no product revenue and management expects operating losses to continue for the foreseeable future**... Management expects to seek additional funds from collaboration partners...Because those plans have not been finalized, **receipt of additional funding is not considered probable**... If the Company does not obtain sufficient funds when needed, the Company expects it would scale back its operating plan by deferring or limiting some or all of its research, development or clinical projects...Because, under the new standard, neither receipt of future collaboration payments, nor management's contingency plans to mitigate the risk and extend cash resources through March 3, 2018, are considered probable, **substantial doubt is deemed to exist about the Company's ability to continue as a going concern**.

For further details about Ernst & Young's audit report and ImmunoGen's 10-K, see: https://www.sec.gov/Archives/edgar/data/855654/000155837017001331/imgn-20161231x10k.htm

ImmunoGen's Temporary Reprieve: A Deal with Jazz Pharmaceuticals

On July 29, 2017 shares of ImmunoGen rose 17.5% when the company announced a deal with Jazz Pharmaceuticals relating to three antibody drugs that work to attack blood cancers. So, management's dire warnings in its 10-K Note A did not become a sad reality. It turns out that management was able to obtain the additional funding that the company required to continue operations.

It is informative to witness the market's reaction to all this drama. Note the lows associated with the market's negative expectations in late 2016 (as a result of weak predictions from stock analysts), the 10-K filing March, and the subsequent increase in the share price with the positive news relating to Jazz Pharmaceuticals in late July 2017.

For a link to the stock price data, see *https://www.google.com/search?q=immunogen+stock+chart&ie=utf-8&oe=utf-8*

It is also interesting to consider the expectations of the six stock analysts who follow ImmunoGen. You can see their weak expectations in late 2016, continued pessimism in March and April of 2017, hopefulness increasing during June and July of 2017, and the ultimate revelation of the Jazz Pharmaceuticals cash infusion leading to much more encouraging analysts' estimates going forward.

For a link to the analyst following data, see https://www.tipranks.com/stocks/imgn

Key takeaways from this example include:

- Managers are responsible for providing disclosures so that users can reasonably understand the risks that they face in interacting with the company (e.g., as a shareholder or debtholder).

- Auditors provide external, independent validation that management's assertions are reliable.

- External parties such as stock analysts collectively use these disclosures to make predictions about likely movements in the company's stock market performance.

For Classroom Discussion

What Do You Think?

Based on the disclosures and assertions made by ImmunoGen management, the opinion of its auditor, and the predictions of the stock analysts, would you invest in ImmunoGen? What data would you gather to help you make that decision? Suppose that you, as an investor, lose money on ImmunoGen stock because it turns out that the company's business model was not as strong as previously believed. Who is to blame for your loss?

The auditor's conclusion about the entity's ability to continue as a going concern should be expressed through the use of the phrase "substantial doubt about its (the entity's) ability to continue as a going concern" (or similar wording that includes the terms substantial doubt *and* going concern). Example language follows:

> The accompanying financial statements have been prepared assuming that the Company will continue as a going concern. As discussed in Note X to the financial statements, the Company has suffered recurring losses from operations and has a net capital deficiency that raise substantial doubt about its ability to continue as a going concern. Management's plans in regard to these matters are also described in Note X. The financial statements do not include any adjustments that might result from the outcome of this uncertainty. (Source: *PCAOB Release No. 2017-001, June 1, 2017*)

The additional paragraph should not include conditional language. Examples of conditional language that are inappropriate include:

- If the Company continues to suffer recurring losses from operations and continues to have a net capital deficiency, there may be substantial doubt about its ability to continue as a going concern.
- The Company has been unable to renegotiate its expiring credit agreements. Unless the Company is able to obtain financial support, there is substantial doubt about its ability to continue as a going concern. (Source: *AU-C 570, revised February 2017*)

Furthermore, the auditor can issue a disclaimer of opinion for uncertainties, such as a going concern uncertainty.

Why It Matters   Going Concern Warnings

This feature provides some interesting insights related to going concern warnings—where auditors signal there is reasonable doubt the company can survive.

Company annual report filings with the SEC for 2015 showed the highest number of auditor going-concern warnings for large companies (market cap of $700 million or more in public float) since 2008, when 20 large companies received a going concern warning. In 2015, 10 large public companies—including three pharmaceutical and four energy companies—reported a going-concern warning from their auditor. For large oil and gas companies, liquidity concerns were one of the most common reasons for the going-concern warning. For large pharmaceutical companies, concerns about operating losses prevailed.

In 2014, 48% of the 530 new going concern warnings issued by auditors were for companies filing for an IPO, not for established companies. In 2013, the number of IPOs receiving an auditors' going-concern warning was even higher, at 59%.

The top two reasons auditors cite for giving a going-concern opinion, are "net losses since inception" or an "absence of significant revenues." Almost 6% of new going-concern opinions given to IPOs in 2015 occurred because the company had "not commenced or had limited or no operations." Warnings about potential going-concern problems and the ultimate bankruptcy filings are unpredictable; a company and/or its auditor may determine that a going-concern warning is prudent, but the company might not go bankrupt. In contrast, a company and/or its auditor might *not* issue a going-concern warning, and the company might still go bankrupt.

In 2017, Sears's management notified users that the company faced very serious cash flow problems and that, despite management's efforts, the company might not remain a going concern. Of interest, Sears's auditor, Deloitte, reached the opposite conclusion and did not issue a going concern report.

Issues around going-concern will likely continue to be a focus, particularly for retailers, into the foreseeable future. The disequilibrium that online retailers have created in the market is most evident when you contrast the stock market charts for Sears as compared to Amazon:

Sears stock price (last 5 years):

See the link to this stock chart at: https://www.google.com/search?q=sears+stock+price+charts&ie=utf-8&oe=utf-8

Amazon stock price (last 5 years):

See the link to this stock chart at: https://www.google.com/search?q=amazon+stock+price+charts&ie=utf-8&oe=utf-8

It will be interesting over time to witness the transformation of the retail sector following this period of rapid change and financial uncertainty for some companies.

For Classroom Discussion

What Do You Think?

How might a going-concern warning from the auditor be a self-fulfilling prophecy causing a company to fail?

In addition, consider several undesirable potential situations:

1. The auditor issues a going-concern warning, and the company fails.
2. The auditor issues a going-concern warning, but the company does not fail.

3. The auditor does not issue a going-concern warning, and the company fails.

   a. Which of these situations would users prefer? Why?
   b. Which of these situations would managers prefer? Why?
   c. Which of these situations would auditors prefer? Why?

Client Correction of a Material Misstatement in Previously Issued Financial Statements

U.S. auditing standards require that the auditor's report recognize a correction of a material misstatement in previously issued financial statements through an additional paragraph. The additional paragraph should include: (1) a statement that the previously issued financial statements have been restated for the correction of a misstatement in the respective period and (2) a reference to the note disclosure describing the correction of the misstatement.

The following is an example of appropriate language when there has been a correction of a material misstatement in previously issued financial statements:

> As discussed in Note X to the financial statements, the 20X2 financial statements have been restated to correct a misstatement. (Source: *PCAOB Release No. 2017-001, June 1, 2017*)

Why It Matters

The Causes and Consequences of Internal Control Material Weaknesses and Restatements

This feature provides an example of a company that disclosed a misstatement and associated restatement of the financial statements, the effect of those actions with respect to the auditor's report, and users' reactions.

Disclosure of the Restatement

Westmoreland Coal Company made the following disclosure relating to its FYE 2016 10-K.

"ENGLEWOOD, Colo., Feb. 24, 2017 (GLOBE NEWSWIRE) — Westmoreland Coal Company (Nasdaq:WLB) today announced that it will restate financial information stemming from changes in the accounting for its customer reclamation receivables. This change has no impact on Westmoreland's cash flow, the economic value of its contracts or its ability to collect cash for reclamation from customers. Westmoreland understands the inconvenience this creates and the team is working diligently to process this change so year-end earnings and the 10-K can be released expeditiously.

Westmoreland's Annual Report on Form 10-K for the year ended December 31, 2016 will include restated consolidated financial statements for the years ended December 31, 2015 and 2014, and all interim periods during 2016 and 2015. Westmoreland does not intend to file amendments to previous filings with the Securities and Exchange Commission. Investors are advised to no longer rely upon previously issued financial statements, earnings releases or other financial communications.

Based on a preliminary assessment, Westmoreland expects the following changes to its financial statements as a result of this restatement:

- For the year ended December 31, 2015, an increase in revenue of $9.5 million, an increase in accretion expense (reflected in cost of sales) of $9.1 million, and an increase in depletion expense of $9.6 million.

- For the nine months ended September 30, 2016, an increase in revenue of $3.4 million, an increase in accretion expense (reflected in cost of sales) of $8.7 million, and an increase in depletion expense of $11.8 million.

- The third-party reclamation receivable will now be recognized on the balance sheet as land and mineral rights. There is no impact on Westmoreland's ability to be reimbursed for reclamation from its customers."

Effect of the Restatement on the Audit Opinion

The following quote includes the auditor's report on the FYE 2016 financial statements and internal controls, which highlight the restatement and the accompanying adverse opinion on the state of Westmoreland's internal controls (emphasis added):

"As discussed in Note 2 to the consolidated financial statements, the December 31, 2015 and 2014 consolidated **financial statements and schedule have been restated to correct errors in the Company's accounting for reclamation receivables, with related effects on revenues, expenses and mineral rights, as well as other immaterial adjustments**.

We have also audited, in accordance with the standards of the Public Company Accounting Oversight Board (United States), the Company's internal control over financial reporting as of December 31, 2016, based on the criteria established in *Internal Control-Integrated Framework* issued by the Committee of Sponsoring Organizations of the Treadway

Commission (2013 framework) and our report dated March 28, 2017 **expressed an adverse opinion thereon.**"

/s/ Ernst & Young LLP

Denver, Colorado
March 28, 2017

Management's Discussion of the Proposed Remediation Process

Management provided the following disclosure with respect to how they anticipate remediating the internal control material weakness (ICMW):

> "As of the date of this filing, the Company has assigned personnel with the appropriate level of asset retirement obligation and technical accounting experience to review the accounting for asset retirement obligations in accordance with GAAP. We are committed to maintaining a strong internal control environment, and believe that these

remediation efforts represent significant improvements in our control environment. The identified material weakness in internal control will not be considered fully remediated until the internal controls over these areas have been in operation for a sufficient period of time for our management to conclude that the material weakness has been fully remediated. The Company will continue its efforts to implement and test the new controls in order to make this final determination."

To review the 10-K, which contains both management's disclosures and Ernst & Young's report, see: https://www.sec.gov/Archives /edgar/data/106455/000010645517000012/wlb-123116_10k.htm

Stock Market Reaction to the Restatement, Management's Disclosures, and the Audit Opinion

The stock market reaction to this series of events was as follows:

Westmoreland Coal Company
NASDAQ: WLB—20 Sep., 12:55 pm EDT

Open	2.48
High	2.56
Low	2.46

Mkt cap 58.60M
P/E ratio —
Div yield —

15.16 Feb 24, 2017

2.47 USD ▼ 0.04 (1.59%)

For further details on the market's pricing of Westmoreland's stock, see: https://www.google.com/search?q=stock+price+chart+f or+westmoreland+coal+company&ie=utf-8&oe=utf-8

The key takeaways from this example include:

- There was an ICMW relating to reclamation receivables and accompanying effects on revenues and expenses.

- The ICMW and accompany effects required that Westmoreland: (a) disclose the ICMW, (b) establish remediation plans, and (c) restate its previously issued financial statements.

- Ernst & Young was then required to alert users to the restatement and express an adverse opinion on the company's internal controls.

- The stock market reaction was initially negative based on all of these "bad news" events, and the market continued to downgrade the company well into 2017.

The following remain unclear: the ultimate resolution of the ICMW, the remediation plans, and the future financial performance of Westmoreland Coal.

For Classroom Discussion

What Do You Think?

Be prepared to give an update to Westmoreland Coal's financial condition.

- Did Westmoreland ultimately remediate the ICMW by FYE 2017?

- What was the nature of the audit report for FYE 2017, and any available subsequent years?

- How is the market valuing the company's stock? What do the analysts following the stock have to say in terms of a buy/hold/sell recommendation?

Check Your Basic Knowledge

15-9 If an auditor decides to include additional language in the audit report because of concerns about the client's ability to remain a going concern, the additional language should include the terms *material doubt* and *going concern*.   (T/F)

15-10 International auditing standards generally permit the auditor to refer to other auditors in the auditor's report, while the U.S. auditing standards allow this reference only if required by law or regulation.   (T/F)

15-11 In which of the following situations would an auditor typically issue an unqualified opinion, but modify the audit report to include additional language?

a. The client has changed an accounting principle, has reasonable justification for the change, and has followed GAAP in accounting for and disclosing the change.

b. The auditor has substantial doubt about the client being a going concern.

c. The client has had significant transactions with related parties that the auditor wants to emphasize.

d. An auditor would typically issue an unqualified opinion, but include additional language, in all of the above situations.

15-12 Eagle Company's financial statements contain a departure from GAAP because, due to unusual circumstances, the statements would otherwise be misleading. Which of the following is descriptive of the type of audit report the auditor should provide?

a. Unqualified opinion, with no mention of the departure in the auditor's report.

b. Unqualified opinion, with a description of the departure in the audit report.

c. Either a or b

d. Neither a nor b

LO 4

Describe financial statement audits resulting in a qualified opinion, an adverse opinion, or a disclaimer of opinion, and identify the appropriate audit report modifications.

Qualified Opinions, Adverse Opinions, and Disclaimers of Opinion

Circumstances may require that the auditor depart from an unqualified/unmodified opinion. The issuance of other than an unqualified opinion is unusual. In the U.S. for example, the SEC, with limited exceptions, will not accept financial statements where the audit opinion is other than unqualified. As a result, the auditor has significant advantage to encourage the client to make corrections that would allow for an unqualified audit opinion. When the auditor is not able to give an unqualified opinion, the auditor will provide a qualified opinion, an adverse opinion, or a disclaimer of opinion.

Qualified Opinions

A qualified opinion states that, except for the effects of the matter(s) relating to the qualification, the financial statements present fairly, in all material respects, the financial position, results of operations, and cash flows of the entity in conformity with generally accepted accounting principles. Auditors will issue a qualified report when:

- The auditor believes that the financial statements contain a departure from generally accepted accounting principles, the effect of which is material but not pervasive, and the auditor has concluded not to express an adverse opinion

- There is a lack of sufficient appropriate evidential matter or there are restrictions on the scope of the audit that have led the auditor to conclude that he or she cannot express an unqualified opinion and concluded not to disclaim an opinion

It's Your Turn!

Prompt for Critical Thinking #3

According to the SEC's Division of Corporate Finance Financial Reporting Manual (paragraph 4115, p. 201), an SEC registrant faces the prospect of needing to obtain a *replacement* audit if its original audit firm has its registration revoked by the PCAOB, that is, an involuntary PCAOB deregistration. According to the Manual, "If the PCAOB revokes the registration of an audit firm, audit reports issued by that firm may no longer be included in a registrant's filings made on or after the date the firm's registration is revoked, even if the report was previously issued before the date of revocation. Financial statements previously audited by a firm whose registration has been revoked would generally need to be reaudited by a PCAOB registered firm prior to inclusion in future filings or if included in a registration statement that has not yet been declared effective."

To access the Manual for further details, see:

https://www.sec.gov/divisions/corpfin/cffinancialreportingmanual.pdf

- What might be the economic rationale for the SEC imposing such a requirement with respect to the demand for audit assurance?
- Speculate on whether and how the replacement audit and associated audit opinion might differ from the original opinion, if at all.
- What power does this rule provide to issuer clients of auditing firms in terms of their demand for quality audits?

When an auditor expresses a qualified opinion, the auditor should disclose all of the substantive reasons for the qualified opinion in one or more separate paragraph(s). The auditor should also include, in the opinion paragraph, the appropriate qualifying language and a reference to the paragraph that discloses all of the substantive reasons for the qualified opinion. A qualified opinion should include the word *except* or *exception* in a phrase such as *except for* or *with the exception of*. Phrases such as *subject to* and *with the foregoing explanation* are not clear or forceful enough; the auditor should not use such phrases.

Qualified Opinion: Departure from GAAP

When financial statements contain a material departure from generally accepted accounting principles the auditor should express a qualified or an adverse opinion. Examples of departures from GAAP include: (1) inadequate disclosure (including the omission of a statement of cash flows, or inadequate disclosure about the client's ability to continue as a going concern for a reasonable period of time); (2) departures from generally accepted accounting principles involving risks or uncertainties (including inadequate disclosure, inappropriate accounting principles, and unreasonable accounting estimates); and (3) departures from generally accepted accounting principles related to changes in accounting principle.

In deciding whether the effects of the departure require a qualified or an adverse opinion, one factor the auditor will consider is the dollar magnitude of such effects. However, the auditor will also consider qualitative factors, such as the:

- significance of an item to a particular entity (e.g., inventories to a manufacturing company)
- pervasiveness of the misstatement (such as whether it affects the amounts and presentation of numerous financial statement items)
- effect of the misstatement on the financial statements taken as a whole

When an auditor expresses a qualified opinion, the auditor should include a paragraph listing all of the substantive reasons that have led to the conclusion that there has been a departure from generally accepted accounting principles. This paragraph should also disclose the principal effects of the subject matter of the qualification on financial position, results of operations, and cash flows, if practicable. Furthermore, the opinion paragraph should include the appropriate

Exhibit 15.4

Example of an Excerpt from a Qualified Audit Report Related
to a Departure from GAAP: PCAOB Audit

NOTE: The format of the audit report depends on the auditing standards the auditor is following.

We have audited the accompanying balance sheets of X Company (the "Company") as of December 31, 20X2 and 20X1, the related statements of [*titles of the financial statements, e.g., income, comprehensive income, stockholders' equity, and cash flows*] for each of the years then ended, and the related notes [*and schedules*] (collectively referred to as the "financial statements"). In our opinion, except for the effects of not capitalizing certain lease obligations as discussed in the following paragraph, the financial statements referred to above present fairly, in all material respects, the financial position of the Company as of December 31, 20X2 and 20X1, and the results of its operations and its cash flows for the years then ended in conformity with accounting principles generally accepted in the United States of America.

The Company has excluded, from property and debt in the accompanying balance sheets, certain lease obligations that, in our opinion, should be capitalized in order to conform with accounting principles generally accepted in the United States of America. If these lease obligations were capitalized, property would be increased by $_____ and $_____, long-term debt by $_____ and $_____, and retained earnings by $_____ and $_____ as of December 31, 20X2 and 20X1, respectively. Additionally, net income would be increased (decreased) by $ and $ and earnings per share would be increased (decreased) by $_____ and $_____, respectively, for the years then ended.

Source: *PCAOB Release No. 2017-001, June 1, 2017*

qualifying language and a reference to the paragraph(s) that describe the substantive reasons for the qualified opinion. *Exhibit 15.4* provides an excerpt from a report in which the opinion is qualified because of the client's use of an accounting principle that departs from generally accepted accounting principles.

Qualified Opinion: Scope Limitations

An auditor can give an unqualified opinion only when the auditor has been able to conduct the audit in accordance with professional auditing standards. Restrictions on the scope of the audit, whether imposed by the client or by circumstances beyond the auditor's or client's control, may require the auditor to qualify an opinion.

In some situations, as discussed below, the circumstances may be such that a disclaimer would be more appropriate. The auditor's decision to qualify the opinion or disclaim an opinion because of a scope limitation depends on the importance of the omitted procedure(s) to his or her ability to form an opinion on the financial statements being audited. This decision depends on the nature and magnitude of the potential effects of the matters in question and on their significance to the financial statements. If the potential effects are **pervasive** and relate to many financial statement items, this significance is likely to be greater than if only a limited number of items is involved.

Examples of circumstances that may limit the audit scope are the timing of the fieldwork, such as being engaged to do the audit after year-end, the inability to gather sufficient appropriate evidence, or an inadequacy in the accounting records. For example, when a company is audited for the first time, the audit firm is often appointed during the year to be audited. In such a case, the auditor may not be able to obtain sufficient appropriate evidence concerning the fairness of the beginning inventory, which affects the current year's income, or of the accounting principles used in the prior year. This may be a scope limitation that is beyond the auditor's control. If the auditor can gather sufficient appropriate evidence without being engaged prior to the beginning of the year, then the scope limitation no longer exists, and the auditor can render whatever would be the appropriate audit opinion.

When a qualified opinion results from a scope limitation or an insufficiency of evidence, the auditor's report should describe the basis for departure from an unqualified opinion in a separate paragraph and refer to that description in Basis for Opinion section and opinion paragraphs of the auditor's report.

It is not appropriate for the auditor to explain the scope of the audit in a note to the financial statements, since the description of the audit scope is the responsibility of the auditor and not that of the client. *Exhibit 15.5* provides an example of a qualified opinion related to a scope limitation concerning an investment in a foreign affiliate (assuming the effects of the limitation are such that the auditor has concluded that a disclaimer of opinion is not appropriate).

Exhibit 15.5

Example of an Excerpt from a Qualified Audit Report Related to a Scope Limitation Concerning an Investment in a Foreign Affiliate: PCAOB Audit

NOTE: *The format of the audit report depends on the auditing standards the auditor is following.*

Opinion on the Financial Statements

We have audited the accompanying balance sheets of X Company (the "Company") as of December 31, 20X2 and 20X1, the related statements of [*titles of the financial statements, e.g., income, comprehensive income, stockholders' equity, and cash flows*] for each of the years then ended, and the related notes [*and schedules*] (collectively referred to as the "financial statements"). In our opinion, except for the effects of the adjustments, if any, as might have been determined to be necessary had we been able to examine evidence regarding the foreign affiliate investment and earnings, as described below, the financial statements present fairly, in all material respects, the financial position of the Company as of December 31, 20X2 and 20X1, and the results of its operations and its cash flows for the years then ended in conformity with accounting principles generally accepted in the United States of America.

We were unable to obtain audited financial statements supporting the Company's investment in a foreign affiliate stated at $_____ and $_____ at December 31, 20X2 and 20X1, respectively, or its equity in earnings of that affiliate of $_____ and $_____, which is included in net income for the years then ended as described in Note X to the financial statements; nor were we able to satisfy ourselves as to the carrying value of the investment in the foreign affiliate or the equity in its earnings by other auditing procedures.

Basis for Opinion

These financial statements are the responsibility of the Company's management. Our responsibility is to express an opinion on the Company's financial statements based on our audits. We are a public accounting firm registered with the Public Company Accounting Oversight Board (United States) ("PCAOB") and are required to be independent with respect to the Company in accordance with the U.S. federal securities laws and the applicable rules and regulations of the Securities and Exchange Commission and the PCAOB.

Except as discussed above, we conducted our audits in accordance with the standards of the PCAOB. Those standards require that we plan and perform the audit to obtain reasonable assurance about whether the financial statements are free of material misstatement, whether due to error or fraud. Our audits included performing procedures to assess the risks of material misstatement of the financial statements, whether due to error or fraud, and performing procedures that respond to those risks. Such procedures included examining, on a test basis, evidence regarding the amounts and disclosures in the financial statements. Our audits also included evaluating the accounting principles used and significant estimates made by management, as well as evaluating the overall presentation of the financial statements. We believe that our audits provide a reasonable basis for our opinion.

Source: *PCAOB Release No. 2017-001, June 1, 2017*

Adverse Opinions

An auditor issues an adverse opinion when, in the auditor's judgment, the financial statements taken as a whole are not presented fairly in conformity with generally accepted accounting principles. An adverse opinion is appropriate when the auditor concludes that misstatements, individually or in the aggregate, are both material and pervasive to the financial statements.

As an example, AU-C 570 notes that if the financial statements have been prepared using the going concern basis of accounting but, in the auditor's judgment, management's use of the going concern basis of accounting in the preparation of the financial statements is inappropriate, the auditor should express an adverse opinion.

When expressing an adverse opinion, the auditor should disclose in a separate paragraph(s): (1) all the substantive reasons for the adverse opinion, and (2) the principal effects of the subject matter of the adverse opinion on financial position, results of operations, and cash flows, if practicable.

When the auditor expresses an adverse opinion, the opinion paragraph should include a direct reference to a separate paragraph that discloses the basis for the adverse opinion. *Exhibit 15.6* provides an example of this situation.

Exhibit 15.6

Example of an Excerpt from an
Adverse Audit Report: PCAOB Audit

NOTE: *The format of the audit report depends on the auditing standards the auditor is following.*

Opinion on the Financial Statements

We have audited the accompanying balance sheets of X Company (the "Company") as of December 31, 20X2 and 20X1, the related statements of [*titles of the financial statements, e.g., income, comprehensive income, stockholders' equity, and cash flows*] for each of the years then ended, and the related notes [*and schedules*] (collectively referred to as the "financial statements"). In our opinion, because of the effects of the matters discussed in the following paragraphs, the financial statements do not present fairly, in conformity with accounting principles generally accepted in the United States of America, the financial position of the Company as of December 31, 20X2 and 20X1, or the results of its operations or its cash flows for the years then ended.

As discussed in Note X to the financial statements, the Company carries its property, plant and equipment accounts at appraisal values, and provides depreciation on the basis of such values. Further, the Company does not provide for income taxes with respect to differences between financial income and taxable income arising because of the use, for income tax purposes, of the installment method of reporting gross profit from certain types of sales. Accounting principles generally accepted in the United States of America require that property, plant and equipment be stated at an amount not in excess of cost, reduced by depreciation based on such amount, and that deferred income taxes be provided.

Because of the departures from accounting principles generally accepted in the United States of America identified above, as of December 31, 20X2 and 20X1, inventories have been increased $_____ and $_____ by inclusion in manufacturing overhead of depreciation in excess of that based on cost; property, plant and equipment, less accumulated depreciation, is carried at $_____ and $_____ in excess of an amount based on the cost to the Company; and deferred income taxes of $_____ and $_____ have not been recorded; resulting in an increase of $ and $_____ in retained earnings and in appraisal surplus of $_____ and $_____, respectively. For the years ended December 31, 20X2 and 20X1, cost of goods sold has been increased $_____ and $_____, respectively, because of the effects of the depreciation accounting referred to above and deferred income taxes of $_____ and $_____ have not been provided, resulting in an increase in net income of $_____ and $_____, respectively.

Source: *PCAOB Release No. 2017-001, June 1, 2017*

Do Illegal Acts by the Client Affect the Auditor's Opinion?

Why It Matters:
An International Perspective

This feature provides guidance on the effect of illegal acts by the client on the audits report for companies, both in the U.S. and internationally.

Illegal Acts and the Auditor's Responsibilities

ISA 250 includes a helpful characterization about audit procedures that the auditor should conduct if and when they suspect an illegal act:

"If the auditor becomes aware of information concerning an instance of non-compliance or suspected non-compliance with laws and regulations, the auditor shall obtain: (a) an understanding of the nature of the act and the circumstances in which it has occurred; and (b) further information to evaluate the possible effect on the financial statements. If the auditor suspects there may be non-compliance, the auditor shall discuss the matter, unless prohibited by law or regulation, with the appropriate level of management and, where appropriate, those charged with governance. If management or, as appropriate, those charged with governance do not provide sufficient information that supports that the entity is in compliance with laws and regulations and, in the auditor's judgment, the effect of the suspected non-compliance may be material to the financial statements, the auditor shall consider the need to obtain legal advice" (p. 9).[3]

With respect to reporting for U.S. companies, if the auditor concludes that an illegal act has a material effect on the financial statements, and the act has not been properly accounted for or disclosed, the auditor should express a qualified opinion or an adverse opinion on the financial statements taken as a whole, depending on the materiality of the effect on the financial statements. Furthermore, if the auditor is precluded by the client from obtaining sufficient appropriate audit evidence to evaluate whether an illegal act that could be material to the financial statements has, or is likely to have occurred, the

auditor generally should disclaim an opinion on the financial statements.

If the client refuses to accept the auditor's report for the above modifications, the auditor should withdraw from the engagement and indicate the reasons for withdrawal in writing to the audit committee or board of directors, and (for public clients) to the appropriate regulatory agency, e.g., the SEC via Form 8-K in the U.S.

The Power of Regulatory Reporting Regarding Auditor Changes

Of course, the auditor does not want to withdraw from an engagement, and she/he also does not want the client to dismiss the auditor; in either case, the auditor loses the audit client. Similarly, managers do not want their auditor to withdraw from the engagement, nor do they want to dismiss the auditor; in either case, management still needs to obtain an audit opinion. In addition, users do not think highly of involuntary auditor changes, whether initiated by the auditor or the client.

In fact, all auditor changes for publicly traded organizations in the U.S. must be disclosed within four days to the SEC via a Form 8-K to alert users to these material, unplanned events; in the case of an auditor change (i.e., dismissal or resignation), users will be very interested to learn the details. The Form 8-K filing requirement gives the auditor power over managers who are hesitant to cooperate (i.e., based on the illegal act or problem that is causing the auditor to consider issuing a qualified, adverse, or disclaimer opinion). The fact that management knows that the disagreement and subsequent fallout will require an 8-K disclosure gives the auditor power in interactions with management. The message is clear: if management does not want the disagreement to be made public, they will need to concede to the auditor's demands with respect to the quality of financial reporting, which will then enable the auditor to avoid having to issue a qualified, adverse, or disclaimer opinion, or having to withdraw from the audit altogether.

Disclaimers of Opinion

A disclaimer of opinion states that the auditor does not express an opinion on the financial statements. A disclaimer of opinion should not be expressed because the auditor believes, on the basis of the audit, that there are material departures from generally accepted accounting principles. Rather, the auditor should disclaim an opinion when the auditor is unable to obtain sufficient appropriate audit evidence on which to base the opinion, and the auditor concludes that the possible effects on the financial statements of undetected misstatements, if any, could be both material and pervasive. A disclaimer of opinion is appropriate when:

- A scope limitation exists, and a qualified opinion is not appropriate
- Substantial doubt exists about the client being a going concern, and an unqualified opinion with an additional paragraph is not appropriate
- The auditor lacks independence

Disclaimer: Scope Limitation

When a scope limitation exists, the auditor may decide that a qualified audit opinion is not appropriate, and may choose to disclaim an opinion. In this situation, the auditor should state in a separate paragraph or paragraphs, all of the substantive reasons for the disclaimer. He or she should state that the scope of the audit was not sufficient to warrant the expression of an opinion.

The auditor should not identify the procedures that were performed nor include the paragraph describing the characteristics of an audit (i.e., the scope paragraph of the auditor's standard report); doing so may overshadow the disclaimer.

In addition, the auditor should also disclose any other reservations he or she has regarding fair presentation in conformity with generally accepted accounting principles. *Exhibit 15.7* provides an example of a report disclaiming an opinion resulting from an inability to obtain sufficient appropriate evidence due to a scope limitation.

What Do You Think?

For Classroom Discussion

Obtain a copy of the FYE August 31, 2016 audit report of Sibannac, Inc. at *https://www.sec.gov/Archives/edgar/data/1313938 /000168316816000946/sibannac_10k-083116.htm*

- What type of audit opinion did the auditor issue?
- Why was this type of opinion issued?
- Identify some possible reasons as to why the auditor was not able to obtain sufficient appropriate audit evidence.

- How common do you think it is for an audit firm to issue this type of opinion?
- What actions will Sibannac need to take given that a disclaimer opinion will not suffice for its SEC filing?

Exhibit 15.7

Example of an Excerpt from an Audit Report with a Disclaimer of Opinion Due to Scope Limitation: PCAOB Audit

NOTE: *The format of the audit report depends on the auditing standards the auditor is following.*

Disclaimer of Opinion on the Financial Statements

We were engaged to audit the accompanying balance sheets of X Company (the "Company") as of December 31, 20X2 and 20X1, and the related statements of [titles of the financial statements, e.g., income, comprehensive income, stockholders' equity, and cash flows], and the related notes [and schedules] (collectively referred to as the "financial statements"). As described in the following paragraph, because the Company did not take physical inventories and we were not able to apply other auditing procedures to satisfy ourselves as to inventory quantities and the cost of property and equipment, we were not able to obtain sufficient appropriate audit evidence to provide a basis for an audit opinion on the financial statements, and we do not express, an opinion on these financial statements.

The Company did not make a count of its physical inventory in 20X2 or 20X1, stated in the accompanying financial statements at \$_____ as of December 31, 20X2, and at \$_____ as of December 31, 20X1. Further, evidence supporting the cost of property and equipment acquired prior to December 31, 20X1, is no longer available. The Company's records do not permit the application of other auditing procedures to inventories or property and equipment.

Basis for Disclaimer of Opinion

These financial statements are the responsibility of the Company's management. We are a public accounting firm registered with the Public Company Accounting Oversight Board (United States) ("PCAOB") and are required to be independent with respect to the Company in accordance with the U.S. federal securities laws and the applicable rules and regulations of the Securities and Exchange Commission and the PCAOB.

Source: *PCAOB Release No. 2017-001, June 1, 2017*

Disclaimer: Substantial Doubt about the Client Being a Going Concern

In some reporting situations, doubt about the client continuing as a going concern is such that the auditor does not believe that an additional paragraph to an unqualified opinion is appropriate. In such cases, the auditor may issue a disclaimer of opinion.

Disclaimer: Auditor Lacking Independence

In rare circumstances, an auditor may lack independence, yet be required by law or regulation to report on the financial statements. In these circumstances, the auditor should issue a disclaimer of opinion. The disclaimer should specifically state that the auditor is not independent. The auditor may choose to provide the reasons for the lack of independence, but is not required to do so. If the auditor does choose to provide the reasons, the auditor should include all the reasons causing a lack of independence.

For Classroom Discussion

What Do You Think?

The bankruptcy of Lehman Brothers in 2008 was the largest in U.S. history and it resulted from and contributed to the Global Financial Crisis of 2007–2008. Ernst & Young (EY) was Lehman's auditor, and issued unqualified audit opinions for seven years prior to and including the bankruptcy. During this time, EY collected approximately $150 million in audit fees from Lehman. EY approved Lehman's use of "Repo 105" transactions to record what was, in substance, a short-term borrowing arrangement as a sale of assets (the purpose of which was to create a misleading picture of Lehman's financial position). This financial accounting treatment eliminated billions of dollars of debt from Lehman's balance sheet and made the bank look less leveraged than it was in reality.

There existed allegations that EY was complicit in enabling financial reporting fraud, and the State of New York initiated a $150 million lawsuit against EY as a result. However, neither the SEC nor the PCAOB ever pressed charges against EY regarding their supposed oversight failure in the case of Lehman. EY ultimately settled the State of New York case for $10 million. However, EY paid $99 million in a class-action lawsuit filed by investors who claimed that their losses were attributable to EY's inappropriately positive assurance on Lehman's financial statements and disclosures therein.

This is a very complex case, and there are many unanswered questions that you might ponder.

- Who is more at fault—Lehman Brothers who used questionable accounting treatments to make their financial statements look "better", or EY for reassuring investors with unqualified audit opinions on Lehman's financial statements?
- Is $150 million in audit fees over seven years a reasonable sum?
- Did the size of those audit fees threaten the firm's independence?
- If the financial crisis in 2008 had not happened, would Lehman's questionable accounting ever have become an issue?

Check Your Basic Knowledge

15-13 The primary reason for issuing an adverse audit opinion is that the client's financial statements contain a pervasive and material unjustified departure from GAAP. (T/F)

15-14 When the auditor issues a disclaimer because of a lack of independence, the audit report must state the lack of independence, and must describe the reasons for the lack of independence. (T/F)

15-15 Tech Company has an uncertainty because of pending litigation. The auditor decided to issue a qualified opinion rather than an unqualified opinion. Which of the following factors most likely influenced this decision?

a. Inconsistent application of GAAP.
b. Inability to estimate the amount of loss.
c. The client's lack of experience with such litigation.
d. Adequacy of the disclosures.

15-16 Which of the following phrases should an auditor not use when qualifying the audit opinion?

a. With the exception of
b. Except for
c. Subject to
d. Any of the above phrases would be appropriate.

Critical Audit Matters and Key Audit Matters

Auditing standards differ in their requirements related to reporting important audit matters—referred to as a **key audit matter** by the IAASB and the ASB of the AICPA, and as a **critical audit matter** by the PCAOB.

Key Audit Matters (KAMs)

ISA 701, *Communicating Key Audit Matters in the Independent Auditor's Report*, requires that key audit matters be included in the audit report, effective for audits of financial statements for periods ending on or after December 15, 2016. *Exhibit 15.8* outlines the components and structure of an audit report, including KAMs, based on guidance in the ISAs. In July 2017, the ASB voted to consider aligning its guidance with ISA 701, and requiring auditors to include a discussion of key audit matters in the audit report.

Key audit matters (KAMs) are matters that the auditor considers to be the most significant in the current audit. KAMs are a subset of the matters communicated to those charged with governance, for example, the audit committee. As examples of the matters that might rise to this level of importance, one audit firm reported that the top six KAM topics for its clients included revenue, IT applications and controls, management override of controls, taxation, recoverability of loans and receivables, and goodwill and intangibles.

The nature of a KAM will vary according to the client's industry. Revenue recognition is likely to be a KAM for software and telecommunications companies, for example, because of their complicated revenue recognition policies. Mining companies, meanwhile, may have licensing rights to mine a particular piece of ground, but it can be difficult for both managers and the auditor to determine the value of that license, as it will depend on the cash flows generated by the mine in future. Therefore, the audit in this case is likely to focus closely on license impairments. Areas of significant *auditor* judgment often relate to areas of complexity and significant *management* judgment.

Exhibit 15.8
Components and Structure of the Audit Report: ISA 701 Requirements

Section	Required
Opinion	Yes
Basis for Opinion	Yes
Emphasis of Matter	If necessary
Material Uncertainty Related to Going Concern	If necessary
Key Audit Matters	Yes, for listed companies
Other Matter	If necessary
Responsibilities of Management and TCWG* for the Financial Statements *(including going concern)*	Yes
Auditor's Responsibilities for the Audit of Financial Statements *(including going concern)*	Yes

*Those Charged With Governance

The number and nature of key audit matters to be included in the auditor's report will depend on the size and complexity of the entity, the nature of its business and environment, and the facts and circumstances of the audit engagement. In general, the greater the number of matters initially determined to be key audit matters, the more the auditor may need to reconsider whether each of these matters meets the definition of a key audit matter. Lengthy lists of key audit matters may be contrary to the notion of such matters being those of most significant in the audit. Therefore, an important challenge to the auditor lies in determining whether a matter rises to the level of a KAM. A KAM does not necessarily mean an account with a large balance or an area where the auditor spent a lot of time. For example, an acquisition of a subsidiary might require a lot of effort; but, if it is a straightforward transaction, it might not be a KAM.

Auditing standards require that the auditor will report KAMs in the audit report. The order of presentation of individual KAM is a matter of professional judgment. For example, KAMs may be organized in order of relative importance, based on the auditor's judgment, or may correspond to the order in which matters are disclosed in the financial statements. The auditor shall describe each key audit matter, using an appropriate subheading, in a separate section of the auditor's report under the heading "Key Audit Matters." The description should explain why the matter was considered a KAM and how it was addressed. There should also be a reference to the related disclosure elsewhere in the financial statements.

When KAMs are included in the audit report, auditors are required to include the following introductory language under the heading "Key Audit Matters" in a separate section of the auditor's report:

Key Audit Matters

Key audit matters are those matters that, in our professional judgment, were of most significance in our audit of the financial statements of the current period. These matters were addressed in the context of our audit of the financial statements as a whole, and in forming our opinion thereon, and we do not provide a separate opinion on these matters. (Source: *https://www.ifac.org/system/files/ publications/files/IAASB-Auditor-Reporting-Toolkit-Illustrative-Key-Audit-Matters.pdf*)

The following paragraph provides an example of how the auditor might describe why a matter is a KAM:

Under IFRSs, the Group is required to annually test the amount of goodwill for impairment. This annual impairment test was significant to our audit because the balance of XX as of December 31, 20X1 is material to the financial statements. In addition, management's assessment process is complex and highly judgmental and is based on assumptions, specifically [describe certain assumptions], which are affected by expected future market or economic conditions, particularly those in [name of country or geographic area]. (Source: *https:// www.ifac.org/system/files/publications/files/IAASB-Auditor-Reporting-Toolkit-Illustrative-Key-Audit-Matters.pdf*)

The following paragraph provides an example of how the auditor might describe how a KAM was addressed in the audit:

Our audit procedures included, among others, using a valuation expert to assist us in evaluating the assumptions and methodologies used by the Group, in particular those relating to the forecasted revenue growth and profit margins for [*name of business line*]. We also focused on the adequacy of the Group's disclosures about those assumptions to which the outcome of the impairment test is most sensitive, that is, those that have the most significant effect on the determination of the recoverable amount of goodwill. (Source: *https://www .ifac.org/system/files/publications/files/IAASB-Auditor-Reporting-Toolkit-Illustrative-Key-Audit-Matters.pdf*)

The following paragraph provides an example of how the auditor might refer to the client's related disclosure:

> The Company's disclosures about goodwill are included in Note 3, which specifically explains that small changes in the key assumptions used could give rise to an impairment of the goodwill balance in the future. (Source: *https://www.ifac.org/system/files/publications/files/IAASB-Auditor-Reporting-Toolkit-Illustrative-Key-Audit-Matters.pdf*)

In certain limited circumstances, if there are no KAMs, the auditor's report includes a statement to that effect. The following illustrates the presentation in the auditor's report for this situation:

> Key Audit Matters
>
> [Except for the matter described in the *Basis for Qualified (Adverse) Opinion* section or *Material Uncertainty Related to Going Concern* section,] We have determined that there are no [other] key audit matters to communicate in our report. (Source: *ISA 701*)

Critical Audit Matters (CAMs)

Under AS 3101 (approved in 2017), audit reports for large U.S. public companies will include critical audit matters (CAMs) for fiscal years ending on or after June 30, 2019. Audit reports for smaller U.S. public companies will include these matters for fiscal years ending on or after December 15, 2020.

Once these requirements are effective, the auditor's report must disclose whether any CAM arose during the current period audit, or state that there was none. A CAM is:

- Any matter that was communicated or required to be communicated to the audit committee, and
- Relates to accounts or disclosure material in regard to financial statements, and
- Involves especially challenging, subjective, or complex auditor judgment.

To determine whether a matter involved especially challenging, subjective, or complex auditor judgment, the auditor takes into account various factors, including:

- The auditor's assessment of the risks of material misstatement, including significant risks
- The nature and timing of significant unusual transactions and the extent of audit effort and judgment related to requisite transactions
- The degree of auditor subjectivity in applying audit procedures to address the matter or in evaluating the results of those procedures

Matters Relating to Accounts and/or Disclosures   It is important to consider the fact that CAM disclosures depend on whether the matter being considered relates to accounts and/or disclosures. *Matters that are material to the financial statements, but that do not relate to accounts or disclosures are not critical audit matters.* For example, if the auditor communicated a potential loss contingency to the audit committee, but the auditor determined that the likelihood of the contingency coming to fruition was remote and management did not record it in the financial statement accounts or disclose it under the applicable financial reporting framework, it is not a critical audit matter, even if the contingency involved especially challenging auditor judgment.

The disclosure of CAMs under PCAOB guidance is similar to the guidance in ISA 701. Once an auditor decides that a CAM needs to be included in the report, the auditor will: (a) identify the CAM; (b) describe the principal considerations that led the auditor to determine that the matter is a CAM; (c) describe how the auditor addressed the CAM in the audit; and (d) refer to the relevant financial statement accounts or disclosures. If no critical audit matters arose, the audit report must state that there were no critical audit matters.

It's Your Turn!

Prompt for Critical Thinking #4

Identify other matters that might be material to the financial statements, but that do not relate to accounts or disclosures (and thus are *not* critical audit matters).

* _____

* _____

The following paragraph provides an example of CAM-related language that would be included in an audit report:

Critical Audit Matters

The critical audit matters communicated below are matters arising from the current period audit of the financial statements that were communicated or required to be communicated to the audit committee and that: (1) relate to accounts or disclosures that are material to the financial statements, and (2) involved our especially challenging, subjective, or complex judgments. The communication of critical audit matters does not alter in any way our opinion on the financial statements, taken as a whole, and we are not, by communicating the critical audit matters below, providing separate opinions on the critical audit matters or on the accounts or disclosures to which they relate.[4]

[*Insert each CAM*]

Insights on Enhanced Reporting

Why It Matters:
An International Perspective

This feature provides a well-known example of KAM disclosures by Rolls-Royce and KPMG and specific risks identified in the KAM disclosures.

While critical audit matters are new to the U.S. reporting environment, some country-specific ISAs already require enhanced auditor reporting. For example, in June 2013, revisions to ISA 700 (UK and Ireland) "The Independent Auditor's Report on Financial Statements" were approved and auditors reporting on companies which apply the U.K. Corporate Governance Code were required to explain more about their work. Specifically, auditors need to:

* Provide an overview of the scope of the audit, showing how this addressed the risk and materiality considerations
* Describe the risks that had the greatest effect on:
  * The overall audit strategy
  * The allocation of resources in the audit
  * Directing the efforts of the engagement team
  * Provide an explanation of how they applied the concept of materiality in planning and performing the audit

The startling thing about these auditor disclosures is the significant level of detail about the client's financial reporting, the risks identified by the auditor, and the auditor's responses to the identified risks; this level of detail is a fundamental shift from prior auditor reporting disclosure conventions.

One of the earliest, and now famous, audit reports including these disclosures was issued by KPMG relating to its audit of the December 31, 2013, financial statements of Rolls-Royce Holdings, plc (Rolls-Royce). That audit report was six pages in length, and included the identification of 11 separate risk areas, along with a description of the auditor response and conclusion with respect to each risk area. In addition, and unlike disclosure in the U.S., an individual auditor employed by KPMG personally signs the audit report with his/her name.

Since that time, KPMG's audit of Rolls-Royce continues to highlight interesting and important disclosures for users. For example, the FYE 2016 audit report contains a list 19 key risks, which are summarized in the following illustration of the risks that KPMG is facing with respect to the audit in terms of the likelihood of material misstatement and the potential impact on the financial statements.

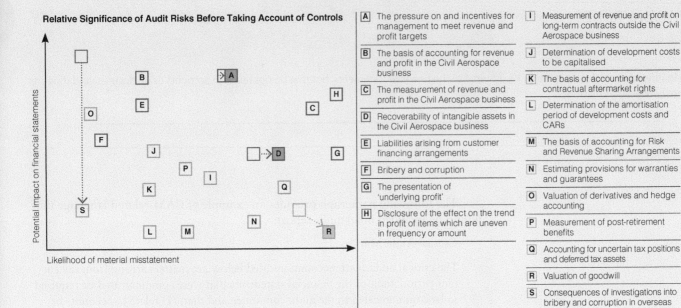

Relative Significance of Audit Risks Before Taking Account of Controls

Potential impact on financial statements

Likelihood of material misstatement

A The pressure on and incentives for management to meet revenue and profit targets	**I** Measurement of revenue and profit on long-term contracts outside the Civil Aerospace business
B The basis of accounting for revenue and profit in the Civil Aerospace business	**J** Determination of development costs to be capitalised
C The measurement of revenue and profit in the Civil Aerospace business	**K** The basis of accounting for contractual aftermarket rights
D Recoverability of intangible assets in the Civil Aerospace business	**L** Determination of the amortisation period of development costs and CARs
E Liabilities arising from customer financing arrangements	**M** The basis of accounting for Risk and Revenue Sharing Arrangements
F Bribery and corruption	**N** Estimating provisions for warranties and guarantees
G The presentation of 'underlying profit'	**O** Valuation of derivatives and hedge accounting
H Disclosure of the effect on the trend in profit of items which are uneven in frequency or amount	**P** Measurement of post-retirement benefits
	Q Accounting for uncertain tax positions and deferred tax assets
	R Valuation of goodwill
	S Consequences of investigations into bribery and corruption in overseas markets

You will note that Risk A poses significant risk on both of these dimensions, reflecting the pressure on and incentives for management to meet revenue and profit targets. KPMG describes Risk A and its response as follows:

"Rolls-Royce Holdings plc Annual Report 2016

Risk A. The pressure on and incentives for management to meet revenue and profit targets Refer to pages 18 to 35 (Business review) and pages 98 and 99 (Audit Committee report—Financial reporting)

The risk

— In recent years the Group has published a number of revisions to its revenue and profit guidance with a generally decreasing trend in profit and revenue and there have been significant associated decreases in the Group's share price. The Group's employee incentive schemes include profit targets. Clear instructions were given to the Executive Leadership Team and the senior finance executives on more than one occasion not to take any account of the pressure to meet forecasts in preparing the financial results and to manage and be alert to how this pressure might affect personnel across the wider Group. Nevertheless, the continuing pressure on and incentives for management to meet targets increases the inherent risk of manipulation of the Group financial statements. The financial results are sensitive to significant estimates and judgements, particularly in respect of revenues and costs associated with long-term contracts, and there is a broad range of acceptable outcomes of these that could lead to different levels of profit and revenue being reported in the financial statements. Relatively small changes in the basis of those judgements and estimates could result in the Group meeting, exceeding or falling short of forecasts, guidance or

targets. The significance of this risk increased marginally following changes to the Group's employee incentive schemes that involved the introduction of individual business profit targets as well as a Group profit target.

Our response

— We have: (i) extended our enquiries designed to assess whether judgements and estimates exhibited unconscious bias or whether management had taken systematic actions to manipulate the reported results; (ii) compared the results to forecasts, guidance and targets, and challenged variances at a much lower level than we would otherwise have done based on our understanding of factors affecting business performance with corroboration using external data where possible; and (iii) applied an increased level of scepticism throughout the audit by increasing the involvement of the senior audit team personnel, with particular focus on audit procedures designed to assess whether revenues and costs have been recognised in the correct accounting period, whether central adjustments were appropriate and whether the segmental analysis has been properly prepared" (p. 177).

This is an extensive disclosure, and it is about just one of the 19 risks that KPMG has identified! The importance of these disclosures by KPMG is undeniable in terms of helping users understand the potential for material misstatement in Rolls Royce's financial statements, and to price that risk appropriately in terms of the market value of the stock (*for information about movements in the stock price, see: https://www.rolls-royce.com/investors/share-price.aspx*).

For further details, see *https://www.rolls-royce.com/~/media/Files/R/Rolls-Royce/documents/annual-report/rr-2016-full-annual-report.pdf*

For Classroom Discussion

On December 9, 2016, Rolls Royce switched auditors from KPMG to PwC, as required by new governance requirements with respect to auditor tenure (KPMG had been Rolls Royce's auditor for 26 years). On May 4, 2017, the U.K. Financial Reporting Council launched an investigation into KPMG's audits of Rolls Royce. On November 7, 2017, the U.S. Department of Justice indicted five Rolls Royce executives, accusing them of various violations of the Foreign Corrupt Practices Act of 1977.

- Investigate the resolution of these situations. What has transpired?

- Look back to KPMG's Dynamic Audit Tool. How did KPMG rank the risks associated with bribery and corruption? Comment on how accurate those risk assessments turned out to be in the end.

- How might the litigation environment in the U.S. versus the U.K play into how auditors assess their own risks associated with a given audit client?

KAMs or CAMs?

The list below summarizes relevant facts with respect to KAMs and CAMs.

Relevant Standard Setter	Applicable Jurisdiction	Title and Abbreviation
International Accounting and Auditing Standards Board	Outside the U.S. listed entities, for which ISAs are applicable	Key Audit Matter (KAM)
Auditing Standards Board	U.S. private entities for which AU-C are applicable	In July 2017, the ASB voted to consider aligning its guidance with ISA 701, and requiring auditors to include a discussion of KAMs in the audit report.
Public Company Accounting Oversight Board	U.S. public entities for which AS are applicable	Critical Audit Matter (CAM)

For Classroom Discussion

Users of financial statements have called for additional transparency about significant audit matters for some time, criticizing the audit report for lacking incremental value because it simply yields a "pass/fail" outcome, that is, a clean opinion or not. For example, users have expressed particular interest in understanding significant judgments that auditors make when forming the opinion on the financial statements. In other words, they are interested in the process of *how* the auditor reached his or her opinion, in addition to the outcome of the audit.

In 2017, when the PCAOB released its updated standard on audit reporting, the PCAOB Chairman at the time, James Doty, prominently noted that the new audit report, which requires CAMs, gives investors the information about the audit that they have been demanding.

In contrast, many companies do not support the new CAM requirements, alleging that critical audit matters will not provide important information to investors, will duplicate the companies' disclosures, may result in disclosing unimportant or overly qualitative information, may increase the cost of the audit, and/or may result in delays in completing the audit.

- Which view do you think is most convincing? Why?
- Will CAMs benefit investors?
- What motivations might managers have that lead to their lack of support for the new standard?
- Will CAMs make the audit report more relevant and useful?
- What would an investor learn by comparing CAMs across companies within an industry and over time?
- Do you think that required CAM reporting will result in management taking more or fewer actions to benefit users?

Check Your Basic Knowledge

15-17 All audit reports issued under the guidance of ISA 701, *Communicating Key Audit Matters in the Independent Auditor's Report*, will include one or more KAMs. (T/F)

15-18 ISA 701, *Communicating Key Audit Matters in the Independent Auditor's Report*, mandates the order of presentation of KAMs. (T/F)

15-19 Which of the following items would <u>not</u> be included in a PCAOB audit report that includes CAMs?
a. Identification of the CAM.
b. Description of the principal considerations that led the auditor to determine that the matter is a CAM.
c. Indication as to whether management agreed that the matter was a CAM.
d. Description of how the CAM was addressed in the audit.

e. Reference to the relevant financial statement accounts or disclosures.

15-20 As part of identifying CAMs, which of the following factors would an auditor consider when determining whether a matter involved especially challenging, subjective, or complex auditor judgment?
a. The auditor's assessment of the risks of material misstatement, including significant risks.
b. The nature and timing of significant unusual transactions and the extent of audit effort and judgment related to requisite transactions.
c. The degree of auditor subjectivity in applying audit procedures to address the matter or in evaluating the results of those procedures.
d. The auditor would consider all of the above factors.

LO 6

For U.S. public companies, describe the information included in an auditor's report on internal control over financial reporting.

Audit Reports on Internal Control Over Financial Reporting for U.S. Public Companies

In determining the appropriate opinion on internal control over financial reporting (ICFR), the auditor evaluates identified control deficiencies individually, and in the aggregate, to assess whether there is a material weakness in ICFR. The auditor will issue an unqualified opinion on ICFR when the auditor determines that there are no material weaknesses in ICFR, and will issue an adverse opinion when there are one or more material weaknesses in ICFR. *Exhibit 15.9* provides example language for a combined report expressing an unqualified opinion on financial statements and an unqualified opinion on internal control over financial reporting

The auditor may choose to issue a separate report on internal control over financial reporting. In that case, the auditor would add the following language to the report on the financial statements immediately following the opinion paragraph:

> We also have audited, in accordance with the standards of the Public Company Accounting Oversight Board (United States) ("PCAOB"), the Company's internal control over financial reporting as of December 31, 20X8, based on [*identify control criteria*] and our report dated [*date of report, which should be the same as the date of the report on the financial statements*] expressed [*include nature of opinion*]. (Source: PCAOB Release No. 2017-001, June 1, 2017)

The auditor would also add the following paragraph (immediately following the opinion paragraph) to the report on internal control over financial reporting:

> We also have audited, in accordance with the standards of the Public Company Accounting Oversight Board (United States) ("PCAOB"), the [*identify financial statements*] of the Company and our report dated [*date of report, which should be the same as the date of the report on the effectiveness of internal control over financial reporting*] expressed [*include nature of opinion*]. (Source: PCAOB Release No. 2017-001, June 1, 2017)

Exhibit 15.9
Combined Report Expressing an Unqualified Opinion
on Financial Statements and an Unqualified Opinion on
Internal Control Over Financial Reporting: PCAOB Audit

NOTE: The format of the audit report depends on the auditing standards the auditor is following.

Report of Independent Registered Public Accounting Firm

To the shareholders and the board of directors of W Company

Opinions on the Financial Statements and Internal

Control over Financial Reporting

We have audited the accompanying balance sheets of W Company (the "Company") as of December 31, 20X8 and 20X7, and the related statements of [*titles of the financial statements, e.g., income, comprehensive income, stockholders' equity, and cash flows*] for each of the years in the three-year period ended December 31, 20X8, and the related notes [*and schedules*] (collectively referred to as the "financial statements"). We also have audited the Company's internal control over financial reporting as of December 31, 20X8, based on [*Identify control criteria, for example, "criteria established in Internal Control - Integrated Framework: (20XX) issued by the Committee of Sponsoring Organizations of the Treadway Commission (COSO)."*].

In our opinion, the financial statements referred to above present fairly, in all material respects, the financial position of the Company as of December 31, 20X8 and 20X7, and the results of its operations and its cash flows for each of the years in the three-year period ended December 31, 20X8 in conformity with accounting principles generally accepted in the United States of America. Also in our opinion, the Company maintained, in all material respects, effective internal control over financial reporting as of December 31, 20X8, based on [*Identify control criteria, for example, "criteria established in Internal Control - Integrated Framework: (20XX) issued by COSO."*].

Basis for Opinion

The Company's management is responsible for these financial statements, for maintaining effective internal control over financial reporting, and for its assessment of the effectiveness of internal control over financial reporting, included in the accompanying [*title of management's report*]. Our responsibility is to express an opinion on the Company's financial statements and an opinion on the Company's internal control over financial reporting based on our audits. We are a public accounting firm registered with the Public Company Accounting Oversight Board (United States) ("PCAOB") and are required to be independent with respect to the Company in accordance with the U.S. federal securities laws and the applicable rules and regulations of the Securities and Exchange Commission and the PCAOB.

We conducted our audits in accordance with the standards of the PCAOB. Those standards require that we plan and perform the audits to obtain reasonable assurance about whether the financial statements are free of material misstatement, whether due to error or fraud, and whether effective internal control over financial reporting was maintained in all material respects.

Our audits of the financial statements included performing procedures to assess the risks of material misstatement of the financial statements, whether due to error or fraud, and performing procedures that respond to those risks. Such procedures included examining, on a test basis, evidence regarding the amounts and disclosures in the financial statements. Our audits also included evaluating the accounting principles used and significant estimates made by management, as well as evaluating the overall presentation of the financial statements. Our audit of internal control over financial reporting included obtaining an understanding of internal control over financial reporting, assessing the risk that a material weakness exists, and testing and evaluating the design and operating effectiveness of internal control based on the assessed risk. Our audits also included performing such other procedures as we considered necessary in the circumstances. We believe that our audits provide a reasonable basis for our opinions.

Definition and Limitations of Internal Control Over Financial Reporting

A company's internal control over financial reporting is a process designed to provide reasonable assurance regarding the reliability of financial reporting and the preparation of financial statements for external purposes in accordance with generally accepted accounting principles. A company's internal control over financial reporting includes those policies and

(Continues)

Exhibit 15.9 *Continued*

procedures that (1) pertain to the maintenance of records that, in reasonable detail, accurately and fairly reflect the transactions and dispositions of the assets of the company; (2) provide reasonable assurance that transactions are recorded as necessary to permit preparation of financial statements in accordance with generally accepted accounting principles, and that receipts and expenditures of the company are being made only in accordance with authorizations of management and directors of the company; and (3) provide reasonable assurance regarding prevention or timely detection of unauthorized acquisition, use, or disposition of the company's assets that could have a material effect on the financial statements.

Because of its inherent limitations, internal control over financial reporting may not prevent or detect misstatements. Also, projections of any evaluation of effectiveness to future periods are subject to the risk that controls may become inadequate because of changes in conditions, or that the degree of compliance with the policies or procedures may deteriorate.

Source: *PCAOB Release No. 2017-001, June 1, 2017*

Why It Matters   Situations Requiring a Modification to the Audit Report on ICFR

This feature summarizes situations in which the auditor may issue an audit report on ICFR containing an opinion other than an unqualified opinion or an adverse opinion on ICFR.

- If there are restrictions placed on the scope of the engagement, the auditor will either withdraw from the engagement or disclaim an opinion (thereby stating that the auditor does not express an opinion on ICFR effectiveness).

- If the auditor determines that management's report on ICFR is incomplete or not properly presented, the auditor's report will include an explanatory paragraph that describes the reasons for this determination.

- The auditor may choose to include a reference in the audit report to work performed by another auditor. Such a reference would occur if the auditor were relying on work of another auditor who might be performing the ICFR audit work at a subsidiary, division, branch, or component of the company. The decision about whether to make reference to another auditor in the report on the audit of ICFR might differ from the corresponding decision as it relates to the audit of the financial statements. For example, the audit

report on the financial statements may make reference to the audit of a significant equity investment performed by another auditor, but the report on ICFR might not make a similar reference because management's assessment of ICFR did not include controls at the equity method investee.

- If management chooses to provide information in its report on ICFR in addition to the information required to be provided, the auditor will disclaim an opinion on that additional information.

- If matters come to the auditor's attention as a result of the audit of ICFR that would cause the auditor to believe that modifications to the disclosures about changes in ICFR (addressing changes in ICFR occurring during the fourth quarter) are necessary for the annual certifications to be accurate and to comply with the requirements of Section 302 of Sarbanes-Oxley, the auditor should modify the report on ICFR to include an explanatory paragraph describing the reasons the auditor believes management's disclosures should be modified.

What Do You Think?   For Classroom Discussion

In Walmart's September 9, 2015 10-Q (i.e., quarterly report), management revealed an internal control material weakness (ICMW) relating to its accounting for leases:

> "During the second quarter of fiscal 2016, we identified a material weakness in our controls over accounting for leases, as described below. Based upon that discovery, our Chief

Executive Officer and Chief Financial Officer have concluded that our disclosure controls and procedures are not effective at a level that provides reasonable assurance as of the last day of the period covered by this report.

The material weakness in internal control over financial reporting resulted from the lack of controls which allowed for the misinterpretation and historical misapplication of Accounting Standards Codification ("ASC") 840, Leases, regarding sale-leaseback accounting, including lessee involvement in the construction of leased assets. Specifically, we did not have adequate controls in place to properly identify and account for leases that were subject to the sale-leaseback accounting guidance, including leases in which we made payments for certain structural components included in the lessor's construction of the leased assets, which should have resulted in the Company being deemed the owner of the leased assets for accounting purposes."

For further details, see: https://www.sec.gov/Archives/edgar /data/104169/000010416915000039/wmtform10-qx7312015.htm# s28CB6E634B5CE93892ABD3EC75948676

The stock market was quick to penalize Walmart relating to the implications of this ICMW:

By the time the FYE and 10-K (i.e., annual report) were filed, management disclosed that internal control was effective:

"Management has assessed the effectiveness of the Company's internal control over financial reporting as of January 31, 2016. In making its assessment, management has utilized the criteria set forth by the Committee of Sponsoring Organizations ("COSO") of the Treadway Commission in Internal Control-Integrated Framework (2013). Management concluded that based on its assessment, Walmart's internal control over financial reporting was effective as of January 31, 2016. The Company's internal control over financial reporting as of January 31, 2016, has been audited by Ernst & Young LLP as stated in their report which appears in this Annual Report to Shareholders" (p. 62).

In addition, Ernst & Young corroborated this management assertion:

"In our opinion, the financial statements referred to above present fairly, in all material respects, the consolidated financial position of Wal-Mart Stores, Inc. at January 31, 2015 and 2014, and the consolidated results of its operations and its cash flows for each of the three years in the period ended January 31, 2015, in conformity with U.S. generally accepted accounting principles" (p. 60).

"In our opinion, Wal-Mart Stores, Inc. maintained, in all material respects, effective internal control over financial reporting as of January 31, 2016, based on the COSO criteria" (p. 61).

For further details, see: http://s2.q4cdn.com/056532643/files /doc_financials/2015/annual/2015-annual-report.pdf

The stock market was equally quick to reward Walmart for remediating the ICMW between the quarterly report and the annual report:

- As a user of the financial statements, do you find Walmart's 10-Q disclosure of an ICMW to be troubling?

- If there was an ICMW in September 2015, why didn't management and the auditor ultimately issue an adverse opinion on internal controls in the annual report?

- What do you infer about users' reactions to ICMW remediation based upon the stock market value of Walmart's stock as of March 30, 2016 (the date of the auditor's report)?

Check Your Basic Knowledge

15-21 The auditor issues an adverse opinion on ICFR if the client has one or more significant deficiencies in ICFR. (T/F)

15-22 If the auditor is conducting an integrated audit, the auditor must provide both opinions in the same report. (T/F)

15-23 The auditor of a large U.S. public company is conducting an integrated audit and has determined that a material weakness exists in the client's ICFR. Which of the following statements is <u>true</u>?

a. The auditor is required to issue an adverse opinion on the financial statements.

b. The auditor should express an adverse opinion on internal controls only if a material misstatement was found in the financial statements.

c. The auditor should express an adverse opinion on ICFR, even if no material misstatements were found in the financial statements.

d. The auditor is not required to express an opinion on internal controls.

15-24 Refer to the *Why It Matters* feature "Situations Requiring a Modification to the Audit Report on ICFR." In which of the following situations would the auditor modify the audit report on ICFR?

a. The auditor identifies multiple unrelated significant deficiencies in ICFR.

b. The auditor concludes that management's report on ICFR is not complete or is improperly presented.

c. The unaudited financial statements did not contain any misstatements.

d. The auditor would modify the audit report on ICFR in all of the above situations.

Omitted Audit Procedures

LO 7

Respond to situations in which omitted procedures come to the auditor's attention after the audit report has been issued.

After the audit report has been issued, the auditor may discover an **omitted procedure**, which is an important audit procedure that was not performed. For example, an auditor may have failed to follow up on a material accounts receivable confirmation response indicating a difference between the client's recorded balance and the customer's recorded balance.

When an omitted procedure is discovered, the auditor should decide whether the previously issued audit report can still be supported. A review of the working papers, discussion of the circumstances with engagement personnel and others, and a reevaluation of the overall scope of the audit may be helpful in making this assessment. The auditor may conclude, for example, that the results of other procedures that were performed may compensate for the omitted procedure or make its omission less important.

Prompt for Critical Thinking #5   It's Your Turn!

Identify ways in which you think that omitted procedures might be discovered after the audit report has been issued.

• _____

• _____

Proper Documentation Reduces the Risk of Omitted Procedures

This feature explains how proper audit documentation can aid auditors in mitigating the risk of accidentally omitting audit procedures.

By complying with the requirements of AU-C 230, *Audit Documentation*, the auditor can help address the risk of omitted procedures. While the auditor primarily uses audit evidence to form a basis for the opinion, and to provide evidence that the audit was planned and performed according to professional standards, documentation can also be useful in ensuring that planned work was, indeed, performed and reviewed, that is, there were no "forgotten" tasks to complete. Such documentation will be helpful in reducing the risk of omitted procedures by:

- Enabling the engagement team to demonstrate that they have reliable evidence that proves they have been accountable in performing procedures, examining evidence, and reaching appropriate conclusion

- Helping members of the engagement team that are responsible for reviewing the work of others to discharge their responsibilities properly

- Enabling the engagement team to demonstrate that they have reliable evidence that proves they have been accountable in performing procedures, examining evidence, and reaching appropriate conclusion

- Ensuring that matters of importance to the audit in the current period, and potentially future periods, are retained

- Enabling potential reviewers of the work (internal to the firm, or external to the firm in terms of peer review or regulatory review) to understand the work that the engagement team performed

Consider an example where the auditor failed to confirm receivables and discovered that omission after issuing the audit report. In that case, the auditor could extend the previous work done on subsequent collections to help determine that the receivables existed and were properly valued at the balance sheet date. If the results of these new procedures indicate that the previously issued statements and audit report should be modified, the auditor should take action to prevent future reliance on the audit report. Otherwise, no further action is necessary.

15-25 An example of a situation in which the auditor discovers omitted procedures after the audit report was issued would be one in which the auditor failed to confirm receivables, and this fact comes to light as part of an internal review program.　(T/F)

15-26 If after the audit report was issued, the auditor discovers that an important audit procedure was not performed, SOX requires that the auditor file a Form 8-K with the SEC.　(T/F)

15-27 Which of the following statements is <u>true</u> when an omitted audit procedures is discovered after the audit report was issued?

　a. After the audit report has been issued, the auditor may discover that an important audit procedure was not performed.

　b. Such an omission may be discovered when audit documentation is reviewed as part of an external or internal review program.

　c. The auditor should decide whether the previously issued audit report can still be supported in light of the omitted procedures.

　d. All of the above.

15-28 If it is discovered after the audit report is issued that the auditor failed to confirm receivables, which of the following statements is <u>true</u>?

　a. The auditor should try to examine subsequent collections of accounts receivable to help determine whether the accounts receivables existed and whether they were properly valued at the balance sheet date.

　b. The auditor must resign immediately.

　c. The auditor must notify the SEC immediately.

　d. The auditor must notify users of the financial statements immediately.

LO 8

Apply the frameworks for professional decision making and ethical decision making to audit reporting situations.

Applying Decision-Making Frameworks

The following *End of Chapter* materials provide you an opportunity to apply the frameworks for professional decision making and ethical decision making for decisions made when conducting an audit: *15-28.*

Let's Review

- The auditor forms an opinion on the financial statements based on an evaluation of the audit evidence obtained, and expresses that opinion in a written report. (LO 1)

- Although specific requirements differ across standards, the basic elements of an unqualified/unmodified report include the title, addressee(s), opinion on the financial statements, basis for opinion, along with the audit firm's signature, tenure, location, and the date that the auditor signed the opinion. (LO 2)

- An auditor issues an unqualified/unmodified report when there are no material violations of generally accepted accounting principles (GAAP), disclosures are adequate, the auditor was able to perform all of the necessary procedures, there was no change in accounting principles that had a material effect on the financial statements, the auditor does not have significant doubt about the client remaining a going concern, and the auditor is independent. (LO 2)

- The following are common situations when the auditor will issue an unqualified/unmodified audit opinion with report modifications:
    - The auditor chooses to emphasizes some matter in the financial statements
    - The auditor opts to include information about audit participants in the audit report (applicable only for PCAOB audits)
    - The auditor decides to refer to other auditors as the basis, in part, for the auditor's own report
    - There is a lack of consistency in the financial statements
    - There is a justified departure from GAAP
    - Substantial doubt about the client being a going concern exists
    - The client had a material misstatement in previously issued financial statements that it has corrected (LO 3)

- When the auditor is not able to give an unqualified opinion, the auditor will provide either a qualified opinion, an adverse opinion, or a disclaimer of opinion, depending on the facts and circumstances. (LO 4)

- A critical audit matter is any matter that was communicated or required to be communicated to the audit committee, relating to accounts or disclosures material to the financial statements, and involving especially challenging, subjective, or complex auditor judgment. (LO 5)

- Key audit matters are those matters that, in the auditor's professional judgment, were of most significance in the audit of the financial statements of the current period. Key audit matters are selected from matters communicated to those charged with governance. (LO 5)

- In determining the appropriate opinion on internal control over financial reporting (ICFR), the auditor evaluates identified control deficiencies individually, and in the aggregate, to assess whether there is a material weakness in ICFR. The auditor will issue an unqualified opinion when the auditor determines that there are no material weaknesses in ICFR, and will issue an adverse opinion when there are one or more material weaknesses in ICFR. Refer to *Exhibit 15.8* for an example report. (LO 6)

- When an omitted procedure is discovered, the auditor should decide whether the previously issued audit report can still be supported. The auditor may conclude, for example, that the results of other procedures that were performed may compensate for the omitted procedure or make its omission less important. Alternatively, the audit may need to extend previous work. If the results of these new procedures indicate that the previously issued statements and audit report should be modified, the auditor should that action to prevent future reliance on the audit report. Otherwise, no further action is necessary. (LO 7)

Significant Terms

Audit scope   The range of accounts and transactions that the auditor evaluates, along with the amount of evidence that they gather, assessments of which accounts and transactions are material, as well as the critical areas where the auditor employed significant assumptions and made associated professional judgments.

Component   An entity or business activity for which group or component management prepares financial information that is required by the applicable financial reporting framework to be included in the group financial statements.

Component auditor   An auditor who performs work on the financial information of a component that will be used as audit evidence for the group audit. A component auditor may be part of the group engagement partner's firm, a network firm of the group engagement partner's firm, or another firm.

Critical audit matter   Any matter that was communicated or required to be communicated to the audit committee, relating to accounts or disclosures material to the financial statements, and involving especially challenging, subjective, or complex auditor judgment.

Emphasis-of-matter paragraph   A paragraph included in the auditor's report that is required by GAAS, or is included at the auditor's discretion, and that refers to a matter appropriately presented or disclosed in the financial statements that, in the auditor's professional judgment, is of such importance that it is fundamental to users' understanding of the financial statements.[2]

Group   All the components whose financial information is included in the group financial statements. A group always has more than one component.

Group audit   The audit of group financial statements.

Group audit opinion   The audit opinion on the group financial statements.

Group engagement partner   The partner or other person in the firm who is responsible for the group audit engagement and its performance, and for the auditor's report on the group financial statements that is issued on behalf of the firm.

Group financial statements   Financial statements that include the financial information of more than one component. The term *group financial statements* also refers to combined financial statements aggregating the financial information prepared by components that have no parent but are under common control.

Key audit matter   A matters that, in the auditor's professional judgment, was of most significance in the audit of the financial statements of the current period. Key audit matters are selected from matters communicated to those charged with governance.

Omitted procedure   After the audit report has been issued, the auditor may discover that an important audit procedure was not performed; these are called omitted procedures.

Other-matter paragraph   A paragraph included in the auditor's report that is required by GAAS, or is included at the auditor's discretion, and that refers to a matter other than those presented or disclosed in the financial statements that, in the auditor's professional judgment, is relevant to users' understanding of the audit, the auditor's responsibilities, or the auditor's report.

Pervasive   A term used in the context of misstatements to describe the effects or the possible effects on the financial statements of misstatements that are undetected due to an inability to obtain sufficient appropriate audit evidence.

Positive assurance   An explicit statement as to whether the financial statements are presented fairly.

Unmodified opinion   See *unqualified opinion.*

Unqualified opinion   The opinion expressed by the auditor when the auditor concludes that the financial statements are presented fairly, in all material respects, in accordance with the applicable financial reporting framework.

Prompts for Critical Thinking

Prompt for Critical Thinking #1

NOTE: Answers are based on accessing the database on September 19, 2017.

Example 1.

a.   Douglas Edward Hunter
b.   Polaris Retirement Savings and Proto Labs, Inc.
c.   These clients are quite different; Target is a major retailer, Polaris is a financial institution, and Proto Labs makes 3-D printer equipment. In thinking critically about this data, a user might question whether Mr. Hunter is an expert in auditing retailers, and why it makes sense for Ernst & Young to have him audit these other clients.

Example 2.

a.   1,880
b.   1,195
c.   69

A critical user will be able to determine which audit firms occupy various niches and sizes in the market for audit services.

Example 3.

Deloitte audits six clients in Brazil: Energy Company of Minas Gerias, Brazilian Distribution Company, Energy Company of Parana, Ultrapar Holdings, CPFL Energy, Inc., and Ambev S.A.

A critical user might use this data to question whether the audit failures at Gol Intelligent Airlines might transfer over to the audits of these particular issuers.

Prompt for Critical Thinking #2

- One inference may be that BHP Billiton has multiple physical locations that KPMG and its affiliates needed to visit to obtain sufficient assurance regarding certain line items or transaction cycles. Another inference may be that KPMG—Australia used another affiliated office, for example, Singapore to conduct portions of the audit that can be completed by lower-level staff on a routine basis to yield cost savings.
- A benefit to having multiple offices participate in the audit is that the overall audit firm keeps the profits, both monetary and reputation-wise, to itself rather than sharing them across competing audit firms. In addition, using multiple offices might yield efficiencies in terms of conducting audit work at geographically dispersed locations, or might yield the ability to incorporate the insights from specialists that are located away from the main portion of the audit.
- Disadvantages might include coordination challenges, differential work quality, and lack of continuity of the entire engagement team over time.

Prompt for Critical Thinking #3

- The economic rationale for imposing the requirement that a registrant obtain a second audit opinion when the original auditor has been deregistered by the PCAOB is likely due to the notion that if the audit firm did a very low-quality audit that brought their firm to the attention of the PCAOB, then that firm may have also provided sub-par audit quality to other clients.
- The replacement audit and associated audit opinion might differ from the original opinion, but not necessarily. Just because the audit firm did a sub-par audit on one engagement does not mean it performed a sub-part audit on another client engagement. Then again, a second (i.e., replacement) auditor might be quite skeptical of the original auditor's work, and might conduct an especially stringent audit with relatively low levels of acceptable materiality to ensure that the audit opinion issued is correct and justifiable.
- The power that this rule provides to issuer clients of auditing firms in terms of their demand for quality audits lies in the fact that clients demand audit quality for the firm's entire portfolio of clients; if they do not, then everyone involved with that sub-part audit has the potential to suffer.

Prompt for Critical Thinking #4

- If an auditor determined that a potential illegal act required no disclosure on the financial statements, the matter would not relate to an account or disclosure that is material to the financial statements.
- If the auditor determined that there is a significant deficiency in internal control over financial reporting that is not a critical audit matter because it does not, in itself, relate to an account or disclosure that is material to the financial statements
- Forward-looking information and disclosures that management makes in its Management, Discussion, & Analysis (not audited) in the annual report
- The evaluation of significant risks facing the organization as part of audit planning

Prompt for Critical Thinking #5

- When audit documentation is reviewed as part of a PCAOB inspection, the firm's internal review program, a peer review program, and/or subsequent year audit
- When news comes to light publicly after year-end about a significant uncertainty that has been resolved, but that the auditor did not consider as part of the audit procedures

Review Questions and Short Cases

15-1 **LO 1** Why is the audit report important to the audit opinion formulation process?

15-2 **LO 1** What are the AICPA's basic principles regarding audit reporting?

15-3 **LO 2** What conditions must be present for an auditor to be able to issue an unqualified audit report similar to the one presented in *Exhibit 15.2*?

15-4 **LO 2** Review *Exhibit 15.1* and identify the timing requirements for U.S. public companies to file audited financial statements with the SEC.

15-5 **LO 2** List the components of a standard unqualified audit report for a U.S. public company.

INTERNATIONAL

15-6 **LO 2** Auditors following the ISAs would refer to ISA 700 for relevant guidance on audit reports. The format of an ISA audit report is similar to the PCAOB's report format under the reporting standard, AS 3101, adopted in 2017. Describe the terminology difference between the two standards.

INTERNATIONAL

15-7 **LO 2** How would the auditor's opinion differ if the financial statements of a company that was a foreign private issuer were prepared in conformity with IFRS and filed with the SEC rather than prepared in conformity with U.S. GAAP?

15-8 **LO 2** Refer to Panel A of *Exhibit 15.2*. What words and phrases in an unqualified audit report imply that there is a risk that the audited financial statements may contain a material misstatement?

INTERNATIONAL

15-9 **LO 3** Refer to *Exhibit 15.3* and the *Why It Matters* feature "Differing Guidance on Referring to Other Auditors." How do the requirements for referring to other auditors differ between U.S. auditing standards and the ISAs?

15-10 **LO 3** You are in charge of the audit of the financial statements of Parat, Inc. and consolidated subsidiaries, covering the two years ended December 31, 2018. Another firm is auditing Nuam, Inc., a major subsidiary of Parat that accounts for total assets, revenue, and net income of 30%, 26%, and 39%, respectively, for 2017, and 28%, 20%, and 33%, respectively, for 2018. The audits are being conducted in accordance with PCAOB standards.

a. What is meant by the term *principal auditor*? What term can be used in place of *principal auditor*?

b. Write the opinion paragraph(s) of the audit report referring to the other audit firm and expressing an unqualified opinion. Refer to *Exhibit 15.3* for guidance.

15-11 **LO 3** A staff accountant of Turner & Turner, CPAs drafted the audit report at the completion of the audit of the financial statements of Lyon Computers, Inc. (a public company) for the year ended March 31, 2018.

It was submitted to the engagement partner, who reviewed matters thoroughly and properly concluded that Lyon's disclosures concerning its ability to continue as a going concern for a reasonable period of time were adequate, but there is substantial doubt about Lyon being a going concern.

a. The partner is concerned that the audit report description on the going concern matter (presented below) is not appropriate. Identify any deficiencies.

The accompanying financial statements have been prepared assuming that the Company will continue as a going concern. As discussed in Note X to the financial statements, the Company has suffered recurring losses from operations and has a net capital deficiency that raises substantial doubt about its ability to continue as a going concern. We believe that management's plans in regard to these matters, which are also described in Note X, will permit the Company to continue as a going concern beyond a reasonable period of time. The financial statements do not include any adjustments that might result from the outcome of this uncertainty.

b. Furthermore, the staff auditor provided suggested wording for the opinion. An excerpt of that wording follows. Identify any deficiencies.

In our opinion, subject to the effects on the financial statements of such adjustments, if any, as might have been required had the outcome of the uncertainty referred to in the preceding paragraph been known, the financial statements referred to above present fairly, . . .

15-12 **LO 3** The accounting and auditing literature discusses several different types of accounting changes. For each of the changes listed below as a–d indicate whether the auditor should add a paragraph to the audit report, assuming that the change had a material effect on the financial statements and was properly justified, accounted for, and disclosed. Assume that the organization is a U.S. nonpublic company.

a. Change from one GAAP to another GAAP
b. Change in accounting estimate not affected by a change in accounting principle
c. Change in accounting estimate affected by a change in accounting principle
d. Change from non-GAAP to GAAP

15-13 **LO 3, 4** Various types of accounting changes can affect the auditor's report.

a. Briefly describe the rationale for having accounting changes affect the auditor's report and the auditor's responsibility in such cases.
b. For each of the changes listed below, as 1 through 7, indicate the type of change and its effect on the audit report for U.S. companies.

1. A change from the completed-contract method to the percentage-of-completion method of accounting for long-term construction contracts.
2. A change in the estimated useful life of previously recorded fixed assets. (The change is based on newly acquired information.)
3. Correction of an inventory error in previously issued financial statements.
4. A change from full absorption costing to direct costing for inventory valuation (which is non-GAAP).
5. A change from presentation of statements of individual companies to presentation of consolidated companies.
6. A change from deferring and amortizing preproduction costs to recording such costs as an expense when incurred, because future benefits of the costs have become doubtful. (The new accounting method was adopted in recognition of the change in estimated future benefits.)
7. A change from including the employer's share of FICA taxes with other taxes to including the employer's share of FICA taxes as retirement benefits on the income statement.

15-14 **LO 3** Under what circumstances must the audit report refer to the consistency, or the lack of consistency, in the application of GAAP? What is the purpose of such reporting?

15-15 **LO 3** When a client has a justified departure from GAAP, how should the auditor modify the audit report?

15-16 **LO 3** Provide examples of matters that auditors may choose to emphasize when issuing an unqualified opinion.

INTERNATIONAL

PROFESSIONAL SKEPTICISM

15-17 **XL Leisure Group, MovieLink (LO 3)** In September 2008, XL Leisure Group, Britain's third-largest tour operator, filed for bankruptcy. A few months prior to filing for bankruptcy, the company had issued its audited financial statements. Neither the financial statements nor the auditor's opinion contained any explicit warning that the company was in financial difficulty.

In contrast, in 2007, the auditors of MovieLink expressed substantial doubt that MovieLink, which offers movies that can be downloaded from the Internet, would be able to continue as a going concern. The basis for the auditors' concern included MovieLink's recurring losses from operations, negative cash flows from operating activities, and an accumulated deficit that had risen to $145 million.

A company's financial statements are prepared and audited under the assumption that the company is a going concern, meaning that that company will continue to operate for a reasonable period of time, for example, one year. However, during times of financial crisis, it is expected that many companies will find themselves facing financial difficulties, even to the point of filing for bankruptcy. Financial difficulties can arise when companies fund their operations through debt, ranging from overdrafts to credit lines to large loans. If companies need these sources of funds to continue to operate, yet banks are unwilling to commit to providing these loans, many companies face the prospect of not being able to continue their operations. During times of financial crisis, banks may not be willing to continue providing the lending they have in the past or to commit to new lending. In these situations, auditors may have substantial doubt about a company's ability to continue as a going concern.

a. How does the auditor's substantial doubt about a client's ability to remain a going concern affect the format of the audit opinion?

b. What are the implications to the company and to the audit firm when the audit firm's report expresses substantial doubt about a company's ability to remain a going concern?

c. Why might the auditors of XL Leisure Group and MovieLink have arrived at two different decisions?

d. How might professional skepticism affect the auditor's decision to issue a going-concern opinion?

15-18 **LO 4** Identify the situations in which an auditor issues a qualified opinion.

15-19 **LO 4** On February 28, 2019, Stu & Dent, LLP completed the audit of ShyLO Ranch, Inc. (a public company) for the year ended December 31, 2018. A recent fire destroyed the accounting records concerning the cost of ShyLO's livestock. These were the only records destroyed. The auditors are unable to obtain sufficient appropriate evidence concerning the cost of the livestock, which represents about 8% of total assets. These are GAAP-based financial statements, and the auditors found no other problems during the audit. The audit report is to cover the 2018 financial statements only. The audit partner has indicated that a qualified opinion is more appropriate than an adverse opinion. Draft the opinion and basis of opinion paragraphs for the audit report.

15-20 **LO 4** In what situations would an auditor issue an adverse opinion?

15-21 **LO 4** What is the purpose of a disclaimer of opinion? In what situations would an auditor issue a disclaimer of opinion?

15-22 **LO 4** Why should the auditor ordinarily disclaim an opinion if the client imposes significant scope limitations on the audit procedures?

15-23 **LO 3, 4** Identify the types of audit reports other than an unqualified/unmodified audit report and explain the circumstances each type of report would be issued.

15-24 **LO 4** The following table outlines various scenarios in which an auditor will determine the appropriate audit opinion to issue. Note that the auditor's professional judgment about the nature of the matter giving rise to the modification and the pervasiveness of its effects or possible effects on the financial statements affect the type of opinion to be expressed. Complete the following table to identify the report that the auditor should issue.

Nature of Matter Giving Rise to the Modification	Auditor's Professional Judgment About the Pervasiveness of the Effects or Possible Effects on the Financial Statements	
	Material but Not Pervasive	**Material and Pervasive**
Financial statements are materially misstated		
Inability to obtain sufficient appropriate audit evidence		

15-25 **LO 2, 3, 4** Several independent audit situations are presented below and labeled a-i. Assume that everything other than what is described would have resulted in an unqualified/unmodified opinion on the company's financial statements. Indicate the type of opinion and audit report you believe the auditor should issue in each situation and explain your choice. Assume that these are U.S. companies.

a. The auditor was unable to obtain confirmations from two of the client's major customers that were included in the sample. These customers wrote on the confirmation letters that they were unable to confirm the balances because of their accounting systems. The auditor was able to achieve satisfaction through other audit procedures.

b. The client treated a lease as an operating lease, but the auditor believes the client should have accounted for it as a capital lease. The effects are material.

c. The client changed from FIFO to LIFO this year. The effect is material. Address the following two situations:
   i. The client properly accounted for, justified, and disclosed the change.
   ii. The client properly accounted for and disclosed the change, but did not properly justify the change.

d. The client restricted the auditor from observing the physical inventory. Inventory is a material item and has pervasive effects on the financial statements.

e. The client is engaged in a product liability lawsuit that is properly accounted for and adequately described in the footnotes. The lawsuit does not threaten the going-concern assumption, but an adverse decision by the court could create a material obligation for the client.

f. The status of the client as a going concern is extremely doubtful. The problems are properly described in the footnotes.

g. One of your client's subsidiaries was audited by another audit firm, whose opinion was qualified because of a GAAP violation. You do not believe that the GAAP violation is material to the consolidated financial statements on which you are expressing an opinion.

h. You are convinced that your client is violating another company's patent in the process of manufacturing its only product. The client will not disclose this because it does not want to wave a red flag and bring this violation to the other company's attention. A preliminary estimate is that the royalty payments required would be material to the financial statements.

i. The client, with reasonable justification, has changed its method of accounting for depreciation for all factory and office equipment. The effect of this change is not material to the current-year financial statements, but is likely to have a material effect in future years. The client's management will not disclose this change because of its immaterial effect on the current-year statements. You have been unable to persuade management to make the disclosure.

15-26 **LO 2, 3, 4** The following are independent audit situations for which you are to recommend an appropriate audit report. For each situation, listed as 1 through 6 below, identify the appropriate type of audit report from the list below (a through e) and briefly explain the rationale for selecting the report.

Appropriate type of audit report:
a. Unqualified opinion, with no report modifications
b. Unqualified opinion, with report modification
c. Qualified opinion
d. Disclaimer of opinion
e. Adverse opinion

Audit Situations
1. An audit client has a significant amount of loans receivable outstanding (40% of assets), but has an inadequate internal control system over the loans. The auditor cannot obtain sufficient appropriate evidence to prepare an aging of the loans or to identify the collateral for about 75% of the loans, even though the client states that all loans are collateralized. The auditor sent confirmations to verify the existence of the receivables, but only 10 of the 50 sent were returned. The auditor attempted to verify the other loans by looking at subsequent receipts, but only eight had remitted payments during the month of January, and the auditor wants to wrap up the audit by February 15. The auditor estimates that if only 10 of the 50 loans were correctly recorded, loans would need to be written down by $7.5 million.

2. During the audit of a large manufacturing company, the auditor did not observe all locations of physical inventory. The auditor chose a random number of sites to visit, and the company's internal auditors visited the other sites. The auditor has confidence in the competence and objectivity of the internal auditors. The auditor personally observed only about 20% of the total inventory, but

neither the auditor nor the internal auditors noted any exceptions in the inventory process.

3. During the past year, Network Computer, Inc. devoted its entire research and development efforts to develop and market an enhanced version of its state-of-the-art telecommunications system. The costs, which were significant, were capitalized as research and development costs. The company plans to amortize these capitalized costs over the life of the new product. The auditor has concluded that the research to date will likely result in a marketable product. A full description of the research and development, and the costs, is included in a note. The note also describes that basic research costs are expensed as incurred, and the auditor has verified the accuracy of the statement.

4. During the course of the audit of Sail-Away Company, the auditor noted that the current ratio had dropped to 1.75. The company's loan covenant requires the maintenance of a current ratio of 2.0, or the company's debt is immediately due. The auditor and the company have contacted the bank, which is not willing to waive the loan covenant because the company has been experiencing operating losses for the past few years and has an inadequate capital structure. The auditor has substantial doubt that the company can find adequate financing elsewhere and may encounter difficulties staying in operation. Management, however, is confident that it can overcome the problem. The company does not deem it necessary to include any additional disclosure because management members are confident that they will find an alternative source of funds by pledging their personal assets.

5. The Wear-Ever Wholesale Company has been very profitable. It recently received notice of a 10% price increase for a significant portion of its inventory. The company believes it is important to manage its products wisely and has a policy of writing all inventory up to current replacement cost. This assures that profits will be recognized on sales sufficient to replace the assets and realize a normal profit. This operating philosophy has been very successful, and all salespeople reference current cost, not historical cost, in making sales. Only inventory has been written up to replacement cost, but inventory is material because the company carries a wide range of products. The company's policy of writing up the inventory and its dollar effects is adequately described in a footnote to the financial statements. For the current year, the net effect of the inventory write-up increased reported income by only 3% and assets by 15% above historical cost.

6. The audit of NewCo was staffed primarily by three new hires and a relatively inexperienced audit senior. The manager found numerous errors during the conduct of the audit and developed very long to-do lists for all members of the audit to complete before the audit was concluded. Although the manager originally doubted the staff's understanding of the audit procedures, by the time the audit was finished, he concluded that the new auditors did understand the company and the audit process and that no material errors existed in the financial statements.

15-27 **LO 2, 4** Each of the following phrases, listed as 1 through 5 below, is from a paragraph in an auditor's report. Assume that except for the information indicated in the phrase, the report would have been an unqualified opinion with no report modifications. Select from the following list (a through d) the most likely opinion for the indicated phrase. Each choice in the list may be used once, more than once, or not at all.

a. Unqualified opinion
b. Qualified opinion
c. Adverse opinion
d. Disclaimer of opinion

    1. In our opinion, except for the omission of the statement of cash flows ...
    2. We are not independent with respect to KC Company . . .
    3. . . . based on our audit and the report of other auditors . . .
    4. . . . presents fairly, in all material respects ...
    5. . . . the scope of our work was not sufficient to enable us . . .

15-28 `LO 3, 8` Assume that you are in a situation where you had doubts about your client's ability to continue as a going concern. Furthermore, assume you have decided that, after performing all the required audit procedures, you can issue an unqualified opinion but need to modify the audit report to indicate substantial doubt about the client's ability to continue as a going concern. You have to let the CFO, who is a long-time friend of yours, know of your decision. When you do this, the CFO tries to explain to you that if the company receives a going-concern opinion, it will go under—that the opinion is a self-fulfilling prophecy. The CFO tries to convince you that if your firm does not issue a going-concern opinion, it is very likely the company will be able to weather its financial difficulties and survive. Furthermore, the CFO notes that this is really a matter of professional judgment and believes that many other auditors would not see the need to issue a going-concern opinion. Should you issue a standard unqualified audit report or an unqualified audit report with a going-concern explanatory paragraph?

Use the framework for ethical decision making introduced in *Chapter 1* to address the dilemma you face regarding what type of opinion to issue. Recall that the steps in the framework are as follows: (1) identify the ethical issue(s), (2) determine who are the affected parties and identify their rights, (3) determine the most important rights, (4) develop alternative courses of action, (5) determine the likely consequences of each proposed course of action, (6) assess the possible consequences, including an estimation of the greatest good for the greatest number, and (7) decide on the appropriate course of action.

15-29 `LO 5` Assume that an auditor has identified a number of CAMs.

a. What are CAMs?
b. For each CAM, what should the auditor include in the audit report?

`INTERNATIONAL` **15-30** `LO 5`

a. What are KAMs?
b. In what order should the auditor present the identified KAMs?

15-31 `LO 6` Under what circumstances must the auditor of a public company express an adverse opinion on the client's ICFR?

15-32 `LO 6` Identify the conditions under which an auditor would modify the opinion or report on ICFR (for situations other than the presence of a material weakness).

15-33 `LO 7` During the course of an interoffice quality review, it was discovered that the auditors had failed to consider whether inventory costs of a wholesale client exceeded their market value. The review took place six months after the audit report had been issued. Some prices had apparently been falling near year-end. Inventory is a major item in the financial statements, but the auditors do not know whether the market price declines were material.

a. What procedures could the auditors now perform to resolve this audit problem?

b. What should the auditors do if it turns out that inventory was materially overstated in the audited financial statements?

Fraud Focus: Contemporary and Historical Cases

ETHICS

PROFESSIONAL SKEPTICISM

INTERNATIONAL

15-34 **PCAOB, AWC Limited, Kandi Technologies Group, Inc. (LO 1, 3)**

This case is based on facts included in PCAOB's Inspection Report of AWC Limited (#104-2010-027), the PCAOB Enforcement Release No. 105-2016-016 against AWC, and financial disclosures from AWC's audit client, Kandi Technologies Group, Inc. This case represents a setting whether the audit firm issued an unqualified audit opinion without adequate evidence and exhibited weak professional skepticism.

The PCAOB 2010 Inspection and 2016 Enforcement Action

On March 31, 2010, the PCAOB issued a routine inspection report of AWC (#104-2010-027), which expressed the following concerns about the firm's audit quality:

"PCAOB standards require a firm to take appropriate actions to assess the importance of audit deficiencies identified after the date of the audit report to the firm's present ability to support its previously expressed opinions.

The matters were of such significance that it appeared to the inspection team that the Firm did not obtain sufficient competent evidential matter to support its opinion on the issuer's financial statements.

Those deficiencies, in each of these two audits, were:

1. the Firm's failure to identify, or to address appropriately, departures from GAAP that related to potentially material misstatements in the audited financial statements concerning the amortization of a beneficial conversion feature and the calculation of earnings per share;

2. the failure to perform sufficient procedures to audit the issuer's accounting for the issuance of preferred shares and related warrants; and

3. the failure to appropriately test and evaluate the accounting for a reverse merger" (p. 4).

For further details, see https://pcaobus.org//Inspections/Reports /Documents/2010_Albert_Wong.pdf

These PCAOB inspection concerns provided an early warning sign about a subsequent 2016 enforcement action against AWC relating to its audit of Kandi Technologies Group, Inc. (Kandi). On May 18, 2016, the PCAOB Enforcement Release No. 105-2016-016 articulated further criticisms about the quality of AWC's audit conduct. The enforcement release revoked AWC Limited's (AWC) registration, censured its two top partners, Albert Wong and Martin Wong, and imposed civil monetary penalties on both individuals.

The PCAOB's criticisms include the following issues with respect to the Kandi audit: *https://pcaobus.org/Enforcement/Decisions/Documents/105-2016-016-AWC-CPA.pdf*

"This matter concerns Respondents' violations of PCAOB rules and standards in connection with the issuance of audit reports on the consolidated financial statements of Kandi Technologies Group, Inc. ('Kandi' or the 'Company') for the years ended December 31, 2010, 2011, and 2012. As detailed below, Respondents, among other things, failed repeatedly to exercise due professional care and professional skepticism, to obtain sufficient appropriate audit evidence with respect to financial statement assertions, to include procedures designed to provide reasonable assurance of detecting fraud or illegal acts that would have a direct and material effect on the determination of financial statement amounts, and to prepare and maintain adequate audit documentation.

8. As the auditor with final responsibility and the engagement partner on the Kandi Audits, Albert Wong also failed to supervise the engagement staff.

9. Throughout the Kandi Audits, the Firm repeatedly violated PCAOB Auditing Standard No. 7, Engagement Quality Review ('AS No. 7'), by failing to have an engagement quality review performed with objectivity. As described below, the engagement quality reviewer in the Kandi Audits did not maintain objectivity because while serving in this capacity, he was an active member of the engagement team and performed audit procedures with respect to the audit of Kandi's deferred taxes and related disclosures.

10. In addition, the Firm and Albert Wong violated Section 10A(g) of the Exchange Act, Exchange Act Rule 10A-2, and PCAOB rules and standards that require a registered public accounting firm and its associated persons to be independent of the firm's audit client throughout the audit and professional engagement period. The Firm and Albert Wong were not independent of Kandi for the 2012 audit because a partner of AWC LLP, an affiliate and associated entity of the Firm, provided prohibited non-audit services to Kandi by accepting a Power-of-Attorney from Kandi and representing Kandi before a New York State regulatory agency.

11. Finally, the Firm failed to comply with PCAOB quality control standards in connection with the audits described herein, when it did not establish policies and procedures to provide the Firm with reasonable assurance that its personnel maintained independence in all required circumstances; the work performed by the engagement personnel met applicable professional standards, regulatory requirements, and the firm's standards of quality; and the policies and procedures established by the firm for the elements of quality control were suitably designed and were being effectively applied. Albert Wong, as the sole-proprietor and person ultimately responsible for the design, implementation and maintenance of the Firm's system of quality control took, or omitted to take, actions that he knew, or was reckless in not knowing, would directly and substantially contribute to the Firm's violation of PCAOB quality control standards, in contravention of PCAOB Rule 3502, Responsibility Not to Knowingly or Recklessly Contribute to Violations" (para. 7, p. 4).

One month prior to the issuance of the Enforcement Action (April 13, 2016), AWC's audit client, Kandi Technologies Group, Inc. (Kandi), dismissed AWC as its independent accountant, and affirmed the appointment of BDO China to take over the prior firm's responsibilities.

Kandi Technologies Group, Inc. Business Model and Stock Performance

As Kandi management articulates in its FYE 2015 Form 10-K (filed March 14, 2016), the Company's business model has evolved as follows:

> "Before the year 2013, the Company had been mainly engaged in the design, production and distribution of the off-road vehicle products. Due to various market factors and the environment with positive government supports, starting from the year 2013, the Company gradually shifted its main focus towards the development on pure electric vehicles ("EV") products and manufacturing electric vehicles parts. Also in the year 2013, the Company set up a Joint Venture with Geely Automobile Holdings Ltd. ("Geely") to focus on EV production, based on the agreement, EV production should be transferred to the Joint Venture. At the end of 2014, this transfer had been completed. Starting from 2015, the majority of the Company's revenue and profit were generated from the sale of EV parts" (p. 1)

For more details, see *https://www.sec.gov/Archives/edgar /data/1316517/000106299316008324/form10k.htm*

The Company's stock price has seen numerous fluctuations over the years, resulting from users' reactions to shifts in the overall economy, the Company's business model with respect to electric vehicles, subsidy payments from the Chinese government, internal control difficulties, and weak assurance on the part of its auditor, AWC Limited. The following chart illustrates these fluctuations:

Kandi Technologies Group, Inc. (KNDI)
NasdaqGS–NasdaqGS Delayed Price, Currency in USD

The Sub-Standard Audits

Kandi hired AWC just after the Company went public. The original auditing firm, Weinberg & Co., was responsible for conducting the audits prior to 2009, along with filing Kandi's registration statements with the SEC. That firm was paid $270,400 for its services in 2008, when the stock first started trading on the NASDAQ (symbol KNDI). Below is a table that reveals the yearly audit fees paid by Kandi to AWC for from the FYE audits 2009–2015, illustrating an over 300% increase in audit fees during the period:

Year	2015	2014	2013	2012	2011	2010	2009
Audit Fee ($)	364,000	310,000	261,000	160,000	111,000	104,850	85,000

Over the course of the firm's tenure auditing Kandi, AWC always issued unqualified audit opinions on the financial statements. The firm did so despite a variety of red flags present in the Company's business dealings, including potentially overstated revenue and accounts receivable, questionable loans and cash balances, and (initially hidden) related party transactions. It is a matter of professional judgment as to whether the financial statements of Kandi were ever materially misstated. The PCAOB's enforcement action does not indicate concerns about any potential material misstatements. Rather, the PCAOB expressed concerns about the Firm's sub-standard audits, and the processes by which AWC reached its audit conclusions prior to issuing its unqualified audit reports.

a. In March 2010, the PCAOB issued an inspection report about AWC with various findings illustrative of low audit quality. At that time, the firm had 10 issuer clients, one engagement partner, and 22 professional staff. Why would a company that has just gone public want to hire an audit firm with those kinds of problems in terms of how it conducts its audits?

b. Explain why the PCAOB's allegations about AWC's sub-standard audits reveal egregious conduct on the part of AWC's engagement team.

c. In addition to lacking independence because one of AWC's employees performed prohibited non-audit services for Kandi, what does the pattern of audit fees reveal to you, particularly with respect to the (likely low) level of effort that AWC likely put into conducting the audit?

d. Comment on why you think that Kandi's audit committee dismissed AWC and hired BDO just prior to the release of the PCAOB's enforcement action?

e. While the PCAOB criticized AWC for sub-standard audits, the SEC did not take any formal action to charge Kandi management with any wrongdoing. However, the SEC did issue numerous comment letters to Kandi regarding questions about the Company's accounting judgments. Comment letters are formal discussions between the SEC staff and issuer clients. As one example, see the concerns the SEC staff express in the following comment letter:
https://www.sec.gov/Archives/edgar/data/1316517 /000000000014018486/filename1.pdf
Do you believe that AWC had a reasonable basis for issuing unqualified opinions on Kandi's financial statements during the period 2008–2015? Explain.

f. Access SEC filings for FYEs subsequent to 2016, to update your knowledge about Kandi's financial statements, and BDO's assurance therein.

Application Activities

NOTE: Completing *Application Activities* requires students to reference additional resources and materials. Some *Application Activities* will require the student to reference relevant professional auditing standards. We make special note of these as *Auditing Standards Application Activities*.

15-35 **LO 3** In the chapter, we learned about the going-concern uncertainties that the following companies have faced:

a. ImmunoGen
b. Sears

Use online resources to determine the ultimate fate of these companies. Comment on which are still in existence (and perhaps why) as compared to others.

AUDITING STANDARDS
APPLICATION ACTIVITY

AUDITING STANDARDS
APPLICATION ACTIVITY

INTERNATIONAL

INTERNATIONAL

15-36 **Forest Oil Company**
(LO 3, 4) Obtain the 10-K/A for Forest Oil Company for FYE December 31,2013 (filed 10/1/2014). Refer to Note 1 to the financial statements (page page 63 of the 10-K/A). Based on management's discussion in the note, what type of audit report did Forest Oil's audit firm likely issue? In this situation, what options did the audit firm have?

15-37 **LO 2** Assume that you are preparing audit report with an unqualified opinion and no report modifications for a nonpublic U.S. company and are not sure how to describe the audit that was performed. Which standard would provide details on what should be included in the auditor's report related to the description of the audit? Refer to the *Auditing Standards Exhibit* inside the front cover of this textbook. Obtain the standard, and identify the relevant paragraph(s) in that standard.

15-38 **IAASB**
(LO 2, 3, 4, 5) Refer to *Exhibit 15.8*. For each of the eight sections, identify the ISA that provides relevant guidance. You may find it helpful to refer to the *Auditing Standards Exhibit* inside the front cover of this textbook.

15-39 **Diageo**
(LO 2, 5) Obtain a copy of the 2017 Annual Report of Diageo.

    a. What information did the auditors provide about:
       i. The audit approach?
       ii. The auditing standards that the auditors followed?
       iii. KAMs?
       iv. Materiality?
       v. Responsibilities for the financial statements and the audit?
    b. Do you think that investors in U.S. public companies would like to see similar information?

Academic Research Cases

NOTE: Completing *Academic Research Cases* requires students to reference additional resources and materials.

SEARCH HINT

It is easy to locate these academic research articles! Use a search engine such as Google Scholar or an electronic research platform such as ABI Inform, and search using the author names and part of the article title.

15-40 **LO 3** Locate and read the article listed below.

Chen, Yu, J. D. Eshleman, and J. S. Soileau. (2017). Business strategy and auditor reporting. *Auditing, A Journal of Practice and Theory* 36(21): 63-86.

    a. What is the purpose of the study?
    b. Describe the design/method/approach used to conduct the study.
    c. What are the primary findings of the study?

15-41 **LO 3** Locate and read the article listed below.

Carson, E., N. L. Fargher, M. A. Geiger, C. S. Lennox, K. Raghunandan, and M. Willekens. (2013). Audit reporting for going-concern uncertainty: A research synthesis. *Auditing: A Journal of Practice & Theory* 32(Supp.): 353–384.

    a. What is the purpose of the study?
    b. Describe the design/method/approach used to conduct the study.
    c. What are the primary findings of the study?

Due to ACL software updates, the following may differ in appearance from the current version of ACL, but the vast majority of the content remains the same. Please keep in mind that you will now **download** ACL instead of **installing** it via a CD.

ACL is a data analytics tool widely used by audit firms and internal auditing organizations to access, analyze, and manipulate electronic data contained in client systems. This ACL tutorial is designed to help you learn how to use many of the important features of this tool, as well as to provide you with hands-on experience of using GAS to help perform audits. You are likely to use this or a similar program in your professional career. The ACL program is contained on a computer resource (CD) that comes with your textbook. It is recommended that you install ACL on your own computer if it has a Windows operating system. (A Mac will not work unless it is configured to act as a Windows operating system.) If this is not possible, check with your instructor to see if Windows is available in a computer lab.

Data Files

The data files for the ACL cases in selected chapters are found on the textbook's website under "Student Resources." If you install ACL on your own computer, it is recommended that you download the data files to your hard drive. If you use ACL on a network, download the files to whatever input/output device can be used on the lab's computers. The files created by ACL are stored on the same device with the data files.

Working on a Project

This section provides directions on how to create a new project or work on an existing project. The first step is to start the ACL program. The ACL icon should appear on your desktop after you install the program from the CD found at the back of your textbook. If the icon does not appear, look under *programs* to locate and start using the software.

Note the menu options on the standard toolbar and the options under each item. Move your cursor along the icons and note what each one stands for as a way to familiarize yourself with the overall setup of the program. Notice that the functionalities of ACL look and behave in a manner that is very similar to an Excel program. The first step in using ACL is to: (1) create a new project or (2) open an existing project.

All figures sources are ACL Services Ltd.
Source: ACL Services Ltd.

(1) Create a New Project

To start a new project (such as a case), select **FILE | NEW | PROJECT** and give the project a name. Or click the **Create a New Project** link on the screen. *Be sure to save the project in the directory with the data files.* The files that are created when using ACL are saved on the same drive with the data files.

You then need to import one or more files to work on:

Import a Table (file)

Click on **FILE | NEW |TABLE** and follow the on-screen instructions.

(2) Open an Existing Project

To open an existing project, select **FILE | OPEN PROJECT** and click on the file name in the directory in which it was saved. Or click the **Open an Existing Project** link on the screen. Then continue working on the project; you can import additional files as needed.

Basic Features of ACL Projects

Following are some basic activities that can be performed on a file that is either a new or existing project. These activities are presented in alphabetical order.

Add a Column

You can add one or more columns with new information you create based on the data in the table. For example, you could calculate the difference between two fields. Either click the **Add Column** icon on the toolbar or place the cursor where you want the column to be inserted, right-click the mouse, and select **Add Columns**. Click the **Expr** button, and build the expression needed to calculate the data for the new column (e.g., Amount–Confirmed). Type a column name in the **Save as** box (e.g., *Difference*). Click **OK** and **OK** again. You may need to move the screen to the right to see the new column.

Age

Select **ANALYZE | AGE** or click the **Age** icon on the toolbar. Select the field on which to age (such as INVDATE). Click the button next to the **Cut-off date** window and select the appropriate date. You can accept the default aging categories or change them. Choose the field to subtotal by aging category (such as AMOUNT) in the right window. Click the **Output** tab at the top and select where you want the output. If the output is saved to a file, give it a name. Click on that category (e.g., >45) to get a list of items in a specific aging category.

Close Projects

To close a project (it is saved in the directory with the data files), either select **FILE | CLOSE PROJECT**, or click the **Close the Open Project** icon on the toolbar.

Delete Files

Files created in a current project can be deleted by right-clicking on the file name in the left window and then choosing **Delete**. To completely delete files you created with ACL, go into the directory with the data files and delete the files created by ACL, including those with the .fil extension.

Extract

Select **DATA | EXTRACT DATA | IF**. You can then create an expression to select the items to extract. For example, if you want to extract all unpaid invoices over a certain age based on the field INVDATE, the expression would be INVDATE < (click on **DATE** and select the appropriate date). Fields can be entered into the expression either by typing or double-clicking on the field in the **Available fields** window. If you want to extract all amounts over $100,000, the expression would be AMOUNTS > 100000. Click **OK** when the expression is complete. Type a name for the extracted file in the **To** window.

Expressions for extracting data can include specific text. For example, if there is a column labeled COMMENT with explanations of confirmation exceptions including "Confirmed–OK" and you want to extract all of those that do not have that explanation, the expression would be COMMENT < > "Confirmed–OK." The words must be within quotes.

> **Note:** When records are extracted from a file, you must create a new file and you should save that file. ACL describes this as creating a filter because we have filtered the data to create a new file. To get back to the original file, click on the original file name in the left window.

File Statistics

There are several ways to get statistics about the data in the file.

1. Click on the icon with the % sign. Choose the field(s) on which you want statistics. Click on the **Output** tab and choose where you want the output (screen, graph, print, or file).
2. Select **ANALYZE | STATISTICAL** and either **STATISTICS** or **PROFILE**. If you choose **STATISTICS**, you have the same choices as in step 1 above. The statistics provided with **STATISTICS** are numbers; totals; and averages for positive, negative, zero items; overall totals; and highest and lowest values for the field(s) selected. The statistics that are provided with **PROFILE** are total, absolute, minimum, and maximum values for the field(s) selected.

Filters

Filters may be used to query the data in a table that have been imported without adding a new field or creating a new table. For example, a filter can identify customer unpaid invoices over $50,000 as follows. Using the data from the Husky Unpaid Inventory Excel file, do the following:

1. Click on the **GREEN EDIT FILTER** button (the icon that looks like a funnel with a green stripe just above the first column of data).
2. The cursor is available under the word Filter at the top of the screen. Type in AMOUNT > 50000.
3. The results appear as below.

Filter: amount>50000

	CUSTNUM	INVNUM	INVDATE	AMOUNT
11	100	168651	11/22/2013	66480.30
19	70	168732	11/25/2013	79374.82
42	143	168925	11/29/2013	57509.74
46	114	169001	11/30/2013	89230.46
65	37	169152	12/04/2013	57340.64
72	184	169186	12/05/2013	143853.83
89	141	169298	12/10/2013	153129.75
91	11	169309	12/10/2013	116936.56
102	121	169349	12/13/2013	58503.00
120	180	169470	12/18/2013	126816.73
124	107	169489	12/19/2013	61809.83
138	123	169551	12/21/2013	121562.18
150	81	169617	12/25/2013	76230.44
159	224	169707	12/26/2013	129494.41
178	172	169969	12/28/2013	82454.77
180	166	169971	12/28/2013	155198.43
188	181	169979	12/29/2013	151012.89

Welcome husky_unpaid_1

<< End of File >>

4. To go back to the unfiltered Excel file, click on the **RED EDIT FILTER** button.

Join Files

To join two tables (files), be sure the fields on which the files are to be matched (e.g., invoice numbers) are in the same format, such as numeric. To join files use a particular field, such as customer number; the field must be in ASCII format. To change the format from numeric to ASCII, select **EDIT | TABLE LAYOUT,** or click the **Edit Table Layout** icon on the toolbar. Double-click on the field to be reformatted, and select **ASCII** from the drop-down menu under **TYPE.** Click on the green check mark in the left margin to accept the change, and then **OK.**

Select one of the files as the primary file by making it active on the screen. If the active file is not to be the primary file, click on the file you want to be the primary file in the left window of the screen. Click the **Join** icon that looks like an upside-down organization chart or select **DATA | JOIN TABLES.** Click on the secondary file you want to join with the primary file. Click on the field name for the primary and secondary file keys (fields on which the files are matched, such as invoice numbers). Click on the primary and secondary fields you want in the combined file. To select more than one field in a window, hold down the Ctrl key. Type a name for the combined files next to the **To** button, and then **OK.**

Move a Column/Change Column Widths

Columns can be rearranged by left-clicking on the column heading, holding the mouse button down, and dragging the column where you want it.

Column widths can be changed by placing the cursor to the right side of the column heading and moving it in either direction.

Prepare and Print Reports

You can tailor a report of the information on the active screen and get column totals. Select **Data | Report** or click the **Report** icon on the toolbar (looks like three pieces of paper stacked upon one another). Type any information you want in the header and/or footer of the report, such as the client's name or your name, a date, and the nature of the information. On the **OUTPUT** tab, choose where you want the output (e.g., screen or file). The report can be previewed by choosing **File | Print Preview** or clicking the **Print Preview** icon. You can change the page layout from portrait to landscape by clicking the **Setup** button. The report displays and prints totals for all numeric fields. You may need to adjust the column widths to see entire column headings.

If you do not want to add headers or footers to the report, you can simply click the **Print** icon or select **File | Print** on the menu. All numeric fields are automatically totaled.

Saving Files

Files created by ACL are automatically stored on the same storage device with the data files. Therefore, you can end an ACL session and come back later. The files will still be there until you delete them.

Search for Duplicates

Select **ANALYZE | Look for Duplicates** and then select the field to be searched (e.g., **Invoice Number**). In the **LIST FIELDS** window, select the fields you want identified with the duplicate entries.

Sort

Right-click on the column heading you want sorted and choose whether you want it sorted in ascending or descending order. All other columns will be included in the sort.

Stratify

Select **ANALYZE | STRATIFY** or click on the **Stratify** icon (looks like the numbers 123). Choose the field on which to stratify in the **Stratify On** window (such as **AMOUNT**). Choose the field to subtotal (such as **AMOUNT**). Type in the minimum and maximum values for the intervals (such as *0* and *100000*) and the number of intervals (such as *10*). Click the **Output** tab and choose where you want the output.

Summarize

Records can be summarized based on some key (e.g., customer number to get customer balances from an unpaid invoice file). The field to be summarized, such as CUSTNUM, must be in ASCII format. Select **ANALYZE | SUMMARIZE** or click on the **Summarize** icon (looks like a green arrow). Choose the field on which to summarize in the **Summarize On** window (such as **CUSTNUM**). Choose the field to subtotal in the **Subtotal Fields** window (such as **AMOUNT**). Choose the other fields you want in the output file in the **Other Fields** window. Click on the **Output** tab at the top and select **Screen** or **File**.

Husky Practice Case

The following case, along with the data files contained in Excel, enables you to practice using the various functions of ACL. The first step is to go to the textbook website and access the student resources. Next, locate the ACL resources, and download the zip file to your desktop. Finally, look in the folder to locate the various Excel files that you will use to complete the case.

For this case, assume that you are auditing the accounts receivable records of Husky Corp. and that the general ledger control account shows a balance of $4,263,919.52. Use ACL to help perform some audit procedures.

There are four related data files you need to download for this tutorial:

- *husky_unpaid* contains the unpaid invoices as of 12/31/13.
- *husky_shipping* contains the shipment numbers and shipment dates for those invoices. You have verified that the last shipment number used in 2013 is 62050.
- *husky_credit* shows the credit limit for each customer.
- *husky_confirm* shows the confirmation results.

Audit Procedures

This tutorial shows you how to perform the following audit procedures using ACL:

1. Foot the unpaid invoice file and agree to the general ledger.
2. Identify any unpaid invoices older than 45 days.
3. Identify customer balances greater than their credit limit or for which there are no credit limits.
4. Perform a sales cutoff test.

Data files and *typed input* are shown in *italics*. **ACL icons, commands,** and **equations** are shown in **bold**. FIELD NAMES are in ALL CAPS.

Step 1—Start a new project

Select **File | New, Project** on the menu bar. Select the location of the data files in the **Save New Project As** window; enter *Husky AR* as the name for the project. Click **Save**.

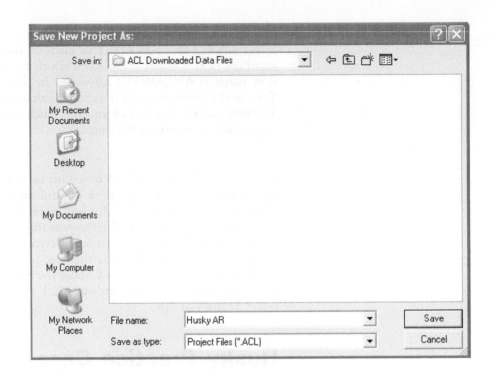

Step 2—Import a table (file)

To import a file (ACL refers to them as tables), click **File | New | Table**.

Follow the onscreen commands and import the Excel file *Husky Unpaid Invoices*. Save it to your computer using the name *Husky_Unpaid*. The file appears as follows:

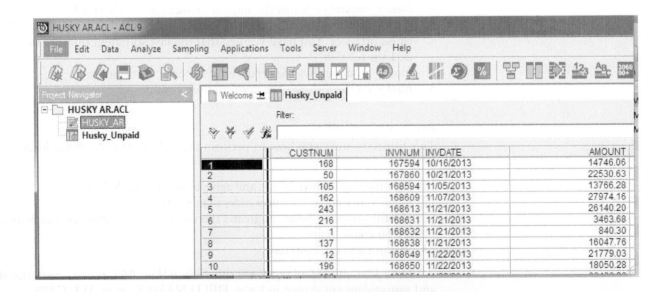

Step 3—Foot the file and agree to the general ledger

With the *Husky_Unpaid* table in the active window, select **ANALYZE | STATISTICAL | STATISTICS** on the menu bar and click on **AMOUNT** to foot the file.

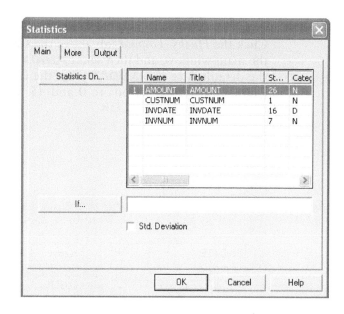

Click **OK**.

The next screen shows several things. The first matrix shows the total value, which agrees with the general ledger balance ($4,263,919.52), and the number and amount of positive and negative values. The second matrix shows on the first line the value of the largest ($155,198.43) and smallest amount ($−22,659.74) of the unpaid invoices. Print the statistics by clicking on the **Print** icon or selecting **File | Print** on the menu bar.

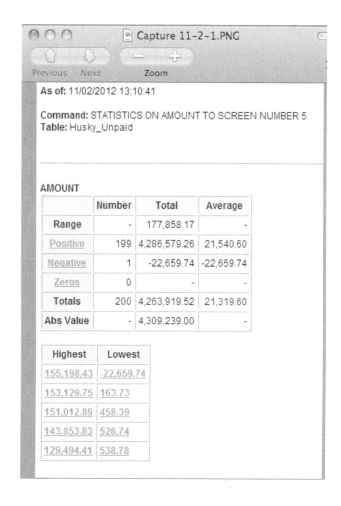

Step 4—Identify any unpaid invoices older than 45 days

Click the *Husky_Unpaid* tab above the statistics to make the table active in the main window, and then select **ANALYZE | AGE** on the menu bar. Accept the default **Age on INVDATE**. Set the cutoff date to December 31, 2013. Change the aging periods to 0 and 45. Click **AMOUNT** under **Subtotal Fields** to subtotal. Click **OK**.

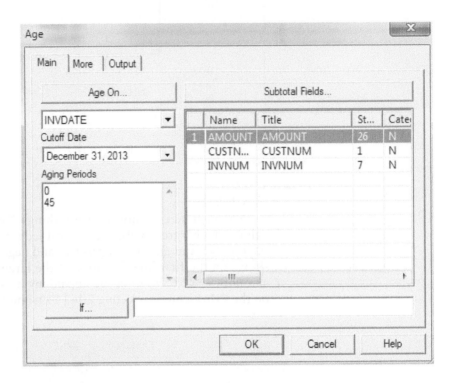

As noted in the following tables, there are four invoices amounting to $79,017.13 that are over 45 days old.

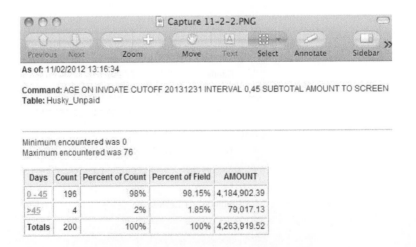

As of: 11/02/2012 13:16:34

Command: AGE ON INVDATE CUTOFF 20131231 INTERVAL 0,45 SUBTOTAL AMOUNT TO SCREEN
Table: Husky_Unpaid

Minimum encountered was 0
Maximum encountered was 76

Days	Count	Percent of Count	Percent of Field	AMOUNT
0 - 45	196	98%	98.15%	4,184,902.39
>45	4	2%	1.85%	79,017.13
Totals	200	100%	100%	4,263,919.52

Click on > 45 under the column headed **Days**; ACL will retrieve those four invoices from the unpaid file.

Print the page showing the details for these four invoices by clicking on the **Print** icon or selecting **File | Print** on the menu bar. Notice the total of the AMOUNT column is printed. These totals should be investigated to determine their collectibility.

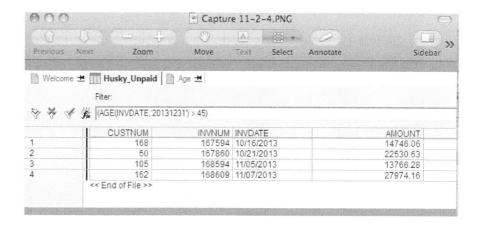

Note: If you want to save this information as a file to retrieve later, make the *Husky_Unpaid* table active and select **DATA | EXTRACT DATA** on the menu and click on **IF**. Enter an expression by double-clicking on **INVDATE**, click <, select **DATE** and scroll to November 16, 2013, on the date selector, and click **OK**. Click **OK** again. Enter a file name such as *Over 45 Days* next to the **TO** button. Click **OK**. The screen will look like the one above but will not have anything showing in the **Filter** window.

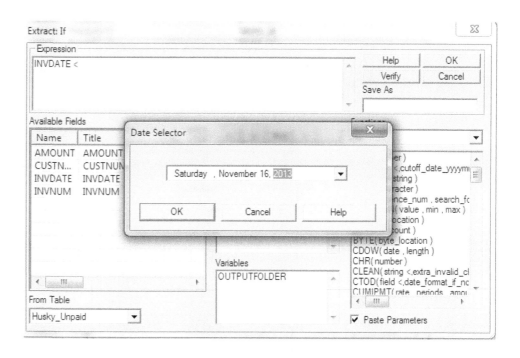

Step 5—Identify customers' balances greater than their credit limit or for which there are no credit limits

First, access the entire *Husky_Unpaid* table. Then, to determine each customer's balance, change the field type of **CUSTNUM** from **NUMERIC** to **ASCII**. Select **Edit |Table Layout** on the menu bar and double-click on **CUSTNUM**.

Click the down arrow in the **Type** window, and locate and click on **ASCII** in the window (it is located above NUMERIC). Click the green arrow at the left of the screen and then the red X in the upper-right corner to exit this window. Also change **INVNUM** to **ASCII**.

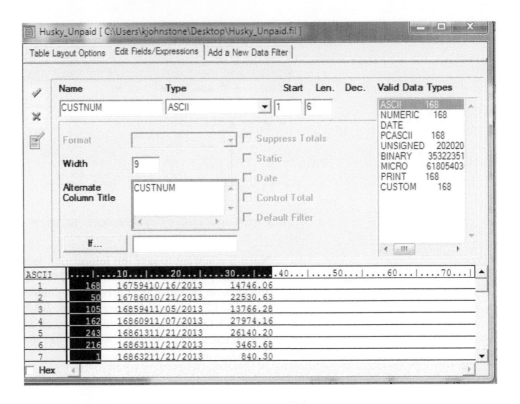

Select **Analyze | Summarize** on the menu bar. Click to summarize on **CUSTNUM** and subtotal on **AMOUNT**. If **CUSTNUM** does not appear in the **Summarize On** window, change the field type to **ASCII**. Click the **Output** tab and choose **FILE**.

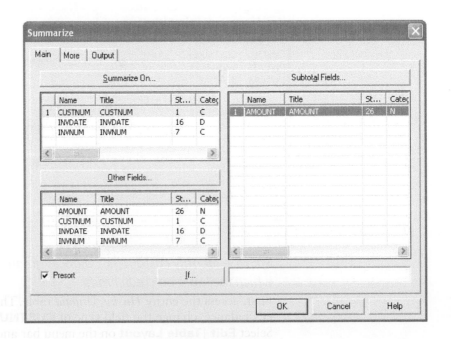

Name the new file *Customer_Balances*.

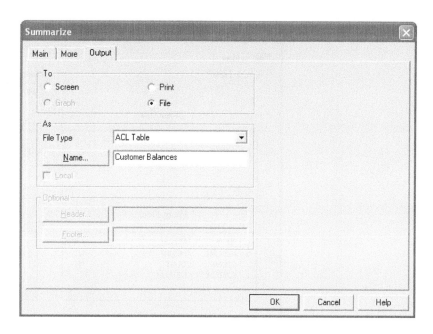

The window will show each customer's balance and the number (count) of unpaid invoices.

	CUSTNUM	AMOUNT	COUNT
1	1	840.30	1
2	2	17249.87	1
3	3	20261.90	1
4	4	22316.02	1
5	6	22937.50	1
6	7	19677.39	2
7	10	22185.45	2
8	11	116936.56	1
9	12	56934.85	3
10	13	24110.44	1
11	16	31495.94	2
12	19	1857.33	1
13	24	526.74	1
14	25	20410.08	1
15	28	9258.93	1
16	30	22709.38	2
17	32	23689.30	2
18	33	39835.72	2
19	36	21164.47	1

Import the *Husky_Credit* file by selecting **File | New | Table** on the menu bar. Save the imported table as *Husky_Credit*. Change **CUSTNUM** from numeric format to ASCII by selecting **Edit | Table Layout** on the menu. Double-click on **CUSTNUM** and change the format to ASCII (as described at the beginning of this step) so the files can be matched on this field.

Make *Customer_Balances* the active table by double-clicking on that name in the left window. Select **Data | Join Tables** on the menu bar or click on the **Join** icon. Choose *Husky_Credit* as the secondary table. Click **CUST-NUM** in both the **Primary Keys** and **Secondary Keys** windows to match the two tables based on CUSTNUM. Click **CUSTNUM** and **AMOUNT** under **Primary Fields** using the **Ctrl** key on the keyboard to select more than one field in the window. Click **CRLIMIT** under **Secondary Fields** to print. Select **Presort Secondary Table**. Type the name *Balances and Credit Limit* in the **To** box. Click **OK**.

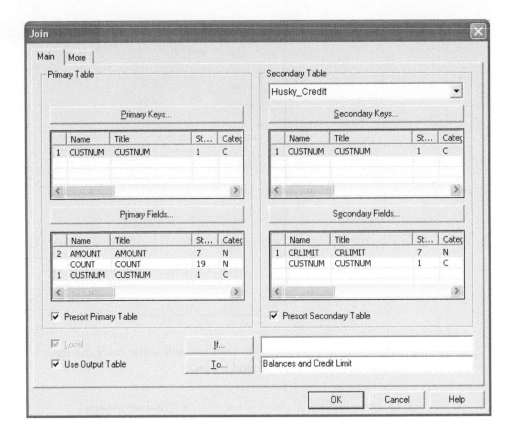

The joined files now show the balances and credit limits for each customer.

Create a filter to show those customers with balances that exceed their credit limit. Click on the **Edit Filter** icon next to the **Filter** window. Enter the expression *AMOUNT > CRLIMIT*. Click **OK**.

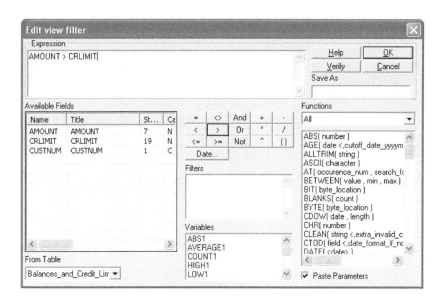

The results show that there are five customers who have exceeded their credit limits and one for whom there is no credit limit. The accounts for these customers should be investigated to determine collectibility.

	CUSTNUM	AMOUNT	CRLIMIT
69	121	68645.17	50000
79	141	161031.79	150000
93	166	155198.43	150000
98	174	83738.44	0
101	181	155986.66	150000
104	184	168611.35	150000
	<< End of File >>		

Print this table by clicking on the **Print** icon or selecting **File | Print** on the menu bar. Notice the total of each numeric column is printed.

Step 6—Perform a sales cutoff test

Import the *husky_shipping* file by selecting **File | New |Table** on the menu bar. Save the table with the name *Husky_Shipping*. Click **Finish | OK**. Change the **INVNUM** field from numeric to ASCII using **Edit |Table Layout** as you have done previously.

Make *Husky_Unpaid* the active table. Join the *Husky_Shipping* table with the *Husky_Unpaid* file. Click **INVNUM** as primary key and secondary key to join on this field. Select the fields to show in the new table by selecting all of the fields in the **Primary Fields** window (remember to hold the **Ctrl** key down) and select the **SHIPNUM** and **DATESHIP** fields under **Secondary Fields**. Click to presort the secondary file. Give the new table the name *Unpaid with ship number*. Click **OK**.

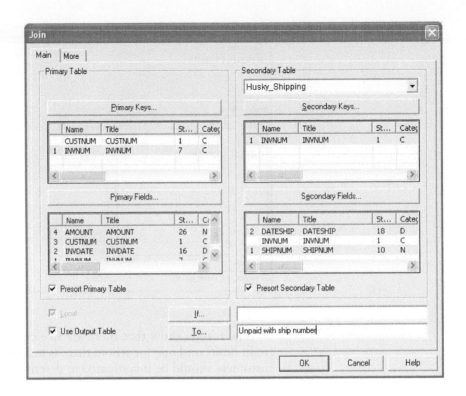

A new table is created that shows the results of combining these two tables (adjust column widths to see all columns):

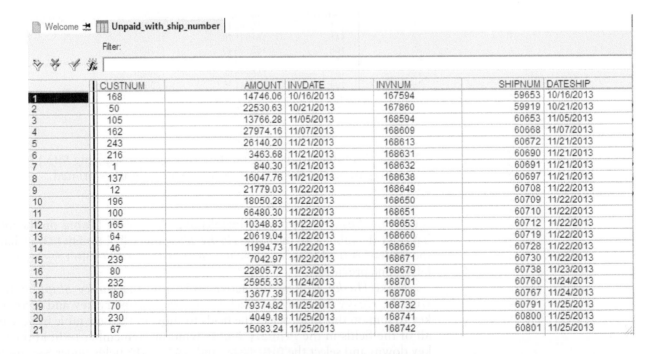

The last shipping number used in 2013 as confirmed by you was 62050. Create a filter with the expression *SHIPNUM > 62050* to see if there are any shipments after year-end.

Welcome ⊞ 🏢 **Unpaid_with_ship_number**

Filter:

SHIPNUM>62050

	CUSTNUM	AMOUNT	INVDATE	INVNUM	SHIPNUM	DATESHIP
189	202	5891.46	12/30/2013	169980	62069	01/01/2014
190	214	6522.71	12/30/2013	169981	62070	01/03/2014
191	45	14315.54	12/30/2013	169982	62071	01/02/2014
	<< End of File >>					

The results show three shipments after year-end. Follow up on these to determine whether the accounts should be corrected for this apparent cutoff error.

Print this table by clicking on the **Print** icon or selecting **File | Print** on the menu. Notice the total of each numeric column is printed.

References

Chapter 1

1. Auditing Concepts Committee. (1972). Report of the Committee on Basic Auditing Concepts. *The Accounting Review*, 47, Supp. 18.
2. *United States v. Arthur Young & Co.* et al, U.S. Supreme Court, No. 82–687 [52 U.S.L.W.4355 (U.S., Mar. 21, 1984)].
3. Government Accountability Office (GAO). (2003). Public Accounting Firms: Required Study on the Potential Effects of Mandatory Audit Firm Rotation. GAO Report 04–216 (November).
4. U.S. Securities and Exchange Commission, Final Rule: Revision of the Commission's Auditor Independence Requirements, February 5, 2001.
5. Op. cit.
6. The 2016 IESBA Handbook contains the entire Code of Ethics for Professional Accountants. International Ethics Standards Board for Accountants. https://www.ethicsboard.org/iesba-code

Chapter 4

1. *Credit Alliance Corp. v. Arthur Andersen & Co.*, 483 N.E. 2d 110 (N.Y. 1985).
2. The *Restatement (Second) of Torts* is published by the American Law Institute. Courts may refer to this treatise when considering an issue of outdated precedent. It offers a unique perspective on the law because its purpose is to state the law as the majority of courts would decide it today. It does not necessarily reflect the rules of the common law as adopted by the courts. Rather, it represents principles of common law that the American Law Institute believes would be adopted if the courts reexamined their common-law rules.
3. *Citizens State Bank v. Timm, Schmidt & Co.*, 335 N.W. 2d 361 (Wis. Sup. Ct. 1983).
4. *Rosenblum, Inc. v. Adler*, 461 A. 2d 138 (N.J. 1983).
5. *Herzfeld v. Laventhol, Krekstein, Horwath & Horwath* [1973–1974] Transfer Binder CCH FED. Sec. Law Reporter #94,574, at 95,999 (S.D.N.Y. May 29, 1974).

Chapter 7

1. The Phoenician was so lavishly constructed that a regulator estimated that just to break even, the resort would have to charge $500 per room per night at a 70% occupancy rate. Similar resort rooms in the area were available at $125 a night.

Chapter 14

1. E. Altman, *Corporate Financial Distress* (New York: John Wiley & Sons, 1983).

Chapter 15

1. https://pcaobus.org/Standards/Auditing/Pages/AU110.aspx
2. AU-C 706, http://www.aicpa.org/Research/Standards/AuditAttest/DownloadableDocuments/AU-C-00706.pdf.
3. http://www.ifac.org/system/files/downloads/a013-2010-iaasb-handbook-isa-250.pdf
4. https://pcaobus.org/Rulemaking/Docket034/2017-001-auditors-report-final-rule.pdf

Case Index

Index

"Why It Matters" Feature Content

PCAOB Standards

General Auditing Standards

1000 General Principles and Responsibilities
- AS 1001: Responsibilities and Functions of the Independent Auditor
- AS 1005: Independence
- AS 1010: Training and Proficiency of the Independent Auditor
- AS 1015: Due Professional Care in the Performance of Work

1100 General Concepts
- AS 1101: Audit Risk
- AS 1105: Audit Evidence
- AS 1110: Relationship of Auditing Standards to Quality Control Standards

1200 General Activities
- AS 1201: Supervision of the Audit Engagement
- AS 1205: Part of the Audit Performed by Other Independent Auditors
- AS 1210: Using the Work of a Specialist
- AS 1215: Audit Documentation
- AS 1220: Engagement Quality Review

1300 Auditor Communications
- AS 1301: Communications with Audit Committees
- AS 1305: Communications About Control Deficiencies in an Audit of Financial Statements

Audit Procedures

2100 Audit Planning and Risk Assessment
- AS 2101: Audit Planning
- AS 2105: Consideration of Materiality in Planning and Performing an Audit
- AS 2110: Identifying and Assessing Risks of Material Misstatement

2200 Auditing Internal Control Over Financial Reporting

- AS 2201: An Audit of Internal Control Over Financial Reporting That Is Integrated with An Audit of Financial Statements

2300 Audit Procedures in Response to Risks—Nature, Timing, and Extent

- AS 2301: The Auditor's Responses to the Risks of Material Misstatement
- AS 2305: Substantive Analytical Procedures
- AS 2310: The Confirmation Process
- AS 2315: Audit Sampling

2400 Audit Procedures for Specific Aspects of the Audit

- AS 2401: Consideration of Fraud in a Financial Statement Audit
- AS 2405: Illegal Acts by Clients
- AS 2410: Related Parties
- AS 2415: Consideration of an Entity's Ability to Continue as a Going Concern

2500 Audit Procedures for Certain Accounts or Disclosures

- AS 2501: Auditing Accounting Estimates
- AS 2502: Auditing Fair Value Measurements and Disclosures
- AS 2503: Auditing Derivative Instruments, Hedging Activities, and Investments in Securities
- AS 2505: Inquiry of a Client's Lawyer Concerning Litigation, Claims, and Assessments
- AS 2510: Auditing Inventories

2600 Special Topics

- AS 2601: Consideration of an Entity's Use of a Service Organization
- AS 2605: Consideration of the Internal Audit Function
- AS 2610: Initial Audits—Communications Between Predecessor and Successor Auditors

2700 Auditor's Responsibilities Regarding Supplemental and Other Information

- AS 2701: Auditing Supplemental Information Accompanying Audited Financial Statements
- AS 2705: Required Supplementary Information
- AS 2710: Other Information in Documents Containing Audited Financial Statements

2800 Concluding Audit Procedures

- AS 2801: Subsequent Events
- AS 2805: Management Representations
- AS 2810: Evaluating Audit Results
- AS 2815: The Meaning of "Present Fairly in Conformity with Generally Accepted Accounting Principles"
- AS 2820: Evaluating Consistency of Financial Statements

2900 Post-Audit Matters

- AS 2901: Consideration of Omitted Procedures After the Report Date
- AS 2905: Subsequent Discovery of Facts Existing at the Date of the Auditor's Report

Auditor Reporting

3100 Reporting on Audits of Financial Statements
- AS 3101: Reports on Audited Financial Statements
- AS 3110: Dating of the Independent Auditor's Report

3300 Other Reporting Topics
- AS 3305: Special Reports
- AS 3310: Special Reports on Regulated Companies
- AS 3315: Reporting on Condensed Financial Statements and Selected Financial Data
- AS 3320: Association with Financial Statements

Matters Relating to Filings Under Federal Securities Laws

- AS 4101: Responsibilities Regarding Filings Under Federal Securities Statutes
- AS 4105: Reviews of Interim Financial Information

Other Matters Associated with Audits

- AS 6101: Letters for Underwriters and Certain Other Requesting Parties
- AS 6105: Reports on the Application of Accounting Principles
- AS 6110: Compliance Auditing Considerations in Audits of Recipients of Governmental Financial Assistance
- AS 6115: Reporting on Whether a Previously Reported Material Weakness Continues to Exist

IAASB Standards

- ISA 200 *Overall Objectives of the Independent Auditor and the Conduct of an Audit in Accordance with International Standards on Auditing*
- ISA 210 *Agreeing the Terms of Audit Engagements*
- ISA 220 *Quality Control for an Audit of Financial Statements*
- ISA 230 *Audit Documentation*
- ISA 240 *The Auditor's Responsibilities Relating to Fraud in an Audit of Financial Statements*
- ISA 250 *Consideration of Laws and Regulations in an Audit of Financial Statements*
- ISA 260 *Communication with Those Charged with Governance*
- ISA 265 *Communicating Deficiencies in Internal Control to Those Charged with Governance and Management*
- ISA 300 *Planning an Audit of Financial Statements*
- ISA 315 *Identifying and Assessing the Risks of Material Misstatement through Understanding the Entity and Its Environment*
- ISA 320 *Materiality in Planning and Performing an Audit*

- ISA 330 *The Auditor's Responses to Assessed Risks*
- ISA 402 *Audit Considerations Relating to an Entity Using a Service Organization*
- ISA 450 *Evaluation of Misstatements Identified during the Audit*
- ISA 500 *Audit Evidence*
- ISA 501 *Audit Evidence-Specific Considerations for Selected Items*
- ISA 505 *External Confirmations*
- ISA 510 *Initial Audit Engagements-Opening Balances*
- ISA 520 *Analytical Procedures*
- ISA 530 *Audit Sampling*
- ISA 540 *Auditing Accounting Estimates, Including Fair Value Accounting Estimates, and Related Disclosures*
- ISA 550 *Related Parties*
- ISA 560 *Subsequent Events*
- ISA 570 *Going Concern*
- ISA 580 *Written Representations*
- ISA 600 *Special Considerations-Audits of Group Financial Statements (Including the Work of Component Auditors)*
- ISA 610 *Using the Work of Internal Auditors*
- ISA 620 *Using the Work of an Auditor's Expert*
- ISA 700 *Forming an Opinion and Reporting on Financial Statements*
- ISA 705 *Modifications to the Opinion in the Independent Auditor's Report*
- ISA 706 *Emphasis of Matter Paragraphs and Other Matter Paragraphs in the Independent Auditor's Report*
- ISA 710 *Comparative Information-Corresponding Figures and Comparative Financial Statements*
- ISA 720 *The Auditor's Responsibilities Relating to Other Information in Documents Containing Audited Financial Statements*
- ISA 800 *Special Considerations-Audits of Financial Statements Prepared in Accordance with Special Purpose Frameworks*
- ISA 805 *Special Considerations-Audits of Single Financial Statements and Specific Elements, Accounts or Items of a Financial Statement*
- ISA 810 *Engagements to Report on Summary Financial Statements*
- International Standard on Quality Control (ISQC) 1, *Quality Controls for Firms that Perform Audits and Reviews of Financial Statements, and Other Assurance and Related Services Engagements*

AICPA Standards

Section	Title
Preface	*Principles Underlying an Audit Conducted in Accordance with Generally Accepted Auditing Standards*
200–299	**General Principles and Responsibilities**
• 120	*Defining Professional Requirements in Statements on Auditing Standards*
• 150	*Generally Accepted Auditing Standards*
• 200	*Overall Objectives of the Independent Auditor and the Conduct of an Audit in Accordance with Generally Accepted Auditing Standards*
• 201	*Nature of the General Standards*

The Audit Opinion Formulation Process

| I. Making Client Acceptance and Continuance Decisions **Chapter 1** | II. Performing Risk Assessment **Chapters 2, 3, 7, and 9–13** | III. Obtaining Evidence About Internal Control Operating Effectiveness **Chapters 8–13** | IV. Obtaining Substantive Evidence About Accounts, Disclosures, and Assertions **Chapters 8–13** | V. Completing the Audit and Making Reporting Decisions **Chapters 14 and 15** |

Quality Auditing and the Need for Quality Auditor Judgments and Ethical Decisions
Chapter 1

Professional Liability
Chapter 4

The Audit Opinion Formulation Process and a Framework for Obtaining Audit Evidence
Chapters 5 and 6

Exhibit 4.3
A Framework for Professional Decision Making

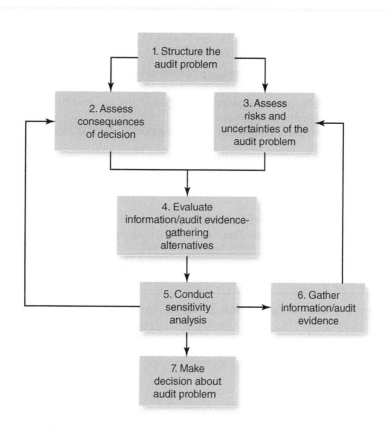

1. Structure the audit problem

2. Assess consequences of decision

3. Assess risks and uncertainties of the audit problem

4. Evaluate information/audit evidence-gathering alternatives

5. Conduct sensitivity analysis

6. Gather information/audit evidence

7. Make decision about audit problem

Source: Adapted from *Judgment and Choice* by Robin Hogarth.

Exhibit 4.4
A Framework for Ethical Decision Making

Step 1
Identify the ethical issue(s).

Step 2
Determine the affected parties and identify their rights.

Step 3
Determine the most important rights.

Step 4
Develop alternative courses of action.

Step 5
Determine the likely consequences of each proposed course of action.

Step 6
Assess the possible consequences, including an estimation of the greatest good for the greatest number.
Determine whether the rights framework would cause any course of action to be eliminated.

Step 7
Decide on the appropriate course of action.

Exhibit 4.5
AICPA Principles of Professional Conduct

Responsibilities In carrying out their responsibilities as professionals, members should exercise sensitive professional and moral judgments in all their activities.
Public interest Members should accept the obligation to act in a way that will serve the public interest, honor the public trust, and demonstrate commitment to professionalism.
Integrity To maintain and broaden public confidence, members should perform all professional responsibilities with the highest sense of integrity.
Objectivity and independence A member should maintain objectivity and be free of conflicts in discharging professional responsibilities. A member in public practice should be independent both in fact and in appearance when providing auditing and other attestation services. A member not in public practice does not need to maintain independence.
Due care A member should observe the profession's technical and ethical standards, strive continually to improve competence and the quality of services, and discharge professional responsibility to the best of the member's ability.
Scope and nature of services A member in public practice should observe the principles of the *Code* in determining the scope and nature of services to be provided.

Source: *http://www.aicpa.org/Research/Standards/CodeofConduct/DownloadableDocuments/2014December15ContentAsof2016August31 CodeofConduct.pdf*

Additional Resources

The Audit Opinion Formulation Process

| I. Making Client Acceptance and Continuance Decisions **Chapter 1** | II. Performing Risk Assessment **Chapters 2, 3, 7, and 9–13** | III. Obtaining Evidence About Internal Control Operating Effectiveness **Chapters 8–13** | IV. Obtaining Substantive Evidence About Accounts, Disclosures, and Assertions **Chapters 8–13** | V. Completing the Audit and Making Reporting Decisions **Chapters 14 and 15** |

Quality Auditing and the Need for Quality Auditor Judgments and Ethical Decisions
Chapter 1

Professional Liability
Chapter 4

The Audit Opinion Formulation Process and a Framework for Obtaining Audit Evidence
Chapters 5 and 6

Exhibit 4.3
A Framework for Professional Decision Making

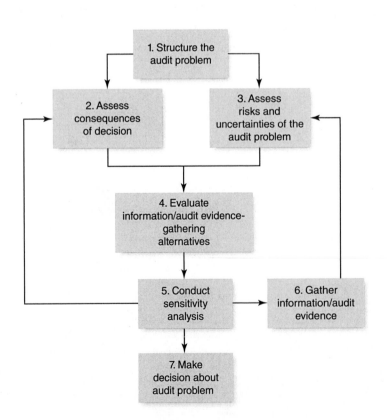

1. Structure the audit problem

2. Assess consequences of decision

3. Assess risks and uncertainties of the audit problem

4. Evaluate information/audit evidence-gathering alternatives

5. Conduct sensitivity analysis

6. Gather information/audit evidence

7. Make decision about audit problem

Source: Adapted from *Judgment* and Choice by Robin Hogarth.